Portfolio Theory and Management

Portfolio Theory and Management

EDITED BY H. KENT BAKER

and

GREG FILBECK

OXFORD
UNIVERSITY PRESS

Oxford University Press is a department of the University of Oxford.
It furthers the University's objective of excellence in research, scholarship,
and education by publishing worldwide.

Oxford   New York
Auckland   Cape Town   Dar es Salaam   Hong Kong   Karachi
Kuala Lumpur   Madrid   Melbourne   Mexico City   Nairobi
New Delhi   Shanghai   Taipei   Toronto

With offices in
Argentina   Austria   Brazil   Chile   Czech Republic   France   Greece
Guatemala   Hungary   Italy   Japan   Poland   Portugal   Singapore
South Korea   Switzerland   Thailand   Turkey   Ukraine   Vietnam

Oxford is a registered trademark of Oxford University Press in the UK and certain other
countries.

Published in the United States of America by
Oxford University Press
198 Madison Avenue, New York, NY 10016

Library of Congress Cataloging-in-Publication Data
Baker, H. Kent (Harold Kent), 1944–
Portfolio theory and management / edited by H. Kent Baker, Greg Filbeck.
    p. cm.
Includes bibliographical references and index.
ISBN 978–0–19–982969–9 (cloth : alk. paper)   1. Portfolio management.
I. Filbeck, Greg.   II. Title.
HG4529.5.P677 2013
332.6—dc23   2012011184

[ISBN: 978–0–19–982969–9]

9 8 7 6 5 4 3 2 1
Printed in the United States of America
on acid-free paper

Contents

Section Seven   SPECIAL TOPICS

Acknowledgments

Many individuals contributed to bringing *Portfolio Theory and Management* from the idea stage to final publication. The chapter authors deserve special thanks for their substantial efforts in writing and revising chapters. Our expert team at Oxford University Press, including but certainly not limited to Terry Vaughn, Joe Jackson, and Jaimee Biggins, exhibited a high level of professionalism in bringing the manuscript to final form as did Molly Morrison, our production editor from Newgen North America, and Doug Sanders, our copy editor. The Kogod School of Business at American University provided financial support. Linda Baker deserves special thanks for her careful review of parts of the manuscript as well as for her patience and encouragement. Janis, Aaron, Kyle, Grant, Mickey, and Judy Filbeck deserve special thanks for their support and encouragement. The authors dedicate this book to Linda Baker and Janis Filbeck.

List of Tables

List of Figures

About the Editors

H. Kent Baker is a University Professor of Finance in the Kogod School of Business at American University. Professor Baker has written or edited 20 books including *Survey of International Finance, Survey Research in Corporate Finance, The Art of Capital Restructuring, Capital Budgeting Valuation, Behavioral Finance—Investors, Corporations, and Markets,* and *Corporate Governance—A Synthesis of Theory, Research, and Practice.* As one of the most prolific finance academics, he has published more than 150 refereed academic journal articles in such journals as the *Journal of Finance, Journal of Financial and Quantitative Analysis, Financial Management, Financial Analysts Journal, Journal of Portfolio Management,* and *Harvard Business Review.* He has consulting and training experience with more than 100 organizations. Professor Baker holds a BSBA from Georgetown University; MEd, MBA, and DBA degrees from the University of Maryland; and an MA, MS, and two PhDs from American University. He also holds CFA and CMA designations.

Greg Filbeck holds the Samuel P. Black III Professor of Insurance and Risk Management at Penn State Erie, the Behrend College and serves as Program Chair for Finance. He formerly served as Senior Vice President of Kaplan Schweser and held academic appointments at Miami University (Ohio) and the University of Toledo, where he served as the Associate Director of the Center for Family Business. Professor Filbeck is an author or editor of two books and has published more than 70 refereed academic journal articles that have appeared in journals such as *Financial Analysts Journal, Financial Review,* and *Journal of Business, Finance, and Accounting.* Professor Filbeck conducts consulting and training worldwide for candidates for the Chartered Financial Analyst (CFA), Financial Risk Manager (FRM), and Chartered Alternative Investment Adviser (CAIA) designations as well as holding all three designations. Professor Filbeck holds a BS from Murray State University and a DBA from the University of Kentucky.

About the Contributors

Nanne Brunia is a Lecturer in Finance at the University of Groningen. His current interests are in the fields of corporate valuation and corporate performance assessment. He developed econometric models of the largest OECD countries and the Dutch social security system. He has lectured in finance and in general economics. Professor Brunia holds a BA in naval architecture from the University of Applied Science of Haarlem and an MSc and PhD in economics from the University of Groningen.

Axel Buchner is an Assistant Professor of Finance and the DekaBank Chair in Finance and Financial Control at Passau University, Germany. His research focuses on issues in private equity, venture capital, and asset pricing. His teaching interests are in derivatives, empirical finance, portfolio theory, and asset pricing. He holds a PhD in finance from Technical University of Munich and a masters degree in business administration from Munich University.

Arnaud Cavé is a PhD student at the University of Rochester. He formerly was a research and teaching assistant in the Department of Finance of HEC, University of Liège. His current research area is the investment funds industry. He holds a masters degree in business engineering from HEC, University of Liège.

Riccardo Cesari is a Professor of Mathematical Finance at the University of Bologna. He has published books and articles on asset allocation, performance measurement, term structure of interest rates, utility theory, and asset pricing. His articles have appeared in such journals as the *Journal of Economics Dynamics and Control*, *Journal of Banking and Finance*, *Applied Economics Letters*, and *Asian Journal of Mathematics and Statistics*. Professor Cesari is a referee for the *Journal of Economics Dynamics and Control*, *Journal of Banking and Finance*, *Journal of Futures Markets*, and *Frontiers in Finance and Economics*. Between 1984 and 1994 he was a research officer at the Bank of Italy. He holds a PhD in Philosophy from the University of Oxford and a BS from the University of Bologna.

Joshua M. Davis is a Senior Vice President in the global quantitative portfolio group in the Newport Beach office of PIMCO. He focuses on portfolio solutions and quantitative strategy including asset allocation, tail risk hedging, foreign exchange, and variable annuities. Before joining PIMCO in 2008, he was a consulting strategist with Prime International Trading in Chicago. He has four years of investment experience and holds a PhD in economics with an emphasis on macroeconomics and finance from Northwestern University, where he also earned his masters degree. He holds undergraduate degrees in pure mathematics and management science from the University of California–San Diego.

James Farrell Jr. is the Chairman of the Institute for Quantitative Research in Finance (the Q Group), one of the premier investment forums in the world. He was the Managing Director of Research and Development at Ned Davis Research. Before joining the firm, Dr. Farrell was managing director and principal of Morse Williams, a New York City-based investment advisory firm. He also founded Farrell-Wako Global Investment Management, a joint venture with Wako Securities, a mid-sized Japanese brokerage firm. The firm eventually grew to $700 million in assets, while generating top quartile performance. Dr. Farrell also worked as a portfolio manager at TIAA-CREF, Citibank, and MPT Associates. He has been widely published in investment journals such as the *Journal of Portfolio Management* and *Financial Analysis Journal*, and is the author of several textbooks on portfolio management including *Portfolio Management: Theory and Application*. His writings and lectures cover asset allocation, security valuation, portfolio analysis, international investing, and the merits of introducing greater discipline and structure in the investment process. He holds a PhD in finance and economics from New York University, an MBA from the Wharton School of Business at the University of Pennsylvania, and a BS degree from the University of Notre Dame. He also holds the Chartered Financial Analyst (CFA) designation.

Michael S. Finke is a Professor and PhD Coordinator of Personal Financial Planning at Texas Tech University. He served as President of the American Council on Consumer Interests, and is the editor of the *Journal of Personal Finance*, Academic Peer Review Committee Co-Chair for the *Retirement Management Journal*, and an editorial board member of the *Journal of Consumer Affairs*. His primary research interests are household financial decision making, analysis of individual investment performance, the value of financial planning advice and the importance of contracts among financial service agents. He holds doctoral degrees in family resource management from the Ohio State University and in finance from the University of Missouri.

Reto Forrer is a research associate and PhD student at the Department of Financial Management at the University of Basel. Previously, he was a Senior Consultant in the M&A department of PricewaterhouseCoopers. His research focuses on applications of fractal structures in finance particularly for listed venture capital. He holds a master's degree in business economics from the University of St. Gallen (HSG).

Roland Füss is a Professor of Finance at the Swiss Institute of Banking and Finance. His research focuses on applied econometrics, risk management, and

Maastricht University (the Netherlands) and Affiliate Professor at EDHEC (France, Singapore) and Solvay Brussels School of Economics and Management (Belgium). Professor Hübner regularly teaches in executive programs in various European institutions including preparation seminars for the GARP (Global Association of Risk Professionals) certification. He has published numerous books and research articles about credit risk, hedge funds, and portfolio performance. He received the best paper award 2002 of the *Journal of Banking and Finance*, and the Operational Risk and Compliance Achievement Award 2006 for the best academic paper. Professor Hübner developed the Generalized Treynor Ratio, a popular portfolio performance measure. He is also co-founder and scientific director of Gambit Financial Solutions, a spin-off company of HEC Liège that produces sophisticated software solutions for investor profiling, portfolio optimization, and risk management. He received his PhD from INSEAD.

Eric Jacquier is Visiting Professor of Finance at the Sloan School of Management at Massachusetts Institute of Technology (MIT), on leave from HEC Montreal. Before joining HEC, he taught at Cornell, Wharton, and Boston College. Professor Jacquier consults and teaches executive education seminars in financial econometrics, quantitative risk, and portfolio management. His research is in empirical asset pricing and financial econometrics and has been published in major academic and practitioners' journals. Specifically, he is interested in the forecasting of risk parameters, such as betas and volatilities, crucial for derivative pricing and risk and portfolio management. He is a specialist of Bayesian and Markov Chain Monte Carlo methods in finance. Professor Jacquier's received his MBA from UCLA and his PhD from the University of Chicago's Booth School.

Christoph Kaserer is a Full Professor of Finance at the School of Management at Technische Universität München (TUM). He heads the Department of Financial Management and Capital Markets and is also a Co-Director of the Center for Entrepreneurial and Financial Studies at TUM. Before joining TUM he was a Full Professor of Finance and Accounting the Université de Fribourg, Switzerland. Professor Kaserer's research has been published in the *Journal of Business Finance and Accounting, European Financial Management, Journal of Risk, Journal of Alternative Investing*, and *International Review of Finance* among others. He is among the top 1 percent downloaded authors on the Social Science Research Network. He is also active as an advisor for large private companies and associations, private equity funds, and public institutions including the Swiss and German government. Professor Kaserer earned his degree in economics from University of Vienna and his PhD in finance from the University of Würzburg.

Matthieu Leblanc heads the Financial Research Department at Edmond de Rothschild Asset Management. Previously, he was quantitative analyst on volatility trading, hedge funds analyst, and head of financial engineering. He also teaches at ENSAI (National School for Statistics and Information Analysis in France), University of Paris, and University Denis Diderot. His research focuses on risk management and investment strategies. His teaching interests are in quantitative asset allocation and derivatives. Dr. Leblanc holds a masters degree of stochastic modeling and a PhD in applied mathematics from University of Paris, and a masters degree in finance from the Conservatoire National des Arts et Métiers.

Thomas Lejeune is an FRS-FNRS research fellow and PhD student at the Finance Department of HEC, University of Liège. His areas of research are macroeconomics and monetary economics, fixed income securities, and financial risk management. His doctoral thesis focuses on frictions in financial markets and their effects on monetary policy. He holds a master's degree in economics from the University of Liège.

Abraham Lioui is a Professor of Finance at EDHEC Business School, Nice, France. His research interests in finance focus on the valuation of financial assets, portfolio management, and risk management. His economics research investigates the relationship between monetary policy and the stock market. Professor Lioui has published widely in and refereed for leading finance and economic journals including *Management Science, Journal of Banking and Finance, Journal of Economic Dynamics and Control,* and *Journal of International Money and Finance* and is regularly invited to the program committee of the European Finance Association's annual conference. He holds a PhD in finance from the Sorbonne.

Harald Lohre is Portfolio Manager in the Quantitative Asset Allocation Team of Deka Investment. Before joining Deka he completed his doctoral studies in finance summa cum laude at the University of Zurich while working as a Quantitative Analyst at Union Investment. He holds a diploma in mathematical finance from the University of Konstanz. Dr. Lohre has published in such journals as *Applied Financial Economics, European Journal of Finance,* and *Journal of Investing.* He won The Sir Clive Granger Memorial Best Paper Prize in 2011 for "Data Snooping and the Golbal Accrual Anomaly."

Massimiliano Marzo is Associate Professor of Microstructure of Financial Markets at the University of Bologna. His research focuses on issues in interbank market, price discovery mechanisms across trading venues, and optimal execution methods. He has published in international peer-reviewed journals including the *Journal of Economics Dynamics and Control, Applied Economics, Structural Change and Economic Dynamics,* and *Journal of Policy Modelling.* He acts as a referee for the *Journal of Money, Credit and Banking, American Economic Review,* and *Structural Change and Economic Dynamics.* He acts as consultant for several trading and banking institutions both of national and international importance. He holds a PhD in economics from Yale University and a BS from University of Bologna.

Andrew Mason is a Lecturer in Finance at the University of Surrey. His research interests include style analysis and investment performance. He has more than 20 years' experience in investment, including positions as economist and investment strategist at Nomura Research Institute and Citicorp before moving into investment management. He held senior investment management roles at USS, one of the United Kingdom's largest pension funds, US mutual fund company Kemper, and was formerly the Head of Equities at Philips Pension Fund, one of the largest pension funds in Europe. He recently returned to academia and obtained a PhD in finance from Southampton University.

Sarah Müller is a doctoral candidate at EBS Business School in Wiesbaden, Germany. Her research lies in the field of hedge funds, with a strong focus on applied econometrics. During her studies, she spent a semester at the ESCP-EAP in Paris, France. Ms. Müller is a CFA charterholder and a member of the Germany CFA society. She works as an asset manager for the pension fund of a large German corporation where she is responsible for the asset classes UK and emerging markets equities as well as alternative assets. Ms. Müller holds an MS from BI Norwegian School of Management, Norway, and a Vordiplom (Bachelor equivalent) from the University of Bamberg, Germany.

Thorsten Neumann is Managing Director for Quant and Risk Management at Union Investment. As an expert in quantitative asset management techniques, he specializes in risk management, portfolio construction, rule-based alpha generation, and the design of investment processes and investment solutions. Prior positions at Deka Investment include Head of Quant Research and Investment Process Consulting, and at DZ Bank as a quantitative analyst. He holds a PhD in econometrics from Christian-Albrechts-University of Kiel and has published in journals such as, *Economic Inquiry, European Journal of Finance, Empirical Economics, Advances in Statistical Analysis,* and *Financial Markets and Portfolio Management.*

Sébastien Page is an Executive Vice President and Global Head of the Client Analytics in the Newport Beach office of PIMCO. Before joining PIMCO in 2010, he was a senior managing director and head of the portfolio and risk management group at State Street Associates, where he managed the firm's asset allocation advisory and currency management activities. Mr. Page has written and spoken extensively on issues pertaining to investing and risk management throughout his career. He won Bernstein-Fabozzi/Jacobs Levy Awards from the *Journal of Portfolio Management* in 2003 and 2010, as well as the Graham and Dodd Scroll Award for excellence in research from the *Financial Analysts Journal* in 2010. He has more than 10 years of experience and holds a masters degree in finance and a bachelors degree in business administration from Sherbrooke University in Quebec, Canada. Mr. Page holds the CFA designation.

Auke Plantinga is an Associate Professor in Finance at the University of Groningen. He specializes in performance measurement and attribution methodology, with a specialist interest in performance measurement in the context of asset liability management. He previously worked as an Associate Professor at the Vrije Universiteit Amsterdam and as a senior ALM consultant at Fortis Investments. He holds an MSc in finance and a PhD in economics from the University of Groningen.

Patrice Poncet is a Distinguished Professor of Finance at ESSEC Business School, Paris, France. He primarily teaches topics related to financial markets and the theory of finance. His research interests mostly focus on financial markets, asset pricing, portfolio management, and monetary economics. He has co-authored 12 books and has published more than 60 referred articles appearing in such journals as *Management Science, Journal of Banking and Finance, Journal of Economic Dynamics and Control, Journal of International Money and Finance*, and *European Economic Review*. Professor Poncet is associate editor of *Banks, Markets & Investors*, and a referee for a dozen international academic journals. He has been a Professor at the Sorbonne and a Visiting Scholar at New York University. Professor Poncet is a former President of the French Finance Association, and has been on the Board of the Parisian Stock Option Market. He holds a PhD from Northwestern University (Kellogg School), an MBA from ESSEC, and a Master in Law from Paris University (Panthéon-Assas).

Dianna C. Preece is a Professor of Finance at the University of Louisville where she has taught for more than 20 years. She teaches undergraduate classes in corporate finance, investments, and financial markets and institutions and MBA courses in corporate finance. Professor Preece also teaches in several banking schools including the Kentucky School of Banking and the Iowa School of Banking. She has published articles in investments and banking in such journals as the *Journal of Banking and Finance* and *Journal of Business Finance and Accounting*. Professor Preece received her DBA from the University of Kentucky and also holds the CFA designation.

Juliane Proelss is a Professor of Finance at the Trier University of Applied Sciences. She was a consultant for the Santander Consumer Bank in Risk Management. Her focus is on alternative investments, refinancing, and defaulted loans. She studied business administration at the University of Eichstaett-Ingolstadt and got a postgraduate diploma in commerce from the Lincoln University, Canterbury. She completed her PhD at the European Business School.

Eric J. Robbins is a Portfolio Manager and Senior Investment Analyst with Robbins Wealth Management in Erie, Pennsylvania. He specializes in strategic asset allocation and options-based strategies. His typical clients are retirees, who are in need of ongoing management of their investment portfolio, and professionals who are planning for their future retirement. Mr. Robbins has more than 13 years of experience in investment management. He is also a Lecturer in Finance at Penn State Erie. He has been married to his wife for 14 years and together they have two children. He holds a BA in accounting from Asbury University and an MBA from Gannon University. Mr. Robbins is also a CFA charterholder.

Cesare Robotti is a financial economist and Associate Policy Adviser with the financial group of the research department of the Federal Reserve Bank of Atlanta and an Affiliate Professor at EDHEC Business School. Dr. Robotti concentrates his research on empirical asset pricing and portfolio management. Before joining the Atlanta Fed in 2001, he was a teaching fellow at Boston College and an adjunct faculty member at Brandeis University. Dr. Robotti has also worked in the dealing room of Novara International Bank in Luxembourg and as a financial analyst at Cariplo Bank in Milan, Italy. He has published works in several leading academic journals and has presented papers and served as a discussant at various professional conferences. He holds a PhD in economics from Boston College, and a BA and an MA in economics from L. Bocconi University.

Gerasimos G. Rompotis is an Assistant Manager at International Certified Auditors in Greece and also a PhD candidate at the Faculty of Economics of the National and Kapodistrian University of Athens. His main area of research covers the evaluation of mutual fund managers' selection and market timing skills, the performance of ETFs, calendar effects on the performance and volatility of equity investments, and intervaling effects on the systematic risk of ETFs. His work has been published in various industry journals including the *Journal of Alternative Investments, Journal of Index Investing, Journal of Asset Management*, and the *Guide to Exchange Traded Funds and Indexing Innovations* issued by Institutional Investor Journals, including conferences held by the European Financial Management Association and the Hellenic Financial and Accounting Association.

Timothy P. Ryan, CIPM, is a Vice President and Head of Performance Measurement at Hartford Investment Management Company. In this role, Mr. Ryan is the department head responsible for GIPS compliance, return calculation, composite maintenance, peer ranking, and performance attribution support for this $100 billion-plus asset manager. For more than seven years, he was affiliated with Fidelity Management and Research Co. in Boston, culminating in the role of Director of Attribution Analysis following stints as Manager of Attribution Analysis and Fixed Income Performance Attribution Analyst. He is a frequent speaker and author on performance topics, serves on the editorial advisory board of the *Journal of Performance Measurement,* and also serves on the CIPM Association Advisory Council. Mr. Ryan is the 2004 recipient of the Dietz Award for Performance Measurement Literature and editor of the book *Portfolio Analysis*. He holds a BSBA cum laude from Suffolk University and earned entry into the Golden Key Honor Society during his MBA studies at Babson College.

Gabriele Sabato is an experienced risk management professional who has worked and researched in this field for more than 12 years. Currently, he is a Senior Manager in RBS Group Risk Management responsible for the oversight and coordination of policies, strategies, models, and governance of consumer and SMEs portfolios across the Group. Before joining RBS, Dr. Sabato worked three years in ABN AMRO Group Risk Management heading up the Group retail analytics team. He led several Basel II projects including models independent validation, Pillar I compliance, stress testing and ICAAP. Before joining the banking world, he spent four years in Experian as a business consultant developing and implementing credit risk models and strategies for several financial institutions across Europe. Dr. Sabato holds a PhD in finance from the University of Rome "La Sapienza" and during his doctoral studies, he spent one year at New York University Stern School of Business working with Prof. Edward Altman. He has published on risk management in such academic journals as the *Journal of Banking and Finance, Journal of Financial Services Research, Journal of Credit Risk,* and *ABACUS.*

Panagiotis Schizas is a Lecturer of Finance at the University of Peloponnese and Fixed Income Portfolio Manager of Marfin Asset Management in Greece. He was a visiting researcher at the B. Baruch Zicklin School of Business of City University of New York. His interests focus on quantitative trading strategies based on exchange traded funds where he created a novel market timing strategy. His research based on his doctoral work was among the all-time top 10 papers downloaded in the financial market category at SSRN. He holds a BA in economics from University of Athens, an MSc in financial management from University of Essex, and a PhD in applied financial econometrics from the University of Peloponnese in association with The Graduate Center of City University of New York.

Denis Schweizer is Assistant Professor of Alternative Investments at WHU–Otto Beisheim School of Management. His research interests include alternative investments and their economic consequences. He has published in such journals as *European Financial Management, International Journal of Theoretical and Applied Finance,* and *Review of Quantitative Finance and Accounting.* Before joining WHU, he studied business administration at the University of Frankfurt am Main and worked for UBS Investment Bank and as a Research Assistant at European Business School.

Hersh Shefrin is the Mario L. Belotti Professor of Finance at Santa Clara University. He has been studying the influence of psychology on economic and financial behavioral since the mid-1970s. His work with Meir Statman, published in the *Journal of Financial Economics* and the *Journal of Finance* represented the first applications of prospect theory to finance. He has authored several books. *Beyond Greed and Fear* provides a systematic treatment of behavioral finance, and was noted by JP Morgan Chase as one of the top 10 books published between 2000 and 2010. *A Behavioral Approach to Asset Pricing* develops a general unified behavioral pricing kernel treatment of asset pricing. *Behavioral Corporate Finance* is the first textbook with the purpose of teaching students the relevance of behavioral concepts to corporate finance. Professor Shefrin completed his PhD at the London School of Economics, holds a masters in mathematics from the University of Waterloo, and a bachelor of science from the University of Manitoba. He also holds an honorary doctorate from the University of Oulu, Finland.

J. Clay Singleton is the Cornell Professor of Finance at the Crummer Graduate School of Business at Rollins College. Before joining the Crummer faculty, he was Vice President of Ibbotson Associates and Senior Vice President for Curriculum and Examinations at the CFA Institute. Professor Singleton's research has been published in the *Journal of Finance, Financial Management,* and *Journal of Portfolio Management* among others. He is the author of *Core-Satellite Portfolio*

Management (McGraw-Hill) and co-author of *Survey Research in Corporate Finance* (Oxford University Press). Professor Singleton earned his BAS in political science from Washington University in St. Louis and his MBA and his PhD in business from the University of Missouri–Columbia, respectively. He holds the CFA designation.

Remus D. Valsan is a lecturer in corporate law at the University of Edinburgh and a doctoral candidate at McGill University. His research interests include corporate law, equity and trusts, and legal history. In his doctoral thesis, Mr. Valsan analyzes the development of fiduciary relationships from a historical and comparative perspective. He received his JD from Nicolae Titulescu University, Bucharest, Romania, and his LLM from the University of Alberta. Mr. Valsan also studied comparative law in Strasbourg, European antitrust law in Turin, and · Austrian Economics in New York.

Niklas Wagner is Professor of Finance at the DekaBank Chair in Finance and Financial Control at Passau University, Germany. His research interests cover asset pricing, market microstructure, risk management, and applied financial econometrics. Professor Wagner has published in various internationally recognized journals, such as the *Journal of Banking and Finance* and the *Journal of Empirical Finance*, and regularly serves as a referee to the finance community. His industry background is in asset management with HypoVereinsbank in Munich. He holds a PhD in finance from the University of Augsburg and previously held visiting positions at University of California–Berkeley and Stanford University.

Thomas Winterfeldt is a Risk Controller (Market Risk and Liquidity Risk) for Deutsche Genossenschafts-Hypothekenbank (DG HYP). Before moving to DG HYP he was a Credit Risk Controller for HSH Nordbank AG. He holds a diploma in business mathematics from the University of Rostock and a masters degree in quantitative finance from the Frankfurt School of Finance and Management.

Moin A. Yahya is an Associate Professor of Law at the University of Alberta. Currently, he is on leave to the Alberta Utilities Commission where he is one of the Commissioners. His research focuses on the law of economics of corporate law, antitrust law, securities law, and criminal law. He obtained his BA (Hons) in economics from the University of Alberta, where he also obtained his MA in economics. Professor Yahya received his PhD in economics from the University of Toronto, and his JD is from George Mason University School of Law, where he graduated summa cum laude and was the Robert A. Levy Fellow in Law and Liberty.

Paolo Zagaglia is a postdoctoral researcher at the University of Bologna, Department of Economics. He previously held positions at the Central Bank of Sweden, European Central Bank, and Bank of England. His research focuses on price discovery mechanisms, trade duration and forecasting models in finance and economics. He has published in international peer-review journals including

Energy Economics, Journal of Policy Modeling, and *Structural Change and Economic Dynamics* and *Applied Economics.* He has acted as a referee for *Macroeconomic Dynamics, Journal of Futures Markets, Energy Economics,* and the *Scandinavian Journal of Economics.* He holds a BS from the University of Ancona and a PhD in economics from Stockholm University.

Portfolio Theory and Management

1

Portfolio Theory and Management

An Overview

H. KENT BAKER
University Professor of Finance, Kogod School of Business,
American University

GREG FILBECK
Samuel P. Black III Professor of Insurance and Risk Management,
Penn State Erie, The Behrend College

Introduction

Portfolio management is an ongoing process of constructing portfolios that balances an investor's objectives with the portfolio manager's expectations about the future. This dynamic process provides the payoff for investors. In portfolio management, individual assets or investments are evaluated by their contribution to the risk and return of an investor's portfolio rather than in isolation. This is called the *portfolio perspective*. In this process, by constructing a diversified portfolio, a portfolio manager can reduce risk for a given level of expected return, compared to investing in an individual asset or security. According to modern portfolio theory (MPT), investors who do not follow a portfolio perspective bear risk that is not rewarded with greater expected return. Portfolio diversification works best when financial markets are operating normally, compared to periods of market turmoil, such as during the financial crisis of 2007–2008. During periods of turmoil, correlations tend to increase, thus reducing the benefits of diversification. *Correlation* is a standardized measure of comovement between returns of two securities or markets.

Portfolio Management Process

The *portfolio management process* consists of an integrated set of steps that a portfolio manager undertakes in a consistent manner to create and maintain an appropriate portfolio to meet a client's objectives. The objectives of different types of investors vary, reflecting their diverse needs and characteristics. That the objectives of individuals and other types of investors, such as banks, endowments, insurance companies, pension funds, mutual funds, and others, vary widely is not surprising. Thus, portfolio managers must tailor portfolios to meet the different objectives of their clients.

The portfolio management process consists of three major steps: planning, execution, and feedback (Maginn, Tuttle, Pinto, and McLeavey, 2007). Planning involves four major tasks: (1) understanding the client's needs, circumstances, and constraints; (2) creating an investment policy statement (IPS); (3) developing an investment strategy consistent with the IPS; and (4) specifying a performance benchmark. A portfolio manager is unlikely to produce good results for a client without understanding the client's needs, circumstances, and constraints. Thus, the planning step begins by analyzing an investor's risk tolerance and return objectives within the context of a variety of *constraints*, both *internal* (the client's liquidity needs, time horizon, and unique circumstances) and *external* (his tax situation and legal and regulatory requirements). *Risk tolerance* refers to an investor's capacity to accept risk. A client's overall risk tolerance depends not only on his ability to take risk, which relates to financial factors, but also on his willingness to take risk, which relates to psychological factors.

This analysis results in the portfolio manager creating an *investment policy statement*, which is a document clearly detailing the investor's investment objectives, constraints, and risk preferences. An IPS contains the following components: (1) a description of the client's circumstances, (2) the purpose of the IPS, (3) the duties and responsibilities of all parties, (4) procedures to update the IPS and to resolve problems, (5) the client's investment objectives and constraints, (6) investment guidelines, (7) an evaluation of performance, including a benchmark, and (8) appendices detailing the strategic asset allocation, permitted deviations, and rebalancing procedures.

The portfolio manager then needs to determine an overall investment strategy that is consistent with the IPS. An IPS provides a plan for achieving investment success through forcing investment discipline and ensuring that objectives are realistic. In devising a strategy, the portfolio manager forms long-term expectations about the capital markets, including forecasts of the risk-and-return characteristics of various asset classes. Part of this strategy entails developing a *strategic asset allocation* (SAA) specifying the percentage of allocations to each of the asset classes to be included in the portfolio. SAA provides the basic structure of a portfolio that the portfolio manager uses to determine the long-term policy for asset weights in a portfolio, which are modified infrequently. The SAA is based on the risk, returns, and correlations (comovements) of the asset classes. The final planning task is to identify or create a *benchmark*, which is a standard of comparison, or a comparison portfolio.

The second step in the portfolio management process is execution, which involves the following key tasks: (1) analyzing the risk-and-return characteristics of asset classes, (2) analyzing market conditions to identify attractive asset classes, (3) identifying attractive securities within asset classes (security selection), and (4) constructing the portfolio. During this step, the portfolio manager turns plans into reality. He examines the risk-and-return characteristics of each asset class and then considers how these characteristics interact from a portfolio per-spective. Given that capital-market conditions affect asset classes, the manager needs to form expectations about which market conditions are likely to prevail. These tasks involve considerable research on the part of the portfolio manager. Next, the manager identifies and selects attractive securities that fall within the asset classes specified by the IPS. In constructing a portfolio, the manager considers such factors as target or strategic asset allocations, individual security weightings, and risk management. As Madhavan, Treynor, and Wagner (2007, p. 637) note, "The portfolio decision is not complete until securities are bought and sold."

The portfolio manager sometimes temporarily moves away from the SAA either to reflect an investor's current circumstances that differ from the norm or because of changes in short-term capital-market expectations. In *tactical asset allocation* (TAA), the asset class mix in the portfolio is adjusted in an attempt to take advantage of changing market conditions. For example, the portfolio manager may engage in *market timing*, which involves shorter-term tactical deviations than the SAA. In TAA, perceived changes in the relative values of the various asset classes solely drive these adjustments (Reilly and Brown, 2000).

The final step in the portfolio management process is feedback, which consists of four components: (1) monitoring and updating an investor's needs, (2) moni-toring and updating market conditions, (3) rebalancing the portfolio as needed, and (4) evaluating and reporting performance. Over time, the investor's needs and circumstances and market and economic conditions change. Additionally, differences between a portfolio's current asset allocation and its SAA result from fluctuations in the market value of assets. Thus, the portfolio manager period-ically reviews and updates the IPS and rebalances the portfolio accordingly. *Rebalancing* involves adjusting the actual portfolio to the current SAA because of price changes in portfolio holdings.

Portfolio evaluation has three components: performance measurement, per-formance attribution, and performance appraisal (Bailey, Richards, and Tierney, 2007). *Performance measurement* involves calculating the portfolio's rate of return. Because many concepts and techniques are available for measuring returns, the portfolio manager must decide on the most appropriate ones for a given port-folio. *Performance attribution* involves comparing a portfolio's performance with that of a valid benchmark identified in the IPS and identifying and quantify-ing the sources of differential returns. In general, a portfolio's overall perfor-mance may be attributed to three main sources: decisions involving the SAA, security selection, and market timing (Maginn et al., 2007). Of these sources, studies suggest that long-term asset allocation decisions best explain investment performance over time (Brinson, Hood, and Beebower, 1986; Brinson, Singer, and Beebower, 1991; Ibbotson and Kaplan, 2000; Xiong, Ibbotson, Idzorek, and Chen, 2010). *Performance appraisal* involves a quantitative assessment of the manager's *investment skill*, which refers to his ability to outperform a spe-cific benchmark consistently over time. Typically, the portfolio manager uses risk-adjusted performance-appraisal measures. Once the investment's performance is evaluated, the portfolio manager needs to report the results. The *Global Investment Performance Standards (GIPS)* offer a recognized approach to providing performance information (Lawton and Remington, 2007).

MODERN PORTFOLIO THEORY

The world of portfolio management has expanded greatly especially during the past three decades, and along with it, so have the theoretical tools necessary to appropriately service the needs of both private-wealth and institutional clients. While the foundations of modern finance emerged during the 1950s and asset-pricing models were developed in a portfolio context in the 1960s, portfolio management has further expanded into more complex models. With respect to modern finance, the mean-variance efficient frontier framework (Markowitz, 1952, 1959), a bottom-up model for portfolio construction, has seen top-down approaches emerge. With respect to asset-pricing models, one-factor models using a single broad-market index for the basis of pricing, such as the capital-asset pricing model (CAPM; Sharpe, 1964; Lintner, 1965), have been replaced by more complex models that include other factors such as market capitalization, style, and momentum (Jagadeesh and Titman, 1993; Carhart, 1997; Fama and French, 2004; Asem and Tian, 2010).

Traditional finance models, such as the efficient market hypothesis (EMH) (Fama, 1970, 1991), are based on the assumption that the market as a whole acts rationally although some individual investors may not. In an efficient financial market, security prices always fully reflect the available information. Thus, an average investor cannot hope to consistently beat the market. If this condition holds, then expending vast resources to analyze, select, and trade securities is a wasted effort. Investors are better served by passively holding the market portfolio and ignoring active money management. As Shleifer (2000, p. 1) notes, "If the EMH holds, the market truly knows best." However, the inefficient market makes many mistakes in pricing securities (Haugen, 2001). Haugen (2004) makes the case for an inefficient stock market, where the complexity and uniqueness of investor interactions have important market-pricing implications.

The traditional assumption of rational investor behavior with decisions made on the basis of statistical distributions has expanded to consider the behavioral attributes of clients (Kahneman and Tversky, 1979; Kahneman, Slovic, and Tversky, 1982) as well as goals-based strategies (Shefrin and Statman, 2000). For example, in assessing risk tolerance for a private-wealth client, portfolio managers must consider not only the client's ability but also the client's risk tolerance in determining an appropriate asset allocation.

Behavioral finance applies psychology to financial behavior and examines its effects on financial markets (Shefrin, 2000). As Nofsinger (2005, p. 5) remarks, "Even the smartest people are affected by psychological biases, but traditional finance has considered this irrelevant." In inefficient markets, securities prices can deviate from their rational levels and be based on biased estimates of intrinsic value. Behavioral finance can help explain not only how investors actually behave and how markets function but also how improvement can occur. Baker and Nofsinger (2010) provide a comprehensive discussion of behavioral finance.

Over time, a larger menu of investment options has been another factor that has expanded choices beyond traditional asset classes (e.g., stocks and bonds), taking them into alternative investments (e.g., commodities, hedge funds, private equity, and real estate). *Alternative investments* are groups of investments with risk-and-return characteristics that differ markedly from those of traditional stock and bond investments. Because investors now have greater access to the international markets, a strong case also exists for global asset allocations. Moreover, with the rapid expansion of the derivatives market, more liquid, synthetic exposure to asset classes and risk management strategies have become more accessible and sophisticated.

Performance evaluation and presentation have taken on greater importance since the 1990s. As the development of multifactor models to explain portfolio performance emerged, the portfolio management community began to recognize the importance of appropriate benchmarking for performance so that "apples-for-apples" comparisons could be made (Bailey, 1992a, 1992b). As Bailey (1992a) points out, an appropriate benchmark should be unambiguous, reflective of current investment opinions, specified in advance, investible, measurable, and appropriate based on similarity of style. Style analysis and ultimately custom benchmarking allow managers to be evaluated using a fairer representation of portfolio performance (Sharpe, 1992; Bailey and Tierney, 1993). Style analysis can be performed in a top-down (e.g., a returns-based style analysis) or a bottom-up (e.g., a holdings-based style analysis) manner. Top-down style analysis typically involves the use of multiple regression models, with the portfolio return serving as the dependent variable and asset-class benchmarks serving as the independent variables. Bottom-up analysis consists of a security-by-security classification approach. A custom, or "normal," benchmark represents a vendor-constructed passive representation of an active manager's style. Risk management in a portfolio context is often accomplished through the use of derivative securities. Chance (2003) presents an overview of using forwards, futures, options, and swaps as a basis of altering the risk profile to desired levels for a portfolio.

GIPS, which are offered by the CFA Institute (2010), provide a standardized set of performance presentation guidelines that allows investors to compare portfolio performance once returns are properly evaluated and attributed. Beyond the impact of turnover on after-tax returns and with advancements in technology, key pieces of this assessment now include more emphasis on efficient trade execution and trading strategies as well as the analysis of implicit and explicit transaction costs (Wagner and Edwards, 1993).

Recent financial crises have called into question whether the theories developed by the financial pioneers were correct and whether practitioners "got it right" in managing assets. Alternative investments have received increased attention as investors look to benefit from eliminating or altering their systematic risk exposure in portfolios (Anson, 2006). Exchange-traded funds (ETFs), with origins going back to the late 1970s and early 1980s, are one of the most successful financial innovations of the last two decades (Gastineau, 2001). The majority of

ETFs seek to replicate the performance of specific domestic, sector, regional, or international indexes. Another innovation has been the development of socially responsible investing in an attempt to generate long-term, competitive financial returns and positive societal impact (Sparkes, 2002). As portfolio management continues to develop, foundational theoretical tools, financial innovation, and increasingly more sophisticated methods of analysis will assist academics and practitioners as they address the concerns of the investing public.

PURPOSE OF THE BOOK

Portfolio management today emerges as a dynamic process, which is continuing to evolve at a rapid pace. The purpose of *Portfolio Theory and Management* is to take readers from the foundations of portfolio management, reviewing the contributions of the financial pioneers, up to the latest trends emerging within the context of special topics. The book includes discussions of portfolio theory and management both before and after the financial crisis of 2007–2008. This volume provides a critical reflection of what worked and what did not work viewed from the perspective of the crisis. Further, the book is not restricted to the US market but takes a more global focus by highlighting cross-country differences and practices.

Readers of this book will have the opportunity to gain a historical grounding as well as an understanding of the latest trends within the field of portfolio theory and management. Those interested in a broad survey of portfolio management will benefit as well as those looking for more in-depth presentations of specific areas within the field of study. Both financial theory and empirical work are also featured. Cited research studies are presented in a straightforward manner focusing on the key findings, rather than the details of mathematical frameworks. Contributions emerge from a group of noted authors, featuring the work of a mix of academics and practitioners. The vast majority of authors hold advanced degrees, mainly doctorates, and some hold the Chartered Financial Analyst (CFA) designation, which is the industry standard for excellence in the areas of security analysis and portfolio management.

FEATURES OF THE BOOK

Portfolio Theory and Management has several distinguishing features:

- Perhaps the book's most distinctive feature is that it provides a comprehensive discussion of portfolio theory and management and empirical work and practice within the various areas covered. The book attempts not only to blend the conceptual world of scholars with the pragmatic view of practitioners in the field but also to synthesize important and relevant research studies in a succinct and clear manner, including those on recent developments.
- The book contains contributions from distinguished scholars, both academics and practitioners, from around the world. The breadth of contributors assures a variety of perspectives and a rich interplay of ideas.

- When discussing the results of empirical studies that link theory and practice, the authors' objective is to distill them to their essential content so that they are understandable to readers. The book includes theoretical and mathematical derivations to the extent that they may be necessary and useful to readers.
- Each chapter ends with a summary and conclusions that provide the key lessons of the chapter.
- All chapters except this chapter contain discussion questions that help to reinforce key principles and concepts. Guideline answers are presented at the end of the book. This feature should be especially relevant to faculty and students using the book in classes.

INTENDED AUDIENCE

Given its features, *Portfolio Theory and Management* should be of interest to a wide audience, including students, academics, practitioners, and investors. However, this book is not intended for the novice, in that it assumes readers have a good grounding in investments, economics, and quantitative methods. In fact, some chapters require a more advanced knowledge of statistics to fully grasp the mathematics underlying the content. The core audience that this book is written for is upper-level business undergraduates and graduate students (primarily those earning an MBA or an MSF (Master of Science in Finance), but doctoral students in finance are also likely to find this book useful in providing an overview of this field. Academics may use this book not only in their advanced undergraduate and graduate portfolio theory and management courses but also to understand the various strands of research emerging in this area. Practitioners can use the book to navigate through the key areas in portfolio management. Individual investors will also benefit as they attempt to expand their knowledge base and apply the concepts contained within the book to the management of their own portfolios.

Structure of the Book

The remaining 29 chapters are organized into seven sections. A brief synopsis of each chapter by section follows.

SECTION I. PORTFOLIO THEORY AND ASSET PRICING

Chapters 2 through 4 provide the foundations of modern portfolio theory and asset pricing from both traditional and behavioral finance perspectives.

Chapter 2 Modern Portfolio Theory (Eric Jacquier)
This chapter surveys modern portfolio theory, which is one of the most spectacular developments of finance in the last 50 years. It starts with the basic one-period setup, which is based on the assumption of normality, reviewing the successive contributions of Markowitz and Sharpe. The chapter then discusses

the multiperiod extension and Merton's concept of optimal asset allocation. The second part of the chapter shows how to extend the framework to allow for parameter uncertainty. In the discussion, the chapter also briefly reviews needed concepts, such as predictive density, shrinkage, and how the Bayesian framework allows the incorporation of prior views to improve on the precision of estimates necessary in the portfolio construction process.

Chapter 3 Asset Pricing Theories, Models, and Tests (Nikolay Gospodinov and Cesare Robotti)

An important but still partially unanswered question in the investment field is why various assets earn substantially different returns on average. Financial economists have typically addressed this question in the context of theoretically or empirically motivated asset-pricing models. Since many of the proposed "risk" theories provide plausible explanations, a common practice in the literature is to apply the models to the data and perform "horse races" among competing asset-pricing specifications. A "good" asset-pricing model should produce small-pricing (expected-return) errors based on a set of test assets and should deliver reasonable estimates of the underlying market and economic-risk premia. This chapter provides an up-to-date review of the statistical methods that are typically used to estimate, evaluate, and compare competing asset-pricing models. The analysis also highlights several pitfalls in the current econometric practice and offers suggestions for improving empirical tests.

Chapter 4 Asset Pricing and Behavioral Finance (Hersh Shefrin)

Behavioral asset pricing focuses on the manner in which investor psychology can create gaps between the market prices of securities and their corresponding fundamental values. This chapter describes the main tenets of behavioral asset pricing by tracing its history both empirically and theoretically. Because of its focus on the gap between price and value, the behavioral framework has come to be viewed as an alternative to the neoclassical-based efficient market framework. The debate between behaviorists and neoclassicists has shed light on weaknesses in both approaches. The chapter discusses these weaknesses and concludes that going forward, the field of finance would benefit by bringing together the psychological insights from behavioral finance and the rigorous approach of neoclassical finance.

SECTION II. THE INVESTMENT POLICY STATEMENT AND FIDUCIARY DUTIES

The four chapters in this section focus on topics that are part of the first step in the portfolio management process—planning. Chapter 5 deals with risk tolerance, which is one of the key elements addressed in constructing an IPS. Chapters 6 and 7 discuss the development of an IPS from individual and institutional perspectives, respectively. Chapter 8 focuses on the responsibilities and legalities of managers of investment portfolios. When portfolio managers serve as fiduciaries, they have a special relationship of trust and responsibilities with respect to other parties.

Chapter 5 Assessing Risk Tolerance (Sherman D. Hanna, Michael A. Guillemette, and Michael S. Finke)

Assessing risk tolerance is an important part of advising clients about portfolio selections. The expected utility approach underlying portfolio advice assumes that a household has some level of risk aversion by which its utility is determined based on different wealth or consumption levels. Therefore, a household's risk aversion or the inverse—its risk tolerance—is a key factor in determining the optimal portfolio for a household. However, risk capacity, based on wealth and the investment horizon, is also crucial in determining the optimal portfolio advice. This chapter provides a discussion of methods for estimating risk tolerance and the limitations of alternative measures.

Chapter 6 Private Wealth Management (Dianna Preece)

Private wealth management is a specialized field focused on investment management for high net-worth individuals and families. The process is complex and must be customized to the individual or family. Historically, the assumption that investors were risk averse resulted in forecasts based on rational expectations, with their assets considered in a portfolio context. Increasingly, accepted behavioral models indicate that investors do not necessarily follow the tenets of modern portfolio theory but are instead loss averse, have biased expectations, and do not integrate assets. These models assume that individual financial circumstances are unique, and constructing an IPS is a critical step in understanding the investor's goals. The risk-and-return objectives of the individual or family are specified in the IPS along with constraints that are relevant to their portfolio. Liquidity needs and taxation are especially important. The portfolio asset allocation is a function of risk-and-return objectives and the investor's constraints. Retirement planning and estate planning are also part of the process.

Chapter 7 Institutional Wealth Management (Eric J. Robbins)

An *institutional investment policy statement* (IIPS) is a formal document designed to help guide the investment process for institutions. Although this document is not currently required by regulation, it is a very useful tool in managing a pool of assets in the best interests of the beneficiaries. In the volatility of modern markets, letting emotions and short-term trends dictate an investment strategy can easily happen. The IIPS is designed to help mitigate this natural tendency and instead focus on long-term goals. The primary factors considered in creating an IIPS are the company's objectives, risk tolerance, and unique constraints. Each type of institutional investor will have a different blend of needs within this framework and will require a customized plan for investing.

Chapter 8 Fiduciary Duties and Responsibilities of Portfolio Managers (Remus D. Valsan and Moin A. Yahya)

The rules governing persons occupying a fiduciary role form a dynamic area of law. With deep historical roots, fiduciary relations have expanded beyond the established categories, such as trust-beneficiary, agent-principal, or director-corporation, to include any person who has power or discretion over another's interests coupled with an express or implied undertaking to act exclusively in the other's service. Managers of investment portfolios, such as trustees, agents, financial advisers, or corporate directors, may be subject to the strict requirements of fiduciary law in various capacities. Although the default fiduciary rules are very strict, courts and legislators have proven willing to take into account commercial realities and relax the standard prohibitions of conflict of interest by imposing lower benchmarks and by allowing parties in a fiduciary relation to contract out proscriptive rules.

SECTION III. ASSET ALLOCATION AND PORTFOLIO CONSTRUCTION

The six chapters in this section deal with elements of the first and second steps in the portfolio management process—planning and execution. Chapter 9 provides an introduction to asset allocation and examines both SAA and TAA. Chapters 10 and 11 discuss various types of asset allocation models, with chapter 10 being a mathematically intensive chapter. Chapters 12 and 13 examine portfolio construction and asset allocation with an emphasis on downside risk. Chapter 14 discusses the role of alternative investments in a portfolio and focuses on their risk-and-return profiles.

Chapter 9 The Role of Asset Allocation in the Investment Decision-Making Process (James L. Farrell, Jr.)

This chapter focuses on asset allocation, which is an important aspect in the investment decision-making process. Asset allocation has the potential to add the most to longer-term performance if executed properly or to detract greatly if done poorly. SAA takes a longer-term approach. One approach to SAA, called the *historic approach*, is to simply extrapolate the risk and return of asset classes experienced over, say, a period starting 80 years prior and extending into the future. Over such a long period, the economy experiences many different economic episodes. An alternative is the *scenario approach*, which forecasts for a shorter three- to five-year period and allows for accommodating such economic episodes. The scenario approach requires greater skill and analysis to execute than the historic approach. TAA is a complementary approach to the scenario approach and looks at a much shorter-time horizon of, say, one to three years. TAA has potential to add value by taking advantage of shorter-term opportunities. At the same time, this approach presents greater risk, which the portfolio manager or investor needs to consider.

Chapter 10 Asset Allocation Models (J. Clay Singleton)

Actively managing a portfolio involves three main activities: asset allocation (designing and maintaining the relative asset-class weights), asset selection (selecting assets to match the allocation), and market timing (deciding when and how much to invest). This chapter looks at asset allocation models—theoretical and practical templates that active asset managers use to make the asset allocation decision. Many observers, influenced by a continuum of research, believe that asset allocation is by far the most influential factor explaining the variability in portfolio performance. Only recently has research supported the roughly equal importance of asset selection with asset allocation, with market timing a distant third. Regardless of the precise influence accorded to any of the three activities of active management, asset allocation is an essential ingredient in portfolio design and performance.

Chapter 11 Preference Models in Portfolio Construction and Evaluation (Massimo Guidolin)

This chapter reviews the role of preference-, or utility-, based asset allocation models in normative portfolio theory. After presenting relevant definitions and tools from the theory of decision making under uncertainty, the chapter surveys moment-based preference functionals and introduces concepts from the literature on portfolio decisions made by ambiguity-averse, robust optimizers. An illustrative back-testing exercise reveals that preference-based models may fail to deliver an ex-post–realized performance that outperforms typical benchmarks. However, this is unlikely for medium-term (6- and 12-month) risk-averse investors, who are characterized by having preferences such as power utility of smooth, ambiguity-averse preferences that overweight higher-order moments and the tail dynamics of the distribution of terminal wealth, in comparison with standard mean-variance preferences.

Chapter 12 Portfolio Construction with Downside Risk (Harald Lohre, Thorsten Neumann, and Thomas Winterfeldt)

In portfolio construction, an optimal trade-off is sought between a portfolio's mean return and its associated risk. Since risk may not be properly described by return volatility, portfolios are optimized in this chapter with respect to various measures of downside risk in an empirical out-of-sample setting. These optimizations are successful for most of the investigated measures when assuming the perfect foresight of expected returns. Moreover, some of these findings continue to hold when using more naïve return estimates. The reductions in downside risk are most convincing for semivariance, semideviation, and conditional value at risk (VaR), while VaR and skewness appear rather useless for portfolio construction purposes.

Chapter 13 Asset Allocation with Downside Risk Management (Joshua M. Davis and Sebastien Page)

The financial crisis of 2007–2008 has sparked a renewed skepticism of portfolio theory and financial engineering. As a result, key changes are taking place in how investors manage risk, now looking at it from the top down. Asset allocators have become increasingly aware of the pitfalls of a naïve approach to portfolio engineering that relies on the normal distribution and that fails to address downside risk. Additionally, asset classes are no longer the optimal way to look at diversification; instead, risk-factor diversification is becoming the focus. This chapter concentrates on these key changes. It presents the theoretical foundations behind the risk-factor approach to asset allocation, demonstrates how risk concentration leads to tail risk, and analyzes the costs and benefits of tail-risk hedging in practice.

Chapter 14 Alternative Investments (Lars Helge Hass, Denis Schweizer, and Juliane Proelss)

The monthly return distributions of alternative assets are generally not normally distributed and typically show significantly smoothed returns, which can lead to an underestimation of risk. Furthermore, portfolio optimization in the mean-variance framework that includes alternative assets is suboptimal. This is because the variance of the return distributions for these investments fails to adequately capture all risks. This chapter provides an estimate of the efficient frontier for portfolios, consisting of numerous alternative assets as well as traditional asset classes, such as equities and bonds. This estimation enables incorporating the special characteristics of alternative investments, especially downside risk, in the optimization procedure for mixed-asset portfolios. Within this approach, mixed-asset portfolios containing a majority of alternative investments can be used to illustrate the previously unknown effects of skewness and excess kurtosis on the efficient frontier. The evidence shows that alternative investments are ideally suited to reduce portfolio risk and enhance risk-adjusted performance.

SECTION IV. RISK MANAGEMENT

This section consists of two chapters. Chapters 15 and 16 examine various types of risk that portfolio managers need to consider as well as how to manage these risks.

Chapter 15 Measuring and Managing Market Risk (Christoph Kaserer)

Market risk, which is caused by fluctuating market prices, is an extremely important risk not only for all institutional investors but also for large corporations and wealthy individuals. Therefore, the appropriate measurement and management of this risk is of considerable importance. This chapter examines measurement models for market risk including their extensions that have been contributed by the recent literature. In this context, the primary stylized facts emerging from this literature are discussed, such as the fat-tails phenomenon, volatility clustering, and serial correlation. Moreover, the necessity of integrating liquidity risk into risk management models is discussed as well. Finally, the impact of model risk is investigated, pointing out that model risk is both a statistical problem and a management problem.

Chapter 16 Measuring and Managing Credit and Other Risks (Gabriele Sabato)

During the last 40 years, risk management has evolved tremendously. The technologies and methodologies to measure risks have reached impressive levels of sophistication and complexity. However, the financial crisis of 2007–2008 clearly demonstrates that substantial improvements in the way financial institutions measure and manage risks are still urgently needed. This chapter provides an analysis and discussion of risk management as well as several proposals on how the financial industry should evolve. In particular, it suggests that financial institutions need to improve their capital-allocation strategies to define a clear risk-appetite framework by taking the following actions: (1) implementing true enterprise risk management programs, which measure and aggregate all risk types; and (2) redefining the role of the risk function within the governance of financial organizations. Improving the methods used to measure risks and implementing the proposed changes in risk management would allow financial institutions to restore the trust of markets and customers and to move forward into a new risk management era.

SECTION V. PORTFOLIO EXECUTION, MONITORING, AND REBALANCING

Having created the IPS and determined the appropriate asset allocation strategy, the portfolio manager moves on to step 1, planning. In step 2, he must analyze the appropriate method for executing the strategy, and in step 3, he monitors the strategy over time and determines the parameters necessary to justify portfolio rebalancing. Chapters 17 and 18 apply quantitative-based techniques in executing trading strategies, while chapter 19 introduces successful market-timing methods based on technical analysis techniques.

Chapter 17 Trading Strategies, Portfolio Monitoring, and Rebalancing (Riccardo Cesari and Massimiliano Marzo)

Trading strategies translate the goals and constraints of asset management into dynamic, intertemporal, and coherent portfolio decisions. Under special assumptions, myopic portfolio policies are shown to be optimal and constant over time. In general, however, both optimal theoretical portfolios and current portfolio positions are subject to random movements, making periodic monitoring and rebalancing necessary. Transaction and monitoring costs create a trade-off between the cost of not being at the optimal allocation (a tracking error) and the cost of swapping a current portfolio for an optimal one. Optimal rebalancing results in the replacement of the optimal allocation with a no-trade region delimited by rebalance boundaries. The factors influencing the boundaries and the rebalancing decisions can be analytically and numerically explained. Popular rebalancing rules imply a substantial amount of excess trading costs, but they can generate positive net returns in the case of mean-reverting market regimes.

Chapter 18 Effective Trade Execution (Riccardo Cesari, Massimiliano Marzo, and Paolo Zagaglia)

This chapter examines the role of algorithmic trading in modern financial markets. Additionally, it describes order types, characteristics, and special features of algorithmic trading under the lens provided by the large development of high-frequency trading technology. Special order types are examined together with an intuitive description of the implied dynamics of the order book conditional to special orders (iceberg and hidden). The chapter provides an analysis of the transaction costs associated with trading activity and examines the most common trading strategy employed in the market. It also examines optimal execution strategy, with the description of the efficient trading frontier. These concepts represent the tools needed to understand the most recent innovations in financial markets and the most recent advances in microstructures research.

Chapter 19 Market Timing Methods and Results (Panagiotis Schizas)

This chapter provides an overview of market-timing methods and explains the concepts that modelers and finance practitioners use professionally in the world of investments. The beauty of trading is the ease of applying a predefined set of rules in order to identify market trends. The chapter also describes the set of indicators and conditions needed for each strategy to be profitable and the outcome of each of strategy. In recent years, quantitative trading has been one of the most applicable ways of investing. Recent evidence shows that a successful quantitative strategy is linked to relative pricing. Thus, this chapter focuses on several mean-reversion strategies that depend on time-varying relative returns and volatilities.

SECTION VI. EVALUATING AND REPORTING PORTFOLIO PERFORMANCE

Chapters 20, 21, and 22 discuss how portfolio performance and attribution analysis are important aspects of the portfolio management process in determining whether constructed portfolios achieve target returns on a macro level and are the drivers of that performance on a micro level. Style analysis, discussed in chapter 23, allows for portfolios to be evaluated against a benchmark of similar style. Portfolios must be constructed within the risk-tolerance constraints often achieved through the use of derivative securities, discussed in chapter 24. Chapter 25 presents industry standards for performance presentation, which allow clients to evaluate portfolio performance in a standardized manner.

Chapter 20 Evaluating Portfolio Performance: Reconciling Asset Selection and Market Timing (Arnaud Cavé, Georges Hübner, and Thomas Lejeune)

This chapter presents the major approaches for assessing portfolio performance in the presence of asset selection and market-timing skills. Given the difficulty of reconciling these two performance drivers, several ways to get a synthetic measure are proposed, but they do not fully reflect the joint qualities displayed by the portfolio manager. In a recently suggested option-replication approach, the linear and quadratic coefficients of the Treynor and Mazuy regression are combined to assess performance in the presence of market timing. This new correction has the potential to overcome the "artificial timing" bias and delivers encouraging results on a sample of 1,413 US mutual funds selected for an empirical analysis. Unlike alternative approaches proposed in the literature, most positive market timers seem to be rewarded for the convexity they add to their portfolio while negative market timers are penalized, and a correlation between abnormal performance and the convexity parameter is found.

Chapter 21 Benchmarking (Abraham Lioui and Patrice Poncet)
The practice of benchmarking is booming in the delegated portfolio management
industry. As an asset-allocation tool, benchmarking is a reference to be followed
by the manager in a more or less strict manner. As a tool for measuring relative
performance, benchmarking helps in assessing the manager's skills involving market timing and/or security selection, and allows for meaningful definitions of the
tracking error and the information ratio. The closely related issues of principal-
agent contracting, compensation schemes and implicit incentives, and optimal
benchmarking are discussed at length. The evolution in the design of appropriate
benchmarks is also analyzed.

Chapter 22 Attribution Analysis (Nanne Brunia and Auke Plantinga)
This chapter discusses performance-attribution models that allow the observer
to identify the timing and selection skills of portfolio managers. The focus is on
holdings-based attribution models, because they generate more precise measurements of managers' skills than return-based models. The discussion starts with the
basic attribution model and how to extend this model to accommodate internationally diversified portfolios. The basic model can also be extended to improve
the precision of the measurements by allowing the user to create a risk-adjusted
performance attribution without the need to run a time-series regression model.
In order to capture the impact of investor timing, performance-attribution models
can be extended further by including a component based on the internal rate of
return.

Chapter 23 Equity Investment Styles (Andrew Mason)
Establishing a meaningful peer group or benchmark is crucial to those involved
in selecting and evaluating investment funds and for those studying the risk-
return profiles of those funds. This chapter outlines the developments in theoretical and empirical studies of equity-investment styles. The review considers
equity-investment styles, the classification of stocks, multidimensional classification, growth-value orientation, funds styles, and the performance of investment
funds. *Investment styles* are groups of portfolios sharing common characteristics
that behave similarly under varying conditions. Style analysis focuses on two key
areas: portfolio holdings and portfolio returns. This type of analysis has evolved
toward using more sophisticated growth-value orientation methods, although
there is no universally accepted approach. Such developments allow more differentiated analysis of investment-fund styles and improve the identification of peer
groups and appropriate benchmarks. The recent developments in performance
analysis underline the importance of establishing the appropriate benchmark or
peer group, and that is the role of style analysis.

Chapter 24 Use of Derivatives (Matthieu Leblanc)
Derivatives are an ancient commercial practice. In the financial world, those products have become essential tools for any professional investor. Asset managers use
them in their investment processes to take advantage of leverage, reactivity, hedging, and low transaction costs. However, the features of these instruments require

technical expertise that is not always part of managers' backgrounds. Investors often fear derivatives because they are poorly understood and sometimes misused. This chapter reaffirms the importance of futures and options and presents the main uses for risk and performance management.

Chapter 25 Performance Presentation (Timothy P. Ryan)

Performance presentation is highly important to investment managers, regulators, and existing clients, as well as prospective clients and their intermediaries. Through performance presentations, portfolio or strategy performance and implementation are clarified in a direct and insightful manner. Presentation content may include the absolute performance of portfolios or strategies, peer-relative performance, index-relative performance, key drivers of performance, asset allocations or exposure weights, ex-post risk-reward characteristics, style analysis, and weighted-average-portfolio characteristics. Performance presentations that are widely distributed and used by prospective clients or their intermediaries usually have specific content and a presentation format that is consistent with industry guidelines and/or required by rules-based regulators. One-on-one presentations and presentations for existing clients on their portfolios typically involve content that is less specific and based on fewer rules and regulator requirements.

SECTION VII. SPECIAL TOPICS

Financial innovations and strategies continue to emerge over time. Chapter 26 shows that exchange-traded funds (ETFs) have provided investors with an alternative to mutual funds as a means of gaining broad market exposure. Chapters 27, 28, and 29 discuss the growing importance of specific alternative investments— hedge funds, private equity funds, and venture capital—in achieving portfolio goals. Chapter 30 focuses on socially responsible investing.

Chapter 26 Exchange Traded Funds: The Success Story of the Last Two Decades (Gerasimos G. Rompotis)

This chapter discusses ETFs, which are one of the most successful financial innovations of the last two decades. A brief historical analysis of the evolution in the ETF market is provided. Next, the unique characteristics and benefits that made ETFs proliferate among investors worldwide are discussed. Several types of ETFs are described as well as the various trading strategies available with ETFs. Then, the chapter focuses on the empirical findings of the literature regarding the competition between ETFs and traditional mutual funds, the tracking ability for ETFs and the factors that usually affect their replication efficiency, and whether the divergence between the trading prices and net-asset values of ETFs indicates future returns.

Chapter 27 The Past, Present, and Future of Hedge Funds (Roland Füss and Sarah Müller)

The finance literature documents that investors can benefit from adding hedge funds as part of the alternative asset class to their asset allocation. By outlining the most important literature, this chapter gives a comprehensive overview on the fundamental characteristics of hedge funds and provides evidence supporting their use in a tactical and strategic portfolio-allocation context. Because the return properties of hedge funds differ from those of traditional asset classes, this chapter discusses appropriate performance measures as well as enhanced portfolio-optimization approaches that can be used when considering hedge funds in mixed-asset portfolios. It also includes information on relevant organizational and regulatory issues. This chapter also focuses on the increased systemic relevance of hedge funds for financial markets, the complex connections they have with other financial institutions, and the implications for future regulatory developments in this industry.

Chapter 28 Portfolio and Risk Management for Private Equity Fund Investment (Axel Buchner and Niklas Wagner)

Private-equity investments make up large portions of institutional investors' risky asset allocations. Hence, the risk of the asset class needs to be properly understood and managed. As private equity represents a relatively opaque and illiquid asset class, standard models are inapplicable. This chapter provides a novel framework based on modeling the stochastic cash flow dynamics of private-equity funds. The model consists of a mean-reverting square-root process, which represents a fund's capital drawdowns, and a geometric Brownian motion with a time-dependent drift, which captures the typical time pattern of capital distributions. The empirical analysis reveals that the model can be calibrated to a given fund's cash flow data. The chapter presents several application examples of the model in the portfolio and risk-management areas.

Chapter 29 Venture Capital (Pascal Gantenbein, Reto Forrer, and Nils Herold)

The venture capital industry has seen tremendous growth over the past two decades. However, research provides mixed results for its investment outcomes and reveals several methodological challenges and constraints arising from the lack of a comprehensive historical data set. Strong evidence suggests that a small number of funds perform extremely well while the majority of venture-capital funds underperform in public stock markets. Furthermore, academic research points out several distinct determinants of investment outcomes. Various studies, for instance, indicate that the experience and skills of both the general and the limited partners behind the fund have a strong effect on its performance. Additionally, evidence of performance persistence exists as well as of the strong impact of macroeconomic conditions. The venture-capital industry exhibits a cyclical pattern characterized by repeated periods of dramatic growth followed by slumps. Yet, whether booms are caused by fundamental factors or constitute an overreaction to perceived investment opportunities is unclear.

Chapter 30 Socially Responsible Investing: From the Fringe to the Mainstream (Hunter Holzhauer)

This chapter provides an introduction into the growing field of socially responsible investing (SRI), which has emerged over the last few decades from a fringe investment activity into the mainstream. With the amount of attention and investment SRI funds have begun to receive, navigating these waters has become extremely important for portfolio managers, pension advisers, charity trustees, corporate executives, and even individual investors. The first half of the chapter analyzes the changing tides of SRI by providing a concise portrayal of the progression of the SRI market, with special attention given to the South African–apartheid and subsequent divestments. The second half of the chapter includes a literature review of empirical findings of SRI performance compared to conventional benchmarks. The review focuses on evidence from equity funds, fixed-income funds, international funds, indices, and "sin" stocks. The chapter concludes with a brief summary of the SRI literature including critiques.

Summary and Conclusions

Since the 1950s and especially during the last few decades, portfolio management has become a more science-based discipline. Numerous theoretical advances combined with empirical research have provided portfolio managers with new concepts, insights, and techniques for making sound investment decisions. Additionally, portfolio managers now have a much larger array of investment products available to them than in the past. Enhancements in technology and evolving market structures have provided new challenges to professional money managers. These changes pose not only challenges but also opportunities for portfolio managers and investors alike.

Both the theory and practice of portfolio management have been moving ahead at a dizzying pace. Thus, gaining an understanding of the key principles and concepts of portfolio management and relevant empirical evidence is more important than ever. Although this is a formidable task, reading this book can help provide a better understanding about the existing state of knowledge and the challenges remaining in the area of portfolio theory and management. Enjoy the journey!

References

Anson, Mark J. P. 2006. *Handbook of Alternative Investments*, 2nd ed. Hoboken, NJ: John Wiley and Sons.

Asem, Ebenezer, and Gloria Y. Tian. 2010. "Market Dynamics and Momentum Profits." *Journal of Financial and Quantitative Analysis* 45:6, 1549–1562.

Bailey, Jeffrey V. 1992a. "Are Manager Universes Acceptable Performance Benchmarks?" *Journal of Portfolio Management* 18:3, 9–13.

Bailey, Jeffrey V. 1992b. "Evaluating Benchmark Quality." *Financial Analysts Journal* 48:3, 33–39.

Bailey, Jeffrey V., Thomas M. Richards, and David E. Tierney. 2007. "Evaluating Portfolio Performance." In *Managing Investment Portfolios: A Dynamic Process*, 3rd ed., edited by John L. Maginn, Donald L. Tuttle, Jerald E. Pinto, and Dennis W. McLeavey, 717–782. Hoboken, NJ: John Wiley & Sons.

Bailey, Jeffrey V., and David E. Tierney. 1993. "Gaming Manager Benchmarks." *Journal of Portfolio Management* 19:4, 37–40.

Baker, H. Kent, and John R. Nofsinger. 2010. *Behavioral Finance: Investors, Corporations, and Markets.* Hoboken, NJ: John Wiley & Sons.

Brinson, Gary P., L. Randolph Hood, and Gilbert L. Beebower. 1986. "Determinants of Portfolio Performance." *Financial Analysts Journal* 42:4, 39–44.

Brinson, Gary P., Brian D. Singer, and Gilbert L. Beebower. 1991. "Determinants of Portfolio Performance II: An Update." *Financial Analysts Journal* 47:3, 40–48.

Carhart, Mark M. 1997. "On Persistence in Mutual Fund Performance." *Journal of Finance* 52:1, 57–82.

CFA Institute. 2010. *Global Investment Performance Standards (GIPS).* Last modified March 29, 2010, Available at http://www.cfapubs.org/doi/pdf/10.2469/ccb.v2010.n5.1.

Chance, Don M. 2003. *Analysis of Derivatives for the CFA Program.* Charlottesville, VA: Association for Investment Management and Research.

Fama, Eugene F. 1970. "Efficient Capital Markets: A Review of Theory and Empirical Work." *Journal of Finance* 25:2, 383–417.

Fama, Eugene F. 1991. "Efficient Capital Markets: II." *Journal of Finance* 46:5, 1575–1618.

Fama, Eugene F., and Kenneth R. French. 2004. "The Capital Asset Pricing Model: Theory and Evidence." *Journal of Economic Perspectives* 18:3, 25–46.

Gastineau, Gary L. 2001. "Exchange-Traded Funds: An Introduction." *Journal of Portfolio Management* 27:3, 88–96.

Haugen, Robert A. 2001. *The Inefficient Stock Market: What Pays Off and Why,* 2nd ed. Upper Saddle River, NJ: Pearson Education.

Haugen, Robert A. 2004. *The New Finance: Overreaction, Complexity, and Uniqueness,* 3rd ed. Upper Saddle River, NJ: Pearson Education.

Ibbotson, Roger G., and Paul D. Kaplan. 2000. "Does Asset Allocation Explain 40, 90 or 100 Percent of Performance?" *Financial Analysts Journal* 56:1, 26–33.

Jagadeesh, Narasimhan, and Sheridan Titman. 1993. "Returns to Buying Winners and Selling Losers: Implications for Stock Market Efficiency." *Journal of Finance* 54:1, 65–91.

Kahneman, Daniel, Paul Slovic, and Amos Tversky. 1982. *Judgment under Uncertainty: Heuristics and Biases.* Cambridge, UK: Cambridge University Press.

Kahneman, Daniel, and Amos Tversky. 1979. "Prospect Theory: An Analysis of Decision Making under Risk." *Econometrica* 47:2, 263–292.

Lawton, Philip, and W. Bruce Remington. 2007. "Global Investment Performance Standards." In *Managing Investment Portfolios: A Dynamic Process,* 3rd ed., edited by John L. Maginn, Donald L. Tuttle, Jerald E. Pinto, and Dennis W. McLeavey, 783–863. Hoboken, NJ: John Wiley & Sons.

Lintner, John. 1965. "The Valuation of Risky Assets and the Selection of Risky Investments in Stock Portfolios and Capital Budgets." *Review of Economics and Statistics* 47:1, 13–37.

Madhavan, Anath, Jack L. Treynor, and Wayne H. Wagner. 2007. "Execution of Portfolio Decisions." In *Managing Investment Portfolios: A Dynamic Process,* 3rd ed., edited by John L. Maginn, Donald L. Tuttle, Jerald E. Pinto, and Dennis W. McLeavey, 637–681. Hoboken, NJ: John Wiley & Sons.

Maginn, John L., Donald L. Tuttle, Jerald E. Pinto, and Dennis W. McLeavey. 2007. "The Portfolio Process and the Investment Policy Statement." In *Managing Investment Portfolios: A Dynamic Process,* 3rd ed., edited by John L. Maginn, Donald L. Tuttle, Jerald E. Pinto, and Dennis W. McLeavey, 1–19. Hoboken, NJ: John Wiley & Sons.

Markowitz, Harry M. 1952. "Portfolio Selection." *Journal of Finance* 7:1, 77–91.

Markowitz, Harry M. 1959. *Portfolio Selection: Efficient Diversification of Investments.* New Haven, CT: Yale University Press.

Nofsinger, John R. 2005. *The Psychology of Investing,* 2nd ed. Upper Saddle River, NJ: Pearson Education.

Reilly, Frank K., and Keith C. Brown. 2000. *Investment Analysis and Portfolio Management,* 6th ed. Orlando, FL: Dryden Press.

Sharpe, William F. 1964. "Capital Asset Prices: A Theory of Market Equilibrium under Conditions of Risk." *Journal of Finance* 19:3, 425–442.

Sharpe, William F. 1992. "Asset Allocation: Management Style and Performance Measurement." *Journal of Portfolio Management* 18:2, 7–19.

Shefrin, Hersh. 2000. *Beyond Greed and Fear: Understanding Behavioral Finance and the Psychology of Investing.* Boston: Harvard Business School Press.

Shefrin, Hersh, and Meir Statman. 2000. "Behavioral Portfolio Theory." *Journal of Financial and Quantitative Analysis* 35:2, 127–151.

Shleifer, Andrei. 2000. *Inefficient Markets: An Introduction to Behavioral Finance.* Oxford and New York: Oxford University Press.

Sparkes, Russell. 2002. *Socially Responsible Investment: A Global Revolution.* Chichester, UK: John Wiley & Sons.

Wagner, Wayne H., and Mark Edwards. 1993. "Best Execution." *Financial Analysts Journal* 49:1, 65–71.

Xiong, James X., Roger G. Ibbotson, Thomas M. Idzorek, and Peng Chen. 2010. "The Equal Importance of Asset Allocation and Active Management." *Financial Analysts Journal* 66:2, 22–30.

PORTFOLIO THEORY
AND ASSET PRICING

2

Modern Portfolio Theory

ERIC JACQUIER
Professor of Finance, HEC Montreal,
Visiting Professor of Finance, MIT
Sloan School of Management

Introduction

Portfolio theory refers to the design of optimal portfolios and its implication for asset pricing. The theory has undergone tremendous development since Markowitz (1952) first laid out the initial mean-variance framework. Numerous outstanding review articles and textbooks are now available on portfolio theory, such as Bodie, Kane, and Marcus (2011). The purpose of this chapter is to review the foundations of modern portfolio theory and its application when one must estimate parameters such as the expected returns (means) and covariance matrix.

The remainder of the chapter is organized as follows: The first part introduces the fundamentals of the efficient frontier, the capital asset pricing model (CAPM), and the theory of active management. For example, the chapter shows that beta, β, is the sole measure of a security's contribution to the risk of the portfolio that contains it. This result, often associated with the CAPM and believed to apply to large portfolios, is true no matter how small the portfolio and does not require the CAPM to hold. The chapter then reviews how the capital allocation line (CAL) and its slope (the Sharpe ratio) arise. The first part concludes by showing how the CAPM and the theory of active management arise from the same logic, albeit with different assumptions.

A large body of academic research has tackled increasingly complex intertemporal portfolio problems to incorporate realistic features, such as multiperiod investments, transaction costs, or the impossibility of trading in continuous time. In an attempt to improve the fit of the models, researchers also specified alternative utility functions, requiring increasingly complex mathematical tools. Intertemporal dynamic asset allocation hinges on the predictability of the investment opportunity set. The empirical literature documents the predictability of financial asset returns, such as the momentum effect observable for holding periods up to one year in length, the reversal of winners and losers at longer horizons, and the predictive power of some variables such as the dividend yield. Most of these effects are still the subject of disagreements in the literature. The results are somewhat mixed, sometimes strong in sample, albeit with low R squares, but often less convincing in out-of-sample experiments.

In contrast, an uncontested fact is that the investor does not know the parameters used to optimize the portfolio, such as the mean vector and the covariance matrix and sometimes the coefficients of predictive regressions used by quantitative portfolio managers. Parameter uncertainty alters the optimal portfolio allocation. While the pursuit of manageable dynamic asset allocation strategies is of great interest, one must absolutely incorporate parameter uncertainty into the optimization. Therefore, the second part of this chapter extends portfolio optimization to the case of unknown parameters. It first shows that increasing the frequency of sampling improves the estimation of the variance but not the mean. It then explains the predictive density of returns that needs to be considered under parameter uncertainty. In this light, the chapter discusses shrinkage, which reduces the dispersion of estimates, and the use of Bayesian priors to incorporate private views in the optimization. The chapter concludes by demonstrating how to optimally estimate future long-term returns for the purpose of asset allocation.

Optimal Portfolios with Known Parameters

This section first reviews optimal portfolio design in the one-period mean-variance framework, with the key combinations of a risk-free asset and several risky assets, where investors know the values of the relevant parameters. It then derives equilibrium (the CAPM) and active management implications. Finally, the chapter reviews the irrelevance of the horizon in a multiperiod setup with identically independently distributed returns.

BASIC MARKOWITZ MEAN-VARIANCE FRAMEWORK

The basic mean-variance framework assumes a single investment period, risky assets with normally distributed returns, and possibly a risk-free asset whose return is known ex-ante. In this framework, one can derive efficient sets agreed upon by all investors, sharing the same information, and investor-specific optimal portfolios depending on each investor's aversion to risk. A *risk-averse investor* dislikes risk. Given a choice between two investments with equal expected returns, a risk-averse investor chooses the one with less risk, as measured by standard deviation (σ). Normally distributed asset returns are fully characterized by their mean vector and covariance matrix. Therefore, investors only care about the mean and variance of their risky wealth. This is the mean-variance framework, actually plotted in mean versus standard deviation, as the figures in this chapter will demonstrate.

Investors' Preferences
Rational investors are risk averse. That is, they prefer a higher expected (mean) return and a lower variance or standard deviation. To rank all available risky assets, one needs to quantify an investor's trade-off between risk and expected return. The foundations of utility theory rely on fundamental axioms of rational

behavior for risky prospects with any general distribution. The investor's *utility function* represents the investor's preferences in terms of risk and return (i.e., her degree of risk aversion). Hence, investor preferences along with the risk-and-return characteristics of available portfolios, serve as the basis for selecting an optimal portfolio for a given investor, the portfolio that maximizes the investor's expected utility.

One can show that under the assumption of normally distributed returns, the risk premium (i.e., the amount of mean return an investor is willing to give up in order to eliminate variance) is proportional to the product of a measure of relative risk aversion (RRA) by variance. The RRA could vary, possibly inversely, with the investor's wealth. Most financial applications assume a constant RRA, which is a reasonable approximation for portfolio applications that do not involve enormous variations in wealth. This is the case for most investments over most horizons.

In summary, with a constant RRA, denoted as γ, the certainty equivalent return (CE) of an asset with mean return μ and variance σ^2 is written as shown in Equation 2.1:

$$CE(\mu,\sigma) = \mu - 0.5\gamma\sigma^2,\tag{2.1}$$

where the term after the minus sign is the Arrow-Pratt risk premium due to the investor's risk aversion. The investor with risk aversion γ is indifferent between a risk-free CE return and the portfolio with mean μ and variance σ^2. In the mean-versus-standard deviation plot for a given CE, this is a parabola with intercept CE, known as an *indifference curve*. In Equation 2.1, a given value of CE generates one indifference curve, plotted in Figure 2.1. All the combinations of μ and σ on the indifference curve are worth CE to the investor. The investor wants to invest in assets with the highest-possible CE lying on the highest-possible indifference curve. Various key combinations of risky and risk-free assets will now be considered.

One Risky Asset and the Risk-Free Asset

Consider a single risky asset P with mean and variance (μ_p, σ^2) and a risk-free asset with return R_f. An asset allocation with weight w in P has a mean $R_f + w(\mu_p - R_f)$ and standard deviation $|w|\sigma_p$. By the constraint of full investment, the weight in R_f is $1 - w$. Both the mean and the standard deviation are linear in w. Therefore, in the typical case when μ is larger than R_f, the possible combinations with $w > 0$ lie on a straight line, with an intercept R_f and a positive slope $w(\mu_p - R_f)/(w\sigma_p)$; for instance, $(\mu_p - R_f)/\sigma_p$. This investment opportunity set is denoted the *capital allocation line* (CAL). The CAL is the line of possible portfolio risk-and-return combinations given the risk-free rate and the risk and return of a portfolio of risky assets. Negative weights span a mirroring line with a negative slope, which is of no interest because the CAL dominates it everywhere. Figure 2.1 shows CALs for several portfolios, P_1, P_2, and others, in the mean-versus-standard deviation space.

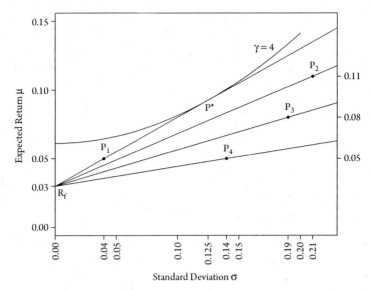

Figure 2.1 Capital allocation lines and Merton's optimal allocation. The figure shows the CALs for four portfolios and the optimal allocation P* in P_1 and R_f for a risk aversion, γ, of 4. The curved line (labeled $\gamma = 4$) is the indifference curve that is tangent the most steeply sloped CAL at P*, which represents the optimal allocation.

If these portfolios are mutually exclusive, investors must choose between mutually exclusive CALs. In Figure 2.1, the choice is unanimous because one of these lines, CAL_1, has a steeper slope than the others: it offers more expected return per unit of risk. For any allocation on another CAL, there are allocations on CAL_1 that dominate it unanimously; that is, with lower variance and an equal or higher mean (or with a higher mean and equal or lower variance). All investors agree, irrespective of their risk aversion, to rank mutually exclusive portfolios by the slope of their CAL, also known as the Sharpe ratio (Sharpe, 1966), denoted here as *Sh*:

$$Sh(P)=\frac{\mu_p-R_f}{\sigma_p}. \tag{2.2}$$

The *Sharpe ratio* is the mean return earned in excess of the risk-free rate per unit of standard deviation. It has become the industry-standard risk-adjusted performance measure due to its simplicity and conceptual appeal. Although the Sharpe ratio is restricted to mutually exclusive investments, later discussion in this chapter will show how to modify the analysis if portfolios can be combined. The Sharpe ratio is also only valid with no transaction cost in the risk-free asset. If the borrowing rate, R_b, is higher than the lending rate, R_l, borrowers ($w > 1$) face a lower Sharpe ratio than lenders ($w < 1$). This difference between the borrowing and lending rates causes a break in the CAL. When the investor has less than 100 percent of her wealth invested in the risky portfolio P ($w < 1$), she is effectively lending at the risk-free rate R_L. To invest beyond 100 percent in the risky asset P ($w > 1$), the investor switches to the higher borrowing rate, and, therefore, is on a CAL with a lower Sharpe ratio. Thus, differential borrowing and lending rates break down the unanimity of portfolio ranking. For example, in Figure 2.1, some investors may prefer P_2 to P_1. The more risk-averse investors and regulated funds that do not use margins are generally unaffected by this problem.

Given the CAL with the highest Sharpe ratio, which optimal allocation w^* does an investor with risk aversion γ select? She maximizes her CE in Equation 2.1, where the mean and variance are the functions of the weight w seen above. The straightforward first-order condition yields the well-known optimal asset allocation in mean-variance, also known as Merton's formula (1969), shown in Equation 2.3:

$$w^* = \frac{\mu_p - R_f}{\gamma \sigma^2} \qquad (2.3)$$

The curve at the top of Figure 2.1 is the best indifference curve (as in Equation 2.1) achievable by the investor. Its intercept is the maximized CE, which is obtained by investing w^* (from Equation 2.3) in P_1 and $1 - w^*$ in R_f. The indifference curve in Figure 2.1 is that of an investor with a risk aversion γ of 4. A more risk-averse investor would have a steeper indifference curve, and her optimal allocation w^* in Equation 2.3 would be smaller. However, all investors would agree to invest somewhere on CAL_1 because it has the highest Sharpe ratio.

Beta Is the Sole Relevant Measure of Risk

Consider two risky assets with means μ_1 and μ_2, standard deviations σ_1 and σ_2, and correlation ρ_{12}. The mean and standard deviation of a portfolio of these assets can be written as a function of the weight w_1, incorporating the constraint of full investment as $w_2 = 1 - w_1$. One can verify that the possible combinations of μ and σ span a hyperbola in mean versus standard deviation, often referred to as the *bullet*. A remarkable portfolio, located on the nose of the bullet, is the global *minimum variance portfolio* (MVP). In Figure 2.2, the portfolio that is farthest to the left (that has the least risk) is the global MVP.

Figure 2.2 plots the achievable investment frontiers and locations of the MVP for three cases of ρ_{12}. The MVP is remarkable because it marks the start of the positively sloped segment of the investment frontier, the only one of interest for any investor. The weight w_1 of asset 1 in the MVP is shown in Equation 2.4:

$$w_1 = \frac{\sigma_2^2 - \sigma_{1,2}}{\sigma_1^2 + \sigma_2^2 - 2\sigma_{1,2}}, \qquad (2.4)$$

where $\sigma_{12} = \sigma_1 \sigma_2 \rho_{1,2}$. Equation 2.4 follows from the minimization of the variance of the portfolio of two assets.

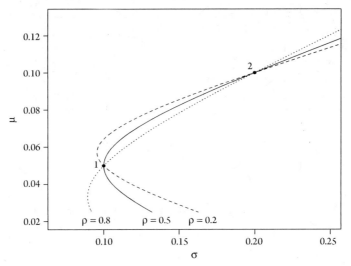

Figure 2.2 Effect of correlation on the minimum variance portfolio. The figure shows the returns and standard deviation for combinations of two assets for three values of their correlation, ρ. The value ρ = 0.5 is equal to the ratio of the two standard deviations, 0.1 and 0.2.

Now, take the view that asset 2 is in fact the investor's current portfolio containing many individual securities. Rename it *P* for convenience. Also rename asset 1 as *i* to denote an individual security, possibly already present in *P*. Then, w_i in Equation 2.4 is the amount of i added to *P*. The investor wants to know whether adding some *i* to her portfolio *P* will increase or decrease its variance. To determine this, one must quantify the effect of a change in the amount of i in P on the variance of *P*. Figure 2.2 shows that ρ, the correlation, is the key. For a low ρ, adding some i to P reduces variance; for a high ρ, it increases it. In a middle case, ρ is such that P is the MVP and there is no need to add or remove any *i*. To find ρ so that adding some i decreases the variance of P, set $w_i > 0$ in Equation 2.4. Note that the denominator is positive because it is the variance of the zero-investment long-short portfolio $R_1 - R_2$. Therefore, a simple manipulation of Equation 2.4 shows that ρ must be smaller than σ_P / σ_i, or σ_{iP} / σ_P^2 must be smaller than 1. This ratio is the beta of stock i with respect to portfolio P, denoted β_{iP}.

To summarize, if the beta of a stock with the current portfolio is larger (smaller) than 1, then increasing its weight increases (decreases) the portfolio variance. The argument is local because β_{iP} changes with w_i. Nevertheless, the beta of a stock with the investor's portfolio is the sole measure of its contribution to the portfolio variance. This powerful result has nothing to do with diversification and does not require portfolio P to be large. Even with a portfolio of two stocks, their beta with the current portfolio is the sole relevant measure of their contribution to its risk.

Another simple way to highlight the role of beta as the sole measure of risk is to note that the portfolio variance is the weighted average of the covariances of each stock i with the portfolio P: $\sigma_p^2 = \Sigma\, w_i\, \sigma_{iP}$. This implies that $\Sigma\, w_i\, \beta_{iP} = 1$. The weighted average of the security betas is 1 by construction for any portfolio. If some stocks have betas above 1, others must have betas below 1. To minimize variance, one decreases (increases) the weights in the high (low) beta stocks. Recall that the betas themselves change with the weights. Then, at the MVP, all the stocks have a beta of 1 with the portfolio.

Key Results in the Mathematics of the Efficient Frontier

The *efficient frontier* can be viewed as a set of minimum variance portfolios, each constrained to produce a desired level of mean return, only considering means above the MVP. While constructing the frontier would seem to require an optimization for each desired mean return, a key result is that if short sales are allowed, the efficient frontier is spanned by any two portfolios on it (Brandt 2009). Indeed, the weight vector of a minimum variance portfolio given a desired expected return μ_0 can be written as shown in Equation 2.5:

$$W_0^* = g + h\mu_0 = (1-\mu_0)g + \mu_0(g+h), \tag{2.5}$$

where g and h are vector functions of μ and V. The first equality in Equation 2.5 is a key result of the efficient frontier: When short sales are allowed, the efficient portfolio weights are linear in the desired expected return. The second equality is a simple manipulation showing that one can choose any two frontier

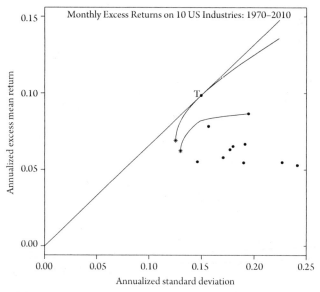

Figure 2.3 Effect of short sales restrictions on the efficient frontier. The figure shows two efficient frontiers for a set of ten US industry portfolios. The mean and standard deviations are annualized estimates. The lower frontier is constrained by a no–short sales restriction. The higher frontier allows short sales. The vertical axis is in excess returns over the risk-free rate.

portfolios (here, with weights g and $g + h$) to span the entire frontier. The efficient portfolio with desired mean μ_0 has weights $1 - \mu_0$ and μ_0 in the two spanning portfolios. In turn, any portfolio of several frontier portfolios is itself a frontier portfolio.

This result breaks down if short sales are not allowed. In this case, most frontier portfolios contain only a subset of the N assets in nonzero weights. Further, each asset appears with nonzero weight in a different subset of the frontier. Consequently, two frontier portfolios cannot possibly span the entire efficient frontier. Only two frontier portfolios (that are close to each other) containing the same assets can span the subset of the frontier between them. The frontier is said to have kinks; at each kink, an asset leaves the frontier and another one may enter. Whether or not short sales are allowed has a strong effect on the efficient frontier. Figure 2.3 shows a plot of the frontiers with and without short sales for 10 US industry portfolios.

Now, consider investors' choices. Even if they all agree on the frontier, each investor selects a personal frontier portfolio that maximizes her CE in Equation 2.1. When short sales are allowed, the first-order conditions of the optimization show that the vector of optimal weights is $(1/\gamma)V^{-1}(\mu - \lambda i)$, where λ is a scalar function of V, μ, and the investor's risk aversion is γ.

The introduction of a risk-free rate dramatically alters the previous decision-making process. Investors now consider all possible CALs between the risk-free rate and efficient risky portfolios. They all select the same frontier portfolio resulting in the CAL with the highest Sharpe ratio: portfolio T in Figure 2.3.

In a second step, investors select their individual optimal Merton allocation on the same CAL_T as seen in Equation 2.3. The introduction of the risk-free asset resulted in a two-fund separation, whereby all investors invest in the risk-free asset and the same tangency portfolio T, albeit in different amounts.

THE EFFICIENT FRONTIER AND ASSET PRICING

The previous section detailed the various scenarios of portfolio optimization available to an investor. The chapter now adds the assumptions of homogeneous information about μ, V, R_f, market efficiency, and frictionless and costless trading to show the implications for equilibrium of portfolio theory.

Recall the case with N risky assets and a risk-free asset. This section now shows how the Sharpe-Lintner CAPM (Sharpe, 1964) follows directly. If all investors have the same information μ, V, they all agree on the tangency portfolio, which is T in Figure 2.3. In equilibrium, demand meets supply and this tangency portfolio must be the capitalization-weighted portfolio of all risky assets, also known as the *market portfolio*. Therefore, the cap-weighted market portfolio is the tangency portfolio on the efficient frontier. It is the mean-variance efficient portfolio because no other portfolio has a higher Sharpe ratio. This is the basis for indexing investment. The CAL defined by the market is called the *capital market line* (hereafter, the CML). It is the optimal CAL given the assumptions made at the beginning of the section.

Consider now a risk-free rate R_f and a frontier of two risky assets, i and M. Quadratic optimization shows that the portfolio with the maximum Sharpe ratio, the tangency portfolio, has a weight as shown in Equation 2.6:

$$w_i^* = \frac{(\mu_i - R_f)\sigma_M^2 - (\mu_M - R_f)\sigma_{iM}}{(\mu_i - R_f)\sigma_M^2 + (\mu_M - R_f)\sigma_i^2 - (\mu_i + \mu_M - 2R_f)\sigma_{iM}} \tag{2.6}$$

Let us apply this result to the context of equilibrium, with M representing the market portfolio, and i representing any security. In equilibrium, M already contains i in the optimal amount because it is already the mean-variance efficient, tangency portfolio of the frontier of all securities in the economy. Therefore, the weight w_i^* must be zero in equilibrium. Now set the numerator in Equation 2.6 to equal to zero. This immediately yields the well-known CAPM equation

$$\mu_i = R_f + (\mu_M - R_f)\beta_{iM}, \tag{2.7}$$

where beta (β_{iM}) is now considered with respect to the market portfolio. In Figure 2.4, the solid lines show a two-asset frontier of the market and a security P_1. M is the tangency portfolio of that frontier because the expected return of P_1 was set equal to the CAPM.

With no risk-free rate, Black (1972) derives a similar CAPM. With no CAL available, investors choose individual efficient risky portfolios by maximizing their CE. If short sales are allowed, a portfolio of frontier portfolios is on the frontier. Therefore, the demand portfolio of investor portfolios weighted by investors' wealth is on the frontier. In equilibrium, this demand portfolio equals the

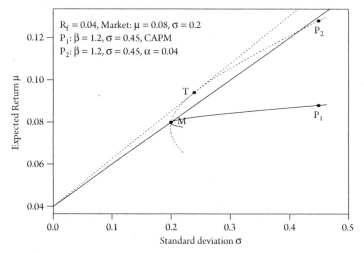

Figure 2.4. The CAPM versus active allocation.
The portfolios P_1 and P_2 have the same beta and standard deviation, but the expected return of P_1 is the CAPM expected return, while P_2 has a Jensen alpha of 0.04. When combining M and P_1, M is the tangency portfolio and has the highest Sharpe ratio. Combining M and P_2 results in attaining a Sharpe ratio higher than M's Sharpe ratio.

supply portfolio, the capitalization-weighted portfolio of all assets. The market portfolio is again on the efficient frontier. But investors do not need to hold it.

Black (1972) then obtains his version of the CAPM pricing equation by invoking two other results of the mathematics of the efficient frontier, given here without proof. First, for any efficient portfolio P, one can find a frontier portfolio with zero covariance with P, denoted Z_p , located on the negatively sloped segment of the frontier. Second, for any security i, one can show that

$$\mu_i = \mu_Z + \beta_{iP}(\mu_P - \mu_Z).$$
(2.8)

Clearly, a different initial P results in different β_{ip}, μ_p, Z_p, and μ_Z. However, it leads to the same μ_i. Black applies these results, using the market portfolio M as P since M is on the efficient frontier in equilibrium. This yields a CAPM in the absence of a risk-free rate, where excess-expected returns are also linear in β_{iM} but are computed in excess of the expected return of the zero-beta portfolio. Note that Black's CAPM is important in situations where investors do not believe that there is a truly risk-free security.

ACTIVE MANAGEMENT AND THE INFORMATION RATIO

This section discusses active management and portfolio performance evaluation. The best-known measure of performance, the Sharpe ratio, discussed in the previous sections, is only valid to rank mutually exclusive investments. The Sharpe ratio does not indicate how to optimally combine competing funds.

The previous section explains how in equilibrium, the capitalization-weighted market portfolio M achieves the best Sharpe ratio. In the active asset allocation framework, the manager identifies securities that may help improve upon the market portfolio's Sharpe ratio. This section introduces the *information ratio*, widely used in quantitative active asset management, which indicates how a security contributes to the Sharpe ratio of a portfolio. The reasoning will parallel the Sharpe-Lintner CAPM proof seen above, incorporating the fact that the expected returns of some securities differ from the CAPM prediction and therefore will improve upon the Sharpe ratio of the market. Departures from the CAPM are modeled via Jensen's (1968) apha, *a*, as shown in Equation 2.9:

$$E(R_i) = \alpha_I + R_f + \beta_i E(R_M - R_f)$$
(2.9)

Equation 2.9 nests the CAPM, in which case *a* is 0. To estimate alpha and beta, Jensen runs the time series regression shown in Equation 2.10:

$$R_{it} - R_{ft} = \alpha_i + \beta_i(R_{Mt} - R_{ft}) + \varepsilon_{it},$$
(2.10)

where R_{it} is the return on the asset i; R_{ft} is the risk-free rate; R_{Mt} is the market index return; and ε is the random error of the regression, also known as the *unsystematic* or *idiosyncratic return*. The regression in Equation 2.10 also estimates the standard deviation of the idiosyncratic return σ_{ε}. In fact, it performs the variance decomposition for security i, shown in Equation 2.11:

$$\sigma_i^2 = \beta_i^2 \sigma_M^2 + \sigma_{\varepsilon,i}^2. \tag{2.11}$$

This decomposition highlights the fundamental intuition of diversification. Adding securities to the portfolio while keeping the beta constant reduces idiosyncratic risk and hence reduces the total variance of the portfolio. In the limit, a fully diversified portfolio bears no idiosyncratic risk. Under the Sharpe-Lintner CAPM, one holds securities in their capitalization weights to eliminate idiosyncratic risk. The active manager departs from this diversified portfolio to increase the weight on securities with an attractive alpha. The cost of this strategy is an increase in idiosyncratic variance. The intuition is readily extended to multifactor models.

The active portfolio manager, with superior information on security i in the form of α_i, maximizes her Sharpe ratio by adding some i to M. The answer is again in Equation 2.7, but the manager does not assume an equilibrium, or w_i, equal to zero. Rather, she uses her superior information by substituting Equations 2.9 and 2.11 into 2.6. The resulting optimal portfolio of M and i can be shown in Equation 2.12 to have a Sharpe ratio S^* such that:

$$S^{*2} = S_M^2 + \left[\frac{\alpha_i}{\sigma_{\varepsilon i}}\right]^2. \tag{2.12}$$

The second term, $\alpha/\sigma_{\varepsilon}$, is the information ratio. The maximum contribution of a security to the improvement on the market portfolio Sharpe ratio is proportional to its alpha and inversely proportional to its idiosyncratic risk. This is because the optimal active position on α leads the manager to depart from M and to bear the idiosyncratic risk, ε_i. The label i can also denote a large active portfolio composed of a number of securities with nonzero alphas.

The dotted lines shown in Figure 2.4 contrast the CAPM and the active allocation. Portfolio P_2 only differs from P_1 by its expected return, equal to the CAPM plus an alpha. The combination of P_2 and M leads to a portfolio T with a higher Sharpe ratio than M. Note how P_2 helps improve on M's Sharpe ratio while it has a Sharpe ratio inferior to that of M. This example illustrates that the Sharpe ratio of a security does not predict how that security will contribute to the Sharpe ratio of a portfolio.

Merton's Allocation: Irrelevance of the Investment Horizon
This section concludes by showing the full extent of the Merton optimal allocation result. This result is later revisited to incorporate measurement uncertainty in the mean. Merton (1969) derives the optimal asset allocation between one risky and one riskless asset in continuous time, a generalization of the one-period result in Equation 2.3. Consider an independent and identically distributed lognormal risky asset, where $log(1 + R) \sim N(\mu,\sigma)$.: Its H-period compound return

can be shown to be lognormal, with mean μH and variance $\sigma^2 H$. Introduce a risk-free return r_0 and a classic power utility of final wealth per dollar invested, $U(V_H) = [1 + R_H]^{1-\gamma}/(1-\gamma)$, where γ is the constant relative risk aversion. Consider an allocation w in the risky asset and $(1 - w)$ in the risk-free asset. The assumption of continuous rebalancing guarantees that the portfolio of the two assets is lognormal. Equation 2.13 can then show that the expected utility of this allocation is

$$E[U(V_H)] = \frac{1}{1-\gamma}\exp[(1-\gamma)H(r_0 + w(\alpha - r_0) - 0.5w^2\sigma^2 + 0.5(1-\gamma)w^2\sigma^2)], \quad (2.13)$$

where $a = \mu + 0.5\ \sigma^2$. The maximization of the expected utility in Equation 2.13 over w gives the well-known Merton allocation in Equation 2.14:

$$w^* = \frac{\alpha - r_0}{\gamma\sigma}. \quad (2.14)$$

The allocation in Equation 2.14 offers an added insight over its one-period counterpart, Equation 2.3, even though they appear similar. Here, Merton works in a truly multiperiod framework. Yet, the horizon H, presented in the expected utility in Equation 2.13, drops out of the optimal solution in Equation 2.14. This finding is the well-known irrelevance of the horizon in the optimal asset allocation, when returns are independent and identically distributed and there is no estimation risk.

If the returns are predictable, with predominantly negative autocorrelations, the variance grows with the horizon at a slower rate than the mean. One, therefore, optimally allocates more to the risky asset in the long than in the short run. Further, in a dynamic strategy, the investor can reallocate her optimal weight within the investment horizon, benefitting further from the long horizon if the investment opportunity set is predictable. Brandt (2009) discusses these intertemporal dynamic strategies, which are beyond the scope of this chapter.

Parameter Uncertainty

Parameter uncertainty, especially in the mean, is a reality for the quantitative portfolio manager. Therefore, the chapter now turns to the extensions of the optimal portfolio theories that incorporate parameter uncertainty.

IMPACT OF DATA SAMPLING FREQUENCY ON MEAN AND VARIANCE ESTIMATES

Consider the estimation of the mean log return of an index of small firms. Suppose an investor collects T = 70 annual log returns from 1926 to 1995. She estimates the mean and standard deviation as m = 0.19 and s = 0.4. Assuming the approximate normality of the estimator of μ, a 95 percent confidence interval for the mean is written as $[m \pm 1.96 \, \sigma/\sqrt{T}]$ = [0.10, 0.28]. With seventy years of returns, one barely discriminates statistically between 10 and 19 percent annual returns. How can one draw conclusions from a manager's alpha of, say, 5 percent, estimated with five years of data? The precision of the mean's estimation is proportional to the sample size T. One way to increase the sample size is to sample more frequently. A sample of daily returns has 250 times more observations, which should increase any t-statistic by a factor of $\sqrt{250}$, or about 16.

This reasoning is a fallacy because using higher-frequency data does not improve the precision of the estimates of the mean returns of financial assets. This follows directly from the known aggregation formulas for the mean and variance as well as their estimates. Consider the logarithms of returns with one-period mean μ and variance σ^2. Then, the H-period log return has mean $H\mu$. Further, if the returns are not autocorrelated, the H-period variance is $H\sigma^2$.

Consider, for example, an estimate of the annual mean from annual returns and for the same calendar span, an estimate of the daily mean from annual returns. First, one can show that the two t-statistics, of the annual and daily mean, are equal. Alternatively, one can build a confidence interval for the daily mean. This interval can be converted into an implied confidence interval on the annual mean by simply aggregating its bounds. One can show that the two intervals are identical.

What about the variance? In the classic option pricing models, the agents observe asset prices and trade in continuous time, and they know the variance. In fact, the agents know the instantaneous variance because they observe prices continuously. Contrary to the case of estimating the mean, one can show that sampling returns more frequently increases the precision of the estimation of the variance. For example, the confidence interval on the standard deviation narrows with the square root of the sampling horizon.

In practice, measurement errors in prices and microstructure noise limit the gains in precision that can be achieved by merely increasing the sampling frequency. However, there is a fundamental difference between inference on the mean and on the variance. One can to a large extent mitigate the uncertainty in variance by using a higher-sampling frequency of returns. This approach is, however, totally ineffective for the mean.

MARKOWITZ FRAMEWORK WITH PARAMETER UNCERTAINTY: PREDICTIVE DENSITY

This section reviews decision theory and shows how to obtain the relevant density of future returns when the parameters are unknown. Early practice involved substituting estimates of the parameters μ and V into the standard optimal portfolio formulas or into an optimizer.

Practitioners quickly recognized that portfolios optimized with these sample estimates could have unstable weights. Clearly, parameter uncertainty should be reflected in the optimization. In fact, decision theory shows that conditioning returns on point estimates of parameter, as good as they may be, leads to sub-optimal portfolios. In fact, to properly account for estimation error, one must compute the predictive density of future returns. Predictive density is best intro-duced after briefly reviewing the Bayesian framework of estimation and predic-tion, whose popularity is on the rise in quantitative portfolio management. The remainder of this chapter surveys important results. Jacquier and Polson (2011) provide further discussion of this topic.

Brief Overview of the Bayesian Process for Stock Returns

An investor may have prior views on parameters even before conducting an empirical analysis. The views can be, for example, that betas are likely to be close to 1, that returns on some risky assets are likely to be equal to the CAPM for lack of better information, or that variances or correlations could be equal. These views are summarized in a prior density, $p(\mu, V)$ for the means and covariance matrix, and could be quite vague. The investor may not have any views, in which case the prior distribution is made very vague so as to have no impact on the analysis. This is referred to as a *diffuse* prior.

In a standard analysis, one typically estimates parameters by maximizing the likelihood function, which is the density of the data—here the returns R—given a value of the parameters $p(R \mid \mu, V)$. This process yields the clas-sic maximum likelihood (ML) estimator. In the Bayesian setup, the likelihood and the priors are combined and result in the so-called *posterior* density of the parameters $p(\mu, V \mid R)$. This density represents the investor's knowledge after observing the data. Quantitatively, this combination is done in an optimal way with the use of Bayes theorem: One can show that the posterior $p(\mu, V \mid R)$ is proportional to the product $p(\mu, V) p(R \mid \mu, V)$. The posterior density is found by simply multiplying the likelihood by the prior density. Estimates of the param-eters typically reported can include the mean and the standard deviation of the posterior distribution. Now, the investor wants to represent the density of future returns, summarizing her knowledge. To do so, she could simply use the distribution of the returns, such as normal or lognormal, substituting her best ML estimate of the parameters, $p(R_{T+1} \mid \mu_{MLE}, V_{MLE})$. Decision theory shows that this is suboptimal. Instead, she must rely on the predictive density of the future returns, which averages out the uncertainty in the parameters. Formally, the predictive density of the asset returns for time T + 1 is shown in Equation 2.15:

$$P(R_{T+1} \mid R) = \int p(R_{T+1} \mid R, \mu, V) p(\mu, V \mid R) d\mu dV, \qquad (2.15)$$

where the integration is done on the range of the mean and variance param-eters. The first term in the integral is the density of the future return, given the mean and variance. This is what the substitution approach uses, simply replac-ing the parameter with an estimate. However, it does not incorporate the fact that these estimates are uncertain. Therefore, it overstates the investor's preci-sion about the future returns. The second term is the posterior distribution of the parameters. It represents the knowledge on the parameters after observing the data.

The reader does not need to know integral calculus to understand the intuition in Equation 2.15; one simply needs to view the integral as a summation for convenience. It then appears that the predictive density is a weighted average of the density of future returns for all the possible values of the parameters. The weights used are the posterior density of the parameters. The intuition is that there should be a high (low) weight when the parameter is viewed as likely (unlikely).

Bayesian Portfolio Optimization with Diffuse Priors (No Views)

Klein and Bawa (1976) show that computing and then optimizing expected utility around the predictive density is the optimal strategy. The chief reason is that the mere substitution of point estimates of the parameters in the variance of a portfolio, in its CE or its Sharpe ratio, clearly omits the uncertainty about these estimates, which must be accounted for, especially by risk-averse investors. Bawa, Brown, and Klein (1979) incorporate parameter uncertainty into the optimal portfolio problem. They mostly use diffuse priors to compute the predictive density of the parameters and maximize expected utility for that predictive density.

For the case of N assets, the main result is that the predictive density of returns has a larger variance than the sample estimate of μ and V suggests. In fact, it is larger by a factor $(1 + 1/T) (T + 1) (T - N - 2)$. This factor modifies the optimal allocation, especially when N is sizable relative to T. Relative to portfolios based on point estimates, Bayesian optimal portfolios take smaller positions on the assets with a higher risk. The term $(1 + 1/T)$ is the correction due to the uncertainty in the mean. Consider, for example, the risky versus risk-free asset allocation. With a diffuse prior, the predictive density of the (single) future return is normal with mean m (the estimate) and variance $s^2(1 + 1/T)$, where s is the sample estimate. Intuitively, the future variance faced by the investor is the sum of the return's variance given the mean s^2 and the variance of the estimate s^2/T. Computing the Merton allocation with respect to this predictive density of returns lowers the allocation on the tangency portfolio in Equation 2.3 by the factor $1 + 1/T$.

These corrections did not appear important initially for the one-period model, when N was deemed small enough relative to T. At that time, the practice of substituting point estimates of μ and V into the theoretical solutions remained common with both practitioners and academics. However, practitioners eventually recognized that this plug-in approach was sensitive to estimation error (Michaud, 1989). Consider an investor who minimizes variance subject to a given desired mean return and uses a point estimate of the mean vector. The highest individual point estimates are such because the corresponding mean may be high but also because the sample of data used may have led to a positive estimation error. The next sample, corresponding to the investment period, will likely lead to lower point estimates for these means. This investor will find himself overinvested in these estimation errors. Using 25 years of monthly returns, Jobson and Korkie (1981) show that the realized Sharpe ratio of a portfolio that optimizes on the basis of point estimates of μ and V is 0.08

versus 0.34 for a portfolio using the true quantities. The substitution approach is clearly costly.

OPTIMAL PORTFOLIOS WITH SHRINKAGE AND EMPIRICAL BAYES

The optimization process tends to put higher (lower) weights on the assets with higher (lower) means. Due to parameter uncertainty, the extreme estimates in the mean vector for one period (estimation) are likely to be closer to the central estimates for the next period, which is the investment period. An optimizer that merely uses point estimates takes extreme positions and experiences poor performance during the investment period. The phenomenon is more serious for the more risk-tolerant investors who load up more on the extreme mean returns.

Frost and Savarino (1986) show that although optimization based on diffuse priors is an improvement over the classical substitution approach, the uncertainty in the mean is still too high to make the Markowitz framework more appealing than passive indexing strategies. The estimates and resulting portfolio weights still vary too much from period to period. This section discusses how portfolio performance can be improved with informative priors.

James and Stein (1961) introduce shrinkage estimators, which although they are biased are more efficient than the standard, maximum likelihood estimator (MLE) for estimating multivariate means. Their shrinkage estimator is:

$$\mu_{JS} = (1-\alpha)m + \alpha\mu_0 i, \tag{2.16}$$

where m is the MLE, μ_0 is a single central value toward which shrinkage occurs, and i is a vector of ones. The scalar coefficient, α, is designed to optimally pull the estimate to a common value μ_0. Shrinkage reduces the impact of parameter uncertainty in a vector of means by bringing extreme estimates closer to a central value. It replaces the sample estimates of the mean vector with a linear combination of this estimate and the central value, thereby reducing the cross-sectional dispersion of these means.

The same result can be achieved in the Bayesian setup with an appropriate prior. A type of priors, denoted conjugate, have the feature that the posterior mean is a linear combination of the prior mean and the MLE. The weights are the respective precisions of these two components. This is exactly as per Equation 2.16. Therefore, a given shrinkage estimation is consistent with some Bayesian prior. The Bayesian framework is more general, as individual prior means need not be equal and the individual means do not have to be shrunk to the same single value, such as μ_0 in Equation 2.16. Classic shrinkage corresponds to *empirical Bayes*, where the prior parameters, based on the data, are a convenience to reduce parameter uncertainty, not a representation of the investor's actual subjective prior views.

A key choice is that of the central value μ_0, toward which one shrinks the initial estimates m. Initial work proposed shrinking it toward the grand mean of all N asset returns. In contrast, Jorion (1986) makes the crucial point that, under basic assumptions, μ_0 should be the mean of the MVP. The intuition is as follows: First, the MVP is robust to uncertainty in the mean because it can be found without estimating the mean. Second, the mean of the MVP is subject to the least uncertainty because it has by definition the smallest variance of all portfolios. Shrinking toward a mean with the smallest possible uncertainty is precisely the desired objective. Jorion writes an empirical Bayes estimator based on a prior that reflects the investor's degree of confidence in the sample estimates. He finds that the mean of the predictive density of the future returns is then:

$$E(R_{T+1}\,|\,R) = (1-\alpha)m + \alpha m_{MVP}i, \tag{2.17}$$

where m_{MVP} is the sample mean of the MVP. The weight α increases to 1 if the investor is not very confident with the maximum-likelihood estimates. Then, the cross-sectional dispersion of $E(R_{T+1}\,|\,R)$ vanishes and the means shrink toward the global MVP. Jorion shows that this empirical Bayes method dominates those approaches based upon the basic sample estimates. The portfolio weights are more stable through time, as they do not make large bets on point estimates.

Frost and Savarino (1986) shrink both the mean vector and the covariance matrix using empirical Bayes. Their priors are centered on equal means, variances, and covariances. This amounts to a shrinkage of the optimal portfolio toward the equal-weighted portfolio since no asset has preferred characteristics in the prior. With an investment universe of 25 randomly selected securities, they compare the realized returns of optimized portfolios based on the classical point estimates, the Bayesian predictive densities with diffuse priors, and their empirical Bayes priors. Their results show that the empirical Bayes estimator leads to a vast additional improvement over the diffuse prior.

INCORPORATING ECONOMIC INFORMATION IN THE PRIOR

The investor may want to incorporate her own subjective views and economic considerations into the prior density. This may also result in posterior mean estimates with a smaller cross-sectional dispersion than that of the sample means. For example, the prior views can center the mean returns on the CAPM. In the absence of additional information on specific returns, capitalization weights are good weights toward which to shrink an optimal portfolio. Indeed, an extreme of the passive investment framework involves simply replacing expected returns with betas, because the CAPM states that expected excess returns are proportional to betas. This reduces the uncertainty in the mean because betas are generally estimated more precisely than sample means.

An investor may have private information on some of the assets arising from proprietary analysis. She views the CAPM prediction for expected returns as prior information. She may have an econometric model to predict abnormal expected returns in excess of the CAPM for some but not all assets. In this spirit, Black and Litterman (1991) specifically account for the fact that active managers do not have private information on every asset in their investment universe. These authors notice that portfolio managers often modify only a few elements of the vector of means for which they have private information. They show that this practice has a large and undesirable impact on the entire vector of weights. Instead, they show how to incorporate both the private views and market equilibrium into the optimization.

Black and Litterman (1991) do not compute prior expected returns using the equilibrium model. Instead, they reverse engineer them from the observed capitalization weights of the different assets. That is, they assume that these weights are consistent with the market's optimization of these expected returns and invert the formula for the optimal weights, finding the implied expected return. The authors combine this economic-based prior view with the investor's private views on (a subset of) the assets. The private views must include an error term that models the investors' confidence in the view. Assumedly, these views come from some data analysis, but this assumption is unnecessary. The posterior views, in Black and Litterman's sense, result from combining the prior, asset pricing–based view with the private view. In their formulation, the posterior mean is a simple weighted average of the economic and private means.

Another productive approach is to actually model expected returns so as to nest the asset pricing model and its deviation, as in Equation 2.10. Reasonable investors assume that the model is neither perfect ($\alpha = 0$) nor totally useless (α unconstrained). Priors on α are a convenient way to model the degree of belief in the model. This approach differs from the earlier literature that argues as to whether an asset pricing model, such as the CAPM, can or cannot be rejected by the data, with no really useful implication for the investor. Jacquier and Polson (2011) provide a detailed discussion of this approach.

IMPACT OF UNCERTAINTY ON LONG-TERM ASSET ALLOCATION

Estimates of expected long-term returns are crucial to long-term investment, for example in retirement policy. This section discusses the impact of uncertainty in the mean on the estimation of compound returns and on the long-run optimal allocation. Suppose one seeks to estimate the expected compound return over H periods, $E(V_H) = exp(H\mu + 0.5H\sigma^2)$.

Denote m, the annual sample mean, computed from T annual log-returns, with annual variance σ^2. For long-term forecasts, practitioners have tended to estimate $E(V_H)$ by compounding the sample geometric return $G = 1/T \; log(P_T/P_1)$. This amounts to estimating $E(V_H)$ using e^{mH}. Academics, however, often substitute m in the expectation $E(V_h)$, estimating is as $e^{(Hm+0.5\sigma^2)}$. That is, they compound at the arithmetic mean return. The difference between these approaches is large. Using the geometric and arithmetic averages of 0.07 and 0.085 per year for the US stock market from 1926 to 1996, the two approaches grow $1 to $160, versus $454, over 75 years.

Jacquier, Marcus, and Kane (2003, 2005) show that both approaches are biased and inefficient. They derive unbiased (U) and minimum mean-squared error (M) estimators of $E(V_H)$ in the form shown in Equation 2.18:

$$C = e^{H(m+0.5\sigma^2(1-kH/T))},$$

$$(2.18)$$

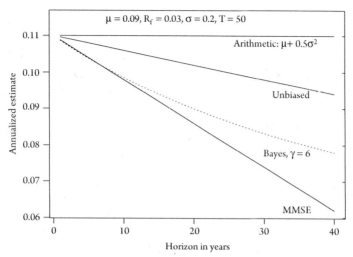

Figure 2.5 Optimal long-term compounding factor with mean uncertainty. The figure shows the arithmetic return (horizontal line), the unbiased minimum mean squared error (MMSE), and Bayesian estimates of the compounding factor, each plotted against the forecasting horizon.

where $k = 1$ for U and $k = 3$ for M. The downward penalty, $-k\,H/T$, counteracts a Jensen effect due to the uncertainty in m, which worsens with the horizon H. Figure 2.5 plots the compounding factor in U and M versus the horizon H. The figure shows that the penalty is severe.

To see how the rational Bayesian investor incorporates uncertainty in the mean into her long-horizon asset allocation, one repeats the Merton long-term asset allocation seen in the first part of the chapter, this time with estimation error. The density of V_H in Equation 2.13 is now conditional on μ, a parameter which must be integrated out to produce the predictive density of V_H, reflecting the full uncertainty. Jacquier et al. (2005) compute this predictive utility and optimize it. They find the optimal asset allocation in Equation 2.19:

$$w^* = \frac{\hat{\alpha} - r_0}{\sigma^2 \left[\gamma + \dfrac{H}{T}(\gamma - 1) \right]}. \tag{2.19}$$

The optimal weight in the risky asset decreases in the horizon H and in the investor's risk aversion. The numerical effect is very large for long horizons. Figure 2.6 compares this Bayesian optimal allocation with the allocation with a known mean. As the horizon H increases, the Bayesian allocation decreases drastically, even for a moderate risk aversions of 3 or 6.

One can reconcile the allocation in Equation 2.19 with a Merton allocation by inputting an estimate of the annual compound factor, already adjusted for

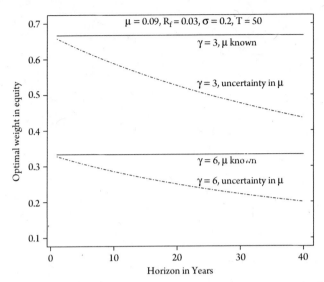

Figure 2.6 Optimal long-term asset allocation with mean uncertainty. The figure plots the Merton allocation (horizontal line) and the optimal allocation that accounts for estimation uncertainty in the mean for two values of the risk aversion.

estimation risk. As shown in Jacquier and Polson (2011), this estimate is a^*, illustrated in Equation 2.20:

$$\alpha^* - r_0 = \frac{\hat{\alpha} - r_0}{1 - \left(1 - \dfrac{1}{\gamma}\right)\dfrac{H}{T}} \tag{2.20}$$

This estimate is decreasing in H as well as in the investor's risk aversion. Figure 2.5 displays it as a dotted line for a risk aversion of 6, typical of a reasonably risk-averse investor. The estimate strongly penalizes uncertainty for long horizons, not as much as the classical M but far more than the unbiased estimator (U). Finally, a^* never implies negative estimates of the risk premium because it follows from the investor's optimal asset allocation in Equation 2.19, which cannot be negative.

In summary, the estimation error in the mean has a far greater effect on long-term than short-term optimal allocation. Because of mean uncertainty, investors should have drastically smaller optimal weights for the long run than for the short run. This is consistent with the fact that optimal estimates of long-term returns all include some form of penalty for estimation risk, which is increasing in the investment horizon.

SUMMARY AND CONCLUSIONS

This first part of this chapter reviews the major stages of optimal portfolio design when the parameters (the means and covariances) are known. The first important result reviewed is that the beta of a security with a portfolio is the sole relevant measure of the contribution of that security to the risk of the portfolio. This result is not predicated on whether or not the CAPM holds. The second important result reviewed is that in equilibrium and when a risk-free rate is available, the capitalization-weighted market portfolio is mean-variance efficient. It has the highest possible Sharpe ratio. In the active management framework, when some securities have alphas, that is, their expected returns are not equal to the CAPM, one can improve on the market's Sharpe ratio. The key statistics showing how this is done is the information ratio, which is the ratio of the security's alpha to its idiosyncratic standard deviation. The final result reviewed in the first part of the chapter is that with known parameters and independent and identically distributed asset returns, the optimal allocation is independent of the investment horizon.

The second part of the chapter revisits this theory, accounting for uncertainty in the means and covariances. The chapter describes how decision theory proves that it is not effective for one to simply proceed with the results of portfolio theory by substituting estimates into optimal portfolio formulas. In practice, this approach results in unstable portfolio weights and poor performance. One must instead consider the predictive density of asset returns. A key tool that is used to improve performance is the prior density on the parameters.

This prior density can be left vague (i.e., diffuse) and the predictive density approach will still result in improved performance over the substitution approach. However, even better performance can be attained by incorporating information in the prior density. Namely, the chapter reviews how the technique of shrinkage drastically reduces the variation of individual mean estimates. Shrinkage combines the individual estimates with a single, central estimate, such as the mean of the MVP. Then, the chapter shows that the investor can use the prior density to incorporate her own economic views into the optimization, with a resulting improvement in performance. Although the chapter does not discuss similar issues arising with the uncertainty in the covariance matrix, Jacquier and Polson (2011) provide such a discussion. The chapter concludes by demonstrating the impact of the uncertainty in the mean on estimating future long-term expected returns and asset allocation. Contrary to conventional wisdom, the optimal asset allocation in the risky asset decreases with the investment horizon. The chapter demonstrates estimates that are either unbiased or consistent with optimal asset allocation.

Discussion Questions

1. A market timer predicts a negative risk premium $\mu - R_f$ for the upcoming investment period. What should be the optimal allocation to the risky asset?
2. Assuming a case in which the risk-free borrowing rate, R_B, is higher than the lending rate, R_L, explain why some investors may prefer P_2 to P_1 in Figure 2.1. Which investors are these likely to be?
3. In the risk frontier of many assets, as shown in Figure 2.3, what is the link between the MVP's expected return and the risk-free rate?

4. When combining an active portfolio P with a beta of 1 and the market portfolio to maximize the Sharpe ratio, the optimal weight in the active portfolio is:

$$w^* = \frac{\alpha_p / \sigma_{\varepsilon,P}}{[E(R_M) - R_f]/\sigma_M^2}.$$

Discuss this result.

5. Consider P_1 and P_2 in Figure 2.4. Find the Sharpe ratio for M. Why cannot P_1 help improve this Sharpe ratio? Find the Sharpe ratio for P_2. Is it better or worse than M's Sharpe ratio? Explain why P_2 can improve on the Sharpe ratio of M.

6. Show that the precision of estimating the mean does not change with the sampling frequency. Also show that the precision of estimating the standard deviation increases with the square root of the sampling frequency in contrast.

Acknowledgment

The author acknowledges financial support from the HEC Montreal professorship in derivative products and the Sloan School of Management.

References

Bawa, Vijay S, Stephen J. Brown, and Roger W. Klein. 1979. *Estimation Risk and Optimal Portfolio Choice*. Amsterdam: North Holland.

Black, Fischer. 1972. "Capital Market Equilibrium with Restricted Borrowing." *Journal of Business* 45:3, 444–455.

Black, Fisher, and Robert Litterman. 1991. "Asset Allocation: Combining Investor Views with Market Equilibrium." *Journal of Fixed Income* 1:2, 7–18.

Bodie, Zvi, Alex Kane, and Alan J. Marcus. 2011. *Investments*, 9th ed. New York: McGraw-Hill and Irwin.

Brandt, Michael. 2009. "Portfolio Choice Problems." In *Handbook of Financial Econometrics*, edited by Yacine Aït-Sahalia and Lars Peter Hansen, 269–336. Amsterdam: North-Holland.

Frost, Peter A., and James E. Savarino. 1986. "An Empirical Bayes Approach to Efficient Portfolio Selection." *Journal of Financial and Quantitative Analysis* 21:3, 293–305.

Jacquier, Eric, Alan Marcus, and Alex Kane. 2003. "Geometric or Arithmetic Mean: A New Take on an Old Controversy." *Financial Analysts Journal* 59:6, 46–53.

Jacquier, Eric, Alan Marcus, and Alex Kane. 2005. "Optimal Estimation of the Risk Premium for the Long-Term and Asset Allocation: A Case of Compounded Estimation Risk." *Journal of Financial Econometrics* 3:1, 37–56.

Jacquier, Eric, and Nicholas Polson. 2011. "Bayesian Methods in Finance." In *The Oxford Handbook of Bayesian Econometrics*, edited by John Geweke, Gary Koop, and Herman K. van Dijk, 437–512. Oxford: Oxford University Press.

James, Willard, and Charles Stein. 1961. "Estimation with Quadratic Loss." In *Proceedings of the Fourth Berkeley Symposium on Mathematical Statistics and Probability*. Vol. 1, *Contributions to the Theory of Statistics*, edited by John Neyman, 361–379. Berkeley, CA: University of California Press.

Jensen, Michael C. 1968. "The Performance of Mutual Funds in the Period 1945–1964." *Journal of Finance* 23:2, 389–416.

Jobson, J. D., and Robert M. Korkie. 1981. "Putting Markowitz Theory to Work." *Journal of Portfolio Management* 7:3, 70–74.

Jorion, Philippe. 1986. "Bayes-Stein Estimation for Portfolio Analysis." *Journal of Financial and Quantitative Analysis* 21:3, 279–292.

Klein, Roger W., and Vijay S. Bawa. 1976. "The Effect of Estimation Risk on Optimal Portfolio Choice." *Journal of Financial Economics* 3:3, 215–31.

Markowitz, Harry M. 1952. "Portfolio Selection." *Journal of Finance* 7:1, 77–91.

Merton, Robert C. 1969. "Lifetime Portfolio Selection under Uncertainty: The Continuous Time Case." *Review of Economics and Statistics* 51:3, 247–257.

Michaud, Richard. 1989. "The Markowitz Optimization Enigma: Is 'Optimized' Optimal." *Financial Analysts Journal* 45:1, 31–42.

Sharpe, William. 1964. "Capital Asset Prices–A Theory of Market Equilibrium under Conditions of Risk." *Journal of Finance* 19:3, 425–442.

Sharpe, William. 1966. "Mutual Fund Performance." *Journal of Business* 39:1, 119–138.

3

Asset Pricing Theories, Models, and Tests

NIKOLAY GOSPODINOV
Professor, Concordia University and CIREQ

CESARE ROBOTTI
Financial Economist and Associate Policy Adviser, Federal
Reserve Bank of Atlanta, Affiliate Professor, EDHEC Risk
Institute

Introduction

Many asset pricing theories predict that the price of an asset will be lower (and its expected return higher) if the asset provides a poor hedge against changes in future market conditions (Rubinstein, 1976; Breeden, 1979). The classic capital asset pricing model (CAPM) of Sharpe (1964) and Lintner (1965) considers the case in which investment opportunities are constant and investors hold efficient portfolios in the desire to maximize their expected return for a given level of variance. The CAPM predicts that an asset's risk premium will be proportional to its beta—the measure of return sensitivity to the aggregate market-portfolio return. The considerable empirical evidence against the CAPM points to the fact that variables other than the rate of return on a market-portfolio proxy command significant risk premia. The theory of the intertemporal CAPM (ICAPM; Merton, 1973; Long, 1974) suggests that these additional variables should serve as a proxy for the position of the investment opportunity set. Although the ICAPM does not identify the various state variables—leading Fama (1991) to label the ICAPM as a "fishing license"—Breeden (1979) shows that Merton's ICAPM is actually equivalent to a single-beta consumption model (CCAPM) since the chosen level of consumption endogenously reflects the various hedging-demand effects of the ICAPM.

Over the years, researchers have made many attempts to refine the theoretical predictions and improve the empirical performance of the CAPM and CCAPM. Popular extensions include internal and external habit models (Abel, 1990; Constantinides, 1990; Ferson and Constantinides, 1991; Campbell and Cochrane, 1999), models with nonstandard preferences and rich consumption dynamics (Epstein and Zin, 1989, 1991; Weil, 1989; Bansal and Yaron 2004), models that allow for slow adjustment of consumption to the information driving asset returns (Parker and Julliard, 2005), conditional models (Jagannathan and Wang, 1996; Lettau and Ludvigson, 2001), disaster-risk models (Berkman, Jacobsen, and Lee, 2011), and the well-known "three-factor model" of Fama and French (1993). Although empirical observation primarily motivated the Fama-French model, its size and book-to-market factors are sometimes viewed as proxies for more fundamental economic variables.

In order to be of practical interest, the asset pricing theories listed above need to be confronted with data. Two main econometric methodologies have emerged to estimate and test asset pricing models: (1) the generalized method of moments (GMM) methodology for models written in stochastic discount factor (SDF) form and (2) the two-pass cross-sectional regression (CSR) methodology for models written in beta form.

The SDF approach to asset pricing indicates that the price of a security is obtained by "discounting" its future payoff using a valid SDF, so that the expected value of the payoff is equal to the current price. In practice, finding a valid SDF, i.e., an SDF that prices each asset correctly, is impossible, and researchers have to rely on candidate SDFs to infer the price of an asset. Although testing whether a particular asset pricing model literally holds true is interesting, a more useful task for empirical researchers is to determine how wrong a model is and to evaluate the relative performance of competing asset pricing models. The latter task requires a scalar measure of model misspecification. While many reasonable measures can be used for this purpose, the one introduced by Hansen and Jagannathan (1997) has gained tremendous popularity in the empirical asset pricing literature. Many researchers have used their proposed measure, called the Hansen-Jagannathan distance (HJ-distance), both as a model diagnostic and as a tool for model selection. Examples include Jagannathan and Wang (1996), Jagannathan, Kubota, and Takehara (1998), Campbell and Cochrane (2000), Lettau and Ludvigson (2001), Hodrick and Zhang (2001), Dittmar (2002), Farnsworth, Ferson, Jackson, and Todd (2002), Chen and Ludvigson (2009), Kan and Robotti (2009), Li, Xu, and Zhang (2010), and Gospodinov, Kan, and Robotti (2011a). Asset pricing models in SDF form are generally estimated and tested using GMM methods. Importantly, the SDF approach and the HJ-distance metric are applicable whether or not the pricing model is linear in a set of systematic risk factors.

When a model specifies that asset expected returns are linear in the betas (beta-pricing model), the CSR method proposed by Black, Jensen, and Scholes (1972) and Fama and MacBeth (1973) has been the preferred method in empirical finance given its simplicity and intuitive appeal. Although there are many variations of the CSR methodology, the basic approach always involves two steps or passes. In the first pass, the betas of the test assets are estimated using the usual ordinary least squares time series regression of returns on some common factors. In the second pass, the returns on the test assets are regressed on the betas estimated from the first pass. Running this second-pass CSR on a period-by-period basis enables obtaining the time series of the intercept and the slope coefficients. The average values of the intercept and the slope coefficients are then used as estimates of the zero-beta rate (the expected return for risky assets with no systematic risk) and factor risk premia, with standard errors computed from these time series as well. Given its simple intuitive appeal, the most popular measure of model misspecification in the CSR framework has been the R^2 for the cross-sectional relation (Kandel and Stambaugh, 1995; Kan, Robotti, and Shanken, 2012). This R^2 indicates the extent to which the model's betas account for the cross-sectional variation in average returns, typically for a set of asset portfolios.

After reviewing the SDF and beta approaches to asset pricing, this chapter describes several pitfalls in the current econometric analyses and provides suggestions for improving empirical tests. Particular emphasis is given to the role played by model misspecification and to the need for more reliable inference procedures in estimating and evaluating asset pricing mode's

Stochastic Discount Factor Representation

The SDF approach to asset pricing provides a unifying framework for pricing stocks, bonds, and derivative products and is based on the following fundamental pricing equation (Cochrane, 2005):

$$p_t = E_t[m_{t+1}x_{t+1}]. \qquad (3.1)$$

Here, p_t is an N-vector of asset prices at time t; $x_{t+1} = p_{t+1} + d_{t+1}$ is an N-vector of asset payoffs, with d_{t+1} denoting an asset's dividend, interest, or other payment received at time $t + 1$; m_{t+1} is an SDF, which depends on data and parameters; and E_t is a conditional expectation given all publicly available information at time t.

Dividing both sides of the fundamental pricing equation by p_t (assuming nonzero prices) and rearranging, we get

$$E_t[m_{t+1}(1+R_{t+1})-1_N]=0_N, \qquad (3.2)$$

where $R_{t+1} = \frac{x_{t+1}}{p_t} - 1 = \frac{p_{t+1} + d_{t+1}}{p_t} - 1$ is an N-vector of asset returns and 1_N and 0_N are N-vectors of ones and zeros, respectively.

Portfolios based on excess returns $R^e_{t+1} = R_{t+1} - R^f_t 1_N$, where R^f_t denotes the risk-free rate at time t, are called zero-cost portfolios. Since the risk-free rate is known ahead of time, it follows that $E_t[m_{t+1}(1+R^f_t)] = E_t[m_{t+1}](1+R^f_t) = 1$ and $E_t[m_{t+1}] = \frac{1}{(1+R^f_t)}$. In this case, with zero prices and payoffs R^e_{t+1}, the fundamental pricing equation is given by

$$E_t[m_{t+1}R^e_{t+1}]=0_N. \qquad (3.3)$$

As an example of the SDF approach, consider the problem of a representative agent maximizing her lifetime expected utility,

$$\sum_{t=1}^{\infty} \beta^t E_0[u(c_t)]$$

(3.4)

subject to the budget constraint

$$a_{t+1} = (a_t + y_t - c_t)(1 + R_{t+1}),$$

(3.5)

where β, c_t, a_t and y_t denote the time preference parameter, consumption, asset amount, and income at time t, respectively. The first-order condition for the optimal consumption and portfolio choice is given by

$$E_t\left[\beta \frac{u'(c_{t+1})}{u'(c_t)}(1 + R_{t+1}) - 1_N\right] = 0_N,$$

(3.6)

where $u'(c)$ denotes the first derivative of the utility function $u(c)$ with respect to c. This first-order condition takes the form of the fundamental pricing equation, with SDF given by the intertemporal marginal rate of substitution, i.e.,

$$m_{t+1} = \beta \frac{u'(c_{t+1})}{u'(c_t)}.$$

(3.7)

While the SDF in Equation 3.7 is positive by construction, it is possible for an SDF to price assets correctly and at the same time take on negative values, especially when the SDF is linear in a set of risk factors. Although a negative SDF does not necessarily imply the existence of arbitrage opportunities, dealing with positive SDFs is generally desirable, especially when the interest lies in pricing derivatives (positive payoffs should have positive prices). Therefore, a common practice in the derivative pricing literature is to consider Equation 3.1 with $m_{t+1} > 0$, which implies the absence of arbitrage. In some situations, however, imposing this positivity constraint can be problematic. For example, if one is interested in comparing the performance of competing asset pricing models on a given set of test assets using the distance metric proposed by Hansen and Jagannathan (1997), constraining the admissible SDF to be positive is not very sensible. Gospodinov, Kan, and Robotti (2010) provide a rigorous analysis of the merits and drawbacks of the no-arbitrage HJ-distance metric.

Beta Representation

Using the law of iterated expectations, the conditional form of the fundamental pricing equation for gross returns can be reduced to its unconditional counterpart:

$$E[m_{t+1}(1+R_{t+1})]=1_N. \tag{3.8}$$

From the covariance decomposition (suppressing the time index for simplicity), the pricing equation for asset i can be rewritten as

$$1= E[m(1+R^i)]= E[m]E[1+R^i] + Cov[m,(1+R^i)]. \tag{3.9}$$

Then, dividing both sides of Equation 3.9 by $E[m]>0$ and rearranging, we get

$$E[R^i]=\frac{1}{E(m)}+\frac{Cov[m,R^i]}{Var[m]}\left[-\frac{Var[m]}{E[m]}\right]=\gamma_0 +\beta_{i,m}\lambda_m, \tag{3.10}$$

using $\frac{1}{E[m]}=1+R^f =1+\gamma_0$ from above. Note that $\beta_{i,m}=\frac{Cov[m,R^i]}{Var[m]}$ is the regression coefficient of the return R^i on m and $\lambda_m =-\frac{Var[m]}{E[m]}<0$ denotes the price of risk.

Recall that the SDF m is a function of the data and parameters. Suppose now that m can be approximated by a linear function of K (risk) factors, denoted by f, which serve as proxies for marginal utility growth:

$$m= \tilde{f}'\theta, \tag{3.11}$$

where $\tilde{f}=(1,f')'$. Then, substituting for m into the fundamental pricing equation and rearranging (see Cochrane, 2005, pp. 107–108), we get

$$E[R^i]= \gamma_0 + \gamma_1'\beta_i, \tag{3.12}$$

where the β_i's are the multiple regression coefficients of R^i on f and a constant, γ_0 is the zero-beta rate and γ_1 is the vector of risk premia on the K factors. The *beta* representation of a factor pricing model can be rewritten in compact form as

$$E[R]= B\gamma, \tag{3.13}$$

where $B=[1_N, \beta]$, $\beta=Cov[R,f]Var[f]^{-1}$ is an ($N\times K$) matrix of factor loadings and $\gamma=(\gamma_0, \gamma_1')'$. Kan, Robotti, and Shanken (2012) show how to incorporate portfolio characteristics into the beta-pricing relation. For ease of exposition, the following analysis will mostly focus on the case of linear asset pricing models, but the techniques in this chapter are applicable to nonlinear seems desirable.

GMM Estimation and Evaluation of Asset Pricing Models in SDF Form

Using Equation 3.11, the pricing errors of the N test assets can be expressed as

$$g(\theta)= E[m(1+R)]-1_N = E[(1+R)\tilde{f}'\theta]-1_N = D\theta-1_N, \tag{3.14}$$

where $D= E[(1+R)\tilde{f}']$. Let $t = 1, 2,..., T$ denote the number of time series observations on the test assets and the factors. The sample analog of the pricing errors is given by

$$g_T(\theta)=\frac{1}{T}\sum_{t=1}^{T}(1+R_t)\tilde{f}_t'\theta-1_N. \tag{3.15}$$

For a given weighting matrix W_T, the GMM estimator of θ minimizes the quadratic form

$$g_T(\theta)'W_Tg_T(\theta) \tag{3.16}$$

and solves the first-order condition

$$D_T'W_T(D_T\theta-1_N)=0, \tag{3.17}$$

where $D_T =\dfrac{\partial g_T(\theta)}{\partial\theta'}=\dfrac{1}{T}\sum_{t=1}^{T}(1+R_t)\tilde{f}_t'$. Solving this system of linear equations for θ yields

$$\hat{\theta}=(D_T'W_TD_T)^{-1}(D_T'W_T1_N). \tag{3.18}$$

The optimal GMM estimator (under the assumption that the model is correctly specified) sets $W_T =V_T^{-1}$, where $V_T = Var[T^{\frac{1}{2}}g_T(\theta)]$. In this case,

$$\hat{\theta}=(D_T'V_T^{-1}D_T)^{-1}(D_T'V_T^{-1}1_N), \tag{3.19}$$

where V_T is evaluated at some preliminary (consistent) estimator $\tilde{\theta}$ (typically obtained using $W_T = I_N$). If the model is correctly specified, i.e., it explains the test assets correctly, the pricing errors $g(\theta)= E[(1+R)\tilde{f}'\theta]-1_N$ are zero and the model's restrictions can be tested using the statistic

$$Tg_T(\hat{\theta})'V_T^{-1}g_T(\hat{\theta})\to^d \chi^2_{(N-K-1)}. \tag{3.20}$$

If the model is misspecified, the value of the test statistic depends on the choice of W_T. Therefore, for model comparison, using the same W_T across models seems desirable.

Hansen and Jagannathan (1997) suggest using $W = U^{-1}$, where $U = E[(1+R)(1+R)']$ is the second-moment matrix of the gross returns with a sample analog U_T. Then, the sample HJ-distance is defined as

$$\delta_T(\theta) = \sqrt{g_T(\theta)' U_T^{-1} g_T(\theta)} \qquad (3.21)$$

and

$$\hat{\theta} = \arg\min_{\theta \in \Theta} \delta_T^2(\theta) = (D_T' U_T^{-1} D_T)^{-1}(D_T' U_T^{-1} 1_N) \qquad (3.22)$$

is the resulting GMM estimator. The HJ-distance has an interesting economic interpretation in that: (1) it measures the minimum distance between the proposed SDF and the set of valid SDFs, and (2) it represents the maximum pricing error of a portfolio of returns with a second moment equal to 1.

The HJ-distance test of correct model specification is based on

$$T\delta_T^2(\hat{\theta}) \rightarrow^d \sum_{j=1}^{N-K-1} \xi_j v_j, \qquad (3.23)$$

(Jagannathan and Wang, 1996; Parker and Julliard, 2005), where the v_j's are independent χ_1^2 random variables and the ξ_j's are the nonzero eigenvalues of the matrix

$$V^{1/2} U^{-1/2} [I_N - (U^{-1/2})' D(D' U^{-1} D)^{-1} D' U^{-1/2}](U^{-1/2})'(V^{1/2})'. \qquad (3.24)$$

If $T\delta_T^2(\hat{\theta})$ exceeds the critical value from this weighted chi-squared distribution, then the model is misspecified. In this case, the traditional standard errors of the estimates $\hat{\theta}$ proposed by Hansen (1982) need to be adjusted for model misspecification (Kan and Robotti, 2009; Gospodinov et al., 2011a). Even if all candidate asset pricing models are misspecified, knowing which model provides the smaller pricing errors is still interesting. The statistical comparison of the HJ-distances of two or more competing models depends on whether the models are correctly specified or misspecified and nested or nonnested. Kan and Robotti (2009) and Gospodinov et al. (2011a) provide model selection tests to compare the performance of linear and nonlinear asset pricing models.

Beta-Pricing Models and Two-Pass Cross-Sectional Regressions

From Equation 3.13, the expected-return errors of the N assets are given by

$$e = E[R] - B\gamma. \qquad (3.25)$$

A popular goodness-of-fit measure used in many empirical studies is the cross-sectional R^2. Following Kandel and Stambaugh (1995), this is defined as

$$R^2 = 1 - \frac{Q}{Q_0}, \qquad (3.26)$$

where $Q = e'We$, $Q_0 = e_0'We_0$, $e_0 = [I_N - 1_N(1_N'W1_N)^{-1}1_N'W]E[R]$ represents the deviations of mean returns from their cross-sectional average and W is a positive-definite weighting matrix. Popular choices of W in the literature are $W = I_N$ (ordinary least squares [OLS]), $W = Var[R]^{-1}$ (generalized least squares [GLS]), and $W = \Sigma_d^{-1}$ (weighted least squares [WLS]), where Σ_d is a diagonal matrix containing the diagonal elements of Σ, the variance-covariance matrix of the residuals from the first-pass time series regression. In order for R^2 to be well defined requires assuming that $E[R]$ is not proportional to 1_N (the expected returns are not all equal) so that $Q_0 > 0$. Note that $0 < R^2 < 1$ and it is a decreasing function of the aggregate pricing-error measure Q. Thus, R^2 is a natural measure of goodness of fit.

As emphasized by Kan and Zhou (2004), R^2 is oriented toward expected returns whereas the HJ-distance evaluates a model's ability to explain prices. With the zero-beta rate as a free parameter, the most common approach in the asset pricing literature, Kan and Zhou show that the two measures need not rank models the same way. Thus, both measures are of interest, with the choice depending on the economic context and perhaps the manner in which a researcher envisions applying the models.

The estimated multiple regression betas of the N assets with respect to the K factors are defined as

$$\hat{\beta} = \hat{V}_{Rf}\hat{V}_f^{-1}, \qquad (3.27)$$

where $\hat{V}_{Rf}$ and $\hat{V}_f$ are consistent estimators of $Cov[R, f]$ and $Var[f]$, respectively. Some studies allow the β's to change throughout the sample period. For example, in the original Fama and MacBeth (1973) study, the authors estimated the betas used in the CSR for month t using data before that month. A more customary practice in recent decades is to use full-period beta estimates for portfolios formed by ranking stocks according to various characteristics. Then, the estimated β's are used as regressors in the second-pass CSR.

Then, the estimated risk premia, γ, are given by

$$\hat{\gamma} = (B_T'W_TB_T)^{-1}B_T'W_T\overline{R}, \qquad (3.28)$$

where $B_T = [1_N, \hat{\beta}]$ and $\overline{R} = \frac{1}{T}\sum_{t=1}^{T}R_t$. Under the correctly specified model, the asymptotic standard errors of the risk premia estimates in Equation 3.28 are provided by Shanken (1992) and Jagannathan and Wang (1998). Further,

Shanken (1992) shows that when the factors are portfolio returns, the most efficient estimates of the factor risk premia are the time-series means of the factors. He also demonstrates how to incorporate the portfolio restriction in the
cross-sectional relation when some of the factors are traded and others are not.

The vector of sample pricing errors is given by

$$\hat{e} = \bar{R} - B_T\,\hat{\gamma} \tag{3.29}$$

and the sample R^2 is

$$\hat{R}^2 = 1 - \frac{\hat{Q}}{\hat{Q}_0}, \tag{3.30}$$

where $\hat{Q} = \hat{e}'W_T\hat{e}, Q_0 = \hat{e}_0'\,W_T\hat{e}_0, \hat{e}_0 = [I_N - 1_N(1_N'\,W_T1_N)^{-1}1_N'\,W_T]\bar{R}$. To determine
whether the model is correctly specified, one can test if the CSR R^2 is equal to 1.
Kan et al. (2012) show that if the expected returns are exactly linear in the betas,
then the limiting distribution of $T(\hat{R}^2-1)$ is that of a linear combination of $N -$
$K - 1$ independent χ_1^2 random variables. Further, the researchers characterize the
asymptotic distribution of the sample R^2 when the true R^2 is zero (i.e., the model
has no explanatory power for expected returns) and the true R^2 is between zero
and one (i.e., the model is misspecified and contains some explanatory power
for the expected returns on the test assets). Shanken (1985); Gibbons, Ross, and
Shanken (1989); and Kan et al. (2012) provide alternative tests of the validity of
the beta-pricing relation.

When the beta-pricing model is misspecified, the asymptotic standard errors
proposed by Shanken (1992) and Jagannathan and Wang (1998) are incorrect.
Shanken and Zhou (2007) and Kan et al. (2012) show how to compute misspecification-robust standard errors of the risk-premia estimates. Finally, Kan et al. (2012)
develop the necessary econometric techniques to compare the cross-sectional R^2s of
two or more beta-pricing models. As for the HJ-distance measure, the asymptotic
distributions of their tests depend on whether the models are correctly specified or
misspecified and nested or nonnested.

Conditional Asset Pricing Models and Return Predictability

Recall that the fundamental pricing equation (Equation 3.2) is defined in terms
of conditional expectations. Although the law of iterated expectations permits
the estimation of the model in terms of unconditional moments, some relevant
information may get lost in the process. This section explains how to incorporate
conditioning information in a linear asset pricing model, describes the underlying
assumptions, and provides an interpretation of the zero-beta rate and risk premia
in the cross-sectional regression.

Let z_t be an L-vector of observed conditioning variables (instruments) that belongs to the information set at time t and define $F_{t+1} = [z_t', f_{t+1}', z_t' \otimes f_{t+1}']'$ as a $\tilde{K} = (K+1)(L+1)-1$ vector of scaled factors. Recently, many empirical studies (see, for example, Shanken, 1990; Lettau and Ludvigson, 2001; Lustig and Van Nieuwerburgh, 2005; Santos and Veronesi, 2006) have considered a cross-sectional regression of unconditional expected returns on their unconditional betas with respect to F_{t+1}:

$$E[R_{t+1}] = 1_N \gamma_0 + \beta \gamma_1, \qquad (3.31)$$

where

$$\beta = Cov[R_{t+1}, F_{t+1}] Var[F_{t+1}]^{-1}. \qquad (3.32)$$

There are two ways for obtaining the unconditional relationship between $E[R_{t+1}]$ and β in Equation 3.31. The first approach is a time-varying SDF coefficients approach, which assumes that the SDF is linear in a set of risk variables, i. e.,

$$m_{t+1} = a_t + b_t' f_{t+1}. \qquad (3.33)$$

The linearity of the SDF in f_{t+1} allows obtaining the following conditional asset pricing model:

$$E[R_{t+1} | z_t] = 1_N \gamma_{0,t} + \beta_t \gamma_{1,t}, \qquad (3.34)$$

where $\beta_t = Cov[R_{t+1}, f_{t+1} | z_t] Var[f_{t+1} | z_t]^{-1}$ is the matrix of conditional betas and

$$\gamma_{0,t} = \frac{1}{E[m_{t+1} | z_t]} - 1, \qquad (3.35)$$

$$\gamma_{1,t} = -\frac{Var[f_{t+1} | z_t] b_t}{E[m_{t+1} | z_t]}. \qquad (3.36)$$

If a zero-beta asset exists with a raw return of $R_{0,t+1}$ (with $R_{0,t+1}$ being conditionally uncorrelated with m_{t+1}), it follows that

$$\gamma_{0,t} = 1 + E[R_{0,t+1} | z_t]. \qquad (3.37)$$

The SDF coefficients, a_t and b_t, are often assumed to be linear functions of the instruments z_t:

$$a_t = a_0 + a_1' z_t \qquad (3.38)$$

and

$$b_t = b_0 + B_1 z_t. \tag{3.39}$$

Then, m_{t+1} can be written as

$$m_{t+1} = a_0 + \tilde{b} F_{t+1}, \tag{3.40}$$

where $\tilde{b} = [a_1', b_0', vec(B_1)']'$. As a result, assuming that the coefficients of the SDF are linear in z_t is equivalent to assuming that the SDF is linear in the scaled factors. For example, in a model with one risk factor and one conditioning variable, the SDF is given by

$$m_{t+1} = (a_0 + a_1 z_t) + (b_0 + b_1 z_t) f_{t+1} = a_0 + a_1 z_t + b_0 f_{t+1} + b_1 (z_t f_{t+1}). \tag{3.41}$$

This suggests that going from a one-factor model with time-varying coefficients to a three-factor model with fixed coefficients is possible. Therefore, one can use the new (scaled) factors with the unconditional moment procedure developed above.

However, the γ_0 in Equation 3.31 should not be interpreted as the unconditional expected return on the zero-beta asset. The reason is that, using Equation 3.37, Jensen's inequality and the fact that $E[m_{t+1} | z_t]$ is a positive random variable (positivity of m_{t+1} is required here), it follows that

$$E[R_{0,t+1}] \geq \gamma_0. \tag{3.42}$$

The equality holds if and only if $E[m_{t+1} | z_t]$ is constant over time. This result suggests that if a risk-free asset exists, then γ_0 tends to be less than the average risk-free rate. Similarly, the elements of γ_1 that correspond to the original K factors should not be interpreted as unconditional risk premia.

The second approach that can deliver Equation 3.31 is a time-varying regression-coefficients approach (Shanken, 1990) with data-generating process given by

$$R_{t+1} = \alpha_t + \beta_t f_{t+1} + \varepsilon_{t+1}, \tag{3.43}$$

where β_t is the matrix of conditional betas defined above and $\alpha_t = E[R_{t+1} | z_t] - \beta_t E[f_{t+1} | z_t]$. When the conditional K-factor beta-pricing model holds,

$$E[R_{t+1} | z_t] = 1_N \gamma_{0,t} + \beta_t \gamma_{1,t}. \tag{3.44}$$

Assuming the conditional expectation of Equation 3.43 holds, the conditional K-factor beta-pricing model imposes the following restrictions on a_t:

$$\alpha_t = 1_N \gamma_{0,t} + \beta_t (\gamma_{1,t} - E[f_{t+1} | z_t]) = 1_N \gamma_{0,t} + \beta_t \varphi_t, \tag{3.45}$$

where $\varphi_t = \gamma_{1,t} - E[f_{t+1}|z_t]$. The betas, the zero-beta rate, and the risk premia in Equation 3.45 are time varying. Since these restrictions are too general to test, some ancillary assumptions are needed. One possibility is to assume that $\gamma_{0,t}$ and φ_t are constant over time and that a_t and β_t are linear functions of z_t:

$$\alpha_t = a_0 + A_1 z_t, \tag{3.46}$$

$$vec(\beta_t) = b_0 + B_1 z_t. \tag{3.47}$$

The restriction in Equation 3.45 then becomes:

$$a_0 + A_1 z_t = 1_N \gamma_0 + (\varphi' \otimes I_N)(b_0 + B_1 z_t). \tag{3.48}$$

This restriction implies that

$$a_0 = 1_N \gamma_0 + (\varphi' \otimes I_N) b_0 \tag{3.49}$$

and

$$A_1 = (\varphi' \otimes I_N) B_1. \tag{3.50}$$

The return-generating process can be written as

$$R_{t+1} = a_0 + A_1 z_t + (f'_{t+1} \otimes I_N)(b_0 + B_1 z_t) + \varepsilon_{t+1}, \tag{3.51}$$

which has $N(K+1)(L+1)$ parameters. This result is the same as running a regression of R_{t+1} on a constant term and the scaled factors F_{t+1}:

$$R_{t+1} = \tilde{\alpha} + \tilde{\beta}_1 z_t + \tilde{\beta}_2 f_{t+1} + \tilde{\beta}_3 (z_t \otimes f_{t+1}) + \varepsilon_{t+1}. \tag{3.52}$$

Comparing Equations 3.51 and 3.52 yields

$$\tilde{\alpha} = a_0, \quad \tilde{\beta}_1 = A_1, \quad vec(\tilde{\beta}_2) = b_0, \quad vec(\tilde{\beta}_3) = vec(B_1). \tag{3.53}$$

Taking the unconditional expectation of Equation 3.52, we get

$$E[R_{t+1}] = \tilde{\alpha} + \tilde{\beta}_1 E[z_t] + \tilde{\beta}_2 E[f_{t+1}] + \tilde{\beta}_3 E[z_t \otimes f_{t+1}]. \tag{3.54}$$

Using the asset pricing restrictions

$$\tilde{\alpha} = 1_N \gamma_0 + \tilde{\beta}_2 \varphi, \tag{3.55}$$

it follows that

$$E[R_{t+1}]=1_N\,\gamma_0+\tilde{\beta}_1 E[z_t]+\tilde{\beta}_2(\varphi+E[f_{t+1}])+\tilde{\beta}_3 E[z_t\otimes f_{t+1}]. \qquad (3.56)$$

The risk premia associated with $\tilde{\beta}$ in the regression setup are not unrestricted, which differs from the time-varying SDF coefficients setup. In the regression framework, γ_0 indeed has a zero-beta interpretation and the risk premia associated with $\tilde{\beta}_2$ are indeed equal to the risk premia on the original factors. However, this relationship comes at the expense of assuming that γ_0 and φ are constant over time. Additionally, imposing the restriction $A_1=(\varphi'\otimes I_N)B_1$, which is equivalent to $\tilde{\beta}_1=\tilde{\beta}_3(I_L\otimes\varphi)$ results in a simpler cross-sectional regression:

$$E[R_{t+1}]=1_N\,\gamma_0+\tilde{\beta}_2(\varphi+E[f_{t+1}])+\tilde{\beta}_3 E[z_t\otimes(\varphi+f_{t+1})]. \qquad (3.57)$$

In summary, both approaches can lead to the unconditional relationship in Equation 3.31. However, the time-varying regression coefficients approach requires many assumptions (linearity assumptions on $N(K+1)$ regression coefficients together with constant γ_0 and φ). In contrast, the SDF approach requires far fewer assumptions (linearity assumption on $K+1$ SDF coefficients) and does not assume that the zero-beta rate and the risk premia are constant over time. In the regression approach, the γ_0 and γ_1 associated with the original factors retain the zero-beta rate and risk premia interpretation. Conversely, in the SDF approach, the γ_0 and γ_1 associated with the original factors cannot be interpreted as unconditional zero-beta rate and risk premia. Finally, Equation 3.57 shows that in the regression approach, the cross-sectional regression should be run only with a constant, $\tilde{\beta}_2$ and $\tilde{\beta}_3$. Although the risk premia associated with $\tilde{\beta}_1$ are in general not zero (unless the information variables are de-meaned), including $\tilde{\beta}_1$ does not provide additional explanatory power in the cross-sectional regression.

Conditional asset pricing models presume the existence of some return predictability. For the conditional restriction in Equation 3.2 to be empirically relevant, there should exist some instruments z_t for which the first and second moments of the SDF and of the returns vary over time. A typical predictive regression model of stock returns has the form:

$$R_{t+1}=\alpha+z_t'\beta+e_{t+1}, \qquad (3.58)$$

where e_{t+1} is a martingale difference sequence. The vector of financial and macro predictors z_t includes valuation ratios (dividend-price ratio, dividend yields, earnings-price ratio, dividend-earnings ratio, and book-to-market ratio); interest and inflation rates (short-term rates, yield spreads, default premium, and inflation rate); consumption and wealth-income ratio; and stock return volatility (realized or implied volatility), among others.

The main drawback of this approach is the reliance on a small number of conditioning variables, which is unlikely to span the information set of market participants (Ludvigson and Ng, 2007). Furthermore, the predictive ability of individual conditioning variables, if there is any, is only short-lived (Timmermann, 2008), unstable, and subject to structural breaks over longer time periods (Lettau and Van Nieuwerburgh, 2008). To a large extent, these drawbacks can be remedied by estimating a few common factors from a large panel of economic time series that are believed to span the information set of investors (Ludvigson and Ng, 2007).

To introduce the main idea behind the estimation of common factors, suppose that the researcher has access to the large panel of data x_{it} ($i = 1,\ldots, M$; $t = 1,\ldots, T$), where M represents the number of variables (financial and macro variables) and T represents the number of time-series observations. Assume that x_{it} admits an approximate factor structure of the form:

$$x_{it} = \omega_i' f_t + e_{it}, \tag{3.59}$$

where f_t is a K-vector of latent factors, ω_i is a K-vector of factor loadings, and e_{it} are errors uncorrelated with the factors. Let $X = [x_1 x_2 \cdots x_M]$ and $F = [f_1 f_2 \cdots f_K]$ denote the stacked matrices for the data and the factors. Then, under some technical conditions, the latent factors can be estimated with the method of principal components by minimizing the objective function

$$\frac{1}{MT} \sum_{i=1}^{M} \sum_{t=1}^{T} (x_{it} - \omega_i' f_t)^2, \tag{3.60}$$

subject to the identifying restriction $\frac{F'F}{T} = I_K$. The problem of estimating f_t is identical to maximizing $\operatorname{tr}(F'(XX')F)$, and the estimated factors $\hat{f}_t$ are $\sqrt{T}$ times the K eigenvectors corresponding to the K largest eigenvalues of the matrix XX'.

The evaluation of the predictability of stock returns is performed either in sample or out of sample using statistical or economic criteria. The in-sample predictability is assessed in terms of the time series R^2 of the model and of the statistical significance of the coefficient on a particular predictor. Typically, predictive regressions of stock returns are characterized by a statistically small but possibly economically relevant R^2 (Campbell and Thompson, 2008). As discussed later in this chapter, the statistical significance of the slope parameter (based on the standard normal approximation) may be misleading if the predictor is highly persistent.

The out-of-sample prediction is performed by dividing the sample into two subsamples, with the first subsample used for parameter estimation and the second subsample used for out-of-sample forecast evaluation. The statistical evaluation is based on the out-of-sample R^2 coefficient and mean-squared or absolute errors that compare the actual and predicted values of the returns. Conversely, the profit-based evaluation involves computing returns from a trading strategy for stocks and bonds, depending on whether the predicted excess returns from the model are positive (position in stocks) or negative (position in bonds). Then, the Sharpe ratio of the model-based trading strategy is compared to the Sharpe ratio of a buy-and-hold benchmark strategy over the out-of-sample evaluation period. Welch and Goyal (2008) provide a comprehensive study of the out-of-sample performance of various financial and macroeconomic variables for predicting stock returns.

Nonlinear Asset Pricing Models

The generality of the SDF representation and GMM estimation based on the HJ-distance becomes obvious in the case, for example, of nonlinear consumption-based asset pricing models. As discussed above, the SDF for a representative agent model can be written as the product of the time-preference parameter β and the ratio of the marginal utilities of consumption at times $t + 1$ and t, respectively.

Consider the constant relative risk aversion (CRRA) or power utility function

$$u(c_t) = \frac{c_t^{1-\rho} - 1}{1 - \rho}, \tag{3.61}$$

where $\rho > 0$ is the coefficient of relative risk aversion. For example, when $\rho \to 1$, $u(c_t) = \log(c_t)$. The Arrow-Pratt coefficient of relative risk aversion $\frac{c_t u''(c_t)}{u'(c_t)}$ is ρ, suggesting that relative risk aversion is constant.

Substituting for $m_t = \beta \left(\frac{c_{t+1}}{c_t} \right)^{-\rho}$ in the fundamental pricing equation delivers the following set of moments:

$$E_t \left[\beta \left(\frac{c_{t+1}}{c_t} \right)^{-\rho} (1 + R_{t+1}) - 1_N \right] = 0_N. \tag{3.62}$$

For a vector of instruments (conditioning variables) z_t that belongs to the information set at time t, the sample analog of the above population moment condition is

$$g_T(\theta) = \frac{1}{T} \sum_{t=1}^{T} \left[\beta \left(\frac{c_{t+1}}{c_t} \right)^{-\rho} (1 + R_{t+1}) - 1_N \right] \otimes z_t = 0_m, \tag{3.63}$$

where $m = \dim(R_{t+1}) \dim(z_t)$ and $\theta = (\beta, \rho)'$. The unknown parameters θ are then estimated by GMM.

Several drawbacks of the CRRA utility function are worth mentioning. First the equity premium puzzle (Mehra and Prescott, 1985) implies unrealistically large values for risk aversion (having a ρ as high as 30–50) in order to fit US data. For example, in a gamble that offers a 50 percent chance to double one's wealth and a 50 percent chance to cut one's wealth in half, a value of risk aversion parameter of 30 implies that one would be willing to pay 49 percent of her wealth to hedge against the 50 percent chance of losing half of her wealth (Siegel and Thaler, 1997). Second, in the CRRA framework, ρ is inversely related to the elasticity of intertemporal substitution (EIS). This is inappropriate because EIS is related to the willingness of an investor to transfer consumption between time periods, whereas CRRA is about transferring consumption between states of the world. The nonexpected and time nonseparable (habit persistence) utility functions described below separate risk aversion and intertemporal substitution.

The nonexpected Epstein-Zin-Weil (Epsein and Zin, 1989, 1991; Weil, 1989) utility is given by

$$u(c_t) = \left[(1-\beta)c_t^{1-\eta} + \beta(E_t[u_{t+1}^{1-\rho}])^{(1-\eta)/(1-\rho)} \right]^{1/(1-\eta)},\qquad (3.64)$$

which gives rise to the following pricing equation (conditional moment restriction):

$$E_t\left[\beta^\lambda \left(\frac{c_{t+1}}{c_t} \right)^{-\eta\lambda} (1+R_{m,t+1})^{\lambda-1}(1+R_{t+1})-1_N \right] = 0_N,\qquad (3.65)$$

where $\lambda = \dfrac{1-\rho}{1-\eta}$ and R_m denotes the market return. Note that for $\lambda = 1$ (or, equivalently, $\eta = \rho$), this equation reduces to the one corresponding to the time-separable (CRRA) utility. The sample analog of the moment condition above is given by

$$g_T(\theta) = \frac{1}{T}\sum_{t=1}^{T}\left[\beta^\lambda \left(\frac{c_{t+1}}{c_t} \right)^{-\eta\lambda} (1+R_{m,t+1})^{\lambda-1}(1+R_{t+1})-1_N \right]\otimes z_t = 0_m,\qquad (3.66)$$

where the parameter vector is $\theta = (\beta, \eta, \lambda)'$.

Another popular extension of the CRRA framework is the utility function with habit persistence and durability,

$$u(c_t, c_{t-1}) = \frac{s_t^{1-\rho}}{1-\rho},\qquad (3.67)$$

where $s_t = c_t + \tau c_{t-1}$ and τ is the habit persistence parameter. The conditional moment restrictions are given by

$$E_t\left[\beta(s_{t+1}^{-\rho}+\beta\tau s_{t+2}^{-\rho})(1+R_{t+1})-(s_t^{-\rho}+\beta\tau s_{t+1}^{-\rho})\right]=0_N,\qquad(3.68)$$

and their sample analog takes the form

$$g_T(\theta)=\frac{1}{T}\sum_{t=1}^{T}\left[\beta\left(\frac{s_{t+1}^{-\rho}+\beta\tau s_{t+2}^{-\rho}}{s_t^{-\rho}(1+\beta\tau)}\right)(1+R_{t+1})-\left(\frac{s_t^{-\rho}+\beta\tau s_{t+1}^{-\rho}}{s_t^{-\rho}(1+\beta\tau)}\right)1_N\right]\otimes z_t=0_m,$$

where $\theta=(\beta,\rho,\tau)'$ and the original moment conditions are divided by the term $s_t^{-\rho}(1+\beta\tau)$ to produce stationary variables and rule out trivial solutions (note that if $\rho = 0$ and $\beta\tau=-1$, the moment conditions are trivially satisfied). As in the case of nonexpected utility, the time-separable (CRRA) utility is a special case of Equation 3.69 for $\tau=0$. While estimating the set of moment conditions for the habit persistence model and testing the implied model restrictions are possible, Equation 3.69 does not have a clear pricing error interpretation. One possibility is to make lognormality assumptions, as done in Balduzzi and Kallal (1997), cast the restrictions in pricing error form, and use the HJ-distance metric for model evaluation and comparison. To conclude, all linear and nonlinear asset pricing models that have been proposed in the literature can be written in terms of the fundamental asset pricing equation (Equation 3.2) and can be estimated using GMM-type techniques.

Pitfalls in the Current Practice and Suggestions for Improving Empirical Work

One empirical finding that consistently emerges from the statistical tests and comparisons of competing asset pricing models is that the data are too noisy for a meaningful and conclusive differentiation among alternative SDF specifications. Given the large noise component in returns on risky assets, explaining the cross-sectional variability of asset returns by using slowly changing financial and macroeconomic variables appears to be a daunting task. Even if the asset pricing theories provide guidance for the model specification, the properties of the data and some limitations of the standard statistical methodology can create further challenges in applied work. This section discusses several pitfalls that accompany the estimation of risk premia and the evaluation of competing asset pricing models using actual data. Particular attention is paid to the possibility of model misspecification, the presence of useless factors, highly persistent conditioning variables, working with a large number of test assets, the potential lack of invariance to data scaling, and the interpretation of risk premia.

MISSPECIFIED MODELS

A widely held belief is that asset pricing models are likely to be misspecified and should be viewed only as approximations of the true data-generating process. Nevertheless, empirically evaluating the degree of misspecification and the relative pricing performance of candidate models through the use of actual data is useful.

There are two main problems with the econometric analyses performed in the existing asset pricing studies. First, even when a model is strongly rejected by the data (using one of the model specification tests previously described, for example), researchers still construct standard errors of parameter estimates using the theory developed for correctly specified models. This process could give rise to highly misleading inferences, especially when the degree of misspecification is large. Kan and Robotti (2009) and Gospodinov et al. (2011a) focus on the HJ-distance metric and derive misspecification-robust standard errors of the SDF parameter estimates for linear and nonlinear models. In contrast, Kan et al. (2012) focus on the beta representation of an asset pricing model and propose misspecification-robust standard errors of the second-pass risk premia estimates. For example, for linear SDF specifications, the misspecification adjustment term, which is associated with the misspecification uncertainty surrounding the model, can be decomposed into three components: (1) a pure misspecification component, which captures the degree of misspecification; (2) a spanning component that measures the degree to which the factors are mimicked by returns; and (3) a component that measures the usefulness of the factors in explaining the variation in returns. The adjustment term is zero if the model is correctly specified (component (1) is zero) and/or the factors are fully mimicked by the returns (component (2) is zero). If the factors are weakly correlated with the returns, the adjustment term could be very large. This issue will be revisited in the discussion of the case involving useless factors in the next section.

Second, many researchers are still ranking competing models by simply eyeballing the differences in sample HJ-distances or sample R^2's without the use of a formal statistical criterion that accounts for the sampling and model misspecification uncertainty. Kan and Robotti (2009), Kan et al. (2012), and Gospodinov et al. (2011a) develop a complete statistical procedure for comparing alternative asset pricing models. These model selection tests take into account the restrictions imposed by the structure of the competing models (nested, nonnested, and overlapping) as well as the estimation and model misspecification uncertainty. Gospodinov et al. (2011a) also propose chi-squared versions of these tests that are easy to implement and that enjoy excellent finite-sample properties.

One recommendation for empirical work that emerges from this discussion is that the statistical inference in asset pricing models should allow for the possibility of potential misspecification. This will ensure robust and valid inference in the presence of model misspecification as well as when the models are correctly specified.

USELESS FACTORS

Consistent estimation and valid inference in asset pricing models crucially depends on the identification condition in which the covariance matrix of asset returns and risk factors is of full rank. Kan and Zhang (1999a, 1999b) study the consequences of the violation of this identification condition. In particular, they show that when the model is misspecified and one of the included factors is useless (i.e., independent of asset returns), the asymptotic properties of parameter and specification tests in GMM and two-pass cross-sectional regressions are severely affected.

The first serious implication of the presence of a useless factor is that the asymptotic distribution of the Wald test of statistical significance (a squared t-test) of the useless factor's parameter (in the HJ-distance case) is chi-squared distributed with $N–K–1$ degrees of freedom instead of one degree of freedom, as in the standard case when all factors are useful. The immediate consequence of this result is that the Wald test that uses critical values from a chi-squared distribution with one degree of freedom will reject the null hypothesis too frequently when the null hypothesis is true. The false rejections are shown to become more severe as the number of test assets N becomes larger and as the length of the sample increases. As a result, researchers may erroneously conclude that the useless factor is priced when, in reality, it is pure noise, uncorrelated with the stock market.

Another important implication of the presence of a useless factor is that the true risk premium associated with the useless factor is not identifiable and the estimate of this risk premium diverges at rate $\sqrt{T}$. In this case, the standard errors of the risk-premium estimates associated with the useful factors included in the model are also affected by the presence of a useless factor and the standard inference is distorted. Similar results also arise for optimal GMM estimation (Kan and Zhang 1999a) and two-pass cross-sectional regressions (Kan and Zhang 1999b).

The useless factor problem is particularly serious because the traditional model-specification tests previously described cannot reliably detect misspecification in the presence of a useless factor. This manifests itself in the failure of the specification tests to reject the null hypothesis of correct specification when the model is indeed misspecified and contains a useless factor.

More generally, similar types of problems are symptomatic of a violation of the crucial identification condition in which the covariance matrix of asset returns and risk factors must be of full rank. Therefore, a rank restriction test (see, for example, Gospodinov, Kan, and Robotti, 2012) should serve as a useful pretest for possible identification problems in the model (see also Burnside, 2010). However, this test cannot identify which factor contributes to the identification failure. Kleibergen (2009) proposes test statistics that exhibit robustness to the degree of correlation between returns and factors in a two-pass cross-sectional regression framework. In the SDF framework, Gospodinov, Kan, and Robotti (2011b) develop a simple (asymptotically χ_1^2-distributed) misspecification-robust test that signals the direction of the identification failure. Only after the useless factor is detected and removed from the analysis, the validity of the (misspecification-robust) inference and the consistency of the parameter estimates can be restored.

ESTIMATING MODELS WITH EXCESS RETURNS

When excess returns (R^e) are used to estimate and test asset pricing models, the moment conditions (pricing equations) are

$$E(mR^e) = 0_N.$$

Let $m = \theta_0 - (\theta_1 f_1 + \cdots + \theta_K f_K)$. In this case, the mean of the SDF cannot be identified or, equivalently, the parameters θ_0 and $(\theta_1, \ldots, \theta_K)$ cannot be identified separately. This requires a particular choice of normalization. One popular normalization is to set $\theta_0 = 1$, in which case $m = 1 - (\theta_1 f_1 + \cdots + \theta_K f_K)$. An alternative (preferred) normalization is to set $\theta_0 = 1 + \theta_1 E(f_1) + \cdots + \theta_K E(f_K)$, in which case $m = 1 - \theta_1[f_1 - E(f_1)] - \cdots - \theta_K[f_K - E(f_K)]$ with $E(m) = 1$. These two normalizations can give rise to very different results (see Kan and Robotti, 2008; Burnside, 2010).

Kan and Robotti (2008) argue that when the model is misspecified, the first (raw) and the second (de-meaned) normalizations of the SDF produce different GMM estimates that minimize the quadratic form of the pricing errors. Hence, the pricing errors and the p-values of the specification tests are not identical under these two normalizations. Moreover, the second (de-meaned) specification imposes the constraint $E(m) = 1$ and, as a result, the pricing errors and the HJ-distances are invariant to affine transformations of the factors. This is important because in the first normalization, the outcome of the model specification test can be easily manipulated by simple scaling of factors and changing the mean of the SDF. This problem is not only a characteristic of linear SDFs but also arises in nonlinear models. The analysis in Burnside (2010) further confirms these findings and links the properties of the different normalizations to possible model misspecification and identification problems discussed in the previous two subsections.

In a two-pass CSR framework, Kan et al. (2012) explore an excess returns specification with the zero-beta rate constrained to equal the risk-free rate. Imposing this restriction seems sensible since when the beta-pricing models are estimated with the zero-beta rate as a free parameter, the estimated zero-beta rate is often too high and the estimated market premium is often negative, contrary to what economic theory suggests. The zero-beta restriction in the CSR context can be implemented by working with test portfolio returns in excess of the T-bill rate, while excluding the constant from the expected return relations. As is typical for regression analysis without a constant, the corresponding R^2 measure involves (weighted) sums of squared values of the dependent variable (mean excess returns) in the denominator, not squared deviations from the cross-sectional average.

With the zero-beta rate constrained in this manner, it follows from the results found in Kan and Robotti (2008) that the equality of generalized least squares (GLS) R^2's for two models is equivalent to the equality of their HJ-distances, provided that the SDF is written as a linear function of the de-meaned factors as mentioned above. No such relation exists for the ordinary least squares (OLS) R^2.

CONDITIONAL MODELS WITH HIGHLY PERSISTENT PREDICTORS

The usefulness of the conditional asset pricing models crucially depends on the existence of some predictive ability of the conditioning variables for future stock returns. While a large number of studies report statistically significant coefficients for various financial and macro variables in in-sample linear predictive regressions of stock returns, several papers raise the concern that some of these regressions may be spurious. For example, Ferson, Sarkissian, and Simin (2003) call into question the predictive power of some widely used predictors, such as the term spread, the book-to-market ratio, and the dividend yield. Spurious results arise when the predictors are strongly persistent (near unit root processes) and their innovations are highly correlated with the predictive regression errors. In this case, the estimated slope coefficients in the predictive regression are biased and have a nonstandard (nonnormal) asymptotic distribution (Elliott and Stock, 1994; Cavanagh, Elliott, and Stock, 1995; Stambaugh, 1999). As a result, t-tests for statistical significance of individual predictors based on standard normal critical values could reject the null hypothesis of no predictability too frequently and falsely signal that these predictors have predictive power for future stock returns. Campbell and Yogo (2006) and Torous, Valkanov, and Yan (2004) develop valid testing procedures when the predictors are highly persistent and revisit the evidence on the predictability of stock returns.

Spuriously significant results and nonstandard sampling distributions also tend to arise in long-horizon predictive regressions, where the regressors and/or the returns are accumulated over r time periods so that two or more consecutive observations are overlapping. The time overlap increases the persistence of the variables and renders the sampling distribution theory of the slope coefficients, t-tests and R^2 coefficients, nonstandard. Campbell (2001) and Valkanov (2003) point out several problems that emerge in long-horizon regressions with highly persistent regressors. First, the R^2 coefficients and t-statistics tend to increase with the horizon, even under the null of no predictability, and the R^2 is an unreliable measure of goodness of fit in this situation. Furthermore, the t-statistics do not converge asymptotically to well-defined distributions and need to be rescaled to ensure valid inference. Finally, the estimates of the slope coefficients are biased and, in some cases, not consistently estimable. All these statistical problems provide a warning to applied researchers and indicate that the selection of conditioning variables for predicting stock returns should be performed with extreme caution.

MODEL EVALUATION WITH A LARGE NUMBER OF ASSETS

A common practice is to evaluate the empirical relevance of different asset pricing models using a relatively large cross-section of returns on 25, 50, or 100 portfolios at monthly or quarterly frequencies over a period of 30 years (Fama and French, 1992; Jagannathan and Wang, 1996). Since the size of the cross-section, N, determines the dimensionality of the vector of moment conditions in the GMM estimation, the small number of time series observations per moment condition renders the asymptotic approximations for some specification and model comparison tests inaccurate.

For instance, Ahn and Gadarowski (2004) report substantial size distortions of the specification test based on the HJ-distance for combinations of N and T that are typically encountered in practice. In particular, in some of their simulation designs, the HJ-distance test rejects the null hypothesis when the null hypothesis is true 99 percent (51 percent) of the time for $N = 100$ and $T = 160$ ($T = 330$) at the 1 percent nominal level. This indicates that the researcher will erroneously conclude with high probability that the asset pricing model under investigation is misspecified. These simulation results suggest that the weighted, chi-squared asymptotic approximation (for a fixed N and T approaching infinity) is inappropriate when the number of test assets is large.

Several testing procedures for correct model specification with improved finite-sample properties are available in the literature. Kan and Zhou (2004) derive the exact distribution of the sample HJ-distance that can be obtained by simulation. On the other hand, Gospodinov et al. (2011a) continue to use the weighted, chi-squared asymptotic approximation but compute the weights for this asymptotic distribution not from the covariance matrix of the pricing errors that are computed under the null hypothesis but from its analog computed under the alternative of misspecification. While these covariance matrices are asymptotically equivalent under the null of correct specification, the covariance matrix computed under the alternative tends to be larger in finite samples, thus rendering the too-frequent rejection problem less severe. Finally, Gospodinov et al. (2011a) propose an alternative model specification test that measures the distance of the Lagrange multipliers, associated with the pricing constraints imposed by the model, from zero. This new test is easy to implement (critical values are based on a chi-squared distribution with $N-K-1$ degrees of freedom) and is characterized by excellent size and power properties.

BETA OR COVARIANCE RISK?

Historically, researchers have almost exclusively focused on the price of beta risk to infer whether a proposed factor is priced. However, a potential issue exists with using multiple regression betas when $K > 1$: in general, the beta of an asset with respect to a particular factor depends on what other factors are included in the first-pass time-series OLS regression. As a consequence, the interpretation of the risk premia given in Equation 3.28 in the context of model selection can be problematic. For example, suppose that a model has two factors:

f_1 and f_2. Interest often lies in determining whether f_2 is needed in the model. Some researchers have tried to answer this question by performing a test of $H_0 : \gamma_2 = 0$, where γ_2 is the risk premium associated with factor 2. When the null hypothesis is rejected by the data, they typically conclude that factor 2 is important, and when the null hypothesis is not rejected, they conclude that factor 2 is unimportant.

Kan et al. (2012) provide numerical examples illustrating that the test of $H_0 : \gamma_2 = 0$ does not answer the question of whether factor 2 helps to explain the cross-sectional differences in expected returns on the test assets. They also provide two solutions to this problem. The first remedy they suggest is to use simple regression betas instead of multiple regression betas in the second-pass CSR. The second solution consists in running the second-pass CSR with covariances instead of betas. Kan and Robotti (2011) derive the asymptotic theory for the case of simple regression betas, while Kan et al. (2012) provide inference techniques for second-pass regressions that are run with covariances instead of betas. Therefore, researchers should focus on the price of covariance risk and not on the price of beta risk. Finding a statistically significant price of covariance risk is indeed evidence that the underlying factor is incrementally useful in explaining the cross-section of asset returns.

Summary and Conclusions

This chapter provides an up-to-date review of the two most popular approaches for estimating, testing, and comparing potentially misspecified asset pricing models: the stochastic discount factor and the beta methods. The analysis points out various pitfalls in the implementation of these methodologies that could lead to erroneous conclusions. Special emphasis is given to the role played by model misspecification in tests of unconditional and conditional asset pricing models, to the important issue of selecting information variables that truly predict future returns, and to different ways of incorporating the predictions of asset pricing theory into competing empirical specifications.

Although the recommendations in this chapter are specifically designed to sharpen asset pricing tests and increase the challenge to the existing models, much remains to be done. On the one hand, given the limited number of time-series observations for stocks and bonds, the asymptotic methods summarized in this chapter should be complemented with more reliable finite-sample procedures. Conversely, whether researchers should use individual assets or aggregated portfolios in tests of asset pricing theories is not entirely clear. Although the finance profession seems to favor the idea of working with portfolios instead of individual assets, justifying the almost exclusive reliance on the 25 size and book-to-market Fama-French portfolio returns is rather difficult. How many portfolios should be considered and how should they be formed are certainly open questions that future research will hopefully address.

Discussion Questions

1. Discuss the advantages and the drawbacks of the HJ-distance and cross-sectional R^2 for evaluating and comparing possibly misspecified asset pricing models.
2. Some studies suggest that the predictive power of different financial and macro variables for forecasting future stock returns should be evaluated only out-of-sample, i.e., by using information only up to the time when the forecast is made. List several reasons that could justify the preference for out-of-sample over in-sample evaluation of predictive power.
3. The SDF approach discussed in this chapter can be used for evaluating the performance of mutual and hedge funds. Describe briefly how the SDF approach can be implemented in practice for this task if mutual/hedge fund data are available.
4. Despite the recent developments in asset pricing theory and practice, many statistical problems can still potentially compromise some of the empirical findings reported in the literature. Discuss some of the pitfalls in the empirical analysis of asset pricing models.

References

Abel, Andrew B. 1990. "Asset Prices under Habit Formation and Catching Up with the Joneses." *American Economic Review* 80:2, 38–42.

Ahn, Seung C., and Christopher Gadarowski. 2004. "Small Sample Properties of the GMM Specification Test Based on the Hansen-Jagannathan Distance." *Journal of Empirical Finance* 11:1, 109–132.

Balduzzi, Pierluigi, and Hédi Kallal. 1997. "Risk Premia and Variance Bounds." *Journal of Finance* 52:5, 1913–1949.

Bansal, Ravi, and Amir Yaron. 2004. "Risks for the Long-Run: A Potential Resolution of Asset Pricing Puzzles." *Journal of Finance* 59:4, 1481–1509.

Berkman, Henk, Ben Jacobsen, and John B. Lee. 2011. "Time-Varying Rare Disaster Risk and Stock Returns." *Journal of Financial Economics* 101:2, 313–332.

Black, Fischer, Michael C. Jensen, and Myron Scholes. 1972. "The Capital Asset Pricing Model: Some Empirical Tests." In *Studies in the Theory of Capital Markets*, edited by Michael C. Jensen, 79–121. New York: Praeger.

Breeden, Douglas T. 1979. "An Intertemporal Asset Pricing Model with Stochastic Consumption and Investment Opportunities." *Journal of Financial Economics* 7:3, 265–296.

Burnside, Craig. 2010. "Identification and Inference in Linear Stochastic Discount Factor Models." Working Paper No. 16634. Cambridge, MA: National Bureau of Economic Research.

Campbell, John Y. 2001. "Why Long Horizons? A Study of Power against Persistent Alternatives." *Journal of Empirical Finance* 8:5, 459–491.

Campbell, John Y., and John H. Cochrane. 1999. "By Force of Habit: A Consumption-Based Explanation of Aggregate Stock Market Behavior." *Journal of Political Economy* 107:2, 205–251.

Campbell, John Y., and John H. Cochrane. 2000. "Explaining the Poor Performance of Consumption-Based Asset Pricing Models." *Journal of Finance* 55:6, 2863–2878.

Campbell, John Y., and Samuel B. Thompson. 2008. "Predicting Excess Stock Returns Out of Sample: Can Anything Beat the Historical Average?" *Review of Financial Studies* 21:4, 1509–1531.

Campbell, John Y., and Motohiro Yogo. 2006. "Efficient Tests of Stock Return Predictability." *Journal of Financial Economics* 81:1, 27–60.

Cavanagh, Christopher L., Graham Elliott, and James H. Stock. 1995. "Inference in Models with Nearly Integrated Regressors." *Econometric Theory* 11:5, 1131–1147.

Chen, Xiaohong, and Sydney C. Ludvigson. 2009. "Land of Addicts? An Empirical Investigation of Habit-Based Asset Pricing Models." *Journal of Applied Econometrics* 24:7, 1057–1093.

Cochrane, John H. 2005. *Asset Pricing*, rev. ed. Princeton, NJ: Princeton University Press.

Constantinides, George M. 1990. "Habit Formation: A Resolution of the Equity Premium Puzzle." *Journal of Political Economy* 98:3, 519–543.

Dittmar, Robert F. 2002. "Nonlinear Pricing Kernels, Kurtosis Preference, and Evidence from the Cross-Section of Equity Returns." *Journal of Finance* 57:1, 369–403.

Elliott, Graham, and James H. Stock. 1994. "Inference in Time Series Regression when the Order of Integration of a Regressor is Unknown." *Econometric Theory* 10:3–4, 672–700.

Epstein, Larry G., and Stanley E. Zin. 1989. "Substitution, Risk Aversion, and the Temporal Behavior of Consumption and Asset Returns: A Theoretical Framework." *Econometrica* 57:4, 937–968.

Epstein, Larry G., and Stanley E. Zin. 1991. "Substitution, Risk Aversion, and the Temporal Behavior of Consumption and Asset Returns: An Empirical Investigation." *Journal of Political Economy* 99:2, 263–286.

Fama, Eugene F. 1991. "Efficient Capital Markets: II." *Journal of Finance* 46:5, 1575–1617.

Fama, Eugene F., and Kenneth R. French. 1992. "The Cross-Section of Expected Stock Returns." *Journal of Finance* 47:2, 427–465.

Fama, Eugene F., and Kenneth R. French. 1993. "Common Risk Factors in the Returns on Stocks and Bonds." *Journal of Financial Economics* 33:1, 3–56.

Fama, Eugene F., and James D. MacBeth. 1973. "Risk, Return, and Equilibrium: Empirical Tests." *Journal of Political Economy* 81:3, 607–636.

Farnsworth, Heber, Wayne E. Ferson, David Jackson, and Steven Todd. 2002. "Performance Evaluation with Stochastic Discount Factors." *Journal of Business* 75:3, 473–503.

Ferson, Wayne E., and George M. Constantinides. 1991. "Habit Persistence and Durability in Aggregate Consumption." *Journal of Financial Economics* 29:2, 199–240.

Ferson, Wayne E., Sergei Sarkissian, and Timothy T. Simin. 2003. "Spurious Regressions in Financial Economics?" *Journal of Finance* 58:4, 1393–1413.

Gibbons, Michael R., Stephen A. Ross, and Jay Shanken. 1989. "A Test of the Efficiency of a Given Portfolio." *Econometrica* 57:5, 1121–1152.

Gospodinov, Nikolay, Raymond Kan, and Cesare Robotti. 2010. On the Hansen-Jagannathan Distance with a No-Arbitrage Constraint. Federal Reserve Bank of Atlanta Working Paper 2010–4. http://www.frbatlanta.org/documents/pubs/wp/wp1004.pdf.

Gospodinov, Nikolay, Raymond Kan, and Cesare Robotti. 2012. *Further Results on the Limiting Distribution of GMM Sample Moment Conditions.* Journal of Business and Economic Statistics, forthcoming.

Gospodinov, Nikolay, Raymond Kan, and Cesare Robotti. 2011a. *Chi-Squared Tests for Evaluation and Comparison of Asset Pricing Models.* Federal Reserve Bank of Atlanta Working Paper 2011–8. http://www.frbatlanta.org/documents/pubs/wp/wp1108.pdf.

Gospodinov, Nikolay, Raymond Kan, and Cesare Robotti. 2011b. *Robust Inference in Linear Asset Pricing Models.* Unpublished manuscript.

Hansen, Lars Peter. 1982. "Large Sample Properties of Generalized Method of Moments Estimators." *Econometrica* 50:4, 1029–1054.

Hansen, Lars Peter, and Ravi Jagannathan. 1997. "Assessing Specification Errors in Stochastic Discount Factor Models." *Journal of Finance* 52:2, 557–590.

Hodrick, Robert J., and Xiaoyan Zhang. 2001. "Evaluating the Specification Errors of Asset Pricing Models." *Journal of Financial Economics* 62:2, 327–376.

Jagannathan, Ravi, Keiichi Kubota, and Hitoshi Takehara. 1998. "Relationship between Labor-Income Risk and Average Return: Empirical Evidence from the Japanese Stock Market." *Journal of Business* 71:3, 319–347.

Jagannathan, Ravi, and Zhenyu Wang. 1996. "The Conditional CAPM and the Cross-Section of Expected Returns." *Journal of Finance* 51:1, 3–53.

Jagannathan, Ravi, and Zhenyu Wang. 1998. "An Asymptotic Theory for Estimating Beta-Pricing Models Using Cross-Sectional Regression." *Journal of Finance* 53:4, 1285–1309.

Kan, Raymond, and Cesare Robotti. 2008. "Specification Tests of Asset Pricing Models Using Excess Returns." *Journal of Empirical Finance* 15:5, 816–838.

Kan, Raymond, and Cesare Robotti. 2009. "Model Comparison Using the Hansen-Jagannathan Distance." *Review of Financial Studies* 22:9, 3449–3490.

Kan, Raymond, and Cesare Robotti. 2011. "On the Estimation of Asset Pricing Models Using Univariate Betas." *Economics Letters* 110:2, 117–121.

Kan, Raymond, Cesare Robotti, and Jay Shanken. 2012. "Pricing Model Performance and the Two-Pass Cross-Sectional Regression Methodology." *Journal of Finance*, forthcoming.

Kan, Raymond, and Chu Zhang. 1999a. "GMM Tests of Stochastic Discount Factor Models with Useless Factors." *Journal of Financial Economics* 54:1, 103–127.

Kan, Raymond, and Chu Zhang. 1999b. "Two-Pass Tests of Asset Pricing Models with Useless Factors." *Journal of Finance* 54:1, 203–235.

Kan, Raymond, and Guofu Zhou. 2004. "Hansen-Jagannathan Distance: Geometry and Exact Distribution." Unpublished manuscript.

Kandel, Shmuel, and Robert F. Stambaugh. 1995. "Portfolio Inefficiency and the Cross-Section of Expected Returns." *Journal of Finance* 50:1, 157–184.

Kleibergen, Frank. 2009. "Tests of Risk Premia in Linear Factor Models." *Journal of Econometrics* 149:2, 149–173.

Lettau, Martin, and Sydney C. Ludvigson. 2001. "Resurrecting the (C)CAPM: A Cross-Sectional Test When Risk Premia are Time-Varying." *Journal of Political Economy* 109:6, 1238–1287.

Lettau, Martin, and Stijn van Nieuwerburgh. 2008. "Reconciling the Return Predictability Evidence." *Review of Financial Studies* 21:4, 1607–1652.

Li, Haitao, Yuewu Xu, and Xiaoyan Zhang. 2010. "Evaluating Asset Pricing Models Using the Second Hansen-Jagannathan Distance." *Journal of Financial Economics* 97:2, 279–301.

Lintner, John. 1965. "The Valuation of Risky Assets and the Selection of Risky Investments in Stock Portfolios and Capital Budgets." *Review of Economics and Statistics* 47:1, 13–37.

Long, John, Jr. 1974. "Stock Prices, Inflation, and the Term Structure of Interest Rates." *Journal of Financial Economics* 1:2, 131–170.

Ludvigson, Sydney C., and Serena Ng. 2007. "The Empirical Risk-Return Relation: A Factor Analysis Approach." *Journal of Financial Economics* 83:1, 171–222.

Lustig, Hanno N., and Stijn van Nieuwerburgh. 2005. "Housing Collateral, Consumption Insurance, and Risk Premia: An Empirical Perspective." *Journal of Finance* 60:3, 1167–1219.

Mehra, Rajnish, and Edward C. Prescott. 1985. "The Equity Premium: A Puzzle." *Journal of Monetary Economics* 15:2, 145–161.

Merton, Robert C. 1973. "An Intertemporal Capital Asset Pricing Model." *Econometrica* 41:5, 867–87.

Parker, Jonathan A., and Christian Julliard. 2005. "Consumption Risk and the Cross-Section of Expected Returns." *Journal of Political Economy* 113:1, 185–222.

Rubinstein, Mark. 1976. "The Valuation of Uncertain Income Streams and the Pricing of Options." *Bell Journal of Economics* 7:2, 407–425.

Santos, Tano, and Pietro Veronesi. 2006. "Labor Income and Predictable Stock Returns." *Review of Financial Studies* 19:1, 1–44.

Shanken, Jay. 1985. "Multivariate Tests of the Zero-Beta CAPM." *Journal of Financial Economics* 14:3, 327–348.

Shanken, Jay. 1990. "Intertemporal Asset Pricing: An Empirical Investigation." *Journal of Econometrics* 45:1–2, 99–120.

Shanken, Jay. 1992. "On the Estimation of Beta-Pricing Models." *Review of Financial Studies* 5:1, 1–33.

Shanken, Jay, and Guofu Zhou. 2007. "Estimating and Testing Beta Pricing Models: Alternative Methods and their Performance in Simulations." *Journal of Financial Economics* 84:1, 40–86.

Sharpe, William. 1964. "Capital Asset Prices: A Theory of Market Equilibrium under Conditions of Risk." *Journal of Finance* 19:3, 425–442.

Siegel, Jeremy J., and Richard H. Thaler. 1997. "Anomalies: The Equity Premium Puzzle." *Journal of Economic Perspectives* 11:1, 191–200.

Stambaugh, Robert F. 1999. "Predictive Regressions." *Journal of Financial Economics* 54:3, 375–421.

Timmermann, Allan. 2008. "Elusive Return Predictability." *International Journal of Forecasting* 24:1, 1–18.

Torous, Walter, Rossen Valkanov, and Shu Yan. 2004. "On Predicting Stock Returns with Nearly Integrated Explanatory Variables." *Journal of Business* 77:4, 937–966.

Valkanov, Rossen. 2003. "Long-Horizon Regressions: Theoretical Results and Applications." *Journal of Financial Economics* 68:2, 201–232.

Weil, Philippe. 1989. "The Equity Premium Puzzle and the Risk-Free Rate Puzzle." *Journal of Monetary Economics* 24:3, 401–421.

Welch, Ivo, and Amit Goyal. 2008. "A Comprehensive Look at the Empirical Performance of Equity Premium Prediction." *Review of Financial Studies* 21:4, 1455–1508.

4

Asset Pricing and Behavioral Finance

HERSH SHEFRIN
Mario L. Belotti Professor of Finance, Santa Clara University

Introduction

Behavioral finance focuses on the manner in which psychology impacts financial decisions and financial markets. This chapter provides a broad, nontechnical overview of the behavioral approach to asset pricing, whose roots go back at least as far back as Keynes's *The General Theory of Employment, Interest, and Money* (1936).

Keynes (1936) uses the word "psychology" extensively in describing the workings of financial markets, with many references to concepts that are now central to behavioral finance, such as optimism, confidence, and sentiment. Slovic (1972) describes how specific psychological concepts have natural applications to finance. During the 1970s, financial academics largely ignored Slovic's article. However, the article did attract the attention of value manager David Dreman, who had been arguing that because of investor overreaction, low price-to-earnings (PE) stocks would outperform high PE stocks (Dreman, 1982).

Dreman did not draw on a specific body of psychological research to analyze overreaction. However, his work did inspire De Bondt and Thaler (1985) to apply the psychology of prediction, as developed by Kahneman and Tversky (1973), to a study of long-term return reversals stemming from investor overreaction. De Bondt and Thaler report a long-term reversal pattern whereby long-term losers subsequently outperform long-term winners.

During the late 1980s and 1990s, behavioral finance scholars were at work developing psychologically-based explanations for a variety of asset pricing phenomena, some of which apply to the cross-section of stocks and others which apply to the overall market. Examples include the coexistence of long-term reversals and short-term momentum, the tendency for closed-end funds to trade at a discount relative to net asset value (NAV), the equity premium puzzle, and excess volatility. In most cases, the behavioral approach has focused on explaining how investors' psychological traits cause market prices to deviate from fundamental values.

In neoclassical finance, investors are assumed to be fully rational, in the sense of being Bayesian-expected utility maximizers. In behavioral finance, some investors, called *noise traders*, are assumed neither to be Bayesians nor expected utility maximizers. The use of the term noise trader to connote investors who are not fully rational stems from Black (1986), who suggests that irrational investors trade on noise as if it were information. Barberis and Thaler (2003) characterize behavioral asset pricing as having two distinguishing building blocks—psychology and the limits to arbitrage. By "psychology," Barberis and Thaler mean the psychological elements that interfere with Bayesian updating and expected utility maximization. *Bayes rule* is a method for updating probabilities based on new information. Probability updating that violates Bayes's rule is inconsistent with the laws of probability. In typical behavioral models, heuristics and biases replace Bayes rule, and prospect theory replaces expected utility maximization. *Heuristics* are rules of thumb, and *biases* are predispositions toward particular types of errors (Kahneman, Slovic, and Tversky, 1982). *Prospect theory* (Kahneman and Tversky, 1979) is a choice framework in which preferences are defined over gains and losses instead of final asset position, with losses looming larger than gains (loss aversion). It features an S-shaped valuation function, which is concave in gains and convex in losses, and weighting functions for substituting probability weights for probabilities.

The concept *limits to arbitrage* refers to obstacles such as risk or liquidity that prevent arbitrage by perfectly rational agents from eliminating price inefficiencies. Shleifer and Vishny (1997) discuss several reasons for these limits. One reason involves the margin investors must post in order to trade futures and options. An investor who attempts to exploit an opportunity involving mispricing may find that in the course of executing his strategy the mispricing worsens, which requires that he contribute additional margin. If he lacks capital, the investor may have to liquidate his position at a loss. This is a risk he faces, and the knowledge of that risk may be sufficient to induce him to limit his arbitrage activity. A similar result may occur if the investor is a money manager whose investors may withdraw their funds and the manager's risk capital if they perceive him to be losing money when mispricing worsens.

Whereas rational investors cause prices to move closer to their efficient levels, noise traders cause prices to move away from their efficient levels. In this respect, equilibrium prices reflect a weighted average of the different investors' beliefs. Whereas the neoclassical paradigm relies on rational investors to eliminate mispricing through arbitrage, the behavioral paradigm argues that there are limits to arbitrage.

The literature in behavioral asset pricing has grown so quickly that providing a comprehensive treatment of the subject is virtually impossible. Given the space constraints, the chapter is intentionally selective with the information it provides about these issues. The chapter is organized as follows: Winner-loser effects and closed-end funds are the first major topics of discussion. These two topics were central to behavioral asset pricing from the mid-1980s through the 1990s. In this chapter, these topics are reviewed from both empirical and theoretical perspectives. This leads to a discussion of how winner-loser effects and closed-end fund discounts relate to the cross-section of stock returns and to neoclassical factor models. The next topic involves behavioral insights into resolving the equity premium puzzle. This is followed by a section describing some of the debates around behavioral explanations of asset pricing phenomena, especially weaknesses in some of the behavioral frameworks. These weaknesses are a feature of particular models rather than of the behavioral perspective as a whole. The fact that the weaknesses are model specific can be seen in the section involving the application of neoclassical asset-pricing kernel techniques to study behavioral issues. The last major topic in the chapter describes behavioral asset pricing papers that developed in response to the global financial crisis. The chapter ends with a summary and conclusions.

Winner-Loser Effects

Kahneman and Tversky's (1973) representativeness-based theory of prediction provides the psychological framework underpinning De Bondt and Thaler's (1985) winner-loser effect. *Representativeness* involves an overreliance on characteristics representative of a population, thereby leading to unwarranted stereotyping. Kahneman and Tversky find evidence that intuitive predictions are insufficiently regressive to the mean, which they explain in terms of a representativeness-based heuristic. They suggest that because people become focused on the representative features of singular data, they tend to ignore base rate data, such as the tendency for regression to the mean.

Investors predict future earnings and returns based on prior earnings and returns. In the context of winning and losing stocks, representativeness leads investors to stereotype firms with low earnings as being perpetual losers and firms with high earnings as being perpetual winners. In this context, *regression to the mean* implies that future earnings and returns will gravitate toward their historical means than to the most recent earnings and returns. Therefore, investors who, because they rely on representativeness, fail to take proper account of regression to the mean will find themselves surprised when prior losers outperform their predictions and prior winners underperform their predictions.

De Bondt and Thaler (1985) hypothesize that noise traders relying on representativeness would be unduly pessimistic about the prospects of firms that are prior losers and unduly optimistic about the prospects of firms that are prior winners. As a result, noise traders would cause the stocks of prior losers to become undervalued and the stocks of prior winners to become overvalued. However, De Bondt and Thaler suggest that noise traders would find themselves surprised over time as the performance of losers reverts to the mean from below and the performance of winners reverts to the mean from above.

Using return data for the period January 1926–December 1982, De Bondt and Thaler (1985) sort stocks based on their prior three-year performance and form two portfolios. One is a loser portfolio consisting of the bottom 10 percent of stocks and the other is a winner portfolio consisting of the top 10 percent. On average, they find that losers cumulatively outperform winners by about 40 percent over the subsequent five years. Transaction costs aside, this means that a long-short portfolio, which shorted prior winners and purchased prior losers, generated a return of roughly 8 percent a year.

According to De Bondt and Thaler (1985), this differential cannot be explained by differential risk premiums, in which risk is measured by capital asset pricing model (CAPM) betas that are constant over time. Yet, the CAPM beta varies with the degree of leverage, which in turn varies with the market value of equity. To test for the effects of time-varying risk, De Bondt and Thaler construct an arbitrage portfolio that finances the purchase of prior losers by short selling prior winners. In the arbitrage portfolio, the subsequent increase in market value for prior losers offsets the decline for prior winners. A regression of the excess return to the arbitrage portfolio on the market risk premium produces an alpha of 5.9 percent and a beta of 0.22. Hence, prior losers appear to be riskier than prior winners, but the 0.22 difference in betas is insufficient to explain the 5.9 percent return differential.

Think about what would happen if the difference in betas tends to be high at the same time that the market risk premium tends to be high and low when the risk premium is tending to be low. In this case, the small difference in betas can be a misleading indicator as far as the return on the arbitrage portfolio is concerned. Yet, De Bondt and Thaler (1985) find that for periods when the market has been up, the loser portfolio has a higher beta than the winner portfolio, and when the market has been down, the loser portfolio has a lower beta. They suggest that such a pattern does not support the contention that prior losers outperform prior winners, because losers are riskier than winners.

A surprising element of the 8 percent differential is that it appears to have been generated entirely in the month of January. There is nothing in the representativeness-based theory of prediction to account for a seasonal pattern. Nor was seasonality the only surprise. Jegadeesh and Titman (1993, 2001) find that if winners and losers are defined using six-month past performance instead of three-year past performance, their subsequent six-month performance displays momentum rather than reversal. That is, over short horizons winners outperform the losers.

Using data for the period 1965–1989, Jegadeesh and Titman (1993) find that a zero-cost portfolio earned more than 10 percent a year. A long-short momentum strategy earned 1.17 percent a month between 1965 and 1989. Interestingly, between 1990 and 1998, the same strategy earned 1.39 percent, suggesting that it was not an artifact (Jegadeesh and Titman, 2001). Interestingly, Jegadeesh and Titman find long-term reversal as well as reversals in January, so there appears to be no empirical conflict with the findings of De Bondt and Thaler (1985).

Modeling Winner-Loser Effects

Whereas reversals are associated with overreaction, momentum is associated with underreaction. Reconciling the coexistence of short-term momentum and long-term reversals, overreaction and underreaction presented a modeling challenge to behavioral finance academics. Three choices for modeling emerged and are discussed below.

The first model was developed by Barberis, Shleifer, and Vishny (1998) (BSV). BSV develop an explanation that combines insights from the psychology literature on conservatism, representativeness, and salience with the literature in accounting on postearnings announcement drift. *Postearnings announcement drift* is the tendency for stock prices to exhibit a positive drift after positive earnings surprises and a negative drift after negative earnings surprises. The BSV model features an underreaction phenomenon underlying short-term momentum and an overreaction phenomenon underlying long-term reversals.

Consider the psychology. Edwards (1968) documents that in particular situations people underreact to recent evidence, meaning they tend to be conservative. Yet, the contribution by Kahneman and Tversky (1973) shows that in other situations representativeness leads people to overreact to recent evidence and ignore base rates. What distinguishes situations in which people underreact to recent evidence from situations in which they overreact to that evidence?

Barberis, Shleifer, and Vishny (1998), who developed a model that crudely captures an argument developed by Griffen and Tversky (1992), postulate that investors believe earnings growth is determined in one of two regimes: (1) a mean-reverting regime that applies most of the time and (2) a trend regime. A representative investor never knows exactly which regime applies but uses Bayes's rule to infer the likelihood of the prevailing regime from the history of earnings growth.

In the BSV model, actual earnings growth follows a random walk. A *random walk* is a time series in which the value of the series in one period equals the value of the series in the previous period plus an unpredictable random error. Thus, when the representative investor holds the strong belief that earnings growth is mean reverting, he will underreact to an earnings surprise. Yet, consider what happens after a string of earnings surprises. In this case, the representative investor adjusts his belief about the prevailing regime, believing that earnings growth is more likely determined in the trend regime. Since actual earnings follow a random walk without trend, the representative investor overreacts to the most recent surprise.

In the second model, Daniel, Hirshleifer, and Subrahmanyam (DHS; 1998) provide a behaviorally based explanation for short-term momentum/long-term reversals that is different in character from that of Barberis, Shleifer, and Vishny (1998). The DHS framework emphasizes the roles of overconfidence and biased self-attribution in the way investors react differently to private and public information. *Overconfidence* is the tendency for people to believe that they are smarter than they actually are and that they know more than they actually do. *Biased self-attribution* refers to individuals taking credit for positive events, attributing them to their own skill, but attributing negative events to bad luck or others.

In the DHS model, informed investors receive noisy signals about the true value of a security. If the signal is private, they react to it with overconfidence, overestimating its precision. Think of the private signal an investor receives as the outcome of his own security analysis. If the signal is public, it can be assumed that the investor is not overconfident and correctly estimates its precision. Biased self-attribution operates as a result of the investor rendering the degree of overconfidence *endogenous*, which means having an internal cause or origin. When an investor makes an assessment and a subsequent public signal confirms that initial assessment, he becomes even more overconfident.

The DHS model has two important features: The first concerns the security price impulse function associated with a private signal. If the signal is positive, informed investors immediately overreact and the security becomes overpriced. However, because of biased self-attribution, the security will tend to become even more overpriced, on average, as public information continues to arrive shortly thereafter. But as public information continues to flow, investors will see that their initial optimism was unfounded. Hence, a correction phase will ensue and the price will subsequently reverse. The resulting time series for price features initial momentum, meaning positive autocorrelation, and then a reversal pattern, as public information fails to corroborate the initial assessment.

Although this price pattern is the same as that described by Barberis, Shleifer, and Vishny (1998), the valuation profile is markedly different. Consider an event that leads to a price rise with momentum. In Barberis, Shleifer, and Vishny, the momentum phase features underreaction, as investors are slow to react to good news. Hence, the security is undervalued during the early stage when momentum builds. In the DHS framework, the dynamic is different because the momentum phase stems from overreaction. Underreaction does occur, but it takes place during the correction phase. Underreaction is why the market takes a long time to correct the initial overreaction, which is a feature discussed earlier in connection with the De Bondt and Thaler (1985) winner-loser effect.

The second important feature in Daniel, Hirshleifer, and Subrahmanyam (1998) involves the relationship between the character of information (private or public) and the market reaction. In the DHS model, investors may underreact to public information about a firm, and yet this need not lead to drift. This situation happens when the public information is received simultaneously by the firm's managers and the investors. However, if the firm's managers previously received the information privately and chose to release it publicly at a later date, then the resulting underreaction by investors will typically occur in conjunction with price drift.

Hong and Stein (1999) develop the third model. They focus on the interaction between two groups of traders who rely on different heuristics. The two groups are "news watchers" (fundamentalists) and "momentum traders" (technical analysts). Notably, news watchers do not condition their beliefs on past prices, and momentum traders do not condition their beliefs on fundamental information.

In the Hong-Stein framework, news watchers base their trades on information that slowly diffuses through the trading population. Momentum traders base their trades on simple trend extrapolation rules. Because information diffuses slowly, news watchers underreact to new fundamental information. Their underreaction leads to price drift, a pattern that momentum traders perceive and trade upon. Hence, the actions of momentum traders reduce the degree of underreaction in the market, up to a point. Because they use crude extrapolation rules, the behavior of momentum traders ultimately produces overreaction, and price reversals occur as a correction to the overreaction.

Closed-End Funds

Closed-end funds are professionally managed pools of investor money that do not take new investments into the fund or redeem investor shares. The shares of these funds are similar to equity shares, such as common stock, because they trade on exchanges or over the counter. Closed-end funds are a subject of study in behavioral asset pricing because their prices typically deviate from their corresponding net asset values (NAV). This divergence is part of a phenomenon called the *closed-end fund puzzle*. Lee, Shleifer, and Thaler (1991) describe the closed-end fund puzzle as consisting of the following four parts:

1. On average, closed-end funds are initially priced at a premium of 10 percent over their NAVs.
2. Within 120 days of their initial public offer (IPO), the average fund trades at a discount of 10 percent to its NAV.
3. The magnitude of the discount varies over time.
4. When a closed-end fund is liquidated, or is converted into an open-end fund (i.e., a mutual fund in which investors can buy newly issued shares at the NAV from the issuer), the share price rises, on average, and the discount shrinks.

The typical explanation for parts 1 and 2 of the puzzle is that the premium is the equivalent of a disguised load, which investors pay when buying the initial issue. In this respect, the fund manager will typically support the fund price in the market for a short while after the offering and reduce that support gradually to mask the nature of the initial premium.

As for part 3, the removal of support does not explain why funds typically trade at a discount. Lee, Shleifer, and Thaler (1991) suggest that the explanation involves investor sentiment, whereby pessimism drives up the magnitude of the discount. However, investor pessimism is more pronounced at some times than others. Therefore, even rational investors face risk when buying at a discount. In fact, closed-end funds may need to trade at a discount most of the time in order to compensate rational investors for the risks associated with holding these funds.

Modeling Closed-End Fund Discounts

A series of papers by DeLong, Shleifer, Summers, and Waldmann (DSSW; 1990a, 1990b, 1991) set out a behavioral asset pricing framework for explaining the closed-end-fund–puzzle and similar pricing phenomena. The model involves overlapping generations, with two types of investors—rational investors and noise traders. At each date, there are only two generations of investors—old and young. The young investors come into financial existence with physical endowment but no financial securities. Think of endowment as agricultural seed that can be consumed directly or planted in order to produce a yield in the form of a future harvest. The older investors possess financial securities but no physical endowment, which is especially important because investors are assumed only to consume the physical endowment once they become old. In this respect, investors all possess the same utility function $u(c) = exp(-ac)$, where $a > 0$ denotes the coefficient of absolute risk aversion and c is the level of consumption. Formally, the degree of absolute risk aversion is measured by the Arrow-Pratt formula $ARA = -u''/u'$. Although absolute risk aversion can vary with c in general, for $u(c) = exp(-ac)$, it is equal to a, a constant.

A competitive market is held at each date, allowing for the exchange of a physical asset and two financial securities. The first security is a storage technology that converts a unit of physical asset at date t into $(1 + r)$ units at date $t + 1$. The second security is a stock that pays a fixed dividend r per share with certainty. The price of the security associated with the storage technology—call it a bond—is normalized to one unit of physical asset. The price of the stock is determined in equilibrium.

In the DSSW model, the storage technology and stock both generate a certain cash flow r per share at each date. If all investors were rational, then the price of the stock would equal 1, the price of the bond. In other words, the fundamental value of the stock is 1. However, noise traders' beliefs about the future stock price are assumed to be normally distributed. DSSW show that the equilibrium price of the stock is the sum of fundamental value 1 and a nonzero term that is proportional to the proportion of wealth held by noise traders. This decomposition is DSSW's main pricing equation.

The DSSW pricing equation supports the intuitive notion that noise traders' beliefs are responsible for moving prices away from their fundamental value and that the magnitude of the distortion varies with the relative size of noise traders' wealth. DSSW describe this phenomenon as noise traders creating their own space.

DSSW apply their model to explain closed-end fund discounts by associating a closed-end fund with the stock and its NAV with the price of the bond. Notice that the underlying cash flows of the two securities are equal (to r), and in the absence of noise traders, the prices of the two securities will be equal. Therefore, when noise traders are absent, the price of the closed-end fund will equal its NAV. However, the presence of noise traders typically leads the price and the NAV to differ from one another, with price being random over time.

Cross-Section of Returns

The emergence of behavioral asset pricing occurred as neoclassical asset pricing theorists were grappling with the discovery of empirical phenomena related to size and scaled price ratios that appeared to be inconsistent with the joint hypothesis of the CAPM and market efficiency. In the finance literature, these phenomena came to be called anomalies because they appeared to be inconsistent with the efficient market hypothesis (EMH), which asserts that stocks are always in equilibrium and investors cannot "beat the market" by consistently earning a higher rate of return than is justified by the stock's risk, as measured by the CAPM. The size anomaly features stocks with low market capitalization, having subsequently earned higher returns than stocks with high market capitalization (Banz, 1981). The scaled price-ratio anomalies feature stocks with high ratios for book-to-market (BM) and earnings-to-price (EP) having subsequently outperformed stocks associated with lower ratios (Rosenberg, Reid, and Lanstein, 1985).

A connection surely exists between these anomalies and behavioral asset pricing phenomena, such as the winner-loser effect. Since the market values of prior losers tend to fall and those of prior winners tend to rise, a natural question to ask is whether the winner-loser effect is a manifestation of the size effect. If it were, then extreme losers would correspond to the firms with the lowest market capitalizations. De Bondt and Thaler (1987) investigate this issue and find that extreme losers are not the smallest firms. In this regard, the market value of equity for the extreme losers is in the fourth size quintile, not the fifth, and has a magnitude of about thirty times that of the smallest firms.

What De Bondt and Thaler (1987) point out is that the winner-loser effect is closer to the BM effect. *Book-to-market* is the ratio of book value of equity to the market value of equity. Firms featuring higher BM ratios have historically earned higher returns when adjusted for risk, as measured by the CAPM beta. De Bondt and Thaler argue that both the winner-loser effect and the BM effect stem from misvaluation. Proponents of market efficiency offer the counterargument that these effects reflect risk that is not captured by the CAPM beta.

Fama and French (1992, 1996) develop a three-factor model that empirically captures many of the anomalies, such as the De Bondt-Thaler effect, for which they provide a neoclassical risk-based interpretation. The factors relate to the market return, the difference in returns between small firms and large firms, and the difference in returns between high and low stocks ranked by BM equity. Notably, Fama and French do not present a formal theory to underlie their framework. Instead, they provide the intuition that size and BM equity serve as proxies for risk associated with financial distress that is not captured by empirical beta, because empirical beta is backward-looking, not forward-looking. For example, an empirical beta might underestimate risk for a firm that recently became financially distressed, whereas such distress would tend to drive down a firm's market value of equity and drive up its BM ratio.

Many view the Fama-French framework as the extension of the CAPM, with its three factors representing fundamental risk. The view of it as an extension has led to competing explanations for pricing phenomena in which the three-factor model is used to provide a risk-based explanation and a behavioral framework has been used to provide a mispricing-based explanation.

Daniel and Titman (1997) raise the question of whether firm characteristics or factor loadings can explain returns. More recently, the debate has become more nuanced, focusing on whether factors serve as proxies for both fundamentally based risk and sentiment.

Barberis and Thaler (2003) raise two concerns in connection with the Fama-French risk-based explanation. First, they suggest that the return on low BM stocks tends to be below the risk-free rate. Second, they propose that neoclassical theory measures risk by the covariance between returns and the marginal utility of aggregate consumption growth. In this regard, the risk of a security is that it will pay a low return in bad times when the marginal utility of consumption growth is high. Therefore, a security earns a risk premium for generating a low return in bad times when aggregate consumption growth is low. However, little if any empirical evidence supports the contention that stocks earning above-average returns perform especially poorly during periods of low aggregate consumption growth.

Sentiment

Lee, Shleifer, and Thaler (1991) suggest that discounts on closed-end funds reflect the sentiment of individual investors. They note that individual investors as a group hold more than 90 percent of closed-end fund shares, and in this regard they suggest that the narrowing of discounts stems from increased investor optimism.

According to Lee, Shleifer, and Thaler (1991), individual investors, rather than institutional investors, mainly hold small stocks. In this regard, individuals hold about 75 percent of the smallest firms (lowest decile). For this reason, the return on small stocks can be expected to increase when individual investors become more optimistic. Indeed, the authors find that a narrowing of these discounts occurs together with an increase in the return on small stocks.

Optimism also appears to affect new issues and repurchases of stocks. Loughran and Ritter (1995) find that stocks of firms that have issued new equity have subsequently underperformed stocks of a control group of firms matched on size and BM equity over a five-year period. Likewise, Ikenberry, Lakonishok, and Vermaelen (1995) find that stocks of firms that have repurchased equity have subsequently outperformed those of a control group of firms matched on size and BM equity over a four-year period.

The connection between closed-end fund discounts and small stocks extends to IPOs. Lee, Shleifer, and Thaler (1991) find that when the number of new IPOs increases, individual investors become more optimistic and closed-end discounts narrow.

Sentiment also appears to affect the market response to dividend initiations and omissions. Stocks associated with dividend initiations have subsequently outperformed the market for a year after the announcement, whereas stocks associated with dividend omissions have subsequently underperformed the market.

Baker and Wurgler (2006, 2007) use a principal components analysis to develop a single measure of sentiment based on the following six specific measures: (1) the closed-end fund discount, (2) the number of IPOs, (3) the first-day return on IPOs, (4) the dividend premium, (5) the equity share in new issues, and (6) de-trended log turnover. The authors suggest that sentiment will affect prices of some stocks more than others. They also suggest that the returns on stocks that are difficult both to value and to arbitrage will be more sensitive to sentiment than stocks that are both easier to value and easier to arbitrage.

The heart of the Baker-Wurlger argument involves the concept of a *sentiment seesaw*. They suggest that when sentiment is high, stocks that are speculative and difficult to arbitrage become overvalued and stocks that are safe and easy to arbitrage become undervalued. When sentiment is low, the reverse occurs. A notable feature of the analysis is the authors' suggestion that because of mispricing, stocks that appear to be riskier in terms of fundamentals can feature lower expected returns than safer stocks.

Baker and Wurgler (2007) measure a stock's sensitivity to sentiment in terms of a *sentiment beta*, which explains the sentiment component of the risk premium. The authors report that from an empirical standpoint, returns are predictable, conditional on the value of sentiment in the prior month. When past sentiment has been high, subsequent returns on speculative stocks, which are more difficult to arbitrage, are indeed lower than returns on safer stocks that are easier to arbitrage. Conversely, when past sentiment has been low, subsequent returns on speculative stocks and stocks that are more difficult to arbitrage are higher than on safer stocks that are easier to arbitrage.

The Equity Premium Puzzle and Excess Volatility

The equity premium puzzle is an important example of the application of behavioral ideas to explain aggregate stock market movements. Mehra and Prescott (1985) coined the term *equity premium puzzle* after finding that the neoclassical intertemporal CAPM (ICAPM) was unable to explain the historical premium that equities earned over Treasuries in US financial markets. This puzzle actually constitutes a triplet of puzzles involving the equity premium, the risk-free rate, market volatility, and the predictability of returns and is based on the notion that plausible parameters in the Mehra-Prescott model cannot explain the magnitude of the historical equity premium, return volatility, and return predictability in the US market. Campbell, Lo, and MacKinlay (1996) point out that the neoclassical model implies an equity premium of 0.1 percent, not the historical 3.9 percent; a return standard deviation of 12 percent, not the historical 18 percent; and the absence of predictability in returns, not the predictability observed in practice.

The main behavioral approach to explaining the equity premium involves the work of Benartzi and Thaler (1995) and Barberis, Huang, and Santos (2001). Both approaches feature a representative investor whose preferences are based on prospect theory, which is briefly described in the introduction. While neoclassical expected utility theory emphasizes risk aversion in respect to total consumption or wealth on the part of investors, prospect theory emphasizes loss aversion in respect to changes in consumption or wealth. Behavioral theories of the equity premium puzzle focus on how short investment-time horizons might induce loss-averse investors to behave as if they were extremely averse to risk, thereby inducing a high equity premium in the market. Additionally, if investors are concerned that they have ambiguous beliefs about stock market returns, suggesting that they realize their subjective beliefs might be in error, then they might demand an additional premium to be compensated not just for what they regard as risk but also for the discomfort of knowing that their estimates of risk are imprecise. This additional premium, known as an *ambiguity aversion premium*, puts additional upward pressure on the equity premium.

A quick way of introducing the main issue is through the well-known Gordon Growth Model, which can be stated as $P_t/D_{t+1} = 1/(r - g)$, where P denotes price, D denotes dividend, r denotes required return, and g denotes the expected dividend growth rate, also called the *sustainable growth rate*. This formula indicates that the price-dividend ratio is driven by the required return and the expected dividend growth. The neoclassical theory predicts that if these factors are stable over time, the price-dividend ratio should also be stable.

In practice, the price-dividend ratio is quite volatile, thereby prompting the question of whether volatility in the dividend growth rate or required return is sufficient to explain the puzzle. Although little evidence suggests that the long-run dividend growth rate is volatile, the required return on stocks is a function of the risk-free rate, degree of market risk, and overall risk aversion. Barberis and Thaler (2003) point out the difficulty of reconciling the volatility of the price-dividend ratio in terms of volatile interest rates or volatile risk.

Representativeness is a heuristic principle involving excessive reliance on stereotypes. Barberis and Thaler (2003) contend that behavioral explanations based upon representativeness suggest that investors' expectations about future dividend growth and risk display excessive volatility relative to recent events. For example, investors might view a recent spurt in dividend growth as "representative" of the long-run sustainable future growth rate, thereby leading the subjective g to exceed the objective g. A similar statement might apply to perceived risk.

A behavioral explanation of the volatility puzzle based on preferences is similar in spirit to the behavioral explanation of the equity premium puzzle. In contrast to neoclassical expected utility theory, in which investors are assumed to be risk averse and have stable attitudes toward risk, prospect theory emphasizes that the attitude toward risk is nonconstant and varies according to whether outcomes are registered as gains or as losses. Barberis, Huang, and Santos (2001) develop a model featuring a representative investor whose preferences conform to prospect theory with hedonic editing (Thaler, 1985). In *hedonic editing*, the investor decomposes variables such as total cumulative returns into constituent components in order to experience higher utility with segregated return components than he would with an integrated total return. In this model, investors become more tolerant of a loss after a rise in the market has generated gains for them and more averse to a loss after a drop in the market reduces that gain. Moreover, in line with hedonic editing, if the drop in the market leads investors to experience losses relative to the amount they originally invested, then they will become much more averse to further loss.

Critiques and Counterarguments

The behavioral perspective continues to evolve along with associated debates. Some of these debates involve behavioral proponents on one side and neoclassical proponents on the other. Other debates feature differing behavioral explanations for particular empirical phenomena. The following sections offer some illustrative examples.

CLOSED-END FUNDS

An early debate about closed-end funds involved Chen, Kan, and Miller (1993) on the neoclassical side and Chopra, Lee, Shleifer, and Thaler (1993) on the behavioral side. Chen, Kan, and Miller suggested that the relationship between fund discounts and small firm returns is neither robust over time nor affected by the degree of institutional ownership. In response, Chopra et al. demonstrated that for 90 percent of small-firm stocks, when discounts narrow, lower institutional ownership stocks do better than higher institutional ownership stocks.

OVERREACTION AND UNDERREACTION

Fama (1998) presents a critique of the literature on over- and underreaction. He points out that instances of overreaction appear about as often as instances of underreaction and suggests that this feature is consistent with market efficiency. According to this view, a market is efficient when price and fundamental value coincide on average, with any deviations due solely to chance. In this respect, the mean abnormal return is zero; however, random fluctuations give rise to nonzero deviations (anomalies) in both directions.

Fama (1998) provides a critical assessment of some of the key articles discussed above, including De Bondt and Thaler (1985); Jegadeesh and Titman (1993); Barberis, Shleifer, and Vishny (1998); and Daniel, Hirshleifer, and Subrahmanyam (1998). Fama's criticisms vary in nature. He points out that the Fama and French (1992, 1996) three-factor risk model can explain the effects reported by both De Bondt and Thaler (1985) and Ikenberry, Lakonishok, and Vermaelen (1995). Hence, he argues that the efficient market paradigm can accommodate these effects. He dismisses both Barberis, Shleifer, and Vishny (1998) and Daniel, Hirshleifer, and Subrahmanyam (1998) for a lack of robustness, asserting that these theories may explain the anomalies they were built to address but fail to explain others sharing similar traits. Fama finds that the studies that pose the most significant challenge to the EMH pertain to postearnings announcement drift (Bernard and Thomas, 1990). The finding concerning postearnings announcement drift is that earnings surprises appear to be positively autocorrelated, suggesting that analysts underreact to earnings announcements. Moreover, there is drift in the associated stock returns, suggesting that investors as a whole underreact. Notably, the drift is short term and is followed by a long-term reversal.

Thus far, all the behavioral arguments advanced to explain momentum have involved investor errors. Grinblatt and Han (2004) provide a different behavioral explanation, one that is rooted in investor emotions and preferences. Their argument is based on the *disposition effect*, which stipulates that outside of the month of December, investors sell their winners too early but hold onto their losers too long. It is notable that the direction might reverse in December, when investors concentrate on tax-loss selling (Shefrin and Statman, 1985). To understand the gist of the Grinblatt-Han argument, keep in mind that the behavioral position accepts the idea that in the long term, price reverts to fundamental value. Therefore, if stock price eventually moves toward fundamental value, consider how the disposition effect will affect the speed of adjustment. The answer is that it will slow the speed of adjustment, thereby resulting in short-term momentum.

Grinblatt and Han (2004) develop a variable called the capital gains overhang, which captures the potential strength of the disposition effect. *Capital gains overhang* is a measure of net paper gains in investors' portfolios (i.e., gains relative to the original purchase price). The authors find that for US stocks, the capital gains overhang completely explains short-term momentum. The disposition effect also explains why the momentum effect reverses at the turn of the year.

Frazzini (2005) develops a trading strategy based on the Grinblatt-Han analysis. The strategy calls for going long in good-news stocks with the largest paper gains because these will feature the largest expected future return drift. Correspondingly, the strategy calls for shorting bad news stocks with the largest paper losses. Frazzini finds that the return on this strategy was 2.4 percent a month for stocks featuring a positive capital gains overhang. However, for stocks with a negative overhang, the return was zero. Why zero? Good news stocks with a loss overhang means disposition prone investors do not rush to sell, so the speed of adjustment to the good news is rapid.

FRAGILITY OF DSSW MODELS

DeLong et al. (1990a, 1990b, 1991) develop their models to formalize the key intuitive behaviorally based insights. In this respect, DSSW models demonstrate that noise traders can create their own space, that closed-end fund prices can deviate from their NAVs, and that rational traders need not eliminate noise traders in the long run. The DSSW models are exceptionally frail, and some of the DSSW claims appear to be in error.

Loewenstein and Willard (2006) carefully analyze the DSSW overlapping generation noise trader model. They find that DSSW's conclusions depend on unrealistic assumptions built into the model and that the conclusions fail to hold when the assumptions are relaxed. DSSW assume that noise traders' beliefs about the future price of stock are normally distributed. This assumption implies that noise traders can believe that stock prices take on unbounded values both above and below zero. It also implies that equilibrium stock prices can take on unbounded values. Of course, negative prices are inconsistent with limited liability, and limited liability is a feature of publicly traded stocks. Positively unbounded values reflect an asset pricing bubble, which, given finite endowments, raise the question of how investors will be able to afford to purchase the stock as time evolves.

Loewenstein and Willard (2006) prove that when the stock price is bounded from above and below, as opposed to being normally distributed, price must equal fundamental value at every date. Therefore, pricing bounds prevent noise traders from creating their own space in an overlapping DSSW model. Notably, closed-end funds trade on public exchanges and therefore feature limited liability. Loewenstein and Willard also prove that imposing limited liability in a DSSW framework prevents the existence of closed-end fund discounts relative to fundamental value. In this regard, they criticize the notion that NAV correctly measures fundamental value.

A different line of argument challenges DSSW's claim that noise traders can survive the presence of rational traders in the long run because noise traders mistakenly take on more risk than rational investors and benefit from the associated higher expected returns. Blume and Easley (2008) find that this claim is inconsistent with general theories (i.e., those that characterize the conditions under which different types of investors survive or vanish in the long run) and suggest that the DSSW claim is false.

Behavioral Pricing Kernel Approach

The Loewenstein and Willard (2006) critique makes it clear that the main conclusions in the DSSW framework depend on model artifacts rather than on the presence of robust assumptions. Moreover, they apply pricing kernel techniques to analyze the DSSW framework. These techniques, while standard tools in neoclassical asset pricing theory (Cochrane, 2005), receive little attention in behavioral finance. This section describes a behavioral pricing kernel approach developed by Shefrin (2008).

A pricing kernel is often represented as a stochastic discount factor (SDF). The fundamental SDF-based asset pricing equation is:

$$p = E(mx) \tag{4.1}$$

Equation 4.1 states that the price p of an asset with random payoff x is the expected value of its discounted payoff, where m is a discount factor used to capture the effects of both time value of money and risk. In Equation 4.1, both m and x are random variables. That is, the discount factor m typically varies across payoff levels in order to reflect that risk is priced differently across payoff levels.

In neoclassical finance, the expectation in Equation 4.1 is assumed to be the objective probability density function (pdf) governing the coevolution of m and x. This assumption is reasonably innocuous in a neoclassical setting, where assets are assumed to be priced by a representative investor whose beliefs correspond to the correct pdf. Most neoclassical asset pricing treatments begin with this assumption about a representative investor, without inquiring about the kind of conditions necessary to produce such a situation. Of course, if all investors are rational and hold correct beliefs, then assuming that the representative investor also holds correct beliefs is natural.

Needless to say, the behavioral view allows for both rational investors with correct beliefs and noise traders with erroneous beliefs. Therefore, in a behavioral setting, assuming that the representative investor holds correct beliefs would be inappropriate. In a behavioral setting, this means clearly distinguishing as to whether the specification of SDF m in Equation 4.1 corresponds to objective beliefs or to the beliefs of a representative investor. Although both approaches are possible, the use of objective beliefs is more insightful, and therefore that is the approach followed.

MODELING SENTIMENT

In the behavioral finance literature, sentiment refers to erroneous beliefs. In this regard, think of security x as having a pdf that is objectively correct but about which individual investors only possess subjective beliefs. The beliefs of an investor whose subjective beliefs are correct are said to feature *zero sentiment*. The beliefs of an investor whose subjective beliefs are incorrect are said to feature *nonzero sentiment*.

Because of Equation 4.1, the SDF m is the core concept in a pricing kernel framework. Therefore, if noise trader sentiment is to affect prices, it must do so through the SDF. To characterize a SDF, which reflects noise trader sentiment, consider a complete market ICAPM-type model in which all investors have constant relative risk aversion (CRRA) utility functions and heterogeneous beliefs about the future growth rates of gross aggregate consumption g. To keep things simple, assume just two dates, $t = 1, 2$.

Denote the true pdf of aggregate consumption growth g at date 2 by the symbol π and investor j's subjective pdf by the symbol π_j. If $\pi_j = \pi$, then investor j is rational. If $\pi_j \neq \pi$, then investor j is a noise trader. The function defined as the likelihood ratio π_j/π is a change of measure. Beginning with π and multiplying by the change of measure converts π into π_j. The log-change of measure $\ln(\pi_j/\pi)$ specifies, for each value of aggregate consumption growth g, the percentage by which $\pi(g)$ is to be adjusted in order to generate $\pi_j(g)$. Suppose that the log-change of measure is positive at a particular value of g. Then, the probability mass shifts toward g when converting π into π_j. Likewise, the negative log-change of measure at g, shifts the probability mass away from g when converting π into π_j.

The shape of the graph of the log-change of measure against g is informative. When the log-change of measure is the zero function, then converting π into π_j involves no change, so that investor j is fully rational. When the log-change of measure is positively sloped throughout, then the conversion of π into π_j features probability mass being reduced at the left and increased at the right. A positive log-change of measure corresponds to investor j being excessively optimistic, or bullish, about aggregate consumption growth. Likewise, a negatively sloped log-change of measure corresponds to investor j being excessively pessimistic, or bearish, about aggregate consumption growth.

The shape of the log-change of measure need not be monotone. Suppose it has the shape of an inverted U. This implies that in converting π into π_j, probability mass is decreased at the tails and increased in the middle. An inverted U-shaped log-change of measure implies that investor j underestimates tail risk, and is therefore over confident. Conversely, a U-shaped log-change of measure implies that investor j is underconfident.

A log-change of measure function also applies at the level of the market. Shefrin (2005, 2008) establishes the existence of a representative investor whose beliefs π_R correspond to generalized weighted Hölder average of the individual investors' pdfs, with the weights reflecting relative wealth or consumption and the exponents being inverse coefficients of relative risk aversion. As a general matter, Hölder averages involve exponentiation, as for example with standard deviation. A standard deviation is an average deviation, defined as the square root of a sum of squared deviations, thereby featuring an exponent of 2.

The existence of π_R gives rise to a well-defined concept of market sentiment, based upon the log-change of measure π_R/π. Market sentiment can be a bit more complicated than simply applying a change of measure, as aggregation involves both risk aversion and time preference. However, these tend to be secondary relative to beliefs.

CONNECTION BETWEEN SENTIMENT AND SDF

In a neoclassical framework involving a representative investor with CRRA preferences, the SDF has the following form:

$$m = \delta g^{-\gamma} \tag{4.2}$$

where δ is the rate of time preference and γ is the coefficient of relative risk aversion. Typically, δ and γ are nonnegative, so m is a monotone-decreasing function. When all investors are fully rational, then the SDF will conform to Equation 4.2, possibly with state dependent risk aversion, and market prices will depend only on fundamentals.

What makes an SDF behavioral is that it reflects market sentiment as well as fundamentals. Shefrin (2005) establishes that when all investors have CRRA utility, the log-SDF can be expressed as the sum of two terms—one reflecting market fundamentals and the other reflecting market sentiment. This decomposition establishes the channel by which sentiment affects market prices through Equation 4.1. Implicit in this discussion is that the expectation in Equation 4.1 is taken with respect to π.

If market sentiment is small, then fundamentals dominate pricing. If market sentiment is large, then sentiment dominates pricing. In the latter case, the shape of the graph of the SDF (m vs. g) will reflect the shape of sentiment. If sentiment is positively sloped, implying sufficiently high bullishness, the SDF will be upward sloping. Likewise, if the log-change of measure for market beliefs has the shape of an inverted U, then so too will the shape of the SDF.

Equation 4.1 implies the *law of one price*, which states that two securities with identical cash flows will have identical prices in equilibrium. However, the Hölder average result for market beliefs implies that the presence of rational investors does not guarantee that market sentiment will be zero and therefore that noise traders will cause prices to move away from fundamental values.

EMPIRICAL ESTIMATION OF THE SDF

Using options data from the early 1990s, Aït-Sahalia and Lo (2000) and Rosenberg and Engle (2002) estimate the empirical SDF or, more precisely, its projection in respect to returns on the Standard & Poor 500 (S&P 500). Both studies find that the empirical SDF is not monotone decreasing but instead features a hump. Rosenberg and Engle estimate the SDF in two ways. First, they restrict the SDF to have the traditional neoclassical shape implied by Equation 4.2. Second, they use a free-form Chebyshev polynomial procedure that involves no such restriction. This approach can be viewed as an inadvertent test of whether or not the empirical SDF is behavioral. The empirical findings provide strong support that the SDF is behavioral.

Barone-Adesi, Engle, and Mancini (2008) apply a different methodology to estimate the empirical SDF during the period 2002–2004. They find a less pronounced hump than in the earlier studies, although their estimates do not conform to Equation 4.2.

BEHAVIORAL MEAN-VARIANCE PORTFOLIOS, RISK PREMIUMS, AND COSKEWNESS

A mean-variance (MV) portfolio is a portfolio of assets that maximizes expected return for a specified return variance. In neoclassical asset pricing, where sentiment is zero, the risk premium for a security is based on its return covariance with the return on any risky mean-variance (MV) portfolio. For example, in the CAPM, the market portfolio is MV efficient, which is why risk premiums are based on the covariance between the security's returns and the returns on the market portfolio.

How does sentiment affect the relationship between risk and return? The short answer is that it affects it in the same way as it does in neoclassical asset pricing. Because risk premiums for all securities are based on return covariance with MV portfolios, even when sentiment is nonzero, the key lies in understanding how sentiment affects the nature of the return distributions for both MV portfolios and individual assets. In this respect, risk has both a fundamental component and a sentiment component.

The SDF can be used to price all assets, including portfolios. Hence, the SDF is used to price all MV-efficient portfolios, and therefore the SDF can be used to generate the return distribution for an MV portfolio. In fact, the return on an MV portfolio is a linear function of the SDF with a negative coefficient (Cochrane, 2005). This relationship implies that the shape of the graph MV return vs. g is essentially the mirror image of the graph of the SDF vs. g.

In the neoclassical case, the SDF is loglinear and negatively sloped. As a consequence, the MV return is log-linear and positively sloped, giving rise to the neoclassical ICAPM result that the MV-efficient frontier can be approximated by portfolios that combine the risk-free asset and market portfolio. The neoclassical SDF has no hump. In contrast, a behavioral SDF might well feature a hump. If so, then the shape of the MV return will feature a mirror-image hump. As a result, the MV-efficient frontier cannot be approximated by portfolios that combine the risk-free asset and market portfolio.

A hump-shaped SDF will lead MV portfolios to be more volatile than they otherwise would be. The difference in volatility has important implications for the magnitudes of risk premiums and Sharpe ratios. Sharpe ratios are bounded from above by the coefficient of variation of the SDF. As a result, the more volatile behavioral SDF admits higher risk premiums and Sharpe ratios than does the less volatile neoclassical SDF.

A nonmonotone-shaped SDF can give rise to a natural factor structure. For example, consider the case when the SDF has a U shape that is approximately quadratic. In this case, the MV return can be expressed as a function of g and g^2 along with an intercept. This implies that the risk premium for any security can be expressed as a two-factor model, with the factors corresponding to the market portfolio and the square of the market portfolio. The covariance between the return of a security and the square of the market return is known as the security's *coskewness*.

Harvey and Siddique (2000) contrast their coskewness analysis to a four-factor model, where the factors are, respectively, the market return, size, BM equity, and momentum. They find that the correlation between coskewness and mean returns of portfolios sorted by size, BM equity, and momentum is −0.71. This means that much of the explanatory power of size, BM equity, and momentum in the returns of individual stocks plausibly derives from coskewness.

Financial Crisis–Related Research

A decade-long bubble in US housing prices played a central role in the financial crisis that erupted in 2008. Although the study of asset pricing bubbles began to intensify during the dot-com bubble of the 1990s, bubbles have historically been a focal point in the behavioral asset pricing literature. Keynes (1936) provides a lengthy discussion of the psychological underpinnings of the business cycle, especially the manner in which excessive optimism and overconfidence generate bubbles. Shiller (2000) suggests a series of conditions under which bubbles emerge, and subsequently applied these ideas to warn at the time that a housing price bubble was underway.

On the theoretical side, Scheinkman and Xiong (2003) develop a model of heterogeneous beliefs, in which frenzied trading caused by intensive fluctuations of investors' beliefs can lead to a significant price bubble. Their approach can incorporate a variety of important features of bubbles and crises, such as over-investment (Bolton, Scheinkman, and Xiong, 2005) and stock market crashes (Abreu and Brunnermeier, 2003; Hong and Stein, 2003).

Asset pricing bubbles are associated with excessive optimism and overconfidence. Barone-Adesi, Mancini, and Shefrin (2011) use an SDF-based approach to estimate sentiment for the S&P 500 during the period 2002–2009, which encompasses the financial crisis. Recall from the discussion in the previous section that the empirical SDF can be decomposed into a fundamental component consistent with Equation 4.2. The methodology involves applying the procedure developed in Barone-Adesi, Engle, and Mancini (2008) to estimate the empirical SDF together with an unconstrained estimate of an SDF that satisfies Equation 4.2. Given the decomposition result, the two estimates can be used to infer sentiment.

Barone-Adesi, Mancini, and Shefrin (2011) find that market optimism is small, if not negative, during the recessions that mark the beginning and end of the sample period but increases markedly during the expansion in the middle of the period. Moreover, the authors find that optimism is highly correlated with housing prices. Overconfidence is low, if not negative, during the two recessions but increases markedly during the expansion. As per the behavioral SDF-based approach, they state that hump patterns in the SDF are weakest during the recessions and strongest during the economic expansion.

Some but not all bubbles are associated with financial crises. In the last fifteen years, the housing bubble was associated with a financial crisis, but the dot-com bubble was not. The difference is that a financial crisis typically involves the markets for credit rather than those for equity. Geanakoplos (2010) provides an insightful analysis of the leverage cycle, meaning the manner in which time-varying optimism and overconfidence affect bubbles through decisions about leverage. Geanakoplos's framework is particularly illuminating about the role that collateral plays in magnifying price volatility. Collateral was a key issue in the events that led to the collapse of Bear Stearns and Lehman Brothers during the onset of the financial crisis as well as the near collapse of AIG.

Many of the financial institutions that failed during the financial crisis had borrowed short term in order to purchase long-term assets, such as mortgage-backed securities. The performance of this long-short strategy depends on the dynamics of the yield curve. In neoclassical theory, the EMH satisfies the expectations hypothesis, with the term structure of interest rates providing efficient forecasts of future short-term rates. For example, when the yield curve is upwardly sloped, the expectations hypothesis predicts that the price of long-term bonds will fall and their yields will rise. This relationship is necessary to equalize the returns from two alternative strategies: (1) holding long bonds and (2) rolling over a series of short-term bonds. Empirically, however, the price of long-term bonds tends to rise in this situation, not fall (Campbell, 1995).

Xiong and Yan (2010) offer a behavioral explanation of the expectations hypothesis. To understand their main argument, suppose that excessive optimism in the aggregate leads investors' forecast of future short rates to be biased upward. In this case, the yield curve will be upwardly sloped and the market's use of short-term rates to discount future payoffs of long-term bonds will result in excessive discounting of those payoffs. Therefore, the prices of long bonds will be driven below their associated fundamental values. However, over time, dissipation of the unwarranted optimism will lead the prices of long bonds to rise and their yields to decline, in contradiction to the expectations hypothesis.

Summary and Conclusions

Concerning the influence of investor psychology on asset pricing, behavioral finance has contributed intuition, empirical analysis, and theory. Much of the intuition derives from the literature on behavioral decision making about the way psychology influences judgment and choice. Although empirical findings in the behavioral finance literature have withstood the test of time, the same cannot be said about behavioral theory. The DSSW framework has been shown to lack robustness. There is still no generally accepted theory about what causes winner-loser effects. Further, no model explains why long-term reversals appear only to occur in January.

Whereas the most frequently cited behavioral asset pricing theories lack robustness and rigor, neoclassical asset pricing theory does have rigor. Unfortunately, neoclassical theory also rests on assumptions that are unrealistic from a behavioral standpoint. The last portion of the chapter describes how neoclassical pricing kernel theory can be extended to accommodate the psychological features emphasized by behavioral asset pricing theorists. This extension offers a new approach to studying both the time series of risk and return as well as the cross-section, which combines the insights from behavioral finance with the rigor of neoclassical finance. Additionally, the asset pricing bubbles and financial crisis that have marked the last fifteen years have spawned a series of new models to explain the role psychology plays in these types of events, which are also described.

Discussion Questions

1. Kahneman and Tversky (1973) postulate that the concept of representativeness explains why people are prone to underestimate regression to the mean. For example, in a regression of the height of a son on the height of a father, the estimated slope coefficient tends to be positive but less than one. Nevertheless, people are prone to predict that sons will be as tall as their fathers, in effect treating the slope coefficient as one. Explain how representativeness might account for this prediction error and then extend the analysis to explain how representativeness might underlie the De Bondt-Thaler winner-loser effect.
2. In the DSSW noise trader model, the younger generation possesses physical endowment e but does not consume, while the older generation possesses no physical endowment but consumes. Portfolios consist of two securities: a risk-free security paying a fixed rate of interest r and a stock paying a certain dividend of r per share. The price of the stock is P per share, in units of endowment, and the price of the risk-free security is normalized to 1. Let W denote the value of investors' portfolios at the end of a period. Suppose one share of stock is available, which is perfectly divisible. Because a perfectly elastic storage technology underlies the risk-free security, the supply of the risk-free security is also perfectly elastic. Let δ denote the net holdings of the risk-free security. Use the aggregate budget constraint to develop an equation that relates P to W and δ, and W to e. Then, use these equations to describe what happens along a bubble

in the DSSW framework. Analyze whether a bubble can occur if the risk-free asset were available in zero net supply and if a bubble can grow without limit.

3. As Fama (1998) points out, instances of overreaction appear about as often as instances of underreaction. He suggests that this feature is consistent with market efficiency because the mean abnormal return is zero, with random fluctuations giving rise to nonzero deviations (anomalies) in both directions. Evaluate Fama's position.

4. Excessive optimism involves overestimating the mean of returns, while overconfidence involves underestimating the standard deviation of returns. Suppose that excessive optimism and overconfidence are positively correlated in the investor population. In this respect, assume that bearish investors tend to be underconfident, while bullish investors tend to be overconfident. Consider the change of measure associated with market sentiment. How will this positive correlation affect the shape of the sentiment function and the shape of the SDF, when graphed against consumption growth?

Acknowledgement

Professor Shefrin acknowledges the financial support of a Leavey Research Grant from Santa Clara University.

References

Abreu, Dilip, and Markus K. Brunnermeier. 2002. "Synchronization Risk and Delayed Arbitrage." *Journal of Financial Economics* 66:2–3, 341–360.

Aït-Sahalia, Yacine, and Andrew W. Lo. 2000. "Nonparametric Risk Management and Implied Risk Aversion." *Journal of Econometrics* 94:1–2, 9–51.

Baker, Malcolm, and Jeffrey Wurgler. 2006. "Investor Sentiment and the Cross-Section of Stock Returns." *Journal of Finance* 61:4, 1645–1680.

Baker, Malcolm, and Jeffrey Wurgler. 2007. "Investor Sentiment and the Stock Market." *Journal of Economic Perspectives* 2:2, 129–152.

Banz, Rolf W. 1981. "The Relationship between Return and Market Value of Common Stocks." *Journal of Financial Economics* 9:1, 3–18.

Barberis, Nicholas, Ming Huang, and Tano Santos. 2001. "Prospect Theory and Asset Prices." *Quarterly Journal of Economics* 116:1, 1–53.

Barberis, Nicholas, Andrei Shleifer, and Robert W. Vishny. 1998. "A Model of Investor Sentiment." *Journal of Financial Economics* 49:3, 307–344.

Barberis, Nicholas, and Richard Thaler. 2003. "A Survey of Behavioral Finance." In *Handbook of the Economics of Finance,* edited by George M. Constantinides, René Stulz, and Milton Harris, 1052–1120. Amsterdam: Elsevier.

Barone-Adesi, Giovanni, Robert F. Engle, and Loriano Mancini. 2008. "A GARCH Option Pricing Model with Filtered Historical Simulation." *Review of Financial Studies* 21:3, 1223–1258.

Barone-Adesi, Giovanni, Loriano Mancini, and Hersh Shefrin. 2011. "Systemic Risk and Sentiment." In *Handbook on Systemic Risk*, edited by Joe Langsam and Jean-Pierre Fouque. Cambridge, UK: Cambridge University Press, forthcoming.

Benartzi, Shlomo, and Richard H. Thaler. 1995. "Myopic Loss Aversion and the Equity Premium Puzzle." *Quarterly Journal of Economics* 110:1, 75–92.

Bernard, Victor L., and Jacob K. Thomas. 1990. "Evidence That Stock Prices Do Not Fully Reflect the Implications of Current Earnings for Future Earnings." *Journal of Accounting and Economics* 13:4, 305–340.

Black, Fischer. 1986. "Noise." *Journal of Finance* 41:3, 529–543.

Blume, Lawrence, and David Easley. 2008. "Market Selection and Asset Pricing." In *Handbook of Financial Markets: Dynamics and Evolution*, edited by Thorsten Hens and Karl Schenk-Hoppé, 403–438. Amsterdam: Elsevier.

Bolton, Patrick, Jose A. Scheinkman, and Wei Xiong. 2005. "Pay for Short-Term Performance: Executive Compensation in Speculative Markets." *Review of Economic Studies* 73:3, 577–610.

Campbell, John Y. 1995. "Some Lessons from the Yield Curve," *Journal of Economic Perspectives* 9:3, 129–152.

Campbell, John Y., Andrew W. Lo, and A. Craig MacKinlay. 1996. *The Econometrics of Financial Markets*. Princeton, NJ: Princeton University Press.

Chen, Nai-Fu, Raymond Kan, and Merton H. Miller. 1993. "Are the Discounts on Closed-End Funds a Sentiment Index?" *Journal of Finance* 48:2, 795–800.

Chopra, Navin, Charles M. C. Lee, Andrei Shleifer, and Richard H. Thaler. 1993. "Yes, Discounts on Closed-End Funds Are a Sentiment Index." *Journal of Finance* 48:2, 801–808.

Cochrane, John H. 2005. *Asset Pricing*, rev. ed. Princeton, NJ: Princeton University Press.

Daniel, Kent, David Hirshleifer, and Avanidhar Subrahmanyam. 1998. "Investor Psychology and Security Market Under- and Overreactions." *Journal of Finance* 53:6, 1839–1885.

Daniel, Kent, and Sheridan Titman. 1997. "Evidence on the Characteristics of Cross Sectional Variation in Stock Returns." *Journal of Finance* 52:1, 1–33.

De Bondt, Werner F. M., and Richard H. Thaler. 1985. "Does the Stock Market Overreact?" *Journal of Finance* 40:3, 793–808.

De Bondt, Werner F. M., and Richard H. Thaler, 1987. "Further Evidence on Investor Overreaction and Stock Market Seasonality." *Journal of Finance* 42:3, 557–581.

DeLong, James Bradford, Andrei Shleifer, Lawrence H. Summers, and Robert J. Waldmann. 1990a. "Noise Trader Risk in Financial Markets." *Journal of Political Economy* 98:4, 703–738.

DeLong, James Bradford, Andrei Shleifer, Lawrence H. Summers, and Robert J. Waldmann. 1990b. "Positive Feedback Investment Strategies and Destabilizing Rational Speculation." *Journal of Finance* 45:2, 375–395.

DeLong, James Bradford, Andrei Shleifer, Lawrence H. Summers, and Robert J. Waldmann. 1991. "The Survival of Noise Traders in Financial Markets." *Journal of Business* 64:1, 1–20.

Dreman, David N. 1982. *The New Contrarian Investment Strategy*. New York: Random House.

Edwards, Ward. 1968. "Conservatism in Human Information Processing." In *Formal Representation of Human Judgement*, edited by Benjamin Kleinmutz and Raymond Bernard Cattell, 17–52. New York: Wiley & Sons.

Fama, Eugene F. 1998. "Market-Efficiency, Long-Term Returns, and Behavioral Finance." *Journal of Financial Economics* 49:3, 283–306.

Fama, Eugene F., and Kenneth R. French. 1992. "The Cross-Section of Expected Stock Returns." *Journal of Finance* 47:2, 427–465.

Fama, Eugene F., and Kenneth R. French. 1996. "Multifactor Explanations of Asset Pricing Anomalies." *Journal of Finance* 51:1, 55–84.

Frazzini, Andrea. 2006. "The Disposition Effect and Underreaction to News." *Journal of Finance* 61:4, 2017–2046.

Geanakoplos, John. 2010. *The Leverage Cycle*. NBER Macroeconomics Annual 2009, 24, 1–65.

Griffin, Dale, and Amos Tversky. 1992. "The Weighing of Evidence and the Determinants of Overconfidence." *Cognitive Psychology* 24:3, 411–435.

Grinblatt, Mark, and Bing Han. 2004. "Prospect Theory, Mental Accounting and Momentum." *Journal of Financial Economics* 78(2): 311–33.

Harvey, Campbell R., and Akhtar Siddique. 2000. "Conditional Skewness in Asset Pricing Tests." *Journal of Finance* 55:3, 1263–1295.

Hong, Harrison, and Jeremy C. Stein. 1999. "A Unified Theory of Underreaction, Momentum Trading, and Overreaction in Asset Markets." *Journal of Finance* 54:6, 2143–2184.

Hong, Harrison, and Jeremy C. Stein. 2003. "Differences of Opinion, Short-Sales Constraints, and Market Crashes." *Review of Financial Studies* 16:2, 487–525.

Ikenberry, David, Josef Lakonishok, and Theo Vermaelen. 1995. "Market Underreaction to Open Market Share Repurchases." *Journal of Financial Economics* 39:2–3, 181–208.

Jegadeesh, Narasimhan, and Sheridan Titman. 1993. "Returns to Buying Winners and Selling Losers: Implications for Stock Market Efficiency." *Journal of Finance* 48:1, 65–91.

Jegadeesh, Narasimhan, and Sheridan Titman. 2001. "Profitability of Momentum Strategies: An Evaluation of Alternative Strategies." *Journal of Finance* 56:2, 699–720.

Kahneman, Daniel, and Amos Tversky. 1973. "On the Psychology of Prediction." *Psychological Review* 80:4, 237–251.

Kahneman, Daniel, and Amos Tversky. 1979. "Prospect Theory: An Analysis of Decision Making under Risk." *Econometrica* 47:2, 263–291.

Kahneman, Daniel, Paul Slovic, and Amos Tversky. 1982. *Judgment under Uncertainty: Heuristics and Biases.* Cambridge, UK: Cambridge University Press.

Keynes, John Maynard. 1936. *The General Theory of Employment, Interest, and Money.* London: McMillan.

Lee, Charles, Andrei Shleifer, and Richard Thaler. 1991. "Investor Sentiment and the Closed-End Puzzle." *Journal of Finance* 46:1, 75–109.

Loewenstein, Mark, and Gregory A. Willard. 2006. "The Limits of Investor Behavior." *Journal of Finance* 61:1, 231–258.

Loughran, Tim, and Jay R. Ritter. 1995. "The New Issues Puzzle." *Journal of Finance* 50:1, 23–51.

Mehra, Rajnish, and Edward Prescott C. 1985. "The Equity Premium: A Puzzle." *Journal of Monetary Economics* 15:2, 145–161.

Rosenberg, Joshua V., and Robert F. Engle. 2002. "Empirical Pricing Kernels." *Journal of Financial Economics* 64:3, 341–372.

Rosenberg, Barr, Kenneth Reid, and Ronald Lanstein. 1985. "Persuasive Evidence of Market Inefficiency." *Journal of Portfolio Management* 11:3, 9–17.

Scheinkman, Jose A., and Wei Xiong. 2003. "Overconfidence and Speculative Bubbles." *Journal of Political Economy* 111:6, 1183–1219.

Shefrin, Hersh. 2005. *A Behavioral Approach to Asset Pricing.* Boston: Elsevier Academic.

Shefrin, Hersh. 2008. *A Behavioral Approach to Asset Pricing,* 2nd ed. Boston: Elsevier Academic.

Shefrin, Hersh, and Meir Statman. 1985. "The Disposition to Sell Winners Too Early and Ride Losers Too Long: Theory and Evidence." *Journal of Finance* 40:3, 777–790.

Shiller, Robert J. 2000. *Irrational Exuberance.* Princeton, NJ: Princeton University Press.

Shleifer, Andrei, and Robert W. Vishny. 1997. "The Limits of Arbitrage." *Journal of Finance* 52:1, 35–55.

Slovic, Paul. 1972. "Psychological Study of Human Judgment: Implications for Investment Decision Making." *Journal of Finance* 27:4, 779–801.

Thaler, Richard. 1985. "Mental Accounting and Consumer Choice." *Marketing Science* 4:3, 199–214.

Xiong, Wei, and Hongjun Yan. 2010. "Heterogeneous Expectations and Bond Markets." *Review of Financial Studies* 23:4, 1433–1466.

THE INVESTMENT POLICY STATEMENT AND FIDUCIARY DUTIES

5

Assessing Risk Tolerance

SHERMAN D. HANNA
Professor, Consumer Sciences Department
The Ohio State University

MICHAEL A. GUILLEMETTE
Doctoral Candidate, Division of Personal Financial
Planning, Texas Tech University

MICHAEL S. FINKE
Professor, Division of Personal Financial
Planning, Texas Tech University

Introduction

Risk tolerance is a crucial part of portfolio selection. The standard presentation of risk versus return (Bodie and Merton, 1998) implies that investors should just pick the level of risk that corresponds to their risk tolerance and obtain the expected return that matches that level of risk on the efficient frontier. There are, however, few clear guidelines for measuring personal risk tolerance. The financial planning industry uses various assessment instruments when determining the risk tolerance level of clients. Financial planners typically choose questionnaires based on validity and reliability or psychometric testing, with no careful discussion of financial economic theory. This chapter discusses the standard economic view of risk aversion, which is the inverse of risk tolerance (Barsky et al., 1997), and demonstrates how many suggested ways of measuring risk tolerance are inconsistent with the normative economic theory related to optimal portfolio choice.

The chapter proceeds as follows: The first section describes the economic concept of risk aversion. The second section discusses how risk preferences affect household portfolios. The third section describes the measurement of risk tolerance, and the fourth section discusses behavioral factors that may explain risk-related household behavior. The final section provides a summary and conclusions.

Risk Tolerance, Normative Finance, and Expected Utility

Normative household finance derives optimal behavior for financial choices from economics (Campbell, 2006) and often uses the economic expected utility theory (Schoemaker, 1982). In that approach, risk aversion is an important preference to consider in determining what is optimal in terms of investment choices, insurance decisions, saving for emergencies, using credit, and saving for retirement (Campbell, 2006). There are conflicting approaches to the measurement of risk tolerance in financial research and practice. Bodie and Merton (1998, 271) note that they would not "distinguish between capacity to bear risk and attitude toward risk." However, other authors suggest that risk capacity should be separated from pure risk tolerance (Malkiel, 1990; Hanna and Chen, 1997; Cordell, 2002). It is necessary to separate risk tolerance from risk capacity to be consistent with the standard normative analysis based on expected utility models.

PLAUSIBLE UTILITY FUNCTIONS

A vital part of normative household finance is choosing plausible utility functions and parameters of utility functions in order to conduct a reasonable normative analysis (Campbell, 2006). As Poterba et al. (2003) note, an important issue is how to estimate the utility function parameters. The key preference parameter for static evaluations of the expected utility of wealth levels is the household's relative risk aversion level. The original concept of risk aversion was developed to explain how insurance could be rational given that people purchased actuarially unfair insurance (Ciecka, 2010). The underlying concept, the decreasing marginal utility of consumption, is intuitive; it can be thought of in terms of a case in which one is given a huge serving of dessert—the fifth bite is likely to give less satisfaction than the first. The basis of the life cycle model of saving is the assumption of decreasing marginal utility, suggesting that a household would prefer smoothing consumption over the life cycle (Modigliani and Brumberg, 1954).

Pratt (1964) and Arrow (1971) discuss properties of utility functions, including the relative risk aversion of a utility function. Consider a utility function U (W), where W represents consumption or wealth. Presumably, the slope of a utility function will be positive, as more consumption is preferred to less consumption. These authors discuss the coefficient of relative risk aversion as a measure of how averse a consumer is to risk, or if extended to consumption over time, how averse a consumer is to fluctuations in consumption. If a consumer has a utility function U (W), then Equation 5.1 defines relative risk aversion:

$$WU''/U', \tag{5.1}$$

where U' is the first derivative of the utility function and U'' is the second derivative of the utility function. If a consumer's marginal utility is constant as wealth or consumption increases, then the relative risk aversion will be zero.

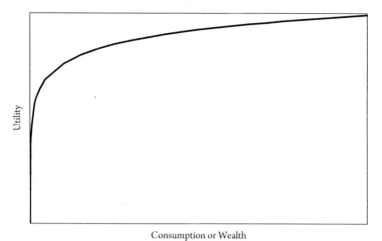

Figure 5.1. Natural log utility function. This figure shows a risk-averse utility function, with decreasing marginal utility as consumption or wealth increases.

Consumers with a positive relative risk aversion are considered to be *risk averse*; those with zero relative risk aversion are deemed to be *risk neutral*; and those with negative relative risk aversion are regarded as *risk seeking*. Figure 5.1 illustrates a risk-averse utility function, the natural log. Utility increases with wealth or consumption but at a rapidly decreasing rate. The utility function for a risk-neutral consumer, with a relative risk aversion of zero, would be a straight line. For example, a $1000 increase in wealth would result in the same increase in utility or satisfaction whether the wealth of the consumer was initially $10,000 or $1 billion. The utility function for a risk-seeking consumer, with a negative relative risk aversion, would be a line of increasing slope. Thus, a $1000 increase in wealth would result in less of an increase in utility or satisfaction for a consumer whose wealth was initially at $10,000 than for one at $1 billion. As Bailey, Olson, and Wonnacott (1980) point out, few consumers are likely to be risk seekers on a consistent basis.

How can relative risk aversion be measured? Kimball (1988) discusses one method involving hypothetical income gambles in regard to the chance to take a new job. Barsky et al. (1997) report analyses of an implementation of this method in the US Health and Retirement Study. The basic concept involves some assumptions, including that the consumer's utility function has a constant relative risk aversion as wealth increases. For instance, a billionaire would receive the same utility gain as a poor person based on a 1 percent increase in wealth. Hanna, Gutter, and Fan (2001) discuss some limitations of the questions asked by Barsky et al. in terms of the respondents not understanding the assumptions about the alternatives in the hypothetical income gambles and test an alternative set of hypothetical questions posed as pension alternatives. Hanna and Lindamood (2004) add graphical presentations of the pension gambles in Hanna, Gutter, and Fan in order to reduce ambiguity for respondents. The series of questions in Hanna and Lindamood (40–45) starts with this initial question: Suppose that you are about to retire and have two choices for a pension: pension A gives you an income equal to your preretirement income. Pension B has a 50 percent chance your income will be double your preretirement income, and a 50 percent chance that your income will be 20 percent less than your preretirement income. You will have no other source of income during retirement, no chance of employment, and no other family income ever in the future. All incomes are stated on an after-tax basis. Which pension would you choose?

The sequence of hypothetical questions is designed to narrow the range of relative risk aversion for consistency with the answers. The assumption is that respondents understand the alternatives and realize, for each set of pension choices, that if they end up with the less favorable pension level, there will be no chance in the future of receiving more income. Table 5.1 shows how the maximum percent of loss accepted corresponds to the respondents' relative risk aversion, assuming their indifference between the final alternatives, based on the discussion in Hanna, Gutter, and Fan (2001). If a person chooses the less risky pension choice from each graph presented, the relative risk aversion will be at least 14.5. If a person chooses the riskier pension choice from each graph presented, the relative risk aversion will be no more than 1.0.

Table 5.1 **Relative risk aversion inferred from maximum loss in hypothetical pension gamble questions**

Maximum percent loss accepted (%)	Relative risk aversion
100.00	0.00
50.00	1.00
33.33	2.00
24.41	3.00
20.00	3.76
15.99	4.76
13.20	5.76
11.19	6.76
10.00	7.53
9.38	8.00
8.00	9.29
6.51	11.29
5.48	13.29
5.00	14.51

Source: Hanna, Gutter, and Fan (2001).

Note: This table shows the relationship between relative risk aversion and the largest percentage loss that a respondent is willing to risk in order to attain a 50 percent chance of doubling his income.

The alternatives presented in Hanna and Lindamood (2004) do not include one corresponding to risk neutrality. However, Table 5.1 shows that risk neutrality (where the relative risk aversion is equal to 0) would mean accepting a 50 percent chance of zero income, which, given the stated conditions, would mean death, because there would be no other resources possible. Therefore, risk neutrality and risk seeking are implausible for rational individuals because a risk-seeking or risk-neutral individual would be willing to accept a substantial risk of death for small gains.

People may appear to be risk neutral in decisions where small amounts of wealth are at risk, even though they are really risk averse. Kahneman and Tversky (1979) found that some individuals who are risk averse under gain domains may be risk-seeking under equivalent loss domains. Yet, in modern economies with social safety nets, not saving and other risky behaviors may be rational for risk-averse people (Hubbard, Skinner, and Zeldes, 1995). Hanna and Lindamood (2004) extrapolate from student responses to the pension gamble questions that the average relative risk aversion in the United States is at least 5.5, although there is a wide range of levels based on responses.

Some complications are present in interpreting the estimates of relative risk aversion in response to the hypothetical income gamble questions, including whether individuals understand the assumptions and whether they answer consistently (Kimball, Sahm, and Shapiro, 2005, 2007; Sahm, 2007). Empirical patterns of responses to the questions regarding income gamble in the *Health and Retirement Study* show some understandable patterns. For instance, female respondents have a lower risk tolerance than otherwise similar male respondents. Further, college-educated respondents have a higher risk tolerance than otherwise similar respondents without a college background. Other results are difficult to explain, such as immigrants having a lower risk tolerance than otherwise similar nonimmigrants (Fang and Hanna, 2007). A plausible explanation is that the effects of education and the effects of immigration could be related to differences in understanding the hypothetical income gamble questions. The gender differences in risk tolerance could be attributed to a genetic component (Little, 2008; Barnea, Cronqvist, and Siegel, 2010), while the different socialization of boys and girls could also have an effect (Croson and Gneezy, 2009).

Estimates of relative risk aversion for static risky decisions can be compared to estimates of the elasticity of intertemporal utility functions, as some people often assume that mathematically the intertemporal utility function has the same form as the utility function of wealth. To evaluate intertemporal savings/consumption decisions, another important preference parameter to consider is the *personal discount rate*, which is the rate at which the utility of future consumption is discounted. Some economists assume that the same utility function and parameters can be used for both risky choices and intertemporal savings and consumption decisions, while others suggest allowing for different preference parameters (Epstein and Zin, 1989). Although some analyses investigate the variance in risky choices over time, considering spending consequences of investment and saving choices in a life cycle investment context, a simpler approach is to first consider intertemporal spending choices with certain income and investment return projections. The recursive utility function in the Epstein-Zin preferences has the primary advantage of making intertemporal portfolio optimization tractable, but it also increases the complexity of analyses.

In the original life-cycle model for savings, the objective is specified as maximizing the lifetime utility of spending in each remaining period, and the typical assumption is that the utility of spending in each period is additive and independent. The assumption of independence is not as restrictive as one might think, because with typical utility functions, such as the natural log, allowing spending to drop to zero in one period has a utility of minus infinity. The original life cycle model and the many analyses based on it over the past 50 years assume maximization of lifetime utility. Freyland (2004) provides an example of the optimization framework, starting with the lifetime budget constraint shown in Equation 5.2:

$$\sum_{t=1}^{T} C_t (1+r)^{-t} \le A_0 + \sum_{t=1}^{T} Y_t (1+r)^{-t}, \tag{5.2}$$

where C_t is consumption in period t; Y_t is income in period t; and r is the real interest rate.

Equation 5.3 shows the maximization problem:

$$\max_{\{C_1...C_T\}} \sum_{t=1}^{T} (1+\rho)^{-t} U(C_t), \tag{5.3}$$

where ρ is the personal discount rate. Freyland (2004) expresses the optimal condition for the spending growth rate, as shown in Equation 5.4:

$$\frac{U'(C_{t+1})}{U'(C_t)} = \left(\frac{1+\rho}{1+r}\right). \tag{5.4}$$

A common assumption is that the utility function has constant elasticity, which is mathematically identical to assuming a constant relative-risk-aversion utility function for risky investment choices. Some authors (e.g., Evans, 2005) refer to the elasticity of marginal utility with respect to consumption, which is denoted as elasticity, ε, and other authors refer to the intertemporal substitution elasticity (e.g., Barsky et al., 1997), which is sometimes denoted as θ. Equation 5.5 shows the relationship between θ and ε.

$$\varepsilon = -\frac{1}{\theta}. \tag{5.5}$$

Hanna, Fan, and Chang (1995) show that if the intertemporal utility function has constant elasticity, ε, the optimal growth rate in spending can be approximated by Equation 5.6:

$$G_c \approx \frac{r-\rho}{-\varepsilon}. \tag{5.6}$$

Hanna, Fan, and Chang (1995) review estimates of ε and ρ, using various studies involving macroeconomic data, household data, and introspective thinking. Barsky et al. (1997), working with a small sample of adults over fifty, and Hanna, Gutter, and Fisher (2003), working with a sample of 252 students, both estimate the mean value of -ε as approximately equal to 5, each using different hypothetical scenarios. These estimates are consistent with the projection by Hanna and Lindamood (2004) of a relative risk aversion of 5.5. The scenarios of Hanna, Gutter, and Chang (1995) and Hanna, Gutter, and Fisher assume a life expectancy of 100 years and a state of perfect health, with no change in household situation and constant real after-tax noninvestment income until death. With the additional assumption of a certain 6 percent real after-tax rate of return on investments, the choice of a consumption path might reveal intertemporal elasticity, assuming that respondents imagine zero discounting of the utility of future consumption. Those who choose a relatively flat consumption path presumably have very high values of −ε, and those who choose very steep consumption paths (e.g., their consumption at age one hundred being over ten times that at age twenty) presumably have very low values of −ε. Hanna, Gutter, and Fisher report that the interquartile range (25th–75th percentiles) for −ε is between 3 and 5 and for relative risk aversion is between 3 and 8, but in the student sample there is not a significant correlation between responses on the two measures.

Authors who have analyzed optimal portfolios by using EZ utility functions can allow for the elasticity of marginal utility, with respect to consumption, to have a magnitude inconsistent with the magnitude of the assumed value of relative risk aversion. Sometimes, however, the assumption involves consistent values. For instance, Gomes and Michaelides (2005) present analyses assuming a value of relative risk aversion of 5 and an elasticity of marginal utility with respect to consumption of −5. They also discuss letting the elasticity have other values. An important consideration is that both relative-risk-aversion and the intertemporal-elasticity parameters are related to the curvature of the utility function. Because utility is assumed to be a function of consumption, both parameters could plausibly be of similar magnitude.

Portfolio Implications of Estimates of Relative Risk Aversion

Standard portfolio theory implies that an investor should choose a mixture of risk-free and risky assets based on personal risk tolerance, ignoring issues of human wealth and holding period. The observed superiority of the long-run performance characteristics of stocks make them a dominant choice for the long-run goals for all but the most risk-averse households. However, the consideration of human wealth and of shorter holding periods makes the role of investor risk tolerance crucial. Assessing behavioral risk tolerance characteristics provides insight into portfolio construction that incorporates preference deviations from standard economic theory.

The concave utility function described in the previous section has important implications for a household considering buying assets that have an uncertain future payout. Uncertainty in asset payout implies uncertainty in future consumption. Since risk-tolerant investors are more willing to accept variation in consumption, they will place a higher value on an asset with a more volatile payout profile. Market participants will trade among themselves in order to create an equilibrium in which those more tolerant of risk choose a portfolio composed of assets that have a higher variation in expected future consumption, while the more risk averse choose a portfolio with less expected variation.

An optimal portfolio consists of a mix of risk-free and risky assets (Bodie and Merton, 1998). Since the marginal investor is risk averse, asset prices will include a risk premium that induces price-taking individuals to allocate a portion of their portfolio to risky assets. An investor will choose the proportion of risky assets that maximizes his expected future utility from consumption. At equilibrium, an additional dollar of expected utility from a risk-free investment will equal the expected utility of a risky investment.

An advisor who is suggesting an optimal portfolio will assess the risk tolerance of the investor and recommend an appropriate portfolio to perfectly balance risky and risk-free investments. Theoretically, recommending an optimal portfolio is a straightforward process that involves estimating the slope of the household's utility function and the risk premium that exists in the market for risky assets. In practice, estimating risk tolerance is complicated by the inability of households to self-evaluate investment risk tolerance, imprecise risk tolerance assessment methods, time-varying changes in the appetite for risk, and risky asset performance idiosyncrasies. Standard economic theory suggests that this portfolio mix is independent of age or time horizon. As discussed in the following sections, this perspective may be incomplete if risky assets exhibit more favorable risk-and-return characteristics with longer holding periods and if households deplete their stock of human wealth over time.

DOMINANT PORTFOLIOS FOR LONG-TERM GOALS

Some advice on portfolio construction is based on a long-run return history of different categories of financial assets. For instance, according to Siegel (1994), for 30-year holding periods going back to the early 1800s in the United States, a diversified stock portfolio would have had the highest mean return, at a level of risk comparable to any other possible combination of stocks and bonds. For a 30-year holding period, Siegel suggests that investors unwilling to take any risk should have 72 percent of their portfolio in stocks, while investors with moderate risk tolerance should have a portfolio with over 115 percent in stocks; in other words, they should buy on margin. However, Siegel does not define risk tolerance.

Other authors ignore risk tolerance and consider the dominance of stocks over less volatile financial investments for long holding periods. As Kish and Hogan (2000) report, for 620 overlapping 240-month holding periods between January 1926 and June 1998, portfolios with a 100 percent allocation to stocks would have been better than bonds or selected mixed portfolios. About 95 percent of the time, a small stock portfolio would have been better than a large stock portfolio. Hanna and Chen (1999) report that for holding periods of twenty-nine years or more, a small stock portfolio would have been better than a large stock portfolio. A limitation of both studies is that they do not consider the possibilities of stock returns that are worse than those observed during the specific historical period. Yet, results through 2007 show a similar dominance of stocks over other financial investments (Morningstar, Inc., 2008).

The financial marketplace allows households in different life cycle stages and with different intertemporal preferences to trade assets in order to achieve an equilibrium that maximizes the discounted expected utility of participants. Intuitively, households that apply a lower rate of discounting on future consumption will place a greater weight on long-run payout characteristics. While US equities have historically provided a high rate of return given their long-run payout variation (Mehra and Prescott, 1985), the historical equity risk premium corresponds to an evaluation period of roughly one year (Benartzi and Thaler, 1995). The average equity holding period of individual investors using a discount brokerage firm is 378 days (Coval, Hirschleifer, and Shumway, 2005). If households make intertemporal investment decisions based on expectations of consumption from future portfolio payout characteristics, a reasonable assumption is that households placing a greater weight on consumption in the more distant future will prefer assets whose long-run payout performance is more favorable.

Observed mean reversion in historical equity returns implies lower risk in equity investment for those with a long-run time horizon (Poterba and Summers, 1988; Campbell and Viceira, 1999). Barberis (2000) estimates that longer time horizons favor equity allocation even if investors are uncertain of the true risk-and-return parameters. Even with a high likelihood that stock returns are independent and identically distributed and the time horizon is irrelevant (Samuelson, 1969), a rational long-term investor will weigh the nonzero possibility that the future will resemble the past and favor equities (Xia, 2001). Although some scholars, such as Bodie (1995), question whether observed prior return characteristics should guide household portfolio selection in the absence of a theoretical rationale for return predictability, conventional wisdom among investment advisers and the popular press is that portfolio allocation to equities rises with the intended length of the holding period. As such, the average investor saving for long-term consumption should favor equity investment.

THE ROLE OF HUMAN WEALTH

Various authors analyze optimal financial portfolios in the context of other components of household wealth, including human wealth or capital, the ability to continue earning money from employment, government social welfare benefits, or pensions such as Social Security. Gutter (2000), for example, estimates that in 1998 75 percent of US households had investment assets representing less than 10 percent of household wealth, which is defined as including the present value of future earnings and other noninvestment income. For a household with an investment portfolio representing a low proportion of their total wealth, the tradeoff between return and risk in an expected utility framework is very different compared to a household whose wealth is composed almost entirely of investment assets.

OPTIMAL PORTFOLIO MODELS WITH HUMAN WEALTH

Various authors, such as Viceira (1999); Campbell and Viceira (2002); and Cocco, Gomes, and Maenhout (2005), analyze optimal portfolio choices in the context of investment portfolios that represent only a part of total household wealth. As Chen et al. (2006, 97) state, "Financial planners and advisors increasingly recognize that human capital must be taken into account when building optimal portfolios for individual investors."

Hanna and Chen (1997) present an approach to optimal portfolio choice that is simpler to understand than that of some other studies. They suggest basic patterns for expected utility analyses of optimal portfolios, taking into account risk aversion and human wealth. The authors assume household utility depends on total wealth, including nonportfolio wealth (e.g., human wealth) and the value of portfolio wealth at the end of the holding period. They also assume that nonportfolio wealth is unrelated to the ending value of portfolio wealth. The authors calculate the expected utility for different allocations of financial assets based on five major categories of financial assets in the United States: large stocks, small stocks, corporate bonds, intermediate government bonds, and Treasury bills. Based on all twenty-year holding periods between 1926 and 1995, even very risk-averse households—those with a relative risk aversion level of at least ten—would maximize expected utility with a 100 percent small stock portfolio, even if the investment portfolio comprised all of the household's wealth. They suggest that households with long holding periods have high objective risk tolerance. This term corresponds to what other authors, such as Malkiel (1990) and Cordell (2002), define as risk capacity.

Hanna and Chen (1997) also try all possible portfolio allocations for the five investment categories for five-year holding periods. For this shorter holding period, the investment-to-total-wealth ratio along with the relative risk aversion is key in determining optimal portfolio allocations. For households with relative risk aversion levels of ten or less, if the initial ratio of investment assets to total wealth is less than 12 percent, 100 percent of the investment portfolio should be placed in small and/or large stocks. For relative risk aversion levels of six or less, if the ratio of investment assets to total wealth is less than 20 percent, 100 percent of the portfolio should also be in small and/or large stocks. Hanna and Chen suggest that households with an investment-to-total-wealth ratio of less than 20 percent have high objective risk tolerance, or high risk capacity.

In terms of a typical household's life cycle pattern of accumulating financial investments for retirement, the Hanna and Chen (1997) results imply that typical young investors should have 100 percent of their retirement accounts in stocks, even if they have low risk tolerance, such as a relative risk aversion of at least 10. Investment assets in the retirement account will typically grow as human wealth decreases, so as retirement gets closer, the combination of a shorter time horizon and a ratio of investment assets to total wealth of more than 20 percent implies that the stock allocation should be reduced and the bond allocation in the retirement account increased.

The Hanna and Chen (1997) analysis implies that most US households should have 100 percent stock portfolios for long-term goals, given the Gutter (2000) results that most households have investment portfolios that are very low proportions of their total wealth. In other words, most households have high objective risk capacity. The other important result from the Hanna and Chen analysis along with more complex analyses using an expected utility approach of optimal portfolios is that the optimal proportion of stock allocation of investment portfolios decreases as retirement approaches, even with an explicit assumption that risk tolerance remains the same. Therefore, even though a rational household decreases the stock proportion of the retirement account as retirement approaches, that does not necessarily mean that the household is becoming less risk tolerant. Stigler and Becker (1977) suggest that economists should refrain from resorting to explanations based on changing preferences unless other explanations are found inadequate. This idea seems reasonable in observing household portfolios. The fact that younger households have riskier retirement portfolios than older households does not necessarily mean a difference in risk tolerance.

The expected utility models of most authors are more complex than the Hanna and Chen (1997) approach and have more complicated implications. For instance, Viceira (1999) obtains results based on assumptions about typical life cycle patterns of asset accumulation. He shows that a household with high risk tolerance (a relative risk aversion of two or less) should have an extremely aggressive investment portfolio until five years from retirement, buying on margin to have a stock allocation of more than 100 percent. For households with moderate risk tolerance (a relative risk aversion of five), allocations should depend on the correlation between human wealth and stock returns. For a correlation of 0.25 between human wealth and stock returns, a household with moderate risk tolerance should start at age thirty with a 60 percent stock allocation and steadily decrease the percentage to about 35 percent at age sixty-five.

The typical result of analyzing optimal portfolios using an expected utility framework is that the effect of risk tolerance on the portfolio allocation depends on the size of the financial investment portfolio relative to other components of household wealth, including human wealth and the personal residence along with the correlations between returns on different components of household wealth. For instance, for a stock broker, a high correlation exists between human wealth and stock returns, whereas for a teacher, there may be a low correlation. In the early part of the teacher's career, holding a very high proportion of the financial investment portfolio in stocks may be reasonable. As retirement approaches, the optimal allocation may depend more on the teacher's risk tolerance.

Optimal Models Allowing for Labor Flexibility

Households may have considerable flexibility in varying their work effort, including the choice of when to retire. The ability of a household to vary labor supply allows the household to assume greater risk in its investment portfolio (Bodie,

Merton, and Samuelson, 1992). Given the same level of risk aversion, a household that has greater labor supply flexibility should normatively accept greater variation in asset payout. This relationship exists because labor market flexibility acts as a hedge against bad outcomes. Cocco, Gomes, and Maenhout (2005) conclude that even though labor income is risky, labor income that is uncorrelated with equity returns is a close substitute for a risk-free asset compared to equities. Earning a labor income should increase the demand for risky assets, especially early in life, due to greater flexibility. However, a small probability of a disastrous labor-income draw substantially decreases the mean allocation to equities. The penalty for ignoring labor-income risk declines as individuals become more risk tolerant.

OTHER FACTORS IN PORTFOLIO CHOICE

In order to give appropriate investment advice, an individual's risk tolerance along with his risk capacity should be estimated. Besides the hypothetical income gamble questions, other approaches attempt to measure risk tolerance by observing behavior, asking about hypothetical investment choices, or asking a series of questions related to both attitudes and hypothetical choices (Hanna, Gutter, and Fan, 2001). An important issue to consider in interpreting actual or hypothetical investment choices is that risk tolerance, risk capacity, and other factors might affect an individual's behavior or answers. Figure 5.2, a conceptual model of choices involving wealth, shows that besides risk tolerance and risk capacity, expectations and feelings about volatility also influence investment choices. Some observers believe that current investor behavior may indicate that investor risk tolerance has increased or decreased. For instance, Lahart (2007, C1) notes, "The risk tolerance of investors had been rising for many months." However, such trends do not indicate that risk tolerance as discussed by economists has changed. Those same investors (Lahart, 2007, C1) might decide to invest in risky assets if expectations change. Some individuals may experience lower utility due to worrying about volatility, even for investments that are not needed for many years. As a result, they might prefer to choose more stable investments even if, based on their risk tolerance and risk capacity, a risky

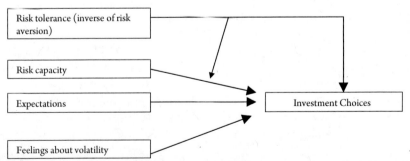

Figure 5.2. Conceptual model of investment choices involving risk. This figure shows a simple model of investment choices that depend on risk tolerance, risk capacity, expectations, and feelings about volatility.

Source: Hanna, Waller, and Finke (2008), used with permission of the editor.

investment would seem appropriate. In considering some of the literature discussing patterns of risk tolerance, the content of Figure 5.2 is important, as are interpreting measures in terms of whether they really include factors other than pure risk tolerance.

Other Measures of Risk Tolerance

Risk-related household behavior may offer an indication of investor risk preferences. However, this type of assessment is only accurate if households have full information and can make highly complex choices consistent with their risk preferences. The Federal Reserve Board's *Survey of Consumer Finances* (SCF) has used a risk tolerance question since 1983, and numerous studies show the relationship between that measure and portfolio choices as well as household characteristics. Risk assessment measures devised for use by financial planners generally include a variety of questions and capture not only the economic concept of risk tolerance but also risk capacity and expectations.

INFERRING RISK TOLERANCE FROM HOUSEHOLD BEHAVIOR

If households are assumed to be informed, rational, and able to freely invest, then their portfolio choices might be a valid indication of their risk tolerance. Friend and Blume (1975) attempt to infer a household's relative risk aversion from its portfolio choices. The *equity premium*, which is the excess return of equities over other investment types, implies that relative risk aversion is extremely high. Yet, explanations for the equity premium paradox other than high relative risk aversion are also available in the literature, such as in Benartzi and Thaler (1995). US households substantially changed their investment choices between 1983 and 1998, with the proportion owning stock assets increasing from 37 percent in 1992 to 52 percent in 2001 (Hanna and Lindamood, 2009). Demographic changes, especially the aging of the "baby boom" generation, affected typical household life cycle savings decisions. Further, the increasing popularity of Individual Retirement Accounts (IRAs) and employer-sponsored retirement accounts influenced investment choices. Thus, concluding that changing portfolio choices indicate changing levels of risk tolerance is not necessarily valid. Wang and Hanna (1997) use assumptions similar to those of Friend and Blume to analyze the risky asset proportion of total wealth. Controlling for other household characteristics, the researchers find that the risky asset proportion increased with age, so they conclude that risk tolerance also increased with age. However, this result might have resulted partly from life cycle factors as human wealth decreases with age. Thus, an elderly household reluctant to spend down financial assets might maintain a relatively high ratio of risky assets. Despite this limitation, the Wang and Hanna results might be consistent with true risk tolerance being relatively constant over the life cycle.

THE SURVEY OF CONSUMER FINANCES RISK TOLERANCE QUESTION

The Federal Reserve Board sponsors the SCF, which includes interviews with thousands of US households every three years. Starting with the 1983 SCF, the survey has included the following question, X3014 (reproduced in Grable and Lytton, 2001, 43), which was intended to measure risk tolerance:

> Which of the statements on this page come closest to the amount of financial risk that you and your (spouse/partner) are willing to take when you save or make investments?
> 1. Take substantial financial risks expecting to earn substantial returns.
> 2. Take above average financial risks expecting to earn above average returns.
> 3. Take average financial risks expecting to earn average returns.
> 4. Not willing to take any financial risks.

No formal research studies asking questions similar to this appear to have occurred before the Federal Reserve Board adopted this one (Yao, Hanna, and Lindamood, 2004). The response to the SCF question is a measure of an attitude reflecting stock market expectations and not a stable measure of risk aversion (Hanna, Waller, and Finke, 2008). Hanna and Lindamood (2009) find that risk tolerance, as measured by the SCF risk attitude question, generally rises after stock market increases and falls after stock market decreases. Yao, Hanna, and Lindamood (2004) report that the willingness to take some financial risk generally decreases with age, increases with education and household income, and is higher for whites than for other racial/ethnic groups. Note, however, that the SCF measure reflects the investment choices that the respondent would make. Therefore, in relation to Figure 5.2, the measure reflects not only risk tolerance but also risk capacity, expectations, and feelings about volatility. The SCF measure is not necessarily a good measure of risk tolerance, as the term is used in economic analyses based on expected utility models.

Evidence also shows that the SCF risk-attitude question is related to ownership of risky assets, such as stocks, but not in a completely consistent way. For instance, Hanna and Lindamood (2008) find that if household characteristics and levels of the SCF risk attitude had remained the same between 2001 and 2004, the likelihood of owning stock assets would not have changed for white households but would have decreased for black, Hispanic, and other/Asian households. Furthermore, the likelihood of white households owning stock assets was higher for those respondents who said they would take average risks than for those who said they would take no risks and also higher for those who responded that they would take above-average risks than for those who claimed average risks, but was lower for those who suggested taking substantial risks than for those who suggested taking above-average risks. The SCF risk-tolerance question has reasonable validity (Grable and Lytton, 2001) but obviously reflects factors other than risk tolerance, such as risk capacity and expectations.

RISK ASSESSMENT INSTRUMENTS USED BY FINANCIAL PLANNERS

Ideally, assessments of risk aversion should incorporate questions that have a strong theoretical basis related to normative portfolio theory. Financial planners and investment advisors have proposed various tolerance measures but none that are strictly consistent with the concept of risk tolerance as the inverse of relative risk aversion. Several measures are described and discussed in the following paragraph.

Droms and Strauss (2003, 75) use the six-item Global Portfolio Allocation Scoring System (PASS) for Individual Investors to determine a client's risk tolerance score. Clients were asked to agree or disagree with the following statements:

1. Earning a high long-term total return that will allow my capital to grow faster than the inflation rate is one of my most important investment objectives.
2. I would like an investment that provides me with an opportunity to defer taxation of capital gains to future years.
3. I do not require a high level of current income from my investments.
4. I am willing to tolerate some sharp down swings in the return on my investments in order to seek a potentially higher return than would normally be expected from more stable investments.
5. I am willing to risk a short-term loss in return for a potentially higher long-run rate of return.
6. I am financially able to accept a low level of liquidity in my investment portfolio.

Respondents can choose from a five-point Likert scale ranging from "strongly agree" to "strongly disagree." The score, combined with a time horizon, provides advisors with a starting point for portfolio allocation recommendations, including a breakdown of recommended asset class percentages. It has not been tested for validity and reliability. In terms of Figure 5.2, the items measure not only risk tolerance but also risk capacity and feelings about volatility.

Grable and Lytton (2003) use a thirteen-item financial risk tolerance assessment instrument to test the relationship between this risk tolerance measure and the proportion of household portfolios held in nonequity investments. Some questions from the thirteen-item assessment (Grable and Lytton, 271) follow:

- In general, how would your best friend describe you as a risk-taker?
  a. A real gambler
  b. Willing to take risks after completing adequate research
  c. Cautious
  d. A real risk avoider
- You have just finished saving for a "once-in-a-lifetime" vacation. Three weeks before you plan to leave, you lose your job. You would:
  a. Cancel the vacation
  b. Take a much more modest vacation

    c. Go as scheduled, reasoning that you need the time to prepare for a job search
    d. Extend your vacation, because this might be your last chance to go first-class

- Given the best and worst case returns of the four investment choices below, which would you prefer?
    a. $200 gain best case; $0 gain/loss worst case
    b. $800 gain best case; $200 loss worst case
    c. $2,600 gain best case; $800 loss worst case
    d. $4,800 gain best case; $2,400 loss worst case

- In addition to whatever you own, you have been given $1,000. You are now asked choose between:
    a. A sure gain of $500
    b. A 50 percent chance to gain $1,000 and a 50 percent chance to gain nothing

- In addition to whatever you own, you have been given $2,000. You are now asked choose between:
    a. A sure loss of $500
    b. A 50 percent chance to lose $1000 and a 50 percent chance to lose nothing

Grable and Lytton (2003) find a statistically significant inverse relationship between their risk tolerance score and the nonequity proportion of household portfolios, which demonstrates the criterion-related and construct-related validity of the instrument. *Criterion-related validity* refers to how accurate an item or index is in multiple situations. *Construct-related validity* refers to how meaningful an item or index is in multiple situations. However, the questions are related to both risk tolerance and risk capacity, as the importance of gains and losses will be different for households of different wealth levels.

Callan and Johnson (2003) contend that *The ProQuest Risk Profiling System* (now *FinaMetrica*) is a scientifically validated test that can help advisors form a more accurate assessment of their clients' risk tolerance levels. FinaMetrica's risk-profiling system is a proprietary, commercially available risk tolerance measurement tool comprised of twenty-five questions that generate a standardized Risk Tolerance Score (RTS) on a scale of one to one hundred, with higher scores indicating greater risk tolerance. The questions are similar to those used in Grable and Lytton (2003). Hallahan, Faff, and McKenzie (2004) find that respondents' choices of portfolios seem to be generally consistent with their RTSs. However, the authors do not rigorously relate the RTS to the normative finance models, and as with the Grable and Lytton research, what is identified as risk tolerance also includes risk capacity and, presumably, expectations.

Unlike the hypothetical income gamble questions (Barsky et al., 1997; Hanna, Gutter, and Fan, 2001, 2004), composite risk tolerance measures (e.g., Grable and Lytton, 2003; Hallahan, Faff, and McKenzie, 2004) neither specify the consumption results of gambles nor put choices in the context of other wealth and of investment horizons. Thus, there is no way of linking the results of these composite measures to relative risk aversion levels in the standard expected utility approach to optimal portfolios.

Limitations of the Standard Normative Portfolio Approach

Although evidence suggests that the standard normative portfolio model does not describe how people actually make decisions, it may be appropriate as a basis for advice if advisors can help people overcome their cognitive limitations. Prospect theory has been proposed as a better model than the standard normative model for explaining investor behavior.

FAILURES OF RATIONAL CHOICE MODELS TO EXPLAIN BEHAVIOR

Tversky and Kahneman (1986) provide evidence that the assumptions about how investors make rational choices underlying the standard normative portfolio model may not describe how people actually make decisions about risky choices. Therefore, the standard normative model may be inappropriate for positive household finance, such as to describe how households actually make decisions (Campbell, 2006). Does that mean that the standard model is an inappropriate basis for advice for households? Tversky and Kahneman suggest thinking of optical illusions as analogies for the cognitive limitations. They give the example that people may be fooled into thinking that one line is longer than another, but if the lines are framed by a grid, the framing can help people overcome the optical illusions. They suggest that in a similar manner, financial advisors might be able to help people overcome their cognitive limitations. However, no agreement exists as to whether normative models based on rational choice should be the basis of prescriptions for households.

PROSPECT THEORY

Rabin (2000) as well as Rabin and Thaler (2001) shows that human behavior cannot be easily reconciled with traditional economic theory. People tend to care less about how risky outcomes affect utility from consumption and more about the pain they feel about losses. For example, the demand for substantial amounts of low-deductible auto insurance and noncatastrophic health insurance translates into improbably high risk aversion levels over larger stakes (Finke, Belasco, and Huston, 2010). Prospect theory modifies traditional expected utility theory by overweighting the disutility experience from losses from an arbitrary reference point, otherwise known as *loss aversion*. Individuals tend to be more sensitive to reductions in their levels of wealth from the amount they initially invested or the amount on their most recent quarterly statement than to gains. Tversky and Kahneman (1992) estimate that losses have approximately 2.25 times the impact on an individual's perceived welfare than does an equal dollar amount of gains. The size of the equity premium is consistent with prospect theory if investors are loss averse and myopic (Benartzi and Thaler, 1995).

The influence of time horizon on investment preference is magnified when households weigh expected utility declines from losses more than those from gains. Dierkes, Erner, and Zeisberger (2010) show that the investment horizon heavily influences optimal portfolio choice among investors with a prospect theory utility function. Because the holding period decreases the likelihood of a decline when an investor buys and holds equities from an investment reference point, long-run investors and those who place a greater weight on future utility will hold a portfolio that is much more heavily weighted toward equities. Investors who heavily weight short-run outcomes (of less than two years) will not prefer stock investment given historical US asset performance characteristics, as suggested in Benartzi and Thaler (1995).

Summary and Conclusions

Assessing risk tolerance is a crucial element when devising appropriate portfolio recommendations for clients. The expected utility approach underlying standard normative portfolio advice of financial economics assumes that a household has some level of risk aversion that determines its utility according to different wealth or consumption levels. Therefore, a household's risk aversion is a key factor in determining the optimal portfolio for a household. The only measures of risk tolerance that are rigorously linked to the standard expected utility approach are based on hypothetical income gambles that carefully specify alternatives in terms of possible consumption available to respondents. Most investors are likely to have a relative risk aversion level between three and eight and therefore should hold some stocks as part of their long-term goals.

Risk tolerance measures that offer choices without providing respondents context as to how their potential consumption would change do not provide estimates that measure the concept of risk aversion assumed in standard expected utility analyses of portfolio choices. Behavioral finance approaches, including prospect theory, may better explain household investment choices, but a consensus does not exist regarding how to incorporate these approaches into rigorous portfolio recommendations. Normative models should be used to assist households to approach outcomes that are closer to the maximization of their expected lifetime utility.

Discussion Questions

1. *The Survey of Consumer Finance*'s financial risk tolerance question is widely used in the academic literature to measure the risk aversion level of households. Why might this not be the best measure to use according to the normative view of measuring risk tolerance?

2. Most risk tolerance surveys contain questions that are not explicitly grounded in theory. Why is having a theoretical basis important when determining which type of questions should be included in a questionnaire?
3. What is human capital and how is it measured? How should human capital and labor flexibility influence an optimal portfolio allocation?
4. What role should investment horizon play, if any, when determining an optimal portfolio allocation?

References

Arrow, Kenneth J. 1971. *Essays in the Theory of Risk-Bearing.* Chicago: Markham.

Bailey, Martin J., Mancur Olson, and Paul Wonnacott. 1980. "The Marginal Utility of Income Does Not Increase: Borrowing, Lending, and Friedman-Savage Gambles." *American Economic Review* 70:3, 372–79.

Barberis, Nicholas. 2000. "Investing for the Long Run When Returns Are Predictable." *Journal of Finance* 551: 225–64.

Barnea, Amir, Henrik Cronqvist, and Stephan Siegel. 2010. "Nature or Nurture: What Determines Investor Behavior?" *Journal of Financial Economics* 98:3, 583–604.

Barsky, Robert B., F. Thomas Juster, Miles S. Kimball, and Matthew D. Shapiro. 1997. "Preference Parameters and Behavioral Heterogeneity: An Experimental Approach in the Health and Retirement Study." *Quarterly Journal of Economics* 112:2, 537–79.

Benartzi, Shlomo, and Richard H. Thaler. 1995. "Myopic Loss Aversion and the Equity Premium Puzzle." *Quarterly Journal of Economics* 110:1, 73–92.

Bodie, Zvi. 1995. "On the Risk of Stocks in the Long Run." *Financial Analysts Journal* 51:3, 18–22.

Bodie, Zvi, and Robert C. Merton. 1998. *Finance.* Upper Saddle River, NJ: Prentice-Hall.

Bodie, Zvi, Robert C. Merton, and William F. Samuelson. 1992. "Labor Supply Flexibility and Portfolio Choice in a Life Cycle Model." *Journal of Economic Dynamics and Control* 16:3–4, 427–49.

Callan, Victor J., and Malcolm Johnson. 2003. "Some Guidelines for Financial Planners in Measuring and Advising Clients about Their Levels of Risk Tolerance." *Journal of Personal Finance* 1:1, 31–44.

Campbell, John Y. 2006. "Household Finance." *Journal of Finance* 61:4, 1553–1604.

Campbell, John Y., and Luis M. Viceira. 1999. "Consumption and Portfolio Decisions When Expected Returns Are Time Varying." *Quarterly Journal of Economics* 114:2, 433–95.

Campbell, John Y., and Luis M. Viceira. 2002. *Strategic Asset Allocation: Portfolio Choice for Long-Term Investors.* New York: Oxford University Press.

Chen, Peng, Roger G. Ibbotson, Moshe A. Milevsky, and Kevin X. Zhu. 2006. "Human Capital, Asset Allocation, and Life Insurance." *Financial Analysts Journal* 62:1, 97–109.

Ciecka, James. 2010. "Daniel Bernoulli on the Measurement of Risk." *Journal of Legal Economics* 16:2, 83–93.

Cocco, João F., Francisco J. Gomes, and Pascal J. Maenhout. 2005. "Consumption and Portfolio Choice over the Life Cycle." *Review of Financial Studies* 18:2, 491–533.

Cordell, David M. 2002. "Risk Tolerance in Two Dimensions." *Journal of Financial Planning* 15:5, 30–36.

Coval, Joshua D., David A. Hirschleifer, and Tyler Shumway. 2005. "Can Individual Investors Beat the Market?" Working paper, School of Finance, Harvard University. Available online.

Croson, Rachel, and Uri Gneezy. 2009. "Gender Differences in Preferences." *Journal of Economic Literature* 47:2, 448–74.

Dierkes, Maik, Carsten Erner, and Stefan Zeisberger. 2010. "Investment Horizon and the Attractiveness of Investment Strategies: A Behavioral Approach." *Journal of Banking and Finance* 34:5, 1032–46.

Droms, William G., and Steven N. Strauss. 2003. "Assessing Risk Tolerance for Asset Allocation." *Journal of Financial Planning* 16:3, 72–77.

Epstein, Larry G., and Stanley E. Zin. 1989. "Substitution, Risk Aversion, and the Temporal Behavior of Consumption and Asset Returns: A Theoretical Framework." *Econometrica* 57:4, 937–969.

Evans, David J. 2005. "The elasticity of marginal utility of consumption: estimates for 20 OECD countries." *Fiscal Studies* 26:2, 197–224.

Fang, Mei-chi, and Sherman D. Hanna. 2007. "Racial/Ethnic Differences in Risk Tolerance in the 2004 Health and Retirement Study." *Proceedings of the Academy of Financial Services.*

Finke, Michael S., Eric Belasco, and Sandra J. Huston. 2010. "Individual Property Risk Management." *Journal of Probability and Statistics 2010.* Article ID 805309. Accessed on 17 June, 2011.

Freyland, Felix. 2004. "Household Composition and Savings: An Overview." Working paper 04–69, Sonderforschungsbereich 504, University of Mannheim.

Friend, Irwin, and Marshall E. Blume. 1975. "The Demand for Risky Assets." *American Economic Review* 65:5, 900–22.

Gomes, Francisco, and Alexander Michaelides. 2005. "Optimal Life-Cycle Asset Allocation: Understanding the Empirical Evidence." *Journal of Finance* 60:2, 869–904.

Grable, John E., and Ruth H. Lytton. 2001. "Assessing the Concurrent Validity of the SCF Risk Tolerance Question." *Financial Counseling and Planning* 12:2, 43–52.

Grable, John E., and Ruth H. Lytton. 2003. "The Development of a Risk Assessment Instrument: A Follow-Up Study." *Financial Services Review* 12:3, 257–74.

Gutter, Michael S. 2000. "Human Wealth and Financial Asset Ownership." *Financial Counseling and Planning* 11:2, 9–19.

Hallahan, Terrence A., Robert W. Faff, and Michael D. McKenzie. 2004. "An Empirical Investigation of Personal Financial Risk Tolerance." *Financial Services Review* 13:1, 57–78.

Hanna, Sherman D., and Peng Chen. 1997. "Subjective and Objective Risk Tolerance: Implications for Optimal Portfolios." *Financial Counseling and Planning* 8:2, 17–26.

Hanna, Sherman D., and Peng Chen. 1999. "Small Stocks Versus Large: It's How Long You Hold That Counts." *AAII Journal* 21:6, 26–27.

Hanna, Sherman D., Jessie X. Fan, and Regina Chang. 1995. "Optimal Life Cycle Savings." *Financial Counseling and Planning* 6: 1–15.

Hanna, Sherman D., Michael S. Gutter, and Jessie X. Fan. 2001. "A Measure of Risk Tolerance Based on Economic Theory." *Financial Counseling and Planning* 12:2, 53–60.

Hanna, Sherman D., Michael S. Gutter, and Patricia J. Fisher. 2003. "Risk Aversion and the Elasticity of Marginal Utility with Respect to Consumption." *Consumer Interests Annual* 49. Available at http://hec.osu.edu/people/shanna/sh/RiskAversion_03.pdf. Accessed on 10 June, 2011.

Hanna, Sherman D., and Suzanne Lindamood. 2004. "An Improved Measure of Risk Aversion." *Financial Counseling and Planning* 15:2, 27–38.

Hanna, Sherman D., and Suzanne Lindamood. 2008. "The Decrease in Stock Ownership by Minority Households." *Journal of Financial Counseling and Planning* 19:2, 46–58.

Hanna, Sherman D., and Suzanne Lindamood. 2009. "Risk Tolerance: Cause or Effect?" *Proceedings of the Academy of Financial Services.* Available at http://www.academyfinancial.org/09Conference/09Proceedings/(1C)%20Hanna,%20Lindamood.pdf. Accessed on 17 July, 2011.

Hanna, Sherman D., William Waller, and Michael S. Finke. 2008. "The Concept of Risk Tolerance in Personal Financial Planning." *Journal of Personal Finance* 7:1, 96–108.

Hubbard, R. Glenn, Jonathan Skinner, and Stephen P. Zeldes. 1995. "Precautionary Saving and Social Insurance." *Journal of Political Economy* 103:2, 360–99.

Kahneman, Daniel and Amos Tversky. 1979. "Prospect Theory: An Analysis of Decision under Risk." *Econometrica* 47:2, 263–291.

Kimball, Miles S. 1988. "Farmers' Cooperatives as Behavior toward Risk." *American Economic Review* 78:1, 224–32.

Kimball, Miles S., Claudia R. Sahm, and Matthew D. Shapiro. Forthcoming. "Using Survey-Based Risk Tolerance." *Journal of the American Statistical Association.*

Kimball, Miles S., Claudia R. Sahm, and Matthew D. Shapiro. 2007. "Imputing Risk Tolerance from Survey Responses." Working Paper 13337, National Bureau of Economic Research, Cambridge, MA.

Kish, Richard J., and Karen M. Hogan. 2000. "Small Stocks for the Long Run." *Financial Counseling and Planning* 11:2, 21–32.

Lahart, Justin. 2007. "Investors' View of Risk Returns to Normal." *Wall Street Journal*, September 10, C1.

Little, Anthony C. 2008. "Testosterone and Financial Risk Preferences." *Evolution & Human Behavior* 29:6, 384–90.

Malkiel, Burton Gordon. 1990. *A Random Walk Down Wall Street.* New York: W. W. Norton.

Mehra, Rajnish, and Edward C. Prescott. 1985. "The Equity Premium: A Puzzle." *Journal of Monetary Economics* 15:2, 145–61.

Modigliani, Franco, and Richard Brumberg. 1954. "Utility Analysis and the Consumption Function: An Interpretation of Cross-Section Data." In *Post-Keynesian Economics*, edited by Kenneth K. Kurihara, 388–436. New Brunswick, NJ: Rutgers University Press.

Morningstar, Inc. 2008. *Ibbotson SBBI 2008 Classic Yearbook: Market Results for Stocks, Bonds, Bills, and Inflation, 1926–2007.* Chicago: Morningstar.

Poterba, James M., Joshua Rauh, Steven F. Venti, and David A. Wise. 2003. "Utility Valuation of Risk in Retirement Saving Accounts." Working Paper 9892, National Bureau of Economic Research, Cambridge, MA.

Poterba, James M., and Lawrence H. Summers. 1988. "Mean Reversion in Stock Prices: Evidence and Implications." *Journal of Financial Economics* 22:1, 27–59.

Pratt, John W. 1964. "Risk Aversion in the Small and in the Large." *Econometrica* 32:1–2, 122–36.

Rabin, Matthew. 2000. "Risk Aversion and Expected-Utility Theory: A Calibration Theorem." *Econometrica* 68:5, 1281–92.

Rabin, Matthew, and Richard H. Thaler. 2001. "Anomalies: Risk Aversion." *Journal of Economic Perspectives* 15:1, 219–32.

Sahm, Claudia. 2007. "How Much Does Risk Tolerance Change?" Finance and Economics Discussion Series 2007–66. Washington, DC: Board of Governors of the Federal Reserve System. Available at https://federalreserve.gov/Pubs/FEDS/2007/200766/200766abs.html. Accessed on 10 June, 2011.

Samuelson, Paul A. 1969. "Lifetime Portfolio Selection by Dynamic Stochastic Programming." *Review of Economics and Statistics* 51:3, 239–46.

Schoemaker, Paul J. H. 1982. "The Expected Utility Model: Its Variants, Purposes, Evidence and Limitations." *Journal of Economic Literature* 20:2, 529–63.

Siegel, Jeremy J. 1994. *Stocks for the Long Run: A Guide to Selecting Markets for Long-Term Growth.* Burr Ridge, IL: Irwin.

Stigler, George J., and Gary S. Becker. 1977. "De Gustibus Non Est Disputandum." *American Economic Review* 67:2, 76–90.

Tversky, Amos, and Daniel Kahneman. 1986. "Rational Choice and the Framing of Decisions." *Journal of Business* 59:4, S251–78.

Tversky, Amos, and Daniel Kahneman. 1992. "Advances in Prospect Theory: Cumulative Representation of Uncertainty." *Journal of Risk and Uncertainty* 5:4, 297–323.

Viceira, Luis M. 1999. Optimal Portfolio Choice for Long-Horizon Investors with Nontradable Labor Income. Working Paper 7409, National Bureau of Economic Research. Cambridge, MA.

Wang, Hui, and Sherman Hanna. 1997. "Does Risk Tolerance Decrease with Age?" *Financial Counseling and Planning*, 8:2, 27–31.

Xia, Yihong. 2001. "Learning about Predictability: The Effects of Parameter Uncertainty on Dynamic Asset Allocation." *Journal of Finance* 56:1, 205–46.

Yao, Rui, Sherman D. Hanna, and Suzanne Lindamood. 2004. "Changes in Financial Risk Tolerance, 1983–2001." *Financial Services Review* 13:4, 249–66.

6

Private Wealth Management

DIANNA C. PREECE
Professor of Finance, University of Louisville

Introduction

As of September 2010, private wealth exceeded $55 trillion in the United States alone, down from a pre–financial crisis high of nearly $66 trillion in June 2007 (Fernando, 2010). In a recent report on global wealth, Credit Suisse performs wealth analysis on 160 countries and forecasts that worldwide private wealth will increase from its level of approximately $200 trillion in late 2010 to $315 trillion by 2015 (Shorrocks and Davies, 2010). Private wealth management (PWM) is a multibillion dollar industry. Further, many individuals have become more sophisticated in recent years and have a better understanding of how their funds are, or should be, managed. As such, an understanding of PWM is critical to both high–net worth individuals and the financial advisors assisting them.

PWM is a specialized field focused on investment management for high–net worth individuals and families. The field has become increasingly more technical, with mathematical and computer modeling playing a larger role in all aspects of wealth management. PWM is highly complex and must be customized to the individual. Private-wealth individuals are usually taxable investors with unique circumstances that shape their financial needs and requirements. Taxes are especially relevant to individuals and affect asset allocation decisions as well as the implementation of those decisions. Also, both an individual's on-and-off balance-sheet assets and his liabilities must be considered in the decision-making process. For example, a defined-benefit pension plan, while not part of the asset pool, is still important to wealth-management decisions related to retirement. Therefore, the approach must be comprehensive and thorough, with little room for standardization.

Individuals in the private wealth domain are broadly classified into three groups from least to most wealthy: (1) mass affluent, (2) high net worth, and (3) ultra-high net worth. "High net worth" is the catchall phrase that is used to encompass all of these individuals in much of the PWM literature. Investments and portfolio management textbooks have traditionally devoted little attention to the management of the wealth of high–net worth individuals. However, academics and practitioners have written much on the subject, some of which will be discussed in the following sections.

This chapter is organized as follows: First, sources of wealth and wealth creation are discussed. Second, the investment policy statement (IPS) is described. While the factors that make up the IPS are the same for individuals and institutions, the focus often differs. Third, the asset allocation decision is considered, including a description of the role human capital plays in the PWM discussion. Recent academic and practitioner research is described in the context of specific PWM topics. The final section includes a summary and conclusions.

Wealth and the Individual

Individuals can be broadly classified based on their stage of life and economic circumstances. This classification scheme is called *situational profiling*. The goal of the financial advisor is to understand his clients and their unique circumstances. This means understanding their preferences, financial goals, life styles, and desires for the future. Situational profiling is a first step in understanding an individual in the wealth management process. The aim is to better appreciate where and how individuals have accumulated their wealth, their perceptions or measures of that wealth, and their stage of life.

WEALTH CREATION

Individuals create wealth actively through entrepreneurial activities as well as through work that involves the willingness and ability to move between jobs and take risks to increase income. Individuals may also receive wealth passively via windfalls such as inheritances or through long-term, secure work and conservative investments. An investor's views of risk and return are in part determined by how wealth has been accumulated.

Individuals have a psychological makeup that makes them more or less willing to assume risk. *Psychological profiling* is one of the methods by which an advisor determines an individual's propensity to tolerate risk. Examples of this propensity include entrepreneurs being more likely to have a higher risk tolerance than those who have created wealth in other manners. Entrepreneurs are known for risk taking and often move from successful companies and high-paying jobs to start-up companies with much less financial security. Such risk-seeking behavior in business theoretically translates into a willingness to assume risk in an investment setting. However, Palich and Bagby (1995) find that, consistent with previous research, entrepreneurs do not see themselves as more predisposed to risk taking than are nonentrepreneurs. However, using a scenario analysis approach, they find that entrepreneurs do categorize business opportunities more positively than nonentrepreneurs. Where a nonentrepreneur sees risk, an entrepreneur sees opportunity. Thus, in the absence of evidence to the contrary, situational profiling of an entrepreneur would initially assume a higher willingness to take investment risk.

In contrast, an individual who has accumulated wealth through years of work and conservative spending and investing is likely to have a lower risk tolerance. These individuals have shown their disinclination toward risk via life decisions. Thus, they are likely to duplicate this unwillingness to assume substantial risks in their portfolio decision making. Investors who have achieved wealth through a windfall such as an inheritance or winning the lottery are also likely to have lower risk tolerance due to a fear of losing their unexpectedly accumulated wealth. Further, these individuals are often unfamiliar with the concepts of risk and return, making them more hesitant to venture into unknown territory. Conversely, an investor's confidence in his own abilities, despite how he accumulated wealth, plays a role in his tolerance for risk. In a PWM case study, Bronson, Scanlan, and Squires (2007) consider psychological profiling along with situational profiling as important inputs in assessing an investor's willingness to take risks.

Behavioral Finance Versus Traditional Models

Modern portfolio theory (MPT) assumes that investors prefer to maximize return for a given level of risk. According to this theory, investors make decisions based on (1) risk aversion, (2) rational expectations, and (3) asset integration. Risk aversion implies that investors prefer to avoid unnecessary risk and will maximize their return for a given level of risk or minimize their risk for a given level of return. In other words, investors like return but dislike risk. Rational expectations imply that investors' forecasts are unbiased and reflect available information about an investment's worth or true value. If assets are integrated, investors take into consideration how the returns on their investments' will interact or correlate with other assets in their portfolio. Harry Markowitz (1952), the father of MPT, first explored this idea of asset integration in a seminal article that ultimately led the author to the Nobel Memorial Prize in Economic Sciences. Markowitz was the first to show that increasing the number of holdings in a portfolio reduces the overall variance or standard deviation of the portfolio's returns.

Another important advance in MPT was the development of the capital asset pricing model (CAPM) during the 1960s (Sharpe, 1964; Lintner, 1965). In recent years, behavioral financial models have posed a challenge to the basic assumptions of MPT (Kahneman and Tversky, 1979; Barberis, Shleifer, and Vishny, 1998; Daniel, Hirshleifer, and Subrahmanyam, 1998). In contrast to the mathematical approach of MPT, behavioral models use social, emotional, and cognitive factors to explain investor behavior and suggest that some people act irrationally at least some of the time. Originally developed to explain market anomalies, the field of behavioral finance has garnered much attention in the last decade or so. Its popularity partly stems from the assumption that investors do not act based on risk aversion, rational expectations, and asset integration, as suggested by decades of financial research and thought beginning with Markowitz (1952). Three common principles of behavioral finance are: (1) loss aversion, (2) biased expectations, and (3) asset segregation.

Prospect theory, developed by Kahneman and Tversky (1979), describes how investors evaluate potential gains and losses. Prospect theory can be used to explain the principle of loss aversion, which suggests that investors focus on gains and losses rather than on risk and return. Kahneman and Tversky (1979) show that investors prefer certain gains but are fine with uncertain losses. For example, given the choice of a certain gain (e.g., $5,000), or a 50–50 chance of a larger gain (e.g., $10,000) or breakeven, an investor will choose the certain gain. In contrast, if an investor is given a choice of a certain loss (e.g., $5,000) versus a 50–50 chance of a larger loss (e.g., $10,000) or a breakeven, he will invariably choose the gamble. Thus, investors are risk averse regarding returns and risk seeking (rather than risk averse) regarding loss avoidance.

Consistent with the individual investor focus on losses rather than volatility, Jacobsen (2006) and Leibowitz and Bova (2010) contend that downside risk measures such as semivariance may be more relevant in a PWM setting than traditional measures such as variance or standard deviation. Jacobsen shows how to use downside risk measures in constructing tax-efficient portfolios for individual investors. Leibowitz and Bova maintain that return targets and shortfall limits may better help investors to express portfolio objectives than traditional mean-variance objectives.

Biased expectations imply that investors do not use all relevant information and learn from their mistakes but instead put too much confidence in their abilities to forecast economic events related to investments. Investors are likely to discount information that does not conform to their views of the world. Thus, expectations are not rational but biased.

Rather than looking at how an investment will interact with their portfolio, as assumed by MPT, the principle of *asset segregation* implies that investors consider assets on a stand-alone basis. In asset integration, the risk-reduction benefits of adding a security to a portfolio result from the correlation of the security's returns with the returns of the other securities in the portfolio. If an investor builds a portfolio one asset at a time and ignores asset correlations, as occurs in asset segregation, he may be inadvertently increasing the portfolio's overall risk due to a lack of diversification.

PERSONALITY TYPES

As previously described, an investor's psychological makeup is reflected in how he generates wealth (i.e., entrepreneurial activities versus passive wealth generation). Personal factors such as whether an investor grew up rich or poor, his job experiences, his current level of wealth, and even his current frame of mind may all affect his investment goals and strategies. An investment professional may use personality questionnaires to determine an individual's investment-related personality type. For instance, the Myers-Briggs Type Indicator (MBTI) helps determine whether an investor is more cautious or daring, methodical or spontaneous, or individualistic or group oriented. These classifications may then help the investor understand potential shortcomings, such as trading too frequently and incurring high transactions costs or being paralyzed by data and unable to make timely decisions.

Understanding a client's investment personality type is important in that it can facilitate identifying potential strengths, such as the willingness to conduct research, and weaknesses, such as overconfidence in personal abilities. It can also provide a starting point for discussion. For example, if an investor knows via a personality questionnaire that he invests spontaneously, he can monitor trading and transactions costs to see if the costs are excessive and perhaps modify his trading behavior. However, ascertaining an investor's personality type is only a starting point in identifying the investor's risk tolerance and return expectations/requirements. The IPS is another critical step.

The Investment Policy Statement

The *investment policy statement* (IPS) is a document that defines the investor's return objectives, risk tolerance, and constraints. Developing an IPS is important for both the investor and the investment advisor. If an individual chooses to manage his own wealth, an IPS should be developed for him to guide the investment process. Bronson, Scalan, and Squires (2007) focus on the development of the IPS in an extended case study. In the process of developing the IPS, the following components are taken into consideration:

- **Risk and return.** The IPS should identify an individual's risk tolerance and return objectives.
- **Constraints.** The document should identify an investor's constraints, such as time horizon or liquidity needs.
- **Strategy.** The IPS should delineate the investment strategy that fits an investor's overall objectives and constraints.
- **Asset Allocation.** The appropriate asset allocation should be determined based on an investor's objectives and constraints.
- **Portfolio decisions.** Investment decisions should be executed based on the defined strategy and asset allocations.
- **Evaluation.** The IPS will be revisited at least annually to identify changes in the client's personal and financial position that affect the IPS. Evaluation of a portfolio's performance takes place after an agreed-upon time period.
- **Modifications.** As necessary, modifications to the portfolio should be made to ensure that an investor's objectives and constraints are being honored.

RETURN OBJECTIVES

Determining an investor's required rate of return is a function of several factors. First, the growth objective for the portfolio is critical and must be realistic and achievable given the limits of the portfolio. Both the size of the portfolio and the investor's time horizon affect the potential portfolio return. Additionally, the individual's expected expenditures, either required or desired, may affect the return that is necessary for the investor. *Required expenditures* are those that the individual is obligated to make. They include living expenses and medical expenditures for dependents as well as bequests and educational expenses for children. *Desired expenditures* are those that are voluntary. Examples include vacation homes, expensive vacations, and large charitable contributions that would potentially necessitate an unreasonably large return from a portfolio.

The return on a portfolio typically includes both growth and income components. Expecting the income component to cover all required expenses is unreasonable in most situations. For this to occur, the asset allocation would necessarily contain a high proportion of income-producing investments, such as fixed-income securities and dividend-paying stocks. As a result, the risk profile would be low, which is appropriate for some investors but not all of them. A total return perspective, one where both growth and income components are used to cover expenditures, is appropriate for most investors.

As an example, assume that Kevin Finney, a single, retired human resources officer at a Fortune 500 company has accumulated a $2.5 million portfolio. He has become accustomed to a fairly high standard of living while working but is willing to reduce that standard in order to retire. Finney no longer has a mortgage on his house and does not plan to buy another property. As such, he estimates that he will require $80,000 on a before-tax basis next year to maintain his new lifestyle. He is partially responsible for the nursing home care of his mother, which will require an additional $20,000 on a before-tax basis next year. Both of these expenses are expected to increase at the 3 percent historical rate of inflation. How much must the portfolio earn annually (nominal, before-tax) in order to cover Finney's expenses? The necessary real before-tax return would be ($80,000 + $20,000)/$2,500,000 = 4 percent. Although the real before-tax return is 4 percent, Finney expects expenses will grow at an annual rate of 3 percent. Thus, the nominal before-tax return is about 4 percent + 3 percent inflation = 7 percent. A more exact return would involve making the following calculation: $(1.04)(1.03) - 1 = 1.0712 - 1 = 0.0712$, or 7.12 percent.

Another way to look at the required return is over a specific time horizon. For example, assume that Sarah Johnson currently has $25,000 in savings. She is twenty-five years old and wants to retire at age sixty-five. She believes that she could have the retirement of her dreams if she could accumulate $3 million by retirement. Assuming that Johnson does not add to her savings over the next forty years, what annual rate must she earn to reach her savings goal?

The solution is structured as a problem involving the time value of money. Using a financial calculator (such as the Texas Instruments BAII Plus), the inputs are: N = 40; PV = − $25,000; FV = $3,000,000; PMT = 0; so CPT I/Y → 12.71 percent, where N stands for number of periods, PV stands for present value, FV stands for future value, PMT stands for payment, CPT stands for compute and I/Y stands for required rate of return. Thus, in order to meet Johnson's goal, the portfolio must earn 12.71 percent annually. She determines, with the help of her financial advisor, that this is an unrealistic return expectation and decides that the most she can earn is 10 percent. Johnson can also add to her portfolio and would like to know how much she must add each year in order to reach her $3 million goal. The inputs are N = 40; PV = −$25,000; FV = $3,000,000; I/Y = 10; so CPT

PMT → $4,221.76, where CPT stands for compute and PMT stands for payment. Thus, Johnson would need to add $4,221.76 per year to her savings in order to reach her $3 million goal, assuming she can earn a 10 percent annual return.

If Johnson's portfolio can only earn 10 percent and she cannot add to her savings, how much will she be able to accumulate in forty years? The inputs are N = 40; PV = −$25,000; PMT = $0; I/Y = 10; so CPT FV → $1,131,481.39. In this case, Johnson would only accumulate $1,131,481.39 if she can earn 10 percent and cannot add to her savings over the forty-year horizon.

Returns are not independent of each other. If an investor loses everything in year one, he will have nothing to invest in year two. This means that the arithmetic average (calculated as the sum of the returns divided by N) may lead the investor to the wrong conclusion regarding his long-term wealth accumulation. As a simple example, assume the return is −100 percent in year one and 120 percent in year two. The arithmetic for the average return is (−100 percent + 120 percent)/2 = 10 percent. In reality, if the investor lost 100 percent in year one, there would be no way to make 120 percent in year two because all of his capital would be gone. As such, the geometric mean is a better measure of return for investors than the arithmetic average. The *geometric mean* is the average annualized return and takes compounding into consideration. The geometric mean return formula is calculated as the nth root of the product of 1 plus each year's holding period return minus 1. As equation 6.1 shows, given a time series of holding period returns R_i, i = 1, 2, ..., n, the geometric mean return, R_G, over the time period spanned by the returns R_1 through R_n is:

$$R_G = \left[\prod_{i=1}^{n} (1+R_i) \right]^{\frac{1}{n}} - 1. \tag{6.1}$$

The arithmetic mean return and the geometric mean return of an asset or portfolio of assets can be quite different (DeFusco, McLeavey, Pinto, and Runkle, 2007). The arithmetic average return will always be greater than the geometric average if volatility in the returns is present. As such, the arithmetic mean return is often used in advertisements for mutual funds and other types of investments. Consider the following example:

Year	Return (%)
2008	50
2009	−20
2010	30
2011	−20

Arithmetic average return = (50% − 20% + 30% − 20%)/4 = 10 percent

Geometric average return = $(1.5)(0.8)(1.3)(0.8)^{1/4} - 1$ = 5.695 percent

If an investor who started with $1,000 of capital calculated his ending wealth based on the arithmetic average, he assume he would have an ending portfolio value of $1,464.10, or $1,000 $(1.1)^4$ = $1,464.10. However, because of the variability of returns over the four years, he would actually have only $1,248.01 at the end of the fourth year. This is calculated as $1,000(1.05695)^4$ = $1,248.01. To check the answer, find the portfolio value year by year. That is: $1000(1.5) = $1,500(0.8) = $1,200(1.3) = $1,560(0.8) = $1,248. The geometric mean return clearly determines the individual's ending wealth. The greater the volatility of returns, the greater the difference between the arithmetic and geometric means (Messmore 1995). This difference is referred to as "variance drain" or "risk drag." The effect is more pronounced if the individual is making periodic withdrawals, such as in retirement, or if the individual has a large concentration in one or a few equity positions.

PORTFOLIO RISK

Risk in a PWM context is multifaceted and complex. Although obvious risk factors such as portfolio risk and inflation risk are present, more subtle risks are also at work. The health of the individual is a risk factor. Poor health may mean higher liquidity requirements due to higher medical costs, while poor health ending in death (i.e., mortality risk) means an end to earning power. Longevity risk (the risk of living longer than expected) and mortality risk (the risk of dying sooner than expected) are relevant to the individual and his heirs. If an individual lives longer than expected, few assets may be available for the heirs. If he dies sooner than expected, insufficient earnings may not cover family expenses. Changes in tax laws are of particular interest to individuals engaged in wealth accumulation and estate planning. Thus, many varied risk factors must be considered in the development of the IPS.

WILLINGNESS VERSUS ABILITY TO TOLERATE RISK

Risk tolerance has two components: the investor's willingness to tolerate risk and his ability or capacity to tolerate risk. These two components may be in conflict. An investor's financial characteristics largely define the ability to take on risk. Factors such as an investor's age and earning capacity affect the ability to tolerate risk. Also, the size of the portfolio and the financial demands on the portfolio (e.g., liquidity requirements for living expenses, health care, and education costs) relative to the portfolio size affect the ability to tolerate risk. Smaller expenses typically mean a greater ability to tolerate risk. Longer time horizons in relation to the investor's life usually imply a greater ability to assume risk. If expenses are large relative to the size of the portfolio, the investor has a lower risk tolerance. The key issue that the investor and his financial advisor must consider is the ability of the portfolio to sustain losses and still meet the investor's goals. In general, an inverse relationship exists between an investor's ability to tolerate risk and his required expenditures. Investors who have more flexibility with respect to expenditures also have a greater ability to tolerate risk.

The willingness to take risk is rooted in the investor's psychological makeup and is related to such factors as how the investor accumulated his wealth and his fears of losing it. Sometimes an investor does not understand his own willingness and ability to assume risk. A client may have substantial assets and minimal liquidity requirements but states that he has a below-average risk tolerance. Distinguishing between the investor's willingness and ability to tolerate risk is important when developing the IPS.

The more wealth an investor has, or believes he has, the more investment risk the investor is likely to assume. The perception of wealth generally affects the investor's choice between lower or higher volatility investments. In some cases, the perception of wealth is more important than the actual wealth for an individual in investment decision making.

RISK AND STAGE OF LIFE

Time horizon is relevant to risk taking, and thus the investor's stage of life is important in determining risk tolerance. Conventional wisdom is that younger investors have more time to recover losses in the event of a substantial downturn in the economy, such as the financial crisis of 2007 and 2008. Not only will their investments have time to recover, but also they can generate employment-related income over many years to supplement savings.

Investors who are in the middle of their earning years still have a long time horizon and can tolerate higher levels of risk. However, as they get closer to retirement, these investors may begin to shift from higher-risk to lower-risk assets. In general, retired investors have the lowest risk tolerance because they have neither the time nor the earning power to make up losses that arise from economic downturns. However, other factors, such as the level of wealth, the demands on the portfolio to generate income, and the psychological makeup of an investor, temper these broad generalizations about the stage of life and risk tolerance.

INVESTOR CONSTRAINTS

An IPS should address the following five constraints of an investor: (1) time horizon, (2) tax considerations, (3) liquidity issues, (4) legal and regulatory factors, and (5) unique circumstances.

Time Horizon

The time horizon of different investors varies considerably and may be multistage. For example, an investor's first stage could encompass the period until his children complete their formal education, and the second stage could cover the period between his children's completion of their formal education and his retirement. In this case, the investor is likely to have high liquidity needs while the children are in school but is probably earning a salary to offset expenses. The investor's liquidity needs may increase again after retirement (the third stage) when the portfolio must cover living expenses, gifts, charitable contributions, entertainment, travel expenses, and so on. At this point, the portfolio's assets should be reallocated to account for the investor's new life stage and the coincident portfolio objectives and constraints.

Tax Considerations

Tax considerations are important to individual investors, and tax planning is a critical part of the IPS process. Investors potentially face various types of taxes on income, capital gains taxes, inheritances, gifts, and other assets that are transferred to children and others, as well as sales, value-added, property, and wealth taxes. In the United States, a progressive income tax system exists for citizens. This means that the more income a person makes, the higher is his tax rate. For example, in the United States, dividends, interest income, and long-term capital gains receive some favorable treatment relative to ordinary income. While considerable variation exists in the treatment of investment income across countries, common progressive systems, as seen in many countries, including the United States and China, generally provide for favorable tax treatment of dividends, interest, and capital gains.

Investors may engage in several tax-management strategies in relation to their investments, including:

- **Tax avoidance.** Investors can invest in nontaxable securities, such as municipal bonds, or put money in special tax-free savings accounts.
- **Tax reduction.** Individuals may invest in growth stocks rather than income stocks to benefit from lower capital gains taxes. *Loss harvesting*, which is the process of selling securities at a loss to offset capital gains taxes, may also be an effective strategy.
- **Deferring taxes.** Investors may hold securities longer to benefit from the tax treatment of long-term capital gains as well as to adopt low turnover strategies and loss harvesting by recognizing gains and losses concurrently.
- **Wealth transfer taxes.** Investors may seek to minimize taxes in the wealth transfer process. For example, in some countries, tax advantages result from gifting part of an individual's assets before death to avoid estate taxes upon death. Limits exist to the amount of tax-free gifts that an individual may make in a year. Also, this strategy often has specific jurisdictional requirements and differs between countries.

Taxes are important to long-term wealth accumulation. For example, Siegel and Montgomery (1995) recreate the well-known return series by Ibbotson and Sinquefield (2009), which finds that the historical returns of small-cap stocks, large-cap stocks, and bonds have been approximately 17, 12, and 6 percent, respectively. However, in this study Siegel and Montgomery find that the actual returns are much lower on an after-tax, inflation-adjusted basis than those demonstrated by Ibbotson and Sinquefield. They find that the difference is most pronounced for equity investors.

Tax drag, which is stated in currency or percentage terms, refers to the amount of an investment's gain that is lost to taxes. It can be substantial depending on the tax treatment of investment income and gains. If individuals pay taxes periodically, called accrued taxes, the tax drag percentage is greater than the percentage tax rate. Further, tax drag increases as both the return and investment horizon increases. One strategy to avoid tax drag is to invest in growth assets that allow the deferral of taxes until the investor sells the asset. While investors typically want to avoid losses, as mentioned previously, loss harvesting is beneficial in PWM. Harvesting losses to offset taxable gains provides a useful tax shield for investors, especially for those who have concentrated holdings in low-basis stocks. *Basis* (also called *cost basis* or *tax basis*) refers to the amount paid for a purchased investment. If an individual receives the investment as a gift, the basis is the amount paid by the giver. If an individual inherits an asset, the basis "resets" to the asset's value at the date of the original owner's death. Employees who receive stock options as part of executive compensation packages may also have high concentrations in low-basis stock because the exercise price on employee stock options is generally low relative to the current market price of the stock. Many high–net worth individuals have received stock from relatives as gifts and have a low to nearly zero cost basis in the stock. These individuals may be disinclined to sell the low-basis stock because taxes on the gains would be substantial.

The case for selling concentrated holdings of stock is strong (Messmore, 1995; Boyle, Loewy, Reiss, and Weiss, 2004; Odegaard, 2009), based on individual stock holdings being riskier than diversified holdings. Loss harvesting allows for a tax-free gain on assets that have increased in value if investors can offset such gains with losses of the same magnitude in other securities. Loss harvesting can also be helpful when most of the selling price is a gain, as is the case with low-basis stock.

Liquidity Issues

Individuals have routine expenses such as living expenses, medical costs, entertainment, and travel expenses. These required expenditures are often recurring in nature and may be met with wages depending on the person's stage of life. Individuals may also have desired (but not required) expenditures, such as vacation homes or large charitable contributions.

Individuals should also have accessible liquid assets in case of an emergency. Typical emergency savings range from three to twelve months of recurring expenses. In the future, this number may need to be increased given the extended period of unemployment many individuals have suffered as a result of the recent economic downturn. However, with the exception of emergency savings, the amount of cash placed in the portfolio should be minimized because the overall portfolio return is reduced when the investor holds higher levels of cash. This reduction in return is referred to as "cash drag."

An investor's liquidity constraints are important in determining a portfolio's asset allocation. Illiquid assets may pose a problem for investors with high liquidity needs. Thus, venture capital and angel investing are typically ill suited for these investors. *Angel investors* are high–net worth individuals who invest in private companies, usually start-up ventures. Because the money is invested in a start-up and not a publicly traded company, the investment is illiquid and best suited for those investors who do not have high liquidity needs. Private equity generally is inappropriate for investors with high liquidity needs due to the lack of a public market in which to sell the holdings. Additionally, investments that are subject to wide value changes, such as highly volatile investments, may not provide the liquidity some investors need. For example, if an investor holds a portfolio consisting primarily of equities, liquidity requirements may dictate selling those assets at a loss. Finally, assets whose sale requires high transaction costs, such as direct real estate investments, may be inappropriate for investors with high liquidity needs because to generate liquidity, investors will incur substantial costs.

Legal and Regulatory Factors

Tax and wealth transfer issues are the primary concerns in PWM. An individual who has set up a trust to provide for children or other family members must consider legal issues. For example, if an individual sets up an *irrevocable trust*, which cannot be canceled or changed once created, a professional trustee manages the assets. Tax returns must be filed and taxes paid for the trust. In general, the legal and regulatory factors are unique to the individual and cannot be generalized.

Unique Circumstances

The unique circumstances category is a catchall for anything not included in the other constraints of investors previously discussed. For example, some investors prefer to avoid certain investments because they find them objectionable. An investor may have a policy of investing only in socially responsible firms, green firms, or family-friendly firms. An individual may also have a desired level of wealth that he wants to obtain or a bequest that he wants to make. These unique factors must be considered when formulating the investor's risk-and-return objectives.

Benefits to Individuals and Wealth Managers of the IPS

The IPS is beneficial to both the individual/client and the financial advisor. While the investor's goals and objectives are of primary concern, a realistic assessment of those goals is realized by the advisor's analysis of specific constraints. This analysis allows the financial advisor to point out why an investor's objective may be unrealistic or unobtainable. Also, the IPS process lends itself to change. If, for instance, an individual must unexpectedly care for an ailing parent resulting in increased liquidity needs, the IPS can be changed to reflect the evolving circumstances. Assets may be reallocated and risk exposures may be adjusted. The IPS is designed to reflect the long-term goals of the investor. Also, if an individual moves or changes investment advisors, subsequent managers can implement a thorough and well-written IPS.

For the financial advisor, the IPS helps guide investment decision making. It provides a starting point for communication with the client about decisions that are or will be made regarding asset allocation and performance. The IPS also contains a process for review that allows the manager to identify potential problems and resolve disputes.

Strategic Asset Allocation

A key component in the IPS process is the determination of the portfolio's asset allocation. At the inception of a portfolio, a base policy mix is established in accordance with the investor's goals and constraints, called the *strategic asset allocation* (SAA). Over time, asset values change, causing portfolio weights to diverge from the initial allocation. Periodically, perhaps monthly or quarterly, the portfolio is rebalanced back to the original strategic weights to maintain the long-term goals of the portfolio. In contrast, *tactical asset allocation* (TAA) seeks to increase returns from short-term and intermediate-term market inefficiencies by shifting portfolio weights to take advantage of market anomalies or strong market sectors. Once the profit has been realized, the allocation is returned to the strategic, long-term mix.

In determining the SAA, all allocations that do not meet the investor's risk-and-return objectives are eliminated. Once this criterion is satisfied, the individual's constraints are used to remove additional potential allocations. To minimize "cash drag," allocations that contain too much cash should be eliminated. Allocations that have too little cash must also be avoided. In order to maintain *purchasing power* (i.e., earn a return that is at least equal to inflation), Campbell (2004) suggests that long-horizon individuals looking to save for retirement use securities such as Treasury Inflation-Protected Securities (TIPS) as their default risk-free assets. Inflation-indexed annuities might also be considered for retirees because the annuity payment the investor receives increases with inflation.

Alternative assets are investments outside traditional asset classes (stocks, bonds, and cash). Alternative assets, such as real estate, commodities, or hedge funds, should be considered for the portfolio although the issues involved are complex in a PWM setting. Brunel (2006) considers the asset allocation and tax implications of alternative assets in portfolios and concludes that taxable investors may benefit from adding alternative assets to the portfolio. For instance, *fund-of-funds* (FOF), which are mutual funds that are invested in other mutual funds, offer diversification but are expensive for individual investors because the expenses are essentially doubled. The underlying funds incur operating expenses, which reduce investor returns. A FOF also charges fees.

Brunel (1999), uses multiperiod, after-tax portfolio optimization software to analyze the role alternative investments should play in an individual portfolio. He concludes that investors with at least average risk tolerance can benefit more from alternative asset classes than can tax-exempt investors. In other words, portfolio optimization results in a higher allocation to alternative assets for taxable investors than for nontaxable investors.

ASSET LOCATION

Asset location involves placing different assets in specific accounts to manage/optimize after-tax returns. For example, including municipal bonds in an Individual Retirement Account (IRA) is inappropriate in most instances because individuals would be giving up the tax advantage offered by the municipal bond. Assuming the same risk level, taxable bonds would offer higher after-tax returns than tax-free municipal bonds. Reichenstein (2001) finds that the same asset held in two different types of accounts (i.e., taxable and tax deferred) essentially becomes two distinct after-tax assets because after-tax returns and standard deviations are different depending on the account in which the asset is held. Shoven and Sialm (1998) find that individuals should exhaust their tax-advantaged savings each year before putting assets in taxable accounts, regardless of the asset class. Although no definitive rules exist on asset location, a general conclusion is that tax-inefficient assets, such as bonds and real estate investment trusts (REITs), belong in tax-advantaged accounts (Dammon, Spatt, and Zhang, 2004; Reichenstein, 2001).

BEHAVIORAL ASSET ALLOCATION

Behavioral asset allocation complements traditional mean-variance portfolio analysis by considering the sometimes irrational human behavior in the allocation decision-making process. According to behavioral finance, humans engage in *mental accounting*, which means they compartmentalize aspects of their life. In an investment context, this means compartmentalizing savings for different purposes rather than looking at the portfolio as a whole, as suggested by MPT. For instance, a family might have a college savings account, vacation home investment plan, retirement fund, and so on. Brunel (2003) uses this idea to the advantage of the investor by creating subportfolios for investment. Each subportfolio has a different investment objective. For example, some funds are managed for growth, income, liquidity, and capital preservation. Different portfolios also have varying time horizons. Brunel's idea is to take advantage of mental accounting to benefit the investor.

In *Integrated Wealth Management: The New Direction for Portfolio Managers*, a seminal private wealth management reference book, Brunel (2006) examines the asset allocation issues for individual portfolios. He advocates an integrated approach to wealth management and emphasizes the human aspect of PWM and the asset allocation decision. Brunel uses a total portfolio approach (rather than managing the individual pieces of the portfolio) and concludes that an integrated, total portfolio approach is necessary to maximize wealth accumulation. Brunel indicates that individuals should focus on wealth accumulation rather than focusing on periodic returns, as suggested by the more traditional portfolio management approach.

HUMAN CAPITAL

Wealth consists of more than just the financial assets that someone has accumulated over time, which is known as *financial capital*. Human capital, which is an important component of an individual's total wealth, refers to an individual's lifetime earning capacity. Technically, an individual's human capital is the present value of the expected income over the individual's remaining lifetime.

A younger person typically has little financial capital but substantial human capital because she has a long preretirement time horizon in which to earn wages.

In contrast, as a worker moves closer to retirement, her financial assets typically increase but her preretirement time horizon grows shorter. Therefore, an inverse relationship exists between an individual's human capital and financial capital. The relative amounts of human and financial capital influence the asset mix of the portfolio. For example, a younger individual with large amounts of human capital (i.e., future earnings) can assume more risk in her portfolio than someone approaching retirement. The assets of a retired person should be protected because little time and potential earnings are available to offset losses. Thus, as the individual gets older and the size of the portfolio increases, the individual's risk exposure is tied more to her financial capital, and a greater proportion of the financial assets should be shifted to lower risk assets.

The correlation between human capital and financial asset classes is also important because both affect portfolio diversification. In general, the risk-and-return characteristics of human capital are more similar to equity securities than to debt because of high expected returns and high variability. Individuals in commission-only sales jobs may have highly variable incomes. Also, for some people, a high correlation may exist between their human capital and equity market returns because the firms for which they work do well when the economy does well and poorly when the economy is weak. For example, individuals who were working in the financial sector during the financial crisis of 2007 and 2008 were subject to a greater likelihood of losing their jobs at the same time that the stock market was falling dramatically. Those individuals saw a high positive correlation between their own incomes and equity market returns.

The individual's willingness (based on behavioral characteristics) and ability (based on time horizon and liquidity needs relative to portfolio size) to tolerate risk are used to construct his asset allocation. However, when considering an individual's human capital as part of his total wealth, the optimal allocation may be quite different, because of a high correlation between human and financial capital. For example, consider a salesperson working on commission with a highly variable income who has an all-equity portfolio based on an assumed high risk tolerance. This scenario would not represent an optimal asset allocation because both the financial assets and the human capital have equity-like characteristics. In contrast, a tenured professor who is risk averse and whose income is fairly certain should not have a portfolio made up entirely of fixed-income securities, because the human capital and financial capital would play the same role in the portfolio (i.e., conservative income generation). The risk of the portfolio might be increased without exceeding the professor's overall risk tolerance if human capital is considered as part of total wealth. Both the financial and human capital components should be considered in accordance with the investor's risk-and-return objectives in determining the optimal asset allocation.

EARNINGS, MORTALITY, AND LONGEVITY RISKS

Mortality risk is the unexpected loss of future earnings due to a sudden death. Unexpected death can result in hardship for dependents even if the deceased was a high wage earner with a high savings rate. An obvious way to protect against

mortality risk is with life insurance. Because life insurance is negatively correlated with mortality, it provides an optimal hedge.

In some cases, individuals live longer than expected and hence outlive their
financial assets. This is called *longevity risk*. The most effective way to hedge longevity risk is by having a lifetime-payout annuity, which life insurance companies
typically offer.

Products such as life insurance and annuities may be used to mitigate threats
associated with the risk of a loss of earnings, mortality risk, and longevity risk.
Investors earn income to support their lifestyles in their early years and plan to
accumulate enough financial assets to support a similar or modified lifestyle in
retirement. However, risks are associated with attaining these goals. An individual may become unemployed or be unable to work due to a disability or other
problem. Disrupted earnings affect not only current consumption but also future
savings and earnings.

Investors have several ways to mitigate earnings risk. First, individuals may
increase their savings rate to reduce earnings risk. Thus, they will put financial
capital to work sooner and it will grow at a faster rate with the higher contributions. This change in strategy should increase the capital available at retirement. Further, an individual can reduce earnings risk by lessening the correlation
between human capital and financial capital. While investors are often comfortable investing in the firm for which they work, diversification is crucial. Individual
investors should not have all of their savings tied up in their company's stock
because this increases the correlation between human and financial capital and
increases overall risk. Diversification is important regardless of whether investors
understand their firms, believe in the stock of their employer, and want to hold
only that stock.

RISKS IN RETIREMENT: FINANCIAL MARKETS, LONGEVITY, AND SAVINGS

Three major factors that can jeopardize an individual's lifestyle in retirement and
any desired bequests upon death are financial market risk, longevity risk, and savings risk. *Financial market risk* is the risk of loss that results from fluctuations in
security prices. *Longevity risk* is the risk of outliving one's financial assets. *Savings
risk* is the desire to consume today rather than postpone consumption in favor of
retirement.

As witnessed in 2008, financial markets can exhibit high volatility. If an
investor is nearing retirement and a downturn occurs in financial markets, this
downturn can severely impair his financial capital. If this scenario occurs, the
individual may be unable to meet his living expenses in conjunction with his
planned bequests.

Savings risk, also known as spending uncertainty, also affects long-term financial well-being. Many individuals spend more and save less than they should during the accumulation phase of life. Some may use historical stock market return
data, such as the often-quoted 12 percent return rate of large-cap stocks over
the last seventy-five years, to determine the value of their savings in the future

(Ibbotson and Sinquefield, 2009). They may rely more on growth and less on savings for their long-term financial health, often to their own detriment. Also, social security replaces less of a high-income individual's earnings than it does of a lower-income individual. Ibbotson, Xiong, Kreitler, Kreitler, and Chen (2007), who develop savings guidelines for individuals based on age, income, and other factors, show that higher-income individuals need higher savings rates to replace 80 percent of their income than do lower-income individuals due to social security ceilings.

Actuarial life expectancies are based on population averages. Half of the population outlives the median while the other half dies before it. If someone outlives his life expectancy, he may have insufficient financial assets to cover his spending needs, resulting in longevity risk. Government plans such as social security pay for a lifetime and mitigate longevity risk. These plans often provide for a surviving spouse. Defined benefit pension plans also pay for a lifetime but are becoming less common as states and other organizations have accumulated large pension liabilities that they can no longer afford. Most US corporations have also stopped providing defined benefit plans, where firms promise to make periodic payments to employees after retirement, making longevity risk a more important consideration for a greater proportion of the population. As noted, individuals can also invest in annuity products to hedge against longevity risk.

Estate Planning

Many individuals face the decision of how to transfer wealth to family, charities, caretakers, or friends. *Estate planning* is the process associated with the transfer of assets to others either before or after death. The estate of an individual is larger than just his investment holdings. It includes his home(s) and other real estate, art, collections, businesses, and intangible assets such as patents or copyrights, as well as the individual's financial assets. A will (or testament) is the most common tool used to transfer assets. If assets are transferred via a will, the individual is necessarily deceased. *Probate* is the process in which the court determines the validity of the will, inventories the property, resolves claims, and distributes property in line with the terms of the will.

Estate planning involves more than just managing investments. Tax planning is critical. In many cases, transferring assets is more efficient from a tax standpoint before death. In this case, the individual transfers assets through gifts or bequests. Gifts may be subject to gift taxes. Bequests may be subject to estate taxes, paid by the grantor, or inheritance taxes, paid by the recipient.

Life insurance is another efficient means of transferring assets to beneficiaries. The probability of death, which is based on such factors as age, health, and occupation; desired bequests at death; the individual's risk aversion; financial capital; and volatility of human capital are all important variables in determining a person's demand for life insurance. Life insurance is often used in conjunction with a trust and may be used to assist heirs in paying taxes. In some instances where the beneficiary is young, disabled, or in some other way unable to manage assets appropriately, the life insurance proceeds may be paid directly into the trust, making the trust a direct beneficiary of the life insurance policy.

DETERMINISTIC MODELS VERSUS MONTE CARLO SIMULATION

Individuals may use deterministic or probabilistic models in investment and retirement planning. The *deterministic method of retirement planning* involves specifying the required dollar amount needed for liquidity purposes in retirement and then working backward to solve for the portfolio value that will be necessary to meet the requirement. Alternately, the expected return may be used as a point estimate and the ending portfolio value, given the expected return, is then calculated. These models use single values for relevant economic and financial variables, such as inflation, expected return, and interest rates. In a time-value analysis, the current portfolio value, the ending or required portfolio value, and the number of years to retirement are used to solve for the return needed to provide the spending desired by the investor. An advantage of this approach is that backing out the required return clarifies if the person can actually reach his retirement spending goal. The answer is basically a Yes or No—the goal is either attainable or unattainable. The problem with a deterministic model is that it does not provide the individual with a clear understanding of the risk inherent in the strategy needed to meet the return and thus the spending objectives.

In contrast, a *Monte Carlo simulation* is a probabilistic approach. Individual assets and asset-class returns are assigned a probability distribution. Economic variables such as inflation, growth in the gross domestic product (GDP), and Federal Reserve policy are included in addition to the individual assets and asset-class returns as input variables in the model and are assigned probability distributions. Each distribution includes an expected value and standard deviation for the input variable. The simulation then pulls values from the distribution of each input variable and combines them to determine the portfolio return, repeating the process several thousand times. The approach allows investors to see the many possible scenarios that could happen between now and retirement given different economic conditions and portfolio allocations. The investor can then choose the best asset allocation given the potential risk. The model is very flexible and allows the investor to consider different tax scenarios as well as factors such as the reinvestment of current income. In general, academics and practitioners prefer probabilistic models such as Monte Carlo simulation to deterministic models because of the added insights that these models provide.

PWM Literature

PWM is complex, dynamic, and specific to the individual. In it, both an individual's actual and implied assets and liabilities must be considered, such as his expected future inheritances or expected expenses for children's educations. An individual's tax issues, psychological makeup, and behavioral preferences all influence the PWM process. Traditional investment management, risk management, estate planning, tax planning, and personal financial planning are all relevant to the individual and to the financial advisor working with the individual. Since the IPS is critical to both institutions and individuals but is distinct for each group, practitioners and academics have gone on to study the nuances and complexities of PWM. Jennings, Horan, Reichenstein, and Brunel (2011) provide an extensive review of the PWM literature. They update and expand the review conducted by Jennings and Reichenstein (2006) by linking the various studies in a cohesive way and expanding the coverage of issues related to governance and portfolio management.

The PWM literature continues to evolve, in many cases taking the behavioral aspects of human nature into account. Also, family governance issues have become of increasing interest. For example, Gray (2011) broadens the definition of family wealth to include such areas as intellectual, social, emotional, and artistic capital. Hughes (2007) contends that those who inherit financial assets must honor not only themselves but also the dreams and aspirations of the earlier generations who created the wealth. These broader issues of behavioral finance and family governance continue to evolve.

Summary and Conclusions

PWM is multifaceted and complex. It requires an understanding of the financial landscape as well as human behavior. The psychological makeup of the individual is important to understanding his propensity for risk. Situational and psychological profiling help to identify factors that may influence an individual's investment decision making (Bronson et al., 2007). How an individual creates wealth and how he sees himself (i.e., as wealthy or poor) influences his willingness to tolerate investment risk. In some cases, the investor's willingness to tolerate risk may be at odds with his ability to tolerate risk.

While MPT assumes that investors choose to maximize return and minimize risk, behavioral models developed by Kahneman and Tversky (1979) and others indicate that these principles do not necessarily guide all investment decision making. Investors tend to be risk seeking when faced with possible losses but risk averse when faced with potential gains. This is known as prospect theory. Prospect theory and the individual's inclination toward mental accounting must be considered when creating an investment strategy.

The IPS is a document that defines the investor's return objectives, risk tolerance, and constraints. Both the individual and the investment advisor need to develop a well thought-out and thorough IPS. Liquidity needs and tax issues are two of the most important factors affecting the allocation of the portfolio. The investor's time horizon and the size of his portfolio influence both the return that is obtainable as well as the risk that is tolerable.

Both strategic and tactical asset allocation decisions stem from the IPS and are used to guide both the long-term goals and the short-term (tactical) deviations in the portfolio. A total portfolio approach, as suggested by Brunel (2006), is important in maximizing wealth accumulation. Both human capital and financial capital must be considered in a total portfolio approach.

Retirement planning and estate planning are both essential components of PWM. Probabilistic models such as Monte Carlo simulation are replacing deterministic models in investment and retirement planning. These models are more flexible and allow individuals to better understand the risks of a specific investment strategy. Probabilistic models provide information on different economic scenarios and portfolio allocations.

The PWM process is dynamic and ever evolving. Information is readily available and investor sophistication continues to increase. Those involved with PWM need to be well versed in a multitude of topics from tax management, to alternative assets, to behavioral finance. Jennings et al. (2011) provide an extensive review of the PWM literature. They link the many studies by academics and practitioners in a cohesive way and update older reviews to include behavioral finance and governance issues.

Discussion Questions

1. Chris Wilson is conducting a situational profile of James Cho, her client. What should Wilson focus on in the profile?
2. How may an individual's willingness to tolerate risk differ from his ability to tolerate risk?
3. Compare and contrast traditional financial models with those of behavioral finance.
4. Explain three constraints that may be more relevant to individual investors than to institutional investors.

References

Barberis, Nicholas, Andrei Shleifer, and Robert W. Vishny. 1998. "A Model of Investor Sentiment." *Journal of Financial Economics* 49:3, 307–343.

Boyle, Patrick S., Daniel J. Loewy, Jonathan A. Reiss, and Robert A. Weiss. 2004. "The Enviable Dilemma: Hold, Sell, or Hedge Highly Concentrated Stock?" *Journal of Wealth Management* 7:2, 30–44.

Bronson, James W., Matthew H. Scanlan, and Jan R. Squires. 2007. "Managing Individual Investor Portfolios." In *Managing Investment Portfolios: A Dynamic Process*, 3rd ed., edited by John L. Maginn, Donald L. Tuttle, Jerald E. Pinto, and Dennis W. McLeavey, 20–62. Hoboken, NJ: John Wiley & Sons.

Brunel, Jean L. P. 1999. "The Role of Alternative Assets in Tax-Efficient Portfolio Construction." *Journal of Private Portfolio Management* 2:1, 9–25.

Brunel, Jean L. P. 2003. "Revisiting the Asset Allocation Challenge through a Behavioral Finance Lens." *Journal of Wealth Management* 6:2, 10–20.

Brunel, Jean L. P. 2006. *Integrated Wealth Management: The New Direction for Portfolio Managers*, 2nd ed. London: Euromoney.

Campbell, John Y. 2004. "Measuring the Risks of Strategic Tilts for Long-Term Investors." *The New World of Pension Fund Management* 6, 12–23. Charlottesville, VA: Association for Investment Management Research.

Dammon, Robert M., Chester S. Spatt, and Harold H. Zhang. 2004. "Optimal Asset Location and Allocation with Taxable and Tax-Deferred Investing." *Journal of Finance* 59:2, 311–334.

DeFusco, Richard A., Dennis W. McLeavey, Jerald E. Pinto, and David E. Runkle. 2007. *Quantitative Investment Analysis*, 2nd ed. Hoboken, NJ: John Wiley & Sons.

Fernando, Vincent. 2010. "American Wealth Is Actually Still Ridiculously Enormous—It's the Government That's Broke." *Business Insider*, September 24. http://articles.businessinsider. com/2010-09-24/markets/29998983_1_wealth-fair value-housing-prices.

Gray, Lisa. 2011. "The Three Forms of Governance: *A New Approach to Family Wealth Transfer and Asset Protection, Part III*." *Journal of Wealth Management* 14:1, 41–54.

Daniel, Kent, David Hirshleifer, and Avanidar Subrahmanyam. 1998. "Investor Psychology and Security Market Under- and Overreaction." *Journal of Finance* 153:6, 1839–1885.

Hughes, Charles E., Jr. 2007. *Family: The Compact among Generations*. New York: Bloomberg.

Ibbotson, Roger, and Rex Sinquefield. 2009. *Ibbotson SBBI … Classic Yearbook: Market Results for Stocks, Bonds, Bills, and Inflation 1926–2008*. Chicago: Morningstar.

Ibbotson, Roger, James Xiong, Robert P. Kreitler, Charles F. Kreitler, and Peng Chen. 2007. "National Savings Rate Guidelines for Individuals." *Journal of Financial Planning* 20(4): 50–61.

Jacobsen, Brian J. 2006. "The Use of Downside Risk Measures in Tax-Efficient Portfolio Construction and Evaluation." *Journal of Wealth Management* 8:4, 17–26.

Jennings, William W., Stephen M. Horan, William Reichenstein, and Jean L. P. Brunel. 2011. "Perspectives from the Literature of Private Wealth Management." *Journal of Wealth Management* 14:1, 18–40.

Jennings, William W., and William Reichenstein. 2006. *The Literature of Private Wealth Management*. Charlottesville, VA: The Research Foundation of CFA Institute.

Jennings, William W. and William Reichenstein. 2006. *The Literature of Private Wealth Management*. Charlottesville, VA: Research Foundation Literature Reviews. 1:3, 1–29.

Kahneman, Daniel, and Amos Tversky. 1979. "Prospect Theory: An Analysis of Decision under Risk." *Econometrica* 47:2, 263–291.

Leibowitz, Martin L., and Anthony Bova. 2010. "Return Targets and Percentile Fans." *Financial Analysts Journal* 66:1, 28–40.

Lintner, John. 1965. "The Valuation of Risky Assets and the Selection of Risky Investments in Stock Portfolios and Capital Budgets." *Review of Economics and Statistics* 47:1, 13–37.

Markowitz, Harry M. 1952. "Portfolio Selection." *Journal of Finance* 7:1, 77–91.

Messmore, Thomas E. 1995. "Variance Drain." *Journal of Portfolio Management* 21:4, 104–110.

Ødegaard, Bernt Arne. 2009. "The Diversification Cost of Large, Concentrated Equity Stakes. How Big Is It? Is It Justified?" *Finance Research Letters* 6:2, 56–72.

Palich, Leslie E., and D. Ray Bagby. 1995. "Using Cognitive Theory to Explain Entrepreneurial Risk-Taking: Challenging Conventional Wisdom." *Journal of Business Venturing* 10:6, 425–438.

Reichenstein, William R. 2001. "Asset Allocation and Asset Location Decisions Revisited." *Journal of Wealth Management* 4:1, 16–26.

Sharpe, William. 1964. "Capital Asset Prices: A Theory of Market Equilibrium under Conditions of Risk." *Journal of Finance* 19:3, 425–442.

Shorrocks, Anthony, and Jim Davies. 2010. *Global Wealth Report*. Zürich: Credit Suisse Research Institute.

Shoven, John B., and Clemens Sialm. 1998. "Long Run Asset Allocation for Retirement Savings." *Journal of Private Portfolio Management* 1:2, 13–26.

Siegel, Laurence B., and David Montgomery. 1995. "Stocks, Bonds and Bills after Taxes and Inflation." *Journal of Portfolio Management* 21:2, 17–25.

7

Institutional Wealth Management

ERIC J. ROBBINS

Portfolio Manager, Robbins Wealth Management, and Lecturer
in Finance, The Behrend College, Penn State Erie

Introduction

The term *institutional investor* refers to entities such as pension plans, foundations, endowments, life insurance companies, non–life insurance companies, and commercial banks. These entities have diverse objectives and constraints. Applying a one-size-fits-all approach to investment allocation in this broad category would be inappropriate.

An *institutional investment policy statement* (IIPS) is a formal document that functions as a customizable road map to success for each type of institutional investor. In this chapter, the discussion focuses on understanding the specific objectives and constraints that apply to each of these organizations. Investment objectives should be described in terms of required return and risk tolerance. Constraints involve liquidity, time horizon, legal and regulatory factors, tax considerations, and unique circumstances.

Because an IIPS is not mandated by regulation, the order in which items appear does not matter. The order should be logical for its intended users and can be adjusted to benefit the application. Table 7.1 provides an outline of the basic form of an IIPS to guide in its creation. The document should clearly define who is responsible for the operations of the plan. It should also specify how investment managers are selected and how their performance will be evaluated relative to a blended benchmark crafted to reflect their investment mandate. The IIPS should also clearly state that investment managers have a fiduciary responsibility to vote by proxy on any shareholder rights in order to promote the best interest of their clients. Many IIPS documents expressly include adopting a code of ethics statement. Sometimes, they simply adopt an appropriate ethics statement such as the *CFA Institute Code of Ethics and Standards of Professional Conduct* (University of California Retirement Savings Program, 2006). Beyond this list of standard inclusions, each institutional investor will customize the other variables to its own situation.

The remainder of this chapter outlines the specific objectives and constraints that apply to pension plans, foundations, endowments, life insurance companies,

Table 7.1 **Generic outline for an institutional investment policy statement**

1. Executive summary
2. Introduction: includes a statement of the purpose of the document
3. Duties and responsibilities: specifies who has authority for oversight and responsibility to conduct various activities
4. Objectives (should be specific)
5. Estimate of the investor's risk tolerance
6. Investment allocation a. Any allocation constraints along with tolerance bands b. Investment choices available for a DC plan c. Investment monitoring process for a DC plan d. Relevant benchmarks for evaluating the investments
7. Constraints a. Liquidity b. Time horizon c. Legal and regulatory constraints d. Tax considerations e. Unique constraints
8. Investment managers a. Selection process b. Monitoring process c. Termination process
9. Ethics statement (consider adopting the CFA Institute Code of Ethics and Standards of Professional Conduct [University of California Retirement Savings Program 2006]) in the absence of a company ethics statement)

Note: This outline serves as a rough guideline for the creation of an IIPS.

non–life insurance companies, and commercial banks. The final section provides a summary and conclusion.

Pension Plans

The two primary stakeholders in the world of pension plans are the companies (the plan's sponsors) and their employees (the participants). The *funded status*, which refers to the difference between the present value of the plan's assets and the present value of the plan's liabilities, is an imperative consideration in

Table 7.2 **Summaries of the characteristics of defined benefit and defined contribution pension plans**

Plan type	Employer impact	Employee impact
Defined benefit plan	• Pension benefits are a liability for the plan's sponsor and thus funded status matters. • Benefits are determined using a preestablished formula that factors in tenure and salary. • The plan's sponsor bears 100 percent of the responsibility for managing the plan's assets. • The plan can serve as a possible source of "income" if pension assets perform better than expected. • The plan is highly regulated, primarily by ERISA in the United States.	• The employee receives periodic payments during retirement (or some other eligibility period as specified by the plan). • The employee may lose benefits through early termination of employment (investing period applies). • There is no risk from investment selections. • Both job and retirement are linked to the success of the same entity.
Defined contribution plan	• The employer matches contributions made by the employee up to a prespecified limit. • The employer deposits contributions to be held by the plan custodian. • The only liability for the employer is making the matching contribution—the employer bears no investment risk. • The employer has the responsibility to offer sufficient investment choices to employees (participants). • Lower liquidity is needed because plan contributions are capped. • A defined contribution plan features much less regulation than a defined benefit plan. • The employer is typically required to have IPS identify how the plan will help employees prepare for retirement.	• The employee makes tax-deductible contributions that the employer matches up to a specific limit. • The employee has direct ownership of assets in the plan, which are held in an account in his name. • The assets are portable if employment is terminated. • The employee makes all investment selections, and the outcome, either good or bad, directly affects the his retirement prospects. • The employee has complete control over asset diversification, which can be a challenge for those who do not understand the principles of investing. • The employee is still subject to a vesting schedule.

developing an IIPS. The plan's liabilities are estimated by calculating the *pension benefit obligation* (PBO), which is the present value of all pension liabilities based on the current benefits accumulated and on the projected future benefits of both existing employees and planned hires. While the logic behind the PBO may appear tenuous to apply, its assumption that the firm will remain a *going concern* is most appropriate for calculating the funded status. The going concern assumption suggests that the firm is presumed to remain in operation.

The pension plan category can be divided into four primary subcategories: (1) defined benefit plans, (2) defined contribution plans, (3) cash balance plans, and (4) profit-sharing plans. This chapter focuses on defined benefit (DB) plans and defined contribution (DC) plans because cash balance plans and profit-sharing plans are subsets of these first two and are less common. A *cash balance plan* is very similar to a defined benefit plan with the exception that assets are broken down into a separate account for each employee. A *profit sharing plan* is closely related to the defined contribution plan, the difference being that the contributions are directly linked to the profitability of the plan's sponsor and are not based on a percentage of compensation. Table 7.2 summarizes the characteristics of DB and DC pension plans.

Defined Benefit Pension Plans

In a *defined benefit plan*, the employer promises to make a certain payment to retired employees upon retirement based upon a predetermined formula linked to years of service and salary level. The assets in a DB plan are held within one large omnibus account that is linked to the company and not to any individual employee. In a DB plan, the plan's sponsor assumes all investment risk. This reality coupled with increasing market volatility has led many employers to stop offering DB plans and instead to favor the defined contribution plans, which will be discussed in a later section (Daley, 2004).

DB PLAN OBJECTIVES AND RISK TOLERANCE

In a DB plan, the employer makes predetermined payments to its retirees. As long as the firm remains in operation, these current and future payments are a liability. With this reality in mind, the primary goal of a DB plan should be to pay the promised benefits when they are due. This objective is best served when the plan's assets exceed the payments being made to existing retirees and the benefits owed to future retirees in the PBO. A positive funded status, or simply a *surplus*, exists whenever plan's assets exceed its liabilities. A reasonable secondary goal is to minimize contributions to the plan so that the firm can deploy its cash to other productive uses. In practice, this secondary goal sometimes takes precedence. Employer contributions are based on actuarial estimates of the returns for the plan's assets. One unethical way sometimes used to minimize current contributions is to overestimate the return on the plan's assets. A tertiary goal is to increase corporate earnings. Any income for the plan that exceeds its expenses can be recorded as income to the sponsor and therefore increases reported earnings. This tertiary goal should be viewed as a positive ancillary benefit should it occur, but focusing on this goal and ignoring the primary objective of a positive plan surplus is unwise.

An actuary determines the pension plan's required rate of return to accomplish the objective of meeting its liabilities. Periodic adjustments are made to this actuarially determined rate. Often this percentage is stated as a certain premium over the consumer price index (CPI), which is a widely used measure of inflation. Managers use this policy because preserving the *real purchasing power*, which is the inflation-adjusted spending ability, is very important to the long-term health of a DB plan. A long-term average rate of return should be the focus because for some years the DB plan will exceed this expectation and for some years the DB plan will underperform it, but the long-term viability is what matters most.

The plan's sponsor will determine a desired strategic allocation for the plan's assets, which may include such categories as domestic large caps, domestic mid caps, domestic small caps, international, fixed income, commodities, and cash. This focus at the asset class level gives the investment manager flexibility within these broad categories to apply their own thinking related to industry exposure. The desired allocation should include a tolerance band around each category. As an example, if the strategic allocation for a sector is 20 percent, the tolerance band might be between 15 percent and 25 percent. This provides the investment manager with flexibility in fluctuating markets. The tolerance band could drop down to 0 percent, giving the investment manager further flexibility if an asset class becomes inappropriate in certain circumstances (Bismarck Firefighter's Relief Association, 2008). This revised tolerance band is the most appropriate for noncore asset classes such as commodities.

The risk tolerance portion of any IIPS begins with a standard disclaimer stating that the plan's trustees recognize the risk inherent in investing and that they are willing to assume reasonable investment risks in pursuit of their objectives. Additionally, a DB plan needs to specifically state the current funded status and how the plan's sponsor will adjust its risk tolerance based upon the potential of the funded status to change in the future. If a plan has a surplus, then it has a greater ability to accept reasonable investment risk. The irony is that when a surplus exists, the plan's sponsor does not need the assets to perform at a higher level except to inflate earnings and buffer future periods of investment shortfalls. If the plan is underfunded, which implies that its assets fall short of its PBO, then it has a decreased ability to accept reasonable investment risk. In this scenario, the plan's assets should be made less risky until contributions made by the firm correct the underfunded status. Managers of an underfunded plan may feel the psychological urge to increase the risk level in an attempt to correct the funded status without requiring additional contributions from the plan sponsor's operations. This action would be incorrect as the increased risk could worsen the situation just as easily as it could bring benefit. As such, an IIPS is useful in the daily operations of a DB plan.

The risk tolerance for the plan's assets should be stated in concrete terms. One method used in practice is to establish an acceptable percentage loss. This method has been used in such plans as the *Invesment Policy Statement for Bismarck*

Firefighter's Relief Association Pension Plan (Bismarck Firefighter's Association, 2008), for which a maximum tolerable loss of 7.2 percent was selected. A percentage this high permits greater flexibility in allocating the plan's assets because investment values fluctuate over time through various business cycles. Another suggested method is called *value at risk* (VAR) (Daley, 2004). Under this method, the plan's sponsor selects a certain dollar loss that it would be comfortable assuming in a worst-case scenario. The sponsor would then statistically determine, with a desired percentage confidence level, the probability of achieving this objective. While this method is mathematically sound, VAR is more cumbersome to apply than a straight maximum percentage loss rule.

The plan's sponsor should estimate the correlation between the plan's assets and the company's operations (Daley, 2004). Psychologically, investors tend to feel comfortable investing in securities in which a level of familiarity exists. A natural tendency exists for a plan to be invested within its own industry because the board understands what drives its growth. However, if a plan's sponsor is perhaps an airline operator, then investing a plan's assets into other airline operators would be unadvisable. The logic behind this advice is that if the industry experiences a downtrend, then the plan assets would suffer and require more contributions at the exact time when the plan sponsor's operations may be unable to support additional contributions. As the correlation between the plan's assets and the sponsor's operations increases, the plan's sponsor should decrease its risk tolerance.

Blending the information involved in the actuarially provided required return and the risk tolerance based upon the funded status, one will arrive at the desired mix of fixed income and equities. Higher required returns and a funding surplus will enable a greater concentration of equities.

DB PLAN CONSTRAINTS

Some constraints of a DB plan are specific to that plan, while others are imposed on all pension plans in this category. *Liquidity* refers to the amount of assets that can be turned into cash on very short notice at a reasonable price. Most assets can be sold at any point in time, but if they do not also retain reasonable value, then such assets have lower liquidity. The need for liquidity in a DB plan depends entirely upon the characteristics of the workforce. A pool of workers who have a high average age means that the plan's sponsor will potentially need access to funds more quickly, as employees will retire in a shorter time frame. Another consideration is the percentage of *retired lives*, which is the ratio of existing retirees to current employees. Liquidity becomes more important as the average age and percentage of retired lives increase.

Time horizon refers to the length of time the plan's sponsor intends to hold the plan's assets before needing to liquidate them in order to meet the plan's disbursement needs. Assuming that a company intends to remain in operation, its time horizon can be relatively long. If the plan is considered to be a *terminating plan* because the company is insolvent, then the time horizon is relatively short.

The primary regulation in the United States for DB plans comes from the Employee Retirement Income Security Act of 1974 (ERISA). This act preempts any governing state or local laws. ERISA imposes a higher standard of due diligence on the investment selection process and also mandates that the DB plan must be operated for the sole benefit of the plan's participants and not the sponsor.

No direct tax consequences typically apply to the assets of a DB plan, but the assets do have a few unique constraints. A DB plan must not only focus on the funded status of the plan and applicable regulatory requirements but also must be concerned with the financial health of the plan's sponsor. Lower levels of debt of the plan's sponsor and higher levels of overall profitability increase the probability that the plan's sponsor will be able to meet its pension liabilities. In this scenario, the risk tolerance of the plan's assets could be adjusted upward.

Defined Contribution Pension Plans

In contrast to a DB plan, a *defined contribution plan* involves the employer promising a certain amount of current contribution to match an employee's contribution, not a future benefit. The participant's contributions into a DC plan are deducted, tax-deferred, from his or her paycheck. The employer's contribution is considered a *matching contribution* based on the amount that the participant deducts from his or her pay. The assets in a DC plan are held in the name of each individual employee, and as such, the plan's sponsor does not need to be concerned with either the PBO or the effect of the plan's assets on company earnings since the assets belong to the participants, not the sponsor. Typically, a vesting schedule is applied to the employer's contributed portion of the plan's balance. This means that employer contributions do not become a transferable asset owned by the participant until after a participant has been employed with the sponsor for a specified period of time. The plan's sponsor may also make a self-directed component available to participants. The Virginia retirement system is a good example of this option, which enables the employees to transfer a portion of their plan's balance into an account at a separate brokerage firm, whereby they may choose from a considerably broader pool of investments (Virginia Retirement System Defined Contribution Plans, 2004). Participants should engage in this option when they possess a solid understanding of investment risks and principles.

The IIPS for a DC plan will declare which representative of the plan's sponsor has operational oversight of the plan's assets. This representative is usually either a committee for larger companies or a selected office of the plan's sponsor for smaller companies. The representative will be responsible for selecting core investment offerings and for appointing investment professionals to help manage the operations and present core offering choices. These offerings are typically mutual funds, and the fund managers will handle the shareholder voting rights.

DC PLAN OBJECTIVES AND RISK TOLERANCE

The purpose of a DC plan is to assist participants in preparing themselves for retirement. Assets only accrue in a DC plan to the extent that participants arrange for savings to be deducted from their payroll. A plan-required minimum return target does not exist. However, the plan's sponsor is responsible for selecting a group of core funds that will be offered in the DC plan from which the participants can choose. The responsibility for selecting the core fund offerings rests with either the sponsor's designated officer or a committee. The number of core holdings offered is entirely at the discretion of the designated officer or committee. However, a common practice is to limit this pool to ten to fifteen different mutual funds across a broad selection of categories to permit the participants an opportunity to diversify their holdings appropriately.

The University of California's IIPS references a few specific risks applicable to a DC plan's assets. These include the capital market risk, the total active risk, the total investment risk, and the participant asset allocation risk (University of California Retirement Savings Program, 2006). All of these risks should be disclosed to participants before they enroll in the plan. *Capital market risk* includes the general market risks that are assumed by the participant. *Total active risk* refers to the difference between the return of the sponsor-selected core investment and its relevant benchmark. The participants share this risk with the sponsor, but it does not potentially require additional employer contributions. However, the sponsor does bear the responsibility to select competitive investments for the purpose of creating choices for participants. *Total investment risk* is the overall volatility of the chosen investment. This category blends both capital market risk and total active risk and therefore has blended responsibilities. *Participant asset allocation risk* refers to the fact that ultimate responsibility for investment selections rests with the participant. Participants need to be aware of this responsibility through appropriate disclosures. Often, the plan's sponsor will provide education to participants in helping them select an appropriate asset allocation mix, but the selection responsibility always rests with the participant.

DC PLAN CONSTRAINTS

A DC plan has few explicit constraints. Both liquidity and time horizon are unique to each plan participant. The sponsor has no constraint in either area, except that it maintains enough operational liquidity to make the promised matching contributions. In the United States, DC plans are subject to the same ERISA oversight as are DB plans. Taxes are not a consideration until the participant draws funds out of the plan, theoretically in retirement, but this creates a participant-level constraint.

Most constraints of DC plans are considered at the participant level. However, several unique factors may affect the plan at large. The sponsor needs to determine if it will permit participants to take loans out of the plan. If the sponsor is a publically traded company, the sponsor must decide if it will enable participants to hold company stock as part of the plan. Employee ownership of company stock gives employees greater buy-in to the operational success of the firm. Conversely, if the employer suffers difficulties, then the employees' paycheck may be in jeopardy at the same time that the balance of their DC plan is declining due to the duplicate exposure to company operations through both payroll and their investment in the DC plan. Additionally, the sponsor may impose an investment constraint on investment managers limiting them to investment selections in socially responsible companies.

Foundations

Foundations are nonprofit grant-writing organizations that are established to fund some form of charitable enterprise. They are highly customizable in terms of their source of funds, charitable purposes, and time horizons. *Private foundations* are established by an individual, a family, or a corporation. An example of a private foundation is the Alfred P. Sloan Foundation. Private foundations have a regulatory requirement to spend 5 percent of their assets each year. Management expenses do not count toward the 5 percent spending rule. Conversely, *public foundations* are funded by the general public. Community foundations are common examples of public foundations. Although they do not have any specific spending requirement, their board of trustees will likely establish a foundation-specific spending rule to entice new donors.

The duties and roles portion of the IIPS should state that the board of trustees is the governing body with oversight over the foundation's assets. Sometimes, foundations will delegate a subcommittee to have operational oversight and then report its progress back to the full board of trustees (Erie Community Foundation, 2010). The foundation IIPS should also establish selection criteria for objectives for investment managers who will conduct the day-to-day investing of the foundation's assets.

FOUNDATION OBJECTIVES AND RISK TOLERANCE

As stated in the previous section, private foundations must spend at least 5 percent of their assets. However, they can set higher spending rates if it better suits their purposes. The return objective is to establish a minimum-required return equal to the target spending rate plus an adjustment for expected inflation and management expenses. The inflation adjustment allows for maintaining the real purchasing power of the assets. This adjustment becomes more important the longer the time horizon of the foundation's goals. A desired strategic asset allocation should also be selected with a realistic tolerance band.

The risk tolerance for foundations is typically high because they do not have a contractually defined liability. The primary factor in determining their risk tolerance is time horizon. A longer time horizon will permit a higher risk tolerance level. Another factor is the source of contributed funds. If the source of funds is a one-time gift, then the risk level should be lower than if there is an ongoing stream of contributions. This guideline must be considered in the context of the size of the gift relative to the charitable effort. If the one-time gift was for $100 million with the intent of giving $200,000 grants for a given charitable service, then the risk level can be higher than a $10 million dollar one-time gift with the same purpose.

A higher risk tolerance enables foundations to focus more on equities and alternative assets, such as commodities and hedge funds, than on fixed-income investments in their asset allocation. A reasonable representation of income-producing assets is recommended to help fund the spending requirement. The board of trustees will be responsible for determining the portion of the foundation's assets to be allocated to speculative investments. The IIPS should also indicate a certain percentage of the foundation's assets that could be allocated within the fixed-income portion across investment-grade and speculative issues. Foundations are not restricted to fixed-income securities that are investment-grade issues. A higher risk tolerance enables them to move down the rating scale to pick up higher-yielding securities. For example, they might select an issue with a BB rating (speculative grade) instead of an A rating (investment grade) to earn extra yield.

Once the desired return objective and risk tolerance level are selected, the board of trustees will select a specific asset allocation to help accomplish these goals. If the board does not have sufficient expertise, then a consultant may be hired to help with this task. The allocation will be stated in percentages assigned to each asset class along with a tolerance band.

FOUNDATION CONSTRAINTS

Many foundations have an infinite time horizon and can therefore assume a higher degree of risk. Exceptions occur when a foundation is established to accomplish a short-term charitable purpose. In this case, the risk tolerance should be adjusted downward. However, assuming that its time horizon is infinite, the foundation is available to select investments that can help preserve the real purchasing power of the foundation's assets. Large-cap stocks are a good example of an asset class that can typically preserve purchasing power better than standard fixed-income instruments.

The liquidity needs of a foundation are directly linked to its spending requirement. While a private foundation is required to spend at least 5 percent of its assets on a charitable purpose each year, it is not constrained by regulation from spending a higher amount. Public foundations are free to select any spending requirement that meets the desires of their sources of funds. In a volatile market, the foundation would not want to be forced to sell an asset at the wrong time. They also would not want to tie up funds in the current lower-yielding money markets unnecessarily when other more profitable selections are available.

Tax considerations are a negligible concern for foundations. Under the Pension Protection Act of 2006, the net investment income of foundations is subject to a 2 percent excise tax (Department of Labor, 2006). If a donor gifts or bequeaths a for-profit business to a foundation, then the normal tax constraints for that business would apply. However, the typical scenario for a foundation is that only a nominal tax rate applies to net investment income. This advantage enables the foundation to invest in derivatives and stocks where high capital gains potentially exist and makes lower-yielding tax-free fixed income instruments such as municipal bonds less appropriate.

Since 1972, foundations in the United States have been regulated by the Uniform Management of Institutional Funds Act (UMIFA). In 2006, a new law was enacted to revise the previous act. This new law is called the Uniform

Prudent Management of Institutional Funds Act (UPMIFA). This newer law generally states that foundations are obligated to give primary consideration to donor intent, act in good faith with the care an ordinarily prudent person would exercise, incur only reasonable costs in investing and managing charitable funds, and diversify assets whenever possible (National Conference on Commissioners on Uniform State Laws, 2006).

Foundations may also have donor-specified constraints. Donors may limit grants to a focused type of charitable organization. They may also exclude certain asset classes from consideration or impose an investment mandate to only purchase assets of socially responsible organizations, requiring that the board of trustees cannot invest in certain industries, such as gambling or tobacco. The board of trustees may also impose investment manager-level constraints, such as limiting the percentage of the portfolio that may be invested in any given security.

Endowments

Endowments are very similar to foundations with the structural exception that they are intended to be permanent in nature. Many universities, hospitals, museums, and local community organizations rely upon endowments for a substantial portion of their funding. The degree of reliance on the endowment is a major consideration in establishing the risk tolerance level.

Investment oversight for an endowment is virtually identical to that for a foundation. As with a foundation, the board of trustees will be named in the IIPS as the entity with oversight over the endowment's assets. The board will also establish objective selection criteria for choosing investment managers.

ENDOWMENT OBJECTIVES AND RISK TOLERANCE

Most endowments share a similar investment objective, such as that for the endowment assets of Georgetown University, which is to "produce the highest expected investment return while controlling risk" (Georgetown University, 2011). Unlike a foundation, endowments do not have a specific spending rule mandated by regulation. However, because their funding typically makes a substantial contribution to the operations of the target organization, one of three smoothing techniques are usually applied to arrive upon an endowment-specific spending rule.

The first method for calculating the spending rule is called the *simple spending rule* (SSR). Under this method, the board of trustees for the endowment selects an arbitrary spending percentage. This percentage is then applied, using equation 7.1, to the beginning market value of the endowment's assets, as follows:

$$\text{SSR Spending}_t = (S)(MV_{t-1}), \tag{7.1}$$

where S = spending rate, MV = market value, and t = time. The spending rate should be both realistic and below the expected return on the endowment's assets. A good benchmark to use is the 5 percent rule imposed on private foundations. If the spending rate selected is above the 5 percent threshold, then the probability increases that the endowment's assets will be depleted over time.

The second method is called a *rolling three-year average spending rule* (R3ASR). This method, shown in equation 7.2, modifies the simple spending rule by applying the selected spending percentage to the arithmetic average of the ending asset balances for the prior three years, as follows:

$$\text{R3ASR spending}_t = S\left[MV_{t-1} + MV_{t-2} + MV_{t-3})/3\right],\qquad (7.2)$$

where S = spending rate, MV = market value, and t = time.

The purpose of the rolling three-year average spending rule is to adjust for volatility in the value of the endowment's assets. Some years are better than others, and this method allows the better years to smooth out the effect of the not-so-good years. Under this approach, a large movement in asset prices can result in a dramatic shift in funding to the endowment's target, albeit with a lesser impact than the simple spending rule alone.

The third method is called the *geometric spending rule* (GSR). This method, shown in equation 7.3, is more complex than the R3ASR and is theoretically based on spending across periods of time. It follows:

$$\text{GSR Spending}_t = \left[(R)(\text{spending}_{t-1})(1+\text{Infl}_{t-1})\right] + \left[(1-R)(S)(MV_{t-1})\right],\quad (7.3)$$

where R = smoothing rate, Infl = inflation rate, S = spending rate, MV = market value, and t = time. The GSR explicitly adjusts for inflation and places a much higher weighting on the previous period's spending levels. The smoothing rate is a simple weighting measure and typically ranges between 0.6 and 0.8. Both the smoothing and spending rates are at the discretion of the board of trustees.

Given that an endowment is intended to be a permanent source of funds for the target organization, the organization's real purchasing power must be taken into consideration to calculate its required return. The GSR calculation most directly adjusts for inflation. One technique for meeting both potentially high needs for current cash generation and the inflation protection of long-term capital gains is called the *total return approach*. Under this approach, the organization's current cash needs can be met not only with dividends and interest from the endowment's assets but also by selling assets, hopefully at a gain. This approach enables the endowment to use nondividend-paying, growth-oriented stocks in its portfolio. The total return framework is vital in order to succeed in providing a long-term stream of cash flow to a target charitable organization.

The risk tolerance for an endowment is directly linked to its relative importance in the budget of the target charitable organization. If the endowment's contributions constitute a substantial portion of the charitable organization's budget, then the risk tolerance should be lowered according to the percentage of reliance. The typically infinite time horizon of an endowment increases the risk tolerance relative to pension plans and foundations. As with the assets of a foundation, the board of trustees for an endowment selects the asset allocation percentages with a tolerance band to guide the investment process.

ENDOWMENT CONSTRAINTS

Because an endowment's purpose is to fund a portion of a charitable organization's needs indefinitely, its time horizon is assumed to be infinite. This assumption permits a higher risk tolerance and a total return approach. The liquidity needs of an endowment are not one size fits all. As a rule of thumb, an endowment is presumed to have low liquidity requirements sufficient to meet the chosen spending rule. However, if capital projects, such as the construction of a building, are part of the endowment's donor-specified purpose, then higher liquidity requirements are appropriate until the capital expenditure is completed.

As with foundations, tax considerations are negligible for endowments. Tax-exempt securities are therefore not usually appropriate inclusions in the investment mix. The same regulatory framework applies to both foundations and endowments. They both must comply with UPMIFA and apply prudence in investment decision making.

Endowments are likely to have donor-specified constraints. Those constraints may limit the available asset classes in the investment pool or impose limitations to invest only in the assets of socially responsible organizations, which can be very specific and diverse. These donor-specified constraints must be factored into the IIPS and the investment selection process.

Life Insurance Companies

A life insurance company sells insurance policies that provide a cash benefit at the death of the insured person. Sometimes these policies are very small in nature and are used simply to cover burial costs. In other situations, they are used to create an estate where one did not previously exist. Policies may also be structured to pay estate and/or inheritance taxes when a sizeable estate did pre-exist. The more complex uses of life insurance policies are beyond the scope of this chapter.

The four primary types of life insurance are whole life, term life, universal life, and variable life. *Whole life insurance* features a level death benefit that remains in force over the entire life of the insured. While the death benefit remains unchanged, the cash value does not. The *cash value* is essentially the initial premium paid plus any accrued interest on that premium. In many circumstances, the insured can borrow against the cash value, but the borrowed funds reduce the ultimate benefit paid at his death.

Term life insurance provides a level death benefit for a given tenure. Typically, term policies do not have the benefit of a cash value, but they do offer substantially reduced premiums. This type of insurance is used less for estate planning purposes than it is by individuals who want protection until a goal is attained, such as a home mortgage being paid off or a child completing college.

The remaining two types of insurance are universal life and variable life. *Universal life insurance* is a variation of the whole life policy, which also features a savings account component with an adjustable death benefit. The policyholder benefits from tax-deferred interest on the savings account portion of their policy. *Variable life insurance* is a completely unique policy where the death benefit and the cash value are both linked to investment selections made by the policyholder.

LIFE INSURANCE COMPANY OBJECTIVES AND RISK TOLERANCE

Life insurance companies need a certain minimum required return on their investments in order to meet the liability created by potential death benefit payouts. Any return earned beyond this minimum level represents profit for the life insurance company. Intense competition in the industry has been driving down insurance premiums and therefore making extra profits harder to realize.

The return objective for a life insurance company falls into one of three categories: (1) a minimum return, (2) an enhanced margin, and (3) a surplus return. The *minimum return* focuses on achieving an actuarially determined minimum growth rate necessary for the life insurance company's reserves to meet its anticipated liabilities based on mortality rate expectations. The *enhanced margin* focuses on attempting to earn a positive interest rate spread on the assets of life insurance companies. Essentially, the life insurance company may need to earn a return of perhaps 5 percent in order to meet their obligations but endeavors to yield something higher in an attempt to make additional profit. The *surplus return* is comprised of any life insurance assets that exceed planned liabilities. In this portion of the assets, the goal is to achieve as much growth as possible. Excess returns in the enhanced margin and surplus categories give a life insurance company a competitive advantage by enabling it to lower its insurance premiums to better compete with rival life insurance companies.

When writing the return objectives for the IIPS of a life insurance company, each category should be enumerated separately, with the respective return requirements. Fixed income and preferred stocks are most appropriate for the minimum return and enhanced margin portions, while the surplus return portion should be more equity oriented.

The risk tolerance of life insurance companies is framed by the fact that their purpose in society involves a sense of trust with the public. A policyholder will pay premiums to the life insurance company only because he believes that when the time comes, the life insurance company will be able to make good on its part of the bargain. The violation of this trust results in grave consequences for the respective life insurance company and to some extent for the entire industry. The National Association for Insurance Commissioners (NAIC), the national regulator in the United States over life insurance companies, requires life insurance companies to maintain a cushion to guard against substantial losses (National Association for Insurance Commissioners, 2002). This cushion is called an *asset valuation reserve* (AVR). The AVR pertains to default and credit risk for fixed income and to variability with equities.

Market volatility can adversely affect the assets of a life insurance company. Life insurance companies need as much stability as possible within the minimum return and enhanced margin portions of their portfolios. Sizeable declines may require accounting write-offs that will damage both their surplus position and public image. For this reason, life insurance companies have a low risk tolerance in their minimum return and enhanced margin categories. Life insurance companies also require cash flow certainty. They have little tolerance for an investment that does not pay cash flows as planned. A good example of this circumstance would be either a preferred stock or an equity that delays or eliminates a dividend payment. In theory, a cumulative preferred stock may eventually repay the missed dividend, but since the life insurance company made the initial investment based on its planned cash budget, life insurance companies do not find this acceptable.

Credit risk relates closely with cash flow risk. Intensive credit analysis to determine both the terminal cash flow of a target investment and if it is likely to repay its periodic payments is essential for life insurance companies. This risk is managed by careful analysis and by diversifying the holdings within the portfolio. Credit risk is so important to the healthy functioning on a life insurance company that it is directly addressed by the AVR (National Association for Insurance Commissioners, 2002).

Another major risk for life insurance companies that affects their risk tolerance is called reinvestment risk. *Reinvestment risk* is the risk of being forced to reinvest cash from an interest payment or a matured fixed income position at a lower interest rate than that of the previous investment. This risk is particularly acute in financial environments with declining interest rates, such as the one observed in 2009 and 2010. In a financial environment with a low interest rate, the fixed-income investments will have either higher current yields with increased risk of loss in value or lower interest rates with less risk of loss in value. These lower rates create a challenge for life insurance companies in earning their required return and reaching for a positive interest rate spread above that of the required rate.

The potential for rising interest rates also presents challenges for life insurance company investments. As interest rates rise, fixed-income investments decline in value. Investments with higher-yielding longer-term maturities decline in value at a more rapid rate than do lower-yielding shorter-term investments.

LIFE INSURANCE COMPANY CONSTRAINTS

Given that the timely payment of obligations is essential to a life insurance company's reputation, liquidity is a vital constraint. The uncertain timing of cash demands due to either the death of an insured party or the potential for policy loans directly contributes to this increased need for liquidity, which is greatest in the minimum return category. To help with the constraint of high liquidity, life insurance companies should limit their investment pool to only highly marketable investments. Purchasing less marketable investments, such as venture capital or private placements, in search of higher yields would be undesirable because the life insurance company may be unable to sell the asset at a reasonable price if it needs to generate liquidity. Investments with staggered maturities should be selected to maximize yield potential and to provide for liquidity on a just-in-time basis.

The time horizon for life insurance companies has traditionally been viewed as being long term, with a focal point between twenty to forty years (World Finances 2011). The marriage of staggered maturities and interest rate volatility has shortened the time horizon somewhat. Each segment of the life insurance company's portfolio should have a different time horizon. For example, the minimum return segment should have a shorter time horizon than does the surplus segment.

Because life insurance companies are taxable entities, they must maximize after-tax returns. Taxes for life insurance companies are divided into two subsections: those on the company's excess returns and those on its cash value accumulations. The company's excess returns are taxed as normal income to the life insurance company. The cash value accumulations are a tax-deferred investment for the policyholder. These accumulations are based on the minimum return determined by the actuary. Periodically legislators consider removing the tax-deferred status of cash value accumulations (World Finances, 2011).

The regulatory landscape for life insurance companies is highly important. In the United States, each state has its own insurance department that heavily regulates the industry. The primary goal of the regulation is to preserve the solvency of the insurer (Jerry, 2002). A secondary goal is to promote fairness for the consumer. From an investment perspective, the regulations limit the available investment choices so as to meet specific constraints, such as interest coverage ratios and ratings. Regulators limit every asset class, from fixed income and common stock to foreign investment. These constraints limit the pool of investment choices and may trigger the selling of an asset if a threshold is breached. Greater flexibility has been added to the regulatory landscape by enabling the *prudent investor rule*, which refocuses the investment decision-making process applicable to a fiduciary. This rule stipulates that a fiduciary, such as a life insurance company, should apply prudence to analyzing investment choices and then renders the company harmless from the ultimate outcome. Fiduciaries are now free to invest for others in the same way they would invest for themselves given the same objectives and constraints.

The NAIC, a nongovernmental organization comprised of insurance regulators, both elected and appointed at the state level, attempts to minimize regulatory disparities between the states. The NAIC has an office called the Securities Valuations Office (SVO), whose purpose is to evaluate investment holdings of member insurance companies to assess both the investments' stability and suitability for inclusion in the investment portfolio. Despite this useful service, the regulatory impact of the NAIC has been called into question because it is nongovernmental. Further, the NAIC is seen as being too closely linked to the insurance industry that it regulates (Randall, 1999). As a consequence, its authority is limited.

The unique constraints of life insurance companies are highly customized to their operations. They involve such matters as expressly distinguishing the company's core holdings from its surplus holdings, the diversity of its product offerings, its size, and the strength of its balance sheet.

Non-Life Insurance Companies

A non-life insurance company (NLIC) focuses primarily on health insurance and property and casualty insurance. NLICs differ substantially from life insurance companies in terms of liabilities and risk factors. While a life insurance company's claims process is fairly quick, it may take years to completely settle a claim with an NLIC. Thus, the cash flow timing for an NLIC is less certain with a little more flexibility. An NLIC's blend of insured products, such as homes, cars, recreational vehicles, and personal health, determines the planned duration of liabilities, which is fairly short. The duration of liabilities for an NLIC is determined by its *underwriting cycle*, which is the cycle of positive cash inflows and negative cash outlays. Research suggests that from 1965 to 1991, the average for this underwriting cycle lasted six years, with three years of gains and three years of losses (Rosenblatt 2004).

NLIC OBJECTIVES AND RISK TOLERANCE

As with a life insurance company, an NLIC segregates its assets into core holdings, which are its fixed-income portion and a surplus portion. The goal for the core holdings is to maximize the fixed-income return in order to pay liabilities. Core holdings for an NLIC constitute a smaller percentage of assets than for a life insurance company, because an NLIC does not have the same mandate to meet a minimum return requirement. An NLIC invests its surplus portion in equities and convertible bonds with the goal of capital appreciation to enable competitive pricing on policy premiums. This goal is highly important, as policies not involved with life insurance have been turned into a commodity where consumers are more concerned about price than quality because all policies are very similar in their function.

Safety of principal is another major concern for NLICs. Similar to their life insurance company cousins, their risk tolerance is very low. NLICs must have assets available to pay liabilities when they are presented. The uncertain timing of potential claims is the reason behind this low risk tolerance.

NLIC CONSTRAINTS

Liquidity requirements are high for an NLIC and are highest toward the end of the underwriting cycle, when claims are most likely to be paid. An NLIC needs to plan for the unexpected. For example, the storms and tornadoes that rattled the United States in May 2011 are estimated to have caused between $4 billion and $7 billion of insured losses (Holm, 2011). An investment in a *private placement*, which is a direct investment in a company in which liquidity is low, would be inappropriate for the needs of an NLIC. Short time horizons are implied by the short time frame of the underwriting cycle. Holding a longer-duration bond or municipal bond in the core holdings would be permissible, assuming that it is both marketable and according to a reasonabe expectation, hold its value during the relevant time period. Longer-term bonds are typically used to gain a higher yield and may be sold before maturity to meet liquidity needs.

Unlike for a life insurance company, where only a portion of the investment assets are taxable, all invested assets of an NLIC are taxable, and as such, taxes are a material consideration. The regulatory backdrop for an NLIC is a little less restrictive than for a life insurance company. An NLIC is not required to maintain an AVR, but it does need to maintain minimum capital requirements. The primary unique circumstance affecting an NLIC is the financial status of the company. Weaker financial health requires more caution in the investment portfolio.

Commercial Banks

Commercial banks are in the business of taking deposits, which represent a liability, and making loans, which are assets. A fundamental mismatch in asset-liability durations exists because the liabilities are usually short term, while the assets are usually long term. Funds that have not been loaned out are available for investment. Loans can become geographically concentrated or risk-factor concentrated, and the securities portfolio is the most direct way for a bank to diversify its overall holdings.

COMMERCIAL BANK OBJECTIVES AND RISK TOLERANCE

The return objective for commercial banks is to earn a positive interest spread. They pay interest on their short-term deposit liabilities and receive interest on the longer-term loan assets. Their primary goal is to earn more in interest than they pay. The goal of their excess holdings is to maximize return and therefore company profits. Commercial banks have no meaningful investment limitations except that they should pay attention to diversifying the risks in their loan portfolio.

The risk tolerance of commercial banks is below average because they must be certain that they can pay their liabilities when they come due. As mentioned previously, banks must diversify their geographic and credit risk through their securities portfolio. Because of the mandate to earn a positive interest rate spread, they also must focus on *interest rate risk*, which is the impact that interest rate changes will have on interest rate–sensitive assets, such as fixed income investments.

COMMERCIAL BANK CONSTRAINTS

Liquidity needs for stocks held by commercial banks are high and are driven by withdrawal of deposits, demand for new loans, and regulatory requirements. If banks cannot monetize their loan portfolio by packaging them into vehicles such as a mortgage-backed security, then they must rely on their securities portfolio for their liquidity needs. The time horizon for a bank is linked to the duration of its liabilities. This typically means that the time horizon will be less than ten years and the average maturity of securities in the investment portfolio needs to be lower than this threshold. As with NLICs, commercial banks are taxable entities and taxes are a material concern.

In light of the mortgage meltdown in the 2000s, banks are subject to greater scrutiny. This trend is likely to intensify as governments worldwide seek increased oversight of commercial banks because of their pivotal position to global economic

Table 7.3 **Summary of objectives for an IIPS**

IPS Component	DB pension plans	DC pension plans	Foundations	Endowments	Life insurance company	Non–life insurance company	Commercial banks
Return	Determined by an actuarial rate designed to meet plan liabilities	At the discretion of each individual participant and their personal goals	Private foundations are required to yield 5 percent plus expenses	Offer a balance between need for current income and long-term principal protection	Based upon actuarial assumptions; the surplus segment can focus on capital gains	• Maximizes return while meeting claim liabilities • Surplus segment focuses on capital gains.	• Focus is on earning a positive interest rate spread • Required return is entirely linked to interest rate levels
Risk tolerance	Depends on funded status, age of workforce, time horizon, and plan sponsor's balance sheet	Depends on each participant's preferences and financial capacity	Moderate to high based upon spending and time constraints	Moderate to high based upon spending and time constraints.	• Conservative for core assets • Moderate to high for the surplus segment	• Conservative for core assets. • Moderate to high for the surplus segment	• Below average due to requirement to meet high liquidity needs

Note: This table summarizes various objectives applied to each type of institutional investor.

Table 7.4 **Summary of constraints for an IIPS**

IPS component	DB pension plans	DC pension plans	Foundations	Endowments	Life insurance company	Non-life insurance company	Commercial banks
Liquidity	Depends on age of workforce and percentage of retired lives	Based on participant's circumstances	Meet 5 percent spending requirement for private foundations	• Linked to spending requirements • Default is low	• Core portion of holdings relatively high • Surplus portion of holdings negligible	• Core portion of holdings relatively high • Surplus portion of holdings negligible	• Liquidity needs high and relative to liabilities and demand for new loans
Time horizon	Long if company is a going concern	Based on participant's circumstances	Assumed to be infinite	Assumed to be infinite	Short	Short	Short to Intermediate depending on duration of liabilities
Legal/ regulatory	ERISA	ERISA	• Low • Prudent investor rule applies	• Low • Prudent investor rule applies	• High • Prudent investor rule applies	• Moderate • Prudent investor rule applies	• Moderate to high • Likely increasing scrutiny
Taxes	None	None	Few	None	A material concern	A material concern	A material concern
Unique needs	Consideration of funded status and company balance sheet	Plan sponsor must provide sufficient investment choices	Foundation-specific constraints imposed by donor	Some restricted asset classes	• Distinguishes between core holdings and surplus • Company balance sheet	• Distinguishes between core holdings and surplus • Company balance sheet	• Specific to each bank • May use investments to diversify risks in loan pool

Note: This table summarizes the constraints carried by each type of institutional investor.

health. The specific regulations are beyond the scope of this chapter. Unique constraints for a bank typically focus on the loan portfolio.

Summary and Conclusions

The IIPS provides a guideline for the unique objectives and constraints that apply to each type of institutional investor. Table 7.3 summarizes the objectives for different institutional investors, and table 7.4 summarizes the constraints. This formal document helps guide the investment process and keeps the focus on long-term objectives as the stock market moves through its various phases of boom and bust.

The outline shown in table 7.1 is provided as a reference. The order is not as important as the substance of what is included. The exact wording and general inclusions in each section will change based on the type of institution involved. The most important element for any IIPS is that it is structured in a way that is useful and actionable for the entity it covers.

Discussion Questions

1. Phil Johnson, President of Johnson Pharmaceuticals, has hired a consultant to help develop an IIPS for his company's defined benefit plan. Johnson provides the consultant with the following relevant details:

    -   The company routinely maintains a profit margin of 15 percent and has virtually no debt. The average profit margin of the industry is 12.6 percent with a total debt-to-equity ratio of 0.5
    -   The average age of the workforce is forty years old. The average age in the industry is forty-seven years old.
    -   A total of 25 percent of the pension plan's participants are currently retired. The industry average of workers retired at a company is 32 percent.
    -   The company's pension plan currently has $75 million in assets and is 15 percent overfunded.
    -   The actuarial required rate of return is 6 percent.
    -   The trustees want to maintain a 5 percent cash balance.
    -   He, Phil Johnson, wants to earn at least 7.5 percent per year so that future contributions can be minimized.

    Based on the information provided, answer the following questions:

    a. What should be used as the return objective?
    b. What should be the fund's risk tolerance level? Provide three points of evidence for your answer.
    c. Identify two specific constraints.

2. Phil Johnson returns to the consultant ten years after the initial consultation. He wants a reassessment of the defined benefit plan given the following information:

- The profitability and debt position of Johnson Pharmaceuticals remain similar to those ten years ago.
- The average age of the workforce is now fifty-two years old.
- Those who have retired in the company now make up 45 percent.
- The pension plan currently has $140 million in assets and is now 10 percent underfunded.
- The actuarial rate has been adjusted upward to 8 percent.
- The trustees have not altered the previous minimum cash balance mandate.
- He, Phil Johnson, wants to eliminate the underfunded status as quickly as possible, proposing that half of the shortfall will be made up in a two $4 million dollar contributions—one occurring in one month and the second occurring in one year.

As the hired consultant, Phil would like the IIPS refreshed. Based on this new information, answer the following questions:

    a. What should be used as the return objective?
    b. What should be the fund's risk tolerance level? Provide three points of evidence for your answer.
    c. Identify two specific constraints of the fund.

3. The Fisher Foundation was established by the estate of a wealthy industrial tycoon. Its sole purpose is to provide grants to improve literacy in low-income demographics in Alabama. Its trustees are targeting a required return of 8 percent, which adds a 3 percentage point inflation adjustment on top of the 5 percent spending rule. The fund has assets totaling $75 million.

    The Fisher Foundation asks for assistance in developing an IIPS to guide the investment of their assets. Based on the information provided, answer the following questions:

    a. What should be the foundation's risk tolerance level?
    b. What is the foundation's time horizon?

4. The Eagle University Endowment was established with $75 million dollars. The endowment has two major goals: to build a $25 million dollar library and to provide scholarships to environmental science majors. The environmental science program is not reliant upon this endowment to remain viable. The endowment has opted to use a simple spending rule with a 5 percent spending rate. Those responsible for the endowment intend to adjust the required return by an allotment for education inflation, which they assume to be 5 percent.

    The Vice President of Finance for Eagle University has asked for recommendations to help construct an IIPS for the endowment fund. Answer the following questions based on the information provided:

    a. What should be used as the return objective?
    b. What should be the fund's risk tolerance level?
    c. Identify two specific constraints.

5. Omaha Life, a regional life insurance company, provides all forms of life insurance coverage. The company's actuaries have calculated a 4.5 percent minimum return is necessary to meet its obligations. Omaha Life has $950 million in assets and $750 million in known liabilities.

Omaha Life needs assistance in answer the following questions::

a. What should be used as the return objective?
b. What should be the risk tolerance level?
c. Identify one constraint relative to Omaha Life's liabilities and one relative to its regulatory framework.

References

Bismarck Firefighters Relief Association. 2008. "Investment Policy Statement for Bismarck Firefighter's Relief Association Pension Plan." Last modified February 26. http://www.bismarckfirefighters.com/pdf/Bis.FirefightersIPS.pdf.

Daley, Erik. 2004. "Risk Management: Proper Management of Defined Benefit Plan Assets & Liabilities." The Multnomah Group. http://www.multnomahgroup.com/articles/Managing%20Defined%20Benefit.pdf.

Department of Labor. 2006. *Pension Protection Act of 2006.* Last modified August 17. http://frwebgate.access.gpo.gov/cgi-bin/getdoc.cgi?dbname=109_cong_public_laws&docid=f:publ280.pdf.

Erie Community Foundation. 2010. "Investment Policy Statement." Approved by the board of trustees December 7. http://www.eriecommunityfoundation.org/files/investment-policy-12.7.10.pdf.

Georgetown University. Retrieved on May 31, 2011. "Investment Policy Statement for the Endowment Fund Georgetown University." Available at http://investments.georgetown.edu/files/endowment%20ips%202007%20pdf.pdf.

Holm, Erik. 2011. "May Storms Caused Up to $7 Billion in Insured Losses." *Wall Street Journal,* June 6. http://professional.wsj.com/article/SB10001424052702304474804576369671738856368.html?mg=reno-wsj.

Jerry, Robert H. 2002. *Understanding Insurance Law,* 3rd ed. Newark, NJ: LexisNexis.

National Association for Insurance Commissioners. 2002. "Asset Valuation Reserves and Interest Maintenance Reserves." Last modified December. http://www.naic.org/documents/svo_avr_imr_blue_book.pdf.

National Conference of Commissioners on Uniform State Laws. 2006. "Uniform Prudent Management of Institutional Funds Act. Retrievved on May 21, 2011" Last modified July 7–14. http://www.law.upenn.edu/bll/archives/ulc/umoifa/2006final_act.pdf.

Randall, Susan. 1999. "Insurance Regulation in the United States: Regulatory Federalism and the National Association of Insurance Commissioners." *Florida State University Law Review* 26:3, 625–699.

Rosenblatt, Alice. 2004. "The Underwriting Cycle: The Rule of Six." *Health Affairs* 23(6): 103–9. http://content.healthaffairs.org/content/23/6/103.full.

University of California Retirement Savings Program. 2006. "Investment Policy Statement; Appendix 4: Core Option Investment Guidelines." Last modified May 2. http://www.ucop.edu/treasurer/invpol/RetSavIPS_Appendix_v9April24.pdf.

Virginia Retirement System Defined Contribution Plans. 2004. "Investment Policy Statement." Revised May 20. http://www.fascore.com/PDF/vadcp/InvestmentPolicy.pdf.

World Finances. 2011. "Life Insurance Companies. Time Horizon. Tax Concerns." Last modified May 11. http://world-finances.com/portfolio-managment/what-is-it-portfolio/institutional-investment/548.pdf.

8

Fiduciary Duties and Responsibilities of Portfolio Managers

REMUS D. VALSAN
Lecturer in Corporate Law, University of Edinburgh

MOIN A. YAHYA
Associate Professor of Law, University of Alberta

Introduction

A portfolio manager is a professional who is responsible for administering a collection of financial assets belonging to individual or institutional investors. Portfolio managers are usually associated with large financial institutions such as mutual funds, pension funds, bank trust departments, or insurance companies. Their main responsibility is to exercise professional judgment in the service of their clients by combining different assets, such as stocks, bonds, cash equivalents, or real estate, into a portfolio that suits the investors' risk-reward preference, time frame, and investment objectives.

Insofar as they enjoy discretion concerning how to promote the investors' best interests, portfolio managers are fiduciaries and assume a series of stringent duties, generally referred to as "fiduciary duties." Portfolio managers owe fiduciary duties to their clients in various capacities, serving in such roles as trustees, agents, partners, brokers, financial advisers, or directors of corporate entities involved in financial administration. Although the requirements for becoming a fiduciary and the content of fiduciary duties are controversial, several fundamental fiduciary law principles have been established across common law jurisdictions. When qualifying as a fiduciary, a portfolio manager becomes bound by the general rules of fiduciary law as well as by the special rules created to meet the particularities of the special fiduciary relation that exists in a given case, such as the relation between the trustee and beneficiary, the broker and client, or the director and corporation.

This chapter is an overview of the general duties and responsibilities associated with the fiduciary position and of several special legal provisions incident on portfolio managers. The remainder of the chapter is organized as follows: The first section introduces the concept of fiduciary relations and the general principles governing fiduciaries in the main common law jurisdictions. The second section addresses several specific fiduciary rules governing portfolio managers, with a focus on US law. The final section provides a summary and conclusions.

General Principles Governing Fiduciary Relations

The general principles of fiduciary law form the background against which the duties and responsibilities of any person holding a fiduciary position are determined. In cases where specific legal rules exist for a fiduciary position, they have primacy over general principles. Thus, insofar as they are not regulated by special provisions, portfolio managers who enjoy discretion over the administration of their clients' assets are bound by the general rules of fiduciary law.

The necessary and sufficient conditions for the existence of a fiduciary relation as well as the normative content of fiduciary duties have been the subject of continuous debates across common law jurisdictions. Although elusive, the fiduciary concept has deep historical roots. The law of fiduciary relationships originated several centuries ago in the jurisprudence of the English Court of Chancery. The traditional fiduciary relationships include trustee-beneficiary, guardian-ward, principal-agent, and attorney-client. Over time, new fiduciary relationships have been recognized by analogy to the established categories. As the courts moved from a categorized view of the fiduciary relationship to a fact-driven approach, the family of fiduciary relationships became open ended.

The unprincipled expansion of fiduciary relations has brought along major conceptual difficulties. First, scholars disagree as to the definition of a fiduciary (Millet, 1998). Fiduciary relations are commonly defined by reference to the "trust" and "confidence" that one party places in another (Glusman and Ciociola, 2006). Trust and confidence, however, are concepts that exceed the limits of fiduciary law. They occur in other circumstances that do not always involve fiduciary duties, such as mortgage or insurance contracts, family relations, public services, or liberal professions. A more useful approach to fiduciary relations focuses on the power or discretion that one party to a legal relation holds over the interests of the other coupled with a duty to use such power or discretion for the other's benefit (Black, 1891).

The affirmation that a person is a fiduciary because he has undertaken to use powers or discretion exclusively for another only begins to deconstruct the fiduciary principle. Another thorny question that needs to be addressed is: what is the normative content of fiduciary duties?

The adjective "fiduciary" is often used as an umbrella term that encompasses all the duties that persons occupying a fiduciary position may have. This non-technical and overly broad use of the term has created confusion as to the proper meaning of "fiduciary duties" by including duties that extend beyond the limits of fiduciary law, such as the duty of good faith or the duty of confidentiality. Instead of applying it to all duties that a fiduciary owes, the adjective "fiduciary" should be used strictly to refer to the specific duty (or duties) owed by a person in a fiduciary position. General agreement exists that the core of the fiduciary duties is the duty of loyalty, which imposes on a fiduciary the obligation to act exclusively in the best interests of the beneficiary, as he perceives them to be. This obligation is protected by the "prophylactic" or "proscriptive" duties, which forbid the fiduciary to be in a position of conflict of interest (Smith, 2003). Besides the duty of loyalty and the prophylactic duties, a fiduciary is bound by the duty of care, imposing a certain threshold of prudence and diligence. Although frequently associated with a fiduciary position, the qualification of the duty of care as "fiduciary" is controversial.

As a consequence of the open-ended approach that courts and commentators have taken to categories of fiduciary relations, portfolio managers may find themselves subject to fiduciary duties, although they do not fit into one of the traditionally recognized fiduciary positions, such as trustee or agent. If the core legal requirements for the existence of a fiduciary relation are present (i.e., the manager's express or implied undertaking to use a power or discretion exclusively in the client's service), portfolio managers are liable to fall under the strict standard of conduct imposed by fiduciary law.

THE "PROSCRIPTIVE" OR "PROPHYLACTIC" DUTIES

The concept of fiduciary duty is often used in a proscriptive sense to designate a set of prohibitions encapsulated in the rule against conflicts of interest (the proscriptive duties). The proscriptive duties are commonly divided into four fiduciary rules: (1) the profit rule, (2) the conflict rule, (3) the self-dealing rule, and (4) the fair-dealing rule.

The *profit rule* forbids a fiduciary from retaining an unauthorized benefit acquired by virtue of his fiduciary position. The *conflict rule* states that a fiduciary is not allowed to place himself in a position where his personal interest, or interest involved in another fiduciary capacity, conflicts or possibly may conflict with his duty. The *self-dealing rule* renders a fiduciary's purchases of property during his administration voidable at the beneficiary's will, irrespective of the honesty of the transaction. The *fair-dealing rule* renders transactions between a fiduciary and a beneficiary voidable unless the fiduciary demonstrates that the transaction is entirely fair and honest and the beneficiary gives his informed consent (Mowbray and Lewin, 2008).

The vast majority of legal scholars agree that the proscriptive duties are very strict. Both self-interested conduct and potential self-serving behavior can be punished. Fiduciaries have been held liable for the breach of conflict rule both in cases of an actual conflict between interest and duty and in cases where a reasonable possibility of such a conflict exists. In some cases, an argument can be made that even the remote possibility of conflict is sufficient to find a breach, as one judge argues in the British case of *Boardman v. Phipps* (1967).

Liability for the breach of the proscriptive rules is also very strict in the sense that it does not depend on the fiduciary's good faith or actual motives. As one British judge explains in *Regal (Hastings) Ltd. v. Gulliver* (1967, p. 145), a landmark fiduciary law case, "The liability arises from the mere fact of a profit having, in the stated circumstances, been made. The profiteer, however honest and well intended, cannot escape the risk of being called upon to account."

When faced with an actual or potential conflict of interest, a fiduciary falls under an obligation to avoid or manage such conflict. When a conflict cannot be avoided, the fiduciary must manage it by disclosing the conflict situation to the interested beneficiaries and seeking their informed consent before proceeding to exercise discretion. When disclosure and informed consent are not a possible or practical option, the fiduciary must abstain from acting in the conflict situation, or resign his position if no other option is available.

THE CORE DUTY OF LOYALTY

The case *Bristol & West Building Society v. Mothew* (1998) points out that the only fiduciary duty is the duty of loyalty. In line with this observation, some scholars separate the duties specific to persons in a fiduciary position into two main groups. First, there are the traditional proscriptive duties that were previously discussed. Second, a core duty is binding on fiduciaries, referred to by some authors as the "duty of loyalty," which differs from the proscriptive duties and justifies their existence.

The proscriptive duties are connected with the core duty in the sense that they play a protective or prophylactic role: they aim to prevent violations of the fundamental fiduciary duty. The views differ, however, regarding the content of this core duty of loyalty. Various authors define this duty as the duty to act (or to refrain from acting) with the proper motive (Smith, 2003), the duty to preserve and promote the interests of the beneficiary (Birks, 2000), or the duty to look after the beneficiary's interests (Burrows, 2002).

THE DUTY OF CARE

Although general agreement exists that persons occupying a fiduciary position owe their beneficiaries a duty of care, common law jurisdictions diverge over how to apply the label "fiduciary" to this duty. In the United Kingdom and Canada, a firmly established belief is that the duty of care owed by fiduciaries is not a "fiduciary duty" in the sense of being a duty specific only to fiduciaries. The liability of a fiduciary for the negligent discharge of his duties is regarded as a consequence of the general duty to act with care imposed by tort law on those who choose to act for or advise others (Smith, 2003; Conaglen, 2010). US courts and legal scholars do, however, include the duty of care in the category of fiduciary duties (Frankel, 2011).

In general terms, the duty of care requires fiduciaries to display reasonable care, skill, and diligence in performing their tasks. The standard of care expected from fiduciaries varies according to the type of fiduciary relation and the specific provisions of the state- or federal-level legislation governing such relations.

Unless other special rules apply, portfolio managers who act as trustees are under a duty "to invest and manage the funds of the trust as a prudent investor would, in light of the purposes, terms, distribution requirements, and other circumstances of the trust" (Prudent Investor Rule, 1992, s. 227). The standards of care and skill set forth by the prudent investor rule require trustees to exercise reasonable effort and diligence in making and monitoring trust investments in line with the trust's objectives. Trustees must display care by giving reasonably careful consideration to the formulation and the implementation of an appropriate investment strategy. Besides the exercise of care, a trustee must display the skill of an individual of ordinary intelligence. If the trustee possesses a greater degree of skill, he may be held liable for the losses resulting from failure to make a reasonably diligent use of that skill (American Law Institute, 1992, § 227, comment *d*). Furthermore, trustees must manage the investment portfolio with the caution of a prudent investor managing similar funds for similar purposes.

The duty of caution requires the trustee to preserve the real value of the trust property while ensuring a reasonable return. This duty does not call for complete avoidance of risk by trustees but for their prudent management of risk. Trustees' duties with respect to risk management require them to minimize nonmarket (or diversifiable) risk through proper diversification of the investment portfolio and to exercise reasonable prudence regarding market (or nondiversifiable) risks.

Special Rules Applicable to Portfolio Managers

Having described fiduciary duties in general terms, the application of those duties to portfolio managers comes next. The most stringent fiduciary duties apply to trust managers, with brokers and investment advisers having less stringent duties and hedge fund managers having the least stringent duties, if any, applied to them.

TRUST MANAGERS

Many families set up trusts for their members in order to make sure that an adequate amount of money is available to provide for the beneficiaries, who are typically their children. Some of these trusts continue even when the children become adults. Reasons for setting up these trusts range from not trusting family members, to the desire to have the money properly managed, to the desire to legally avoid taxes. Regardless of motivation, if a trust is set up for the benefit of a family member, the first type of trust, the manager of the trust faces numerous strict legal obligations. Another example of a trust arrangement that is closely related to the first example is the charitable trust. Many charitable organizations are established on the basis of assets donated by individuals and corporations, which are then managed as trusts.

A third example of a trust concerns pensions. Pension plan managers face legal requirements to act in a certain manner when managing employees' pensions and other benefits plans. In the United States, the Employee Retirement Income Security Act of 1974 (ERISA) (ERISA 1974) governs the obligations of such pension plan managers. ERISA is a federal law. In the United States, state law governs trusts, both familial and charitable. Two main sources of governance for trusts are the *Restatement of the Law, Third: Trusts* by the American Law Institute (1992) and the Uniform Prudent Investor Act (UPIA 1994). Both of these standards are simply model codes that each state adopts with its own customized specifications.

Trust managers have fiduciary duties to the beneficiaries of trusts. Similarly, the pension plan manager is declared a trustee by the applicable legislation, such as ERISA in the United States. The imposition of fiduciary duties on trust managers or pension plan managers could be justified by the vulnerable position in which the trust beneficiaries and future retirees are placed with respect to the managers. This fiduciary requirement ensures adequate safeguards and protection through regular contracting. In the case of a child or even an adult for whom a trust fund is created, this individual is usually not as sophisticated as the trustee. The sophistication mismatch is even more obvious for pension planning. While some individuals have self-directed pension plans, most citizens today rely on their employer or the state to plan for their retirement years.

In both examples, the managers are fiduciaries who, therefore, become obligated to strictly act according to the duties of a fiduciary. With respect to the proscriptive duties, the trust manager must avoid all conflicts of interest. With respect to the duty of skill and care, the manager must act according to the prudent man rule, the prudent investor rule, or the prudent expert standard. The first two terms are used when discussing the duties required of a trust manager, while the last term is more specific to pension plan managers. The standards are described in the following paragraphs.

Historically, the courts required those managing trust assets to do so in very safe investments. Some states only allowed the trust managers to place funds in investments on an approved list. These investments were typically safe but low yielding. Even in states that did not have such an approved list, many courts scrutinized the individual performance of each investment, not just the overall performance of the portfolio. In a now infamous case, In re Bank of New York (1974), one court found that the trust manager had possibly violated their fiduciary duty in that even though the portfolio as a whole had performed positively, a subset of the portfolio's investments had not. Trust managers, back then, were not even allowed to delegate the management of some or all of the assets to other financial advisers, such as mutual fund managers. The security of the investments was the main concern of the law of trusts. The obvious concerns were that if trust managers could deviate beyond strict controls, the financial safety of the beneficiaries would be compromised (Droms, 1992; Aalberts and Poon, 1996).

These restrictive views, however, were not universal. As far back as 1830, one court in Massachusetts recognized the need to allow trust managers some flexibility in how they managed the assets. The court stated that those managing the trust's assets should "observe how men of prudence, discretion and intelligence manage their own affairs, not in regard to speculation, but in regard to the permanent disposition of their funds, considering the probable income, as well as the probable safety of the capital to be invested" (Harvard College v. Amory 1830, 461). This case created the *prudent man standard* (also known today as the *prudent person standard* or *prudent investor standard*), which suggests that the manager should be allowed to diversify the trust's investments in order to achieve growth, stability, and income. The implication of the rule, however, did not catch on. More than a hundred years passed before most states dropped the approved list of investments. Only in the 1980s and 1990s did most states start paying attention to modern portfolio theory and diversification and the directions from the case.

By the mid-1990s, most states had adopted the UPIA, and this finally allowed trust managers the freedom to engage in more sophisticated investing strategies. Section 2(b) of the UPIA now states, "A trustee's investment and management decisions respecting individual assets must be evaluated not in isolation but in the context of the trust portfolio as a whole and as a part of an overall investment strategy having risk and return objectives reasonably suited to the trust." In fact, section 3 of the UPIA now requires the trust manager to diversify the portfolio as the default option, absent compelling circumstances not to diversify. This duty is a nod to the ideas of modern finance showing that portfolio managers can achieve a much higher return by investing along the capital asset line (Merton, 1972) than investing only in risk-free assets. In diversifying the portfolio, the trust manager can now delegate some investment decisions to other financial managers, such as a mutual fund manager. The trust manager, however, must take care in investigating the bona fides of the mutual fund manager as well as monitoring the fund's performance.

The courts will no longer look at the individual performance of each investment in the portfolio but at the overall performance. Some authors suggest that trust managers may be required to hold some of their portfolio in riskier investments than in the trusts in which they were traditionally held. These investments would include options, futures, and foreign investments (Bendremer, 2001).

Regarding pension plans, the courts applying the dictates of ERISA have been more forward thinking than their counterparts in dealing with trusts. Pension plan managers have long been expected to diversify their clients' portfolios and take reasonable risks in order to achieve a good balance of income, growth, and stability for the plan's assets. Pension plan managers are given great deference in how they are expected to manage the asset mix of the plan as long as their strategies are within the norm of what financially sophisticated managers would do. Pension plan managers are also allowed to delegate some of their investments to other financial managers.

For both the trust and pension plan managers, the law still requires a duty of loyalty. This means that managers must act in the best interests of the beneficiaries for whom the trust is established and never engage in any conflict of interest. It would not be acceptable, for example, for the manager to invest in a business or company owned by the manager. Such managers are expected to avoid any appearance of conflict of interest, such as making a profit by using information obtained in the course of managing the funds, even if it did not compromise the fund's value.

Interestingly, the official comments in the UPIA state that no form of social investing is permitted, as this mandate would be a conflict of interest unless the particular social investments yielded returns comparable to other investments. In other words, the manager could not choose his favorite cause and invest in it simply because the cause was socially desirable. Socially desirable funds, as the implication of the official comments would suggest, have lower returns than do other assets with similar risk characteristics, and this would lower the overall return of the portfolio below the efficient frontier.

BROKERS

The relationship between individuals who trade in stocks, bonds, or other assets for their own personal portfolios and their brokers is not obviously a fiduciary relationship. Day-trading individuals who purchase individual stocks for personally directed retirement plans, for personal portfolios that are meant for long-term income and security, or just for short-term speculation have a very different view of their brokers than do trust beneficiaries or future retirees. Some of these individuals may consider themselves, and actually may be, more sophisticated than their brokers. Conversely, how these individuals view their abilities may be vastly exaggerated, which is as almost guaranteed by the efficient markets hypothesis. Nonetheless, many individuals choose to pick specific assets as opposed to investing in mutual funds or diversified portfolios.

The question, therefore, becomes: what are the duties of brokers or investment advisers toward their clients? If brokers or financial advisers are fiduciaries, then they will be bound by strict fiduciary duties. Brokers that are fiduciaries would not be allowed to sell stock that they personally owned to their clients because the transaction would create a conflict of interest. Moreover, brokers serving as fiduciaries would have to advise clients against making certain trades if they believed those trades were adverse to their clients' interest. In a way, any time a broker sold an asset from his own vault to a client, the broker would be implicitly stating that he thought the asset would decline or stay flat in value. He would be obligated to alert the client to any trade he felt was improper. Brokers would even have to watch out for their client's behavior, similar to a bartender cutting off an extremely drunk patron. A client who persists in making bad investments would have to be denied any more trades if the broker observed losses accumulating.

Customers deal with two types of brokers: pure brokers and investment advisers. Pure brokers, also known as broker-dealers, simply execute their clients' sales and purchase orders (Laby 2010). They tend to charge a commission for each transaction. Broker-dealers, on the other hand, are likely to provide some advice to their clients, especially if oral communication exists between the two. Investment advisers only give advice, but in reality they are active managers who manage the client's assets. These advisers, who charge fees that are related to the size of the assets, are best known as managing mutual funds or hedge funds.

The Securities Exchange Act of 1934 (SEA) outlines some basic requirements for brokers. The SEA, however, allows self-regulating organizations to impose their own rules in order to govern the conduct of its members. These are known as *self-regulatory organizations* (SROs). One such SRO is the Financial Industry Regulatory Authority (FINRA), formerly known as the National Association of

Securities Dealers (NASD). At present, the legal provisions concerning the fiduciary duties of brokers are in a state of transition. The uncertainty may be compounded or reduced depending on the outcome of many new proposals by the Securities and Exchange Commission (SEC). The Dodd-Frank Wall Street Reform and Consumer Protection Act (2010; also known as the Dodd-Frank Act, or Dodd-Frank) requires the SEC to examine the state of legal obligations for these two types of brokers. In response, the SEC issued "Study on Investment Advisers and Broker-Dealers" in January 2011; in it, the SEC recommends a uniform fiduciary standard for both broker-dealers and investment advisers (SEC 2011).

What will happen to these recommendations is anyone's guess. The SEC will have to act upon its studies and issue new regulations, which ultimately will be challenged in the courts. If the courts strike down an SEC regulation, all that happens is that the regulation returns to the SEC for further study and action. Then another round of litigation starts all over again. Therefore, how these recommendations will affect the legal provisions governing brokers remains to be seen.

Broker-dealers live in a world of ambiguity on many fronts. They are not explicitly deemed to be fiduciaries, but that situation is subject to change depending on the circumstances. Broker-dealers are required to deal with their clients in a fair and honest manner. These requirements stem mostly from the SEA, which, when passed, were primarily concerned about disclosure. As Ribstein (2010) points out, the state laws were meant to deal with the substantive aspects of the relationship between the various interested parties, such as whether or not certain parties are fiduciaries and the nature of their fiduciary duties, while the federal securities laws were all about disclosure. That line of distinction has become and is becoming even blurrier today.

Broker-dealers are not considered fiduciaries unless they play an active role in managing their clients' accounts. SROs impose additional requirements regarding records and fair play on broke-dealers, but they do not elevate the nature of their duties to that of a fiduciary. That being said, because the federal regulations of brokers are not exclusive, broker-dealers are required to register with a state agency and are subject to various state regulations. A few states, such as California, have held that brokers could be fiduciaries, while others have not. This means that depending on the state from which the broker operates, he may be required to, at the very least, disclose personal interests or duties in other capacities that may conflict with their fiduciary duties toward their clients. Even if the relationship between the broker and the client is passive, the broker may be required to disclose adverse information he has about a security at the time that the client wants to buy or sell it. Additionally, a broker may have a duty to stop a client from engaging in certain trading practices if the broker knew or ought to have known that this would have negative financial consequences.

Even in those states where broker-dealers are not fiduciaries by default, brokers may find themselves in quasi-fiduciary roles. The most obvious one is when brokers recommend particular investments or investment strategies to their clients, which then trigger what is known as suitability requirements. Brokers, under these requirements, must understand their client's specific financial situation and needs beyond understanding the investment or strategy they are recommending.

Conceptually, these requirements can be related back to the capital allocation line and investors' tolerance for risk. An investor who has preference for higher returns and more tolerance for risk will invest more of his investments in the risky portfolio, while an investor with less tolerance for risk will shift the investments toward the risk-free asset. Brokers engaged in recommending investments are therefore expected to understand and explain what exactly the efficient frontier is to a client, whose utility curve they are expected to also understand.

In practice, brokers are required to determine whether the client is more income oriented or more growth oriented. This requirement would, for instance, dictate that the stereotypical aged widow who is investing to keep up her retirement income should not receive the same recommendation as a young high-income professional. Nonetheless, these suitability requirements suffer from many flaws when benchmarked against modern portfolio theory. Root (1991) shows that suitability requirements have been interpreted as focusing on individual investments and not the entire portfolio. Even a highly risk-averse individual who desires stability rather than return will invest some proportion of the overall investments in the risky portfolio located on the efficient frontier. Hence, more courts are looking at the overall investment strategy and not just the individually recommended investments. Many commentators, such as Rapp (1998), have advocated that modern portfolio theory should be the basis for evaluating whether brokers have complied with their suitability requirements.

However, suitability requirements are not strict fiduciary duties. They do not require a disclosure of conflict of interest or even that the broker does not believe that the investment being recommended is contrary to the client's best interest. Rather, suitability requirements are mechanical rules that require that the broker to ensure some sort of welfare of the client. Hence, a tension exists between the lack of fiduciary duties and certain obligations, such as the suitability requirements. This tension is a source of uncertainty for broker-dealers. As Laby (2010) points out, only a few disputes concerning brokers' fiduciary obligations reach the courts. Most such disputes are handled by arbitration, and arbitral awards seldom provide detailed reasons for their decisions. Even when the cases are litigated, they usually settle. Consequently, little concrete guidance is available from the courts as to the exact circumstances in which brokers owe fiduciary duties to their clients.

INVESTMENT ADVISERS

Investment advisers, conversely, live in a slightly less strict legal environment. Generally speaking, investment advisers who manage less than a certain amount of assets, currently $100 million, are regulated at the state level, while those managing more than that are regulated federally. The Investment Advisers Act of 1940 (Investment Advisers Act, 1940), which lays out the obligations of those managing other people's money, serves as the regulatory framework at the federal level. The Investment Company Act of 1940 (Investment Company Act, 1940) lays out the duties of investment companies that manage other people's money. With respect to investment advisers, the Investment Company Act of 1940, §

36(b) states, "The investment adviser of a registered investment company shall be deemed to have a fiduciary duty with respect to the receipt of compensation for services, or of payments of a material nature, paid by such registered investment company, or by the security holders thereof, to such investment adviser or any affiliated person of such investment adviser."

This means that duties of disclosure come with any transaction that the investment adviser conducts on behalf of the client. According to the SEC (2011, 4), the commission requires registration for the more than 11,000 investment advisers who manage "more than $38 trillion for more than 14 million clients." The majority of these investment advisers "reported that over half of their assets under management related to the accounts of individual clients" (SEC 2011, 4). In contrast to broker-dealers, who charge transaction-based commission, "most investment advisers charge their clients fees based on the percentage of assets under management" (SEC 2011, 4). Investment advisers' clients, according to the SEC, include "individuals", "high net worth individuals", "banking institutions", "investment companies (including mutual funds)", "pension and profit-sharing plans", and "hedge funds" (SEC 2011, 6). Investment advisers engage in activities such as financial planning services and portfolio management as well as the publication of investment bulletins for investors.

Investment advisers are fiduciaries, and hence must, at the very least, disclose conflicts of interest if not eliminate these conflicts. Besides the antifraud provisions of the SEA, which require disclosure of material facts that could defraud their clients, investment advisers must also advise their clients of any information that could even be seen as a conflict of interest. So, for example, if the investment adviser has one arrangement with a set of clients and other arrangements with more preferred clients, both sets of clients must be informed.

Another duty of the adviser is that of best execution. Best execution means that the adviser must make a transaction on behalf of the client on the best possible terms. The adviser must seek out the lowest brokerage fee, all other things being equal. As such, any material payments received by the investment adviser from other brokers, for example, must also be disclosed. These payments could be in either hard cash or soft dollars. *Hard cash* means that the investment adviser is paid outright for each trade that he executes with a specific broker. *Soft-dollar payments* involve a broker paying the investment adviser in credits; say, free research or even free financial software or hardware. In return, the adviser pays a higher brokerage fee for executing the trades (Johnsen, 2009).

Investment advisers must avoid conflicts of interest, such as selling clients' securities from their own accounts, especially if the effect of such a transaction is that the price of the security gets manipulated (SEC 2011). Disclosure, and in some cases the consent of the client, may be required to legally cure such a conflict. Investment advisers are also required to look at the suitability of the advice that they give their clients depending on similar factors as those that govern broker-dealers, as discussed above.

An area that has generated much litigation but very little change in the law is that of mutual fund management fees. Investment advisers who are also the managers of the mutual funds are paid a management fee that is typically related to the size of the assets managed. The mutual fund is usually structured as an investment company with a board of directors. These directors have their own set of fiduciary duties (Valsan and Yahya, 2010). They must ensure that the management fees paid to the investment adviser-manager are reasonable.

Ribstein (2010) surveys the history and latest developments in the law concerning investment advisers' fiduciary duties, especially as they relate to management fees. Regarding mutual funds, the most common of these funds regulated under the investment company act, Ribstein (p. 302) notes that the law holds that for a manager to have violated § 36(b) of the Investment Company Act of 1940, the fee charged by the mutual fund adviser-manager must be "so disproportionately large that it bears no reasonable relationship to the services rendered and could not have been the product of arm's-length bargaining." The United States Supreme Court recently reaffirmed this rule in *Jones v. Harris Associates L.P.* (2010). The practical effect of this rule is to make it impossible for a party to prevail during a trial in a case against a mutual fund manager on the charge of breaching fiduciary duty through the use of fees. As Ribstein (2010) points out, however, most of the lawsuits that concern the excessive fees never reach trial and are usually settled. The average annual settlement works out to an average of $125,000 for each of the approximately 8,000 mutual funds in the United States.

Freeman, Brown, and Pomerantz (2008) point out that while the Supreme Court seems to have kept the status quo, the subject of advisers' fees continues to stoke academic controversy. The authors survey some of the earlier studies that debate whether mutual fund advisers' fees are unjustified based on actual performance. A study commissioned by the SEC in the early 1960s, known as *The Wharton Report* as well as another study by the SEC shortly thereafter shows that advisers' fees on mutual funds were "unusually high" (Freeman et al., pp. 103–104). These advisers charged higher fees on their mutual funds than the fees they would charge for simply selling investment advice services to nonmutual fund investors, such as institutional investors. Freeman and Brown (2001) conduct an extensive study using two major datasets and find that advisers' fees on mutual funds are higher than the fees they charge to other clients, such as those investing in pension funds. This, they argue, shows that the fees are excessive.

Coates and Hubbard (2007) respond to the Freeman and Brown (2001) study by arguing that the market disciplines bad investment managers by enabling those investing their money in mutual funds to easily sell their shares in the funds and invest in other mutual funds. While mutual fund boards seldom fire investment managers, investors' ability to redeem their investments in subperforming funds and reinvest in better-performing funds shows that the need for regulating fees is overblown (Ribstein, 2010).

Judge Easterbrook, himself a law and economics scholar, also points out that many sophisticated investors pay much higher fees when they invest their money in hedge funds (*Jones v. Harris Associates L.P.*, 2008). He additionally notes that mutual funds and pension plans differ in the nature and liquidity of their investments, making any inference on reasonableness meaningless.

Using additional data analysis, Freeman and Brown (2008) claim to reestablish the case, that they had established earlier in 2001, for excessive fees still stands. As a legal matter, however, when courts evaluate mutual fund fees and almost always find them reasonable, they seek to benchmark the fees against other mutual fund adviser's fees. Examples of studies critical of these fees propose that the courts not only benchmark the fees against other mutual funds but also against those fees charged to institutional investors (Johnson, 2009) or that the rules governing such lawsuits be eased (Langevoort, 2005).

SOFT DOLLAR PAYMENTS

Another area involving disclosure that has generated both regulatory and academic commentary is soft dollar brokerages. Over the years, the SEC has tried to restrict soft dollar payments. Johnsen (2009) is one of the leading critics of the SEC's attack on soft dollar practices. To understand the potential issues, consider the typical soft dollar setup. A mutual fund consists of a portfolio of shares and securities, which an adviser manages on behalf of its investors. The manager uses different brokers to execute trades for the portfolio. Some brokers charge less for services while others charge more. The more expensive broker may pay a vendor directly to provide the manager with research. On this basis, the broker executes the manager's trades at a much higher commission than that of less expensive brokers (Johnsen, 2009).

These soft dollar arrangements have been criticized for generating conflicts of interest and self-regarding incentives. According to its critics, managers overuse the research and engage in excessive trading using expensive brokers. These actions lower the overall return for the investors. Johnsen (2009) argues that soft dollar arrangements are a credible commitment by high-quality dealers. He suggests that low-quality brokers may be cheap, but the investment manager has difficulty knowing which broker is high quality. Quality of brokers refers to the ability of the broker to achieve the manager's objectives in an efficient manner. Investment managers have many objectives in mind when executing a trade. Besides price, the manager may want relative anonymity in the market, given that rival mutual funds could mimic the manager's strategy. The trade must be executed flawlessly, as complications in execution may have negative consequences for the portfolio as a whole.

The high-quality brokers' upfront payment to the research vendors on behalf of the manager to signal the quality of execution is a performance bond that cannot be recovered if the manager stops using the broker due to executing low-quality trades (Johnsen, 2009). The provision of research services overcomes the principal-agent economic incentive problem. In the standard economic model, the agent is expected to invest an optimal amount of effort on behalf of the principal, which in this case is research. But because the agent only receives a percentage of his output as compensation, he likely only invests in effort where the percentage multiplied by the marginal output is equal to marginal cost of the research. Hence, if the investment manager has to do his own research, he is likely to underinvest. Conversely, the high-quality broker, who receives commissions for each executed trade, has an incentive to invest in more research in order to incentivize the manager to execute more trades.

The manager will not, however, overinvest in trades, because any diminution in value of the portfolio will result in investors exiting the fund. The SEC, however, appears to be skeptical of such efficiency-enhancing arguments. As such, they continue to pursue the disclosure of soft dollar arrangements under the belief that they are a breach of investment managers' fiduciary duties (Johnsen, 2009; SEC, 2011).

HEDGE FUNDS

Hedge funds present another set of legal issues. Sklar (2009, p. 3256) defines a hedge fund as "an entity that holds a pool of securities and perhaps other assets, whose interests are not sold in a registered public offering and which are not registered as an investment company under the Investment Company Act." Hedge funds, which have grown enormously in terms of the size of their assets, have the potential to create large returns and losses. They also have the potential to pose a threat to the financial system in the event that a trading strategy goes awry. Long Term Capital Management (LTCM) is the most famous example of a hedge fund that failed long before the current subprime mortgage meltdown (Lowenstein, 2000).

Hedge funds typically seek to exploit potential market mispricing using leveraged positions. These positions can profit handsomely if the market corrects itself in the direction the hedge fund manager anticipates, but the opposite is also true. Unlike mutual funds, which are organized as corporations with a board of directors and an investment adviser-manager, hedge funds are usually set up as a limited partnership with the hedge fund manager being the general partner and manager and the investors being the limited partners (Sklar, 2009). In a typical limited partnership, the general partner owes the limited partners fiduciary duties, just as the investment adviser does. Further, the partnership agreement may have some other clauses that outline the nature of the manager's duties. The investors are usually rich individuals looking for a profitable investment vehicle. Most hedge funds are registered in the state of Delaware, which is also the state of choice for most corporations in the United States.

Because Delaware allows the partnership agreement to dilute the fiduciary duty protections, possible conflicts of interest may arise. Because the investment clients are typically very wealthy and because of the way such funds are set up, hedge funds are not regulated to the same degree as are mutual funds. While hedge fund managers must avoid fraudulent dealings with their investors, the managers are generally exempt from direct supervision by the SEC. This allows them to engage various financial strategies that are not allowed for mutual fund managers. It also creates the potential for conflicts of interest to arise. Because hedge funds not only contain stocks but also financial instruments such as options and derivatives (things mutual funds are not allowed to have), valuing the assets is not so straightforward. The manager has an incentive to inflate the value, which can inflate the management fee, but the value-inflating financial instruments could expose the fund as a whole to risk and ruin (Sklar, 2009). In other words, a hedge fund may only have a high valuation at a particular point in time because the mix of debt, derivatives, and stocks or currencies is highly valued at the moment. A sudden unanticipated change in interest rates could, however, turn the highly valued assets into worthless pieces of paper, as happened to LTCM. The tug between high valuation and risk creates a set of conflicts that is not easy to cure.

Conflicts arise if the hedge fund manager manages two different hedge funds and the financial strategies involved in one conflict with the other (Sklar, 2009). One fund may take long positions in stocks plus a long position in the put options on the stocks, while the other may take short positions plus a short position in the call options. This situation would be a clear conflict of interest and breach of fiduciary duty. Similarly, the hedge fund may have two classes of investors. The manager may want to give one class preferential treatment in terms of better (higher return but more risk) investment strategies but also better (easier) redemption (exit) terms. As Sklar (pp. 3270–3271) notes, the less preferred customers would not be pleased if they knew about a much more privileged class of investors. Yet, hedge fund managers can potentially hide the existence of one group from another.

Hedge funds have been largely exempt from any supervisory role by the SEC. In 2004, the SEC attempted to regulate hedge funds using "the hedge fund rule," which would have required most hedge fund advisers to register with the SEC. This would have allowed the SEC to gather some basic information about the hedge fund advisers in order to oversee the industry and prevent fraud. The rule was overturned by an appeals court on the ground that the SEC did not follow the proper procedure in enacting the rule. The Dodd-Frank Bill gives the SEC more legislative teeth to enact such supervisory rules. Thus, the SEC has enacted a new hedge fund rule as of June 2011. The fate of this new rule is now in the hands of the courts for the next few years. The current rules are modest in what they require, which mostly consists of disclosure of basic operational information and registration with the SEC. Whether this will start a more extensive form of regulation is unclear, but it is a response to the growing work calling for such oversight (Hall, 2008; Schneider, 2009).

Summary and Conclusions

Portfolio managers can become subject to fiduciary duties in various roles, such as that of trustee, agent, corporate director, broker, financial adviser, and partner. Each of these roles is governed by a set of common principles. When deemed fiduciaries, portfolio managers have a general duty to act exclusively in the interests of their clients, avoid conflicts of interest, and refrain from seeking unauthorized profits. Portfolio managers have the discretion to determine the most appropriate way to advance the beneficiary's interests. Portfolio managers are also bound by duties of care, skill, and diligence, measured according to the various benchmarks of the role's the specific legislation. These duties are a constantly evolving legal area, as each financial crisis spurs a call to action by academics and activists alike.

Discussion Questions

1. What are the proscriptive duties to which fiduciary portfolio managers may be bound?
2. What are the fiduciary duties by which trust managers must abide?
3. Are broker-dealers fiduciaries, and if so, what specific duties must they perform?
4. Should mutual fund managers be classified as fiduciaries? If so, what are the practical implications of being fiduciaries for their fee structure?
5. What is soft dollar brokerage, and why does it present a potential breach of fiduciary duties?
6. Are hedge fund managers bound by fiduciary duties to their investors? Explain.

References

Aalberts, Robert J., and Percy S. Poon. 1996. "The New Prudent Investor Rule and the Modern Portfolio Theory: A New Direction for Fiduciaries." *American Business Law Journal* 34:1, 39–72.

American Law Institute. *Restatement of the Law, Third: Trusts*. 1992. St. Paul, MN: American Law Institute.

Bank of New York. 1974. 323 N.E. 2d 700 (NY).

Bendremer, Fredric J. 2001. "Modern Portfolio Theory and International Investments under the Uniform Prudent Investor Act." *Real Property, Probate and Trust Journal* 35(4): 791–809.

Birks, Peter. 2000. "The Content of Fiduciary Obligation." *Israel Law Review* 34(3): 3–38.

Black, Henry C. 1891. *A Dictionary of Law: Containing Definitions of the Terms and Phrases of American and English Jurisprudence, Ancient and Modern*. St. Paul, MN: West.

Boardman v. Phipps. 1967. [1967] 2 AC 46 at 111.

Bristol & West Building Society v. Mothew. 1998. [1998] Ch 1 at 18.

Burrows, Andrew. 2002. "We Do This at Common Law but That in Equity." *Oxford Journal of Legal Studies* 22:1, 1–16.

Coates, John C., and R. Glenn Hubbard. 2007. "Competition and Shareholder Fees in the Mutual Fund Industry: Evidence and Implications for Policy." *Journal of Corporation Law* 33:1, 151–222.

Conaglen, Matthew. 2010. *Fiduciary Loyalty: Protecting the Due Performance of Non-Fiduciary Duties*. Oxford, UK: Hart.

Dodd-Frank Wall Street Reform and Consumer Protection Act. 2010. H.R. 4173, Pub. L. No. 111–203.

Droms, William G. 1992. "Fiduciary Responsibilities of Investment Managers and Trustees." *Financial Analysts Journal* 48:4, 58–64.

ERISA (Employee Retirement Income Security Act of 1974). 1974. 29 U.S.C. 1001–1461.

Frankel, Tamar. 2011. *Fiduciary Law*. Oxford, UK: Oxford University Press.

Freeman, John P., and Stewart L. Brown. 2001. "Mutual Fund Advisory Fees: The Cost of Conflicts of Interest." *Journal of Corporation Law* 26:3, 609–673.

Freeman, John P., Stewart L. Brown, and Steve Pomerantz. 2008. "Mutual Fund Advsiory Fees: New Evidence and a Fair Fiduciary Duty Test." *Oklahoma Law Review* 61:1, 83–153.

Glusman, David H., and Gabriel D. Ciociola. 2006. *Fiduciary Duties and Liabilities: Tax and Trust Accountant's Guide*. Chicago: CCH.

Hall, Dustin G. 2008. "The Elephant in the Room: Dangers of Hedge Funds in Our Financial Markets." *Florida Law Review* 60:1, 183–227.

Harvard College v. Amory. 1830. 26 Mass. (9 Pick.) 446, 461.

In re Bank of N.Y. 1974. 323 N.E.2d 700 (NY).

Investment Advisers Act of 1940. 1940. 15 U.S.C. § 80b-1–80b-21.

Investment Company Act of 1940. 1940. 15 U.S.C. § 80a-1–80a-64.

Johnsen, D. Bruce. 2009. "The SEC's 2006 Soft Dollar Guidance: Law and Economics." *Cardozo Law Review* 30(4): 1545–1613.

Johnson, Emily D. 2009. "The Fiduciary Duty in Mutual Fund Excessive Fee Cases: Ripe for Reexamination." *Duke Law Journal* 59:1, 145–181.

Jones v. Harris Associates L.P. 2008. 527 F.3d 627, 634–635 (7th Cir.).

Jones v. Harris Associates L.P. 2010. 130 S. Ct. 1418.

Laby, Arthur B. 2010. "Fiduciary Obligations of Broker-Dealers and Investment Advisers." *Villanova Law Review* 55:3, 701–742.

Langevoort, Donald C. 2005. "Private Litigation to Enforce Fiduciary Duties in Mutual Funds: Derivative Suits, Disinterested Directors and the Ideology of Investor Sovereignty." *Washington University Law Review* 83:4, 1017–1044.

Lowenstein, Roger. 2000. *When Genius Failed: The Rise and Fall of Long-Term Capital Management*. New York: Random House.

Merton, Robert C. 1972. "An Analytic Derivation of the Efficient Portfolio Frontier." *Journal of Financial and Quantitative Analysis* 7:4, 1851–1872.

Millet, Peter J. 1998. "Equity's Place in the Law of Commerce." *Law Quarterly Review* 114:2, 214–227.

Mowbray, William John, and Thomas Lewin. 2008. *Lewin on Trusts*. London: Sweet & Maxwell.

Rapp, Robert N. 1998. "Rethinking Risky Investments for That Little Old Lady: A Realistic Role for Modern Portfolio Theory in Assessing Suitability Obligations of Stockbrokers." *Ohio Northern University Law Review* 24:1, 193–279.

Regal (Hastings) Ltd. v. Gulliver. 1967. [1967] 2 AC 134 at 144.

Ribstein, Larry E. 2010. "Federal Misgovernance of Mutual Funds." *Cato Supreme Court Review* 2009–2010, 301–331.

Root, Stuart D. 1991. "Suitability—The Sophisticated Investor—and Modern Portfolio Management." *Columbia Business Law Review* 1991:3, 288–357.

Schneider, David. 2009. "If at First You Don't Succeed: Why the SEC Should Try and Try Again to Regulate Hedge Fund Advisers." *Journal of Business & Securities Law* 9(2): 261–310.

SEC (Securities and Exchange Commission). 2011. "Study on Investment Advisers and Broker-Dealers." Last modified January. http://sec.gov/news/studies/2011/913studyfinal.pdf.

Securities Exchange Act. 1934. 15 U.S.C. § 78a-78–lll.

Sklar, Ryan. 2009. "Hedges or Thickets: Protecting Investors from Hedge Fund Managers' Conflicts of Interest." *Fordham Law Review* 77:6, 3251–3323.

Smith, Lionel D. 2003. "The Motive, Not the Deed." In *Rationalizing Property, Equity, and Trusts: Essays in Honour of Edward Burn*, edited by Joshua S. Getzler, 53–81. London: LexisNexis.

UPIA (Uniform Prudent Investor Act). 1994. Chicago: National Conference of Commissioners on Uniform State Laws.

Valsan Remus D., and Moin A. Yahya. 2010. "Fiduciary Duties and Financial Distress." In *Capital Structure and Corporate Financing Decisions: Theory, Evidence, and Practice*, edited by H. Kent Baker and Gerald S. Martin, 371–386. Hoboken, NJ: John Wiley & Sons.

ASSET ALLOCATION AND PORTFOLIO CONSTRUCTION

9

The Role of Asset Allocation in the Investment Decision-Making Process

JAMES L. FARRELL JR.
Chairman, Institute of Quantitative Research
in Finance (the Q-Group)

Introduction

Determining the asset mix that best suits an investor's risk-return objective is the most important decision in meeting the longer-range goals of the investment plan. Studies by leading pension fund consulting firms show that approximately 90 percent of differential performance, such as a passive 60/40 stock-bond allocation, is related to asset class selection, with the remainder related to manager selection and other factors (Brinson, Hood, and Beebower 1986; Brinson, Singer, and Beebower, 1991). Yet, Ibbotson and Kaplan (2000) note that the influence of asset allocation on the investment's performance depends on the question asked, although their findings fail to account for the pervasive influence of the market. Xiong, Ibbotson, Idzorek, and Chen (2010) conduct a study that controls for the influence of the market. Their empirical evidence shows that market return and asset allocation policy return in excess of market return are collectively the most important determinants of total return variations.

Asset allocation encompasses selecting asset classes, proper blending of the asset classes in a portfolio, and managing the asset mix over time. Because of its focus on the longer range, this aspect of the process is also referred to as *strategic asset allocation* (SAA). Once the longer-range asset mix is established, investors can then attempt to identify pricing discrepancies among asset classes and change the mix opportunistically over the interim. This aspect is known as *tactical asset allocation* (TAA) and by nature has a shorter-term orientation. TAA has the potential of adding value over time but also presents substantial risks that investors should consider. TAA is another way of managing the asset mix over time.

The purpose of this chapter is to discuss asset allocation and its differing aspects. The chapter begins by describing a structured approach for SAA. The second part of the chapter deals with TAA and its implementation. Along the way, the chapter shows how this analysis is especially pertinent in the economic environment following the financial crisis of 2008 and 2009, where an unusually high degree of risk of either deflation or, alternately, inflation exists. The chapter ends with a summary and conclusions.

Strategic Asset Allocation

The purpose of the SAA process is to select assets for a portfolio in such a way as to maximize return at a level of risk consistent with the investor's objective. This process involves four key elements. First, the investor needs to determine the assets that are eligible for the portfolio. Second, the investor needs to assess the risk and to estimate the expected return for these eligible assets over a holding period or planning horizon. Third, an investor can use optimization techniques to find the portfolio mixes that provide the highest return for each level of risk. The final step is to choose the portfolio.

The next section begins by giving special emphasis to determining the expected risk and return for assets of interest to the portfolio manager. Essentially, two methods of estimating the risk-return relationship among securities are available. The *historical approach* assumes that the future will be like the past and extrapolates past experience into the future. By contrast, the *scenario approach* involves establishing appropriate economic scenarios and then assessing the risks and returns associated with these scenarios. Generally, forecasts using this latter approach have a three-to-five year planning horizon. Forecasting by extrapolating the past into the future implicitly presumes an infinite planning, or forecasting, horizon. The next section describes the historical approach and also covers the more complex scenario approach to forecasting risk-return relationships.

Using the Past to Forecast the Future

Table 9.1 shows the risks and returns associated with asset classes based on the analysis of past data. Because this table considers only three asset classes (common stocks, long-term bonds, and short-term Treasury bills), the analysis is simplified, improving the illustration. The risks and returns associated with the assets involve the period 1926–2010. The returns are realized and include income and capital gains, whereas the risks are measured by the standard deviation of return and correlation among the asset classes.

Table 9.1 indicates that stocks have exhibited the highest return, followed by bonds, and then Treasury bills. The risk of the assets, as measured by the standard deviation of return, is consistent with the realized return in which stock returns are the most variable and Treasury bills the least. Stocks show virtually zero correlation with Treasury bills over the period and a slightly positive correlation with bonds, whereas Treasury bills show a moderately positive correlation with bonds.

In forecasting, investors ordinarily assume that the standard deviations and correlations among assets realized in the past will persist in the future. Investors

Table 9.1 **Risk and Return Characteristic of Major Asset Classes, 1926 to 2010**

			Correlation		
Asset Class	Return (%)	Risk (standard deviation) (%)	Stocks	Bonds	Treasury bills
Stocks	9.40	19.40	1.00		
Bonds	5.40	8.00	0.14	1.00	
Treasury bills	3.90	0.90	0.05	0.24	1.00

Note: This table describes the risks and returns associated with major asset classes between 1926 and 2010.

Source: SBBI, Ibbotson Associates, Chicago.

will, however, adjust projected returns for the current levels of inflation, as theory and empirical research indicate they are primarily concerned with real rather than nominal returns (Fama, 1975). Projections, then, assume that the real return earned in the future will be the same as that earned in the past. Nominal returns projected into the future will differ from past returns by the differences in the assumed future level of inflation and by the inflation rates realized in the past.

Table 9.2 shows the inflation rate for the period 1926–2010, the realized real return for the three asset classes, and the projected nominal returns incorporating current levels of inflation. Over this period, the annual inflation rate averaged 3.1 percent, so that the real return (removing the impact of inflation) on stocks was 7.2 percent, on bonds 1.9 percent, and on Treasury bills close to zero. Adding an assumed current inflation rate of 3 percent to the real returns of the historical period 1926–2010 provides projected nominal returns only slightly lower than the past rates of 9.4 percent for stocks, 5.4 percent for bonds, and 3.9 percent for Treasury bills.

Table 9.2 **Risk and Return Profiles of Three Major Asset Classes, 1926 to 2010**

Asset class	Return (%)	Standard deviation (%)	Consumer price index (%)	Real return (%)	Expected inflation 2009 (%)	Projected nominal return (%)
Stocks	9.4	19.4	3.2	7.2	3.0	9.2
Bonds	5.4	8.0	3.2	2.2	3.0	5.2
Treasury bills	3.9	0.9	3.2	0.7	3.0	3.7

Note: This table illustrates a projection of risk/returns on asset classes from the past into the future.

Source: Farrell (1998).

Economic Eras

To best evaluate how asset classes perform over shorter periods, Table 9.3 divides the overall 80-year period from 1929 to 2009 into three major economic eras: (1) growth/low inflation, (2) inflation/stagflation, and (3) deflation. It shows that growth/low inflation occurs when productivity is strong, inflation is low (below 3 percent), and profitability is good.

The postwar period contains two longer secular periods (1946–1965 and 1982–1999) and three shorter periods (1934–1938, 1939–1945, and 2004–2007). The interim period 1966–1981 represents a longer secular period of stagflation-rising prices with little real growth, which led to high rates of inflation at the end of the period. Deflation characterizes some other periods, most notably the five-year period of the Depression (1929–1933) and two recent shorter periods (2000–2003 and 2008–2009)

Variations in Return

Table 9.4 shows returns in percent experienced by each of the three asset classes over the three different economic eras, growth/low inflation, inflation/stagflation, and deflation. Returns for stocks in the growth/low-inflation overall period are

Table 9.3 **Economic Eras, 1929–2009**

Growth/Low Inflation: 1934–1938, 1939–1945, 1946–1965, 1982–1999, and 2004–2007
Inflation/Stagflation: 1966–1981
Deflation: 1929–1933, 2000–2003, and 2008–2009

Note: This table illustrates the three major economic eras and corresponding asset class performance between 1929 and 2009.

Source: Modified from Farrell (1998).

Table 9.4 **Variation in Returns, 1928 to 2009**

Asset Class	Growth/low inflation (%)	Inflation/ stagflation (%)	Deflation (%)
Stocks	13.6	6.7	−12.3
Bonds	6.0	3.0	8.8
Treasury bills	3.4	6.6	2.3
Consumer price index	4.1	6.9	−2.0
Frequency	70.0	20.0	10.0

Note: This table describes returns experienced by each of the three asset classes over three different economic eras.

Source: Farrell (1998).

Table 9.5 **Inflation vs. Productivity, Real GDP, and Stock Prices March 31, 1947 to March 31, 2010**

Year-to-Year Change in the Consumer Price Index	Gain/Annum in Non-Farm Productivity	Gain/Annum in Real Gross Domestic Product	Gain/Annum in the S&P 500 Index
Below 1%	3.85	4.65	20.05
1% to 4%	2.69	3.67	8.77
4% to 9%	1.33	2.57	1.24
Above 9%	0.98	1.03	0.69

Note: GDP and related data are revised. This table shows how inflation and productivity interact to generate higher or lower real GNP growth and hence, higher or lower stock returns.

generated by splicing together the returns over the five subperiods 1934–1938, 1939–1945, 1946–1965, 1982–1999, and 2004–2007. Similarly, the returns for bonds for the overall deflation period are generated by splicing together the returns for the three deflation periods 1929–1933, 2000–2003, and 2008–2009. The inflation/stagflation rate simply represents the long, continuous period 1966–1982. The bottom row shows the frequency with which these episodes occurred over the total period: 70 percent for growth/low inflation, 20 percent for stagflation/inflation, and 10 percent for deflation. Note that stocks show the highest return of 13.6 percent, as might be expected over the growth/low inflation cycles.

Table 9.5 illustrates that stocks perform best when inflation as measured by changes in the consumer price index (CPI) is low and productivity is high but perform poorly with high inflation and low productivity. Although not shown in Table 9.5, stocks perform dismally during periods of deflation (−12.3 percent). Conversely, bonds perform very well during deflation, averaging 8.8 percent, and even better on a real-return basis of 10.8 percent. Treasury bills exhibit the best performance during the inflation/stagflation period by maintaining pace with the CPI.

Stock-Bond Correlation

Figure 9.1 illustrates the correlations between stocks and bonds using a rolling monthly period. As Figure 9.1 shows, the stock-bond correlation is slightly positive at 0.14 using the longer period 1929–2009, implying no long-term trend in the relationship. At the same time, time periods exist when the correlation is both markedly above and below the overall average: two extended subperiods where the stock-bond correlation are more strongly positive (the period of the 1970s and into the early 1980s) as well as the period post 1982–1983.

Table 9.6 shows the returns for stocks and bonds as well as the relationship between the two periods of above-average correlation. The earlier period is one of stagflation, which affected both bonds and stocks negatively. Hence, a positive

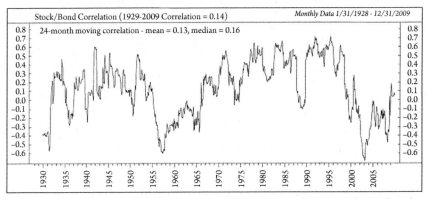

Figure 9.1 Rolling two-year monthly stock-bond correlation. This chart shows that the correlation between stocks and bonds varies greatly between positive and negative over shorter intervals. The mean of the correlation = 0.13 and the median = 0.16. The stock-bond correlation for 1929–2009 is 0.14.

Table 9.6 **Asset Returns and Positive Correlations**

Start Date	End Date	Stocks	Bonds	Correlation
5/31/1975	6/30/1980	4.54	5.39	0.39
9/30/1982	3/31/1986	21.61	22.76	0.55
12/31/1990	4/30/1998	18.00	10.68	0.47

Source: Ned Davis Research, Inc.

Note: This table illustrates the relationship between stocks and bonds during periods of above average correlation.

correlation exists between the two asset classes. Conversely, the second period represents a strong disinflationary environment. The declining inflation rate along with favorable economic growth and declining interest rates led to strong returns for both stocks and bonds, especially in the first part of the period. As a result, these trends led to a positive correlation, which is due to the exposure of stocks and bonds to positive rather than negative fundamentals.

In comparison, the periods of negative stock-bond correlation are much shorter, and are generally associated with periods of high market and/or economic stress. These factors can be seen by the extreme downward dips in Figure 9.1 where the correlation becomes negative at −0.5 and less. A total of 13 noteworthy periods occur in which the stock-bond correlation becomes meaningfully negative.

Table 9.7 shows the beginning and ending dates for the period of negative price action for each of 13 periods beginning in 1929 and ending in 2008, the duration of the negative stock-bond correlation, and the amount of negative correlation. The average correlation for each of the 13 periods is −0.35 with a range between −0.13 and −0.70. The duration of these negative periods ranges from a low of five months in 1998 to a high of 26 months from 2001 to 2003.

Table 9.7 **Asset Returns and Negative Correlations, 1929 to 2008**

Start Date	End Date	Stocks	Bonds	Correlation
9/30/1929	5/31/1931	−39.61	7.91	−0.55
4/30/1936	1/31/1937	40.74	5.90	−0.13
1/31/1956	9/30/1958	5.12	−2.38	−0.40
8/31/1961	5/31/1962	−16.22	7.20	−0.15
3/31/1965	12/31/1965	9.77	−0.50	−0.25
1/31/1968	11/30/1968	21.35	0.25	−0.29
12/31/1972	1/31/1974	−16.90	−0.13	−0.25
7/31/1980	2/28/1981	13.97	−15.61	−0.18
3/31/1987	11/30/1987	−9.78	−8.40	−0.70
6/30/1989	12/31/1989	23.31	9.59	−0.20
5/31/1998	10/31/1998	1.73	22.08	−0.53
1/31/2001	3/31/2003	−19.79	10.13	−0.64
12/31/2006	9/30/2008	−10.57	8.19	−0.37

Note: This table shows the beginning and ending dates for negative price action for thirteen periods beginning in 1929 and ending in 2008.

Source: Ned Davis Research, Inc.

Table 9.8 illustrates how negative bond/stock correlation relates to bear markets. These bear markets exhibit durations from four months to more than three years (during the Great Depression) and as short as less than six months in 1987 and 1998. The table also shows the magnitude of losses during a bear market, with the longest and greatest losses associated with the Depression, whose market lasted for more than three years. Although bear markets, such as the one in 1987 can be brief, they can be quite devastating in the long run.

Most bear market events are associated with recession periods. Some began coincidentally or close to the start of a recession, while most others precede one. This correlation is especially so in the post–World War II period.

There are three instances where no official recession occurs with a market decline: in 1962, 1987, and 1998. These declines were relatively short lived but nevertheless destructive over relatively short periods, especially in 1987. The 1962 bear market is associated with a growth slowdown, overvaluation of growth stocks, and a high degree of political uncertainty, as was occurring that year with the Kennedy showdown with the steel industry. In 1987, international turmoil along with currency weakness compounded by the failure of portfolio insurance led to a short but severe bear market. In 1998, international turmoil, including a Russian bond default and the uncertain future of a large, highly leveraged hedge fund especially affecting many emerging markets, created severe pressure over a short bear market. The latter two bear markets, in 1987 and 1998, may reflect investor fears of financial collapse portending the advent of deflation.

Table 9.8 **Lead-lag Effect to Bull Top and Loss for Bear Markets**

Bull top	Bear bottom	Stocks (%)	Bonds (%)	Amount of time negative correlation begins before the top of the bull market
10/31/1929	2/28/1933	−35.31	4.59	One month
2/28/1937	3/31/1938	−50.15	0.21	Nine months
3/31/1956	10/31/1957	−9.94	−3.76	Two months
12/30/1961	6/30/1962	−41.71	8.18	Four months
1/31/1966	9/30/1966	−5.28	−0.31	Eleven months
11/30/1968	5/31/1970	−20.70	−8.37	Ten months
12/31/1972	11/30/1974	−23.90	1.33	Coincident
4/30/1981	7/31/1982	−5.80	15.99	Nine months
8/31/1987	10/30/1987	−80.11	16.33	Five months
7/30/1990	11/30/1990	−25.88	9.99	Six months
6/30/1998	9/30/1998	−35.04	35.13	One month
9/30/2000	10/31/2002	−20.70	12.05	Post-top
9/30/2007	2/28/2009	−40.31	12.72	Nine months

Note: This table illustrates how a negative stock-bond correlation relates to bear markets.

Source: Ned Davis Research, Inc.

Scenario Forecasting

Besides using the historical approach, scenario forecasting is another major way to develop returns and assess risk for securities. It differs from the historical approach regarding both the analytical difficulty in developing the forecast and the appropriate time horizons for the forecast. The scenario approach requires greater analytical effort and forecasting skill. The tradeoff is, of course, the greater flexibility it offers in dealing with changing environments and, hence, the possible derivation of more effective forecasts of future returns.

Although forecasting based on the historical approach implies an infinite forecasting horizon, the scenario approach requires a more explicit statement of the forecast period. Generally, forecasters choose an intermediate-term forecasting horizon of, say, three to five years. This time horizon forces planners to look beyond seasonal and cyclical events and focus on socio-politico-economic trends and their implications for stock prices and interest rates. At the same time, because this planning horizon is not remote, it is not beyond the capability of developing objective and useful forecasts of value.

Further, this lesser time horizon provides the appropriate perspective for shorter-term portfolio decision making. Once longer-term benchmark yields and price levels for security classes are established, tactical portfolio decisions flow naturally from the interaction between (1) short-term fluctuations in these benchmark yields and price levels and (2) a predetermined long-term investment plan. In composing the latter, TAA (a shorter-term approach) can be differentiated from SAA (a longer-term approach) to determine and change the composition of the portfolio. TAA and its integration with the SAA process are discussed later in this chapter.

The final task in the scenario approach is to identify the possible range of economic environments that could exist. Three scenarios would seem to cover the major kinds of economic environments. The first scenario reflects the mainline economic environment of low inflation and steady growth that occurs most often over time. It diverges greatly when output falls and recession and deflation emerge, which represents the second scenario. Third, inflation can develop when output is insufficient to meet demand. The last two scenarios represent extreme and negative environments. Focusing on three scenarios simplifies the analysis.

Role of Asset Classes in the Allocation

Table 9.9 illustrates another way to look at historic data: to view asset classes as a way to participate in certain favorable economic environments or a way to hedge against adverse economic conditions. For example, if asset classes are being looked at as a way to produce strong growth, stocks would obviously present the best opportunities. By contrast, bonds perform best in a deflationary environment and in a sense provide a good hedge in such a dismal economic environment. Similarly, Treasury bills that track changes in the CPI rather closely can provide a hedge against both stagflation and inflation. With the introduction of Treasury Inflation-Protected Securities (TIPS), investors have an even better vehicle for hedging against inflation.

Table 9.9 **Asset Allocation, 2010–2014**

Asset class	Reflation/recovery	Deflation	Inflation/stagflation
Stocks	++	−	−
Bonds	+	++	−
Tips	+	−	++
Probability	?	?	?

Note: This table illustrates alternate ways to view the historic data: to view asset classes as a way to participate in certain favorable economic environments or a way to hedge against adverse economic conditions.

Source: Farrell (1998).

Generating an Asset Class Forecast

Reasonably good data are available on stocks, bonds, and Treasury bills since about the 1920s. This period encompasses numerous episodes: high growth, stagflation/inflation, and deflation, along with a major war, political upheavals, and social changes. With a long history, one might project that the future will look reasonably similar to the past, where growth occurred 70 percent of the time and inflation and deflation occurred 20 and 10 percent of the time, respectively. For an investor with a long planning horizon, say of ten–twenty years, this is likely to make sense.

Using the period 1929-2008 of risk-and-return measures, Table 9.10 shows selected asset mixes of stocks, bonds, and Treasury bills, along with their associated risks and returns. Risk and return varies with allocation to stocks compared with bonds and Treasury bills. Also, the portfolio return is lowest when stocks comprise 40 percent of the mix, whereas it is highest at a 70 percent allocation. A direct trade-off exists between risk and return: higher return is accompanied by higher risk. The range is generally consistent with common recommendations of asset mixes for long-term investors.

Assessing Risk

Assessing the degree of risk for an asset allocation is useful when either deflation and/or inflation occur at a materially greater rate than experienced historically. To assess the effects of either of these scenarios, the possibilities of scenarios can be changed from those occurring during the past, over the longer time horizons. For example, in such conditions an investor could assume that the probability of deflation is 40 percent rather than the historic average of 10 percent. By contrast, an investor could assume that the probability of inflation is 60 percent rather

Table 9.10 **Asset Allocation: Persistence of Longer-term Trends, 1929–2008**

	Return (%)	Risk (standard deviation) (%)	Allocation		
			Low risk (%)	Medium risk (%)	High risk (%)
Stocks	10.3	19.0	40.0	55.0	70.0
Bonds	5.4	7.6	35.0	30.0	20.0
Treasury bills	3.9	1.0	25.0	15.0	10.0
Return to allocation			7.0	7.9	8.7
Risk to allocation (standard deviation)			10.5	12.7	14.6

Note: This table shows selected asset mixes of stocks, bonds, and Treasury bills, along with their associated risks and returns.

Source: Farrell (2011).

than the historic 20 percent. In either case, deflation or inflation is plausible and worth testing to show the risk of adverse economic conditions.

To illustrate the case for deflation, assume a 40 percent probability of deflation, a 30 percent probability of inflation, and a 30 percent probability of growth. Over a five-year forecast period, this would imply two years of deflation, 1.5 years of inflation, and 1.5 years of growth. Calculating returns for these outcomes involves using historic data and applying the forecast weights. For example, the deflation period receives a 40 percent weight, while growth receives a 30 percent weight rather than a 70 percent weight. Similarly, reweighting would also occur for the covariance matrixes to accord with the forecast weightings rather than the eighty-year average of occurrences.

Regarding inflation, assume a probability of 60, 20, and 20 percent for inflation, growth, and deflation, respectively. Using a five-year forecast period, this could imply a year of deflation, followed by a year of reflation that results in three years of stagflation/inflation. Calculating returns involves using historic data and applying the forecast weights; for example, inflation would receive a 60 percent weight, while the growth weight would decrease from 70 percent to 20 percent. Similarly, the covariance matrixes would be reweighted according to the forecast weighting rather than the -80 year average.

Table 9.11 makes a comparison between the risk-return profile for the asset classes of stocks, bonds, and Treasury bills using the weights for a deflationary and an inflationary environment and that for the case of growth assuming that the past repeats itself. In the growth scenario, stocks have the highest return and risk, as measured by the standard deviation. In the deflation scenario, stocks provide the lowest return while showing the highest volatility. Returns for stocks in the stagflation scenario are better than under the deflation scenario but only do about as well as bonds and Treasury bills. Yet, risk under the stagflation and growth scenario remains similar but without compensation returns under stagflation.

Hedging the Risk

The previous section illustrates the risk of maintaining a standard longer-term allocation when assuming a pessimistic yet realistic view of the potential for inflation and/or deflation. With this potential, or even worse, at this especially uncertain time, developing some hedge against adverse outcomes would be reasonable. As illustrated, over the past eighty years of financial history, long-term (10 year) government bonds provide the best hedge against deflation, while T-bills are best in stagflation/inflation environments. With the introduction of TIPS in January 1997, these instruments should provide an even-better hedge in a rising price environment but suffer more greatly with deflation, as occurred in 2008.

Assuming that a high degree of uncertainty will characterize the financial environment over the next three to five years, hedging against these scenarios would be prudent. For example, one could increase the probability of inflation to 30 percent from the long-term average of 20 percent, while also increasing the

Table 9.11 **Risk-and-Return Trade-offs for Three Scenarios**

	Growth		Deflation		Stagflation	
Asset class	Return (%)	Risk (standard deviation) (%)	Return (%)	Risk (standard deviation) (%)	Return (%)	Risk (standard deviation) (%)
Stocks	10.3	19.0	2.8	22.4	5.3	18.9
Bonds	5.4	7.6	5.4	8.6	5.1	9.3
Treasury bills	3.9	1.0	3.8	0.7	5.4	0.8

Note: This table shows risk-return trade-offs when the probability of differing scenarios changes markedly from the past.

Source: Farrell (2011).

deflation probability to 20 percent from the 10 percent average. The allocation to growth then drops to 50 percent.

These assessed probabilities imply 1 year of deflation, 1.5 years of inflation, and 2.5 years of growth over the five-year planning horizon. This possibility might seem to be a reasonable but somewhat pessimistic scenario. This scenario could follow several patterns over the period, such as deflation at the start, followed by reflation, and then stagflation/inflation.

Using these probabilities, Table 9.12 indicates asset mixes that show various risk-return trade-offs. These asset combinations are the same as shown in Table 9.10. The stock allocation ranges between 40 and 70 percent. Returns are lower at all asset allocations, except Treasurey bills, than in Table 9.10. While the risk is lower at lower stock allocations, it is considerably higher at high allocations: the reward to risk is lower than in Table 9.10. Higher allocations to bonds and

Table 9.12 **Asset Allocation: Hedged**

			Allocation		
	Return (%)	Risk (standard deviation) (%)	Low risk (%)	Medium risk (%)	High risk (%)
Stock	8.25	18.50	40.0	55.0	70.0
Bond	5.39	8.14	35.0	30.0	20.0
Treasury bills	4.16	0.73	25.0	15.0	10.0
Return to allocation			6.2	7.0	7.3
Risk to allocation (standard deviation)			10.4	12.8	14.7

Note: This table gives an example of hedging an allocation when great uncertainty exists about the direction of deflation or inflation.

Source: Farrell (2011).

Treasury bills provide the hedging mechanism and reduce relative risk exposure. The allocations provide a more balanced posture toward risk and return.

Meanwhile, opportunities may be available to pursue a more activist approach as markets overshoot with respect to the prospect for inflation, or deflation, or growth. An investor could attempt to determine the degree of overshoot and attempt to tilt the asset mix away from a perceived bias toward a certain scenario. As long as markets continue to be highly volatile, these opportunities may abound. Over time, the market is likely to gravitate toward a more normalized course.

Tactical Asset Allocation (TAA)

As noted previously, the expected return, standard deviation, and covariance inputs to the asset allocation process are of a longer-term nature, which can be defined as a period of more than three years. However, these longer-term asset class expectations embody short-term risk-return parameters. Yet, the short-term return (say, the one-year return) will likely diverge from the average return to be realized over the longer period. In the absence of special information, proceeding as if the year-by-year results will be identical to the longer-term average is likely to be the best course of action. For example, if the expected return on stocks is 13 percent over a four-year forecasting period, the return realized each year could be assumed to be 13 percent.

Conversely, the position can be taken that an investor has special knowledge about the return from an asset class that differs from the average return expected over the longer period. The investor can vary the asset mix from the position established on the basis of longer-term projections to take advantage of the short-term forecast. For example, if for long-term planning purposes an organization is using the expected 13 percent return on stocks but forecasts a declining market for the coming 12 months, the investor could use this judgment to reduce his exposure to stocks to a level below that of its long-term view.

TAA is the process of forecasting shorter-term return movements and varying the asset mix accordingly. This activist management style is analogous to company or industry group selectivity. An investor using TAA is consciously taking an incremental risk in order to achieve incremental return. Engaging in this activity, however, presumes some sort of predictive capability with respect to market movements.

Forecasting the Market

This section reviews indicators that research shows are useful in providing insights into forecasting the market. First, two indicators are described that use a risk premium approach to assess the valuation status of the market at given time. Next, a description is provided that indicates how the correlation behavior of stocks and bonds not only can act as a hedge in portfolio construction but also can provide a leading indicator for the direction of stocks and bonds. Correspondingly, one could

attempt to deduce from the price action of stocks and bonds the likely expectations of investors for the stocks and bonds and adjust the asset mix accordingly.
Further, some economic and technical indicators that can provide insight into the
relative positioning of asset classes are discussed. Finally, this section concludes by
discussing how to use data about historic stock market returns to illustrate how
market environments can affect the potential for success of TAA.

Valuation: Risk Premium Approach

Assessing valuation can simply involve comparing current market returns with
those in other periods to develop some perspective on the current level. However,
comparing the current absolute returns with the returns on alternative investments,
such as bonds and Treasury bills, is also useful in order to develop the attractiveness measure, commonly referred to as *a risk premium valuation indicator.*

Evaluating the longer-range productivity of the risk-premium (expected stock
returns minus short-term rates) valuation indicator is possible by referencing the
data shown in Table 9.13. This table shows the relationship, which is measured
over the period 1951–1990, between risk premiums and realized returns. The risk
premium is segmented into seven brackets ranging from a low of 2 percent or less
to a high of 10 percent or greater. The table also shows the number of months during the period in which the premium was in a particular bracket. The risk premium

Table 9.13 **Risk Premiums and Realized Returns, 1951–1990**

Risk premium range (%)	Number of monthly obser- vations	Average subsequent excess return (stock return minus treasury bill return) (%)			Percentage of positive excess returns (stock returns minus treasury bill return) (%)		
		Months			Months		
		1	3	12	1	3	12
>10.0	10.0	2.5	6.8	26.1	80	80	100
8–9.9	64.0	1.9	4.8	16.7	66	78	89
6–7.9	102.0	0.5	2.0	6.1	57	63	63
5–5.9	64.0	0.7	1.6	4.8	61	70	67
4–4.9	107.0	0.4	1.8	2.7	60	64	62
2–3.9	96.0	−0.1	−1.4	2.8	48	42	60
< 2.0	2.5	−1.8	−1.7	−6.9	32	36	40
Total	468	0.5	1.5	5.7	57	61	66

Note: This table shows how the size of the equity risk premium correlates with the magnitude of realized returns.

Source: Arnott and Fabozzi (1992).

exceeds 10 percent for only ten months of the period and is at the low extreme of less than 2 percent for only 2.5 months. The risk premium is more frequently observed and evenly distributed across the brackets between 2 and 10 percent.

Again, Table 9.13 also shows the percentage of stock returns realized for 1, 3, and 12 months after the observed risk premium, as well as the percentage of times that the realized return is positive. When the risk premium exceeds 10 percent, subsequent stock returns are much larger and positive, with the percentage positive increasing from 80 percent after one month to 100 percent after one year for the period of measurement. Conversely, for months in which the risk premium was low (2 percent or less), the subsequent stock returns are negative and increasingly negative as the time period increases from one month to one year. Correspondingly, the percentage of positive subsequent returns is low, implying a high probability of subpar returns when the risk premium is low.

Further, data in Table 9.14 indicate a strong positive relationship between the size of the risk premium and subsequent stock returns. Realized returns are consistently higher as the risk premium increases, and conversely, the realized returns are lower or negative as the risk premium decreases. These return differences are statistically significant.

Figure 9.2 illustrates another approach to risk-premium analysis. In this case, a Moody's Baa bond yield provides the base return against which stocks should be measured. These bonds reflect a certain degree of risk but not to the extent of stocks. Many investors use the bonds as a relative benchmark. These bonds also tend to move in tandem with stocks over time. The bottom panel of figure 9.2 shows this relationship. The middle panel of the figure shows volatility, as measured by the standard deviation, reflecting changes in the S&P 500 over time. Volatility moves in concert with investor changes in risk aversion, moving high when great concern exists and moving down when investor concerns are low. The top panel shows the price action of the S&P 500 over the period 1930–2009.

As shown as shaded periods in Figure 9.2, the volatility index is generally elevated in bear market years. Volatility spikes in periods of declining economic

Table 9.14 **Perspectives on Investor Expectations**

Indicator	12/31/07 (%)	12/31/08 (%)	6/30/09 (%)
Ten-year Treasury bond yield	4.1	2.4	3.7
Treasury bond return		20.0	−8.7
S&P 500 return		−37.0	4.0
S&P 500 return/Treasury bond return		−57.0	12.7
Implied inflation (TIPS)	2.3	0.3	1.9

Note: This table shows the relationship between the size of the risk premium and subsequent stock returns.

Source: Farrell (2011).

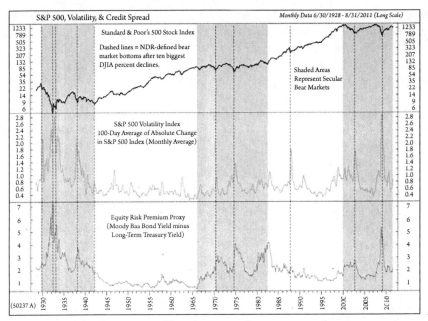

Figure 9.2 Equity risk premiums. This chart provides a measure of equity attractiveness or unattractiveness.

activity or elevated inflation, most notably in the depression period and from the 1970s to the early 1980s. Correspondingly, the risk premium increases along with volatility during these periods and again most notably in the 2007–2010 time frame. Both risk and expected return are high. During other periods, when volatility is low, the risk premium reflects a lower investor demand for return.

Stock-Bond Correlation: Leading Indicator or Hedge

Table 9.8 shows the tops of bull markets (bull market tops) and the bottoms of bear markets ((bear market bottoms as well as losses associated with bear markets. The table also shows the dates where a negative correlation began relative to each of the bull market tops. The final column shows the degree of lead, lag, or coincident action of negative correlation around bull market tops.

For 11 of the 13 periods on Table 9.8, the beginning stage of negative correlation precedes the bull market tops. These leads range from short as one to two months to as long as nine to 11 months, with the others falling between four to six months. The two periods of coincidence and lag are relative to extended periods of negative correlation that span essentially the full period of the bear market. In analyzing the period 2000–2003, some confusion may exist in dating the bear market because of the catastrophe of September 11, 2001, and shocks that occurred around the beginning of the bear market. Two other periods of short leads of one month in 1929–1933 and 1956–1957 were followed by longer-lasting bear markets where the negative correlation persisted over an extended period. One short lead of one month in June to September 1998 is also associated with the shortest bear market (less than four months) over the study period.

The other eight periods of negative correlation precedent to bear markets range from four to six months to as long as nine months to 11 months. Of the eight associated bear markets, six are relatively short in duration and last less than a year, although some are quite severe in speed and depth: those of 1937–1938, 1961–1962, and August to October 1987. The most recent bear market in 2007–2009 is both extended, at 17 months, and financially destructive, with a decline of 54 percent over the period. The possibility of a financial meltdown leading to a severe breakdown of economic activity with deflation becoming palpable, rather than simply an underlying fear as in 1987 and 1998, led to the severity and length of this bear market. At a minimum, periods of negative correlation appear to provide useful information on the state of the market, with the possibility of providing some insight into possibly adjusting the risk exposure of an asset allocation. Naturally, implementing this information successfully depends on the analytical skill and judgment of the portfolio manager.

Table 9.8 also illustrates that long-term Treasury bonds provide effective diversification (hedging) over the 13bear markets of the study period. In all 13 cases, bonds outperform stocks over the full range of each of the bear markets, with bond returns negative in only three instances, and then only moderately so. The spread between large losses for stocks and generally positive returns for bonds is quite substantial, with the exception of the bear market of 1956–1957, which was long lasting but moderate in its degree of loss. Inflationary pressures building toward the long period of stagflation of the 1970s and early 1980s may have partially driven the relative large loss of 8.37 percent for bonds in 1968–1970

Investor Expectations

Analyzing how economic environments interact with capital market returns can be useful to provide perspective on what investors might be expecting with respect to deflation, growth, or inflation at any given point in time. The 14-month period from the end of 2007 to the end of the first quarter of 2009 provides a good illustration of this situation. This period is most notable because of its recovery and extreme volatility, from a peaking at the end of 2007 to a year-end decline that was the most severe of the postwar periods. One of the strongest stock market rebounds followed, throughout 2009.

Table 9.14 shows some relevant economic and financial data for December 2007, December 2008, and June 2009, which can be used to characterize how expectations changed over that period. For example, this table shows returns for stocks (on the S&P 500) and bonds (-10-year Treasuries).

At the beginning of the period measured in table 9.14 (December 2007), the yield on the 10-year Treasury bond is 4.1 percent, but at the end of the year, the yield declines

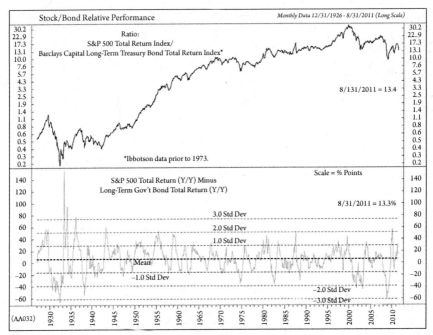

Figure 9.3 Stock-bond relative performance. This chart provides perspective on the relative attractiveness of stocks versus bonds that can reach extremes at certain times.

to a postwar low of 2.4 percent. Correspondingly, the bond return is 20 percent for the year, while stocks decline by 37 percent, showing a strong negative counteraction.

By the end of the first quarter in the table (2009), the spread between bonds and stocks is at three standard deviations below the mean and in line with the all-time low in the early 1930s (during the depression), as Figure 9.3 shows. The relative market action of stocks and ten-year Treasuries along with TIPS pricing imply that the market expectations for a deflationary environment moving forward are strong. Conversely, expectations for inflation/stagflation are exceptionally low, as are prospects for growth and stock returns.

Table 9.14 also shows how these variables responded after the market bottoming at the end of 2009. The 10-year Treasury bond yield declines in price, resulting in a yield of 3.7 percent from a major low of 2.4 percent the year before. Correspondingly, the implied inflation rate, as shown by TIPS pricing, recovers to a more normal rate of 1.9 percent. Stocks recover dramatically from a March 2009 low as the return rose by 37 percent, one of the strongest over a long financial history.

Economic and Technical Indicators

Although a multitude of indicators can be helpful in providing perspective on the market, giving a comprehensive review of these many indicators is beyond the scope of this chapter. Consequently, this section classifies these indicators into broad categories of economic and technical types and defines subsets of these categories. Additionally, this section offers examples of indicators that may be useful for gaining perspective on category type.

ECONOMIC INDICATORS

As a general guideline, recognizing that the stock and bond markets are efficient discounting mechanisms is important in order to assume that reported economic data are generally impounded in market prices. Thus, looking for economic indicators that can offer insights into subsequent price action is important.

Economic indicators could include the following examples:

- **Rate of change indicators.** Changes in the rate of the unemployment may serve as a leading indicator of the economy and, at a minimum, reflect the current state of the economy.
- **Cyclical indicators.** The ratio of coincident to lagging indicators can provide some insights into the current status and future course of the business cycle.
- **Expectations surveys.** Surveys conducted with bank loan officers can provide insights into whether a future easing or tightening of credit will occur.

TECHNICAL INDICATORS

Whereas economic indicators are external to the stock and bond markets, technical indicators help investors develop insights from the current action of stock or bond markets and serve as internal indicators. These technical indicators can be broadly categorized as momentum or mean reversion types.

Momentum indicators include the following:

- **Trend.** The 200-day moving average of a broad index such as the S&P 500 is generally considered positive when rising and negative when declining.
- **Breadth.** This indicator tends to be positive when broad participation occurs across industries and global markets. It is typically negative when the participation is narrow, indicating that few industries or global markets are rising.

Mean reversion indicators include the following:

- **Volatility.** When volatility, as measured by standard deviation or the VIX Index, reaches extremes, it can signal extreme pessimism when high or extreme optimism when low. Investors should show caution when volatility is low and be prepared to buy when it is high, reflecting pessimism.
- **Liquidity.** When money growth is low and demand is high, stocks tend to be under pressure. Alternatively, when money growth is high, stocks tend to do well. These changes in liquidity especially affect small-cap stocks.
- **Sentiment.** When investors are overly optimistic or pessimistic, this can be reflected in some gauges. Being cautious is appropriate when excessive optimism is present in the market. Investors can look for opportunities when pessimism abounds.

Stock Market: Cyclical and Secular Behavior

Figure 9.4 shows stock history from 1900 to 2010, which is classified into phases of
secular bull and secular bear markets determined by Ned Davis Research (NDR).
For example, the period from 1982 to 2000 represents a secular bull phase, whereas
the following period from the beginning of 2000 to the end of 2010 represents a
bear phase that may continue into the future. Both bull and bear phases can persist for fairly extended periods, averaging about 15 years. Alternating phases, with
bull markets followed by bear markets and vice-versa, also occur. Nevertheless,
the trend in the market is upward over time, with bull markets showing higher
returns than the losses in bear markets and lasting longer than bear markets.

Table 9.15 shows the average performance of cyclical bull as well as cyclical
bear markets spanning over the longer period, as determined by researchers at
NDR. The table shows 34 cases of cyclical bull markets and 34 total cases of
cyclical bear markets, which alternate over time (bear following bull and vice-
versa). The average gain during the bull phase of all markets was 85.6 percent and
the average duration 751 days. Conversely, bear markets lasted roughly about half
as long at an average of 410 days, with a mean loss of 31.5 percent, or roughly
about one-third, offsetting the average bull market gain.

Table 9.15 shows the average duration and gains or losses from cyclical bull
and bear markets in secular markets. During secular bull markets, the average
duration of 508 days and a mean gain 64.3 percent. Within secular bear markets,
the average duration is 472 days days and the mean losses are 36.3 percent.

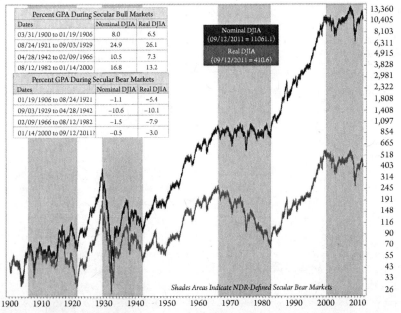

Figure 9.4 Equity Performance during Secular Bull and Bear Markets. This chart
defines periods of secular bull markets as well as secular bear markets and shows
equity returns (or losses) during those periods.

Table 9.15. **Cyclical Markets during Secular Bull and Bear Markets**

All cyclical bull markets

Statistic	# Cases	% Gain	% GPA	Days
Mean	34	85.6	194.9	751
Median	34	69.1	36.8	614

All cyclical bear markets

Statistic	# Cases	% Loss	% GPA	Days
Mean	34	−31.5	−36.1	410
Median	34	−27.0	−29.9	375

Cyclical bull markets

Statistic	# Cases	% Gain	% GPA	Days
Mean	16	109.5	31.7	1,024
Median	16	77.2	27.4	870

Cyclical bear markets

Statistic	# Cases	% Loss	% GPA	Days
Mean	12	−22.8	−37.7	295
Median	12	−19.4	−23.4	245

Within secular bull markets

Statistic	# Cases	% Gain	% GPA	Days
Mean	18	64.3	340.0	508
Median	18	55.4	41.9	371

Within secular bear markets

Statistic	# Cases	% Loss	% GPA	Days
Mean	22	−36.3	−35.3	472
Median	22	−33.7	−30.0	521

Note: This table shows the average performance of cyclical bull as well as bear markets for various periods.

Source: Ned Davis Research, Inc.

The changing behavior of the market, bull to bear and back again, has relevance to the ease of implementing a strategy of TAA. For example, using TAA strategies would have been more difficult during the 1950s and early 1960s, and again in the early 1980s–2000. These periods of unusually favorable market experience produce returns that are high on average and market declines that are relatively short lived. Investors attempting to forecast the market and who recommend selling would have had to be quite nimble to successfully time a sale

and repurchase. This problem would have been especially severe for large investors because establishing positions requires substantial time. For example, 18
months in 1969 and 1970 and 21 months in 1973 and1974 are more severe and
contracted than in the previous period. Investors purchasing funds in an attempt
to protect against a market decline would have had greater opportunity to successfully time a sale and repurchase over a period of 18 to 21 months than in the
9-month interval of the earlier period.

Summary and Conclusions

Despite being highly important to long-term investors, making asset allocation
decisions can often be difficult. For example, at the beginning of the twenty-first
century, making a strong case for a heavy portfolio weighting of large-cap US
stocks might have been considered easy. This would have been well supported
by the strong performance of these equities during the secular bull market that
had begun in the early 1980s. Unfortunately, this asset class proved disappointing, generating virtually no positive return throughout most of the decade; other
classes showed strong performance. Yet, a decision in early 2009 to commit to
equities would have been very difficult because of palpable fear, strong emotions,
and the strongly negative consensus among investors at that time. The indicators
discussed in this chapter suggested that equities in that period were attractively
valued both absolutely and relatively. In retrospect, a decision to commit to equities should have been "easy."

Currently, much uncertainty exists in the market. Hence, making a decision on
asset allocation is not "easy" either emotionally or based on objective indicators. Thus,
developing portfolio balance and waiting for opportunities to emerge seem prudent.

Discussion Questions

1. Compare and contrast the historic approach to the scenario approach in generating inputs to the asset allocation process.
2. How does the status of the secular market (bull or bear) affect the difficulty
   of implementing a TAA strategy?
3. Describe how the risk premium approach provides perspective on the relative
   attractiveness of asset classes.
4. Compare the underlying "concepts" driving the different technical indicators.
   Give an example with a description for each.

References

Arnott, Robert D., and Frank J. Fabozzi. 1992. *Active Asset Allocation: State-of-the-Art Portfolio
   Policies, Stategies, and Tactics*, 2nd ed. Chicago: Probus.

Brinson, Gary P., L. Randolph Hood, and Gilbert L. Beebower. 1986. "Determinants of Portfolio Performance." *Financial Analysts Journal* 42:4, 39–44.

Brinson, Gary P., Brian D. Singer, and Gilbert L. Beebower. 1991. "Determinants of Portfolio Performance II: An Update." *Financial Analysts Journal* 47:3, 40–48.

Fama, Eugene F. 1975. "Short-Term Interest Rates as Predictors of Inflation." *American Economic Review* 65:3, 269–282.

Farrell, James L., Jr. 2011. "Asset Allocation under Extreme Uncertainty." *Journal of Portfolio Management* 37:2, 72–82.

Farrell, James L., Jr., 1998. *Portfolio Management: Theory and Application*, 2nd ed. New York: McGraw-Hill.

Ibbotson, Roger G., and Paul D. Kaplan. 2000. "Does Asset Allocation Explain 40, 90 or 100 Percent of Performance?" *Financial Analysts Journal* 56:1, 26–33.

Ned Davis Research, Inc. Venice, FL.

Xiong, James X., Roger G. Ibbotson, Thomas M. Idzorek, and Peng Chen. 2010. "The Equal Importance of Asset Allocation and Active Management." *Financial Analysts Journal* 66:2, 22–30.

10

Asset Allocation Models

J. CLAY SINGLETON
George D. and Harriet W. Cornell Professor of Finance
Crummer Graduate School, Rollins College

Introduction

Interest in asset allocation models is motivated by an intuition suggesting that how much weight a portfolio assigns to different assets has a strong influence on that portfolio's risk and return. The common phrases "Don't put all your eggs in one basket" and "Nothing ventured, nothing gained" capture the sense that asset allocation is important. Investors understand that a portfolio constructed with 70 percent equity and 30 percent fixed income will have very different performance characteristics from a portfolio with 30 percent equity and 70 percent fixed income. This introductory section discusses the importance of asset allocation to portfolio performance.

Not content to rely on intuition alone, a series of researchers investigated how much asset allocation contributes to portfolio performance. Brinson, Hood, and Beebower (1986) and Brinson, Singer, and Beebower (1991) are among the first to empirically measure the relative influence of asset allocation. These authors' most quoted conclusion is that more than 90 percent of the variability in a typical portfolio's performance is due to asset allocation Brinson, Hood, and Beebower (1986, 137). As will be discussed, some readers reach conclusions that this research cannot actually support.

In a follow-up article, Ibbotson and Kaplan (2000) point out that the influence of asset allocation depends on the question asked. The Brinson research (1986 and 1991) asks how much of the variability of a portfolio's returns over time is explained by asset allocation. Ibbotson and Kaplan confirm that the answer to this question is around 90 percent. They then suggest the research question could be posed as how much of the variation in a cross-section of portfolio returns at a point in time is explained by asset allocation. The authors find that the answer to this question is about 40 percent. Ibbotson and Kaplan go on to investigate the question many readers incorrectly thought the Brinson research asked: What portion of a portfolio's historical return is explained by asset allocation? They cannot answer this question using return data alone. Ibbotson and Kaplan point out that by definition the weighted average performance of all portfolios is the market return. Because active managers charge fees, their performance, on average, will be less than the market return by the amount of their fees.

While Ibbotson and Kaplan's (2000) research helps clarify and extend the scope of the original Brinson studies, their findings are incomplete because the study does not control for the pervasive influence of the market. Ibbotson and Kaplan (p. 29) acknowledge, almost as an aside, that their results stem "primarily from the funds' [portfolios'] participation in the capital markets in general, not from the specific asset allocation policies of each fund. In other words, the results of the Brinson et al. studies and our results...are a case of a rising tide lifting all boats."

Xiong et al. (2010, pp. 27–28) return to this observation and control for the influence of the market and conclude:

> By decomposing a portfolio's total return into its three components—(1) the market return, (2) the asset allocation policy return in excess of the market return, and (3) the return from active portfolio management— we found that market return dominates the other two return components. Taken together, market return and asset allocation policy return in excess of market return dominate active portfolio management. This finding confirms the widely held belief that market return and asset allocation policy return in excess of market return are collectively the dominant determinant of total return variations, but it clarifies the contribution of each. More importantly, after removing the dominant market return component of total return, we answered the question, Why do portfolio returns differ from one another within a peer group? Our results show that within a peer group, asset allocation policy return in excess of market return and active portfolio management are equally important.

This clarification does not diminish the importance of asset allocation as a determinant of portfolio performance. Rather, this stream of research confirms the intuition that asset allocation is an essential ingredient in portfolio management. Even without this empirical confirmation, theoreticians have pursued asset allocation models for almost as long as assets have been assembled into portfolios.

Before discussing the organization of the remainder of the chapter, the reader should note that the literature reviews in this chapter do not include all the related research. Such a project would be encyclopedic and would not serve the purpose of discussing the asset allocation models most relevant to investment practice. This approach is not intended to slight any particular stream of research but rather to focus on asset allocation models that have practical applications.

The rest of the chapter includes four sections. The first section explores the asset allocation models that have guided the practice of portfolio construction and maintenance. The one dominant model is Markowitz's mean-variance efficient approach. Other models have been advanced and this section reviews their attempts to improve upon the Markowitz model, including variations proposed by Markowitz himself. The second section returns to the premise of this chapter, which is that a good asset allocation model can be defined as one that is used by investors to construct and manage their portfolios. This section describes new research, first published in this chapter, on the asset allocation model revealed by the US wealth portfolio, which measures how US investors actually allocate their wealth between the broad categories of equity, fixed income, and real estate. By relying on the wisdom of crowds, the aggregate US wealth portfolio reveals characteristics of the underlying asset allocation models investors employ. This section adds to the previous literature by calculating the investor return expectations that are consistent with this aggregate portfolio. The return expectations revealed by in the aggregate wealth portfolio appear to be more reasonable than a Markowitz model's theoretical allocations, suggesting that the Markowitz model is not being used by investors. The third section is concerned with asset allocation maintenance or rebalancing. Any asset allocation will be revised by market action over time. A complete asset allocation model, therefore, must provide guidance on when to rebalance a portfolio back to its design specifications. Too much rebalancing generates unnecessary transactions costs, while too little rebalancing allows the portfolio to deviate materially from the risk-return trade-off inherent in its original design. Rebalancing is complex. This section, however, identifies one unifying research study that clarifies how much to rebalance and puts other studies in perspective. The chapter concludes with a final section summarizing asset allocation models.

History of Asset Allocation Models

Two publications by Markowitz (1952, 1959) mark the beginning of modern portfolio theory. The investment problems Markowitz addresses, however, were not new. Bernstein (2002, pp. 13–14), who spent more than 50 years as an investment professional, recalls what portfolio management was like in the 1950s: "We did understand the importance of diversification, in both individual positions and in asset allocation. The diversification we provided, however, was determined by seat-of-the-pants deliberations, with no systematic evaluation beyond hunch. Although risk was an ever-present consideration, in our shop at least, the idea of attaching a number to investment risk was inconceivable." Markowitz marked a turning point in asset allocation models and this section begins with a brief review of his contributions. The discussion then turns to a review of other models that attempt to address the theoretical or practical shortcomings in Markowitz's model.

THE MARKOWITZ MODEL

Markowitz, as an economist, was careful to situate his model within the economic canon of utility theory and probability analysis. The contribution for which he is most remembered, however, is his mathematical solution to the problem of constructing a portfolio by minimizing the expected variance for a specified level of expected return. Given forecasts of asset returns, their standard deviations, and correlations, as well as the investor's risk tolerance, Markowitz's algorithm leads to the *efficient frontier*, which is that set of portfolios having the minimum expected variance for the entire range of expected returns. These portfolios differ in their asset allocation as a function of their expected risk and return. From an investment perspective, portfolios not in the efficient set should not attract any funds because there is always an efficient portfolio with less risk and the same return or with the same risk and more return. The necessary and sufficient assumptions for the Markowitz model to hold are that all investors:

1. measure returns with the probability distribution of expected returns over a single investment horizon;
2. maximize their expected utility of wealth over a single investment horizon with diminishing marginal utility;
3. measure portfolio risk with variance;
4. construct portfolios based on expected return and variance alone; and
5. seek return and avoid risk.

These assumptions produce many now-familiar results that were a revelation at the time they were written. One is that the expected return for a portfolio is the weighted average of the expected returns of the constituent securities, but the risk of a portfolio is not the weighted average of the variances of the constituent securities, because variance depends on both the constituent variances and the pair-wise correlations. Another result is that the variance of a portfolio depends more on the average pair-wise correlation than on the average variance. That is, the risk of individual securities is not so much dependent on their variances as it is on their average pair-wise correlation with other securities in the portfolio. A third result is that all investors will avoid holding individual securities and prefer portfolios because diversification controls risk.

Mean-variance optimization, a form of quadratic programming, is usually used to calculate Markowitz portfolios. This algorithm traces the efficient frontier—represented as the right branch of a hyperbola in expected return, standard deviation space—consisting of portfolios that have the highest expected return for every level of standard deviation risk or, equivalently, the lowest risk for every level of expected return. Markowitz assumed that investors would choose a portfolio from the efficient set based on their risk tolerance. These and other implications of this model are the subject of subsequent research, described in the discussion that follows.

The discussion of Markowitz's asset allocation model is not complete without including William F. Sharpe's contributions. Sharpe's publication, "A Simplified Model for Portfolio Analysis" (Sharpe 1963), which was based on his PhD dissertation, paved the way for a simpler solution to the then computer-constrained application of the Markowitz algorithm. Beyond saving computer time, Sharpe shows that in the presence of a risk-free asset the efficient frontier shifts to a line connecting the risk-free asset (the intercept) and one risky portfolio (a point of tangency on the original efficient frontier). Sharpe's work led to the capital asset pricing model (CAPM), a theory of the relationship between risk and return in the capital markets, which is beyond the scope of this chapter.

RELAXING THE MARKOWITZ MODEL ASSUMPTIONS

The academic investment literature offers many examples of alternatives to the Markowitz model. In tribute to the enduring stature of the Markowitz model, however, many of these should be labeled elaborations because they attempt to address perceived shortcomings in either the model's assumptions or results. This section reviews each of the five Markowitz assumptions by highlighting a few of the more prominent studies associated with each assumption. The section concludes with some examples of the real-world challenges inherent in using the Markowitz model to manage portfolios.

Single Investment Horizon (Assumptions One and Two)

The framework for investigating multiple investment horizons can be traced to Merton's (1973) work on lifetime portfolio choice and continuous time models (see also Fama and Schwert 1977).

Research by Brennan, Schwartz, and Lagnado (1997) provides one possible solution to the problem posed by multiple horizons. These authors suppose a three state-variable world in which short- and long-term bond rates as well as the dividend yield follow a joint Markov process. Because the authors use a stochastic optimal control algorithm, they address the potential dimensionality problem of too many variables by limiting the model to three known state variables. They generate a large number of mean-variance optimal portfolios and observe that given a long investment horizon, the optimal portfolio invests significantly more in the risky asset classes than does the optimal portfolio with a short horizon. The embedded assumption is mean reversion in returns, which makes stocks less risky than bonds in the long term. While the authors cite computational restrictions that constrain the number of state variables as a limitation of their study, the real constraint is their formulation of the asset allocation problem in a world with more than one investment horizon. A realistic model with multiple horizons requires many more state variables. Even so, the authors conclude that extending their asset allocation model to allow for more uncertainty would reduce leverage and turnover in the optimal portfolio, both commonsense results.

Campbell and Viceira's (2002) summary work provides the most detailed analysis of the consequences of extending Markowitz's single investment horizon. In this monograph, the authors introduce markets with short- and long-term investors, inflation, mean reversion in returns, intertemporal hedging, and labor income. They cite the research of Brennan, Schwartz, and Lagnado (1997); Balduzzi and Lynch (1999); Brandt (1999); and Barberis (2000), as well as the theoretical work of Modigliani and Sutch (1966) and Fama and Schwert (1977) as precedents.

Campbell and Viceira (2002) begin by noting that using extant utility theory and assuming that relative risk aversion is independent of wealth, long-term investors should construct the same portfolios as short-term investors. The authors point out that this conclusion holds only in the absence of labor income and with constant investment opportunities. More realistically, investment opportunities are time varying, if only because the real rate of interest changes. This observation allows the authors to argue that mean-variance optimal portfolios will depend on an investor's horizon.

In successive chapters, the authors introduce more realistic assumptions by including a variable risk premium, time variation in excess returns on stocks and bonds, mean reversion in stock and bond returns, and labor income that follows the investor's life cycle. Predictably, all of these variables affect the portfolios that short- and long-term investors find optimal. In general, long-term investors prefer portfolios that reflect their age—favoring risky assets when young—and the riskiness of their labor income—with more income risk leading to safer financial assets.

Munk and Sørenson (2010) are among several researchers who build on the Campbell and Viceira (2002) results. They tie labor income to the business cycle and use *The Panel Study of Income Dynamics*, an annual survey of US personal income, to calibrate their model. Most importantly for purposes here, their model shows that Campbell and Viceira's results—suggesting that asset allocation is a function of variations in labor income—hold under income uncertainty and over the business cycle.

Expanding Markowitz's model to accommodate multiple investment horizons is anything but straightforward. Many years of research using a plethora of complex mathematical tools shows that the answer corresponds to what many financial planners recommend: the appropriateness of risky assets depends on time horizon and the income requirements. Relaxing the assumptions about preferences (that investors maximize their expected utility of wealth over a single investment horizon with diminishing marginal utility) and beliefs (that investors measure portfolio risk with variance and construct portfolios based on expected return and variance alone) is fortunately not as complex but no less important.

Preferences and Beliefs (Assumptions Three, Four, and Five)

Specifying the parameters of portfolio construction in terms of mean and variance is equivalent to restricting investors' beliefs about the probability distributions of expected returns (Rothchild and Stiglitz, 1970). Invoking utility theory means making assumptions about investor preferences. Under the fifth assumption, Markowitz investors seek return and avoid risk in the form of variance.

Markowitz (1952) recognized that portfolio choice based on expected return and variance required a quadratic utility function. He also acknowledged that a quadratic utility function was a reasonable description of rational behavior only over a portion of its range. This range depends on the function's inherent maximum value and the largest return expected for the portfolio. When this expected return is less than the utility function's maximum, the function indicates a decreasing utility of wealth, which implies investors no longer prefer more to less (contradicting common sense and assumption two). As Meyer (1987) notes, the amount of literature on utility theory and portfolio choice has grown considerably since Markowitz's original publications, and other authors such as Bigelow (1993) and Mathews (2004) do not disagree. Little would be served by rehashing this literature here. Sharpe (2007) provides a contemporary perspective in an article in which he reviews the three conditions that justify considering only mean and variance as the basis for an asset allocation model, either:

1. all relevant probability distributions have the same form and the mean and variance are sufficient statistics to identify the full distribution (e.g., a normal distribution), or
2. investors have quadratic utility functions (implausible over a wide range of returns for most investors), or
3. a quadratic utility function is an adequate approximation of the investors' true utility function over the range of probability distributions to be evaluated.

Sharpe (1987) first proposed an improved algorithm assuming the perspective of maximizing expected utility. In this article he uses a swapping procedure to replace the traditional quadratic programming solution and shows that if the investor's utility is quadratic then mean-variance optimization maximizes expected utility. He then uses the same swapping approach to investigate the optimal portfolio for investors with utility functions that exhibit hyperbolic absolute risk aversion (HARA). These functions are important because they can be used to describe investors who have a minimum required return or constant relative risk aversion. In this case, optimal portfolios are different from mean-variance optimal portfolios when investors have something other than quadratic utility. Sharpe (2007) points out that his swapping procedure requires specifying discrete distributions for all potential scenarios, which is less general than the continuous distributions used by the mean-variance approach. For our purposes here, however, the most important result is that Markowitz-style optimal asset allocation models are valid without insisting on the quadratic utility functions that have bedeviled academic theorists for so many years.

The academic jury is still out on which utility function or functions fulfill all the requirements of rational behavior. Evidence shows, however, that the quadratic function is not the first choice.

In the preface to the second printing of Markowitz (1959), the author acknowledges the objections of Mandelbrot (1961), Fama (1963), and Mandelbrot and Taylor (1967) suggesting that the distribution of stock prices does not have a defined second moment (for example, stable Paretian distributions) or, equivalently, has tails that are too fat to be consistent with a normal (Gaussian) distribution. In response, Markowitz says that the embedded assumption that leads to the "strange conclusion" of these authors is that the probability distribution of fluctuations in stock prices is invariant to time, so that the probability distribution of tick-by-tick fluctuations is the same as the distribution of year-to-year fluctuations. He is also suspicious of the analysis that leads to the stable Paretian distribution on the basis that, by assumption, either stock price fluctuations are normally distributed or they have an infinite variance, excluding from empirical consideration all bounded and most unbounded distributions.

Many subsequent authors investigate the empirical distribution of stock prices. Most are not reviewed here because a few illustrations are sufficient to suit the current purpose of considering the historical role of beliefs in asset allocation models. Ghose and Kroner (1995, p. 225), for example, find that the stable Paretian distribution is consistent with autoregressive conditional heteroskedascity (GARCH) models, implying that "many of the findings of fat-tailed distributions in finance since Mandelbrot (1963) could be caused by temporal clustering of volatility" and that "the GARCH model characterizes the [financial] data better than the stable Paretian model."

More recently, Garcia, Renault, and Veredas (2011) illustrate their indirect method of detecting stable distributions of the S&P 500 Index returns over five-minute intervals. They find, once again, that the index displays fat tails that are inconsistent with normal distributions. In an intriguing twist on stock return distribution research, Brada, Ernst, and Van Tassel (1966) observe that when stock price changes are defined by differencing based on the volume of transactions rather than elapsed time, they do not have an excessive number of extreme events. Further, as the number of transactions increases to the largest number of transactions over which the price has remained unchanged, the distribution approaches the normal distribution. Finally, according to an interview in Kaplan (2009), Mandelbrot continues to insist that stock prices have an unbounded variance. Despite many years of research, the debate continues. More relevant to this chapter, however, are the implications for alternative asset allocation models.

ALTERNATIVE ASSET ALLOCATION MODELS

The non-Gaussian (non-normal) stock price distributions most studied in the context of asset allocation models exhibit skewness and kurtosis. Researchers, therefore, propose asset allocation models that incorporate these higher moments. As before, Markowitz (1959) anticipates some of these models when he considers investors who measure risk by semivariance instead of standard deviation. By using the semivariance, Markowitz supposes that investors have a downside loss limit and calculate the average of the squared observations below that limit rather than around the mean like the standard deviation. Anticipating behavioral finance by several decades, the concept of semivariance is consistent with that of loss aversion developed by Kahneman and Tversky (1979). Markowitz, however, confines his observations to the class of utility functions that would be consistent with preferences for limiting losses. From a beliefs perspective, semivariance implies a preference for right-skewed distributions.

Skewness Asset Allocation Models

Various authors, such as Jean (1971, 1973), Arditti and Levy (1975), Bawa and Lindenberg (1977), Simkowitz and Beedles (1978), and Harlow and Rao (1989), all present versions of a three-moment asset allocation model. This research continues through explorations of coskewness by Harvey and Siddique (2000), Adesi, Gagliardini, and Urga (2004), and Xu (2007). Despite the popularity of this research, Harlow and Rao's (1991, p. 39) claim that asset allocation models that are based on downside risk "offer the potential for portfolios that are more attractive than mean-variance portfolios" cannot be sustained. One problem is that these models lack generality because every investor's downside loss limit is potentially different. Similar problems arise with safety-first asset allocation models, such as those proposed by Arzac and Bawa (1977). According to Singleton and Wingender (1986), another problem is that skewness in individual stock returns and equity portfolios does not persist. As Singleton and Wingender (p. 341) point out, skewness can be reliably created with options or other assets, so the search for asset allocation models based on skewness in individual assets or portfolios is a "misallocation of resources."

Stochastic Dominance Asset Allocation Models

Stochastic dominance is a tool for decision making under uncertainty. This technique provides a ranking of probabilistic outcomes, such that A is preferred to B if and only if A provides at least as good an outcome as B (and involves less risk) in every possible future state. This approach avoids the complications of specifying preferences or beliefs and, as such, is an alternative to rather than a substitute for the Markowitz approach. Instead, stochastic dominance skirts the necessity to specify either preferences or beliefs by relying on historical probability distributions embedded in states of nature, assumed to occur with equal (or known) probabilities.

Bawa, Lindenberg, and Rafsky (1979) defend this approach by asserting that (1) investors typically choose between portfolios based on historical data; (2) the stochastic dominance criteria reduce to the mean-variance rule, assuming a continuous distribution (i.e., normal); and (3) using observed distributions is consistent with a Bayesian perspective. Stochastic dominance is not a popular technique—either in theory or in practice—because it does not allow analysts to enumerate efficient sets. Because the number of possible portfolios that are possible for even two securities is infinite (assuming security positions are infinitely divisible), determining efficient portfolios based on stochastic dominance is a formidable problem. From a purely economic perspective, a dominated asset would have no market value. Despite more recent work by Kuosmanen (2004) that uses discrete states of nature, as an asset allocation model stochastic dominance continues to promise more than it delivers.

Ad Hoc Asset Allocation Models

Asset allocation models used by professional investment practitioners are often more ad hoc than they are based on any theoretical model. Conventional wisdom, such as that which suggests that the equity allocation percentage should be 100 (or now 120 as people live longer) minus the beneficiary's age, is popular with financial planners and reflects the idea that portfolios should become less risky as investors age. The rationale is that younger investors have more time to recoup losses in risky investments. Like all generalities, however, this approach has some serious drawbacks. Consider the young investor who starts investing in a drawn-out bear market. The early losses are very difficult to make up. Financial planners are fond of constructing examples in which an individual who begins to invest at age 21 has far more capital at retirement than someone who invests twice as much every year and begins at age 31. These examples can be easily contradicted by choosing a starting date when the market turns down dramatically.

The other problem with these ad hoc rules is that people can live a long time in retirement—often thirty years or more. Conservative investment portfolios heavily weighted to bonds have little resistance to inflation and may not serve retirees well. Regardless of these problems, target date funds that are designed to become more conservative over time are popular with investors. According to Tom Idzorek (2011), chief investment officer of Ibbotson Associates, a Morningstar company, "Total assets in mutual fund-based Target Maturity Funds rose to $340 billion at the end of 2010, their highest level. The new cash flows into these funds averaged about $45 billion per year over the last five years."

Despite decades of research on alternative models—theoretical and ad hoc—the Markowitz approach continues to dominate discussions of theory. In practice, however, this model faces widely recognized and formidable challenges.

REAL-WORLD CHALLENGES OF IMPLEMENTING MARKOWITZ ASSET ALLOCATION MODELS

The appeal of using mean-variance optimization to calculate Markowitz efficient portfolios lies in its mathematical rigor. No judgment is required to run the mean-variance algorithm. Unfortunately, practitioners must overcome four major problems in deciding on the appropriate forecasts to satisfy the model's requirements for expected returns, variances, and correlations. First, these expected values are not easy to estimate. While security analysts' opinions of expected returns, such as those found in First Call and the Institutional Brokers' Estimate System (I/B/E/S), are widely available, few researchers publish estimates of volatility. By far the biggest practical challenge in implementing the Markowitz approach, however, is correlation. The problem is that if security A is positively correlated with security B and security B is positively correlated with security C, then A must be positively correlated with security C. In general, given the correlations between A and B, and B and C, the correlation between A and C is bounded. While keeping these bounds in mind might seem easy, forecasting correlations for just ten securities and producing 45 consistent pair-wise correlations is a formidable task. Technically, if the correlation matrix is mathematically singular with one or more columns linearly related, no mean-variance optimal solution is possible. Even worse, if the matrix is not singular but one or more columns are weakly linearly related, the optimization can be solved but will result in unstable efficient frontiers. Most practitioners substitute the historical correlation matrix, which is always consistent. The problem with this approach is that it assumes the future will be like the past and only produces portfolios that would have been optimal.

The second problem with the mean-variance approach is that the algorithm can only use the information it has. The illustrative case is private equity. If private equity has a very high expected return and a low correlation with other assets, the algorithm will naturally add a substantial amount to the optimal portfolios.

The problem is that private equity is illiquid over short investment horizons, and portfolios with substantial amounts of illiquid assets would be suitable for very few investors.

The third problem arises because most optimal portfolios are judged to be unsuitable either because they fail to include some of the assets or the allocations are extreme. In many cases, the portfolio manager responds to poor diversification by constraining the weights to make the asset allocation more attractive. Too many constraints make optimization irrelevant. While this problem is more a symptom than a cause, it is a function of the algorithm lacking information that the manager considers material.

The final practical problem is that small changes in inputs may result in large changes in the optimal portfolios. This problem is not mathematical, because the solution is always optimal. The problem is credibility and transactions costs. When capital market conditions change, a portfolio manager's estimated security returns, variances, and correlations are likely to change. The efficient portfolios also change. Managers who maintain efficient portfolios are then left to explain to their clients why they generated transactions costs to rebalance the portfolio when the forecasts did not change significantly.

Revealed Asset Allocation Models

This chapter focuses on asset allocation models that are relevant to investment practice. A survey of mutual fund prospectuses turns up very few investment managers referring to their portfolios as mean-variance optimal. Canner, Mankiw, and Weil (1997) view investment advisors' asset allocation advice as a puzzle because the advice is contrary to Markowitz's theory. These authors hypothesize that either the managers' advice is wrong or the Markowitz model is inadequate. Canner et al. (p. 184) also note that the advice is common enough that "academic financial economists may be able to learn from popular advisors." The next section of this chapter follows that advice by investigating asset allocation at the capital market level. Before moving on, however, reviewing some of the research that is based on Canner et al. is appropriate.

Bajeux-Besnainou, Jordan, and Portait (2001) investigate two factors that imply that the Markowitz model is inadequate: its absence of a truly risk-free asset and its lack of the possibility of rebalancing because it has only one investment horizon. Although the Markowitz (1952) model does not require a risk-free asset, Sharpe's (1963) extension does. Bajeux-Besnainou et al. note that Treasury bills, a common surrogate for the risk-free asset, are not risk free when the investment horizon exceeds the instrument's maturity. They also show that rebalancing can produce an asset allocation that is both theoretically correct and similar to popular advice. Bajeux-Besnainouet al. (pp. 1178–1179) conclude: "Portfolio theory unambiguously supports the popular advice about allocations to stocks, bonds, and cash under two conditions: (1) complete markets, and (2) the investor's horizon exceeding the maturity of cash." The authors' results suggest that under these two conditions there is no asset allocation puzzle because both theory and popular advice agree that the ratio of bonds to stocks should vary directly with an investor's risk aversion.

Amenc, Goltz, and Lioui (2011) provide some recent evidence of professional portfolio manager practice. In a survey of 229 institutions based in Europe conducted in 2007, they ask respondents about their portfolio construction methods. While the authors do not ask respondents directly if they use Markowitz portfolios, questions such as "When implementing portfolio optimization, do you set *absolute* risk objectives?" elicit positive responses from 60 percent of the sample. The actual sample size is difficult to determine because even though the authors say that they surveyed 229 institutions, the number of responses to their questions ranged from 242 to 329. The authors do not reveal the distribution of responses among institutions.

Amenc et al. (2011) find that 46 percent of their sample assumes the distribution of future returns is normal and ignores tail risk. Contrary to Markowitz's original theory, 23 percent of the sample explicitly considers semivariance or lower partial moments. A majority of their sample reports using the sample covariance matrix to implement portfolio optimization, which the authors point out exposes the portfolios to considerable sample risk but, as discussed elsewhere in this chapter, assures the optimization routine does not suffer from estimation problems. Amenc et al. (p. 45) observe: "The conclusion that emerges...is that both average risk and extreme risk are measured with simplistic tools that expose institutions to both estimation risk (when the sample estimator is used for the covariance matrix) and model risk (when VaR relies on the assumption of normal distributions)." They also note that portfolio managers report using unsophisticated methods to remedy shortcomings in the model, including 68 percent of their sample who manage estimation risk by subjective allocation constraints. Amenc et al. (p. 48) summarize by saying: "Investment managers at financial institutions know, in principle, that basic mean-variance portfolio theory has its limits, but our findings clearly show that, in practice, *mean-variance analysis is still the industry workhorse*" [emphasis added].

An alternative interpretation of these results is that the mean-variance approach is still widely used but not as a primary tool for constructing portfolios. In this author's experience as a consultant to many major portfolio managers in the United States, Asia, and Europe, mean-variance optimization is rarely used to design portfolios but often used to check portfolios constructed by ad hoc methods. The large percentage of survey responses that acknowledge the shortcomings of mean-variance optimization suggests this alternative explanation is a strong possibility among the respondents. If these survey results reflect that the respondents do not use mean-variance optimization in portfolio design, then the conclusion by Amec et al. suggesting that the respondents do not find its shortcomings important is not surprising. Unfortunately, the authors do not pose a question about mean-variance optimization directly enough to shed much light on the role of mean-variance optimization in the respondents' portfolio design. Most likely, the practical problems discussed elsewhere in this chapter contribute to the scarcity of theoretical Markowitz portfolios guiding investment practice.

The following section explores another possibility—that when investors allocate their wealth, the resulting relative asset class market values approximate a Markowitz asset allocation. That is, market values might resemble a Markowitz portfolio if investors follow the Markowitz process of constructing their portfolios without realizing it explicitly.

THE US WEALTH PORTFOLIO

Ibbotson and Fall (1979) calculate the market values of six asset classes in the United States: common and preferred stocks, corporate, Treasury and municipal bonds, and real estate. Their interest is primarily in estimating the weights of these asset classes in the market portfolio, a key component of the CAPM. The market portfolio is the tangency portfolio that Sharpe (1963) derives by adding a risk-free asset to Markowitz's efficient frontier. As Ibbotson and Fall make clear, no individual investor would be expected to hold the market portfolio, because the sum of all investors' individual decisions creates the market capitalization of the asset classes. By deriving the relative weights of these asset classes, the market's asset allocation can be inferred and therefore can provide insight into the asset allocation models in use. At the least, the market-capitalization-weighted portfolio can be compared with the Markowitz efficient portfolio. The expected returns that investors would have used to make the market portfolio an optimal portfolio can also be extracted.

Ibbotson and Fall (1979, p. 87) provide the following estimate of the relative values of capital market securities in a US market portfolio at the beginning of 1978: common stocks 20.77 percent, corporate bonds and preferred stock (6.97 percent), real estate (51.65 percent), U.S. government bonds (14.42 percent), and municipal bonds (6.18 percent).

The availability of data has improved dramatically since 1979. Although no one appears to be tracking the US wealth portfolio directly, the Federal Reserve Flow of Funds Accounts table Z.1 provides the necessary data. The levels table, L.5, includes the total value of public corporate stock and private equity interests (table FL893064105) and credit market instruments, including corporate and government bonds (table FL894104005) and real estate at market value in the hands of corporations, noncorporate business, farms and households and nonprofit organizations (tables FL105035085, FL115035085, FL155035005 and FL135035003, respectively). These statistics do not capture every investment opportunity. Neither Ibbotson and Fall (1979) nor this analysis consider commodities, for example, although they are probably immaterial to the aggregate wealth represented by the Federal Reserve's totals.

Data from the Federal Reserve's tables previously listed show less equity and more real estate than Ibbotson and Fall (1979) at the beginning of 1978: with equity at 9.68 percent, corporate bonds at 19.08 percent, US government bonds at 6.24 percent, state and local bonds at 2.81 percent, other liabilities at 5.11 percent, and real estate at 57.09 percent

The differences between the Federal Reserve data and Ibbotson and Fall's (1979) numbers are probably due to different definitions and data sources. For

Table 10.1 **Allocations of US wealth portfolio, 1977–2010**

	Equity	Corporate bonds	US government bonds	State and local bonds	Other liabilities	Real estate
Average (%)	11.24	19.04	7.29	2.71	12.14	47.57
Range (+/–)	3.70	4.28	5.06	1.38	15.56	18.44

Note: This table describes the allocation of invested wealth among equity, bonds, and real estate in the United States between 1977 and 2010.

Source: Data derived from Federal Reserve (June 2011) tables FL893064105, FL894104005, FL105035085, FL115035085, FL155035005 and FL135035003.

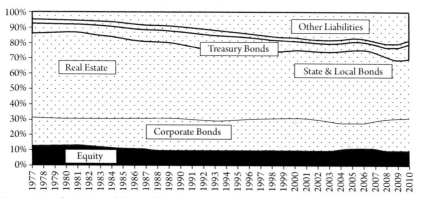

Figure 10.1 The US wealth portfolio from 1977 through 2010 in percentages.
This graph shows the average allocation of the US wealth portfolio measured in market values, as published by the Federal Reserve. The vertical distance measures the percent allocated to the asset class. For example, in 1977 real estate has the largest allocation (55 percent) as measured between the 30 percent and 85 percent marks on the vertical axis. Similarly, state and local bonds had the smallest allocation (3 percent), measured between the 91 percent and 94 percent marks.

example, only the Federal Reserve data include proprietors' equity in private companies as well as public corporate stock. One advantage of the data used here is consistency over time.

Figures 10.1 and 10.2 show the trends in these allocations from 1977 through 2010. These figures suggest that the asset allocation of the US wealth portfolio changes only slightly over time.

Table 10.1 shows the average allocations and ranges of US wealth portfolios between 1977 and 2010. The allocations did not deviate much in these years, except in the categories of other liabilities and real estate. Other liabilities are tied to real estate through mortgage-related securities and consumer debt. Their volatility is evidence of the magnitude of the real estate boom and bust. The point

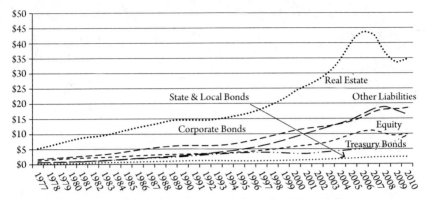

Figure 10.2 The US wealth portfolio from 1977 through 2010 in dollar amounts. This graph presents the same data as in figure 10.1 except here the allocations are shown in dollar amounts. The real estate boom and bust of the last decade is visible, as is the dominance of debt over equity in dollar values.

of this table is that the relatively constant asset allocation suggests investors' asset allocation model have been stable.

MARKOWITZ PORTFOLIOS

The first analyses based on these data employ historical data as inputs to a mean-variance optimization. Despite the earlier overview of the drawbacks of using historical data, assuming investor forecasts would add unwanted speculation to the analysis. Figure 10.3 shows the Markowitz portfolios that result from using historical data as inputs. The optimal portfolios shown in figure 10.3 have some obvious drawbacks. Of the six asset classes used in the analysis, only four appear in any of the portfolios. The asset class "Other Liabilities" dominates the portfolios. Not surprisingly, mortgage-backed assets included in Other Liabilities by the Fed appear to do well (before the crash), but few analysts would recommend them in 2011 for every portfolio across the risk spectrum. From this illustration, one can easily see why professional portfolio managers might not use mean-variance analysis to design portfolios.

BLACK-LITTERMAN ANALYSIS

The second analysis of the market capitalization data uses the Black and Litterman (1992) reverse optimization algorithm. The Black-Litterman model starts by assuming that the market is in equilibrium and derives expected returns using reverse optimization. That is, this approach answers the question of what expected returns must have been assumed for the market to have assigned these relative market weights to the asset classes. The following historical data are used to supply the inputs: a risk-free rate of 3.01 percent, a market premium of 4.68 percent, market capitalization and standard deviation for each asset class, and asset class correlations. The expected returns extracted from the US wealth

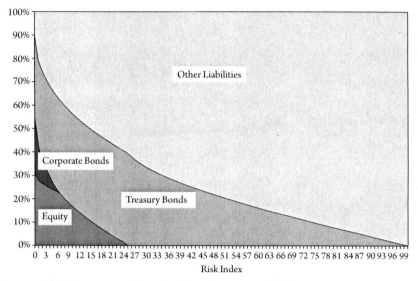

Figure 10.3 Markowitz portfolios based on the US wealth allocation.
This graph shows the results of a mean-variance analysis of US equity; bonds (corporate bonds, Treasury bonds, state and local bonds, and other liabilities); and real estate. Historical returns from 1978 through 2010 are used to produce mean-variance optimal portfolios. The horizontal axis is a risk index, arbitrarily scaled from 0 to 100. The vertical axis represents the percentage of the portfolio allocated to the assets classes, labeled from 0 to 100 percent. Every Markowitz portfolio is depicted. For example, the Markowitz portfolio at risk index 50 is made up of 20 percent Treasury bonds and 80 percent other liabilities, reading from the vertical scale. Note that other liabilities are part of every portfolio, regardless of risk level.

portfolio from 1977 to 2010 are: equity (8.77 percent), corporate bonds (6.64 percent), US government bonds (0.48 percent), state and local bonds (5.00 percent), other liabilities (8.28 percent), and real estate (9.74 percent). Based on the inputs and assumptions, the Black-Litterman reverse optimization results suggest that at the end of 2010 the markets were especially pessimistic about the prospect for returns on US government bonds. Given the low level of interest rates at the end of 2010, this expectation appears justified. Overall, these results appear reasonable.

This analysis of the US wealth portfolio suggests that investors are not following the Markowitz model when they design their portfolios. If they did, the market capitalization of the asset classes would more closely reflect the relative value of the portfolios shown in figure 10.3. Thus, despite the elegance of Markowitz's argument and the sophistication of the mathematics of mean-variance optimization, not many investors appear to be using Markowitz portfolios to guide their investment selections.

A review of asset allocation models is incomplete without considering how portfolios are maintained in the face of market movements that change the asset allocations. The next section addresses the question of portfolio rebalancing.

Portfolio Rebalancing

The Markowitz model is a single period model and does not envision any rebalancing. If the portfolio accurately forecasts return, risk, and correlation and investors have a one-period investment horizon, rebalancing is unnecessary. Even Campbell and Viceira (2002), as discussed elsewhere in this chapter, who work in the context of dynamic markets with both short- and long-term investors, inflation, mean reversion in returns, intertemporal hedging, and labor income, have no specific advice for portfolio rebalancing.

Other research on the topic of rebalancing appears to have become the province of operations research. This research is prone to losing touch with the underlying economics. For example, Yu and Lee (2011) use fuzzy multi-objective programming in the context of multiple criteria portfolio rebalancing models to study the effect of transaction cost, risk, return, short selling, skewness, and kurtosis on rebalancing. In results typical of this genre, their conclusions are mixed without much practical application. Yu and Lee's (p. 173) call for future research includes the suggestion that "rather than a portfolio selection based on historical return, a portfolio selection that is able to predict future return can be developed in order to meet this fast-changing environment." Of course, if investors had a reliable forecasting model, they would not need to rebalance. In contrast, the Perold and Sharpe (1988) study of rebalancing clarifies that the most important factors depend on market conditions and investor risk tolerance.

DYNAMIC STRATEGIES FOR ASSET ALLOCATION

From a practical perspective, rebalancing needs a consistent definition. Changes in a portfolio can stem from changes in capital market forecasts, which would require redesigning the portfolio's asset allocation, or from differences between the portfolio's actual allocation and the intended asset allocation. Perold and Sharpe (1988) provide a framework for thinking about rebalancing, whether it is based on changes in expectations or deviations from an established policy. While this framework is more than 20 years old, it remains the best explanation for the difficulty in determining the single-best rebalancing model.

Perold and Sharpe (1988) examine rebalancing in the context of the most basic asset allocation decision: the split between risky and riskless assets. Their approach is simple and generalizable because it reduces the asset allocation decision to its essence and applies to any asset allocation model. The authors identify four possible strategies for portfolio rebalancing between risky and riskless assets: (1) buy and hold, (2) constant mix, (3) constant-proportion portfolio insurance, and (4) option-based portfolio insurance. The authors show that these strategies differ in terms of performance depending on market volatility and that investors' preferences for one strategy over another depend on their risk tolerance.

No matter what happens to relative values, a buy-and-hold strategy never rebalances. The worst case result is limited to the return on the risk-free asset, and investors can invest enough in the risk-free asset to establish a cushion consistent with their risk aversion. The upside potential of this strategy is linearly related to the investment in the risky asset. In an oscillating market that comes back to its original value, the buy-and-hold portfolio's value will return to its initial value. A constant mix strategy, however, will do relatively better in such a market.

Constant-mix strategies set the allocation to the risky asset as a constant percentage of wealth. Investors who follow this strategy exhibit risk tolerances that vary proportionally with their wealth. Unlike buy and hold, this strategy requires trading whenever the actual proportions deviate from the design. This strategy is contrarian in the sense that a portfolio's exposure to a risky asset is increased when that asset falls in value. Constant-mix strategies also require a rule of avoiding excessive transaction costs that dictates how far from the design the actual value must be to trigger a trade. By buying stocks when a market trends downward in a flat but oscillating market, the constant-mix strategy makes more money than the buy-and-hold strategy as it buys low and sells high. Perold and Sharpe (1988) observe that the amount of trend will make a big difference in results. When the trend is stronger than the short-term variations, a buy-and-hold strategy does better that a constant-mix strategy. The converse is also true in an oscillating market.

In constant-proportion portfolio insurance, the amount of money that should be committed to the risky assets is computed as a percentage of the difference between the portfolio's value and the floor, the lowest acceptable portfolio value. For example, this strategy might start with a cushion equal to the difference between the value of the portfolio and the floor. The strategy then keeps the exposure to the risky asset at some multiple of this cushion. Investors who use this strategy have a zero risk tolerance when portfolio values reach the floor value. In this rebalancing strategy, assets are shifted into the risky asset as it rises and into the risk-free asset as the risky asset falls. This strategy will do better than the constant mix in up markets, offer good downside protection (down to the value of the floor), and do poorly in flat but oscillating markets. If everyone tried to use constant-proportion portfolio insurance at the same time it would fail, because for every investor who sells the risky asset as it falls (constant-proportion strategies), there must be another investor who buys that risky asset (constant mix strategies).

Option-based portfolio insurance is the final rebalancing strategy. This strategy differs from the others in that an investment horizon must be specified, just as standard options have an expiration date. As with the constant-proportion strategy, a floor is set and the investor has zero risk tolerance for values that reach the floor. This strategy invests 100 percent in the risk-free assets whenever the value of the risky asset falls to the floor value. When the value of the risky asset is above the floor, the exposure to the risky asset rises with the difference between the risky asset value and the floor, reaching 100 percent at the investment horizon. One considerable drawback to this strategy is resetting the floor once the horizon has been reached.

Perold and Sharpe (1988, p. 28) conclude by observing that "ultimately, the issue concerns the preferences of the various parties that will bear the risk and/or enjoy the reward from investment. There is no reason to believe that any particular type of dynamic strategy is best for everyone (and, in fact, only buy-and-hold strategies could be followed by everyone)."

Sharpe (2010a) observes that many institutional investors have an asset allocation policy that invests fixed percentages of the portfolio in asset classes, such as 60 percent in equities and 40 percent in bonds. Moreover, target date funds not only use percentages but also have an announced reallocation from risky equity to less risky bonds over time, presumably as the investor ages. These investors must follow a contrarian strategy, moving more funds into the relatively poorest performing asset classes to maintain the predetermined asset allocation. The author stresses that these rebalancing strategies can accommodate only a limited number of investors, as not everyone can buy the same asset—buyers who want to buy poorly performing assets must trade with investors who want to sell poorly performing assets. According to Sharpe, adopting this strategy requires that portfolio managers believe the market is efficient and that their investors' preferences and beliefs are materially different from those of the average investor, or that the market is inefficient and that enough foolish investors will take the other side of the manager's trade when it is not in their best interests to do so. Sharpe (2010b, p. 13) summarizes his views as follows: "My personal experience is that the historical relative efficacy of rebalancing strategies depends on the time period, country, and asset classes chosen. And, of course, the relevant time period for investment decisions is the future." Further, he concludes that the question of which rebalancing strategy is best depends on the risk preferences of investors and their forecast of market trends. Sharpe's work makes clear that because of the codependency between contrarian and traditional strategies, no one strategy is unlikely to dominate the others over time.

ASSET ALLOCATION REBALANCING

The insight to be gleaned from this research is that many of the attempts to address portfolio rebalancing from an operations research perspective are bound to be incomplete. Because it is a purely quantitative perspective, operations research ignores the underlying economic questions of risk, return, and market environment, and has little potential to add to our understanding of rebalancing.

If Sharpe is correct, however, the practical implications of asset allocation are straightforward: First, from a rebalancing perspective, the asset allocation model used to design the portfolio is not as important as the investors' risk tolerance and market forecast. Second, risk tolerance is an important factor in selecting a model portfolio. Last, most models accommodate a range of risk tolerances. Therefore, portfolio design and portfolio rebalancing, while related, are not sufficiently dependent for a unified solution. Conventional wisdom, such as the perceived necessity of rebalancing whenever the asset allocation varies by more than 10 percent from its target, is widely followed and has some justification. The best answer, however, is that rebalancing depends on both the investor's risk tolerance and market forecast, so that no one rebalancing model, a priori, will be better than the accuracy of that forecast and the validity of the investors' perceived risk tolerance.

Summary and Conclusions

Markowitz's portfolio theory has dominated the discussion of asset allocation models since its origin in 1952. Portfolios that offer the highest expected return for a given level of risk are appealing. Most investors would gladly accept such a portfolio. Unfortunately, Markowitz's portfolios remain a theoretical ideal rather than a practical reality. Most practitioners realize that Markowitz's portfolios exist only in expected return-variance space and that using historical experience to construct these portfolios falls far short of the ideal. Problems with accurate forecasts, consistency of inputs, and optimal but unappealing results have kept the Markowitz asset allocation model from being widely applied in practice.

Alternative models using three moments or stochastic dominance have their own problems. These models remain popular with academics but are rarely used in practice. Some authors even suggest that such models will never be practical because they are based on individual preferences, skewness that does not persist, faulty economics, or algorithms that cannot handle rebalancing.

Portfolio models recommended by financial advisors based on conventional wisdom continue to have a strong appeal. When using the US market portfolio to observe what model might be motivating the distribution of aggregate wealth among asset classes, the underlying expected returns appear reasonable but the portfolio itself does not match any Markowitz portfolio.

This chapter concludes by reviewing rebalancing strategies designed to keep portfolios consistent with their risk-and-return design specifications. Despite a wealth of academic literature on the topic, the solution, if there is only one, is simple and intuitive. The appropriate rebalancing strategy depends on the investor's risk tolerance and expectations for the market climate.

Despite the practical problems with the Markowitz model and its apparent lack of popularity as a practical investment guide, the portfolio management profession owes a huge debt to Markowitz. His model serves as a constant reminder of what is important. Expected return, risk, and pair-wise correlations will always be part of parametric asset allocation models. Investors would like to have portfolios that offer the highest expected return for the least expected risk. Markowitz should not be blamed for the fact that the future is unknowable. He should, instead, be honored for showing us how to think about best building portfolios for the future, regardless of what it brings.

Discussion Questions

1. Adopting Markowitz's assumptions means that investors either have quadratic utility or believe all investments follow a normal distribution. Markowitz acknowledges that neither of these assumptions is likely to reflect the preferences or beliefs of real investors. Identify and discuss one shortcoming of assuming quadratic utility and a normal distribution.

2. Investors who want to construct Markowitz-based mean-variance optimal portfolios face several challenges. List and discuss two of these challenges.

3. The US wealth portfolio is used to gain insight into how US investors allocate their assets. Explain why the market value of the wealth portfolio's asset classes is a reasonable proxy for the collective optimal portfolio. Cite one example of why investors might be motivated to change their asset allocation.

4. The research presented in this chapter compares how US investors have allocated their funds with how a Markowitz portfolio would allocate funds among the same asset classes. Identify and discuss two differences between the actual US wealth portfolio and the Markowitz portfolio.

5. Portfolio rebalancing is necessary to keep every portfolio as close as practical to its original risk-return specifications. Perold and Sharpe (1988) classify all rebalancing strategies into four types. Identify each of these four strategies and discuss how they behave in a trendless market.

References

Adesi, Giovanni Barone, Patrick Gagliardini, and Giovanni Urga. 2004. "Testing Asset Pricing Models with Coskewness." *Journal of Business & Economic Statistics* 22:4, 474–485.

Amenc, Noel, Felix Goltz, and Abraham Lioui. 2011. "Practitioner Portfolio Construction and Performance Measurement: Evidence from Europe." *Financial Analysts Journal* 67:3, 39–50.

Arditti, Fred D., and Haim Levy. 1975. "Portfolio Efficiency Analysis in Three Moments: The Multiperiod Case." *Journal of Finance* 30:3, 797–809.

Arzac, Enrique R., and Vijay S. Bawa. 1977. "Portfolio Choice and Equilibrium in Capital Markets with Safety-First Investors." *Journal of Financial Economics* 4:3, 277–288.

Bajeux-Besnainou, Isabelle, James V. Jordan, and Roland Portait. 2001. "An Asset Allocation Puzzle: Comment." *American Economic Review* 91:4, 1170–1179.

Balduzzi, Pierluigi, and Anthony W. Lynch. 1999. "Transactions Costs and Predictability: Some Utility Cost Calculations." *Journal of Financial Economics* 52:1, 47–78.

Barberis, Nicholas. 2000. "Investing for the Long Run when Returns Are Predictable." *Journal of Finance* 55:1, 225–264.

Bawa, Vijay S., and Eric B. Lindenberg. 1977. "Capital Market Equilibrium in a Mean-Lower Partial Moment Framework." *Journal of Financial Economics* 5:2, 189–200.

Bawa, Vijay S., Eric B. Lindenberg, and Lawrence C. Rafsky. 1979. "An Efficient Algorithm to Determine Stochastic Dominance Admissible Sets." *Management Science* 25:7, 609–622.

Bernstein, Peter L. 2002. "Then and Now in Investing and Why Now is So Much Better." In Ralph E. Badger, Harold W. Torgerson, and Harry G. Guthmann (ed.), *Investment Principles and Practices*, 6th edition. Englewood Cliffs, NJ: Prentice-Hall, Inc.

Bigelow, John P. 1993. "Consistency of Mean-Variance Analysis and Expected Utility Analysis: A Complete Characterization." *Economics Letters* 43:2, 187–192.

Black, Fischer, and Robert Litterman. 1992. "Global Portfolio Optimization." *Financial Analysts Journal* 48:5, 28–43.

Brada, Josef, Harry Ernst, and John van Tassel. 1966. "The Distribution of Stock Price Differences: Gaussian after All?" *Operations Research* 14:2, 334–340.

Brandt, Michael W. 1999. "Estimating Portfolio and Consumption Choice: A Conditional Euler Equations Approach." *Journal of Finance* 54:5, 1609–1645.

Brennan, Michael J., Eduardo S. Schwartz, and Ronaldo Lagnado. 1997. "Strategic Asset Allocation." *Journal of Economic Dynamics and Control* 21:8–9, 1377–1403.

Brinson, Gary P., L. R. Hood, and Gilbert L. Beebower. 1986. "Determinants of Portfolio Performance." *Financial Analysts Journal* 42:4, 39–48.

Brinson, Gary P., Brian D. Singer, and Gilbert L. Beebower. 1991. "Determinants of Portfolio Performance II: An Update." *Financial Analysts Journal* 47:3, 40–48.

Campbell, John Y., and Luis M. Viceira. 2002. *Strategic Asset Allocation: Portfolio Choice for Long-Term Investors.* New York: Oxford University Press.

Canner, Niko, N. Gregory Mankiw, and David N. Weil. 1997. "An Asset Allocation Puzzle." *American Economic Review* 87:1, 181–191.

Fama, Eugene F. 1963. "Mandelbrot and the Stable Paretian Hypothesis." *Journal of Business* 36:4, 420–429.

Fama, Eugene F., and G. William Schwert. 1977. "Asset Returns and Inflation." *Journal of Financial Economics* 5:2, 115–130.

Garcia, René, Eric Renault, and David Veredas. 2011. "Estimation of Stable Distributions by Indirect Inference." *Journal of Econometrics* 161:2, 325–337.

Ghose, Devajyoti, and Kenneth F. Kroner. 1995. "The Relationship between GARCH and Symmetric Stable Processes: Finding the Source of Fat Tails in Financial Data." *Journal of Empirical Finance* 2:3, 225–251.

Harlow, W. V. 1991. "Asset Allocation in a Downside-Risk Framework." *Financial Analysts Journal* 47:5, 28–40.

Harlow, W. V., and Ramesh K. S. Rao. 1989. "Asset Pricing in a Generalized Mean-Lower Partial Moment Framework: Theory and Evidence." *Journal of Financial and Quantitative Analysis* 24:3, 285–311.

Harvey, Campbell R., and Akhtar Siddique. 2000. "Conditional Skewness in Asset Pricing Tests." *Journal of Finance* 55:3, 1263–1295.

Ibbotson, Roger G., and Carol L. Fall. 1979. "The United States Market Wealth Portfolio: Components of Capital Market Values and Returns, 1947–1978." *Journal of Portfolio Management* 6:1, 82–92.

Ibbotson, Roger G., and Paul D. Kaplan. 2000. "Does Asset Allocation Explain 40, 90 or 100 Percent of Performance?" *Financial Analysts Journal* 56:1, 26–33.

Idzorek, Tom. "Ask an Expert–Target Date Funds." 2011. Interview by The Center for Due Diligence. Available at http://www.thecfdd.com/askanexpert/targetdatefunds. Retrieved June 15, 2012.

Jean, William H. 1971. "The Extension of Portfolio Analysis to Three or More Parameters." *Journal of Financial and Quantitative Analysis* 6:1, 505–515.

Jean, William H. 1973. "More on Multidimensional Portfolio Analysis." *Journal of Financial and Quantitative Analysis* 8:3, 475–490.

Kahneman, Daniel, and Amos Tversky. 1979. "Prospect Theory: An Analysis of Decision under Risk." *Econometrica* 47:2, 263–292.

Kaplan, Paul D. 2009. "Roger Ibbotson, Benoit Mandelbrot, and George Cooper: Our Distinguished Economics Panel Debates the Value of Current Risk Models." *Morningstar Advisor*, February 2. http://publishing.ramp.com/advisor/theme/5735/t/42990755/roger-ibbotson-benoit-mandelbrot-and-george-cooper.htm.

Kuosmanen, Timo. 2004. "Efficient Diversification According to Stochastic Dominance Criteria." *Management Science* 50:10, 1390–1406.

Mandelbrot, Benoît. 1961. "Stable Paretian Random Fluctuations and Multiplicative Variation of Income." *Econometrica* 29:4, 517–543.

Mandelbrot, Benoît. 1963. "The Variation of Certain Speculative Prices." *Journal of Business* 36:4, 394–419.

Mandelbrot, Benoît, and H. M. Taylor. 1967. "On the Distribution of Stock Price Differentials." *Operations Research* 15:6, 1057–1062.

Markowitz, Harry. 1952. "Portfolio Selection." *Journal of Finance* 7:1, 77–91.

Markowitz, Harry M. 1959. *Portfolio Selection: Efficient Diversification of Investments.* New Haven, CT: Yale University Press.

Mathews, Timothy. 2004. "Portfolio Selection with Quadratic Utility Revisited." *Geneva Papers on Risk and Insurance Theory* 29:2, 137–144.

Merton, Robert C. 1973. "An Intertemporal Capital Asset Pricing Model." *Econometrica* 41:5, 867–887.

Meyer, Jack. 1987. "Two-Moment Decision Models and Expected Utility Maximization." *American Economic Review* 77:3, 421–430.

Modigliani, Franco, and Richard Sutch. 1966. "Innovations in Interest Rate Policy." *American Economic Review* 56:1/2, 178–197.

Munk, Claus, and Carsten Sørenson. 2010. "Dynamic Asset Allocation with Stochastic Income and Interest Rates." *Journal of Financial Economics* 96:3, 433–462.

Perold, Andre, and William Sharpe. 1988. "Dynamic Strategies for Asset Allocation." *Financial Analysts Journal* 44:1, 16–27.

Rothchild, Michael, and Joseph Stiglitz. 1970. "Increasing Risk: I. A Definition." *Journal of Economic Theory* 2:3, 225–243.

Sharpe, William F. 1963. "A Simplified Model for Portfolio Analysis." *Management Science* 9:2, 277–93.

Sharpe, William F. 1987. "An Algorithm for Portfolio Improvement." In Kenneth D. Lawrence, John B. Gueward, and Gary D. Reeves (ed.), *Advances in Mathematical Programming and Financial Planning*, Volume 1, 155–170. Greenwich, CT: JAI Press.

Sharpe, William F. 2007. "Expected Utility Asset Allocation." *Financial Analysts Journal* 63:5, 18–30.

Sharpe, William F. 2010a. "Adaptive Asset Allocation Policies." *Financial Analysts Journal* 66:3, 45–59.

Sharpe, William F. 2010b. "Adaptive Asset Allocation Policies: Author Response." *Financial Analysts Journal* 66:5, 13–14.

Simkowitz, Michael A., and William L. Beedles. 1978. "Diversification in a Three Moment World." *Journal of Financial and Quantitative Analysis* 13:5, 927–941.

Singleton, J. Clay, and John Wingender. 1986. "Skewness Persistence in Common Stock Returns." *Journal of Financial and Quantitative Analysis* 21:3, 335–341.

Xiong, James X., Roger G. Ibbotson, Thomas M. Idzorek, and Peng Chen. 2010. "The Equal Importance of Asset Allocation and Active Management." *Financial Analysts Journal* 66:2, 22–30.

Xu, Jianguo. 2007. "Price Convexity and Skewness." *Journal of Finance* 62:5, 2521–2552.

Yu, Jing-Rung, and Wen-Yi Lee. 2011. "Portfolio Rebalancing Model Using Multiple Criteria." *European Journal of Operational Research* 209:2, 166–175.

11

Preference Models in Portfolio Construction and Evaluation

MASSIMO GUIDOLIN
Professor of Finance, IGIER, Bocconi University and CAIR,
Manchester Business School

Introduction

What role should the preferences of an investor play in optimal portfolio decisions? If one adds a qualifier that the optimal portfolio decision concerns the very investor whose preferences are under investigation, the question seems trivial. Everyone would answer that preferences are crucial or at least very important ingredients, alongside other factors such as the asset menu, the dynamics of investment opportunities, and the relevant constraints. Modern portfolio theory affirms that such a question is far from trivial for two reasons: First, various asset allocation frameworks often disregard the role of preferences. This omission is often justified by results in asset pricing theory; for instance by the separation result of the celebrated capital asset pricing model (CAPM) implying that, independently of preferences, investors ought to simply demand a multiple of the market portfolio. Second, critical differences between ex-ante versus ex-post optimal portfolios exist, and preferences are often downplayed on an ex-ante basis. Strategies that seem to be optimal ex-ante may turn gravely disappointing ex-post. Further, strategies that in principle are suboptimal (e.g., ones disregarding the preferences of decision makers) may yield ex-post robust performance. This chapter investigates whether and how preference-based optimal asset allocation models may potentially contribute to producing appealing ex-ante and ex-post performances.

This chapter mixes the goals and methods of a review of the methodological literature with the objective of offering novel insights on whether and how the tools described herein may work in practice. The chapter is organized as follows: It begins by setting up the typical portfolio problem, providing relevant definitions and notations. Next, the chapter introduces the main types of preference frameworks used in the portfolio literature and, to a lesser extent, in the practice of applied wealth management, often borrowing from microeconomic theory. Because various researchers have proposed that Taylor approximations applied to the functional representation of standard preferences may replace more complex mathematical constructs, the chapter includes an in-depth discussion of the advantages and disadvantages of using Taylor approximations, which emphasize the role played by statistical moments (mean, variance, skewness, and kurtosis) of either terminal wealth or portfolio returns. Some discussion is then devoted to new and exciting developments that have recently occurred at the intersection between decision theory and portfolio management in the form of frameworks that emphasize the concepts of robust decisions and ambiguity aversion. We provide an illustrative example that aims at investigating some aspects of the interaction between preferences and statistical models of investment opportunities is undertaken. In particular, optimal portfolio decisions are computed under regime-switching models that capture various features of time-varying investment opportunities.

Preliminaries and Definitions

In the economic literature, a standard practice is to model the choices of economic agents among several goods using the concept of a utility function. In its cardinal form, a utility function, $u(\cdot)$, is used to assign a numeric value to all possible choices (e.g., bundles of goods) faced by an economic agent. These values, often referred to as the *utility index*, have the property that bundle r^1 is (weakly) preferred to r^2 if and only if the utility of r^1 is higher than that of r^2, as in $u(r^1) \geq u(r^2)$. The higher the value of a particular choice, the greater the utility derived from that choice. Utility functions can represent a broad set of preference orderings.

The literature on utility functions, such as Elton, Gruber, Brown, and Goetzmann (2010), widely explores the precise conditions under which a preference ordering can be expressed through a utility function. At least at a superficial level, the properties of such conditions are usually held to imply several things. First, when a utility index is written as a function of either the wealth or the consumption of an agent, the condition implies that $u(\cdot)$ should be monotonically increasing in its argument(s); this increase is known as the *nonsatiation property*, meaning that investors always prefer more to less. Second, the conditions necessary for a preference ordering imply that $u(\cdot)$ should be concave, which can be proven to be equivalent to risk aversion. Risk aversion involves that investors prefer the expected value of a gamble (risky investment) to the risky gamble itself.

In portfolio theory, investors are faced with a set of choices under uncertainty. Different portfolios have different levels of risk, κ, and expected return, μ, where risk may be measured in various ways. Besides variance, examples of alternative measures of risk are dispersion measures, such as mean absolute deviation of portfolio returns or wealth and downside risk measures. Investors are faced with the decision of choosing a portfolio from the set of all possible risk-return combinations, and obtain different levels of utility from different combinations. The utility obtained from a risk-return combination is expressed by the utility function, implicitly or explicitly capturing preferences in regard to perceived risk and expected return. When such dependence is assumed to be explicit, the result is Equation 11.1,

$$V \equiv U(\mu, \kappa) \quad \partial U / \partial \mu > 0, \partial U / \partial \kappa < 0 \qquad (11.1)$$

where $\partial U / \partial \mu > 0$ derives from nonsatiation and $\partial U / \partial \kappa < 0$ from risk aversion. These preference representations may be particularly simple and enlightening, giving rise to classical derivations, for instance of the CAPM in asset pricing theory. However, in such cases, how this risk-return preference is derived from an underlying preference ordering concerning bundles of goods and services under uncertainty is often unclear. When the agent has simple preference structures directly defined according to expected risk and returns, a utility function can be presented in graphical form by a set of indifference curves.

More often, such dependence is modeled in an indirect, implicit fashion, so that the links with the underlying, micro-founded preference ordering are easy to formalize, but the analysis tends to be more involved. In this case, the general idea is that a rational investor with utility $u(\cdot)$ and initial wealth W_t chooses his portfolio γ_t at time t so as to maximize his expected utility of either of the terminal wealth T periods ahead, as shown in Equation 11.2,

$$\max_{\omega_t} E_t[u(W_{t+T})] \; s.t. (\mathrm{i}) W_{t+T} = \exp\left[\sum_{n=1}^{N} \omega_t^n \sum_{i=1}^{T} r_{t+i}^n + (1 - \sum_{n=1}^{N} \omega_t^n) Tr^f \right]$$

$$W_n; (\mathrm{ii}) \omega_t' 1_N = 1. \qquad (11.2)$$

or of the stream of consumption flows between t and $t+T$, as shown in Equation 11.3:

$$\max_{\{\omega_{t+i}, C_{t+i}\}_{i=0}^{T-1}} \sum_{i=0}^{T} E_t[u(C_{t+i})] \; s.t.$$

$$(\mathrm{i}) W_{t+i} = \exp\left[\sum_{n=1}^{N} \omega_t^n \sum_{i=1}^{T} r_{t+i}^n + (1 - \sum_{n=1}^{N} \omega_t^n) Tr^f \right] (W_{t+i-1} - C_{t+i});$$

$$(\mathrm{ii}) \omega_{t+i}' 1_N = 1 \quad i = 0, 1, \ldots, T-1;$$

$$(\mathrm{iii}) C_{t+i} \geq 0 \quad i = 0, 1, \ldots, T-1.$$

$$(11.3)$$

In both Equations 11.2 and 11.3, the constraint in (i) is the dynamic law of motion of wealth (the net of consumption withdrawals in the case of Equation 11.3). Equation 11.2 illustrates the problem of an investor who commits her initial wealth W_t to a vector of weights $\{\omega_t^n\}_{n=1}^{N}$ in order to maximize the expected utility of her final wealth, $u(W_{t+T})$, without the possibility of any interim withdrawals or consumption. This is also called a *buy-and-hold problem*. Of course, most investors are not concerned with the level of wealth for its own sake but with the standard of living that their wealth can support. In other words, they consume out of wealth and derive utility from consumption rather than wealth. Therefore, Equation 11.3 illustrates the problem of an investor who selects a vector of weights, $\{\omega_{t+i}^n\}_{n=1}^N$, as well as of interim consumption levels C_{t+i} and who does this repeatedly over time to maximize her utility of the flow of consumption. However, in both equations 11.2 and 11.3, the utility indices play a key role.

The Arrow-Pratt coefficients of (local) absolute and relative risk aversion are two key measures describing the (local) properties of utility functions $u(W_{t+T})$ and/or $u(C_{t+i})$, usually abbreviated as $CARA(x)$ and $CRRA(x)$, respectively. They are illustrated in the equations shown in 11.4:

$$CARA(x) \equiv -\frac{u'(x)}{u''(x)} \quad CRRA(x) \equiv -\frac{u'(x)}{u''(x)}x = CARA(x)x. \qquad (11.4)$$

where x is either terminal wealth W_{t+T} or consumption C_{t+i}. These properties give important insights into the nature and behavior of cardinal utility functions, as described in the following: $CARA(x)$ is a scaled, normalized measure of an individual's risk aversion in a small neighborhood of her current (initial) wealth or consumption. Notice that if $u'(x)>0$ and $u''(x)<0$, as normally required of utility functions used in portfolio theory, then $CARA(x)>0$. $CRRA(x)$, on the other hand, is a normalized measure of an individual's risk aversion in a small neighborhood of her current (initial) wealth or consumption per unit of wealth or consumption. Because $CRRA(x) = CARA(x) \cdot x$, when $CARA$ $(x)>0$, $CRRA$ $(x)>0$. Pratt (1964) shows that for a small degree of risk, the CARA coefficient determines the absolute dollar amount that an investor is willing to pay to avoid such a small risk. A common view is that CARA should decrease, or at least not increase, with wealth. Instead, CRRA determines the fraction of wealth than an investor will pay to avoid a small risk of a given size relative to wealth. Another common belief is that plausible preferences should imply that relative risk aversion should be independent of wealth (LeRoy and Werner, 2001). Moreover, Campbell and Viceira's (2002) discussion of the long-run behavior of most economies, characterized by substantial growth in real consumption but also by real interest rates and consumption-wealth ratios that fail to be trending, is consistent with relative risk aversion levels that are independent of wealth.

This chapter examines relatively simple portfolio selection problems under a variety of alternative assumptions concerning the preferences (objectives) of an atomistic investor who is not necessarily representative of the market. Therefore, the analysis is of a partial-equilibrium nature. In particular, unless otherwise stated, the chapter deals with an investor who has to choose a portfolio comprised of N risky assets, described by a vector $\mathbf{r}_t$ of continuously compounded returns. If a riskless asset exists, its risk-free yield is denoted as r^f and the asset is indexed as 0. To keep things simple, the assumption is made not only that the riskless asset exists but also that the risk-free rate is constant over time. In fact, these assumptions are not far from describing how very–short-term interest rates behave in reality, over the investment horizons of interest in this chapter. The investor's choice is embodied in an $N \times 1$ vector, $\omega \equiv [\omega^0 \omega^1 \omega^2 \cdots \omega^N$ of weights, where each weight ω^n represents the percentage of the nth asset held in the portfolio, and the sum of the weights, including the riskless asset weight ω^0 must be equal to 1 (i.e., no money should be left on the table, which derives from non-satiation). Although, in general, short selling (the case in which weights can be negative or can exceed 1 is possible. In the illustrations given later, the restriction prohibiting short selling is imposed because this is realistic and often simplifies numerical optimization when short selling is undertaken.

Subjective Expected Utility Preferences: Main Functional Classes

To get comfortable with the previously described frameworks and concepts, listing the most commonly used assumptions made in the literature about $u(W_{t+T})$ and $u(C_{t+i})$ and discussing their connections are useful. As a rule, examples are provided with explicit reference to the case of utility depending on terminal wealth, unless the presentation requires dealing with consumption.

AD-HOC MEAN-VARIANCE UTILITY FUNCTIONS

The development of the classical theory of finance has been characterized by using simple but ad-hoc mean-variance (MV) objective functions with structure, as shown in Equation 11.5:

$$MV \equiv E[W_{t+T}] - \frac{1}{2}\lambda Var[W_{t+T}]. \tag{11.5}$$

However, Equation 11.5 does not define a utility function in a technical sense. Instead of writing a mapping from either terminal wealth or consumption streams into investor's welfare, Equation 11.5 pins down a mapping between the final investor's objective—say, expected utility—and the first two moments of the distribution of wealth (i.e., mean and variance). For a long time, this representation has been just perceived as a convenient shortcut. Using Equation 11.5 generates problems that stem from its lack of microfoundations. For instance, Equation 11.5 does not allow computing either $CARA(W_t)$ or $CRRA(W_t)$ and therefore formally characterizing MV. However, finding interpretations of λ that assimilate this coefficient to a CARA measure is common. Although this interpretation is not formally correct, it is approximately the case under some special assumptions.

Interestingly, these remarks concerning Equation 11.5 do not apply to Markowitz's classical risk minimization framework that is sometimes referred to as being based on MV, although this labeling may be misguiding. Markowitz (1952) argues that for any given level of expected return, $\bar{\mu}_p$, a rational investor would choose the portfolio with minimum variance from among the set of all possible portfolios, as illustrated in Equation 11.6:

$$\min_{\omega} \omega' Var[r_t]\omega \ \text{s.t.} \ (\text{i}) \omega' E[r_t] = \bar{\mu}_p; (\text{ii}) \omega' 1_N = 1. \tag{11.6}$$

The set of all possible portfolios that can be constructed is called the *feasible set*. MV portfolios are called *mean-variance efficient portfolios*. The set of all MV efficient portfolios, for different desired levels of expected return, is called the *efficient frontier*. Clearly, this algorithm does not lead to selecting a unique optimal portfolio but instead to locating the efficient frontier, represented by the set $\hat{\omega}$ seen as a function of $\bar{\mu}_p$. However, a well-known alternative to Markowitz's risk minimization framework, shown in the optimization problem 11.6, is to explicitly model the trade-off between risk and return in the objective function using a fictitious risk-aversion coefficient, λ, which is commonly called the risk-aversion formulation of the efficient frontier problem, as shown in Equation 11.7:

$$\min_{\omega} \omega' E[r_t] - \lambda \omega' Var(r_t)\omega \quad \text{s.t.} \ \omega' 1_N = 1. \tag{11.7}$$

If λ is gradually increased from zero to infinity, and for each increase, the optimization problem is solved, the result is that all portfolios along the efficient frontier can be calculated . Equation 11.7 differs from Equation 11.5 in that the MV trade-off is explicitly formulated in terms of the expectation and variance of portfolio returns. Although useful in the development of the CAPM, this relationship cannot represent a benchmark in portfolio choice applications. In fact, the objective in Equation 11.7 is even more problematic than the one in Equation 11.5. When returns are discretely compounded, as in $W_{t+T} = (1 + R_{t,T}^p(\omega_t))W_t$, where $R_{t,T}^p$ is the total portfolio return (from an investment strategy characterized by ω_t) between time t and time T, many researchers often plug this accounting into Equation 11.5 and obtain an equivalent objective, as shown in Equation 11.8:

$$
\begin{aligned}
MV^R &\equiv E[(1 + R_{t,T}^p(\omega_t))W_t] - \frac{1}{2}\lambda Var[(1 + R_{t,T}^p(\omega_t))W_t] \\
&= W_t + E[R_{t,T}^p(\omega_t)]W_t - \frac{1}{2}W_t^2 \lambda Var[R_{t,T}^p(\omega_t)].
\end{aligned}
\tag{11.8}
$$

If one further standardizes initial wealth to be 1 and observes that adding a constant to the objective of a maximization problem does not change the nature of the problem or affect the set of controls, then Equation 11.9 results:

$$MV^R \propto E[R_{t,T}^p(\omega_t)] - \frac{1}{2}\lambda Var[R_{t,T}^p(\omega_t)], \tag{11.9}$$

which is a new, ad-hoc objective functional in which the mean and variance are no longer defined with reference to terminal wealth but directly in terms of portfolio returns over the horizon $[t,T]$. However, the absence of a precise microfoundation is simply concealed by the deceivingly intuitive nature of the objective

11.9, as defining $CARA(R_{t,T}^P)$ or $CRRA(R_{t,T}^P)$ remains impossible. An additional problem is caused by that fact that because of Equation 11.10,

$$R_{t,T}^P = \prod_{i=0}^{T-1}(1+R_{t+i,t+i+1}^P)-1 = \prod_{i-0}^{T-1}\left(1+\sum_{n=0}^{N}\omega_t^n r_{t+i,t+i+1}^n\right)-1. \qquad (11.10)$$

$Var[R_{t,T}^P(\omega_t)]$ has a complicated expression unless one assumes, usually in contrast with the data, that the returns on all risky assets are independent over time with zero cross-serial correlations. Probably as a result of this simple fact, Equation 11.9 has been most often employed only after setting $T=1$, when $Var(R_{t+1}^P) = \omega_t Var(\mathbf{r}_{t+1})\omega_t$.

Both equations 11.5 and 11.9 are frequently used in portfolio management, and, at least to some extent, in practice this is because they lead to a closed-form expression (Fabozzi, Focardi, and Kolm, 2006). For instance, in the case of Equation 11.5, Equation 11.11

$$\max_{\omega_t} E[R_{t+1}^P(\omega_t)]-\frac{1}{2}\lambda Var[R_{t+1}^P(\omega_t)]$$

$$\text{s.t. (i) } R_{t+1}^P = \omega_t'\mathbf{r}_{t+1} +(1- \omega_t'\mathbf{1}_N)r^f W_t; \text{ (ii) } \omega_t'\mathbf{1}_N =1, \qquad (11.11)$$

leads to the first-order conditions $(\mathbf{r}_{t+1} -r^f \mathbf{1}_N)- \lambda Var(\mathbf{r}_{t+1})\,\hat{\omega}_t =0_N$ that yield the classical MV formula in Equation 11.12:

$$\hat{\omega}_t = \lambda^{-1}[Var(\mathbf{r}_{t+1})]^{-1}(\mathbf{r}_{t+1} -r^f \mathbf{1}_N). \qquad (11.12)$$

LINEAR UTILITY

Even though the case of linear utility, which is better known as maintaining risk-neutral preferences, can be easily derived from Equation 11.5 by setting $\lambda=0$, different than that done in both equations 11.5 and 11.9, linear utility has clean microfoundations, as shown in Equation 11.13:

$$u_{lin}(W_{t+T})=W_{t+T}, \qquad (11.13)$$

which implies that $E[u_{lin}(W_{t+T})]= E[W_{t+T}]$, implying that an investor ought to simply maximize her expected terminal wealth. Because the case of risk neutrality derives from an assumption of preferences for terminal wealth, then $u'_{lin}(W_{t+T})=1>0$, $u''_{lin}(W_{t+T})=0$, which imply $CARA(W_t)= CRRA(W_t)=0$. Even though this specification lacks an assumption of risk aversion, much commentary about market performance implicitly assumes that a simple, linear objective may characterize the behavior of important portions of investors, especially those with short-term goals.

QUADRATIC UTILITY

One of the most traditional assumptions concerning $u(W_{t+T})$ or $u(C_{t+i})$ is that this relationship is a quadratic utility function (Hanoch and Levy, 1970). For instance, focusing on the simpler case of no interim consumption yields Equation 11.14:

$$u_{quad}(W_{t+T}) = W_{t+T} - \frac{1}{2}\lambda W_{t+T}^2.$$

(11.14)

In this case, risk aversion holds as $u''_{quad}(W_{t+T}) = -\lambda < 0$, but issues exist with nonsatiation because $u_{quad}(W_{t+T}) = 1 - \lambda W_{t+T}$, which is positive if and only if $W_{t+T} < 1/\lambda$, putting an upper bound on the domain for wealth levels and therefore the portfolio choices. $W_{t+T}^* = 1/\lambda$ is often also called the *bliss point* of quadratic utility. Notice that in the case of Equation 11.15, we have

$$E[u_{quad}(W_{t+T})] = E[W_{t+T}] - \frac{1}{2}\lambda E[W_{t+T}^2] = E[W_{t+T}] - \frac{1}{2}\lambda\{Var[W_{t+T}] + (E[W_{t+T}])^2\}$$

$$= \left\{E[W_{t+T}] - \frac{1}{2}\lambda(E[W_{t+T}]^2)\right\} - \frac{1}{2}\lambda Var[W_{t+T}],$$

(11.15)

which shows that quadratic utility is of a MV type. Even though under quadratic utility $E[u_{quad}(W_{t+T})]$ declines in the variance of terminal wealth, some ambiguity remains over the behavior of $E[u_{quad}(W_{t+T})]$ as a function of expected terminal wealth, as shown in Equation 11.16:

$$\frac{\partial E[u_{quad}(W_{t+T})]}{\partial E[W_{t+T}]} = 1 - \lambda E[W_{t+T}].$$

(11.16)

The expression in Equation 11.16 is positive if and only if $E[W_{t+T}] < 1/\lambda$, which means that expected wealth is below the bliss point. However, this issue is only an apparent one, as $W_{t+T} < 1/\lambda$ is sufficient for $E[W_{t+T}] < 1/\lambda$ to hold, so that quadratic utility preferences are truly based on the MV framework. As a result, the decomposition in 11.15 indicates the way in which the portfolio objective in 11.5 may suffer from an ad-hoc nature. If Equation 11.5 derives from a quadratic utility function, then its functional form is misspecified, because Equation 11.5 differs from Equation 11.15 in the absence of the term $-0.5\lambda(E[W_{t+T}])^2$. Additionally, if the objective in 11.5 derives from a quadratic utility function, then one should emphasize that this representation is only valid for $W_{t+T} < 1/\lambda$, something that users of Equation 11.5 often forget.

As $u_{quad}(W_{t+T})$ has a precise microfoundation, computing CARA and CRRA measures in Equation 11.17 is useful:

$$CARA_{quad}(W) \equiv -\frac{1-\lambda W}{-\lambda} = \frac{1}{\lambda} - W \quad CRRA_{quad}(W) = W\left(\frac{1}{\lambda} - W\right).$$

(11.17)

Clearly, as long as wealth is below the bliss point, $CARA_{quad}(W) > 0$, but CARA is decreasing in wealth so that as wealth approaches the bliss point, then $CARA_{quad}(W)$ converges to zero from the right, $CARA_{quad}(W) \to 0^+$ and the investor stops being risk averse. Moreover, Equation 11.17 shows that in this case CRRA is decreasing in wealth. The finding that scaled, normalized risk aversion is declining as investors grow wealthier is an unrealistic feature of quadratic preferences, as is the property that utility may be defined only below the bliss point. In fact, while Equation 11.5 is often employed in practice because of the attractiveness of closed-form expressions such as Equation 11.12, its microfounded version in Equation 11.15 is hardly ever used. These relationships imply that the microfoundations of the portfolio objective in 11.5 have to be found elsewhere.

NEGATIVE EXPONENTIAL UTILITY

This utility function is as popular as the quadratic utility function, both in its own right—for implying a rather realistic constant coefficient of absolute risk aversion for small risks—and because it provides an alternative to and more compelling microfoundation than Equation 11.5 under the specific assumptions shown in Equation 11.18:

$$u_{exp}(W_{t+T}) = -\exp(-\lambda W_{t+T}) \qquad (11.18)$$

Because $u'_{exp}(W_{t+T}) = \lambda \exp(-W_{t+T})$ and $u''_{exp}(W_{t+T}) = -\lambda^2 \exp(-W_{t+T})$, Equation 11.19 results in:

$$CARA_{exp}(W) \equiv -\frac{-\lambda^2 \exp(-W_{t+T})}{\lambda \exp(-W_{t+T})} = \lambda \quad CRRA_{quad}(W) = \lambda W, \quad (11.19)$$

which means that CARA is constant and independent of wealth, with λ being the CARA coefficient, while CRRA is monotone, increasing in wealth. Of course, this latter property is unrealistic, and concerns about the usefulness of this utility function have stemmed from this CRRA behavior.

When using expected utility as an objective in portfolio optimization, $u_{exp}(W_{t+T})$ fails to yield particularly enlightening insights, such as $E[u_{exp}(W_{t+T})] = -E[\exp(-\lambda W_{t+T})]$, because the convexity of the exponential function prevents the claim that $E[\exp(-\lambda W_{t+T})] = \exp(-\lambda E[W_{t+T}])$. However, when W_{t+T} has a lognormal distribution, the function in Equation 11.20 results from the properties of the moment generating function of terminal wealth:

$$E[\exp(-\lambda W_{t+T})] = \exp(-\lambda E[W_{t+T}]) \exp\left(\frac{1}{2}\lambda^2 Var[W_{t+T}]\right). \qquad (11.20)$$

Because the standard features of convex optimization ensure that when $\lambda > 0$, then choosing ω_t to maximize $-E[u_{exp}(W_{t+T}(\omega_t))]$ is identical to maximizing

$-\ln E[-\lambda^{-1}u_{\exp}(W_{t+T}(\omega_t))]$. Thus, maximizing the function in Equation 11.21,

$$-\ln E[-\lambda^{-1}u_{\exp}(W_{t+T}(\omega_t))]=E[W_{t+T}(\omega_t)]-\frac{1}{2}\lambda Var[W_{t+T}(\omega_t)], \qquad (11.21)$$

delivers the same optimal weights as the maximization of the original expected utility functional $E[u_{\exp}(W_{t+T})]$. In turn, for any given choice of weights ω_t, it follows that the expression in Equation 11.22,

$$W_{t+T}(\omega_t)=\exp(\omega_t'\mathbf{r}_{t,T})=\exp\left(\omega_t'\sum_{i=1}^{T}\mathbf{r}_{t+i}\right), \qquad (11.22)$$

has a lognormal distribution (i.e., $\ln W_{t+T}(\omega_t)=\omega_t'\sum_{i=0}^{N}\mathbf{r}_{t+i}$ has a normal distribution) if and only if $\mathbf{r}_{t+i}$ has a multivariate normal distribution for all cases of $i\geq 1$. Therefore, under negative exponential utility, the fact that $\mathbf{r}_{t+i}$ has a multivariate, joint normal distribution is sufficient to lead to an expected utility functional with a structure identical to Equation 11.5. In that case, the parameter λ in Equation 11.5 can be interpreted as a constant CARA coefficient.

LOGARITHMIC UTILITY

As discussed later in this chapter, the case of logarithmic utility corresponds to a special limit parameterization of power, known as isoelastic preferences. The structure of this utility function is shown in Equation 11.23:

$$u_{\log}(W_{t+T})=\ln W_{t+T}, \qquad (11.23)$$

which implies $u_{\log}'(W_{t+T})=1/W_{t+T}$ and $u_{\log}''(W_{t+T})=-1/W_{t+T}^2$, so that the expressions in Equation 11.24 are obtained:

$$CARA_{\log}(W)\equiv-\frac{1/W^2}{-1/W}=\frac{1}{W} \quad CRRA_{\log}(W)=1, \qquad (11.24)$$

which reveals that a logarithmic utility function implies a monotone decreasing CARA coefficient (i.e., the investor becomes decreasingly risk-averse as she gets wealthier) and a constant unit CRRA coefficient.

POWER UTILITY

This functional generalizes the logarithmic case in the utility function 11.25,

$$u_{power}(W_{t+T})=\frac{W_{t+T}^{1-\gamma}}{1-\gamma} \quad \gamma\neq 1, \qquad (11.25)$$

which implies $u'_{power}(W_{t+T}) = W_{t+T}^{-\gamma}$ and $u''_{power}(W_{t+T}) = -\gamma W_{t+T}^{-\gamma-1}$ so that expressions in Equation 11.26,

$$CARA_{power}(W) \equiv -\frac{-\gamma W^{-\gamma-1}}{W^{-\gamma}} = \frac{\gamma}{W} \quad CRRA_{power}(W) = \gamma, \quad (11.26)$$

confirm the same properties obtained under logarithmic utility. Yet, in this case, all the results concerning CARA and CRRA appear to have been scaled by a factor of $\gamma \neq 1$. However, one notable limit result applied to Equation 11.26 leads to.

$$\lim_{\gamma \to 1} u_{power}(W_{t+T}) = \ln W_{t+T} = u_{\log}(W_{t+T}). \quad (11.27)$$

Unless one is ready to resort to some form of approximations, power utility preferences, of which the logarithmic case may be simply interpreted as a special case for $\gamma \to 1$, generally do not lead to closed-form expressions for optimal portfolio weights. Hence, one has to resort to numerical methods to compute optimal allocations.

EPSTEIN-ZIN PREFERENCES

Despite the many attractive features of the power utility model, it has one highly restrictive feature, which is that power utility implies that the consumer's elasticity of intertemporal substitution, ψ, is the reciprocal of the coefficient of relative risk aversion, γ. Yet, whether these two concepts should be linked so tightly is unclear. Risk aversion describes the consumer's reluctance to substitute consumption across states of the world and is meaningful even in a temporal setting. By contrast, the elasticity of intertemporal substitution describes the consumer's willingness to substitute consumption over time and is meaningful even in a deterministic setting. Epstein and Zin (1989) offer a more flexible version of the basic power utility model. The Epstein-Zin model retains the desirable scale independence of power utility (i.e., the fact that CRRA does not depend on wealth) but breaks the link between the parameters ψ and γ. In this section, the assumption is made that utility is defined over a stream of consumption. This is the only case for which the recursive structure of Epstein-Zin preferences is sensible, because defining utility over consumption streams drives a wedge between ψ and γ. The Epstein-Zin objective function is defined recursively, as shown in Equation 11.28:

$$V_t = \left\{ (1-\delta)C_t^{\frac{1-\gamma}{\theta}} + \delta\left(F_t[V_{t+1}^{1-\gamma}]\right)^{\frac{1}{\theta}} \right\}^{\frac{\theta}{1}\frac{1}{\gamma}}, \quad (11.28)$$

where $\delta \in (0,1)$ is the subjective discount rate that reflects the impatience of investors and $\theta \equiv (1-\gamma)/(1-1/\psi)$. When $\gamma = 1/\psi$, $\theta = 1$ and the recursion in Equation 11.28 becomes linear, so that it can be solved forward to yield the familiar (time-separable) power utility model.

The nonlinear recursion in Equation 11.28 is generally difficult to work with in consumption/portfolio problems. However, when risky returns are IID (identically and independently distributed, i.e., investment opportunities are constant), then consumption is a constant fraction of wealth and covariance with consumption growth equals covariance with portfolio return. In this case, showing that if $\gamma = 1$, then $\theta = 0$ is straightforward, so that the standard myopic MV portfolio rule in Equation 11.12 results.

MOMENT-BASED APPROXIMATIONS

Both power and, at least under general dynamics for portfolio returns, negative exponential utility fail to lead to a closed-form solution for optimal portfolio weights, while MV preferences do not account for skewness and kurtosis in either the (portfolio) return distribution or in interim or terminal wealth under models of time-varying predictive densities. To compensate for these weaknesses, a growing body of literature that goes back to seminal papers by Arditti and Levy (1975) and Kraus and Litzenberger (1976) has adopted a different approach. The key idea of this strand of papers is that expanding one of the utility functions (e.g., power utility or negative exponential) previously specified is useful to obtain a tractable expression that depends only on the first M moments of the wealth or portfolio return distribution. In fact, although in the classical development of financial economics, MV-based portfolio selection and performance evaluation have been dominant, some papers (Arditti, 1967; Samuelson, 1970) stress that, unless either asset returns are multivariate and normally distributed or utility functions are quadratic, higher moments cannot be neglected. Indeed in the 1960s, the literature shows that security returns were hardly Gaussian (Fama, 1965). More recently, Harvey and Siddique (2000) show that skewness in stock returns is relevant to portfolio selection based on asset pricing fundamentals. If asset returns exhibit nondiversifiable coskewness (the covariance between portfolio returns and the variance of market returns), investors must be rewarded for coskewness, resulting in increased expected returns. In fact, in the presence of positive coskewness, investors may be willing to accept a negative return. Guidolin and Timmermann (2008) extend these intuitions to international asset allocation applications and derive results that explain why US investors may hesitate before aggressively diversifying their equity portfolios internationally.

In particular, Samuelson (1970) shows that the possibility of using MV preferences to approximate any properly defined utility function (as discussed by Tsiang, 1972, and Levy and Markowitz, 1979) extends to all finite Mth moment approximations (obtained by taking a Taylor expansion) and to the generic utility of final wealth functions, $u(W_{t+T})$. The approximation will work and will generate a sensible representation of preferences (for instance, in terms of global nonsatiation and risk aversion) only when riskiness is limited in a very precise sense. Assume that the $t+T$ period returns on the N risky assets are drawn from a family of compact (small-risk) distributions; for instance, a multivariate distribution illustrated in Equation 11.29

$$F(\mathbf{r}_{t \to t+T}) = P\left(\frac{r_{t,T}^{1} - r^{f} - \sigma_{1}T}{\sigma_{1}\sqrt{T}}, \frac{r_{t,T}^{2} - r^{f} - \sigma_{2}T}{\sigma_{2}\sqrt{T}}, \cdots, \frac{r_{t,T}^{N} - r^{f} - \sigma_{N}T}{\sigma_{N}\sqrt{T}} \right), \quad (11.29)$$

such that the condition will do (in other words, this condition will only be sufficient). Intuitively, compactness implies that as the time horizon vanishes asset returns all converge to the riskless rate. Samuelson shows that an Mth moment approximation of a utility function $u(W_{t+T})$ has a precision that increases as the horizons gets small. Furthermore, given the order of M of the approximation in Equation 11.30,

$$\lim_{T \to 0^+} \frac{\partial \hat{w}_n^M(T)}{(\partial T)^m} = \frac{\partial \hat{w}_n(T)}{(\partial T)^m} \qquad m = 0, 1, \ldots, M \text{ and } n = 1, \ldots, N, \qquad (11.30)$$

where $\partial \hat{w}_n^M(T)/(\partial T)^0 = \hat{w}_n^M(T)$, the apex indicates that an optimal portfolio weight has been computed from an Mth order approximation and $\hat{w}_n^M$ is the optimizing weight under the utility function $u(W_{t+T})$ The implication is that the gain in taking expansions that go beyond the simple MV model is that not only portfolio weights but also their overall behavior as a function of the time horizon can be better approximated the higher that the expansion order M is. These local approximations involving derivatives of the control variable are referred to as being high contact. Conversely, notice that the result holds only asymptotically and irrespective of the order m: if T is too large even under a high M, the resulting $\hat{w}_n^M$ may have nothing to do with the correct $\hat{w}_n$. Samuelson's paper stresses that two components are needed for approximations to work in asset allocation problems: (1) the asset returns must be drawn from well-behaved distribution families (such as normals), and/or (2) the investment horizon must be very short, in principle infinitesimal.

Tsiang (1972) seems to offer the deepest theoretical background to finite-order Taylor expansions of generally accepted utility functions. Tsiang notes that although rigorous, Samuelson's (1970) asymptotic results could be improved, so that risk would be nonnegligible and small enough in a relative sense for Taylor approximations (possibly MV analysis) to be sufficiently accurate. Finite-order Taylor expansions may be applied to utility functions that display these properties, provided that the power series converges (equivalently, provided the remainder term can be ignored). Tsiang carefully considers this aspect for two classes of utility functions. First, in the case of negative exponentials shown in Equation 11.31,

$$u_{app}^M(W_{t+T}; E_t[W_{t+T}]) = -\exp(-\lambda E_t[W_{t+T}]) + \lambda(W_{t+T} - E_t[W_{t+T}])\exp(-\lambda E_t[W_{t+T}]) +$$
$$-\frac{1}{2}\lambda^2(W_{t+T} - E_t[W_{t+T}])^2 \exp(-\lambda E_t[W_{t+T}]) +$$
$$+\frac{1}{6}\lambda^3(W_{t+T} - E_t[W_{t+T}])^3 \exp(-\lambda E_t[W_{t+T}]) + \cdots +$$
$$-(-1)^M \frac{1}{M!}\lambda^M(W_{t+T} - E_t[W_{t+T}])^M \exp(-\lambda E_t[W_{t+T}])$$
$$= -\exp(-\lambda E_t[W_{t+T}])\Big[1 + \lambda(W_{t+T} - E_t[W_{t+T}]) -$$
$$\frac{1}{2}\lambda^2(W_{t+T} - E_t[W_{t+T}])^2 + \frac{1}{6}\lambda^3(W_{t+T} - E_t[W_{t+T}])^3 + \cdots$$
$$-(-1)^M \frac{1}{M!}\lambda^M(W_{t+T} - E_t[W_{t+T}])^M\Big].$$

$$(11.31)$$

which gives an approximation to the expected utility in Equation 11.32 of

$$
\begin{aligned}
E_t[u_{app}^M(W_{t+T};E_t[W_{t+T}])] &= -\exp(-\lambda E_t[W_{t+T}]) \\
&\left[1+\frac{1}{2}\lambda^2 Var_t[W_{t+T}]+\frac{1}{6}\lambda^3(Var_t[W_{t+T}])^{3/2}\right. \\
&\left.\times Skew_t[W_{t+T}]+\cdots-(-1)^M\frac{1}{M!}\lambda^M E_t[(W_{t+T}-E_t[W_{t+T}])^M]\right]
\end{aligned}
$$
(11.32)

From well-known mathematical results, the series emerging in Equation 11.33

$$
1+\lambda h-\frac{1}{2}\lambda^2 h^2+\frac{1}{6}\lambda^3 h^3+\cdots-(-1)^M\frac{1}{M!}\lambda^M h^M,
$$
(11.33)

converges for all hs (provided they are finite). This relationship also guarantees that the approximation can be accurate provided M is high enough ($M\to\infty$). In particular, Tsiang argues that if λ is bounded by $1/E_t[W_{t+T}]$, then setting $M=2$ or 3 may be enough.

With reference to power utility, and when the approximation is taken around $v\equiv E_t[W_{t+T}]$, $v=E_t[W_{t+T}]$ as shown in Equation 11.34,

$$
\begin{aligned}
E[u_{app}^M(W_{t+T};E_t[W_{t+T}])] &= \frac{(E_t[W_{t+T}])^{1-\gamma}}{1-\gamma}-\frac{1}{2}\gamma(E_t[W_{t+T}])^{-\gamma-1}Var_t[W_{t+T}]+ \\
&+\frac{1}{6}\gamma(\gamma+1)(E_t[W_{t+T}])^{-\gamma-2}(Var_t[W_{t+T}])^{3/2}Skew_t[W_{t+T}]+ \\
&+\cdots-(-1)^M\frac{1}{M!}\prod_{j=0}^{M-2}(\gamma+j)(E_t[W_{t+T}])^{-\gamma-M+1}E[(W_{t+T}-E_t[W_{t+T}])^M].
\end{aligned}
$$
(11.34)

Tsiang (1972) shows that the condition $|h|=|W_{t+T}-E_t[W_{t+T}]|\le E_t[W_{t+T}]$ is required for the series in Equation 11.35,

$$
\begin{aligned}
\frac{(E_t[W_{t+T}])^{1-\gamma}}{1-\gamma}&+h(E_t[W_{t+T}])^{-\gamma}-\frac{1}{2}(E_t[W_{t+T}])^{-\gamma-1}h^2 \\
&+\frac{1}{6}(E_t[W_{t+T}])^{-\gamma-2}h^3+\ldots+-(-1)^M\frac{1}{M!}(E_t[W_{t+T}])^{-\gamma-M+1}h^M,
\end{aligned}
$$
(11.35)

to converge. In general, convergence is much slower than in the exponential utility case, and it turns out to depend on T. For large values of T, $Pr\{|W_{t+T}-E_t[W_{t+T}]|\le E_t[W_{t+T}]\}=1$ is unlikely to hold (depending on the distribution of asset returns), and as such approximations may not be viable. Moreover, from an asset allocation perspective, Equation 11.34 has the disadvantage of being taken around expected time $t+T$ wealth, which depends on a portfolio choice that is supposed to be derived endogenously from the maximization of Equation 11.34, which is a circular reasoning (Kane, 1982).

Of course, moment-based expansions developed around points that differ from conditional expected wealth can also be considered. In the case of power utility, suppose $W_t = 1$ and consider a fourth-order Taylor series expansion, such as a polynomial approximation arrested to the fourth-term of a standard power function $W_{t+T}^{1-\gamma}/(1-\gamma)$ ($\gamma > 0$) around $v \equiv \exp(r^f T)$ (i.e., a 100 percent investment in the riskless asset), as shown in Equation 11.36:

$$u(W_{t+T}) \cong \frac{v^{1-\gamma}}{1-\gamma} + v^{-\gamma}(W_{t+T}-v) - \frac{1}{2}\gamma v^{-(\gamma+1)}(W_{t+T}+v)^2 +$$

$$+ \frac{1}{6}\gamma(\gamma+1)v^{-(\gamma+2)}(W_{t+T}-v)^3 - \frac{1}{24}\gamma(\gamma+1)(\gamma+2)v^{-(\gamma+3)}(W_{t+T}-v)^4,$$

$$(11.36)$$

where $u'(v)=v^{-\gamma}$, $u''(v)=-\gamma v^{-(\gamma+1)}$, $u'''(v)=\gamma(\gamma+1)v^{-(\gamma+2)}$, and $u''''(v)=-\gamma(\gamma+1)(\gamma+2)v^{-(\gamma+3)}$. Expanding the powers of $(W_{t+T}-v)$ and taking the expectation conditional on information up to time t, one obtains the expression for a fourth-order approximation in Equation 11.37:

$$E_t[u_{app}^4(W_{t+T})] \cong \kappa_0(\gamma) + \kappa_1(\gamma)E_t[W_{t+T}] + \kappa_2(\gamma)E_t[W_{t+T}^2]$$

$$+ \kappa_3(\gamma)E_t[W_{t+T}^3] + \kappa_4(\gamma)E_t[W_{t+T}^4].$$

$$(11.37)$$

Here, variable definitions are shown in the following expressions:

$$\kappa_0(\gamma) \equiv v^{1-\gamma}\left[(1-\gamma)^{-1} - 1 - \frac{1}{2}\gamma - \frac{1}{6}\gamma(\gamma+1) - \frac{1}{24}\gamma(\gamma+1)(\gamma+2)\right]$$

$$\kappa_1(\gamma) \equiv \frac{1}{6}v^{-\gamma}[6+6\gamma+3\gamma(\gamma+1)+\gamma(\gamma+1)(\gamma+2)]>0$$

$$\kappa_2(\gamma) \equiv -\frac{1}{4}\gamma v^{-(1+\gamma)}[2+2(\gamma+1)+(\gamma+1)(\gamma+2)]<0 \qquad (11.38)$$

$$\kappa_3(\gamma) \equiv \frac{1}{6}\gamma(\gamma+1)(\gamma+3)v^{-(2+\gamma)}>0$$

$$\kappa_4(\gamma) \equiv -\frac{1}{24}\gamma(\gamma+1)(\gamma+3)v^{-(3+\gamma)}<0.$$

Equation 11.37 has highly intuitive implications: the (conditional) expected utility from final wealth increases in $E_t[W_{t+T}]$ and $E_t[W_{t+T}^3]$, i.e., the higher the expected portfolio returns are and the more skewed to the right the induced distribution of final wealth is. These are all signed statistics measuring the location of the distribution of final wealth. By contrast, expected utility is a decreasing function of even noncentral moments, such as $E_t[W_{t+T}^2]$ and $E_t[W_{t+T}^4]$, which are statistics related to the thickness of the tails of the distribution of time $t+T$ wealth.

As for the economic interpretation of the coefficients $\kappa_3(\gamma)$ and $\kappa_4(\gamma)$ in the expressions in Equation 11.39, in the former case (with reference to a third-order Taylor expansion of power utility around expected future wealth W_{t+T}), Kraus and Litzenberger (1976) observe that as long as the bound is imposed, a three-moment Taylor expansion has three desirable properties besides the existence of expected utility: (1) positive marginal utility of wealth, (2) decreasing marginal utility (risk aversion), and (3) nonincreasing absolute risk aversion, which implies $\kappa_3(\gamma)>0$. Scott and Horvath (1980) show that a strictly risk-averse individual who always prefers more to less and who consistently (i.e., for all wealth levels) likes skewness will necessarily dislike kurtosis, $\kappa_4(\gamma)<0$. Since global risk aversion and nonsatiation seem plausible and preference for skewness may be obtained under very weak assumptions, assuming kurtosis aversion may be justified.

MV PREFERENCES AS A SPECIAL CASE

As a special case of Equation 11.35, one can obtain a MV objective function that can be interpreted as a two-moment approximation to a power utility objective, the argument of which is time $t+T$ wealth, similarly to that done by Tsiang (1972) and Levy and Markowitz (1979) in Equation 11.39:

$$E_t[u_{app}^2(W_{t+T})] \cong \kappa_0(\gamma) + \kappa_1(\gamma)E_t[W_{t+T}] + \kappa_2(\gamma)E_t[W_{t+T}^2]. \qquad (11.39)$$

This result derives from the fact that $E_t[W_{t+T}^2] = Var_t[W_{t+T}] + \{E_t[W_{t+T}]\}^2$, implying the following expression:

$$E_t[u_{app}^2(W_{t+T})] \cong \kappa_0(\gamma) + \kappa_1'(\gamma)E_t[W_{t+T}] + \kappa_2(\gamma)Var_t[W_{t+T}] \propto E_t[W_{t+T}] - \lambda Var_t[W_{t+T}]. \qquad (11.40)$$

The expressions in the former equation are defined in Equation 11.41,

$$\kappa_1'(\gamma) \equiv \kappa_1(\gamma) + \kappa_2(\gamma)E_t[W_{t+T}] = \frac{1}{6}v^{-\gamma}[6+3\gamma+3\gamma(\gamma+1)+\gamma(\gamma+1)(\gamma+2)] +$$

$$-\frac{1}{4}\gamma v^{-(1+\gamma)}[2+2(\gamma+1)+(\gamma+1)(\gamma+2)]E_t[W_{t+T}]$$

$$= \frac{1}{12}v^{-(1+\gamma)}\{2v[6+3\gamma+3\gamma(\gamma+1)+\gamma(\gamma+1)(\gamma+2)]$$

$$-3\gamma[2+2(\gamma+1)+(\gamma+1)(\gamma+2)]E_t[W_{t+T}]\},$$

$$(11.41)$$

while $\kappa_2(\gamma)$ has a definition identical to Equation 11.38. $\kappa_1'(\gamma)$ can be shown to be positive provided γ is not too high. However, the sign of $\kappa_1'(\gamma)$ is hard to assess, as it depends on $E_t[W_{t+T}]$ and hence on the portfolio strategy implemented by the investor.

Exotic, Nonstandard Preferences

A new strand of research that straddles the empirical finance, theoretical microeconomics, and portfolio management literatures develops techniques of robust portfolio management. This work contributes to establishing important connections between the role played by preferences in the practice of asset allocation and applications of optimal decisions under ambiguity. Traditional models assume the following: (1) that investors maximize (subjective) expected utility ([S]EU), (2) that agents are perfectly of aware their own preferences, and (3) that investors' expectations are not systematically biased and are made up of rational expectations. However, a growing body of empirical evidence suggests that this traditional paradigm does not well describe investors' behavior in that actual choices are incompatible with (S)EU predictions. As a result, a new line of research entertains agents whose choices are consistent with models that are less restrictive than the standard (S)EU framework in the sense that the underlying axioms are less demanding. In this area, particular attention has recently been dedicated to ambiguity. Under (S)EU, if preferences satisfy certain axioms, numerical utilities and probabilities are used to represent decisions under uncertainty by a standard weighted sum of the utilities, where the weights are (subjective) probabilities for each of the states. As innocuous as this basic principle may seem, a long, rich tradition questions whether it adequately describes behavior. Knight (1921) distinguishes risk, or known probability, from uncertainty. He suggests that economic returns could be earned for bearing uncertainty but not for bearing risk. However, Ellsberg's (1961) paradox most directly provides the modern attack to (S)EU as a descriptive theory. Ellsberg's thought-provoking article led researchers to assemble massive experimental evidence indicating that people generally prefer the least ambiguous acts. Such a pattern is inconsistent with Savage's (1954) *sure-thing principle*, the axiom by which a state with a consequence common to a pair of acts is irrelevant in determining preference between the acts. The implication for portfolio management would be that investors would select optimal portfolios not only by taking the risk of portfolios into account but also by considering their overall uncertainty, which cannot be simply measured as risk.

Although a brief survey of this literature follows, a more complete discussion is available in textbooks devoting chapters to the topic of robust portfolio decisions, such as Fabozzi et al. (2006), or in papers reviewing applications of ambiguity to finance, such as Guidolin and Rinaldi (2010).

MV ANALYSIS UNDER AMBIGUITY

As previously shown, under the assumption that $\mathbf{r}_t$ follows a joint multivariate normal distribution with known variance-covariance matrix $\Sigma \equiv Var[\mathbf{r}_t]$ and known mean $\mu \equiv E[\mathbf{r}_t]$, a MV investor will invest using the well-known formula in Equation 11.12. Kogan and Wang (2003) extend this result to the case in which $\mathbf{r}_t$ the investor does not have perfect knowledge of the distribution of the risky returns; specifically, the case in which follows a joint multivariate normal distribution with a known variance-covariance matrix and an unknown vector of mean returns, μ. Here, the agent displays a special kind of preferences, which Gilboa and Schmeidler (1989) call the multiple priors type (MPP). In this classification, a rational decision maker evaluates expected utility using a multivalued set of priors to capture the existence of ambiguity on the distribution of the set of random outcomes that may affect either the wealth or consumption of the investor. In this case, Schmeidler (1989) proves that standard SEU optimization may be replaced by max-min problems, in which an investor minimizes her maximum expected utility with reference to a set of candidate probability measures, as defined by the multiple priors. Assuming a unique source of information, so that the agent is able to derive only a reference joint normal distribution of asset returns, $\hat{\mathbf{f}} \sim N(\mu, \Sigma)$, the set of effective priors $\wp(\hat{\mathbf{f}})$ is shown in Equation 11.42:

$$\wp(\hat{\mathbf{f}}) = \left\{ q : E[z \ln z] \leq \eta z \equiv \frac{dq}{d\hat{\mathbf{f}}} \right\}, \qquad (11.42)$$

where η captures ambiguity aversion (a larger η means higher aversion). The investment problem can then be reformulated as a typical max-min problem illustrated in Equation 11.43:

$$\max_{\omega} V(W, \wp(\hat{\mathbf{f}})) = \max_{\omega} \min_{q \in \wp(p)} \{E_q[u(W)]\} \quad \text{s.t.} \quad W = [\omega'(\mathbf{r} - r^f \iota_N) + (1 + r^f)], \quad (11.43)$$

(under the standard constraint that portfolio weights sum to one, $\omega' \iota_N = 1$) where W is final wealth, and the set $\wp(\hat{\mathbf{f}})$ constrains the statistical models for the vector process $\mathbf{r}$ to be not too distant from the benchmark $\hat{\mathbf{f}}$, with maximum distance given by η. Letting $\theta \equiv \mu - \hat{\mu}$ be the divergence between one of the possible mean vectors under MPP and the vector of expected returns under the benchmark model, the problem in Equation 11.43 can be rewritten in Equation 11.44 as

$$\max_{\omega} \min_{\theta \in \left\{ \theta : \frac{1}{2} \theta \Sigma^{-1} \theta \leq \eta \right\}} E(z(\mathbf{r})u(W)) \quad z(\mathbf{r}) \equiv \exp \left\{ \frac{1}{2} \theta \Sigma^{-1} \theta - \theta' \Sigma^{-1} \theta(\mathbf{r} - \mu + \theta) \right\}, \quad (11.44)$$

subject to a budget constraint, which is a transformation of the constraint on the set of admissible models under the parameter η into a (multiplicative) factor that appears in the objective function.

Garlappi, Uppal, and Wang (2007) extend these early results and show how to use a confidence interval framework that appears to be natural in the portfolio literature. Their starting point is that the parameters of the joint normal density characterizing the ambiguous asset returns **r** have to be estimated. Assuming that a time series of length T of past asset returns $\mathbf{h}_t$ is available, the conditional density distribution of returns $g(\mathbf{r}|\mathbf{h}_t)$ must be derived. Assuming that the returns depend on some unknown parameters θ, whose prior is $\pi(\theta)$, the predictive density $g(\mathbf{R}|\mathbf{h}_t)$ is $g(\mathbf{r}|\mathbf{h}_t) = \int g(\mathbf{r}|\theta)p(\theta|\mathbf{h}_t)d\theta$, where $p(\theta|\mathbf{h}_t)$ is the data posterior. If an investor solves the classical MV problem using the predictive density of the data, Equation 11.45 emerges:

$$\max_{\omega} \omega' \int \mathbf{r} g(\mathbf{r}|\mathbf{h}_t) d\mathbf{r} - \frac{1}{2}\gamma\omega'\Sigma\omega \tag{11.45}$$

The resulting portfolio is of a Bayesian type, taking into full account the existence of parameter uncertainty (Barberis, 2000). The portfolios in which only parameter uncertainty is considered often perform poorly out of sample, even in comparison to portfolios selected according to some simple ad-hoc rules (De Miguel, Garlappi, and Uppal, 2009). One reason for this result is that the vector of expected asset returns μ is hard to estimate with any precision. This induces Garlappi et al. (2007) to introduce ambiguity on the appropriate statistical model, as identified here by the vector of expected returns μ. When using MPP, the optimization takes the form shown in Equation 11.46:

$$\max_{\omega} \min_{\mu} \omega'\mu - \frac{1}{2}\gamma\omega'\Sigma\omega \quad \text{s.t. } \mathbf{f}(\mu,\hat{\mu},\Sigma) \le \eta \quad \omega'1 = 1 \tag{11.46}$$

where $\mathbf{f}$ is a vector-valued function and $\hat{\mu}$ is the estimate of μ derived from the predictive density $g(\mathbf{r}|\mathbf{h}_t)$. One can prove that the max-min problem in Equation 11.46 is equivalent to the simpler maximization problem in Equation 11.47:

$$\max_{\omega} \omega'(\hat{\mu}-\mu^{adj}) - \frac{1}{2}\gamma\omega'\Sigma\omega, \tag{11.47}$$

where $\hat{\mu}-\mu^{adj}$ is the adjusted estimated expected return (the adjustment has the role of incorporating ambiguity), and define a vector μ^{adj} to satisfy Equation 11.48,

$$\mu^{adj} = \left[\text{sgn}(\omega_1)\frac{\sigma_1}{\sqrt{T}}\sqrt{\eta_1} \; \text{sgn}(\omega_2)\frac{\sigma_2}{\sqrt{T}}\sqrt{\eta_2} \cdots \text{sgn}(\omega_N)\frac{\sigma_N}{\sqrt{T}}\sqrt{\eta_N} \right]. \tag{11.48}$$

The adjustment depends on the precision with which parameters are estimated, the length of the data series, and the investor's aversion to ambiguity (η).

Additional papers have recently shown that using ambiguity aversion to solve realistic, large-scale portfolio problems is possible. Boyle et al. (2009), who study the role of ambiguity in determining portfolio underdiversification and the flight to familiarity episodes, offer the simplest of such papers. Consider a MV portfolio problem in which the asset menu is composed of N identical risky assets and one riskless asset. Each asset has (unknown) expected excess return μ_i and common volatility σ. Using the framework developed by Boyle et al., the authors write the optimization problem as shown in Equation 11.49:

$$\max_{\omega} \min_{\mu} \omega'\mu - \frac{\gamma}{2}\omega'\Sigma\omega \quad \text{s.t.:} \frac{(\mu_i - \hat{\mu}_i)^2}{\sigma_{\hat{\mu}_i}^2} \leq \eta_i \quad \omega'_{nN} = 1. \tag{11.49}$$

Under this specification, the ambiguity problem can be interpreted in terms of classical statistical analysis, because by letting $\hat{\mu}_i$ represent the estimated value of the mean return of asset $i = 1,\ldots,N$ and $\sigma_{\hat{\mu}_i}^2$ represent the variance of $\hat{\mu}_i$, defining the confidence interval $\{T(\mu_i - \hat{\mu}_i)^2 / \sigma_{\hat{\mu}_i}^2 \leq \eta_i$ for expected returns is possible. Hence $\sqrt{\eta_i}$, is the critical value determining the size of the confidence interval, which can be interpreted as a measure of the amount of ambiguity of the estimate of expected returns. The authors find that an investor holds familiar assets but balances this investment by also holding a portfolio of all the other assets (as advocated by Markowitz 1952), which remains biased toward more familiar assets.

SMOOTH RECURSIVE PREFERENCES

One novel approach to modeling ambiguity in asset allocation decisions exploits a generalization of Klibanoff, Marinacci, and Mukerji's (2005; hereafter, KMM) class of smooth preferences. These authors propose that the ambiguity of a risky act or decision can be characterized by a set $\wp = \{P_1,\ldots,P_n\}$ of subjectively plausible cumulative probability distributions. They give the hypothetical example that letting W_j denote the random variable distributed as P_j, $j = 1, \ldots, n$ the decision maker, based on her subjective information, associates a distribution $q_1, \ldots, q_n$ over $\wp$, where q_j is the subjective probability of P_j being the true distribution of W. They that show that resulting preferences have the following representation:

$$\sum_{j=1}^{n} q_j \varsigma \left(\int u(W) dP_j \right), \tag{11.50}$$

where $\varsigma(\cdot)$ is an increasing real-valued function whose shape describes the investor's attitude toward ambiguity. Using Equation 11.50, the decision maker first evaluates the expected utility of W with respect to all the priors in $\wp$: each prior P_j is indexed by j, so in the end, a set of expected utilities results, each being indexed by j. Then, instead of taking the minimum of these expected utilities, as MPP would, the investor takes an expectation of distorted expected utilities. The role ς of is crucial here: If ς were linear, the criterion would simply reduce to (S) EU maximization with respect to the combination of the qs representing the probabilities, and the P_js, representing the possible distributions. When ς is not linear, one cannot combine qs and P_js to construct a reduced probability distribution. In this event, the decision maker takes the expected ζ-utility (with respect to q) of the expected u-utility (with respect to the Ps). A concave ζ will reflect ambiguity aversion, in the sense that it places a larger weight on poor expected u-utility realizations. One important implication of the two-stage approach is that the decision maker is not forced to be so pessimistic as to select the act that maximizes the minimum expected utility as a consequence of the separation between ambiguity and her attitude toward ambiguity. In this sense, KMM preferences may be interpreted as a smooth extension of Gilboa and Schmeidler's (1989) classical MPP. MPP is a limiting case of Equation 11.50. Up to ordinal equivalence, MPP is obtained in the limit as the degree of concavity of ζ increases without bound. Although the type of portfolio problems that have been analyzed so far, assuming simple KMM's preferences, remain limited, this smooth class will acquire increasing weight in the asset allocation literature.

An Illustrative Application

To illustrate the effects of preferences on optimal portfolio decisions, providing an empirical example is useful. Assume the following two experiments: The first experiment involves calculating optimal weights under a range of alternative utility functions (preferences). Such optimal weights are computed over a range of alternative scenarios describing the state of the economy, where the state is defined through the lenses of a simple but powerful two-state Markov switching model (henceforth, MSM). The second experiment illustrates the power of alternative preference frameworks as tools to evaluate performance. To keep things simple, a recursive evaluation of three portfolio strategies is undertaken. The first strategy is the optimal recursive strategy computed under a given preference framework. The second strategy is an equally weighted strategy (also called 1/N after De Miguel et al., 2009) that has been shown to be highly performing in spite of its complete disregard for any kind of utility optimization. The third strategy involves deriving the value-weighted market portfolio implied by the CAPM. Notice that 1/N basically results in a simple 50–50 allocation between stocks and cash. This result avoids both estimation and model specification errors that are implicit when relying on the CAPM. The following are the preference frameworks employed in the examples:

- The linear utility framework characterizes the behavior of a risk-neutral investor.
- Ad-hoc MV preferences are defined over portfolio returns.
- Ad-hoc MV preferences are defined over terminal wealth.
- Three- and four-moment ($M = 3$ and $M = 4$) Taylor expansions approximate the expected power utility of terminal wealth as a function of the first three and four moments of terminal wealth. In this case, calculations are performed around two approximation points, $v = r^f T$ and $v = E_{t-1}[W_t]$.
- Additional frameworks include:

- The power utility function characterizes the behavior of a risk-averse investor with constant relative risk-aversion.
- The negative exponential utility function characterizes the behavior of a risk-averse investor with constant absolute risk-aversion; entertaining this utility function as a separate framework from the standard MV one is advisable when stock returns do not follow an IID Gaussian distribution.
- A KMM smooth ambiguity functional characterized by $u(W_{t+T})$ set to be a power utility function and $\zeta(E_t[u(W_{t+T})])=-\exp(-E_t[u(W_{t+T})])$ captures aversion to ambiguity; the set $\wp=\{P_1,...,P_n\}$ of plausible cumulative probability distributions is specified to correspond to the set of possible states/scenarios according to the estimated MSM along a grid $\{0,0.1,0.2,\cdots,1\}$ with each of the regimes being equally weighted.

This list delivers a total of 10 alternative preference frameworks, in which alternative choices of the approximation points v are taken into account. In fact, each such framework is implemented with three alternative values for the unique parameter characterizing the degree of risk aversion: $\zeta = 0.5, 2,$ and 4 in the case of MV and negative exponential utility and $\gamma=2, 5,$ and 10 in the case of power utility and KMM. Finally, calculations are performed for four horizons of 1, 3, 6, and 12 months. Short sales are ruled out throughout. However, calculations that are done without imposing the short sales restriction have been performed, obtaining results that are qualitatively similar.

ECONOMETRIC ESTIMATES

Monthly data from the Center for Research in Security Prices (CRSP) at the University of Chicago from July 1926 through December 2010 on value-weighted stock returns on the New York Stock Exchange (NYSE), American Stock Exchange (AMEX), and NASDAQ markets are employed to estimate two alternative statistical models that describe the dynamics of stock returns. The first model is a simple Gaussian IID model that is consistent with the hypothesis of geometric random walk in (cum dividend) stock index prices and with the absence of predictability (robust standard errors are in parenthesis) shown in the estimated model 11.51:

$$r_t = 0.920 + 5.465\varepsilon_t \quad \varepsilon_t \sim \text{IID } N(0,1). \tag{11.51}$$
$$\underset{[0.172]}{}$$

Moreover, a simple, two-state MSM is estimated in model 11.52:

$$r_t = -1.223S_t + 1.293(1-S_t) + [10.607S_t + 3.801(1-S_t)]\varepsilon_t \quad \varepsilon_t \sim \text{IID } N(0,1).$$
$$\underset{[0.920]}{} \quad \underset{[0.152]}{} \tag{11.52}$$

Regime 1 $(S_t =1)$ is a bear state with negative expected returns and high volatility, while regime 0 $(S_t =0)$ is a bull state with positive expected return and moderate equity volatility. The estimated persistence on the main diagonal of the transition probability matrix is $p_{11} = 0.984$ and $p_{22} = 0.907$. These imply an average duration of eleven months for the bear regime and sixty-three months for the bull regime. As a result, the ergodic, long-run probabilities (that one would obtain from an infinite sample from the process) of the two regimes are 0.147 and 0.853, respectively. Figure 11.1 plots the full-sample, smoothed-state probabilities of the two regimes. In the bear state plot, various episodes of declining and turbulent aggregate stock prices can be singled out: two spikes corresponding to the Great Depression in the 1930s, two spikes for the oil shocks of 1974–1975 and 1980, and one spike each for the crash of late 1987, the Asian crisis of the summer 1998, the dot-com bubble crash of 2000–2001, and more recently the great financial crisis of 2008–2009.

The reason the MSM is entertained as an alternative statistical framework is that dynamic econometric frameworks from this family are well known to capture,

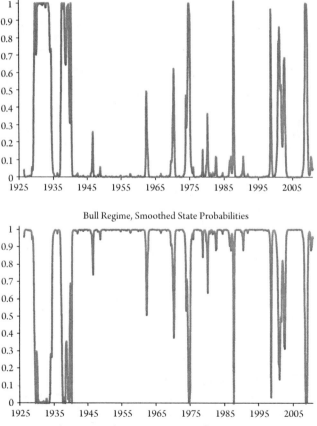

Figure 11.1 Smoothed (full-sample) probabilities from two-state Markov switching model. These two plots show the full-sample smooth probabilities derived from a two-state Markov switching model in which means, variances, and covariances are assumed to be a function of the Markov state.

in an intuitive way, the most salient features of the dynamics of investment opportunities. MSM also has rich implications for the time variation of means, variances, and especially skewness and kurtosis (Timmermann, 2000). Guidolin and Timmermann (2008) and Guidolin (2011) provide additional details on the role of MSMs in dynamic portfolio selection and estimation. These authors also show how to derive closed-form expressions for the first four noncentral moments of the time $t+T$ wealth. Guidolin and Timmermann prove that when the risky asset return follows a Markov switching process, conditional expectations of the type $E_t[\exp(m\sum_{i=1}^{T} r_{t+i})]$ can be calculated in a recursive fashion.

OPTIMAL PORTFOLIO WEIGHTS UNDER ALTERNATIVE SCENARIOS

Table 11.1 reports optimal weights computed under different preferences, risk aversion parameters, and investment horizons. The optimal allocation to US stocks in five representative scenarios has been computed: (1) when at time t the regime is bull, (2) when it is bear, (3) when the investor is in a state of ignorance on the nature of the regime and guesses that each state carries a current probability equal to its ergodic frequency, (4) when the investor is in such a state of ignorance to understand only the presence of two regimes but is unable to compute the ergodic frequencies and she attributes equal probabilities to both, and (5) when the investor ignores regimes altogether. Notice that in scenarios (1)-(4), even when knowledge of the starting regime is assumed in the scenario simulation, this never implies that the regime is known in advance or observable at times $t+1$, $t+2$,...,$t+T$. Under scenario (5), optimal weights are computed assuming (counterfactually) that stock returns are generated by a simpler single state, Gaussian IID model, when only one regime is possible at all times.

Independent of the preference framework for low risk aversion (i.e., $\varsigma = 0$, 0.5, and 2; moreover $\gamma = 2$), in the IID case, a common finding is that an investor ought to invest 100 percent of her wealth in stocks. Equivalently, the market portfolio advocated by the CAPM is ex-ante optimal. This result is easy to understand because over the sample period, the US market portfolio yielded a handsome average monthly return of 0.9 percent, which exceeds the 0.3 percent average monthly return on one-month Treasury bills. The difference of about 7 percent per year is called the *equity premium*, which appears to be sufficiently high to lead any moderately risk-averse investor to bet all of her wealth on stocks. Under some preference assumptions such as power utility and KMM, higher risk aversion levels would induce an investor to a much more balanced approach, in which the optimal share invested in US stocks might be as low as 30 percent, independent of the horizon.

For zero- or low-risk-aversion coefficients and especially for short investment horizons of one and three months, all asset allocations simulated under alternative MSM scenarios reveal the following: Investors ought to aggressively time the market in a simple way. They should invest 100 percent in stocks in bull markets when limited uncertainty leads them to think that the current state does not depart much from ergodic probabilities. During bear markets, they should invest 0 percent in stocks (100 percent in cash). The case of 50–50 uncertainty is of some interest because this

Table 11.1 Optimal portfolio weights under alternative preferences, risk aversion coefficients, and investment horizons

Preferences	State/model	Risk aversion coefficient/investment horizon			
		T = 1	T = 3	T = 6	T = 12
Linear (risk neutral)	Bull regime	1.000	1.000	1.000	1.000
	Ergodic probabilities	1.000	1.000	1.000	1.000
	Equal probabilities	0.000	0.000	0.000	1.000
	Bear regime	0.000	0.000	0.000	0.000
	Gaussian IID	1.000	1.000	1.000	1.000

Preferences	State/model	λ = 0.5				λ = 2				λ = 4			
		T = 1	T = 3	T = 6	T = 12	T = 1	T = 3	T = 6	T = 12	T = 1	T = 3	T = 6	T = 12
(Ad-hoc) mean-variance in portfolio returns	Bull regime	1.000	1.000	1.000	1.000	1.000	1.000	1.000	1.000	1.000	1.000	0.916	0.695
	Ergodic probabilities	1.000	1.000	1.000	1.000	0.799	0.766	0.728	0.680	0.400	0.383	0.364	0.340
	Equal probabilities	0.000	0.000	0.000	0.107	0.000	0.000	0.000	0.027	0.000	0.000	0.000	0.013
	Bear regime	0.000	0.000	0.000	0.000	0.000	0.000	0.000	0.000	0.000	0.000	0.000	0.000
	Gaussian IID	1.000	1.000	1.000	1.000	1.000	1.000	1.000	1.000	1.000	1.000	1.000	1.000

(Continued)

Table 11.1 (Continued)

Preferences	State/model	Risk aversion coefficient/investment horizon											
		γ = 2				γ = 4				γ = 10			
		T = 1	T = 3	T = 6	T = 12	T = 1	T = 3	T = 6	T = 12	T = 1	T = 3	T = 6	T = 12
(Ad-hoc) mean-variance in terminal wealth	Bull regime	1.000	1.000	1.000	1.000	1.000	1.000	1.000	0.955	1.000	0.895	0.760	0.590
	Ergodic probabilites	1.000	1.000	1.000	1.000	0.700	0.680	0.660	0.610	0.420	0.410	0.395	0.365
	Equal probabilities	0.000	0.085	0.200	0.380	0.000	0.040	0.100	0.190	0.000	0.025	0.060	0.115
	Bear regime	0.000	0.000	0.000	0.000	0.000	0.000	0.000	0.000	0.000	0.000	0.000	0.000
	Gaussian IID	1.000	1.000	1.000	1.000	1.000	1.000	1.000	1.000	1.000	1.000	1.000	0.985
		γ = 2				γ = 4				γ = 10			
		T = 1	T = 3	T = 6	T = 12	T = 1	T = 3	T = 6	T = 12	T = 1	T = 3	T = 6	T = 12
Three-moment preferences (approximate past exponen-tial wealth)	Bull regime	1.000	1.000	1.000	1.000	1.000	1.000	1.000	1.000	0.575	0.545	0.520	0.595
	Ergodic probabilites	1.000	1.000	1.000	1.000	0.535	0.535	0.540	0.595	0.215	0.210	0.215	0.150
	Equal probabilities	0.000	0.065	0.155	0.305	0.000	0.030	0.075	0.150	0.000	0.015	0.030	0.060
	Bear regime	0.000	0.000	0.000	0.000	0.000	0.000	0.000	0.000	0.000	0.000	0.000	0.000
	Gaussian IID	1.000	1.000	1.000	1.000	1.000	1.000	1.000	1.000	1.000	1.000	1.000	1.000

Three-moment preferences (approximately r^2T)

	$\gamma = 2$				$\gamma = 4$				$\gamma = 10$			
	T = 1	T = 3	T = 6	T = 12	T = 1	T = 3	T = 6	T = 12	T = 1	T = 3	T = 6	T = 12
Bull regime	1.000	1.000	1.000	1.000	1.000	1.000	1.000	1.000	0.575	0.560	1.000	1.000
Ergodic probabilities	1.000	1.000	1.000	1.000	0.535	0.535	0.545	0.670	0.215	0.210	0.215	1.000
Equal probabilities	0.000	0.065	0.155	0.305	0.000	0.030	0.075	0.150	0.000	0.015	0.030	0.060
Bear regime	0.000	0.000	0.000	0.000	0.000	0.000	0.000	0.000	0.000	0.000	0.000	0.000
Gaussian IID	1.000	1.000	1.000	1.000	1.000	1.000	1.000	1.000	1.000	1.000	1.000	1.000

Four-moment preferences (approximately past exponential wealth)

	$\gamma = 2$				$\gamma = 4$				$\gamma = 10$			
	T = 1	T = 3	T = 6	T = 12	T = 1	T = 3	T = 6	T = 12	T = 1	T = 3	T = 6	T = 12
Bull regime	1.000	1.000	1.000	1.000	1.000	1.000	0.910	0.695	0.540	0.460	0.375	0.285
Ergodic probabilties	1.000	0.965	0.910	0.840	0.520	0.495	0.470	0.440	0.210	0.200	0.190	0.180
Equal probabilities	0.000	0.065	0.150	0.290	0.000	0.030	0.075	0.145	0.000	0.015	0.030	0.060
Bear regime	0.000	0.000	0.000	0.000	0.000	0.000	0.000	0.000	0.000	0.000	0.000	0.000
Gaussian IID	1.000	1.000	1.000	1.000	1.000	1.000	1.000	1.000	1.000	1.000	1.000	1.000

(Continued)

Table 11.1 **(Continued)**

		γ = 2				γ = 4				γ = 10			
		T = 1	T = 3	T = 6	T = 12	T = 1	T = 3	T = 6	T = 12	T = 1	T = 3	T = 6	T = 12
Four-moment preferences (approximately r^2T)	Bull regime	1.000	1.000	1.000	1.000	1.000	1.000	0.880	0.640	0.540	0.455	0.365	0.270
	Ergodic probabilities	0.520	0.960	0.900	0.810	0.520	0.495	0.470	0.430	0.210	0.200	0.190	0.175
	Equal probabilities	0.000	0.065	0.150	0.290	0.000	0.030	0.075	0.145	0.000	0.015	0.030	0.060
	Bear regime	0.000	0.000	0.000	0.000	0.000	0.000	0.000	0.000	0.000	0.000	0.000	0.000
	Gaussian IID	1.000	1.000	1.000	1.000	1.000	1.000	1.000	1.000	1.000	1.000	1.000	1.000
Power utility (CRRA)	Bull regime	1.000	1.000	1.000	1.000	1.000	1.000	1.000	0.990	0.930	0.710	0.550	0.430
	Ergodic probabilities	1.000	1.000	1.000	1.000	1.000	1.000	0.940	0.870	0.420	0.400	0.390	0.360
	Equal probabilities	0.250	0.420	0.520	0.660	0.130	0.210	0.260	0.330	0.050	0.080	0.100	0.130
	Bear regime	0.000	0.000	0.000	0.000	0.000	0.000	0.000	0.000	0.000	0.000	0.000	0.000
	Gaussian IID	1.000	1.000	1.000	1.000	0.890	0.890	0.890	0.890	0.350	0.350	0.350	0.350

Negative exponential utility (CARA)

	λ = 0.5				λ = 2				λ = 4			
	T = 1	T = 3	T = 6	T = 12	T = 1	T = 3	T = 6	T = 12	T = 1	T = 3	T = 6	T = 12
Bull regime	1.000	1.000	1.000	1.000	1.000	1.000	1.000	1.000	1.000	1.000	1.000	0.990
Ergodic probabilities	1.000	1.000	1.000	1.000	1.000	1.000	1.000	1.000	1.000	1.000	0.940	0.870
Equal probabilities	1.000	1.000	1.000	1.000	0.250	0.420	0.520	0.660	0.130	0.210	0.260	0.330
Bear regime	0.000	0.000	0.000	0.020	0.000	0.000	0.000	0.000	0.000	0.000	0.000	0.000
Gaussian IID	1.000	1.000	1.000	1.000	1.000	1.000	1.000	1.000	0.890	0.890	0.890	0.890

Klibanoff, Marinacci, and Mukerji's smooth ambiguity preferences (power/negative exponential utility)

	γ = 2				γ = 4				γ = 10			
	T = 1	T = 3	T = 6	T = 12	T = 1	T = 3	T = 6	T = 12	T = 1	T = 3	T = 6	T = 12
Bull regime	1.000	1.000	0.980	0.910	0.990	0.920	0.860	0.780	0.930	0.710	0.550	0.430
Ergodic probabilities	1.000	0.970	0.860	0.780	0.960	0.900	0.830	0.750	0.420	0.400	0.390	0.360
Equal probabilities	0.250	0.420	0.520	0.660	0.110	0.195	0.245	0.305	0.050	0.080	0.100	0.130
Bear regime	0.000	0.000	0.000	0.000	0.000	0.000	0.000	0.000	0.000	0.000	0.000	0.000
Gaussian IID	1.000	1.000	1.000	1.000	0.810	0.810	0.810	0.810	0.295	0.295	0.295	0.295

Note: The table shows optimal portfolio weights under alternative assumptions concerning the investment horizon, coefficient that captures risk-aversion, regime scenario under which the calculation has been performed, and preference framework.

is when different preferences lead to heterogeneous indications. For example, linear utility, MV, and all moment-based preference models suggest exiting the stock market. Power utility and KMM favor mixed portfolios, and negative exponential utility oddly indicates a 100 percent optimal investment in stocks. Instead, for higher risk aversion and especially longer investment horizons, most preference frameworks give balanced indications in which the optimal share of stocks is not zero or one, although it remains the case that starting from a bear regime, all preferences and horizons indicate the optimality of exiting the stock market. This strategy is not only sensible, because in a bear regime, US stocks yield negative expected returns, but also plausible, in the light of the finding that the average duration of a bear regime is 11 months. Thus, even an investor with $T = 12$ may expect to remain, on average, in the bear regime over her entire horizon. However, in the remaining three switching scenarios, the heterogeneity in optimal portfolio weights across preferences is remarkable. Unlike the case of constant investment opportunities, an investor should pin down a preference framework that accurately describes her risk attitudes in order to be able to employ quantitative frameworks of portfolio optimization.

BACK-TESTING THE REALIZED PERFORMANCE OF ALTERNATIVE PREFERENCES

Table 11.1 cannot be used to show that modeling portfolio decisions in a utility-maximizing setup give investors any advantage. A simple recursive back-testing exercise was implemented for each month between January 1980 and December 2010, both econometric models (IID and MSM) were recursively reestimated, and the resulting parameter estimates were used to compute optimal portfolio weights for the same range of preferences, the same risk aversion coefficients, and the same horizons as those in Table 11.1. After computing the weights, realized wealth (or portfolio returns) over the assumed horizons were computed from the data, such as the actual value-weighted CRSP stock returns and one-month Treasury bill yields. This yields a total of $372 - T$ measures of realized wealth for each combination of preferences, risk aversion parameter, and horizon. Such time series of realized wealth were converted in time series of realized utility using the assumed structure for preferences and for instances in the case of power utility, so that Equation 11.53 emerges:

$$u_{power}(\hat{\omega}_{t,T}) = \frac{[W_{t+T}(\hat{\omega}_{t,T})]^{1-\gamma}}{1-\gamma} \qquad (11.53)$$

For the time index t that ranges between January 1980 and December 2010 . Finally, such time series of realized utility were averaged and converted into certainty equivalent returns (CERs), as illustrated in Equation 11.54:

$$\frac{[(1+CER_{power}^{\gamma,T})W_t]^{1-\gamma}}{1-\gamma} = \frac{1}{372-T} \sum_{t=1980:01}^{2010:12-T} u_{power}(\hat{\omega}_{t,T}) \Rightarrow$$

$$CER_{power}^{\gamma,T} = [(1-\gamma)\bar{u}_{power}(\hat{\omega}_{t,T})]^{\frac{1}{1-\gamma}} - 1 , \qquad (11.54)$$

where $\bar{u}_{power}(\hat{\omega}_{t,T}) \equiv (372-T)^{-1} \sum_{t=1980\,:\,01}^{2010\,:\,12-T} u_{power}(\hat{\omega}_{t,T})$. The CER represents the certain return that one investor would be ready to accept in replacement of the risky portfolio strategy defined by $\{\hat{\omega}_{t,T}\}_{t=1980\,:\,01}^{2010\,:\,12-T}$ because it gives her the same average realized utility. Obviously, the better a strategy is, the higher its CER. Moreover, the CER has the additional advantage of converting the realized performance of potentially heterogeneous strategies into a comparable measure. Obviously, in the case of simple MV frameworks, the ranking provided by the CER is identical to rankings based on Sharpe ratios. In the case of linear utility, the CER is identical to average realized portfolio returns. However, in other cases, including moment-based preferences, power utility, and KMM, the CER is likely to give indications that significantly differ from simple Sharpe ratios (Guidolin and Ria, 2011).

Table 11.2 presents the realized certainty equivalent returns (CERs) for the three alternative strategies. Corresponding to each combination of preferences and risk aversion coefficients/horizon, the best performing CER is shown in boldface. The table shows that preference-based, optimizing asset allocation models may help investors to maximize their realized performance but may also occasionally provide disappointing results. Although a detailed analysis of the point estimates of the CERs in Table 11.2 is beyond the scope of this illustration, the usefulness of preference-based asset allocation seems to be "U-shaped" with respect to both risk aversion and horizon. The utility-based CER outperforms the benchmarks for risk-neutral investors and for highly risk-averse investors, while it underperforms the benchmarks for investors who display intermediate levels of risk aversion. The utility-based CER outperforms the benchmarks for shorter (one-month) and especially longer (6- and 12-month) horizons. However, when preferences are MV or MV skewness, utility-based CERs are never superior to those of the benchmarks. The equally weighted portfolio does not perform as well as expected in light of the recent academic literature. However, its realized performance tends to be strong for long-horizon investors whose risk aversion is relatively high. Yet, even when the utility-optimizing framework fails to turn out the best realized performance, the distance to the benchmarks remains modest. For instance, consider the case of a three-month investor favoring MV skewness whose approximation is taken around a power utility function with $\gamma = 4$. Independent of the details of the Taylor approximation, her CER is 6.3 percent per year from the utility-maximizing framework, 7.1 percent from 1/N, and 7.2 percent from the market portfolio that always invests 100 percent in stocks. One final finding is intriguing. The ex-ante preference-optimizing strategy is ex-post the most successful strategy under KMM's ambiguity-averse preferences. This finding confirms the importance of performing quantitative portfolio optimization in the case where investors are sensitive to parameter and model uncertainty.

Summary and Conclusions

Surveying the portfolio theory literature that uses preference-based frameworks to compute optimal portfolios, this chapter's key empirical result is that basing

Table 11.2 **Realized, recursive back-tested certainty equivalent return performance of alternative portfolio strategies**

Risk aversion coefficient/investment horizon

Preferences	State/model	T=1	T=3	T=6	T=12
Linear risk neutral	Optimal strategy	**10.903**	**11.682**	**12.096**	**12.760**
	Market portfolio	-0.359	7.813	9.718	10.468
	1/N	8.273	8.504	8.589	8.703

Preferences	State/model	λ = 0.5				λ = 2				λ = 4			
		T=1	T=3	T=6	T=12	T=1	T=3	T=6	T=12	T=1	T=3	T=6	T=12
(Ad-hoc) mean-variance in portfolio returns	Optimal strategy	10.323	10.819	11.174	11.736	8.644	8.989	8.912	9.011	6.708	6.270	5.864	5.741
	Market portfolio	**12.338**	**12.705**	**12.808**	**12.907**	**10.404**	**10.489**	**10.420**	**10.216**	**7.732**	**7.353**	6.975	6.399
	1/N	8.115	8.325	8.397	8.487	7.637	7.781	7.814	7.830	6.989	7.037	**7.010**	**6.925**
(Ad-hoc) mean-variance in terminal wealth	Optimal strategy	9.311	9.719	9.876	10.339	7.657	7.702	7.422	7.506	4.630	3.359	3.158	5.125
	Market portfolio	**11.049**	**11.248**	**11.274**	**11.288**	**9.055**	**8.908**	**8.688**	**8.449**	4.796	3.547	2.133	1.565
	1/N	7.797	7.969	8.025	8.091	7.315	7.421	7.441	7.451	**6.326**	**6.272**	**6.193**	**6.080**

		γ = 2				γ = 4				γ = 10			
		T = 1	T = 3	T = 6	T = 12	T = 1	T = 3	T = 6	T = 12	T = 1	T = 3	T = 6	T = 12
Three-moment preferences (approximate past exponential wealth)	Optimal strategy	8.783	9.085	9.110	9.529	6.611	6.293	5.823	5.647	2.493	-3.445	-10.220	-8.635
	Market portfolio	**10.393**	**10.488**	**10.449**	**10.385**	**7.678**	**7.235**	**7.037**	**7.007**	-1.644	-5.667	-10.715	-8.595
	1/N	7.637	7.788	7.833	7.881	6.988	7.045	7.037	7.007	**4.947**	**4.609**	**4.303**	**4.063**
Three-moment preferences (approximate i around r²t)	Optimal strategy	8.783	9.086	9.105	9.534	6.611	6.296	5.839	5.647	2.493	-3.746	-10.201	-8.635
	Market portfolio	10.393	10.488	10.449	10.385	7.678	7.235	6.744	6.328	-1.644	-5.667	-10.715	-8.595
	1/N	7.637	7.788	7.833	7.881	6.988	7.045	7.037	7.007	4.947	4.609	4.303	4.063
Four-moment preferences (approximate past exponential wealth)	Optimal strategy	8.770	9.076	9.088	9.373	**6.681**	6.240	5.778	**6.568**	3.562	3.793	**4.329**	**4.814**
	Market portfolio	**9.728**	**9.709**	**9.588**	**9.439**	6.261	5.454	4.575	4.025	-2.527	-7.024	-12.595	-9.757
	1/N	7.477	7.605	7.639	7.668	6.659	**6.663**	**6.622**	6.551	**4.770**	**4.389**	4.045	3.798
Four-moment preferences (approximate past exponential wealth)	Optimal strategy	8.770	9.075	9.085	9.369	**6.681**	6.245	5.915	**6.717**	3.562	3.884	**4.492**	**4.873**
	Market portfolio	**9.728**	**9.709**	**9.588**	**9.439**	6.261	5.454	4.575	4.025	-2.527	-7.024	-12.595	-9.757
	1/N	7.477	7.605	7.639	7.668	6.659	**6.663**	**6.622**	6.551	**4.770**	**4.389**	4.045	3.798

(Continued)

Table 11.2 (Continued)

		γ = 2				γ = 4				γ = 10			
		T = 1	T = 3	T = 6	T = 12	T = 1	T = 3	T = 6	T = 12	T = 1	T = 3	T = 6	T = 12
Four-moment preferences (approximate i around r²t)	Optimal strategy	8.742	9.030	9.059	9.324	6.554	6.305	5.731	5.654	2.311	2.857	3.549	4.307
	Market portfolio	**9.924**	**10.160**	**10.410**	**10.001**	**7.293**	**6.993**	**6.730**	**6.615**	-1.631	-5.286	-10.325	-7.846
	1/N	7.365	7.524	7.831	7.710	6.774	6.352	6.281	6.008	**4.491**	**4.185**	**4.115**	**3.885**
Power utility (CRRA)	Optimal strategy	10.326	10.939	11.228	11.692	8.704	9.046	9.002	9.100	6.738	6.346	6.382	6.593
	Market portfolio	**12.338**	**12.705**	**12.808**	**12.907**	**10.404**	**10.489**	**10.420**	**10.216**	**7.732**	**7.353**	6.975	6.399
	1/N	8.115	8.325	8.397	8.487	7.637	7.781	7.814	7.830	6.989	7.037	**7.010**	**6.925**
Negative exponential utility (CARA) I	Optimal strategy	8.437	8.274	**7.662**	**8.690**	**6.046**	5.172	4.744	4.139	2.523	2.980	**4.064**	**4.450**
	Market portfolio	**8.575**	**8.793**	7.587	6.931	5.814	4.973	4.561	3.980	-3.416	-8.051	-13.901	-10.271
	1/N	6.207	7.420	6.561	7.183	5.843	**5.726**	**5.869**	**5.930**	**4.338**	**3.934**	3.574	3.209

Note: The table reports the annualized certainty equivalent return (CER) corresponding to average realized utility under alternative assumptions concerning the investment horizon, the coefficient that captures risk-aversion, the regime scenario under which the calculation has been performed, and the preference framework. Average realized utilities are computed with reference to the back-testing period 1980:01–2010:12. The best-performing CERs are shown in bold-face.

asset allocation decisions on preferences may pay off not only in ex-ante but also ex-post terms under two important conditions: First, asset returns must be generated from non-Gaussian frameworks characterized by nonlinear predictability dynamics, which translates into rich time variation in skewness and kurtosis. Second, the preferences must overweight the importance of higher-order moments and of the (conditional) tails of the distribution of portfolio returns, such as power utility or ambiguity-averse preferences.

Although this finding fits the key results in the literature, its characterization under Markov switching dynamics when ambiguity aversion is called into play appears novel. For instance, Kallberg and Ziemba (1983) already report that in many practical applications, one can choose the utility function that allows for the most efficient numerical solution. As the utility function that is most easily tractable in terms of computation, finding that quadratic utility is by far the most commonly used in practice is not surprising. These authors note, however, that they performed most of their calculations using assets exhibiting return distributions not too far away from normality; for instance, in the case of the so-called elliptical distributions (such as the normal, Student t, and Levy distributions). This chapter further emphasizes that when such elliptical properties are absent, results for MV preferences may differ from those derived under more complex and arguably realistic preferences.

Discussion Questions

1. What are the possible combinations of assumptions about individual's preferences and about the statistical distribution of asset (portfolio) returns that may justify a simple MV approach to portfolio optimization, such as that in Equation 11.5?
2. Why is computing the standard (small) risk measures CARA(W) and CRRA(W) impossible in the case of MV preferences? Explain the source from which deficiencies stem.
3. Describe the intuition underlying Klibanoff, Marinacci, and Mukerji's (2005) smooth ambiguity-averse preferences. Explain how these smooth preferences can nest both Gilboa and Schmeidler's (1989) max-min type, multiple priors preferences, and the standard subjective expected utility case.
4. Why is a dynamic model of risky asset returns such as a Markov switching model likely to bring out the power of smooth ambiguity preferences to improve realized performance?

References

Arditti, Fred D. 1967. "Risk and the Required Return on Equity." *Journal of Finance* 22(1): 19–36.

Arditti, Fred D., and Haim Levy. 1975. "Portfolio Efficiency Analysis in Three Moments: The Multi-Period Case." *Journal of Finance* 30:3, 797–809.

Barberis, Nicholas. 2000. "Investing for the Long Run When Returns Are Predictable." *Journal of Finance* 55:1, 225–264.

Boyle, Phelim, Lorenzo Garlappi, Raman Uppal, and Tan Wang. 2009. "Keynes Meets Markowitz: The Trade-Off between Familiarity and Diversification." Working Paper, London Business School, London.

Campbell, John Y., and Luis M. Viceira. 2002. *Strategic Asset Allocation: Portfolio Choice for Long-Term Investors.* Oxford, UK: Oxford University Press.

DeMiguel, Victor, Lorenzo Garlappi, and Raman Uppal. 2009. "Optimal Versus Naive Diversification: How Inefficient Is the 1/N Portfolio Strategy?" *Review of Financial Studies* 22:5, 1915–1953.

Ellsberg, Daniel. 1961. "Risk, Ambiguity, and the Savage Axioms." *Quarterly Journal of Economics* 75:34, 643–669.

Elton, Edwin, J., Martin J. Gruber, Stephen J. Brown, and William N. Goetzmann. 2010. *Modern Portfolio Theory and Investment Analysis,* 8th ed. London: John Wiley & Sons.

Epstein, Larry G., and Stanley E. Zin. 1989. "Substitution, Risk Aversion, and the Temporal Behavior of Consumption and Asset Returns: A Theoretical Framework." *Econometrica* 57(4): 937–969.

Fabozzi, Frank J., Sergio M. Focardi, and Petter N. Kolm. 2006. *Financial Modeling of the Equity Market: From CAPM to Cointegration.* New York: John Wiley and Sons.

Fama, Eugene F. 1965. "The Behavior of Stock Market Prices." *Journal of Business* 38(1): 34–105.

Garlappi, Lorenzo, Raman Uppal, and Tan Wang. 2007. "Portfolio Selection with Parameter and Model Uncertainty: A Multi-Prior Approach." *Review of Financial Studies* 20:1, 41–81.

Gilboa, Itzhak, and David Schmeidler. 1989. "Maxmin Expected Utility with Non-Unique Prior." *Journal of Mathematical Economics* 18:2, 141–153.

Guidolin, Massimo. 2011. "Markov Switching Models in Empirical Finance." in David M. Drukker (ed.) *Missing Data Methods: Time-Series Methods and Applications* (Advances in Econometrics, Volume 27), Emerald Group Publishing Limited,1-86.

Guidolin, Massimo, and Federica Ria. 2011. "Regime Shifts in Mean-Variance Efficient Frontiers: Some International Evidence." *Journal of Asset Management* 12:5, 322–349.

Guidolin, Massimo, and Francesca Rinaldi. 2010. "Ambiguity in Asset Pricing and Portfolio Choice: A Review of the Literature." Working Paper No. 2010–028A, Federal Reserve Bank of St. Louis, St. Louis, MO.

Guidolin, Massimo, and Allan Timmermann. 2008. "International Asset Allocation under Regime Switching, Skew and Kurtosis Preferences." *Review of Financial Studies* 21:4, 889–935.

Hanoch, Giora, and Haim Levy. 1970. "Efficient Portfolio Selection with Quadratic and Cubic Utility." *Journal of Business* 43:2, 181–189.

Harvey, Campbell R., and Akthar Siddique. 2000. "Conditional Skewness in Asset Pricing Tests." *Journal of Finance* 55:3, 1263–1295.

Kallberg, Jerry G., and William T. Ziemba. 1983. "Comparison of Alternative Utility Functions in Portfolio Selection Problems." *Management Science* 29:11, 1257–1276.

Kane, Alex. 1982. "Skewness Preference and Portfolio Choice." *Journal of Financial and Quantitative Analysis* 17:1, 15–25.

Klibanoff, Peter, Massimo Marinacci, and Sujoy Mukerji. 2005. "A Smooth Model of Decision Making under Ambiguity." *Econometrica* 73:6, 1849–1892.

Knight, Frank H. 1921. *Risk, Uncertainty, and Profit.* Boston and New York: Houghton Mifflin.

Kogan, Leonid, and Tan, Wang. 2003. "A Simple Theory of Asset Pricing under Model Uncertainty." Working Paper, Massachusetts Institute of Technology, School of Management.

Kraus, Alan, and Robert Litzenberger. 1976. "Skewness Preference and the Valuation of Risk Assets.Assets" *Journal of Finance* 33:2, 303–310.

LeRoy, Stephen F., and Jan Werner. 2001. *Principles of Financial Economics*. Cambridge, UK: Cambridge University Press.

Levy, Haim, and Harry M. Markowitz. 1979. "Approximating Expected Utility by a Function of Mean and Variance." *American Economic Review* 69:2, 308–317.

Markowitz, Harry. 1952. "Portfolio Selection." *Journal of Finance* 7:1, 77–91.

Pratt, John W. 1964. "Risk-Aversion in the Small and in the Large." *Econometrica* 32:3, 122–136.

Samuelson, Paul A. 1970. "The Fundamental Approximation Theorem of Portfolio Analysis in Terms of Means, Variances and Higher Moments." *Review of Economic Studies* 37:3, 537–542.

Savage, Leonard J. 1954. *The Foundations of Statistics*. New York: John Wiley & Sons.

Schmeidler, David. 1989. "Subjective Probability and Expected Utility without Additivity." *Econometrica* 57:3, 571–587.

Scott, Robert C., and Philip A. Horvath. 1980. "On the Direction of Preference for Moments of Higher Order than Variance." *Journal of Finance* 35:4, 915–919.

Timmermann, Allan. 2000. "Moments of Markov Switching Models." *Journal of Econometrics* 96:1, 75–111.

Tsiang, S. C. 1972. "The Rationale for the Mean-Standard Deviation Analysis, Skewness Preference and the Demand for Money." *American Economic Review* 62:2, 354–371.

12

Portfolio Construction with Downside Risk

HARALD LOHRE
Portfolio Manager, Deka Investment GmbH

THORSTEN NEUMANN
Managing Director, Union Investment
Institutional GmbH

THOMAS WINTERFELDT
Risk Controller, DG HYP Deutsche
Genossenschafts-Hypothekenbank

Introduction

The mean-variance paradigm of Markowitz (1952) is the classical approach to portfolio optimization. As with any classical approach, numerous shortcomings have been discussed in the finance literature. The main issues claimed in regard to this approach are its static one-period character, its high sensitivity of optimization outcomes regarding small changes in the inputs, and its use of volatility as the measure of risk. Given that volatility encompasses negative and positive surprises, this measure hardly conforms to investors' risk perception as the danger of ending up with less than expected.

Tobin (1958) shows that volatility is only an appropriate risk measure for quadratic utility functions or, equivalently, normally distributed returns. Both assumptions are not sustainable. Rubinstein (1973) and Neumann and Morgenstern (1944) discuss the properties of utility functions, and Mandelbrot (1963) and Fama (1965) discuss the nonnormality of returns. Of course, alternative concepts that account for the asymmetric nature of risk have also been proposed. For example, Roy (1952) adds a criterion to Markowitz's (1952) efficient frontier, called Roy's safety first ratio, in which the efficient portfolio with the lowest probability to fall short of a given target return is selected. Markowitz (1959) proposes a portfolio optimization procedure based on the semivariance measure. Fishburn (1977) employs a utility function model that translates downside risk depending on a risk aversion parameter and a target return. His findings indicate that investors' risk perception significantly changes below this individual threshold. However, downside risk is not only meaningful from an individual investor's perspective but also from an asset pricing perspective. Bali, Demirtas, and Levy (2009) demonstrate a strong, positive risk-return trade-off using downside risk measures, whereas the mean-variance tradeoff is less robust. Hence, broad consensus exists among both researchers and practitioners that asymmetry is a reasonable property for any risk measure.

Whatever the choice of risk measure, any optimizer will certainly find risk-minimized portfolios given that perfect information is provided. In practice, however, portfolio construction takes place in an ex-ante context relying on forecasts of the respective risk measure that have to be derived from historical data. Therefore, predictability of a risk measure is a prerequisite in practice. This is an important challenge because risk structures (e.g., correlations) are known to be unstable over time. For instance, numerous studies, such as Ebner and Neumann (2005), document the instability of beta factors and, as a consequence, covariance matrices and other correlation-based risk measures. Although comparing alternative risk measures in an empirical out-of-sample setting is important, the literature lacks such a study.

The main contribution of this chapter is to empirically examine whether asymmetric risk measures are useful to define risk in the context of portfolio construction. Therefore, the authors substitute volatility in the objective function of portfolio optimization with various alternative risk measures and compare their out-of-sample performance characteristics to those of the mean-variance investment strategy in an empirical backtest. To assess whether downside risk measures are of any value in portfolio optimization, the case of perfect foresight with respect to returns is first considered. Since mean-variance optimization is typically confounded by estimation risk, especially the one embedded in estimates of expected returns (Chopra and Ziemba, 1993), this assumption allows for isolating portfolio construction from the return-forecasting problem. Given perfect foresight, minimizing downside risk is promising for six out of eight investigated measures. To also judge whether these risk reductions can be achieved in absence of a crystal ball, the authors then imitate a more naïve portfolio manager who employs historical means to estimate expected returns. While the results are noisier, they qualitatively confirm the prior findings. Hence, downside risk measures can successfully be used for portfolio optimization as long as they are sufficiently persistent over time.

The chapter is structured as follows: The next section presents various measures of downside risk and discusses their strengths and weaknesses with respect to portfolio optimization. In the third section, a motivation is presented for the methodology of the empirical backtest, which is pursued in the fourth section. Therein, the portfolio characteristics of the various downside risk strategies are thoroughly described. The final section concludes with a brief summary.

Measuring Downside Risk

Positive and negative deviations equally contribute to risk when measured by volatility using the standard deviation of returns. However, downside events typically have a greater effect on investors' risk perception. In a world of symmetric returns, volatility control coincides with downside risk control. However, empirical evidence shows that returns exhibit asymmetry. In particular, return distributions exhibiting equal volatility may entail different downside risk. In the following sections, appropriate risk measures focusing on downside risk are discussed, which will be used in the subsequent portfolio optimization study. All of the measures capture downside risk by considering negative deviations as the sole source of risk.

VALUE AT RISK AND CONDITIONAL VALUE AT RISK

Given the random return R of a portfolio for a certain holding period, value at risk (VaR) at the confidence level p is used to determine the loss corresponding to the lower quantile of its distribution. If $p = 99$ percent, then

$$VaR_p(R) = -F_R^{-1}(1-p) = -F_R^{-1}(0.01), \qquad (12.1)$$

where F_R is the cumulative distribution function of R. Thus, VaR represents a loss value that is not breached with a certain (high) probability. However, VaR ignores extreme events below the specified quantile. If optimization is not limited to certain distribution families, the optimizer may even provide optimized portfolios with a low VaR but possibly fat tails beyond that threshold. Alexander and Baptista (2002) also point out that mean-VaR optimization does not necessarily improve upon mean-variance. In fact, one may end up with more volatile portfolios when switching from variance to VaR as a measure of risk. Finally, VaR is not a coherent risk measure because the subadditivity property is not satisfied. That is, the VaR of a portfolio may be larger than the sum of its constituents' VaRs. Artzner, Delbaen, Eber, and Heath (1999) discuss the concept of coherent risk measures.

These drawbacks of VaR are mitigated by a related risk measure, the conditional VaR (CVaR). While VaR is basically a quantile, CVaR is simply a conditional expectation that gives the expected loss beyond a specific threshold such as the VaR. Therefore, CVaR is often referred to as expected shortfall. CVaR is defined as follows:

$$CVaR_p(R) = -E(R \mid R < F_R^{-1}(0.01)). \qquad (12.2)$$

Bertsimas, Lauprete, and Samarov (2004) show that CVaR exhibits convexity with respect to portfolio weights under fairly weak continuity assumptions, thus facilitating mathematical optimization and contributing to the risk measure's coherence. Also, Alexander and Baptista (2004) theoretically compare CVaR and VaR in a portfolio selection context and contend that imposing a CVaR constraint is more effective than imposing a VaR constraint. However, optimization with respect to CVaR requires either an assumption about the return distribution or numerous observations below the target. Rockafellar and Uryasev (2000, 2002) provide a discussion of computational issues of CVaR optimization.

LOWER PARTIAL MOMENTS

The next risk measure discussed is semideviation, which is related to CVaR in that it also entails a linear evaluation of below-target returns. Semideviation belongs to the broader class of risk measures involving lower partial moments (LPMs) that only take downside events below a given target into account. Returns below this threshold are evaluated by a penalty function that increases polynomially with the distance from the target return.

Two parameters determine an LPM risk measure. One is the exponent or degree k and the other is the target return τ. Given the return distribution R of a portfolio, its lower partial moment is defined by

$$LPM_{\tau,k}(R) = E((\tau-R)^k \,|\, R < \tau)P(R < \tau). \tag{12.3}$$

Common parameter choices are $k = 1$ and $\tau = E(R)$, yielding the semideviation

$$SD(R) = E((R-E(R))\,|\,R < E(R))P(R < E(R)) \tag{12.4}$$

and $k = 2$ and $\tau = E(R)$, yielding the semivariance

$$SV(R) = E((R-E(R))^2 \,|\, R < E(R))P(R < E(R)). \tag{12.5}$$

Other common values of τ are the risk-free rate and a zero return. These choices refer to the risk of falling behind opportunity costs and the risk of realizing an absolute loss, respectively. The parameter k serves as a risk aversion parameter—losses are penalized with power k. Porter (1974) and Bawa (1978) show that the semivariance measure is consistent with the concept of stochastic dominance, Ogryczak and Ruszczyński (2001) give analogous proof for semideviation, and Harlow and Rao (1989) provide a detailed discussion of further LPM properties. LPMs entail considerable computational difficulties. For instance, a portfolio's LPM cannot be expressed as a function of security LPMs unlike volatility. This shortcoming contributes to the limited application of these risk measures in practice. However, both semideviation and semivariance are included in the empirical investigation contained in this chapter. Let $(R_t)_{t=1,\ldots,T}$ denote the sample of return (vector) realizations and let x be the vector of portfolio weights. The vector of portfolio returns $(X_t)_{t=1,\ldots,T}$ then obtains as $X_t = x'R_t$. Semideviation and semivariance of this portfolio are computed as follows:

$$f(x) = SD(x) = \frac{1}{T}\sum_{t=1}^{T} \min\{(X_t - \bar{X}), 0\} \quad \text{and} \tag{12.6}$$

$$f(x) = SV(x) = \frac{1}{T}\sum_{t=1}^{T} \{\min[(X_t - \bar{X}), 0]\}^2, \tag{12.7}$$

where $\bar{X}$ denotes the mean of X estimated by $\bar{X} = \frac{1}{t}\sum_{t=1}^{T} X_t$.

LOSS PENALTY

Mean-variance optimization is often set in a utility maximization framework. The investor maximizes the expected utility u of his portfolio return distribution by maximizing

$$f(x) = E[u(x'R)] \tag{12.8}$$

for a given random vector of market returns R. The approach builds on the work of Neumann and Morgenstern (1944). For ease of deduction, the utility function is assumed to be quadratic (or fitting its quadratic approximation very well), giving rise to consistency of mean-variance optimization and utility maximization (Tobin, 1958). Again, this approach addresses downside risk only in a world of symmetric returns. However, the properties of u allow definitions of utility functions that match an investor's downside risk attitude. Therefore, the negative exponential is chosen as a utility function given by

$$u(x, R) = -\exp(-(x'R - E(x'R))). \tag{12.9}$$

Adjusting for the mean gives a reasonable threshold below which the outcomes are penalized more than positive deviations. Therefore, this measure will be hereafter referred to as *loss penalty*. Although the investor's utility function is not claimed to be known, this chapter optimizes a function having returns as arguments that fit the goal of mitigating downside risk and can coincidentally be interpreted as one possible utility function.

Again, the computation of investor utility is not as convenient as that for volatility. For a given time series vector $(R_t)_{t=1,\dots,T}$ and a specific vector x of portfolio weights, the authors determine

$$X = (X_t)_{t=1,\dots,T}, X_t = x'R_t \quad \text{and} \tag{12.10}$$

$$E[u(x, R)] = \frac{1}{T} \sum_{t=1}^{T} -\exp(-X_t + \overline{X}). \tag{12.11}$$

SKEWNESS

The skewness of a return distribution R captures its deviation from symmetry and is defined as

$$\gamma(R) = \frac{E[(R - E(R))^3]}{\sigma(R)^3}. \tag{12.12}$$

The more positive the skewness measure is, the heavier are the upper tails as compared to the lower tails of a distribution. Figure 12.1 shows how downside risk decreases with positive skewness. This is because the positively skewed (or right-skewed) distribution has fewer events at the far lower tail, at the cost of more events slightly below the mean, than does a symmetric distribution.

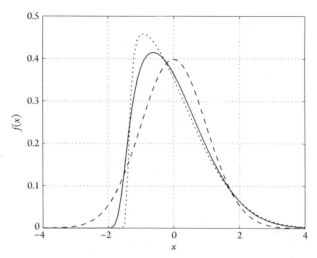

Figure 12.1 Some density functions of skewed distributions. The graph gives sample density functions for skewed distributions. All plotted density functions have a zero mean and are scaled to have volatility equal to 1. The more right-skewed density functions refer to random variables that have significantly less mass at the lower tail and are represented by the dotted and the solid line. Accordingly, for a downside risk-oriented investor, the symmetric curve (dashed) corresponds to having more risky assets.

However, skewness alone does not add value, and volatility has to be limited as well. Otherwise, optimized portfolios might exhibit favorable skewness and fat downside tails due to an overall rise in volatility. This issue is illustrated in Figure 12.2 in a comparison of two graphs showing equally skewed distributions with different volatilities. Apparently, this effect also holds for left-skewed distributions. Therefore, portfolio optimization will additionally require a nonlinear constraint that limits volatility to a fixed level while testing for the performance effects of alternative skewness levels.

As for skewness, consider the standard skewness estimator given by

$$\hat{\gamma}=\frac{1}{T}\sum_{t=1}^{T}\left(\frac{X_t-\hat{\mu}}{\hat{\sigma}(X)}\right).$$ (12.13)

However, the literature repeatedly mentions that the straightforward estimator is not only biased but also highly sensitive to sample outliers (Harvey and Siddique, 2000; Kim and White, 2004). A few more robust skewness estimators have been discussed, and the following one proposed by Bowley (1920) is chosen in the current study:

$$S_B(X)=\frac{Q_3(X)+Q_1(X)-2Q_2(X)}{Q_3(X)-Q_1(X)},$$ (12.14)

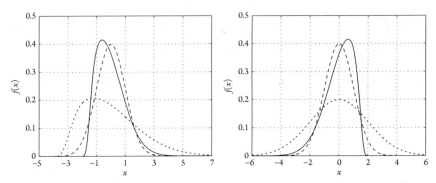

Figure 12.2 Skewness versus volatility. The left graph gives two equally right-skewed distribution functions with volatility 1 (solid line) and volatility 2 (dotted line) and compares with a symmetric distribution with volatility 1 (dashed line). The right graph compares two symmetric density functions—one with volatility 1 (dashed line) and the other with volatility 2 (dotted line)—to a left-skewed density function with volatility 1 (solid line).

where $Q_i(X)$ is the i-th quartile of the sample $(R_t)_{t=1,...,T}$. This estimator is less sensitive to outliers than the traditional one, which is of particular relevance in portfolio construction given that return data exhibit fat tails.

MAXIMUM DRAWDOWN

The maximum drawdown (MDD) measure defines risk as the maximum percentage of loss that an asset or portfolio has suffered from its top valuation to its bottom valuation within a given sample period. An important advantage of this risk measure is its independence from the underlying return distribution because it entirely relies on historical returns. For a given return time series of a security S, $\left(R_t^{(S)}\right)_{t=1,...,T}$, the corresponding time series of a portfolio value that solely consists of security S can be easily computed. This value is given as

$$V_0^{(S)} = 1, \quad V_t^{(S)} = V_{t-1}^{(S)}(1 + R_t^{(S)}), \quad t = 1,...T. \tag{12.15}$$

In order to retrieve the worst period of investment in security S, the MDD for period $[0,T]$ is calculated recursively in this study. Given the MDD for the time period $[0,T-1]$, $MDD_{[0,T-1]}(S)$, the following equation is obtained:

$$MDD_{[0,T]}(S) = \min\left\{\frac{V_T - V_{\hat{t}}}{V_{\hat{t}}}, MDD_{[0,T-1]}(S)\right\}, \tag{12.16}$$

where $V_{\hat{t}}$ is the maximum value of the security held within $[0,T-1]$. Setting $MDD_{[0,0]}(S)$ to a sufficiently large number, $MDD_{[0,T]}(S)$ is computed by stepping through the sample and applying Equation 12.16. Figure 12.3 illustrates the MDD of a portfolio that has been optimized with respect to the MDD and compares it to the MDD realized by holding the benchmark. For ease of presentation, the time index is neglected.

Portfolio optimization techniques for drawdown constraints have been demonstrated by Checklov, Uryasev, and Zabarankin (2005) by means of linear programming and by Karatzas and Cvitanic (1994) in a continuous time framework. Johansen and Sornette (2001), Burghardt, Duncan, and Liu (2003), and Hamelink and Hoesli (2004) provide empirical results on maximum drawdown as a portfolio risk measure.

Empirical Methodology

The characteristics of the previously mentioned portfolio construction approaches that arise from active benchmark-oriented management of a European equity portfolio are now investigated. Discrete weekly return data of the Dow Jones EURO STOXX 50 constituents from January 1992 to November 2009 are examined. In untabulated results, the evidence shows that almost 60 percent of the sample stocks exhibit significantly skewed returns. Hence, this asymmetry in returns obviously calls for appropriate downside risk control.

PREDICTABILITY OF RISK MEASURES

Predictability is a key for any risk measure to be of practical value in portfolio optimization. To judge the persistence of downside risk measures, the stability

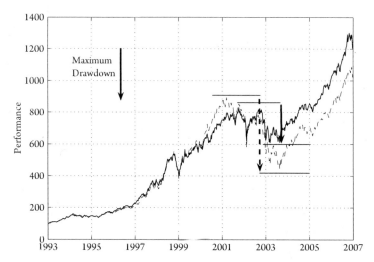

Figure 12.3 Visualizing Maximum Drawdown (MDD). In this figure, the dashed line gives the time series of portfolio value that arises from a benchmark investment. The solid line represents the respective time series according to a portfolio optimized with respect to MDD (given perfect foresight of return). The arrows indicate the MDD. The dashed arrow is for the benchmark while the solid arrow is for the optimized portfolio.

of the respective stock rankings is examined. In particular, the stock universe is ranked yearly according to the respective risk measure, and Spearman's rank correlation coefficient is computed for all pairs of consecutive years in Table 12.1. For instance, the stocks included in this study are first sorted by their volatility observed in 1991, and then the same set of stocks is sorted by their volatility observed in 1992. These two rankings have a correlation of 0.69. Over all pairs of years, volatility exhibits a mean correlation of 0.62, suggesting considerable persistence. Next to volatility, semideviation and semivariance also have high correlation over the years that one may well exploit when minimizing the respective risk dimensions. In contrast, the VaR correlation is less stable—an observation that does not translate to CVaR. Table 12.1 also reveals that skewness is rather unstable, suggesting that portfolio optimization with respect to skewness may fail. The results for loss penalty and MDD show more stability.

FORMULATION OF PORTFOLIO OPTIMIZATION TASKS

The empirical examination adopts the following investment strategy: It minimizes risk according to the respective definition of downside risk while requiring all optimization solutions to exceed the benchmark return expectation and to satisfy a certain maximum tracking error limit.

Imposing quarterly rebalancing, the necessary optimization inputs are computed every three months as follows: The respective measures of downside risk are estimated using two years of historical data, amounting to 104 weekly observations. As for the estimation of expected returns, two approaches are considered. First, perfect foresight of returns is assumed, and second, a simple return forecast is considered by computing the historical mean. At first glance, assuming perfect foresight seems inappropriate, but it allows for isolating the portfolio construction problem from the return forecasting problem. This issue is important because a well-known empirical finding is that mean-variance optimization typically suffers more from estimation risk embedded in expected returns than from estimation risk in (co-)variances. Because the intention is to focus on the risk dimension, perfect foresight of returns represents a natural base case for testing portfolio construction methods. Any method failing in this base case may be discarded immediately. Any method succeeding in this base case may be subjected to a further test. A reasonable further test is given in the second approach of estimating expected returns. Instead of using the perfect foresight estimate, a simple one is employed, which is given as the historical mean over the two-year estimation window.

All in all, eight portfolio strategies are examined based on the objective functions introduced in the last section together with the traditional mean-variance approach. Setting $X = x'R$, the optimization problems are as follows:

1. Volatility:
$$f(x) = \sigma(x) = \sqrt{(x'Cx)} \to \min$$

Table 12.1 **Rank correlation of various risk measures**

Years	Volatility	VaR	CVaR	Semi-		Loss	Skewness	MDD
				Deviation	Variance	Penalty		
1991 vs. 1992	0.69	0.51	0.63	0.66	0.69	0.33	0.22	0.50
1992 vs. 1993	0.79	0.63	0.71	0.80	0.79	0.62	0.26	0.65
1993 vs. 1994	0.87	0.48	0.74	0.87	0.87	0.77	−0.03	0.45
1994 vs. 1995	0.76	0.25	0.54	0.79	0.76	0.58	0.31	0.08
1995 vs. 1996	0.85	0.56	0.72	0.86	0.85	0.62	−0.04	0.22
1996 vs. 1997	0.58	0.59	0.52	0.58	0.58	0.26	0.07	0.39
1997 vs. 1998	0.35	0.21	0.19	0.36	0.35	0.31	0.22	0.11
1998 vs. 1999	0.37	0.13	0.04	0.31	0.37	0.16	0.01	0.03
1999 vs. 2000	0.35	−0.40	0.09	0.37	0.35	0.24	−0.05	−0.10
2000 vs. 2001	0.57	−0.23	0.03	0.56	0.57	0.47	0.05	−0.01
2001 vs. 2002	0.63	0.57	0.60	0.65	0.63	0.46	−0.05	0.42
2002 vs. 2003	0.59	0.63	0.60	0.63	0.59	0.12	0.17	0.58
2003 vs. 2004	0.80	0.73	0.78	0.81	0.80	0.59	0.18	0.56
2004 vs. 2005	0.80	0.69	0.78	0.85	0.80	0.59	0.12	0.49
2005 vs. 2006	0.51	0.10	0.48	0.51	0.51	0.27	0.13	0.21
2006 vs. 2007	0.45	0.18	0.34	0.49	0.45	0.22	0.15	0.41
2007 vs. 2008	0.52	0.23	0.44	0.53	0.52	0.32	−0.07	0.12
2008 vs. 2009	0.56	0.51	0.58	0.58	0.56	0.33	−0.25	0.54
Mean correlation	0.62	0.35	0.49	0.62	0.62	0.40	0.08	0.31
Standard deviation of correlation	0.17	0.32	0.25	0.18	0.17	0.19	0.14	0.24

Note: The table reports Spearman rank correlation coefficients of estimated risk measures using pairs of consecutive years.

2. VaR:

$$f(x)=VaR_p(X)\to\min$$

3. CVaR:

$$f(x)=CVaR_p(X)\to\min$$

4. Semideviation:

$$f(x)=SD(X)=E((X-E(X))|X<E(X))\cdot P(X<E(X))\to\min$$

5. Semivariance:

$$f(x)=SV(X)=E((X-E(X))^2\,|\,X<E(X))\cdot P(X<E(X))\to\min$$

6. Loss penalty:

$$f(x)=-E[u(x'R-E(x'R))]\to\min$$

7. (Robust) skewness:

$$f(x)=-S_B(X)=-\frac{Q_3(X)+Q_1(X)-2Q_2(X)}{Q_3(X)-Q_1(X)}\to\min$$

8. MDD:

$$f(x)=MDD(X)\to\min$$

To complete the formulation of the optimization tasks, the following constraints are added: First, the tracking error (TE) is restricted. For a given vector of benchmark portfolio weights $X_t = x'R_t$ and (optimized) weights x, the tracking error is constrained by

$$TE(x)=\sqrt{(x-x_{BM})'C(x-x_{BM})}\le TE_{max}\,. \qquad (12.17)$$

Considering N assets, C is the $N\times N$ sample covariance matrix of the vector of asset returns. An annual tracking error limit of 5 percent is set, which provides the optimizer with a fairly large discretion in determining the portfolio weights and allows for a clear picture about the impact of the optimization process.

The second constraint requires the expected portfolio return to reach at least the benchmark, as done in

$$\mu'x\ge\mu'x_{BM}. \qquad (12.18)$$

The expected mean return of the optimized portfolio (which coincides with the realized return in the case of perfect foresight) is therefore greater or equal to the expected benchmark return. This constraint avoids optimization solutions that reduce risk at the cost of return. Conversely, this constraint sets no incentive for the optimizer to go for higher returns.

Also, the following linear (in-)equalities must be met:

$$\sum_{i=1}^{N}x_i=1 \quad\text{and}\quad x_i\ge 0i, \qquad (12.19)$$

representing the full investment and nonnegativity constraints, respectively.

As for optimization problems 2 and 3, for VaR and CVaR, the quantile level p equals 0.75 because a lack of data may hamper the optimization for higher values of p. Hence, the first quartile of the return distribution is the quantile of choice.

Volatility is also restricted when skewness is the objective; thus, the following constraint is added for optimization problems 7 and 8:

$$\sigma(x) = \sqrt{x'Cx} \le \sigma_{BM}. \tag{12.20}$$

To sum up, these assumptions and restrictions imitate a portfolio manager who adjusts his portfolio every three months to meet a certain risk objective, considering data of a revolving two-year-period. Regarding the optimization process, the approach used is quite pragmatic. Optimization routines embedded in standard software packages are employed, especially applying to the case when the focus is not on streamlining the optimization but on setting the objectives and interpreting the outcome.

Minimizing Downside Risk

In this section, the effectiveness of the different downside risk optimizations is evaluated for two settings. The first setting assumes perfect foresight of expected returns in order to isolate the forecasting of risk and return. Because this knowledge is unavailable in practice, this assumption is dropped in the second setting to obtain a reasonable reality check.

OPTIMIZING WITH PERFECT FORESIGHT OF RETURNS

The value of downside risk minimization should reveal when optimizing with perfect foresight of returns. To investigate the degree to which the different optimization approaches succeed in mitigating downside risk, the optimized strategy is compared with two competing strategies in the following two steps: First, a check is made on whether each can outperform the benchmark in terms of the risk dimension that is to be minimized. Second, the risk measure of the optimal strategy is computed—assuming perfect foresight, which results in obtaining both returns and risk—providing an upper boundary that allows for judging the optimization efforts.

Consider, for example, the traditional mean-variance optimization in Table 12.2. The average weekly volatility of the benchmark across all holding periods is 2.71 percent, while the optimized portfolio exhibits a lower volatility of 2.33 percent. Given perfect information, one would have even been able to achieve an optimal volatility as low as 2.02 percent, which corresponds to an annual volatility of 14.55 percent.

In Table 12.2, the column headed "Gain" indicates the fraction of risk reduction that results for portfolio optimization under imperfect information compared to the risk reduction under perfect information. In the case of volatility, 55.17 percent of the feasible spread is exploited by portfolio optimization.

While scaling the average gain to percentages allows for a comparison across measures, care is needed in interpreting differences because percentage reductions of risk measures with different growth characteristics are being compared. More precisely, semideviation grows linearly, semivariance exhibits a quadratic increase, loss penalty grows exponentially, and robust skewness is bounded by the interval [-1,1]. Instead, a hit rate is computed that indicates the fraction of optimization periods in which the optimized portfolio exhibits more favorable risk figures than the benchmark. The last column of Table 12.2 gives a highly significant hit rate of 94.52 percent for volatility, on the basis that 69 out of 73 holding periods are successful in that respect. For significance testing of the hit rate, the number of intended objective changes that will result from a random guess is assumed, in statistical terms, to be a realization of a binomially distributed variable $Y \sim B(Z,p)$, with $p = 0.5$ and $Z = 73$. For the hit rate to be significant at the 0.05 (0.01) level, Y has to be greater or equal to 44 (47).

Having examined the traditional mean-variance case, attention is now focused on the results for the optimization with respect to downside risk measures. The results show that all of the optimization tasks providing optimized portfolios exhibit more favorable downside risk figures than the benchmark.

Table 12.2 **Downside risk reduction with perfect foresight of returns**

	Strategy	Risk			Gain	Hit
		Benchmark	Optimized	Optimal	Average (%)	Rate (%)
1	Volatility	2.71	2.33	2.02	55.17	**94.52**
2	VaR	1.54	0.85	−0.43	35.03	**93.15**
3	Conditional VaR	3.18	2.24	1.22	47.68	**90.41**
4	Semideviation	2.17	1.88	1.35	35.47	**80.82**
5	Semivariance	4.33	3.11	2.63	71.85	**94.52**
6	Loss penalty	2099.24	476.83	231.29	86.85	**78.08**
7	Skewness	0.04	0.02	−0.93	1.85	50.68
8	Maximum draw-down	7.80	5.50	2.70	44.98	**89.04**

Note: The first column contains the weekly average value of the respective risk measure obtained from holding the benchmark portfolio. The second column gives the respective value according to a portfolio optimized in regard to that measure given a perfect foresight of returns. The optimal values are obtained when optimizing with respect to that measure given a perfect foresight of risk and return. The fourth column gives the average gain of the optimization efforts; that is, the degree to which the maximum risk spread between the benchmark and optimal strategy is translated into the optimized portfolios. The last column gives the hit rate, which is computed as the percentage of holding periods that exhibit more favorable risk figures than the benchmark; hit rates that are significant at the 0.05 level are in boldface.

The average values of CVaR, volatility, VaR, semideviation, semivariance, loss penalty, and maximum drawdown of optimized portfolios are far below those of the benchmark. For instance, the weekly maximum drawdown of the benchmark is 7.8 percent, while the optimized portfolio only exhibits 5.5 percent, thereby exploiting almost half of the spread to the optimal strategy, which has a maximum drawdown of 2.7 percent. Regarding loss penalty, the best performance observed has an average gain of 86.85 percent. Given the low persistence in skewness, finding that the average improvement for skewness is close to zero is not surprising. This observation indicates that skewness is an unreliable property for the assets under scrutiny. Despite the obvious effect of skewness on downside risk, this result adds to the rather-weak empirical evidence of a skewness premium in asset prices, as reported in the empirical study of Post, van Vliet, and Levy (2008).

For six out of eight investigated downside risk measures, the results show significant hit ratios reinforcing the evidence given by the average gain figures. The maximum hit ratio of 94.52 percent occurs for semivariance. Unsurprisingly, the hit ratio for the skewness optimization is indistinguishable from a random guess.

Next, given quarterly rebalancing, the resulting 73 optimization outcomes are examined, and Figure 12.4 plots the optimized strategies' risk measures over time together with that occur for the benchmark and for the optimal strategy. Thereby, intuition is fostered about the time-varying characteristics of the portfolios' downside risk and about the degree to which the spread in the optimal downside risk strategies can be exploited.

In particular, Figure 12.4 illustrates the spread between the risk measure of the benchmark and the optimal portfolio (given perfect foresight of returns and risk) as the shaded areas in the graphs. This figure provides a general idea of the feasible risk levels that can be expected from a given optimization routine. For example, the weekly volatility ranges between 1 percent and 7 percent over time, usually exhibiting bandwidth of 1 percent. The realized volatility of the optimized mean-variance strategy is shown as a solid line. Note that this line is not confined to the shaded spread area because it may be that the optimized strategy is more risky than the benchmark at a given time. In the figure, the evolution of the according gain figures over time is also plotted. For instance, if the optimized strategy's VaR equals the one of the optimal strategy, the corresponding gain is 100 percent, and if the former equals the VaR of the benchmark, the gain is 0 percent. As a consequence, the gain may also turn negative when the optimized strategy's VaR is higher than the one of the benchmark. The latter behavior most often applies to the skewness strategy. Moreover, the benchmark's skewness is hardly worse than that of the optimized strategy. As a result, the gain figures are rather disappointing. Considering the case of mean-variance, i.e., volatility, the results are more convincing, with few periods of negative gain. The gain profiles of volatility and semivariance almost coincide, while semideviation has a more volatile one. The gain profile of CVaR is especially desirable, being consistently above 0, and is closely followed by the gains of loss penalty, VaR, and MDD.

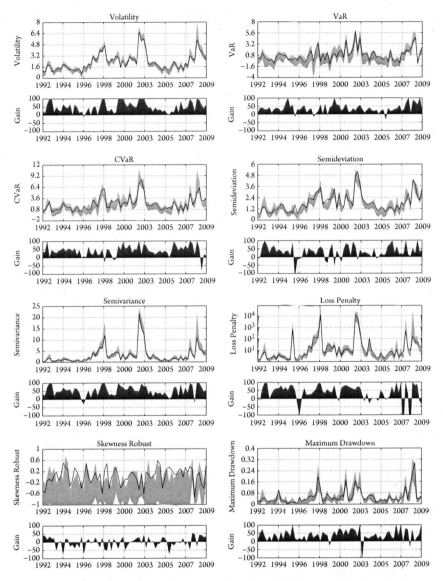

Figure 12.4 Downside risk over time with perfect foresight. The upper graphs give the evolution of downside risk over time. The light-shaded area indicates the spread between the optimal portfolio (given perfect foresight of risk and return) and the benchmark. The solid line represents the optimized portfolio's realized downside measure. The lower graphs quantify the degree of spread exploitation that results in the respective optimization.

OPTIMIZING WITH FORECASTED RETURNS

Lacking a crystal ball, the practical value of the previous results may be rather limited. Therefore, the issue examined next is whether a less skilled investor is also able to significantly reduce his exposure to downside risk. To imitate the estimation of such an investor, a simple estimate of expected returns, as represented by their historical mean, is used.

Table 12.3 gives the respective results for this scenario, and, of course, the degree of risk reduction is muted when compared to the base case. The observed setback is most severe for VaR and CVaR. The latter experiences a decrease in the gain average of 19.24 percentage points, and VaR actually has a gain average close to zero. Obviously, the according hit rates are no longer statistically significant. Given that the skewness measure has already failed in the base case, the conclusions do not change when using less perfect information. However, the hit rates still prove to be significant for volatility and for five downside risk measures—namely, CVaR, semideviation, semivariance, loss penalty, and MDD. Among these five measures, the performances of loss penalty, semideviation, and semivariance are very similar to the performances in the findings for perfect foresight.

In Figure 12.5, the corresponding seventy-three optimization outcomes are again evaluated by inspecting the optimized strategy's risk measure over time together with the risk measures that are obtained for the benchmark and for the optimal strategy. Confirming the above average gain figures, the according gain profiles for volatility, semivariance, semideviation, and loss penalty are similar to

Table 12.3 **Downside risk reduction with forecasted returns**

		Risk			Gain	Hit
	Strategy	Benchmark	Optimized	Optimal	average (%)	rate (%)
1	Volatility	2.71	2.33	2.02	54.73	**93.15**
2	VaR	1.54	0.85	−0.35	3.04	54.79
3	CVaR	3.18	2.61	1.18	28.44	**89.04**
4	Semideviation	2.17	1.86	1.35	37.84	**79.45**
5	Semivariance	4.33	3.16	2.63	69.07	**93.15**
6	Loss penalty	2099.24	411.35	231.29	90.36	**78.08**
7	Skewness	0.04	0.03	−0.92	1.29	54.79
8	Maximum drawdown	7.80	6.80	2.70	19.18	**75.34**

Note: The first column contains the weekly average value of the respective risk measure obtained from holding the benchmark portfolio. The second column gives the respective value according to a portfolio optimized with respect to that measure. The optimal values are obtained when optimizing with respect to that measure given perfect foresight of risk and return. The fourth column gives the average gain of the optimization efforts; that is, the degree to which the maximum risk spread between benchmark and optimal strategy is translated into the optimized portfolios. The last column gives the hit rate, which is computed as the percentage of holding periods that exhibit more favorable risk figures than the benchmark; hit rates that are significant at the 0.05 level are in boldface.

the case of perfect foresight. However, the VaR gain profile is almost completely neutralized for the whole sample period. The weak performance of the CVaR at the end of the 1990s is in line with its poor predictability in the same time period, as shown by the according rank correlations in Table 12.1. This observation also applies to the MDD strategy for which the underperformance in the first half of the total sample period is more severe.

To visualize the return characteristics of portfolios optimized with respect to downside risk, the corresponding performance time series is plotted in Figure 12.6. The shaded areas indicate the spread between the strategies' best and worst cumulative return for a given month. This spread is quite narrow, highlighting that downside risk control does not necessarily come at the cost of return. In fact, all strategies do outperform the benchmark over the whole sample period. Nevertheless, in this setting, downside risk control is not identical to hedging market risk; thus, one is not immune to sudden market shocks. The MDD strategy is the worst in terms of return, while the VaR and CVaR strategies perform quite convincingly. The strategies that are driven by volatility and semivariance exhibit mediocre performance. Surprisingly, robust skewness exhibits a favorable return path.

COMPARISON OF DOWNSIDE STRATEGIES

Given the five measures that succeed in significantly reducing downside risk, one may wonder which to choose, particularly since the different measures of risk may ultimately lead to very similar portfolios. As a metric of strategy similarity, mutual tracking errors computed in relation to the various strategies are displayed in Table 12.4. Along the diagonal, tracking errors of the downside risk strategy with perfect foresight versus the downside risk strategy with forecasted returns are given. As expected, these figures are highest for VaR, CVaR, and MDD, all of which suffer the most when the assumption of perfect foresight is dropped. Tracking errors are given for the case of perfect foresight above the diagonal and for the case of forecasted returns below the diagonal. While the latter figures appear noisier, the results are quite similar in both cases; thus, attention will focus on the case of forecasted returns. The first column gives the realized tracking errors in regard to the benchmark. While the ex-ante tracking error has been restricted to 5 percent, the ex-post figures only slightly exceed this boundary for most of the strategies. However, the CVaR and MDD strategies are most different to the benchmark, given the corresponding tracking errors of 6.58 percent and 6.54 percent, respectively. Concerning the remaining strategies, there is a cluster consisting of strategies driven by volatility, semideviation, and semivariance. The remaining strategies exhibit tracking errors mostly in excess of 4 percent.

The similarity of strategies can also be judged by computing the mutual downside risk measures of the various downside strategies. Panel A of Table 12.5 gives the mutual risk measures obtained in the optimal case, whereas panels B and C cover the results for the portfolios optimized with perfect foresight and forecasted returns. In each row, one specific risk measure is computed over the

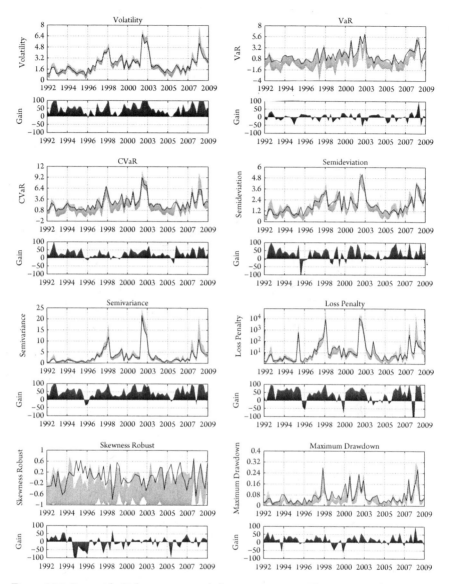

Figure 12.5 Downside Risk over time with forecasted returns. The upper graphs give the evolution of downside risk over time. The light-shaded area indicates the spread between the optimal portfolio (given perfect foresight of risk and return) and the benchmark. The solid line represents the optimized portfolio's realized downside measure. The lower graphs quantify the degree of spread exploitation that results from the respective optimization.

whole sample period for all of the downside strategies together with that for mean-variance one and the benchmark. For instance, in panel A representing the optimal case the benchmark volatility is 3.10 percent, while the maximum value is 3.11 percent based on the skewness strategy. As expected, the most favorable volatility figure results from the mean-variance strategy, Therefore, the outcome

Table 12. 4 **Mutual tracking errors of strategies**

	BM	Volatility	VaR	CVaR	Semi-Deviation	Semi-Variance	Loss Penalty	Skewness	MDD
BM	**0.00**	5.87	7.56	7.39	5.93	6.05	5.75	4.96	6.35
Volatility	6.03	**2.18**	7.17	5.82	3.09	2.08	3.76	6.91	6.11
VaR	5.51	5.90	**7.86**	5.78	7.08	7.25	7.27	8.06	6.82
CVaR	6.58	3.17	6.10	**6.53**	6.17	5.87	6.16	7.98	6.23
Semideviation	5.94	3.04	5.85	4.15	**3.44**	3.32	4.64	6.80	6.56
Semivariance	6.17	1.94	6.15	2.87	3.34	**2.11**	3.05	6.96	6.14
Loss penalty	5.89	3.35	6.34	4.14	4.38	2.68	**2.49**	6.83	5.92
Skewness	5.07	7.07	6.05	7.23	6.69	7.08	7.27	**5.41**	7.19
MDD	6.54	4.72	6.71	4.53	5.48	4.57	4.77	7.58	**7.18**

Note: The diagonal of the table gives numbers in boldface, which refer to the mutual tracking errors pertaining to strategies with perfect foresight versus the one with forecasted returns. Above the diagonal are the tracking errors for the case of perfect foresight. The mutual tracking errors for the case of forecasted returns are noted below the diagonal. The tracking errors along the diagonal are in boldface to enhance readability of the table. BM denotes benchmark and MDD, maximum drawdown.

Table 12.5 **Mutual downside risk**

	BM	Volatility	VaR	CVaR	Semi-Deviation	Semi-Variance	Loss Penalty	Skewness	MDD
Panel A. Optimal									
Volatility	3.10	**2.55**	2.96	2.74	2.65	2.62	2.67	3.11	2.77
VaR	-0.37	-0.51	**-1.36**	-1.02	-0.46	-0.35	-0.38	-0.08	-1.03
CVaR	2.01	1.36	0.72	**0.59**	1.40	1.40	1.45	1.95	0.67
Semideviation	1.12	**0.86**	0.96	0.92	0.87	0.88	0.91	1.15	0.94
Semivariance	9.61	**6.52**	8.77	7.49	7.01	6.85	7.12	9.66	7.66
Loss penalty	4071	1178	2689	754	1906	755	**477**	4432	558
Skewness	0.05	0.09	-0.06	-0.22	0.11	0.02	0.07	**-0.28**	-0.17
MDD	61.2	49.6	21.2	17.5	50.2	48.8	48.4	59.9	**15.3**
Mean ranking	7.88	3.75	4.88	3.25	5.13	4.25	4.63	7.75	3.50
Panel B. Perfect Foresight									
Volatility	0.08	2.64	2.96	2.80	2.70	**2.64**	2.75	3.08	2.84
VaR	0.40	-0.44	-0.83	**-0.84**	-0.45	-0.42	-0.41	-0.44	-0.64
CVaR	0.98	1.58	1.25	**1.18**	1.62	1.57	1.65	1.87	1.36
Semideviation	0.11	0.95	1.06	1.00	0.97	**0.94**	0.99	1.10	1.02
Semivariance	0.50	6.99	8.74	7.81	7.26	**6.95**	7.54	9.46	8.06
Loss penalty	434	1474	2292	2622	2702	2016	**1072**	10504	1229

Table 12.5 (Continued)

	BM	Volatility	VaR	CVaR	Semi-		Loss Penalty	Skewness	MDD
					Deviation	Variance			
MDD	0.2	50.5	26.3	**24.9**	51.0	52.2	54.8	58.7	43.3
Mean ranking	8.50	3.88	4.13	3.38	5.00	4.00	4.88	7.38	3.88
Panel C. Forecasted									
Volatility	3.08	**2.64**	2.95	2.65	2.70	2.64	2.73	3.06	2.73
VaR	0.40	−0.38	−0.34	−0.36	**−0.41**	−0.37	−0.36	−0.39	−0.32
CVaR	1.98	**1.64**	1.85	1.64	1.68	1.64	1.71	1.93	1.74
Semideviation	1.11	**0.95**	1.07	0.96	0.97	0.95	0.98	1.10	0.98
Semivariance	9.50	**6.95**	8.70	7.00	7.29	6.96	7.45	9.38	7.44
Loss penalty	5434	1399	2083	1782	2673	1873	**998**	10964	1418
Skewness	0.09	0.09	0.03	0.05	0.11	0.10	0.06	0.08	**0.03**
MDD	1.2	53.7	56.1	**52.1**	54.4	56.2	59.9	62.8	59.7
Mean ranking	7.50	2.38	5.88	3.25	4.50	4.00	5.00	7.25	5.25

Note: Each row contains the risk measure as given in the first column for the downside strategies together with the mean-variance strategy (column 'Volatility') and the benchmark. The downside measure of the best strategy according to the respective dimension is given in boldface. BM denotes benchmark, and MDD, maximum drawdown.

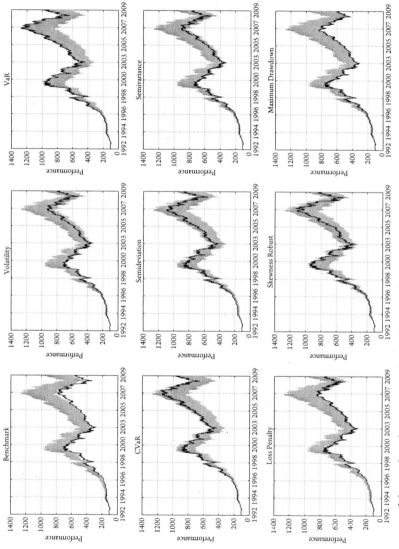

Figure 12.6 Performance of downside risk strategies. The graphs give the cumulative return of several strategies. The shaded area indicates the spread between the highest cumulative return and the lowest cumulative return among the downside risk strategies. The solid line represents the cumulative return of one particular strategy as indicated by the graph's title.

of 2.55 percent volatility is in boldface, highlighting the strategy with the lowest volatility. Only in two cases do these figures not belong to the downside strategy that seeks to minimize the respective risk dimension. To judge the overall performance of strategies, their mean ranking is computed, which equals 1 if the strategy always entails the lowest downside risk among the alternatives and which equals 9 if the strategy always entails the highest downside risk. In panel A, CVaR ranks first, with a mean ranking of 3.25, closely followed by MDD with 3.50 and semivariance with 4.25. Notably the benchmark is the worst, with a mean ranking of 7.88.

Continuing with the case of perfect foresight in panel B of Table 12.5, the CVaR and MDD strategies are quite robust with respect to their mean ranking. The VaR strategy also fares relatively well, as reflected by an increase in its ranking to 4.13. The semivariance strategy has a mean ranking of 4.00 and, moreover, its volatility, semideviation and semivariance figures are the lowest.

Finally, panel C of Table 12.5 gives the results for the case of forecasted returns. The benchmark continues to be the worst-performing strategy, with a mean ranking slightly below the one of skewness. Interestingly, volatility ranks first with a mean ranking of 2.38, now exhibiting the lowest values for three downside dimensions. Also, the CVaR and semivariance strategies exhibit consistent performance across various measures.

Summary and Conclusions

Because investors are mostly concerned about downside risk, volatility may not be an appropriate risk measure. In this chapter, the characteristics of asymmetric risk measures have been empirically examined in an out-of-sample context, employing stock return data of European large-cap companies. Overall, the results indicate that portfolio optimization techniques can more successfully reduce asymmetric risk in equity portfolios than can a strategy of buying and holding the benchmark portfolio. This is particularly true for semideviation, semivariance, loss penalty, and CVaR. While this result is first derived assuming a perfect foresight of returns, it remains valid when using estimated forecasts of the expected returns. Skewness risk is the hardest one to control, even when using a robust estimator. Given the instability of the associated measure, skewness risk cannot be predicted properly and optimization fails to reduce skewness risk ex-post. Of course, the predictability of risk measures is key for their successful implementation in a portfolio optimization process.

However, based on the empirical results reported here, a conclusion is that some alternative risk measures do a good job in equity portfolio optimization. To demonstrate their added value over traditional approaches, future research should improve the forecasting techniques for these asymmetric measures and should examine their characteristics in the presence of asset returns facing stronger asymmetry than do equities.

Discussion Questions

1. Give several shortcomings of the Markowitz paradigm and provide a rationale to account for downside risk in portfolio optimization.
2. Discuss several downside risk metrics.
3. Describe the employed methodology of comparing different downside metrics in portfolio construction.
4. What are the main findings and implications of the empirical study for portfolio management presented in this chapter?

REFERENCES

Alexander, Gordon J., and Alexandre M. Baptista. 2002. "Economic Implications of Using a Mean-VaR Model for Portfolio Selection: A Comparison with Mean-Variance Analysis." *Journal of Economic Dynamics & Control* 26:7–8, 1159–1193.

Alexander, Gordon J., and Alexandre M. Baptista. 2004. "A Comparison of VaR and CVaR Constraints on Portfolio Selection with the Mean-Variance Model." *Management Science* 50:9, 1261–1273.

Artzner, Philippe, Freddy Delbaen, Jean-Marc Eber, and David Heath. 1999. "Coherent Measures of Risk." *Mathematical Finance* 9:3, 203–228.

Bali, Turan G., K. Ozgur Demirtas, and Haim Levy. 2009. "Is There an Intertemporal Relation between Downside Risk and Expected Returns?" *Journal of Financial and Quantitative Analysis* 44:4, 883–909.

Bawa, Vijay S. 1978. "Safety-First, Stochastic Dominance and Optimal Portfolio Choice." *Journal of Financial and Quantitative Analysis* 13:2, 255–271.

Bertsimas, Dimitris, Geoffrey J. Lauprete, and Alexander Samarov. 2004. "Shortfall as a Risk Measure: Properties, Optimization and Applications." *Journal of Economic Dynamics & Control* 28:7, 1353–1381.

Bowley, Arthur L. 1920. *Elements of Statistics*, 4th ed. New York: Charles Scribner's Sons.

Burghardt, Galen, Ryan Duncan, and Lianyan Liu. 2003. "Deciphering Drawdowns." *Risk Magazine*, September, 16–20.

Chekhlov, Alexei, Stanislav P. Uryasev, and Michael Zabarankin. 2005. "Drawdown Measure in Portfolio Optimization." *International Journal of Theoretical and Applied Finance* 8:1, 13–58.

Chopra, Vijay K., and William T. Ziemba. 1993. "The Effect of Errors in Mean and Co-Variance Estimates on Optimal Portfolio Choice." *Journal of Portfolio Management* 19:2, 6–11.

Ebner, Markus, and Thorsten Neumann. 2005. "Time-Varying Betas of German Stock Returns." *Financial Markets and Portfolio Management* 19:1, 29–46.

Fama, Eugene F. 1965. "The Behavior of Stock Market Prices." *Journal of Business* 38:1, 34–105.

Fishburn, Peter C. 1977. "Mean-Risk Analysis with Risk Associated with Below-Target Returns." *American Economic Review* 67:2, 116–126.

Hamelink, Foort, and Martin Hoesli. 2004. "Maximum Drawdown and the Allocation to Real Estate." *Journal of Property Research* 21:1, 5–29.

Harlow, W. V., and Ramesh K. S. Rao. 1989. "Asset Pricing in a Generalized Mean-Lower Partial Moment Framework: Theory and Evidence." *Journal of Financial and Quantitative Analysis* 24:3, 285–311.

Harvey, Campbell R., and Akhtar Siddique. 2000. "Conditional Skewness in Asset Pricing Tests." *Journal of Financial Economics* 55:3, 1263–1295.

Johansen, Anders, and Didier Sornette. 2001. "Large Stock Market Price Drawdowns Are Outliers." *Journal of Risk* 4:2, 69–110.

Karatzas, Ioannis, and Jaksa Cvitanic. 1994. "On Portfolio Optimization under Drawdown Constraints." *IMA Volumes in Mathematics & Applications* 65:March, 77–88.

Kim, Tae-Hwan, and Halbert White. 2004. "On More Robust Estimation of Skewness and Kurtosis." *Finance Research Letters* 1:1, 56–70.

Mandelbrot, Benoit. 1963. "The Variation of Certain Speculative Prices." *Journal of Business* 36:4, 394–419.

Markowitz, Harry M. 1952. "Portfolio Selection." *Journal of Finance* 7:1, 77–91.

Markowitz, Harry M. 1959. *Portfolio Selection: Efficient Diversification of Investments.* New York: John Wiley & Sons.

Neumann, John von, and Oskar Morgenstern. 1944. *Theory of Games and Economic Behavior.* Princeton, NJ: Princeton University Press.

Ogryczak, Wlodzimierz, and Andrzej Ruszczyński. 2001. "On Consistency of Stochastic Dominance and Mean-Semideviation Models." *Mathematical Programming* 89:2, 217–232.

Porter, R. Burr. 1974. "Semivariance and Stochastic Dominance: A Comparison." *American Economic Review* 64:1, 200–204.

Post, Thierry, Pim van Vliet, and Haim Levy. 2008. "Risk Aversion and Skewness Preference." *Journal of Banking and Finance* 32:7, 1178–1187.

Rockafellar, R. Tyrrell, and Stanislav Uryasev. 2000. "Optimization of Conditional Value-at-Risk." *Journal of Risk* 2:3, 21–41.

Rockafellar, R. Tyrrell, and Stanislav Uryasev. 2002. "Conditional Value-at-Risk for General Loss Distributions." *Journal of Banking and Finance* 26:7, 1443–1471.

Roy, Andrew D. 1952. "Safety-First and the Holding of Assets." *Econometrica* 20:3, 431–449.

Rubinstein, Mark E. 1973. "A Comparative Statics Analysis of Risk Premiums." *Journal of Business* 46:4, 605–616.

Tobin, James. 1958. "Liquidity Preference as Behavior towards Risk." *Review of Economic Studies* 25:2, 65–86.

Asset Allocation with Downside Risk Management

JOSHUA M. DAVIS
Senior Vice President, Portfolio Manager,
Quantitative Strategies, PIMCO

SÉBASTIEN PAGE
Executive Vice President, Global Head of
Client Analytics, PIMCO

Introduction

At the grocery store, food labels reveal that everything people eat is ultimately a combination of carbohydrates, proteins, and fats. Similarly, most asset classes offer exposure to common risk factors. For example, corporate bonds, hedge funds, private equity, and real estate can all be expressed as different combinations of interest rate, yield curve, equity, and liquidity risk. Therefore, risk factors—as opposed to asset classes—should be the building blocks for portfolio construction.

If asset classes are simply linear combinations, or "containers," of risk factors, then diversifying across risk factors should lead to lower and more stable portfolio risk (Page and Taborsky 2011). Equity risk dominates most portfolios, and thereby, most portfolios are exposed to unexpectedly large losses (also called "tail risk"). Accordingly, asset allocators should not focus strictly on asset class diversification. Instead, they should diversify across risk factors and carefully analyze the costs and benefits of hedging downside risk.

THEORETICAL FOUNDATIONS

The theory behind the risk factor approach to asset allocation begins with the capital asset pricing model (CAPM). Treynor (1961, 1999), Sharpe (1964), Lintner (1965), and Mossin (1966) independently developed this model. The CAPM states that under equilibrium conditions, returns on a security should be proportional to how it varies in relation to the market as a whole, as shown in Equation 13.1:

$$R_i = R_F + \beta_i(R_M - R_F) + \epsilon_i,$$

(13.1)

where R_i is the return on a given security i; R_F is the risk-free rate; β_i is the security's beta with respect to the market portfolio; R_M is the expected return of the market portfolio; and ϵ_i is the return unexplained by the factor model. The security's beta can be measured as the correlation between the security and the market portfolio multiplied by the ratio of the security's volatility to the market portfolio's volatility, or as the coefficient of a regression between historical security returns and market returns.

Elton and Gruber (1995, p. 301) call Equation 13.1 "one of the most important discoveries in the field of finance." From a risk perspective, β_i indicates that if the market returns 1 percent, the security can be expected to return β_i x 1 percent. Securities with betas greater than 1 are riskier than the market, and securities with betas less than 1 are less risky than the market. From an asset allocation perspective, the CAPM states that security-specific risk (ϵ_i) can be diversified away, and therefore, beta risk is the only risk that matters. In other words, to model a portfolio's (or security's) volatility, all the investor needs to know is its beta and the volatility (standard deviation) of the market portfolio. For example, suppose the investor holds a portfolio with a beta of 1.5 and the market portfolio has a volatility of 10 percent; then the model's factor-based volatility forecast is 1.5 x 10 percent = 15 percent.

In the same vein, the model states that for asset allocation, the only choice that matters is how much to allocate between the "risk-free" asset and the market portfolio, which in theory should contain all tradable assets in proportion to their market capitalization. Risk factor-based asset allocation cannot get any simpler than that. All securities are exposures to one risk factor (market risk), and the investor should simply choose how much to allocate to this single risk factor based on his risk tolerance. Any other portfolio will be suboptimal.

Unfortunately, the CAPM relies on a long list of unrealistic assumptions, including that investors are rational, markets are frictionless, and investors can easily lend and borrow at the risk-free rate. In practice, the model's empirical performance has been less than stellar. Fama and French (1992), for example, show that CAPM betas have little relation with long-run average returns. The authors' findings open the door to multifactor models. They introduce size and value factors as important drivers of the risk and return of securities. This leads to a three-factor model (beta, size, and value), where size is related to the company's market capitalization and value is related to the ratio of the firm's book value relative to its market value. Carhart (1997) introduces momentum as a fourth factor, which relies on a security's prior-year return as an additional explanatory variable.

In such multifactor models, risk becomes more complicated to estimate. In the single-factor world of the CAPM, the model simply multiplies the beta by the market's volatility. In contrast, in a multifactor world, the model must account for multiple sources of volatility as well as correlations between risk factors. Hence, the model must add risk contributions from each factor as well as correlation effects. Consider a two-factor model, with factors A and B. Portfolio volatility (σ_p) is given by Equation 13.2:

$$\sigma_p = w_A^2\sigma_A^2 + w_B^2\sigma_B^2 + 2w_Aw_B\sigma_A\sigma_B\rho_{A,B}. \tag{13.2}$$

Equation 13.2 is the same as the standard portfolio risk calculation. However, instead of asset class weights, w denotes risk factor weights, and σ and P denote risk factor volatilities and correlation. Factor weights are often referred to as factor "loadings," and investors typically use regression models, such as those presented in Fama and French (1992) and Carhart (1997), to calculate them.

For asset allocation purposes, risk factor models usually capture the sources of risk in asset classes quite accurately, because security-specific risk gets diversified away. Therefore, the important implication is that investors who want to focus on risk factor diversification can substitute asset classes for risk factors and use the same risk measurement and optimization tools they use to allocate across asset classes. A mathematical trick to make this framework effective is that risk factor loadings are linearly additive. For example, the equity beta of a portfolio of two asset classes is the weighted sum of the two betas.

However, in certain asset allocation situations, Equation 13.2 will not suffice. Concentrated portfolios and portfolios where active management plays an important role, such as hedge funds, will require the addition of a so-called "idiosyncratic" term. This idiosyncratic term is usually uncorrelated with the portfolio, and it represents the residual volatility not captured by the risk factor model. The simplest approach to estimate it is to calculate the volatility of the difference between the historical portfolio returns and the returns generated by multiplying the current risk factor exposures by historical risk factor returns.

This difference must be scaled to account for the diversification effect with the rest of the portfolio (idiosyncratic risk should have zero correlation with the portfolio), such that when the idiosyncratic risk is added, the total portfolio volatility rises to a level similar to historical volatility.

Overall, risk factor models seek to explain as much of the portfolio's volatility as possible without overfitting the data. While the three- and four-factor models improve upon the CAPM, they remain too equity-centric to be useful for asset allocation. They fail to capture important drivers of returns across assets classes, such as the impact of interest rates on bonds, real estate, and other asset classes.

Ross (1976) introduced a more general framework, called the arbitrage pricing theory (APT), which allows for multiple risk factors and takes an agnostic view on which risk factors should drive returns. This model can be summarized as Equation 13.3:

$$R_i = \alpha + b_{i1}F_1 + b_{i2}F_2 + \cdots + \epsilon_i, \qquad (13.3)$$

where R_i is the return on security i, α is the mean return assuming all risk factor returns are zero, b_{i1} is the sensitivity of security i returns to the returns of risk factor 1 $(F1)$, and ϵ_i is the unexplained or diversifiable return. The APT does not specify a priori which risk factors matter. Instead, the model (typically) relies on principal component analysis, which is a type of factor analysis, to extract risk factors that are completely independent of each other ("orthogonal"). These factors are expressed as linear combinations of exposures to individual securities ("eigenvectors").

While allocating across eigenvectors would in theory produce superior portfolio diversification compared to other risk factor models, decision makers have been reluctant to adopt the approach because such purely statistical factors are often difficult to interpret. Asset allocators find it a challenging task to go to their board with the recommendation to increase allocation to a specific eigenvector. Financial economists often try to relate principal components to observable factors, such as equity risk and interest rates, but so far the approach has had little practical appeal. Moreover, perhaps the most important limitation of principal components is that they are highly unstable; hence confidence around the eigenvector-based approach is lacking because correlations and volatilities move around.

In practice, asset allocators must compromise between principal components and asset classes. Figure 13.1 illustrates the practitioner approach, which is also referred to as the fundamental factor approach. On the right-hand side of Figure 13.1, asset classes are shown to offer poor and unstable diversification, but strong investability. For example, domestic equities and global equities are often considered two separate asset classes. But consider this example from Chua, Kritzman, and Page (2009):

- From January 1970 to February 2008, when both the U.S. and World ex-U.S. stock markets—as represented by monthly returns for the Russell 3000 and MSCI World Ex-U.S. indexes, respectively—were up more than one standard deviation above their respective full-sample mean, the correlation between them was −0.17.
- In contrast, when both markets were down more than one standard deviation, the correlation between them was +0.76.

In this context, asset class diversification might feel like having one's head in the freezer and feet in the oven: while the average temperature is perfect, the chances of survival are low. In risk factor space, these two asset classes would represent mostly equity risk.

On the left hand side of Figure 13.1, principal components offer superior diversification but with little practical appeal. Therefore, when practitioners build their risk factor sets, they focus on investable factors that are as diversified as possible.

The Barra platform offers perhaps the most widely used set of risk factors in equity space. Barra cleans and quality checks data on more than 8,000 securities globally. The system compiles weekly data on a comprehensive list of factors, including more than 55 counties, 20 currencies, 34 industries, and eight style factors. The models embedded in Barra have sound theoretical foundations, including those mentioned in this chapter, and the methodologies are designed to make the factors as independent as possible. The platform is mainly used for active management of equity portfolios. For asset allocation purposes, practitioners may modify this platform to focus on a few key risk factors, such as world equity risk, currency factors, regional factors, volatility, size, value, liquidity, and momentum.

For fixed-income asset classes, most practitioners use proprietary models. Robust fixed-income platforms calibrate pricing models to observed market prices daily.

Once a calibration is made, these models extract risk factor exposures via simulated shocks. For example, to calculate a bond's exposure to the interest rate risk factor (its duration), such models shock the interest rate by one basis point and then measure the change in the security's price. This approach is superior to regression-based models because it provides a live (sometimes referred to as "forward-looking") picture of risk exposures. The most important risk factors in fixed income are: interest rates (duration), the slope of the yield curve, spreads, and currencies.

While a relatively good industry consensus exists on how to map equities and bonds to risk factors, private and illiquid assets classes present a major challenge. Dimson (1979), for example, discusses biases in beta estimates. A lack of market-to-market data often lures investors into the misconception that these asset classes represent a free lunch. However, a growing consensus in the practitioner community suggests that a reasonable approach to modeling the risk in private and illiquid asset classes should involve the use of public proxies. From an asset allocation perspective, real estate, for example, can be expressed as a linear combination of duration, real duration (duration net of the effect of inflation), equity, and liquidity risk. The bottom line is that to build risk factor models for private and illiquid asset classes requires both art and science.

Once all asset classes have been mapped to risk factors, Equation 13.2 can be applied to produce a portfolio risk estimate. A simple approach is to calculate the covariance matrix of the risk factors, which can be estimated from a time series of historical returns for each risk factor.

Overall, the risk factor approach reveals that risk allocations are quite different from asset allocations. To view the world through the risk factor lens leads to the inescapable conclusion that equity risk is the single most important source of downside risk in most portfolios.

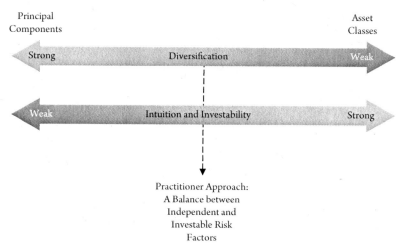

Figure 13.1 Illustration of the practitioner approach to risk factor diversification. The figure shows the trade-off between ease of use and statistical purity of the risk factors. Practitioners usually compromise somewhere between asset classes, which are the easiest to use but which do not provide strong and stable diversification, and principal components, which are statistically independent but difficult to use in practice.

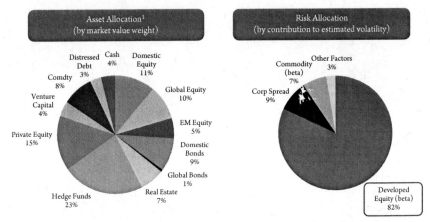

Figure 13.2 Risk allocation vs. asset allocation for a "diversified" portfolio. The pie chart on the left shows a typical asset allocation for university endowments. The chart on the right shows the percentage contribution to total portfolio risk for each risk factor, which is a function of the portfolio's exposure to a given risk factor, the risk factor's volatility, and its contribution to the rest of the portfolio.

EQUITY RISK EVERYWHERE

One of the most frequently quoted phrases in asset allocation discussions recently has been "equity risk represents X percent of your risk," with X being an alarmingly large number, usually in the order of 80–99 percent. Bhansali (2010), for example, demonstrates that equity risk contributes approximately 97 percent of the volatility of a typical 60/40 portfolio (modeled as 60 percent in the S&P 500 and 40 percent in Barclays Capital Aggregate indexes). Even seemingly well-diversified portfolios contain a substantial amount of equity risk. Figure 13.2 shows the difference between asset allocation and risk allocation for the average US endowment, based on a covariance matrix of risk factor returns from January 1997 to June 2011. This portfolio only has 26 percent directly invested in equities, yet equity risk contributes 82 percent of its volatility.

How is the 82 percent number obtained? The model behind Figure 13.2 calculates equity risk contributions as shown in Equation 13.4:

$$x_i = \beta_i \sigma_i \rho_{i,p},\qquad(13.4)$$

where x_i is the risk contribution for factor i, β_i is the risk factor's beta (exposure), and $\rho_{i,p}$ is the correlation between the risk factor and the rest of the portfolio. These three components contribute to the high percentage of equity risk in the following ways:

- The equity risk factor is more volatile than most if not all other risk factors. Suppose the rock band AC/DC (representing equities) is playing in the same room as a string quartet (representing bonds). Which song would be the most audible, "Back in Black" or Vivaldi's "The Four Seasons"? In a similar way, equity volatility dominates the volatility of other risk factors in the portfolio.

- Equity beta is often greater than investors assume because other asset classes contain equity risk. For example, corporate bonds, real estate, hedge funds, commodities, and private equity all contain indirect equity exposures.
- Investors have long recognized that economic conditions frequently undergo regime shifts (Hamilton 1989; Goodwin 1993; Luginbuhl and Vos 1999; Lam 2004). Due to this on-off effect for risks, the equity risk factor typically exhibits positive correlations with other sources of risk premia in the portfolio.

Important caveats apply to these analyses, such as:

- The percentage of portfolio risk contributed by the equity risk factor does not relate directly to the actual riskiness of the portfolio. Imagine a portfolio with 95 percent cash and 5 percent equity. Almost all of this portfolio's risk would come from equities, but its volatility would be lower than, say, a long government bond portfolio (especially these days with increased sovereign risk!).
- The model ignores nonlinearities: correlations and volatilities change through time, and therefore equities' contribution to risk also changes. The bad news is that if nonlinearities are included, then equity contributes even more to portfolio volatility than it does under normal assumptions.
- The model decomposes volatility; but to the extent that returns are not normally distributed, volatility may be a poor measure of risk. A superior approach to risk decomposition would be to decompose tail risk directly.

Also note that when a risk factor helps decrease portfolio risk, the correlation effect can generate negative risk contributions, which cannot be shown in pie charts, and which makes the interpretation of risk contributions less intuitive. The attribution of this diversification effect across risk factors can be open to metaphysical interpretation.

In terms of investment implications, such risk decomposition models ignore expected returns and the dynamic nature of markets. The optimal risk factor allocation at any point in time may not be the "risk parity" portfolio. The *risk parity portfolio* allocates assets equally across risk factors and typically uses leverage to make the contribution to risk from bonds equal to the contribution to risk from equities. Only under a restrictive set of assumptions—namely, that risk-return ratios and correlations are all the same—will the risk parity portfolio be optimal. These assumptions are not necessarily "bad" assumptions because in the absence of informed inputs, they provide robustness to the portfolio construction process. For a passive investor, the risk parity portfolio may indeed be optimal. But if the expected returns on risk factors vary through time and if the investor possesses some foresight on the markets, then the optimal risk factor diversification should trade off time-varying return opportunities for risk.

FAT TAILS AND BLACK SWANS

Unforeseen market crises are often referred to as "tail risk events" because of the way they appear on the bell-shaped curves often used to illustrate market outcomes. That is, the most likely outcomes are at the center of the curve, whereas the unforeseen, less likely events are plotted at either end—or tail—of the curve. Black swans (undesirable left tail events) can wreak havoc on portfolio performance.

The value of tail risk hedging comes to be seen as the most important investment implication of risk factor analysis. The framework reveals that most portfolios cannot be diversified in a way that directly reduces downside risk because equity risk dominates and equity returns exhibit fat tails.

As a powerful illustration of fat tails, Caldwell (2010, 1) quotes this interesting statistic from Benoit Mandelbrot:

> The 20th century saw 48 days in which the Dow Jones Industrial Average swung more than 7 percent. "Normal" statistical modeling predicts such swings should happen once every 300,000 years. We forget the explosiveness of the market at our peril.

The presence of fat tails in markets has led Taleb (2010, p. 277) to qualify some of the theoretical foundations presented in this chapter as "pseudoscience and phony mathematics," which is far from Elton and Gruber's (1995, p. 301) qualification of the CAPM as "one of the most important discoveries in the field of finance." In practice, sophisticated investors have long recognized the presence of fat tails and they have adapted models to account for them.

For example, to measure tail risk in a portfolio, practitioners often use block bootstrap simulations. *Bootstrapping* is a procedure by which new samples are generated from an original data set by randomly selecting observations from the original data set (Efron and Tibshirani 1993). Bootstrapping differs from a Monte Carlo simulation in that it draws randomly from an empirical sample, whereas a Monte Carlo simulation draws randomly from a theoretical distribution. A major advantage of bootstrapping is that it captures fat tails in asset returns. *Block bootstrapping* uses contiguous blocks of data, which in addition to the nonnormality of asset returns also capture serial correlation effects such as momentum and reversal.

Figure 13.3 shows the distribution generated from a block bootstrap of risk factor returns for the portfolio shown in Figure 13.2. The box highlights the "fat tail." To generate this distribution:

1. The model first randomly selects four three-month blocks of risk factor returns from a monthly risk factor data set ranging from January 1997 to June 2011;
2. The model then calculates an annual return by connecting the four three-month blocks.
3. The model goes on to multiply the portfolio's current factor exposures by the simulated annual risk factor returns. For example, assume the portfolio has a duration of five years and an equity beta of 1.0, and the simulated risk factor returns show a change in interest rates of +20 basis points (BPS) and

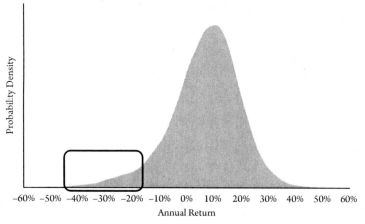

Figure 13.3 Return distribution of the average endowment allocation. The graph shows the portfolio return distribution obtained from performing block bootstrapping on three-month risk factor returns, creating one-year paths, and multiplying each outcome by the portfolio's current risk factor exposures.

an equity return of −5 percent. Then, the simulated one-year portfolio return would be −5 x 20 bps + 1.0 x −5 percent = −6 percent.

4. The model proceeds to put the selected returns back in the distribution.
5. Finally, the model repeats steps 1 to 4 to generate thousands of scenarios.

This simulation also accounts for initial conditions, such as the current level of rates and spreads. For example, if current interest rates are at 1.5 percent, the model cannot assume a decline in interest rates of more than 1.5 percent. Additionally, to make the model forward looking, investors may program the computer to oversample from periods that are more likely to be representative of future market conditions. For example, to account for rising rates, the model may be programmed to increase the probability, so that in step 1, the samples are selected from periods of rising rates. Lastly, investors may add scenarios that have not occurred in the past but that represent possible risks going forward. For example, the possibility is available to specify, qualitatively, what would happen to the various risk factors under a European Monetary Union breakup. Investors may proceed to add this scenario to the distribution based on a qualitative assessment of its probability of occurrence.

In summary, risk factor analysis helps to provide an understanding of the sources of tail risk in portfolios. The most important implication for asset allocators is the decision of whether to hedge tail risk. In their analysis, investors should look beyond the impact of direct hedging costs and conduct a complete analysis of the portfolio's return distribution with and without tail risk hedging, including the impact of hedging on the decision to hold more high-returning risk assets. In practice, tail risk hedging is not just about playing defense. It can also add returns.

TAIL RISK HEDGING IN PRACTICE

The long-run consequences of a severe tail risk event may take years to overcome. Consider an investor who has been talented for nine years in a row, generating a 10 percent return every single year. Assume that in the tenth year, the investor turns out to be "unlucky" and generates a −25 percent return. (A cynic may argue there are only two types of investors: those who are talented and those who are unlucky.) Simple compounding mathematics reveals that this investor's 10-year track record now stands at 5.9 percent.

As investors react to a tail risk event, they typically run for cover and sell risky assets. They place their capital "under the mattress" until their confidence rises to a level that justifies rerisking. But during these stressful times, expected returns on risky assets may be at their highest, simply because valuations are cheap and risk premiums are high. Therefore, the opportunity to increase risk exposures in a tail event may improve the return distribution on most investment portfolios.

From a strategic perspective, many long-horizon investors assume that investors need not purchase tail risk hedges against rare but severe events. Even when tail risk hedges are justified, investors often interpret these "hedges" as a cost that reduces the expected return of the portfolio. But while a tail risk hedge may have negative expected return outright, it may also allow the investor to buy risky securities that have a higher expected return, which can offset the cost. Bhansali and Davis (2010a) call this approach "offensive risk management." Ultimately, combining tail risk hedges with offsetting risky trades can increase expected return and produce more certainty around portfolio returns in rare but severe events.

The implicit value of the tail hedge, therefore, depends both on its explicit price and its impact on the subjective expected return of the portfolio. Consider the case of an investor who finds the risk/reward of a 60 percent stock–40 percent bond allocation to be optimal. This allocation has implicitly revealed the investor's risk tolerance.

To apply a tail risk hedge to this hypothetical portfolio will truncate the extreme left portion of its return distribution. A comparison of the original 60/40 portfolio with the tail-hedged 60/40 portfolio places the two on different scales because the tail profiles of the two asset allocations are different. Thus, an investor who is comfortable with the risks in the original 60/40 portfolio should also be comfortable with a riskier portfolio, say 70/30, incorporating a tail hedge. Although both portfolios display similar behavior on the downside, which is the ultimate concern of the investor, the 70/30 portfolio takes more equity risk and is positioned to harvest more equity risk premium but incurs the cost of the tail risk hedge. Thus, the investor's asset allocation and attitude toward risk imply a value for the tail hedge. This implicit value should be compared with the market prices of the hedges.

The "shadow value" of the tail risk hedge, a measure of the implicit value obtained from adding return to the portfolio by taking more risk, allows investors to augment the return distribution in ways that deviate from the usual bell-shaped pattern. Consider the two annual portfolio return probability distributions shown in Figure 13.4. The appendix describes the model used to generate these distributions. The first distribution is a fat-tailed distribution whose shape is derived based on the assumption that 60 percent of capital is allocated to stocks and

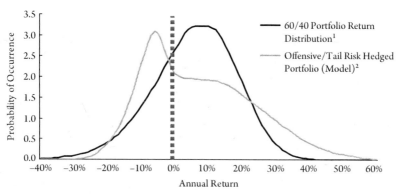

Figure 13.4 Comparison of portfolio return distributions with and without tail risk hedging. The first distribution is based on an allocation of 60 percent equities in the S&P 500 and 40 percent in Treasuries in the Citigroup 3-Month Treasury Bill, with a risk premium on equities of 5 percent per year. The second distribution is derived based on an iterative optimization (varying increases of equity allocation above 60 percent and different strikes on an S&P put option hedge) to match estimated value of losses greater than 5 percent in the unhedged portfolio. The estimated value of losses is defined as the probability of losses greater than 5 percent, multiplied by the magnitude of those returns. While the median return of the tail-hedged portfolio is lower, its estimated return (probability multiplied by magnitude of returns) is higher, with a fatter right tail compensating for the shift of the median to the left.

40 percent to Treasury bills. The second distribution is derived based on the following assumptions: (1) the investor cares about losses that exceed 5 percent, and (2) the investor increases exposure to risky assets and finds an equity option that equates the expected value of losses greater than 5 percent in the second portfolio with the expected value of losses greater than 5 percent in the first portfolio. *The expected value of losses greater than X percent* is a metric similar to conditional value-at-risk except that it measures expected loss beyond a fixed threshold instead of a confidence level. Both distributions assume that the risk premium on equities is 5 percent per annum, a number broadly consistent with the 4–7 percent range found in surveys such as Graham and Harvey (2005). Also, both distributions assume that Treasury bills are completely risk free. Davis, Moore, and Pedersen (2011) relax this assumption and introduce a correlation term between rates and equities.

The shape of the second distribution is derived from an iterative optimization procedure that specifies different allocations to equities and different strikes to the option hedge. The cost of the option is included in the distribution. In this example, the optimizer settles on a 96 percent allocation to equities and a 4 percent allocation to an option with an at-the-money strike price. This result means that if the investor cares about exposure to losses greater than 5 percent, then 96 percent equities and a 4 percent at-the-money equity put investment is equivalent to 60 percent equities and 40 percent in Treasury bills.

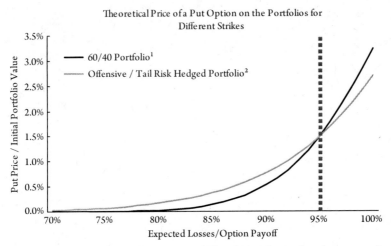

Figure 13.5 Theoretical prices of put options. This figure shows that the expected payoff (also the theoretical price of a put option) of the tail-hedged portfolio matches the 60/40 portfolio at the 95 percent loss threshold.

Even though the median return of the tail-hedged portfolio is lower, its expected return is higher (expectations require averaging all outcomes and letting the fatter right tail compensate for the shift of the median to the left). The 60/40 portfolio exhibits a larger tail than the tail-hedged portfolio with a higher probability of severe losses but compensates by much lower probability of smaller losses. On average, these severities, weighted by the probability of occurrence, are the same.

Figure 13.5 compares the expected value of losses on the two portfolios for different thresholds. The two portfolios have an equivalent tail risk at the −5 percent threshold. In other words, the two portfolios have the same "conditional value-at-risk" beyond −5 percent.

Table 13.1 contrasts additional statistical characteristics of the two return distributions. For the same level of risk, the tail-hedged portfolio offers greater expected return than the 60/40 portfolio. While the tail-hedged portfolio's volatility is greater, this volatility, similar to good and bad cholesterol, comes in two forms: Good and bad and volatility correspond to upside and downside volatility in the tables. Downside volatility is much larger in the 60/40 portfolio, while upside volatility is much larger in tail-hedged portfolio. Similarly, the 10th and 90th percentiles of the two distributions reveal that the downside tail on the 60/40 portfolio is greater, whereas the upside tail on the tail-hedged portfolio is greater.

A FRAMEWORK FOR ASSET ALLOCATION WITH TAIL RISK HEDGING

Tail risk hedging allows investors to reduce exposure to losses and increase exposure to gains, but it can be expensive. The previous example shows that asset allocators must evaluate the cost of the hedge against its overall impact on the portfolio's return distribution, including its ability to increase exposure to risk assets. To assess the

Table 13.1 **Comparison of return, volatility, and percentiles between a 60/40 portfolio and a tail-hedged portfolio**

	60/40 portfolio (%)	*Offensive/tail risk portfolio (%)*
Expected return	6	7
Volatility	12	16
Downside volatility	8	5
Upside volatility	8	12
10th percentile	−11	−11
90th percentile	21	30

Source: PIMCO (Bhansali and Davis 2010a).

Note: Column 1 shows the 60/40 portfolio (made up of S&P 500 and the Citigroup US 3-Month Treasury Bill) for January 1, 1990–March 1, 2010. Column 2 shows offensive/tail risk hedged portfolio (model). Fees and/or expenses are excluded when calculating the annual return. The table shows the differences in summary statistics between the 60/40 portfolio and the tail-hedged portfolio. The 60/40 portfolio shown differs from the "traditional" 60/40 portfolio referenced earlier in this chapter. Bonds in this portfolio are represented by short-maturity T-bills rather than the intermediate investment-grade bonds in the "traditional" portfolio. Different indexes would produce different results. This hypothetical example is for illustrative purposes only for the period January 1, 1990–March 1, 2010.

net benefit of tail risk hedging, asset allocators may adopt the following seven-step strategy:

1. Specify a starting asset allocation that does not include a tail hedge.
2. Measure the portfolio's exposure to key risk factors.
3. Based on the portfolio's risk factor exposures, build a model to generate realistic fat-tailed return distributions.
4. Decide on a "utility function," usually specified as a threshold beyond which losses should be minimized.
5. Solve for the portfolio's exposure to risk assets and option notional exposure (and strike price) that generate the same loss exposure as the starting asset allocation.
6. Calculate the net benefit of tail risk hedging as follows: Assume the expected benefit of tail risk hedging equals theexpected return (or "payoff") on the hedge plus its "shadow value" from its increased exposure to risk assets.
7. If the net benefit after cost is positive, invest in the tail-hedged asset allocation. Otherwise, find ways of reducing the cost of hedging or invest in the unhedged allocation.

STEPS 1, 2 AND 3: ESTIMATING THE PORTFOLIO'S PROBABILITY DISTRIBUTION

Consider the example with 60 percent equities and 40 percent Treasury bills as the starting allocation. As shown in the introduction of this chapter on risk factor analysis, most portfolios contain a heavy concentration in the equity risk factor, and block bootstrapping often reveals fat-tailed distributions. In this example, the problems with risk concentration and fat tails become obvious because nearly all of the portfolio's volatility comes from the equity risk factor.

The framework requires the following inputs, all of which are derived from the distribution of equity returns:

- **Expected return payoff on the hedge.** This is the probability-weighted loss amount below the threshold. This metric is a function of the shape of the distribution and its mean. The higher the equity risk premium, the lower is the expected return on the hedge.
- **"Shadow value" of the hedge.** This is the incremental expected return gained from increasing exposure to the risk asset in the tail-hedged portfolio, holding tail risk exposure constant.
- **Market price of hedge.** This is the price of the equity put option. Basic option theory specifies that this market price depends on the shape of the distribution but not its mean. In other words, the market price of the hedge should vary with volatility but not with the equity risk premium.

As equity risk is the only source of risk in this portfolio, a full block bootstrap is unnecessary to estimate its probability distribution. Instead, an analytical model enables illustrating the framework and price options on a forward-looking basis as well as deriving the implicit value of the tail hedge. To remain consistent with the findings from the block bootstrap, the analytical model must incorporate fat tails as well as the real-world features of option prices, in particular the fact that out-of-the-money equity put options, which are a common tail risk hedge to an equity-heavy portfolio, should have a negative expected return. The appendix to this chapter presents this model.

STEPS 4 AND 5: CONSTRUCTING THE TAIL-HEDGED PORTFOLIO

Once the return distribution has been estimated, the next step is to construct the tail-hedged portfolio. To do so, the model solves simultaneously for the allocation to equities and the tail hedge value and strike. The goal is to match expected losses below a given threshold (K) for the tail hedge portfolio with those of the 60/40 starting portfolio. This expected loss metric measures the tails of distributions in terms of a risk measure that is familiar to investors. As mentioned, it consists of the product of two components: the probability of the scenario times the severity of the scenario.

The expected returns on the 60/40 ($E[r_1]$) and the tail-hedged portfolios ($E[r_2]$) are expressed as Equations 13.5 and 13.6, respectively:

$$E[r_1]=0.6\times(rp+r_f)+0.4\times r_f \tag{13.5}$$

$$E[r_2]=(1-Tail\ cost)[w_s(rp+r_f)+(1-w_s)r_f]+E[Tail\ Payoff]-Tail\ Cost, \tag{13.6}$$

where rp is the risk premium, r_f is the risk-free rate, and w_s is the allocation to equities. Defining $Port_1$ as the value of the 60/40 portfolio in one year with an initial value of one dollar and $Port_2$ as the tail-hedged portfolio in one year with an initial investment of one dollar, the constraint on the portfolio construction algorithm can be expressed as in Equation 13.7:

$$E[\max(K - Port_1), 0] = E[\max(K - Port_{2,0})], \qquad (13.7)$$

where K is the threshold beyond which the expected loss must provide a match between the 60/40 portfolio and the tail-hedged portfolio.

STEPS 6 AND 7: PUTTING IT ALL TOGETHER

The overall expected return to the tail hedge is the sum of the explicit expected return $E[Tail\,Payoff]$ plus the "shadow" expected return, $E[r_2] - E[r_1]$, which is the gain that the investor expects from investing more heavily in risk assets and earning a greater risk premium. Without adding the tail hedge, the investor could not increase the allocation to risky assets and still hold the overall risk, as measured by expected loss below K, to be the same. Thus, this shadow return should be incorporated when thinking about the overall value added of a tail hedge.

Table 13.2 breaks down the net benefit of tail risk hedging into its components, as follows: the expected benefit of tail risk hedging equals the expected payoff on the hedge plus the shadow value from increased exposure to risk assets. The table shows the sensitivity of the benefit of tail risk hedging as a function of the loss threshold (K), and the assumed equity risk premium. The benefits of increasing exposure to risk assets and hedging the tails increase as the equity risk premium increase, as expected. Also, the benefits of this approach increase as the loss threshold ("utility function") moves further into the tails.

Overall, tail risk hedging has the potential to improve the return profile of portfolios. Such strategies may impose deadweight costs, but they allow investors to implement strategies that more heavily weight risk assets, which presumably have higher expected returns. On balance, hedges may improve the overall return profiles of return distributions.

DOWNSIDE RISK AND LIQUIDITY

Another benefit of tail risk hedging is that active monetization of hedges may provide liquidity that might be used to purchase cheap assets in periods of crisis, thus further improving the ex-ante long-term return potential of the portfolio (Bhansali and Davis 2010b). When traders buy and sell securities in large quantities, they care deeply about liquidity. Traders must constantly balance the need to act fast—before prices move away from them—with the risk that their own trading will push prices. Considerable resources are spent in managing liquidity from this bottom-up security-level perspective.

Table 13.2 **Decomposition of the benefits of tail risk hedging**

		Expected return (Payoff) on tail hedges Equity (S & P 500) risk premium (%)				
K		3.00	4.00	5.00	6.00	7.00
	80	0.88	0.87	0.83	0.78	0.72
	85	1.47	1.35	1.27	1.18	1.10
	90	2.23	2.02	1.89	1.77	1.63
	95	3.01	2.90	2.66	2.54	2.37
	100	4.07	3.92	3.72	3.58	3.43
		Shadow value of tail hedges Equity (S & P 500) risk premium				
K		3.00	4.00	5.00	6.00	7.00
	80	1.14	1.52	1.91	2.30	2.69
	85	1.10	1.48	1.87	2.24	2.64
	90	1.05	1.42	1.80	2.17	2.55
	95	1.00	1.35	1.72	2.08	2.45
	100	0.92	1.26	1.61	1.95	2.29
		Market costs of tail hedges Equity (S & P 500) risk premium (%)				
K		3.00	4.00	5.00	6.00	7.00
	80	1.09	1.15	1.18	1.19	1.19
	85	1.79	1.76	1.77	1.76	1.77
	90	2.69	2.58	2.59	2.58	2.55
	95	3.59	3.65	3.58	3.61	3.60
	100	4.84	4.93	5.00	5.10	5.21
		Expected net benefit of tail hedges Equity (S & P 500) risk premium (%)				
K		3.00	4.00	5.00	6.00	7.00
	80	0.93	1.24	1.56	1.89	2.22
	85	0.78	1.07	1.37	1.66	1.97
	90	0.59	0.86	1.10	1.36	1.63
	95	0.42	0.60	0.80	1.01	1.22
	100	0.15	0.25	0.33	0.43	0.51

Source: PIMCO (Bhansali and Davis 2010a).

Note: These tables show that tail risk hedging can add value after accounting for the cost of hedging. A substantial amount of value is added from the investor's ability to increase exposure to risky assets once the tails have been hedged. This hypothetical example is for illustrative purposes only for the period January 1, 1990–March 1, 2010.

Surprisingly, investors pay little attention to how liquidity should influence the choices that precede execution. The further away the investment choice is from execution, the less liquidity appears to matter. Asset allocation decisions, for example, are often made without serious consideration of liquidity risk. If an asset class offers an attractive expected Sharpe ratio (or if it helps elevate the portfolio's Sharpe ratio), then it should receive a higher allocation, as asset allocators often reason. Unfortunately, because such events occur outside of the bell curve for probability distribution, Sharpe ratios mask the impact that systemic liquidity crises have on asset class returns.

Page, Simonian, and He (2011) contend that investors should care about liquidity from bottom-up and top-down perspectives. From the top down, liquidity should be viewed as an important risk factor that drives asset prices, and investors should decide how much to allocate to this risk factor. Unfortunately, unlike other risk factors, liquidity risk is highly nonlinear. It often manifests itself during "risk-off" panics, similar to a virus that lays dormant until the body weakens.

Bhansali (2010) argues that any excess yield comes from implicitly selling an option. He urges investors to move away from the linear assumptions that plague investment thinking. Selling an out-of-the-money liquidity option might look attractive on the surface, for example, in terms of Sharpe ratio, which is a linear measure; yet, the important questions are whether the option is currently attractively valued and whether investors can use hedges to offset most of the risk (or all of the risk in the case of pure liquidity arbitrage opportunities, which are rare).

To decide how much to allocate to the liquidity risk factor, investors should be suspicious of liquidity lunches that appear to be free, while at the same time looking for opportunities to harvest inexpensive liquidity premiums. This process should take place with careful consideration for tail risk exposures.

Lo (2001, 21) provides an intuitive example of how allocations to nonlinear risk premiums can mislead investors. He presents a simulated investment strategy with the following attractive track record, measured from 1992 to 1997:

> an average monthly return of 3.7% versus 1.4% for the S&P 500; a total return of 2,721.3% over the eight-year period versus 367.1% for the S&P 500; a Sharpe ratio of 1.94 versus 0.98 for the S&P 500; and only 6 negative monthly returns out of 96 versus 36 out of 96 for the S&P 500.

Not bad. Aside from strategies designed by Bernard Madoff or inexperienced quantitative analysts running "out-of-sample" back tests, investment strategies are rarely expected to deliver such risk-adjusted returns over the long run. This statement is especially true in light of the fact that Lo's (2001) simulated strategies consist of selling out-of-the-money put options on the S&P 500.

The bottom line is that when asset allocators strategically allocate to the liquidity premium through real estate, private equity, and hedge fund investments, they implicitly sell an out-of-the-money put option on liquidity risk. When the option becomes in the money, the strategy must be able to survive the storm and pay up. In such markets, a strategic allocation to a tail risk hedging strategy may provide liquidity when it is needed the most.

Summary and Conclusions

The following conversation is said to have taken place in the halls of the Massachusetts Institute of Technology (MIT) Sloan School of Management during the market crash of the fall of 2008. The conversation was between Mark Kritzman, the managing partner and Chief Investment Officer of Windham Capital Management, who teaches a financial engineering class at MIT, and Paul Samuelson, who was arguably one of the greatest economists of the century (and who sadly has passed away).

Mark Kritzman: Paul, can you tell me why the market crashed?

Paul Samuelson: Mark, I hate to say this, but I'm afraid it's a consequence of financial engineering.

Samuelson's reply must have been disheartening for Kritzman, who was on his way to teach a financial engineering class.

For the last sixty years, portfolio theory has received both praise and criticism. To balance return against risk at the portfolio level is a worthy objective, but the models used to achieve this objective can be misleading. The recent financial crisis has reinforced the importance of a number of key developments in the field of asset allocation. As robust postcrisis asset allocation, pension plans, foundations, endowments, and individuals should pay close attention to developments in risk factor analysis and tail risk hedging.

Risk factor analysis reveals that most portfolios are poorly diversified because they are mostly exposed to equity risk. This lack of diversification at the risk factor level leads to exposure to tail risk. When investors evaluate the benefits of tail risk hedging, they should consider the impact of the hedges on their ability to invest in risk assets. In other words, tail risk hedging is an asset allocation decision. This cost-benefit analysis helps integrate downside risk management into the asset allocation decision.

APPENDIX: ANALYTICAL MODEL TO GENERATE
FAT-TAILED DISTRIBUTIONS AND PRICE OPTIONS

To estimate the expected payoff on the hedge, assume log stock returns exhibit time-varying volatility, as shown in Equation 13.8:

$$r_t \sim N\left[\left(r_t^f + rp_t\right) \times dt, \sigma_{t-1}\sqrt{dt}\right], \tag{13.8}$$

where r_t^f is the annualized short term interest rate, rp_t is the annualized risk premium of the asset (the excess return of equities minus the risk-free rate), dt is the amount of time over which the return is measured (for example, in years $dt = 1/52$ for weekly spacing), and σ_{t-1} is the annualized volatility of the stock return conditional on the information at time t−1. Under this notation, the expected return of the asset over the horizon given by dt is approximately $(r_t^f + rp_t) \times dt$, and the volatility of that return is $\sigma_{t-1}\sqrt{dt}$. When $\sigma_{t-1} \equiv \sigma$, a constant, this model exhibits constant volatility as in the standard Black-Scholes framework.

What differentiates this model from the simple constant volatility in the log-normal process underlying the theory of Black and Scholes (1973) is that the conditional volatility of the log stock return is allowed to vary. In particular, the annualized variance of the stock return at time t is related to the variance of stock returns last period, time t–1, through the following relationship (Heston 1993) in Equation 13.9:

$$\tilde{\sigma}_t^2 = \tilde{\sigma}_{t-1}^2 + \kappa(\theta - \tilde{\sigma}_{t-1}^2)dt + \gamma\tilde{\sigma}_{t-1}\sqrt{dt} \times \mu_i, \qquad (13.9)$$

with the additional criteria that $corr(\mu_t, r_t) = \rho$ and $\mu_t \sim N(0,1)$. The correlation between the stock's return and the stock's return volatility allows the model to match the negative skewness of the block-bootstrapped stock return distribution. This negative skewness is an important feature to include in accurately modeling portfolio tails because it implies that larger negative outcomes are more likely than larger positive outcomes. Furthermore, the time variation in the volatility of stock returns allows the model to exhibit excess kurtosis relative to a constant volatility distribution, which is a feature consistent with empirical return distributions whereby large outcomes are more likely relative to the normal distribution.

To estimate the market price of the hedge, the model must derive option prices that are consistent with the absence of arbitrage opportunities. According to this risk-neutral model, option prices do not depend on the risk premium and therefore the model for log stock returns excludes rp_t, as follows:

$$r_t \sim N(r_t^f \times dt, \sigma_{t-1}\sqrt{dt}). \qquad (13.10)$$

Removing rp_t from the equation shifts the distribution to the left. This adjustment makes the market price of the option higher than its expected payoff, which in turn translates into a negative expected return from buying the option.

Note that the volatility model is the same for both the expected payoff on the hedge and its market price, as described in Equation 13.6. The calibration of this volatility model matches the characteristics of historical equity returns, based on a weekly return frequency. To begin, the long-term, option-implied volatility is set to $\sqrt{\theta} = 20$ percent and $\sigma_0 = \sigma_0 = 20$ percent, which implies, along with the parameters below, that at-the-money equity put options trade at 20 percent volatility, a value close to the long-run average of the VIX Index. The correlation parameter between equity returns and changes in equity volatility can be roughly calibrated by comparing the returns on the S&P 500 Index and the changes in the VIX Index (squared). Because implied volatility and realized volatility generally track one another well over time, this estimate provides a reasonable approximation of the correlation and volatility of volatility parameters. Equations 13.11, 13.12, and 13.13 summarize the calibration model:

$$\tilde{\sigma}_t^2 \approx \left(\frac{VIX}{100}\right)^2. \qquad (13.11)$$

$$\mu_t \approx \frac{\sigma_t^2 - \sigma_{t-1}^2}{\gamma \sigma_{t-1}}. \tag{13.12}$$

$$\gamma \approx stdev\left(\frac{\sigma_t^2 - \sigma_{t-1}^2}{\sigma_{t-1}}\right) \tag{13.13}$$

Here, the parameter describing the volatility of volatility is approximately $\gamma = 0.41$, and the correlation is found to be about $corr(\mu_t, r_t) = -0.75$. Finally, a simple regression using the squared VIX Index reveals that $\kappa = 4.7$ is approximately the rate at which the conditional variance mean reverts to its long-run level.

Discussion Questions

1. To diversify across risk factors may lead to better portfolio diversification and lower downside risk than would allocating across asset classes. While allocation across principal components would be a theoretically superior approach to risk factor diversification, practitioners typically prefer to use fundamental risk factors. Explain at least two challenges of principal component analysis and enumerate four of the key risk factors commonly used by practitioners.
2. Duration represents a security's sensitivity to changes in interest rates; in other words, a security's exposure to the interest rate risk factor. Explain two ways to measure duration and recommend the preferred methodology.
3. Discuss three reasons that risk factor decompositions often show a substantial allocation to the equity risk factor.
4. Explain why the decision to hedge tail risk may change the asset allocation decision.
5. Provide another example of an indirect benefit of tail risk hedging.

Acknowledgements

The authors would like to thank Jim Moore, Peter Matheos, Suzanne Oden, John Tran, and Antoan Nikolaev for helpful comments, as well as Vineer Bhansali for his thought leadership behind the concepts presented in this chapter.

References

Bhansali, Vineer. 2010. *Bond Portfolio Investing and Risk Management.* New York: McGraw Hill.
Bhansali, Vineer, and Joshua M. Davis. 2010a. "Offensive Risk Management: Can Tail Risk Hedging Be Profitable?" *PIMCO Viewpoints,* February. http://www.pimco.com.
Bhansali, Vineer, and Joshua M. Davis. 2010b. "Offensive Risk Management II: The Case for Active Tail Hedging." *Journal of Portfolio Management* 37:1, 78–91.

Black, Fischer, and Myron Scholes. 1973. "The Pricing of Options and Corporate Liabilities." *Journal of Political Economy* 81(3): 637–654.

Caldwell, Christopher. 2010. "Maldelbrot Tips off the Markets." *Financial Times*, October 22. http://www.ft.com/intl/cms/s/0d0da878-de0f-11df-88cc-00144feabdc0,Authorised=fals e.html?_I_location=http%3A%2F%2Fwww.ft.com%2Fcms%2Fs%2F0%2F0d0da878-de0 f-11df-88cc-00144feabdc0.html&_I_referer=http%3A%2F%2Fsearch.ft.com%2Fsearch%3F queryText%3Dmandlebrot%2Btips%2Boff%2Bthe%2Bmarkets#axzz1w6QmbZlz.

Carhart, Mark M. 1997. "On the Persistence in Mutual Fund Performance." *Journal of Finance* 52(1): 57–82.

Chua, David B., Mark Kritzman, and Sébastien Page. 2009. "The Myth of Diversification." *Journal of Portfolio Management* 36(1): 26–35.

Davis, Josh, Jim Moore, and Niels K. Pedersen. 2011. "Tail Risk Hedging Strategies for Corporate Pension Plans." *Journal of Derivatives & Hedge Funds* 17: 237–252.

Dimson, Elroy. 1979. "Risk Measurement When Shares are Subject to Infrequent Trading." *Journal of Financial Economics* 7(2): 197–226.

Efron, Bradley, and Robert J. Tibshirani. 1993. *An Introduction to the Bootstrap*. New York: Chapman & Hall/CRC.

Elton, Edwin J., and Martin J. Gruber. 1995. *Modern Portfolio Theory and Investment Analysis*, 5th ed. Hoboken, NJ: John Wiley and Sons.

Fama, Eugene F., and Kenneth R. French. 1992. "The Cross-Section of Expected Stock Returns." *Journal of Finance* 47(2): 427–465.

Goodwin, Thomas H. 1993. "Business-Cycle Analysis with a Markov-Switching Model." *Journal of Business and Economic Statistics* 11(3): 331–339.

Graham, John R., and Campbell R. Harvey. 2005. "The Long-Run Equity Risk Premium." Working Paper 79, Fuqua School of Business, Duke University, Durham, NC.

Hamilton, James D. 1989. "A New Approach to the Economic Analysis of Nonstationary Time Series and the Business Cycle." *Econometrica* 57(2): 357–384.

Heston, Steve L. 1993. "A Closed-Form Solutions for Options with Stochastic Volatility with Applications to Bond and Currency Options." *Review of Financial Studies* 6(2): 327–343.

Lam, Pok-sang. 2004. "A Markov-Switching Model of GNP Growth with Duration Dependence." *International Economic Review* 45(1): 175–204.

Lintner, John. 1965. "The Valuation of Risk Assets and the Selection of Risky Investments in Stock Portfolios and Capital Budgets." *Review of Economics and Statistics* 47(1): 13–37.

Lo, Andrew A. 2001. "Risk Management for Hedge Funds: Introduction and Overview." *Financial Analysts Journal* 57(6): 16–33.

Luginbuhl, Rob, and Aart de Vos. 1999. "Bayesian Analysis of an Unobserved-Component Time Series Model of GDP with Markov-Switching and Time-Varying Growths." *Journal of Business and Economic Statistics* 17(4): 456–465.

Mossin, Jan. 1966. "Equilibrium in a Capital Asset Market." *Econometrica* 34(4): 768–783.

Page, Sébastien, Joseph Simonian, and Fei He. 2011. "Asset Allocation: Systemic Liquidity as a Risk Factor." *Trading* 2011:1, 19–23.

Page, Sébastien, and Mark Taborsky. 2011. "The Myth of Diversification: Risk Factors vs. Asset Classes." *Journal of Portfolio Management* 37(4): 1–2.

Ross, Stephen A. 1976. "The Arbitrage Theory of Capital Asset Pricing." *Journal of Economic Theory* 13(3): 341–60.

Sharpe, William F. 1964. "Capital Asset Prices: A Theory of Market Equilibrium under Conditions of Risk." *Journal of Finance* 19(3): 425–442.

Taleb, Nassim Nicholas. 2010. *The Black Swan: The Impact of the Highly Improbable*, 2nd ed. New York: Random House.

Treynor, Jack L. 1961. "Market Value, Time, and Risk." Unpublished Manuscript.

Treynor, Jack L. 1999. "Toward a Theory of Market Value of Risky Assets." In *Asset Pricing and Portfolio Performance: Models, Strategy and Performance Metrics*, edited by Robert A. Korajczyk, 15–22. London: Risk.

14

Alternative Investments

LARS HELGE HASS
Lancaster University

DENIS SCHWEIZER
Assistant Professor of Alternative Investments, WHU—
Otto Beisheim School of Management

JULIANE PROELSS
Professor of Finance, Trier University of Applied Sciences

Introduction

Alternative investments have gained much public attention due to announce-ments such as those announcing a "commodities boom," a strong price increase of precious metal prices in the aftermath of the financial crisis of 2007 and 2008, and concerns in 2011 about the creditworthiness of countries such as Greece, Portugal, Spain, and the United States. In comparison, publicly listed real estate investment trusts (REITs) around the world reached $568 billion in 2010, which was up 230 percent from the previous year (Ernst & Young 2010). Admittedly, during the financial crisis of 2007 and 2008, the value of REITs was roughly halved but recovered strongly, showing annualized returns for the FTSE National Association of Real Estate Investment Trusts (NAREIT) Real Estate 50 Index Fund of 27.8 percent in 2009, 27.6 percent in 2010, and 10.1 percent as of July 2011. Additionally, the total assets increased to an all time high in 2010 of about $2 trillion and net inflows remained stable in first half of 2011 (Hedge Fund Research, 2011). The only outlier in the alternative invest-ment universe at the moment is private equity. The transaction flow of private equity funds reached record lows in 2009. A constrained debt supply and drop in risk appetite ushered in a more prudent attitude, which resulted in a global fundraising of about $200 million in 2010, compared to $800 billion in 2007 and 2008 (Credit Suisse, 2011).

Despite the current trend toward alternative investments, this asset class does not represent a financial innovation. The first hedge fund started in 1949. The first (modern) trade of standardized commodity futures contracts occurred with the formation of the Chicago Board of Trade (CBOT) in 1848. The formation of the first venture capital firm occurred in 1946. Given this history, why are alternative investments attracting such attention now? This question is appropriate considering the many failures and crises such as the collapse of Long-Term Capital Management (LTCM) in 1998 and Bernard Madoff's infamous $50 billion–plus Ponzi scheme.

This chapter limits its discussion of alternative investments to commodities, hedge funds, private equity, and real estate. It identifies two major interconnected reasons for increased attention to alternative investments: First, expanding globalization leads to a greater correlation among international financial markets, especially the correlations between industrial and emerging countries because of the interconnectedness of the economies. Thus, structuring a well-diversified portfolio with international stocks and bonds as the sole diversifier of domestic financial assets becomes more difficult. Second, worldwide changes in regulation and accounting standards encourage diversification as a means to improve the portfolio risk-return profile. Consequently, investors are searching for return drivers with low or even negative correlations with traditional assets, such as alternative investments, to enhance their risk-adjusted portfolio performance.

Alternative investments offer investors exposure to risk-return profiles that are often not replicable using traditional assets for regulatory reasons. Mutual funds and traditional investors face prohibitions or limitations on using strategies such as leverage, which includes investments in risky assets such as derivatives and short selling. On the other hand, most alternative investments involve a level of complexity that requires special skills and long-term experience. Regulatory authorities acknowledge the advantages of further diversification with laws encouraging diversification such as Basel II and Basel III and the Employee Retirement Income Security Act of 1974 (ERISA), which opens up the possibility of using certain alternative investments.

Surprisingly, while alternatives are becoming a substantial part of a mixed institutional portfolio, little literature exists about how to incorporate such investments. Investors need answers to such questions as: To what extent should institutional investors move into alternative asset classes to achieve the goal of enhanced risk-adjusted performance? What does an optimal allocation involving alternative investments look like? These questions are not easily answered. What is clear is that the observed asset allocation is no longer optimal under the current market and regulatory environment (Greenwich Associates, 2007). Thus, determining the composition of an optimal portfolio allocation that accounts for recent diversification changes is important.

This chapter first considers two major questions: (1) Which alternative asset classes should investors and portfolio managers include in a mixed-asset portfolio? (2) In what proportion should these classes be involved in a portfolio? Both questions are essential because the assets included in a strategic asset allocation determine both the diversification potential and the variability of the portfolio return.

To assess which alternative investments are the most efficient portfolio diversifiers requires considering the risk-return characteristics as well as the other factors unique to commodities, hedge funds, private equity, and real estate. Using these characteristics, the aim is to identify an adequate asset allocation model that is flexible enough to incorporate the return characteristics of alternative investments. This enables us to determine how much to allocate to alternative investments. If the chosen model does not sufficiently capture the risk-return characteristics, then the suggested mixed-asset optimal portfolio may include only alternative assets (Terhaar, Staub, and Singer, 2003).

The extant literature focuses on the effects of including only one alternative investment class in a traditional mixed-asset portfolio, or how including more than one alternative investment tends to make the respective model too inflexible or fails to capture the risk-return profiles adequately (Schneeweis, Karavas, and Georgiev, 2002; Conner, 2003; Winkelmann, 2004; Hocht, Ng, Wolf, and Zagst, 2008; Huang and Zhong, 2012). Consequently, a satisfactory answer to the allocation question is unavailable in the literature.

The remainder of the chapter is organized as follows: The next section reviews the risk-return characteristics of alternative investments to determine which should be considered in a mixed-asset portfolio allocation. The risk-return profiles of the chosen alternative investments are adjusted for selection biases. Based on these return characteristics, a model is presented that is flexible enough to incorporate different alternative investments as well as traditional investments such as stocks and government bonds. Next, an optimal strategic mixed-asset allocation is computed using Conditional Value-at-Risk (CVaR) as a risk measure to account for the special characteristics of alternative investments. The results are compared with a traditional mean-variance optimal allocation to identify potential misallocations. The chapter ends with a summary and conclusions.

Risk-and-Return Profiles of Alternative Investments

Markowitz's (1952) seminal paper on portfolio theory shows that diversification can increase a portfolio's expected returns while reducing volatility. However, investors should not add an additional asset class to their portfolios without carefully considering its properties in the context of the portfolio. An added asset class may not improve the risk-return profile, and may even worsen it. Therefore, the first step should be to assess which alternative asset classes (e.g., commodities, hedge funds, private equity, or real estate) can be effective portfolio diversifiers.

Following Kat (2007), this chapter examines (1) the expected return of the asset class, (2) the variation of the returns around their mean as well as the higher moments of the return distribution, (3) the correlation with traditional assets in the existing portfolio, and (4) the liquidity of this asset class as well as any fees. A benchmark is also identified to serve as a representative approximation for the asset classes. Before determining whether to include any given asset class in a portfolio, potential biases in the return time series are identified that may affect the risk-return profile and necessary adjustments are made.

COMMODITIES

Compared to other asset classes, the existence of a risk premium for commodities remains an ongoing question. The literature provides mixed evidence: Bodie and Rosansky (1980) and Gorton and Rouwenhorst (2006) find stocklike historical returns for unleveraged commodity futures indices. Conversely, Erb and Harvey (2006), Kat (2007), and Kat and Oomen (2007) find no evidence of time-persistent risk premiums for single commodities (except in regard to energy commodities, including natural gas, crude oil, unleaded gasoline, and heating oil). These results may be explained by the fact that a well-diversified portfolio of commodities offers a reliable source of returns, which Erb and Harvey refer to as the diversification return.

Unlike the risk premium discussion, the literature is consistent about the second through fourth moments of the return distribution (namely, variance, skewness, and kurtosis) of commodities. Researchers such as Erb and Harvey (2006) and Gorton and Rouwenhorst (2006) show that most single commodity return distributions are positively skewed and have a kurtosis greater than three, which is often referred to as positive excess kurtosis or leptokurtosis (Fama and French, 1987). This means that a higher probability of "fat tails" exists; that is, higher (lower) positive (negative) returns compared to a normal distribution. At the same time, the excess kurtosis implies the existence of high extreme risks. The reasoning is that commodity market shocks are generally associated with price spikes. However, this is not the case for well-diversified commodity portfolios, whose return distributions often follow a normal distribution (see Table 14.3).

Single commodity returns have a low or negative correlation with nonrelated commodities. This is a favorable characteristic that permits structuring a well-diversified commodity portfolio. Additionally, the generally positive correlation of most single commodities with inflation makes them a good investment during periods of high inflation. Finally, and most importantly for diversifying a traditional portfolio, commodities often exhibit a correlation of close to zero with bonds and equity (Bodie and Rosansky, 1980; Georgiev, 2006; Gorton and Rouwenhorst, 2006; Idzorek, 2006).

Thus far, diversified commodity portfolios have met all the criteria necessary to be considered effective diversifiers when combined with portfolios of traditional assets. However, the question remains as to how best to gain exposure to commodities. Also, the issues of liquidity and possible fees need to be considered.

As Fabozzi, Fuess, and Kaiser (2007) discuss, the commodity futures index with the largest invested capital may be a suitable proxy for asset class commodities. Therefore, the S&P GSCI Total Return Index for commodities is included in the mixed-asset portfolio optimization, as its total return indices best replicate an investment in a diversified commodity portfolio. The liquidity of this investable index is generally high. Furthermore, the fees for those passive products are low. However, the investor bears the default risk of the issuer because investable indices are usually structured as bearer bonds.

HEDGE FUNDS

Like most alternative investments, hedge funds are a heterogeneous asset class. This results from the high variability of instruments such as derivatives, which can take advantage of investing in hedge funds, selling short, and using leverage, as well as a host of even more complex investment strategies. Depending on the specific hedge fund's strategy, investors and portfolio managers can use these possibilities to a greater or lesser extent. Also, these possibilities are the reason hedge funds have special risk-return characteristics. Brooks and Kat (2002) provide more details on the different strategies and how they influence a hedge fund strategy's return distribution.

Many empirical studies, such as that by Jagannathan, Malakhov, and Novikov (2006), find statistically and economically significant persistence in the performance of hedge funds relative to their benchmarks. However, those figures are often subject to biases, so the risk premium may be lower and the variance underestimated. For example, Brown, Goetzmann, and Ibbotson (1999) find no evidence of a consistent risk premium for an unbiased hedge fund time series. As Eling (2009) notes, the use of different research periods and databases can often explain the differences in the risk premium estimates.

Hedge fund substrategy return distributions also tend to exhibit significant negative skewness and leptokurtosis. This is because many substrategies are based on nonlinear investments, such as derivatives and nontraditional asset classes including credit derivatives. They may also follow investment strategies with high event risk or be invested in illiquid assets, such as distressed securities (Ackermann, McEnally, and Ravenscraft, 1999; Amin and Kat, 2003; Agarwal and Naik, 2004; Anson, Ho, and Silberstein, 2007).

Although additional risks are associated with the higher moments, compensation occurs for taking such risks. For example, the low or negative correlation among several substrategies makes structuring a well-diversified hedge fund portfolio with more favorable moment characteristics possible (Proelss and Schweizer, 2011). Also, hedge fund managers are not subject to the same level of restrictions as mutual fund managers (Kahan and Rock, 2007), so their strategies may also exhibit low correlation with bonds and equities and offer institutional investors the opportunity to gain exposure to the risk-return profiles of nontraditional investment instruments or strategies, as shown in Table 14.3.

Nevertheless, the cost of gaining exposure to hedge funds should not be underestimated. The annual management fee is usually about 2 percent, and the incentive fee can be 20 percent or higher (Cottier, 2000; Mietzner, Schweizer, and Tyrell, 2011). Because of their sophisticated investment approaches, hedge funds often have long lock-up periods as well, which can range from an average of between one to five years. Hedge funds often have minimum investment requirements in the range of $100,000–$500,000. Alternatives to single hedge fund investments are investable index products and diversified funds of hedge funds. While the minimum investment for funds of hedge funds is usually much lower than for single hedge funds, additional management fees (about 1.5 percent a year) and incentive fees (about 10 percent) apply.

In summary, the discussion of consistent performance persistence for hedge funds remains ongoing, and some hedge fund substrategies exhibit unfavorable statistical return distribution characteristics, such as negative skewness combined with positive excess kurtosis. This disadvantage is expected to be lower for diversified hedge funds. However, hedge funds still offer institutional investors access to new return drivers that may have low correlations with those in their existing portfolios. This makes hedge funds a promising asset class for mixed-asset portfolios.

The HFRI Fund of Funds Composite Index represents a good proxy for the performance of the hedge fund asset class. The index might not cover the entire hedge fund market, but the performance by fund of fundmanagers, ensures reporting accuracy and transparency requirements. Furthermore, many data biases apparent in indexes for single hedge funds, such as the Dow Jones Credit Suisse or Eurekah Hedge, do not exist or are reduced.

The returns of some hedge fund strategies and single hedge funds exhibit autocorrelation in their returns due primarily to illiquidity and smoothed returns (Getmansky, Lo, and Makarov, 2004; Avramov et al., 2008). Positive autocorrelation causes the standard deviation of hedge fund return distributions to be underestimated, which can lead to an overallocation of hedge funds (Kat, 2003). However, a test provided in this chapter using the HFRI Fund of Funds Composite Index reveals no evidence of this potential bias.

PRIVATE EQUITY

Private equity as an asset class exhibits very low transparency. Each private equity fund has some unique characteristics, and the target companies of the private equity funds are generally not publicly traded, with the exception of listed private equity (Bergmann et al., 2009). Consequently, the lack of available data and the granularity (often only quarterly returns are provided) complicates a meaningful comparison with other asset classes on an aggregate level. Empirical research in private equity usually calculates returns by using reported cash flows and the appraised values of unrealized investments.

Several researchers attempt to quantify the risk-return characteristics of private equity on a fund level or on an individual portfolio company level (Gompers and Lerner, 1997; Moskowitz and Vissing-Jørgensen, 2002; Cochrane, 2005; Kaplan and Schoar, 2005). These studies, however, have some drawbacks: Researchers conduct most analyses using data from data vendors, which rely on self-reporting. These studies also do not provide a consensus of the reported returns, so annual returns range from −1.5 percent to 17.0 percent. Additionally, the reported returns are subject to biases induced by including unrealized and realized investments and different accounting treatments.

Phalippou and Gottschalg (2009) conclude that the dramatic growth in private equity cannot be attributed to genuinely high past net performance. They find an average annual underperformance of 3 percent for private equity funds with respect to the S&P 500. While disagreement exists about the existence of a risk premium for private equity, the literature offers consistent evidence of positive skewness and positive excess kurtosis in the return data.

Although the literature offers no ultimate conclusion on private equity returns, their correlation with other asset classes is an important property that investors and portfolio managers should consider. Private equity returns exhibit a low to negative correlation with bonds and a low correlation with equity (Chen, Baierl, and Kaplan, 2002). Thus, investors should include private equity in a portfolio to enhance the risk-return profile if they are willing to assume some risk (Lamm and Ghaleb-Harter, 2001; Schmidt, 2004; Ennis and Sebastian, 2005). The costs of a private equity investment, however, should not be underestimated. Annual management fees usually range from 1.5 percent to 2.5 percent plus an incentive fee (carry) of about 20 percent (Metrick and Yasuda, 2010). Similar to hedge funds, the possibility also exists of investing in funds of funds that typically charge an additional 1 percent management fee and a 10 percent incentive fee.

In summary, even without high past returns, the return drivers for private equity differ from those for traditional asset classes. Private equity offers positive diversification benefits because of lower correlation coefficients with traditional asset classes. Therefore, considering buyouts as the major private equity "strategy" in the mixed-asset portfolio optimization is appropriate.

The heterogeneity and lack of data for private equity make identifying a suitable benchmark difficult. Hence, this chapter uses a new benchmark index for buyouts introduced by Cumming, Hass, and Schweizer (2010). This benchmark, which is updated monthly, adjusted for autocorrelation (desmoothing), and available contemporaneously, enables superior quantitative portfolio optimizations.

REAL ESTATE

Before analyzing the diversification properties of REITs, REITs are examined to determine if they are (1) representative of the real estate market, (2) more suitable as a substitute for stocks, or (3) an asset class of their own. Evidence suggests that common factors affect both the return series of REITs and direct real estate as well as REITs and the stock market time series (Myer and Webb, 1993; Barkham and Geltner, 1995; Li and Wang, 1995; Ling and Naranjo, 1999).

However, the literature reports that the sensitivity of REIT returns to the stock market declined significantly in the 1990s, which Clayton and MacKinnon (2000) attribute to the growth and maturity of the REIT market. In addition, they show that the relationship between REITs and direct real estate strengthened in the 1990s. This insight is valuable because the sample time period used in this chapter begins in the 1990s.

Clayton and MacKinnon (2000) conclude that both REITS and direct real estate have a place in optimal, short-term portfolios. But in the long term, only one should be included, because each is a substitute for the other. Evidence also suggests that REITs are a "unique" asset class with price behavior unequal to stocks, fixed-income securities, direct real estate, or combinations thereof (Liang and McIntosh, 1998; Stevenson, 2001). Based on these results, REITs appear to be a reasonable but incomplete proxy for the real estate market.

Although REITs seem to be unequal to stocks and are not a substitute for them, this finding does not imply that REITs are a good portfolio diversifier. The risk-and-return characteristics of REITs as an asset class need to be assessed.

The literature reports annualized mean returns for REITs of between 11.6 percent and 17.9 percent and standard deviations ranging from about 13.3 percent to 14.1 percent (Myer and Webb, 1993; Jinliang, Mooradian, and Yang, 2005; Cotter and Stevenson, 2007). Regarding the higher moments, the evidence is mixed. Myer and Webb find no significant skewness or kurtosis using an equally weighted equity REIT index, whereas Cotter and Stevenson report significant negative skewness and excess kurtosis for different research periods. In summary, REITs offer a large risk premium, which makes them an interesting asset class. However, investors and portfolio managers must consider the higher moments of REITs because they can pose an additional source of risk.

REITs offer an adequate risk premium and diversification potential. The literature provides evidence that the correlation between REITs and bonds is low or even negative. Yet, the correlation between REITs and US equity is not. As a result, the evidence about the diversification advantages of REITs in mixed-asset portfolios is inconclusive and often depends on the research period.

For example, Kuhle (1987) finds no significant benefits from including REITs in a stock portfolio. Other researchers report that REITs can be beneficial in mixed-asset portfolios and can improve the risk-adjusted performance (Mueller, Pauley and Morrill, 1994; Mull and Soenen, 1997; Hudson-Wilson, Fabozzi, Gordon, and Gilberto, 2004; Lee and Stevenson, 2005). Others claim that REITs may enhance the efficient frontier (Chen et al., 2005; Chiang and Lee, 2007). Thus, most evidence suggests that REITs are a good diversifier in a mixed-asset portfolio.

REITs are a unique asset class and differ dramatically from stocks. Because REITs are publicly traded, gaining exposure to them is fairly easy, fees tend to be low, and liquidity tends to be high. Therefore, this chapter includes REITs in its mixed-asset portfolio optimization, which is discussed later.

As a proxy for REITs, the FTSE EPRA/NAREIT Global Real Estate Index is used in the portfolio optimization process because it provides REIT returns using transaction data, which are representative of market value. The index includes leverage of about 50 percent, which is beneficial because real estate investments are often leveraged. Therefore, the volatility of NAREIT reflects higher and more realistic return volatility.

Data Set Description

The previous section provided a discussion of the risk-return profiles and the potential advantages involved with including several alternative investments in a mixed-asset portfolio. It also highlighted data biases in the private equity return distributions that might affect portfolio optimization if not properly taken into account. This section provides an empirical investigation of alternative investments in a mixed-asset portfolio. This investigation uses two major traditional asset classes (each represented by three indices) and four alternative asset classes.

Equity markets are included in this analysis, as represented by the Nikkei 500 Total Return, the S&P 500, and the DJ Stoxx 600. Government bonds are represented by the J.P. Morgan Government Bond Indices for Japan, the US, Europe, and the UK, as well as the money market represented by the London Interbank Offered Rate (LIBOR). As a proxy for the alternative investments, the S&P GSCI Commodity (commodities) is included for a diversified exposure to commodities, the HFRI Fund of Funds Composite Index (hedge funds) for a multistrategy hedge fund exposure, the FTSE EPRA/NAREIT Global Real Estate Index for a diversified exposure to US REITs, and the Private Equity U.S. Buy Out Benchmark, as computed by Cumming, Hass, and Schweizer (2010), to proxy for an exposure to buyout funds. All indices are total return indices, and including reinvested distributions. Conversions are made from the indices denominated in non-US dollars into US dollars.

The sample consists of 156 monthly index returns from January 1998 to December 2010, with a January 1998 inception date. Because the Private Equity U.S. Buy Out Benchmark starts from the inception date, no data are available earlier. The sample includes several international returns for periods of market crises, such as the 1994 bond market crash, the 1997 Asian crisis, the 1998 Russian and Long-Term Capital Management (LTCM) crisis, the 2000–2001 NASDAQ crash, the September 11 terrorist attacks, and the current financial crisis. The data set includes both up and down markets and therefore satisfies the recommendations for robustness of Capocci and Hübner (2004) and for reliability of Fung and Hsieh (2000).

As mentioned in the previous subsection, raw data hedge funds and private equity from data vendors can suffer from several biases. Obtaining an "adequate" data set requires correcting the raw time series. This correction is highly important because the data feed the models, and if the input data are biased, the implications will be as well. The reasons for the biases and how they can be handled to obtain an "adequate" data set are now outlined.

Despite these many advantages, a point of criticism of appraisal-based private equity indices is that smoothed returns result from the deformation—which could occur through appraisal smoothing (the estimated-value method for determination of net asset values [NAVs] of portfolio companies) and quarterly data availability and/or stale pricing (prices are distorted due to illiquid positions that are not evaluated daily)—and statistically cause a positive autocorrelation. These occurrences are common among illiquid investments, such as private equity, individual hedge funds strategies, and real estate. They typically arise due to (1) irregular price determination, (2) long time periods between price determination, and (3) the use of book value instead of market prices (Geltner, 1991; Gompers and Lerner, 1997). The resulting autocorrelation causes a significant underestimation of risk, such as volatility.

In comparison, using individual hedge fund index data may have some major drawbacks in addition to causing a positive autocorrelation. These include databases not ensuring accuracy because funds are not subject to reporting requirements and, as a consequence, the possibility of index data suffering from biases, such as liquidation bias, survivorship bias, and attrition rate. Estimates for survivorship bias vary from 0.16 percent (Ackermann et al., 1999) to 6.22 percent (Liang, 2002).

Furthermore, the backfill bias or instant history bias arises when a new hedge fund is added to a database at a later stage than the original launch date. Good track records of hedge fund managers can be assumed to be more likely to be backfilled than bad ones because the probability of raising capital for a hedge fund is higher with a good track record than with an average one. Fung and Hsieh (2000) show for the TASS Database, the hedge fund return series are biased upward by 1.4 percent due to backfill bias.

In comparison to private equity, hedge fund managers can invest in illiquid assets whose value may not be marked to market. Some hedge fund strategies exhibit autocorrelation (Agarwal and Naik, 2004; Getmansky et al., 2004; Avramov et al., 2008). The analysis included in this chapter uses a fund of fund index for which most of the biases do not apply because performances are "replicable" by investing in the underlying fund of hedge funds. For that reason, positive autocorrelation is tested to avoid underestimating the inherent "risk."

Given possible biases in the raw data, the autocorrelation structure should be examined. Controls should account for statistically significant effects. This process requires testing all indices for autocorrelation effects up to lag 12. As mentioned above, a positive first-order autocorrelation between the hedge fund and private equity return time series is expected due to illiquid trading strategies and appraisal smoothing. Interestingly, the results do not show a significant autocorrelation structure for hedge funds, which is not unusual for a diversified hedge fund portfolio (Eling, 2006) but is unusual for our Private Equity U.S. Buy Out Benchmark, as shown in Table 14.1.

To adjust for appraisal smoothing and illiquidity, the current study uses the method of Getmansky et al. (2004). This method incorporates the whole autocorrelation structure of the monthly return distribution (as shown in Table 14.1) and improves on Geltner's (1991) approach by considering the entire lag structure simultaneously. Also, no need exists for a desmoothing parameter (Byrne and Lee, 1995) for the problematic determination of the desmoothing parameter.

Table 14.1 **Autocorrelation structure of Private Equity U.S. Buy Out Benchmark**

Lag	1	2	3	4	5	6	7	8	9	10	11	12
	0.810	**0.620**	**0.431**	**0.388**	**0.345**	**0.302**	0.263	0.224	0.186	0.165	0.143	0.122

Note: This table shows the autocorrelation coefficient for lags 1 through 12 of the monthly return distributions for the period January 1998–December 2010 for the Private Equity U.S. Buy Out Benchmark (using the index of Cumming, Hass, and Schweizer 2010), before applying the (desmoothed) method of Getmansky, Lo, and Makarov (2004). The values in bold indicate statistical significance at the 99 percent confidence level.

The intuition behind this method is as follows: The measurable return, R_t^0, is not the true return. Rather, it is a combination of the true return in previous periods, R_t:

$$R_t^0 = \Theta_0 R_t + \Theta_1 R_{t-1} + \cdots + \Theta_k R_{t-k}, \Theta_j \in [0,1], \quad j = 0, \cdots k \quad and \quad 1 = \Theta_0 + \Theta_1 + \cdots + \Theta_k.$$

$$(14.1)$$

Therefore, the measurable return is the weighted sum of the true returns of the previous periods, in which the weighting factors, Θ_k, determine the contributions by the specific periods. The mean of the observable returns is equal to the mean of the true returns, and the standard deviation of the measurable returns is smaller than that of the true returns. Equation 14.2 describes the relationship between the standard deviations of the true and observable returns:

$$Std[R_t^0] = \frac{1}{\Theta_0^2 + \Theta_1^2 + \cdots + \Theta_k^2} \sigma \leq \sigma,$$

$$(14.2)$$

Table 14.2 Descriptive statistics of the monthly return distributions of the Private Equity U.S. Buy Out Benchmark before and after desmoothing

	US buy out	US buy out (desmoothed)
Mean (%)	0.51	0.51
Standard deviation (%)	1.34	2.36
Kurtosis	3.46	3.51
Skewness	−0.78	−0.80
LPM (%)	0.33	0.68
CVaR (%)	−2.80	−5.31
MDD (%)	23.34	35.03
Jarque-Bera statistic	17***	18***

Note: A Jarque-Bera value of 1 means that the assumption of the normal distribution at the 0.05 level can be rejected. This table gives the mean, standard deviation, skewness, kurtosis, and square root of lower partial moment (LPM) 2 with threshold 0 (LPM), conditional value-at-risk (CVaR) with a 95 percent confidence level, and maximum drawdown (MDD) for the monthly return distribution for the Private Equity U.S. Buy Out Benchmark with and without autocorrelation after applying the method (desmoothing) of Getmansky, Lo, and Makarov (2004). The period is January 1998–December 2010. All indices are total return (or their distributions are reinvested), and all are denominated in US dollars. The Jarque-Bera test (Jarque and Bera 1980) is used to test the assumption of normally distributed monthly returns. The notations ***, **, and * indicate that the assumption of a normal distribution of monthly returns is rejected at the 0.01, 0.05, and 0.10 significance levels, respectively. All statistics are based on continuous returns.

where σ represents the standard deviation of the true returns. Table 14.2 indicates the effect on the risk measures after desmoothing.

In order to calculate the true returns, the weighting factors Θ_k can be estimated by using maximum likelihood estimation because the measurable returns can be considered as a moving-average process with constant weighting factors. Finally, the true returns can be calculated using the estimated weighting factors.

Table 14.2 illustrates the influence of the autocorrelation on the descriptive statistics for the Private Equity US Buy Out Benchmark. All risk measures (standard deviation, LPM, CVaR, and MDD) clearly show a considerable increase in the risk level for the same expected return. Furthermore, the higher moments (skweness and kurtosis) indicate a greater magnitude of losses with a higher probability, which means that the drawdown or tail risks increase.

As mentioned previously, the illiquidity of private equity investments could also be driving the positive autocorrelation. Further, the value of liquidity can be quite large. As Benveniste, Capozza, and Seguin (2001) show, claims on illiquid assets can increase by as much as 12 to 22 percent.

Illiquidity can also have a major impact on portfolio composition. Anglin and Gao (2011) analyze how an asset's liquidity (autocorrelation and trading inability) can affect an individual's investment decision when that individual has an uncertain need to liquidate. The authors find that in this instance illiquidity can change the risk profile dramatically.

This chapter models illiquidity implicitly by desmoothing the private equity return series, which increases all risk measures (see Table 14.2). This increase in risk also affects optimal portfolio holdings negatively, as noted in the literature cited in this section, where illiquidity is considered explicitly. The current analysis follows Cumming, Hass, and Schweizer (2010) and Cavenaile, Coen, and Hubner (2011) by using the "corrected" return series in the asset allocation.

During the sample period, from January 1998 to December 2010, REITs and US equity had the highest average monthly returns at 1.13 percent and 0.91 percent, respectively. Interestingly, the standard deviation of the REIT return distribution is 3.75 percent, which is far below the standard deviations of the NIKKEI and DJ STOXX 600 indexes (which are 6.69 percent and 6.07 percent, respectively) but is the highest among all investment opportunities. The high standard deviations are partially caused by the conversion from the yen and the euro to the US dollar. Skewness and kurtosis are additional potential sources of risk and return. While J.P. Morgan Europe shows the highest observed skewness (generally a favorable return distribution characteristic), it also exhibits the highest kurtosis, which is undesirable because it indicates a high probability of extreme risks. In contrast, three out of four alternative investments (REITs, hedge funds, and private equity) show a considerable negative skewness combined with a high kurtosis, which can be interpreted as a higher likelihood of negative tail events compared to a normal distribution.

As indicated in Table 14.3, the results of the Jarque-Bera test (Jarque and Bera, 1980), which assesses whether a given probability distribution can be regarded as a normal distribution, show that the returns of alternative investments must be considered as nonnormally distributed. The risk-return characteristics of

Table 14.3 **Descriptive statistics for monthly return distributions**

	Equity markets			Bond markets and money markets					Alternative investments			
	NIKKEI	S&P 500	DJ STOXX 600	JPM Japan	JPM US	JPM Europe	JPM UK	MM	S&P GSCI	HFRI FoHF	REITs	PEBuyOut
Mean (%)	0.52	0.91	0.21	0.67	0.53	0.43	0.78	0.45	0.81%	0.72%	1.13%	0.51%
Standard deviation (%)	6.69	3.99	6.07	2.77	1.35	3.65	2.64	0.09	5.60	1.68	3.75	2.36
Kurtosis	3.12	3.31	4.35	3.31	3.82	8.72	3.04	2.12	3.07	6.90	4.51	3.51
Skewness	0.56	-0.29	-0.09	0.30	-0.46	1.13	0.11	-0.05	0.14	-0.25	-0.54	-0.80
LPM (%)	2.41	1.19	2.15	0.76	0.32	1.08	0.68	0.00	1.81	0.33	1.00	0.68
CVaR	-10.29	-8.24	-13.81	-4.73	-2.63	-6.90	-4.79	0.29	-10.40	-2.92	-7.30	-5.31
MDD (%)	66.69	43.07	77.12	23.16	4.84	31.45	11.22	0.00	47.51	13.08	26.32	35.03
Jarque-Bera statistic	8.3	2.7	12.0***	2.9	9.8**	245***	0.3	5.1	0.50	100***	22***	18***

Note: This table gives the mean, standard deviation, skewness, kurtosis, and square root of lower partial moment (LPM) 2 with threshold 0 (LPM), the conditional value-at-risk (CVaR) with a 95 percent confidence level, and the maximum drawdown (MDD) for the monthly return distribution for the period January 1998–December 2010. The assets considered are equity markets (the Nikkei 500, the S&P 500, and the DJ Stoxx 600); bond markets (J.P. Morgan in Japan; US, Europe, and UK government bond indices); money markets (MM; LIBOR); and alternative investments (the S&P GSCI Total Return Index, the HFRI Fund of Funds Composite Index, and the FTSE EPRA/NAREIT Global Real Estate Index); and the Private Equity US buyout (using the index of Cumming, Hass, and Schweizer 2010). All indices are for total return (or their distributions are reinvested), and all are denominated in US dollars. The results show no autocorrelation effects for the time series of equity and bond markets or for alternative investments. A test by Jarque-Bera test (Jarque and Bera 1980) is used to test the assumption of normally distributed monthly returns. The notations ***, **, and * indicate that the assumption of a normal distribution of monthly returns is rejected at the 0.01, 0.05, and 0.10 significance levels, respectively. All statistics are based on continuous returns.

commodities are the only ones considered here for which the normality hypothesis cannot be rejected. Therefore, standard deviation (variance) as a risk measure does not sufficiently describe the return distribution of these asset classes. Relying on a mean-variance framework while ignoring the higher moments will not cover the risk-return profile adequately. As a result, in this model higher moments must be considered when the investors do not have quadratic utility functions. Otherwise, a high probability exists of having portfolio allocations that investors do not desire (Proelss and Schweizer, 2012).

Portfolio optimization, however, is not only about risk-return characteristics but also about diversification. Gaining more insight into the diversification potential of the asset classes requires calculating the correlation matrix in Table 14.4.

According to the correlation coefficients, alternative investments have the highest diversification potential. In most cases, they show insignificant correlations from zero with other alternative investments and other investment opportunities, or even a negative (statistically significant) correlation. In contrast, bond and equity markets show a significant positive intermarket correlation (low diversification potential) but low correlation between both markets (high diversification potential).

After reviewing the descriptive statistics of the return distributions and correlations for all asset classes, determining that one can substitute for another a priori is impossible. Therefore, all asset classes are considered in the portfolio construction. The next section presents a framework for an optimal portfolio construction that accounts for the distribution characteristics. The results are compared with the mean-variance framework in order to assess the influence of the higher moments.

Introducing the Methodology

Markowitz (1952) developed the theoretical basis for efficient portfolio theory. The theory is based on the idea that portfolio risk as a whole is smaller than the sum of the risks of the single assets. Financial economists initially used variance, or rather standard deviation, to measure risk and defined the diversification advantage by the correlation or covariance of the investment opportunity in the portfolio. Markowitz's portfolio optimization aims for the combination of assets that will result in an expected portfolio return with the lowest portfolio risk as measured by variance.

Because most returns are not normally distributed (see Table 14.3), higher moments and downside risk measures must be considered. Any skewness effects as well as the effects of extreme returns (positive excess kurtosis), such as those measured for alternative investments, will be neglected otherwise. The optimization procedure should incorporate additional risk measures besides variance in a downside risk framework. This will also help to reduce the likelihood of biased and suboptimal portfolio weights.

For this purpose, three alternate risk measures (RM) are considered. The last two are suitable for covering the risk in the tail (downside) of the distribution: (1)

Table 14.4 **Correlation matrix**

	NIKKEI	S&P 500	DJ STOXX 600	JPM Europe	JPM US	JPM U.K	JPM Japan	REITs	S&P GSCI	HFRI FoHF	PE Buy out	MM
NIKKEI	**1.00**	**0.40**	**0.26**	0.02	-0.09	**0.40**	0.01	0.02	**0.25**	0.06	-0.01	-0.12
S&P 500	**0.40**	**1.00**	**0.58**	-0.09	-0.04	0.09	0.00	**0.28**	0.06	-0.04	-0.06	0.14
DJ STOXX 600	**0.26**	**0.58**	**1.00**	**-0.40**	**-0.23**	-0.06	**-0.22**	0.13	0.05	0.13	0.00	0.14
JPM Europe	0.02	-0.09	**-0.40**	**1.00**	**0.47**	**0.41**	**0.79**	0.09	0.12	-0.15	-0.07	-0.03
JPM U.S.	-0.09	-0.04	**-0.23**	**0.47**	**1.00**	0.15	**0.52**	0.12	0.06	-0.10	-0.08	**0.18**
JPM U.K.	**0.40**	0.09	-0.06	**0.41**	0.15	**1.00**	**0.29**	-0.04	0.08	-0.10	0.03	0.02
JPM Japan	0.01	0.00	**-0.22**	**0.79**	**0.52**	**0.29**	**1.00**	0.11	0.07	0.00	-0.08	0.05
REITs	0.02	**0.28**	0.13	0.09	0.12	-0.04	0.11	**1.00**	0.02	0.01	**-0.22**	-0.08
S&P GSCI	**0.25**	0.06	0.05	0.12	0.06	0.08	0.07	0.02	**1.00**	0.01	-0.13	-0.15
HFRI FoHF	0.06	-0.04	0.13	-0.15	-0.10	-0.10	0.00	0.01	0.01	**1.00**	**-0.16**	0.02
PE Buy Out	-0.01	-0.06	0.00	-0.07	-0.08	0.03	-0.08	**-0.22**	-0.13	**-0.16**	**1.00**	0.11
MM	-0.12	0.14	0.14	-0.03	**0.18**	0.02	0.05	-0.08	-0.15	0.02	0.11	**1.00**

Note: This table shows the correlations between the asset classes from table 14.3. Values in boldface differ significantly from zero at the 0.05 level.

standard deviation (Markowitz, 1952), (2) lower partial moment (LPM; Harlow, 1991), and (3) conditional value-at-risk (CVaR; Rockafellar and Uryasev 2000, 2002). LPM, CVaR, and maximum drawdown (MDD) implicitly incorporate higher moments due to their calculation methods and can be regarded as a robustness check on the validity of the results when higher moments are ignored.

Next, the three risk measures are used to calculate efficient mixed-asset portfolios. A portfolio is characterized as efficient when no other combination of assets provides lower risk for the same expected return. For the following portfolio optimizations, risk (for every risk measure separately) is minimized for the given expected portfolio return $E[r_p]$. The optimization problem is formulated in Equation 14.3:

$$\min_{x} RM(\tilde{r}_p),$$ (14.3)

subject to the restrictions in Equation 14.4:

$$E[r_p]=r, \quad 0 \le x_i \le 25\% \quad and \quad x_1 + \cdots + x_n = 1, \quad \forall i = 1, \cdots, n, \cdots, \quad (14.4)$$

where r_p is the portfolio return and x_i is the percentage weight invested in security i. The optimization is restricted by budget constraints (full investment) and by nonnegative weights (no short sales involved). Furthermore, a minimum diversification constraint of 25 percent is imposed for the alternative asset classes only. Thus, no investment opportunity portfolio weight x_i may exceed 25 percent. This restriction aims to avoid having a single alternative asset class dominate the portfolio. Investments can be made in all assets considered in Table 14.3.

Empirical Results

Following the procedure outlined in the previous section, the efficient frontiers are estimated for the different risk measures. Figure 14.1 shows the efficient frontiers and the portfolio weights for the asset classes in the portfolios on the efficient frontier. The ordinate shows the expected monthly return of the efficient portfolios, and the abscissa shows the "risk" of the respective portfolio measured.

Considering the minimum-standard-deviation portfolio weights (7.0 percent return and 2.1 percent standard deviation), the results show that bonds, the money market, and hedge funds are the most important portfolio stabilizers. The portfolio weights are 29 percent for bonds (made up of 3 percent J.P. Morgan Europe, 25 percent J.P. Morgan US, and 1 percent J.P. Morgan UK), 25 percent for the money market, and 23 percent for hedge funds. For further diversification, private equity has a major portfolio weight of about 14 percent, and equity markets, commodities, and REITs have only minor portfolio weights of 3 percent.

Considering the minimum CVaR and LPM portfolio weights (the latter equaling 7.0 percent return, 2.1 percent CVaR, and 1.2 percent LPM), the evidence shows "similar" portfolio weights for both. Yet, some differences to the minimum-standard-deviation portfolio weights occur. The first noticeable difference is the five-percentage-point-higher portfolio weight for bond investments. This increase in portfolio weight accompanies a reduction in the portfolio weights for hedge funds and private equity.

Thus, the evidence shows that mean-variance optimization fails to properly capture the higher-moment characteristics. Hedge funds and private equity have more unfavorable higher-moment characteristics and higher tail risks in comparison to bonds. But the mean-variance optimization ignores these higher-moment characteristics. In contrast, bonds have more favorable higher-moment characteristics, resulting in higher allocations when CVaR or LPM is the risk measure of choice (see Figure 14.1). This evidence illustrates that standard deviation does not capture extreme risks adequately. Thus, classical mean-variance leads to an overallocation to risky assets, increasing the downside risk to an unnecessarily high level. This conclusion holds even in light of findings by Cheng and Wolverton (2001). The CVaR-efficient frontier converges strongly with the mean-variance efficient frontier when using variance as a risk measure. Variance also measures upside potential, unlike the CVaR, which is solely a downside risk measure.

By increasing the expected return, the portfolio weight of stocks and REITs increases significantly, at the cost of money market investments, to achieve higher returns. Interestingly, the portfolios' weight allocation for private equity is zero, for an expected return of about 10 percent a year, but bond investments remain at a higher return level of about 20 percent, regardless the considered risk measure. This exchange can at least partially be explained by the fact that private equity has comparable historical returns and standard deviation but more disadvantageous higher-moment properties. Remarkably, the allocation to hedge funds remains stable at more than 20 percent—regardless of the expected return—reaching an upper bound of 25 percent in most portfolios. In comparison, commodity investments are part of all efficient portfolios but are more an intermixture in the range of 3 percent–7 percent. In sum, the allocation of alternative investments is in the range of 35 percent–50 percent of the portfolios, making them an essential building block for investors' portfolios. The findings in Table 14.4 also support this conclusion. Thus, including alternative investments not only enhances the statistical significance of the expected return but also reduces the risk, as measured by standard deviation and CVaR, resulting in higher risk-adjusted portfolio returns. Figure 14.2 shows this effect. The Monte Carlo simulation shows that including alternative investments only slightly reduces the probability of "extreme" high annual returns. In exchange, the downside risk is reduced substantially. The worst case annual return in the simulation is about 1.5 percent for alternative investments and −5.5 percent for traditional investments.

In general, as the riskiness of the portfolios increases, the optimal portfolios weights derived from the mean CVaR or mean LPM and the mean-variance

Table 14.5 **Differences in the risk-return profile for portfolios with and without alternative investments**

Portfolio weights for private equity proxies	Mean %	Standard deviation %	LPM %	CVaR %	VaR %	MDD %	Sharpe ratio
Without alternative investments							
Low risk	6.64***	3.84***	0.01	−1.37***	−1.37***	1.79 ***	1.21***
Medium risk	7.62***	4.50***	0.01	−1.45***	−1.45***	1.89 ***	1.36***
High risk	8.75***	5.97***	0.01	−2.23***	−2.23***	3.08 ***	1.13***
With alternative investments							
Low risk	7.22***	1.97***	0.00	−0.39***	−0.39***	0.50 ***	2.65***
Medium risk	7.89***	2.19***	0.00	−0.45***	−0.45***	0.55 ***	2.69***
High risk	9.45***	3.57***	0.01	−1.03***	−1.03***	1.27 ***	2.09***

Note: This table gives the mean, standard deviation, and square root of lower partial moment (LPM) 2 with threshold 0; the conditional value-at-risk (CVaR) with a 95 percent confidence level; the value at risk (VaR) with a 95 percent confidence level; the maximum drawdown (MDD); and the Sharpe ratio (the LIBOR risk-free rate equals 2.13 percent) for optimal portfolios with and without alternative investments. The three portfolios without alternative investments are the minimum risk portfolio, the maximum return portfolio, and a portfolio with an expected return that is the arithmetic mean of the two former portfolios. Portfolios with alternative investments that have an equal mean to the portfolios without alternative investments are then selected. Calculations are based on Efron and Tibshirani's (1994) standard block-bootstrap Monte Carlo simulation for the period from January 1999 to December 2008 with five lags and 1,000 runs. For the tests in differences for the mean and the risk measures, t-values are used. For the Sharpe ratio, the tests proposed by Jobson and Korkie (1981) and Ledoit and Wolf (2008) are used. ***, **, and * indicate the statistical significance at the 0.01, 0.05, and 0.10 levels, respectively, that the mean, standard deviation, LPM, CVaR, VaR, MDD, and Sharpe ratio for the portfolio with alternative investments differ from the portfolio without alternative investments for each risk level (low, medium, and high) separately.

optimization converge somewhat. This finding can be explained as greater amounts of money are allocated to the assets with the highest returns, independent of the level of riskiness (see Figure 14.1).

The analysis of the skewness of the efficient frontier portfolios for different risk measures indicates that the resulting skewness estimates of the minimum-CVaR/minimum-LPM portfolios differ from the minimum standard deviation (see Figure 14.3). For the downside approach, the minimum-risk portfolios exhibit higher positive skewness, which investors usually desire. The reason for this is

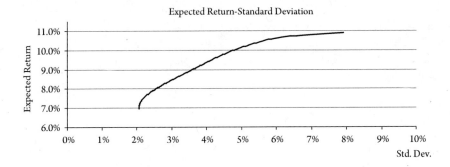

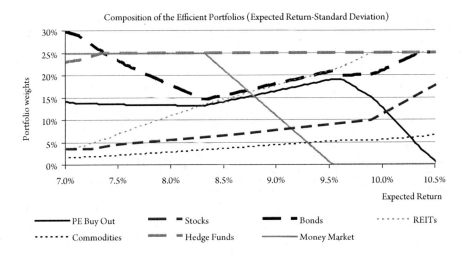

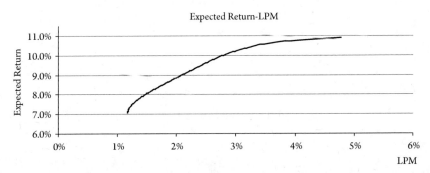

Figure 14.1 Efficient portfolios and the respective portfolio holding. These figures illustrate the following about the asset classes in the portfolios on the efficient frontier: (1) the efficient frontiers, using standard deviation, LPM, and CVaR as the risk measures of choice, and (2) the portfolio weights for the asset classes in the portfolios on the efficient frontier, with LPM, CVaR, and MDD as the risk measures dependent on the expected return. All calculations are subject to the weight limits discussed in the chapter. The observation period is January 1998–December 2010. (Continued)

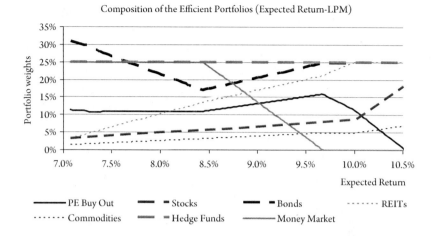

Composition of the Efficient Portfolios (Expected Return-LPM)

PE Buy Out · Stocks · Bonds · REITs · Commodities · Hedge Funds · Money Market

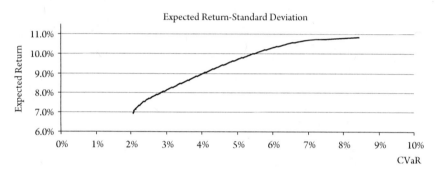

Expected Return-Standard Deviation

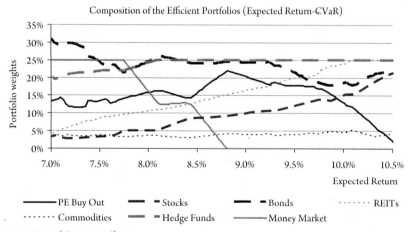

Composition of the Efficient Portfolios (Expected Return-CVaR)

PE Buy Out · Stocks · Bonds · REITs · Commodities · Hedge Funds · Money Market

Figure 14.1 (Continued)

that the implicit downside portfolio optimization accounts for skewness. When comparing the mean downside and the mean standard deviation optimization results, the largest difference in skewness is in the low-risk portfolios with a –7.5 percent expected return. As the portfolio returns increase, the higher-moment statistics for both optimizations tend to converge. The intuition is that with

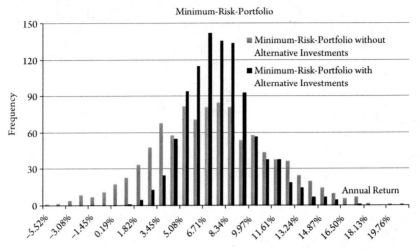

Figure 14.2 Efficient multiasset portfolios and optimal private equity portfolio weights. This figure shows the distribution of the annual return for the minimum-risk portfolios with and without alternative investments. The distribution is based on Efron and Tibshirani's (1994) standard block-bootstrap Monte Carlo simulation for the period from January 1999 to December 2008, with five lags and 1,000 runs.

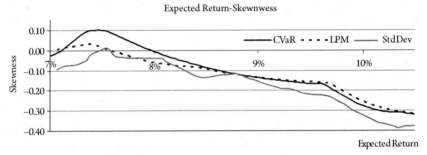

Figure 14.3 Skewness of efficient portfolios for different risk measures. This figure shows the skewness of optimal portfolios along the efficient frontier for the mean-standard deviation, mean-LPM, and mean-CVaR optimization.

increasing expected returns, the focus in both optimizations is on the expected return rather than on the "risk" (see Figure 14.2). This again highlights the fact that the mean-standard-deviation approach captures the risk arising from higher moments only to an inadequatel extent.

Summary and Conclusions

Analyzing the return-distribution characteristics of alternative assets is important to do before considering them as portfolio diversifiers. Estimates of their returns vary markedly in the literature, often with mixed results for performance persistence.

However, alternative investments exhibit favorable diversification properties. Consequently, investors should include them in a portfolio allocation optimization if the biases are considered and the optimization allows for higher moments.

The results of CVaR and LPM optimizations when compared with a mean-standard deviation allocation imply that composing a superior mixed-asset portfolio is possible. Because standard deviation or variance as a risk measure does not properly capture the risk-return properties of most alternative investments, investors may overallocate to assets that do not offer enough downside protection, and for that reason the portfolios show unfavorable higher-moment properties. Alternative assets show allocations between 35 and 50 percent of the mixed-asset portfolios, making them an essential building block for investors' portfolios. Ultimately, alternative investments can significantly improve the risk-return characteristics of traditional portfolios. However, bonds are an especially important portfolio component in all portfolios as a proper protection for tail events.

Discussion Questions

1. Alternative investments can offer exposure to risk-return profiles not replicable by traditional asset classes. Discuss why this is the case for hedge funds.
2. What should be considered when including private equity indices in asset allocation models?
3. Why is using the Markowitz approach inappropriate for asset allocation with alternative investments?
4. What are the performance consequences of including alternative investments in the asset allocation?

References

Ackermann, Carl, Richard McEnally, and David Ravenscraft. 1999. "The Performance of Hedge Funds: Risk, Return, and Incentives." *Journal of Finance* 54:3, 833–874.

Agarwal, Vikas, and Narayan Y. Naik. 2004. "Risks and Portfolio Decisions Involving Hedge Funds." *Review of Financial Studies* 17:1, 63–98.

Amin, Guarav S., and Harry M. Kat. 2003. "Hedge Fund Performance 1990–2000: Do the 'Money Machines' Really Add Value?" *Journal of Financial and Quantitative Analysis* 38:2, 251–274.

Anglin, Paul M., and Yanmin Gao. 2011. "Integrating Illiquid Assets into the Portfolio Decision Process." *Real Estate Economics* 39:2, 277–311.

Anson, Mark J. P., Ho Ho, and Kurt Silberstein. 2007. "Building a Hedge Fund Portfolio with Kurtosis and Skewness." *Journal of Alternative Investments* 10:1, 25–34.

Avramov, Doron, Robert Kosowski, Narayan Y. Naik, and Melvyn Teo. 2008. "Investing in Hedge Funds When Returns Are Predictable." Paper presented at the Annual Meeting of the American Finance Association 2008, New Orleans.

Barkham, Richard, and David Geltner. 1995. "Price Discovery in American and British Property Markets." *Real Estate Economics* 23:1, 21–44.

Benveniste, Lawrence, Dennis R. Capozza, and Paul J. Seguin. 2001. "The Value of Liquidity." *Real Estate Economics* 29:4, 633–660.

Bergmann, Bastian, Hans Christophers, Matthias Huss, and Heinz Zimmermann. 2009. "Listed Private Equity." In *Private Equity: Fund Types, Risks and Returns, and Regulation,* edited by Douglas J. Cumming, 53–70. Hoboken, NJ: John Wiley & Sons.

Bodie, Zvi, and Victor I. Rosansky. 1980. "Risk and Returns in Commodity Futures." *Financial Analysts Journal* 36:3, 27–39.

Brooks, Chris, and Harry M. Kat. 2002. "The Statistical Properties of Hedge Fund Index Returns and Their Implications for Investors." *Journal of Alternative Investments* 5:2, 22–44.

Brown, Stephen J., William N. Goetzmann, and Roger G. Ibbotson. 1999. "Offshore Hedge Funds: Survival and Performance, 1989–95." *Journal of Business* 72:1, 91–117.

Byrne, Peter, and Stephen Lee. 1995. "Is There a Place for Property in the Multi-Asset Portfolio?" *Journal of Property Finance* 6:3, 60–83.

Capocci, Daniel P. J., and Georges Hübner. 2004. "Analysis of Hedge Fund Performance." *Journal of Empirical Finance* 11:1, 55–89.

Cavenaile, Laurent, Alain Coën, and Georges Hübner. 2011. "The Impact of Illiquidity and Higher Moments of Hedge Fund Returns on Their Risk-Adjusted Performance and Diversification Potential." *Journal of Alternative Investments* 13:4, 9–29.

Chen, Peng, Gary T. Baierl, and Paul D. Kaplan. 2002. "Venture Capital and Its Role in Strategic Asset Allocation." *Journal of Portfolio Management* 28:2, 83–89.

Cheng, Ping, and Marvin L. Wolverton. 2001. "MPT and the Downside Risk Framework: A Comment on Two Recent Studies." *Journal of Real Estate Portfolio Management* 7:2, 125–131.

Chiang, Kevin C. H., and Ming-long Lee. 2007. "Spanning Tests on Public and Private Real Estate." *Journal of Real Estate Portfolio Management* 13:1, 7–15.

Clayton, Jim, and Greg MacKinnon. 2000. "What Drives Equity REIT Returns? The Relative Influences of Bond, Stock and Real Estate Factors." Working Paper, Real Estate Research Institute (RERI).

Cochrane, John H. 2005. "The Risk and Return of Venture Capital." *Journal of Financial Economics* 75:1, 3–52.

Conner, Andrew. 2003. "Asset Allocation Effects of Adjusting Alternative Assets for Stale Pricing." *Journal of Alternative Investments* 6:3, 42–52.

Cotter, John, and Simon Stevenson. 2007. "Uncovering Volatility Dynamics in Daily REIT Returns." *Journal of Real Estate Portfolio Management* 13:2, 119–128.

Cottier, Phillipp. 2000. *Hedge Funds and Managed Futures: Performance, Risks, Strategies and Use in Investment Portfolios.* Bern, Switzerland: Haupt Verlag.

Credit Suisse. 2011. *Hedge Fund Monitor August 2011.* Available at https://www.credit-suisse.com/ch/en/. Accessed on August 30, 2011.

Cumming, Douglas J., Lars Helge Hass, and Denis Schweizer. 2010. "Private Equity Benchmarks and Portfolio Optimization." Last modified October 4. http://ssrn.com/abstract=1687380.

Efron, Bradley, and Robert J. Tibshirani. 1994. *An Introduction to the Bootstrap.* New York: Chapman & Hall.

Eling, Martin. 2006. "Autocorrelation, Bias, and Fat Tails: Are Hedge Funds Really Attractive Investments?" *Derivatives Use, Trading & Regulation* 12:1, 28–47.

Eling, Martin. 2009. "Does Hedge Fund Performance Persist? Overview and New Empirical Evidence." *European Financial Management* 15:2, 362–401.

Ennis, Richard M., and Michael D. Sebastian. 2005. "Asset Allocation with Private Equity." *Journal of Private Equity* 8:3, 81–87.

Erb, Claude B., and Campbell R. Harvey. 2006. "The Strategic and Tactical Value of Commodity Futures." *Financial Analysts Journal* 62:2, 69–97.

Ernst & Young. 2010. *Global Real Estate Investment Trust Report 2010: Against all Odds.* http://www.ey.com/Publication/vwLUAssets/Global-REIT-report-2010_Against-all-odds/$FILE/Global_REIT_report_2010_Against_all_odds.pdf. Accessed on August 30, 2011.

Fabozzi, Frank J., Roland Fuess, and Dieter Kaiser. 2007. "A Primer on Commodity Investing." In *The Handbook of Commodity Investing,* edited by Frank J. Fabozzi, Roland Füss, and Dieter G. Kaiser, 3–37. Hoboken, NJ: John Wiley and Sons.

Fama, Eugene F., and Kenneth R. French. 1987. "Commodity Futures Prices: Some Evidence on Forecast Power, Premiums, and the Theory of Storage." *Journal of Business* 90:1, 55–73.

Fung, William, and David A. Hsieh. 2000. "Performance Characteristics of Hedge Funds and Commodity Funds: Natural vs. Spurious Biases." *Journal of Financial and Quantitative Analysis* 35:3, 291–307.

Geltner, David Michael. 1991. "Smoothing in Appraisal-Based Returns." *Journal of Real Estate Finance & Economics* 4:3, 327–345.

Georgiev, Georgi. 2006. "The Benefits of Commodity Investment: 2006 Update." Working Paper, Center for International Securities and Derivatives, Isenberg School of Management, University of Massachusetts Amherst.

Getmansky, Mila, Andrew W. Lo, and Igor Makarov. 2004. "An Econometric Model of Serial Correlation and Illiquidity in Hedge Fund Returns." *Journal of Financial Economics* 74:3, 529–609.

Gompers, Paul A., and Josh Lerner. 1997. "Risk and Reward in Private Equity Investments: The Challenge of Performance Assessment." *Journal of Private Equity* 1:2, 5–12.

Gorton, Gary B., and K. Geert Rouwenhorst. 2006. "Facts and Fantasies about Commodity Futures." *Financial Analysts Journal* 62:2, 47–68.

Greenwich Associates. 2007. "New Products and Strategies Shake Up 'Traditional' Asset Allocation for U.S. Institutions." http://www.securitization.net/knowledge/article.asp?id=363&aid=7192. Accessed on August 30, 2011.

Harlow, W. Van. 1991. "Asset Allocation in a Downside-Risk Framework." *Financial Analysts Journal* 47:5, 28–40.

Hedge Fund Research. 2011. *Hedge Fund Monitor.* http://www.hedgefundresearch.com/. Accessed on August 30, 2011.

Hocht, Stephan, Kah Hwa Ng, Jürgen Wolf, and Rudi Zagst. 2008. "Optimal Portfolio Allocation with Asian Hedge Funds and Asian REITs." *International Journal of Services Sciences* 1:1, 36–68.

Huang, Jing-zhi, and Zhaodong Zhong. 2012. "Time-Variation in Diversification Benefits of Commodity, REITs, and TIPS." *Journal of Real Estate Finance and Economics,* forthcoming.

Hudson-Wilson, Susan, Frank J. Fabozzi, Jacques N. Gordon, Mark J. P. Anson, and S. Michael Giliberto. 2004. "Why Real Estate?" *Journal of Portfolio Management* 31:5, 12–21.

Idzorek, Thomas M. 2006. "Strategic Asset Allocation and Commodities." Working Paper, Ibbotson Associates, Chicago.

Jagannathan, Ravi, Alexey Malakhov, and Dmitry Novikov. 2006. "Do Hot Hands Persist among Hedge Fund Managers? An Empirical Evaluation." Working Paper 12015, National Bureau of Economic Research (NBER), Cambridge, MA.

Jarque, Carlos M., and Anil K. Bera. 1980. "Efficient Tests for Normality, Homoscedasticity and Serial Independence of Regression Residuals." *Economics Letters* 6:3, 255–259.

Jinliang, Li, Robert M. Mooradian, and Shiawee X. Yang. 2005. "Economic Forces, Asset Pricing, and REIT Returns ." Working Paper, American Real Estate Society, Monterey, CA.

Jobson, J. Dave, and Bob M. Korkie. 1981. "Performance Hypothesis Testing with the Sharpe and Treynor Measures." *Journal of Finance* 36:4, 889–908.

Kahan, Marcel, and Edward B. Rock. 2007. "Hedge Funds in Corporate Governance and Corporate Control." *University of Pennsylvania Law Review* 155:5, 1021–1093.

Kaplan, Steve N., and Antoinette Schoar. 2005. "Private Equity Performance: Returns, Persistence, and Capital Flows." *Journal of Finance* 60:4, 1791–1823.

Kat, Harry M. 2003. "10 Things Investors Should Know about Hedge Funds." *Journal of Wealth Management* 5:4, 72–81.

Kat, Harry M. 2007. "How to Evaluate a New Diversifier with 10 Simple Questions." *Journal of Wealth Management* 9:4, 29–36.

Kat, Harry M., and Roel C. A. Oomen. 2007. "What Every Investor Should Know about Commodities, Part II: Multivariate Return Analysis." *Journal of Investment Management* 5:3,1–25.

Kuhle, James L. 1987. "Portfolio Diversification and Return Benefits—Common Stock vs. Real Estate Investment Trusts (REITs)." *Journal of Real Estate Research* 2:2, 1–9.

Lamm, R. McFall, Jr., and Tanya E. Ghaleb-Harter. 2001. "Private Equity as an Asset Class: Its Role in Investment Portfolios." *Journal of Private Equity* 4(4): 68–79.

Ledoit, Oliver, and Michael Wolf. 2008. "Robust Performance Hypothesis Tests with the Sharpe Ratio." *Journal of Empirical Finance* 15:5, 850–859.

Lee, Stephen, and Simon Stevenson. 2005. "The Case for REITs in the Mixed-Asset Portfolio in the Short and Long Run." *Journal of Real Estate Portfolio Management* 11:1, 55–80.

Li, Yuming, and Ko Wang. 1995. "The Predictability of REIT Returns and Market Segmentation." *Journal of Real Estate Research* 10:4, 471–482.

Liang, Bing. 2002. "Hedge Funds, Fund of Funds, and Commodity Trading Advisors." Working Paper, Case Western Reserve University, Weatherhead School of Management, Cleveland, OH.

Liang, Youguo, and Willard McIntosh. 1998. "REIT Style and Performance." *Journal of Real Estate Portfolio Management* 4:1, 69–78.

Ling, David C., and Andy Naranjo. 1999. "The Integration of Commercial Real Estate Markets and Stock Markets." *Real Estate Economics* 27:3, 483–515.

Markowitz, Harry M. 1952. "Portfolio Selection." *Journal of Finance* 7:1, 77–91.

Metrick, Andrew, and Ayako A. Yasuda. 2010. "The Economics of Private Equity Funds." *Review of Financial Studies* 23:6, 2303–2341.

Mietzner, Mark, Denis Schweizer, and Marcel Tyrell. 2011. "Intra-Industry Effects of Shareholder Activism in Germany—Is There a Difference between Hedge Fund and Private Equity Investments?" *Schmalenbach Business Review* 63:2, 151–185.

Moskowitz, Tobias J., and Annette Vissing-Jørgensen. 2002. "The Returns to Entrepreneurial Investment: A Private Equity Premium Puzzle?" *American Economic Review* 92:4, 745–778.

Mueller, Glenn R., Keith R. Pauley, and William K. Morrill. 1994. "Should REITs Be Included in a Mixed-Asset-Portfolio?" *Real Estate Finance* 11:1, 23–28.

Mull, Stephen R., and Luc A. Soenen. 1997. "U.S. REITs as an Asset Class in International Investment Portfolios." *Financial Analysts Journal* 53:2, 55–62.

Myer, F. C. Neil, and James R. Webb. 1993. "Return Properties of Equity REITs, Common Stocks, and Commercial Real Estate: A Comparison." *Journal of Real Estate Research* 8:1, 87–106.

Phalippou, Ludovic, and Oliver Gottschalg. 2009. "Performance of Private Equity Funds." *Review of Financial Studies* 22:4, 1747–1776.

Proelss, Juliane, and Denis Schweizer. 2012. "Polynomial Goal Programming and the Implicit Higher Moment Preferences of U.S. Institutional Investors in Hedge Funds." *Financial Markets and Portfolio Management*, forthcoming.

Rockafellar, R. Tyrrell, and Stanislav Uryasev. 2000. "Optimization of Conditional Value-at-Risk." *Journal of Risk* 2:3, 21–41.

Rockafellar, R. Tyrrell, and Stanislav Uryasev. 2002. "Conditional Value-at-Risk for General Loss Distributions." *Journal of Banking and Finance* 26:7, 1443–1471.

Schmidt, Daniel M. 2004. "Private Equity-, Stock- and Mixed Asset-Portfolios: A Bootstrap Approach to Determine Performance Characteristics, Diversification Benefits and Optimal Portfolio Allocations." Working Paper 2004–12, Center of Private Equity Research (CEPRES), Munich.

Schneeweis, Thomas, Vassilios N. Karavas, and Georgi Georgiev. 2002. "Alternative Investments in the Institutional Portfolio." Working Paper, Alternative Investment Management Association (AIMA), University of Massachusetts, Amherst, MA.

Stevenson, Simon. 2001. "Evaluating the Investment Attributes and Performance of Property Companies." *Journal of Property Investment & Finance* 19:3, 251–266.

Terhaar, Kevin, Renato Staub, and Brian Singer. 2003. "Appropriate Policy Allocation for Alternative Investments: A Factor Approach and Simulation Techniques." *Journal of Portfolio Management* 29:3, 101–110.

Winkelmann, Kurt. 2004. "Improving Portfolio Efficiency: Risk Budgeting, Implied Confidence Levels, and Changing Allocations." *Journal of Portfolio Management* 30:2, 23–38.

Section Four

RISK MANAGEMENT

15

Measuring and Managing Market Risk

CHRISTOPH KASERER
Professor of Finance, Head of the Department of Financial
Management and Capital Markets, TUM School of Management,
Technische Universität München

Introduction

Market risk is caused by the uncertainty of future movement in market prices. Any asset portfolio is exposed to market risk, which is due both to different risk factors, such as fundamental factors driving the valuation of assets, and to the fact that markets consist of different segments. The typical categories of market risk follow:

- *Equity risk* is the risk associated with equity (stock) prices. Fundamental risk factors such as growth expectations, interest rates, and risk premia drive equity risk.
- *Interest rate risk* is the risk associated with any interest-sensitive instrument, such as bonds. Changes in expected interest rates and interest rate structure are the primary contributors to interest rate risk.
- *Property risk* is the risk associated with real estate prices. Its nature is similar to the equity risk.
- *Foreign exchange risk* is the risk associated with movements in the exchange rate between two currencies. Fundamental factors such as the relative movement of interest rates in the underlying currencies and the trade balance of the respective countries drive foreign exchange risk.
- *Commodity price risk* is the risk associated with commodity prices. Fundamental risk factors associated with the expected supply and demand of specific commodities and their extraction or production costs drive commodity price risk.
- *Liquidity risk* is the risk associated with adverse price changes when selling or buying a financial asset. This risk is related to the depth of the market, such as the contemporaneous movement of bid and ask volumes and trading technology.
- *Credit risk* is the risk associated with a change in the assessment of the probability of default by a bond issuer.

Two other points are worth noting about market risk: First, no consensus exists in the literature about whether credit risk is a category within the market risk framework or a separate type of risk. Based on the general definition of market risk previously given, credit risk should be considered as a part of it (Dowd, 2005). However, in practice market risk and credit risk are often treated as two separate types of risk. This chapter follows this distinction and focuses on a narrow definition of market risk that doesn't include credit risk, with a special focus on equity risk. Credit risk will be addressed in the next chapter.

Second, market risk exists regardless of whether an asset is traded in an organized marketplace such as a stock exchange. In fact, over the last decade, private equity has become an asset class that has attracted interest among many investors. In its traditional form, private equity funds are constructed as limited partnerships investing in unlisted companies. Therefore, the net asset value of such a fund cannot directly be observed. This situation, however, does not mean that an investment in this asset class is free of any market risk. It is rather a question of how this market risk can be extracted from available empirical data.

Market risk is an important decision-making parameter used by institutional investors, large corporations, and wealthy individuals. In fact, in mutual funds a fund's market risk is benchmarked against the market risk displayed by their benchmarks. For pension funds and life insurance companies, the market risk of their investment portfolio is an extremely important parameter, as it determines the probability by which a promised or, at least, targeted retirement income will not be achieved. In fact, insurance regulations force life insurance companies to fulfill a capital requirement that depends on the market risk assumed by the company among other factors. A comprehensive regulatory reform in the insurance sector recently introduced in the European Union rests upon the idea that insurance companies should have sufficient equity in order that the probability of default over a one-year period is below 0.5 percent, where an insurance company, on average, defaults less than once over a 200-year period (Sandström, 2011).

Banks are also highly concerned about market risk. As far as their credit book is concerned, they measure and manage the credit risk associated with their loan portfolio. Moreover, banks, especially the larger ones, are also engaged in trading financial instruments. These positions, labeled as the trading book of the bank, are exposed to all the different types of market risk. After all, banks can be considered as being *risk traders*, in that they accept risk in exchange for a premium paid by the client (Alexander, 2008). Therefore, measuring risk is an essential tool in bank management. Regulatory rules according to the Basel II framework force banks to hold sufficient equity in order to be able to cover at least 99 percent of the portfolio losses expected over a 10-day interval (Freixas and Rochet, 2008). Therefore, banks must carefully monitor their market risk.

Besides financial companies, corporations are also required to have sophisticated risk management tools in place to measure and manage market risk, especially those that are active traders on financial or commodity markets; for instance, large utility corporations that act as big traders in energy markets. Corporations hedge their foreign-exchange or interest-rate risk with over-the-counter (OTC) derivatives. Airlines hedge their oil price risk by assuming appropriate hedging positions in oil futures. Individuals also have to decide how much market risk they are willing to bear in their private portfolios. In this respect, the measurement and management of market risk has an important interface with personal finance, even though risk management techniques in this area are less developed.

Measures of Risk: the Mean-Variance Framework

Starting with the Markowitz (1952) model of portfolio selection, the mean-variance framework for risk management has become very popular. As Alexander (2008) notes, many risk management models are build on the Markowitz set of assumptions. For example, the capital asset pricing model (CAPM), the nucleus of the broad area of capital market research, rests on those assumptions (Sharpe, 1964). Specifically, the mean-variance framework assumes that the return r of any risky asset (i.e., any asset exposed to market risk) or portfolio of assets is normally independently and identically distributed (i.i.d.), as shown in Equation 15.1:

$$r \overset{iid}{\sim} N(\mu, \sigma^2). \tag{15.1}$$

These assumptions are important if the interest focuses on how risk evolves over time. The implications are that subsequent returns represent independent drawings (commonly known as a *random walk*) and that the underlying distribution of these drawings does not change over time. In this assumption, an important consequence is that the variance (σ^2) of an asset's return increases linearly over time, which implies that the standard deviation increases by the square root of the time interval. Hence, if the standard deviation of an i.i.d. return over a period t is σ, it follows that the standard deviation over the time interval nt is $\sigma\sqrt{n}$.

The rationale behind the normality assumption is three-fold: First, as in many other types of risky environments such as weather or other natural phenomena, a normal distribution might be an intuitive way to describe the behavior of a random variable. Second, normality is appealing because its explanation of the whole distribution in two parameters, the mean (μ) and standard deviation (σ), allows investors to make decisions under uncertainty by describing the 'riskiness' of the portfolio without using any additional information. Third, normality makes the analytic treatment of risk relatively easy so that in most cases simple closed-form solutions result. A *closed-form solution* is any formula that can be evaluated in a finite number of standard operations. Thus, an equation is said to be a closed-form solution if it solves a given problem in terms of functions and mathematical operations with a generally accepted set. For instance, important portfolio risk metrics, such as value at risk, can easily be calculated under this assumption, as shown later on in this chapter. Nevertheless, many have challenged the normality assumption over the last two decades.

Measures of Risk: The Asset Level

Investors are interested in more than just the overall riskiness of their investment portfolios. When taking particular investment decisions, investors might also be interested in the relative contribution of a single asset to the overall portfolio risk. In order to assess the relative risk contribution, a model is needed to indicate how the individual asset returns are interrelated with the returns on the *market port-folio*, that is, the portfolio of all risky assets. Hence, a return-generating process is needed. Return-generating models are used to estimate the expected returns on risky securities based on one or more specific factors. The most frequently used model for the return-generating process of an equity instrument is the *market model*, which is a single-factor (sometimes termed single-index) model. As an alternative, more general factor models have been developed, which are also discussed in this section.

THE MARKET MODEL

The market model, shown in Equation 15.2, assumes that for every security i and j, the following condition holds:

$$r_{it} = \alpha_i + \beta_i r_{mt} + \varepsilon_{it}, E[\varepsilon_{it}]=0, E[\varepsilon_{it}^2]=\sigma_e^2, E[\varepsilon_{it}\varepsilon_{it-1}]=0, E[\varepsilon_{it}\varepsilon_{jt}]=0, \qquad (15.2)$$

where r_i is the asset's return, r_m is the return on the market portfolio, and t refers to any period of time. The term α_i is an asset-specific constant return component, while β_i is the asset's return sensitivity with respect to the return of the market portfolio. It is called the beta factor of an asset. Therefore, the market model assumes that a single asset's return depends linearly on the return of the market portfolio. Moreover, an idiosyncratic factor, such as the ε_i in Equation 15.2, forces the return to deviate randomly from this linear relationship. Because the expectation of this factor, expressed as $E[\varepsilon_i]$, this is a pure randomly driven noise term. The market model builds on the i.i.d. assumption, as the distribution of the idiosyncratic risk is assumed to be constant over time and there is no serial dependence that occurs. This is expressed by the conditions that the variance of the idiosyncratic factor σ_e^2 has no time index and the realization of this idiosyncratic factor in a period t does not depend on its realization in period $t-1$, which implies that their autocorrelation coefficient is zero. Moreover, the market model also assumes no cross-sectional dependence in the idiosyncratic risk. This is reflected in the condition that the realization of the idiosyncratic factor of an asset i does not depend on the realization of another asset j at the same time.

On the basis of this assumption, the individual risk of a stock (also called its *total risk*, as measured by the standard deviation) can be divided into two components: (1) the market risk, also called nondiversifiable risk, and (2) an idiosyncratic component, also called the unsystematic, unique, diversifiable, or firm-specific risk. In fact, using the market model, the individual asset's return variance can be decomposed, as shown in Equation 15.3:

$$\sigma_i^2 = \beta_i^2 \sigma_m^2 + \sigma_\varepsilon^2, \qquad (15.3)$$

where σ_i^2 is the return variance of a stock i, σ_i is its beta factor according to Equation 15.2, σ_m^2 is the return variance of the market portfolio, and σ_ε^2 is the variance of the idiosyncratic factor, according to Equation 15.2. Because of the assumption that idiosyncratic risk is uncorrelated among assets, this part of the risk can be diversified through portfolio combination. In market equilibrium, only the individual asset's market risk should be priced. That is, an investor should not expect to receive additional return for bearing idiosyncratic risk because such risk can be diversified away in a well-diversified portfolio. Thus, equilibrium security returns depend on the market risk of a stock or a portfolio as measured by beta, not its total risk as measured by standard deviation. An implication of this conclusion is that a stock with the greatest total risk does not necessarily have the greatest expected return. This relationship is an empirically testable hypothesis that has earned much attention in the asset pricing literature. Despite clear evidence that market risk is a factor that is priced at the individual asset level, this risk is not the only priced risk factor, as the next section will discuss (Fama and French, 2004).

FACTOR MODELS

The more recent literature indicates that the one-factor market model should be extended to a three- or even four-factor model (Jegadeesh and Titman, 1993; Carhart, 1997; Fama and French, 2004; Asem and Tian, 2010). According to extensive empirical research conducted during the last 20 years, the following four-factor model in Equation 15.4, also known as the Carhart four-factor model, which is based on the Fama-French three-factor model, has emerged to capture cross-sectional variation in stock returns:

$$r_{it} - r_{ft} = \alpha_i + \beta_{im}(r_{mt} - r_{ft}) + \beta_{is}SMB_t + \beta_{ih}HML_t + \beta_{iw}WML_t + \varepsilon_{it}, \quad (15.4)$$

where r_f is the risk-free rate of return, SMB_t is the return difference between a portfolio of small and large stocks, HML_t is the return difference of a portfolio of stocks with high and low book-to-market values, and WML_t is the return difference between one portfolio of stocks that outperformed in the past and one that underperformed. The average return of the SMB portfolio is labeled as the size effect; the average return on the HMB portfolio is called as the value effect; and the average return on the WML portfolio is referred to as the momentum effect.

Although the Fama-French-Carhart four-factor model appears suitable in explaining cross-sectional variation in stock returns, even at an international level (Antoniou, Lam, and Paudyal, 2007), it does not have a convincing theoretical foundation. Therefore, discussion continues about whether its mentioned size, value, and momentum effects are driven by fundamental risk factors or just related to mispricing (Fama and French, 2004). If the latter is the case, there is the possibility of observing the effect from hindsight, such as when analyzing past stock returns, but the effect would not be present ex-ante. A new strand in the asset pricing literature has evolved indicating that the value effect, and to some extent also the size effect, is reflected in ex-ante stock pricing and should, therefore, be interpreted as compensation for some specific market risk factors (Lee, Ng, and Swaminathan, 2009).

From a theoretical perspective, the market should only price relevant risk factors. In the CAPM framework, the only relevant risk factor is the market risk, while in the Fama-French-Carhart model, the size, value, and momentum effects are three additional market-relevant risk factors. A common belief is that these risk factors could only be identified by analyzing historical stock returns, as actual market expectations regarding stock returns cannot be observed because of the noise in stock price data and therefore that the relationship between expected returns and fundamental risk factors is contaminated and thus hard to detect (Elton, 1999).

Gebhardt, Lee, and Swaminathan (2001) propose a method to extract market expectations from realized stock prices. According to their method, a firm's implicit cost of capital can be observed. This cost is nothing more than the market's return expectation with respect to a particular company. The return-generating process in its ex-ante form can thereby be tested. A first result emerging from this strand of literature using the implicit cost of capital is that the value effect is also present at the level of expected returns. The results for the size effect are less clear, while the momentum effect seemingly disappears once expected returns are used. The momentum effect may thus be related to mispricing and does not reflect a fundamental market-related risk factor. This literature serves as confirmation of the robustness of the Fama and French (2004) three-factor model.

DURATION MODELS

While the market model and the different types of factor models focus on modeling equity risk, and to some extent also property and commodity price risk, a different type of framework has been developed for modeling interest rate risk. In this context, the concept of duration is important. One can show that the relative (percentage) change in the price B of a fixed-income instrument for a small change in the annually compounded interest rate r is given as shown in Equation 15.5:

$$\frac{\Delta B}{B} \approx -\frac{D}{1+r}\Delta r, \qquad (15.5)$$

where Δ stands for the difference in the price or the interest rate and D stands for the duration. If c_t represents the coupon paid by the bond at time t and T

represents the maturity of the bond, the duration of this bond is calculated as shown in Equation 15.6:

$$D=\frac{1}{B}\sum_{t=1}^{T}tc_{t}\left(1+r\right)^{-t}.\qquad(15.6)$$

Economically, the duration can be interpreted as being the weighted average of the times when payments are made, where the weight is equal to the present value of the respective payment divided by the present value of all payments. Bond duration can be viewed as an estimate of the average maturity of a bond. The important insight of this approach is that the interest rate risk, shown by the sensitivity to an interest rate change, increases with duration.

A commonly neglected issue is that every financial instrument has a duration. For instance, the duration of a zero bond is equal to its maturity. Stocks also have duration, even though the measure depends critically on the assumption one has about the future dividend stream. However, if one assumes that a stock has a constantly growing dividend with a current dividend yield of d, the duration of the stock is $1/d$.

Duration is only a *first-order approximation*, suggesting that it rests on such assumptions as that a linear relationship exists between the price of the financial instrument and the interest rate. In reality, this is not true. While for small changes in the interest rate (r), the error resulting from this assumption may be negligible, this approximation is certainly not true for larger changes in r, which involve what is called a *second-order effect*. This effect is based on the claim that even though it is assumed that the relationship between two variables is linear, they are in actuality nonlinear. In order to take such second-order effects into account, Fabozzi (2006) discusses the concept of convexity. *Convexity* is a measure of the curvature of the price-yield curve. The more curved the price-yield relation is, the greater the convexity, where price-yield relations that consist of straight lines have a convexity of zero. Investors care about convexity because a greater curvature of the price-yield relation leads to worse duration-based estimates of a financial instrument's price changes in response to changes in yield. Thus, duration assumes a *flat-term structure*, where interest rates do not differ depending on the maturity of a payment. For other than flat-yield curves, a broader term structure theory should be used, which is beyond of the scope of this chapter (Cox, Ingersoll, and Ross, 1985; Fabozzi, 2006).

Measures of Risk: the Portfolio Level

Only under the assumption of a normal distribution the parameters μ and σ are appropriate to describe the overall distribution, and so more specific risk measures have evolved. Value at risk (VaR) is one of the most prominent among them. This measure is of special importance for institutions holding assets and liabilities that are exposed to market risk. The framework was initially developed in the banking sector and later spread to the insurance sector as well as to large corporations. Apart from VaR, other frequently used risk measures exist. The most important among them are discussed in this section.

VaR AND PROBABILITY OF DEFAULT

Starting from the current market value of a portfolio, VaR represents a critical loss value for a given probability p assuming that the probability that the realized loss will be higher than the VaR is p%. As a specific example, assume that an investment bank holds a portfolio of financial instruments with an initial value of $100 million. Then, suppose that the portfolio returns follow a normal distribution with a standard deviation of 10 percent over the following ten trading days. Because of the short time period, the expected return is assumed to be zero. Figure 15.1 gives the probability distribution of the returns of this portfolio. This figure also shows a second density function (dotted line) representing a standard deviation of 20 percent.

The probability that the realized return is worse than −16.4 percent is 5 percent. This result is represented by the black shaded area under the normal density function. Hence, the 5 percent VaR for this portfolio is $16.4 million. If the standard deviation is 20 percent, the 5 percent VaR is $32.9 million. Therefore, if this financial instrument's portfolio is partly financed with debt and the bank management—or the supervisor—would like to have a probability of default of 5 percent over a ten-day interval at the maximum, the bank should not be allowed to have more than $83.6 million of debt in case the return's standard deviation is

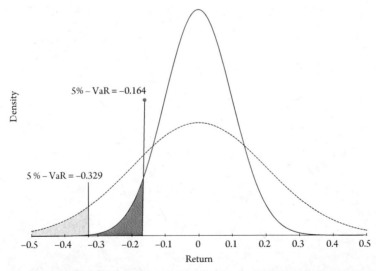

Figure 15.1. Illustration of the VaR. This figure gives a graphical interpretation of the VaR. The black lines represent the normal density function for parameters $\mu = 0$ and $\sigma = 0.1$, while the dashed line stands for $\mu = 0$ and $\sigma = 0.2$. The shaded areas under the density function represent 5 percent of total probability mass.

10 percent. If the standard deviation is 20 percent, the debt should not be larger than \$67.1 million if the default probability is still to be below 5 percent.

VaR can be interpreted as the negative of the p-quantile of a given profit-and-loss distribution. Therefore, the VaR can be defined according to the Equation 15.7:

$$VaR_p = N^{-1}(1-p)\sigma - \mu. \qquad (15.7)$$

Here, N^{-1} denotes the inverse of the standard normal distribution function. As the standard deviation and the expected return increase with the holding period under consideration, the VaR must be specified as a given quantile for a given holding period. For instance, the VaR at the 5 percent quantile for a ten-day holding period was calculated in the preceding example. The VaR can easily be scaled under the i.i.d. assumption. Under this assumption, the standard deviation increases with the square root of the time length. Hence, the relationship between the VaR over a t-day interval and the VaR over an n*t-day interval is shown in Equation 15.8:

$$VaR_{p,t\times n} = N^{-1}(1-p)\sigma_{t\times n} - \mu_{t\times n} = N^{-1}(1-p)\sigma_t\sqrt{n} - \mu_t n. \qquad (15.8)$$

Based on the previous example, VaR can be used as an instrument to manage the probability of default for liability-bearing institutions. For this purpose, banking and insurance supervision rely heavily on this instrument, forcing these institutions to determine their equity holdings on the basis of a VaR calculation. According to the Basel II framework, banks must calculate VaR in their trading book at the 1 percent level over a 10-day interval (Freixas and Rochet 2008). Under the Solvency II framework instituted by the European Union, European insurance companies will be forced to hold a solvency capital ratio equal to a VaR at the 0.5 percent level over a one-year interval (Sandström, 2011).

BENCHMARK VaR AND TRACKING ERROR

Despite the wide use of VaR, the measure has several limitations. For example, one practical limitation is that it includes only a straightforward interpretation for liability-bearing institutions, such as banks, insurance companies, and to some extent pension funds. The framework must be adapted for a mutual fund or other purely equity-financed investments. Two cases must be distinguished here. The first case involves a fund that follows a pure passive investment strategy, such as one that approximates the performance of a predefined benchmark. In this situation, further risk characterization may be superfluous because an investor should be aware that by investing in this fund, he has to accept the market risk of the benchmark. Whether his personal risk preferences and his portfolio allocation allow him to accept this risk is another issue.

The second case involves an investment in an actively managed fund. In this case, the fund manager's portfolio does not mimic the benchmark, creating a risk for the investor that the return of this investment strategy will deviate from the benchmark return. As a measure for this risk, the concept of the tracking error has been developed. Characterizing the active return as the difference between the return of the fund manager's investment strategy and the benchmark return, the *tracking error* can be defined as the standard deviation of this active return.

The concept of the benchmark VaR is closely related to this concept of the tracking error (Alexander 2008). In fact, the benchmark VaR informs the investor about the difference of the return between the active investment strategy and the benchmark that will only be exceeded with a probability equal to the quantile specified for VaR. More specifically, the tracking error of an active investment strategy can assumed to be 4 percent per year. An investor having invested $1 million in the fund wants to calculate the benchmark VaR at the 1 percent level, which is given as follows: $N^{-1}(0.99)$ (0.04) ($1,000,000$) = 2.3264 (0.04) ($1,000,000$) = $93,056. Therefore, the investor knows that only with a probability of 1 percent would the return difference between the active investment strategy and the benchmark exceed $93,056.

CONDITIONAL VAR AND EXPECTED TAIL LOSS

Another problem of VaR is that this number contains no information about the losses that may occur if a tail event is realized, such as in the case that the VaR is exceeded. For that purpose, the conditional VaR, or the expected tail loss (ETL), has been developed. It gives the expected loss under the condition that the realized loss is larger than the predefined VaR. More precisely, the ETL is defined in Equation 15.9 as:

$$ETL_p = -E\left[r \middle| r < \frac{-VaR_p}{V} \right] V , \qquad (15.9)$$

where V is the market value of the portfolio. Of course, this ETL can also be defined relative to a benchmark, in which case it is called an *expected shortfall*.

After the 2007–2008 financial crisis, conditional VaR received new attention in the risk management literature. One important application, for instance, is related to the measurement of systemic risk. A bank is defined as being systemically relevant if in the case of a systemic crisis its loss contribution is relatively high. This loss contribution can be measured as an ETL (Kaserer and Lahmann, 2011).

COHERENT RISK MEASURES

From a more general perspective, one can raise the normative question about what properties a meaningful risk measure should satisfy. The literature contains a consensus that if a risk measure is used to rank different risky alternatives, it should, at least, satisfy the condition of weak stochastic dominance. *Stochastic dominance* is a term referring to a set of relations that may hold between a pair of distributions. For example, investment A would exhibit weak stochastic dominance over investment B if the probability that the return will exceed any fixed value is never greater for investment B than with investment A. Therefore, any rational investor should rank investment A higher than investment B. Risk measures are said to be coherent if they preserve weak stochastic dominance. The literature has developed a set of axioms, for instance *subadditivity*, which involves the requirement that the risk of a portfolio should never be larger than the weighted average risk of its constituents to be satisfied by a coherent risk measure (Arztner, Delbaen, Eber, and Heath; 1999; Alexander, 2008).

The VaR risk measure is only coherent under certain specific assumptions, such as normally distributed returns. By contrast, the conditional VaR is a coherent risk measure that holds true in any situation. The lack of universal coherence does not mean, however, that using VaR is flawed. In many practical applications, VaR is an adequate instrument to manage the risk or the default probability of an institution.

Estimating Market Risk

In order to implement risk management systems, market risk has to be measured. Therefore, forming a reliable estimation of market risk is an issue that has been extensively investigated over the last two decades. This section discusses some of the most important challenges arising in this context.

PARAMETRIC APPROACHES AND THEIR PROBLEMS

Estimating market risk is less complex under the assumption of normally distributed returns. In this case, historical observations can be made in order to estimate the expected return as well as its standard deviation. Once these parameters are known, every risk measure, such as VaR, can be straightforwardly calculated.

One should, however, be careful when using the normality assumption in market risk calculations. A long history of empirical research shows that observed asset returns deviate consistently from the normality assumption (Dowd, 2005; Alexander, 2008). One stylized fact emerging from the literature is that empirical distributions are leptokurtic instead of normal. *Leptokurtic* describes a distribution that is more peaked and has fatter tails than does a normal distribution. This relationship is true regardless of whether single assets or asset portfolios are considered. Figure 15.2 gives an impression of this phenomenon. The figure shows the empirical distribution of daily returns of the S&P 500 over the period 1950–2011, which is characterized by the grey vertical lines. These empirical observations are later used to estimate the average daily return as well as the daily standard deviation. The dotted line in the figure shows the normal density function, using this information. The figure shows a nonnegligible difference between the empirical and the theoretical distribution.

The following deviations in Figure 15.2 are worth noting: First, average return realizations (returns near the average) occur far more frequently than under the normality assumption. Second, extreme return realizations (returns far below or

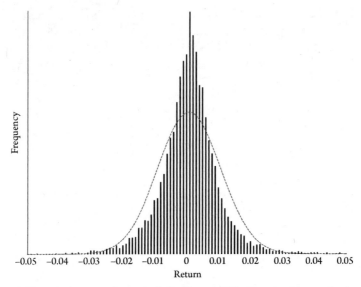

Figure 15.2 Empirical versus theoretical distribution. The bars in this graph give the empirical distribution of the S&P 500 daily returns over the period 1950–2011. The dotted line shows the theoretical distribution, which was calculated using the normality assumption on the basis of the mean and variance of the empirical distribution.

above the average) also happen much more frequently than predicted by the normality assumption. Because of scaling in Figure 15.2, this fact is hard to see but becomes much more evident in Figure 15.5. This latter *fat tail phenomenon* has gained much attention in the literature. This phenomenon is important in risk management applications because it indicates that by assuming a normal distribution, one is underestimating the probability of extreme losses. Therefore, a 1 percent VaR calibrated under the normality assumption, may, in fact, correspond with a realized default probability that is greater than 1 percent.

A second assumption that is relevant for assessing market risk is how this risk evolves over time. As previously stated, the i.i.d. assumption is important in determining the risk's evolution; in this case, the standard deviation of the return increases with the square root of the length of the time period. Consistent evidence shows that the i.i.d. assumption might be violated by empirically observed returns (Campbell, Low, and MacKinlay, 1997). In fact, consensus exists that returns in the short term (one week or less) suffer from positive serial correlation. Whether serial correlation is eliminated if longer-term returns (one year and longer) are considered is less clear (Dimson, Marsh, and Staunton, 2006).

Nevertheless, a large difference might exist between countries. Figure 15.3 provides some corroboration of this statement and shows the autocorrelation coefficients for a US, German, and worldwide market portfolio. The data used for this exercise are from Global Financial Data (GFD), which provides long-term time series. In some cases, monthly returns go back to 1869. As Figure 15.3

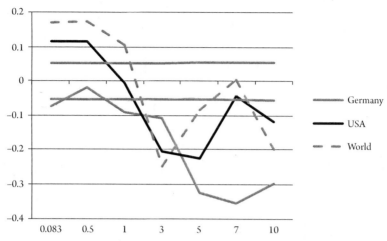

Figure 15.3 Serial correlation in stock prices. This figure reports the coefficient of autocorrelation (y-axis) for different lags. Lags are shown on the x-axis and measured in years. The solid grey horizontal lines characterize the 95 percent confidence interval; autocorrelation coefficients within these two grey lines in a statistical sense are not different from zero.

Source: Monthly return figures for different stock markets are from Global Financial Data (GFD). GFD provides long-term time series, with some of them going back to 1869.

shows, some evidence supports a positive serial correlation in the short term and a negative serial correlation in the long term. In any case, the figure corroborates the warning that using the i.i.d. assumption could result in problems.

Volatility clustering, which refers to the fact that volatility does not seem to change randomly over time, is a more empirically robust phenomenon (Dowd, 2005). Volatility clustering exists in periods in which volatility stays at a relatively moderate level. Suddenly, however, volatility often jumps and tends to stay at this elevated level for a while. Figure 15.4 depicts a typical example of this volatility clustering using S&P 500 returns. Using the yearly volatility on the basis of rolling 60-day windows shows that volatility seems to have a strong autoregressive component. Moreover, periods of elevated volatility go along with a stressed market situation. This observation is an important phenomenon because, for instance, risk measures such as VaR are linear in their volatility. Therefore, a VaR calculation based on long-term average volatility may be too low during periods of market stress.

Volatility clustering has gained much attention over the last decade, despite Engle (1982) having addressed it as a fundamental problem many years earlier. Today, a large number of generalized autoregressive conditional heteroskedasticity (GARCH) models are available (Bauwens, Laurent, and Rombouts, 2006). These models can capture the autoregressive behavior of prices of financial instruments in a far better way than the i.i.d. models have done. Although a detailed discussion of these models is beyond the scope of this chapter, the reader nevertheless should be aware of their ubiquitous adoption.

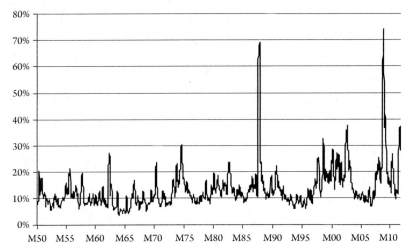

Figure 15.4 Volatility clustering. This figure reports the yearly standard deviation of the S&P 500. The figure is calculated based on rolling windows of sixty days over the period 1950–2011.

The stylized facts reported here strongly suggest that market risk assessment should not be based on normality and i.i.d. assumptions, as the literature contains many alternatives. For instance, one might use a parametric risk assessment approach, which requires substituting the normality assumption with some other more sophisticated distributional assumption (Alexander 2008). This option is not discussed here. Instead, two other alternatives, which seem to be more relevant in practice, are examined in the following section.

HISTORICAL SIMULATION AND MONTE CARLO ANALYSIS

Historical simulation is a method that reflects the fact that empirical return distributions are more irregular than any parametric distribution, such as a normal distribution (Alexander, 2008). In a historical simulation, one relies solely on empirically observed distributions. For instance, in order to estimate the 5 percent VaR over a ten-day interval, one can take a given number of ten-day return realizations, identify the 5 percent quantile (i.e., the best out of the 5 percent worst realizations), and use this as the relevant VaR observation.

For example, Figure 15.5 uses the historical daily return distribution of the S&P 500 Index over the period 1950–2011. In this figure, the grey vertical lines represent the frequency of historical tail realizations, while the dotted line characterizes the theoretical frequency assuming normality. As the figure shows, extreme negative returns occur much more frequently than predicted by the normality assumption. Consequently, the risk assessment of such an investment considerably differs when using theoretical distributions instead of historical distributions. In fact, the 5 percent VaR, based on the assumption of normally distributed returns, is –2.24 percent, while the historical VaR is –2.59 percent. Hence, the VaR is roughly 16 percent, underestimated by the parametric method.

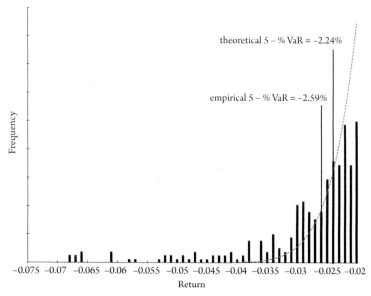

Figure 15.5 The Empirical VaR versus the theoretical VaR. The bars in this graph give the empirical tail distribution of the S&P 500 daily returns over the period 1950–2011. The dotted lines show the theoretical tail distribution, which is calculated using the normality assumption on the basis of the mean and variance of the empirical distribution.

Although this method seems to be appealing because no parametric assumptions are needed, it suffers from several drawbacks (Alexander, 2008). First, no obvious way is available to define the appropriate sample size. As the length of the historical observation period increases, so does the number of observations and risk. Because of structural breaks, the historical distribution deviates systematically from the current unknown return distribution. Second, the method may encounter data limitation problems due, for instance, to an insufficient return history for a specific asset. Actually, this is a problem if risk management is done on a longer-term basis. As an example, one can think of life insurance companies where the VaR calculation typically refers to a one-year period. Now, if one wants to identify the 1 percent historical VaR even in the case of a 100-year return history, the VaR calculation is based on a single observation. One can circumvent this problem by calculating the VaR on a lower frequency such as on a daily basis and from there derive the yearly VaR. In this case, however, one needs a distributional assumption with respect to risk evolvement over time; for instance the i.i.d. assumption. But this situation is exactly what the historical simulation method claims to avoid.

An alternative approach that can address this data limitation problem is the *Monte Carlo simulation*. Although this method has a long history in science and engineering, it has only become more widely used in finance over the last two decades. The idea underlying Monte Carlo simulation is to define a model for specific random variables, including their mutual dependencies. Once this model is defined, one can simulate return paths by making random drawings based on the distributions defined in the model. This approach has two advantages. First, the Monte Carlo simulation can handle very complex structural dependencies of specific random variables (Dowd, 2005). Modeling path dependencies or fat tails is not a problem using this approach. Therefore, it is much more powerful than relying on pure parametric distributions. The second advantage is that data limitation problems can be overcome because the number of simulations is unlimited.

Monte Carlo simulation, however, suffers from model risk. Misspecification risk can occur because the multivariate distribution of the random variables has to be specified in order to simulate the paths. Although Monte Carlo simulation is an important tool in risk measurement and management, it cannot overcome the model risk issue.

Liquidity Risk as a Part of Market Risk

Although researchers and practitioners did not focus on liquidity risk for a long time, such risk has gained renewed attention since the 2007–2008 financial crisis. Because banks need to reduce their risk exposure and mutual funds have to make payments to investors, both can be forced to liquidate large positions during times when this is hardest to do, such as during economic turmoil. Traditional risk management concepts such as VaR may fail if they do not account for market liquidity under a stress scenario. Because reduced liquidity may affect an asset's selling price, risk management models should account for liquidity risk.

When liquidating an asset, the most important cost component is the *spread*, which is the difference between the achievable transaction price and the stock's fair price. In this context, the bid-ask spread is a commonly used cost measure. However, only small positions can be traded at bid or ask prices. The market maker quoting the spread is only required to trade positions up to a certain size, called the *quote depth*. When trading larger positions, liquidity costs increase substantially. This increase is also known as the *price impact*, which is a liquidity cost. Liquidity costs are presumed to increase with order size.

Measuring the price impact is difficult given that one is looking for counterfactual evidence, such as what the price of an asset would have been if an order of a given size would have been placed on the market at a given point in time. However, as stock exchanges (e.g., the London Stock Exchange, the NASDAQ, the Deutsche Börse AG, the Euronext, and the Australian Stock Exchange) increasingly use transparent electronic limit order books, recent research has gained new insights into this issue (Stange and Kaserer, 2011; Ernst, Stange, and Kaserer 2012). Figure 15.6 summarizes information emerging from the limit order books.

When transacting a small position, liquidation costs are measured as half of the bid-ask spread. When transacting a larger position, however, this approach has to be generalized. If a market order of larger size is submitted, it is executed not only against the bid-ask limit orders because the quoted size is too small but also against the next-best limit orders in the book. The market order is matched against limit orders in the book until the full position size is liquidated. Therefore, the resulting liquidity cost can be calculated as half the *weighted spread*, which is the spread of all consumed limit orders weighted with their specific size.

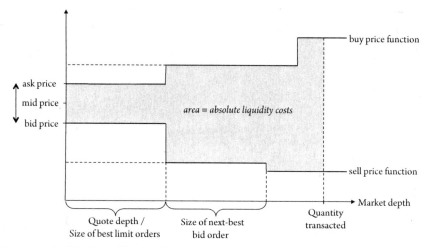

Figure 15.6 Calculating the liquidity cost from using limit order book information. This figure gives a graphical interpretation of how to calculate the liquidity cost from limit order book information. For a round-trip transaction, the liquidity cost is equal to the shaded area. The liquidity cost per transaction, therefore, is half the shaded area.

As Stange and Kaserer (2011) show, liquidity risk is not negligible. They use a unique data set provided by the Deutsche Börse AG, the German stock exchange, for the 160 most liquid stocks over the period 2002–2008. Their evidence shows that, on average, the 10-day 99 percent VaR of such stocks would have been underestimated by 10 percent had liquidity risk not been taken into account. Evidently, this liquidity impact differs depending on order size and the liquidity of the stock. But even for the 30 most liquid German stocks, liquidity risk can increase VaR by more than 20 percent if the order size is beyond €3 million. Even more interesting is that price and liquidity risk are not perfectly correlated, suggesting that liquidity cost is not highest when prices are lowest. Stange and Kaserer show that the average correlation between liquidity cost and price return is between 0.4 and 0.6, which clearly indicates some degree of diversification. Therefore, the overall impact on VaR of a portfolio should be smaller than the 10 percent mentioned above. Yet, the period analyzed does not consider the financial crisis of 2007-2008. Especially during the period between September 2008 and March 2009, liquidity costs may have behaved differently than during other periods.

A pure mean-variance framework may not describe liquidity costs. In fact, like equity risk, liquidity risk does not seem to be normal (Ernst et al., 2012). If that is the case, alternative approaches should be implemented in order to correctly assess the price impact generated by varying market liquidity.

MODEL RISK

Model risk refers to the problem that risk assessment is biased either because the model calibration, i.e., the parameter estimation, is defective or because inappropriate models are applied for measuring the risk or the model calibration, i.e., parameter estimation, is defective. While the second problem is more of a management problem, the first problem is more a statistical issue, which has been extensively analyzed.

According to Alexander (2008), estimation risk is related to such questions as: What is the impact of sample size on parameter calibration? What is the impact of choosing different calibration periods? How does the frequency of observed realizations affect the outcome? By contrast, model risk is related to the question of whether the model is correctly specified and whether it is correctly applied and implemented (Dowd, 2005). Incorrect specifications could be caused by the stochastic processes being misspecified, the relevant risk factors being neglected, and important interdependencies among the risk factors being ignored or misspecified. Most important, they could be caused by relevant market imperfections being ignored.

These misspecification problems are important to address in a model validation process. However, model validation also has its limitations. Model validation mostly involves *backtesting*, which refers to analyzing the performance of a model over periods that have not been used for calibrating the parameters. Because of data limitation issues, such out-of-sample tests are often difficult to implement and may have limited power from a statistical perspective. Moreover, to the extent that an economic turmoil goes along with structural breaks, backtesting will be of limited help.

A lesson gleaned from the financial crisis of 2007–2008 is that model risk is not only a statistical issue but also a management issue. As risk management models are getting increasingly complex, senior management needs to have an understanding of the most important risk factors and the interdependencies among them driving the risk position of their institution. In some cases, however, board members were unaware of the risk a company was taking with its financial markets transactions before the financial crisis (OECD, 2009). Although large banks had complex information systems in place, the aggregation of divisional risk positions to form a comprehensive risk assessment was defective. This specific area of model management risk appears underresearched when compared with other statistical issues of risk analysis.

Summary and Conclusions

Although market risk is a topic that has been comprehensively analyzed over the last fifty years, several issues still need further investigation. The need for further exploration has become even more significant in light of the financial crisis of 2007–2008, which showed that sound risk management systems are essential for the stability of financial markets.

The major topics addressed in this chapter can be summarized as follows: First, despite some consensus about what constitute the most important market risk metrics, such as VaR or the ETL, discussion continues about what the best risk metric is to apply under specific conditions. This discussion suggests a lack of a "one-size-fits-all" solution; that is, the most appropriate risk metric may differ depending on the specific needs of the different types of investors, including institutions, large corporations, and individuals.

Second, concerning risk measurement at the individual asset level, this chapter suggests that the literature corroborates the relevance of market risk; the so-called value effect; and, to some extent, the size effect. Thus, when modeling individual returns, these latter two risk-factors should be considered combined with market risk.

Third, the deficiencies of using the normality and i.i.d. assumptions when modeling market risk are well known at the portfolio level. Empirical returns display fat tails and are serially correlated, and their variance is clustered over time. Since the 1990s, a vast literature has evolved dealing with these stylized facts, which has come up with remarkable results. Because of data limitation problems and structural breaks, however, the risk of model misspecification is still an important issue.

Fourth, the integration of liquidity risk into the market risk assessment is not yet common despite recent literature showing that liquidity risk makes a relevant risk contribution. Because of better data availability, ongoing research is likely to influence the design of future risk management models.

The final suggestion is that in the aftermath of the 2007–2008 financial crisis, the deficiencies of risk management models became apparent. These deficiencies are related to both calibration problems and the management process. The chapter discusses some of these issues despite having little academic evidence on this subject.

Discussion Questions

1. Identify and discuss at least three different types of market risk.
2. What is meant by the mean-variance framework? Under the i.i.d. assumption, how does the return variance of a portfolio evolve over time? How is this related to what is empirically observed?
3. What is the market model and what is its relation to market risk? What is the Fama-French model? Discuss some recent empirical findings regarding the Fama-French model.
4. What is VaR? Who uses VaR and what are some alternative risk measures?
5. Define liquidity risk and discuss whether it is a relevant component in the overall riskiness of a portfolio.
6. Define model risk and explain whether it is mainly a pure statistical problem or a management problem.

References

Alexander, Carol. 2008. *Market Risk Analysis*. Vol. 4, *Value at Risk Models*. Chicester, UK: John Wiley & Sons.

Antoniou, Antonios, Herbert Y. T. Lam, and Krishna Paudyal. 2007. "Profitability of Momentum Strategies in International Markets: The Role of Business Cycle Variables and Behavioral Biases." *Journal of Banking and Finance* 31:3, 955–972.

Artzner, Philippe, Freddy Delbaen, Jean-Marc Eber, and David Heath. 1999. "Coherent Measures of Risk." *Mathematical Finance* 9:3, 203–228.

Asem, Ebenezer, and Gloria Y. Tian. 2010. "Market Dynamics and Momentum Profits." *Journal of Financial and Quantitative Analysis* 45:6, 1549–1562.

Bauwens, Luc, Sébastien Laurent, and Jeroen V. K. Rombouts. 2006. "Multivariate GARCH Models: A Survey." *Journal of Applied Econometrics* 21:1, 79–109.

Campbell, John Y., Andrew W. Lo, and Archie Craig MacKinlay. 1997. *The Econometrics of Financial Markets*. Princeton, NJ: Princeton University Press.

Carhart, Mark M. 1997. "On Persistence in Mutual Fund Performance." *Journal of Finance* 52:1, 57–82.

Cox, John C., Jonathan E. Ingersoll Jr., and Stephen A. Ross. 1985. "A Theory of the Term Structure of Interest Rates." *Econometrica* 53:2, 385–407.

Dimson, Elroy, Paul Marsh, and Mike Staunton. 2006. "The Worldwide Equity Premium: A Smaller Puzzle." Last modified April 2006. http://ssrn.com/abstract=891620.

Dowd, Kevin. 2005. *Measuring Market Risk*, 2nd ed. Chicester, UK: John Wiley & Sons.

Elton, Edwin J. 1999. "Expected Return, Realized Return, and Asset Pricing Tests." *Journal of Finance* 54:4, 1199–1220.

Engle, Robert F. 1982. "Autoregressive Conditional Heteroskedasticity with Estimates of the Variance of United Kingdom Inflation." Econometrica 50:5, 987–1007.

Ernst, Cornelia, Sebastian Stange, and Christoph Kaserer. 2012. "Accounting for Non-Normality in Liquidity Risk." *Journal of Risk* 14:3, 3–21.

Fabozzi, Frank J. 2006. *Fixed-Income Mathematics: Analytical and Statistical Techniques*. New York: McGraw-Hill.

Fama, Eugene F., and Kenneth R. French. 2004. "The Capital Asset Pricing Model: Theory and Evidence." *Journal of Economic Perspectives* 18:3, 25–46.

Freixas, Xavier, and Jean-Charles Rochet. 2008. *Microeconomics of Banking*. Cambridge, UK: MIT Press.

Gebhardt, William R., Charles M. C. Lee, and Bhaskraran Swaminathan. 2001. "Toward an Implied Cost of Capital." *Journal of Accounting Research* 39:1, 135–176.

Jegadeesh, Narasimhan, and Sheridan Titman. 1993. "Returns to Buying Winners and Selling Losers: Implications for Stock Market Efficiency." *Journal of Finance* 54:1, 65–91.

Kaserer, Christoph, and Wolfgang Lahmann. 2011. "Measuring Systemic Risk and Assessing Systemic Importance in Global and Regional Financial Markets Using the ESS-Indicator." Last modified January 2012. http://ssrn.com/abstract=1906682.

Lee, M. C. Charles, David Ng, and Bhaskraran Swaminathan. 2009. "Testing International Asset Pricing Models Using Implied Costs of Capital." *Journal of Financial and Quantitative Analysis* 44:2, 307–335.

Markowitz, Harry M. 1952. "Portfolio Selection." *Journal of Finance* 7:1, 77–91.

OECD (Organisation for Economic Co-Operation and Development). 2009. *Corporate Governance and the Financial Crisis: Key Findings and Main Messages*. Paris: OECD.

Sandström, Arne. 2011. *Handbook of Solvency for Actuaries and Risk Managers: Theory and Pracitce*. London: CRC Press.

Sharpe, William F. 1964. "Capital Asset Prices: A Theory of Market Equilibrium under Conditions of Risk." *Journal of Finance* 19:3, 425–442.

Stange, Sebastian, and Christoph Kaserer. 2011. "The Impact of Liquidity Risk: A Fresh Look." *International Review of Finance* 11:3, 269–301.

16

Measuring and Managing Credit and Other Risks

GABRIELE SABATO
Senior Manager, Royal Bank of Scotland
Group Risk Management

Introduction

Financial markets play an essential function in the economy, by allowing funds to move from people who lack productive investment opportunities to those who have such opportunities. These markets are critical for producing an efficient allocation of capital, which contributes to higher production and efficiency for the overall economy. Well-functioning financial markets also directly improve the well-being of consumers by allowing them to time their purchases, which leads to improving the economic welfare of everyone in the society.

In *direct finance*, borrowers obtain funds directly from lenders in financial markets by selling them securities (also called financial instruments), which are claims on the borrower's future income or assets. However, borrowers can obtain funds from lenders by a second route, called *indirect finance*, which involves a financial intermediary that stands between the lender-savers and the borrower-spenders and helps transfer funds from one to the other. Thus, a financial intermediary borrows funds from the lender-savers and then uses these funds to make loans to borrower-spenders.

The process of indirect finance using financial intermediaries, called *financial intermediation*, is the primary and often the only available route for moving funds from lenders to borrowers. In fact, due to the opaqueness of the information available on the market, the time and expertise that lenders would need to assess and monitor borrowers, and the high costs that lenders would need to face, households generating excess savings do not often find investing directly in the securities issued by companies very attractive.

Financial institutions (FIs) play an important role in the economy because they provide liquidity services, promote risk sharing, and solve information problems. The success of financial intermediaries in performing this role is evidenced by the fact that most households invest their savings using their services and obtain loans through them. A well-functioning set of financial intermediaries is a necessary condition to allow an economy to reach its full potential.

Several different types of FIs operate in the markets, such as depository institutions, insurance companies, pension funds, mutual funds, and securities firms. Each sells different products and faces different risks. Entering the twenty-first century, the light regulatory barriers, technology, and financial-innovation changes enabled single financial-services firms to offer a full set of financial services, weakening the boundaries between traditional industry sectors. Products and risks faced by modern FIs were becoming increasingly similar. However, in 2009, after the most recent financial crisis, discussions resurfaced in several countries regarding whether financial-services–holding companies should still be allowed to offer a full range of financial services. The increased level of disclosure and separation between investment and commercial banking activities seem to be the common themes of the review of the current FIs (Institute of International Finance, 2007; Basel Committee on Banking Supervision, 2008; Financial Services Authority, 2008; Walker, 2009).

Commercial banks' primary business activity is related to extending credit to borrowers, generating loans, and growing credit assets. A major component of a bank's risk, therefore, lies in the quality of its assets, which need to be in line with the bank's risk appetite. *Risk appetite* is defined as the maximum risk the bank is willing to accept in executing its chosen business strategy and to protect itself against events that may have an adverse impact on its profitability, capital base, or share price. In order to manage risk efficiently, quantifying it with the most appropriate and advanced tools is an extremely important factor in determining the bank's success.

Credit risk is the risk that a borrower will be unable to make payments of interest or principal in a timely manner. It represents the main risk by far that most FIs face in the everyday business. Credit risk is a necessary consequence of a vibrant economy where producers need to borrow funds to finance the production that they will then hopefully sell to pay back the loan and generate profits.

Originally, credit risk was essentially local. Credit suppliers would know everything about their customers and would base their decisions on reputation and direct observation of these customers who were often local farmers. Credit analysis used to rely exclusively on knowledge of the specific business and local conditions. Financial statements were unavailable as a basis on which to form the decisions and compare different applicants. Experience and judgment were the only acceptance criteria used.

This situation began to change in the United States in the mid-nineteenth century. Railroads required huge capital investments, thousands of miles away from providers of capital. As such, railroad creditworthiness could not be determined by local observation but required knowledge of overall transportation infrastructure and the economics of all goods that are shipped by rail. Potential creditors could not get this information from companies directly because consistent and reliable financial statements were still unavailable.

Encouraged by the aforementioned conditions, Lewis Tappan founded the Mercantile Agency—which became Dun & Bradstreet—in 1841. This company provided commercial information on businesses throughout the United States to subscribers. At about the same time, a specialized financial press emerged. When Henry Varnum Poor became owner and editor of the *American Railroad Journal* in 1849, he began publishing financial and operating data of US railroads. The publisher of the journal, Poor's Publishing Company, later merged with a competitor, Standard Statistics, to become Standard & Poor's. John Moody's innovation in 1909 was to combine the credit reporting of Dun & Bradstreet with the investor focus of Standard & Poor's. Moody's quickly expanded to cover almost all bond issuers. John Fitch jumped into the ratings business in 1913, and Standard & Poor's got its official credit ratings start in 1916.

Due to a lack of data for estimating reliable default probabilities, ratings remained mainly qualitative. The study of consumer credit risk, which never had the historical baggage that has weighed down the corporate credit risk, provided important cross-fertilization especially due to the bigger samples and higher number of defaults. Beaver (1967) and Altman (1968), who introduced multivariate discriminant analysis (MDA), provided the first major attempt at quantification. MDA was the most popular statistical methodology used to estimate credit risk models until Ohlson (1980), for the first time, applied the conditional logit model to the default prediction's study. Since Ohlson's research emerged, analysts have used several other statistical techniques, such as linear regression, probit analysis, Bayesian methods, and neural networks to improve the prediction power of credit-scoring models, but logistic regression still remains the most popular method.

Credit risk modeling has gained new importance with the New Basel Capital Accord (Basel Committee on Banking Supervision, 2004). The so-called Basel II replaced the Basel Accord, or Basel I, signed in 1988, and focused on techniques that allowed banks and supervisors to properly evaluate the various risks that banks face. Since credit risk modeling contributes broadly to the internal risk assessment process of an institution, regulators have enforced more strict rules about the model development, implementation, and validation to be followed by banks that want to use their internal models in order to estimate capital requirements (Altman and Sabato, 2005, 2007).

Since the financial crisis of 2007–2008, FIs have reconsidered all methods and processes related to measuring and managing credit and other risks in the belief that has proven true that these did not work as expected. Regulators are leading this review. New rules are being imposed and tougher controls are being applied with the aim of trying to avoid or mitigate another banking crisis.

This chapter provides an analysis and discussion of risk management as well as several proposals on how the financial industry should evolve. Several aspects are assessed in terms of how to improve the measurement of risk and provide a quantitative metric that could summarize different risk types, such as credit, market, and operational risk. Enterprise risk management (ERM) and economic capital (EC) are old concepts that are finally getting more attention. However, having the best tools to measure and aggregate different risks, such as these, will be insufficient to reduce the damages of financial crises in the future. Risk management and governance are other key elements that need to be addressed.

The ability to quantitatively assess risk and take appropriate actions together with the power to enforce these actions will be the main drivers of a new risk management function. New risk management leaders will need to have a strong analytical background and the ability to drive a bank's strategy. Ultimately, risk management has the opportunity to redefine itself as the main driver of FIs' profitability (Aebi, Sabato, and Schmid, 2011).

The remainder of this chapter has the following organization: The next section analyzes the most common methodologies used to measure credit and other risks. In particular, for credit risk, measures at the customer and portfolio level are discussed separately in order to provide a more detailed examination. The following section provides a discussion of the most important topics currently under scrutiny in the area of risk management evolution, such as capital allocation, ERM, and risk governance. The last section provides a summary and conclusions.

Measuring Risk

A fully objective measure of risk cannot be derived. Risk is a mix of perceptions, expectations, and probabilities, which is based on a subjective assessment. Each individual can use different methods to assess risks, but even using the same methods, the results can still be different. For this reason, regulators have tried to enforce rules that would aim to align methodologies applied to measure risks (Basel Committee on Banking Supervision 1988, 2004, 2006). Complexity and sophistication have increased tremendously, and some kind of alignment has now been reached. However, measuring risks still remains a highly subjective process that markedly affects the success of FIs.

In this section, attention is placed on credit risk because it represents the main threat for most FIs. Both old and new methodologies that are used to measure credit risk are discussed and analyzed. Then, the other risk types are considered with a special focus on market, liquidity, and operational risk.

CREDIT RISK

This section assesses the processes and methodologies that are used to measure credit risk at different levels of aggregation. Aggregation is an important part of the risk-measuring process. Credit risk is usually first assessed at the contract level and then aggregated at the customer or client level. The following aggregation levels (country, sector, product, or asset class level) depend on the strategy that is used to manage risk groupings. The most common levels of aggregation for credit risk at the customer and portfolio level are discussed next.

Customer Level

Credit risk measurement has evolved dramatically. Originally, financial institutions would rely almost exclusively on subjective analysis to assess the credit risk on corporate and retail loans. Credit underwriters would analyze various borrower characteristics to reach a largely subjective judgment (often thought of as an "expert judgment") as to whether to grant credit. Based on this decision, ranking the risk of counterparties and associating a potential loss to them were impossible.

Slowly, toward the end of the 1960s, academics started to build the link between credit risk and the probability of default of a borrower. The need existed to create new methods to assign an objective rating/scoring to each borrower that could be translated into a probability that a customer would not repay the loan.

The statistical techniques used for credit scoring are based on the idea of discrimination among discriminating between several groups within a data sample. These procedures originated in the 1930s and 1940s (Fisher, 1936; Durand, 1941). At that time, some of the finance houses and mail order firms were having difficulties with their credit management. Credit analysts made subjective decisions about whether to give loans or send merchandise to the applicants. Because the decision procedure was nonuniform and opaque, assessment depended on the rules of each financial house and on the personal and empirical knowledge of each clerk. With the rising number of people applying for a credit card, relying only on credit analysts was impractical if not impossible. Thus, an automated system was necessary. During the late 1950s, Bill Fair and Earl Isaac formed the first consultancy in San Francisco, known as Fair Isaac, to provide such a system.

After the first empirical solutions, academic interest in the topic rose, and researchers started to focus on loans to small- and medium-sized enterprises (SMEs). Beaver (1967) and Altman (1968), who developed univariate and multi-variate models to predict business failures using a set of financial ratios, provide the seminal works in this field.

Beaver (1967) uses a dichotomous classification test to determine the error rates a potential creditor would experience, classifying firms on the basis of individual financial ratios as failed or nonfailed. He analyzes 14 financial ratios using a matched sample consisting of 158 firms (79 failed and 79 nonfailed).

By contrast, Altman (1968) uses MDA to solve the inconsistency problem linked to Beaver's (1967) univariate analysis and to assess a more complete financial profile of firms. Altman based his analysis on a matched sample containing 66 manufacturing firms (33 failed and 33 nonfailed) that filed a bankruptcy petition during the period 1946–1965. He examined 22 potentially helpful financial ratios and selected the following five as doing the best overall job in the prediction of corporate bankruptcy: (1) working capital to total assets, (2) retained earnings to total assets, (3) earnings before interest and tax (EBIT) to total assets, (4) market value of equity to book value of total debt, and (5) sales to total assets. Altman classified the variables into five categories of standard ratios: liquidity, profitability, leverage, solvency, and activity ratios.

For many years thereafter, MDA was the prevalent statistical technique applied to the default prediction models. Many authors, such as Deakin (1972), Edmister (1972), Blum (1974), Taffler and Tisshaw (1977), Altman, Haldeman, and Narayanan (1977), Micha (1984), Gombola, Haskins, Ketz, and Williams (1987), and Lussier (1995), used this technique. In most of these studies, the respective authors note that researchers and others often violated the following two basic but restrictive assumptions when applying MDA to default prediction problems: (1) the independent variables included in the model should be normally distributed in a multivariate sense, and (2) the group dispersion matrices (or variance-covariance matrices) should be equal across the failing and the nonfailing group (Barnes, 1982; Karels and Prakash, 1987; McLeay and Omar 2000). Moreover, in MDA models, the standardized coefficients cannot be interpreted like the slopes of a regression equation and hence do not indicate the relative importance of the different variables.

Considering these problems of MDA, Ohlson (1980) applies the conditional logit model when studying default prediction. This model is a type of regression analysis used for predicting the outcome of a categorical (a variable that can take on a limited number of categories) criterion variable based on one or more predictor variables. When applied to default prediction problems, the dependent variable is generally defined as binomial (default/nondefault).

The practical benefits of the logit methodology are that it does not require the restrictive assumptions of MDA and allows working with disproportional samples. Ohlson used a data set including 105 bankrupt firms and 2,058 nonbankrupt firms over the period 1970–1976. He chose nine predictors (seven financial ratios and two binary variables) to conduct his analysis mainly because they appeared to be the ones most frequently mentioned in the literature.

The performance of Ohlson's models, in terms of classification accuracy, were lower than the ones reported in the previous studies based on MDA (Altman, 1968; Altman, Haldeman, and Narayanan, 1977), but he points out some reasons that the logistic analysis is preferable. He suggests that from a statistical point of view, logit regression seems to fit well the characteristics of the default prediction problem, where the dependent variable is binary (default/nondefault) and with the groups being discrete, nonoverlapping, and identifiable. Also, the logit model yields a score between zero and one, which conveniently can be transformed in the probability of default (PD) of the client. Additionally, the estimated coefficients can be interpreted separately as the importance or significance of each of the independent variables in the explanation of the estimated PD. After the work of Ohlson (1980), most of the academic literature (Zavgren, 1983; Gentry, Newbold, and Whitford, 1985; Aziz, Emanuel, and Lawson, 1988; Platt and Platt, 1990; Ooghe, Joos, and Bourdeaudhuij, 1995; Mossman, Bell, Swartz, and Turtle, 1998; Becchetti and Sierra, 2002) used logit models to predict the risk of default. Researchers have also tested several other statistical techniques to improve the prediction accuracy of credit scoring models, such as linear regression, probit analysis, Bayesian methods, and the neural network, but the empirical results have never shown highly significant benefits.

Toward the end of the 1990s, when the focus on the New Basel Capital Accord was growing, academics and practitioners agreed that in order to quantify credit risk at the customer level, the PD was insufficient. They also agreed that a measure of the potential severity of the loss in the case of default was needed. The concept of loss given default (LGD) was finally defined.

Empirical studies reporting LGD for different categories of influence factors (e.g., Asarnow and Edwards, 1995; Felsovalyi and Hurt, 1998; Eales and Bosworth, 1998; Araten, Jacobs, and Varshney, 2004) provided a first step toward forecasting the LGDs of individual customers in relation to bank loans. More recent studies analyze the main drivers of LGD via linear regressions (e.g., Caselli, Gatti, and Querci, 2008; Sabato and Schmid, 2008; Grunert and Weber, 2009); log regressions (e.g., Caselli et al., 2008); and log-log regressions (e.g., Dermine and Neto de Carvalho, 2006; Bastos, 2010). Bellotti and Crook (2007) compare the performance of different models, constructed as combinations of different modeling algorithms and different transformations of the recovery rate, such as ordinary least squares (OLS) regressions or decision trees, on the one hand, and log or probit transformations on the other hand. Bastos proposes modeling LGDs with nonparametric and nonlinear regression trees.

Additionally, exposure at default (EAD) is important to mention because it measures the expected exposure that a customer will have at the moment the default would occur. This will generally be a certain percentage of the limit and is typically calculated through simple regression models based on the observation of the history of similar customers.

Although several forces, including regulators, competition, and markets, have convinced banks to adopt increasingly sophisticated methods to estimate PD, LGD, and EAD, many financial institutions still use judgmental/expert methods to determine these parameters at the customer level. Expert judgment can be the only solution in some cases but should be a temporary solution because it risks undermining the trust in the outputs of several portfolio management tools, which will be discussed in the next section and that affect the overall credit risk management process (Sabato, 2008, 2010).

Portfolio Level

Credit risk is conventionally defined using the concepts of expected loss (EL) and unexpected loss (UL). The previously discussed customer-level metrics, PD, LGD, and EAD, are the inputs to calculate both values. Because EL can be anticipated, it should be regarded as a cost of doing business and not as a financial risk. Obviously, credit losses are not constant across the economic cycle due to the substantial volatility (unexpected loss) associated with the level of expected loss. Credit portfolio models are designed to quantify this volatility. Two factors drive the volatility of portfolio losses: concentration and correlation.

Correlation is mainly an exogenous factor that depends on the customer type, geography, and macroeconomic factors, while *concentration* is (or should be) the result of conscious decisions of an FI's senior management through a well-defined risk appetite framework as discussed in the next section. However, optimal concentration limits cannot be defined without an appropriate measure of capital/risk concentration such as economic capital (EC), and correlations are the most important input for EC.

In order to calculate regulatory capital (RC; e.g., the internal rating based approach of Basel II), correlations are also used, which are given by the regulator (e.g., the Bank for International Settlements) and are equal for all banks. Additionally, these correlations cover only intraproduct, not interproducts correlations (correlations between defaults in different products). This difference is a very strong assumption that fully excludes diversification benefits.

Accurately modeling portfolio credit risk requires first measuring the correlation between exposures. Complexity arises when calculating credit risk correlations directly. The task of calculating such correlations is extremely difficult. The simplest solution is to use an aggregate time series to infer credit risk correlations. However, a more attractive possibility is to apply a causative default model (e.g., the Merton model) that takes more observable financial quantities as inputs and then transforms them into a default probability. This solution is the most frequently applied method for identifying corporate exposures. For retail exposures, correlations are best measured using factor models in the same way that an equity beta is estimated. Factor models usually produce better prospective correlation estimates than does direct observation and have the additional benefit, if macroeconomic factors are chosen, of enabling intuitive stress testing and scenario analysis of the credit portfolio.

In 1999, a few years before the publication of the first version of Basel II, several credit portfolio models, such as CreditMetrics, Credit Risk Plus, and Moody's KMV portfolio model, were developed. Although all of the models have different correlation structures and risk measures, the ultimate scope for all of them is to quantify the volatility around the expected losses. Currently, several FIs still use these generic models to estimate EC, while others have tried to move to more bespoke models that use internal data to estimate correlations.

As mentioned previously, measuring concentration using the exposure balance of a portfolio to determine regulatory capital (RC) or EC can make a huge difference in the results of the analysis and on the required actions. Regulators have slowly started to realize this benefit, and they are now forcing FIs to develop and implement sophisticated internal EC models subject to regulatory validation. EC is calculated from the tails of the credit-risk distribution by determining the probability that a reduction in portfolio value will exceed a critical value (e.g., 99.95 percent). Thanks to the correlation structures included in its estimation, EC allows large, well-diversified banks to take full advantage of asset diversification. This opportunity is increasingly important in times when the regulatory capital ratio is rising (as it is the case with the new Basel III regulation). Moreover, EC allows FIs to include all risks types, such as liquidity risk, pension risk, and business risk, not just credit, market, and operational risk.

OTHER RISKS

Risk takes many forms. Individuals and enterprises face risks every time they act. The focus is generally on financial risks, as these are the ones that generate the most significant losses. The list of financial risks is long and includes risks associated with every aspect of business. The list of financial risks used to include three types: credit, market, and operational risk, where operational risk would include all other possible risks than credit and market risk.

Basel II has changed the way of categorizing risks by assigning a stand-alone, clear definition to operational risk and separating from it all other risks. Today, business risk, interest rate risk, funding (liquidity) risk, reputational risk, pension risk, tax risk, and many other risks need to be measured, assessed, and covered separately from operational risk. All firms, not just FIs, generally face these "minor" risk types. This section limits the focus to the market, liquidity, and operational risks, which represent the three major risks, together with credit risk, that FIs have to face in their daily activity on the markets.

Market Risk

Market risk refers to the possibility of incurring large losses from adverse changes in financial asset prices. Standard risk management involves using statistical models to forecast the probabilities and magnitudes of large, adverse price changes. Value-at-risk (VaR) models are used to establish capital standards that protect against potential losses. In practice, while models provide a convenient methodology for quantifying market risks, limitations exist in regard to their ability to predict the magnitude of potential losses. To address these limitations, firms also use stress tests that examine the impact of large hypothetical market movements on portfolio values.

The VaR figure has two important characteristics: The first is that it provides a common, consistent measure of market risk across different positions and risk factors. It enables measuring the risk associated with a fixed-income position in a way that is comparable to and consistent with a measure of the risk associated with equity positions. This common risk standard established when using VaR models enables institutions to manage their risks in new ways that were not previously possible. The other characteristic of VaR is that it takes account of the correlations between different risk factors. If two or more risks offset each other, VaR accommodates this offset.

Liquidity Risk

Liquidity, or *funding, risk* is the risk that a firm cannot obtain the funds necessary to meet its financial obligations, such as short-term loan commitments. Three common techniques for mitigating funding risk are diversifying across funding sources, holding liquid assets, and establishing contingency plans, such as backup lines of credit. Generally, firms set funding goals as benchmarks to measure their current funding levels and take mitigating actions when they are below certain thresholds. This risk, which historically was underestimated, has now gained new interest and attention from academics and practitioners alike due to the liquidity shock that invaded the markets during the 2007–2008 financial crisis. Currently, new, more sophisticated methodologies to measure and manage liquidity risk are being developed and tested together with new rules enforced by regulators (e.g., Basel Committee on Banking Supervision, 2008).

Operational Risk

Operational risk is the risk of monetary loss resulting from inadequate or failed internal processes, people, and systems or from external events. Basel II, together with efforts by researchers and risk managers at major banks, has helped to shape emerging risk management practices for operational risk. Operational risk measurement should combine both qualitative and quantitative techniques for assessing risks. For example, settlement errors in a trading operation's back office happen with sufficient regularity that they can be modeled statistically. Many other contingencies affect FIs infrequently and are of a nonuniform nature, which makes modeling difficult. Examples include acts of terrorism, natural disasters, and trader fraud.

Quantitative techniques have been developed primarily for the purpose of assigning capital charges for banks' operational risks. Regulators developing Basel II performed much of the work in this field. The final Basel II rules on operational risk were first released in 2004 and then revised in 2010 (Basel Committee on Banking Supervision, 2004, 2010). These rules allow banks to measure operational risks using a standardized or advanced measurement approach (AMA).

The AMA allows large banks to base operational risk capital requirements on their own internal models. This has spawned considerable independent research into methods for measuring operational risk. Techniques have been borrowed from fields such as actuarial science and engineering. However, few FIs apply the AMA due to the lack of internal data on operational losses. Data collection started quite recently at most financial organizations and improvements will be seen in the near future.

Managing Risk

Risk management is a science that is continuously evolving. Even assuming that risk has been measured correctly, managing it appropriately requires considerable experience and knowledge. Moreover, the governance structure of FIs needs to allow risk managers to enforce their decisions and strategies. This section provides a discussion of the most advanced risk management techniques currently in use together with a brief analysis of what is the most appropriate risk governance structure.

CAPITAL ALLOCATION STRATEGY

Portfolio selection strategies have been a major topic in the literature during the last 60 years, especially after Markowitz (1952). However, few studies analyze how to apply these strategies to FIs. This situation may seem strange considering that financial organizations are among the main investors in the financial markets; the reasons stem from several peculiarities that may have distracted the attention from FIs.

First, during most of the last 30 to 40 years capital tended to be cheap and easy to raise. This opportunity created the belief that every deal that looked profitable could be executed by letting market demand drive asset growth. Second, many viewed banking organizations as having the social function of providing funds to companies in order to start or grow their business and to consumers in order to buy homes or goods. Although this social function was prevalent as a capital allocation strategy, the opinion of shareholders, especially since the 1990s, tended to be that banks should be a profit-making institution. Thus, to please shareholders and to outperform peers, chief executive officers (CEOs) in banking aggressively invested in complex assets, mixing their traditional lending culture with a more speculative equity one (Blundell-Wignal, Atkinson, and Lee, 2008).

The business model for FIs moved toward an equity culture with a focus on faster share price growth and earnings expansion. Because the previous model, based on balance sheets and old-fashioned spreads on loans, was not conducive to FIs becoming "growth stocks," the strategy switched more toward an activity-based framework, rendered on trading income and fees via securitization. This change enabled FIs to grow earnings while at the same time economizing on capital by gaming the Basel system.

In implementing this cultural change, most FIs focused mainly on the expected return side of their investment, omitting the risk side. Concentrations in highly correlated assets increased markedly without any consideration of the volatility of their losses. Portfolio diversification became a purely theoretical and easily sacrificed concept to allow the market share to grow. Pricing was mainly set to be competitive in the market and not to guarantee an appropriate return.

Ultimately, the 2007–2008 financial crisis provided FIs with the right incentives to correct the shortfalls previously mentioned. Yet, to achieve this, having a well-defined and fully embedded risk appetite strategy is essential to ensure that accepted risks and rewards are aligned with shareholders' expectations.

In his seminal study, Markowitz (1952) explains how to build the most efficient investment portfolio to find the right balance between expected returns and volatility of losses. He demonstrates that diversification is the best tool to reduce the risk of the entire portfolio.

The risk function of a FI cannot define a risk appetite framework by itself; it needs the help of its business (sales) department to model the expected returns. Articulating a consistent and effective risk appetite framework requires joining the efforts of those involved in risk management with those of others in business through a top-down approach. Ultimately, the board of directors, interpreting shareholders' views, needs to steer the way forward in terms of acceptable risks and required returns. Then, following these guidelines, the risk and the business functions can define risk appetite at different levels, such as the group, divisional, and portfolio level.

A good risk appetite framework should consist of two parts. The first part presents a picture of the current situation by clarifying how capital is currently allocated among portfolios and identifying the main concentrations and portfolios that are below the expected minimum return. Clarifying this picture also requires defining the required metrics.

Following Markowitz (1952), the standard deviation (σ) of the losses and the return on equity (ROE) for each portfolio should be calculated. Expected returns can also be measured by more sophisticated metrics or risk-adjusted performance measures (RAPM), such as risk-adjusted return on capital (RAROC), return on risk-adjusted capital (RORAC), or risk-adjusted return on equity (RAROE). For example, a bank that offers just three products, such as mortgages (P1), credit cards (P2), and small- and medium-sized enterprise (SME) loans (P3), can be represented by using "bubbles" of different sizes indicating how much capital is allocated in each portfolio, as shown in Figure 16.1.

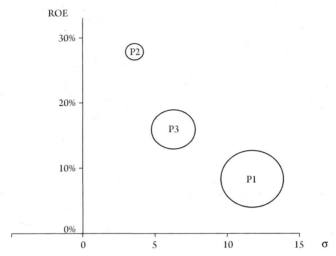

Figure 16.1. Portfolio selection for banks. This figure shows the possible distribution of three portfolios in a bank's risk appetite picture: mortgages (P1), credit cards (P2), and SME loans (P3). The two axes show the expected return on equity (ROE) and the expected volatility of losses. The size of the bubble indicates the quantity of capital such as risk-weighted assets (RWA) or economic capital (EC) absorbed by the specific portfolio.

After developing the picture, the second part that a good risk appetite framework should consist of involves building the framework. Following the guidelines of a company's board of directors in terms of expected return and volatility of losses, four lines can be drawn to separate different areas in the model. Two lines should show the minimum expected return and the maximum acceptable risk, defining the *risk capacity* (or risk tolerance) of the institution. The other two lines indicate the desired expected return and the desired acceptable risk, defining the bank's *risk appetite*.

Distinguishing risk capacity from risk appetite is important in several respects. First, these two concepts differ substantially. Confusing them could lead to generating uncertainty around what is possible and what is desired. Second, each concept has a specific time horizon. While risk capacity is a long-term statement, risk appetite should change frequently, adapting to the market and economic situation.

Drawing the risk appetite and risk capacity lines (thresholds) in the graph allows limits to be implemented in order to classify assets/portfolios in the different areas and specific concentration strategies to be defined based on them (e.g., the goal of increasing, decreasing, or keeping growth stable). Figure 16.2 describes how the risk appetite and risk capacity limits should be represented in a visual framework.

As indicated for the previous figure, the size of the bubbles in Figure 16.2 represent the concentration in the specific product, portfolio, sector, or country. Several metrics can be used to define the bubble size, such as balance, RC, or EC. The choice depends on the level of sophistication that the FI has reached in measuring the allocated capital.

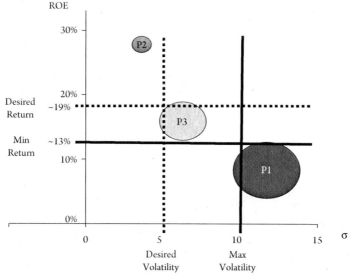

Figure 16.2. Definition of the risk appetite framework. This figure shows how a risk appetite framework can be defined. Following the guidelines of a company's board of directors, the risk tolerance and the risk appetite lines can be drawn in the picture and the different portfolios (P1, P2, and P3) can be classified in the appropriate areas. The step that follows this one consists of defining the mitigating actions to be implemented so that portfolios move to desired levels of returns and volatility.

The risk appetite framework should describe how the capital allocation strategy should change when the components of portfolios end up in the different areas, as determined by the defined limits, but it should not set the specific concentration limits for each product, portfolio, country, or sector. These limits should be decided in a limit concentration framework using a top-down approach. Separating the risk appetite framework from the concentration framework is important mainly from the implementation point of view. Concentrations are more difficult to influence and slower to change than the parameters that influence expected returns and volatility of losses.

Once the risk appetite framework is fully embedded, debate is motivated and it is ensured that risks are made explicit. To change behaviors in relation to risk in a company, interventions through additional training or changing personnel may be needed. Yet, in most organizations, the tone set by senior management tends to have the greatest impact. Risk appetite is not only a framework but also a deep cultural change that will ensure that FIs are more solid in the next future.

ENTERPRISE RISK MANAGEMENT

FIs and the academic world have extensively discussed enterprise risk management (ERM) for at least the last ten years. The numerous papers and books written on this topic provide clear guidelines and theoretical background to support this fundamental change in risk management (e.g., Doherty, 2000; D'Arcy, 2001; Lam, 2003; Olson and Wu, 2008). However, today, few FIs have tried to implement ERM and even fewer have been successful in embedding it in their management culture.

The ERM concept is relatively simple: Risks that may affect the value of an organization are all of a different nature, and their sum does not give the total risk. Several correlations and covariance should be considered when different risks are aggregated. ERM is a rigorous approach to assessing and addressing the risks from all sources that threaten the achievement of an organization's strategic objectives. A well-implemented ERM approach should be able to provide a comprehensive and coherent view of the risks that an institution is facing, allowing senior management to focus on the full picture and not on a single "silo."

The first step in operationalizing ERM is to identify the risks to which a firm is exposed. A common approach is to identify the types of risks to be measured. Many firms have gone beyond measuring market, credit, and operational risks. In particular, in recent years, firms have also attempted to measure liquidity, reputation, tax, pension, and strategic risks.

Organizations that have grown through acquisitions or without centralized information technology (IT) departments typically face the problem of having some systems that are incompatible with the others. Firms need to be able to aggregate common risks across all of their businesses to analyze and manage those risks effectively. The goal is to capture and quantify all risks by employing a consistent approach and then aggregate individual risk exposures across the entire organization and proceed to analyze the aggregate risk profile considering the risk correlations.

Ideally, a good ERM framework should be able to summarize all risks into one metric: the optimal level of available capital. A firm that practices ERM may have an amount of capital that substantially exceeds its regulatory requirements because it maximizes shareholder wealth by doing so. In this case, the regulatory requirements are not binding and would not affect the firm's decisions. The firm would be in a more difficult situation if its required RC exceeds the amount of capital it should hold to maximize shareholder wealth. RC for banks is generally defined in terms of regulatory accounting. For ERM, banks should focus on EC. An exclusive focus on RC is likely to be mistaken because it does not correctly reflect the buffer stock of available equity.

In summary, how to aggregate different risks remains the main challenge for all firms willing to implement an ERM approach and for FIs in particular. Often, forming a dialogue between IT systems, and the methodologies used to evaluate their respective risks is exceptionally difficult. They differ so much that reconciling them in one single number is almost impossible. Ignoring these main issues by providing ERM reports that address risks "by silos" is useless and dangerous. Some time may be needed to build the right infrastructure to implement an ERM framework, but FIs should be convinced that this is the best way to avoid mistakes that could potentially threaten their existence.

RISK GOVERNANCE STRUCTURE

The lack of an appropriate risk governance structure dissolves any benefit generated by a first-class risk management team. Before the financial crisis of 2007–2008, the role of risk management was extremely marginal at most institutions, leaving the ability of influencing business decisions to the persuasive skills of each risk manager and not to his authority.

The role of the chief risk officer (CRO) and the importance of risk governance in the financial industry have been highlighted in newspapers and in various reports (e.g., Brancato, Tonello, Hexter, and Newman, 2006), as well as in practitioner-oriented studies (e.g., Banham, 2000). Yet, the academic literature has largely neglected these areas so far.

A few recent academic studies (e.g., Erkens, Hung, and Matos, 2010; Minton, Taillard, and Williamson, 2010; Beltratti and Stulz, 2011; Fahlenbrach and Stulz, 2011) have addressed some other aspects of corporate governance in banks, such as board characteristics and CEO pay structure. However, the literature on corporate governance and its valuation effect in financial firms is still very limited. Moreover, FIs have particularities such as higher opaqueness as well as heavy regulation and intervention by the government (Levine, 2004) that require a distinct analysis of corporate governance issues. Adams and Mehran (2003) as well as Macey and O'Hara (2003) highlight the importance of taking into consideration differences in governance between banking and nonbanking firms.

In particular, in most FIs the CRO is still not a board member and the risk managers in the divisions often have only dotted lines for reporting to him and solid ones for the business heads. This structure means that risk managers can discuss issues with the bank's CRO, but their boss, the one who will assess their performance and set their objectives, is the head of business, whose objectives are usually in contrast with risk management objectives. This kind of organizational structure has clearly proved to be inappropriate because it precludes the possibility for risk to influence strategic decisions when needed. The independence of the risk function must be ensured, and supervisory authorities need to continuously monitor this to avoid having FIs focus again on short-term speculative investments to generate unsustainable results (Aebi et al., 2011).

Yet, empowering risk management and ensuring its independence will not solve all problems if the quality of the function does not improve accordingly. Senior management needs to drive the improvement, moving toward a more effective and efficient role of risk by increasing its involvement in daily decisions substantially and ensuring the stability and soundness of the overall process. The board needs to pay more attention to risk in general, approving and monitoring in regard to the risk appetite framework through good ERM reporting.

Summary and Conclusions

The topics covered in this chapter reflect the current status of risk management. Much work has been done and quite often in the right direction, but a new era has just started. Beyond the immediate pressures of global markets, more demanding customers, and dramatic industry change is a growing recognition that FIs have an opportunity to drive competitive advantage with their risk management capabilities, enabling long-term profitable growth and sustained future profitability. These changes mean that risk management at the top-performing organizations is now more closely integrated with strategic planning and is conducted proactively, with an eye on how such capabilities might help a company move into new markets faster or pursue other evolving growth strategies. At its best, risk management is a matter of balance—the balance between a company's appetite for risks and its ability to manage them.

Methodologies and tools applied to measure risks have evolved tremendously since the 1990s. Credit and market risk have led the evolution and have now reached a more advanced status. At present, the focus is moving toward operational and the other "minor" risk types. Also, risk aggregation is the next challenge for most financial organizations.

In terms of risk management, three main topics have emerged after the last financial crisis: (1) capital allocation, (2) ERM, and (3) risk governance structure. FIs that can address these issues effectively will have a competitive advantage and will be rewarded by financial markets. Risk management is now a priority at most financial and nonfinancial companies that are investing substantially in systems and people. This is a great opportunity for risk management to finally find the appropriate leading role in the changing financial culture.

Discussion Questions

1. Identify the original first (in time) methodology applied to estimate default in a prediction model and describe its weaknesses.
2. Explain the benefits of using a logit methodology to develop default prediction models.
3. Discuss the approaches that can be used to quantify operational risk under Basel II.
4. What is the difference between risk capacity and risk appetite? Why is distinguishing between the two concepts important?
5. What is the main objective of ERM?
6. How is risk appetite defined?

References

Adams, René B., and Hamid Mehran. 2003. "Is Corporate Governance Different for Bank Holding Companies?" *Federal Reserve Bank of New York Economic Policy Review* 9:1, 123–142.

Aebi, Vincent, Gabriele Sabato, and Markus Schmid. 2012. "Risk Management, Corporate Governance, and Bank Performance in the Financial Crisis." *Journal of Banking and Finance* 36:12, 3213–3226.

Altman, Edward I. 1968. "Financial Ratios, Discriminant Analysis and the Prediction of Corporate Bankruptcy." *Journal of Finance* 23:4, 589–611.

Altman, Edward I., Robert Haldeman, and Paul Narayanan. 1977. "ZETA Analysis: A New Model to Identify Bankruptcy Risk of Corporations." *Journal of Banking and Finance* 1:1, 29–54.

Altman, Edward I., and Gabriele Sabato. 2005. "Effects of the New Basel Capital Accord on Bank Capital Requirements for SMEs." *Journal of Financial Services Research* 28:1/3, 15–42.

Altman, Edward I., and Gabriele Sabato. 2007. "Modeling Credit Risk for SMEs: Evidence from the US Market." *ABACUS* 43:3, 332–357.

Araten, Michel, Michael Jacobs Jr., and Peeyush Varshney. 2004. "Measuring LGD on Commercial Loans: An 18-Year Internal Study." *RMA Journal*, May, 28–35.

Asarnow, Elliot, and David Edwards. 1995. "Measuring Loss on Defaulted Bank Loans: A 24-Year Study." *Journal of Commercial Lending* 77:7, 11–23.

Aziz, Abdul, David C. Emanuel, and Gerald H. Lawson. 1988. "Bankruptcy Prediction—An Investigation of Cash Flow Based Models." *Journal of Management Studies* 25:5, 419–437.

Banham, Russ. 2000. "Top Cops of Risk." *CFO* 16:10, 91–98.

Barnes, Paul. 1982. "Methodological Implications of Non-Normally Distributed Financial Ratios." *Journal of Business Finance and Accounting* 9:1, 51–62.

Basel Committee on Banking Supervision. 1988. *International Convergence of Capital Measurement and Capital Standards.* Basel: Bank for International Settlements.

Basel Committee on Banking Supervision. 2004. Basel II: *International Convergence of Capital Measurement and Capital Standards: A Revised Framework.* Basel: Bank for International Settlements.

Basel Committee on Banking Supervision. 2008. *Principles for Sound Liquidity Risk Management and Supervision.* Basel: Bank for International Settlements.

Basel Committee on Banking Supervision. 2010. *Recognising the Risk-Mitigating Impact of Insurance in Operational Risk Modelling.* Basel: Bank for International Settlements.

Bastos, João A. 2010. "Forecasting Bank Loans Loss-Given-Default." *Journal of Banking and Finance* 34:10, 2510–2517.

Beaver, William. 1967. "Financial Ratios Predictors of Failure. Empirical Research in Accounting: Selected Studies 1966." *Journal of Accounting Research*, no. S4, 71–111.

Becchetti, Leonardo, and Jaime Sierra. 2002. "Bankruptcy Risk and Productive Efficiency in Manufacturing Firms." *Journal of Banking and Finance* 27:11, 2099–2120.

Bellotti, Tony, and Jonathan Crook. 2007. "Modelling and Predicting Loss Given Default for Credit Cards." Working Paper, Qualitative Financial Risk Management Centre, University of Edinburgh.

Beltratti, Andrea, and René M. Stulz. 2011. "The Credit Crisis around the Globe: Why Did Some Banks Perform Better during the Credit Crisis?" *Journal of Financial Economics*, forthcoming.

Blum, Marc. 1974. "Failing Company Discriminant Analysis." *Journal of Accounting Research* 12:1, 1–25.

Blundell-Wignall, Adrian, Paul Atkinson, and Se Hoon Lee. 2008. "The Current Financial Crisis: Causes and Policy Issues." *OECD Financial Market Trends* 95:2, 1–21.

Brancato, Carolyn, Matteo Tonello, Ellen Hexter, and Katharine R. Newman. 2006. *The Role of U.S. Corporate Boards in Enterprise Risk Management.* New York: Conference Board.

Caselli, Stefano, Stefano Gatti, and Francesca Querci. 2008. "The Sensitivity of the Loss Given Default Rate to Systematic Risk: New Empirical Evidence on Bank Loans." *Journal of Financial Services Research* 34:1, 1–34.

D'Arcy, Stephen P. 2001. "Enterprise Risk Management." *Journal of Risk Management of Korea* 12:1, 23–37.

Deakin, Edward B. 1972. "A Discriminant Analysis of Predictors of Business Failure." *Journal of Accounting Research* 10:1, 167–179.

Dermine, Jean M., and Cristina Neto de Carvalho. 2006. "Bank Loan Losses-Given-Default: A Case Study." *Journal of Banking and Finance* 30:4, 1291–1243.

Doherty, Neil A. 2000. *Integrated Risk Management: Techniques and Strategies for Managing Corporate Risk*. New York: McGraw-Hill.

Durand, David. 1941. *Risk Elements in Consumer Installment Lending. Studies in Consumer Installment Financing*, vol. 8. New York: National Bureau of Economic Research.

Eales, Robert, and Edmund Bosworth. 1998. "Severity of Loss in the Event of Default in Small Business and Large Consumer Loans." *Journal of Lending & Credit Risk Management* 80:9, 58–65.

Edmister, Robert O. 1972. "An Empirical Test of Financial Ratio Analysis for Small Business Failure Prediction." *Journal of Financial and Quantitative Analysis* 7:2, 1477–1493.

Erkens, David H., Mingyi Hung, and Pedro Matos. 2010. "Corporate Governance in the 2007–2008 Financial Crisis: Evidence from Financial Institutions Worldwide." *Journal of Corporate Finance* 18:2, 389–411.

Fahlenbrach, Rüdiger, and René M. Stulz. 2011. "Bank CEO Incentives and the Credit Crisis." *Journal of Financial Economics* 99:1, 11–26.

Felsovalyi, Akos, and Lew Hurt. 1998. "Measuring Loss on Latin American Defaulted Bank Loans: A 27-Year Study of 27 Countries." *Journal of Lending & Credit Risk Management* 81:2, 41–46.

Financial Services Authority. 2008. *Strengthening Liquidity Standards*. London: Financial Services Authority.

Fisher, Ronald Aymer. 1936. "The Use of Multiple Measurements in Taxonomic Problems." *Annals of Eugenic* 7:7, 179–188.

Gentry, James A., Paul Newbold, and David T. Whitford. 1985. "Classifying Bankrupt Firms with Funds Flow Components." *Journal of Accounting Research* 23:1, 146–160.

Gombola, Michael J., Mark E. Haskins, J. Edward Ketz, and David D. Williams. 1987. "Cash Flow in Bankruptcy Prediction." *Financial Management* 16:4, 55–65.

Grunert, Jens, and Martin Weber. 2009. "Recovery Rates of Commercial Lending: Empirical Evidence for German Companies." *Journal of Banking and Finance* 33:2, 505–513.

Institute of International Finance. 2007. *Principles of Liquidity Risk Management*. Washington, DC: Institute of International Finance.

Karels, Gordon V., and Arun J. Prakash. 1987. "Multivariate Normality and Forecasting of Business Bankruptcy." *Journal of Business Finance & Accounting* 14:4, 573–593.

Lam, James. 2003. *Enterprise Risk Management: From Incentives to Control*. New York: John Wiley and Sons.

Levine, Ross. 2004. "The Corporate Governance of Banks: A Concise Discussion of Concepts and Evidence." Policy Research Working Paper 3404, World Bank, Corporate Governance Department, Global Corporate Governance Forum, Washington, DC.

Lussier, Robert N. 1995. "A Non-Financial Business Success versus Failure Prediction Model for Young Firms." *Journal of Small Business Management* 33:1, 8–20.

Macey, Jonathan R., and Maureen O'Hara. 2003. "The Corporate Governance of Banks." *Federal Reserve Bank of New York Economic Policy Review* 9:1, 91–107.

Markowitz, Harry. 1952. "Portfolio Selection." *Journal of Finance* 7:1, 77–91.

McLeay, Stuart, and Azmi Omar. 2000. "The Sensitivity of Prediction Models to the Non-Normality of Bounded and Unbounded Financial Ratios." *British Accounting Review* 32:2, 213–230.

Micha, Bernard. 1984. "Analysis of Business Failures in France." *Journal of Banking and Finance* 8:2, 281–291.

Minton, Bernardette A., Jérôme Taillard, and Rohan G. Williamson. 2010. "Do Independence and Financial Expertise of the Board Matter for Risk Taking and Performance?" Working Paper 2010–03–014, Fisher College of Business, Ohio State University, Columbus, OH.

Mossman, Charles E., Geoff G. Bell, Mick L. Swartz, and Harry Turtle. 1998. "An Empirical Comparison of Bankruptcy Models." *Financial Review* 33(2): 35–54.

Ohlson, James A. 1980. "Financial Ratios and the Probabilistic Prediction of Bankruptcy." *Journal of Accounting Research* 18:1, 109–131.

Olson, David Louis, and Desheng Dash Wu, eds. 2008. *New Frontiers in Enterprise Risk Management*. Berlin: Springer.

Ooghe, Hubert, Philip Joos, and Carl de Bourdeaudhuij. 1995. "Financial Distress Models in Belgium: The Results of a Decade of Empirical Research." *International Journal of Accounting* 30:3, 245–274.

Platt, Harlan D., and Marjorie B. Platt. 1990. "Development of a Class of Stable Predictive Variables: The Case of Bankruptcy Prediction." *Journal of Business Finance & Accounting* 17:1, 31– 51.

Sabato, Gabriele. 2008. "Managing Credit Risk for Retail Low-Default Portfolios." In *Credit Risk: Models, Derivatives and Management*, edited by Niklas Wagner, 269–288. Boca Raton, FL: Chapman & Hall.

Sabato, Gabriele. 2010. "Credit Risk Scoring Models." In *Encyclopedia of Quantitative Finance*, edited by Rama Cont, Chapter 19, vol. 3. Chichester, UK: John Wiley & Sons.

Sabato, Gabriele, and Markus M. Schmid. 2008. "Estimating Conservative Loss Given Default." Working Paper, University of St. Gallen, Swiss Institute of Finance and Banking, St. Gallen, Switzerland.

Taffler, Richard J., and Howard J. Tisshaw. 1977. "Going, Going, Gone: Four Factors Which Predict." *Accountancy* 88:1003, 50–54.

Walker, David. 2009. *A Review of Corporate Governance in UK Banks and Other Financial Industry Entities: Final Recommendations*. London: Walker Review Secretariat.

Zavgren, Christine V. 1983. "The Prediction of Corporate Failure: The State of the Art." *Journal of Accounting Literature* 2:1, 1–37.

PORTFOLIO EXECUTION, MONITORING, AND REBALANCING

17

Trading Strategies, Portfolio Monitoring, and Rebalancing

RICCARDO CESARI
Professor of Mathematical Finance, University of Bologna

MASSIMILIANO MARZO
Professor of Economics, University of Bologna

Introduction

All trading strategies are defined in terms of goals and constraints and specify the necessity of continuous monitoring in order to assess the effectiveness of the strategy in achieving the portfolio's stated objective. Rebalancing is the result of portfolio monitoring, consisting of a set of trading rules aimed at repositioning the portfolio in order to better accomplish goals and constraints. Various reasons exist according to which rational investors trade in financial markets and adjust their financial portfolios, including: (1) market price movements, to be distinguished in noisy (transitory) and structural (persistent) movements; (2) the modification of individual characteristics, among which personal wealth is of the greatest importance; (3) the receipt of new information, expectations, and learning, suggesting the need for improving portfolios; and (4) the passage of time, making previous portfolio positions no longer optimal (as in portfolio insurance or life-cycle investments). Figure 17.1 illustrates the circular interactions between trading strategies, monitoring, and rebalancing decisions.

Suppose that a portfolio manager has selected an optimal asset allocation, represented by the vector w*(t) of percentage holdings in m risky assets. Possible portfolio adjustments will need to be evaluated in subsequent periods. If w_t(t+1) is the portfolio allocation obtained with time t quantities and time t+1 prices, the allocation dynamics from t to t+1 are reflected in Equation 17.1:

$$W_{t+1}(t+1) = W_t(t) + \left[W_t(t+1) - W_t(t)\right] + \left[W^*(t) - W_t(t+1)\right]$$
$$+ \left[W^*(t+1) - W^*(t)\right] + \left[W_{t+1}(t+1) - W^*(t+1)\right] \quad (17.1)$$

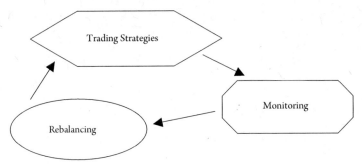

Figure 17.1 Trading, monitoring, and rebalancing. The figure illustrates the circular interactions between trading strategies, monitoring, and rebalancing decisions.

where the four components in brackets represent, respectively, the change in allocation due to price movements (*passive rebalancing*), the distance from the old target w*(t), the change in the optimal target (*target rebalancing*), and the distance between the new portfolio and the new target w*(t+1) (*portfolio rebalancing*).

As documented in Calvet, Campbell, and Sodini (2009), for about one half of a large sample of Swedish households, passive rebalancing in the period 1999–2002 has been offset by the other kinds of rebalancing (target rebalancing plus portfolio rebalancing). The offsetting adjustments have been greater in the case of affluent investors in terms of wealth, education, and income. Cremers and Mei (2004) estimate that risk management concerns motivate about 75 percent of trading activity.

Equation 17.2 simplifies the first component in Equation 17.1, thus obtaining:

$$W_{t+1}(t+1) = W^*(t) + \left[W^*(t+1) - W^*(t)\right] + \left[W_{t+1}(t+1) - W^*(t+1)\right], \quad (17.2)$$

so that even in the case of a constant target w*, portfolio rebalancing is required to offset price movements.

In many situations, rebalancing is defined simply as the trading activity by which an optimal (strategic) allocation among different asset classes (target constant mix [CM]), altered by the market movements of relative prices, is restored by selling (buying) the asset class that is increasing (decreasing) in value ("sell high and buy low").

Two questions arise concerning this meaning of rebalancing for an investor. First, is restoring the target asset mix a good idea? That is, is the original asset allocation still optimal, or are market-relative movements void of useful information and just an effect of noise and randomness? A negative answer to this question would imply the need to move from a static to a dynamic asset allocation, considering target rebalancing as an endogenous choice in an allocation process in which adjustments are costly. Second, what trade-offs exist between transaction costs and tracking errors (so that rebalancing becomes a proper optimization problem)?

Clearly, in the ideal situation of frictionless markets, continuous rebalancing would be costless, guaranteeing a zero tracking error with respect to any target mix. With transaction costs, rebalancing must jointly take into account two negative elements: the distance from the target and the cost of reducing such a distance.

The purpose of this chapter is to review the implementation of trading strategies that is done when asset prices fluctuate randomly and both monitoring costs and transaction costs impede continuous adjustments. The remainder of the chapter is organized as follows: The first section is devoted to two cornerstone results of asset allocation theory, the Markowitz (1959) static optimal portfolio and the Merton (1971) dynamic extension, showing the conditions required to obtain their equivalence (myopic portfolios). The second section introduces transaction costs and their effects on optimal decisions for portfolios. The general result of a no-trade region induced by transaction costs is analyzed both in the simple two-asset case (involving a risk-free and a risky asset) and in the more complex multiasset case. Moreover, the cases of an absolute target (in mean-variance terms) and a relative target (a benchmark) are discussed. The empirical literature on simple rebalancing rules is reviewed and the allocation consequences of monitoring costs evaluated. The third section considers two important examples of target rebalancing, portfolio insurance and life-cycle investments, in which rebalancing is directed to the protection of the future value of the portfolio, a goal particularly appreciated by investors in times of highly volatile markets. A final section summarizes and concludes the chapter.

Myopic Portfolios and the Case for Rebalancing

Trading strategies (TS), both static and dynamic, can be classified, with respect to their objectives, into two broad classes: absolute and relative TS. *Absolute trading strategies* have an absolute goal that can be expressed in terms of risk or returns. Those absolute TS with a target risk maximize the portfolio return under the constraint of a given (maximum) risk, and those with a target return minimize the portfolio risk under the constraint of a given (minimum) return. *Relative trading strategies* have a goal that is often expressed in terms of a benchmark portfolio.

Figure 17.2 illustrates this simple taxonomy of TS.

Markowitz's (1952, 1959) work on mean-variance portfolio selection is the seminal reference on static, absolute trading strategies. According to his static analysis,

Figure 17.2 Absolute and relative trading strategies. The figure shows a simple taxonomy of TS.

considering one single-period (0–T) horizon and just two assets for simplicity, one riskless and one risky, the optimal risky position is given by Equation 17.3:

$$w_{0,T} = \frac{\mu_{0,T} - r_{0,T}}{\vartheta \sigma^2_{0,T}},$$

(17.3)

where ϑ is the investor's risk aversion parameter; $\mu_{0,T}$ ($r_{0,T}$) is the expected value of the risky (riskless) rate of return over the 0 to T horizon; and $\sigma^2_{0,T}$ is its variance.

If the 0–T horizon is composed by T-unit periods (e.g., months), in which the investor has full access to the financial markets to buy and sell securities (see Longstaff 2009, for major effects of nonmarketability and blackout periods), the same analysis would produce an optimal risky position weight for the first period, as shown in Equation 17.4:

$$w_{0,1} = \frac{\mu_{0,1} - r_{0,1}}{\vartheta \sigma^2_{0,1}},$$

(17.4)

and under the assumption of (serially) independent, identically distributed $D(\mu, \sigma^2)$ rates of returns (the IID hypothesis), the same allocation (called the Markowitz portfolio) would be optimal for every single period and for the overall period, as illustrated in Equation 17.5:

$$w^* = \frac{\mu - r}{\vartheta \sigma^2} = \frac{T\mu - Tr}{\vartheta T \sigma^2} = \frac{\mu_{0,T} - r_{0,T}}{\vartheta \sigma^2_{0,T}}.$$

(17.5)

This relationship implies that no target rebalancing is required from one period to the next and that the initial one-period allocation is optimal across time. In an intertemporal setting with a long-run horizon, this policy is called *myopic*, focusing on the near term, despite the longer-term target. If returns are not IID, this policy is suboptimal, with room for optimally rebalancing the allocation from one period to the next, up to the final time horizon.

One famous exception, pointed out by Mossin (1968) and Fama (1970), is represented by the investor with log utility in final wealth. As shown in Cesari (2010), the portfolio value at time T, W(T), can be expressed as shown in Equation 17.6:

$$W(T) = W(0) \prod_{t=0}^{T-1} \sum_{j=1}^{N} w_{j,t} \left(1 + R_j(t+1)\right),$$

(17.6)

where $R_j(t+1)$ is the rate of return of asset j between t and t+1, and $w_{j,t}$ is the weight of asset j at time t, so that the expected log utility is the sum of T expected logs, which can be maximized separately (i.e., myopically), as shown in Equation 17.7:

$$
\max_{w_0, w_1, \dots} \left\{ E_o\left(\log(W(T)) \right) \right\} \Rightarrow \max_{w_0, w_1, \dots} \left\{ \sum_{t=0}^{T-1} E_0 \left(\log\left(\sum_{j=1}^{N} w_{j,t}\left(1+R_j(t+1)\right) \right) \right) \right\}
$$

$$
\Rightarrow \sum_{t=0}^{T-1} \max_{w_t} \left\{ E_t\left(\log\left(\sum_{j=1}^{N} w_{j,t}\left(1+R_j(t+1)\right) \right) \right) \right\} . \qquad (17.7)
$$

This relationship implies that in each period t, the investor has to maximize $E_t \log(W(t+1)/W(t))$, which is the expected continuously compounded rate of growth of wealth ("growth-optimal policy"). Rebalancing should take place from one period to the next, but under the additional hypothesis of lognormal distribution for values, the Equation 17.8 applies (see Equation 17.5 for the symbol definitions):

$$
E_t \log\left(\frac{W(t+1)}{W(t)} \right) = r + w(\mu - r) - \frac{1}{2} w^2 \sigma^2, \qquad (17.8)
$$

and the optimal myopic policy is again the constant Markowitz portfolio w^* with $\vartheta = 1$ (isoelastic utility).

Merton (1969, 1971) generalizes this result under the now-classical setting of continuous time, continuous trading, and diffusion processes. With only two assets, Merton assumes that asset prices are governed by the general dynamics in Equation 17.9:

$$
\frac{dP_1(t)}{P_1(t)} = \mu(t)dt + \sigma(t)dZ(t)
$$
$$
\frac{dP_0(t)}{P_0(t)} = r(t)dt \qquad , \qquad (17.9)
$$

where $\mu(t)$ is the expected rate of return, $\sigma(t)$ is the return volatility, and $r(t)$ is the short-term interest rate and that the investor maximizes the expected lifetime discounted utility of consumption and final wealth $W(T)$. He thereby shows that the optimal portfolio is given by Equation 17.10:

$$
w^*(t) = \frac{J_W}{-J_{WW}W(t)} \frac{\mu(t)-r(t)}{\sigma^2(t)} + \frac{J_{1W}P_1(t)}{-J_{WW}W(t)}, \qquad (17.10)
$$

where $J(W, P_1, t)$ is the maximized indirect utility function (Bellman's value function) and J_W, J_{WW}, J_{1W} are the partial derivatives with respect to wealth W and price P_1. Under price lognormality, J is no longer function of prices, the hedging demand for price movements is zero, and the optimal allocation is in Equation 17.11:

$$w^*(t) = \frac{J_W}{-J_{WW}W(t)} \frac{\mu - r}{\sigma^2}, \qquad (17.11)$$

where time dependence of w^* comes only from the (indirect) relative risk aversion coefficient, that is $-J_{ww}(W,t)\,W(t)/J_w(W,t)$.

Using the general class of discounted hyperbolic absolute risk aversion utilities (HARA), as in Equation 17.12:

$$U(W,t) = e^{-\rho t} \frac{1-\gamma}{\gamma} \left(\frac{\beta W}{1-\gamma} + \eta \right)^\gamma, \qquad (17.12)$$

the dynamics of the optimally invested wealth are given by Equation 17.13:

$$dW(t) = \left(r + w^*(t)(\mu - r) - \frac{c^*(t)}{W(t)} \right) W(t)dt + \sigma w^*(t)W(t)dZ(t), \qquad (17.13)$$

and the optimal portfolio is shown in Equation 17.14:

$$w^*(t) = \frac{\mu - r}{(1-\gamma)\sigma^2} \left(1 + \frac{(1-\gamma)\eta}{rW(t)\beta}\left(1 - e^{-r(T-t)}\right) \right), \qquad (17.14)$$

so that continuous rebalancing is required. Some possible time paths of the portfolio allocation and its time changes (target rebalances) are given in Figure 17.3 for values of parameters $\mu = 5$ percent, $\sigma = 30$ percent, $\gamma = -4$, $r = 1$ percent, and monthly time steps.

Figure 17.3 shows that, under general conditions, the optimal target portfolio is changing over time and requires a substantial amount of rebalancing activity in order to maintain the correct diversification of investments.

With constant relative risk aversion (CRRA) utility $\eta = 0$, the optimal intertemporal allocation is again the Markowitz constant portfolio, requiring portfolio rebalancing only to offset price movements. As Campbell and Viceira (2002) contend, CRRA is, in fact, a plausible assumption given that from a long-run perspective, per capita wealth has increased greatly in many countries during the last century, while risk premia have not shown any long-term trend. This empirical observation implies that relative risk aversion (RRA) as percentage compensation for bearing the risk (Pratt, 1964) is, *prima facie*, independent of wealth and other trended state variables.

Portfolio Allocation and Rebalancing with Transaction Costs

In the final, applied chapter of his seminal book *Portfolio Selection: Efficient Diversification of Investments*, Markowitz (1959, 300) recognizes the issue of

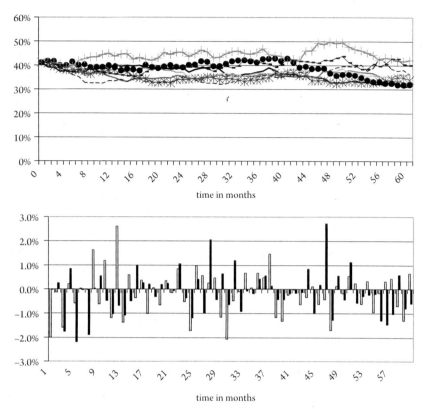

Figure 17.3 Simulated values and changes of optimal portfolios with the HARA utility. Assuming hyperbolic absolute risk aversion, the upper figure shows eight possible paths of the optimal risky asset allocation in a five-year time window, and the lower figure shows the required rebalancing from one month to the next.

illiquidities and transaction costs, arguing that "The Rational Investor must move more slowly toward his desired portfolio because of the existence of these illiquidities." Suggesting this critical area for important future development, in the introduction of the book, Markowitz (p. xii) states: "My own chief theoretical worry remains with the gap between a theory based on perfect liquidity and the existence of illiquidities." Bid-ask spreads, brokerage fees, trading taxes (e.g., Tobin's tax and capital gain tax), and the price impact of sales/purchases represent the main sources of illiquidity (Demsetz, 1968; Collins and Fabozzi, 1991).

Classical research on this subject distinguishes differences between liquidity and marketability. As Hicks (1962, 789) points out, following Keynes (1930), the characteristic of a liquid asset is that it can be "certainly realizable at short notice without loss." The first part of this definition ("certainly realizable at short notice") is specific to the wider class of marketable assets; the second part ("without loss") identifies the subset of liquid assets. A liquid asset is marketable but not vice versa. The presence of transaction costs generates illiquidities even if it is compatible with perfect marketability. Longstaff (2009) provides recent developments and references on this issue.

Various researchers provide early contributions on portfolio selection and transaction costs. For example, Smith (1968) compares, in a simulation experiment, buy and hold (BH), constant mix (CM), and two other kinds of dynamic adjustment strategies. Leland (1974) and Goldsmith (1976) consider fixed transaction costs in a single-period model. However, in the wake of Merton's (1969, 1971, 1973) dynamic approach, Magill and Constantinides (1976) produced a pathbreaking paper and a cornerstone result on the subject. Apart from a technical error pointed out by Darrell Duffie and corrected in Constantinides (1986), in their text Magill and Constantinides provide for the first time a general framework to endogenize consumption and trading decisions when transactions are costly in proportion to the monetary size of trade.

PORTFOLIO DECISIONS WITH CONSUMPTION: TWO-ASSET CASE

In Magill and Constantinides's (1976) model, a competitive market in continuous time is characterized by m risky assets with lognormal price dynamics, as illustrated in Equation 17.15:

$$\frac{dP_j(t)}{P_j(t)} = \mu_j dt + \sigma_j dZ_j(t),$$

(17.15)

where, μ_j is the expected (total) rate of return of asset j, and σ_j is the volatility parameter, amplifying the random shocks dZ_j and a riskless bank account, with constant interest rate r ($m+1$ assets in total), and price dynamics as shown in Equation 17.16:

$$\frac{dP_0(t)}{P_0(t)} = rdt.$$

(17.16)

In this model, assets are perfectly marketable but transaction costs are incurred in the purchase or sale of each risky security and paid by the bank account. The latter is increased (decreased) by sales (purchases) and decreased by transaction costs, proportional to the amount exchanged but with possibly different coefficients, k_s, k_b, respectively.

For the decision maker maximizing his lifetime (T-period) expected utility of consumption, the problem is a case of stochastic optimal control and the solution is the optimal trading-consumption policy, indicating at any time t the buying and selling decisions for each asset and the amount to consume $c(t)$.

A manageable case is obtained assuming just two assets, one risky and one risk free, and a power utility $u(c) = c^\gamma/\gamma$, with CRRA = $1 - \gamma$. In this case, Merton's (1973) result, in absence of transaction costs, provides a constant optimal asset allocation (myopic trading strategy or Markowitz-Merton portfolio), as in Equation 17.17:

$$w*(t)=w*=\frac{\mu-r}{(1-\gamma)\sigma^2},\qquad(17.17)$$

and, therefore, a constant risky/riskless asset ratio $w*/(1-w*)$.

The solution obtained by Magill and Constantinides (1976), amended in Constantinides (1986), and extended by Davis and Norman (1990), is the identification of a no-trade region between $w*_{min}$ and $w*_{max}$ (geometrically, a segment with just one risky asset, $m = 1$, an area for $m = 2$, and the like). The optimal trading strategy becomes the following: (1) if $w(t) < w*_{min}$ buy the risky asset up to $w*_{min}$; (2) if $w(t) > w*_{max}$ sell the risky asset down to $w*_{max}$; or (3) if $w*_{min} \le w(t) \le w*_{max}$ do not trade.

This finding means that the optimal allocation is no longer a point value but an entire region. A graphical representation of the no-trade wedge is shown in Figure 17.4, where the classical Markowitz-Merton allocation is seen as a special case (when transaction costs are zero) inside the no-trade area.

The critical points $w*_{min}$ and $w*_{max}$ depend on the transaction cost parameters k_s and k_b and the other parameters (mean, variance, and interest rate) of the model. As Davis and Norman (1990) report, by setting $k_s = k_b = 1.5$ percent, r = 7 percent, μ = 12 percent, σ = 40 percent, and γ = −1, you get the results in the Markowitz-Merton allocation of $w* = 15.6$ percent and in the no-trade interval of $w*_{min} = 9.0$ percent and $w*_{max} = 19.8$ percent. The optimal trading strategy is to stay inside the interval, preceded by an immediate transaction to the closest boundary if the initial endowment (e.g., 100 percent cash) is outside of the no-trade region.

As Magill and Constantinides (1976) observe, without transaction costs, the benefit from improved diversification would always induce the investor to continually

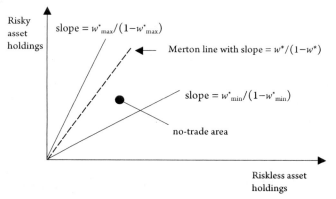

Figure 17.4 No-trade wedge in the case of one risky asset. The figure shows the space of possible asset holdings in the simple case of two assets, one risky and one risk-free. The dashed line represents Merton's optimal allocation (zero transaction costs), in which the two assets are in fixed proportions to one another. The continuous lines represent the boundaries (min and max allocation) of a no-trade region inside which it is optimal not to trade.

rebalance the portfolio to the optimal w*. As soon as the investor faces (proportional) transaction costs, this incessant trading would completely drain the portfolio. Thus, he must match the benefits of optimal diversification with the associated transaction costs. The no-trade area identifies the region in which the allocation is not "too distant" from the optimal portfolio to justify trading, or, equivalently, the region in which transaction costs exceed the benefits of improved diversification.

Technically, the optimally controlled portfolio inside the wedge is a stochastic process called "reflecting diffusion," and the buying and selling policies, $L(t)$ and $U(t)$, represented in monetary terms as cumulative (right continuous, nondecreasing, adapted) processes of all $0-t$ purchases and sales (respectively), are the "local times" of the asset value reaching the lower (buy) and upper (sell) boundaries of the wedge.

In fact, in absence of transaction costs (the Merton case), the optimization problem can be conditioned to the dynamics of the total wealth process $W(t)$ (budget constraint), as shown in Equation 17.18:

$$\frac{dW(t)}{W(t)} = \left(w(t)\mu + (1-w(t))r - \frac{c(t)}{W(t)} \right) dt + w(t)\sigma dZ(t)$$

$$W(t) \equiv V_1(t) + V_0(t) \equiv P_1(t)Q_1(t) + P_0(t)Q_0(t) \tag{17.18}$$

$$w(t) \equiv \frac{P_1(t)Q_1(t)}{W(t)},$$

where $V_j(t)$ is asset j (monetary) value, $Q_j(t)$ is asset j quantity in t (number of shares), and the decision variables can be identified in the portfolio allocation, $w(t)$, and the consumption rate, $c(t)$.

In the presence of transaction costs, the representation in Equation 17.18 is no longer possible. Three decision variables emerge with transaction costs: (1) the purchase of the risky asset (and the sale of the riskless asset), (2) the sale of the risky asset (and the purchase of the riskless asset), and (3) consumption.

The representation is shown in Equation 17.19:

$$dV_0(t) = (rV_0(t) - c(t))dt - (1+k_b)dL(t) + (1+k_s)dU(t)$$

$$dV_1(t) = \mu V_1(t)dt + \sigma V_1(t)dZ(t) + dL(t) - dU(t), \tag{17.19}$$

where, in the first line, both consumption and transaction costs deplete the current account, and in the second line, the value of the risky asset is increased by the purchases, $dL(t)$, and decreased by the sales, $dU(t)$. The triple $(L^*(t), U^*(t), c^*(t))$ (instantaneous control) represents the optimal trading-consumption policy.

Market practice defines $P_1^{ask} \equiv (1 + k_b)P_1$ as the ask price (buying price) and $P_1^{bid} \equiv (1 + k_s)P_1$ as the bid price (selling price). Asset quantity at time t is obtained as the initial quantity plus purchases less sales in Equation 17.20:

$$Q_1(t) = Q_1(0) + \int_0^t \frac{1}{P_1(s)}(dL(s) - dU(s)). \tag{17.20}$$

The distinguishing feature of Magill and Constantinides's (1976) paper is that it reaches the substantially correct result without all the required technical devices now available. As Davies and Norman (1990, p. 678) note:

> The paper was in fact well ahead of its time, in that an essential ingredient of any rigorous formulation, namely the theory of local time and reflecting diffusion, was unavailable to the authors, being at that time (1976) the exclusive property of a small band of pure mathematical votaries. Needless to say, Magill's and Constantinides' paper is far more valuable than many others of unimpeachable mathematical rectitude.

The model is of partial equilibrium in nature in the sense that asset price dynamics are exogenously given (see Equation 17.13). At a more theoretical level, an interesting issue to investigate is if transaction costs are compatible with a general equilibrium framework in which asset prices involve processes of unbounded variation (diffusions or semimartingales) as in the case of no trading costs (Amihud, Mendelson, and Pedersen, 2005).

With proportional trading costs, even in the simple two-asset case, no closed-form solutions are available. However, numerical methods, under appropriate conditions on the parameters (e.g., $0 < r < \mu < r + (1 - \gamma)\sigma^2$), can give the unique boundaries w^*_{min} and w^*_{max} (Dumas and Luciano, 1991).

Figure 17.5 provides a graphical representation of the optimal allocation $w(t)$ as a function of the level k ($= k_s = k_b$) of proportional transaction costs.

As unit transaction costs k in the figure increase, the no-trade area widens but not symmetrically. The upper boundary is less sensitive and the lower boundary decreases more rapidly, so that the optimal no-trade area is shifted toward the riskless asset and the demand for the risky asset decreases as transaction costs increase.

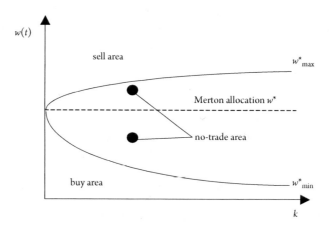

Figure 17.5 Optimal allocation boundaries for the risky asset as function of transaction costs. The figure shows how the level of transaction costs k, assumed to be the same for purchases and sales, affects the no-trade area. For $k = 0$, this represents Merton's allocation; with increasing k, the area widens but not in a symmetrical way.

This finding is a result of the consumption-investment interaction, given that, by construction, the consumption is withdrawn from the current account. High transaction costs reduce the minimum boundary w^*_{min} of the risky asset, given that buying the asset for investment and later reselling it for consumption may not be worthwhile. Overall, investors accommodate larger transaction costs by reducing the frequency and volume of trading.

In a slightly different model, in which consumption is not relevant (e.g., the investor is a financial institution), Dumas and Luciano (1991) find both a wider no-trade area and a more symmetric effect of an increasing transaction cost on the two boundaries (see also Taksar, Klass, and Assaf, 1988). As Dumas and Luciano explain, when consumption must be met from the existing current account, as in Constantinides's (1986) model, there is less room for fluctuations in the amount of available cash and there is more need to bias the portfolio in favor of cash than when consumption is postponed to a distant future.

An increase of the risk aversion parameter $1- \gamma$ has no significant effect on the width of the no-trade area, but it shifts the region toward the riskless asset, given that the demand for the risky asset is decreasing with increased risk aversion. The same sensitivities are obtained in the case of increasing volatility (σ).

Constantinides (1986) also shows that transaction costs have a small, decreasing effect on consumption. This finding combines (1) a positive substitution effect, given that current consumption is less costly in term of transaction costs than future consumption and (2) a negative income effect, given that higher transaction costs reduce disposable wealth.

Transaction costs affect the equilibrium rate of return of the risky asset. With respect to the case of no transaction costs, an (il)liquidity premium occurs as compensation for bearing an asset subject to costs of transaction. This (il)liquidity premium increases with transaction costs and asset volatility, given that the latter increases the frequency of transactions. According to Constantinides (1986), however, illiquidity premia, explained by transaction costs, represent only second-order effects on equilibrium asset returns. Therefore, transaction costs cannot explain large anomalies such as the negative relationship between average return and market size of stocks (Banz 1981). Jang et al. (2007), who build a generalized portfolio model with a risky and a risk-free asset but stochastic investment opportunity set, question this conclusion. In their model, contrary to most other studies, the parameters r, μ, and σ are stochastically changing and the optimal trading policies are significantly affected. In particular, they assume two regimes, the "Bull" (B) and the "bear" (b), so that all the fundamental parameters are regime-dependent and the financial market switches randomly between regimes. Given that σ_B is significantly less than σ_b, an investor can infer the state of the current regime from observing stock return volatility.

One relevant result is that the optimal trading strategy with proportional transaction costs is no longer myopic, with two possibly overlapping no-trade regions, one for a Bull and one for a bear regime. Second, the trading strategy in one regime is affected by the investment opportunity set in the other regime, so that the investor smoothes not only consumption but also trading strategies across regimes. For example, using parameter values (e.g., σ_B = 13 percent,

σ_b = 26 percent, a Bull average duration of 4.25 years, and a bear average duration of 0.58 years), the investor tends to hold more risky assets in the bear regime (with respect to the no transaction cost case) to reduce transaction costs upon regime switching, given the relative shorter duration of the bear than the Bull phase. The effect is increased if the proportional costs of the Bull are higher than the bear costs. In this case, buying the asset in the bear regime, which is expected to last a short time, is less expensive and receives the benefits in the Bull regime.

PORTFOLIO DECISIONS WITH CONSUMPTION: MANY-ASSET CASE

The generalization of the allocation model with transaction costs of $m > 1$ risky assets presents exponentially increasing complexities. In fact, j (between 0 and m) risky securities can be bought or sold in 2^j ways, and j securities can be chosen from the m risky securities in $\binom{m}{j} \equiv \dfrac{m!}{j!(m-j)!}$ ways, so that there are $\binom{m}{j}2^j$ different regions in which only j securities are transacted in all possible ways. Given that j goes from 0 to m, the total number of possible regions is

$$\sum_{j=0}^{m}\binom{m}{j}2^j = \sum_{j=0}^{m}\binom{m}{j}2^j 1^{m-j} = 3^m;$$ for instance, 3 for $m = 1$ (Buy (B), No-Trade

(N), and Sell (S)), 9 for $m = 2$ (BB, BN, BS, NB, NN, NS, SB, SN, SS), ..., and 59,049 for $m = 10$. Notwithstanding these difficulties, Akian, Menaldi, and Sulem (1996) provide a multidimensional version of Davis and Norman (1990) assuming uncorrelated assets, and Liu (2004) includes both fixed and proportional transaction costs. The presence of fixed costs changes the optimal strategy by including discrete, lump-sum trades (impulse control).

Assuming homogeneous costs across assets, the current account dynamics are now as shown in Equation 17.21:

$$dV_0(t) = (rV_0(t) - c(t))dt - \sum_{j=1}^{m}[(1+k_b)dL_j(t) + (1-k_s)dU_j(t) + K_b 1_{dL_j > 0} + K_s 1_{dU_j > 0}],$$

(17.21)

where $1_{A>0}$ is the indicator function of the event $\{A>0\}$, and K_b (K_s) is the fixed cost per buy (sale) trade.

The optimal trading strategy involves four critical points for each asset j: $w^*_{j,min} < w^{**}_{j,min} < w^{**}_{j,max} < w^*_{j,max}$, and can be stated as follows: (1) if $w_j(t) \le w^*_{j,min}$, then buy asset j to jump to $w^{**}_{j,min}$, (2) if $w_j(t) \ge w^*_{j,max}$, then sell asset j to drop the portfolio allocation to $w^{**}_{j,max}$, or (3) if $w^*_{j,min} < w_j(t) < w^*_{j,max}$, then do not trade.

Figure 17.6 depicts the result: As long as the portfolio allocation lies within the outer, signaling boundaries, no trade is made. When it hits one of the boundaries, a lump-sum trade is made toward the nearest inner boundary.

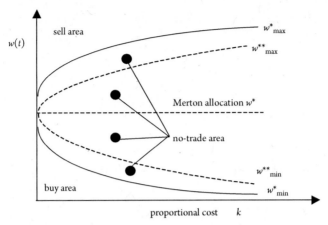

Figure 17.6 No-trade area as function of proportional costs k for fixed costs K > 0. The figure shows the optimal allocation when both proportional and fixed transaction costs are present. In this case, the external boundaries (continuous lines) identify the no-trade region: inside the boundaries, it is optimal not to trade. The inner dashed boundaries represent the optimal allocation to jump in on whenever the portfolio goes out of the no-trade region.

As transaction costs increase, the no-trade area widens and the optimal trans-action frequency decreases, in particular, for buy decisions. Using reasonable estimates ($5 for fixed transaction costs and 1 percent for proportional ones), Liu (2004) finds that the optimal trading frequency, on average, should be one optimal sale per year and one optimal purchase in 2.5 years. Thus, monthly or daily trade frequency would induce a substantial utility loss. The potential net gains from stock picking, market timing, and return predictability (Black and Litterman, 1992; Kandel and Stambaugh, 1996; Barberis, 2000) should be revised accordingly. Note, however, that the level of transaction costs is asset specific, given that different assets have different levels of illiquidity. Clarke (1992) indicates that whenever futures markets are available for certain securi-ties or asset classes, the level of transaction costs can be significantly reduced. Even if the proportional cost k is 0, a small fixed transaction cost K is sufficient to generate a no-trade area, making the Merton allocation w* no longer optimal for continuous maintainance. In this case, the Merton allocation w* is essen-tially the target to reach whenever the current portfolio pierces the boundar-ies. As the proportional cost k increases, both the two upper and the two lower boundaries converge, meaning that the size of a sale (upper case) or purchase (lower case) decreases.

One interesting result of the Liu (2004) model is that, notwithstanding the multiplicity of assets, the investor has to trade, with a probability of 1, at most one asset at a time. This result is not the effect of the assumption of uncorrelated assets but a more general effect of the imperfect substitutability of one asset for any other. Increasing the degree of substitutability (i.e., the correlation) among assets reduces the investment in each asset because of a smaller diversification benefit. Moreover, in contrast with Constantinides's (1986) results, the average long-run allocation in risky assets is increased by transaction costs, and a greater asset volatility σ_j lowers the boundaries and narrows the no-trade area. This relationship emerges because the greater risk reduces the optimal holdings in risky assets and increases its monitoring and rebalancing frequency. The opposite holds in the case of a greater expected return μ_j, which increases the boundaries and widens the no-transaction region.

PORTFOLIO DECISIONS WITH TRADING COSTS AND ABSOLUTE TARGETS

The generalization of the Markowitz (1952, 1959) and Tobin (1958) mean-variance one-period portfolio model to the case of transaction costs is relatively straightforward. The maximizing target is total portfolio return ($m + 1$ assets) adjusted for risk (the covariance matrix Σ) and for transaction costs, measured as a squared function of the distance between the optimal risky portfolio w and the inherited portfolio w_0, as exhibited in Equation 17.22:

$$\max_{w}\left\{w'\mu+(1+w'1)r-\frac{\vartheta}{2}w'\Sigma w-\frac{1}{2}(w-w_0)'\Lambda(w-w_0)\right\}, \qquad (17.22)$$

where the parameter ϑ represents the investor's aversion to risk and the vector $\Lambda/2(w-w_0)$ (with Λ possibly diagonal and related to Σ) represents the transaction costs of exchanging w_0 for w. Gârlenau and Pedersen (2012) provide a microfoundation of this setup.

The first-order conditions give the optimal portfolio shown in Equation 17.23:

$$w^*=(\vartheta\Sigma+\Lambda)^{-1}(\mu-r1+\Lambda w_0), \qquad (17.23)$$

where *1* is the symbol for the m-dimensional column vector of ones, so that r1 is the m-dimensional column vector of *r*. This solution shows that transaction costs have the joint effect of an increase in variance for all risky assets and an increase in expected returns for all inherited positions. The Markowitz portfolio is recovered by assuming that $\Lambda = 0$.

Assuming $\Lambda = \lambda\Sigma$, so that transaction costs (the bid-ask spread) increase with market volatility, as shown in Roll (1984), the resulting w^* is a weighted average of the classical Markowitz portfolio (with no transaction costs) and the old portfolio, as shown in Equation 17.24:

$$w^*=\frac{\lambda}{\vartheta+\lambda}w_0+\frac{\vartheta}{\vartheta+\lambda}(\vartheta\Sigma)^{-1}(\mu-r1)=w_0+\frac{\vartheta}{\vartheta+\lambda}(w_{Mark}-w_0). \qquad (17.24)$$

The portfolio rebalancing is shown in Figure 17.7, indicating that the optimal portfolio is related to the Markowitz portfolio in proportion to risk aversion ϑ and the old position in proportion to transaction costs λ.

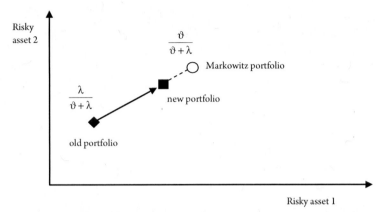

Figure 17.7 Single-period portfolio rebalancing with transaction costs. The figure shows that with transaction costs proportional to asset volatility, the optimal rebalanced mean-variance portfolio is a weighted average of the old portfolio, in proportion to transaction costs λ, and the Markowitz portfolio, in proportion to risk aversion ϑ.

An intertemporal discrete time extension can be obtained as shown in Equation 17.25, following Gârlenau and Pedersen (2012), assuming that the investor is willing to choose the dynamic trading strategy (w_0, w_1, ... ,w_t, ...) to maximize the expected value of all discounted mean-variance utilities:

$$\max_{w_0, w_1, ...} E_0 \left[\sum_{t=0}^{\infty} (1-\rho)^t \left(r + w_t' \eta_t - \frac{\vartheta}{2} w_t' \Sigma w_t - \frac{1}{2} (w_t - w_{t-1})' \Lambda (w_t - w_t) \right) \right]. \quad (17.25)$$

Here, ρ is the time preference discount rate; Σ and Λ are constant symmetric matrices of covariances and transaction costs, respectively; and the excess return vector $\eta_t \equiv \mu_t - r1$ is assumed to exhibit a stationary mean-reverting process according to the dynamics shown in Equation 17.26:

$$\eta_{t+1} - \eta_t = \Phi(\eta - \eta_t) + \varepsilon_{t+1}. \quad (17.26)$$

The intertemporal optimization gives, as before, an intuitive result: the optimal portfolio is a "matrix-weighted average" of previous portfolio w_{t-1} and a dynamic-target portfolio z_t, as illustrated in Equation 17.27:

$$w_t = (I - A)w_{t-1} + Az_t, \quad (17.27)$$

so that the optimal trade is $w_t - w_{t-1} = A(z_t - w_{t-1})$ for an optimal matrix A, nonlinear function of ρ, ϑ, Σ, and Λ.

Equivalently, w_t is a weighted average of the previous portfolio, the Markowitz portfolio, and the expected value of the next target, as shown in Equation 17.28:

$$w_t = Bw_{t-1} + C(\vartheta\Sigma)^{-1} \eta_t + (I - B - C)E_t(z_{t+1}) \quad (17.28)$$

where B and C are functions of the basic parameters.
If $\Lambda = \lambda\Sigma$, the solution is simplified in Equation 17.29:

$$w_t = \left(1 - \frac{a}{\lambda}\right)w_{t-1} + \frac{a}{\lambda}z_t$$

$$= \frac{\lambda}{\lambda + \vartheta + (1-\rho)a}w_{t-1} + \frac{\vartheta}{\lambda + \vartheta + (1-\rho)a}(\vartheta\Sigma)^{-1}\eta_t + \frac{(1-\rho)a}{\lambda + \vartheta + (1-\rho)a}E_t(z_{t+1})$$

$$z_t = (\vartheta\Sigma)^{-1}\left(I + \frac{a(1-\rho)}{\vartheta}\Phi\right)^{-1}\eta_t$$

$$a = \frac{-(\vartheta + \lambda\rho) + \sqrt{(\vartheta + \lambda\rho)^2 + 4\vartheta\lambda(1+\rho)}}{2(1-\rho)}.$$

$$(17.29)$$

The first line of Equation 17.29 states that the optimal portfolio is a balance between the previous portfolio w_{t-1} and an optimal target z_t, with a weight, a/λ. The weight is inversely related to trading costs λ, because higher trading costs imply a penalty for altering the inherited portfolio, and to risk aversion ϑ, because higher risk aversion means a penalty for straying too far from the optimal target z_t. As ρ increases toward a value of 1, the investor becomes increasingly more impatient, discounting the future heavily, up to the limit case (a goes to $\vartheta\lambda/(\vartheta + \lambda)$), in which the optimal portfolio is the (myopic) static portfolio w^*.

The second line provides an equivalent decomposition involving not only the previous portfolio w_{t-1} but also the Markowitz portfolio, optimal under no trading costs, and the expected value of the future target portfolio z_{t+1}. The optimal rebalancing is depicted in Figure 17.8.

One interesting version of the Gârlenau and Pedersen (2012) model is obtained in their main case of predictable returns. A vector of predictors, f_t, stationary and

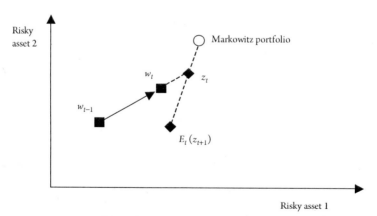

Figure 17.8 Dynamic portfolio rebalancing with transaction costs. This figure shows that the rebalanced portfolio is obtained as a weighted average of the old portfolio w_{t-1}, the Markowitz portfolio, and the expected value of the target portfolio z_{t+1}.

zero-mean reverting, representing the private information of the investor (or asset manager), helps forecast the asset returns, which are reflected in the relationships shown in Equation 17.30:

$$\mu_t = \mu + Bf_t$$
$$f_{t+1} - f_t = -\Phi f_t + \varepsilon_{t+1}.$$

(17.30)

Here, the matrix B includes the predictor loadings, and the vector $\alpha_t \equiv Bf_t$ is the vector of active "alphas" of the asset manager, whose objective is to maximize the expected value of the (discounted) portfolio's alphas, $w_{t+h}'\alpha_{t+h}$, adjusted for portfolio risk and transaction costs. Given that the alphas are expected to converge to zero in the long run, the optimal Markowitz portfolio is expected to converge to the steady-state vector $(\vartheta\Sigma)^{-1}\mu$, and the actual portfolios are optimally driven to exploit the available alphas, taking into account portfolio risks and transaction costs. Figure 17.9 depicts this expected evolution. Gârlenau and Pedersen provide a continuous-time version of their model.

PORTFOLIO DECISIONS WITH TRADING COSTS AND BENCHMARK

From the point of view of asset managers, portfolio decisions could be conveniently set out by assuming an exogenous, fixed target portfolio allocation w* (CM strategic portfolio), which represents the benchmark reference to the fund manager (agent) in the mandate of the investor (principal).

As asset values move randomly, the actual portfolio w(t) diverges from the target w* and the asset manager has to optimally drive the portfolio composition, taking into account both tracking error costs, depending on w(t) − w*, and trading costs, depending on |w(t + 1) − w(t)|. The tracking error is usually measured by the variance (or the standard deviation) of difference in return between the current and the optimal portfolio. Following Leland (1999), the costs of both tracking errors and transactions create utility loss, and the optimal investment policy will minimize the present value of tracking error costs plus transaction costs over the mandate maturity T as shown in Equation 17.31:

$$\min_w E_t \left\{ \int_t^T e^{-r(s-t)} \vartheta(w(s) - w^*)'\Sigma(w(s) - w^*)ds + \int_t^T e^{-r(s-t)} k' |dw(s)| \right\}.$$

(17.31)

Here, ϑ is the parameter representing the manager's "tracking error aversion" and k' is the vector of assets trading costs. All costs are measured per unit of wealth, and the objective function is consistent with expected utility maximization for the instantaneous net utility $U(w^*) - \vartheta(w(s) - w^*)'\Sigma(w(s) - w^*) - k'|dw(s)|$.

Alternatively, as in Sun et al. (2006) and Kritzman, Myrgren, and Page (2009), the tracking error costs for not being at the optimal allocation w* could be measured as the certainty-equivalent loss (in dollar terms) between w(t) and w*.

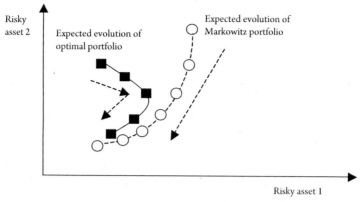

Figure 17.9 Expected evolution of an optimal portfolio with transaction costs and predictable returns. This figure shows the dynamic evolution of optimal asset holdings in the two-asset case, when Markowitz portfolio moves northeast to southwest and the optimal portfolio eventually converges to the former taking into account expected excess returns, risks and transaction costs.

Leland's (1999) approximated results, obtained in the infinite horizon case ($T = \infty$), are qualitatively similar to those of Magill and Constantinides (1976). The optimal policy is represented by a connected, compact no-trade region expressed in the riskless-risky two asset case by the segment $[w_{min}, w_{max}]$, where w_{min} and w_{max} are obtained as a solution of the (ordinary) differential problem, as illustrated in the relationships exhibited in Equation 17.32:

$$\frac{1}{2}w^2(1-w^*)^2\sigma^2 J_{ww} + w(1-w^*)(\mu-r-\sigma^2 w^*)J_w + \vartheta\sigma^2(w-w^*)^2 - rJ = 0$$

$$J_{w|w=w_{min}} = -J_{w|w=w_{max}} = -k \quad (value\,matching\,conditions)$$

$$J_{w|w=w_{min}} = -J_{w|w=w_{max}} = 0 \quad (super\,contact\,conditions).$$

(17.32)

Here, $J(w(t))$ is Bellman's value function, representing the optimal expected utility from t onward (Bellman's principle of intertemporal optimization). A numerical result with $m = 2$ risky assets and the risk-free asset is given in Figure 17.10 for $w^* = (40\text{ percent}, 40\text{ percent})$.

The upper panel of Equation 17.32 compares the no-trade regions in the cases where the two assets have a low (20 percent) or a high correlation (70 percent). Increasing the correlation increases the skewness of the region, given that the two assets are close substitutes in the latter case. In the lower panel, the reduction in trading costs for asset 2 (from 1 percent to 0.1 percent) shrinks the no-trade region in that dimension but also, due to the correlation effect, moves the optimal boundaries of the more expensive asset 1: more (less) of asset 2 implies less (more) of asset 1.

Another interesting result of Leland's (1999) model is that it provides an estimate of the effects of a "Tobin tax." A 2 percent tax on portfolio trades in addition to 0.5 percent of transaction costs would reduce trading volume by about 42 percent.

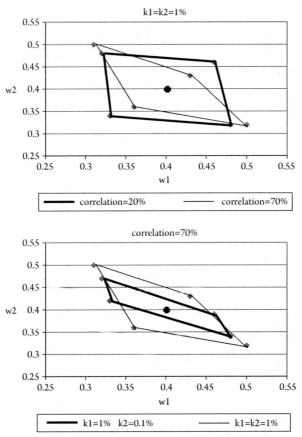

Figure 17.10 No-trade regions with two risky assets. The upper panel of the figure compares the no-trade regions when the two assets have low (20 percent; bold lines) or high (70 percent; thin lines) correlations. Increasing the correlation increases the skewness of the region. In the lower panel, the reduction in trading costs for asset 2 (from 1 percent [thin lines] to 0.1 percent [bold lines]) shrinks the no-trade region in that dimension but also moves the optimal boundaries of the more expensive asset, asset 1, in the opposite direction.

Moreover, using optimal rebalancing would reduce turnover by about 50 percent with respect to suboptimal rules, such as periodic rebalancing with the same tracking error volatility: a significant reduction in costs without any loss in controlling the risks.

SIMPLE REBALANCING RULES: A COMPARISON

A quick review of the literature (Arnott and Lovell, 1993; Buetow et al., 2002; Masters, 2003; O'Brien, 2006) reveals that various simple rules of portfolio rebalancing have been proposed in theory and practice. As Cao (2009) and Hong (2009) document, individual long-term investors are often advised to follow the simple rule of checking at their birthday (once a year) and rebalancing if the portfolio deviates from the target by more than 5 percent, given that "letting a portfolio untended is like leaving a toddler alone in a room with a hot stove" (Hong, 2009, p. 1).

Besides the risk-reduction motivation, rebalancing is often suggested as a tool for yield enhancement, given that, in its usual meaning, it implies the trading rule "buy low, sell high" (a contrarian strategy), which under price mean reversion will improve portfolio performance (Perold and Sharpe, 1988; Cesari and Cremonini, 2003). This phenomenon is sometimes referred to as the "rebalancing bonus." The need for rebalancing depends on the asset characteristics; in particular, it depends (1) on volatility, expected return, and time in a direct way, because they imply a high probability of large deviations of one asset relative to the others; (2) on correlations in an inverse way, because high correlations indicate high asset comovements and less need for rebalancing (Pliska and Suzuki, 2004). For example, more specialized portfolio allocations (e.g., 90/10) should require less rebalancing than mixed ones (e.g., 50/50).

Given a benchmark allocation, w^*, and a prespecified periodic monitoring, some popular rules are the following: (1) *time rebalancing*: rebalance the portfolio to w^* at a given time period (every day or week, month, quarter, year); (2) *fixed rebalancing*: rebalance when $|w_j(t) - w_j^*| > \alpha$; (3) *proportional rebalancing*: rebalance when $|w_j(t) - w_j^*|/w_j^* > \beta$; or (4) *probability rebalancing*: rebalance when $|R_j(t_r,t)| > \gamma \sigma_j(t)$, where $R_j(t_r,t)$ is the annualized rate of return of asset j between the last rebalancing date t_r and current date t and $\sigma_j(t)$ is the estimated annualized volatility up to time t. In this case, the trigger is an "excess return" (in either direction) for asset j, independent from its current or optimal weight.

Time rebalancing (e.g., monthly) is equivalent to periodic (e.g., monthly) monitoring and fixed rebalancing with $\alpha = 0$. The buy and hold strategy (BH), on the other hand, involves fixed rebalancing (or another rule) with $\alpha = 1$, so that rebalancing will never have to occur.

Different rules are obtained by combining the length of monitoring periods with the trigger parameters (α, β, and γ). Moreover, instead of full rebalancing to w_j^*, a rebalance to $w_j^* \pm \delta \le \alpha$ (rebalance boundary) or to $w_j^* \pm q \delta$ (tolerance boundary) could be implemented whenever $|w_j(t) - w_j^*| > \alpha$ (similarly for the other rules).

Notwithstanding the available, mixed evidence, some general results emerge from the cited empirical analyses. First, historical simulation shows that, on average, rebalancing activity provides extra returns (net of transaction costs) with respect to BH, with an important exception in periods of sufficiently strong up- or down-market trends. Second, when market regimes cannot be recognized, higher monitoring frequency is required. Third, with high frequency monitoring (daily or weekly), the best results are obtained with large boundaries (e.g., $\alpha = 15$ percent), yet with a low-frequency monitoring (yearly), narrow boundaries (e.g., 1 percent) are preferred. Fourth, on average, fixed rebalancing and proportional rebalancing provide superior returns (also adjusted for risk) with respect to BH and to the popular time rebalancing. The resemblance of fixed and proportional rebalancing to the optimal theoretical rebalancing policy could explain this result.

PORTFOLIO DECISIONS WITH MONITORING COSTS

Monitoring activity is usually considered costless. In practice, however, monitoring involves various operations and actions (e.g., collecting data, monitoring price, conducting a market analysis, and engaging in back-office reporting) that are time- and resource-consuming and therefore costly. If these activities can be done at will, the proper approach should be to explicitly take into account the possibility of discrete monitoring and finding its optimal time frequency.

In absence of transaction costs, Bukhvalova (2007) analyzes portfolio decisions that have monitoring costs, defined as the fixed proportion v of the beginning of period wealth. Her results show that over a given horizon T, there is an optimal number of periods, N^* (depending on v, r, and T), of equal length in which the investor has to monitor the portfolio. The value of N^* increases with T, and r and decreases with the unit cost v. For example, with a monitoring cost of four basis points, r = 2 percent and a horizon of twenty years, then five rebalancing periods emerge as optimal. Portfolio allocation is affected as well, and the optimal weight $w^*(t)$ is time dependent, below the zero-cost case in previous periods and above it in final periods.

Target Rebalancing for Portfolio Protection

Target rebalancing is defined as the dynamic adjustment of strategic portfolio weights $w^*(t)$. Two kinds of target rebalancing are aimed at protecting the future value of the portfolio: One is portfolio insurance (Black and Jones, 1987; Black and Perold, 1992), and the other is life cycle investment (Campbell and Viceira, 2002).

PORTFOLIO INSURANCE

Portfolio insurance is an automatic rebalancing strategy that tries to "guarantee" (in a probabilistic, noncontractual sense) reaching at least a final-level F(T) (floor) for the portfolio value at time T. In a simplified model, the portfolio is composed of a riskless (current account) and a risky asset, and the portfolio manager must periodically adjust the portfolio composition in order to have a reasonable certainty of reaching the minimum target F(T).

Let V(0) be the initial wealth and $F(0) = F(T)e^{-rT}$ be the initial value of the final floor. The rule suggested by Black and Jones (1987) is to rebalance the risky position in monetary terms, as shown in Equation 17.33:

$$E(t) = \begin{cases} m(V(t) - F(t)) & \text{if } V(t) > F(t) \\ 0 & \text{if } V(t) \le F(t). \end{cases} \qquad (17.33)$$

The parameter m > 1 is called the *multiplier*, and $C(t) \equiv V(t) - F(t)$ is called the *cushion*, so that the rule (constant proportion portfolio insurance [CPPI]) could be expressed—à la Albert Einstein in the Black-Jones original formula—as E = mc. The model implies that the value of the risky asset must be in proportion (at level *m*) with the distance between the portfolio value V(t) and the floor value F(t). The greater (shorter) the distance, the greater (lower) is the risky exposure.

If P(t) is the unit price of the risky asset and $P_0(t) = e^{rt}$ is the unit value of the current account, the optimal quantity is, therefore, shown in Equation 17.34:

$$Q^*(t)=\frac{m\big(V(t)-F(t)\big)}{P(t)} \qquad Q_0^*(t)=\frac{V(t)-m\big(V(t)-F(t)\big)}{e^{rt}}, \qquad (17.34)$$

and the budget constraint is shown in Equation 17.35:

$$V(t) = Q(t)P(t) + Q_0(t)e^{rt} = Q^*(t)P(t) + Q_0^*(t)e^{rt}, \qquad (17.35)$$

so that, since the portfolio is self-financed, Equation 17.36 emerges:

$$dV(t)=Q^*(t)dP(t)+Q_0^*(t)dP_0(t)=\frac{m\big(V(t)-F(t)\big)}{P(t)}dP(t)$$

$$+\frac{V(t)-m\big(V(t)-F(t)\big)}{e^{rt}}e^{rt}rdt. \qquad (17.36)$$

The CPPI rule in Equation 17.33 implies a general solution for V(t) of the form illustrated in Equation 17.37:

$$V(t)=F(t)+hP^m(t)e^{(1-m)}rt, \qquad (17.37)$$

where *h* is a general constant. Equation 17.37 shows that the net asset value (NAV) of the portfolio (the portfolio payoff) is a convex function of the price P(t) of the risky asset. Note that for $0 < m < 1$ and $F(0) = 0$, the NAV is concave and results in the CM strategy.

This convexity, obtained with $m > 1$, is a typical effect of the insurance rebalancing behavior. This behavior can be found, under apparently different forms, in many situations in which the investor is intentionally hedging against adverse movement of the market. Two well-known examples are the market timing activity of the asset manager (Treynor and Mazuy, 1966; Henriksson and Merton, 1981) and the protective put option, both characterized by a convex payoff. In fact, similar results are obtained when the protective rebalancing is defined by the dynamic replication of a put option with strike F(T) (option-based portfolio insurance; see Cesari and Cremonini, 2003).

A second feature of protective rebalancing (and insurance policies in general) is its "momentum" character. In fact, inserting Equation 17.37 into Equation 17.34, Equation 17.38 emerges:

$$\frac{\partial Q^*(t)}{\partial P(t)}=(m-1)\frac{Q^*(t)}{P(t)}>0 \quad for\ m>1, \qquad (17.38)$$

so that the rule is buy (sell) if the risky price goes up (down). This relationship implies that with portfolio insurance, investors trade with the market—"buy high, sell low"—following the market momentum. In fact, a generalized adoption of portfolio insurance rules by market participants could substantially increase market volatility and the probability of booms and crashes, as documented in the case of the global stock market crash that occurred on Black Monday on October 19, 1987 (Rubinstein, 1988).

In actual practice, discrete portfolio rebalancing cannot guarantee the final floor F(T), and the risk of default for the strategy is a direct function of the multiplier m, the price volatility σ, and the distance of time between rebalancings (Etzioni, 1986).

LIFE-CYCLE INVESTMENTS

A second example of target rebalancing for portfolio protection is life-cycle investments. *Life-cycle investment* is a popular expression used to indicate a dynamic asset allocation for long-term investors in which, when a given final date is approaching (typically the retirement date), the investor is advised/committed to progressively reduce his exposure to risky assets (stocks, in particular) in favor of safer, short-term bonds, so that he can reach the end date with a low-risk portfolio. The stated goal for such an age-based asset allocation is twofold: (1) to earn profit from the long-term growth of stocks and (2) to preserve the investor's accumulated wealth over his lifetime, avoiding, in particular, the unpleasant, last-minute surprises from adverse market movements.

The optimal portfolio weights $w^*(t)$ for risky assets are gradually decreased as an investor approaches his retirement date, T. Conventional wisdom implies that $w^*(t) = 100 - \text{age}(t)$, suggesting a risky exposure of about 80 percent for younger investors and 20 percent for older investors. This strategy could be implemented with periodic switches from higher-risk into lower-risk mutual funds or investing in the same target-date fund with time-decreasing risk.

In general, life-cycle investments can be justified whenever there is a "horizon effect" on the optimal portfolio, that is when $w^*(t)$ is a direct function of $T - t$. The rationale supporting the strategy is found in a few "postulates" that have fed a long and lively debate: the risk premium of stocks, their reduced volatility in the long run because of mean reversion (the so-called "time-diversification" effect), and the human capital to be included as personal wealth in the analysis (Viceira, 2008; Cesari, 2011). The actual ability of life-cycle investing to provide excess returns and risk reduction in the long run, in comparison with the more traditional CM, is still under active scrutiny (Soto et al., 2008).

Summary and Conclusions

Both active and passive asset management implies adequate trading strategies, suitably defined in terms of goals and constraints. The intrinsic randomness of financial markets suggests the necessity of periodic monitoring and rebalancing of the portfolio in order to be fully compliant with internal and external rules and in line with expectations and targets. Even in the case of classical, static portfolio results (Markowitz, 1952, 1959)—which, under special assumptions, are also valuable in a dynamic context (Merton, 1969, 1971, 1973)—rebalancing activity is necessary due to the random movements of relative asset prices.

In addition to passive rebalancing, target rebalancing and portfolio rebalancing toward target can also be utilized. Intertemporal models actually show that the target itself could be time dependent, enlarging the scope for a fine-tuning of portfolio weights. The presence of transaction costs makes optimal rebalancing a major issue.

The pathbreaking work of Magill and Constantinides (1976) and Constantinides (1986) shows the effects of transaction costs on rebalancing activity and portfolio-consumption decisions. In their models, the optimal portfolio is replaced by optimal boundaries in the space of asset weights, defining a connected no-trade region. If the current portfolio pierces the boundaries, an instantaneous trade is made to rebalance the portfolio at (in the case of proportional costs) or inside (in the case of fixed costs) the boundaries. In the case of many risky assets, the rebalancing problem is extremely challenging and only numerical solutions are available (Liu, 2004).

From a management point of view, an interesting setup for rebalancing decisions is obtained in the case of a fixed w*, from which it is assumed the actual portfolio will stray because of random market movements (Leland, 1999). The asset manager has to consider the trade-off between the costs of erroneously tracking the target and the costs of trading it against current positions. Even in this case, a no-trade region defines the optimal policy.

In actual practice, financial advisors and fund managers suggest a number of simple rebalancing rules, aiming at both controlling the risk and enhancing the return of the portfolio. Periodic rebalancing or fixed-proportional rebalancing are the most popular rules, implying a "buy low, sell high" trading rule (a contrarian strategy). However, both theoretically and empirically, the rules cannot guarantee positive excess returns under all market regimes (there is no free lunch in the market) with respect to the basic BH rule.

Similar results hold for the opposite strategies (momentum strategies) that fund managers often adopt. Both portfolio insurance and life-cycle investments are aimed at protecting the portfolio using a "buy high, sell low" rule, inducing convexity in the return to hedge the accumulated wealth from downside risks. The actual implementation of these strategies jeopardizes their theoretical optimality, so that their risk-return efficiency with respect to more traditional BH or CM strategies is controversial.

Discussion Questions

1. Discuss the main reasons for rebalancing assets in a financial portfolio.
2. Explain the effects of fixed and proportional trading costs on optimal asset allocation.

3. Discuss the problem of optimal rebalancing with respect to a given benchmark portfolio.
4. Describe the most popular rules of portfolio rebalancing and discuss the relative merits of each.
5. Explain the functioning of two popular trading strategies, portfolio insurance and life-cycle investments, which are aimed at protecting the portfolio.

References

Akian, Marianne, José Luis Menaldi, and Agnès Sulem. 1996. "On an Investment-Consumption Model with Transaction Costs." *SIAM Journal of Control and Optimization* 34:1, 329–364.

Amihud, Yakov, Haim Mendelson, and Lasse Heje Pedersen. 2005. "Liquidity and Asset Pricing." *Foundations and Trends in Finance* 1:4, 269–364.

Arnott, Robert D., and Robert M. Lovell Jr. 1993. "Rebalancing: Why? When? How Often?" *Journal of Investing* 2:1, 5–10.

Banz, Rolf W. 1981. "The Relationship between Return and Market Value of Common Stocks." *Journal of Financial Economics* 9:1, 3–18.

Barberis, Nicholas. 2000. "Investing for the Long Run When Returns Are Predictable." *Journal of Finance* 55:1, 225–264.

Black, Fischer S., and Robert C. Jones. 1987. "Simplifying Portfolio Insurance." *Journal of Portfolio Management* 14:1, 48–51.

Black, Fischer S., and Robert Litterman. 1992. "Global Portfolio Optimization." *Financial Analysts Journal* 48:5, 28–43.

Black, Fischer S., and André Perold. 1992. "Theory of Constant Portfolio Insurance." *Journal of Economic Dynamics and Control* 16:3, 403–426.

Buetow, Gerald W., Jr., Ronald Sellers, Donald Trotter, Elaine Hunt, and Willie A. Whipple Jr.. 2002. "The Benefits of Rebalancing." *Journal of Portfolio Management* 28:2, 23–32.

Bukhvalova, Barbara A. 2007. "Monitoring Costs and Portfolio Choice." Working Paper. Norwegian School of Management, Norwegian Business School, Oslo, Norway.

Calvet, Laurent E., John Y. Campbell, and Paolo Sodini. 2009. "Fight or Flight? Portfolio Rebalancing by Individual Investors." *Quartrely Journal of Economics* 124:1, 301–348.

Campbell, John Y., and Luis M. Viceira. 2002. *Strategic Asset Allocation: Portfolio Choice for Long-Term Investors*. Oxford, UK: Oxford University Press.

Cao, Bolong. 2009. "Testing Generic Rebalancing Policies for Retirement Portfolios." http://www.ssrn.com/abstract=1362006.

Cesari, Riccardo. 2010. "The Algebra of Portfolio Dynamics." http://www.ssrn.com/abstract=1931750.

Cesari, Riccardo. 2011. "All Stocks Half the Time? A Short Account of the Life-Cycle Controversy." http://www.ssrn.com/abstract=1918830.

Cesari, Riccardo, and David Cremonini. 2003. "Benchmarking, Portfolio Insurance and Technical Analysis: A Monte Carlo Comparison of Dynamic Strategies of Asset Allocations." *Journal of Economic Dynamics and Control* 27:6, 987–1011.

Clarke, Roger G. 1992. "Asset Allocation Using Futures Markets." In *Active Asset Allocation: State-of-the-Art Portfolio Policies, Strategies, & Tactics*, edited by Robert D. Arnott and Frank J. Fabozzi, 303–326. Chicago: Probus.

Collins, Bruce M., and Frank J. Fabozzi. 1991. "A Methodology for Measuring Transaction Costs." *Financial Analysts Journal* 47:2, 27–36.

Constantinides, George M. 1986. "Capital Market Equilibrium with Transaction Costs." *Journal of Political Economy* 94:4, 842–862.

Cremers, Martijn K. J., and Jianping Mei. 2004. "Turning over Turnover." Working Paper 03–26, International Center of Finance, Yale University, New Haven, CT. http://www.ssrn.com/abstract=452720.

Davis, Mark H. A., and A. R. Norman. 1990. "Portfolio Selection with Transaction Costs." *Mathematics of Operations Research* 15:4, 676–713.

Demsetz, Harold. 1968. "The Cost of Transacting." *Quarterly Journal of Economics* 82:1, 33–53.

Dumas, Bernard, and Elisa Luciano. 1991. "An Exact Solution to a Dynamic Portfolio Choice Problem under Transactions Costs." *Journal of Finance* 46:2, 577–595.

Etzioni, Ethan S. 1986. "Rebalance Disciplines for Portfolio Insurance." *Journal of Portfolio Management* 13:1, 59–62.

Fama, Eugene F. 1970. "Multiperiod Consumption-Investment Decisions." *American Economic Review* 60:1,163–174.

Gârlenau, Nicolae Bogdan, and Lasse Heje Pedersen. 2012. "Dynamic Trading with Predictable Returns and Transaction Costs." Working Paper DP7392, Center for Economic Policy Research, London. Last modified March. http://pages.stern.nyu.edu/~lpederse/papers/DynamicTrading.pdf.

Goldsmith, David. 1976. "Transaction Costs and the Theory of Portfolio Selection." *Journal of Finance* 31:4, 1127–1139.

Henriksson, Roy D., and Robert C. Merton. 1981. "On Market Timing and Investment Performance II: Statistical Procedures for Evaluating Forecasting Skills." *Journal of Business* 54:3, 513–533.

Hicks, John R. 1962. "Liquidity." *Economic Journal* 72:4, 787–802.

Hong, Hui. 2009. "Portfolio Rebalancing Revisited: What Strategy Optimally Triggers an Adjustment to the Asset Weights? A New Story in Hong Kong Market" http://www.ssrn.com/abstract=1798386.

Jang, Bong-gyu, Hyeng Keun Koo, Hong Liu, and Mark Loewenstein. 2007. "Liquidity Premia and Transaction Costs." *Journal of Finance* 62:5, 2329–2366.

Kandel, Shmuel, and Robert F. Stambaugh. 1996. "On the Predictability of Stock Returns: An Asset-Allocation Perspective." *Journal of Finance* 51:2, 385–424.

Keynes, John M. 1930. *A Treatise on Money.* Vol. 2, *The Applied Theory of Money.* London: Macmillan.

Kritzman, Mark, Simon Myrgren, and Sébastien Page. 2009. "Optimal Rebalancing: A Scalable Solution." *Journal of Investment Management* 7:1, 63–71.

Leland, Hayne E. 1974. "On Consumption and Portfolio Choice with Transaction Costs." In *Essays on Economic Behavior under Uncertainty,* edited by Michael S. Balch, Daniel L. McFadden, and Shih-yen Wu, 184–91. Amsterdam: North Holland.

Leland, Hayne E. 1999. "Optimal Portfolio Management with Transaction Costs and Capital Gains Taxes." Working Paper, Haas School of Business, University of California, Berkeley.

Liu, Hong. 2004. "Optimal Consumption and Investment with Transaction Costs and Multiple Risky Assets." *Journal of Finance* 59:1, 289–338.

Longstaff, Francis. 2009. "Portfolio Claustrophobia: Asset Pricing in Markets with Illiquid Assets." *American Economic Review* 99:4, 1119–1144.

Magill, Michael J. P., and George M. Constantinides. 1976. "Portfolio Selection with Transaction Costs." *Journal of Economic Theory* 13:2, 245–263.

Markowitz, Harry M. 1952. "Portfolio Selection." *Journal of Finance* 7:1, 77–91.

Markowitz, Harry M. 1959. *Portfolio Selection: Efficient Diversification of Investments.* New Haven, CT: Yale University Press.

Masters, Seth J. 2003. "Rebalancing." *Journal of Portfolio Management* 29:3, 52–57.

Merton, Robert C. 1969. "Lifetime Portfolio Selection under Uncertainty: The Continuous-Time Case." *Review of Economics and Statistics* 51:3, 247–257.

Merton, Robert C. 1971. "Optimum Consumption and Portfolio Rules in a Continuous-Time Model." *Journal of Economic Theory* 3:4, 373–413.

Merton, Robert C. 1973. "An Intertemporal Capital Asset Pricing Model." *Econometrica* 41:5, 867–887.

Mossin, Jan. 1968. "Optimal Multiperiod Portfolio Policies." *Journal of Business* 41:2, 205–229.

O'Brien, John. 2006. "Rebalancing: A Tool for Managing Portfolio Risk." *Journal of Financial Service Professionals* 60:3, 62–68.

Perold, André F., and William F. Sharpe. 1988. "Dynamic Strategies for Asset Allocation." *Financial Analysts Journal* 44:1, 16–27.

Pliska, Stanley R., and Kiyoshi Suzuki. 2004. "Optimal Tracking for Asset Allocation with Fixed and Proportional Transaction Costs." *Quantitative Finance* 4:4, 233–243.

Pratt, John W. 1964. "Risk-Aversion in the Small and in the Large." *Econometrica* 32:1, 122–136.

Roll, Richard. 1984. "A Simple Implicit Measure of the Effective Bid-Ask Spread in an Efficient Market." *Journal of Finance* 39:4, 1127–1139.

Rubinstein, Mark. 1988. "Portfolio Insurance and the Market Crash." *Financial Analysts Journal* 44:1, 38–47.

Smith, Keith V. 1968. "Alternative Procedures for Revising Investment Portfolios." *Journal of Financial and Quantitative Analysis* 3:4, 371–403.

Soto, Mauricio, Robert K. Triest, Alex Golub-Sass, and Francesca Golub-Sass. 2008. "An Assessment of Life-Cycle Funds." CRR Working Paper 2008–10, Center for Retirement Research, Boston College, Boston, MA.

Sun, Walter, Ayres Fan, Li-Wei Chen, Tom Schouwenaars, and Marius A. Albota. 2006. "Optimal Rebalancing for Institutional Portfolios." *Journal of Portfolio Management* 32:2, 33–43.

Taksar, Michael, Michael J. Klass, and David Assaf. 1988. "A Diffusion Model for Optimal Portfolio Selection in the Presence of Brokerage Fees." *Mathematics of Operations Research* 13:2, 277–294.

Tobin, James. 1958. "Liquidity Preference as Behavior towards Risk." *Review of Economic Studies* 25:1, 65–86.

Treynor, Jack L., and Kay Mazuy. 1966. "Can Mutual Funds Outguess the Market?" *Harvard Business Review* 44:4, 131–136.

Viceira, Luis M. 2008. "Life-Cycle Funds." In *Overcoming the Saving Slump: How to Increase the Effectiveness of Financial Education and Savings Programs*, edited by Annamaria Lusardi,140–177. Chicago: University of Chicago Press.

18

Effective Trade Execution

RICCARDO CESARI
Professor of Mathematical Finance, University of Bologna

MASSIMILIANO MARZO
Professor of Economics, University of Bologna

PAOLO ZAGAGLIA
Assistant Professor of Economics, University of Bologna

Introduction

The traditional view about financial market organization is that market participants meet to exchange securities in their respective interests and positions. According to this wisdom, intermediaries (brokers or dealers) conduct floor trades with the goal of finding the various matches among market participants. Technological advances represent a critical component relative to the evolution of market organization. The strong development of technology for adoption results in an increased speed of financial transactions by gradually reducing the importance of physical location on the trading floor.

Moreover, the search for liquidity, which results in the tension in the trading industry toward the minimization of execution costs and trade impact, creates room for an increase in the number of competing trading venues. The resulting international trading landscape is characterized by a substantial amount of automated trading technologies and an increase of market fragmentation, with the emergence of several trading venues and the consequent emergence of competition for the order flow. The adoption of algorithmic trading (AT) and high-frequency trading (HFT) are the direct consequence of this competition.

This chapter explores the role of innovation in trading activity and its impact on the various order characteristics, trading strategies, and costs, as shown in in the recent evolution of literature on market microstructure. The rapidly evolving scenario witnessed by the role of trading algorithms results in a very important set of changes in the market architecture regarding optimal order size, market timing strategies, information disclosure, and competition among trading venues and market participants. Existing microstructure theories are being reevaluated as a result of the expanding roles of AT and HFT.

AT results in adopting a set of trading strategies, or "algorithms," that often involve computer-based implementations. An *algorithm* is a set of decision rules and strategies used to satisfy a specific goal. HFT is an evolution of AT. HFT represents the implementation of proprietary trading strategies by agents through the adoption of fast technological computing. This is done to realize trading at very high frequencies and extremely low latencies (below ten microseconds). The main drivers of AT and HFT can be identified according to the following elements: (1) the market access model, (2) the fee structure, and (3) latency reduction and increases in competition and fragmentation of the order flow.

The market access model has evolved in an important way. In the past, designated intermediaries (brokers or market makers) had the role of collecting orders from their customers and allocating them to appropriate market venues. This business model has evolved over time by qualifying the market access, to two ends: (1) direct market access (DMA) and (2) sponsored access (SA). With DMA, investors can directly place their orders in the marketplace by using the broker's infrastructure for accessing the market. In this case, brokers do not intervene in the order placement mechanisms. Their role is only to provide the infrastructure to their clients to gain access to the market, which is done after a pre-trade risk check.

With SA, an agent, which could be an investment firm, a private wealthy client, or a mutual fund, can gain access to the market without being a member of the floor by using the broker's member identification (ID) and doesn't necessarily use the latter's infrastructure. If the trading venue provides filtered SA, then the broker can implement pre-trade risk checks. Conversely, if the market provides "naked access," then the sponsor does a preliminary check to protect his own risk exposure. The main advantage of SA over DMA is the strong reduction of latency, which makes SA more attractive for AT of HFT operators.

The recent evolution of policies implemented at the level of each market exchange has resulted in a strong increase in fee competition among trading venues and attracts the highest possible quantity of order flow. Market participants reducing liquidity from the market are charged a higher fee, while traders increasing liquidity are charged a lower fee or are provided with a rebate. BATS, Chi-X Global, and Turquoise, some specific trading venues used to raise the competition for the order flow, implemented this fee structure for the first time. Given the implementation of these aggressive trading schemes, all European exchanges have lowered their fees to avoid losing order flow. If an order is incorrectly implemented, a substantial risk exists that it will no longer be appropriate in terms of price limit or size based on having been executed at an improper price or even not having been executed at all. In this context, the design of a proper infrastructure that minimizes the communication delay between the market and the traders is crucial in allowing the execution of data receipt, order submissions, and confirmations at the highest possible speed. Further, one of the key drivers of a successful trading strategy is being able to read the full order book in real time and design the more appropriate trading strategy. Latency minimization goals are generally obtained by colocating the servers of market participants that are closest to the market's infrastructure.

Regulation results in an increased role of the algorithmic trader. In many cases, laws encourage market fragmentation and, correspondingly, competition among market venues. In this circumstance, the availability of tools that allow traders to place or cancel orders on multiple venues is essential to the ability to generate profits from arbitrage as a result of the lowest possible trading fees. Gomber, Arndt, Lutat, and Uhle (2011) point out regulatory changes are one of the key drivers of the recent innovations in financial markets.

This chapter provides an overview of the most recent advances in trading systems and strategies together with the cost of benefits of their respective implementations. Unlike the previous chapter, the security and the quantity object of trading are here exogenously given and the analysis is addressed to the optimal way of trade execution using algorithms.

The topics discussed in this chapter are presented in a sequential order. The next section presents the various definitions of AT and HFT and then qualifies their importance in the current evolution of trading technologies. After that, various order types are introduced to provide an appreciation of trading-execution techniques. The third section presents the definitions of basic limit and market orders together with the most common instructions currently adopted in the trading practice, such as *fill or kill* (FOK), *immediate or cancel* (IOC), and *immediate or none* (ION). Having established the general terminology, a special section is then dedicated to describing the main algorithms, classified as impact driven, cost driven, and opportunistic. Within this context, the main characteristics of volume-weighted average price (VWAP), percent of volume (POV), and time-weighted average price (TWAP) algorithms are analyzed. The choice of execution is conditional upon the pre- and posttrade analysis needed to estimate transaction costs involved in trading activity. This is discussed in a separate section, where all the types of transaction costs, both explicit and implicit, are presented, following and extending the concept of implementation shortfall (IS) by Perold (1988). The choice of a trading strategy can be presented as an optimization problem. This is discussed in the section entitled "Optimal Execution Strategies," including a presentation of the approach leading to the trading path that minimizes transaction costs together with the concept of efficient-trading frontier (ETF) highlighted by Almgren and Chriss (2000). Also discussed is the practical implementation of the concept. Next, the execution tactics are divided into the categories of impact driven, price risk driven, and opportunistic. and presented with a special emphasis on hidden and iceberg orders. The final section presents a conclusion.

The first two sections introduce the main terminology and definitions and then provide general descriptions of the algorithms. To efficiently implement an algorithm requires understanding the constraints, which are basically given in terms of transaction costs. The design of an optimal trading strategy delivers a set of alternatives classified according to aggressiveness of trade, and this originates with the efficient trading frontier (ETF). Thus, the presentation starts with definitions and then moves to constructing optimal and implementable trading strategies. This chapter builds on work by Johnson (2010) and Kissel and Glantz (2003).

Trading Algorithms Classification

The first problem in exploring the subject of AT is the lack of a consistent set of definitions regarding algorithmic processes. However, Gomber et al. (2011) contend that HFT may be viewed as a subgroup of AT, being that professional traders observe market parameters or other information in real time and properly design specific trading strategies aimed at achieving specific goals without human intervention. These goals generally apply to DMA or SA technologies for order routing.

The main characteristics of AT include the following: (1) automated order submission, (2) automated order management, and (3) the use of DMA. In contrast, the main characteristics of HFT include the following: (a) the ability to handle a large number of orders, (b) rapid order cancellation, (c) proprietary trading, (d) not having a large position at the end of day, (e) a very short holding period and low latency requirement, and (f) colocation/proximity services. According to Brogaard's (2010) estimates, HFT accounts for more than 50 percent of the overall daily volume of equity markets.

With the massive use of computerized trading systems, market making has experienced further evolution: traders simultaneously quote buy and sell limit orders to profit from bid-ask differences. In some circumstances, this evolution is specifically determined by market regulation, as in the case of the designated market maker at the New York Stock Exchange (NYSE) or the designated sponsor via the trading system Xetra at the Frankfurt Stock Exchange (FRA). Basically, this feature highlights market making with obligations for registered market makers. Therefore, a close link exists between market making and HFT: designated liquidity provisions are a specific subset of rules of the market-making strategies, which can be very efficiently implemented by using HFT. At the same time, nonmandatory market-making strategies not necessarily linked to liquidity provisions can be implemented with HFT. Market fragmentation allows traders to choose the best trading venue in terms of price discovery mechanism and liquidity.

Quantitative portfolio management (QPM) refers to the technical ability of portfolio managers to relate stock movements to other market data. This approach has the main goal of monitoring large securities portfolios for a prolonged period of time, as opposed to HFT where positions tend to be liquidated overnight. Greater human intervention can occur by using QPM. The strategy uses algorithms to generate trading decisions based on statistical calculations and data analysis techniques. QPM tools are built in order to perform automated analysis and decisions related to portfolio selection. The generation of trading signals is a consequence of previous analysis. This process can be automated as well, but the human role intervenes in the verification of the analysis and the trading strategies to be implemented. In principle, QPM differs from HFT in that the latter does not have the goal of portfolio optimization and selection. Conversely, the increasing role of latency and computer speed makes the distinction between HFT and QPM more evanescent.

An interesting aspect emerges as a consequence of both increased fragmentation and transactions in smart-order routing (SOR) systems. SOR systems allow simultaneous access to several venues or liquidity pools to search for the best order destination to optimize order execution in order to minimize implicit and explicit trading costs. In practice, SORs scan predefined markets in terms of bid-ask quotes in real time and direct the order in a dynamic way toward the venue offering the most convenient conditions at the time of order entry. This process is extremely complicated. Achieving the best results requires a routing system that is able to screen in real time the entire order flow/order book composition of each trading venue in the market together with the price evolution and then compute the total execution costs of each trade in each different market by applying the explicit cost dimension (commissions, fees, and taxes). This activity is mainly reserved for fully automated systems for HFT, which have the ability to reduce search costs and increase search speed across trading venues.

Overall, the assessment of AT and HFT misses the fact that both procedures represent some of the most important advances in modern market arena. Given the complexity of actions that traders must implement, including risk exposure analysis, gross position netting, matching order size, and strategies with regulations and market rules, algorithms can be of great help in mitigating the cognitive limits associated with traders' ability in collecting and processing a large mass of information in a few seconds. Another benefit of algorithms consists in their ability to generate liquidity when it is scarce.

According to Biais, Foucault, and Moinas (2010), a problem of adverse selection arose after the introduction of algorithms, where asymmetric information emerged between slow and fast traders: fast traders observe information before other agents. Because fast traders can profit from such knowledge, slow traders lose. The authors show that the increase in algorithm trading might cause an increase of adverse selection costs when slow traders are evicted from the market. Empirically, Jovanovic and Menkveld (2010) verify this finding in the case where a fast algorithm trader enters Chi-X Global (a dark pool listed in the Dutch market). The authors clearly document a fast drop in volume, which is probably due to slow traders pulling away from the market. The risk with AT and HFT arises from a multiplicity of equilibria where identifying positive and negative effects is possible. At the moment, there is no strong evidence to either favor or oppose algorithms.

Order Types and Trading Strategies

A distinction exits between two types of orders in the market: limit orders and market orders. With a *limit order*, a trader specifies and orders the purchase (or sale) of a quantity of securities at a prespecified price. A *market order* is an instruction to trade a given quantity of securities at the best possible price. The main difference between the two types of orders involves the need for immediacy: the market order is a demand of immediacy expressed by a trader, possible because it does not impose a price limit on the transaction. As a result, market orders have a high probability of being executed. Uncertainty surrounding this type of order often relates to the execution price. Conversely, a limit order fixes a price limit above or below which the order should not be executed. For a buy limit order, the execution must occur at or below the limit price, while for sell limit order, the execution must take place at or above the price limit. Limit orders are more uncertain than market orders because if the book does not contain a proper match, the order either will expire or remain unexecuted. If the order is partially executed, a residual quantity can be left on the order book.

Additional instructions can be attached to the main order. Some of the most common include the following:

- **Fill or kill (FOK).** A FOK instruction ensures that either the order gets executed immediately in full or not at all.
- **Immediate or cancel (IOC).** An IOC instruction states that any portion of the order that cannot be executed immediately against any order on the book is cancelled. IOC orders can be associated with both market orders and limit orders. When a limit price is inserted, the order will execute when the required quantity is available.
- **All or none (AON).** This instruction forces a 100 percent completion requirement on an order. After giving this instruction, the focus in not on immediacy. In fact, there might be some persistence of the order on the book.

According to the execution time, orders are classified in the following manner:

- **Good till date (GTD).** This order will remain active until the end of the trading session at a prespecified date, such as *good this week* (GTW) or *good this month* (GTM).
- **Good till cancel (GTC).** This order will stay active until the user specifically cancels it (*good till expiration*).
- **Good after time date (GAT).** This order allows the trader to control when it becomes active. This type of order is useful for broker systems where clients may choose to spread orders over the day. In trading algorithms, this instruction is a start-time parameter initializing the trading process.

Among the different order types, various preferencing and directed instructions may exist. These instructions allow the routing of orders toward a specific broker or dealer or trading venue. The order can contain the routing instructions including the price and quantity instructions. Some specific routing instructions are:

- **Order protection rules in the United States.** This instruction makes brokers and venues responsible for finding the best price. The host venue should either reject or forward the order to the market when achieving a better price is possible.

- **Additional instructions.** These instructions as "do not route" or "intermarket sweep" allow for better control of the order routing.

Flash orders represent a specific and interesting order instruction. These orders display the source venue for a short period before being routed to another destination. The idea underlying such orders involves offering a trader the possibility of achieving the best price. Only AT and HFT can exploit the advantage emerging from flash orders because the technological requirements are binding. These types of orders are under scrutiny because of the advantage assigned to specific traders. In some senses, the asymmetric information phenomenon previously discussed becomes part of the problem.

Hybrid order mechanisms combine features typical of limit orders with those of market orders. *Markets with protection orders* are an example of this combination, whose goal is to offer the immediate execution of a market order with the protection of a price limit. In this type of order, the limit price is established as being different from the last execution price. This type of order balances the certainty of execution and certainty of price.

Sometimes, specifying the conditions for the execution of a given order may be useful. Under these conditions, conditional order types emerge. These types of orders are valid under a given set of conditions usually determined by the limit assigned to the market price. If the specific conditions (say, with respect to the price limit) are met, then the order is effectively executed.

Stop orders (sometimes also called *stop loss orders*) become binding when the market price reaches a given threshold. At this point, they are transformed into market orders. In continuous trading, the triggering price is the last traded price. In an open outcry auction, the triggering price is the closing price. Activation occurs for buy orders when the market price hits the stop price or above. For sell orders, activation occurs when the market price goes below the threshold. For example, suppose an investor initiated a long position at a price of 10 dollars. It the price increases to 11 dollars, a stop sell order is placed at 11 dollars as a means of protection. If the price trend reverts, the stop threshold will be triggered. Alternatively, the stop order is never implemented. These order types are implemented and combined with the market with protection order types in order to increase the probability of execution and to obtain strong price controls.

Next, this chapter discusses hidden and iceberg orders. These types of orders are at the core of the functioning of some specific venues, such as the "dark pools," where the identity of traders is hidden alternately or jointly with the full size of the order book. Transparency in financial markets allows traders to correctly track demand and supply. Conversely, when some traders need to exchange large-size orders, consequences may be too strong, based on the price patterns. For example, a large order might convey wrong information to the whole market and might generate herd behavior, which, in turn, could cause strong oscillations. For these reasons, many trading venues allow the retention of large orders that are hidden in the book. Moreover, a compromise between hidden orders and visible orders is represented by iceberg orders, where only a fraction of the order is made visible to the market. If the market allows hidden orders, traders can participate without revealing their positions to the market. To further illustrate this point, consider the example reported in Table 18.1, which presents the order book for trades of a given stock.

The order book outlined in Table 18.1 represents the situation before the order is sent to the market. As shown in the first row of the table, a market order to purchase 2,000 shares of stock is hidden. The last four columns, representing the sell side of the book, show the order book after it has been routed to the venue and executed; here, the information related to 1,000 shares are matched with the initial order. Note that the order to buy 2,000 shares is not visible on the buy side because it is inserted in the book as a hidden order. As a market order, it does not have price priority and can immediately be matched with the best prices offered by the sell side. Second, after having executed half of the order (1,000 shares), the remaining part becomes latent, sitting on the order book. If an IOC instruction is issued to sell an additional 1,000 shares at $51, the investor can test the presence of liquidity ("ping" the market) to attempt to match with the remaining portion of the order. If an order to sell occurs and is executed, the implication is that the book contained a hidden order ready to be exchanged.

A different pattern can be observed for iceberg orders. In this case, only a small part of the order is visible, with the remaining portion hidden. The visible

Table 18.1 **Example of implementation of a hidden order**

	BUY			SELL (before execution)			
H	Time	Size	Price ($)	Price ($)	Size	Time	Price
B1	10:41:00	2,000	50	51	1,000	10:35:00	S1
B2	10:35:10	1,000	49	52	1,500	10:37:15	S2
B3	10:40:10	8,000	48	52	8,00	10:39:09	S3
B4	10:40:75	3,000	47	52	2,000	10:41:00	S4

	SELL (after execution)		
Price ($)	Size	Time	Price ($)
51	1,000	10:35:00	S1
52	1,500	10:37:15	S2
52	800	10:39:09	S3
52	2,000	10:41:00	S4

Note: This table shows the behavior of the order book when hidden orders are implemented. "H" stands for the hidden orders, before they are sent to the market. The "B" in the column to the left stands for "buy," and the "S" in column to the right stands for "sell."

Table 18.2 **Example of order book after iceberg order**

	Buy		Sell (before execution)			
ID	Size	Price ($)	Price ($)	Size	Time	ID
B1	2,000	50	51	2,000	1020:00	S1
B2	700	49	51	2,000	10:21:15	S2
B3	2,500	48	51	18,000	10:05:10	H1
			52	2,500	10:25:31	S3

	Sell (after execution)		
Price ($)	Size	Time	ID
51	2,000	10:20:00	S1
51	1,000	10:21:15	S2
51	1,000	10:21:15	S2
51	2,000	10:28:30	S4
51	16,000	10:05:10	H1

Note: This table highlights the evolution of the order book after introducing an iceberg order.

portion of the order is virtually nonevident from other types of limit orders. When the visible portion of the order is executed, the trading system slices a new order from the hidden part until the whole order is completed. The visible part has time priority, while the hidden portion has only price priority.

Consider the example of the iceberg order in Table 18.2, adapted from Johnson (2010). On the left side of the table (the sell side of the book), a portion of the sell order S1 has been issued on the order book. The whole order is H1, which is not visible. When order S1 at a price of $51 is executed, a new portion of the hidden order is released from the hidden order H1 and is included in the book in the pace of order S4. If there were two hidden orders at the same price, time priority would indicate which gets executed first.

In actual current market practice, a more granular structure of orders exists. In the present context, the chapter limits its treatment to the most important orders. The next section discusses the main trading strategies and related algorithm selection.

Algorithm Selection

As discussed earlier, an algorithm identifies a set of instructions for accomplishing a specific trading task. Three types of algorithms are described below:

- **Impact-driven algorithms.** These algorithms attempt to minimize the overall market impact. They are created in order to reduce the effect that trading activity might have on the market price.
- **Cost-driven algorithms.** The underlying goal of these algorithms is cost minimization. They do not take into account market impact, timing risk, and other related factors such as the measures of benchmarking and implementation shortfall.
- **Opportunistic algorithms.** These algorithms take advantage of market evolutions.

IMPACT-DRIVEN ALGORITHMS

The most common impact-driven algorithms are the *time-weighted average price* (TWAP) and the *volume-weighted average price* (VWAP). The general feature of these algorithms is that they focus on the behavior of a prespecified benchmark and track it systematically, with limited sensitivity to market conditions.

Time-Weighted Average Price

An example of TWAP can be shown in the two possible strategies for buying ten thousand shares of a given asset: First, a trader could issue regular-sized orders to buy five hundred shares every fifteen minutes for five hours. In a second strategy, the trader could issue an order to buy one thousand shares every fifteen minutes for 2.5 hours. The trade profile is very simple and can be easily forecasted, implying a signaling risk.

After systematically observing the behavior exhibited with such trades, the market can easily forecast the next trade and implement actions that may create adverse price movements. After the trading pattern is discovered, the only unknown for the market is the total size of the order. For the trader, an alternative to this predicted behavior could consist of inserting a tilting factor, acceleration, or deceleration of the order size after an established threshold of the total order has been fulfilled.

As an example, the trader may insert a tilting factor that results in the order executing more quickly after 30 percent of the total order has been executed. Another alternative is the insertion of a randomized approach whose position can be adjusted after the fulfillment of the order has been completed. In general, the tilting factor defines the degree of aggressiveness attached to the algorithm. An *aggressive strategy* occurs when a larger percentage of the order is executed early. A *passive strategy* occurs when the order size is smoothed out over time. The algorithm is generally completed by the inclusion of some parameters, such as an on/off switch that highlights how far the order might be from the benchmark. Another choice parameter is the frequency of trades and the degree of randomization of the trade sizes.

The more aggressive the order strategy, the greater the price impact associated with the trade. The primary shortcoming of the TWAP strategy is associated with a passive strategy. An alternative to the passive strategy involves implementing a trading schedule with a dynamical adjustment path that evolves according to the general market conditions.

Volume-Weighted Average Price

The main property of VWAP is its ability to design trading strategies according to the total market volume. A more general definition of the VWAP is given by Equation 18.1:

$$VWAP = \frac{\sum_{i=1}^{n} V_i P_i}{\sum_{i=1}^{n} V_i}, \tag{18.1}$$

where V_i is the size of the ith trade and P_i is the price associated to the ith trade. VWAP identifies the ratio of total traded value to the total traded quantity. In Equation 18.1, n represents the number of trades. The main way in which VWAP differs from TWAP is by the n variable: in the case of VWAP, it is possible for the total number of trades when the strategy is formulated to remain unknown. Estimation methods based on historical volume can be used to solve for the optimal number of trades. Kissel, Malamut, and Glantz (2003) contend that the optimal trading strategy can be found by using Equation 18.2:

$$x_j = z_j X, \tag{18.2}$$

where z_j is the percentage of daily volume traded, X is the total volume traded, and X_j is the target quantity. Thus, VWAP can be reinterpreted as shown in Equation 18.3:

$$VWAP = \sum_{j=1}^{n} z_j \overline{P}_j, \tag{18.3}$$

where P_j is the average price level in each period. According to Equation 18.3, VWAP is defined as the weighted average value of the prices associated with trades executed to implement a given strategy.

The VWAP trading activity is dependent on the historical pattern of the trading volume, not the actual volume or actual price changes. The performance evaluation of VWAP is given in terms of how closely it tracks the target and predicted market values. If the historical and actual market values do not differ substantially, then the performance of the VWAP strategy will not suffer. The performance of the VWAP strategy is less effective if substantial differences exist between the two volumes.

VWAP can be complemented by special tracking parameters that monitor how closely the algorithm tracks the target together with trending or tilting instructions. The objective of the VWAP strategy is to adjust the path of trade to closely target the execution method.

Percent of Volume

Percent of volume (POV) is an algorithm designed to closely target the market volume. With TWAP and VWAP, the trading schedule is deterministically derived, independent of the market volume. Conversely, the trading schedule based on POV is dynamically adjusted. The deterministic choice involves setting the proportion of market volume, or participation rate, that is to be targeted. For example, by establishing a 10 percent participation rate, the POV algorithm implies an order submission strategy equal to 10 percent of the total market volume (or possibly associated with either the buy or sell side of the order book). As a result, the trader no longer has any certainty about the trade being completed within a specific time period, because trade size is dependent on total market volume. Although POV is similar to VWAP, the difference is that in POV an actual volume is employed as opposed to a historical or estimated volume in VWAP. In practice, POV reacts to repeated trades with a trading target formulated with the observed value of the order's book total volume. Clearly, the trade sizes need to be adjusted to take into account the sequence of orders placed by the ith trade. The adjustment factor is given by $1/(1 - pr)$, where pr is the participation rate.

One of the main problems associated with this algorithm is given by the competition for liquidity. If several traders adopt a similar algorithm for trading illiquid assets, the direct consequence can be a strong price pressure that takes places as liquidity is reduced by absorbing available market volume. Thus, using this algorithm is often accompanied by price limits associated with excessive liquidity tension.

To avoid the risk of the market being able to predict the trading schedule implemented with POV, order aggressiveness and placement is often adjusted by tilting deterministic parameters. Further, some safeguards are often inserted in order to prevent excessive fluctuation of market volume. This is usually obtained by inserting the maximum trade size.

A variant of POV is offered by its price-adaptive version. In this case, the participation rate is adjusted according to how the market price compares to a benchmark, which could be either a market index or an exchange traded fund (ETF)–based index. Trade aggressiveness is reduced when price tension is high and relaxed when price tension is low. Another modification of the POV strategy can be implemented when another type of price condition is added to the algorithm such that orders are not going to receive a price higher than the last trade or the current best bid.

Overall, the dynamical features of POV make this algorithm more attractive and less forecastable than the simple VWAP or TWAP. However, regulatory authorities are now leading market participants to adopt variants of POV that are less likely to endanger the safety of the market as a whole. In this case, including as such variants as an adjustment mechanism toward a market benchmark with mandatory parameters may be possible. Currently, no formal prescriptions by the Securities and Exchange Commission (SEC) or other regulatory agencies exist, so more research needed in this field.

OPPORTUNISTIC ALGORITHMS

Opportunistic algorithms are designed to take advantage of favorable market conditions. Liquidity-driven algorithms that search for liquidity across several market venues play a key role in this process. After the introduction of algorithms, liquidity has become even more central in judging the quality of market status. Traditionally, liquidity has been associated with lower bid-ask spreads, focusing exclusively on the explicit transaction costs. As this chapter will clarify, after the presentation of a transaction-costs analysis, a nonliquid asset implies excessive price volatility after a trade, signaling a trading activity that is even slightly above what the market may expect. The increasing degree of fragmentation occurring in modern markets has delivered a more careful definition of opportunistic algorithms. In this context, liquidity-driven opportunistic algorithms are designed to search for liquidity over multiple execution venues. The most important element is given by liquidity aggregation across venues, and there is technology that is able to collect order-book data from all possible venues for the purpose of assembling everything into a unique order book. The design of a proper opportunistic algorithm should take into account the following: (1) the fee structure associated with each trading venue; (2) the latency, which in this case represents the time lag between orders sent and orders processed from each venue; and (3) the probability of execution associated to each trading venue. Orders are aggregated by using price priority and then by calculating the probability of execution.

Given that algorithms are designed to capture the performance of the entire order book, implementing a way to track the behavior of the order book over time is extremely important. In this context, a historical data analysis and a close monitoring scheme of the order book may help in estimating hidden liquidity. Often, the setup of the opportunistic algorithm includes specific actions such as "pinging for liquidity" in the book of a given trading venue. This practice consists of inserting a specific type of order, such as an IOC or a FOK, to test for liquidity inside the order book. If an IOC or FOK gets executed, then hidden liquidity exists in the book.

In practice, opportunistic algorithms represent a form of liquidity-seeking strategies that do not react to traded volume. Instead, the market depth, reflecting the volume at each favorable price point, represents the indicator leading the algorithm's strategies. When prices are favorable, the algorithm is designed to trade more aggressively to consume liquidity. When market conditions are unfavorable, participation trade falls to zero. Of course, liquidity plays a crucial role in this context. With such types of algorithms, orders do not necessarily get completed. The algorithm often contains a set of warnings about the liquidity situation of a given security in each trading venue. Some of the key parameters to be specified at the order initiation include visibility and benchmark pricing. Visibility specifies how much of the order may actually be displayed at each execution venue. For example, in the case of low visibility, IOC order types are largely employed. An alternative to this type of order is represented by processing the order through dark pools. The role of benchmark pricing is employed to decide if the security's price is favorable enough to measure participation.

Pre-trade and Post-trade Analysis

In trading activity, the role of transactions is crucial, and an accurate quantification of them helps traders to properly decide when and where to make transactions. In this context, pre-trade analysis is very important because it helps traders make informal decisions about the best order execution. *Pre-trade analysis* is conducted by using information coming from data. This type of analysis employs two sources of information. The first source includes information relative to the fundamentals of securities, such as price/earnings for stocks and coupons for fixed income. The second source includes trade-related factors, such as prices, liquidity, and cost estimates.

Information is gathered from trade-related sources related to price ranges, trends, and momentum. Obtaining liquidity information permits getting average daily volume (ADV), volume profile, and indicators of trading stability. Risk indicators include volatility, beta, and risk exposure. Cost estimates are defined by measures of market impact and timing risk. The estimate of transaction costs is an exact implication of the importance and difficulty of executing a given order.

Post-trade analysis delivers results about broker/trader performance in order to make both investment and execution decisions. The key element of the Post-trade analysis is obtained by breaking down costs into several components, including fees and commissions. With post-trade analysis, establishing relative performance and net of costs is possible for the trading activity implemented by a trader. Within this context, the choice of the benchmark becomes essential in performance computations. The average execution price of any given trade has to be compared with a benchmark. Post-trade benchmarks are based on closing prices. The main purpose of these benchmarks is to determine the mark-to-market computation and profit and loss. The problem with closing prices is their scarce power to represent real market conditions. An algorithm can be designed to track closing prices. However, closing prices tend to be more sensitive to the order flow than are those of other periods during the day. This situation implies that orders can be more exposed to timing risk and to more volatile conditions.

Intraday benchmarks are generally given in the following manner: (1) the average of open high price, low close price, (2) the TWAP, and (3) the VWAP. The average of the open high represents an average over only four data points and can be easily distorted by extreme values. The TWAP represents an average of all observed trade prices over a given timing period. Thus, all trades are weighted equally, which has the drawback that smaller trades occurring at extreme prices may markedly affect TWAP calculations. However, the TWAP is generally employed when trade volume data are unavailable. In general, the VWAP is probably the fairest indication of how market prices have changed over a specific time span. The VWAP does not have a strong impact on small trades and can be considered a very good representation of average market conditions. A higher value of VWAP indicates a higher market impact determined by the last trade. Conversely, the VWAP does not deliver good performance when the sample of analysis includes large orders or when the volatility of orders is large.

At the same time, market conditions that include large price reversals do not represent an ideal context in which to apply VWAP.

Pre-trade benchmarks can be separated into those that are directly available and those that not publicly observable. Directly available benchmarks are represented by the previous close and opening prices. These benchmarks do not necessarily reflect actual market conditions during the trading day. Other useful prices include the decision price and arrival price. The *decision price* is the price at which the choice to invest was actually made. The decision price is used in the calculations related to the implementation shortfall, which will be discussed in a later section. The *arrival price* is the price registered at the time when the order was actually traded, which is the time at which the order arrives from the investor. The problem with such information is that the decision/arrival price is not always recorded by the investor.

Kissel, Malamut, Glantz (2003) propose a relative performance measure (RPM) based on the assessment of what the trade achieved in relation to market condition. Equation 18.4 presents the RPM for volume, while Equation 18.5 gives the RPM for trades.

$$RPM(Volume) = \frac{total\ volume\ at\ prices\ less\ favorable\ than\ execution}{total\ market\ volume} \quad (18.4)$$

$$RPM(trades) = \frac{number\ of\ trades\ at\ prices\ less\ favorable\ than\ execution}{total\ number\ of\ trades} \quad (18.5)$$

The advantage of using the RPM is that it is already normalized in percentage terms. For example, a trade achieving 90 percent of the RPM is better than another trade reaching 60 percent.

POST-TRADE TRANSACTION COSTS

The most important measure of performance in post-trade analysis is the *implementation shortfall* (IS), which is the difference between the price that an investor decides to trade at and the average execution price that is actually achieved. The decision price is the benchmark. If the decision price is not specified, the mid-price is generally accepted as the default benchmark. Perold's (1988) measure of IS consists of comparing the return of a "paper" (hypothetical) portfolio with the return obtained in the real, actually traded portfolio, as shown in Equation 18.6:

$$IS = Return_{paper} - Return_{real}. \quad (18.6)$$

The performance of the theoretical or paper portfolio depends on three factors: (1) the price at which the decision to invest was made P_d, (2) the final market price P_N, and (3) the size of the intended investment X. More formally, given

x_j the size of the jth buy order, with achieved price p_j, the IS can be defined as shown in Equation 18.7:

$$IS = X(P_N - P_d) - (XP_N - \sum_j x_j p_j - \text{fixed}).$$ (18.7)

Assuming that the order is fully executed, the IS measure, as shown in Equation 18.8, becomes:

$$IS = \sum_j x_j p_j - XP_d + \text{fixed}.$$ (18.8)

If the order is not fully executed, the IS can be rewritten as shown in Equation 18.9:

$$IS = \frac{\sum_j x_j p_j - \left(\sum_j x_j\right) P_d}{\text{Execution Cost}} + \frac{\left(X - \sum_j x_j\right)(P_N - P_d) + \text{fixed}}{\text{Opportunity Cost}},$$ (18.9)

where $X - \sum_j x_j$ indicates the size of the unexecuted position.

According to Kissel, Malamut, and Glantz (2003), transaction costs can be classified as either: (1) fixed and variable or (2) visible and transparent. Typically, visible costs cannot be managed, while nontransparent components are manageable through an appropriate execution strategy.

Perold's implementation shortfall (IS) measure can be expanded by adding investment-related delay costs, as suggested by Wagner and Glass (2001). In this case, the expanded measure of transaction costs is given in Equation 18.10:

$$TC = \frac{\sum_{j=1}^{n} x_j (P_d - P_o)}{\text{Delay cost}} + \frac{\sum_{j=1}^{n} x_j P_j - \sum_{j=1}^{n} x_j P_o}{\text{Trade Related}} + \frac{\left(X - \sum_{j=1}^{n} x_j\right)(P_n - P_d)}{\text{Opportunity Costs}},$$ (18.10)

where X indicates the total amount of shares traded at jth transaction, P_j is the price of the jth transaction, P_d is the price observed at the time of investment decision, P_o is the price at time when the order is released to the market, P_n is the price at the end of the trading session, and n is the total number of trading periods.

Cost minimization strategies focus on developing analytical methods to manage trade-related transaction costs. Minimization of delay costs and opportunity costs is a natural consequence of adopting a fast trading method, with the ability of minimizing trade latency as much as possible. The rapid increase of HFT techniques and infrastructures is motivated by the need to minimize delay and opportunity costs. The design of an optimal execution method allows reducing the trade-related component of transaction costs.

Optimal Execution Strategies

Trading activity is a complex set of strategies, market conditions, and costs. Trading too aggressively produces a higher market impact. Conversely, trading too passively implies a higher timing risk. In general, optimal execution strategies attempt to find a balance between these two extremes. The optimal execution strategies can be synthetically represented by Figure 18.1.

In Figure 18.1, the market impact is decreasing over time through trading strategies, while the timing risk is increasing over time. The optimal execution strategies mix up the balance between these two cost measures. In general, the optimal solution is determined by the trader's degree of risk aversion. The balance between market impact and timing risk defines the famous optimal trading horizon.

The design of an optimal algorithm has the goal of minimizing total costs related to trading activity. The characteristics of a transparent and efficient algorithm are given by two elements: The first element is the choice of a desired benchmark price: at close, at open, or at arrival. The second element is the choice of a desired trading style—aggressive, normal, or moderate—including the choice about how the algorithm should adapt to market conditions. Algorithms should be built in order to balance the tradeoff between market impact and timing risk over the trading horizon. According to Kissel, Malamut, and Glantz (2003),

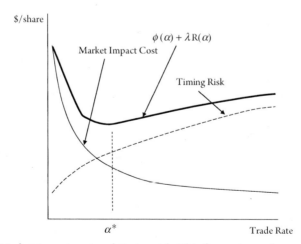

Figure 18.1 Market impact cost and timing risk. This figure shows the market impact cost and the timing risk as functions of the trading rate. The optimal trading rate is obtained from the minimum point on the curve, $\phi(\alpha)+\lambda\mathfrak{R}(\alpha)$.

market impact is the movement in stock caused by the order or the trade. Permanent impact costs are the result of an information leakage.

Almgren and Chriss (2000) focus on designing optimal execution strategies. The problem with their approach is the lack of an approximate market impact function at the trade level that also takes into account price movements. Kissel and Malamut (2006) solve this problem by considering a top-down approach, where the average market impact cost is estimated for aggregated trade imbalance and allocated to trading periods.

According to Kissel and Malamut (2006), the impact cost is defined according to Equation 18.11:

$$I = a_1 \left(\frac{X}{ADV} \right)^{a^2} \sigma^{a3} X P_o,$$ (18.11)

where X is the number of shares contained in the order, ADV is the average daily trading volume, σ is the annualized volatility, and P_0 is the current price. The market impact function is given in Equation 18.12:

$$MI(x_k) = \sum_{j=1}^{n} \underbrace{\frac{b_I I x_j^2}{X(x_j + 0.5v_j)}}_{temporary\ impact} + \underbrace{(1-b_I)I}_{permanent\ impact},$$ (18.12)

where x_j indicates the number of shares transacted in period j, v_j is the expected volume (net of the order) in period j, and b_1 is the percentage of temporary market impact costs. Assuming the existence of a constant trading rate, Equation 18.13 emerges in the following manner:

$$\alpha = \frac{x_j}{v_j}.$$ (18.13)

After rearrangement (Kissel and Malamut 2006), the entire expression can be rewritten for the market impact given in Equation 18.12 as a function of the trading rate shown in equation 18.14:

$$MI(\alpha) = \underbrace{\left(\frac{b_1 I}{X} \right)\left(\frac{2}{3} \right)\alpha^{\frac{1}{2}}}_{l_1} + \underbrace{\frac{(1-b_1)I}{X}}_{l_2},$$ (18.14)

which, after rearrangement, becomes Equation 18.15:

$$MI(\alpha) = l_1 \alpha^{\frac{1}{2}} + l_2.$$ (18.15)

Equation 18.16 provides an alternative formulation for market impact:

$$MI = \underbrace{I(Q,\sigma)}_{I_{bp}}\underbrace{[\mu^{-1}b_1 +(1-b_1)]}_{d(\mu)},$$ (18.16)

where $I(Q,\sigma)$ is the trade impact function whose arguments are market imbalance Q and volatility σ. Function $d(\mu)$ is the dissipation function, where $\mu = V_{side}/Q$ $\mu = {V_{side}}/{Q}$ and $V_{side} = \sum_{i \in Q} \text{sign}(v_i)$ indicate the cumulative amount of the order on the same side of the market (in buy or in sell, according to the sign of v_j).

Given the information contained in the previous paragraph, the problem of optimal trade execution consists in finding the optimal trading rate that minimizes the cost given the risk. Formally, the problem can be stated in Equation 18.17 as such:

$$\begin{cases} \text{Min } \phi(x_k) \\ \text{s.t. } \Re(x_k) \le \Re^*, \end{cases}$$ (18.17)

where $\Re^*$ is the threshold level of timing risk. Following Kissel, Malamut, and Glantz (2003), the timing risk is the uncertainty surrounding the expected market impact cost, which is related with volume and intraday volume patterns. Timing risk, according to its definition, is given in Equation 18.18:

$$\Re(x_k) = P_0 \sqrt{\sum_{j=1}^{n} r_j^2 \frac{t\sigma^2}{n}}.$$ (18.18)

In terms of the trading rate a, the timing risk can be reformulated as shown in Equation 18.19:

$$\Re(\alpha) = P_0 X \sigma \sqrt{\frac{s}{3\alpha}}.$$ (18.19)

The goal of finding optimal execution consists of finding the trading rate a that minimizes the expression in Equation 18.20:

$$\underset{\alpha}{\text{Min}}\{MI(\alpha) + \lambda \Re(\alpha)\}.$$ (18.20)

A crucial parameter in Equation 18.20 is λ, which represents the degree of risk aversion of the trader. In other words, choosing the value of λ can affect the aggressiveness of the trading strategy. A lower λ indicates a patient trader because less weight is assigned to timing risk and more weight is assigned to trading cost.

Conversely, a higher λ implies a more aggressive trading strategy, with higher weights assigned to market impact costs and lower weights assigned to timing risk.

As discussed previously, Figure 18.1 is a pictorial representation of the optimization procedure. The figure illustrates the evolution of market impact cost and timing risk as a function of trading rates. Clearly, the optimal trading rate is obtained as the minimum point of the curve outlined by Equation 18.20 for any given level of risk aversion λ.

Given the optimal strategy, which is defined in terms of the trading rate as a function of the parameters and exogenous variables of the model, Equation 18.20, conditional on the optimal solution, delivers the ETF as defined by Almgren and Chriss (2000). In Figure 18.2, the ETF is shown for two given levels of price benchmarks adopted to study trade performance.

The dashed-line ETF has been constructed adopting the previous close price as a benchmark, while the solid-line ETF is based on the arrival price. In general, the ETF computed using the previous close price can either be above or below the ETF based on the arrival price for two reasons: First, the ETF includes permanent price impacts, not just the temporary component. Second, the ETF includes price movements between the time of investment decisions and the trade starting time.

By definition, the ETF is the locus of all optimal trading strategies, such as the least cost for a given level of timing risk and the lowest timing risk for a specified cost. An efficient strategy is on the ETF. All strategies above the ETF are inefficient in the sense that finding another strategy with lower timing risk is always possible. Movements along the curve are governed by the size of parameter λ. That is, if λ is higher (implying a more aggressive trading strategy), then the optimal trading point will be located in the top left part of the curve, while for lower λ, the solution will be associated with lower expected cost and higher timing risk.

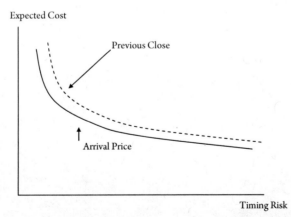

Figure 18.2 Efficient trading frontier. This figure shows two ETFs computed as conditional in relation to two prices: the previous close and the arrival price.

The notion of the ETF has recently expanded to several other optimal trading models that include the uncertainty of prices. Almgren (2012) develops an optimal trading model with an arithmetical Brownian motion process for the stock prices. Gatheral and Schied (2011) expand their optimal trading model on the basis of geometric Brownian motion. This area of research is rapidly expanding, which is not surprising given the strong impact that it will have in the design of trading strategies and on its global market impact.

Execution Tactics

Passive approaches use limit orders priced at or behind the market, whereas aggressive approaches adopt either market or marketable orders. Neutral tactics tend to be more flexible and start passively and seek price improvement. If they fail, these neutral tactics should be replaced with more aggressive ones. A more dynamic tactic strategy considers market conditions and adapts its strategy to it. Broadly speaking, execution tactics may be classified on the basis of the goals that drive their usage. Three common execution tactics include ones that are impact driven, price risk driven, and opportunistic.

IMPACT-DRIVEN TACTICS

Impact-driven tactics seek to further reduce market impact by splitting an order into smaller quantities or by hiding a portion of it. As discussed by Johnson (2010), two types of impact-driven tactics are slicing and hiding.

Slicing
Slicing of an order is the precursor to the early schedule-driven algorithms. Reducing the size of an order can lower its market impact and any associated signaling risk. Randomization is a way of further reducing signaling risk. This reduction applies to both the quantities to be split and the time between each subsidiary (or 'child') order. When adopted sequentially, order slicing effectively acts as a hiding mechanism. The strategy may be adopted to create synthetic iceberg orders for venues that do not natively support this order type. For native iceberg orders, the hidden portion is still part of the order book, so it may still participate in the trade-crossing mechanism, with only price priority.

On the other hand, order slicing relies on execution confirmations to know when to send order slices. These orders are dispatched after a matching process is employed. In this way, a trader may miss some crossing opportunities. For example, consider a requirement to sell 10,000 shares of ABC stock, from which the trader has split an initial order for 1,000 shares at $51 as S1. The main advantage of order slicing is that the trader has much more control of the display size. In this case, the second order can be split with a random size rather than simply splitting 1,000 shares each time. Order slicing can also be applied in parallel, allowing simultaneous trading across several execution venues. The example,

Table 18.3 **An example of slicing execution tactics Panel A. Before execution: Incoming market order to buy 2,200 shares**

	Buy				Sell		
ID	Time	Size	Price	Price	Size	Time	ID
B1	10:25:00	1,000	50	51	1,000	10:20:00	S1
B2	10:20:25	2,000	49	51	800	10:25:25	S2
B3	10:24:20	1,500	48	52	2,500	10:24:09	S3

Panel B. **Effect of market order crosses**

Price ($)	Size	ID
51	1,000	S1
51	800	S2
52	400	S3
52	2,100	S3

Panel C. **Effect of a synthetic iceberg order**

	Buy				Sell		
ID	Time	Size	Price ($)	Price ($)	Size	Time	ID
B1	10:25:00	1,000	50	51	1,000	10:20:00	S1
B2	10:20:25	2,000	49	51	800	10:25:25	S2
B3	10:24:20	1,500	48	52	400	10:24:09	S3
				51	850	10:26:00	S6
				52	2,100	10:24:09	S3

Panel D. **Effect of a native iceberg order**

	Sell	
Price ($)	Size	ID
51	1,000	S1
51	800	S2
51	400	S6
51	600	S6
52	2,500	S3

Note: The panels in this table shows the effect of an order to buy 2,200 shares on the order book.

adapted from Johnson (2010), reported in table 18.3 represents the effect of an order to buy 2,200 shares on the order book.

In panel B of table 18.3, note the effect highlighted in italics, which is due to market order matching. In panel C, note that for a synthetic iceberg order, an immediate cross exists for orders S1 and S2 at 51. The next cross will be in S3 at 52. After the venue sends confirmation for these fills, another split occurs for S6 for 850 shares. Panel D of the table illustrates the effects of a native iceberg order. In this case, the hidden size completes the market order at 51. A new display size would have been split in order S6: 400 shares would complete the market order, and the remaining 600 shares would stay on the order book.

Hiding

Hiding is associated with reducing signaling risk, which is the potential information that a trading pattern relays to other market participants. As in Johnson (2010), the example reported in table 18.4 records large block orders.

In table 18.4, algorithmic orders are implicitly hidden because most of its strategies only release a small portion of the order for immediate trading. Liquidity is another critical variable because even a small order may have important price

Table 18.4 **Example of hiding execution tactics**
Panel A

	Sell	
Price ($)	Size	ID
51	1,000	S1
51	3,000	S2
52	4,000	S3
52	2,000	S4

Panel B

	Sell	
Price ($)	Size	ID
51	2,000	S1
51	3,000	S2
51	1,000	S3
51	7,000	H1
52	4,000	S4

Panel C

Price ($)	Sell	
	Size	ID
51	1,000	S1
51	2,000	S2
51	4,000	H1
52	1,000	S4

Note: This table shows an example of hiding execution tactics for large block orders.

effects in the case of illiquid assets. Discretionary orders allow a trader to hide his actual limit price. In panel A, the intention to execute the order S3 with a limit price 52 exists even though the trader was prepared to trade at 51. The trader could increase his discretionary amount to shift his order deeper in the order book. This change would place more orders in front of the trader in terms of execution priority. Iceberg orders allow the trader to display only a portion of the order, with the remaining portion retaining price priority. For example, in panel B, 1,000 shares are displayed, with the remaining 7,000 shares are hidden until S3 is completed, although its price will maintain priority over S4. This example illustrates the importance of obtaining the right balance between the visible and hidden parts. Smaller trades may take too long to complete, with larger visible portions having greater predictability.

PRICE RISK-DRIVEN TACTICS

Price risk-driven tactics are based on changes in the spread and short-term price trends. As the gap between the best bid and offer narrows, a trader can afford to pay the spread, and the tactics may indicate issuing more-marketable limit or market orders. When the spread widens, a trader uses more passive pricing. Market conditions are also important. In a passive trading style during a favorable price trend, orders tend to be priced away from the market to try to take maximum advantage of price improvements. Conversely, in a passive trading style during unfavorable price trends, orders be may be priced closer to the market in order to reduce potential losses. Aggressive price strategies tend to rely on mean-reverting trends, so that they behave in the opposite fashion.

In risk-driven tactics, the asset's price volatility and how much time is left for execution are considered. The tactics may be combined to create a timing factor, which can be incorporated into order placement decisions. For a liquid asset at the start of the execution, the timing factor is minor but increases over time. For less liquid assets, the timing factor is more important. Other execution tactics are defined as catching, which is based on cutting the losses when the price appears to be trending away.

The layering tactic simultaneously maintains a range of standing limit orders. Orders are spread throughout the order book, usually with different limit prices. This approach attempts to take advantage of favorable price movements. With price/time priority, layering allows for the preservation of time priority for each order. This priority occurs because as the market price moves, a new order can be split, rather than just updating an existing order to match the new level. Time priority is very important for liquid stocks that have a densely populated order book. If time priority is lost, the only way to regain it is with a more aggressive price. In general, layering is useful for highly liquid assets with dense order books, where achieving time priority is difficult. In this way, price moves can be tracked without substantially affecting the overall probability of execution.

OPPORTUNISTIC TACTICS

Opportunistic tactics tend to maximize the benefits from favorable market conditions, such as liquidity. As classified by Johnson (2010), three types of such tactics are:

- **Seeking.** This tactic aims to source additional liquidity from hidden orders. Seeking tactics may also focus on reducing signaling risk. Monitoring the state of the order book can enable creating models to estimate the probability of how much volume is hidden at the various price levels throughout the order book. Another important concern when searching for liquidity is keeping orders hidden. The goal is to fill the orders at the best price possible without giving away information about the actual requirements. The choice is between various fill instructions available for limit orders. Only IOC or FOK are suitable because the others all leave residual orders on the order book. IOC allows partial fills, whereas FOK is a strict execution.
- **Sniping.** This tactic allows the capture of liquidity while minimizing signaling risk. It is a way for liquidity-demanding traders to hide their strategy. As such, sniping is a variation of the tactic for seeking visible liquidity. To reduce signaling risk, traders use marketable limit orders with specific fill instructions. When liquidity becomes available, an aggressive order is used to cross with it.
- **Routing.** This tactic chooses the best destinations unto which to send orders. Many factors have to be analyzed before deciding where to send an order, including: (1) the probability of hidden liquidity, (2) the likelihood of successful execution, (3) latency, and (4) the venue-specific costs or fees. Routing mechanisms are used to make these decisions based on available market data. Liquidity aggregation is the key aspect for trading in a fragmented market. Virtual order books can be formed by collecting data from all possible execution venues.

Summary and Conclusions

The key piece of knowledge presented in this chapter is based on the most recent advances in market evolutions, mainly represented by HFT and AT. The order characteristics and all the variants of the basic limit and market order types are considered for different trading needs. Given that AT and HFT involve using a specific trading strategy, the chapter also presents the main characteristics of the most-often-employed trading strategies, such as VWAP, TWAP, POV, and others. Implicit and explicit transaction costs are also introduced, which are at the core of the choice process of an optimal trading strategy. The optimal trade execution presented by Kissel and Malamut (2006) is also introduced together with a full description of the EFT.

The subject matter that the material in this chapter covers is evolving quickly and is new to the microstructure literature. The authors believe that adopting HFT and AT will radically modify the way in which researchers and practitioners approach the fields of market microstructure and market architecture. Many research areas are now open to these new advances, which challenge traditional concepts about market quality, liquidity, and price discovery. HFT has a role in propagating liquidity shortages and generating market crashes. While limited research exists on this topic, the design of optimal execution methods that do not endanger market conditions will be the challenge for the future.

Discussion Questions

1. Explain the advantages and risks of algorithmic trading.
2. Discuss the most useful instructions that are widely employed in high-frequency trading as well as the role of flash orders.
3. Describe the role of transaction costs in conditioning the design of optimal trading strategies.
4. Discuss the role of slicing an order.

References

Almgren, Robert. 2012. "Optimal Trading with Stochastic Liquidity and Volatility." *SIAM Journal of Financial Mathematics* 3, 163–181. Earlier version released as NYU Mathematics in Finance Working Paper 2009–2, New York University, New York.

Almgren, Robert, and Neill Chriss. 2000. "Optimal Execution of Portfolio Transactions." *Journal of Risk* 3:2, 5–39.

Biais, Bruno, Thierry Foucault, and Sophie Moinas. 2010. "Equilibrium Algorithmic Trading." Working Paper, Toulouse School of Economics, Toulouse, France.

Brogaard, Jonathan A. 2010. "High Frequency Trading and Its Impact on Market Quality." Working Paper, Kellogg School of Management, Northwestern University, Evanston, IL.

Gatheral, Jim, and Alexander Schied. 2011. "Optimal Trade Execution under Geometric Brownian Motion in the Almgren and Chriss Framework." *International Journal of Theoretical and Applied Finance* 14:3, 353–68.

Gomber, Peter, Bjöern Arndt, Marco Lutat, and Tim Uhle. 2011. "High-Frequency Trading: A European Perspective." *HoF Quarterly* 2, 9–10.

Johnson, Barry, C. 2010. "Algorithmic Trading and DMA: an introduction to direct access trading strategies", Myeloma Press, London.

Jovanovic, Boyan, and Albert J. Menkveld. 2010. "Middlemen in Limit Order Markets." Working Paper, New York University, New York.

Kissel, Robert, and Roberto Malamut. 2006. "Algorithmic Decision-Making Framework." *Institutional Investor: Guide to Algorithmic Trading*. Spring, 81–91.

Kissel, Robert, Roberto Malamut, and Morton Glantz. 2003. *Optimal Trading Strategies: Qualitative Approaches for Managing Market Impact and Trading Risk*. New York: AMACOM.

Perold, André F. 1988. "The Implementation Shortfall: Paper versus Reality." *Journal of Portfolio Management* 14:3, 4–9.

Wagner, Wayne H., and Steven Glass. 2001. "What Every Plan Sponsor Needs to Know about Transaction Costs." *Trading* 1, 20–35.

19

Market Timing Methods and Results

PANAGIOTIS SCHIZAS
Lecturer of Finance, University of Peloponnese

Introduction

Market timing is the investment strategy occurring when investors increase their allocation in risky assets in periods of bull markets. By contrast, *volatility timing* is the reaction when investors reduce their exposure in risky assets in periods of high volatility. Market timing or active trading is not a new idea. Keynes (1936) examines the variation on stock returns according to the business cycle and suggests a cyclical trading strategy called active investment policy. He based his strategy on constantly switching between shorter- and longer-maturity assets under forecast estimates following changes in the interest rate. In recent years, market timing requires identifying the correct market trend. Investors and finance professionals look for successful trading strategies that account for different aspects and assumptions about the markets. The triggering variation in the new concept of market timing is often referred to as the diminishing of the trading asset allocation framework. The success or failure of the pattern mainly depends on achieving absolute returns, not on the efficiency of the optimal asset allocation, which indicates the role of relative return. *Absolute return* is the return on an asset or an investment, expressed as a percentage, relative only to the investment itself. Absolute return differs from relative return because it focuses only on an asset's return, and it does not compare returns to any other measure or benchmark. The absolute return approach to a fund is a relatively new investment philosophy. Hedge funds mainly use this approach when they seek positive returns by employing investment strategies such as short selling, futures, options, derivatives, arbitrage, leverage, and using unconventional assets. Traditional mutual funds often are not permitted to use such strategies. The profitable implementation of the absolute return approach requires the existence of asymmetric returns. Although the absence of absolute returns indicates the absence of normally distributed returns, the departure from linearity is the consequence of an asymmetric risk-return profile. Alternative investment vehicles such as hedge funds are responsible for the presence of asymmetric returns by using unconventional investment strategies.

To better understand the role of hedge funds, consider an example of a strategy where the initial wealth is $1000 with $950 invested in a money market instrument yielding the risk-free rate and $50 invested in put options. During the period, the value of the options doubles in value, so that the initial $50 investment is now worth $100. Also, the $950 riskless investment in money market instruments has increased in value to $1000. At the end of the period, the value of the portfolio is $1000 + $100 = $1100, which equates to a return of 10 percent. Now suppose that, instead of buying options, the intrinsic value of the option is zero. In this case, at the end of the period, the terminal value of the portfolio would be $1000 + $0 = $1,000. The investor would still experience a loss. The initial capital of $1000 was preserved. So, the principal capital was safe even though the potential gain was unlimited; the tradeoff between potential gains and potential losses is asymmetric. The sense of optimal market timing corresponds to identifying and exploiting investment opportunities where the risk-reward relationship is asymmetric, so as the potential profit is higher than the potential loss, or the probability of a profit should be higher than the probability of a loss of the same magnitude or a combination of the above.

Active market timing strategies try to identify these asymmetries and achieve a positive "alpha." The traditional asset pricing models, some of which are quite successful, find "alpha" from a linear model, while the exploration of nonlinear models leads to the generation of asymmetric returns. Asymmetry can be split into two basic parts: the frequency of positive versus negative returns and the magnitude of positive versus negative returns.

This chapter focuses on the impact of the existence of asymmetry in the returns and provides an overview of several technical indicators and trading strategies under the spectrum on optimal market timing. The technical indicators discussed are intended: (1) to be able to identify several market trends, (2) to be widespread and applied by the practitioners, and (3) to point out the technical indicators that not only can stand alone but also can be combined or used within advanced trading strategies to achieve profitability. The chapter also presents several quantitative trading strategies that depend on time-varying relative returns and volatilities.

The rest of the chapter is organized as follows. The first section examines the role of hedge funds in market timing. The next section presents the characteristics of trading strategies based on empirical distributions. The chapter then provides a description of the technical patterns and their use in the optimal timing of the market. The next-to-last section demonstrates methodologies based on relative market timing. The final section provides a summary and conclusions.

The Role of Hedge Funds on Market Timing

To illustrate the reactions of the market and the crucial role of the hedge funds, Zuckerman (2009) states:

> After seeing which type of stocks are exploding higher, and just how vicious the moves are, some hedge: ... My gut tells me quant (and other varieties) of hedge funds have been shorting these names, using

fundamental reasons—expecting some pullback after huge runs—only to be run over again and again even in week 6 and 7 of this rally. But much like August 2007 (but in opposite direction back then) we are seeing some very strange moves of magnificent quantity in individual names that do not square up with any reasonable fundamental reason; it just appears to be hedge funds leaning hard and being snared ... in August 2007 the moves were down, now the moves are up.... Unfortunately that only comes with a long delay on the long side via SEC filings, and we have zero visibility on the short side. Some of these quants are turning over hundreds upon hundreds of trades a day, so you just never know what is going on out there. As we posted last year, while the hedges control a relatively moderate amount of assets, they dominate the day-to-day trading and volume in these markets.... I cited August 2007 specifically above because I saw the exact same sort of "markings" in the market—the dislocations looked identical.

Hedge funds that are based on sophisticated computer models are known as *quant funds*. Although quant funds outperformed the market before the credit crunch in 2008, they can suffer great losses in the case of an extreme event for two reasons. First, their objective is to capitalize on shorter-term trends. In shorter time spans, the trading algorithms can provide false alarms while the market is moving in the opposite direction and their behavior is designed to dominate the daily volumes of the markets, so the daily turnover is coming mainly by orders given by the hedge funds. Second, hedge funds could face great losses due to leverage and short exposure. As an example during and after the financial crisis of 2007 and 2008, hedge funds had to reduce their leverage substantially and those that had a short exposure in an upwardly trending market suffered the most.

CRUCIAL FACTORS NEEDED TO IMPLEMENT MARKET TIMING

Regulatory constraints affect the practical implementation of market timing strategies. The most important regulatory concerns are associated with the price impact to block trades, liquidity constraints, and restrictions on short sales and leverage, which affect identifying arbitrage opportunities.

The Importance of Arbitrage

In an era of quantitative strategies, market timing strategies are implicitly grounded in the importance of exploiting arbitrage opportunities. Arbitrage opportunities emerge either under the spectrum of the convergence to long-run trends or the exploitation of extreme price differentials. How do these opportunities affect final profitability of statistical arbitrage strategies? Under extreme market circumstances, arbitrage opportunities diminish such that all arbitrageurs are fully invested, and the profits have to be shared by an extremely limited pool of participants. However, from the pool of the investors, only a small group of specialists can identify and exploit abnormal returns opportunities. When the market becomes aware of these opportunities, such opportunities to earn excess returns diminish. Therefore, knowing when to enter and exit a trade is important to a successful strategy. As Jurek and Yang (2006) point out, historical returns are vital to arbitrage strategies by hedge funds. In general, practitioners are reluctant to increase their allocation in a high volatility environment even when mispricing has widened. The absence of arbitrage opportunities in the market helps predictability power and results in prices converging based on fundamentals.

The Importance of Liquidity and Leverage

Long Term Capital Management (LTCM) is an example of a well-known market-neutral long/short fund established in 1994. LTCM largely used relative value strategies involving global fixed income arbitrage, equity index futures arbitrage, and interest rates derivatives. Because these arbitrage differences are minute, especially for the convergence trades, the fund took highly leveraged positions to enhance profits. During its early years, LTCM was initially successful and achieved an annualized return of more than 40 percent (after fees). Yet, in 1998, the firm lost \$4.6 billion in less than four months after the Russian financial crisis. LTCM closed in early 2000. Before its collapse, LTCM controlled \$120 billion in positions with \$4.8 billion in capital, which represented an extremely high leverage ratio (120/4.8 = 25). LTCM had extremely large positions in areas such as merger arbitrage and S&P 500 options (net short long-term S&P volatility), S&P 500 vega, which had been in demand by companies seeking to essentially insure equities against future declines. Vega is the measurement of an option's price sensitivity to a 1 percent change in volatility in the underlying asset. Lowenstein (2000) notes that because these differences in value were minute, especially for the convergence trades, LTCM had to take highly leveraged positions to make substantial profits, while the financial crisis resulted in extreme losses.

As a result of the financial crisis of 2007 and 2008, the average leverage multiplier for hedge funds dropped to about three times capital (Blundell-Wignall, 2007), as most funds started using far less leverage. Leverage in quantitative funds is essential because these funds focus on earning small gains through mispricing, which are enhanced through leverage. Inherent tradeoffs exist with this strategy between balancing the long and short investments as a safeguard against market risk. Due to their market neutral exposure, without leverage, these funds cannot compete in a bull market with an aggressive, long-only growth manager. Many hedge funds use a market neutral strategy called *pairs trading* to exploit mispricing. An assumption of pairs trading is that prices of selected assets tend to move together, and when they diverge, present an investment opportunity that is exploited by taking a market neutral position. A pairs trading strategy exploits statistical tools such as the concept of distance and the convergence/divergence of prices and is based on this distance, using pairs and distances for formulating combinations of long/short positions. Distances are denoted for the minimum of the price distance between two assets in order to match a pair. Implementing the strategy requires a simultaneous investing in a long and short position within a related sector. Thus, the source of the returns in market neutral funds comes from the mispricing performance differential within the pair. So implementing the strategy leads to the goal of achieving smaller returns, rather than pursuing strategies aimed at earning large returns, but may result in generating large losses.

The Importance of the Day-of-the-Week Effect

The importance of the day-of-the-week effect to the profitable market timing trading strategy has increased due to the growing role of the quantitative hedge funds in the recent years. Historical returns are a crucial factor in the success of this quantitative trading strategy. As Schizas, Thomakos, and Wang (2010) show, specific days of the week (Monday, Wednesday, and Friday) contain embedded historical information that helps one's predictive ability. Monday and Friday are the days that are before or after holidays or weekends, which is known as "weekend effect" or "closed-market effect." French (1980) provides empirical evidence that Monday returns are generally negative, except for the month of January where returns on Monday are positive. The distributions of the returns on Monday exhibits the lowest mean against any other day of the week. Wednesday confirms the existence of several patterns on trades, while returns exhibit significant predictive ability and returns from Wednesday to Wednesday are positively correlated. The distribution of the returns on Wednesday exhibits the highest mean among any other days of the week. Although Friday returns are influenced by the substantial decrease in trading activity and liquidity, the mean is slightly positive. Actions by arbitrageurs and investors who remain off the market due to the soaring uncertainty lead to substantial levels of volatility, which could lead to creating profitable arbitrage strategies.

Quantitative Trading Strategies Based on Empirical Distributions

The financial literature often uses distribution properties in evaluating the performance of strategies and in ranking assets such as mutual funds. For illustrative purposes, this section presents two frequently used metrics—the omega ratio and stochastic dominance—to assess the overall performance of trading strategies.

THE OMEGA RATIO

While performance measurement is traditionally based on mean and variance, these measures do not capture all of the risk and reward features in a distribution of financial returns, unless the returns are normally distributed. Keating and Shadwick (2002) develop a measure known as *omega* that employs all four statistical moments (return, variance or standard deviation, skewness, and kurtosis) of the distribution contained within the returns series. This leads to a more precise evaluation of the "alpha" of the strategy. The omega ratio could be characterized as an improved indicator of the well-known *Sharpe ratio* (1966), which is defined as the measure of the excess return (or risk premium) per unit of risk, as measured by a portfolio's standard deviation, in an investment asset or a trading strategy. The Sharpe ratio considers only the first two moments of the distribution (return and variance or standard deviation). However, the omega ratio considers all four statistical moments. The omega ratio, for a given targeted return (r), calculates the probability weighted gain-loss ratio relative to (r). Equation 19.1 provides the formula for calculating the omega ratio:

$$\Omega(r) = \frac{\displaystyle\int_r^b (1 - F(x))dx}{\displaystyle\int_a^r F(x)dx} \tag{19.1}$$

where (a, b) is the interval of returns and F is the cumulative distribution of returns. Omega is the ratio of the two areas where r is the local threshold between the gain and the loss. The omega ratio takes the value 1 when r is the mean return. Higher ratio values indicate better success in trading. The omega function features important statistical behaviors that can be interpreted in financial terms and provide profitable signs. The most important feature of omega is its nonparametric nature because its calculation is done directly from the observed distribution, using the entire information of the sample.

THE STOCHASTIC DOMINANCE INDICATOR

The stochastic dominance approach provides a robust estimation of the degree of success of market timing approaches. *Stochastic dominance* is defined as a ranking scale over possible outcomes between two assets taking into consideration their probability distribution function. The comparative advantage of stochastic dominance theory is the ability to use risk evaluation and create accurate results under the minimum possible quantity of information. Stochastic dominance includes three orders.

Levy (2006) points out that the first and simplest order exists if the cumulative distribution of returns F(x) dominates the cumulative distribution of returns G(x), then the expected value of F(x) is higher than the expected value of G(x). The second-order stochastic dominance exists if two distributions F(x) and G(x) have the same mean, and F(x) stochastically dominates G(x) for every nondecreasing concave function u: R+ → R+. Equation 19.2 gives the function of stochastic dominance:

$$\int_0^{+\infty} u(x)dF(x) \geq \int_0^{+\infty} u(x)dG(x) \tag{19.2}$$

A concave function exists if every line segment joining two points does not lie above the distribution function at any point. Third-order stochastic dominance exists when Fu(x) > Gu(x) for all increasing, concave utility functions u that are positively skewed, so they have a positive third derivative u''' > 0. The economic interpretation of the third-order stochastic dominance derives investor's behavior to decrease risk-aversion aligned with increasing wealth. To that context, the methodology allows for the observation of decision makers' reaction without knowing their utility function and their sensitivity of an optimal decision to different levels of risk.

The nonparametric nature of stochastic dominance allows investors to distinguish between profits and losses and to understand that the utility function is adequate when making a decision about an optimal investment. This strategy is contrary to traditional asset pricing models that fail to explain momentum profits with respect to nonsatiated and risk-averse investors (Jarrow, 1986). Stochastic dominance provides a distinctive advantage for identifying a profitable strategy, where the accuracy in the optimal portfolio selection is high. The ability of stochastic dominance to identify arbitrage opportunities is effective under the perquisite condition that the prices of a particular contingent claim are not positive.

THE RELATIVE STRENGTH INDEX (RSI) OSCILLATOR

The relative strength index (RSI) is the technical oscillator with the ability to measure the velocity and the magnitude of directional price movements. Wilder (1978) developed the RSI, where the intuition of the indicator is to identify the market trends of the underlying asset mainly from a recent trading period. The RSI is calculated as the upward periods (U) and the downward periods (D). The definition of the U is denoted as the closing price being higher than the previous closing price, and the definition of D is denoted as the closing price being lower than the previous period's closing price. If the last close is the same as the previous one, U and D each equal zero. Thus, the underlying assets that show larger positive changes have a higher RSI than stocks that have larger negative changes.

The regular RSI estimation period usually uses the most recent 14 days, and the index is measured on a scale from 0 to 100. The sell sign occurs when the RSI of a stock rises above 70, which indicates that stock is overbought. According to Kestner (2003), the buy sign occurs when the RSI of a stock moves below 30, which indicates that the stock is oversold. Apart from the customized bounds, practitioners apply several other bounds such as shorter or longer time frames and more extreme RSI thresholds in order to capture stricter momentum trends. Table 19.1 represents the calculations of the RSI indicator for the two different periods, U and D.

The average U and D can be calculated in several ways even though the most common is either using an n-period exponential moving average (EMA) or simple averages using the first n values in the price series. The ratio of these averages is the relative strength (RS) ratio that appears in Equation 19.3:

$$RS = \frac{EMA(U,n)}{EMA(U,n)} \qquad (19.3)$$

Table 19.1 **Relative Strength Indicator (RSI)**

This table represents the calculations of the RSI indicator for the two different states. The up state (U) requires subtracting the last closing price minus the previous closing price. The down state (D) requires subtracting the previous closing price minus the most recent closing price.

	Periods	
UP		*DOWN*
$U = \text{close}_{now} - \text{close}_{previous}$	$U = 0$	
$D = 0$	$D = \text{close}_{previous} - \text{close}_{now}$	

If the average of the D values is 0, then the RSI value is defined as 100. The next step is to convert the RS to a RSI that takes values between 0 and 100. The formula for RSI appears in Equation 19.4:

$$RSI = 100 - \frac{100}{1 + RS} \tag{19.4}$$

RSI is a momentum indicator well known for its ability to identify when an asset reaches extreme levels to the upside (referred to as overbought higher than 70 percent) or downside (referred to as oversold lower than 30 percent) and is therefore due for a reversal.

THE PRICE TECHNICAL PATTERNS

Price technical patterns, also known as momentum patterns, are useful tools in identifying market trends. The patterns are based on local thresholds in a time series, which represent the trading signals for implementing the strategy. Lo, Mamaysky, and Wang (2000) develop the most popular reversal technical patterns.

Head and Shoulders Pattern

The head and shoulders (HS) pattern is the most popular trading pattern among the price technical patterns. Two basic ways are available to identify the pattern either on a sequence of three or five consecutive maximum thresholds. The threshold is the established critical value that determines whether to take an investment position either long or short. Strategy implementation requires the first local threshold as the maximum. However, the different implementation between the two ways is based on the two middle thresholds. So, the alternative strategy with the five thresholds requires the third threshold to be greater than the first and less than the fifth.

The following example describes implementing the pattern with the three thresholds. The first threshold is the left shoulder. Suppose that a stock rises in excess of 50 percent from $30 to $55. At this point, assume that the stock achieves a short-term peak on the heaviest volume in several months. A prerequisite for the left shoulder is that it starts with higher volume than the average volume. Next, the stock trades in a narrow price range between $50 and $55. The second threshold is the head. After several weeks of moving within this range, the stock price breaks out to $58 but with a low volume. So, the head ($58) is clearly above the left shoulder ($55). In terms of volume, the breakout occurs with less volume than the volume of the left shoulder. This volume divergence indicates a negative sign because the tension of the breakout is diminishing. The third threshold is the right shoulder. Following the peak of $58, the stock moves back to $50 in an aggressive volume selloff. Usually, the share price will react to this aggressive move and will bounce back to $55 but with tepid volume.

The formation of the pattern draws a neckline starting with the support level of $50 and going horizontally across the lows of the left and right shoulders. The neckline can also be drawn diagonally, sloping in either direction. When the neckline is broken, the stock price movements display the HS pattern. Practitioners typically apply a "filter" of either 3 percent or two trading days to take their decisions and at least two or three months to complete the pattern. Volume can also serve as an indicator for the pattern. Volume must confirm a peak on the left shoulder, a lower peak at the head, and finally an even lower peak at the right shoulder. Technical analysts regard the HS pattern as the most reliable sign of a bearish trend and consequently to short the market. Figure 19.1 illustrates the HS pattern.

Inverse Head and Shoulders Pattern

The inverse head and shoulders (IHS) pattern is based on at least five consecutive thresholds, where the local threshold is a minimum. The pattern is applied in the following manner: The first price falls to a trough and then rises; next, the price

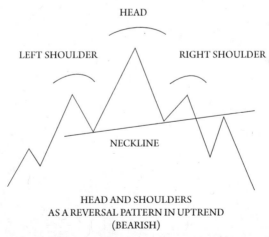

HEAD

LEFT SHOULDER   RIGHT SHOULDER

NECKLINE

HEAD AND SHOULDERS
AS A REVERSAL PATTERN IN UPTREND
(BEARISH)

Figure 19.1 Head and Shoulders Neckline. This figure represents the neckline of the head and shoulders pattern. The neckline is formatted with the left shoulder, head, and right shoulder. The head and shoulders pattern is used as a reversal pattern in an uptrend market.

falls below the former trough and then rises again; and finally, the price falls again but not as far as the second trough. Figure 19.2 illustrates the IHS pattern.

Broadening Tops and Bottoms

The HS and IHS are the most common technical indicators. However, several technical indicators capture the market trend. Broadening tops (BTOP) and bottoms (BBOT) are based on at least five consecutive thresholds. BTOP are based on maximum thresholds, and BBOT are based on minimum thresholds. Within the distribution, at least five local thresholds are distinguished from bottom to top and the reverse. Figures 19.3 and 19.3 illustrate the BTOP and BBOT patterns, respectively.

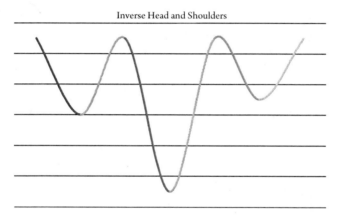

Figure 19.2 Inverse Head and Shoulders. This figure represents the inverse head and shoulders pattern. The pattern is based on at least five consecutive thresholds, where the local threshold is a minimum. The pattern is applied as follows: The first price falls to a trough and then rises, next the price falls below the former trough and then rises again, and finally the price falls again but not as far as the second trough.

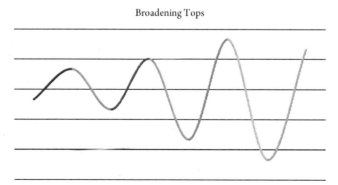

Figure 19.3 Broadening Tops. This figure represents the broadening tops (BTOP) pattern. This pattern is based on at least five consecutive thresholds. Tops are based on maximum thresholds. Within the distribution, at least five local thresholds are distinguished from bottom to top.

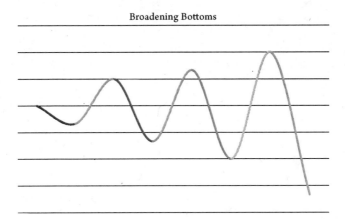

Figure 19.4 Broadening Bottoms
This figure represents the broadening bottoms (BBOT) pattern. This pattern is based on at least five consecutive thresholds. Bottoms are based on minimum thresholds. Within the distribution, at least five local thresholds are distinguished from top to bottom.

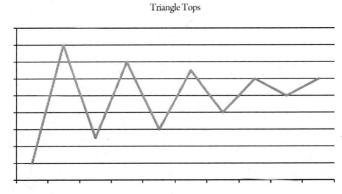

Figure 19.5 Triangle Tops
The triangle tops (TTOP) pattern is characterized by a sequence of a minimum of five consecutive local thresholds. This pattern needs the first threshold to be the maximum. Then, the first threshold is greater than the third threshold, and the third threshold is greater than the fifth threshold.

Triangle Tops and Bottoms

Triangle tops (TTOP) and triangle bottoms (TBOT) are characterized by a sequence of five consecutive local thresholds. The TTOP pattern needs the first threshold to be the maximum. Then, the first threshold is greater than the third threshold, and the third threshold is greater than the fifth. Then, the second threshold is greater than the fourth local minimum. The TBOT pattern stands out as the reversed pattern of the TTOP. Figures 19.6 and 19.7 illustrate the TTOP and TBOT patterns, respectively.

Triangle Bottoms

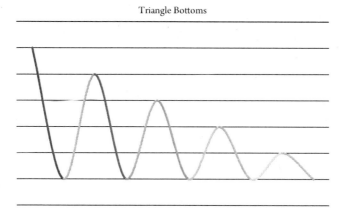

Figure 19.6 Triangle Bottoms. A triangle bottoms (TBOP) pattern is characterized by a sequence of a minimum of five consecutive local thresholds. This pattern needs the first threshold to be the minimum. Then, the first threshold is greater than the third threshold, and the third threshold is greater than the fifth threshold.

Rectangle Tops and Bottoms

Rectangle tops (RTOP) and rectangle bottoms (RBOT) are characterized by a sequence of five consecutive local thresholds. The first top is the maximum, with the maximum tops within 0.75 percent of their average price, bottoms are within 0.75 percent of their average price, and the lowest top is greater than the highest bottom. The average price is defined as the average of the five most recent closing prices. Rectangle bottoms (RBOT) are the reversed pattern of the RTOP where the first threshold is the minimum, tops are within the 0.75 of their average, bottoms are within the 0.75 percent of their average, and the lowest top is greater than the highest bottom. Figures 19.7 and 19.8 illustrate the RTOP and RBOT patterns, respectively.

Double Tops and Bottoms

Double tops (DTOP) and double bottoms (DBOT) are constructed by locating the highest local.

maximum that takes place after the predefined local maximum. The aforementioned two local maximums should be within 1.5 percent and should occur at most within 22 days, even though some technical analysts use a longer period to identify the pattern. The reverse pattern of the DTOP should form with the DBOT. Figures 19.9 and 19.10 illustrate the DTOP and DBOT patterns, respectively.

Uses of Price Technical Indicators

Technical analysts use the aforementioned technical indicators to identify market trends. More precisely, the indicators typically generate the sell and buy decisions. Thus, changes in the trend of the market and the thresholds indicate an investment position. Most traders do not wait for the full pattern to unfold, they

Rectangle Tops

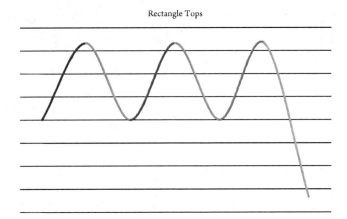

Figure 19.7 Rectangle Tops. A rectangle tops (RTOP) pattern is characterized by a sequence of a minimum of five consecutive local threshold.. The first top is the maximum, and the lowest top is greater than the highest bottom.

Rectangle Bottoms

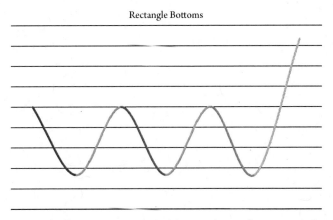

Figure 19.8 Rectangle Bottoms. A rectangle bottoms (RBOT) pattern is characterized by a sequence of a minimum of five consecutive local thresholds where the first threshold is the minimum.

predict that the trend is moving in a specific pattern and take the respective position in the market. These indicators can also be the sign generator or a second filtering of more complex trading strategies.

Lo et al. (2000) evaluate the performance of technical patterns on the New York Stock Exchange (NYSE), American Stock Exchange (AMEX), and NASDAQ between 1962 and 1996. They find that the relative frequencies of the conditional returns are significantly different from those of the unconditional returns for the majority of the patterns. The three exceptions are the BBOT, TTOP, and DBOT patterns. The overall results show that market trends confirm the patterns formation incrementally and that the patterns work more effectively on the NASDAQ stocks. The performance of technical patterns in five-year subperiods

Double Tops

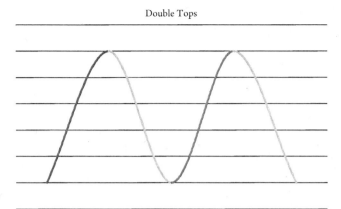

Figure 19.9 Double Tops. This figure shows a double tops (DTOP) pattern. Double tops are constructed by locating the highest local maximum that occurs after a predefined local maximum.

Double Bottoms

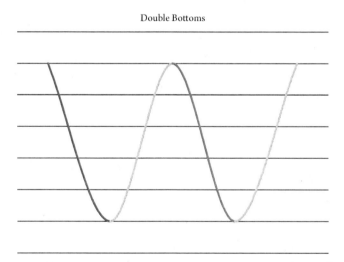

Figure 19.10 Double Bottoms. This figure shows a double bottoms (DBOT) pattern. Double bottoms are constructed by locating the highest local minimum that occurs after the predefined local minimum.

and market-capitalization quintiles are statistically significant for five of the 10 patterns: HS, BBOT, RTOP, RBOT, and DTOP. Trading volume reveals informative dynamics because the declining volume trend leads to the declining success of most patterns. The authors find trading volume to be a vital trend factor, especially in TBOT and BTOP patterns.

Lucke (2003) conducts a different examination on the profitability of chartist trading rules for exchange rates using the HS pattern. Contrary to stocks, the HS pattern earns negative returns when applied to exchange rates.

THE MOVING AVERAGE OSCILLATOR

A *moving average*, also known as the *rolling mean oscillator*, is the average of the finite observations from a larger set of data points. The rolling mean is useful in technical analysis of financial data such as stock prices, returns, or trading volumes. The oscillator is computed by calculating a fix or variable subset of the numbers in a time series data. The fixed subset, which is the most widespread, is calculated by keeping the number of observations in the subset fixed and rolling over to the next subset, which is also averaged. The variable subset is applied with unequal weights in order to emphasize particular values in the subset. Technical analyses commonly use a moving average to smooth out short-run fluctuations and to identify long-run trends or cycles. In practice, several thresholds are available to identify short- and long-run trends, with selected parameters depending on the objective scope of the signal processing. The most popular moving average horizons are 10, 20, 50, and 200 days.

Practitioners apply moving average oscillators as a set of trading rules that combines the link between prices and moving averages. Moving averages also use a subfilter or a trading sign in a trading algorithm. Another variation of the model looks at combinations of two or more moving averages. In general, the trading rules are to buy when the current price crosses above the moving averages and to sell when the current price crosses below the moving averages. When using two moving averages, a buy sign occurs when the current price crosses above both moving averages and a sell signal occurs if the current price crosses below both moving averages.

Bock and Mestel (2008) apply a fixed- and a variable-length rolling average model to stocks listed on the Dow Jones Industrial Average (DJIA) for an extensive period between 1897 and 1986. The implementation consists of shorter- and longer-term moving averages, such as 1–50, 1–150, 5–150, 1–200, and 2–200, where the first number represents the shorter period and the second number represents the longer period. The fixed-length trading rule gives a buy signal when the shorter-moving average shifts from below the longer-moving average to above it. The variable-length trading rule gives a buy signal when the shorter moving average is above the longer moving average. The thresholds based on moving averages confirm the predictive power of the indicator. Practitioners usually apply the aforementioned rules, as they enter a long (short) position when the short-moving average moves above (below) the long.

THE STOCHASTIC OSCILLATOR

According to Kestner (2003), Lane (1984) developed the stochastic oscillator in the late 1950s. This oscillator measures the magnitude of directional price movements. The concept is to compare the current prices to the high and low range over a predefined trading period in order to predict the price turning points. The indicator is defined as shown in Equation 19.5:

$$\%K = 100 - \frac{C - LN}{HN - LN} \tag{19.5}$$

where C represents the latest closing price; HN is the highest price over the n periods; and LN is the lowest price over the n periods. The indicator consists of two lines and %D is smoothed out using a three-period rolling average to form the %K. Thus, %K compares the latest closing price to the recent trading range, while %D is an n-periods simple moving average of %K. Table 19.2 shows an example of this strategy.

Table 19.2 **Stochastic Oscillator of stock AX**

This table represents the 14-day stochastic oscillator for the stock AX. The calculation of the indicator is based on closing prices between January 23 and February 21, 2011. Based on the results, the %K stochastic oscillator ranges between $40.39 up to $98.58

			Stochastic Oscillator				
Stock parameters	AX 14-day smoothing						
Description	14-day high minus 14-day low						
Run dates	January 23, 2011 to February 21, 2011						
No	Date (2011)	High	Low	Highest High (14)	Lowest Low (14)	Current Close	14-day Stochastic Oscillator
1	January 23	127.01	125.36	n/a	n/a	n/a	n/a
2	January 24	127.62	126.16	n/a	n/a	n/a	n/a
3	January 25	126.59	124.93	n/a	n/a	n/a	n/a
4	January 26	127.35	126.09	n/a	n/a	n/a	n/a
5	January 27	128.17	126.82	n/a	n/a	n/a	n/a
6	January 28	128.43	126.48	n/a	n/a	n/a	n/a
7	January 29	127.37	126.03	n/a	n/a	n/a	n/a
8	January 30	126.42	124.83	n/a	n/a	n/a	n/a
9	January 31	126.90	126.39	n/a	n/a	n/a	n/a
10	February 1	126.85	125.72	n/a	n/a	n/a	n/a
11	February 2	125.65	124.56	n/a	n/a	n/a	n/a
12	February 3	125.72	124.57	n/a	n/a	n/a	n/a
13	February 4	127.16	125.07	n/a	n/a	n/a	n/a

(Continued)

Table 19.2 **(Continued)**

		Stochastic Oscillator					
Stock param-eters	AX 14-day smoothing						
De-scrip-tion	14-day high minus 14-day low						
Run dates	January 23, 2011 to February 21, 2011						
No	*Date (2011)*	*High*	*Low*	*Highest High (14)*	*Lowest Low (14)*	*Current Close*	*14-day Stochastic Oscillator*
14	February 5	127.72	126.86	128.43	124.56	127.29	70.44
15	February 6	127.69	126.63	128.43	124.56	127.18	67.61
16	February 7	128.22	126.80	128.43	124.56	128.01	89.20
17	February 8	128.27	126.71	128.43	124.56	127.11	65.81
18	February 9	128.09	126.80	128.43	124.56	127.73	81.75
19	February 10	128.27	126.13	128.43	124.56	127.06	64.52
20	February 11	127.74	125.92	128.27	124.56	127.33	74.53
21	February 12	128.77	126.99	128.77	124.56	128.71	98.58
22	February 13	129.29	127.81	129.29	124.56	127.87	70.10
23	February 14	130.06	128.47	130.06	124.56	128.58	73.06
24	February 15	129.12	128.06	130.06	124.56	128.60	73.42
25	February 16	129.29	127.61	130.06	124.57	127.93	61.23
26	February 17	128.47	127.60	130.06	125.07	128.11	60.96
27	February 18	128.09	127.00	130.06	125.92	127.60	40.39
28	February 19	128.65	126.90	130.06	125.92	127.60	40.39
29	February 20	129.14	127.49	130.06	125.92	128.69	66.83
30	February 21	128.64	127.40	130.06	125.92	128.27	56.73

Table 19.2 represents the high, low, and closing price of stock AX. Using Equation 19.5, the 14-day stochastic oscillator is calculated. The results show that if an investor only focuses on the closing prices, he cannot figure out the correct market trend of the stock. Assume that on February 14, the closing price is almost identical to the closing price of February 20 ($128.71 and $128.69, respectively). However, the oscillator is $98.58 and $66.83, respectively.

Trading Signals

The thresholds of the trading signals are similar to RSI: A buy signal occurs when the indicator rises above 30 and crosses above the %D stochastic, and a sell sign occurs when the indicator falls below 70 and crosses below the % D stochastic. A short-term trend is established when %K and %D each move in the same direction. The shape of a stochastic bottom or top provides a strong indication of the market trend. A narrow bottom indicates that the downward trend is weak and shorter in duration and the market is likely to bounce back. Traders also impose stop-losses in a long position when the trend achieves a minor low. The trading rules are identical in the reverse form. Table 19.3 represents two different market trends, a shorter-term trend indicator and a longer cycle indicator and the characteristics that are needed to indentify each period.

Thus, long trading signals:

- take a long position when the %D stochastic remains below the respective oversold level.
- take a long position when %K and %D each drop below the oversold level and bounce back above the oversold level.
- take a long position when %K crosses %D and remains above the %D stochastic.

Short trading signals:

- take a short position when the %D stochastic remains above the respective oversold level.
- take a short position when %K and %D each rise above the overbought level and drop below the overbought level.
- take a short position when %K crosses %D and remains below the %D stochastic.

Table 19.3 **Stochastic Oscillator**
This table represents two possible scenarios to apply the stochastic oscillator. The scenarios assume different levels of thresholds (80 percent – 20 percent or 70 percent – 30 percent) and the success of each level.

Identification	*%K Periods (days)*	*%D Periods (days)*	*% Overbought*	*% Oversold*	*Outcome*
Trend indicator	5 to 10	3 days	80	20	Extremely sensitive
Longer cycles	14 or 21	3 days	70	30	Effective to sharp U-turns

Quantitative Strategies and Relative Market Timing

Market timing strategies are relatively aggressive strategies that use assumptions and models about market timing, which is the ability to provide accurate signals of when to enter or exit the market and which way (long or short) to invest. Market timing can be cast in the context of market neutral strategies, where no net market exposure is present, or of market exposure. This section introduces the latter as quantitative trading.

PAIRS TRADING

Pairs trading is one of the most compelling and widespread market timing methods. According to Gatev, Goetzmann, and Rouwenhorst (2006), the origins of pairs trading stem from the mid-1980s when Nunzio Tartaglia, head of the quantitative group at Morgan Stanley, developed a high-end trading platform to implement it. In the early 1990s, some market participants attempted to reduce market exposure. The intuition of the strategy uses various underlying assumptions the most important of which involve comovement and mean reversion. That is, prices of selected assets tend to move together and when they diverge, this presents an investment opportunity that can be exploited by taking a market neutral position. The degree of mean reversion of stock markets signals the success of market timing. The pairs trading strategy exploits statistical tools such as the concept of distance and of the convergence or divergence of prices and is based on this distance and the use of pairs and distances for formulating combinations of long or short positions.

Distances denote the minimum of the price distance between two assets in order to match a pair. According to Gatev et al. (2006), this distance should be at least two standard deviations. Implementing the strategy requires a simultaneous investing in a long and short position where investors take positions on a timing signal. So, if the investor owns \$100, he should invest \$50 taking a long position and \$50 taking a short position. Identifying the long and short positions can be achieved through several methods. The original method used by practitioners assumes that if a price divergence occurs by more than two historical standard deviations, then a trade unwinds. Equation 19.6 illustrates the formula for calculating the return to a pairs trading strategy

$$PD_{i,j,m} = \frac{\sum_{t=1}^{T_m} \left(P_t^i - P_t^j \right)^2}{T_m}$$

(19.6)

where P_t^i and P_t^j are the price index of assets i and j at time t.

Before interpreting opportunities for implementing the pairs trading strategy, an investor must construct a cumulative total return index for all the assets (set) during the formation period, when pairs are formed by exhaustive matching in normalized daily "price" space, where price includes reinvested dividends. The next step is to choose a matching partner for each stock by finding the security that minimizes the sum of squared deviations between the two normalized price series. Trading begins on the next trading day of the last day of the pairs formation period. When a position is initialized, traders go long in the asset with the lowest price index and short in the asset with the highest one. Then, they check that each day of the trading period has the same sign. Otherwise, traders liquidate the trade. The hypothesis of optimal time exit argues that statistical arbitrage strategies should be considered a unique factor that affects profitability of a pairs trading strategy. Practitioners usually open a trade for a short period. Implementing the trading assumes a portfolio of L pairs.

Gatev et al. (2006) test pair trading profitability on stocks traded on the NYSE, AMEX, and NASDAQ, using daily closing prices for the period from January 1992 to June 2006. They apply the strategy to the number of L pairs in the top five and top 20 pairs with the smallest historical distance measure, in addition to the 20 pairs after the top 100 (pairs 101 to 120). Their results show that excess returns of the five best-pairs and 20 best-pairs portfolios earned an average excess monthly return of 1.31 percent and 1.44 percent per month, respectively. On a relative basis, they report that excess return is meaningful and provide evidence that using pairs trading is a profitable market timing method. Diversification benefits also exist from combining multiple pairs in a portfolio. As the number of pairs in a portfolio increases, the portfolio standard deviation falls. The diversification benefits are apparent from the range of realized returns. Interestingly, as the number of pairs in the strategy increases, the minimum realized return also increases, while the maximum realized excess return remains relatively stable. Gavet et al. find the strategy's profitability to be uncorrelated with the S&P 500. However, the strategy exhibits low sensitivity to the spreads between small and large stocks and between value and growth stocks in addition to the spread between high grade and intermediate grade corporate bonds and shifts in the yield curve.

Schizas, Thomakos, and Wang (2011) implement the strategy in a different way by incorporating a methodological innovation in identifying the diverging pairs. During the formation period, instead of the sum of squares, the average absolute distance among all pairs is applied as shown in Equation 19.7:

$$PD_{a,b,m} = \frac{\sum_{t=1}^{T_m} |P_t^i - P_t^j|}{T_m} \tag{19.7}$$

Subsequently, the distances are ranked from largest to smallest to identify trading opportunities, where the distances are larger than half standard deviations instead of the previously used two standard deviations. Using absolute distances allows for more trading opportunities when compared to a sum-of-squares measure and is more robust against sudden large discrepancies that quickly disappear. The absolute distances are applied to the first 19 available international exchange traded funds (ETFs) for the period September 1996 to March 2009. The number of pairs used in constructing the portfolio returns is set to L = 2, 5, 10, and 20.

Schizas et al. (2011) discover that increasing the number of the pairs in the portfolio results in a significant deterioration of performance based on terminal wealth. Therefore, reducing the number of pairs by 10 to 25 percent appears to be optimal for the strategy. Increasing the number of pairs reduces the standard deviation and the Sharpe ratio of the strategy. The percentage of successful trades exceeds 50 percent, but more importantly, trades tend to be more accurate in their timing. The comparison between the two distance measures— the sum of squares and the absolute distances—for the top five pairs results in an average monthly excess of 1.49 percent versus a 0.78 percent for the sum-of-squares measure. By contrast, for the top 20 pairs, the results are similar between the two strategies, 0.93 percent and 0.81 percent, respectively.

OTHER PAIRS TRADING TESTED METHODS

A different implementation of pairs trading based on fundamental analysis systematically analyzes companies to identify those on the brink of change, either positive or negative in nature. Jurek and Yang (2007) suggest a type of strategy known as the Siamese twin formula, as the trading rule is formulated between two assets with common fundamentals. This strategy proposes taking a long position in an undervalued security and a short position in an overvalued security. Thus, the fundamentals of a security take the place of price divergence. The pair should have similar levels of systematic and sector risk.

Mitchell and Pulvino (2001) examine fundamentals factors of 4,750 stock swap mergers, cash mergers, and cash tender offers for the period from 1963 to 1998. Their evidence shows that pairs trading arbitrage generates substantial positive excess returns.

Although pairs trading can be a profitable strategy, increased hedge fund activity has led to lower profitability of pairs trading in recent years. However, despite declining raw returns, the risk-adjusted returns have continued to persist.

Quantitative Trading Through Market and Volatility Arbitrage

Quantitative strategies are a family of strategies that use assumptions and models about market timing. In general, quantitative arbitrage market timing strategies require a model selection methodology for generating predictions and a trading rule. In particular, determining "optimal patterns" for detecting certain types of phenomena in financial time series (for example, an optimal shape for detecting stochastic volatility or changes in regime) may be possible. Moreover, patterns that are optimal for detecting statistical anomalies need not be optimal for trading profits and vice versa. Two basic pillars are needed to construct a successful model: one pillar on market and volatility timing and the other on sign and volatility predictability. A quantitative trading system must have an easy user interface. The system must not only be eloquent enough to use easily but also powerful enough to describe more sophisticated trading algorithms. As in forecasting or other applications, trading models rely heavily on the quality of financial data. The architecture of a trading model involves five main components: (1) select the financial data inputs, (2) account for market or volatility arbitrage, (3) generate the trading model, (4) account for the success of sign predictability, and (5) account for the correct criterion of the sign recommendations.

The architecture of a quantitative equity directional strategy depends on a forecasting ability of the underlying assets. The intuition behind the trading models assumes that the prices of the underlying assets are mean reverting and mispricing will be alleviated as they attempt to capture the asymmetric response of the relative returns. The basic mechanism to capture this disequilibrium is based on an arbitrage model where the dependent variable is either the relative return of the underlying assets—arbitrage in returns—or the relative volatility between two assets-volatility arbitrage. The outcome of these asymmetries provides the investing signal.

RELATIVE ARBITRAGE BASED ON RETURNS

The intuition of the relative arbitrage based on returns assumes that past returns of two assets are mean reverting and the relative pricing between the two assets could lead to profitable trading. The asymmetric response of the relative returns is captured by considering relative past returns y_t as both a dependent and a decision variable. So, the relative pricing is defined as $y_t = R_{ti} - R_{tj}$, which is equivalent to the return of relative prices. For the computation of the relative prices the daily closing price for each included asset is used.

VOLATILITY ARBITRAGE

An underlying assumption of the volatility arbitrage model is that the relative volatility of the two underlying assets is bound by the separate volatility of each asset, while any relative mispricing will properly self-correct. Two separate models define relative volatility arbitrage. The first model tries to capture the direct modeling of volatility by dealing with the individual log volatilities, thus using the volatility levels of the two underlying assets $V_t = V_{ti} - V_{tj}$. The second model tries to deal with the volatility ratio, which is defined as the logarithms of the volatility ratio of the two underlying assets as $v_t = \log(V_{ti}) - \log(V_{tj})$.

TRADING BASED ON RELATIVE RETURNS AND VOLATILITY ARBITRAGE

Schizas et al. (2010) develop a basic equity directional strategy as an asset rotation model capturing both the dynamics of the relative return and relative volatility. The algorithm uses the relative pricing of the underlying assets as both a dependent and a decision variable and follows a standard regression specification whose dimension and included variables differ across model specifications. The model is constructed by including a lagged dependent variable, lagged values of the relative volatility, and asymmetric response terms for both of them, as well as cross-terms. Equation 19.8 presents the specification model with a single lag

$$y_t = \beta_0 + \beta_1 y_{t-1} + \beta_2 V_{t-1} + \beta_3 I_t^y + \beta_4 I_t^V + \beta_5 V_{t-1} I_t^V$$
$$+ \beta_6 V_{t-1} I_t^V + \beta_7 y_{t-1} I_t^V + \beta_8 V_{t-1} I_t^y + u_t \qquad (19.8)$$

where $I_t^y = I(y_{t-1} < 0)$ is a dummy variable capturing the asymmetric response of relative returns; $I_t^V = I(V_{t-1} < c)$ is a dummy variable capturing the asymmetric response of relative volatilities; and c is a fixed threshold. In implementing the trading strategy, the threshold is assumed to be 0. This type of specification can capture the potentially different behavior of relative returns in periods when one asset outperforms the other depending on both the asymmetric response of relative returns and relative volatilities. The trading strategy is based on the forecasts generated by Equation 19.8 following autoregressive models and involves a binary decision for the asset on which investment will take place. For this strategy, all available capital rotates when a signal for a switch from one asset to the other is given. The practical implementation starts with a rolling window of 104 observations for the historical evaluation of the strategy and computes the one-week-ahead forecast. Quantitative trading requires a benchmark for the relative comparison. In this context, two simple rotation models are applied, one including only the mean of the relative returns and another one including the dynamics that are present in the regression error term using a moving average.

The Decision Criteria and the Importance of the Correct Sign Predictions

Based on the one-week-ahead forecasts, the trading signal is as follows: If the forecast of the relative return or relative volatility is greater than 0, $\hat{y}_{t+1|t}^{(m)} > 0$, $\log(\hat{V}_{t+1|t,i}) > \log(\hat{V}_{t+1|t,j})$, $\hat{v}_{t+1|t} > 0$, then open a long trade for asset i, otherwise enter a long position for asset j. Note that a switch occurs at time t only if the position is in a different asset at the previous time from the current signal. The model based on the moving averages coincides with a momentum strategy based on local smoothing: The comparison is between two moving averages of the same size because $\hat{y}_{t+1|t} = \hat{\beta}_0 = \overline{y}_{n_0} = \overline{R}_{i,n_0} - \overline{R}_{j,n_0}$.

The success of quantitative strategies depends both on the optimal capturing of the asymmetries and on the percentage of correct sign predictions. Note that the expected return is positive if $(r_{t+1,i}/r_{t+1,j}) > (1 - P^{-1})$. Thus, the relative realized return is greater than a negative threshold that depends on the probability of making a positive prediction. Eventually, the strategy's expected return is positive when both returns are positive. The volatility of the rotation strategy is maximized when the probability of making a positive prediction is close to one-half, when the difference between the two realized returns is increasing or both. Fundamentally, the expected return and volatility of the strategy each depend on the distribution of the models' forecasts. Quantitative trading is subject to pairs' selection of the two assets, while pairs of assets that move together are unsuitable for successful rotation trading.

Results on Quantitative Trading

Schizas et al. (2010) examine the outcome of quantitative trading on four passive index ETFs, the SPDR on the S&P 500 index (ticker: SPY), the SPDR on
Financial Sector (ticker: XLF), the NASDAQ QQQ (ticker: QQQQ), and the
Oil Services HOLDRs trust (ticker: OIH). The four ETFs formatted into three
pairs as SPY-OIH, SPY-XLF, and SPY-QQQ, and the data hold since February
2001, December 2001, and March 1999 for each pair, respectively. The data span
ends on April 4, 2008. The estimations are conducted for three different days of
the week (Monday, Wednesday, and Friday), because the implied information is
different for each day of the week and the performance across the trading models
is subject to the day-of-the-week effect. The results show that the basic piecewise
rotation model is the best performer in terms of the Sharpe ratio, while the models based on the timing of the past returns perform better than the models based
on volatility arbitrage. The relative comparison between the best rotation models
and the best performing asset in each pair in terms of terminal wealth reveals an
outperformance for the rotation strategy.

The comparison based on volatility characteristics shows that the difference
in volatility is the highest for the SPY-OIH pair and the difference in volatility is
the lowest for the pair SPY-QQQ. Volatility timing models perform better than
the piecewise model for the SPY-OIH pair. However, for the SPY-QQQ pair, the
piecewise specification outperforms the alternative specifications. The empirical
evidence shows that the relative performance of the piecewise specification works
better as the volatility of the one asset of the pair is not dominating the other
asset.

The estimations of the quantitative equity directional trading can be summarized as: market and volatility arbitrage can realize substantial profits and
can outperform a buy-and-hold strategy. However, the trading algorithms reveal
higher volatility compared to a buy-and-hold strategy. In this group of strategies,
the success of the sign is important for good trading performance, and a link
exists between good performance in sign prediction and fewer trading signals.

Summary and Conclusions

In recent years, market timing has been dominated by the activity of hedge funds.
Regardless of the indicator or the trading strategy that one could follow, market
timing is a complex procedure. This chapter examines several methods that fall
within a spectrum fulfilling three criteria. First, the strategy can identify market
trends with relative success. Second, the strategy is well known and applied by
practitioners. Third, the strategy cannot only stand alone but also cannot be combined or used within advanced trading strategies to achieve profitability.

The results of several strategy global implementations exploit the fact that
mean reversion is much larger in less broad-based and less sophisticated markets.
Also, mean reversion is more negative for the portfolios of smaller firms and for
the equal-weighted index than for the larger firm portfolios or the value-weighted

index. Quantitative strategies depend on time-varying relative returns, and volatilities can lead to potentially profitable trading strategies. The selection of data inputs and methodology is also a factor that affects final profitability.

Discussion Questions

1. Define the term *asymmetries of returns*.
2. Identify and describe three basic factors that may affect implementing trading strategies.
3. Name two indicators based on empirical distributions that can be used to identify the market trend and indicate the main advantages of these indicators.
4. What is a pairs trading strategy?

References

Blundell-Wignall, Adrian. 2007. "An Overview of Hedge Funds and Structured Products: Issues in Leverage and Risk." *Financial Market Trends* 92:1, 37–57.

Bock, Michael, and Roland Mestel. 2008. "A Regime-Switching Relative Value Arbitrage Rule." Working Paper, Institute for Banking and Finance, University of Graz.

French, Kenneth. 1980. "Stock Returns and the Weekend Effect." *Journal of Financial Economics* 8:1, 55–69.

Gatev, Evan, William Goetzmann, and Geert Rouwenhorst. 2006. "Pairs Trading: Performance of a Relative-Value Arbitrage." *Review of Financial Studies* 19:3, 797–827.

Jarrow, Robert. 1986. "The Relationship Between Arbitrage and First Order Stochastic Dominance." *Journal of Finance* 41:4, 915–921.

Jurek, Jakob, and Halla Yang. 2007. "Profiting from Mean-Reversion: Optimal Strategies in the Presence of Horizon and Divergence Risk." Working Paper, Harvard Business School.

Keating, Con, and William Shadwick. 2002. "An Introduction to Omega." Working Paper, International Development Centre Limited.

Kestner, Lars. 2003. *Quantitative Trading Strategies.* New York: McGraw Hill Companies.

Keynes, John Maynard. 1936. *The General Theory of Employment, Interest, and Money.* Cambridge, UK: Macmillan Cambridge University Press.

Lane, George. 1984. "Lane's Stochastics." *Technical Analysis of Stocks and Commodities* 2, 87–90.

Levy, Haim. 2006. *Stochastic Dominance: Investment Decision Making under Uncertainty.* New York: Springer.

Lo, Andrew, Harry Mamaysky, and Jiang Wang. 2000. "Foundations of Technical Analysis: Computational Algorithms, Statistical Inference, and Empirical Implementation." *Journal of Finance* 55:4, 1705–1765.

Lowenstein, Roger. 2000. *When Genius Failed: The Rise and Fall of Long-Term Capital Management.* New York: Random House.

Lucke, Bernd. 2003. "Are Technical Trading Rules Profitable? Evidence for Head-and-Shoulder Rules." *Applied Economics* 35:1, 33–40.

Mitchell, Mark, and Todd Pulvino. 2001. "Characteristics of Risk and Return in Risk Arbitrage." *Journal of Finance* 56:6, 2135–2175.

Schizas, Panagiotis, and Dimitrios Thomakos. 2010. "Market Timing and Trading Strategies Using Asset Rotation." Working Paper, University of Peloponnese.

Schizas, Panagiotis, Dimitrios Thomakos, and Tao Wang. 2011. "Pairs Trading on International ETFs." Working Paper, City University of New York and University of Peloponnese.

Sharpe, William. 1966. "Mutual Fund Performance." *Journal of Business* 39:1, 119–138.

Wilder, J. Welles. 1978. *New Concepts in Technical Trading Systems*. McLeansville, NC: Trend Research.

Zuckerman, Gregory. 2009. "Once Again, There's Trouble in Quant Land." *Wall Street Journal*, May 11. http://online.wsj.com/article/SB124199541589104765.html.

EVALUATING AND REPORTING
PORTFOLIO PERFORMANCE

20

Evaluating Portfolio Performance

Reconciling Asset Selection and Market Timing

ARNAUD CAVÉ
HEC Management School, University of Liège,

GEORGES HÜBNER
HEC Management School, University of Liège; School of
Business and Economics, Maastricht University; Gambit Financial
Solutions Ltd.

THOMAS LEJEUNE
F.R.S.-FNRS Research Fellow, HEC Management School,
University of Liège

Introduction

Managers of actively managed funds claim to be able to deliver positive abnormal performance through their superior selectivity of securities or asset classes (asset selection) or through their ability to successfully anticipate market movements (market timing). Gauging this assertion appears to be of great importance from both a practitioner and an academic perspective. The ability to claim that active management strategies are successful would provide justification for moving away from passively managed portfolios. Moreover, in their research of optimal allocation, investors who are able to better identify superior funds will acquire a positive advantage. From an academic point of view, the assessment of genuine anticipation skills represents a delicate but important matter as it seriously challenges the efficient market hypothesis (EMH). In order to perform this assessment, adequate tools to measure the performance of actively managed funds are needed.

Traditional performance measurement is based on the work of Sharpe (1966) and his well-known Sharpe ratio. Other measures, such as Jensen's (1968) alpha and the Treynor (1965) ratio, have been derived to cope with performance assessment of stationary returns in a mean-variance environment. Later, with the appearance of nonlinear portfolio strategies, other measures have been proposed to capture nonlinearities. Among other influential measures are the Sortino ratio of Sortino and Price (1994) and the Omega of Keating and Shadwick (2002).

Most classical performance measures provide an assessment of asset selectivity skills. The ability to perform superior selection of assets or asset classes has received much attention in the literature, with performance measures derived from Jensen's alpha and its multifactor extensions (e.g., Kothari and Warner, 2001). Market timing abilities are generally assessed with the extensive use of two return-based approaches: the piecewise linear regression of Henriksson and Merton (1981), henceforth HM, and the quadratic regression of Treynor and Mazuy (1966), henceforth TM.

However, the detection of abilities to time the market is generally not empirically reconciled with the performance of market timers. Even though Jiang, Yao, and Yu (2007) find that an annual average performance of 0.6 percent can be attributable to market timing skills, empirical studies generally provide little support for market timing performance of actively managed funds (Kryzanowski, Lalancette, and To, 1997; Becker, Ferson, Myers, and Schill, 1999; Bollen and Busse, 2004; Comer, Larrymore, and Rodriguez, 2009).

This chapter introduces the major alternative methods for measuring portfolio performance in the presence of asset selectivity and market timing skills. Then, the measurement of both skills is reconciled by introducing several methods to deal with the total performance of a market timer. An empirical investigation is performed on a sample of mutual funds showing the importance of market timing in generating performance.

The remainder of the chapter is organized in the following manner. The next section describes classical methods used to assess mutual fund performance, which is followed by a section focusing on performance measurement in presence of market timing. The next to last section presents an empirical comparison of the methods available to measure market timers' performance, and the last section concludes.

Performance Measurement for Asset Selection

Although initially developed as an equilibrium framework for identifying ex-ante expected returns, the capital asset pricing model (CAPM) soon became useful for evaluating ex-post risk-adjusted (realized) returns. In this perspective, the fair rate of return corresponds to the risk-free rate augmented with the risk premium, and the EMH precludes a systematic gap between the realized and the required return. Then, any positive (negative) difference between a portfolio rate of return and that of a representative passive portfolio with the same risk can be considered as positive (negative) performance if it is economically and statistically significant.

Following the introduction of CAPM, performance measurement took three different directions depending on the type of risk (total, systematic, or specific) considered for the adjustment of returns. Even though performance measures considering these three types of risk arose independently, the decision to select one over the others stems from rational considerations about the "complement portfolio," i.e., the one that the investor holds besides the portfolio to be evaluated (Bodie, Kane, and Marcus, 2010).

The first direction, grandfathered by the Sharpe ratio, builds on the total risk of the portfolio, as depicted in Equation 20.1

$$SR = \frac{\bar{R} - R_f}{\sigma} \tag{20.1}$$

where $\bar{R}$, R_f, and σ represent the mean portfolio return, the risk-free rate, and the total portfolio risk as measured with the standard deviation of returns, respectively.

The second approach of performance measurement works directly with the security market line (SML) and disentangles the systematic and specific components of risk. The seminal performance measures are Jensen's alpha (α), the Black-Treynor ratio (TR), and the information ratio (IR) (also known as the "appraisal ratio"), represented in Equations 20.2 to 20.4, respectively.

$$\alpha = \bar{R} - R_f - \beta(\bar{R}_m - R_f) \tag{20.2}$$

$$TR = \frac{\alpha}{\beta} \tag{20.3}$$

$$IR = \frac{\alpha}{\sigma(\varepsilon)} \tag{20.4}$$

Beta (β) stands for the systematic risk coefficient of the portfolio, while $\bar{R}_m$ represents the expected return of the market portfolio—in practice proxied by a market index. The denominator of the IR, namely $\sigma(\varepsilon)$, reflects the specific risk of the portfolio and is measured by the standard deviation of the residual term of the regression of excess portfolio returns over market returns. In practice, analysts often use IR against a benchmark portfolio, in which case the beta is set to one and the specific risk is equal to the tracking error of the portfolio over its benchmark.

Equation 20.2 represents a convenient way to measure performance for two reasons: (1) it delivers an interpretable abnormal rate of return, and (2) it can be easily extended to the case where the risk premium is not unique, thus escaping the CAPM framework. Therefore, a return generating process belonging to the class of Ross's (1976) arbitrage pricing theory (APT) or empirical CAPM frameworks, which does not require any further adaptation of the measure and has the very same interpretation. The TR ratio bears a proper generalization as well (Hübner, 2005), but it was derived recently while the multi-index alpha, although less robust to the manipulation of portfolio leverage, has been used for more than 30 years and remains extremely popular.

In the US equity mutual funds industry, most funds are benchmarked and thus the notion of systematic risk is highly relevant. Portfolio styles are often distinguished on the basis of their global market exposure as well as their sensitivity to small versus large caps, growth versus value stocks, and momentum versus contrarian investment strategies. The return generating process that best corresponds to this partitioning is the four-factor Carhart (1997) model.

$$R_i = R_f + \beta_1(R_{mt} - R_f) + \beta_2 SMB_t + \beta_3 HML_t + \beta_4 UMD_t + \varepsilon_t \qquad (20.5)$$

According to this framework, a portfolio's realized abnormal return is measured by the multifactor alpha:

$$\alpha_{4F} = \bar{R} - R_f - \beta_1(\bar{R}_m - R_f) - \beta_2 \overline{SMB} - \beta_2 \overline{HML} - \beta_4 \overline{UMD} \qquad (20.6)$$

where SMB and HML are the size (small minus big capitalization) and the book-to-market (high minus low book-to-market ratios) factors, respectively, of Fama and French (1992) and UMD is the momentum factor of Carhart (1997).

Equations 20.5 and 20.6 can potentially identify the ability of the portfolio manager to choose sectors or to pick securities that provide an excess return over the benchmark. As with any other specification corresponding to a model with constant risk exposures, these equations are not suited for estimating market timing skills. The reason is straightforward: As market timing strategies involve the dynamic management of betas depending on market anticipations per se, a model with constant risk factor exposures cannot reflect such an approach.

Performance Measurement for Market Timing

Because they assume constant betas, the classical performance measures discussed in the previous section are not suited to reflect market timing skills, which involve voluntary shifts in risk exposures. This section discusses the major approaches used to overcome this issue proposed within the same family of asset pricing models.

THE HM AND TM MODELS

Still reasoning within the scope of the CAPM as in the previous section, analysts often use three specifications to assess a manager's market timing abilities. First, the Henriksson and Merton (1981) model considers that the manager switches the portfolio's beta depending on the sign of the market return

$$r_t = \alpha_{HM} + \beta_{HM} r_{mt} + \gamma_{HM} \max(-r_{mt}, 0) + \varepsilon_t \qquad (20.7)$$

where $r_t = R_t - R_f$ is the portfolio excess return over the risk-free rate and r_{mt} is the market portfolio excess return. This equation introduces γ_{HM} as the coefficient of the return of a put option on the market portfolio. It reflects the intensity of the manager's market timing efforts. The intercept α_{HM} represents the portfolio return, which is neither explained by the linear exposure β_{HM} nor by the put option exposure γ_{HM}. A good or "positive" market timer can increase her market exposure when the market excess return is positive and can keep this exposure lower otherwise. The HM model translates the behavior of a manager who can change her market beta from a high level equal to β_{HM} when the market return exceeds the risk-free rate to a low level of $(\beta_{HM} - \gamma_{HM})$ in the opposite situation.

Second, the Treynor and Mazuy (TM) (1966) model adds a quadratic term to the traditional one-factor model CAPM:

$$r_t = \alpha_{TM} + \beta_{TM} r_{mt} + \gamma_{TM} r_{mt}^2 + \varepsilon_t \qquad (20.8)$$

As before, the coefficients γ_{TM} and α_{TM} reflect the intensity of market timing and the unexplained portfolio return. More specifically, coefficient γ_{TM} reflects the convexity achieved by the manager in her exposure to the market portfolio. If the coefficient is positive, the manager succeeds in gradually increasing her exposure when the market goes up, which shows that she displays market timing skills. Under both specifications, a negative value of γ_{TM} corresponds to "negative" market timing.

The purpose of HM and TM models is to show a manager's asset selection and market timing skills using only one equation. Under both specifications, the regression intercept is supposed to capture the selection skills of the fund manager while γ_{TM} reflects her ability to time the market. Yet, γ_{TM} does not deliver a measure of excess return due to market timing. As a result, the simple separation between the regression intercept and market timing coefficient, as proposed by Lee and Rahman (1990) is inappropriate when evaluating performance of market timers. The time varying intercept of a conditional asset pricing model is another major approach used for the measurement of market timing skills, but it is not the focus on this chapter (Christopherson, Ferson and Glassman, 1998).

PERFORMANCE CORRECTIONS FOR MARKET TIMING

Many researchers have investigated different ways to measure the contribution of market timing to a fund's performance. In the context of the TM model, three traditional approaches coexist to measure the total performance of market timers. One is based on the variance of the market portfolio, a second relies on the average of squared market returns, and a final approach is based on an option portfolio and referred to as the option portfolio replication approach. Hübner (2010) explores a new development of the option portfolio replication approach with its extension in the framework of multifactor models.

Classical Correction Methods

The work of Admati, Bhattacharya, Pfeiderer, and Ross (1986) characterizes the properties of an active market timing portfolio managed optimally under the standard assumptions of the CAPM, namely if returns are normally distributed and investors exhibits a classical structure of preferences involving constant absolute risk aversion (CARA). Grinblatt and Titman (1994) show that the variance of the market portfolio returns adequately represents the reward for the manager's market timing skills. Formally, the total return attributable to the manager's performance, denoted $\pi_{TM,v}$, corresponds to

$$\pi_{TM,v} = \alpha_{TM} + \gamma_{TM}\sigma_m^2 \qquad (20.9)$$

where σ_m^2 is the variance of the market portfolio returns.

Bollen and Busse (2004) assume that a perfect market timer ex post would make her beta time varying according to market conditions. To find the total performance of a manager combining asset selection and market timing abilities involves averaging the periodic market returns in the model with time varying betas. Bollen and Busse present an equation for total performance, called $\pi_{TM,a}$, which is shown in Equation 20.10

$$\pi_{TM,a} = \alpha_{TM} + \gamma_{TM}\bar{r}_m^2 \qquad (20.10)$$

where $\bar{r}_m^2$ is the arithmetic mean of the squared market returns over the analyzed period.

Merton (1981) introduces the third way to correct for market timing that involves using option trading strategies. He states that the portfolio return obtained in Equation 20.7 can be replicated by simultaneously taking a long position of β_{HM} in the market index and of γ_{HM} in a put on the same index, which will only pay off if the index return is lower than the risk-free rate. The remaining amount $(1-\beta_{HM}-\gamma_{HM})$ is invested (if positive) or borrowed (if negative) at the riskless rate. The cost of adopting such a strategy is the initial put premium. The manager's total performance $\pi_{TM,o}$, combining her selectivity and timing skills, can be represented in Equation 20.11:

$$\pi_{HM,o} = \alpha_{HM} + \gamma_{HM}e^{R_f\Delta t}P(M,\Delta t,e^{R_f\Delta t}) \qquad (20.11)$$

where $P(M,\Delta t,e^{R_f\Delta t})$ is a put written on the market portfolio M, whose price is normalized to 1. The remaining time to maturity is equal to the time interval and the strike price is equal to $e^{R_f\Delta t}$. Ingersoll, Spiegel, Goetzmann, and Welch (2007) adapt Equation 20.11 to the TM framework and get

$$\pi_{TM,o} = \alpha_{TM} + \gamma_{TM}e^{2R_f\Delta t}(e^{\sigma_m^2\Delta t}-1) \qquad (20.12)$$

where R_f is the continuous interest rate and σ_m^2 is the variance of the market index returns. The second term of this expression should be interpreted as the payoff for the fraction γ_{TM} of a derivative security that pays the square of the excess market return.

Integrating the Directional Exposure

None of the corrections for the market timing skills takes into account the portfolio manager's directional exposure. This omission neglects important information because in the absence of any managerial skill, there is a direct link between the beta (β_{TM}) and gamma (γ_{TM}) coefficients of the TM specification and the intercept of the same equation. Hübner (2010) demonstrates that it is possible to build a portfolio consisting of a mix of options and risk-free instruments, which would have the same linear (β_{TM}) and convexity (γ_{TM}) exposures to a market index as those observed in the TM model.

The reasoning for this argument is straightforward. Consider a self-financing investment strategy consisting in creating a long position in a market index with a positive or a negative convexity in returns and lending or borrowing at the risk-free rate. A position involving a long call option written on this index has a positive first order partial derivative with respect to the underlying (option delta) and a positive second order partial derivative with respect to the underlying (option gamma), while a position involving a short put option has a positive option delta and a negative option gamma. In principle, finding an option whose time to maturity and moneyness match the sensitivities to the underlying index observed with the TM regression is possible.

Consider, without loss of generality, a market timer with both a positive β_{TM} and γ_{TM}. Following this approach, Hübner (2010) shows that the solution is given by selecting an option on the market index whose pair (τ^*, κ^*) satisfies the following conditions

$$\alpha^{(\tau^*,\kappa^*)} = \max_{\tau,\kappa} \left(w_{\tau,\kappa} \Theta_{\tau,\kappa} + (1 - w_{\tau,\kappa}) R_f \right) \tag{20.13}$$

$$\text{s.t.} \frac{2\Delta_{\tau^*,\kappa^*}}{\Gamma_{\tau^*,\kappa^*}} = \frac{\beta_{TM}}{\gamma_{TM}} \tag{20.14}$$

$$w_{\tau,\kappa} = \frac{\beta_{TM}}{\Delta_{\tau,\kappa}} > \beta_{TM} \tag{20.15}$$

where τ and κ are the time to maturity and the strike price (expressed as a multiple of the spot price) of the option, respectively, and

$\Delta_{\tau,\kappa} \equiv \dfrac{\partial C(M,\tau,\kappa)}{\partial M}$, $\Gamma_{\tau,\kappa} \equiv \dfrac{\partial^2 C(M,\tau,\kappa)}{\partial M^2}$ and $\Theta_{\tau,\kappa} \equiv \dfrac{\partial C(M,\tau,\kappa)}{\partial t}$ are the option

delta, gamma, and theta, respectively.

The outperformance of the active portfolio that yields the returns over the replicating portfolio is obtained by subtracting the value of $\alpha^{(\tau^*,\kappa^*)}$ from the portfolio "total alpha" (i.e., the intercept of the regression using total returns):

$$\pi_{TM}^* = \alpha_{TM} + (1 - \beta_{TM}) R_f - \alpha^{(\tau^*,\kappa^*)} \tag{20.16}$$

The cases where β_{TM} and/or γ_{TM} are null or negative are governed by a similar logic. If $\beta_{TM} > 0$ and $\gamma_{TM} < 0$, the portfolio replication will involve a short position in a put. If $\beta_{TM} < 0$ and $\gamma_{TM} > 0$, the strategy involves going long in a put option. Finally, if $\beta_{TM} < 0$ and $\gamma_{TM} < 0$, the replicated portfolio contains a short position in a call option. In all four cases, the sign of the ratio β_{TM} / γ_{TM} drives the choice of the option (call or put) and implies the nature of the position to be taken (long or short), or in other words the sign of w_{τ^*, κ^*}. If β_{TM} is null, the difficulty in obtaining an option whose delta is very low with respect to its gamma can be overcome by creating long or short straddles, depending on whether γ_{TM} is positive or negative. Finally, when γ_{TM} is null, there is no market timing to be emphasized, which suggests returning to linear models.

Working in a Multifactor Framework

The model specification is particularly important for the methods involving option strategies. The smaller the specific risk ε_t in the TM regression, the closer the replicated option portfolio can be associated to an arbitrage-free relationship. Decreasing the specific risk is possible by using a multifactor version of the Treynor and Mazuy (1966) model. Therefore, several authors propose extending the original TM model. Lehmann and Modest (1987) consider that the manager can anticipate the changes of a number of K indices. Consequently, they propose adding the same number of squared returns to the specification. Moreover, the authors include all the two-by-two interaction terms. Such a specification leads to a number of $K(K-1)2$ market timing terms to compute. The potentially important number of statistically insignificant variables induces problems of overspecification. Comer (2006) avoids this issue by excluding all interaction terms from the specification. In his eight-factor model (four for stocks and four for bonds), he considers only two market timing factors: one for the stock market and one for the bond market.

Hübner (2010) demonstrates that the portfolio replication approach may be extended to a multifactor specification. Consistent with Comer (2006), he considers that the linear return generating specification features K risk factors but only a subset $L \leq K$ are prone to a market timing behavior. For each of these factors, the linear and quadratic sensitivities can be isolated and the replication process described previously can be reproduced individually for each factor. Formally, the return generating process is expressed as

$$R_t - R_f = \alpha + \sum_{i \in L} \beta_i (R_{it} - R_f) + \sum_{i \in K, L} \beta_i R_{it} + \sum_{i \in L} \gamma_i (R_{it} - R_f)^2 + \varepsilon_t \qquad (20.17)$$

$$\Rightarrow R_t = \alpha + (1 - \sum_{i \in L} \beta_i) R_f + \sum_{i \in K} \beta_i R_{it} + \sum_{i \in L} \gamma_i R_{it}^2 + \varepsilon_t \qquad (20.18)$$

and the market timing adjusted performance is obtained as follows

$$\pi^* = \alpha + (1 - \sum_{i \in L} \beta_i) R_f - \sum_{i \in L} \alpha^{(\tau_i^*, \kappa_i^*)} \qquad (20.19)$$

where

$$\alpha^{(\tau^*,\kappa_i^*)} = w_{\dot{\tau}_i,\kappa_i} \cdot \Theta_{\dot{\tau}_i,\kappa_i} + (1-w_{\dot{\tau}_i,\kappa_i})R_f \qquad (20.20)$$

if the beta in absolute terms associated to the ith factor is above a minimum threshold. In the case of a very small beta but a large gamma, the replicating strategy uses option straddles as before.

Taking the Carhart (1997) four-factor model as in Equation 20.5 and adopting an approach similar to Comer (2006), who considers that most of the managers' timing skills are concentrated on anticipating broad market movements, Hübner (2010) obtains the following

$$r_t = \alpha_{4F-TM} + \beta_1 r_{mt} + \beta_2 SMB_t + \beta_3 HML_t + \beta_4 UMD_t + \gamma r_{mt}^2 + \varepsilon_t . \qquad (20.21)$$

The performance adjusted for selectivity and timing is obtained by a similar formula:

$$\pi^*_{4F-TM} = \alpha_{4F-TM} + (1-\beta_1)R_f - w_{\tau^*,\kappa^*} \cdot \Theta_{\tau^*,\kappa^*} - (1-w_{\tau^*,\kappa^*})R_f . \qquad (20.22)$$

Empirical Analysis

In this empirical part of the chapter, the solutions previously exposed to measure the performance of funds exhibiting market timing behaviors are compared. By applying the various corrections to mutual fund alphas in the context of the TM model, the authors obtain alternative performance measures leading to different rankings. The correlations between these measures are examined, which allows focusing on the relationship between the adjusted performance and the intensity of market timing. The goal is to detect whether there is a link between market timing and performance that can be emphasized and which type of correction makes it possible.

DATA AND MODELS

Using the screener of Bloomberg, a selection of equity mutual funds investing solely in the United States is performed. All funds from the sample selection are located in the United States and are priced in US dollars. Only funds with a net asset value (NAV) calculation realized on a daily basis are retained. Concerning the length of the NAV history, the sample is composed of funds launched before January 1, 1999, and survived at least until January 1, 2005. This screen allows the analysis on a first subperiod with only active funds and to check results on a second subperiod in which both active and defunct funds are kept to overcome a potential survivor bias. A full history of return is not necessarily required but only a time series with at least two years of data points is retained to provide reliable regression estimates. As in Bollen and Busse (2004), index funds are excluded in the selection because market timing is not part of the objectives of their managers. For the selected funds, daily and weekly total returns from January 1, 1999, until May 31, 2011, are downloaded. The selection contains 1,413 funds with about 22 percent of them are still active at the end of the sample period. Risk factors are market, size, and book-to-market factors of Fama and French (1992) as well as the Carhart (1997) momentum factor are downloaded from Kenneth French's website (http://mba.tuck.dartmouth.edu/pages/faculty/ken.french/data_library.html).

Asset Pricing Specifications

In their study, Bollen and Busse (2004) apply the Fama and French (1992) and Carhart (1997) four-factor model rather than the market model corresponding to the CAPM in order to get a more precise return-generating process, and they add a single term to reflect the managers' ability to anticipate variations of the market returns. As in their paper, the four-factor TM model is applied to the mutual fund sample as in Equation 20.21.

Tables 20.1 and 20.2 present descriptive statistics on the mutual fund samples and results of the estimation (Equation 20.21) run on these same samples, respectively. Positive and negative market timers correspond to funds that obtain a gamma significant at the 0.10 level when applying the multifactor TM specification. In Table 20.2, the level of R^2_{adj} is high and sufficiently important given the desire to apply the option portfolio replication method. The proportion of market timers (positive and negative) is higher when using daily data as suggested by Bollen and Busse (2001).

THE PERFORMANCE OF MARKET TIMERS

Given the form of the applied specification (a multifactor model with only one factor prone to market timing behavior), the formulas for the total performance correspond to Equations 20.9, 20.10, 20.12, and 20.16. For the correction based on replicating option portfolios, a maturity of three months for all options is selected.

Next, the authors check some or all of the corrections proposed in the literature attribute a positive total performance to the positive market timers and a negative total performance to negative market timers. Second, they compute the correlations between various performance measures and the gamma coefficient, with an assumption that funds exhibiting a greater convexity would achieve a higher total performance. These analyses are performed with daily and weekly data on the whole period and on two subperiods in order to get an idea about the robustness of results.

Table 20.3 compares a set of performance measures that can be obtained from the multifactor TM specification. The adjustment obtained while applying Grinblatt and Titman (1994), Bollen and Busse (2004), or Ingersoll et al. (2007) methods are almost identical. Unlike Hübner (2010)'s method, the first three leave positive market timers with a negative total performance and negative market timers with a positive total performance when the analysis uses daily

Table 20.1 **Descriptive Statistics of the Dependent and Independent Variables**

				Period			
	1999–2011		1999–2005			2006–2011	
Daily	Mean	Std. Dev.	Mean	Std. Dev.		Mean	Std. Dev.
Mutual funds excess returns	4.53	23.26	5.09	20.80		2.19	20.34
Positive market timers	4.44	22.94	5.37	23.21		4.56	23.31
Negative market timers	4.76	23.06	5.01	22.91		5.10	23.46
Market excess returns	3.76	21.39	2.18	18.77		5.83	24.37
Small minus big	5.73	10.13	7.42	10.28		3.58	9.93
High minus low	4.51	11.25	7.83	11.37		0.37	11.08
Momentum	4.60	17.80	11.45	15.96		-3.63	19.93
Market excess returns squared	0.02	0.05	0.01	0.03		0.02	0.08

(*Continued*)

Table 20.1 **(Continued)**

Weekly	Period					
	1999–2011		1999–2005		2006–2011	
	Mean	*Std. Dev.*	*Mean*	*Std. Dev.*	*Mean*	*Std. Dev.*
Mutual funds excess returns	3.09	24.00	3.85	22.16	2.15	24.39
Positive market timers	3.12	24.05	3.02	23.22	3.36	24.75
Negative market timers	3.47	23.59	2.98	23.08	4.10	24.16
Market excess returns	2.87	19.98	1.34	18.22	4.87	22.08
Small minus big	6.07	10.39	8.06	11.51	3.55	8.75
High minus low	4.56	11.62	8.05	11.91	0.22	11.22
Momentum	5.51	20.44	12.76	18.95	-3.17	22.20
Market excess returns squared	0.08	0.21	0.06	0.15	0.09	0.27

Note: This table reports descriptive statistics on our sample of 1,413 US equity mutual funds and Fama-French (1992) and Carhart (1997) factors (FFCF) used in regressions. Treynor and Mazuy (TM) regressions augmented by FFCF are performed to build a sample of positive and negative market timers. Positive (negative) market timers are funds with positive (negative) and significant (at the 0.10 level) coefficient on the quadratic term for the period under study. Mean and volatility of funds and factors returns are expressed in percentage and annual terms. Statistics for the quadratic terms are not annualized.

Table 20.2 **Summary Results of the Estimation of the Multifactor TM Model**

Daily		Period		
		1999–2011	1999–2005	2006–2011
R^2_{adj}	Mean	0.86	0.83	0.92
	Standard deviation	0.13	0.15	0.11
$a_{4F\text{-}TM}$	Mean	−0.67	−1.03	−1.01
		0.29	0.34	0.29
	% significant	0.12	0.09	0.10
β_1	Mean	0.96	0.97	0.98
	Standard deviation	0.19	0.21	0.18
	% significant	1.00	1.00	0.99
γ	Mean	0.10	0.25	0.02
	Standard deviation	0.70	1.03	0.68
	% significant	0.23	0.25	0.21
β_2	Mean	8.86	7.76	8.48
	Standard deviation	18.36	15.97	15.20
	% significant	0.57	0.58	0.59
β_3	Mean	4.59	6.31	−0.98
	Standard deviation	15.78	13.76	6.56
	% significant	0.58	0.64	0.36
β_4	Mean	0.10	−1.38	0.32
	Standard deviation	6.94	6.72	6.74
	% significant	0.40	0.33	0.42

Weekly		Period		
		1999–2011	1999–2005	2006–2011
R^2_{adj}	Mean	0.84	0.81	0.90
	Standard deviation	0.12	0.14	0.10
$a_{4F\text{-}TM}$	Mean	−0.98	−0.78	−1.59
	Standard deviation	0.54	0.61	0.57
	% significant	0.08	0.08	0.06
β_1	Mean	0.95	0.97	0.99
	Standard deviation	0.18	0.20	0.17
	% significant	1.00	1.00	1.00
γ	Mean	0.19	0.07	0.23
	Standard deviation	0.70	0.80	0.84
	% significant	0.16	0.14	0.22

(Continued)

Table 20.2 **(Continued)**

		Period		
Daily		*1999–2011*	*1999–2005*	*2006–2011*
β_2	Mean	3.79	3.55	4.25
	Standard deviation	9.09	8.13	8.21
	% significant	0.54	0.56	0.56
β_3	Mean	2.45	3.75	−1.05
	Standard deviation	8.24	7.50	3.89
	% significant	0.54	0.61	0.26
β_4	Mean	0.14	−0.77	0.41
	Standard deviation	3.91	3.88	3.54
	% significant	0.36	0.28	0.36

Note: This table reports statistics obtained when running the multifactor Treynor and Mazuy (TM) regression on the whole sample of mutual funds: $r_t = a_{4F\text{-}TM} + \beta_1 r_{mt} + \beta_2 SMB_t + \beta_3 HML_t + \beta_4 UMD_t + \gamma r_{mt}^2 + \varepsilon_t$. The mean and the standard deviation of $a_{4F\text{-}TM}$ are annualized. The mean and standard deviation of the cross-section of estimated parameters are expressed in percentage terms.

data. Average amplitudes of the corrections as well as their standard deviation are always higher with Hübner (2010)'s method, regardless of the data frequency.

Table 20.4 focuses on market timing situations. The results show the tendency for positive market timers to have $\alpha_{4F\text{-}TM} < 0$ and the opposite is true for negative market timers. The sign and the amplitude of the directional exposure are particularly of interest since they drive the choice of the replication strategy. A large majority of market timers have a linear exposure greater than 0.5. Thus, most of positive market timers can be replicated by taking a long position in a call option while most of the negative market timers can be replicated by taking a short position in a put option on the index. Among positive market timers, the proportion of funds having a positive total performance is always much higher with Hübner (2010)'s method, while the opposite is observed with the variance correction approach of Grinblatt and Titman (1994). Concerning negative market timers, the bulk of funds receive a negative total performance with Hübner's method while the results are less obvious with the variance correction approach. These findings confirm those of Hübner (2010) and Cavé, Hübner, and Sougné (2011), who show that traditional approaches tend to underestimate the adjustment to the alpha in order to reflect abnormal returns due to market timing.

Table 20.5 shows the correlations between four performance measures (two nonadjusted and two adjusted for market timing) and the funds' convexity exposure. Although the performance obtained with the variance correction method is sometimes negatively correlated with gamma, the replication approach does not exhibit this relationship. For positive market timers, the performance corrected by the replication approach is always strongly correlated with gamma.

Table 20.3 **Corrections for Market Timing**

Positive Market Timers

Daily	N	a_{4F}	a_{4F-TM}	Variance		Squared Return		Option 1		Option*	
				cor.	π_v	cor.	π_a	cor.	π_o	cor.	π^*
1999–2011	331	-0.58	-3.67	3.48	-0.19	3.47	-0.19	3.48	-0.19	5.50	1.83
		(0.18)	(0.25)	(0.18)	(0.18)	(0.18)	(0.18)	(0.18)	(0.18)	(0.22)	(0.20)
1999–2005	348	0.23	-4.64	4.81	0.17	4.80	0.17	4.81	0.17	7.66	3.03
		(0.23)	(0.27)	(0.16)	(0.23)	(0.16)	(0.23)	(0.16)	(0.23)	(0.20)	(0.23)
2006–2011	249	-1.18	-4.25	3.75	-0.50	3.75	-0.50	3.75	-0.49	5.23	0.98
		(0.20)	(0.23)	(0.21)	(0.23)	(0.21)	(0.23)	(0.21)	(0.23)	(0.33)	(0.33)

Negative Market Timers

Daily	N	a_{4F}	a_{4F-TM}	Variance		Squared Return		Option 1		Option*	
				cor.	π_v	cor.	π_a	cor.	π_o	cor.	π^*
1999–2011	123	0.80	6.09	-5.66	0.43	-5.66	0.43	-5.66	0.42	-8.88	-2.79
		(0.26)	(0.34)	(0.24)	(0.28)	(0.24)	(0.28)	(0.24)	(0.28)	(0.29)	(0.29)
1999–2005	105	0.38	7.28	-6.92	0.36	-6.92	0.36	-6.92	0.36	-11.01	-3.74
		(0.31)	(0.44)	(0.23)	(0.32)	(0.23)	(0.32)	(0.23)	(0.32)	(0.29)	(0.31)
2006–2011	121	-1.29	4.56	-6.60	-2.04	-6.60	-2.04	-6.60	-2.04	-9.35	-4.79
		(0.32)	(0.40)	(0.35)	(0.35)	(0.35)	(0.35)	(0.35)	(0.35)	(0.40)	(0.36)

(Continued)

Table 20.3 **(Continued)**

Positive Market Timers

Weekly	N	a_{4F}	a_{4F-TM}	Variance cor.	π_v	Squared Return cor.	π_a	Option 1 cor.	π_o	Option* cor.	π^*
1999–2011	223	0.62	−2.89	4.50	1.61	4.49	1.61	4.51	1.62	6.93	4.04
		(0.58)	(0.63)	(0.38)	(0.57)	(0.38)	(0.57)	(0.38)	(0.57)	(0.54)	(0.59)
1999–2005	298	0.49	−3.03	3.48	0.45	3.47	0.44	3.49	0.46	6.43	3.40
		(0.52)	(0.60)	(0.32)	(0.52)	(0.32)	(0.52)	(0.32)	(0.52)	(0.47)	(0.54)
2006–2011	150	−1.12	−4.90	5.46	0.56	5.44	0.54	5.47	0.57	7.37	2.47
		(0.49)	(0.61)	(0.66)	(0.60)	(0.66)	(0.60)	(0.66)	(0.61)	(0.82)	(0.69)

Negative Market Timers

Weekly	N	a_{4F}	a_{4F-TM}	Variance cor.	π_v	Squared Return cor.	π_a	Option 1 cor.	π_o	Option* cor.	π^*
1999–2011	116	−0.62	2.18	−3.78	−1.60	−3.78	−1.59	−3.79	−1.60	−6.79	−4.60
		(0.34)	(0.38)	(0.27)	(0.37)	(0.27)	(0.37)	(0.27)	(0.37)	(0.32)	(0.40)
1999–2005	70	−1.01	2.31	−3.80	−1.49	−3.79	−1.48	−3.81	−1.50	−7.27	−4.96
		(0.44)	(0.55)	(0.36)	(0.48)	(0.36)	(0.48)	(0.36)	(0.48)	(0.47)	(0.53)
2006–2011	185	−1.69	1.32	−3.90	−2.58	−3.89	−2.57	−3.90	−2.59	−6.44	−5.13
		(0.47)	(0.51)	(0.36)	(0.51)	(0.36)	(0.51)	(0.36)	(0.51)	(0.41)	(0.54)

Note: This table reports six performance measures for positive and negative market timers. a_{4F} and a_{4F-TM} are intercepts of specifications (20.23) and (20.24), respectively. For "Variance," "Squared Return," "Option 1," and "Option*," the statistics for the adjustments are show as well as the total performance of Grinblatt and Titman (1994), Bollen and Busse (2004), Ingersoll et al. (2007), and Hübner (2010). Average performance and correction are expressed in yearly percent terms. Standard deviations are in parentheses and expressed in yearly terms.

Table 20.4 **Analysis of Market Timing Situations**

Daily	Positive Market Timers			Negative Market Timers		
	1999–2011	1999–2005	2006–2011	1999–2011	1999–2005	2006–2011
$\alpha_{4F\text{-}TM} > 0$	32	39	18	115	93	95
$\alpha_{4F\text{-}TM} < 0$	299	309	231	8	12	26
$0 < \beta_1 < 0.5$	0	3	0	7	11	1
$-0.5 < \beta_1 < 0$	0	0	0	3	0	6
$\beta_1 > 0.5$	331	345	249	113	94	113
$\beta_1 < -0.5$	0	0	0	0	0	1
$\pi_v > 0$	150	173	99	64	54	49
$\pi_v < 0$	181	175	150	59	51	72
$\pi^* > 0$	251	279	153	30	22	19
$\pi^* < 0$	80	69	96	93	83	102

(Continued)

Table 20.4 **(Continued)**

Weekly	Positive Market Timers			Negative Market Timers		
	1999–2011	1999–2005	2006–2011	1999–2011	1999–2005	2006–2011
$\alpha_{4F\text{-}TM} > 0$	50	64	7	93	53	120
$\alpha_{4F\text{-}TM} < 0$	173	234	143	23	17	65
$0 < \beta_1 < 0.5$	5	7	0	2	1	2
$-0.5 < \beta_1 < 0$	0	0	0	0	0	0
$\beta_1 > 0.5$	215	289	147	114	69	183
$\beta_1 < -0.5$	3	2	3	0	0	0
$\pi_v > 0$	146	147	73	26	20	43
$\pi_v < 0$	77	151	77	90	50	142
$\pi^* > 0$	198	251	110	8	6	9
$\pi^* < 0$	25	47	40	108	64	176

Note: This table reports information about the situations of market timing. For positive and negative market timers, counts are made for the number of times statistics of the multifactor Treynor and Mazuy (TM) model or derived performances measures are included in a given interval.

Table 20.5 **Correlation Analysis**

	1999–2011							
	Positive Market Timers				Negative Market Timers			
Daily	a_{4F}	a_{4F-TM}	π_v	π^*	a_{4F}	a_{4F-TM}	π_v	π^*
a_{4F-TM}	0.83***				0.81***			
π_v	0.95***	0.70***			0.97***	0.73***		
π^*	0.86***	0.50***	0.96***		0.93***	0.59***	0.98***	
γ	−0.15***	−0.66***	0.08	0.31***	−0.02	−0.58***	0.14	0.31***
	1999–2005							
	Positive Market Timers				Negative Market Timers			
Daily	a_{4F}	a_{4F-TM}	π_v	π^*	a_{4F}	a_{4F-TM}	π_v	π^*
a_{4F-TM}	0.81***				0.88***			
π_v	1.00***	0.81***			0.99***	0.87***		
π^*	0.97***	0.69***	0.98***		0.96***	0.75***	0.98***	
γ	0.06	−0.52***	0.08	0.25***	−0.31***	−0.72***	−0.28***	−0.10
	2006–2011							
	Positive Market Timers				Negative Market Timers			
Daily	a_{4F}	a_{4F-TM}	π_v	π^*	a_{4F}	a_{4F-TM}	π_v	π^*
a_{4F-TM}	0.85***				0.69***			
π_v	0.88***	0.60***			0.95***	0.57***		
π^*	0.72***	0.36***	0.91***		0.92***	0.46***	0.99***	
γ	0.04	−0.45***	0.45***	0.62***	0.15*	−0.58***	0.35***	0.46***
	1999–2011							
	Positive Market Timers				Negative Market Timers			
Weekly	a_{4F}	a_{4F-TM}	π_v	π^*	a_{4F}	a_{4F-TM}	π_v	π^*
a_{4F-TM}	0.89***				0.87***			
π_v	0.98***	0.81***			0.96***	0.74***		
π^*	0.88***	0.62***	0.93***		0.92***	0.66***	0.99***	
γ	−0.02	−0.46***	0.15**	0.37***	0.09	−0.39***	0.32***	0.43***
	1999–2005							
	Positive Market Timers				Negative Market Timers			
Weekly	a_{4F}	a_{4F-TM}	π_v	π^*	a_{4F}	a_{4F-TM}	π_v	π^*
a_{4F-TM}	0.85***				0.87***			
π_v	0.99***	0.84***			0.95***	0.77***		
π^*	0.93***	0.66***	0.94***		0.89***	0.63***	0.98***	
γ	0.01	−0.50***	0.05	0.29***	−0.06	−0.51***	0.16	0.35***

(Continued)

Table 20.5 **(Continued)**

| | *2006–2011* | | | | | | | |
| | *Positive Market Timers* | | | | *Negative Market Timers* | | | |
Weekly	a_{4F}	a_{4F-TM}	π_v	π^*	a_{4F}	a_{4F-TM}	π_v	π^*
a_{4F-TM}	0.70***				0.88***			
π_v	0.88***	0.40***			0.95***	0.75***		
π^*	0.78***	0.22***	0.97***		0.93***	0.69***	0.99***	
γ	0.16**	−0.55***	0.55***	0.69***	0.13*	−0.33***	0.37***	0.44***

Note: This table reports the correlations between nonadjusted performance measures (a_{4F-TM} and a_{4F}) and performance measures adjusted for market timing (π_v and π^*) and the market timing coefficient (γ). *, **, *** indicate statistical significance at the 0.10, 0.05, and 0.01 levels, respectively.

Figure 20.1 represents two measures adjusted for market timing (π_v and π^*) as functions of the gamma coefficient. For both positive and negative market timers, the slope of the regression line is steeper when the performance is measured with the portfolio replication approach. This means that positive market timers with stronger convexity exposure tend to receive higher performances and negative market timers with more concave returns obtain lower performances.

Summary and Conclusions

Traditional performance measures derived from the CAPM have taken two routes, depending on whether the focus is set on selectivity or anticipation skills. As a result, models such as the HM piecewise regression or TM quadratic regression specifications that aim at measuring market timing must be adjusted to accommodate both types of skills in one single measure.

The intercepts of those regressions cannot be used to measure the total performance of market timers. These coefficients are often negative for funds achieving convexity and positive for funds that cannot time the market. From this counterintuitive fact, researchers have investigated ways to correct the alpha in order to properly measure the performance of market timers. This chapter explores three classical adjustments: one is based on the variance of the market returns, a second is based on the squared market returns, and a third relies on creating an option portfolio to replicate the shape of fund's returns.

This chapter also explores a recent development of the portfolio replication approach and observes its advantages over the classical methods. Unlike its predecessors, this new measure of performance cannot be easily manipulated through the purchase and sale of options. With this new method, most positive market timers get rewarded for their skills measured as the level of convexity that they are able to achieve. These conclusions are verified over three time periods and do not differ based on the use of either daily or weekly data.

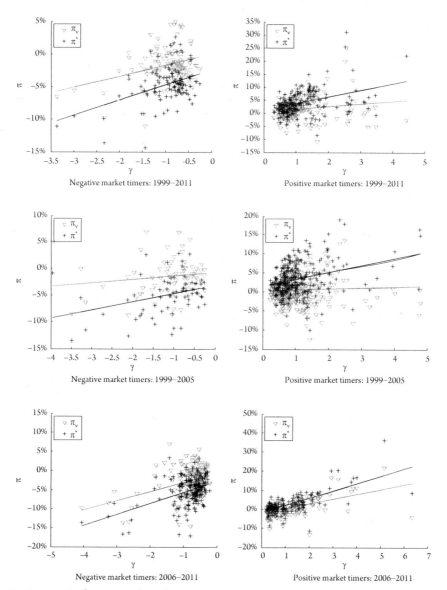

Figure 20.1 Performance of Market Timers as a Function of Their Convexity Exposure

These figures represent the adjusted performance of mutual funds, i.e., the $a_{4F\text{-}TM}$ corrected with the variance method (π_v) and the Hübner (2010) portfolio replication method (π^*) as a function as of their convexity exposure (γ). Performance is expressed in yearly percentage terms. These figures are realized with weekly data.

Discussion Questions

1. Using Carhart's (1997) multifactor model, why is neither using alpha suited to measure market timing skills nor alpha with a quadratic term suited to measure asset selection skills?

2. Under the Treynor and Mazuy (1966) model, four adjustment methods have been proposed to integrate market timing and asset selection in a single, synthetic performance measure. Why are the three classical methods likely to leave a biased measure of performance?
3. Explain the reasoning underlying the replicating option adjustment method to the Treynor and Mazuy (1966) model and apply it to all possible patterns for the sign of the delta and the gamma.
4. Based on the empirical analysis of mutual funds in this chapter, discuss evidence that the intensity of market timing is related to portfolio performance.

References

Admati, Anat R., Sudipto Bhattacharya, Paul Pfeiderer, and Stephen A. Ross. 1986. "On Timing and Selectivity." *Journal of Finance* 41:3, 715–730.

Becker, Connie, Wayne Ferson, David H. Myers, and Michael J. Schill. 1999. "Conditional Market Timing with Benchmark Investors." *Journal of Financial Economics* 52:1, 119–148.

Bodie, Zvi, Alex Kane, and Alan J. Marcus. 2010. *Investments*, 8th edition. New York: McGraw-Hill/Irwin.

Bollen, Nicolas P. B., and Jeffrey A. Busse. 2001. "On the Timing Ability of Mutual Fund Managers." *Journal of Finance* 56:3, 1075–1094.

Bollen, Nicolas P. B., and Jeffrey A. Busse. 2004. "Short-Term Persistence in Mutual Fund Performance." *Review of Financial Studies* 18:2, 569–597.

Carhart, Mark M. 1997. "On Persistence in Mutual Fund Performance." *Journal of Finance* 52:1, 57–82.

Cavé, Arnaud, Georges Hübner, and Danielle M. Sougné. 2012. "The Market Timing Skills of Hedge Funds during the Financial Crisis." *Managerial Finance* 38:1, 4–26.

Christopherson, Jon A., Wayne E. Ferson, and Debra A. Glassman. 1998. "Conditioning Manager Alphas on Economic Information: Another Look at the Persistence of Performance." *Review of Financial Studies* 11:1, 111–142.

Comer, George. 2006. "Hybrid Mutual Funds and Market Timing Performance." *Journal of Business* 79:2, 771–798.

Comer, George, Norris Larrymore, and Javier Rodriguez. 2009. "Controlling for Fixed-Income Exposure in Portfolio Evaluation: Evidence from Hybrid Mutual Funds." *Review of Financial Studies* 22:2, 481–507.

Fama, Eugene F., and Kenneth R. French. 1992. "The Cross-Section of Expected Stock Returns." *Journal of Finance* 47:2, 427–465.

Grinblatt, Mark, and Sheridan Titman. 1994. "A Study of Monthly Mutual Fund Returns and Performance Evaluation Techniques." *Journal of Financial and Quantitative Analysis* 29:3, 419–444.

Henriksson, Roy D., and Robert C. Merton. 1981. "On Market Timing and Investment Performance II. Statistical Procedures for Evaluating Forecasting Skills." *Journal of Business* 54:4, 513–533.

Hübner, Georges. 2005. "The Generalized Treynor Ratio." *Review of Finance* 9:3, 415–435.

Hübner, Georges. 2010. "The Alpha of a Market Timer." Working Paper, HEC Management School, University of Liège.

Ingersoll, Jonathan, Matthew Spiegel, William Goetzmann, and Ivo Welch. 2007. "Portfolio Performance Manipulation and Manipulation-Proof Performance Measures." *Review of Financial Studies* 20:5, 1503–1546.

Jensen, Michael J. 1968. "The Performance of Mutual Funds in the Period 1945–1964." *Journal of Finance* 23:2, 389–416.

Jiang, George J., Tong Yao, and Tong Yu. 2007. "Do Mutual Funds Time the Market? Evidence from Portfolio Holdings." *Journal of Financial Economics* 86:3, 724–758.

Keating, Con, and William F. Shadwick. 2002. "Omega: A Universal Performance Measure." *Journal of Performance Measurement* 6:3, 59–84.

Kothari, S. P., and Jerold B. Warner. 2001. "Evaluating Mutual Fund Performance." *Journal of Finance* 56:5, 1985–2010.

Kryzanowski, Lawrence, Simon Lalancette, and Minh C. To. 1997. "Performance Attribution Using an APT with Prespecified Macrofactors and Time-Varying Risk Premia and Betas." *Journal of Financial and Quantitative Analysis* 32:2, 205–224.

Lee, Cheng-Few, and Shafiqur Rahman. 1990. "Market Timing, Selectivity, and Mutual Fund Performance: An Empirical Investigation." *Journal of Business* 63:2, 261–278.

Lehmann, Bruce N., and David M. Modest. 1987. "Mutual Fund Performance Evaluation: A Comparison of Benchmarks and Benchmark Comparisons." *Journal of Finance* 42:2, 233–265.

Merton, Robert C. 1981. "On Market Timing and Investment Performance I: An Equilibrium Theory of Value for Market Forecasts." *Journal of Business* 54:3, 363–406.

Ross, Stephen A. 1976. "The Arbitrage Theory of Capital Asset Pricing." *Journal of Economic Theory* 13:3, 341–360.

Sharpe, William F. 1966. "Mutual Fund Performance." *Journal of Business* 39:1, 119–138.

Sortino, Frank A., and Lee N. Price. 1994. "Performance Measurement in a Downside Risk Framework." *Journal of Investing* 3:3, 54–69.

Treynor, Jack. 1965. "How to Rate Management Investment Funds." *Harvard Business Review* 43:1, 63–75.

Treynor, Jack, and Kay Mazuy. 1966. "Can Mutual Funds Outguess the Market?" *Harvard Business Review* 44:4, 131–136.

21

Benchmarking

ABRAHAM LIOUI
Professor, EDHEC Business School

PATRICE PONCET
Distinguished Professor, ESSEC Business School

Introduction

Benchmarking is the practice of designing a given portfolio or index as a reference for the portfolio adopted by the fund manager. It serves two main purposes. First, benchmarking is an asset allocation tool for delegated portfolio management. The investor typically designs a strategic portfolio composed of broad classes of assets whose weights reflect her appetite for return and aversion to risk over a given investment horizon. The manager, who is responsible for the actual investment decisions, uses benchmarking as a guideline. Second, benchmarking is a tool for measuring the portfolio manager's performance and compensating her accordingly. A sensible practice is to compensate fund managers on their talents and their skill (or lack of it), which is best estimated after considering the performance of the market or markets in which they trade. For example, earning 8 percent in a given year by investing in US stocks does not have the same meaning and the same implications as to the manager's ability according to whether the S&P 500 index has increased by 15 percent or decreased by 6 percent.

The spectacular growth of the managed funds industry in recent years has elicited extensive academic and professional research on the various aspects of delegated portfolio management, particularly when benchmarking is involved. The objective of this chapter is to address the aim and scope of benchmarking, to analyze its merits and shortcomings from both theoretical and practical viewpoints, and to assess the likely future of the profession in light of its recent evolution.

The chapter is organized as follows. The next section defines the objectives of delegated portfolio management with a benchmarking orientation, presents the concept of tracking error, and provides an analysis of passive and active management. The third section considers the central question of the optimality of benchmarks and compensation schemes commonly encountered in practice. Different types of schemes and the alignment of interests of investors and managers are discussed within a principal-agent framework. Some implicit incentives given to managers are uncovered and the means to mitigate them are discussed. The optimality of exogenously given benchmarks from the investors' viewpoint and the impact of benchmarking on equilibrium asset prices and volatilities are examined. The fourth section provides various methods for assessing the manager's performance relative to a benchmark on an ex-post basis. The fifth section discusses the past, present, and the likely future of the benchmarking industry. The final section briefly summarizes the contents of the chapter.

Aim and Scope of Portfolio Management with Benchmarking

The first and main application of benchmarking is the adoption of a strategic reference portfolio. This portfolio includes a few asset classes (typically stocks, bonds, and money market instruments), the precise weights of which depend essentially on the investor's wealth and risk aversion. Inside each asset class, the risks specific to individual securities tend to be eliminated through diversification. Within this framework, one can distinguish passive from active portfolio management. The passive manager only tries to replicate the benchmark as perfectly as possible. In contrast, the active manager is given more latitude to depart from his reference portfolio and strives to "beat" it in risk-return tradeoff terms, either by modifying the respective weights of the asset classes (*market timing*) or by selecting particular securities within each class (*security selection*).

The *tracking error* measures how much a given portfolio deviates from its benchmark. Consider an investment horizon T. Let Δ_t be the period t difference in returns (R_t) between portfolio P and its benchmark B $(\Delta_t \equiv R_{P,t} - R_{B,t})$, i.e., the portfolio excess return, for $t = 1, \dots, T$. Let $E(\Delta)$ be the expectation of the excess return. The theoretical, or ex-ante tracking error (TE) is generally defined as the *standard deviation* of the portfolio excess returns Δ_t over the horizon T as shown in Equation 21.1:

$$TE = \sqrt{\frac{1}{T}\sum_{t=1}^{T}\left(\Delta_t - E(\Delta)\right)^2} \qquad (21.1)$$

The excess return Δ_t itself and not its standard deviation is sometimes called "tracking error," which is an unfortunate source of misunderstanding. When portfolio managers use a model to predict TE, e.g., to control for the relative risk of the portfolio, they use this ex-ante TE. When, however, TE is used as a tool for reporting performance, it is measured from historical data and is called realized or ex-post TE. It then is computed as Equation 21.2

$$TE^{sp} = \sqrt{\frac{1}{T-1}\sum_{t=1}^{T}(\Delta_t - \overline{\Delta})^2} \qquad (21.2)$$

since one degree of freedom is lost from the computation of the empirical

mean $\bar{\Delta}=\dfrac{1}{T}\sum\limits_{t=1}^{T}\Delta_t$. Most often, TE is computed from weekly observations. The result of the above formula then is multiplied by $\sqrt{52}$ to deliver the annualized TE. In Gaussian models, variance is proportional to time horizon T, thus standard deviation is proportional to the square root of T.

PASSIVE PORTFOLIO MANAGEMENT

Assets invested in passively managed equity funds, whose objectives are merely to reproduce benchmark indices, have enjoyed an accelerating growth in recent years, reaching more than one trillion US dollars as of December 2010 according to Xiong and Sullivan (2011). Thus, passive portfolio management represents a sizeable part of the industry. The commercial success of these funds, despite (or because) of their apparently limited objective, may be attributed to the relative efficiency of the financial market, which makes their performance difficult to beat. In practice, few funds outperform the market in terms of risk-adjusted gross returns in the long run, and, moreover, management fees reduce net returns to investors. Because investors, individuals, and institutions alike do not have trust in the ability of managers to add value to their portfolios, they impose on them both the acceptable universe of relevant assets and the portfolio strategy. Yet, investors do not invest directly because of economies of scale in transaction costs or a lack of time to devote to management. Often, their implicit benchmark is a broad stock market index, and historically, the tracking record of most professional managers has been disappointing. Passive investment then was the logical next step.

Passive investment is, in practice, a relatively heterogeneous style class as the maximum authorized TEs professional managers are subject to by regulation may vary substantially. According to a classification adopted in 2004 by the International Organization of Securities Commissions (IOSCO), index funds and exchange traded funds (ETFs), also routinely called *trackers*, belong to this class. An index fund typically strives to reproduce a return similar to a market index, such as the S&P 500, the FTSE 100, the Nikkei 225, or the CAC40 for stocks; or for bonds, commodities, or a composite index such as the various indices computed by Morgan Stanley. In principle, replicating an index or benchmark is easily obtained by constructing a portfolio whose assets are the same as the index and with identical weights at any point in time. Therefore, a buy-and-hold strategy is all that is required in theory. In practice, however, many events force managers to make transactions that are sources of TEs, such as coupon and dividend payments, equity issues or redemptions, liquidity considerations, and random inflows or outflows imposed by investors.

As a result, professional managers have often pursued synthetic replication or even statistical replication. The former technique uses derivatives, essentially futures or forward contracts when these contracts exist and have sufficient liquidity to replicate the index returns. A long equity position is equivalent to long positions on a corresponding futures or forward contract and on the riskless asset. As the number of instruments comprising the synthetic portfolio is considerably reduced, most difficulties previously mentioned disappear or are alleviated. However, a risk exists associated with rolling over the derivative positions due to random interest rate fluctuations, and transaction costs are not negligible when using options in lieu of futures.

Statistical replication is one additional step away from the purely passive strategy. The portfolio comprises fewer assets than the index to mitigate the said difficulties. Although the portfolio managers select the assets so as to optimally mimic the index, this method leads to TEs that are larger than those obtained with a strict replication.

ETFs or trackers typically reproduce specific sectors, although some replicate a broader market index, in particular when commodities are concerned. ETFs differ from index funds in two ways. First, ETFs are quoted, thus tradable, on a continuous basis as if they were quoted assets themselves. Second, their price is but a fraction of the index, and fees paid by investors to compensate the issuers are reduced to proportional management fees (typically 30 basis points) without entry and/or exit charges. These features make ETFs attractive and explain their booming success.

ACTIVE PORTFOLIO MANAGEMENT

The objective of a delegated portfolio management strategy that compares its performance to a benchmark to which it is more or less strictly linked is no longer to minimize the TE. Rather, the goal is to maximize the expected portfolio return, subject to looser TE constraints. When the constraints are tighter, usually less than 5 percent on an annual basis, the portfolio beta measured against the benchmark is generally closer to one. Recall that the beta measures the portfolio sensitivity to its benchmark (see Equation 21.9 for a formal definition). The fund's outperformance then stems essentially from security selection among the targeted asset classes, and the manager is assumed to exhibit the ability to select winners and avoid (or even to short) losers. When the TE constraint is looser, the manager can additionally build a portfolio whose beta relative to its benchmark departs from one. Then, she can use derivatives or statistical replication to benefit from arbitrage opportunities and strive to outperform the benchmark by market timing and security selection.

The optimization is usually conducted within the standard mean-variance, static framework pioneered by Markowitz (1959) and Sharpe (1964). To illustrate, assume that the manager has access to the riskless asset, yielding r, and to n risky assets where the $(n{\times}1)$ vector of random returns, the $(n{\times}1)$ vector of expected returns, and the $(n{\times}n)$ variance-covariance matrix are denoted by R, μ and $\mathbf{V}$, respectively. The active manager's formal program then becomes Equation 21.3

$$\underset{p}{Max}\ [E(R_p)]\ subject\ to\ \sigma(R_p - R_B) = e \qquad (21.3)$$

where portfolio P is characterized by the vector of weights p (such that $p'\mathbf{1} = 1$, with the prime denoting a transpose); its benchmark by the vector b (with $b'\mathbf{1} = 1$); σ denotes a standard deviation (also called volatility); and e is the maximum TE, or degree of freedom, the manager is authorized.

Defining $\Delta_P = R_P - R_B$ and realizing that, once determined, the benchmark B, hence R_B, is exogenous for the manager who cannot monitor it, this program amounts to maximizing the expectation of $\Delta_P (\Delta_P = R_P - R_B)$ under the TE constraint as shown in Equation 21.4

$$\underset{p}{Max} \ \ [E(\Delta_p)] \ subject \ to \ \sigma(\Delta_p) = e \tag{21.4}$$

where e is a positive constant. Roll (1992) shows that the solution to Equation 21.4 leads to the following main conclusions:

1. The active manager's optimal portfolio P^* is a linear combination of the benchmark B and a portfolio Q independent of the benchmark as shown in Equation 21.5:

$$x^* = b + \lambda q \tag{21.5}$$

where the vector of weights q that define Q is given by Equation 21.6:

$$q = \mathbf{V}^{-1}(\mu - r \ \mathbf{1}) \tag{21.6}$$

and where $\lambda = e / \sigma_q$ is a positive constant proportional to e and inversely proportional to σ_q, the volatility of Q, and $(\mu - r \ \mathbf{1})$ is the vector of excess returns (or risk premia).
2. The optimal portfolio P^* is mean-variance efficient if and only if the benchmark B is itself mean-variance efficient.

The result (1) is a two-fund separation theorem as in Tobin (1958) or Black (1972), which means that both the manager and the investor are indifferent between having access to all $(n + 1)$ assets or access only to two mutual funds, B and Q. Separation theorems constitute the theoretical foundation for active management. Instead of having to trade in all $(n + 1)$ assets, which implies effort, higher transaction costs, and suboptimal diversification for small-sized portfolios, the manager or investor trades in two well-diversified portfolios. There is, of course, no guarantee that the selected benchmark B is mean-variance efficient, but, given B, portfolio P^* is optimal in the sense of Equation 21.3.

The result (2) stems from the fact that any mean-variance efficient portfolio can be obtained from two different efficient portfolios. Note that when e is set to zero (hence λ is also zero), a passively managed portfolio emerges. Also, when σ_q increases, which increases the probability of departing substantially from the benchmark, the manager reduces the weight of portfolio Q.

Another observation leads to a generalization of the familiar Sharpe ratio $\left(\equiv \dfrac{\mu_P - r}{\sigma_P}\right)$. Equation 21.3 can be rewritten as Equation 21.7

$$\max_{p}\left(\frac{E(\Delta_P)}{\sigma(\Delta_P)}\right) \qquad (21.7)$$

such that $\sigma(\Delta_p) = e$. The ratio to be maximized, $(E(\Delta_P)/\sigma(\Delta_P))$, is called the *information ratio* (IR). The IR is useful in practice because it summarizes in a single measure the expected (or mean) excess return of the portfolio and its risk, as measured per unit of TE. It can be computed ex ante (from the theoretical distributions that the portfolio and its benchmark are assumed to follow) or estimated ex-post. In the latter case, the IR provides a quantitative assessment of the manager's performance. Note that the Sharpe ratio is but a particular case of the IR, appropriate only when the (usually implicit) manager's benchmark is the riskless rate. These measures are examined further in the section titled "Performance Evaluation."

An interesting practical issue is worth mentioning. The performance of a fund manager is usually assessed on the basis of the empirical, ex-post TE, simply because her theoretical, ex-ante TE is unobservable. The realized TE, in practice, matters for managers, investors, and regulatory bodies. Thus, TE will require modification over a given time horizon. Assuming that the TE is observed on a weekly basis, the revision of the targeted TE at the beginning of the week as a function of the observed TE at the end of the previous week is a better managerial practice. As a result, the manager minimizes the probability of her ex-post TE measured at the end of the current week by not adhering to the original constraint. Further, one can show that the manager will have to aim at an ex-ante TE smaller, on average, than the targeted TE in order for the empirical TE not to exceed the latter more frequently than authorized. In active management, therefore, the degree of freedom left to the manager is rather large, once the benchmark has been defined and imposed.

DYNAMIC MODELS

As mentioned earlier, Equation 21.3 and its offspring are static by nature, thereby denying any possibility of explicit portfolio rebalancing and leaving open the question of what is the investment horizon. This assumption may not be too severe for short-term investors but is surely untenable in most other situations. This obvious drawback has elicited a more recent and abundant strand of research, pioneered by Merton (1971), devoted to dynamic (asset pricing and) portfolio allocation. These models are grounded on stochastic dynamic programming, whose objective is more general than building a mean-variance portfolio and consists of maximizing the expected utility of the investor's terminal wealth. Time to investment horizon T is divided in subperiods, the length of which is finite in discrete time (from t to $t + 1$) or infinitesimal in continuous time (from t to $t + dt$).

Unfortunately, practical applications are difficult because no closed-form solution for the optimal portfolio strategy can be derived, even in the mathematically more tractable continuous time. However, under the assumption of perfect and complete markets (i.e., any terminal payoff can be replicated by a self-financing dynamic strategy), Karatzas, Lehoczky, and Shreve (1987) as well as Cox and Huang (1989) develop a method that transforms a complex dynamic program into a simpler static one and can be applied, in particular, to active management with benchmarking. This method allows for the determination of the optimal dynamic strategy in a relatively simple manner. However, the model is technically beyond the scope of this chapter and will not be covered.

Clearly, the results of optimal benchmarking (the subject of the next section) depend on the dynamics of asset prices. In static models, asset returns are generally assumed to follow a Gaussian distribution. In dynamic models, the corresponding assumption is that asset prices follow geometric Brownian motions, which implies independently and identically distributed Gaussian returns. Few tractable results are obtained outside of this framework. Yet, some predictability exists in asset returns.

Campbell (1987), Campbell and Shiller (1988a, 1988b), and Fama and French (1989) report that long-term US equity returns can be explained either by a short-term interest rate, some measure of the term premium, and the average dividend yield or by the dividend/price and the earnings/price ratios. Ferson, Heuson, and Su (2006) report that the time variation in expected returns remains economically important even after considering transaction costs. In works more closely related to the topic of this chapter, Pástor and Stambaugh (2002), Jones and Shanken (2005), and Busse and Irvine (2006) show that the predictability embedded in observed managerial skills could be exploited. According to Avramov (2004) and Avramov and Chordia (2006), investment strategies involving individual stocks or benchmarks are more profitable when they incorporate macroeconomic variables as predictors.

Using managers' skills, mutual fund risk loadings, and benchmark returns as predictors, Avramov and Wermers (2006) provide convincing evidence that the predictability reported for single assets carries over to actively managed mutual funds and that portfolio strategies exploiting such predictability significantly outperform those that do not. However, no complete model exists of delegated management with benchmarking where skillful managers can exploit the predictability of asset returns more efficiently than principals do. As buy-and-hold strategies are generally suboptimal, and dynamic ones are difficult or impossible to implement by direct investment, portfolio delegation is warranted. When benchmarking is involved, which is as stated previously often the case, the central issue of what is an appropriate benchmark remains a matter to be discussed.

Optimality of Benchmarks and Compensation Schemes

Under passive management, investors decide what their relevant benchmarks are and impose them on managers. As the compensation of the latter is essentially based on the market value of assets under management, these funds chase after customers to increase volume. Under active management, the problem is different as compensation schemes are more complex, the degree of freedom granted to managers is higher, and agency costs associated with their monitoring by investors are larger. Also, the practice of benchmarking has an impact on the managers' behavior towards risk and expected return as well as on equilibrium asset prices.

So far, nothing has been said about the relationship between the fund managers and their investors, incentives given to parties, link between performance and benchmarking, and possible impact of current practices on market equilibrium. Yet, these issues lie at the heart of the delegated management industry. In particular, the section investigates (1) whether benchmarks are legitimate from the investors' viewpoint; (2) the relationship between managers' actual portfolios and their compensation schemes when the latter are linked to a benchmark; and (3) the practical problems met in the practice of benchmarking.

PRINCIPAL-AGENT CONTRACTS INVOLVING A BENCHMARK

At the theoretical level, the relationship between an investor and his manager is best viewed as a principal-agent problem. The principal (investor) delegates to his agent (manager) the portfolio decisions against fees. The delegation may be motivated by lack of time and/or expertise on the part of the investor, differences in transaction costs, asymmetric information on market conditions and availability of assets, or differential skills in processing available information. These motivations cause a moral hazard problem, as the manager may exert too little effort and sacrifice her client's interests to her own. Adopting optimal compensation schemes mitigates the potential misalignment of the manager's and the customer's interests. One objective is to assess under what conditions a given scheme encountered in practice is optimal or how to design optimal contracts. A closely related problem, in the frequent case where the compensation scheme depends on a benchmark, is the optimality of the latter. Finding the optimal contract that solves the agency problem under benchmarking endogenously yields both the parameters of the compensation scheme and the optimal benchmark.

Before discussing these issues, since most contracts used in practice are linear or piecewise linear, the corresponding compensation schemes in Equation 21.8 are defined (slightly more complicated structures exist but are not essential to the purpose here)

$$F(T) = \phi + aV^P(T) + b[V^P(T) - V^B(T)] + c\, Max[V^P(T) - V^B(T); 0]\,(21.8)$$

where T is the investment horizon; F denotes the total fees paid to the manager; V^P and V^B are the terminal values of the managed portfolio and its benchmark, respectively; ϕ (a flat fee); and a, b, and c are positive constants. In the absence of benchmarking, b and c are set to zero. When b is positive and c is equal to zero, the contract is said to be *symmetric* (this type of fee is also known as *fulcrum* performance fees) and *asymmetric* if b is zero and c is positive. A symmetric scheme implies that the manager receives a bonus if the portfolio return exceeds that of the benchmark but is penalized if the opposite occurs. Asymmetric compensations generate bonuses only when the portfolio outperforms the benchmark.

Within the strand of research devoted to benchmark-adjusted compensation schemes, most of the attention focused on symmetric contracts. This choice was essentially motivated by the regulation in force in the United States (Amendment to the Investment Advisors Act of 1940 passed by the Congress in 1970), as well as in many European countries, which prohibits mutual funds, pension funds, and other publicly registered investment firms from using the asymmetric (bonus only) compensation scheme. Moreover, these institutions still represent the bulk of the delegated portfolio management industry despite the recent success of hedge funds and other alternative management funds.

Following the early lead by Ross (1973) on the principal-agent issue, Holmström and Milgrom (1987), whose work was generalized by Schättler and Sung (1993) and Sung (1995), prove in continuous time that if the principal's and agent's utility functions exhibit constant absolute risk aversion (CARA) and the principal cannot observe the agent's actions, linear contracts are optimal. CARA utility (U) is given by $U(W) = -\exp(-\rho W)$, where W is wealth and the absolute risk aversion coefficient (equal to $-U''/U'$, with the prime ' and double prime " denoting first and second derivatives, respectively) is the positive constant ρ. This restrictive assumption leads to tractable results when made in conjunction with the Gaussian distribution for wealth. It is not, however, realistic as the individual exhibits the same absolute risk aversion whether his decisions make him much richer or poorer.

Slightly more generally, Ou-Yang (2003) proves that the symmetric compensation scheme is efficient in a framework where all processes follow geometric Brownian motions, the investor does not observe the value of the managed portfolio continuously, and the manager has CARA utility. In a much more general stochastic environment, in which the agent controls both the expectation and the volatility of her portfolio returns but assuming perfect information, Cadenillas, Cvitanić, and Zapatero (2007) prove that if the manager and the investor have the same constant relative risk aversion (CRRA) coefficients or possibly different CARA parameters, the optimal contract is (ex post) linear. CRRA utility is given by $U(W) = W^{(1-\gamma)}/(1-\gamma)$, where the relative risk aversion coefficient $((-U''/U')W)$ is the positive constant γ $(\neq 1)$.

Although CRRA and especially CARA utilities are rather restrictive assumptions, those results were encouraging for the profession routinely using linear contracts. However, the benchmark must be found endogenously. A major difficulty then is to interpret the latter as a viable portfolio (e.g., is its value always non-negative?) and to implement the strategy. If, alternatively, the market portfolio is chosen as the benchmark, it is not in general optimal as discussed in the subsection titled "Exogenous, Optimal, and Suboptimal Benchmarks."

Some authors, however, question the optimality of linear contracts. For example, Admati and Pfleiderer (1997) show in a static framework that using a risky benchmark portfolio of the type commonly adopted in practice, such as an index fund, cannot be, in general, rationalized when a linear and symmetric contract binds the investor and the manager. Driving this result is the assumption that, unlike what had been supposed in the section titled "Active Portfolio Management," the manager possesses some private information to which the investor has no access. This information asymmetry, in general, destroys Roll's (1992) separation result and leads to a managed portfolio that is suboptimal for the investor. The latter's expected welfare loss may be substantial. According to Admati and Pfleiderer, this loss can be up to a few hundred basis points depending on the quality of the manager's private information or skill. Thus, commonly used, benchmark-adjusted compensation schemes will (1) be inconsistent with the investor's objective of maximizing expected utility, (2) tend to increase the manager's incentives to shirk, and (3) be of little use in screening out informed (skillful) from uninformed (bad) managers.

Moreover, Li and Zhou (2006) subsequently show that, in general, an optimal contract is an increasing, nonlinear function of final wealth, the shape of which depends on the principal's and the agent's risk aversions, state price density function, and agent's reservation utility level. As noted in the introduction, this criticism has recently elicited a renewed interest for optimal benchmark design.

In a type of "reverse engineering" approach, one may also assume the (linear) contract structure as given and derive the optimal (for the principal) parameters (ϕ, a, b, and c in Equation 21.8) of the contract. For instance, Golec (1992) provides an explicit solution for the latter parameters when performing the optimization in a purely static framework. In Kapur and Timmermann (2005), the agent has superior information and the investor chooses the parameters of the optimal contract subject to the condition that they lie in a range acceptable by the manager (participation constraint). Here again, a major difficulty can arise as to the sign and order of magnitude of the parameters as compared to what is encountered in practice.

IMPLICIT INCENTIVES AND CONSTRAINTS

Another interesting aspect of delegated portfolio management using benchmarks is that, quite often, the actual style of an actively managed fund specifying a self-designated benchmark does not match its prospectus. For instance, Sensoy (2009) reports that about one-third of US equity mutual funds specifying a size and value/growth (S&P or Russell) index fail to track their benchmark and actually follow similar but different ("mismatched") benchmarks.

A plausible explanation of this behavior is grounded in the regulatory environment with two premises. First, the Securities and Exchange Commission (SEC) requires that each fund's prospectus exhibits the fund's historical record together with that of a passive benchmark index but leaves the choice of the latter to the fund's manager. Second, principals (investors) may not be sophisticated enough or have sufficient resources to really distinguish relevant benchmarks from less relevant ones.

Additionally, principals do not seem to react symmetrically to outperformance and shortfall, as new inflows to the fund in the former case tend to be larger than outflows from the fund in the latter. Conversely, managers are given incentives to attract as many inflows as possible, as compensation fees depend positively on the fund value (parameter a in Equation 21.8). Because performance is presumably a key criterion to investors and performance is relative to a benchmark, the manager faces the temptation of designating a benchmark that does not fully capture her exposures to common factors in returns and thereby cannot help to accurately measure her skills or lack thereof. Consequently, using "mismatched" benchmarks is justified from the viewpoint of strategic managers. Empirically, overperformance relative to a self-designated benchmark, even after controlling for performance measures that better reflect the fund's style, seems to significantly determine subsequent cash inflows. This result seems rather robust to changes in methodology and data sets (Chevalier and Ellison, 1997; Musto, 1999; Elton, Gruber, and Blake, 2003; Sensoy, 2009).

Models such as Lynch and Musto (2003) and Berk and Green (2004) are available in which an increasing and, especially, convex relationship between fund flows and relative performance arises endogenously. This convexity has interesting practical implications. For example, as Basak, Pavlova, and Shapiro (2007) and Hugonnier and Kaniel (2010) contend, this convexity creates a strong implicit incentive for the manager to distort her asset allocation so as to maximize the chances that the portfolio value ends up above that of the benchmark. If downside risk materializes, the incurred penalty (in terms of cash outflows) is not too severe due to convexity.

Such risk shifting is ultimately intended to increase the probability of attracting new future inflows into the fund. In general, deviating from the benchmark will increase the managed portfolio risk (as measured by volatility), which makes perfect sense by acknowledging the (partial) optionlike feature of the performance-flows relationship (Carpenter, 2000). Interestingly, however, if the manager's risk aversion is high, she may actually leave unchanged or even decrease the risk of the portfolio upon observing that it currently underperforms its benchmark. This reaction occurs because, should this course continue, it may lead ultimately to hurting future outflows. This is why the manager does not really hold a call.

Under rather restrictive assumptions, namely, CRRA utility and asset prices governed by geometric Brownian motions, offsetting the aforementioned implicit incentive is possible. As Basak, Pavlova, and Shapiro (2008) show, a simple contract provision can help realign the interests of the principal and his agent. It suffices to impose a minimum performance constraint on the manager that prohibits the portfolio return over a given horizon to fall short beyond a predetermined level to that of the benchmark. The financial penalty upon failure should be severe. As a consequence, beyond a certain shortfall, the incentive to deviate from the benchmark to benefit from the convexity in the performance-flow relationship disappears. Note that such a provision is related to other common practices in portfolio management such as the TE limits previously discussed, portfolio insurance, value at risk (VaR), and conditional VaR (or Expected Shortfall). Also note that all these provisions or techniques do not exonerate the manager to design a benchmark that fits the principal's attitude toward risk. As discussed previously, not all benchmarks create value for investors because some of them do not initially exhibit the appropriate risk-return tradeoff.

More generally, the asset management industry is directed by both competition and regulation (or moral suasion) toward using more stringent investment mandates, such as narrower TE bounds, limits on investing in specific securities, and other investment constraints. These practices could be perceived at first sight as inefficient from the investors' viewpoint as they limit the managers' ability to benefit from efficient investment opportunities outside their mandates.

These mandates can, however, be rationalized along the lines suggested by He and Xiong (2011). First, imposing less investment flexibility on a manager strengthens the relationship between the fund relative performance and the manager's (not directly observable) effort in her primary market (that of the benchmark), which decreases the agency cost associated with shirking. This situation occurs because the manager's outperformance could be either due to genuine effort in her own market or to sheer luck in other markets should she be granted a broad or vague mandate.

Second, a narrow mandate limits the manager's ability to gamble on outside (of the benchmark realm) assets with negative skewness, i.e., exhibiting small positive returns most often and a huge negative return infrequently. To the extent that the compensation scheme is asymmetric, the manager is incentivized to take on huge risks in markets outside her own and be rewarded most of the time while the principals are left suffering from the occasional big loss. For example, the recent financial crisis has exposed this kind of behavior on the part of some rogue traders. Stringent mandates help reduce the agency cost associated with this unwarranted risk and should be adopted except when the manager possesses proven unusual skills.

The delegated portfolio management industry exhibits a complex incentive structure, especially when benchmarking is at play, which tends to be now the norm. Explicit incentives are given managers through a compensation scheme such as given by Equation 21.8. Implicit incentives are no less important such as reputation, career concerns, and the ability to attract future flows.

EXOGENOUS, OPTIMAL, AND SUBOPTIMAL BENCHMARKS

In most of the extant literature, the benchmark the manager tracks is given exogenously (typically the market portfolio), which faces the criticism raised by Admati and Pfleiderer (1997), at least when the compensation contract is linear or affine. Alternatively, one could derive the benchmark that is optimal from the investor's viewpoint. For instance, Lioui and Poncet (2010) examine the issue under general Von Neuman-Morgenstern utility functions and diffusion processes for asset returns and the riskless rate. The investor derives the appropriate benchmark (knowing his manager's skills and the fee parameters) so as to maximize the expected utility of his final wealth. The manager (knowing which optimal benchmark will be imposed on her) controls both the drift and the volatility of the managed portfolio so as to maximize her own utility.

Lioui and Poncet (2010) report three specific findings. First, the optimal delegated portfolio almost always differs in a complex way from the optimal benchmark chosen by the investor, which reinforces the view that commonly observed benchmarks are suboptimal. Second, under a symmetric compensation scheme, the managed portfolio can be split in two components: a speculative part that depends on the manager's preferences but not on those of investors and a hedging part that is independent of the manager's utility function hedging against the adverse fluctuations in the value of the imposed benchmark. Third, differences between commonly adopted benchmarks and optimal ones can be substantial, which implies that tangible welfare losses for investors.

A related approach is not to derive an optimal benchmark directly but to maximize expected utility (not expected return) while using a given benchmark and allowing for a predetermined TE. For instance, Basak, Shapiro, and Teplá (2006) impose a prespecified maximum shortfall from the benchmark return (with a given confidence) and show how the manager chooses to optimally over- or underperform the reference return according to her risk aversion, the benchmark sensitivity to changes in the state of the economy, and the actual economic condition (bad or good) that prevails. Then investors are left to choose the optimal combination of the benchmark and the managed portfolio.

Essentially the same idea underlines two recent papers. Zhao (2007) chooses the linear combination of the market portfolio (adopted as the benchmark) and the growth optimum portfolio (the one that maximizes the expected utility of a logarithmic investor: $U(W) = Log(W)$) (Merton, 1971; Long, 1990) that maximizes the risk-adjusted excess return over the benchmark. Risk is measured by the TE in the spirit of Roll (1992). Baptista (2008) takes into account that the investor has other components of wealth (e.g., real estate and human capital) that are difficult or impossible to insure in the financial markets. These additional sources of risk, which are dubbed *background risk*, affect the composition of an investor's optimal portfolio of financial assets in a way not predicted by standard portfolio theory. Because of this, conditions exist under which investors can optimally delegate their portfolio decisions to managers even though, in the absence of such background risk, the objective function in Equation 21.4 adopted by managers would be suboptimal.

The idea of combining an inefficient benchmark B with an inefficient portfolio P so as to maximize the Sharpe ratio or the IR is quite general. One can view the inefficiency of commonly used benchmarks as making legitimate in theory and credible in practice all active portfolio management methods that aim at beating the said benchmarks. To achieve this goal, one has to find the conditions under which portfolio delegation can be optimal when using a criterion based on a TE relative to a predetermined benchmark. How to achieve this goal in practice heavily depends on the assumptions that underlie the manager's and investor's utility functions (and possibly mental attitudes as in behavioral finance), asset return generating processes, and background risk. Alexander and Baptista (2010, 2011), for example, provide some insightful methods.

BENCHMARKING AND EQUILIBRIUM ASSET PRICES

To the extent that the practice of benchmark-linked portfolio management tends to generalize, a legitimate question arises as to its impact on equilibrium asset prices. The influences of passive and active management are discussed separately despite sharing some features. Xiong and Sullivan (2011) contend that the development of trading associated with passive investing implies increased trading commonality among the constituents of frequently adopted benchmarks, as observed in the United States since 1997. Such trade commonality induces increased systematic fluctuations in overall demand and in systematic risk. Consequently, even well-diversified portfolios exhibit a greater risk for all styles of stock portfolios, which, other things being equal, is detrimental to investors' welfare. The decrease of diversification benefits also implies lower Sharpe ratios.

The literature is scant as to the general equilibrium analysis of active management based on benchmarks. As a notable exception, Cuoco and Kaniel (2011) study the impact of the managers' portfolio decisions on asset allocation by fund investors and direct investors and on asset prices. They provide a general equilibrium dynamic model where multiple risky asset classes are available for trade, and the extent of portfolio delegation by investors and the parameters of the compensation scheme (the general structure of which is given by Equation 21.8) are both endogenous. The markets for fund investors and portfolio managers are assumed to be competitive.

Equilibrium prices are variously affected according to which precise compensation scheme such investors and managers actually adopt. Under fulcrum performance fees, the prices of the assets included in the benchmarks unambiguously increase, and consequently, the Sharpe ratios decline. These results occur because the managers are incentivized to tilt their portfolios towards these securities. This empirical evidence and changes in the composition of all major equity indices, such as the S&P 500 or the FTSE 100, vindicate this theoretical construct. Under asymmetric schemes, however, the effects on prices and Sharpe ratios are more complex and ambiguous as the composition of the managers' portfolios depends crucially on their excess performance relative to their benchmarks (see the section "Moral Hazard, Implicit Incentives, and Constraints") and thus varies randomly. Overall, the reported changes in delegated asset management bring about new challenges to risk management in portfolio allocation.

Performance Evaluation and Assessment

Performance measurement aims at evaluating the quality of past asset allocation decisions in risk-return tradeoff terms, assessing whether it is significant and persistent enough so that a forecast is sensible, and comparing competing funds (Sharpe, 1992).

ALPHAS AND BETAS

Benchmarking constitutes a convenient way to evaluate the ex-post performance of a delegated portfolio. To this end, one commonly runs the regression analysis associated with Equation 21.9

$$R_{P,t} = \alpha + \beta R_{B,t} + \varepsilon_t \tag{21.9}$$

where the R_t are returns or (sometimes) returns in excess of the riskless rate; α denotes the under- or overperformance (it is Jensen's alpha if B is the market portfolio and the R_t are excess returns); β the portfolio sensitivity to its benchmark; and ε is a random variable independent of R_B and of zero mean. As explained previously, beta (β) should be one for passive investment but could be different from one under active management.

In the former case ($\beta = 1$), the manager makes no attempt at timing the market and concentrates on security selection to obtain a positive alpha. Equation 21.9 then simplifies to Equation 21.10:

$$R_{P,t} - R_{B,t} \equiv \Delta_t = a + \varepsilon_t. \tag{21.10}$$

The ex-ante IR to be maximized is shown in Equation 21.11:

$$IR = \frac{E(\Delta)}{\sigma(\Delta)} = \frac{\alpha}{\sigma(\varepsilon)}. \tag{21.11}$$

Regressing R_P on R_B yields the estimators $\hat{\alpha}$ and $\hat{\sigma}(\Delta) = \hat{\sigma}(\varepsilon)$ from which the empirical, ex-post IR in Equation 21.12 is computed as:

$$\hat{IR} = \frac{\hat{E}(\Delta)}{\hat{\sigma}(\Delta)} = \frac{\hat{\alpha}}{\hat{\sigma}(\varepsilon)}. \tag{21.12}$$

$\hat{IR} = \dfrac{\hat{\alpha}}{\hat{\sigma}(\varepsilon)}$ is also equal to $\dfrac{t(\alpha, T-1)}{\sqrt{T}}$, where T is the number of observations

and $t(\alpha, T-1)$ is a Student-t random variable centered on α with $(T - 1)$ degrees of freedom. This is a test of the null hypothesis $\hat{\alpha} = 0$ (the portfolio performance is that of the benchmark) when assuming Gaussian returns. Therefore, one can assess, within a given confidence interval, whether the manager's performance has been obtained by chance or by skill. For usual levels of confidence (95 percent or more), a long time (many years of observations) is generally needed to reject the null when the manager is in fact good or bad. This result incidentally casts doubt on the usefulness of fund hit parades routinely advertised in professional publications.

When the manager significantly modifies the portfolio composition, thus its beta, over time in an attempt to time the market, the beta can differ from unity and Equation 21.9 applies. The latter can be rewritten so as to recover the differential return Δ_t as shown in Equation 21.13:

$$R_{P,t} - R_{B,t} \equiv \Delta_t = (\beta - 1)R_{B,t} + (\alpha + \varepsilon_t). \tag{21.13}$$

Then the portfolio's excess return and (squared) TE can be decomposed into the part due to market timing and the part due to security selection into Equations 21.14 and 21.15, respectively:

$$E(\Delta_t) = (\beta - 1) E(R_{B,t}) + \alpha \tag{21.14}$$

$$\sigma^2(\Delta_t) = (\beta - 1)^2 \sigma^2(R_{B,t}) + \sigma^2(\varepsilon). \tag{21.15}$$

Consequently, two IRs can be defined: $IR_s = \alpha / \sigma(\varepsilon)$ measures the manager's security selection ability, which is also related to the Student-t distribution as in the preceding; and $IR_g = E(\Delta_t)/\sigma(\Delta_t)$ measures her global performance.

The manager's market timing ability can be appreciated from the regression analysis emerging from Equation 21.16:

$$R_{P,t} - R_{B,t} = \alpha + \beta_1 \max(0, R_{B,t}) + \beta_2 \max(0, -R_{B,t}) + \varepsilon_t \quad (21.16)$$

Treynor and Mazuy (1966) and Henriksson and Merton (1981) provide alternative but similar regressions. The ability to forecast upward movements in the benchmark translates in a positive β_1, and the capacity to anticipate downward changes in a positive β_2. In case of a genuine market timing ability, the relationship between the portfolio returns and the benchmark returns is convex, an obviously desirable property for investors. In case of failure, however, the relationship is concave.

PERFORMANCE ATTRIBUTION

In many instances, practitioners adopt an alternative method to decompose the spread Δ_t into the market timing and the security selection elements. This method is known as *performance attribution*, as it strives to attribute the sources of the fund under- or overperformance to specific decisions made by the manager. The notion of performance is here reduced to the return dimension alone, without any risk analysis. In this context, *market timing* is defined as the opportunistic weighting of asset classes within the portfolio, and *security selection* is defined as the ability to discriminate individual securities within each asset class. To disentangle these two components, all assets included in the fund and in the benchmark are regrouped in broad asset classes (e.g., stocks, bonds, money market instruments, exchange rates, and commodities).

Assuming n asset classes denoted by i ($i = 1, \ldots, n$), the following notation is used: x_i (respectively, w_i) is the weight of class i in the portfolio (respectively, the benchmark); R_{Pi} (respectively, R_{Bi}) is the class i average return in the portfolio (respectively, in the benchmark); and R_P (respectively, R_B) is the average return of the portfolio (respectively, the benchmark).

By construction, Equations 21.17, 21.18, and 21.19 emerge:

$$\sum_{i=1}^{n} x_i = \sum_{i=1}^{n} w_i = 1 \quad (21.17)$$

$$\sum_{i=1}^{n} x_i R_{Pi} = R_P \quad (21.18)$$

$$\sum_{i=1}^{n} w_i R_{Bi} = R_B. \quad (21.19)$$

Thus, the portfolio relative performance can be decomposed into three elements that measure the respective impact of market timing, security selection, and the interaction between the two.

Market timing measures the manager's ability to overweight (underweight) the more (less) profitable asset classes relatively to the benchmark. It is computed as shown in Equation 21.20:

$$MT = \sum_{i=1}^{n}(x_i - w_i)(R_{Bi} - R_B).$$

(21.20)

Security selection within an asset class measures the manager's capacity to select winners and avoid losers. It is computed as shown in Equation 21.21:

$$SS = \sum_{i=1}^{n} w_i (R_{Pi} - R_{Bi}).$$

(21.21)

The interaction term measures the joint impact on the portfolio return of market timing and security selection and is defined as shown in Equation 21.22:

$$I = \sum_{i=1}^{n}(x_i - w_i)(R_{Pi} - R_{Bi}).$$

(21.22)

Summing up Equations 21.20 to 21.22 and using Equations 21.17 to 21.19 yields Equation 21.23:

$$MT + SS + I = R_p - R_B = \text{over- or underperformance.}$$

(21.23)

Once the benchmark is determined, this method is simple to implement. It can incidentally be generalized to other sources of return, such as the variation in exchange rates for international portfolios. This method should, however, be complemented by a variance decomposition analysis, which is similar albeit slightly more complex. Indeed, market timing and security selection may have led, say, to a superior performance in terms of average return but also to greater risk. The manager's actual ability to add value may then be ambiguous.

Development of the Benchmarking Industry

The benchmarking industry has enjoyed spectacular growth in recent years. During the early stages of benchmarking, the benchmark adopted in practice was a broad index representing the primary market in which the manager operated, such as the S&P 500 for US stock managers. As the manager tends to more or less reproduce her benchmark, the selection of the latter is crucial for the investor. However, a broad stock market index did not always offer the best risk-return tradeoff (Grinold, 1992). Additionally, if the tolerated TE is narrow, the adjustments of the managed portfolio may be too mechanical at times and thus detrimental to principals.

Adopting this kind of benchmark then penalizes investors, while managers are not necessarily hurt. As sophisticated (mostly, institutional) investors become aware of this issue, the fund industry devoted resources and energy to develop and promote alternative indices that could be used as better benchmarks.

The first efforts focused on how individual assets are weighted in stock indices (Arnott, Hsu, and Moore, 2005). Traditionally, these indices are weighted by market capitalizations, which tend to introduce a bias toward large cap stocks. Evidence shows that these indices do not offer the best risk-return tradeoff (Amenc, Goltz, Martellini, and Retkowski, 2010). Indices based on alternative, ad hoc, weighting rules have been proposed, among which is the straightforward equal weights scheme. Weighting rules mitigate or eliminate the bias toward large cap stocks. These alternative frameworks additionally prevent the portfolio allocation from drifting mechanically toward the riskiest assets, which also are the ones that tend to perform better over time. Also, selling the former winners and buying the former losers tends to enhance return on average. Another suggested possibility was to adopt weighting schemes grounded on some firms' fundamentals such as dividend payouts, total book assets, or other accounting variables. The main advantage of such schemes is that they are less sensitive to over- or underpricing than are market weights. At the international level, some suggested building indices where the weight of a country is related to its GDP or another macroeconomic fundamental. The newly offered indices were not biased toward any particular type of stocks.

A second generation of benchmarks provided indices intentionally tilted toward particular stocks or investment styles. The most popular are intended to track value or growth stocks such as the S&P Pure Growth Style Index and Pure Value Style Index. A value stock has a relatively large book-to-market ratio while a growth stock has a relatively small one. As widely documented, value stocks earn, on average, higher expected returns than growth stocks (Fama and French, 1996, 2006). The superior returns are accompanied by increased risk, although the issue of the sources of risk for which the value premium compensates is still hotly debated. Institutional investors are interested in portfolios with a value tilt, and many managers offer such funds. The question of the relevance of the weighting scheme, although less acute, is still open for these types of indices.

The last wave of innovation is more sophisticated and strives at building efficient indices. Efficiency is understood as providing the best risk-return tradeoff within a universe of assets. Such an index, for example, could be the minimum variance portfolio. The idea is inherently sound as, even if the manager simply replicates the index, the investor will still benefit from maximum diversification. The difficult part of the task lies in estimating the inputs, namely the vector of means and the covariance matrix. However, estimation risk may prove fatal to any portfolio strategy.

Summary and Conclusions

Benchmarking is an interesting and useful portfolio management tool. The practice of benchmarking has evolved markedly over time. It is now routinely applied outside the mutual fund and hedge fund industries. For instance, the benchmark for optimal asset allocation of insurers or pension funds could be a function of their liability payments to pension or policyholders (Lim and Wong, 2010).

The actual implementation of portfolio selection with benchmarking involves, however, various issues that are currently being addressed by academia and the investment profession. These issues include but are not limited to the size of the tolerated TE, actual value added by active management, optimal design of principal-agent contracts, appropriate compensation schemes, and construction of optimal benchmarks.

Discussion Questions

1. What is the objective of active portfolio management under benchmarking?
2. Explain the terms *tracking error* and *information ratio*.
3. What is a symmetric incentive fee?
4. Who is the principal, and who is the agent in portfolio delegation?
5. Explain whether benchmarking matters for asset prices.
6. What is an efficient index?

References

Admati, Anat R., and Paul Pfleiderer. 1997. "Does It All Add Up? Benchmarks and the Compensation of Active Portfolio Managers." *Journal of Business* 70:2, 323–350.

Alexander, Gordon J., and Alexandre M. Baptista. 2010. "Active Portfolio Management with Benchmarking: A Frontier Based on Alpha." *Journal of Banking & Finance* 34, 2185–2197.

Alexander, Gordon J., and Alexandre M. Baptista. 2011. "Portfolio Selection with Mental Accounts and Delegation." *Journal of Banking & Finance* 35:10, 2637–2656.

Amenc, Noel, Felix Goltz, Lionel Martellini, and Patrice Retkowski. 2010. "Efficient Indexation: An Alternative to Cap-Weighted Indices." Working Paper, EDHEC Risk Institute.

Arnott, Robert D., Jason C. Hsu, and Philip Moore. 2005. "Fundamental Indexation." *Financial Analysts Journal* 61:2, 83–99.

Avramov, Doron. 2004. "Stock Return Predictability and Asset Pricing Models." *Review of Financial Studies* 17:3, 699–738.

Avramov, Doron, and Tarun Chordia. 2006. "Asset Pricing Models and Financial Market Anomalies." *Review of Financial Studies* 19:4, 1001–1040.

Avramov, Doron, and Russ Wermers. 2006. "Investing in Mutual Funds When Returns Are Predictable." *Journal of Financial Economics* 81:2, 339–377.

Baptista, Alexandre M. 2008. "Optimal Delegated Portfolio Management with Background Risk." *Journal of Banking & Finance* 32:6, 977–985.

Basak, Suleyman, Alexander Shapiro, and Lucie Teplá. 2006. "Risk Management with Benchmarking." *Management Science* 54:4, 542–557.

Basak, Suleyman, Anna Pavlova, and Alexander Shapiro. 2007. "Optimal Asset Allocation and Risk Shifting in Money Management." *Review of Financial Studies* 20:6, 1583–1621.

Basak, Suleyman, Anna Pavlova, and Alexander Shapiro. 2008. "Offsetting the Implicit Incentives: Benefits of Benchmarking in Money Management." *Journal of Banking & Finance* 32:9, 1883–1893.

Berk, Jonathan, and Richard Green. 2004. "Mutual Fund Flows and Performance in Rational Markets." *Journal of Political Economy* 112:6, 1269–1295.

Black, Fischer. 1972. "Equilibrium with Restricted Borrowing." *Journal of Business* 45:3, 444–454.

Busse, Jeffrey A., and Paul J. Irvine. 2006. "Bayesian Alphas and Mutual Fund Persistence." *Journal of Finance* 61:5, 2251–2288.

Cadenillas, Abel, Jakša Cvitanić, and Fernando Zapatero. 2007. "Optimal Risk Sharing with Effort and Project Choice." *Journal of Economic Theory* 133:1, 403–440.

Campbell, John. 1987. "Stock Returns and the Term Structure." *Journal of Financial Economics* 18:2, 373–399.

Campbell, John, and Robert Shiller. 1988a. "The Dividend-Price Ratio and Expectations of Future Dividends and Discount Factors." *Review of Financial Studies* 1:3, 195–228.

Campbell, John, and Robert Shiller. 1988b. "Interpreting Co-Integrated Models." *Journal of Economic Dynamics and Control* 12:2–3, 505–522.

Carpenter, Jennifer. 2000. "Does Option Compensation Increase Managerial Risk Appetite?" *Journal of Finance* 55:5, 2311–2331.

Chevalier, Judith, and Glenn Ellison. 1997. "Risk Taking by Mutual Funds as a Response to Incentives." *Journal of Political Economy* 105:6, 1167–1200.

Cox, John, and Chi-Fu Huang. 1989. "Optimal Consumption and Portfolio Policies When Asset Prices Follow a Diffusion Process." *Journal of Economic Theory* 49:1, 33–83.

Cuoco, Domenico, and Ron Kaniel. 2011. "Equilibrium Prices in the Presence of Delegated Portfolio Management." *Journal of Financial Economics* 101:2, 264–296.

Elton, Edwin J., Martin J. Gruber, and Christopher R. Blake. 2003. "Incentive Fees and Mutual Funds." *Journal of Finance* 58:2, 779–804.

Fama, Eugene F., and Kenneth R. French. 1989. "Business Conditions and Expected Returns on Stocks and Bonds." *Journal of Financial Economics* 25:1, 23–49.

Fama, Eugene F., and Kenneth R. French. 1996. "Multifactor Explanations of Asset Pricing Anomalies." *Journal of Finance* 51:1, 55–84.

Fama, Eugene F., and Kenneth R. French. 2006. "The Value Premium and the CAPM." *Journal of Finance* 61:5, 2137–2162.

Ferson, Wayne E., Andrea Heuson, and Tie Su. 2006. "Weak and Semi-Strong Form Stock Return Predictability Revisited." *Management Science* 51:10, 1582–1592.

Golec, Joseph. 1992. "Empirical Tests of a Principal-Agent Model of the Investor-Investment Advisor Relationship." *Journal of Financial and Quantitative Analysis* 27:1, 81–95.

Grinold, Richard C. 1992. "Are Benchmark Portfolios Efficient?" *Journal of Portfolio Management* 19:1, 34–40.

He, Zhiguo, and Wei Xiong. 2011. "Delegated Asset Management and Investment Mandates." Working Paper, University of Chicago and Princeton University.

Henriksson, Roy D., and Robert C. Merton. 1981. "On Market Timing and Investment Performance of Managed Portfolios (II): Statistical Procedures for Evaluating Forecasting Skills." *Journal of Business* 54:3, 513–533.

Holmström, Bengt, and Paul Milgrom. 1987. "Aggregation and Linearity in the Provision of Intertemporal Incentives." *Econometrica* 55:2, 303–328.

Hugonnier, Julien, and Ron Kaniel. 2010. "Mutual Fund Portfolio Choice in the Presence of Dynamic Flows." *Mathematical Finance* 20:2, 187–227.

Jones, Christopher S., and Jay Shanken. 2005. "Mutual Fund Performance with Learning Across Funds." *Journal of Financial Economics* 78:3, 507–552.

Kapur, Sandeep, and Allan Timmermann. 2005. "Relative Performance Evaluation Contracts and Asset Market Equilibrium." *Economic Journal* 115:506, 1077–1102.

Karatzas, Ioannis, John P. Lehoczky, and Steven E. Shreve. 1987. "Optimal Portfolio and Consumption Decisions for a Small Investor on a Finite Horizon." *SIAM Journal of Control and Optimization* 25:6, 1557–1586.

Li, Tao, and Yuging Zhou. 2006. "Optimal Contracts in Portfolio Delegation." Working Paper, Chinese University of Hong Kong.

Lim, Andrew, and Bernard Wong. 2010. "A Benchmarking Approach to Optimal Asset Allocation for Insurers and Pension Funds." *Insurance: Mathematics and Economics* 46:2, 317–327.

Lioui, Abraham, and Patrice Poncet. 2010. "Optimal Benchmarking for Active Portfolio Managers." Working Paper, EDHEC Business School and ESSEC Business School.

Long, John B. 1990. "The Numeraire Portfolio." *Journal of Financial Economics* 26:1, 29–69.

Lynch, Anthony, and David Musto. 2003. "How Investors Interpret Past Fund Returns." *Journal of Finance* 58:5, 2033–2058.

Markowitz, Harry. 1959. *Portfolio Selection: Efficient Diversification of Investment*. New York: John Wiley & Sons.

Merton, Robert C. 1971. "Optimum Consumption and Portfolio Rules in a Continuous-Time Model." *Journal of Economic Theory* 3:4, 373–413.

Musto, David. 1999. "Investment Decisions Depend on Portfolio Disclosures." *Journal of Finance* 54:3, 935–952.

Ou-Yang, Hui. 2003. "Optimal Contracts in a Continuous-Time Delegated Portfolio Management Problem." *Review of Financial Studies* 16:1, 173–208.

Pástor, Luboš, and Robert Stambaugh. 2002. "Investing in Equity Mutual Funds." *Journal of Financial Economics* 63:3, 351–380.

Roll, Richard. 1992. "A Mean/Variance Analysis of Tracking Error." *Journal of Portfolio Management* 18:4, 13–22.

Ross, Stephen. 1973. "The Economic Theory of Agency: The Principal's Problem." *American Economic Review* 63:1, 134–139.

Schättler, Heinz, and Jaeyoung Sung. 1993. "The First-Order Approach to the Continuous-Time Principal-Agent Problem with Exponential Utility." *Journal of Economic Theory* 61:4, 331–371.

Sensoy, Berk. 2009. Performance Evaluation and Self-Designated Benchmark Indexes in the Mutual Fund Industry." *Journal of Financial Economics* 92:1, 25–39.

Sharpe, William F. 1964. "Capital Asset Pricing: A Theory of Market Equilibrium under Conditions of Risk." *Journal of Finance* 19:2, 425–442.

Sharpe, William F. 1992. "Asset Allocation: Management Style and Performance Measurement." *Journal of Portfolio Management* 18:1, 7–19.

Sung, Jaeyoung. 1995. "Linearity with Project Selection and Controllable Diffusion Rate in Continuous-Time Principal-Agent Problems." *RAND Journal of Economics* 26:4, 720–743.

Tobin, James. 1958. "Liquidity Preference as Behavior Towards Risk." *Review of Economic Studies* 25:1, 65–86.

Treynor, Jack L., and Kay Mazuy. 1966. "Can Mutual Funds Outguess the Market?" *Harvard Business Review* 44:2, 131–136.

Xiong, James X., and Rodney N. Sullivan. 2011. "How Passive Investing Increases Market Vulnerability." Working Paper, Morningstar Investment Management and the CFA Institute.

Zhao, Yonggan. 2007. "A Dynamic Model of Active Portfolio Management with Benchmark Orientation." *Journal of Banking & Finance* 31:11, 3336–3356.

22

Attribution Analysis

NANNE BRUNIA
Lecturer in Finance, University of Groningen

AUKE PLANTINGA
Associate Professor in Finance, University of Groningen

Introduction

Attribution analysis aims to identify the skills of asset managers in managing investment portfolios. Traditionally, the analysis focuses on the distinction between timing and selection skills. *Timing* refers to the ability of someone, such as an asset manager, to forecast the future return of markets or groups of securities. By contrast, *selection* refers to someone's ability to forecast the future return of individual securities. Timing and selection skills are based on different information sets. Timing skills rely more on macroeconomic analysis and the behavior of investors and firms at the aggregate level, whereas selection skills require in-depth knowledge of individual stocks. Both the investor and the asset manager benefit from knowing which type of forecasting skill is likely to generate higher future returns.

Many studies focus on the performance of mutual funds in addressing this issue. Historically, the general conclusion seems to be that the managers of mutual funds have little timing or selection skills. Yet, several studies report that some managers may have selection skills (Daniel, Grinblatt, Titman, and Wermers, 1997). Individual managers have little ability to profit from timing skills because the information used in the analysis is widely available and should be priced in an efficient market. Conversely, selection skills profit from information that is security specific and may not be widely available to all individual investors or may even be exclusively available to the asset manager only in the form of private information.

In calculating and analyzing the performance of portfolios, the focus is on so-called *buy-and-hold returns*. In summarizing returns over multiple periods, buy-and-hold returns implicitly assume no subsequent allocations and/or withdrawals after the initial investment decisions. However, investors usually tend to add or subtract money from an investment portfolio, which can have a major impact on the performance of their portfolios. Analysts use money weighted returns to capture the impact of investor decisions on investment performance.

Money weighted return measures summarize returns over multiple periods by weighting with the amount of money invested in the portfolio at the beginning of each period. Dichev (2007) and Friesen and Sapp (2007) find that investor decisions usually have a negative impact on their performance and result in a lower performance relative to the buy-and-hold returns.

This chapter discusses some of the best known methods of attributing managerial performance to different decisions. The remainder of the chapter has the following five sections. The first section deals with the basic holdings-based attribution models used in practice. The second section examines regression-based attribution models proposed in the academic literature. In the third section, advances in holdings-based attribution models are discussed. The fourth section discusses money weighted returns as a means to extend performance attribution in order to capture investor's decisions. The final section offers a summary and conclusions.

The Basic Holdings-Based Performance Attribution Models

Performance attribution models can be classified according to their data needs. Return-based models exclusively rely on a portfolios time-series of returns and one or more benchmark portfolio, whereas holdings-based models require knowledge of the composition of the portfolio. These methods focus on a portfolio manager's skills and analyze buy-and-hold returns, which exclude any intermediate cash flows to the portfolio.

Brinson, Hood, and Beebower (1986) propose a basic holdings-based model, which is widely applied in practice. Their model calculates the timing and selection components by comparing the performance of a hypothetical timing and selection portfolio with that of a benchmark portfolio. The model is based on a top-down approach in the investment management process, starting from a general investment plan that describes planned portfolio weights for asset classes and assigns benchmarks to asset classes. Although top management authorizes this general investment plan, the plan provides room for the lower levels of the organization to deviate from it in order to capture changing conditions or expectations in financial markets. Many professional investors have monthly or weekly meetings with portfolio managers and researchers to determine tactical strategy in regard to any deviation from the planned asset allocation. This decision-making process is called the *tactical asset allocation decision*. Portfolio managers responsible for a particular asset class can also deviate from their benchmarks, as a result from stock selection decisions.

The analysis is based on the construction of four different portfolios. Portfolio I is the overall benchmark portfolio, which is derived directly from the general investment plan. This portfolio defines the desired asset allocation, which is also known as the *strategic asset allocation*. Additionally, benchmark returns have to be specified for each individual asset class. For example, the benchmark could be the return on the S&P 500 for a US equity portfolio and the return on the MSCI

Europe index for European stocks. Portfolios II and III are the outcomes of a "what if" analysis that tries to measure the impact of decisions in isolation from other decisions. Portfolio IV is the actual portfolio.

The return on portfolio I is the result of investing the portfolio according to the strategic asset allocation and the benchmarks for the asset classes. The return of this portfolio is defined as

$$R(I) = \sum_{i=1}^{n} w_i^s R_i^b,\qquad\qquad(22.1)$$

where w_i^s is the strategic weight of asset class i and R_i^b is the return of the benchmark for asset class i. Portfolio II measures the return of implementing the stock selection decision, while ignoring the tactical asset allocation decision. If the actual return of an investor in asset class i is R_i^a, then the return on portfolio II is:

$$R(II) = \sum_{i=1}^{n} w_i^s R_i^a.\qquad\qquad(22.2)$$

Portfolio III measures the return of implementing the tactical asset allocation decision without the stock selection decision. The asset class weights for this portfolio are equal to the actual weights, w_i^a, and the composition at the level of individual securities for each asset class i is exactly equal to that of the benchmark for asset class i. The return on this portfolio is:

$$R(III) = \sum_{i=1}^{n} w_i^a R_i^b.\qquad\qquad(22.3)$$

Portfolio IV is the actual portfolio and is the subject of the analysis. The return on the actual portfolio is:

$$R(IV) = \sum_{i=1}^{n} w_i^a \times R_i^a.\qquad\qquad(22.4)$$

The difference between the return of portfolio III and the return of portfolio I is the so-called *timing effect*. This difference represents the additional return due to the tactical asset allocation. The actual portfolio weights deviate from those in the strategic plan. The impact of a timing decision will only be measured properly if the decision is implemented at the start of the measurement period when the actual portfolio weights are collected. For example, assume that a portfolio manager has a benchmark weight of 40 percent for US domestic equity. If the manager anticipates a strong month for the US equity markets, he may choose to allocate 50 percent to this asset class. If the realized return of the actual US domestic equity portfolio is 40 percent, then the contribution to the timing effect will be $(0.50 - 0.40)0.4 = 4$ percent. Assuming that the manager has not made any selection decisions, the selection effect will be 0. However, if the manager implements his tactical asset allocation decision one day later, the timing effect will be 0 because the actual allocation to US domestic equity is 40 percent. If the return on the first day is 0, then the actual return for US domestic equity becomes $[(0.5)(0.4)]/0.4 = 50$ percent. The extra return now shows up in the selection effect, which will be $0.4(0.50 - 0.40) = 4$ percent.

The return difference between portfolio II and portfolio I is the so-called *selection effect* and shows the additional return due to the selection of individual securities within each asset class. The implicit assumption in calculating the selection effect is that the systematic risk of the actual returns in each of the individual asset classes is the same as its benchmark. As a result, a manager operating with a beta greater than 1.0 may show on average returns greater than the benchmark. Such returns are due to the higher systematic risk rather than stock selection ability. Another potential problem with this assumption is that a manager may attempt to time the market not by changing the dollar allocation to the market but by changing his portfolio beta instead. In this case, the impact of the manager's timing ability will be revealed as part of the selection effect.

Because the timing effect and selection effect are calculated independently, a joint impact also exists for both decisions, which is called the *interaction effect*. This effect is calculated as the sum of the return of portfolios I and IV minus the sum of the return of portfolios II and III. Because the interaction effect cannot be attributed to a single person or department, some practitioners allocate this effect in equal parts to both the timing and selection effect. Table 22.1 summarizes the definition of the different effects and their calculation.

The main reason for the popularity of Brinson model is that it requires only one observation to calculate an outcome for both the timing and the selection component. Of course, a proper statistical inference would require multiple observations. In practice, however, statistical significance is often regarded as less important relative to the need of informing investors on the up-to-date performance of a portfolio. Also, previous observations may simply not exist in the case of new portfolios.

A disadvantage of the decomposition of Brinson et al. (1986) is that any deviation from the implicit assumptions in the model is classified within the selection effect. Both academics and practitioners have attempted to improve the precision of the selection effect. For example, Ankrim (1992) shows how the basic model can be improved in order to separate the impact of changing betas from the selection effect. A related problem also exists in the management of bond portfolios, where managing the portfolio's duration is another timing activity that is not captured well in the basic model. Fong, Pearson, and Vasicek (1983) propose an attribution model that captures the specific characteristics of bond portfolios and decomposes the return on a portfolio into duration effects, sector effects, and individual bond picking.

Singer and Karnosky (1995) propose a useful extension of the Brinson et al. (1986) model in order to deal with foreign currency exposures in the context of an internationally diversified portfolio. A distinct feature of the model is that

Table 22.1 **Components of the Brinson Model**

Effect	Definition	Calculation
Timing	R(III) − R(I)	$\sum_i \left(w_i^a - w_i^s\right) \times R_i^b$
Selection	R(II) − R(I)	$\sum_i \left(R_i^a - R_i^b\right) \times w_i^s$
Interaction	R(I) − R(II) − R(III) + R(IV)	$\sum_i w_i^s \times R_i^b - \sum_i w_i^s \times R_i^a$ $-\sum_i w_i^a \times R_i^b + \sum_i w_i^a \times R_i^a$
Total	R(IV) − R(I)	$\sum_i w_i^a \times R_i^a - \sum_i w_i^p \times R_i^p$

Note: This table presents the components of the attribution model of Brinson et al. (1986), in terms of the returns of the four portfolios, and the weights and returns of the underlying asset classes. w_i^a is the actual portfolio weight, and w_i^s is the portfolio weight from the strategic plan for asset class i; R_i^a is the actual return and R_i^b the return on the benchmark for asset class i.

local returns are analyzed in terms of risk premia. Singer and Karnosky argue that international interest parity conditions imply that currency returns depend on the interest rate differences among countries. In particular, the pricing of currency forward contracts is determined largely by interest rate differences. For this reason, the authors consider the effects of interest rate differences jointly with currency returns.

The return of a nonhedged internationally diversified portfolio in terms of the base currency equals

$$R_{bc} = \sum_{i=1}^{n} w_i \left(R_{l,i} + \varepsilon_{bc,i}\right), \tag{22.5}$$

where w_i is the weight of country i as a fraction of the total portfolio value measured in terms of base currency; $R_{l,i}$ is the local currency return of an investment in country i; and $\varepsilon_{bc,i}$ the relative value change of the local currency i against the base currency. The base currency can be interpreted as the currency used for reporting purposes. Using currency forward contracts to hedge the currency risk completely results in the following return in terms of base currency

$$HR_{bc} = \sum_{i=1}^{n} w_i \left(R_{l,i} + f_{bc,i}\right). \tag{22.6}$$

where f_i is the base currency return of the currency forward contract. In hindsight, hedging provides the highest return if the realized currency return is lower than the return on the forward contract:

$$f_i > \varepsilon_i. \tag{22.7}$$

According to international interest rate parity, the return of the forward contract is approximately equal to the difference in interest rates between the foreign country and the base currency

$$c = c_i + f_i \tag{22.8}$$

where c is the interest rate for the base currency and c_i the interest rate for the foreign currency i. The return of a nonhedged foreign investment in terms of the base currency can be written as

$$R_{bc} = \sum_{i=1}^{n} w_i \left(R_{l,i} + \varepsilon_{bc,i} \right), \tag{22.9}$$

and using the interest rate parity condition, the return of a hedged foreign investment in terms of the base currency as

$$R_i^H = \left(R_i - c_i \right) + \left(c_i + f_i \right) = \left(R_i - c_i \right) + c. \tag{22.10}$$

The return of any foreign investment in terms of the base currency can be written as a combination of the local risk premium, $\left(R_i - c_i \right)$ and the relative change of an investment in terms of currency effects $c_i + e_i$ and $c_i + f_i$. The second component is determined by the foreign interest rate and, if the foreign currency position is unhedged, the relative change in the value of the foreign currency. If the foreign currency position is fully hedged, the interest rate of the base currency replaces the foreign interest rate and the return of the currency forward contract.

This return decomposition is essential in the attribution model of Singer and Karnosky (1995). Each component can be analyzed in terms of timing and selection attributes resulting in the market attribution and the currency attribution of the investment. Following the method of Brinson et al. (1986), each attribution requires four portfolios to determine the timing and selection effects on the performance of the portfolio. With partial hedging, $100 \times h_i$ percent of each foreign investment is hedged using forward contracts, the return of the portfolio can be written as:

$$R = \sum_{i=1}^{n} w_i \times (R - c_i) + \sum_{i=1}^{n} w_i \times \{(c_i + e_i) + h_i \times (f_i - e_i)\}. \tag{22.11}$$

The portfolio return is a combination of the local risk premiums, the first summation in Equation 22.11, and the currency effects, the second summation in Equation 22.11. This specification also allows the evaluator to assess how actual hedging policies as compared to the hedging policies in the strategic plan have contributed to the performance of the portfolio.

Several other modifications of the Brinson model have been proposed. For example, Hsu, Kalesnik, and Myers (2010) propose an extension of the model in order to measure the performance of a dynamic asset allocation strategy in addition to the static exposure to the strategic asset allocation, which is implicit in the Brinson model. Menchero (2004) discusses how to create consistent linking of multiperiod outcomes of performance attribution models.

Regression-Based Peformance Attribution

Models analyzing time series of returns are usually easier to use because they requires little additional information. Analysts often use asset-pricing regressions such as Fama and French (1993) and Carhart (1999) to estimate the risk-adjusted performance of mutual funds. In these regressions, the coefficients for the independent variables represent the exposures to the fundamental risk factors. Based on this information, the performance of a portfolio can be decomposed into the risk-adjusted return and the return from exposure to the risk factors. A more practitioner-oriented approach of this idea uses market indices and is known as *return-based style analysis* (Sharpe, 1992). The exposure to markets and/or fundamental risk factors allows the evaluator to assess the nature of the investment portfolio and whether the portfolio satisfies its objectives in terms of its stated investment universe. For example, such an analysis enables assessing whether an internationally operating fund manager is investing in more than one country.

In order to identify timing and selection skills, Treynor and Mazuy (1968) and Henriksson and Merton (1981) propose a regression-based attribution model involving nonlinear terms identifying the timing ability. Treynor and Mazuy introduce a quadratic term to the equation for calculating Jensen's alpha to identify timing skills. The theory is that when a portfolio manager has timing ability, he can change his portfolio's beta. For example, if the manager forecasts a negative market return, then he will reduce beta but will increase beta with a positive market outlook. Eventually, this could lead to positive returns if the manager constructs a negative beta portfolio in a market downturn. Based on this assumption, Treynor and Mazuy propose to measure selection and timing abilities by fitting the following curve on the time series of the returns of the portfolio and the returns of the market index

$$R_a - R_f = TM_0 + TM_1\left(R_m - R_f\right) + TM_2\left(R_m - R_f\right)^2 + \varepsilon, \qquad (22.12)$$

where R_a denotes the actual return on the portfolio; R_f is the risk-free rate; R_m is the return on the market portfolio; and ε is the error term; TM_0 is a measure of the portfolio manager's selection ability; TM_1 is the average exposure to the market index; and TM_2 is a measure of the manager's timing ability. The manager exhibits selection abilities if $TM_0 > 0$ and the manager has timing abilities if $TM_2 > 0$.

The HM_2 measure of Henriksson and Merton (1981) is based on viewing timing ability as a (free) put option on the stock market. The degree of timing ability is measured by introducing the returns on a put option on the market portfolio, with the regression coefficient HM_2 in the following equation

$$R_a - R_f = HM_0 + HM_1(R_m - R_f) + HM_2(\max(R_m - R_f, 0)) + \varepsilon, \quad (22.13)$$

where HM_0 is the measure of selection ability; HM_1 is a measure of the manager's exposure to the market portfolio; and HM_2 is the measure of timing ability. The term $(\max(R_m - R_f, 0))$ can be seen as the payoff of a long put option. If HM_2 is significantly positive, then the portfolio manager exhibits superior timing skills. If HM_0 is significantly positive, then the portfolio manager exhibits superior selection skills.

Advances in Performance Attribution Models

A major source of inspiration for new performance attribution models was the creation of portfolio holdings databases. Available information on the holdings of mutual funds has increased over time, which offers more ways to learn from the behavior of its portfolio managers. Daniel et al. (1997) is one of the first studies using holdings information, which proposes a decomposition of performance based on benchmarks that matches the characteristics of the portfolio. This study uses 125 benchmark portfolios that are constructed using a triple sort procedure. Each benchmark portfolio consists of a particular quintile of the asset universe in terms of size, book-to-market ratio, and momentum. Next, each security is linked to the matched benchmark portfolio.

The decomposition of performance of the total return (TR) of a fund, including characteristic selection (CS), characteristic timing (CT), and average style (AS) is calculated as follows:

$$TR_t = CS_t + CT_t + AS_t. \quad (22.14)$$

Characteristic selection is calculated as:

$$CS_t = \sum_{i=1}^{n} w_{i,t} \times (R_{i,t} - R_{i,t}^b), \quad (22.15)$$

where $w_{i,t}$ denotes the portfolio weight of stock i at the beginning of month t; $R_{i,t}$ is the return of stock i in month t; $R_{i,t}^b$ is the return in month t of the benchmark portfolio that is matched to the characteristics of stock i at the beginning of month $t - 1$; and n is the number of securities in the portfolio.

Characteristic timing represents the impact of changing the portfolio's exposure to the 125 style benchmarks relative to its exposure in the previous period. This measure, which is similar to the portfolio change measure proposed by Grinblatt and Titman (1993), is calculated as:

$$CT_t = \sum_{i=1}^{n} (w_{i,t} - w_{i,t-1}) \times R_{i,t}^b. \qquad (22.16)$$

Average style represents the return of the portfolio based on its previous exposure on the 125 style benchmarks. The measure can be interpreted as the benchmark portfolio as revealed by the portfolio manager's behavior in the previous period. It is calculated as:

$$AS_t = \sum_{i=1}^{n} \mathbf{w}_{i,t-1} \times R_{i,t}^b. \qquad (22.17)$$

A major advantage of the matching based on characteristics is that securities in the actual portfolio are benchmarked against securities with approximately the same level of systematic risk.

Table 22.2 illustrates the model with an example. For reasons of simplicity, the characteristics-based benchmarks are created using two characteristics, each with two groups. The benchmarks include the following: large value, small value, large growth, and small growth stocks. Panel A presents the input data necessary for the analysis. The actual portfolio holdings for each group are given at $t = 0$, $t = 1$, and $t = 2$. The returns are given for periods 1 and 2. To simplify the presentation, the results for the actual portfolio are summarized at the level of the characteristics-based benchmark. For example, the individual stocks fitting into the large value category have a 15 percent weight in the overall portfolio at the beginning of the first period and their weighted average return is 13 percent in the first period.

Panel B presents the results of the attribution analysis. The average style return for period 1 is calculated as 0.2(12 percent) + 0.25(14 percent) + 0.30(4 percent) + 0.25(5 percent) = 8.45 percent. This return is what the manager would have achieved if the average exposure to each of the individual characteristic-based benchmark portfolios would have been maintained from the previous period and if the securities had achieved the characteristics-based benchmark returns. The characteristics-based returns using actual portfolio weights is 7.55 percent, and the difference with the average style return is characteristic timing, which equals −0.80 percent for period 1. Finally, characteristic selection is 0.40 percent, which is the difference between the actual return on the portfolio, 9.30 percent, and the characteristics-based returns using actual portfolio weights, 7.55 percent. The results for the second period can be calculated in a similar way.

Table 22.2 **Attribution with Characteristics-Based Benchmarks**

Panel A. Input Data

Holdings	Actual Portfolio (%)		
Period	0	1	2
Large value	20	15	25
Small value	25	20	40
Large growth	30	30	15
Small growth	25	35	20

Returns	Actual Portfolio		Characteristics Based Portfolio	
Period	1(%)	2(%)	1(%)	2(%)
Large value	13.0	11.0	12.0	10.0
Small value	12.0	17.0	14.0	14.0
Large growth	6.0	26.0	4.0	25.0
Small growth	9.0	22.0	5.0	22.0
Return	9.3	17.9	8.9	17.3

Panel B. Attribution Analysis

Period	1(%)	2(%)	Mean(%)
Average style	8.4	19.5	13.9
Characteristic styling	−0.8	−3.2	−2.0
Characteristic selection	1.8	1.6	1.7
Total	9.3	17.9	13.6

Note: Panel A presents the input data including holdings at the beginning of periods 0, 1, and 2, as well as the returns over periods 1 and 2. Panel B presents the outcome of the attribution analysis based on the model of Daniel et al. (1997).

Holdings information creates the opportunity to measure active management in a more precise way than regression-based attribution. Plantinga (1999), who tests this relationship in a simulation experiment, finds that the probability of incorrectly rejecting the presence of active management skills (Type I error) is much larger for techniques based on regression versus a technique using the covariance between portfolio weights and subsequent returns. Similarly, several authors are able to identify specific groups of portfolio managers who seem to have active management skills. For example, Daniel et al. (1997) find that aggressive growth funds have some selection skills. Kacperczyk, Sialm, and Zheng (2005) find that managers with the most concentrated holdings in one particular industry tend to have positive risk-adjusted returns. Cremers and Petajisto (2009) find that managers with the highest active share have positive risk-adjusted returns.

Money Weighted Returns

In order to present and analyze performance, data should be collected for multiple periods. Managers may aggregate performance data by weighting each period equally (or by the length of the period) or by weighting each period with the amount of money invested in the portfolio. The first approach results in a *time-weighted return measure*, and the second approach results in a *money-weighted return measure*. Each approach corresponds to the decision context of a particular actor in the investment process. Time-weighted returns are relevant for evaluating portfolio managers as their decisions about the composition of portfolios impact their period-by-period returns. Money-weighted returns are relevant for evaluating the decisions of investors because they decide when and how much money to allocate to their portfolio managers.

MONEY-WEIGHTED RETURN AND PERFORMANCE ATTRIBUTION

Dietz (1968) proposes using money-weighted return, especially the internal rate of return (IRR), as a measure to determine the return from the investor's perspective. The IRR is a money-weighted return in which the weights depend on the amount of money invested in each period. The idea is that a money-weighted return measure assigns more weight on the returns in periods when assets under management are larger. Money-weighted return measures depend not only on the returns of the securities in individual periods but also on the timing of the buying and selling of these securities.

In the context of delegated asset management, the question arises as to what extent investor and manager decisions drive performance. Dietz (1968) suggests that the difference between the IRR and the average (time-weighted) return is a measure of the timing ability of an investor. Dichev (2007) and Friesen and Sapp (2007) compare money- and time-weighted returns to assess the timing performance of investors. Any difference is interpreted as an estimate of the effects of the timing decisions of investors on performance. This finding suggests that the traditional performance attribution models should be extended with a component identifying the impact of investor timing on his performance.

Consider the following example where a portfolio manager can choose between stocks and bonds over two periods. For the sake of convenience, selection decisions are ignored. The portfolio manager allocates $100 to bonds and $50 to stocks. Panel A in Table 22.3 gives the returns on bonds and stocks in each period separately, indicating that period 1 is a good period for stock performance with a return of 25 percent and period 2 is a good period for bond performance with a return of 6 percent. The value invested in stocks and bonds is indicated as assets under management. The geometric-weighted average of the portfolio equals $[(1.0967)(1.0145)]^{1/2}-1 = 5.48$ percent. This portfolio manager was given a 60/40

Table 22.3 **An Example of Manager and Investor Market Timing**

Panel A. Input Data

	Assets under Management			Single Period Returns		
	Portfolio ($ mil)	Bonds ($ mil)	Stocks ($ mil)	Portfolio (%)	Bonds (%)	Stocks (%)
t = 0	150.00	100.00	50.00			
t = 1	184.50	132.00	52.50	9.67	2.00	25.00
t = 2	187.17	139.92	47.25	1.45	6.00	-10.00

Panel B. Portfolio Weights

	Actual		Benchmark	
	Bonds (%)	Stocks (%)	Bonds (%)	Stocks (%)
t = 0	66.7	33.3	60.0	40.0
t = 1	71.5	28.5	60.0	40.0

Panel C. Performance Attribution

Buy-and-hold benchmark return	5.24%	Manager timing	0.24%
Buy-and-hold actual return	5.48%	Investor timing	−0.24%
Money weighted return	5.24%		

Note: Panel A presents information on the input data for the example: the value of assets under management for the entire portfolio, stock portfolio, and bond portfolio at t = 0, t = 1, and t = 2. The returns of the first period are the returns obtained between t = 0 to t = 1, and the returns of the second period are the returns from t = 1 to t = 2. Panel B presents the actual and benchmark portfolio weights at the beginning of each period. Panel C summarizes the outcome of the performance attribution.

benchmark of bonds and stocks, respectively, resulting in a benchmark performance of 11.2 percent for the first period and −0.4 percent for the second period. The geometric weighted average of these returns is 5.24 percent.

Given no selection effects, the difference in performance between the actual portfolio and the benchmark portfolio is the timing effect realized by the manager, which is 0.24 percent. In other words, the manager was able to successfully time his portfolio allocations by decreasing his exposure in periods when an asset class has lower returns and increasing the exposure to an asset class that has higher returns.

The impact of investor timing can be calculated as the difference between the IRR of the cash flows to and from the portfolio and the geometric weighted average of the portfolio returns. The first cash flow is equal to the investment in the portfolio at the beginning of the first period, in this case −$150. With a return of 9.67 percent the value of this portfolio becomes $164.50. Because the value of the assets under management increased to $184.50, investors deposited an additional $20 in the fund. So the second cash flow is −$20. The last cash flow is the value of the portfolio at the end of the second period, which in this case is $187.17. The IRR of these three cash flows, −$150, −$20, and $187.17, is unique and equals 5.24 percent. The IRR is less than the geometric-weighted average of the portfolio returns, indicating poor investor timing. The poor timing by investors completely eliminates the efforts of the portfolio manager.

SOLVING IRRS IN THE CONTEXT OF ASSET PORTFOLIOS

One of the perceived problems of applying the IRR method is that multiple IRRs may be generated. With multiple IRRs, alternatives cannot be properly ranked without additional information. Hazen (2003) presents the relevant information to rank alternatives consistent with the net present value (NPV) criterion when multiple IRRs exist. The additional computations solve the problem of multiple IRRs but reduce the ease of using the IRRs to rank alternatives. Dichev (2007) and Friesen and Sapp (2007) recognize the potential problem of multiple IRRs. Dichev considers the likelihood of multiple IRRs to be small given the nature of this problem and the stability and the robustness of his computations. Friesen and Sapp suggest that the short-sales constraint in the mutual fund industry implies a unique IRR greater than −100 percent. They discard only a small minority of the mutual funds from their analysis because of multiple IRRs. This subsection shows that a unique IRR always exists in the special case when portfolio values are always positive. This finding is relevant for mutual funds, which can only take long positions in assets with limited liability.

Pratt and Hammond (1979) present a simple method to determine the maximum number of IRRs. The existence of a unique IRR depends crucially on the sign and the magnitude of the cash flows. Restrictions on the sign and the magnitude of the cash flows may reduce the number of internal returns. In Dichev (2007) and Friesen and Sapp (2007), the value of the portfolios is always positive. Positive portfolio values bind the cash flows that can be extracted from a portfolio. As will be seen below, positive portfolio values always result in a unique IRR larger than −100 percent. Investors' returns are therefore unambiguously measured by the IRR of the portfolio cash flows.

The NPV of a series of cash flows $C_0, C_1, ..., C_T$ equals

$$P(d) = \sum_{t=0}^{T} C_t \times d^t \tag{22.18}$$

where $d = (1+k)^{-1}$ denotes the discount factor and k the discount rate. The IRR of these cash flows is a discount rate larger than −100 percent that makes the

NPV of these of cash flows equal to zero. An IRR also makes the future value of the cash flows equal to zero. The future value is defined as:

$$F(a) = \sum_{t=0}^{T} C_t \times a^{T-t} \qquad (22.19)$$

where $a = (1+k)$ denotes the compound factor. The first cash outflow equals the value of the portfolio at the end of period 0, $C_0 = -V_0$, and the last cash inflow equals the value of the portfolio at the end of period T, $C_T = V_T$. Intermediate cash flows are related to portfolio values, V_t, and portfolio returns, R_t, as:

$$C_t = (1 + R_t) \times V_{t-1} - V_t. \qquad (22.20)$$

With only positive portfolio values, investors cannot extract any amount of cash from their portfolios. Intermediate cash outflows cannot be larger than the value of the portfolio just before the selling of any securities, $C_t < (1 + R_t) \times V_{t-1}$. With a buy-and-hold strategy, investors immediately reinvest any cash income derived from their portfolio. They create their own homemade stock dividends; intermediate cash flows are zero.

IRRs correspond to the positive roots of the polynomials $P(d)$ and $F(a)$. Finding positive IRRs corresponds to finding the roots between zero and 1 of the polynomial $P(a)$. Finding negative IRR corresponds to finding the roots between zero and 1 of the polynomial $F(a)$. The number of positive roots is according to Descartes' rule of signs equal to the number of sign changes in the series of coefficients of the polynomial or is less than this number by a multiple of two. Zeros are ignored in counting the number of sign changes, and repeated roots are counted separately. Thus, a necessary condition for a unique IRR is that first and last cash flow have opposite signs. With opposite signs there is an odd number of positive roots, possibly a unique root. With only positive portfolio values, this necessary condition for a unique IRR is met.

Pratt and Hammond (1979) point out that stricter bounds on the number of positive roots can be obtained by inspecting the number of sign changes in the sequence of partial sums of the coefficients. Table 22.4 presents their method to determine the number of unique IRRs using an example. Panel A contains the financial data of a portfolio investment. The sequence of cash flows contains three sign changes. According to Descartes' rule of signs, an odd number of IRRs exists. A unique IRR may be present but the existence of three IRRs cannot be ruled out. Descartes' rule of signs can also be applied to the sequence of cash balances in order to bind the number of positive IRRs (Norstrøm, 1972). The first cash balance is equal to the first cash flow; subsequent cash balances are equal to the cash balance of the previous period plus the cash flow of the current period. The sequence of cash balances contains three sign changes, so there is at least one positive IRR but possibly three.

Panel B of Table 22.4 presents the partial sums to determine the number of positive IRRs. The first row ($i = 0$) of Panel B contains the portfolio cash flows. The other cells of the first column ($j = 0$) are equal to the cell in the first row of this column. The other elements represent so-called partial sums, which are

Table 22.4 **Determining the Number of IRRs**

Panel A. Financial Information Investment

Period	0	1	2	3	4	5
Return on portfolio (%)		30	40	−50	−30	−50
Cash flow	−10.00	5.00	6.00	−1.00	−1.00	1.76
Cash balance	−10.00	−5.00	1.00	0.00	−1.00	0.76
Value of portfolio	10.00	8.00	5.20	3.60	3.52	1.76

Panel B. Bounding the Number of Positive IRRs

i	j	0	1	2	3	4	5
0		−10.00	5.00	6.00	−1.00	−1.00	1.76
1		−10.00	−5.00	1.00	0.00	−1.00	0.76
2		−10.00	−15.00	−14.00	−14.00	−15.00	−14.24
3		−10.00	−25.00	−39.00	−53.00	−68.00	−82.24

Panel C. Bounding the Number of Negative IRRs

i	j	0	1	2	3	4	5
0		1.76	−1.00	−1.00	6.00	5.00	−10.00
1		1.76	0.76	−0.24	5.76	10.76	0.76
2		1.76	2.52	2.28	8.04	18.80	19.56
3		1.76	4.28	6.56	14.60	33.40	52.96

Note: Panel A of contains the financial data of an investment. Panel B (C) contains the partial sums of the cash flows to determine the number of positive (negative) IRRs. The first row of Panel B (C) contains the cash flows (in reverse order) from Panel A. The other entries in the first column in both panels are equal to the entry in the first row of this column. The other cells in both panels are equal to the sum of the cell to the left and the cell above it. The number of sign changes in the sequences of underlined numbers bounds the number of IRRs.

equal to the sum of the cell to the left and the cell above. An upper bound for the number of IRRs is found by counting the number of sign changes along a path starting in a cell in the first column and then moving right and up to the rightmost cell in the second row. The first sequence of partial sums in Panel B corresponds to the sequence of cash balances in Panel A. This first sequence of sums has three sign changes, which indicates the existence of one or three positive IRRs. However, the second sequence of partial sums (italic numbers), which includes the last element of the first sequence ($i = 1$, $j = 5$), has only one sign change. Hence, only one unique positive IRR exists in this example.

Panel C gives the partial sums to determine the number of negative IRRs. The structure of Panel C is similar to Panel B, except that the cash flows are presented in reversed order. The other cells of the first column ($j = 0$) are equal to the cell in the first row of this column. Again, each partial sum is equal to the sum of the cell to the left and the cell above. The first sequence of partial sums in panel C has two sign changes, but the second sequence (italic numbers), which includes the element $i = 1$ and $j = 5$, includes none. So no negative IRR exists, and therefore the above positive IRR is unique. The IRR of the investment in the example turns out to be 4.35 percent and the buy-and-hold strategy equals −20.45 percent. The difference points at superior timing capabilities of the investor. When necessary, the panels can be extended by adding more rows and columns. By adding more rows and columns, the bound always reaches the exact number of IRRs, but usually it suffices to add only a few rows and columns (Pratt, 1979).

Without additional information on the sign and size of the cash flows, no general conclusions can be made about the uniqueness of the IRR. Positive portfolio values bound the net cash flows that can be extracted from the portfolio. Simulations show that with positive portfolio values the numbers in each column of Panel B become smaller and smaller and negative when sufficient rows are added. In Panel C, the numbers in each column gradually become positive when sufficient rows are added. So, one sign change always exists in one of the two panels and none in the other. Positive portfolio values are therefore a sufficient condition for a unique IRR larger than −100 percent. Investors' returns are unambiguously measured by the IRR of the portfolio cash flows.

The partial sums in Panel B are a weighted sum of the original cash flows (Pratt, 1979):

$$S_{i,j} = \sum_{t=0}^{T} \binom{i+j-1-t}{j-t} \times C_t. \qquad (22.21)$$

The weights are the binomial coefficients, which are positive by definition. Expressing the portfolio cash flows in terms of portfolio values and portfolio returns yields after rewriting the following expression for the partial sums in Panel B:

$$S_{i,j} = \sum_{t-1}^{T} \left(R_t - \frac{i-1}{j} \right) \times \binom{i+j-1-t}{j-t} \times V_{t-1}. \qquad (22.22)$$

With positive portfolio values, the sign of a partial sum depends crucially on the sign of the first terms in the summation. Note that the binomial coefficients are always positive. For a sufficiently large i, the first terms become negative, resulting in a negative partial sum. The positive sign of the partial sums in Panel C when sufficient rows are added can be shown in a similar way.

Summary and Conclusions

This chapter has discussed the basic performance attribution model of Brinson et al. (1986). Analysts and others can use this model to analyze the performance of a portfolio in order to detect manager skills. As this model relies on analyzing the portfolio composition in combination with asset class returns, the chapter restricts the use of the model to practitioners. Analysis based on holdings is usually more accurate than time series analysis of returns. However, since the last decade of the twentieth century, databases with portfolio holdings have become available for academics resulting in a further development of holdings-based attribution models. Daniel et al. (1997) propose and use a more elaborate attribution model that accounts for risk in the spirit of the Fama and French (1993) and the Carhart (1999) regression models. Performance measurement based on holdings suggests that groups of portfolio managers have forecasting skills and the potential to "beat the market."

As investors rely more on external managers, their sole responsibility is to select portfolio managers. As Friesen and Sapp (2007) discuss, investors struggle with the selection process. For this reason, the regular performance attribution models should be extended with an additional component based on money-weighted returns in order to identify the impact of investor's decisions on total performance. The additional component is based on calculating the IRR of the cash flows to the portfolio. In the context of an investor who only can take long positions in instruments with minimum returns of −100 percent, a unique IRR exists. Any reports suggesting that such IRRs do not always exist are due to data errors.

Discussion Questions

1. What are the potential pitfalls in the attribution model of Brinson et al. (1986) in interpreting the selection component as a measure of the manager's ability to select superior stocks?
2. If an investor's asset allocation has a major impact on a portfolio's performance, why do various studies show that market timing does not work?
3. What is the fundamental difference between timing as defined in the traditional Brinson model and characteristic timing as defined by Daniel et al. (1997)?
4. The model of Daniel et al. (1997) controls for risk by creating characteristic-based benchmark portfolios. Similar to the Carhart (1999) model, the model uses size, book to market, and momentum as characteristics. Discuss the advantages and disadvantages of using the model developed by Daniel et al. versus Carhart.
5. Finance textbooks typically express concern about the existence of a unique solution for the IRR. Discuss whether this concern is justified for mutual funds and hedge funds.

References

Ankrim, Ernest M. 1992. "Risk-Adjusted Performance Attribution." *Financial Analysts Journal* 48:2, 75–82.

Brinson, Gary P., L. Randolph Hood, and Gilbert L. Beebower. 1986. "Determinants of Portfolio Performance." *Financial Analysts Journal* 42:4, 39–44.

Carhart, Mark M. 1999. "On Persistence in Mutual Fund Performance" *Journal of Finance* 52:1, 57–82.

Cremers, Martijn, and Antti Petajisto. 2009. "How Active Is Your Fund Manager? A New Measure That Predicts Performance." *Review of Financial Studies* 22:9, 3329–3365.

Daniel, Kent, Mark Grinblatt, Sheridan Titman, and Russ Wermers. 1997. "Measuring Mutual Fund Performance with Characteristic Based Benchmarks." *Journal of Finance* 52:3, 1035–1058.

Dichev, Ilia D. 2007. "What Are Stock Investors Actual Historical Returns? Evidence from Dollar-Weighted Returns." *American Economic Review* 97:1, 386–401.

Dietz, Peter O. 1968. "Components of a Measurement Model: Rate of Return, Risk, and Timing." *Journal of Finance* 23:2, 267–275.

Fama, Eugene F., and Kenneth R. French. 1993. "Common Risk Factors in the Returns on Stocks and Bonds." *Journal of Financial Economics* 33:1, 3–56.

Fong, Gifford, Charles Pearson, and Oldrich Vasicek. 1983. "Bond Performance: Analyzing Sources of Return." *Journal of Portfolio Management* 16:3, 46–50.

Friesen, Geoffrey C., and Travis R. A. Sapp. 2007. "Mutual Fund Flows and Investor Returns: An Empirical Examination of Fund Timing Ability." *Journal of Banking & Finance* 31:9, 2796–2816.

Grinblatt, Mark, and Sheridan Titman. 1993. "Performance Measurement Without Benchmarks: An Examination of Mutual Fund Returns." *Journal of Business* 66:1, 47–68.

Hazen, Gordon B. 2003. "A New Perspective on Multiple Internal Rates of Return." *Engineering Economist* 48:1, 31–51.

Henriksson, Roy D., and Robert C. Merton. 1981. "On Market Timing and Mutual Fund Performance. II. Statistical Procedures for Evaluating Forecasting Skills." *Journal of Business* 54:4, 513–533.

Hsu, Jason C., Vitali Kalesnik, and Brett W. Myers. 2010. "Performance Attribution: Measuring Dynamic Asset Allocation Skill." *Financial Analysts Journal* 66:6, 1–10.

Kacperczyk, Marcin, Clemens Sialm, and Lu Zheng. 2005. "On the Industry Concentration of Actively Managed Mutual Funds." *Journal of Finance* 60:4, 1983–2011.

Menchero, Jose. 2004. "Multiperiod Arithmetic Attribution." *Financial Analysts Journal* 60:4, 76–91.

Norstrøm, Carl J. 1972. "A Sufficient Condition for a Unique Nonnegative Internal Rate of Return." *Journal of Financial and Quantitative Analysis* 7:3, 1835–1839.

Plantinga, Auke. 1999. *Performance Evaluation of Investment Portfolios: The Measurement of Forecasting Abilities and the Impact of Liabilities.* Leens, Netherlands: Uitgeverij de Marne B.V.

Pratt, John W. 1979. "Finding How Many Roots a Polynomial Has in $(0,1)$ Or $(0,)$." *American Mathematical Monthly* 84:A, 630–637.

Pratt, John W., and John S. Hammond III. 1979. "Evaluating and Comparing Projects: Simple Detection of False Alarms." *Journal of Finance* 34:5, 1231–1242.

Sharpe, William F. 1992. "Asset Allocation: Management Style and Performance Measurement." *Journal of Portfolio Management* 18:2, 7–19.

Singer, Brian D., and Denis S. Karnosky. 1995. "The General Framework for Global Investment Management and Performance Attribution." *Journal of Portfolio Management* 21:2, 84–92.

Treynor, Jack L., and Kay K. Mazuy. 1968. "Can Mutual Funds Outguess the Market." *Harvard Business Review* 44:4, 131–136.

23

Equity Investment Styles

ANDREW MASON

Lecturer in Finance, University of Surrey

Introduction

The rise to prominence of institutional investors in financial markets over the last 30 to 40 years has been accompanied by the development of pronounced equity investment styles. This development has spawned an industry analyzing and advising on all aspects of portfolio construction and selection. It has also been accompanied by a vast body of academic literature focused on returns to market and returns to stock "styles" following the groundbreaking work of Sharpe (1964), Farrell (1974), and Fama and French (1992) and investment manager style research by Sharpe (1992), Brown and Goetzmann (1997), and Chan, Dimmock, and Lakonishok (2009). Despite general agreement that a range of differing styles exists and similarities between descriptions of investor types, no uniformly accepted classification of equity styles exists. Further, those styles most commonly used allow a wide range of strategies to be employed under the broad umbrella of their classification system. Kaplan, Knowles, and Phillips (2003) observe that equity investment style is a "catch all phrase" referring to a range of factors relating to the behavior of investment portfolios over time, that are closely related to the risk factors embedded in those portfolios, that may lead to performance differences. *Equity investment styles* are defined as portfolios that share common characteristics and behave similarly under varying conditions.

The following is a brief overview of the most discussed investment styles in operation today: Value investors (funds) invest in stocks that are cheap relative to their earnings or assets, offering "intrinsic value," and they are less concerned with growth. Such investors believe these undervalued stocks will revert to more normal values (mean reversion). Often value stocks will be out of favor due to a specific problem with the company, or belong to slower growth or depressed sectors of the market. The most extreme versions of value funds are often called "deep value" or "contrarian" funds as they exploit the behavioral aspect of over-reaction to bad news and their stocks may be experiencing severe problems. Typically, value stocks have a lower price-to-earnings (PE) ratio or price-to-book (PB) ratio than the market average but a higher dividend yield. In the case of deep value, the PE may be very high if earnings are very low or undefined if the firm has negative earnings. The biggest risk for value investors is that they have misinterpreted intrinsic value or bought stock ahead of major future bad news.

Growth investors (funds) invest in stocks with above average prospects for longer term profit and earnings per share (EPS) growth and are willing to pay a premium to market valuations for premium growth. The most extreme versions of growth investors are "aggressive growth" and "momentum." Such stocks may trade on very high multiples and need to sustain very high levels of long-term growth or the momentum of constantly rising profits and analysts' forecasts to justify their valuations. The major risks for growth investors are that forecasted earnings do not materialize, valuation multiples contract, or both. Investors whose universe is a broad market index such as the S&P 500 may be designated market oriented or "blend" investors because they have the ability to alter their growth-value bias or enter into top-down sector rotation, where they overweight or underweight stock market sectors in response to changing economic or market conditions.

Despite having many variants, the analysis of investment management style typically falls into three broad categories: (1) identification of style through portfolio characteristics, (2) identification of style through portfolio returns, and (3) assessment of portfolio performance against an appropriate benchmark or peer group. Through these avenues, many key elements that are important to identifying investment styles may be considered as well as the risks being undertaken by portfolio managers and whether investors are being adequately compensated for the risks taken.

This chapter outlines the developments in theoretical and empirical studies of equity investment style. The remainder of the chapter has the following organization: The first section looks at the classification of stocks and equity investment styles. The second section investigates multidimensional classification and growth-value orientation. The third section explores investment fund styles and the fourth section discusses the performance of investment funds. The final section provides the summary and conclusions.

Classication of Stocks and Equity Investment Styles

Much of the early analysis of equity investment style focused on identifying styles of stocks. Noteworthy contributions include Fama and French's (1992) three-factor model of equity returns, which built on the earlier work of Fama (1972), Sharpe (1967), and others who contributed groundbreaking work on the effect of the market factor (beta), valuations, and size. King (1966) and Farrell (1974) suggest that common or latent factors explain stock price behavior. Farrell supplements King's market, industry, and company factors using a classification according to growth, cyclical, or stable return characteristics. The findings of these early studies give pension plan sponsors an opportunity to reduce volatility within and across style groups within the equity asset class. The importance of this analysis goes beyond diversification and has an important role to play in selecting, benchmarking, and rewarding investment managers. As a result, a whole industry has grown up to provide these services with prominent players including Russell, BARRA, Morningstar, and Lipper.

Following in the footsteps of Fama and French (1992), many academics, consultants, and index providers based their classification on a size and book value to price, or PE metric. Under this approach, stocks are initially ranked by market capitalization (cap) and allocated to groups, such as large, mid, and small cap, subsequently ranked by a single valuation multiple such as PB or PE, and then allocated to a subgroup typically called value, core or blend, and growth. Many viewed growth as meaning high PE or high PB and effectively defined as the absence of value whereas "core" or "blend" was some undefined middle ground.

Speidell and Graves (2003) caution against misunderstanding or misappropriating the basic concepts of growth and value, emphasizing that growth is an important element in assessing value and investment quality. Furthermore as Damodaran (2003) notes, no evidence confirms that growth investors care less about the value of an investment than do value investors. The ultimate objective of both investors is to maximize the value of their investments given the constraints within which they operate. Cunningham (2002, pp. 12–13) quotes Warren Buffet on this issue: "All true investing must be based on an assessment of the relationship between price and value. Strategies that do not employ this comparison of price and value do not amount to investing at all, but to speculation." Growth and value, Buffet says, are not distinct. They are integrally linked since growth must be treated as a component of value. The distinction lies in where growth and value investors focus their efforts to uncover value. Value investors search for undervalued assets in place and invest in mature firms with underperforming assets. By contrast, growth investors search for investments with undervalued growth opportunities.

Much of the academic debate on investment styles focuses on the relative returns of value and growth stocks with high PB being used as a proxy for growth stocks and low PB being taken as a proxy for value stocks. Studies such as de Bondt and Thaler (1987) and Lakonishok, Shleifer, and Vishny (1994) conclude that value-based strategies outperform growth strategies. Fama and French (1992) suggest that the value premium may be due to value stocks being riskier. Lakonishok et al. also suggest that spotting mispricing is easier with value stocks. Studies such as Arshanapalli, Coggin, and Doukas (1998) establish the superior performance of value over growth stocks without considering any growth measure. Speidell and Graves (2003) observe that although growth portfolios may result in higher PB or PE ratios, using this output characteristic as an input variable may be misleading because a high valuation multiple is an inadequate growth measure. Brush (2007) notes that studies based on this premise are only comparing "high book-to-market" stocks with "low book-to-market" stocks not growth and value.

Many proponents of the PB approach such as Davis (2001) are aware of the criticisms leveled at PB for classification of mutual fund performance and manager style. Justification is often offered that a return premium may be gained by investing in a portfolio of stocks that is sensitive to the Fama and French (1992) "high minus low" book to market value factor, whatever it measures. Davis ponders whether funds attempt to capture this value premium and why, over his study period, funds with value exposure performed poorly. These findings are similar to the observations of Chan, Chen, and Lakonishok (2002). Brown and Goetzmann (1997) and Michaud (1998) believe that this simple approach does not capture the diversity of investment styles.

Brown and Goetzmann (1997) and Speidell and Graves (2003) state that a new framework of classification will better differentiate the various investment styles being pursued in the equity market. They agree with Bailey and Tierney (1995) who observe that different styles lead to differentiated portfolios and thus affect performance. Classification of equity investment style is a multidimensional issue reflecting combinations of revealed preference for income, growth, and asset backing. Kaplan et al. (2003) stress that growth orientation and value orientation are distinct concepts. This distinction becomes more apparent when measuring growth directly rather than implied from valuation. The assumption that growth-oriented stocks have weak value orientation and vice versa is sometimes observed to be inaccurate. A stock may possess neither exclusively growth nor value characteristics. As a result, an acknowledged growth or value manager may include the same stock in their respective portfolios. As Sorensen and Lazzara (1995) note, most stocks fall between extreme classifications of pure growth and pure value. They devise two panels of pure growth and pure value stocks based on quantitative characteristics and the subjective judgments of analysts, portfolio managers, and investment strategists. The authors use these characteristics to determine the growth orientation or value orientation of nonpanel stocks.

All major index providers and mutual fund database providers including Russell, Standard & Poor's/Citigroup, MSCI, Dow Jones Wilshire, Morningstar, and Lipper have abandoned ranking by a single valuation multiple for their stock style indices. Instead, reflecting concerns that the traditional model may fail both to capture the diversity and complexity of the range of investment styles and to provide adequate tools for benchmarking or peer group assessment, each provider has established a growth-value orientation based on valuation and growth metrics.

These growth-valuation nuances are widely accepted both in the academic literature and by practitioners although the exact terminology or definition may differ. Christopherson and Williams (1997) outline a typical categorization scheme employed by practitioners when describing Russell's US manager styles comprising four broad categories—value, growth, market oriented, and small capitalization—plus a range of substyles. Value includes low PE, contrarian, and yield. Growth includes consistent growth and earnings momentum. Market-oriented includes managers with a value bias, growth bias, market normal, and growth at a reasonable price (GARP). Brown and Goetzmann's (1997) methodology provides a wider range of mutual fund styles than traditional industry classification and performs well in terms of predicting out-of-sample cross-sectional performance. They identify the following set of styles: growth and income, income, value, growth, glamour, global timing, international, and metal. Their study drew attention to the existence of several types of growth style. This is evidence of mutual fund product differentiation that may be a function of differences in investment philosophy and process. Michaud (1998) uses factor analysis to examine the relationship between fundamental characteristics and stock returns for the US, Japan, and UK equity markets. Michaud focuses on three value style factors: earnings yield, normalized earnings yield, and asset yield. His results indicate that value may be multidimensional and acknowledges the presence of at least three distinct kinds of equity value styles. He concludes that value-growth orientation is not one dimensional and not well represented by PB. He also observes that growth stocks are not the absolute opposite of value stocks and that a multidimensional style factor framework is necessary for style analysis. As such, no single factor fully captures the growth or value orientation of a stock or the investment style of a mutual fund manager. The number of factors used should be large enough to give confidence that the most relevant information has been considered, but small enough to limit the complexity of the classification process.

The literature also considers whether there are style cycles where certain types of stocks or mutual funds systematically outperform. For example, Amenc, Sfeir, and Martellini's (2003) model of tactical style allocation shows evidence that economic and financial factors drive style index returns and that different equity styles perform differently at different stages of the economic and stock market cycle. The variables used in their analysis include interest rates, risk, relative cheapness of stocks, liquidity, and various economic variables such as commodity prices and foreign exchange rates. Chen and de Bondt (2004) add dividend yield to market capitalization and PB in their analysis of style momentum within the S&P 500 index. They conclude that style cycles exist. Strategists at investment bank such as Merrill Lynch regularly publish "style cycle" research. Inflows to certain styles often follow periods of outperformance. Therefore, marketing of funds is easier when a fund's style is in a favorable stage of the style cycle.

Chen (2003) highlights the importance of a firm's characteristics. He analyzes portfolios formed by firm characteristics (size, book to market, and dividend yield) and observes "characteristics momentum" periods when certain firm characteristics are in favor or out of favor. Chen also highlights the slow evolution of changes in firm characteristics that he believes can potentially provide valuable information about future stock returns. Thus, the prior literature and the actions of industry participants indicates that at both the level of stock style analysis and mutual fund style analysis a movement has occurred to incorporate a more complex set of characteristics to determine investment style. PB analysis is generally included as one of a range of more broadly based factors rather than a sole determinant of investment style.

INVESTMENT FUNDS STYLES

Bailey and Tierney (1995) and Damodaran (2003) are among those who believe that investment managers differentiate themselves, their portfolios, and the attendant returns through their investment philosophy, investment process, and investment style. Damodaran as well as Slager and Koedijk (2007) describe an investment philosophy as a coherent way of thinking about financial markets and how they work, including the belief in where to find market anomalies or investment opportunities. Kudish (1995) denounces stock picking as the differentiating factor between investment managers and their performance and discusses the investment philosophy and investment process that determines a fund's performance pattern. The investment process is the method by which an investment philosophy is implemented. This process reduces a universe of stocks through stock screening, fundamental research, stock selection, and portfolio construction into a portfolio that has a certain style. The fundamental difference between investment fund style and investment stock style is that a fund selects a portfolio of stocks in a manner consistent with that manager's chosen style or investment philosophy whereas a stock either has style attributes or does not. Much attention is paid to investment philosophy and process at the manager selection stage in order to ascertain whether manager performance is explainable and repeatable.

During the 1930s to 1950s, Graham and Dodd (1988) and Fisher (2003) document the investment philosophies and processes spawning the wide range of equity investment styles in evidence today. They articulate the value and growth styles, which have been in common usage since the 1930s. Similarities exist in the rigorous investment processes proposed by Graham and Dodd and Fisher. The processes differ, however, as to where the authors think investment opportunities exist. Graham and Dodd espouse a cautious estimate of intrinsic value and building in a margin of safety, which includes a low price to value or a high dividend yield. By contrast, Fisher advocates searching for companies that have disciplined plans to achieve substantial long-term profit growth, which implies a low or no dividend policy.

Studies of investment fund styles tend to take two approaches. The first approach uses simulated portfolios as in the case of Connor and Korajczyk (1991) and Bassett and Chen (2001). The second approach uses actual portfolios as in the case of Sharpe (1992), Brown and Goetzmann (1997), and Vardharaj and Fabozzi (2007). Vardharaj and Fabozzi believe that to better understand the motivations and outcomes of actions taken by fund managers, empirical studies should reflect the constraints faced by investment managers. These constraints may reflect prudent risk management practices, legal requirements, or marketing requirements. Such constraints lead to persistent differences between actual portfolios that are difficult to model in simulated portfolios. Typical constraints may include market capitalization restrictions, sector neutrality relative to a benchmark, or turnover constraints that may affect a fund's character and performance. The next section reviews the two main forms of style analysis: characteristics based style analysis, which is based on stocks held in fund portfolios, and returns based style analysis, which is based on fund returns.

CHARACTERISTICS BASED STYLE ANALYSIS (CBSA)

An important method of analyzing investment style is to consider the portfolio holdings of investment funds and the characteristics of those portfolios. Identifying common factors will facilitate forming style groups and may also provide insights into estimates of expected future performance of such groups. Early analysis of common factors related to investment style by King (1966) and Farrell (1974) suggest that analysts could use common or latent factors to form a cluster based classification according to growth, cyclical, or stable return characteristics. Although these authors restricted their approach to stocks, they paved the way for characteristics based analysis of investment funds. Daniel, Grinblatt, Titman, and Wermers (1997) use characteristics based benchmarks in their work on fund performance. Falkenstein (1996) examines mutual funds revealed preferences for certain stock characteristics based on portfolio holdings. Abarbanell, Bushee, and Raedy (2003) provide an extension of the use of portfolio holdings. They use CBSA to identify behavioral traits in institutional investors in the case of corporate spinoffs.

CBSA is based on empirical investigation of the average weighted portfolio characteristics of stocks held in an investment portfolio. In its simplest form, CBSA might be restricted to average market capitalization of stocks held and a single valuation multiple such as the average PB ratio of all stocks held in the portfolio at a single point in time. More complex versions contain average weighted market capitalization, a range of valuation measures, and dividend yield, as well as historical and forecast growth rates of factors such as earnings, cash flow and other risk or efficiency measures. The desirability and the explanatory power of these variables have long been acknowledged. Yet, the task of collecting and collating variables has been difficult until recently, which may partly explain the willingness to exclude growth metrics from style analysis and to focus on PB.

Abarbanell et al. (2003) analyze the behavior of different types of financial institutions: banks, insurance companies, pensions, and endowments. They base their classification scheme on institutions-revealed preferences for characteristics, which allow them to form style groups defined by size, growth potential, and valuation. The authors also note that an explicit or implicit contract exists between institutions and their clients. This contract includes the assumption that institutions will continue to pursue the investment style or use the selection criteria that they have used in the past.

Radcliffe's (2003) factor based styling (FBS) uses a factor model with a broad range of portfolio characteristics: S&P quality, market capitalization, dividend yield, retention rate, sustainable internal growth, PE, PB, return on equity, earnings growth, and dividend growth. Radcliffe interprets his factors to represent unobservable economic influences and observable portfolio characteristics, which result in fundamental differences in portfolio returns. This approach is similar to the characteristics based models of Morningstar or Mason, Thomas, and McGroarty (2011). Prather, Bertin, and Henker (2004) also incorporate a large range of portfolio characteristics that they organize under four headings: popularity, growth (risk), cost, and management.

Based on his research on factor analysis of returns, Barr Rosenberg established BARRA, one of the best known commercial providers of portfolio analysis, risk, and performance attribution systems (Rosenberg and Rudd, 1982). BARRA takes an innovative "portfolio attributes" approach to create style indexes for mutual funds and BARRA factors are often used in portfolio research. De Allaume (1995), who adapts the BARRA factor model, finds five BARRA factors to be useful in identifying a fund's style: earnings yield, size, growth, book to price, and dividend yield. He constructs style maps for a sample of mutual funds based on size and weighted valuation characteristics and identifies them as belonging to the broad categories of value, growth, and style neutral.

Leinweber, Krider, and Swank (1995) postulate that factor returns (i.e., returns to broad characteristics such as growth, value, interest rate sensitivity, and industry group membership) explain equity returns. They note that factor models of risk and return are the most well-established of all quantitative equity management tools.

According to Christopherson and Williams (1997), under the Russell methodology value funds are likely to be invested in stocks with low PE or PB ratios and high yields, which may be found in cyclical or regulated industries. By contrast, growth managers are likely to be invested in stocks with higher earnings per share growth, higher profitability ratios, and higher valuations. These characteristics are more likely to be found in sectors such as consumer and service sectors, health, and technology. This methodology results in clearly identified styles that are differentiated in terms of portfolio characteristics within broad categories reflecting differing investment philosophies and investment processes.

Speidell and Graves (2003) note that due to the sophisticated methods of analysis undertaken and access to the same news sources and databases, what differentiates investment managers is the emphasis placed on different measures of valuation, growth, and qualitative factors. They list a range of analytical tools for equity style analysis under the following headings: accounting measures, valuation models, subjective fundamentals, growth measures, and change measures. The authors assume that value managers are more likely to focus on the former categories (e.g., accounting measures and valuation models) and growth managers are likely to focus on the latter items (e.g., growth measures and change measures). Speidell and Graves map style on the basis of growth rates and investors time horizons. They illustrate a range of styles and substyles that would be difficult to identify using the traditional size and PB methodology (e.g., deep value, absolute value, traditional value, yield based value, flexible value, relative value, and growth at a reasonable price [GARP], which combines growth and valuation, traditional growth, and earnings momentum growth. Thus, CBSA aims to form style groups based on funds revealed preferences for different combinations of growth, valuation, and income reflecting differentiated investment philosophies, investment processes, and ultimately investment portfolios.

RETURNS BASED ANALYSIS (RBA)

RBA is the other main methodology employed to identify investment management styles. Portfolio returns are analyzed and funds assigned to style groupings on the basis of past performance. The most parsimonious method of RBA is to use a single-factor capital asset pricing model (CAPM) to identify the relationship between the returns of a fund and a range of stock market indices and to select the stock market index providing the best fit against a fund's returns. This methodology has some intuitive appeal because many funds have a specified benchmark against which they are measured. In the light of Chan et al.'s (2002) observation that funds have a tendency to cluster around a broad index, Mason, Thomas and McGroarty (2012) adopt a best fit index (BFI) approach, which is sometimes employed to supplement portfolio analysis or characteristics based analysis by organizations such as Morningstar that specialize in investment fund research. Cremers and Petajisto (2009) highlight the fact that practitioners use stock market indices to benchmark fund manager performance not factor models such as Fama and French (1992), which are widely used in academic studies.

The second method of RBA, which has attracted much attention in the literature, is returns based style analysis (RBSA). Sharpe (1992) pioneered RBSA partly to overcome the problems of portfolio data collection and the lack of suitable investment benchmarks. RBSA is a specialized form of factor analysis where the factors are index returns. Sharpe's model estimates average economic exposure of a fund to selected asset classes based solely on the comovements of the fund's returns relative to those asset classes. The objective of this analysis is to approximate the factors influencing a fund's returns with limited and easily obtainable data. A synthetic style is formed based on an optimized portfolio of index returns, which may be regarded as a fund's style or style benchmark. The model measures the tracking variance between the style benchmark and the fund's actual return. The fund's style is the portion of the return explained by the model. The portion unexplained by the model is regarded as the manager's selection skills or how actively the portfolio is managed with respect to the passive style benchmark.

Some debate exists in the literature about several aspects of RBSA including the interpretation of the results generated. Discussion generally revolves around the selection of the appropriate benchmarks, timeliness of the methodology, and whether constraints (non-negativity and exhaustive coverage) should be applied. Despite some criticism, the RBSA model is still being implemented and refined and has a place to play in style analysis.

Christopherson (1995) notes that a delay may occur in discovering a change in style as the method provides an average economic exposure to factors (asset classes) over a long period of time, initially 60 months. Ben Dor, Jagannathan, and Meir (2003) and others shorten their analysis period to mitigate timeliness effects and manager change. In cases in which style change is thought to be important, they believe adding portfolio analysis can be useful. The RBSA model includes the non-negativity and exhaustive coverage constraints that aid the optimization process and reflect the constraints faced by many fund managers who are not allowed to run short positions in stocks or indices (non-negativity). Asset class coefficients are constrained to be non-negative and to sum to one. That is, the asset classes are assumed to reflect the economic exposure of 100 percent of the portfolio (exhaustive coverage). Ben Dor et al. and others remove the non-negativity constraint when analyzing hedge funds where short selling is permitted. Various modifications or refinements have occurred to the original RBSA model that aim to improve the statistical or functional properties of the model, but they may be outweighed by ease of application and properties noted by ter Horst, Nijman, and de Roon (2004) such as the original model's ability to cope with indices that are highly correlated or where one of the parameters is close to zero, which is common.

Waring and Siegel (2003) advocate RBSA as part of a sophisticated process of portfolio optimization where it could generate a "normal" portfolio or customized benchmark that describes the manager's neutral position with respect to style and market risk exposures. Mason et al. (2012) form equity style groups on the basis of RBSA factors. The original RBSA model was not restricted to equities. Ben Dor, Budinger, Dynkin, and Leech (2008) develop peer groups for funds that do not fit a particular index or benchmark using the example of multisector bond funds.

Other studies imply that funds are misclassified according to broad portfolio investment objectives or fund titles. Ben Dor and Jagannathan (2003) claim that many funds change their style or operate in a manner that is inconsistent with their investment objective. Various authors such as Brown and Goetzmann (1997) and Di Bartolomeo and Witowski (1997) also note the ambiguity of broad style groupings and the potential for misclassification.

Chan et al. (2002) note style drift as a potential problem in the case of some underperforming funds. Style drift occurs when a fund starts to employ a style other than the original selected style. According to Kudish (1995), managers do not change style, even if that style is underperforming, for both business and philosophical reasons. Detzel and Weigand (1998) also support this view.

In summary, RBSA still has a role to play in style analysis, particularly in areas where obtaining timely and transparent data is difficult such as for hedge funds or multisector funds (Ben Dor et al., 2008). Given the abundance of sophisticated style indices, RBSA's appeal may be limited for single asset portfolios such as equity investment funds because the availability of sophisticated style indices or portfolio characteristics data may perform this role more efficiently.

RBSA OR CBSA?

Much debate exists in the literature about the relative merits of RBSA or CBSA (Coggin and Fabozzi, 2003). Ben Dor and Jagannathan (2003) favor RBSA as a means of evaluation of asset allocation and performance measurement allowing investors to evaluate the nature of active style and selection decisions taken by an investment manager. They conclude that RBSA may be useful, especially as a precursor to CBSA, but specifying the correct benchmarks is critical to avoid misinterpreting the degree of active management and the historical nature of the method could lead to a delay in picking up style changes. Ben Dor and Jagannathan also note the risk of indicating false style signals as correlations in the style indices may give the appearance of style changes that have not actually occurred and are merely anomalies caused by index construction and correlation. Surz (2003) suggests that the RBSA and CBSA methodologies could be used to differentiate between skill and style. RBSA being used to identify the style component and CBSA being used to identify the two components of skill: sector allocation and stock selection.

In his review of RBSA and CBSA, Radcliffe (2003) concludes that neither analysis completely dominates the other model in terms of explaining future returns. He also states that using all style information and being aware of the strengths and weaknesses of each model used is important to gain insights into a portfolio's true style characteristics.

Buetow and Ratner (2000) and Rekenthaler, Gambera, and Charlson (2004) conclude that CBSA is a more reliable method of style analysis than RBSA. In a comprehensive review of mutual fund style, Chan et al. (2002) conclude that where the results differ CBSA does a better job of predicting future fund performance than RBSA. Mason et al. (2011) find that RBSA and CBSA may be complementary and may be used on a combined basis. Finally, when comparing benchmarking methods used in academic research and by investment practitioners, Chan et al. (2009) find benchmarking measures using size and value-growth orientation accurately reflect investment styles but more comprehensive measures of portfolio characteristics do a better job of matching equity managers' value-growth orientation than a simple PB rank. Thus, while on balance CBSA may produce more accurate assessment of style, both CBSA and RBSA work best together wherever possible in order to get a more comprehensive assessment of investment style.

PERFORMANCE OF INVESTMENT FUNDS: FACTOR MODELS AND BENCHMARKS

This section concentrates on the recent literature comparing investment managers' returns with a benchmark or model having similar risk and return properties developed in the wake of Fama and French (1992) and Carhart (1997). Their factor models and Jensen's (1968) alpha are still part of a range of models being used to measure risk-adjusted performance in recent studies such as Kosowski, Timmermann, Wermers, and White (2006), Busse, Goyal, and Wahal (2010), and Fama and French (2010), who consider whether funds' performance reflect luck or skill.

Studies of the performance of investment funds focus on four key issues. First, do funds on average outperform an "otherwise equivalent" benchmark? Argon and Ferson (2006) describe an otherwise equivalent benchmark as an investment alternative that offers the same risk-reward characteristics as the fund under review. This alternative may be a model such as the three-factor model of Fama and French (1992), or it may represent a style index such as the Russell 1000 Growth index, which is representative of a designated style's investment universe. Second, are there segments of outperformance at the top or bottom of the performance spectrum that are statistically significant? Third, if abnormal performers exist, do they exist due to luck or skill? Fourth, does performance persist from one period to the next?

Some studies such as Wermers (2000) suggest that elements of skill exist at the pre-cost investment skill level but that does not filter through to the ultimate investor. Grinblatt and Titman (1993) support the view that mutual fund managers have some investment skill to the extent that they have the ability to pick stocks that outperform relevant benchmarks before costs. This evidence is counterbalanced by others who find little evidence of skill, including Lakonishok, Shleifer, Vishny, Hart, and Perry (1992) and Carhart (1997). They find that, where abnormal performance exists and persists, it tends to be prevalent amongst the poorest performers. Carhart also identifies a form of persistence that became the fourth factor in many performance models: the existence of momentum in fund returns. This momentum factor is due to a short-term continuation of stock price momentum generated by stocks already held in the portfolio. Fama and French (2010) report that the momentum factor has the largest impact of all the factors on performance including the market return. Recent literature including Busse et al. (2010) confirms Lehmann and Modest's (1987) finding that mutual fund performance is sensitive to the choice of the benchmark or model chosen, which is an important consideration when evaluating investment skill.

Daniel et al. (1997) construct passive characteristics based benchmarks based on size, PB, and lagged returns of actual portfolio holdings. This approach addresses some concerns that models typically used in performance studies may be unable to identify abnormal performance if a fund's style characteristics differ markedly from the benchmark portfolio. The authors find that when using these characteristics-based benchmarks, some evidence of skill exists before deducting fees, but this excess performance is approximately equal to the fees charged. As a result, at the net level, the average fund is unlikely to add value. Such findings are common in the literature and are consistent with the equilibrium theory of Berk and Green (2004) that mutual fund managers can extract economic rent that cancels out the benefits of skill. Argon and Ferson (2006) define funds that generate excess returns relative to their benchmark at the gross level, i.e., before all costs, as having "investment skill" and funds that generate excess returns relative to their benchmark at the net level as adding value.

Next, the chapter focuses on recent performance literature on the subject of persistence of performance and luck versus skill. Barras, Scalliet, and Wermers (2010) develop a model that controls for "false discoveries" of abnormal performance, i.e., mutual funds that through luck rather than skill generate abnormal return. Their conclusions seem to send mixed signals about the effectiveness of active management as they state that about 75 percent of funds exhibit zero alpha. The authors note, however, that poor overall performance is due to the existence of a minority of extremely poor performing funds with the majority of active funds generating a net alpha that is positive.

Kosowski et al. (2006) introduce a bootstrap methodology to infer what proportion of funds might exhibit skill compared to a random sample, which represents luck. Fama and French (2010) adopt a modified version of this technique for the US mutual fund market and Busse et al. (2010) do the same for the US institutional investment market. These studies focus on the distribution of performance amongst investment funds as well as the overall sample. They pay particular attention to the performance tails, typically the top decile and bottom decile performance, and also the difference between the best and worst performers.

Despite similarities in methodology, the results differ among studies and in some instances across models within the same study.

Kosowski et al. (2006) find that a sizeable minority of equity mutual fund managers add value in terms of performance: The positive alpha generated more than covers their costs, and this is found to persist. When tested with their bootstrap methodology, the authors conclude that the performance of the best and worst managers is not solely due to luck. However, Fama and French (2010) contend that insufficient evidence exists to reject the hypothesis that active management does not create true value added returns.

Bollen and Busse (2005) find evidence of short-term persistence of US mutual funds. When considering the institutional equity investment market, however, Busse et al. (2010) do not find evidence of superior performance in aggregate. Yet, they report that some investment managers may exhibit superior investment returns for long periods of time. Perhaps the most interesting conclusion that they draw is the need to choose an appropriate measure of risk and return as indicated by Lehmann and Modest (1987). Busse et al. explain that interpreting their results depends on the benchmark under consideration. An investor selecting and measuring on the basis of a single factor (CAPM) or three-factor model might interpret their results as providing some support for the existence of superior returns with some evidence of persistence. However, if the same investor factors in momentum, the results from the four-factor model performance would not persist. Busse et al. also find mixed results when using conditional factor models, which leads them to conclude that in aggregate there is no statistical evidence of alpha estimates significantly different to zero.

Cremers and Petajisto (2009) also highlight the concept of identifying the correct index and use a range of indices for their analysis of active management. Using an inappropriate benchmark leads to a built-in tracking error, which hinders evaluation using tools such as the information ratio. Therefore, while the recent literature on investment performance provides mixed evidence on creating added value by active managers, undertaking performance analysis to avoid the worst performers might be rewarded.

Summary and Conclusions

The literature on equity investment styles has evolved towards a more multidimensional growth-value orientation approach. Although the major index and data providers have also adopted this approach, still no universally accepted approach exists. Such developments are allowing more differentiated analysis of investment styles and improving the identification of peer groups and appropriate benchmarks. These improvements greatly aid the selection and evaluation of investment funds. The awareness of style cycles or style behavior could be useful when reviewing managers or undertaking due diligence before selection, as well as enhancing the benefits of diversification and risk-reward attribution. The review of methods of style identification based on portfolio holdings and return based analysis suggests that characteristics based analysis using portfolio holdings may have some advantages over returns based analysis for equity investment style. Still, both may have a part to play in style assessment. In terms of investment performance, no conclusive evidence exists that equity fund managers in aggregate add value, but there may be a case for detailed performance analysis if only to avoid the worst performing managers. The recent developments in performance analysis underline the importance of establishing the appropriate benchmark or peer group and that is the role of style analysis.

Discussion Questions

1. Contrast the key differences between determination of a stock's style and a fund's style.
2. Discuss the ability to evaluate a growth fund without considering growth.
3. Distinguish between RBSA and CBSA.
4. Discuss evidence associated with the outperformance of "otherwise equivalent benchmarks."

References

Abarbanell, Jeffery S., Brian J. Bushee, and Jana S. Raedy. 2003. "Institutional Investor Preferences and Price Pressure: The Case of Corporate Spin-Offs." *Journal of Business* 76:2, 233–261.

Amenc, Noel, Daphne Sfeir, and Lionel Martellini. 2003. "An Integrated Framework for Style Analysis and Performance Measurement." *Journal of Performance Measurement* 7:4, 35–41.

Argon, George O., and Wayne E. Ferson. 2006. "Portfolio Performance Evaluation." *Foundations and Trends in Finance* 2:2, 83–190.

Arshanapalli, Bala, T. Daniel Coggin, and John A. Doukas. 1998. "Multifactor Asset Pricing Analysis of International Value Investment Strategies." *Journal of Portfolio Management* 24:4, 10–23.

Bailey, Jeffery V., and David E. Tierney. 1995. "Controlling Misfit Through the Use of Dynamic Completeness Funds." In Robert A. Klein and Jess Lederman (eds.), *Equity Style Management: Evaluating and Selecting Investment Styles*, 433–478. Chicago: Irwin Professional Publishing.

Barras, Laurent, Olivier Scalliet, and Russ Wermers. 2010. "False Discoveries in Mutual Fund Performance: Measuring Luck in Estimated Alphas." *Journal of Finance* 65:1, 179–216.

Bassett, Gilbert W., and Hsiu-Lang Chen. 2001. "Portfolio Style: Return-Based Attribution Using Quantile Regression." *Empirical Economics* 26:1, 293–305.

Ben Dor, Arik, Vernon Budinger, Lev Dynkin, and Kenneth Leech. 2008. "Constructing Peer Benchmarks for Mutual Funds: A Style Analysis-Based Approach." *Journal of Portfolio Management* 34:2, 65–77.

Ben Dor, Arik, and Ravi Jagannathan. 2003. "Style Analysis: Asset Allocation and Performance Evaluation." In T. Daniel Coggin and Frank J. Fabozzi (eds.), *Handbook of Equity Style Management*, 3rd edition, 1–45. Hoboken, NJ: John Wiley & Sons.

Ben Dor, Arik, Ravi Jagannathan, and Iwan Meir. 2003. "Understanding Mutual Fund and Hedge Fund Styles Using Return-Based Style Analysis." *Journal of Investment Management* 1:1, 94–134.

Berk, Jonathan, and Richard C. Green. 2004. "Mutual Fund Flows and Performance in Rational Markets." *Journal of Political Economy* 112:6, 1269–1295.

Bollen, Nicholas P. B., and Jeffrey A. Busse. 2005. "Short-Term Persistence in Mutual Fund Performance." *Review of Financial Studies* 18:2, 569–597.

Brown, Stephen J., and William. N. Goetzmann. 1997. "Mutual Fund Styles." *Journal of Financial Economics* 43:3, 373–399.

Brush, John S. 2007. "Value and Growth, Theory and Practice: A Fallacy That Value Beats Growth." *Journal of Portfolio Management* 33:3, 22–32.

Buetow, Gerald W., and Hal Ratner. 2000. "The Dangers in Using Return Based Style Analysis in Asset Allocation." *Journal of Wealth Management* 3:2, 26–38.

Busse, Jeffrey A., Amit Goyal, and Sunil Wahal. 2010. "Performance Persistence in Institutional Investment Management." *Journal of Finance* 65:2, 765–790.

Carhart, Mark M. 1997. "On Persistence in Mutual Fund Performance." *Journal of Finance* 52:1, 57–82.

Chan, Louis K. C., Hsui-Lang Chen, and Josef Lakonishok. 2002. "On Mutual Fund Investment Styles." *Review of Financial Studies* 15:5, 1407–1437.

Chan, Louis K. C., Stephen G. Dimmock, and Josef Lakonishok. 2009. "Benchmarking Money Manager Performance: Issues and Evidence." *Review of Financial Studies* 22:11, 4553–4599.

Chen, Hsui-Lang. 2003. "On Characteristics Momentum." *Journal of Behavioral Finance* 4:3, 137–156.

Chen, Hsui-Lang, and Werner de Bondt. 2004. "Style Momentum Within the S&P-500 Index." *Journal of Empirical Finance* 11:4, 483–507.

Christopherson, Jon A. 1995. "Equity Style Classifications: Adventures in Return Pattern Analysis." *Journal of Portfolio Management* 21:3, 32–43.

Christopherson, Jon A., and C. Nola Williams. 1997. "Equity Style: What It Is and Why It Matters." In T. Daniel Coggin, Frank J. Fabozzi, and Robert D. Arnott (eds.), *Handbook of Equity Style Management*, 2nd edition, 1–19. Hoboken, NJ: John Wiley & Sons.

Coggin, T. Daniel, and Frank J. Fabozzi (eds.). 2003. *Handbook of Equity Style Management*, 3rd edition. Hoboken, NJ: John Wiley & Sons.

Connor, Gregory, and Robert A. Korajczyk. 1991. "The Attributes, Behavior, and Performance of U.S. Mutual Funds." *Review of Quantitative Finance and Accounting* 1:1, 5–26.

Cremers, K. J. Martijn, and Antti Petajisto. 2009. "How Active Is Your Fund Manager? A New Measure That Predicts Performance." *Review of Financial Studies* 22:9, 3329–3365.

Cunningham, Lawrence A. (ed.). 2002. *The Essays of Warren Buffet: Lessons for Investors and Managers*, 4th edition. Singapore: John Wiley & Sons.

Damodaran, Aswath. 2003. *Investment Philosophies: Successful Strategies and the Investors Who Made Them Work.* Hoboken, NJ: John Wiley & Sons.

Daniel, Kent, Mark Grinblatt, Sheridan Titman, and Russ Wermers. 1997. "Measuring Mutual Fund Performance with Characteristic-Based Benchmarks." *Journal of Finance* 52:3, 1035–1058.

Davis, James L. 2001. "Mutual Fund Performance and Manager Style." *Financial Analysts Journal* 57:1, 19–27.

de Allaume, William J. D. 1995. "The Sponsor's Perspective." In Robert A. Klein and Jess Lederman (eds.), *Equity Style Management: Evaluating and Selecting Investment Styles*, 49–66. Chicago: Irwin Professional Publishing.

de Bondt, Werner F. M., and Richard H. Thaler. 1987. "Further Evidence on Investor Overreaction and Stock Market Seasonality." *Journal of Finance* 42:3, 557–581.

Detzel, F. Larry, and Robert A. Weigand. 1998. "Explaining Persistence in Mutual Fund Performance." *Financial Services Review* 7:1, 45–55.

Di Bartolomeo, Dan, and Eric Witowski. 1997. "Mutual Fund Misclassification: Evidence Based On Style Analysis." *Financial Analysts Journal* 53:5, 32–43.

Falkenstein, Eric G. 1996. "Preferences for Stock Characteristics as Revealed by Mutual Fund Portfolio Holdings." *Journal of Finance* 51:1, 111–135.

Fama, Eugene F. 1972. "Components of Investment Performance." *Journal of Finance* 27:3, 551–567.

Fama, Eugene F., and Kenneth R. French. 1992. "The Cross-Section of Expected Stock Returns." *Journal of Finance* 47:2, 427–465.

Fama, Eugene F., and Kenneth R. French. 2010. "Luck Versus Skill in the Cross-Section of Alpha Estimates." *Journal of Finance* 65:5, 1915–1947.

Farrell, James L. 1974. "Analyzing Covariation of Returns to Determine Homogenous Stock Groupings." *Journal of Business* 47:2, 186–207.

Fisher, Philip A. 2003. Common Stocks and Uncommon Profits and Other Writings. Hoboken, NJ: John Wiley & Sons.

Graham, Benjamin, and David L. Dodd. 1988. *Security Analysis*. New York: McGraw-Hill.

Grinblatt, Mark, and Sheridan Titman. 1993. "Performance Measurement Without Benchmarks: An Examination of Mutual Fund Returns." *Journal of Business* 66:1, 47–68.

Jensen, Michael C. 1968. "The Performance of Mutual Funds in the Period 1945–1964." *Journal of Finance* 23:2, 389–416.

Kaplan, Paul D., J. A. Knowles, and Don Phillips. 2003. "More Depth and Breadth Than the Style Box: The Morningstar Lens." In T. Daniel Coggin and Frank J. Fabozzi (eds.), *Handbook of Equity Style Management*, 3rd edition, 131–158. Hoboken, NJ: John Wiley & Sons.

King, Benjamin F. 1966. "Market and Industry Factors in Stock Price Behavior." *Journal of Business* 39:1, 139–190.

Kosowski, Robert, Allan Timmermann, Russ Wermers, and Hal White. 2006. "Can Mutual Fund 'Stars' Really Pick Stocks? New Evidence from a Bootstrap Analysis." *Journal of Finance* 61:6, 2551–2595.

Kudish, D. J. 1995. "Reversing Manager-Selection Failure: Using Style Allocation to Improve Fund Returns." In Robert A. Klein and Jess Lederman (eds.), *Equity Style Management: Evaluating and Selecting Investment Styles*, 399–420. Chicago: Irwin Professional Publishing.

Lakonishok, Josef, Andrei Shleifer, and Robert W. Vishny. 1994. "Contrarian Investment, Extrapolation and Risk." *Journal of Finance* 49:5, 1541–1578.

Lakonishok, Josef, Andrei Shleifer, Robert W. Vishny, Oliver Hart, and George L. Perry. 1992. "The Structure and Performance of the Money Management Industry." *Brookings Papers on Economic Activity—Microeconomics*, 1992, 339–391. Washington, DC: The Brookings Institution.

Lehmann, Bruce N., and David M. Modest. 1987. "Mutual Fund Performance Evaluation: A Comparison of Benchmarks and Benchmark Comparisons." *Journal of Finance* 42:2, 233–265.

Leinweber, David J., David Krider, and Peter Swank. 1995. "Evolutionary Ideas in International Style Management." *Investment Management Reflections* No. 1 First Quadrant Corporation.

Mason, Andrew, Thomas, Steve, and Frank J.A. McGroarty. 2012. "Style Analysis for Diversified US Equity Funds" *Journal of Asset Management* 13:3, 170–185.

Mason, Andrew, Steve Thomas, and Frank J. McGroarty. 2011. "Complementary or Contradictory? Combining Returns Based & Characteristics Based Investment Style Analysis." Available at http://papers.ssrn.com/sol3/papers.cfm?abstract_id=1868831.

Michaud, Richard O. 1998. "Is Value Multidimensional? Implications for Style Management and Global Stock Selection." *Journal of Investing* 7:1, 61–65.

Prather, Laurie, William J. Bertin, and Thomas Henker. 2004. "Mutual Fund Characteristics, Managerial Attributes, and Fund Performance." *Review of Financial Economics* 13:4, 305–326.

Radcliffe, Robert C. 2003. "Models of Equity Style Information." In T. Daniel Coggin and Frank J. Fabozzi (eds.), *Handbook of Equity Style Management*, 3rd edition, 75–108. Hoboken, NJ: John Wiley & Sons.

Rekenthaler, John, Michele Gambera, and Joshua Charlson. 2004. "Estimating Portfolio Style in U.S. Equity Funds: A Comparative Study of Portfolio-Based Fundamental Style Analysis and Returns-Based Style Analysis." Morningstar Research Report. Chicago: Morningstar.

Rosenberg, Barr, and Andrew Rudd. 1982. "Factor-Related and Specific Returns of Common Stocks: Serial Correlation and Market Inefficiency." *Journal of Finance* 37:2, 543–554.

Sharpe, William F. 1964. "Capital Asset Prices: A Theory of Market Equilibrium under Conditions of Risk." *Journal of Finance* 19:3, 425–442.

Sharpe, William F. 1967. "Portfolio Analysis." *Journal of Financial and Quantitative Analysis* 2:2, 76–84.

Sharpe, William F. 1992. "Asset Allocation: Management Style and Performance Measurement." *Journal of Portfolio Management* 18:2, 7–19.

Slager, Alfred, and Kees Koedijk. 2007. "Investment Beliefs: Every Asset Manager Should Have Them." *Journal of Portfolio Management* 33:3, 77–83.

Sorensen, Eric H., and Craig J. Lazzara. 1995. "Equity Style Management: The Case of Growth and Value." In Robert A. Klein and Jess Lederman (eds.), *Equity Style Management: Evaluating and Selecting Investment Styles*, 67–84. Chicago: Irwin Professional Publishing.

Speidell, Lawrence S., and John Graves. 2003. "Are Growth and Value Dead? A New Framework for Equity Investment Styles." In T. Daniel Coggin and Frank J. Fabozzi (eds.), *Handbook of Equity Style Management*, 3rd edition, 171–193. Hoboken, NJ: John Wiley & Sons.

Surz, Ronald J. 2003. "Using Portfolio Holdings to Improve the Search for Skill." In T. Daniel Coggin and Frank J. Fabozzi (eds.), *Handbook of Equity Style Management*, 3rd edition, 159–170. Hoboken, NJ: John Wiley & Sons.

ter Horst, Jenke R., Theo E. Nijman, and Frans A. de Roon. 2004. "Evaluating Style Analysis." *Journal of Empirical Finance* 11:1, 29–53.

Vardharaj, Raman, and Frank J. Fabozzi. 2007. "Sector, Style, Region: Explaining Stock Allocation Performance." *Financial Analysts Journal* 63:3, 59–70.

Waring, M. Barton, and Laurence B. Siegel. 2003. "The Dimensions of Active Management." *Journal of Portfolio Management* 29:2, 35–51.

Wermers, Russ. 2000. "Mutual Fund Performance: An Empirical Decomposition into Stock-Picking Talent, Style, Transactions Costs, and Expenses." *Journal of Finance* 55:4, 1655–1695.

24

Use of Derivatives

MATTHIEU LEBLANC
Head of the Financial Research Department,
Edmond de Rothschild Asset Management

Introduction

In the sixth century BCE, a famous Greek geometer named Thales expected a bumper crop of olives in a horizon of nine months. With this scenario in mind, he secured the exclusive use of all the oil presses in the area for a reasonable price, the owners being too happy in the moment to realize an immediate and certain income. In autumn, the harvest was so huge that Thales could fix the rent for the presses at high prices and became wealthy. Before that, in the fourteenth century BCE in Egypt, merchants bought and sold wheat before the flooding of the Nile and sowing seeds. These two examples show that futures and options were already integrated into business practices at least since human antiquity. Through the creation of modern exchanges, derivatives have become essential tools in managing financial risks, as well as agricultural, climatic, and natural resources risks.

The ability of derivatives to provide facilities for hedging, investing, and arbitrage favored their growth. But beyond these uses, derivatives have utility in the function of risk transfer. Before their creation, industrial companies maintained a cash cushion to protect themselves against the changing value of commodities, interest rates, or currencies. Derivatives save substantial capital by removing the risks that are not part of their business model (through the intermediation of a bank to other agents). Moreover, derivatives have allowed for the specialization of market participants. Previously, managing risk in a portfolio could be achieved with diversification that required handling various products, such as equities, bonds, currencies, and commodities, and estimating correlations. Today, a 100 percent equity portfolio manager can control his exposure and finely reduce his risk based on his market expectations.

The purpose of this chapter is to illustrate the use of derivatives in portfolios. While many practices are transferable from one market to another, some of their characteristics will imply investment decisions. For example, the implied volatility curve as a function of the strike price has different characteristics for equity markets than for currency markets. The first one is described by a skewed (or asymmetric) smile (so called skew) that looks like a one-sided parabola; the second is described by a symmetric parabola (a smile) that reflects different risk perceptions from market's participants. Therefore, some strategies are very specific. This chapter focuses only on using equity and index derivatives. The spectrum of products will be reduced to the listed derivatives with no counterparty risk in theory (except that of the clearinghouse): futures, calls, and puts with which the reader is assumed to be familiar. More complex products often have insufficient liquidity to be used in most of the active asset managers' processes. Finally, their value is subject to several levels of uncertainty (modeling and parameters) instead of standard products whose pricing models, even if questionable, are part of standard market practice.

The valuation of futures contracts is not problematic. Because futures contracts are marked to market daily, their value is zero. However the "price" of the contract, which determines the notional principal, is linked to the underlying security's value taking account of the maturity and the income (e.g., dividends or coupons) attached to the security until the contract's maturity. Options valuation is more complex and many works deal with option pricing of which the most famous are Wilmott (2006), Alexander (2008), Kwok (2008), and Hull (2011). Rarer are the books sharing investment strategies related to options in a portfolio of securities.

Options are on the border between two financial activities. The first activity is based on risk-neutral probability that determines the fair price of an option. This price is obtained as the price of a replication strategy of the payoff of the option, based on changes in the value of the underlying asset or security (hereafter also called the underlying). Here, the option seller hedges his strategy by taking a dynamic (and sometimes systematic) position in the underlying security without a particular scenario (on the underlying) in mind. The second activity is based on historical (or real or physical) probability that reflects the conviction of a trend in the movements of the underlying asset and then requires the formulation of a view. The combination of these two approaches is at the heart of constructing investment strategies based on derivatives. The sensitivities of the option price to market parameters (determined with the risk neutrality framework) combining with a view on these parameters (real world) allow selecting the appropriate contracts.

Some books show derivatives as tools to gain exposure to changes in the underlying asset. They are often designed for individual investors rather than professional investors because derivatives offer easier access than the underlying security itself (such as currencies, oil, or wheat). Johnson (1999), McMillan (2002, 2004), Kaeppel (2002), Fontanills (2005), and Yates (2009) explain the important points in selecting an option strategy focusing on the short-term investment through options or portfolio insurance.

In an Undertaking for Collective Investment Schemes in Transferable Securities (UCITS) fund, the core assets are held several months or even more than a year and represent the long-term, called *strategic asset allocation* (SAA). Investment in derivatives is not usually the main source of income but a means for risk management or generation of short-term performance: as a part (or a whole) of the so-called *tactical asset allocation* (TAA). Using derivatives becomes a piece of the investment process of the fund that mixes several securities (diversification of assets) and several time horizons (temporal diversification). Within a fund, derivatives offer a means of reactivity in terms of protecting the value of assets or exposure to risk factors, already present or not in the portfolio. The evolution of the investment process with derivatives requires a good understanding of the impact of introducing them into the structure of the overall portfolio. Scherer (2007) provides an overview of risk budgeting techniques for stocks and asset classes. By smart linearization of the options, these techniques extend to nonlinear patterns asset returns. Wilmott (2006) discusses the delta-gamma approximation that is useful to include options in a risk budgeting approach.

This chapter provides the prerequisites for using derivatives in portfolio management. It also explains how options are used in asset management. The first section is dedicated to the use of futures positions combined with traditional assets. The rest of the chapter features the use of standard options. The second part introduces the options from a static point of view, that is to say, without the use of valuation models. Then, a follow-up section discusses the dynamic point of view of these products, particularly the management of the "Greeks" that measures the options sensitivities with a focus on volatility and passage of time. The last section presents basic options strategies associated with long positions in equity products. The practice of risk budgeting in constructing and analyzing a position is also discussed. The basis of this chapter is a course for professionals of the financial industry (Leblanc, 2010b, 2011).

Futures Contracts in a Portfolio

An investment in a derivative contract requires knowing how it works and how the clearinghouse ensures that the exchange works. For example, clearing conditions of the Eurex Exchange are contained in a 405-page document (Eurex Exchange, 2012).

Buyers and sellers of contracts are subject to future price changes. The price converges to the underlying price at the term of the contract. Basically, in the case of an index future, each party has to provide margin to cover its position, i.e., to ensure its ability to pay for losses. The eligible asset that serves as margin is usually cash, but other securities such as stocks are allowed. In this case, each risky asset category provides a margin amount according to its risk assessment by the clearinghouse. However, at the term of the contract, the settlement is in cash. Every business day, profits and losses arising out of open positions are determined and margin calls are made relative to a reference daily price called the *settlement price*. Because the investor is usually not a clearing member, he adjusts his margin position through a broker-dealer approved by the clearer.

For index futures, the margin is often given as a number of index points. For example, if an index level is 1,000, the margin amount (imposed by the clearer) could be 100 points. The value of one index point depends on underlying assets and is fixed by the exchange: EUR 25 for futures contracts on the Dax index;

CHF 10 for futures contracts on the SMI index; and USD 100 for futures contract on the Dow Jones Sector Titans indices for the Eurex exchange.

Margin mechanisms imply leverage because a small amount of cash (the margin) is enough to expose the trader to the variation of the notional amount of the contract defined as the level of the future multiplied by the index point value. For instance, if the Dax index is at 5,000, the margin amount is 500 points, an investor needs €25(500) = €12,500 to take a notional position of €25(5,000) = €125,000. In this example, the leverage is 10 (€125,000/€12,500).

IMPACT OF A FUTURE POSITION ON THE RETURN OF A PORTFOLIO

The first issue to understand is how a futures position modifies the return of a portfolio. If the value at time t of a portfolio is denoted P_t, its performance between two dates t and T is shown in Equation 24.1

$$R_{t,T}^{P,0} = \sum_{i=0}^{n} w_t^i R_{t,T}^i \qquad (24.1)$$

where w_t^i is the weight of portfolio assets at beginning of period $[t,T]$. The asset i = 0 is the cash of the portfolio from which the *deposit* (i.e., the amount required by the broker for a futures investing) is subtracted (a negative position meaning a borrow), and $R_{t,T}^i$ is the performance of the ith asset. The performance of the portfolio adjusted of K futures is shown in Equation 24.2

$$R_{t,T}^{P,K} = R_{t,T}^{P,0} + K p_t \frac{F_T - F_t}{F_t} \qquad (24.2)$$

where, at time t, $p_t = \dfrac{m F_t}{P_t}$ is the weight (in the sense of exposure) of a future of price F_t; m is the value of the index point; and $m F_t$ the notional amount of investment in one future.

RISK MANAGEMENT OF A PORTFOLIO

The variance of the portfolio performance described by the Equation 24.2 gives a measure of the portfolio risk and the impact of the futures position on it. Taking the variance of Equation 24.2 results in Equation 24.3:

$$\mathrm{var}(R_{t,T}^{P,K}) = \mathrm{var}(R_{t,T}^{P,0}) + (K p_t)^2 \, \mathrm{var}(R_{t,T}^F) + 2K p_t \, \mathrm{cov}\, ar(R_{t,T}^{P,0}; R_{t,T}^F) \quad (24.3)$$

where $R_{t,T}^F$ is the performance of the future during the period $[t,T]$.

The relationship in Equation 24.3 could be used to pick K according to a target level of standard deviation for the portfolio. Further, the minimum risk is achieved as shown in Equation 24.4 for K^* such that

$$K^* p_t = -\frac{\operatorname{cov}ar(R_{t,T}^{P,O};R_{t,T}^{F})}{\operatorname{var}(R_{t,T}^{F})} \tag{24.4}$$

By injecting this term in the expression of the previous variance calculation, the risk of the portfolio is "canceled" with a position in a future if and only if the portfolio and the future are perfectly correlated. Otherwise, residual (or *basis*) risk always exists. This approach can be generalized by optimizing a Markowitz-type utility function (Markowitz, 1952), for example, and then by introducing the manager's expectations (Leblanc, 2011).

MANAGEMENT OF THE EXPOSURE OF A PORTFOLIO

The rigorous identification of the exposure of a portfolio to different risk factors is beyond the scope of this chapter. Several approaches are standard such as the capital asset pricing model (CAPM) and its generalization given by the model resulting from the arbitrage pricing theory (APT). The estimation of these models requires applying statistical techniques, such as ordinary least squares, Kalman filter, or partial least squares, which can provide quite different results. To illustrate this approach and simplify the notation, an assumption is made that CAPM explains the return on assets and portfolios (this assumption is in fact a market practice). A single risk factor will be considered here, but the generalization is immediate. During the period [t,T], the expected return of the ith asset as a function of the reference market (designed by M) is given by Equation 24.5

$$r_{t,T} + \beta_{t,T}^{i}(R_{t,T}^{M} - r_{t,T}) \tag{24.5}$$

where r is a risk-free rate; and β is the sensitivity of the risk premium of the ith asset according to the market's return R^{M}. By comparing performance achieved over a period with this theoretical return, Jensen's alpha (Jensen, 1968) denoted by a is generated as shown in Equation 24.6:

$$R_{t,T}^{i} = \alpha_{t,T}^{i} + r_{t,T} + \beta_{t,T}^{i}(R_{t,T}^{M} - r_{t,T}) \tag{24.6}$$

Applied to a portfolio, this approach provides the manager's alpha, which can be negative or positive. In order to keep the calculations simple, the estimated beta will be carried out directly on performance and not on the risk premium whose definition can vary. Equation 24.7 shows the simplified model:

$$R_{t,T}^{i} = \alpha_{t,T}^{i} + \beta_{t,T}^{i} R_{t,T}^{M} \tag{24.7}$$

Combining Equation 24.1 and Equation 24.7, the portfolio beta with K futures is written as Equation 24.8:

$$\beta_{t,T}^{P,K} = \sum_{i=0}^{n} p_t^{i}\beta_{t,T}^{i} + K p_t^{F} \beta_{t,T}^{F} = \beta_{t,T}^{P,0} + K p_t^{F} \beta_{t,T}^{F} \tag{24.8}$$

Thus, exposure to market fluctuations will be amplified (target beta $\beta^* > 1$) or reduced (target beta $\beta^* < 1$) with K^* future contracts such that $K^* = (\beta^* - \beta_{t,T}^{P,0})/(p_t^F \beta_{t,T}^F)$. From Equation 24.7, it follows that $R_{t,T}^{P,K} = \alpha_{t,T}^P + \beta_{t,T}^{P,K} R_{t,T}^M$. The variance of the portfolio is now shown in Equation 24.9:

$$\text{var}(R_{t,T}^{P,K}) = \text{var}(\alpha_{t,T}^{P,0}) + (\beta_{t,T}^{P,K})^2 \text{var}(R_{t,T}^M) + 2*\beta_{t,T}^{P,K} \text{cov}\,ar(\alpha_{t,T}^{P,0}; R_{t,T}^M). \quad (24.9)$$

From here market risk will be eliminated by imposing the constraint $\beta_{t,T}^{P,K} = 0$.

WHY AND HOW TO USE FUTURES?

As a product with linear payoff, the decision to invest in futures is realized in the same way as stocks or exchange traded funds (ETFs), i.e., based on the antici- pation on the underlying asset. However, two points are worth noting. First, several contracts with different maturities are available for the same underlying exposure. For an investor, the choice between these maturities usually results in the level of liquidity of each contract and a basis risk that grows with time. To maintain a position, the manager sometimes initiates a *rollover* (i.e., he bal- ances his position on a short maturity contract with a contract with more distant maturity). This rollover is usually performed a few weeks before the term of the contract because, during the last month, the future may have (depending on the underlying asset and the type of delivery, physical, or cash) a behavior uncorre- lated with the underlying asset. Second, the impact of anticipated dividends in the future prices is crucial: the (theoretical) price of the future must take into account the present value of dividends whose ex-date is before the maturity of the future contract.

As described in the previous sections, futures allow the asset manager to adjust his position on the risk factors represented by the underlying asset. Although futures contracts exist for individual stocks, the manager usually uses index futures because one operation is enough to cover overall market risk expo- sure (macro hedging). Further, the greater liquidity of index futures contracts provides easy negotiations. Finally, index futures give the manager the ability to temporarily cover the market risk of securities in its portfolio (the *systematic risk*) while retaining the benefit of its stock selection (the *specific risk*). This is proved when using Equations 24.1 and 24.7. As long as Jensen's alpha is greater than the risk-free rate, hedging will be more profitable than the disinvestment. Additionally, transaction costs are much more expensive for securities transac- tions than futures contracts.

Futures pricing is relatively simple to understand because their behavior is similar to the underlying security. However, the manager has to use leverage carefully. Hedging with futures will prevent the need to disinvest the portfolio, if the scenario is bearish in the short term. This contract has no value in contrast to the options discussed in the following sections.

Benefits from Options Investment and Static Analysis

The asymmetric payout profile of options reflects the difference between the buyer of the option, who has the ability (without obligation) to buy (with a call contract) or sell (with a put contract) a certain amount of an underlying asset at a price fixed in advance, and the seller, who has to carry out the terms of the contract upon the exercise of the option. Unlike futures, the options contracts have a nonzero value (called the *premium*) that the seller (option writer) receives to compensate for this asymmetry of rights. If the buyer immediately exercised the option, the value obtained is named *intrinsic value* and the difference between premium and intrinsic value is the *time value* of the option. In the following discussions, *out-of-the-money* (or OTM) options refer to options with zero intrinsic value; *in-the-money* (ITM) options refer to options with positive intrinsic value; and *at-the-money* (ATM) options refer to the case where the price of the underlying asset is equal to the exercise price (also named the moneyness of the option's contract). An option is called European if the right to buy or sell is only exercisable at the maturity of the contract. An option is said to be American if this right is exercisable until the maturity.

In a financial market, different players use options in different ways. Specifically, an investor (especially a nonfinancial buyer) has structurally long positions in options for horizons from several weeks to several months. He has directional position in an underlying asset. A day trader will invest during shorter time horizons such as a few days or one week with long-short strategies. The market maker has a nondirectional strategy on the underlying asset. He tries to anticipate future volatility of the underlying asset relative to the implied volatility (i.e., volatility trading or delta neutral strategy based on the market's current perceptions). Sinclair (2008) discusses this view as well as Natenberg (1994), Rebonato (2004), and Bittman (2009). Market makers have a key role in options markets because they always offer a price for the sale (the *offer*) and purchase (the *bid*) of the main options contracts. Other players in this market are structurers, who hedge complex options by buying listed options. Avellaneda, Levy, and Paras (1995) and Leblanc (2002) provide examples of this approach.

However, a transaction may be successful for the buyer and the seller. Both the buyer and the seller could have the right expectation, the former on the underlying asset and the latter (the market maker) on the volatility of the underlying asset. Thus, both could achieve positive returns over time. Of course, another market participant will lose money, because such exchanges are a zero sum game. Like futures, options trading is subject to clearing conditions with the Eurex Exchange (2012) serving as an example of the appropriate documentation for such conditions.

SELLING OPTIONS

The purchase of a call or put option has obvious advantages: The maximum loss is limited and known in advance while the earning potential is unbounded. Further, by leveraging, a reduced investment is sufficient to obtain exposure to large variations in the value of the underlying asset. So why sell options? Why are there sellers of options for which, by symmetry, the risk is unlimited and gain limited? The distribution of profits between (structural) sellers of options is different. For sellers, the high probability of getting a limited profit outweighs the risk of a potentially unlimited loss, as is the case with insurers or casinos. The following example shows this likelihood in which two bullish positions are illustrated in Figure 24.1: the purchase of one call and the sale of one put, both at the money.

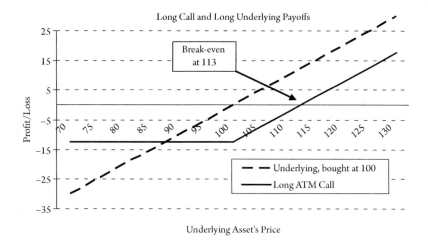

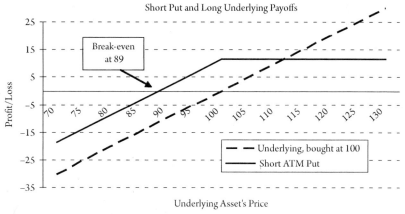

Figure 24.1 A Comparison of Two Bullish Positions. This figure shows two bullish positions. First, the purchase of one call implies paying the premium. In this case, the buyer expects a large rise of the underlying asset. Second, the sale of one put means receiving the premium. In this case, the seller expects that the underlying price will not move downward or that a rise of the underlying price will be small. At maturity, the loss starts only when the underlying value falls below 89 (Panel B), whereas the buyer (Panel A) has to expect an advance of at least 13 percent in order to register a gain. These graphs illustrate the fact that the probabilities favor the options seller because market returns more than 13 percent are less likely than returns less than 11 percent in the few days or weeks after the trade.

The *break-even point* is defined as the level (in unit or percentage terms) that the underlying asset must reach at expiration to reimburse (or offset) the premium of the option. Here, the long call position starts out at a loss (due to the premium that is paid), and the underlying asset must increase by at least 13 percent to obtain a positive return. The short position starts out at a gain (due to the premium that is received) and will experience a loss if the underlying asset drops by more than 11 percent. This example reflects the probability in favor of the option's seller to obtain a moderate gain (the premium or a part of it) because observing a market return above 13 percent is less likely than a market decline in excess of 11 percent in the few days or weeks after the trade.

HEDGING

The sale of a call option generates a gain that will protect the position from a moderate decline in asset value. On the contrary, if the decline is substantial, the purchase of a put or even the sale of a futures contract (if the option premium is considered too high) is recommended. Again, the break-even point of each optional position compared to the scenario of the manager is a way to select the strategy. In all three situations, the underlying exposure is reduced, the probability distribution is modified, and the volatility and the Value at Risk (VaR) are reduced.

TAKING ADVANTAGE OF NEUTRAL MARKETS

When a manager anticipates a tight market, he can use options to take advantage of the expected low volatility of an underlying asset. The *calendar spread* strategy is an example of a position that profits from low market volatility. The strategy consists of buying one call (or put) of a maturity greater than one month and simultaneously selling the same option (same type and strike) but of a shorter maturity. The goal of this strategy is to take advantage of the faster loss in time value of the shorter maturity option when nothing else happens. For example, assume a manager anticipates short-term stability of the Hewlett-Packard (HP) share price currently priced at $40. He could buy a 40 call contract (an ATM call) that expires in August and sell a 40 call on HP expiring in July. Assuming the strategy costs $38 ($0.38 per option x 100 options in a contract), Figure 24.2 illustrates its gain profile.

The strategy results in a net gain if the expiration interval price is between $37.70 and $42.40. The gain increases as the maturity of the sold option approaches.

OPTIONS WITHOUT MATHEMATICAL MODELING

From the definition and characteristics of the contract, certain properties, relations, or inequalities between the prices of options can be established using the principle of no arbitrage. The most famous of these is the *call-put parity* for European options. Many books such as Kwok (2008) and Hull (2011) identify

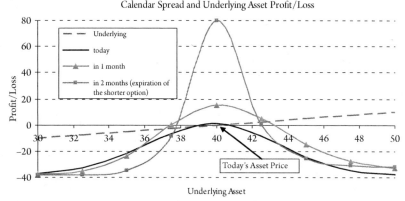

Figure 24.2 Calendar Spread Strategy. The calendar spread strategy presented here consists of buying one call or put and simultaneously selling the same option with a shorter maturity. The payoff at maturity is positive when the underlying price ends between $37.70 and $42.40. This strategy illustrates how to build an options position that profits when a lack of market volatility exists. This graph also illustrates that the carry of such a position is not always comfortable: A small change in the underlying price can lead to an immediate loss. On the figure, the "today" straight line goes less than zero as soon as the underlying asset moves.

this relationship. This subsection gives some option's price characteristics focusing on two parameters, volatility and maturity, both of which play important roles in the dynamics of option prices.

Volatility is a measure of the extent to which a stock's price moves away from its current price over time. The greater a stock's volatility, the more likely a stock's price can exceed the exercise price on the rise (favorable to the call) or the decline (favorable to the put). This scenario implies that the option's price increases with an increase in implied volatility.

The more distant the expiration of the option, the more the underlying has the opportunity to move away from the strike price, which is favorable to option's premiums and therefore increases the prices of calls and puts, European and American. Another effect comes from interest rates. For a call, the more distant the time until expiration, the more the cash payment is late and the more the option is expensive (favoring the option buyer). This effect adds to the volatility effect and the price of a call (European or American) increases with maturity. For a put, the buyer hopes to quickly exercise the option to cash the exercise price as soon as possible, which reduces the price of the put option. This interest rate effect offsets the volatility effect for a European put. For example, for a deep ITM put, the volatility effect is low because the probability of being ITM at maturity is high. The possibility then exists of finding an ITM European put less expensive than a shorter-maturity ITM put. This is impossible for an American put as it is exercisable immediately, which cancels the effect of interest rates. Incidentally, deducing that an increase in interest rates increases the price of calls and reduces the price of puts is easy.

The Reality of Options: Complex Dynamics

Before Black and Scholes (1973) and Merton (1973), buyers of (American and over-the-counter) calls were classified as speculators. As the call could be exercised at any time, sellers held the underlying deliverable assets. This constraint immobilized money and costs interest, while the holder of the option earned interest until the exercise. The premium, established empirically based on maturity, exercise price, and the level of rates, compensated for this loss. In 1973, changes occurred not only from the fair price given by a formula but also from the self-financing dynamic strategy of payoff replication that gave the required number of shares in case of exercise. As a result, holding the exact number of shares of the underlying asset until exercise was no longer necessary when selling an option. If dynamically managed, the premium ensures compliance with the contract. The same year, industrialization began with the creation of the Chicago Board of Exchange (CBOE) and the launch of 911 call contracts on 16 underlying assets. Four years later, the put contracts began trading, and in 1983, the first index options started trading.

THE NEED FOR A MATHEMATICAL MODEL

Figure 24.2 shows the need to understand the dynamics of option prices. Even if the anticipated scenario is realized, the portfolio could support a losing position in the case of small but rapid change (the "today" straight line in Figure 24.2) while the position registers a gain at option expiration. The manager may, therefore, not be comfortable having such long strategies in his portfolio because of the risk of an immediate loss.

To determine the payoff profiles before expiration requires using valuation models. The models help to ensure that the market price is realistic when liquidity is low. But one option is not purchased because its market price is attractive compared to the price given by a model. Too many parameters are involved that can wipe out any theoretical consideration with the passage of time. Contract prices are subject to supply and demand. The market makers fuel the quotations and the bid-ask spread size depends on the volume, option price, and implied volatility. The model allows for a better understanding of the risks involved and for using options based on anticipation on market's moves.

GREEKS: IMPORTANCE OF RISK FACTORS

The purpose of this subsection is to show how an options pricing model allows the investor to assess the dynamics of an option position to be able to adapt its sensitivities (the Greeks) to an anticipated market scenario. The option premium increases with increasing volatility and decreases when the maturity decreases (except for puts deep in the money). For a call (put), the premium increases (decreases) with the increase in the value of the underlying asset. Hence, a dividend detachment is favorable for a long put position but not for a long call position. To be pragmatic, only the most useful Greeks (delta, gamma, vega, and theta) will be considered without providing the mathematical details available in Briys, Mai, Bellalah, and de Varenne (1998), Hull (2011), Wilmott (2006), and Haug (2007). This understanding is essential in order to select the suitable option. The following summarized analysis is performed on long positions (calls or puts):

- *Delta* measures the approximate change in the premium based on the variation of one unit in the price of the underlying asset. Deltas are additive and increase with the value of the underlying asset. All things being equal, the passage of time strengthens the position of the underlying asset relative to the strike price: The delta of a call (put) in-the-money (out-of-the-money) increases when maturity decreases while the delta of a call (put) that is out-of-the-money (in-the-money) decreases. A rise in implied volatility reflects an increase of uncertainty. Thus, assessing whether or not the option will expire in the money becomes more difficult. Delta then approaches the delta of an ATM option (say in the interval $[0.4, 0.6]$ for a call and $[-0.6, -0.4]$ for the put depending on market's conditions). Uncertainty is greatest when the underlying asset is at the strike price: the profit-loss (PL) of the option's strategy may become positive and then negative at any moment. Finally, delta is used to determine the exposure (E) of an options position with respect to a number of input variables as shown in Equation 24.10,

$$E = \frac{NnmS\Delta}{NAV} \qquad (24.10)$$

where N is the number of contracts; n the size of the contract (i.e., the number of options included in an option contract); S is the price of the underlying asset; m is the point value ($1 for a stock but $100 for S&P 500 options contracts); NAV is the net asset value of the considered portfolio; and Δ is the delta of the option. The numerator of Equation 24.10 is the instantaneous notional market value of the position. This equation represents the options position within a portfolio and is essential to assess its impact in terms of performance and risk.

- *Gamma* measures the rate of change in delta associated with changes in the underlying asset price. As with deltas, gammas are additive in nature. Gamma is always positive for a long position. It is at a maximum when the option is close to the option's moneyness (ascending then descending with the level of the underlying asset) and for short maturity options (less than six months). This feature explains the attraction (and hence the high liquidity) for these contracts from market makers.

- *Vega* measures the change in the premium when implied volatility increases by 1 percent. Vega is highest for ATM options (ascending and descending with the increase of the underlying price), where uncertainty is the greatest. Vega increases when implied volatility increases. An option with longer maturity is more sensitive to changes in volatility than the same option with shorter maturity. This situation may affect the choice of a contract. If a decrease in implied volatility is anticipated, a sale of a long-maturity option will generate a bigger PL. Also, purchasing options of long maturity may generate substantial losses if volatility falls.

- *Theta* measures the negative impact on the option premium with changes in time until expiration (except for ITM puts as previously explained). As with gamma, theta is large (in absolute value) for options with short maturities. Theta is at a maximum value in absolute terms when the option is at the money. The loss of time value increases with the increase in implied volatility. The effects of the theta are opposed to those of the gamma. The loss of time value accelerates at the end of the life of the option. Using that property has already been illustrated in the case of an anticipation of a neutral market (see Figure 24.2). Finally, thetas are additive.

HOW TO INVEST IN OPTIONS?

The decision to buy a contract or the comparison of several contracts can be first assessed by estimating if break even is attainable. Assume Boeing is trading at $75 and the call at the strike of $80 and four-month maturity quotes for $3.32. The break even of this OTM call is $83.32, which implies a movement of 11.09 percent within four months. Is this movement feasible? The annual historical volatility (assumed to be 15 percent) can be a first proxy of the future volatility. According to the Black-Scholes approach (Black and Scholes, 1973), which became the standard model to price stocks and index options, the volatility is proportional to the square root of time. From here, the volatility for an option with four months remaining is given by $15 \ percent \left(\sqrt{1/3} \right) = 8.7 \ percent$. This volatility measures the capability of the underlying asset to move away from its actual level in four months. The issue is then to evaluate if this volatility level is sufficient for the underlying asset to reach the break-even (denoted by B). If, following the Black-Scholes model, the underlying return is assumed to follow a Gaussian probability distribution with approximately a zero mean (meaning no bullish or bearish bias) and with a standard deviation of 8.7 percent, the probability of variation greater than or equal to 11.09 percent in four months is evaluated to be 10.13 percent. As a consequence, good timing in the underlying asset is not enough to obtain a profit.

This technique enables comparing the likelihood of different strategies in a simple way. Other measures can be used as well. The delta is the (risk-neutral) probability for the option to expire in the money. As expiration in the money is not enough to ensure a positive PL, using the delta of the option with strike B is best. However, these measures do not compare implied with realizable volatility. Finally, because one achieves a positive return as soon as the break-even is reached, the probability is the one of reaching the barrier B before the four months maturity. This assessment, however, is more complex and could require Monte Carlo simulations. The key is always to use the same approach to select the strategy. The absolute level of probability is secondary because it does not include the investor's expectations.

The proposed approach compares implied volatility (contained in the premium and then in the break-even by definition) against "achievable" volatility of the underlying asset. If implied volatility is expensive, selling options or at least reducing the cost of options investing may be preferable. The current level of implied volatility will be historically appreciated as illustrated in the following situation. From February 12, 2009, to February 12, 2010, the implied volatility of Telefonica was between 13 percent and 43 percent with a level of 28.2 percent on February 12, 2010. This level is high compared to the one-year historical range and the six-month average volatility of 22. As a result, option premiums will be relatively expensive based on current values. An optimal strategy would be to take a short position in the premiums. Assume that during the same day, the implied volatility of Nokia is 29 percent. This volatility level represents the low end of its one-year history (the maximum volatility was 72 percent, with the minimum at 24.8 percent during the same period) and the six-month average volatility of 37. Thus, a long volatility strategy is preferred.

VOLATILITY SKEW

Since the markets crash of October 1987, the implied volatility of equity markets has resembled a skew (compared to a straight line before that time). Two explanations (among others) can be given. First, the demand for extreme risks hedging from institutional investors drove up prices of OTM puts and then implied volatilities on the left side of the curve. A second possibility is that the model is incorrect. As presented by Rebonato (2004, p. 169), the implied volatility is the "wrong number to put into the wrong formula to get the right price of plain-vanilla options."

Based on the shape of this skewed curve, there could be an interest in selling the left side of the curve (i.e., the strike price is away from the moneyness, which implies a low gamma) and in buying the right side (i.e., the strike price is close to moneyness, which implies a higher gamma) to take advantage of the difference between implied volatilities. Recall that gamma is at a maximum for ATM options. These types of positions are named call or put spreads. This approach reduces the cost of buying a hedge (an ATM put) by giving up of the protection beyond a certain level (below the lower strike price). The break-even of this position then becomes lower. This position, if managed with a delta neutral approach, is optimal when the realized volatility is between the two implied volatilities of the options included in the strategy.

VOLATILITY TERM STRUCTURE

For a given strike level, the implied volatility observed in the market generally increases with maturity, which reflects that long-term uncertainty increases. However, risk assessment can be reversed. During the bankruptcy of Lehman Brothers, no one knew the consequences in the short term, but many expected a return to normal in the long term. On September 17, 2008, the two-year implied volatilities before and after the collapse were at the same level whereas the one-month maturity volatility spread between these dates was 15 percent.

SIMPLIFIED RULES OF THUMB OF OPTION INVESTMENT

While each situation is unique, certain principles emerge from this review. The first that the portfolio manager should address is whether to buy or sell the implied volatility of the underlying. Next, the portfolio manager should make a decision about the direction of the position for which greater flexibility is provided through calls and puts, purchased or sold. The choice of the strike should be conducted from the expected move whereas the maturity will be chosen to refine the sensitivity desired by the portfolio manager. Table 24.1 presents a summary of the basic choices.

Using options requires special attention to the limited life of these financial products and the importance of the realization of the selected scenario, as previously mentioned, not only with good timing but also with the right amplitude of variations. Further, the leverage is a mixed blessing because it also applies to the volatility of the position.

Options Strategies for Risk and Performance Management

Given the description of the basics of options in the previous section, several option-based strategies emerge. These strategies allow for generating alpha

Table 24.1 **Simplified Rules of Thumb of Derivatives Investment**

		Scenarios for underlying expectations				
		Large downside	Low downside	Neutral	Low upside	Large upside
Implied	Expensive	Sale of futures	Sall of ITM call	Sale of straddles and strangles	Sale of ITM puts	Purchase of futures
volatility	Normal	Purchase of puts financed by sale of calls	Purchase of puts spreads		Purchase of calls spreads	Purchase of calls financed by sale of puts
levels	Attractive (or cheap)	Purchase of OTM puts	Purchase of ITM putss	Purchase of options if expected rise of implied volatility	Purchase of ITM calls	Purchase of OTM calls
		Large expected volatility	Moderate expected volatility	Very low realized volatility	Moderate expected volatility	Large expected volatility
		Scenarios for realized volatility expectations				

Note: This table shows the simplified investment rules according to implied volatility and expectations on the underlying asset. ITM options are chosen when sensitivity is needed whereas OTM options are selected when leverage is expected. Futures are preferred when implied volatility is estimated too high, which means that option prices are expensive.

by offering the possibility to exploit potential market movements. In this section, options are systematically combined with securities or indices within a portfolio.

HOW TO CALIBRATE AN OPTION POSITION?

Several approaches previously described are available to the portfolio manager to implement an option position. The easiest way to calibrate an option position is to only consider the terminal payoff. The number of contracts is based on the exercise profile: to hedge n shares, n puts (or n/m put contracts where m is the size of the contract) are used. In the short term, dynamically, the choice is based on the exposure (positive or negative) that one wants to include in the portfolio. The main consequence is delta management because exposure will vary in real time. In both cases, if the underlying is not identical to the asset in the portfolio, beta management is added. In the following example, the number of put contracts on an index to purchase is determined by the beta of stock A, which is assumed to be two. Suppose the investor has a portfolio of $100,000 that consists of 2,000 shares of stock A at $50 each. The portfolio manager wants to hedge for losses greater than 10 percent at maturity. The size for the S&P 500 put contract is $100 and the level of the index is 1,000. Hence, the necessary amount of contracts to be hedged at expiration is $[2000(\$50)(2)]/[1000(\$100)] = 2$ puts (see also Equation 24.10 with $\Delta = 1$). The strike price has to be adjusted in order to capture the variation of the S&P Index as soon as it is needed given the reactivity of the stock relative to the index. With the help of Equation 24.7 and since in a short time α of stock A could be estimated at zero, the adjusted strike price (K) verifies -10 percent = 90 percent $-$ 100 percent = β (K $-$ 100 percent) that gives K = 95 percent.

Another approach is to determine a risk budget allocated to the strategy for the fund. For example, in the worst-case scenario, the portfolio manager wants the strategy to cost no more than 0.5 percent of the NAV of the fund, with an assumption that the expected profit will justify such a cost.

In each situation, for a given underlying, once the portfolio manager has chosen his exposure to volatility and the type (i.e., call or put), choosing an option means selecting a maturity and a strike price. At maturity, the strike is the level at which protection begins and the scenario of the investor influences its choice. Because the scenario represents the choice of a point on the surface of volatility, this decision results in the choice of a probability of occurrence of an event as demonstrated previously. Choosing an option also means choosing the Greeks, delta in particular, i.e., sensitivities to risk parameters. Considering the horizon of the scenario, maturity comes to increase or decrease the sensitivity of the strategy.

With options, for example, a position in stocks (or indices) dynamically fully hedged with puts can still benefit from an increase in the underlying asset because the PL is a convex function of the underlying price, which results in downside protection with upside potential. This situation is not the case with a full-hedged position with futures.

The type of hedging may be global (with futures or options on indices, implying a few positions) or individual with options on stocks (implying multiple positions). These choices depend on the amount of time spent for managing derivatives in the investment process. Moreover, the demand for global protection against extreme risks drives up prices (and implied volatility as already seen) of the OTM puts on indices. The same level of protection on the underlying shares may be less expensive.

The calibration comes from the cost of the implemented strategy. Using Black-Scholes pricing (Black and Scholes, 1973), this approach shows the shortcomings of static management. If a manager wants to protect 100 percent of the portfolio beyond an annual decline of 10 percent in purchasing a put at the strike of 90 percent and one-year maturity, the premium costs will be about 3.3 percent of the amount of assets under management to protect the portfolio for an implied volatility of 20 percent. If the volatility is 30 percent, the cost is about 7.4 percent and 10.9 percent for a volatility of 40 percent. This cost represents the starting handicap that must be compensated in performance to simply reimburse for the purchase of insurance. Of course, this pricing is too expensive (i.e., the break even is too high). Moreover, this insurance is static while the portfolio is not: The 90 percent OTM put can become a 70 percent OTM put if the market rises sufficiently. Protection is then virtually useless and worthless. New insurance will generate an additional cost. This observation argues for a short-term management of options strategies in place.

STRATEGY TO PROTECT PROFITS

The protection strategy of selling a call has been previously discussed. The most natural protection is to be long put contracts. From there, any hedging profile can be established. The basic one is the purchase of puts to hedge the underlying at expiration. Dynamic hedging will imply, for instance, buying twice as many ATM puts (each with a delta of 0.5) than shares (with delta of 1) held in portfolio because the delta of this optional position is then equal to the delta of the portfolio (see also Equation 24.10). At maturity, the stock position is hedged twice over. In unfavorable cases, the losses are lower. Intermediate hedging profiles could be possible: One of these profiles consists of reducing costs of the previous hedging strategy by selling OTM puts (see the section "Volatility Skew"). The gamma of the options' position is lower. In counterpart, this reduces the potential profit in heavy decline. Dynamically, these three strategies show different convexities (i.e., different gammas) that will be chosen depending on the expectations on the moves of the underlying security.

STRATEGY OF CASH EXTRACTION

This approach consists of replacing long positions in shares by long positions in calls on the same securities. This exchange is done dynamically, with a short-term view, and helps protect the selloff while being exposed to a potential increase. The risk is limited to the premiums paid. According to the investment process, the cash can be reinvested into less risky assets in order to continue to deliver some income. The worst case emerges when calls and the protection of gains are unnecessary, when the stock moves in a limited range (low realized volatility). For this strategy, the targeted shares are those that performed well for which no dividend is expected, liquidity of options is sufficient, and for which the investor still holds bullish views.

Of course, the act of management is profoundly altered once these strategies are in place because the options have to be monitored much more intensely than stocks. Moreover, this type of movement is not always easy for funds with large amount of assets under management.

STRATEGY OF PERFORMANCE ENHANCEMENT (OVERWRITING)

The principle of this strategy is to sell an unlikely scenario (for which the investor estimates a low probability), while keeping the stocks in the portfolio. When calls are sold on long positions in the underlying asset (the calls are covered), the upside is limited until the expiration of the option position. This approach is attractive when markets are disrupted and pessimistic. With the sale, the investor's portfolio receives the premium (performance improvement) and reduces its volatility (risk reduction): The upside potential is replaced by a smaller certain profit, which is the premium. The unfavorable case is the realization of the unexpected scenario, namely a substantial decline in the underlying asset that is not offset by the premium. Implementing this strategy will be accompanied by a rule limiting the loss (redemption of calls).

Brehon and Mougeot (2008) analyze the development of a systematic strategy of selling calls. Each month, they sell one month calls on the Euro-Stoxx 50 price index such that the underlying position is 100 percent covered. The calls are then held to expiration. The authors show the particular relevance of the strategy in reducing risk in volatile markets.

RISK MONITORING

Once investors include options in a portfolio, they need to understand the risk the portfolio is bearing. The derivatives have to be monitored in the same way a market maker would, which includes calculating aggregate Greeks, especially delta (with all underlying assets of the portfolio), gamma and theta. The addition of vegas is more difficult to handle because of their square root of time-to-maturity dependencies. Taleb (1997) and Haug (2007) are good references on this subject. Moreover, the effects of derivatives strategies on the portfolio's total risk have to be identified. This risk measure will depend on the management company or the market regulation but volatility and VaR appear general choices (even if not always good ones). As those measures (and also conditional VaR and tracking error volatility) are homogeneous of order one according to weights, they are decomposable using Euler's theorem: The risk function is equal to the scalar product of the vector of weights with the gradient of the risk function where derivatives are taken with respect to weights (Leblanc, 2009).

Table 24.2 gives a summary of computations for the portfolio of a manager initially invested in an ETF on the Dow Jones Industrial Index (the benchmark). The NAV is $1,150,000. After taking a new derivatives position, the total volatility is 12.16 percent whereas the index volatility is 15.10 percent. Equation 24.10 gives the derivatives exposures in the third column. The risk contributions are given in the fourth and fifth column.

Table 24.2 A Simplified Risk Analysis

Name/Type	Quantity /Price	Exposure (%)	Volatility Contributions (%)	Tracking Error Contributions (%)
			(Total 12.15%)	(Total 2.97%)
ETF DJIA/Mutual Funds	10,000/$114.10	99.20	14.97	0.19
S&P500 Mini/Future	−3/$1,188.80	−15.55	−2.46	2.43
DJX Sept ATM/Call	20/$2.80	9.10	1.36	−1.31
DJX Dec ATM/Call	−20/$5.00	−9.34	−1.40	1.35
DJX Dec 85%OTM/Put	10/$2.60	−2.14	−0.32	0.31
Cash	13,734/$1.00	1.19	0.00	0.00

Name /Type	Quantity /Price	Exposure (%)	Volatility Contributions after Shock (%)	Tracking Error Contributions after Shock (%)
			(Total 13.33%)	(Total 3.15%)
ETF DJIA/Mutual Funds	10,000/$114.10	99.20	16.48	0.00
S&P500 Mini/Future	−3/$1,188.80	−15.51	−2.76	2.76
DJX Sept ATM/Call	20/$2.80	9.10	1.50	−1.50
DJX Dec ATM/Call	−20/$5.00	−9.34	−1.54	1.54
DJX Dec 85%OTM/Put	10/$2.60	−2.14	−0.35	0.35
Cash	13,734/$1.00	1.19	0.00	0.00

Note: This table contains the risk decomposition of a simplified portfolio with derivatives positions before and after simulated shocks on volatilities and correlation. The net asset value of the portfolio is $1,150,000. The benchmark is the Dow Jones Industrial Average Index (DJIA). The Bloomberg database as of August 17, 2011, is the source of the price quotations. After taking derivatives position, the total volatility is 12.15 percent whereas the index volatility is 14.97 percent. The figures in this table give a picture of the risk of the portfolio in real time (based on estimates obtained from historical data). The tracking error volatility comes essentially from future and options positions and is evaluated to be 2.97 percent. With this methodology, the manager knows at each time where the carrying risks are.

The figures in Table 24.2 give a picture of the risk of the portfolio in real time (based on estimates obtained, for instance, from historical data). The tracking error volatility comes essentially from future and options positions and is evaluated to be 2.96 percent. With this methodology, the manager knows at each time where the carrying risks are. In order to complete this information, the same calculations should be done after stress tests on the underlying asset and market parameters such as volatility and correlation. Table 24.2 also presents the results after a volatility shock of 10 percent and assigning all correlations a value of 1.

Summary and Conclusions

This chapter provides a foundation for active portfolio management with listed derivatives. Futures contracts are a useful tool of reactivity (in exposure or hedging) whose behavior is linear and close to the cash products. In order to provide a full understanding of the use of options, the chapter discusses their main features from the investor's point of view. Options offer portfolio managers unique opportunities to protect their positions as well as to improve the return of their portfolios. This chapter also gives an overview of the analysis a manager should do in order to select the right strategy taking account his expectations and options market conditions.

As a word of warning, no chapter can replace actual practice. Because the complex dynamics of derivatives, managers using futures and options may experience a new investment stress compared to those only used to investing in products without maturity and with well-apprehended variability. Given this situation, investment firms may consider developing the role of a "derivatives manager" who is in charge of implementing and monitoring option strategies in coordination with managers of equity or allocation funds.

Discussion Questions

1. Discuss the main mistakes to avoid in options investing.
2. Discuss good practices of options investing.
3. What kind of information does the options market offer invertors?
4. What are the advantages to using futures in a portfolio?

References

Alexander, Carol. 2008. Market Risk Analysis—Pricing, Hedging and Trading Financial Instruments. Hoboken, NJ: John Wiley & Sons, Inc.
Avellaneda, Marco, Arnon Levy, and Antonio Paras. 1995. "Pricing and Hedging Derivative Securities in Markets with Uncertain Volatilities." Applied Mathematical Finance 2:2, 73–88.
Bittman, James B. 2009. Trading Options as a Professional. New York: McGraw-Hill.

Black, Fischer, and Myron Scholes. 1973. "The Pricing of Options and Corporate Liabilities." Journal of Political Economy 81:3, 637–654.

Brehon, Daniel, and Nicolas Mougeot. 2008. "The Benefits of Overwriting." Working Paper, Global Markets Research, Deutsche Bank.

Briys, Eric, Huu Minh Mai, Mondher Bellalah, and François de Varenne. 1998. Options, Futures and Exotic Derivatives. New York: John Wiley & Sons, Inc.

Eurex Exchange. 2012. "Clearing Conditions for Eurex Clearing AG." Available at http://www.eurexchange.com/download/documents/regulations/clearing_conditions/clearing_conditions_En.pdf.

Fontanills, George A. 2005. Options Course: High Profit and Low Stress Trading Methods, Second Edition. Hoboken, NJ: John Wiley & Sons, Inc.

Haug, Espen Gaarder. 2007. The Complete Guide to Option Pricing Formulas. New York: McGraw-Hill.

Hull, John C. 2011. Options, Futures and Other Derivatives, Eighth Edition. Upper Saddle River, NJ: Prentice Hall, Pearson Education Inc.

Jensen, Michael C. 1968. "The Performance of Mutual Funds in the Period 1945–1964." Journal of Finance 23:2, 389–416.

Johnson, Philip McBride. 1999. Derivatives: A Manager's Guide to the World's Most Powerful Financial Instruments. New York: McGraw-Hill.

Kaeppel, Jay. 2002. The Option Trader's Guide to Probability, Volatility and Timing. New York: John Wiley & Sons, Inc.

Kwok, Yue-Kuen. 2008. Mathematical Models of Financial Derivatives, Second Edition. Berlin and Heidelberg: Springer.

Leblanc, Matthieu. 2002. Super Replication and Uncertain Volatility: European, American and Passport Options. PhD Thesis, University Paris 7 Denis Diderot. Available at http://ssrn.com/abstract=1544617.

Leblanc, Matthieu. 2010a. "Active Risk Budgeting: Volatility Is Not Standard Deviation." Working Paper, Edmond de Rothschild Asset Management. Available at http://ssrn.com/abstract=1407584.

Leblanc, Matthieu, 2010b. "Derivatives Strategies for Asset Management." Lecture. Available at http://ssrn.com/abstract=1649955.

Leblanc, Matthieu. 2011. "Derivatives for Asset Managers." Working Paper, Edmond de Rothschild Asset Management. Available at http://ssrn.com/abstract=1911812.

Markowitz, Harry. 1952. "Portfolio Selection." Journal of Finance 7:1, 77–99.

McMillan, Lawrence G. 2002. Profit with Options: Essential Methods for Investing Success. New York: John Wiley & Sons, Inc.

McMillan, Lawrence G. 2004. McMillan on Options. Hoboken, NJ: John Wiley & Sons, Inc.

Merton, Robert C. 1973. "Theory of Rational Option Pricing." Bell Journal of Economics and Management Science (The RAND Corporation) 4:1, 141–183.

Natenberg, Sheldon. 1994. Option Pricing and Volatility. New York: McGraw-Hill.

Rebonato, Riccardo. 2004. Volatility and Correlation: The Perfect Hedger and the Fox, Second Edition. Hoboken, NJ: John Wiley & Sons, Inc.

Scherer, Bernd, 2007. Portfolio Construction and Risk Budgeting, Third Edition. London: Risk Books.

Sinclair, Euan. 2008. Volatility Trading. Hoboken, NJ: John Wiley & Sons, Inc.

Taleb, Nassim. 1997. Dynamic Hedging: Managing Vanilla and Exotic Options. New York: John Wiley & Sons, Inc.

Wilmott, Paul. 2006. Paul Wilmott on Quantitative Finance, Second Edition. Hoboken, NJ: John Wiley & Sons, Inc.

Yates, Tristan. 2009. Enhanced Indexing Strategies: Utilizing Futures and Options to Achieve Higher Performance. Hoboken, NJ: John Wiley & Sons, Inc.

25

PERFORMANCE PRESENTATION

TIMOTHY P. RYAN
CIPM, Vice President
Hartford Investment Management Company

Introduction

Performance presentations and their content are vitally important to each stake-holder in the investment management relationship and responsibility. Stakeholders include the investment management firm and its personnel, existing clients, pro-spective clients and their intermediaries (such as institutional investment consul-tants and statistical vendors of portfolio/strategy performance, profiles, and peer rankings), as well as regulators where applicable. Performance presentations need to be clear and informative.

The purpose of this chapter is to examine critical aspects of performance pre-sentation. The four remaining sections of the chapter have the following organi-zation. The first section examines purposes and general content of performance presentations. The second section addresses relevant performance standards and guidelines. The third section presents design considerations including ways to opti-mize knowledge conveyance. The fourth section provides a list of best practices. The final section concludes with a brief summary and further discussion topics.

Purpose and General Content of Performance Presentations

The overriding purpose of a performance presentation is to convey knowledge of a portfolio's or composite's investment approach, positioning, performance over recent time frames in absolute as well as index-relative and/or peer-relative terms, and indicative characteristics. For fixed income portfolios, characteristics may include such measures as a portfolio's weighted-average option-adjusted dura-tion and coupon, among others. For equity portfolios, the characteristics may include the price-to-equity (P/E) ratio and dividend yield. Beyond this typical content, performance presentations may have additional components such as pertinent information unique to the portfolio, its strategy, market conditions or time frames under consideration and/or presented. Content varies according to the audience (such as an existing client for its portfolio or prospective clients through marketing presentations or advertisements), the relevant standards and regulations where applicable, and the situation. For example, Ryan (2009/2010) covers the analysis and presentation when returns are outside expectations.

THE MULTIPLE ASPECTS OF PERFORMANCE

Performance is more than just returns. Performance includes the following: (1) a choice of return measures to present; (2) components and drivers of those returns in either an absolute or benchmark-relative context; (3) where applicable, placement of the return measures in the context of a peer universe; and (4) measurement of the risk or volatility assumed to achieve the returns. Beyond the general perspective that performance is more than just returns, some products such as insurance portfolios have particular performance needs and measures. While the specific performance needs for insurance portfolios are beyond the scope of this chapter, Hahn and Saf (1997) as well as Galdi (2006) provide a discussion of insurance portfolio performance needs. In the following subsections, each of the four aspects of performance is covered individually.

RETURN MEASURES

As is widely covered in the investment performance measurement literature, more than one return is available for a portfolio in a specific period. Two particular paths are available: (1) time-weighted returns and approximations thereof and (2) money-weighted or dollar-weighted returns and approximations thereof.

Most commonplace pooled investment products such as mutual funds use time-weighted returns for the purposes of advertising returns and marketing services to prospective clients. This is because time-weighted returns more approximately measure the portfolio manager's return on the portfolio when the portfolio manager does not control external capital flows into or out of the portfolio. This is usually the case for most commonplace pooled investment products. As such, the time-weighted return for a portfolio captures more of what was in the portfolio manager's purview. It may, however, capture less than the portfolio manager can control such as the inability to control prevailing market conditions. Time-weighted returns do not capture the collective impacts of the timing and size of the external capital flows into and out of the portfolio controlled by others, specifically shareholders. The size and timing of flows, particularly their confluence with immediately subsequent market or portfolio performance, can have a material impact on actual returns realized by investors or shareholders.

By contrast, money-weighted or dollar-weighted returns take into account the timing, size, and impact of external capital flows into or out of the portfolios. Such returns can be applied to portfolios for which portfolio managers control external capital flows into or out of the portfolio as may be the case in limited partnerships of investment vehicles in which committed capital can be called on at the portfolio manager's discretion. In this latter usage, the money-weighted return may more approximately represent the actual return for investors including the impact of their capital call decisions and timing, particularly in the case of multiple capital call decisions put into effect and their timing and size.

Bailey, Richards, and Tierney (2007) provide a useful summary on the two paths as follows: time-weighted return "reflects the compound rate of growth over a stated evaluation period of one unit of money initially invested in the account," while money-weighted return "measures the compound growth rate in the value of all funds invested in an account over the evaluation period" (724, 726). Thus, time-weighted and money-weighted returns are two distinct return measures and can have very divergent results (for example, one may be positive and the other negative) for a given portfolio for a given time frame. Bailey et al. also provide a good example of such divergent results where the portfolio's time-weighted return was 66.7 percent but its money-weighted return was 87.5 percent for the same time frame. The divergence in this example was a large capital inflow to the port-folio just before a large positive return occurred. Before the inflow during the first third of the analysis period, the portfolio had a lower capital base and a 0 percent return.

COMPONENTS AND DRIVERS OF RETURNS

In addition to presenting a portfolio return of, for example, 5 percent, perfor-mance presentations may also provide the composition of that return. This com-position may be the sum of the contribution to the portfolio return such as 4 percent of the portfolio's 5 percent return is from energy stocks, 1.25 percent of the 5 percent portfolio return is from Stock A, and the like. Presentations can also provide comparable information for benchmark-relative performance through a sundry of performance attribution methodologies and their resulting output. Table 25.1 contains an example of a performance attribution presentation. This example involves an equity portfolio where portfolio and benchmark indicative data are presented as well as return attribution by industry and region.

RETURN MEASURES IN A PEER UNIVERSE CONTEXT

Sometimes returns are presented in the context of a peer universe and listed with a resulting rank or percentile. Vendors provide this information service. Those using such information need to use it appropriately and with caution for several reasons. First, gauging managers in this manner based on returns for commonplace pooled investment products is best done using time-weighted returns for the reason cited previously. Second, running this analysis using gross-of-fees returns is useful because it removes the relative influence of the competitor cost positioning stance that a management firm has assumed in its product lineup. Third, paying attention to the peer universe count and range of returns is useful as the following example explains. For instance, having a 25 basis point range of returns divvied up to derive peer rankings across 1,500 funds would not result in a meaningful differentiator between a top 10th per-centile fund and a top 40th percentile fund; nor would a peer universe totaling eight funds provide a meaningful separator of skill based on percentile rank-ings as could a peer universe encompassing 800 funds. Survivorship bias is also a well-documented concern for peer groups as is the potential misclassifications of funds to peer cohorts.

Table 25.1 **Sample Return and Risk Attribution Presentation**

The following sample attribution analysis report refers to an equity portfolio and is an example of how a performance attribution presentation in compliance with this Guidance could look like. This sample report is absolutely not intended to server as a "best practice" benchmark to present performance attribution in terms of methodology or layout.

Investment Manager ABC
Return Attribution and Risk Attribution Report for Equity Portfolio XYZ as of 31.03.2001

Return and Risk Attribution Report for:	**PORTFOLIO XYZ**
Period:	**1.1.2000 - 30.03.2001**
Reference Currency:	**EUR**
Benchmark:	**Customised (refer to Disclosures)**

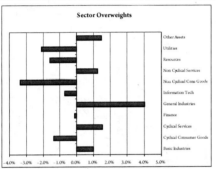

Return	
Portfolio	-4.45%
Benchmark	-2.89%
Active (Relative) Return	-1.56%
Return Attribution Analysis by Industry Sector	
Asset Allocation	-0.79%
Stock Selection	-0.52%
Other Effect	-0.25%
Total	**-1.56%**
Return Attribution Analysis by Region	
Asset Allocation	0.09%
Stock Selection	-2.74%
Other Effect	1.09%
Total	**-1.56%**

Risk Analysis (end of period)	Portfolio	Benchmark
Number of Securities	99	576
Number of Currencies	2	2
Portfolio Value	227'447'728	
Total Risk (ex-ante)	15.76%	15.31%
- Factor Specific Risk	15.53%	15.20%
- Style	4.91%	4.29%
- Industry	11.95%	11.80%
- Stock Selection Risk	2.72%	1.83%
Tracking Error (ex-post)	2.29%	
Tracking Error (ex-ante)	2.35%	
Value at Risk (at 97.7%)	10'878'425	
R-squared	0.98	
Beta-adjusted Risk	15.59%	15.31%
Predicted Beta	1.02	
Predicted Dividend Yield	2.22	2.37

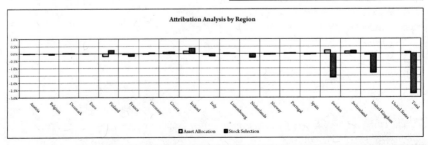

RISK APPROXIMATIONS AND RETURN TO RISK ASSUMED MEASUREMENT

A performance presentation may include the volatility of returns and other risk approximation or risk/reward approximation measures. Such measures for risk approximation may include value at risk (VaR), standard deviation of the returns over a given period or periods, beta to an index, R-squared, tracking error, and various downside risk measures. Risk-to-reward approximation measures may include the information ratio, Sharpe ratio, Sortino ratio, and Jensen's alpha, among others. The usefulness of the resulting output is sensitive to the number of observations used. For example, the greater the number of observations, the more statistically significant is the result, all things equal. Usefulness also depends on the periodicity in each observation. For instance, diBartolomeo (2003) notes that monthly data are generally considered to contain more information and less noise than daily data. Further, periodicity depends on the period under analysis. Some measures have sensitivity to whether the distribution is assumed to be normal. Ryan (2009/2010) discusses analysis in periods of non-normal distributions. As Amenc and le Sourd (2010) note, the Cornish-Fisher VaR has the capability to better capture distributions involving skewness and kurtosis.

AUDIENCE FOR PERFORMANCE PRESENTATIONS

Performance presentations have both internal and external audiences. For an investment advisory firm, internal audiences may include portfolio managers, investment staff, senior management, boards of directors, and compliance departments. External audiences may include the following: existing clients, including their representatives such as mutual fund boards; advisers of mutual funds who sub-advise investment portfolio management; pension boards; investment consultants; and prospective clients to whom the firm is advertising or marketing. The prospective client category also includes intermediaries such as investment consultants and statistical data providers. This latter intermediary group captures investment consultant databases as well as vendors such as Lipper and Morningstar.

Performance presentations provided to prospective clients normally are subject to regulatory oversight if they involve marketing and/or advertising, particularly for the retail marketplace. For the institutional marketplace, which spans investing for pension plans, corporations, governments, and endowments, performance presentations to prospective clients normally follow additional voluntary industry standards such as the Global Iinvestment Performance Standards (GIPS). The institutional marketplace is not without regulatory oversight and requirements. Thus, regulatory compliance is a GIPS prerequisite and component. Still, regulatory compliance, even from solely a US perspective, is too large a subject to be adequately covered in this chapter.

Performance Standards and Guidelines

This next section reviews key voluntary industry guidelines as well as their history and place in the industry. The first standards reviewed are highly accepted in the marketplace. Next, private equity and venture capital reporting guidelines are reviewed.

GLOBAL INVESTMENT PERFORMANCE STANDARDS (GIPS)

Chief among the voluntary industry standards is GIPS. GIPS has a history dating back to 1995 in its Association for Investment Management and Research—Performance Presentation Standards (AIMR-PPS) form. GIPS is maintained and developed by the CFA Institute and its supporting cast of staff and volunteers. As the name implies, GIPS has a global footprint, influence, and acceptance.

GIPS is a robust and well-developed set of standards. It has a five-year full review schedule, an annual conference, and a website (www.gipsstandards.org), which provides details such as a Q&A database, guidance statements, handbooks for proper interpretation, and a help desk. Changes and additions to the standards are transparent and inclusive. Any changes or additions to GIPS are preceded by publishing drafts of the comments and reviews of them. The central focus of GIPS is toward clients and investors. Further, GIPS is based on the principles of fair representation and full disclosure. This is clearly demonstrated in key parts of GIPS that directly benefit prospective clients and investors. As such, the investment industry as a whole is an indirect beneficiary. Investment firms claiming compliance to GIPS pay the direct costs, which are sometimes heavy such as the case for intramonth portfolio valuation for large external cash flows. Additionally, GIPS includes procedures for voluntary, independent verification to these standards, which again fortifies the central focus.

Accordingly, GIPS is a rigorous set of standards that has garnered global acclaim, recognition, and wide support. A survey by ACA Compliance Group's Beacon Verification Services and eVestment Alliance (2009) demonstrates the strong standing of GIPS in the institutional marketplace. This survey's summary report cites 68 percent of investment firms (1,561 total) submitting information to eVestment Alliance as claiming compliance to GIPS with 75 percent of those stating the claim is verified. A firm's claim of GIPS compliance can be verified by a qualified independent third party. At the end of a successful verification process, a qualified independent third party verifier issues a report opining that the firm has complied with all the composite construction requirements of the GIPS standards on a firm-wide basis and that the firm's policies and procedures are designed to calculate and present performance in compliance with the GIPS standards. The 333 firms in this group directly responding to the survey have slightly higher respective percentages of 75 percent claiming compliance to GIPS with 84 percent of those stating the claim is verified. The survey also indicates this supply of GIPS-compliant firms is demand driven given that 83 percent of compliant responding firms indicate more than half of request for proposals (RFPs) ask for a claim of GIPS compliance. Additionally, 95 percent of the investment consultants surveyed note GIPS compliance as "important" or "very important" when evaluating an investment manager.

The provisions contained in GIPS encompass nine sections with sections 0 through 5, respectively addressing fundamentals of compliance, input data,

Table 25.2 **Sample GIPS-Compliant Presentation**

Sample 1 Investment Firm Balanced Growth Composite 1 January 2002 through 31 December 2011

Year	Composite Gross Return (%)	Composite Net Return (%)	Custom Benchmark Return (%)	Composite 3-Yr St Dev (%)	Benchmark 3-Yr St Dev (%)	Number of Portfolios	Internal Dispersion (%)	Composite Assets ($ M)	Firm Assets ($ M)
2002	-10.5	-11.4	-11.8			31	4.5	165	236
2003	16.3	15.1	13.2			34	2.0	235	346
2004	7.5	6.4	8.9			38	5.7	344	529
2005	1.8	0.8	0.3			45	2.8	445	695
2006	11.2	10.1	12.2			48	3.1	520	839
2007	6.1	5.0	7.1			49	2.8	505	1,014
2008	-21.3	-22.1	-24.9			44	2.9	475	964
2009	16.5	15.3	14.7			47	3.1	493	983
2010	10.6	9.5	13.0			51	3.5	549	1,114
2011	2.7	1.7	0.4	7.1	7.4	54	2.5	575	1,236

Sample 1 Investment Firm claims compliance with the Global Investment Performance Standards (GIPS®) and has prepared and presented this report in compliance with the GIPS standards. Sample 1 Investment Firm has been independently verified for the periods 1 January, 2000, through 31 December, 2010. The verification report is available upon request. Verification assesses whether (1) the firm has complied with all the composite construction requirements of the GIPS standards on a firm-wide basis and (2) the firm's policies and procedures are designed to calculate and present performance in compliance with the GIPS standards. Verification does not ensure accuracy of any specific composite presentation.

Notes:

1. Sample 1 Investment Firm is a balanced portfolio investment manager that invests solely in U.-S.-based securities. Sample 1 Investment Firm is defined as an independent investment management firm that is not affiliated with any parent organization. Policies for valuing portfolios, calculating performance, and preparing compliant presentations are available upon request.

Table 25.2 (Continued)

2. The Balanced Growth Composite includes all institutional balanced portfolios that invest in large-cap U.S. equities and investment-grade bonds with the goal of providing long-term capital growth and steady income from a well-diversified strategy. Although the strategy allows for equity exposure ranging between 50–70 %, the typical allocation is between 55–65 %. The account minimum for the composite is $5 million.

3. The custom benchmark is 60% YYY US Equity Index and 40% ZZZ U.S. Aggregate Bond Index. The benchmark is rebalanced monthly.

4. Valuations are computed and performance is reported in US dollars.

5. Gross-of-fees returns are presented before management and custodial fees but after all trading expenses. Composite and benchmark returns are presented net of nonreclaimable withholding taxes. Net-of-fees returns are calculated by deducting the highest fees of 0.83% from the monthly gross composite return. The management fee schedule is as follows: 1.00% on the first $25 million, 0.60% thereafter.

6. This composite was created in February 2000. A complete list of composite description is available upon request.

7. Internal dispersion is calculated using the equal-weighted standard deviation for annual gross returns of those portfolios that were included in the composite for the entire year.

8. The three-year annualized standard deviation measures the variability of the composite and the benchmark returns over the preceding 36-month period. The standard deviation is not presented for 2002 through 2010 because monthly composite and benchmark returns were not available and is not required for periods prior to 2011.

Source: Copyright 2010, CFA Institute. Republished and reprinted from *Global Investment Performance Standards* (GIPS®) with permission from the CFA Institute. All rights reserved.

calculation methodology, composite construction, disclosure, presentation and reporting, regarded as generally applicable, and sections 6 through 8 respectively covering real estate, private equity, and wrap fee/separately managed account (SMA) portfolios. In addition to this thematic overview of GIPS, the details and latest updates are available at www.gipsstandards.org. Table 25.2 provides a sample presentation compliant to these standards. This sample presentation includes the key disclosures, descriptions, returns, and return history, among other items, to quickly convey vital information.

PRIVATE EQUITY AND VENTURE CAPITAL REPORTING GUIDELINES

In addition to prospective client presentation standards, a robust set of reporting guidelines has been developed for existing private equity and venture capital investors. The European Private Equity and Venture Capital Association (EVCA) (2010) developed these guidelines in March 2000 with updates in 2005, 2009, and 2010. These reporting guidelines are thorough, practical, and include a sample report template comprising 13 of the guideline's 30 pages.

SUMMARY REPORTING TO PROSPECTIVE CLIENTS

In addition to fuller prospective client-focused reporting, such as GIPS- or EVCA-compliant presentations, and prospectuses or statements of additional information, summary reporting is also commonly available. Such summary reporting, which comprises one to five pages, may fall under monikers such as a simplified prospectus or product fact sheets. More recently on the European front, such reporting has converged into a Key Investor Information Document (KIID). Content of these reports normally describes a product's investment objective or investment approach. In some cases, these reports describe it tangibly by listing buy or sell criteria, investment personnel of the firm, past performance and distributions, portfolio allocations and characteristics, investment risks, risk and reward profiles, comparisons to relevant benchmarks and/or peers, fees, and other relevant information. Normally such reporting would also indicate how to obtain more complete information.

REPORTING TO EXISTING CLIENTS ON THEIR PORTFOLIOS

Reporting to existing clients on their portfolios can be subject to customization by the client. A general view of this, however, from an institutional client perspective is well covered by the Regional Investment Performance Committee for Europe, Middle East, and Africa (RIPS EMEA, 2006).

The purpose of the following definitions is to provide users with an overview and elaborations on typical components of the investment management reporting clients may expect to receive. As Table 25.3 shows, this overview is illustrative and is not exhaustive. Some of those components may not always be included in the standard reporting package but rather may have to be requested by the client. Reporting to mutual fund boards and individual shareholders is beyond the scope of this chapter.

Table 25.3 **Components of Client Reporting**

Portfolio information	This part of the reporting includes the general portfolio standing data such as client name and portfolio identification, mandate type, reference currency, investment strategy, and the portfolio benchmark.
Portfolio structure	This report may include the following information: • Portfolio asset allocation, which is a breakdown/overview of the portfolio assets by various criteria such as by asset class, country, currency, industry sector, maturity, derivative type, manager, and subadvisor. This may be provided as of the reporting date as well as a dynamic analysis for a particular period. • The largest portfolio positions and their share in the total portfolio. • Asset liability analysis.
Performance report	This report provides a summary of the portfolio and the benchmark performance achieved over the reporting period and may include single period, cumulative, and average returns.
Return and risk analysis	This report may include the following components: • Return analysis for the portfolio and benchmark by various factors such as by asset class, country, industry sector, maturity profile, manager, and sub-advisor. • Return contribution and attribution analysis. • Ex-post and ex-ante analysis of portfolio risk measures such as volatility, tracking error, risk-adjusted performance measures, and value -at -risk.
Portfolio valuation statement	This report provides a total portfolio valuation as of a specific date with a breakdown of the assets by individual securities and investment instruments.
Profit and loss statement	This report provides an analysis of the gains and losses generated during the reporting period. This report may also show an analysis of costs of asset management such as total expense ratio and breakdown of transaction costs and fees. The degree of detail may vary.
Transactions report	This report shows all transactions (purchases and sales of securities) carried out during the reporting period on a trade date basis.
Cash and capital flow report	This report shows cash flows into/out of the portfolio during the reporting period. Cash flows typically include capital contributions and withdrawals by client (both as cash and securities), dividend and interest income payments, and fee charges.

Investment compliance report	This report may include the following information: · • Analysis of compliance with statutory legal requirements application for a particular client such as legal investment exposure. • Analysis of compliance with the client's investment guidelines such as investment restrictions, asset allocation ranges, asset liability parameters, and tracking error targets.
Composite report	GIPS compliant composite report the portfolio belongs to
Descriptive information	This report may include the following information: • Qualitative information on the investment process. • Information on the market developments such as interest rate and currency exchange movements and general macroeconomic situation. • Qualitative information about the portfolio risk-return profile. • Various disclosures and disclaimers.

Design Considerations for Performance Presentations

This section addresses design considerations for performance presentations. Design considerations are important to ensure important knowledge is both conveyed and received. This section provides guidance on how to achieve this essential goal.

TABULAR VERSUS GRAPHICAL PRESENTATIONS

Tabular presentations are commonly used in presentations subject to regulations and other standards. Such a presentation format is particularly useful when the information presented is static, such as a point or period in time or is one-dimensional. Useful tabular information may contain month-end or year-end snapshots of portfolio-weighted characteristics, the top five or 10 positions by portfolio weight, rolling 1-, 3-, 5-year total returns, or portfolio (benchmark) allocations or weightings to one dimension such as quality ratings, countries, or industries.

Graphical conveyance of knowledge is particularly useful for presenting time series data and for communicating with a sophisticated audience. This audience is most frequently an internal audience for an investment management firm. The graphical conveyance of knowledge follows from the raw materials consumed by the firm through its transformation into the resulting product's performance and the risk profile the product assumes. Where permissible and appropriate, those preparing performance presentations should consider graphically conveying knowledge. The following three subsections describe the graphical conveyance of knowledge in more detail.

The Knowledge Continuum

The investment management industry is a knowledge-based industry consuming massive amounts of data. Data are the industry's raw materials entering the intellectual production line. If properly processed, data can be converted into information, which in turn may result in knowledge and occasionally wisdom. Wisdom is recognized in the investment management industry as repeated outperformance spanning market cycles or episodes in time. Thus, the intellectual production line or knowledge continuum proceeds from data to information to knowledge and occasionally to wisdom. This is a seminal, poignant, but not semantic statement.

As Ryan (2010) notes, knowledge is the investment industry's "compete" level, to use a sporting term. *Compete* is the root word of *competency,* which means a level below which sustainable and/or deserving market participants should not be. Information is merely work in progress within the competent investment manager's intellectual production line. Information by definition cannot be the output of a knowledge-based industry's intellectual product line. Experienced and self-aware practitioners know this already. However, a practitioner may be reluctant to state something analogous to the following: "The requestor asked for information on topic A. If the request is completed as stated, the requestor will be provided with so much (so called) information as to be buried in the output until the requested (so called) information ultimately become noise itself or lost in the noise." The thirst for information should be quenched but not with a fire hose. That reluctance is effective and beneficial when repurposed and done in a client partnering rather than customer service approach. In a customer service approach, an order would be received and completed as requested, without clarification of purpose or goals and without further customer interaction apart from delivery. A client partnering approach, however, involves more thought and client interaction to clarify a request's purpose in order to ensure that the intended goal is understood and accomplished.

The request repurposed in an effective and beneficial manner follows this thought process: The requestor ultimately wants an insightful and impactful analysis, which is truly informative because it conveys knowledge. So a manager should ask what insights the requestor ultimately wants to achieve, what intended or unintended scenarios or situations the requestor is trying to uncover, and what questions the requestor desires to answer. Then the manager can begin the intellectual production line, where every data point is an answer to a particular, tactical, and narrowly focused question. By knowing the requestor's purpose and desired outcomes (insights), the manager can gather the appropriate data to form a higher processed level of (intermediate, work-in-progress) material (information) to cull further into an insightful, impactful analysis as requested (knowledge). This final output (also known as the knowledge product) may be a mosaic of disparate but complementary information, which acting as a catalyst in the recipient's mind (intellectual engine), may yield actionable wisdom. That is the goal because value is either added or neglected. The next subsection discusses how to achieve this goal.

Communicating Victory on the Recipient's Terms

After completing the request repurposing, the communication output and the conveyance of knowledge should be considered. The immediate consideration focuses on what the recipient wants and needs to know. Campisi (2011) captures this point in compelling fashion, particularly for an endowment or charitable foundation client base. Campisi notes, "For an analysis of performance based on clients' goals, the actual money earned and spent are what needs to be measured" (34). He illustrates this point through a case study. The next consideration is how to convey this knowledge to the recipient. To fulfill these two considerations, an effective approach is to start with a summary and then provide supporting details and pertinent (even if contradictory) facts.

An illustration may be helpful. ACME Stock Selector Fund, an actively managed equity portfolio, outperformed its benchmark by 0.25 percent for a specific period. The fund's total return was 11.25 percent compared to the benchmark's 11 percent return. A top-down performance attribution methodology indicates this outperformance, or relative value added, consisted of a +0.35 percent industry allocation effect and a −0.10 percent security selection effect. The fund's beta and annualized tracking error for the period is calculated as 1.00 and 0.60 percent, respectively. The fund uses a bottom-up investment style and a concentrated holdings approach. As such, the fund's managers neither make explicit top-down industry allocation overweight or underweight decisions nor design the fund to behave like its benchmark, as a beta value of 1 would imply. Accordingly, fund managers place less value on the industry allocation effect, security selection effect, and beta and more on the overall outperformance and annualized tracking error numbers. In the newspaper industry, this is known as the "don't bury the headline" approach. This approach is useful for both an analytical audience (the client base) and in a time-constrained, multitasking, attention-span-dwindling world (the present). In this time-challenged world, the presentation must be insightful and immediately impactful.

Getting the Point Across

Graphical conveyance of knowledge is ready made to be insightful and immediately impactful, especially for performance and analytics data. As Degroot and Greenwood (2009/2010) state: "Graphical displays of performance and analytics data can transform a page of numbers into a more accessible and easier-to-interpret representation of investment information. By incorporating peer and index comparisons, time dimensions and a visual representation of data, a story that might be missed in a tabular form is uncovered" (77).

Using graphics is the one of the most effective ways to get important messages across and complex points conveyed. In particular, visual learners often are predisposed or prefer this medium. Thus, the graphical conveyance of knowledge has the opportunity to replace fixed income attribution as the "hottest topic" in performance measurement. Various sources such as the Financial Industry Regulatory

Authority (FINRA) (2000), Tufte (2001), Few (2004), Reynolds (2008), Rosling (2009), Ryan (2010), and Wong (2010) provide further discussion of graphical conveyance of knowledge.

Best Practices for Performance Presentations

The first five best practices are from the Regional Investment Performance Subcommittee for Europe, Middle, East, and Africa (RIPS EMEA, 2006):

- Reporting philosophy should be identifiable and transparent. For example, presentation of performance as a part of the client reporting should clearly state if a client return perspective or a portfolio manager return perspective is applied.
- Reporting should take into account the type of client. Institutional clients may have other reporting needs than private retail clients.
- Reporting should present a true and fair picture of the client assets and performance and contain all necessary details relevant to the client.
- Reporting should be timely and accurate.
- Reporting should take into consideration the applicable legal requirements. (CFA Institute [2006]. Republished and reprinted from *Guidance for Recipients of Investment Reporting* with permission from the CFA Institute. All rights reserved.)

The next two best practices are from the European investment Performance Committee (EIPC. 2004a):

- Return and risk attribution analysis must follow the investment decision process of the investment manager and measure the impact of the active management decisions. The attribution analysis must reflect the actual decisions made by the investment manager. Return and risk attribution analysis must mirror the investment style of the investment manager.
- For the attribution of relative return and risk, a benchmark appropriate to the investment strategy must be used. The employed benchmark should be specified in advance and meet such criteria as investability, transparency, and measurability. (Copyright [2004], CFA Institute. Republished and reprinted from *Guidance on Performance Attribution Presentation* with permission from the CFA Institute. All rights reserved.)

The remaining best practices are those based on the experience of the author:

- Reports should have a date and time stamp.
- Reports should facilitate transparency and comparability.
- Reports should specify which content, if any, is preliminary and subject to change.

- Reports should provide insights on the investment approach, performance drivers, relative trends, and time series.
- Report content should be multifaceted and comprehensive.
- Report content should integrate performance, risk, and positioning.
- Reports should have appropriate disclosures and be presented so that their clarity cannot be misunderstood.
- Terms within the report should be defined in an available glossary and/or in an annotated user's guide to the report or report template.
- Reports should be immediately impactful and insightful with cascading tiers of knowledge conveyance.
- Reports should be as straightforward and simple as possible and be stated in "plain English."
- Reports should use the most explanatory formats, which may include a mix of tables, charts, and narratives.

Putting presentations to this best practice's tests in the design phase, or at least before publishing, demonstrates a concerted, thoughtful approach to achieve knowledge conveyance. The best practices listed also ensure critical knowledge is properly received, interpreted, and applied. To that end, the investment industry has assisted through the Guidance for Recipients of Investment Reporting and Guidance on Performance Attribution Presentation resources as well as through EIPC (2002, 2004b). Dimson and Jackson (2001) caution against committing the potential error of overusing frequent observations to one's own detriment because increased frequency is not synonymous with increased effectiveness or insights.

Summary and Conclusions

Performance presentation is more than just listing a return. Performance presentation conveys vital knowledge of a portfolio's or composite's investment approach, positioning, and performance over recent time frames in absolute as well as index-relative and/or peer-relative terms and through indicative characteristics. Performance presentations and their content are critically important to each stakeholder in the investment management relationship and responsibility. Through performance presentations, portfolio or strategy performance and implementation are clarified in a direct and insightful manner. As such, performance presentations are a key component to meeting a required fiduciary duty and to providing fair representation and full disclosure to prospective clients as well as their intermediaries and representatives. The CFA Institute (2010) codifies this duty in its *Standards of Professional Conduct* (III.D—Duties to Clients—Performance Presentation) as follows: "When communicating investment performance information, Members or Candidates must make reasonable efforts to ensure it is fair, accurate, and complete" (2). Thus, the presentation should be used prudently.

Discussion Questions

1. How similar or customized are performance presentations?
2. Who contributes to the process of creating performance presentations?
3. How prevalent is reporting time-weighted returns as compared to dollar-weighted returns?
4. Which performance metric matters more: portfolio absolute return, portfolio benchmark-relative return, portfolio peer-universe ranking, or portfolio risk-adjusted return?

References

ACA Compliance Group's Beacon Verification Services and eVestment Alliance. 2009. "The Value of GIPS' Compliance: An Industry Survey." Available at http://www.beaconvs.com/documents/The%20Value%20of%20GIPS%20Compliance%20-%20an%20Industry%20Survey.pdf.

Amenc, Noel, and Veronique le Sourd. 2010. "An Advanced Methodology for Fund Rating." *Journal of Performance Measurement* 15:1, 16−24.

Bailey, Jeffrey V., Thomas M. Richards, and David E. Tierney. 2007. "Evaluating Portfolio Performance." In John L. Maginn, Donald L. Tuttle, Jerald E. Pinto, and Dennis W. McLeavey (eds.), *Managing Investment Portfolios: A Dynamic Process*, 3rd Edition, 717−782. Hoboken, NJ: John Wiley & Sons, Inc.

Campisi, Stephen. 2011. "Client Goal-Based Performance Analysis." *CFA Institute Conference Proceedings Quarterly*, March, 32−41.

CFA Institute. 2010. "Code of Ethics and Standards of Professional Conduct." Available at http://www.cfapubs.org/doi/pdf/10.2469/ccb.v2010.n14.1.

CFA Institute. 2010. "Global Investment Performance Standards." Available at http://www.cfapubs.org/doi/pdf/10.2469/ccb.v2010.n5.1

Degroot, George, and Paul Greenwood. 2009/2010. "Equity Style Analysis: Beyond Performance Measurement." *Journal of Performance Measurement* 14:2, 64−68.

diBartolomeo, Dan. 2003. "Just Because We Can Doesn't Mean We Should—Why Daily Observation Frequency in Performance Attribution Is Not Better." *Journal of Performance Measurement* 7:3, 30−36.

Dimson, Elroy, and Andrew Jackson. 2001. "High-Frequency Performance Monitoring." *Journal of Portfolio Management* 28:1, 33−43.

European Investment Performance Committee (EIPC). 2002. *Guidance for Users of Attribution Analysis*. Charlottesville, VA: The CFA Institute.

European Investment Performance Committee (EIPC). 2004a. *Guidance on Performance Attribution Presentation*. Charlottesville, VA: The CFA Institute.

European Investment Performance Committee (EIPC). 2004b. *Questionnaire for Investors*. Charlottesville, VA: The CFA Institute.

European Private Equity & Venture Capital Association (EVCA). 2010. *Reporting Guidelines*. Available at http://www.evca.eu/uploadedFiles/Home/Toolbox/Industry_Standards/evca_reporting_guidelines_2010.pdf.

Few, Stephen. 2004. *Show Me the Numbers: Designing Tables and Graphs to Enlighten*. Oakland, CA: Analytics Press.

Financial Industry Regulatory Authority (FINRA). 2000. "Inaccurate Performance Graphs Result in Formal Action." *Regulatory and Compliance Alerts*, Summer. Available at http://www.finra.org/Industry/Regulation/Guidance/RCA/p015307.

Galdi, Philip H. 2006. "Performance Measurement for Insurers and Other Book Income-Oriented Investors." In Timothy P. Ryan (ed.), *Portfolio Analysis: Advanced Topics in Performance Measurement, Risk and Attribution*, 67–102. London: Risk Books.

Hahn, Gregory J., and John C. Saf. 1997. "Measuring Performance of the Insurance Company Portfolio." In Frank J. Fabozzi (ed.), *Managing Fixed Income Portfolios*, 493–526. New Hope, PA: Frank J. Fabozzi Associates.

Reynolds, Garr. 2008. *Presentation Zen: Simple Ideas on Presentation Design and Delivery.* Berkeley, CA: New Riders Press.

Regional Investment Performance Subcommittee for Europe, Middle East, and Africa (RIPS EMEA). 2006. *Guidance for Recipients of Investment Reporting.* Charlottesville, VA: The CFA Institute.

Rosling, Hans. 2009. "Time Series Analysis Tool Speech and Demonstration." TED (Technology, Entertainment, Design). Available at http://www.ted.com/talks/hans_rosling_at_state. html.

Ryan, Timothy P. 2010. "Get Graphic,,, And Your Client's Full Attention." *Performance Measurement & Client Reporting Review* 3:1, 18–23.

Ryan, Timothy P. 2009/2010. "Target Practice." *Performance Measurement & Client Review* 2:2, 41–47.

Tufte, Edward R. 2001. *The Visual Display of Quantitative Information*, 2nd Edition. Cheshire, CT: Graphics Press.

Wong, Dona M. 2010. *The Wall Street Journal Guide to Informational Graphics: The Dos and Don'ts of Presenting Data, Facts, and Figures.* New York: W. W. Norton & Company.

Section Seven

SPECIAL TOPICS

26

Exchange Traded Funds

The Success Story of the Last Two Decades

GERASIMOS G. ROMPOTIS
Assistant Audit Manager, International Certified Auditors,
Greece, and PhD Candidate, National and Kapodistrian
University of Athens

Introduction

Exchange traded funds (ETFs) are one of the most successful financial innovations of the last two decades. The majority of ETFs seek to replicate the performance of specific domestic, sector, regional, or international indexes. To meet their investment goal, ETFs are usually fully invested in the securities of the underlying indexes. However, a small portion of ETFs' assets (up to 5 percent of total funds) might be allocated in other indexes' components or held in cash accounts.

According to Gastineau (2001), the origins of ETFs go back to the late 1970 and early 1980s and to the so-called portfolio or program trading, which involved the idea of trading an entire portfolio consisting of stocks included in the S&P 500 index. Index participation shares (IPS), an S&P 500 proxy that started trading on the American Stock Exchange (AMEX) and the Philadelphia Stock Exchange in 1989, preceded ETFs as they are known today. This ETF initially experienced great success with investors but was short lived, because the Chicago Mercantile Exchange claimed that an ETF was essentially a future contract and, therefore, it could not trade on the exchange as an ordinary stock. The Federal Court of Chicago commanded the withdrawal of IPS, and investors redeemed their shares. An investment product similar to IPS, the Toronto Index Participation Shares (TIPS), was developed in Canada and started trading on the Toronto Stock Exchange (TSE) in 1990. TIPS were initially benchmarked to the TSE 35 index and later to the TSE 100 index and proved to be very popular with Canadian and foreign investors due to their low cost and trading flexibility. However, the TSE decided to cease trading TIPS and their shares were redeemed or absorbed by the BGI 60 fund.

Although the aforementioned ETFs were short lived, they set the foundation for the growth and the spectacular proliferation of ETFs in the following years. After the first two failed efforts, State Street Global Advisors introduced the well-known Standard and Poor's Depository Receipts (SPDRs) on the AMEX in January 1993. This ETF tracked the performance of the S&P 500 index and became the largest ETF in the world. In May 1995, the same company introduced the MidCap SPDRs, which track the S&P Mid-Cap 400 index. Barclays Global Investors entered the ETF universe in 1996 with the launch of World Equity Benchmark Shares (WEBS), which were subsequently renamed iShares MSCI Index Fund Shares. The 17 original WEBS tracked country indexes of Morgan Stanley and enabled casual investors to easily access foreign markets. The so-called DIAMONDS, which follow the Dow Jones Industrial Average, appears in 1998. State Street Global Advisors also developed in 1998 the Sector Spiders, which follow the nine individual sectors of the S&P 500 index. A year later, the so-called CUBES, pursuing the Nasdaq 100 index, entered the ETF marketplace. In early 2000 Barclays Global Investors launched iShares, which track several domestic or foreign broad and sector indexes. Within five years from their inception, the assets held by iShares index funds surpassed the assets of any other ETF competitor in the United States and Europe. Vanguard, which is the biggest provider of traditional open-ended index funds, entered the ETF market in 2005.

Another fast growing trend in the ETF market concerns fixed-income ETFs. In July 2002, Barclays was the first investment company to launch fixed-income ETFs in the US market (Mazzilli, Maister, and Perlman, 2008). Another trend in the ETF universe concerns leveraged and inverse leveraged ETFs, whose investment target is to deliver twice or three times (in a positive or a negative fashion, respectively), the return of a specific index on a daily basis. Proshares introduced the first leveraged ETFs in June 2006. Finally, on April 30, 2008, Invesco PowerShares launched the first equity-linked actively managed ETFs. In the German market, active ETFs have been traded since the beginning of the 21st century. Both leveraged and active ETFs respond to the need of investors for implementing more active strategies with ETFs.

Currently, ETFs invest in whatever an investor could imagine. According to Liz Skinner's report released on InvestmentNews.com on November 21, 2010, 1,049 equity-linked, fixed-income, commodity, and currency ETFs in the United States hold $995 billion in assets. The corresponding figures for active ETF market are 22 funds and $1.23 billion invested in them. The same spectacular growth is observed in the overseas ETF market.

The main body of this chapter describes the features, benefits, and structures of ETFs. ETF trading strategies are also discussed along with empirical findings concerning some key elements of investing with ETFs. These elements are as follows: the competition with traditional mutual funds, the ability of ETFs to efficiently replicate the return of their benchmarks and the factors that affect them, and the divergence between the trading and net asset values (NAVs) of ETFs and whether ETF pricing can be used to predict future returns. A summary and conclusions section highlights the key points of this chapter.

Features and Benefits

ETFs owe their success and worldwide popularity among both institutional and retail investors to their unique trading characteristics and advantages. For example, ETFs have low administrative costs compared to other investment products because the majority of them pursue a passive management investment strategy. Passive management not only leads to low administrative, marketing, distribution and accounting expenses but also allows individual investors to benefit from economies of scale by spreading administration and transaction costs over a large number of investors. Further, most ETFs have no 12b-1 fees (marketing fees) and do not charge investors any front-end or back-end fees as many mutual funds do. Moreover, ETFs do not need to buy and sell securities to meet shareholders purchases and redemptions because these actions are performed through the exchange of ETF shares with the underlying securities without cash deposits. The low cost of ETFs is reflected in their expense ratios, which are considerably lower than those of active mutual funds. The fees charged by ETFs are comparable or lower than those charged by classic index funds. Yet, ETFs must pay brokerage commissions and are subject to costs relating to the bid-ask spread. Both the commissions and the bid-ask spread vary among the various types of ETFs.

The buying and selling flexibility is another advantage of ETFs. In particular, investors can buy and sell ETFs at current market prices at any time throughout the trading day. Traditional mutual funds and unit investment trusts (UITs) do not have such flexibility as they can only be traded at the end of the day. Moreover, just like ordinary stocks, ETFs can be purchased on margin and sold short, enabling their use in hedging strategies and traded using stop-and-limit orders because they are exempt from the "uptick" rule. Such active strategies are unavailable with mutual funds and UITs.

ETFs are considered tax-efficient investment vehicles because they generally generate low capital gains as a result of the low turnover displayed by their portfolio securities. This advantage is also available with traditional index funds, but the tax efficiency of ETFs is further enhanced by the unique "in-kind" creation and redemption process of their shares. In particular, ETF shares are created in creation units, which are large blocks of tens of thousands of ETF shares, by authorized participants (usually large institutional investors) via the deposit of the underlying index's equities to a trustee and the issuance of ETF shares in return to this deposit. These shares are then sold to the secondary market. The shares of an ETF are redeemed by exchanging the shares with the deposited baskets of equities. In this process, no money transaction occurs and no taxable capital gains are realized.

The high degree of liquidity associated with the in-kind creation and redemption process is another attractive feature of the ETF market. In an ongoing process, the authorized participants act as market makers on the open market and whenever arbitrage opportunities relating to the gaps between the trading prices of ETFs and their NAVs are noticed. Authorized participants use their ability to exchange creation units with the underlying baskets of securities to provide liquidity of the ETF shares and to help ensure that their intraday market price approximates the NAV of the underlying assets. The efficient arbitrage execution contributes to eliminating these divergences, which is the reason that ETFs usually trade at slight and short-lasting premiums or discounts to their NAV. Conversely, regular open-ended mutual funds offer no arbitrage opportunities. This is also the case for traditional closed-end funds, which usually trade at larger premiums or discounts to their NAVs because the pricing of their shares is set by supply and demand forces.

Moreover, ETFs are considered an efficient means for investors to implement effective risk diversification strategies. ETFs enable investors to access the hundreds or thousands of stocks comprising an index in an easy and inexpensive way. The cost of individually acquiring the stocks that make up an index would not allow implementing such diversification strategies. Additionally, ETFs offer many options concerning market exposure. In this respect, the exposure to several broad-based indexes, broad-based international and country-specific indexes, industry sector-specific indexes, bond indexes, and commodities is available with ETFs.

A final feature of ETFs concerns their transparency. ETFs are priced at frequent intervals throughout the trading day and, unlike many investment vehicles such as mutual funds that only disclose their holdings quarterly, most of them publish their exact holdings on a daily basis. The publication of ETF holdings helps investors know what they actually own and accordingly respond to the trends in the ETF market. However, full transparency is not a feature available with all ETFs because some ETF families refuse to frequently disclose their holdings. Vanguard is an example in this respect because it usually discloses its ETF holdings every 90 days.

Structure

In general, investment institutions issuing ETFs typically must abide by the Investment Company Act of 1940. Several types of ETF structures exist. In brief, traditional equity-linked and bond ETFs resemble open-ended mutual funds or UITs. Conversely, ETFs that invest in commodities, currencies, and other specialized strategies are usually organized as grantor trusts and exchange-traded notes. Although all types of ETFs share some basic common characteristics, the different types of ETFs imply different tax implications, different frequencies in dividend distribution as well as different treatment of dividends, unequal trading, and investing flexibility. This section describes the various structures of ETFs in more detail.

The most popular structure adopted by various ETF families such as iShares, Sector SPDRs, Powershares, and Vanguard ETFs concerns the open-ended structure, which is assumed to provide ETF investors with the greatest trading flexibility. ETFs of this type are registered under the Investment Company Act of 1940. The open-ended ETFs are managed by an administrator, who is responsible for making all the investment decisions including the decision to reinvest accrued dividends, lend the underlying securities, adopt portfolio optimization techniques, and use derivative products for enhancing the delivery of investment targets. Usually, in the case of open-ended ETFs, the dividends received on the underlying basket securities are immediately reinvested while a monthly or a quarterly dividend distribution applies for open-ended ETFs. Finally, open-ended ETFs have no expiration dates.

The second most popular ETF type is the UIT structure. This is the structure followed by some of the oldest and best known ETFs such as SPDRs, DIAMONDS, and CUBES. The Investment Company Act of 1940 is the relevant legislation for UITs. ETFs structured as UITs do not have an administrator as they are not allowed to invest in securities not included in the tracking index. In other words, the UIT ETFs are usually fully invested in the components of the underlying benchmarks and at the same weights. In the case of UITs, the accrued dividends on the index stocks are not reinvested in the fund, but they are kept in nonbearing accounts until they are paid to shareholders quarterly or annually. The nonreinvestment of dividends triggers the so-called dividend drag effect and is considered as to be one of the factors that negatively affects the replication efficiency of ETFs organized as UITs. Furthermore, the UITs are not permitted to lend the underlying securities (thus, not receiving income from the lending) or to hold positions in derivative securities. Finally, unlike the open-ended ETFs, UITs have expiration dates usually ranging from a period of some years to decades. However, the expiration dates are usually extended.

The third most common ETF structure concerns the grantor trust scheme. These ETFs are significantly different from the traditional mutual funds and not considered as to be investment companies according to the US legislation. In particular, the grantor trusts are registered under the Securities Act of 1933. The investors in these ETFs obtain ownership of a portion of the underlying securities along with voting rights on these securities. Further, the grantor trust ETFs pay dividends directly to the shareholders. Moreover, these ETFs are fully invested in specific securities without rebalancing, but they can lend the underlying securities for a short time, just like traditional mutual funds do. The streetTRACKS Gold Shares, the iShares Silver Trust, and the HOLDRs of Merrill Lynch are some examples of ETFs structured as grantor trusts.

The final structure considered are the so-called exchange traded notes (ETNs) issued as debt instruments by Barclays, whose performance is linked to the return of a specific security or index. ETNs are registered under the Securities Act of 1933. The ETN structure is preferable for specialized asset classes such as commodities and emerging markets. No uniform treatment of dividends exists for the ETNs: Some ETFs of this kind reinvest the dividends in the fund, others do not. Under current tax law, commodity and equity ETNs are taxed as prepaid contracts. This means that any difference between the sale and purchase prices will be classified as capital gain while there are no other distributions with ETNs. Taxable capital gains are also realized upon the maturity of the contract. However, the currency-linked ETNs are treated as ordinary debt for tax purposes. This means that any interest deriving from the note is taxed as ordinary income, even though the interest is reinvested and not paid out until the shareholder sells the ETN shares or the contract matures.

Investing Strategies

The first ETFs mainly addressed the needs of institutional investors who used them for applying sophisticated trading strategies such hedging or for investing dormant cash. Later, however, ETFs became appealing both to institutional and retail investors who wanted to enter the stock markets and receive capital gains while diversifying the risk of their portfolios. The unique features of ETFs—such as the simplicity of the product, low cost, trading flexibility, tax efficiency, and transparency contributed to ETFs—becoming one of the most successful financial innovations of the last two decades.

ETFs serve several needs of investors. In this respect, there are both common and noncommon usages of ETFs by institutional and retail investors. The common usages include the replacement of a high volume of transactions with just one single transaction, equitization of cash (i.e., creating systematic risk exposure from a market-neutral position), asset allocation in buy-and-hold strategies, tactical asset allocation, risk diversification, hedging of short or long positions on market indexes, and acquiring structured portfolios offered at low cost by specialized investment advisors. Some institutional investors such as pension funds use ETFs in order to hedge other investment positions because they are not permitted to use derivative products. By contrast, mutual fund managers use ETFs to enhance their liquidity during periods of massive redemptions by shareholders.

In addition to the general uses of ETFs just described, the various types of ETFs reflect different strategies and possibilities that are feasible with ETFs. The main investment strategies available with ETFs are summarized in this section.

The first option is the passive investment in domestic broad market indexes via the corresponding market index ETFs. This option is available to all ETF markets worldwide while the respective ETFs are usually among the most tradable securities on the exchanges. At the same time, an investor who wants to obtain access to foreign markets or hedge foreign investing risk can choose from the bulk of foreign, regional, or global market ETFs. The iShares in Morgan Stanley country indexes is an example of ETFs offering exposure to foreign markets.

The exposure to broad indexes, either domestic or foreign, is not the only possibility for investors. Investors may want to take advantage of the trends in specific sectors or industries without needing to invest in the entire market. The sector and industry ETFs fulfill this need of investors, who are not required to purchase the plethora of individual stocks comprising the targeted sector or industry.

Style ETFs offer investors the opportunity to invest in specific types of stocks. Style ETFs can be structured to expose investors to securities having a specific level of capitalization such as small cap, mid cap, or large cap. Also, style ETFs may consist of stocks within a specific class such as growth securities, value securities, and blended ones. Style ETFs are suitable for investors with a defined investment orientation who want to diversify their portfolio or hedge other positions.

Risk-averse investors or investors who want to enter the fixed-income market can use fixed-income or bond ETFs to gain access to a wide spectrum of fixed-income investment instruments from sovereign and corporate bonds, covered bonds, credit default swaps as well as alternative securities such as interest rate volatility or inflation swaps. For an ETF investing in stock indexes, the fund is generally composed of all stocks in the underlying index. However, this is not the case for the majority of fixed-income ETFs, which usually apply optimization techniques and consequently hold a fraction of the bonds that comprise the underlying index. Bond prices are relatively straightforward given that they are a function of the risk-free rate, the coupon, the quality of the bond, and the years to maturity. However, investors should bear in mind that tracking failure between bond ETFs and their holdings is probable due to noncurrent trading hours. The foreign currency ETFs is another option. Currency ETFs are investment vehicles that track a foreign currency enabling investors to wager on foreign currencies with simple transactions. In some cases, currency ETF may track a basket of currencies.

The commodity ETFs (ETCs) are another growing component of ETF markets. The commodity ETFs provide access to a wide range of commodities and commodity indices including energy, metals, and agriculture. Commodity ETFs resemble the sector or industry ETFs because they channel their assets to a certain area of the market. However, investors in ETCs should bear in mind that when they obtain shares of a commodity ETF, they do not buy the commodity itself but actually acquire front-month future contracts, which are used by the ETC in order to replicate the price of the underlying commodity. Given the fact that the ETCs are index funds seeking to emulate the performance of nonsecurity indexes and that they do not invest in securities, ETCs are not regulated under the Investment Company Act of 1940 in the United States. However, the Securities and Exchange Commission (SEC) supervises the public offering of commodity ETFs, which are registered under the Securities Exchange Act of 1934.

Derivative ETFs consist of derivative contracts such as futures, forwards, and options. These ETFs still attempt to replicate the performance of a specific investment vehicle but they use other means than the traditional ETFs to do so. Usually, derivative ETFs can invest in individual securities or in derivative products on single securities or indexes.

Moreover, investors wanting to receive regular income from dividends can also use ETFs. For example, some ETFs invest in equities that pay dividends on a regular basis. Such ETFs usually track a dividend index and the assets in the fund and index consist of a diverse range of dividend-paying securities. In some cases, the dividend stocks are segmented according to their capitalization or geographic location.

Another nontraditional type of ETFs is the leveraged (ultra funds) and inverse ETFs (short funds) whose main investment objective is to provide investors with two or three times the performance of an index in a positive (ultra ETFs) or a negative way (short ETFs) on a daily basis. Along with fulfilling the need of investors for implementing more active strategies with ETFs, these ETFs can also be viewed as a means for investors to hedge their exposure to the ETF market in a simpler and cheaper way than the placement in complex and risky index futures or other derivative products would entail. Given their investment philosophy, the leveraged and inverse-leveraged ETFs are suitable for very short-term traders. For more long-run holding periods, the returns of leveraged and inverse-leveraged ETFs will likely differ in amount and/or direction from the target return for the same period due to the compounding of daily returns.

The key element in the operation of these ETFs is the leverage ratio. In particular, the portfolio must be rebalanced at the end of each day in order for the leverage ratio not to change from day to day. In regard to the magnitude of leverage ratio, on a profitable day a long (short) ETF is under- (over-) leveraged for the following day and needs to increase (decrease) its index exposure by acquiring (redeeming) stocks or index derivatives. The opposite action must be taken on a downturn day.

Another recent innovation in the ETF marketplace at least in the United States concerns actively managed ETFs, which combine the benefits and characteristics of regular ETFs and traditional mutual funds. The active and passive ETFs have major structural differences. The main difference between them is that regular, passively managed ETFs are structured to track a specific public market index, while the active ETFs aim at outperforming the market. Active ETFs are assigned a benchmark while they are usually designed to track a popular investment manager's top picks, mirror any existing mutual fund or pursue a particular investment objective, and target to offer investors above-average returns.

Some other differences exist between passive and active ETFs such as the number of market makers required by each type of ETFs (at least two and one market maker for passive and active ETFs, respectively) the minimum size of investment (not required by passive ETFs but required by active ETFs), and the relationship between the market maker and the ETF manager. In particular, these parties are not related in the case of passive ETFs while the market maker and the manager of an active ETF belong to the same company.

Review of Empirical Findings

This section provides a comprehensive analysis of the literature's findings on various core issues relating to ETFs. These issues concern the following areas: competition between ETFs and traditional mutual funds, tracking efficiency of ETFs and the factors that affect it, the gap between the trading and NAV of ETFs, and the ability of one predicting the future returns of ETFs on the basis of trading premiums or discounts.

ETFS VERSUS INDEX FUNDS

The ETFs versus index funds debate has attracted substantial interest in the literature because these two investment products are considered to be strong competitors. The empirical research comparing these products has mainly focused on the costs charged to their investors as well as their performance and ability to efficiently replicate the return of their benchmarks.

Dellva (2001) compares the costs of the most important trackers in terms of assets under management and trading activity of the S&P 500 index, which are the SPDRs and Barclay's iShares S&P from the family of ETFs and the Vanguard 500 Index Fund from the bundle of mutual funds. This comparison reveals a

significant annual expense benefit of ETFs despite ETFs generally bearing transaction costs and paying brokerage commissions while their trading is also subject to the bid-ask spread, which is kind of cost shouldered on investors. Dellva
notes that this cost benefit of ETFs becomes greater when extending an investor's
investment horizon.

Kostovetsky (2003) also supports the cost benefit provided by ETFs compared
to mutual funds. Yet Bernstein (2002) questions the cost advantage of ETFs.
She contends that this advantage is weakened or eliminated by the temptation
of investors to liquidate their shares frequently. The average holding interval for
SPDRs during the first five months of 2001 was 10 days and for the QQQ (which
tracks the Nasdaq 100 Index) only four days. The short holding periods along
with the brokerage commissions can offset the lower expense basis of ETFs.

Elton, Gruber, Comer, and Li (2002) survey the primary trackers of the S&P
500 index. They consider the return of SPDRs compared with the return of corresponding index funds and futures contracts. The authors report that the SPDRs
underperform their counterparts. They attribute the underperformance to the lost
income caused by SPDRs not reinvesting the dividends received on the underlying assets and holding them in nonbearing accounts as a result of them being
structured as a UIT.

In the same spirit, Gastineau (2004) suggests that the pretax return of ETFs is
generally inferior to the return of index funds benchmarked to the same indexes.
Yet, Poterba and Shoven (2002), who focus on the pretax and aftertax returns of
SPDRs and Vanguard 500 Index Fund, find no significant difference between the
returns of these competitive funds.

The findings of Rompotis (2008a, 2008b) also support the similarity in
returns of ETFs and index funds. Rompotis (2008a) uses a sample of 16 pairs of
ETFs and index funds having the same benchmark and finds no significant difference in average daily returns between these two investment products. Using
an extended sample of 23 ETFs and index funds tracking the same benchmark
and employing more recent return data than those in the first study, Rompotis
(2008b) reconfirms his initial conclusion about the equality of performance
between competitive ETFs and index funds. Svetina and Wahal (2008) also draw
the same conclusion.

All the aforementioned studies focus on the competition between ETFs and
mutual funds using cost and return data of US-listed funds. In regard to the
non-US ETF market, Gallagher and Segara (2004) compare corresponding ETFs
and index funds traded on the Australian market and find no difference between
the performances of these competitive products. Zanotti and Russo (2005) examine the risk-adjusted return of ETFs traded on the Italian stock market along with
the return of corresponding mutual funds. The authors find that the risk-adjusted
performance of ETFs is greater than that of mutual funds. Moreover, focusing on
the emerging ETF market in Greece, Rompotis (2011b) examines whether patterns in expenses and returns of ETFs and index funds in this less developed
market differ from those in the developed ones. The author reconfirms the cost
advantage of ETFs relative to index funds. Yet, Rompotis finds that ETFs underperform the mutual funds contrary to evidence by Zanotti and Russo on the

Italian ETF market, which is also an emerging market as far as ETFs are concerned. Overall, the findings on the Greek market are in line with those concerning the US stock market.

Researchers have also addressed the debate involving ETFs versus index funds using fund data from the same investing family. For example, Rompotis (2009a) studies the return and risk attributes of ETFs and index funds managed by Vanguard. His intention is to determine whether a different treatment and philosophy is applied to the two alternative investment products. According to the findings, Vanguard ETFs and index funds perform similarly to each other while having similar risk levels. Thus, an inference of this finding is that Vanguard treats ETFs and index funds in a similar manner.

A final issue relating to the competition between ETFs and index funds concerns the possible substitution of index funds by ETFs. In this respect, Huang and Guedj (2009) report that ETFs and index funds coexist because they are chosen by investors with different liquidity needs. More specifically, investors with high liquidity needs prefer to invest in open-ended mutual funds while ETFs are better suited for investors having longer investment horizons and are willing to invest in narrower and less liquid indexes. Therefore, based on the liquidity needs, ETFs do not seem to replace conventional index funds.

Agapova (2010) examines whether a substitution effect exists between ETFs and index mutual funds managed by Vanguard similar to that observed in the industry in general. Her results indicate that the ETFs and index funds managed by the same family are not substitutes but rather complements because of the presence of a positive spillover effect between them. That is, the asset flows into ETFs and index funds positively affect each other. Yet, evidence by Agapova (2011) reveals a substitution effect between ETFs and index funds when the assets flows to non-relating funds are taken into account. The author reports that an increase in ETF flows by one dollar creates an expectable decrease in conventional index funds' flows by 22 cents. Agapova explains the replacement of index funds with ETFs on the basis of a tax clientele effect, which suggests that the tax-averse investors invest in ETFs whereas the tax-neutral investors are driven to traditional index funds.

TRACKING ETF EFFICIENCY

The core target for the majority of ETFs is to replicate the return of specific benchmarks by pursuing a passive investment strategy. However, the perfect performance replication by ETFs (as well as index funds) is rare, if not impossible. In general, evidence shows that passively managed investment products underperform their benchmarks. This deviation in returns is called tracking error and has drawn much interest from researchers, who suggest several factors that contribute to index funds and ETFs failing to perfectly replicate the return of the underlying indexes.

Empirical evidence on ETFs' tracking error is voluminous. For instance, Elton et al. (2002) reveal an average annual underperformance of SPDRs compared to the return of the S&P 500 index of 0.28 percent between 1993 and 1998. They attribute the tracking error of SPDRs to the lack of dividend reinvestment.

Gastineau (2004) reports that ETFs display inferior returns compared to the underlying indexes. The author believes that the tracking error of ETFs is due to the lack of aggressiveness displayed by ETF managers when faced with changes in the composition of the underlying indexes. He also notes that the ongoing in-kind creation and redemption process of ETFs weakens the ability of their managers to accurately, immediately, and inexpensively respond to the adjustments of the tracking indexes, resulting in lower returns and higher tracking errors.

Johnson (2009) examines the relationship between the return of foreign country ETFs and the underlying index returns. He shows that the positive excess returns of foreign indexes relative to the US index and the nonoverlapping trading hours between the different markets explains the tracking error of country ETFs. Various studies conducted by Rompotis (2008a, 2008b, 2010a, 2011a) confirm that US-listed ETFs are subject to significant tracking error. In these studies, the author investigates various factors that induce the tracking error of ETFs. He empirically demonstrates that the expenses, volatility, nonfull replication strategies frequently adopted by several ETFs, geographical focus (namely whether they are domestically or internationally allocated), and age of ETFs significantly affect their tracking efficiency. Further, Rompotis shows that the tracking error strongly persists on an annual basis.

Other studies on ETFs traded on various exchanges overseas show that non-US ETFs are also subject to significant tracking failure. For example, Gallagher and Segara (2004) find that the Australian ETFs fail to perfectly replicate the performance of the selected indexes. Rompotis (2008c) reveals a similar with situation with XTRA funds traded on the board of Deutsche Boerse. In the case of German ETFs, the positive correlation of ETFs' tracking error with expenses and risk found in the US market applies to the German market too. Rompotis demonstrates that the bid-ask spread also introduces tracking error. Furthermore, Blitz, Huij, and Swinkels (2009) find that the European ETFs underperform their benchmarks on an annual basis and suggest that the dividend taxes along with expenses account for this underperformance. Chu (2009) reports that the ETFs listed in the market of Honk Kong suffer from a higher tracking error than that observed in the US and Australian ETF markets. The author reconfirms the positive impact of expenses on the magnitude of tracking error while finding that the size of ETFs in terms of assets under management is negatively related to tracking error. Milonas and Rompotis (2010) show that a tracking error effect applies to the Swiss-listed ETFs. Their evidence also reveals that the tracking error records of ETFs written on non-European indexes are higher than those of ETFs following indexes from the European stock market.

Tracking error of ETFs has been investigated relative to the tracking error of competitive index funds. Gallagher and Segara (2004) find that the Australian ETFs have lower tracking errors than the competitive index funds. Rompotis (2008a) reveals weak statistical evidence that the tracking error of ETFs is higher than that of the corresponding open-ended index funds while Rompotis (2008b) provides stronger evidence on the disadvantage of ETFs with respect to index funds in terms of tracking error. Aber, Li, and Can (2009) verify the findings of Rompotis (2008a, 2008b). The authors indicate that the conventional index funds managed by Vanguard beat the respective iShares when the tracking efficiency in concerned. Finally, Rompotis (2011b) shows that the ETFs in the Greek market have greater tracking error than the corresponding index funds.

All the cited studies on the tracking error of ETFs in both the US and non-US markets concern the equity-linked ETFs. The tracking efficiency of fixed-income ETFs has drawn less attention from the industry literature. Evidence by Rompotis (2010b) reveals that the respective iShares listed in the US market underperform the underlying market benchmarks. However, the magnitude of tracking error of these ETFs is not very high and considerably lower than usually observed in the equity ETF market. Drenovak, Uroševic, and Jelic (2011) report the opposite results for European bond ETFs. In particular, the bond ETFs traded in Europe outperform their bond index benchmarks by a range of 10 to 27 basis points. Moreover, the authors note that the outperformance is more prominent in the case of bond ETFs employing physical replication techniques via the acquisition of the actual securities held in the underlying indexes and not synthetic swaps.

PREMIUMS AND RETURNS

Similar to close-ended funds (CEFs), ETFs trade on stock exchanges at prices that usually differ from their NAV. However, in contrast to CEFs, the magnitude of the premiums or discounts observed in the pricing of ETFs is not significant at normal levels whereas these premiums or discount are short lived as a result of the efficient arbitrage execution by big institutional investors. Researchers have thoroughly investigated the efficiency in the pricing of ETFs.

Ackert and Tian (2000) examine the pricing of SPDRs. They find that SPDRs did not trade at economically significant discounts between 1993 and 1997 despite the primary investors in SPDRs during this period were individual investors. The authors attribute the insignificance of the discounts to the redemption mechanism, which enables the sophisticated investors to take advantage of mispricing and to eliminate it using arbitrage techniques. Moreover, Ackert and Tian find that the MidCap SPDRs had larger and economically significant discounts than the SPDRs as a result of the higher arbitrage costs.

In their study of the pricing of SPDRs, Elton et al. (2002) also find that the daily trading prices of this ETF move closely to the corresponding NAVs. They attribute this result to the efficient arbitrage's execution as evidenced by the increased trading volume triggered by the lagged premiums and intraday volatility of the underlying market index. Curcio, Lipka, and Thornton (2004) provide the same results on CUBES. With respect to iShares, various studies such as these of Cherry (2004) and Rompotis (2009b, 2010c) find that the premiums or discounts of these ETFs are not significant in magnitude and are lacking in persistence.

All the studies above concentrate on US-listed ETFs. In regard to other ETF markets, Gallagher and Segara (2004) find that in the case of ETFs listed on the Australian exchange, the deviation between their trading and NAV is not that frequent and sizeable. Kayali (2007a, 2007b) reports slight but significant discounts in the pricing of local ETFs in the Turkish market. Although these discounts are statistically significant, they are not economically significant whereas they sharply disappear in the next two trading days. Rompotis (2008c) shows that the German ETFs trade at a slight discount to their NAVs, which on average amounts to 27 basis points. The author does not consider this discount to be especially high, which implies that the efficient arbitrage also applies to the German ETF market.

The aforementioned studies basically focus on ETFs that are invested in domestic market indexes. However, the results on the pricing efficiency of ETFs could differ when discriminating between domestic and foreign ETFs. In this respect, the findings of Engle and Sarkar (2002) are enlightening. Although they support the lack of persistence in premiums/discounts of ETFs, the authors point out that the premium/discount of country ETFs is greater and more persistent than that of the domestically allocated ETFs.

Hughen (2003) studies the Malaysian iShares and finds significant premiums and discounts in the pricing of this ETF after the local government poses substantial burdens on arbitrage execution. Jares and Lavin (2004), who study the Japan and Hong Kong iShares that trade on the AMEX, also find significant and frequent deviations between the trading prices and the NAVs of these ETFs. In the same spirit, Ackert and Tian (2008) verify the finding that the country ETFs trade at larger and more consistent deviations from their NAVs.

Another important issue regarding the pricing of ETFs concerns the predictability of future returns on the basis of mispricing. Findings of the literature indicate that the performance of ETFs can be predictable based on information provided by the deviation between their trading values and NAVs. For example, Cherry (2004) finds that discounts are meaningful in explaining future returns. In particular, the author reports that an inverse relationship exists between the lagged discount and the contemporary return of iShares. Cherry also shows that trading strategies based on premium and discounts can beat naïve buy-and-hold strategies, which is inconsistent with the efficient market hypothesis.

Rompotis (2009b, 2009c, 2010c) also finds support for the negative impact of the lagged premium/discount on return. Additionally, he finds that the return of ETFs is positively related to its contemporary premium or discount. Moreover, Rompotis (2010c) provides evidence that ETFs displaying higher discounts (or the lowest premiums) are likely to perform better than ETFs having the highest premium. The findings on the relationship between return and lagged and contemporary premium revealed by Rompotis (2009b, 2009c, 2010c) contrast with those of Jares and Lavin (2004). The latter authors demonstrate that the discounts in the pricing of ETFs can be exploitable for predicting future returns but reported a negative and a positive correlation between return and concurrent and lagged premium, respectively for Japan and Hong Kong iShares. Simon and Sternberg (2004) also report significant predictability of the return of European iShares traded on the AMEX on the basis of the premium to their NAV.

All of the studies previously cited dealing with the pricing of ETFs and the predictability of future return on the basis of the premiums or discounts observed between the trading price and NAV of ETFs concern equity-linked ETFs. Conversely, little work is available on the pricing of fixed-income ETFs

despite them being a fast growing trend in the ETF market. One study, however, concerns the pricing of bond ETFs. Rompotis (2010b) examines the pricing mechanism of iShares listed in the United States and finds that they trade
at a persistent premium to their NAV. The persistence in the premium of bond
ETFs contrasts with the findings on equity ETFs, whose premiums or discounts
are, in general, not persistent. On the question of the relationship between
the returns and premiums or discounts of fixed-income ETFs, the findings of
Rompotis (2010b) are in line with those on equity ETFs. The return is positively and negatively influenced by the contemporaneous and lagged premium,
respectively.

Summary and Conclusions

This chapter introduces ETFs by describing their characteristics and benefits as
well as several key issues relating to ETFs that have been empirically investigated. ETFs experienced a great flourish after the introduction of SPDRs in 1993
and have become one of the most successful financial products of the last two
decades. The proliferation of ETFs is evidenced by the thousands of such products launched in stock markets worldwide during the past two decades and the
trillions of funds globally invested in these products.

The success of ETFs is based on their unique features and the plethora of
choices that they provide investors. This chapter summarizes the trading characteristics and the benefits offered to investors by ETFs. In particular, the low
costs, especially compared with the charges of traditional open-ended mutual
funds, trading flexibility, tax efficiency, high liquidity, wide risk diversification,
and transparency of ETFs are discussed justifying the spectacular popularity of
ETFs with investors. Moreover, the chapter provides a discussion of the various
investing choices offered by ETFs, which make them highly appealing both to
retail and institutional investors. Such strategies include investment in domestic, foreign country, regional or global market indexes; allocation in sectors or
industries, either domestic or international ones; implementation of strategies
focusing on specific style of securities such as small-cap, mid-cap and large-cap
stocks or growth, value and blend securities; choices from the fixed-income and
currency markets; access to commodity and derivative markets via specialized
ETFs; and leveraged and inverse-leveraged strategies as well as actively managed ETFs.

Empirical findings are discussed involving various issues. The first issue discussed concerns the competition between ETFs and traditional mutual funds at
three levels. The first level concerns the cost relating to the investment in each
product. In general, researchers report a cost advantage of ETFs over their mutual
fund counterparts in terms of administrative fees. They also highlight that ETFs
are subject to additional costs such as the bid-ask spread and the commissions
paid to brokerage houses, which do not apply when investing in mutual funds.
At the second level, the empirical investigation reveals that ETFs typically do

not outperform the mutual funds but actually underperform them in some cases. At the third level, the research demonstrates that a substitution effect generally exists between ETFs and index funds considering asset flows. In particular, the ETFs seem to attract a large amount of funds compared to their mutual fund peers.

The chapter also discusses empirical research on tracking efficiency and the factors that affect it. Researchers show that the perfect replication of the underlying portfolio's return is a nonevent for ETFs as for index funds. This failure applies to all the types of ETFs and to all ETF markets worldwide. Researchers offer several explanations for this failure. Some factors that negatively influence the ability of ETFs to deliver the performance of the tracking indexes include expenses, nonfull strategies replication frequently adopted by ETFs, and nonreinvestment of dividends. Other factors include the so-called cash drag effect as well as dividend taxes, bid-ask spreads, and geographical proximity between ETFs and the underlying assets and the resulting nonoverlapping trading hours in the cases of international ETFs. Research shows that ETFs, when compared to index funds in terms of tracking error, usually fall short of them. That is, the tracking error of ETFs is greater than the tracking error of the corresponding index funds.

The last empirical issue discussed concerns the deviation between the trading prices and the NAVs of ETFs. The literature reveals that the equity-linked ETFs trade at slight and nonpersistent premiums or discounts to their NAVs. These gaps are usually easy to observe and can be eliminated via efficient and profitable arbitrage techniques. However, researchers demonstrate that the premiums or discounts of ETFs tracking nondomestic indexes are more prominent and consistent due to frictions to arbitrage strategies posed by the nonoverlapping hours or other burdens raised by the local authorities. Additionally, the premiums and discounts also seem to be persistent in the case of fixed-income ETFs.

On the question of the relationship between premiums or discounts and future returns, research finds that the performance of ETFs is positively affected by the contemporaneous premium or discount while the lagged premium exerts a negative influence on performance. These correlations also apply to fixed-income ETFs. In any case, the performance of ETFs can be predictable on the basis of information included in the deviation between the trading prices and NAVs of ETFs.

Discussion Questions

1. Discuss how ETFs are superior and inferior to traditional open-ended index funds?
2. Can ETFs perfectly replicate the performance of the underlying indexes, and what are the factors that affect their tracking efficiency?
3. What is the relationship between the trading prices and NAVs of ETFs?
4. Can the divergence between the trading prices and NAVs of ETFs be indicative of future returns? If so, how?

References

Aber, Jack, W., Dan Li, and Luc Can. 2009. "Price Volatility and Tracking Ability of ETFs." *Journal of Asset Management* 10:4, 210–221.

Ackert Lucy F., and Yisong S. Tian. 2000. "Arbitrage and Valuation in the Market for Standard and Poor's Depositary Receipts." *Financial Management* 29:3, 71–87.

Ackert Lucy F., and Yisong S. Tian. 2008. "Arbitrage, Liquidity, and the Valuation of Exchange Traded Funds." *Financial Markets, Institutions & Instruments* 17:5, 331–362.

Agapova, Anna. 2010. "Are Vanguard's ETFs Cannibalizing the Firm's Index Funds?" *Journal of Index Investing* 1:1, 73–82.

Agapova, Anna. 2011. "Conventional Mutual Index Funds Versus Exchange Traded Funds." *Journal of Financial Markets*, 14:2, 323–343.

Bernstein, J. Phyllis. 2002. "A Primer on Exchange-Traded Funds." *Journal of Accountancy* 193:1, 38–41.

Blitz, David, Joop Huij, and Laurens A. P. Swinkels. 2009. "The Performance of European Index Funds and Exchange-Traded Funds." Working Paper, Robeco Asset Management, Rotterdam School of Management, and Erasmus University.

Cherry, Josh. 2004. "The Limits of Arbitrage: Evidence from Exchange Traded Funds." Working Paper, University of California, Berkeley.

Chu, Patrick Kuok-Kun. 2009. "Study on the Tracking Errors and their Determinants: Hong Kong Exchange Traded Funds (ETFs) Evidences." Working Paper, Department of Accounting and Information Management, University of Macau.

Curcio Richard J., Joanna M. Lipka, and John H. Thornton, Jr. 2004. "Cubes and the Individual Investor." *Financial Services Review* 13:2, 123–138.

Dellva, L. Wilfred. 2001. "Exchange-Traded Funds Not for Everyone." *Journal of Financial Planning* 14:4, 110–124.

Drenovak, Mikica, Branko Uroševic, and Ranko Jelic. 2011. "European Bond ETFs-Tracking Errors and Sovereign Debt Crisis." Working Paper, European Financial Management Symposium, Alternative Investments, April 7–9, 2011, York University, Toronto, Canada.

Elton, J. Edwin, Martin J. Gruber, George Comer, and Kai Li. 2002. "Spiders: Where Are the Bugs?" *Journal of Business* 75:3, 453–473.

Engle, Robert and Debojyoti Sarkar. 2002. "Pricing Exchange Traded Funds." Working Paper, NYU Stern School of Business.

Gallagher, David R. and Reuben Segara. 2004. "The Performance and Trading Characteristics of Exchange-Traded Funds." Working Paper, University of New South Wales.

Gastineau, L. Gary. 2001. "Exchange-Traded Funds: An Introduction." *Journal of Portfolio Management* 27:3, 88–96.

Gastineau, L. Gary. 2004. "The Benchmark Index ETF Performance Problem." *Journal of Portfolio Management* 30:2, 96–104.

Huang, Jennifer and Ilan Guedj. 2009. "Are ETFs Replacing Index Mutual Funds?" Annual American Finance Association, San Francisco Meetings Paper.

Hughen, J. Christopher. 2003. "How Effective Is Arbitrage of Foreign Stocks? The Case of the Malaysia Exchange Traded Fund." *Multinational Business Review* 11:2, 17–27.

Jares, E. Timothy, and Angeline M. Lavin. 2004. "Japan and Hong Kong Exchange-Traded Funds (ETFs): Discounts, Returns, and Trading Strategies." *Journal of Financial Service Research* 25:1, 57–69.

Johnson, William F. 2009. "Tracking Errors of Exchange Traded Funds." *Journal of Asset Management* 10:4, 253–262.

Kayali, Mustafa Mesut. 2007a. "Do Turkish Spiders Confuse Bulls and Bears?: The Case of Dow Jones Istanbul 20." *Investment Management and Financial Innovations* 4:3, 72–79.

Kayali, Mustafa Mesut. 2007b. "Pricing Efficiency of Exchange Traded Funds in Turkey: Early Evidence from the Dow Jones Istanbul 20." *International Research Journal of Finance and Economics* 10:July, 14–23.

Kostovetsky, Leonard. 2003. "Index Mutual Funds and Exchange Traded Funds." *Journal of Portfolio Management* 29:4, 80–92.

Mazzilli, Paul, Dominic Maister, and David Perlman. 2008. "Fixed-Income ETFs: Over 60 ETFs Enable Portfolios of Bonds to Be Traded Like Stocks." *ETFs and Indexing* 2008:1, 58–73.

Milonas, Nikolaos T., and Gerasimos G. Rompotis. 2010. "Dual Offerings of ETFs on the Same Stock Index: US vs. Swiss ETFs." *Journal of Alternative Investments* 10:4, 97–113.

Poterba, M. James, and John B. Shoven. 2002. "Exchange Traded Funds: A New Investment Option for Taxable Investors." *American Economic Review* 92:2, 422–427.

Rompotis, G. Gerasimos. 2008a. "An Empirical Comparing Investigation on Exchange Traded Funds and Index Funds Performance." *European Journal of Economics, Finance and Administrative Studies* 13:November, 7–17.

Rompotis, G. Gerasimos. 2008b. "Exchange Traded Funds vs. Index Funds." *ETFs and Indexing* 2008:1, 111–123.

Rompotis, G. Gerasimos. 2008c. "Performance and Trading Characteristics of German Passively Managed ETFs." *International Research Journal of Finance and Economics* 15:May, 218–231.

Rompotis, G. Gerasimos. 2009a. "Interfamily Competition on Index Tracking: The Case of the Vanguard ETFs and Index Funds." *Journal of Asset Management* 10:4, 263–278.

Rompotis, G. Gerasimos. 2009b. "Premiums and Returns of iShares." *ETF Funds and Indexing* 2009:1, 135–143.

Rompotis, G. Gerasimos. 2009c. "Performance and the Trading Characteristics of iShares: An Evaluation." *The ICFAI Journal of Applied Finance* 15:7, 24–39.

Rompotis, G. Gerasimos. 2010a. "Investigating the Tracking Error of ETFs." *International Journal of Management Research* 1:1, 23–42.

Rompotis, G. Gerasimos. 2010b. "Penetrating Fixed-Income Exchange-Traded Funds." In Greg Gregoriou (ed.), *The Handbook of Trading*, 213–231. New York: McGraw Hill.

Rompotis, G. Gerasimos. 2010c. "Does Premium Impact Exchange Traded Funds' Returns? Evidence from iShares." *Journal of Asset Management* 11:4, 298–308.

Rompotis, G. Gerasimos. 2011a. "Predictable Patterns in ETFs' Return and Tracking Error." *Studies in Economics and Finance* 28:1, 14–35.

Rompotis, G. Gerasimos. 2011b. "ETFs vs. Mutual Funds: Evidence from the Greek Market." *South Eastern Europe Journal of Economics* 9:1, 27–43.

Simon, David P., and Joel S. Sternberg. 2004. "Overreaction and Trading Strategies in European iShares." Working Paper, Department of Finance, Bentley College and Graduate School of Management.

Skinner, Liz. 2010. "Under the Hood: How to Pick the Right ETFs." InvestmentNews.com, November 21.

Svetina, Marko, and Sunil Wahal. 2008. "Exchange Traded Funds: Performance and Competition." Working Paper, School of Business Administration, University of San Diego and W. P. Carey School of Business, Arizona State University.

Zanotti, Giovanna, and Cristiano Russo. 2005. "Exchange Traded Funds Versus Traditional Mutual Funds: A Comparative Analysis on the Italian Market." Working Paper, Bocconi University.

27

The Past, Present, and Future
of Hedge Funds

ROLAND FÜSS
Professor of Finance, Swiss Institute of Banking
and Finance, University of St. Gallen

SARAH MÜLLER
CFA, EBS Business School

Introduction

Hedge funds are pools of private capital that are typically organized as private partnerships and located offshore for regulatory and tax purposes. They differ from traditional funds in several ways. For example, hedge funds follow an absolute return approach to generating performance by using a variety of instruments and investment techniques, such as leverage, short selling, and derivatives, in addition to trend-following, beta-neutral, contrarian, and arbitrage strategies. In comparison to mutual funds, these instruments allow hedge funds to take a pessimistic view of the markets, to reduce market exposure, and thus to provide an extended risk and return spectrum in a mixed-asset portfolio.

Due to its outperformance, the hedge fund sector has grown continuously over the last two decades and is now among the most systemically important players in financial institutions. Although Hedge Fund Research (HFR, 2011) notes that the 2007–2008 subprime and financial crisis slowed the net inflows to hedge funds, the most recent figures reflect that this specific asset class is again increasing in importance.

At the beginning of 2011, HFR reported that assets under management (AuM) for hedge funds had increased to $1.917 trillion and that inflows during the last quarter of 2010 were nearly $149 billion. Further, the increase in the total volume of funds managed increased along with the number of funds. Until 1990, the overall number of hedge funds was less than 100. A 1984 Tremont Partners survey estimated the number at 68 (Lhabitant, 2002), while the HFR report found a total of 610 in 1990, which had increased to more than 1,000 by 1992 (Hedge Fund Research, 2011). *BusinessWeek* reported 3,000 funds in 1994 (Weiss and Weber, 1994). According to HFR, by 2010, the number of live hedge funds had increased dramatically to about 7,000.

The remainder of the chapter is organized as follows. Section 1 gives a short overview of hedge fund characteristics, strategies, and styles. In this context, section 2 discusses the specific properties of hedge fund data, while section 3 focuses on their risk and return characteristics. Due to the non-normality of hedge fund returns, this section presents adequate performance measures to evaluate the risk and return relationship of hedge fund returns. The section also illustrates the differences between mean-variance and alternative allocation techniques such as mean-shortfall variance and higher moment optimization. Section 4 provides an overview of hedge fund operations, fees, and the relevant regulatory issues. Section 5 analyzes the role of hedge funds in the 2007–2008 financial crisis and notes potential future problems for financial development. Section 6 concludes with predictions for future developments in the hedge fund industry.

Hedge Fund Characteristics

Traditional asset managers, such as mutual fund managers, are primarily responsible for balanced portfolios, i.e., portfolios consisting of bonds and stocks for a large pool of private and institutional investors. In 1949, an extension of this traditional fund concept was introduced to the investment community, so-called absolute return funds, or hedge funds.

Hedge funds are generally comprised of a wide variety of different investment approaches. Hedge fund managers pursue a diverse array of styles, ranging from opportunistic-oriented strategies such as long/short equity, to event-driven and relative value strategies. Reuters Hedgeworld (2011) provides a description of different hedge fund styles based on the Lipper/TASS database.

Because hedge funds are open to institutional investors and high-net-worth individuals, they are now an integral part of the investment universe and are included as part of the alternative asset class allocation. Hedge funds today are also marketed to retail investors through funds of hedge funds and exchange-traded funds (ETFs). ETFs tend to offer enhanced transparency, lower fees, and superior liquidity.

Hedge funds are managed without being confined to specific benchmarks. Managers are free to direct their investments to all assets they consider undervalued to capitalize on any opportunities they perceive in the market. Because managers can also freely engage in all kinds of trading instruments, they are not limited to holding stock, bonds, or cash.

Traditional mutual fund managers, in contrast, usually operate in an investment universe defined by their benchmark, and they are limited to investing in the securities in the benchmark. Hedge fund investments are often referred to as skill-based investments, where managers can implement proprietary trading strategies. However, any excess returns should not be attributed solely to manager skill. These excess returns could also result from a myriad of other factors to which traditional investments are not exposed.

For example, hedge fund managers take both long and short positions in assets according to expected performance (opportunistic strategies) or to reduce market exposure (relative value strategies). While most mutual fund managers are constrained from holding negative positions in their portfolios, shorting securities is an important source of profit for many hedge funds. Hedge funds also make extensive use of leverage to enhance their return potential, but such strategies involve a considerable increase in risk.

Leverage also increases overall systemic risk because of the associated counterparty and credit risk. For example, as opaque and highly leveraged investment partnerships, hedge funds have received prominent attention as a potential source of *contagion*, a transmission channel of risk between different financial institutions and potential amplifiers of systemic risk in financial markets. If highly leveraged hedge funds are forced to liquidate large positions at fire sale prices, the counterparties will sustain heavy losses. This situation may lead to further defaults or threaten systemically important institutions, not only directly as counterparties or creditors but also indirectly through asset price adjustments.

STRATEGIES AND STYLES

The hedge fund asset class comprises a large number of funds that are heterogeneous in their trading strategies. The characteristics noted in the previous section actually provide only a vague structure for categorizing single funds into a larger framework. To fully capture the investment style of each fund vis-à-vis its peers, funds are usually classified into distinct subgroups.

CS/Tremont classifies hedge funds according to their market exposure into the categories of "relative value," "event driven," and "opportunistic." Conversely, Agarwal and Naik (2004) classify hedge funds into directional, nondirectional, and mixed categories, depending on the fund's side of market exposure. Additionally, there is a separate category for managed futures or commodity trading advisers (CTAs). Like hedge funds, managed futures are actively managed pools of private capital. However, they differ from hedge funds in that they trade exclusively in derivative markets, while hedge funds trade in all types of markets and use futures markets for hedging and leverage purposes. Figure 27.1 provides an overview of hedge funds strategies and styles.

Relative value strategies aim to capitalize on temporary valuation discrepancies in the market; *event driven strategies* attempt to benefit from expected or already announced events such as management buyouts, mergers, or restructurings. The distressed securities subcategory describes investments in both the debt and equity of companies in or near bankruptcy. *Opportunistic strategies* depend heavily on a manager's ability to correctly identify market movements and to capitalize on them through long and/or short positions with varying degrees of leverage.

Emerging market hedge funds (EMHF) primarily follow a buy-and-hold strategy. Efficient hedging strategies cannot always be used in these markets because of the lack of derivative instruments and the difficulty in building short positions. Thus, as Fung and Hsieh (2000) argue, little difference exists between emerging market mutual funds and EMHF. However, the latter tend to have lower net returns because of higher performance fees Fuss, Kaiser, and Schindler 2012.

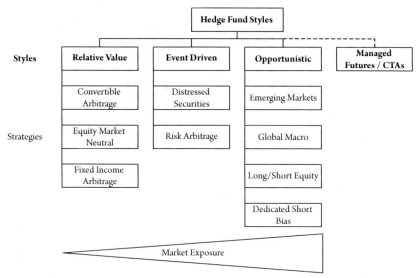

Figure 27.1 Overview of Hedge Fund Strategies and Styles. This figure shows the classification of hedge fund styles (relative value, event driven, and opportunistic) according to CS/Tremont. The strategy Managed Futures/CTA is sometimes related to the opportunistic style, but it is generally considered to be its own strategy.

STYLE DRIFT

The framework used in this chapter to categorize hedge fund strategies depicts only one specific classification. However, each hedge fund data provider uses its own classification based on distinct investment styles and definitions. Because including hedge funds in a database is attributed to one of these style groups, substantial differences can exist in risk and return characteristics between different providers' styles and strategies.

Managers can potentially adjust their actual investment strategies, and hedge funds may thus drift in style. Gibson and Gyger (2007) analyze data from a proprietary database and find two distinct clusters (tactical trading managers and long/short managers), along with two other "fuzzier" clusters. They show that managers who consistently pursue their predefined investment styles do not usually generate higher future performance. Thus, investors must carefully monitor the hedge funds in their asset allocation and adjust their portfolio composition accordingly, if a hedge fund needs to be reclassified from one category to another.

Many researchers find that the style analysis framework of Sharpe (1992) is particularly useful to detect the "true" investment style or composition of an individual hedge fund or fund of hedge funds. Style analysis tries to approximate risk and return characteristics by finding the optimal weights of the underlying factors. The optimization problem is defined as minimizing tracking errors with respect to the weights summing to 1. The weights that provide the best fit in this constrained regression analysis indicate the investment style.

Hedge Fund Data

The decision to include hedge funds in an investor's asset allocation is most often based on the analysis of historical data. However, these data can differ substantially from index series of traditional asset classes. They are also subject to deficiencies in construction that must be considered when evaluating the overall risk/return profile of hedge fund investments. Hedge fund data suffer primarily from survivorship bias, stale price bias, self-reporting bias, and backfill bias. Thus, hedge fund performance among data providers can differ not only by strategy definition and allocation but also by potential data bias.

SURVIVORSHIP BIAS

Survivorship bias in hedge fund databases has probably received the widest attention in the literature. This bias can occur when funds cease reporting to databases and are no longer part of the respective dataset. Two main reasons account for these dropouts: (1) the fund was liquidated, or (2) it simply stopped reporting performance. In this context, hedge fund databases are often separated into live (or active) and graveyard (or inactive) databases. However, "graveyard" does not mean the fund has ceased operations and was liquidated, it just means the fund stopped reporting. Some researchers such as Malkiel and Saha (2005) posit that funds report to databases for purposes of advertising, and they may stop after reaching their target size. Unfortunately, databases rarely provide reasons when a fund suspends reporting its performance.

The literature finds substantial evidence of survivorship bias in hedge fund data but with different results depending on the sample period and data provider. Table 27.1 gives an overview of some relevant articles that highlight how survivorship bias tends to lead to overestimating hedge fund returns.

STALE PRICE BIAS

The amount of academic research on hedge fund returns has increased substantially, and researchers have noticed that hedge fund returns often exhibit significant serial correlation as well (Kat and Lu, 2002; Kat, 2003; Lo, 2005).

For example, Asness, Krail, and Liew (2001) explore the ability of hedge fund managers to smooth returns. They highlight the fact that hedge funds appear to price part of their securities with a lag. The authors use a multiperiod regression approach to estimate the true correlation between hedge fund styles and traditional assets in the presence of stale prices due to illiquidity and managed pricing.

In traditional markets, a lack of liquidity and a lack of marking to market value can result in stale prices. These problems affect hedge funds even more strongly because they invest primarily in such illiquid assets. The prices of the underlying assets are valued infrequently and/or are based on appraisal-based values, which means they are smoothed across time. Consequently, hedge fund returns

Table 27.1 **Empirical Evidence on Survivorship Bias**

Authors	Data	Period	Results
Fung and Hsieh (1997)	TASS	1989 to 1995	Survivorship bias of 3.42 percent per year
Ackermann, McEnally, and Ravenscraft (1999)	MAR/HFR	1988 to 1995	Survivorship bias of 0.16 percent per year
Brown, Goetzmann, and Ibbotson (1999)	Bernheim Offshore	1989 to 1995	Survivorship bias of 3.00 percent per year for offshore hedge funds
Fung and Hsieh (2000)	TASS	1994 to 1998	Survivorship bias of 3.00 percent per year
Liang (2000)	TASS and HFR	1994 to 1998 (TASS), 1994 to 1997 (HFR)	Survivorship bias of 2.24 percent per year (TASS), and 0.60 percent per year (HFR)
Brown, Goetzmann, and Park (2001)	TASS	1994 to 1998	Analyze the time since defunct funds were included in the TASS database
Schneeweis, Kazemi, and Martin (2002)	TASS	1998 to 2000	Survivorship bias depending on strategy, ranging from 0.2 percent (global macro) to 3.8 percent (currency) per year
Amin and Kat (2003)	TASS	1994 to 2001	Survivorship bias of 1.89 percent per year
Malkiel and Saha (2005)	TASS	1996 to 2003	Survivorship bias of 4.42 percent per year, controlling for backfilled data
Hodder, Jackwerth, and Kolova (2008)	ALTVEST	1994 to 2006	Returns of delisted funds (−1.86 percent) are significantly smaller than average hedge fund returns (1.01 percent) but they are not dramatically worse

This table presents an overview of some relevant articles on survivorship bias by providing information on the dataset and time period analyzed in each and their major findings. It highlights the impact of survivorship bias on hedge fund return data and gives an estimate on the resulting upward bias in returns.

are serially correlated, estimated betas might be higher, and standard deviation might be lower, but traditional research methods will essentially fail to reflect the risk and return characteristics of the respective funds.

Table 27.8 reports the autocorrelation coefficients for nine distinct hedge fund style indices as well as for composite index for the January 1994 through September 2011 period. Except for the equity market neutral and global macro indices, all indices exhibit statistically significant autocorrelation to the tenth lag with the autocorrelation coefficients being especially high for the first lag. The empirical results shown in Table 27.2 confirm previous studies on hedge fund returns.

In addition to Geltner's (1991, 1993) desmoothing technique, Conner (2003) provides a methodology for delagging the time series of hedge fund returns for higher-order autocorrelation. The adjusted risks and correlations for the effect of stale pricing allow investors to apply traditional mean-variance optimization tools. Conner shows that the perceived risk of hedge funds increases substantially, while their diversification benefits decrease. However, the optimal portfolios based on adjusted risk and correlation returns do not have a lower allocation to hedge funds.

SELF-REPORTING BIAS

Self-reporting bias, also called self-selection bias, results from whether a particular hedge fund reports its returns to a database. This decision is at the discretion of each hedge fund. Such funds can also choose the database in which they want to be included. Individual databases thus differ considerably both in size and constituent composition.

Agarwal, Fos, and Jiang (2010) analyze a dataset of 11,417 hedge funds from five different databases (CISDM, TASS, MSCI, HFR, and Eureka). They find that less than 1 percent of all funds are included in all databases. Conversely, 17 percent of all funds are included in only the TASS database. Thus, researchers who are analyzing data from only one database will miss out on information in other databases and must consider the impact of any missing data on their specific research. In a similar approach, Fung and Hsieh (2009) analyze the constituents of four different databases (HFR, Lipper/TASS, Barclays Global Investors, and the Center for International Securities and Derivatives Markets). They find that half of the hedge funds in the entire sample are included in only one database. Table 27.3 provides an overview of these two studies that focus explicitly on this self-reporting bias.

The difference in individual dataset composition becomes especially problematic when creating an index. Indices from different providers are comprised of very different constituents, although they are supposed to represent a comparable hedge fund style or strategy. Investors should carefully choose a hedge fund index as a benchmark that matches the characteristics of their respective portfolios. Table 27.4 lists several hedge fund index providers and indicates their data availability.

Amenc and Martellini (2002) and Amenc, Martellini, and Vaissié (2003) list the maximum return differences for different hedge fund indices for different

Table 27.2 **Empirical Evidence on Stale Price Bias**

Authors	Data	Period	Results
Kat and Lu (2002)	TASS	1994 to 2001	Hedge fund returns exhibit serial correlation; merger arbitrage, distressed securities, convertible arbitrage, and emerging markets tend to exhibit particularly high first-order autocorrelation. Kat and Lu (2002) unsmooth data following the Geltner (1991, 1993) approach:
			Thus, the observed value at time t, V_t^*, is the weighted average of the true value V_t and the smoothed value V_{t-1}^* at time $t-1$:
			$$V_t^* = \alpha V_t + (1 - \alpha)V_{t-1}^*$$
			From this equation can be derived an expression that removes first-order autocorrelation:
			$$r_t = \frac{r_t^* - \alpha r_{t-1}^*}{1 - \alpha}$$
			For unsmoothed return data, the standard deviation of returns significantly increases.
Kat (2003)	TASS	1994 to 2001	Significant first-order autocorrelation decreases the actual "true" standard deviation.
Getmansky, Lo, and Makarov (2004)	TASS	1977 to 2001	Serial correlation mainly results from illiquidity and smoothed returns. The authors provide an econometric model for return smoothing and derive estimators for smoothing profiles.
Lo (2005)	CSFB/Tremont, TASS	Various	The study shows high and statistically significant autocorrelation up to six lags.
Bollen and Pool (2008)	CISDM	2003 to 2008	Delaying the reporting of losses, but reporting gains in a timely manner, will result in autocorrelation in hedge fund returns.

This table lists studies that examine stale price bias in hedge fund returns. The serial correlation in Table 27.8 confirms the findings of the studies listed here. The table gives explanations of the potential sources of the autocorrelation and provides solutions on how to remove autocorrelation from the return series.

Table 27.3 **Empirical Evidence on Self-Reporting Bias**

Authors	Data	Date	Results
Fung and Hsieh (2009)	Hedge Fund Research, Lipper/TASS, Barclays Global Investors, and the Center for International Securities and Derivatives Markets	2008	Half the hedge funds in the sample are included in only one of the databases and only 7 percent are listed in all four databases.
Agarwal, Fos, and Jiang (2010)	CISDM, Eureka, HFR, MSCI, and TASS	2008	Younger and medium-sized funds tend to report to databases in order to publicize their funds and attract potential investors. Initiation and termination of reporting is a strategic decision.

This table presents two studies on self-reporting bias for hedge fund databases. Both studies find that only a few hedge funds are included in all databases and that constituents differ considerably for each database.

investment styles. Differences are significant and range up to 20 percent for long/short equity in February 2000. To overcome the problem of nonrepresentativeness of hedge fund indices, Amenc et al. (2003) propose an "index of indexes" for the hedge fund industry. As a benchmark, this summary of hedge fund indexes is more stable in composition and improves the soundness of the strategic asset allocation process.

BACKFILL BIAS (INSTANT HISTORY BIAS)

Because hedge funds voluntarily provide their returns to data providers, managers may only begin reporting when returns are favorable. If historical data are then added to the entire dataset, the results can be biased upward. The size of the backfill bias is estimated to range from 1.3 percent to 3.5 percent, depending on the period under investigation and the index provider analyzed. Table 27.5 shows some of the relevant research on this problem. All studies listed in the table find a backfill bias.

Risk and Returns of Hedge Funds

Hedge funds managers aim at returning positive performance irrespective of the market conditions in which they operate. The following section gives an overview on hedge fund performance identifying specifics of hedge funds data that

Table 27.4 **Hedge Fund Data Provider**

Data Provider	Launch Date	Data Available Since	Calculation Method	Homepage
Hennessee Group	1987	1987	AM	hennesseegroup.com
LJH Global Investments	1992	1989	AM	ljh.com
Van Hedge Fund Advisors International, Inc.	1994	1988	AM	vanhedge.com
Hedge Fund Research, Inc.	1994	1990	AM	hedgefundresearch.com
CISDM/MAR	1994	1990	Median	marhedge.com
HegdeFundNews.com/Bernheim Index	1995	1999	Not communicated	hedgefundnews.com
Evaluation Associates Capital Markets, Inc.	1996	1996	AM	eacm.com
Hedgefund.net/Tuna Indices	1998	1976 to 1995	AM	hedgefund.net
Hedge Fund Intelligence	1998	1998	Median	hedgefundintelligence.com
CS/Tremont LLC	1999	1994	WM	hedgefundindex.com
Investorforce/Altvest	2000	1993	AM	investorforce.com
Zurich Hedge Fund	2001	1998	AM	www1.zindex.com
Standard & Poor's	2002	1998	AM	spglobal.com
Eurekahedge	2002	2000	AM	eurekahedge.com
MSCI Hedge Fund Indices	2002	2002	AM and WM for global indexes	msci.com
Blue Chip Hedge Fund Index	2002	2002	Between 2 percent and 8 percent for a HF, with a maximum of 20 percent for funds from the same organization	bluex.org

(Continued)

Table 27.4 **(Continued)**

Data Provider	Launch Date	Data Available Since	Calculation Method	Homepage
Feri Alternative Assets GmbH	2001	2002	AM and WM for the composite index	feri-alta.de
EDHEC Alternative Indices	2003	1997	Principal component analysis	edhec-risk.com
Mondo Hedge Index	2003	2002	AM and WM	mondohedgeindex.com
Barclay Hedge	2003	1997	AM	barclayhedge.com

This table lists several hedge fund index providers and gives on overview on the data they provide concerning data availability, launch date, calculation method, and the respective Internet addresses. AM denotes the arithmetic mean, i.e., the index is constructed as an equally weighted index; WM denotes the weighted mean, i.e., the index is value weighted according to the net asset value of the funds; and the median denotes the median-weighted index.

Source: Adapted from Amenc, Martellini, and Vaissié (2003) and Heidorn, Hoppe, and Kaiser (2006).

Table 27.5 **Empirical Evidence on Backfill Bias**

Authors	Data	Period	Results
Fung and Hsieh (2000)	TASS	1994 to 1998	Backfill bias of 1.40 percent per year
Capocci, Corhay, and Hübner (2005)	MAR	1994 to 2002	Backfill bias of 1.32 percent per year
Malkiel and Saha (2005)	TASS	1994 to 2003	Backfill bias of more than 500 bps on average is significant at the 0.05 level
Fung and Hsieh (2009)	TASS, Tremont	1999, 2001	Analysis of database merger between TASS and Tremont Before 2001, the median elapsed time until a fund was included was 14 months; in 2001, this number tripled to more than 60 months.
Ibbotson, Chen, and Zhu (2010)	TASS	1995 to 2009	Backfill bias of 1.42 percent per year for live funds, and 3.51 percent per year for live and dead funds

Several studies analyze backfill bias in hedge funds returns. In general, research finds significant backfill bias that results from adding past returns to a database of hedge fund returns. The following table lists a sample of these articles, indicates for which period the data were analyzed, and presents their major findings.

need to be considered in the performance measurement process. Thus, this section provides performance ratios that better capture the characteristics of hedge fund return data and discusses potential issues that arise when hedge funds are included in a portfolio context. Finally, the role of fund of hedge funds is discussed as an addition to (private) investors' asset allocation.

HEDGE FUND ALPHA

Hedge fund managers claim to provide superior returns at low risk levels. Ackermann, McEnally, and Ravenscraft (1999) analyze one of the first comprehensive datasets of hedge fund returns and find that hedge funds consistently outperform mutual funds but not standard market indices. Brown, Goetzmann, and

Ibbotson (1999) examine the performance of offshore hedge funds from 1989 to 1995 and also find little evidence of manager skill-based impact on risk-adjusted returns.

However, Fung and Hsieh (2001) find positive alphas of around 1 percent per month for CTAs. Fung and Hsieh (2002b) find a small but significant alpha for the 1994 to 2002 period for four equally weighted hedge fund indices (HFR, CSFB/Tremont, TASS, and MSCI). Testing the alpha for the 1994 to 1998 and 2000 to 2002 subperiods, however, results in considerably lower alpha values. This empirical evidence raises the question of whether the regression over the entire sampling period creates an alpha illusion.

For later datasets, Capocci, Corhay, and Hübner (2005) find significant outperformance for one-third of the hedge fund strategies analyzed within a capital asset pricing model (CAPM) and 10-factor framework. They confirm the outperformance for both bullish and bearish periods. Fung, Xu, and Yau (2004) also analyze hedge fund returns using both the CAPM and the Dimson model. The Dimson (1979) model can be used to correct the CAPM for the impact of the illiquidity of assets by including additional lagged betas. The authors find small excess returns for hedge funds of 0.384 percent for the CAPM and 0.183 percent for the Dimson model.

Fung et al. (2004) extend their earlier work to include three lagged betas. Fung and Hsieh (2004) support their results, finding significant alphas for US hedge funds. They posit that investors should hedge against systematic market risk factors such as the value to growth factor by investing in hedge funds. They prove that the resulting alpha series is independent of the original systematic risk factors during both normal and crisis times.

In more recent research, Ibbotson, Chen, and Zhu (2010) decompose hedge fund returns into the systematic market exposure, hedge fund fees, and the actual value added by the fund. They find that 3.61 percent of the return is attributable to management skill. Cai and Liang (2010) find positive alphas for the entire 1994 to 2008 period that are largely statistically significant.

Hedge funds can implement dynamic trading strategies and make extensive use of derivatives. Linear factor models thus do not fully capture the features inherent in hedge fund returns. Fung and Hsieh (2001) are among the first to link hedge fund performance to various nonlinear and dynamic factor exposures. They model simple factors by using lookback straddles. A *lookback straddle* is an option strategy composed of two options: a lookback call and a lookback put. A *lookback call option* grants its holder the right to buy an asset at the lowest price observed during the option's lifetime, while a *lookback put option* gives its holder the right to sell the same asset at the highest price observed during the option's lifetime. Thus, a lookback straddle enables the investor to "buy low and sell high." The authors find a positive and statistically significant relationship between the performance of the lookback straddle and that of a representative set of trend-following hedge funds.

Fung and Hsieh (2002c) propose asset-based style factors in their modification of the arbitrage pricing theory (APT) model. They first extract common sources of risk for the fixed-income hedge fund styles and then illustrate how those sources relate to observable market prices. Their factors are standard fixed-income indices representing long-only investments, differences between two index returns for passive spread trading, lookback straddles for trend-following strategies, and, finally, a short position in the lookback straddle strategy that represents convergence trading. All the factors are directly observable from market prices and are thus widely available. The factors can then be implemented into a factor model with time-varying factor loadings (betas).

Fung and Hsieh (2002c) confirm that hedge funds are exposed to the seven factors. In Fung and Hsieh (2002a), they extend their earlier work by implementing the factor model with dynamic factor coefficients on a comprehensive set of hedge funds and hedge fund indices. They find that the seven asset-based style factors explain up to 80 percent of the return variance.

Fung and Hsieh (2002a, 2002c) highlight the fact that the nonlinearity of hedge fund investments results in the limited applicability of simple linear factor models. Bollen and Whaley (2009) note that coefficients in a factor analysis are generally assumed to be constant, when they are actually time varying. The authors implement two different econometric models (the optimal change point regression and the stochastic beta model) that allow for time-varying coefficients and prove that alpha calculations or rankings derived from standard linear regressions are misleading.

Furthermore, Cai and Liang (2010) analyze hedge fund returns by means of a dynamic linear regression model. Compared to the Fung and Hsieh (2002c) seven-factor model, the residuals from their regression exhibit less autocorrelation and the predictive power of this model is also superior.

PERFORMANCE EVALUATION FOR HEDGE FUNDS

Given the findings on abnormal hedge fund returns, this section discusses important issues about performance evaluation in the context of non-normally distributed hedge fund returns. Performance measures and portfolio optimization techniques are then explored that might be better suited to capture the specific risk and return characteristics of hedge funds.

Non-Normality in Hedge Fund Returns

Most hedge fund returns deviate from the assumption of a normal distributions, exhibiting negative skewness and leptokurtosis. They are not symmetrically distributed around the mean, and they are more peaked than the normal distribution, respectively. In the academic literature, negatively skewed payoffs are often attributed to the dynamic trading strategies that, together with the fee structure, enforce the optionlike payoff structure of hedge funds (Goetzmann, Ingersoll, and Ross, 2003; Chan, Getmansky, Haas, and Lo, 2006).

Brooks and Kat (2002) and Kat and Lu (2002) explicitly analyze the statistical properties of hedge fund returns and hedge fund index returns. Brooks and Kat find negative skewness and positive excess kurtosis but also a lower standard deviation for a series of monthly hedge fund index returns. Although the lower standard deviation (i.e., lower riskiness would be desirable from an investor standpoint), the negative skewness is less attractive because risk-averse investors prefer a positively skewed distribution.

Kat and Lu (2002) also find significant excess kurtosis for all individual hedge fund returns, and negative skewness, except for global macro and long/short equity funds. Table 27.8 lists the descriptive statistics for 1994 through 2011. Except for dedicated short bias, all indices exhibit negative skewness and positive excess kurtosis, with the findings for the equity market neutral index especially prominent. The Jarque-Bera test also clearly rejects the assumption that the data are normally distributed.

Mahdavi (2004) proposes a different approach to handle the non-normality in hedge fund returns. He suggests a methodology that first transforms the returns so that their distribution matches the benchmark distribution. The advantage is that the adjusted Sharpe ratios for the hedge funds are directly comparable to those for the benchmark.

Performance Measures

In traditional investment performance measures, risk is given by the standard deviation. However, this measure is only accurate if the data are at least approximately normally distributed. Thus, as Amin and Kat (2003) and Eling and Schuhmacher (2007), for example, note, using measures such as the Sharpe ratio or Jensen's alpha to evaluate hedge fund performance is somewhat questionable. Therefore, alternative performance measures focus especially on the risk of a loss.

One set of performance measures builds on the lower partial moment (LPM) concept. LPMs capture risk through the downward deviations from a minimally acceptable rate of return, τ, such as 0 percent (the nominal preservation of capital), the inflation rate (the real preservation of capital), the risk-free rate, the benchmark return, or any other targeted rate. Equation 18.1 defines the LPM of order n over period T for security i (Bawa, 1975; Bawa and Lindenberg, 1977; Harlow and Rao, 1989; Harlow, 1991; Nawrocki, 1991)

$$LPM_{ni}(\tau) = \frac{1}{\tilde{T}-1} \sum_{t=1}^{\tilde{T}} \max\left[(\tau - r_{it}), 0\right]^n \qquad (27.1)$$

where the sample size $\tilde{T}$ sometimes refers to the number of shortfall observations; however, it may also refer to the total number of observations, which then results in a lower value for downside risk.

According to Sortino and van der Meer (1991) and Eling and Schuhmacher (2007), measures based on LPMs are more intuitive than measures that capture both negative and positive deviations from a target return, i.e., the mean in the case of central moments. Eling and Schuhmacher show that, according to the rank correlation coefficient, the ordering of performance is unaffected by differentiating between downside and dispersion risk measures. However, this effect could be driven mainly by the construction of the Spearman's rank correlation coefficient. This coefficient is based on the assumption of equally spaced ranks, while Kendall's tau is based on ordinal information.

The Omega ratio (Shadwick and Keating, 2002), shown in Equation 27.2, and the Sortino ratio (Sortino and van der Meer, 1991), shown in Equation 27.3, relate the return r_i at time i over the minimal acceptable rate of return τ to the LPM of orders 1 and 2 (Shadwick and Keating, 2002):

$$Omega_i = \frac{r_i - \tau}{LPM_{1i}(\tau)} + 1, \qquad (27.2)$$

$$Sortino_i = \frac{r_i - \tau}{\sqrt{LPM_{2i}(\tau)}} + 1. \qquad (27.3)$$

Other commonly applied performance measures within the hedge fund industry are derived from the concept of drawdowns. Drawdowns do not build on specific assumptions about the statistical properties of the underlying data. They can thus be classified as nonparametric measures. Drawdowns are popular in practice and are less abstract than comparable measures (Lhabitant, 2004). A *drawdown* in a return series occurs when the cumulative return at the respective period of time drops below the maximum cumulative return at this time. The term r_{it-T} denotes the return realized in the period from t to T. The maximum drawdown is the maximum possible loss realized during this specific investment period. It can thus be seen as the worst-case scenario, where MD_{i1} denotes the lowest or maximum drawdown, MD_{i2} is the second lowest drawdown, and so on.

The Calmar and Sterling ratios are used to implement the maximum drawdown as a risk measure in a risk-adjusted performance ratio. Both ratios substitute versions of the maximum drawdown for the Sharpe ratio's standard deviation. The Calmar ratio (Young, 1991) sets the excess return over the risk-free rate relative to the maximum drawdown; the Sterling ratio (Kestner, 1996) replaces the denominator by the average over the N largest drawdowns:

$$Calmar = \frac{r_i - r_f}{-MD_{i1}}, \qquad (27.4)$$

$$Sterling = \frac{r_i - r_f}{\frac{1}{N}\sum_{j=1}^{N} -MD_{ij}}. \qquad (27.5)$$

The inclusion of drawdowns leads to a powerful performance measure for hedge fund return data. However, drawdowns are sensitive to the length of the time period for which they are calculated, as well as to whether the time period is tranquil or volatile.

Füss, Kaiser, Müller, and Zietz (2011) analyze the behavior of maximum drawdowns for single hedge funds according to the observation period and find that drawdowns have predictive power for future fund failure. Heidorn, Kaiser, and Roder (2009) analyze a set of fund of hedge fund data and also find that drawdowns are necessarily larger during times of crisis. Their evidence also shows that the magnitude of the maximum drawdown depends on the age of the fund of hedge funds but not on its size.

Table 27.6 gives an overview of the performance measures and corresponding rankings. These figures clearly show that the different ratios result in contradictory rankings.

Table 27.6 **Performance Ratios and Rankings**

	Sharpe Ratio	Rank	Omega Ratio	Rank	Sortino Ratio	Rank	Calmar Ratio	Rank	Sterling Ratio	Rank
HF Composite	1.108	4	2.401	4	0.289	4	0.419	4	0.829	2
Convertible Arbitrage	1.002	5	2.363	5	0.194	6	0.210	7	0.296	7
Equity Market Neutral	0.280	10	1.988	8	0.051	11	0.066	11	0.080	11
Fixed Income Arbitrage	0.835	7	2.227	6	0.137	8	0.166	8	0.247	8
Distressed Securities	1.477	2	3.088	2	0.297	3	0.438	2	0.777	3
Risk Arbitrage	1.586	1	3.326	1	0.371	1	0.801	1	3.929	1
Emerging Markets	0.399	9	1.455	10	0.114	9	0.126	9	0.159	9
Global Macro	1.193	3	2.636	3	0.302	2	0.420	3	0.656	6
Long/Short Equity	0.869	6	1.997	7	0.248	5	0.380	5	0.677	4
Dedicated Short Bias	-0.257	13	0.878	13	-0.055	13	-0.063	13	-0.074	13
Managed Futures	0.478	8	1.464	9	0.162	7	0.304	6	0.663	5
S&P 500	0.239	11	1.263	11	0.077	10	0.066	10	0.081	10
Barclays US Aggregate	-0.002	12	1.013	12	0.005	12	-0.001	12	-0.004	12

This table shows the Sharpe, Omega, Sortino, Calmar, and Sterling ratios for the different hedge fund indices as well as the S&P 500 and the Barclays US Aggregate Bond Index. The resulting rankings from each ratio are listed in the subsequent column. These calculations are based on 213 observations covering January 1994 through September 2011. The S&P 500 and Barclays US Aggregate represent the U.S. stock and bond market. The risk-free rate for the Sharpe ratio and the minimal acceptable return for the Omega and Sortino ratios are assumed to be 0 percent.

Comovements with Traditional Asset Classes

Most investors select hedge funds for inclusion in their portfolios due to their superior return profile, but more specifically for their risk-return profile. Historical hedge fund returns exhibit low correlation with traditional markets such as stocks and bonds. Kat and Lu (2002), Amin and Kat (2003), Schneeweis, Kazemi, and Martin (2003), and Billio, Getmansky, and Pelizzon (2009) analyze the correlation of hedge fund returns with other standard indices, such as the S&P 500 and the Russell 2000, as proxies for traditional asset classes. Following the standard assumptions for including hedge funds, the return series should exhibit a low or negative correlation with these indices. On average, these studies find low correlations of hedge funds with other asset classes.

Lo (2005) provides a comprehensive overview of the correlation between hedge fund style indices and proxies for the overall market such as the S&P 500. He finds very different correlations, ranging from 0.60 between event driven funds and the small company index to significantly negative correlations between dedicated short bias (short-seller) funds and the large company index (i.e., the S&P 500). Furthermore, Billio et al. (2009) find that the correlations with the S&P declined during the 2007–2008 financial crisis. Based on these findings, hedge funds can be considered as a good addition to traditional asset allocation.

Table 27.7 shows the overall correlations between different hedge fund style indices and the S&P 500 and the Barclays U.S. Aggregate index as proxies for the equity and bond markets. Figure 27.2 graphically depicts the development of the average correlation between the different hedge fund indices and the traditional asset classes, while Table 27.8 gives a comprehensive overview of the descriptive statistics of the indices. The figures show the desirable characteristics of the hedge fund indices from a mean-variance perspective.

Table 27.7 shows the low and even negative correlations of the different hedge fund indices with the US bond market proxy. The correlations between the hedge fund indices and the US stock market proxy, however, are higher and vary considerably for the different indices.

Figure 27.2 illustrates how correlations evolve over time. The correlations had previously been low. However, after the sudden increase in July 2008, the average correlation between hedge funds and traditional asset classes has remained high and the correlations between bond markets and hedge funds and between stock markets and hedge funds are moving in unison. The beneficial effects of hedge funds within the portfolio optimization might thus be limited, at least during the 2007–2008 financial crisis.

Amin and Kat (2003) and Kat (2005) test the effects of including hedge funds in a portfolio context. Both studies find that, in a traditional mean-variance framework, a substantial allocation to hedge funds can improve the characteristics of the resulting portfolio. Amin and Kat (2003) propose an allocation of at least 20 percent. However, the studies also find that the resulting portfolio exhibits a lower skewness and higher kurtosis than it would without the addition of hedge funds. In a later paper, Kat (2005) emphasizes the value of using an optimization algorithm that considers higher moments of the underlying return distributions.

Table 27.7 **Correlation of Hedge Fund Indices and Traditional Assets**

	HF Composite	Convertible Arbitrage	Equity Market Neutral	Fixed Income Arbitrage	Distressed Securities	Risk Arbitrage	Emerging Markets	Global Macro	Long/Short Equity	Dedicated Short Bias	Managed Futures	S&P 500	Barclays US Aggregate
HF Composite	1												
Convertible Arbitrage	0.557 (9.730)	1											
Equity Market Neutral	0.275 (4.151)	0.192 (2.842)	1										
Fixed Income Arbitrage	0.546 (9.479)	0.788 (18.591)	0.310 (4.730)	1									
Distressed Securities	0.690 (13.852)	0.599 (10.866)	0.326 (5.013)	0.500 (8.384)	1								
Risk Arbitrage	0.510 (8.618)	0.476 (7.856)	0.152 (2.238)	0.317 (4.860)	0.595 (10.759)	1							
Emerging Markets	0.708 (14.563)	0.447 (7.262)	0.134 (1.965)	0.412 (6.570)	0.651 (12.442)	0.516 (8.744)	1						
Global Macro	0.810 (20.087)	0.347 (5.368)	0.061 (0.884)	0.406 (6.458)	0.341 (5.269)	0.229 (3.415)	0.448 (7.282)	1					
Long/Short Equity	0.835 (22.001)	0.459 (7.495)	0.181 (2.679)	0.382 (6.010)	0.678 (13.403)	0.600 (10.899)	0.668 (13.055)	0.454 (7.398)	1				
Dedicated Short Bias	−0.490 (−8.158)	−0.267 (−4.022)	−0.141 (−2.065)	−0.201 (−2.975)	−0.570 (−10.090)	−0.473 (−7.788)	−0.540 (−9.316)	−0.116 (−1.699)	−0.694 (−13.990)	1			

Managed Futures	0.185 (2.737)	−0.069 (−1.003)	0.000 (0.001)	−0.060 (−0.869)	−0.040 (−0.577)	−0.037 (−0.533)	−0.032 (−0.467)	0.292 (4.435)	0.080 (1.163)	0.057 (0.830)	1	
S&P 500	0.579 (10.313)	0.388 (6.116)	0.260 (3.914)	0.356 (5.542)	0.631 (11.824)	0.516 (8.742)	0.549 (9.538)	0.247 (3.697)	0.668 (13.036)	−0.752 (−16.590)	−0.087 (−1.263)	1
Barclays U.S. Aggregate	0.136 (2.001)	0.123 (1.796)	−0.142 (−2.091)	0.157 (2.305)	−0.019 (−0.276)	0.023 (0.338)	0.005 (0.075)	0.274 (4.140)	0.073 (1.061)	0.044 (0.641)	0.173 (2.553)	0.050 (0.727) 1

This table shows the correlation coefficients for each of the different hedge fund indices and the S&P 500 as well as the Barclays U.S. Aggregate Bond Index. These calculations are based on 213 observations covering January 1994 through September 2011. S&P 500 and Barclays U.S. Aggregate represent the US stock and bond markets. The *t*-statistics are in parentheses.

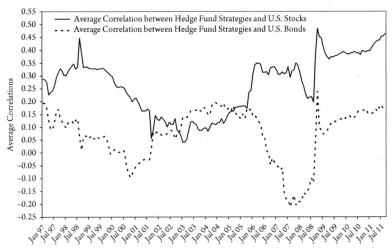

Figure 27.2 Average Correlations Between Hedge Fund Strategies and Traditional Assets. This figure shows the average correlation between the hedge fund composite index and the US stock market and the US bond market. These calculations are based on 213 observations covering January 1994 through September 2011. The S&P 500 and Barclays U.S. Aggregate represent the US stock and bond markets, respectively.

For many of the same reasons, Davies, Kat, and Lu (2009) use polynomial goal programming to set up optimal fund of hedge fund portfolios. Other approaches aim to replace the risk measure of the traditional Markowitz (1952, 1959) portfolio optimization with more comprehensive risk measures such as lower partial moments or measures based on them such as Omega.

Harlow (1991) optimizes the portfolio with respect to minimizing lower partial moments. However, he does not account for potential comovements between the lower partial moments of the assets. Sing and Ong's (2000) approach does account for such movements. They find that an optimization based on lower partial moments is always preferred to a traditional mean-variance optimization. In another approach, Agarwal and Naik (2004) replace variance with conditional value at risk (VaR) and illustrate the extent to which traditional mean variance optimization can underestimate tail risks.

Table 27.9 gives the average allocations for portfolios optimized under the mean-variance versus the mean-shortfall variance framework. Allocations vary significantly depending on the framework chosen: Under the mean-shortfall allocation, average portfolio returns and skewness increase, while excess kurtosis decreases below zero creating a platykurtic rather than leptokurtic distribution. Hence, the risk parameters of the mixed portfolio improve.

Hedge funds are an important addition to the asset allocations of both private and institutional investors. Although they do not offer quite the same magnitude of excess returns independent of market conditions that they did in the past, they continue to provide important diversification benefits through their statistical properties versus other more traditional asset classes. Figure 27.3 graphically depicts the rolling returns of the composite hedge fund index and the stock

Table 27.8 **Descriptive Statistics of Hedge Fund Indices**

Indices		Annual Average Monthly Return (in %)	Max Return (in %)	Min Return (in %)	Annual Standard Deviation (in %)	Skewness	Kurtosis	Jarque-Bera Test	AC1 (LB)	AC2 (LB)	AC3 (LB)	AC5 (LB)	AC10 (LB)
HF Composite		8.44	98.20	−94.19	7.63	−0.33	5.41	55.37***	0.221 (10.51***)	0.111 (13.18***)	0.051 (13.74***)	0.031 (13.98***)	0.052 (16.48***)
Relative Value	Convertible Arbitrage	7.25	67.74	−161.50	7.63	−2.99	20.85	3,145.30***	0.563 (68.52***)	0.298 (87.81***)	0.154 (92.98***)	0.024 (94.37***)	−0.102 (99.22***)
	Equity Market Neutral	4.87	43.11	−622.08	7.63	−12.69	176.65	273,350.80***	0.057 (0.71)	0.032 (0.93)	0.140 (5.21)	−0.015 (5.28)	−0.005 (6,032)
	Fixed Income Arbitrage	5.11	50.92	−181.48	7.63	−4.67	36.13	10,513.66***	0.523 (59.13***)	0.199 (67.68***)	0.112 (70.44***)	−0.049 (72.02***)	−0.050 (74.61***)
Event Driven	Distressed Securities	9.84	48.83	−159.62	7.63	−2.41	15.63	1,621.06***	0.405 (35.37***)	0.241 (48.03***)	0.153 (53.13***)	0.040 (55.91***)	−0.056 (58.61***)
	Risk Arbitrage	6.54	44.88	−76.23	7.63	−1.11	8.09	273.58***	0.298 (19.18***)	0.006 (19.19***)	−0.065 (20.12***)	0.161 (26.30***)	0.070 (31.25***)
Opportunistic	Emerging Markets	7.16	182.39	−314.04	7.63	−1.21	9.69	448.39***	0.311 (20.90***)	0.054 (21.53***)	0.041 (21.89***)	−0.067 (22.92***)	0.019 (28.46***)
	Global Macro	11.58	120.87	−147.29	7.63	−0.26	6.81	131.24***	0.090 (1.74)	0.038 (2.06)	0.070 (3.13)	0.205 (13.15***)	0.111 (22.58***)
	Long/Short Equity	8.80	146.74	−145.72	7.63	−0.23	6.25	95.65***	0.221 (10.56***)	0.090 (12.32***)	−0.001 (12.32***)	−0.141 (17.22***)	0.003 (22.52***)
	Dedicated Short Bias	−3.02	245.60	−143.64	7.63	0.48	3.75	13.01***	0.116 (2.89*)	−0.047 (3.37)	−0.025 (3.51)	−0.092 (6.38)	−0.039 (8.610)

(Continued)

Table 27.8 (Continued)

Managed Futures	6.15	113.85	−117.85	7.63	−0.08	2.98	0.24	0.018 (0.07)	−0.144 (4.59)	−0.114 (7.41)	−0.033 (7.83)	0.039 (18.68··)
S&P 500	4.99	110.79	−222.76	7.63	−0.85	4.36	42.36···	0.124 (3.33·)	−0.017 (3.39)	0.120 (6.53·)	0.034 (8.23)	−0.011 (10.62)
Barclays U.S. Aggregate	0.07	39.69	−48.19	7.63	−0.37	3.96	13.13···	0.142 (4.38···)	−0.140 (8.63··)	0.091 (10.46···)	−0.095 (12.48··)	0.008 (12.68)

This table presents the descriptive statistics of the hedge fund indices as well as the S&P 500 and Barclays U.S. Aggregate Bond Index. The calculations are based on 213 observations covering January 1994 through September 2011. The continuously compounded returns are calculated from the NAV of CS/Tremont indices. S&P 500 and Barclays U.S. Aggregate represent the US stock and bond markets. Average, minimum (min), and maximum (max) returns, as well as standard deviations are annualized and given in percentages. $AC(L)$ and LB stand for the autocorrelation coefficient and the Ljung-Box statistic at specific lag orders L. ···, ··, and · denote significant deviations from normality or from zero autocorrelation, respectively, at the 0.01, 0.05, and 0.10 levels, respectively.

Table 27.9 **Comparative Statistics for Various Allocation Methods**

	Mean-Variance (in percent)	Mean-Shortfall Variance (in percent)
	Average Weight	
Convertible Arbitrage	0.72	0.00
Equity Market Neutral	32.44	39.27
Fixed Income Arbitrage	3.91	0.00
Distressed Securities	19.47	20.92
Risk Arbitrage	23.43	16.53
Emerging Markets	0.00	0.00
Global Macro	7.40	8.64
Long/Short Equity	1.11	0.35
Dedicated Short Bias	7.93	6.63
Managed Futures	3.60	7.66
	Average Portfolio	
Mean	0.004	0.005
Standard Deviation	0.008	0.008
Skewness	−0.802	−0.416
Excess kurtosis	0.699	−0.165

The table shows the average weights as well as the descriptive statistics for portfolios derived under the mean-variance optimization and under the mean-shortfall variance optimization. Calculations are based on 213 observations covering January 1994 through September 2011. Average portfolios are calculated from 70 portfolios derived for 12-year rolling windows. Optimizations include the risk-free asset, which is assumed to be 0 percent. The minimal acceptable return for the LPM is 2 percent.

market. In general, hedge fund returns were higher and standard deviations were lower than the returns and standard deviations of the stock market proxy.

Funds of Hedge Funds

Funds of hedge funds invest in a variety of single hedge funds, typically incorporating from 10 to 30 underlying funds. They are considered a good entry-level investment because of the additional diversification benefits they offer (Ineichen, 2003; Black, 2006). Investing in funds of funds also significantly decreases the due diligence tasks for investors.

However, despite their many benefits, funds of hedge funds come with another layer of fees. Investors must pay fees not only at the single underlying hedge fund level but also to the fund of fund manager. A careful evaluation should also be conducted about the tax effects of these investments. But fund of fund data are

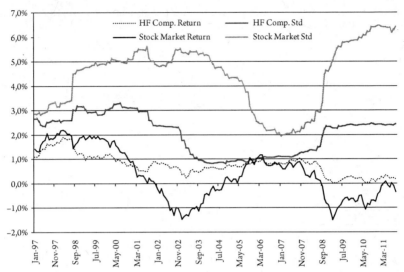

Figure 27.3 Rolling Returns and Standard Deviations of the Hedge Fund Composite Index and the Stock Market. This figure graphically illustrates the development of returns and standard deviations of the hedge fund composite index and the S&P 500. The calculations are based on 213 observations covering January 1994 through September 2011; rolling returns and rolling standard deviations of returns are calculated for a three-year rolling period. The CS/Tremont index and the S&P 500 represent the hedge fund industry and the US stock market, respectively.

not subject to the data biases of single hedge fund data such as survivorship bias, self-reporting bias, and backfill bias. As per Fung and Hsieh (2004), using fund of fund return data will thus reduce the effects of these biases.

Organization, Fees, Operations, and Regulations

Hedge fund managers are compensated on a fee-for-performance basis. A typical fee structure, for example, would be the so-called 2-and-20 setup, where the manager receives a 2 percent fee based on the assets under management and a 20 percent fee based on performance. Hedge funds normally have a *high watermark*. Once a hedge fund experiences a drawdown, it must recover this loss before the manager is allowed to charge performance fees. Some hedge funds also specify a *hurdle rate*, which is a rate that fund management must reach before it can charge performance fees.

But particularly interesting from a portfolio context is whether a fund has a lock-up period, charges a redemption fee, or implements a redemption period. Under these constraints, investors are not allowed to redeem or sell shares. Redemption fees or periods imply that investors will be charged substantial additional sums for capital withdrawals before the redemption date. In some cases, fund withdrawals may not even be possible. Such structures are typically implemented to limit portfolio turnover, but they can severely impact investors' portfolio decisions.

Thus, operational due diligence is especially important when considering investing in hedge funds. Hedge fund operations are opaque to investors, and they obviously bring additional layers of operational risk to an investment. Because hedge funds operate through private placements, with share ownership restricted to institutional and high-net-worth private investors, they are mainly exempt from the disclosure and reporting requirements that apply to other financial institutions.

In 2006, the United States attempted to impose limited public disclosure regulations on hedge fund operations. Under this new regulation, funds with more than 14 investors and assets AuM of more than $25 million were required to register via the standard Form ADV. This new regulation was quickly challenged in court, and a majority of states eventually chose to vacate the regulation. In June 2011, the Securities and Exchange Commission (SEC) enacted a new legislation in response to the Dodd-Frank Act. Beginning in March 2012, investment funds such as venture capital funds and hedge funds with AuM of more than $150 million are required to provide basic organizational and operational information to the SEC and the public, such as size and ownership of assets, adviser services to the fund, and other general fund data.

In general, hedge funds are reluctant to provide investors with sufficiently detailed information on a timely basis about their overall risk profile. They argue that such disclosures would severely impact their future performance potential by attracting copycat traders. Brown and Schwarz (2011) confirm the existence of abnormal market conditions around the disclosure date of Form 13(f) filings, which could indicate imitators. They also find that over the long-term investors are unlikely to be able to benefit from the information contained in these forms. The authors conclude this is due to the delay in reporting (13(f) fillings must be available 45 days after the end of the quarter), as well as to the fact that 13(f) fillings only report on long positions (hedge fund returns may be driven largely by short positions instead).

Until the late 1990s, the focus when assessing the risk of hedge fund investments was clearly financial. Investors acknowledged the existence of operational risk, but their primary goal was to assess market or price risk. Hedge fund performance was extremely positive, and no hedge fund failures had yet occurred. However, this changed dramatically when the first hedge fund failures due to operational risk, such as Bayou in 1998, became public.

The sudden availability of data on hedge fund operations has also increased academic interest and research. Despite the fact that investors were not focused on it, prior studies had already noted the importance of operational risk. For example, Brown, Goetzmann, and Park (2001) find that the attrition rate within the hedge fund universe is high and significant, and they attribute it to operational risk.

As researchers gained access to data they could not analyze previously, they were able to advance more comprehensive theories about the risks inherent in hedge fund returns. Brown, Goetzmann, Liang, and Schwarz (2009) create the so-called omega score to predict fund failures, with operational risk indicators derived from the Form ADV.

Although investors today seem aware of the additional operational risk from hedge funds, they do not seem to fully integrate such risk into their investment decisions (Brown, Goetzmann, Liang, and Schwarz, 2008). Brown, Fraser, and Liang (2008) posit that avoiding operational risk can be a source of alpha generation. They apply their approach to a number of funds of funds and find that larger funds of funds that can absorb the high costs of due diligence and use service providers more efficiently exhibit more stable and higher overall alpha.

Hedge Funds and the 2007–2008 Financial Crisis

As their numbers and size have increased, hedge funds today have become a major liquidity provider for capital markets. Through their models and managerial capability, hedge fund managers seek mispriced securities and accept the short side of market trades. For example, a contrarian hedge fund buys past losing stocks, which most market participants would like to sell. Traditionally, brokers or other market makers have filled this role, but hedge funds have increasingly been entering this market to capitalize on such trades.

Hedge funds have also found another arena from which to earn attractive returns. They have evolved from merely stock picking and block trading to being major players in corporate bonds, i.e., providing credit to corporations as well as indirectly loans to the real estate market. This situation has created a system of underground financing often referred to as a *shadow banking system*. Shadow banking provides funding but is not yet restricted by the same regulations as the traditional banking system. The development of a new style in the hedge fund universe has promoted this shift. Most hedge funds no longer restrict themselves to just one investment style, but have begun to implement a so-called *multistrategy approach*, investing in any market that promises above-average returns.

Contrary to highly regulated banks, hedge funds face almost no restrictions or reporting requirements, despite the fact that the complex interactions between hedge funds and other financial institutions (e.g., commercial or investment banks) might be systemically relevant. This development has major implications for the characteristics of hedge funds, and the effects can best be illustrated by what took place leading up to and during the 2007–2008 financial crisis.

During the second half of 2007, events in the US subprime market were already pointing to potential turmoil in the financial market. Largely unnoticed by the public, however, were the turbulences that unfolded from August 6 to 10, 2007, the so-called quant crisis. During these five days, several of the most prominent quantitative and long/short equity hedge funds experienced unprecedented losses. Khandani and Lo (2007) provide a comprehensive overview and examine the reasons for this event.

Understanding the quant crisis is essential to understand some of the major issues of hedge fund investments for investors. Industry structures and characteristics that may have contributed significantly to the magnitude of the losses are still in place and could result in further severe losses for investors.

CROWDED TRADES

The first hedge fund managers bought or sold stocks based on their assessment of the riskiness of an asset. Advances in the finance industry and especially within the hedge fund industry, however, eventually resulted in using technology and implementing ever more advanced quantitative methods. For example, trades are initiated electronically by signals of underlying algorithms. The underlying data from which trading signals are derived were widely available and so were the factors that consequently produced trades where several hedge funds act on more or less the same signals. Together with the rapid increase in hedge fund volume and AuM, this resulted in *crowded trades* in which large sums of money are being traded on the same assets at the same time. Such a structure might eventually result in so-called *fire sales*. Fire sales occur when large volumes being traded on the same signal depress market prices, which result in further sell signals from the system and so on.

Khandani and Lo (2007) replicate the returns of long/short equity hedge funds by modelling a simple contrarian strategy. They find returns, on average, for this strategy of 1.38 percent per day in 1995, decreasing to 0.13 percent in 2007. This result can be partially attributed to increased competition. Khandani and Lo also find a significant increase in the number of long/short equity hedge funds and in AuM invested in this strategy, which again points to more competition, at least in this specific investment style.

The crowding of factors results not only in increased return correlations among individual hedge funds but also in increased correlations with other asset classes and autocorrelation. The beneficial characteristics of hedge funds with respect to their behavior within and outside the hedge fund industry do not appear to hold during times of crisis. The rapid increase in the number of hedge funds and the crowding of factors eventually results in a decrease in liquidity for these strategies and thus in increased serial correlation. Khandani and Lo (2007) confirm this notion, finding increasing autocorrelations for the 1994 to 2007 period except for a short dip in 2004. They also find increased correlations among different hedge fund styles when comparing the 1994 to 2000 period with the 2001 to 2007 period.

Chan et al. (2006), who find that funds are more highly correlated during crisis times, support Khandani and Lo's (2007) findings. Billio et al. (2009) also find that hedge fund correlations increase during times of crisis. They attribute approximately one-third of this increase to the increased exposure to common classical risk factors.

Füss, Kaiser, and Adams (2007) examine the volatility of hedge fund returns over 2002 to 2006. In comparing different alternative volatility models, they find that incorporating conditional volatility into a GARCH-type VaR more accurately reflects the increased risk. The GARCH-type VaR figures adjust better to time-varying risk, thus allowing for better portfolio protection against downside risk. Their findings also imply that traditional means of portfolio allocation, especially during bearish markets, may not correctly reflect the true risk of the overall portfolio.

Boyson, Stahel, and Stulz (2010) investigate whether contagion occurs in the hedge fund industry. The idea here is that a danger exists of one failing hedge fund affecting other hedge funds and causing them to fail as well. The authors find no evidence of contagion between broad market indices and hedge fund returns. This result is in line with Billio et al. (2009), who also find that the correlation between hedge fund returns and the S&P 500 declines during crisis times. The 2007–2008 financial crisis did not affect hedge funds to the same extent as other financial institutions such as AIG and Fannie Mae. Yet, Boyson et al. find strong evidence of contagion effects between the different hedge fund styles.

Adams, Füss, and Gropp (2010), using their state-dependent sensitivity VaR (SDSVaR) approach, were among the first to quantify the size and duration of risk spillovers between different financial institutions. They find that spillovers tend to be rather small during tranquil times, but they are often significant during times of volatility or crisis. The authors show that hedge funds are a major transmitter of shocks to the financial system.

Contagion in this context can be transmitted in two ways. First is the so-called *prime broker channel*, when poor returns to one hedge fund hurt financial intermediaries, who then are unable to provide credit to other hedge funds. The second channel is the so-called *stock market liquidity channel*. Brunnermeier and Pedersen (2009) find that market and funding liquidity are interrelated. As long as hedge funds have access to funding, they provide liquidity to illiquid markets. However, once funding liquidity dries up, due to higher margins and/or losses on existing positions, funding considerations tend to drive market prices more than other factors.

LEVERAGE

Since the 1990s, hedge funds have experienced declining returns. They have thus had to increase leverage in order to obtain a performance level similar to what investors have come to expect. Quant funds have a particular focus on finding small pricing anomalies that they can turn into superior profits by using leverage. Khandani and Lo (2007) calculate that a simple contrarian strategy would require a 9:1 leverage ratio in August 2006 to deliver the same results that it did in 1998.

However, leverage increases the risk of every investment. This increase occurs because once certain markets drop in value, the value of the collateral will also decrease, and managers will face margin calls from brokers asking for more collateral. Such a chain of events could eventually force managers to sell other parts of their portfolios in order to replenish their collateral. Leverage thus magnifies all events for hedge funds, either positive or negative, and accelerates the level of risk for both the gains and all the capital involved.

Khandani and Lo's (2007) "unwind hypothesis" replicates the strategy of a market-neutral hedge fund. The authors illustrate how the losses of August 7 and 8, 2007, would have resulted in liquidating a considerable part of the overall portfolio of these funds in order to provide for collateral calls and to fund the leverage. Such sudden large liquidations would consequently have affected all strategies that focused on the same factors, for example, long/short equity funds. The "Crowded Trades" subsection shows how such common factor exposures are likely to occur. Thus, funds are more likely to make the same bets on the market but will also be affected by the same movements.

Eventually, these issues lead to the conclusion that hedge funds may be operating at or beyond market capacity. The sheer number and size of hedge funds indicate how crowded some of the strategies must be. Additionally, studies show that hedge funds, through leveraging up their positions, can dominate entire markets (President's Working Group on Financial Markets. 1999).

Summary and Conclusions

Several important issues should be considered before investing in hedge funds or funds of hedge funds. Still, this group of assets provides a combination of characteristics that can be enormously beneficial to the risk and return properties of the overall portfolio. Hedge funds as an asset class cover a wide variety of different investment strategies and apply a broad range of financial instruments. They are often and accurately described as unregulated pools of private capital. Their structure allows them to avoid regulations that would restrict their activities or force them to publish information they prefer not to share. Hedge fund managers are thus able to implement any strategy and investment approach they think best to capture the highest returns at the lowest risk.

This has been the status quo in the hedge fund industry for most of this asset's existence. Managers have more or less been given the opportunity to capitalize on their desired strategies outside the general public's attention. However, the 2007–2008 financial crisis dramatically changed public awareness of the financial industry, in general, and particularly of heretofore unregulated players within the industry, such as hedge funds. The United States has already implemented regulations that require hedge fund firms, beginning in March 2012, to provide more detailed and timely information to the public. The United Kingdom and the European Union will likely follow suit.

This chapter was written at a time when the number of funds is rising and many copycat firms are entering the market. Returns are declining, and the favorable correlations with other asset classes may also be affected. Thus, the next few years will be critical to shaping the future of this industry.

Discussion Questions

1. During the 2007–2008 financial crisis, the question of contagion in the financial industry has received intense attention. Among others, the role of hedge funds in spreading contagion throughout the system has been widely discussed. Discuss whether hedge funds have increased the riskiness in the system and spread increased risks to other participants.

2. Discuss some important aspects to consider for investing in hedge funds irrespective of their distinct characteristics.
3. Hedge fund return data differ from returns of other traditional asset classes such as bonds or stocks. How should investors account for this disparity in their investment process?
4. Name at least three biases that are present in hedge fund return data. Identify the source of each bias, and discuss how each one affects implications drawn from such data.

References

Ackermann, Carl, Richard McEnally, and David Ravenscraft. 1999. "The Performance of Hedge Funds: Risk, Return, and Incentives." *Journal of Finance* 54:3, 833–874.

Adams, Zeno, Roland Füss, and Reint Gropp. 2010. "Modeling Spillover Effects among Financial Institutions: A State-Dependent Sensitivity Value-at-Risk (SDSVaR) Approach." Working Paper, EBS Business School, EBS Universität für Wirtschaft und Recht.

Agarwal, Vikas, Vyacheslav Fos, and Wei Jiang. 2010. "Inferring Reporting Biases in Hedge Fund Databases from Hedge Fund Equity Holdings." Working Paper, Georgia State University.

Agarwal, Vikas, and Narayan Y. Naik. 2004. "Risk and Portfolio Decisions Involving Hedge Funds." *Review of Financial Studies* 17:1, 63–98.

Amenc, Noël, and Lionel Martellini. 2002. "The Brave New World of Hedge Fund Indexes." Working Paper, EDHEC Graduate School of Business and University of Southern California.

Amenc, Noël, Lionel Martellini, and Mathieu Vaissié. 2003. "Indexing Hedge Fund Indexes." Working Paper, EDHEC Risk and Asset Management Research Center, EDHEC Business School, Lille.

Amin, Gaurav, and Harry M. Kat. 2003. "Welcome to the Dark Side: Hedge Fund Attrition and Survivorship Bias over the Period 1994–2001." *Journal of Alternative Investments* 6:1, 57–73.

Asness, Clifford, Robert Krail, and John Liew. 2001. "Do Hedge Funds Hedge?" *Journal of Portfolio Management* 28:1, 6–19.

Bawa, Vijay S. 1975. "Optimal Rules for Ordering Uncertain Prospects." *Journal of Financial Economics* 2:1, 95–121.

Bawa, Vijay S., and Eric B. Lindenberg. 1977. "Capital Market Equilibrium in a Mean-Lower Partial Moment Framework." *Journal of Financial Economics* 5:2, 189–200.

Billio, Monica, Mila Getmansky, and Loriana Pelizzon. 2009. "Crises and Hedge Fund Risk." Working Paper, University of Massachusetts, Amherst.

Black, Keith H. 2006. "The Changing Performance and Risks of Funds of Funds in the Modern Period." In Greg N. Gregoriou (ed.), *Funds of Hedge Funds*, 99–106. Oxford, UK: Elsevier.

Bollen, Nicolas P. B., and Veronika K. Pool. 2008. "Conditional Return Smoothing in the Hedge Fund Industry." *Journal of Financial and Quantitative Analysis* 43:2, 267–298.

Bollen, Nicolas P. B., and Robert E. Whaley. 2009. "Hedge Fund Risk Dynamics: Implications for Performance Appraisal." *Journal of Finance* 64:2, 985–1035.

Boyson, Nicole M., Christof W. Stahel, and René M. Stulz. 2010. "Hedge Fund Contagion and Liquidity Shocks." *Journal of Finance* 65:5, 1789–1816.

Brooks, Chris, and Harry M. Kat. 2002. "The Statistical Properties of Hedge Fund Index Returns and Their Implications for Investors." *Journal of Alternative Investments* 5:2, 26–44.

Brown, Stephen, Thomas Fraser, and Bing Liang. 2008. "Hedge Fund Due Diligence: A Source of Alpha in a Hedge Fund Portfolio Strategy." Working Paper, New York University, Stern School of Business.

Brown, Stephen, William Goetzmann, and Roger Ibbotson. 1999. "Offshore Hedge Funds: Survival and Performance, 1989–1995." *Journal of Business* 72:1, 91–117.

Brown, Stephen, William Goetzmann, Bing Liang, and Christopher Schwarz. 2008. "Mandatory Disclosure and Operational Risk: Evidence from Hedge Fund Registration." *Journal of Finance* 63:6, 2785–2815.

Brown, Stephen, William Goetzmann, Bing Liang, and Christopher Schwarz. 2009. "Estimating Operational Risk for Hedge Funds: The ω-Score." *Financial Analysts Journal* 5:1, 43–53.

Brown, Stephen, William Goetzmann, and James Park. 2001. "Careers and Survival: Competition and Risk in the Hedge Fund and CTA Industry." *Journal of Finance* 56:5, 1869–1886.

Brown, Stephen, and Christopher Schwarz. 2011. "The Impact of Mandatory Hedge Fund Portfolio Disclosure." Working Paper, New York University, Stern School of Business.

Brunnermeier, Markus, and Lasse H. Pedersen. 2009. "Market Liquidity and Funding Liquidity." *Review of Financial Studies* 22:6, 2201–2238.

Cai, Li, and Bing Liang. 2010. "Asset Allocation Dynamics in the Hedge Fund Industry." Working Paper, University of Massachusetts.

Capocci, Daniel, Alexandre Corhay, and Georges Hübner. 2005. "Hedge Fund Performance and Persistence in Bull and Bear Markets." *European Journal of Finance* 11:5, 361–392.

Chan, Nicholas, Mila Getmansky, Shane M. Haas, and Andrew W. Lo. 2006. "Do Hedge Funds Increase Systematic Risk?" Federal Reserve Bank of Atlanta, *Economic Review* 91:4, 49–80.

Conner, Andrew. 2003. "Asset Allocation Effects of Adjusting Alternative Assets for Stale Pricing." *Journal of Alternative Investments* 6:3, 42–52.

Davies, Ryan J., Harry M. Kat, and Sa Lu. 2009. "Fund of Hedge Funds Portfolio Selection: A Multiple-Objective Approach." *Journal of Derivatives and Hedge Funds,* 15:2, 91–115.

Dimson, Elroy. 1979. "Risk Measurement When Shares Are Subject to Infrequent Trading." *Journal of Financial Economics* 7:2, 197–226.

Eling, Martin, and Frank Schuhmacher. 2007. "Does the Choice of Performance Measure Influence the Evaluation of Hedge Funds?" *Journal of Banking and Finance* 31:9, 2632–2647.

Fung, Hung-Gay, Xiaoqing E. Xu, and Jot Yau. 2004. "Do Hedge Fund Managers Display Skill?" *Journal of Alternative Investments* 6:4, 22–31.

Fung, William, and David A. Hsieh. 1997. "Empirical Characteristics of Dynamic Trading Strategies: The Case of Hedge Funds." *Review of Financial Studies* 10:2, 275–302.

Fung, William, and David A. Hsieh. 2000. "Performance Characteristics of Hedge Funds and CTA Funds: Natural Versus Spurious Biases." *Journal of Financial and Quantitative Analysis* 35:3, 291–307.

Fung, William, and David A. Hsieh. 2001. "The Risk in Hedge Fund Strategies: Theory and Evidence from Trend Followers." *Review of Financial Studies* 14:2, 313–341.

Fung, William, and David A. Hsieh. 2002a. "Asset-Based Style Factors for Hedge Funds." *Financial Analysts Journal* 58:5, 16–27.

Fung, William, and David A. Hsieh. 2002b. "Hedge Fund Benchmarks: A Risk-Based Approach." *Financial Analysts Journal* 60:5, 65–80.

Fung, William, and David A. Hsieh. 2002c. "Risk in Fixed-Income Hedge Fund Styles." *Journal of Fixed Income* 12:2, 1–22.

Fung, William, and David A. Hsieh. 2004. "Extracting Portable Alphas from Equity Long/Short Hedge Funds." *Journal of Investment Management* 2:4, 1–19.

Fung, William, and David A. Hsieh. 2009. "Measurement Biases in Hedge Fund Studies: An Update." *Financial Analysts Journal* 65:3, 36–38.

Füss, Roland, Dieter G. Kaiser, and Felix Schindler. 2012. "Dynamic Linkages Between Hedge Funds and Traditional Financial Assets: Evidence from Emerging Markets." EBS Working Paper Series No. 09–19, EBS Universität für Wirtschaft und Recht.

Füss, Roland, Dieter G. Kaiser, and Zeno Adams. 2007. "Value at Risk, GARCH Modeling and the Forecasting of Hedge Fund Return Volatility." *Journal of Derivatives and Hedge Funds* 13:1, 2–25.

Füss, Roland, Dieter G. Kaiser, Sarah Müller, and Joachim Zietz. 2011. "When 'to Fire' an Absolute Return Portfolio Manager? A Systematic Framework for the Hedge Fund Industry." Working Paper, EBS Business School, EBS Universität für Wirtschaft und Recht.

Geltner, David. 1991. "Smoothing Appraisal-Based Returns." *Journal of Real Estate Finance and Economics* 4:3, 327–345.

Geltner, David. 1993. "Estimating Market Values from Appraised Values Without Assuming an Efficient Market." *Journal of Real Estate Research* 8:3, 325–345.

Getmansky, Mila, Andrew W. Lo, and Igor Makarov. 2004. "An Econometric Model of Serial Correlation and Illiquidity in Hedge Fund Returns." *Journal of Financial Economics* 74:3, 529–609.

Gibson, Rajna, and Sébastien Gyger. 2007. "The Style Consistency of Hedge Funds." *European Financial Management* 13:2, 287–308.

Goetzmann, William, Jonathan Ingersoll, and Stephen Ross. 2003. "High-Water Marks and Hedge Fund Management Contracts." *Journal of Finance* 58:4, 1685–1717.

Harlow, W. V. 1991. "Asset Allocation in a Downside Risk Framework." *Financial Analysts Journal* 47:5, 28–40.

Harlow, W. V., and Ramesh K. S. Rao. 1989. "Asset Pricing in a Generalized Mean-Lower Partial Moment Framework: Theory and Evidence." *Journal of Financial and Quantitative Analysis* 24:3, 285–309.

Hedge Fund Research. 2011. Global Hedge Fund Industry Report—Year End 2010. Chicago: Hedge Fund Research.

Heidorn, Thomas, Christian Hoppe, and Dieter G. Kaiser. 2006. "Implikationen der Heterogenität auf das Benchmarking mit Hedgefondsindizes." *Finanz Betrieb* 8:9, 557–571.

Heidorn, Thomas, Dieter G. Kaiser, and Christoph Roder. 2009. "Empirische Analyse der Drawdowns von Dach-Hegdefonds.„ Working Paper, Frankfurt School of Finance.

Hodder, James E., Jens C. Jackwerth, and Olga Kolova. 2008. "Recovering Delisting Returns of Hedge Funds." MPRA Paper, University of Wisconsin, Madison.

Ibbotson, Roger, Peng Chen, and Kevin Zhu. 2010. "The A, B, Cs of Hedge Funds: Alphas, Betas, and Costs." Working Paper, Yale University.

Ineichen, Alexander M. 2003. *Absolute Returns. The Risks and Opportunities of Hedge Fund Investing.* London: John Wiley & Sons.

Kat, Harry M. 2003. "10 Things That Investors Should Know about Hedge Funds." *Journal of Wealth Management* 3:5, 72–81.

Kat, Harry M. 2005. "Integrating Hedge Funds into the Traditional Portfolio." *Journal of Wealth Management* 7:4, 51–57.

Kat, Harry M., and Sa Lu. 2002. "An Excursion into the Statistical Properties of Hedge Fund Returns." Working Paper, Alternative Investment Research Centre, City University.

Kestner, Lars N. 1996. "Getting a Handle on True Performance." *Futures* 25:1, 4446.

Khandani, Amir E., and Andrew W. Lo. 2007. "What Happened to the Quants in August 2007?" *Journal of Investment Management* 5:4, 29–78.

Lhabitant, Francois-Serge. 2002. *Hedge Funds: Myths and Limits.* Chichester, UK: John Wiley & Sons.

Lhabitant, Francois-Serge. 2004. *Hedge Funds: Quantitative Insights.* Hoboken, NJ: John Wiley & Sons.

Liang, Bing. 2000. "Hedge Funds: The Living and the Dead." *Journal of Financial and Quantitative Analysis* 35:3, 309–326.

Lo, Andrew W. 2005. *The Dynamics of the Hedge Fund Industry.* Charlottesville, VA: The Research Foundation of CFA Institute.

Mahdavi, Mahnaz. 2004. "Risk-Adjusted Return When Returns Are Not Normally Distributed: Adjusted Sharpe Ratio." *Journal of Alternative Investments* 6:4, 47–57.

Malkiel, Burton G., and Atanu Saha. 2005. "Hedge Funds: Risk and Return." *Financial Analysts Journal* 61:6, 80–88.

Markowitz, Harry. 1952. "Portfolio Selection." *Journal of Finance* 7:1, 77–91.

Markowitz, Harry. 1959. *Portfolio Selection-Efficient Diversification of Investments*. New Haven, CT: Yale University Press.

Nawrocki, David N. 1991. "Optimal Algorithms and Lower Partial Moments: Ex-Post Results." *Applied Economics* 23:3, 465–470.

President's Working Group on Financial Markets. 1999. "Hedge Funds, Leverage, and the Lessons of Long-Term Capital Management." Available at http://www.treasury.gov/resource-center/fin-mkts/Documents/hedgfund.pdf.

Reuters Hedgeworld. 2011. "Hedge Fund Styles." Available at http://www.hedgeworld.com/education/index.cgi?page=hedge_fund_styles.

Schneeweis, Thomas, Hossein B. Kazemi, and George A. Martin. 2002. "Understanding Hedge Fund Performance, Research Issues Revisited—Part I." *Journal of Alternative Investments* 5:3, 6–22.

Schneeweis, Thomas, Hossein B. Kazemi, and George A. Martin. 2003. "Understanding Hedge Fund Performance, Research Issues Revisited—Part II." *Journal of Alternative Investments* 5:4, 8–30.

Shadwick, William F., and Con Keating. 2002. "A Universal Performance Measure." *Journal of Performance Measurement* 6:3, 59–84.

Sharpe, William F. 1992. "Asset Allocation: Management Style and Performance Measurement." *Journal of Portfolio Management* 18:2, 7–19.

Sing, Tien F., and Seow E. Ong. 2000. "Asset Allocation in a Downside Risk Framework." *Journal of Real Estate Portfolio Management* 6:3, 213–223.

Sortino, Frank A., and Robert van der Meer. 1991. "Downside Risk." *Journal of Portfolio Management* 17:4, 27–31.

Weiss, Gary, and Joseph Weber. 1994. "Fall Guys?" *Businessweek*, April 25, 116–121.

Young, Terry W. 1991. "Calmar Ratio: A Smoother Tool." *Futures* 20:1, 40.

28

Portfolio and Risk Management for Private Equity Fund Investments

AXEL BUCHNER

Assistant Professor of Finance, DekaBank Chair in
Finance and Financial Control, Passau University

NIKLAS WAGNER

Professor of Finance, DekaBank Chair in
Finance and Financial Control, Passau University

Introduction

Over the past 25 years, managers of institutional assets have increasingly allocated funds to the private equity industry. During this period, private equity
yielded relatively high returns as compared to traditional stock and bond market
investments. However, the 2007 to 2008 credit crisis revealed that private equity
may also exhibit substantial risk. The question that arises from the recent financial crisis is how private equity risk can be properly understood and managed.

Given the unique features of the private equity asset class, the answer to this
question is not straightforward. In particular, traditional portfolio and risk management approaches fail to adequately describe this asset class in many situations.
Institutions invest in private equity predominantly through closed-end limited
partnership funds that are illiquid. As such, no public markets are available to
help set the valuations of these vehicles. The only observable variables are usually
the cash flows of the funds. Consequently, returns of private equity funds cannot
be evaluated on the basis of standard time-weighted returns. Returns of private
equity funds have to be evaluated using other performance measures that cannot
be taken into account directly in standard portfolio and risk management models,
such as the internal rate of return (IRR) or cash flow multiples.

Additionally, private equity funds have special cash flow structures that distinguish them from other asset classes. Private equity funds are raised every few
years on a blind pool basis by professional management companies that invest,
manage, and harvest the portfolio companies of the fund. At the onset of the
partnership, investors commit capital that gets drawn over several years. Together
with the illiquid nature of the private equity funds, the uncertain schedule of the
capital drawdowns and unpredictable distributions of cash or securities to the

investors of the fund make accurately managing these partnership interests difficult. For example, estimating expected future cash needed to meet capital commitments, as well as projected distributions that generate liquidity in the future, is challenging for investors.

Following this line of argument, the key to accurate private equity portfolio and risk management is to develop models that explicitly tie the variables of interest to the observable cash flows structures of private equity funds. The contribution of this chapter is to present a novel stochastic model on the cash flow dynamics of private equity funds that fulfills this requirement and can be applied to many portfolio and risk management questions. Although no independent strand of research has developed so far, modeling the cash flow dynamics of private equity funds is one of the latest challenges in the private equity literature.

The stochastic model presented in this chapter differs from the existing work of Takahashi and Alexander (2002) and Malherbe (2004) in that it solely relies on observable cash flow data. Based on cash flow data, the analysis shows that the model is flexible and can well match various drawdown and distribution patterns that are observed empirically. The empirical analysis uses a dataset of 203 mature European private equity funds, of which 95 were fully liquidated during the January 1980 to June 2003 sample period. The analysis shows that the model can easily be calibrated to real-world fund data and is a good fit for historical data.

At the same time, the model is easy to understand and implement and has a variety of applications. First, institutional investors can employ it for the purpose of liquidity planning. Second, such investors can use the model as a tool for many risk management applications. For example, they can measure the sensitivity of some ex–post performance measure, such as the IRR, to changes in typical drawdown or distribution patterns. Third, portfolio managers can use the model to determine to optimal allocation between, for example, the venture capital and buyout segments.

The remainder of this chapter is organized as follows. The next section outlines the methodological problems of using standard portfolio and risk management techniques in the private equity area. The third section introduces the stochastic model for the cash flow dynamics of private equity funds and illustrates the model dynamics by a numerical example. The fourth section evaluates the goodness of fit of the model with empirical data. The fifth section illustrates how the model can be applied in a portfolio and risk management context. The final section concludes with a brief summary and conclusions.

Challenges in Private Equity Portfolio and Risk Management

The illiquid nature of the private equity asset class presents particular challenges for portfolio management and risk management. The application of the standard neoclassical financial models, such as portfolio optimization techniques and value at risk, typically requires the knowledge of the risk-return characteristics of an asset class. Risk-return characteristics for asset classes of publicly traded securities can easily be estimated by standard econometric procedures from historical returns that are derived based on the securities' observable market prices. As private equity fund investments are not traded on secondary markets, observable market prices are unavailable for this asset class.

To circumvent this problem, the performance of private equity funds is typically measured by the internal rate of return (IRR) of the investment. Studies using the IRR or related cash flow–based performance measures include, among others, Burgel (2000), Ljungqvist and Richardson (2003a, 2003b), Kaplan and Schoar (2005), Diller and Kaserer (2009), and Phalippou and Gottschalg (2009). As discussed in the literature, using the IRR as a measure of performance has several drawbacks. First, the IRR may not be unique when future cash flows vary in sign. Second, the IRR is based on the implicit assumption that intermediate cash flows can be reinvested at the IRR. Last but perhaps the most important in the context of portfolio and risk management is the fact that the IRR does not enable estimating a standard deviation of returns and a correlation of private equity returns to other asset classes, such as publicly traded stocks.

Another line of research in the private equity area tries to avoid these drawbacks of the IRR by calculating periodic returns based on the fund's disclosed net asset values (NAVs). Studies in this area include, for example, Rhodes-Kropf and Jones (2004) and Cochrane (2005). The resulting periodic returns are based on the implicit assumption that the fund's assets may be realized (or are at least accurately measured) by the reported NAVs of the fund management. However, as discussed in the literature, reported NAVs frequently suffer from stale and managed pricing. Stale pricing is caused by the fact that the reported NAVs of the fund management do not readily incorporate all available information. Stale pricing leads to a lag time between observable market valuations and valuations in private equity portfolios. Under these conditions, the reported NAVs will only occasionally reflect the true market values, i.e., the price at which the fund's assets could be sold in an open market transaction. Similarly, as private equity fund managers have considerable discretion in their valuations, reported NAVs might suffer from a managed pricing phenomenon. This means that fund managers actively manage the pricing of their portfolios. In this sense, fund managers may mark the values of their portfolios up or down only when doing so is favorable.

Thus, private equity portfolio and risk models need to be based on observable cash flow patterns of the funds, not on possibly biased valuations of the fund management. This need requires models that account for the cash flows dynamics of private equity funds.

A Stochastic Cash Flow Model for Private Equity Funds

This section summarizes the model for the cash flow dynamics of private equity funds. Following the typical construction of private equity funds, the model consists of two independent stages: (1) the stochastic model of the capital drawdowns and (2) the stochastic model of the capital distributions over a fund's lifetime.

MODELING CAPITAL DRAWDOWNS

Investments in private equity are frequently intermediated through *private equity funds*, which are pooled investment vehicles for securities of companies that are usually unlisted. Private equity funds usually represent closed-end funds with a finite lifetime that are organized as a limited partnership. The private equity firm serves as the general partner (GP). Institutional investors, who then act as limited partners (LPs), normally provide the bulk of the capital invested in the fund. The LPs commit to provide a certain amount of capital to the private equity fund, which is the committed capital (C). The GP has an agreed time period (usually five years) in which to invest committed capital, denoted as commitment period T_c. When a GP identifies an investment opportunity, it "calls" money from its LPs up to the amount committed at any time during the prespecified commitment period. Thus, capital calls of the fund occur unscheduled over the commitment period with the exact timing depending only on the investment decision of the GP. In order to model this behavior, Equation 28.1 assumes that cumulated capital drawdowns D_t at any time t during the commitment period can be described by the ordinary differential equation

$$dD_t = \delta_t(C - D_t)dt, \tag{28.1}$$

where $\delta_t > 0$ is the fund's drawdown rate at time t. Under this specification, total capital calls can never exceed C. Further, the typical time pattern of real-world capital drawdowns is reflected in the structure of Equation 28.1. Capital drawdowns of private equity funds tend to be concentrated in the first few years or even first quarters of a fund's life. After high initial investment activity, drawdowns of private equity funds are carried out at a declining rate, as fewer new investments are made, and follow-on investments are spread over a number of years.

As investment opportunities do not arise constantly over the commitment period, capital drawdowns of private equity funds will exhibit some erratic features. Equation 28.2 captures this relationship by assuming that the rate at which capital is drawn over time follows a mean-reverting square root process given by

$$d\delta_t = \kappa(\theta - \delta_t)dt + \sigma_\delta\sqrt{\delta_t}\,dB_{\delta,t}, \tag{28.2}$$

where $\theta > 0$ is the long-run mean of the drawdown rate; $\kappa > 0$ governs the rate of reversion to this mean; $\sigma_\delta > 0$ reflects the volatility of the drawdown rate; and $B_{\delta,t}$ is a standard Brownian motion. The drawdown rate behavior implied by the above square root diffusion ensures that negative values of the drawdown rate are precluded and that the drawdown rate randomly fluctuates around some mean level θ.

MODELING CAPITAL DISTRIBUTIONS

As capital drawdowns occur, the private equity fund immediately invests the available capital in managed assets and the portfolio begins to accumulate. As the underlying investments of the fund are gradually exited, cash or marketable securities are received, and finally returns and proceeds are distributed to the LPs of the fund. Distributions and drawdowns are modeled separately and, therefore, must also restrict capital distributions to be strictly non-negative at any time t during the legal lifetime T_1 of the fund. This is achieved by assuming that capital distributions p_t follow a geometric Brownian motion given by Equation 28.3:

$$d \ln p_t = \mu_t dt + \sigma_p dB_{p,t},$$ (28.3)

where μ_t denotes the time-dependent drift and σ_p is a constant volatility. $B_{p,t}$ is a second standard Brownian motion, which is uncorrelated with $B_{s,t}$.

Defining an appropriate function for μ_t is difficult because this parameter must incorporate the typical time pattern of the capital distributions of a private equity fund. In a fund's early years, capital distributions tend to be of minimal size as investments have not had the time to be harvested. The fund's middle years, on average, tend to display the highest distributions as more and more investments can be exited. Finally, later years are marked by a steady decline in capital distributions as fewer investments are left to be harvested. This behavior is modeled by assuming that the unconditional expectation of the cumulative capital distributions, $E[P_t]$, is given by Equation 28.4

$$E[P_t] = mC\left[1 - \exp\left(-\frac{1}{2}\alpha t^2\right)\right],$$ (28.4)

where m is the fund's expected cash multiple and a governs the speed at which capital distributions occur over time.

MODEL ILLUSTRATION

This section illustrates the model's ability to reproduce important features of the cash flow patterns of private equity funds with a numerical example. Table 28.1 illustrates the model parameters used for this example.

To illustrate the model dynamics, Figure 28.1 compares the expected cash flows (drawdowns, distributions, and net fund cash flows) for two different hypothetical funds. As the different sets of parameter values in Table 28.1 reveal, both hypothetical funds are assumed to have the same long-run multiple m and a committed capital that is standardized to a value of 1. Each fund is assumed to have cumulated capital drawdowns equal to 1 over their lifetime and expected cumulated capital distributions equal to 1.5. However, they differ in the timing of the capital drawdowns and distributions, as indicated by the different values of the other model parameters. For the first fund, the assumption is that drawdowns occur rapidly in the beginning, whereas capital distributions take place

Table 28.1 **Model Parameters**

	Drawdowns			Distributions		
	κ	θ	σ_δ	m	α	σ_p
Fund 1	2.0	1.0	0.5	1.5	0.03	0.2
Fund 2	0.5	0.5	0.2	1.5	0.06	0.2

This table gives the model parameters for the capital drawdowns and distributions of two different hypothetical funds. Both hypothetical funds are assumed to have the same long-run multiple m and a committed capital that is standardized to a value of 1. However, they differ in the timing of the capital drawdowns and distributions. For Fund 1, the assumption is that drawdowns occur rapidly in the beginning, whereas capital distributions take place later. Conversely, for Fund 2, the assumption is that drawdowns occur quicker and that distributions take place sooner. This pattern is mainly achieved for Fund 1 through a lower value of a and a higher value of θ.

later. Conversely, for the second fund, the assumption is that drawdowns occur quicker and that distributions take place sooner. This pattern is mainly achieved for Fund 1 through a lower value of a and a higher value of θ. The effect can be inferred by comparing the different lines in panels A and B of Figure 28.1. For this reason, each fund also has different expected amortization periods, which are given as 8.6 years and 6.1 years, respectively.

The basic patterns of the model graphs of the capital drawdowns, distributions, and net fund cash flows in Figure 28.1 conform to reasonable expectations of private equity fund behavior. In particular, the cash flow streams that the model can generate will naturally exhibit a lag between the capital drawdowns and distributions, thus reproducing the typical development cycle of a fund and leading to the private equity characteristic J-shaped curve for the cumulated net cash flows that can be observed in panel C of Figure 28.1. Furthermore, the model is flexible enough to generate many different patterns of capital drawdowns and distributions. By altering the main model parameters, the timing and magnitude of the fund cash flows can be controlled in the model.

Empirical Calibration and Model Fit

This section addresses the calibration of the model to empirical data and analysis of its goodness of fit. A short description of the empirical data employed for the purpose of this study leads off the section.

DATA SOURCE AND CALIBRATION RESULTS

Thomson venture economics (TVE) is the source of the dataset of European private equity funds used in this study. TVE uses the term *private equity* to describe the universe of all venture, buyout, and mezzanine investing. Kaplan and Schoar (2005) provide a detailed overview on the TVE dataset and a discussion of its

(a)

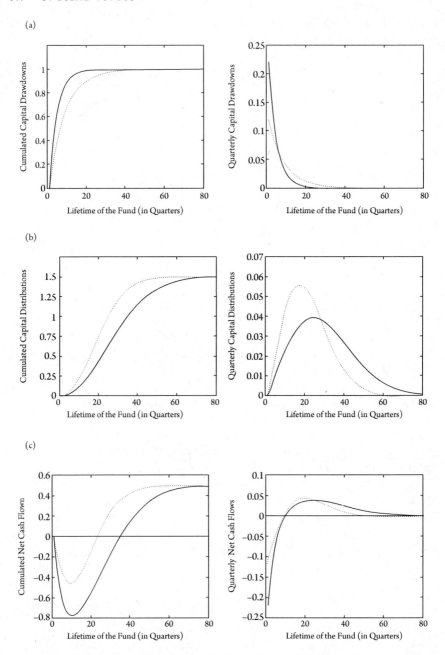

Figure 28.1 Model Expectations for Two Different Funds. This figure shows the model expectations of two different hypothetical funds. The solid lines represent Fund 1 and the dotted lines represent Fund 2. (a) Expected cumulated capital drawdowns (*left*) and quarterly capital drawdowns (*right*); (b) expected cumulated capital distributions (*left*) and quarterly capital distributions (*right*); (c) expected cumulated net fund cash flows (*left*) and quarterly net fund cash flows (*right*).

Table 28.2 **Calibrated Model Parameters**

	Drawdowns			Distributions		
	κ	θ	σ_δ	m	α	σ_p
Total	7.33	0.47	4.70	1.85	0.028	1.42
Venture Capital	13.31	0.46	5.26	2.08	0.023	1.47
Buyout Funds	4.98	0.48	4.56	1.61	0.038	1.20

This table shows the estimated (annualized) model parameters for the capital drawdowns and distributions of the 203 sample funds. The committed capital of all sample funds is standardized to 1.

potential biases. Data on a total of 777 funds with various information related to the exact timing and size of cash flows, residual NAVs, fund size, vintage year, fund type, fund stage, and liquidation status for the funds were collected over the period from January 1, 1980, through June 30, 2003. All cash flows and reported NAVs are net of management fees and carried interest. The empirical analysis draws on the subset of mature private equity funds. The sample of mature private equity funds contains all funds that are either fully liquidated or nearly liquidated. Nearly liquidated funds are selected by using the criterion developed in Diller and Kaserer (2009). Thus, the sample consists of a total of 203 funds and comprises 102 venture capital funds and 101 buyout funds. For the sample of mature funds, model parameters are calibrated by the concept of conditional least squares (CLS). Buchner, Kaserer, and Wagner (2010, 2011) provide a formal description of the estimation methodology. Table 28.2 shows the estimated model parameters for the sample of all (Total), venture capital (VC), as well as buyout (BO) funds.

The results reveal that the venture capital and buyout segment have slightly different cash flow profiles. When comparing venture funds to buyout funds, venture and buyout funds, on average, appear to draw down capital at a relatively similar pace as the coefficients θ are almost equal among the two subsamples. However, venture funds draw down capital with somewhat higher uncertainty than their buyout counterparts, which is indicated by a higher value of the volatility σ_δ for venture funds. For capital distributions, the long-run multiple m for all sample funds is estimated to equal 1.85. That is, on average, funds distribute 1.85 times their committed capital over the total lifetime. The subsample of venture funds returns substantially more capital to the investors than the corresponding sample of buyout funds. A comparison of the a-coefficients further reveals that the average buyout fund tends to pay back its capital much faster than the average venture fund, an observation that is also statistically significant.

MODEL FIT

Assessing the goodness of fit of a new model is essential. A simple way to gauge the specification of the model is to examine whether the model's implied cash

(a)

(b)

(c)

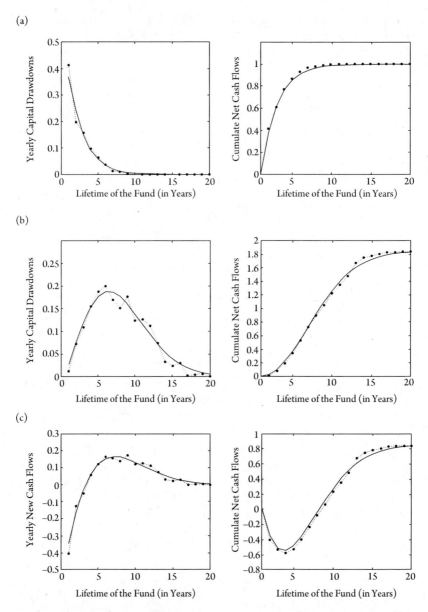

Figure 28.2 Model Expectations and Observations. This figure shows model expectations compared to historical observations for all N = 203 sample funds. The solid lines represent model expectations, and the dotted lines represent historical observations. (a) yearly capital drawdowns (*left*) and cumulated capital drawdowns (*right*) (b) yearly capital distributions (*left*) and cumulated capital distributions (*right*) (c) yearly net fund cash flows (*left*) and cumulated net fund cash flows (*right*).

flow patterns are consistent with those implicit in the time series of the defined data sample. Are the model expectations of the cash flows similar in magnitude and timing to the values derived from their data samples counterparts?

Figure 28.2 compares the historical average capital drawdowns, capital distributions, and net fund cash flows of the overall sample of mature funds to the corresponding expectations that can be constructed from the model by using the calibrated model parameters. Overall, the results from Figure 28.2 indicate an excellent fit of the model with the historical data. As measured by the coefficient of determination, R^2, the model can explain 97.73 percent of the variation in average yearly net fund cash flows. Further, the mean absolute error (MAE) of the approximation is only 1.56 percent annually (as measured in percent of committed capital). Splitting the overall sample for venture and buyout funds, the results show that the quality of the approximation is slightly lower for venture funds (R^2 with 94.69 percent) than for buyout funds (R^2 with 97.02 percent).

Risk and Portfolio Management Applications of the Model

Having shown the excellent fit of the model, the analysis now turns to its possible applications in the risk and portfolio management context. The model can be used in a variety of applications. This section describes the main application areas and provides realistic examples.

CASH FLOW PROJECTIONS

First, the model can be applied for liquidity planning purposes. In this area, an investor can employ the model to estimate expected future cash needed to meet capital commitments, as well as projected distributions that generate liquidity in the future. Table 28.3 illustrates the model's ability to forecast the capital distributions of private equity funds. All calculations are based on quarterly simulated fund cash flows and are standardized, i.e., all calculations show cumulated capital distribution for $1 committed to the corresponding fund.

For example, the results reveal that an investor who commits $1 to a buyout fund can expect to receive $0.61 during the first five years of his investment. In contrast, an investor who commits $1 to a venture capital fund can only expect to receive $0.52 during the same time frame. This result corresponds to the common notion that venture funds invest in young and technology-oriented startups, whereas buyout funds invest in mature and established companies. Growth companies typically do not generate enough cash flows during their first years in business, and more time is usually required until these investments can be successfully exited (e.g., by an initial public offer [IPO] or a trade sale to a strategic investor). In addition to expected cumulated capital distributions, Table 28.3 also gives confidence intervals for the cumulated capital distributions. For example, Table 28.3 reveals that $1 committed to a venture capital fund will lead to cumulated capital

Table 28.3 **Projection of the Cumulated Capital Distributions**

	Cumulated Capital Distributions (per $1 Committed)		
Year	Private Equity Overall	Venture Capital	Buyout Funds
1	0.0260 [0.0031; 0.1156]	0.0237 [0.0024; 0.1057]	0.0303 [0.0063; 0.1371]
2	0.1019 [0.0193; 0.3267]	0.0934 [0.0161; 0.2993]	0.1178 [0.0344; 0.3636]
3	0.2215 [0.0525; 0.6046]	0,2042 [0.0446; 0.5619]	0.2530 [0.0863; 0.6525]
4	0.3752 [0.1034; 0.9250]	0.3490 [0.0888; 0.8743]	0.4220 [0.1591; 0.9724]
5	0.5517 [0.1674; 1.2704]	0.5189 [0.1467; 1.2147]	0.6088 [0.2477; 1.2920]
6	0.7389 [0.2432; 1.6019]	0.7040 [0.2169; 1.5589]	0.7978 [0.3432; 1.5822]
7	0.9255 [0.3239; 1.9042]	0.8947 [0.2964; 1.8862]	0.9758 [0.4398; 1.8365]
8	1.1022 [0.4065; 2.1763]	1.0820 [0.3787; 2.1927]	1.1336 [0.5291; 2.0404]
9	1.2617 [0.4876; 2.4113]	1.2586 [0.4634; 2.4738]	1.2657 [0.6095; 2.2017]
10	1.3999 [0.5631; 2.5978]	1.4192 [0.5430; 2.7089]	1.3708 [0.6760; 2.3195]
12	1.6073 [0.6850; 2.8560]	1.6803 [0.6889; 3.0634]	1.5080 [0.7703; 2.4552]
14	1.7320 [0.7662; 2.9916]	1.8588 [0.7960; 3.2759]	1.5740 [0.8189; 2.5130]
16	1.7975 [0.8110; 3.0519]	1.9674 [0.8686; 3.3927]	1.6007 [0.8380; 2.5339]
18	1.8277 [0.8333; 3.0786]	2.0268 [0.9105; 3.4488]	1.6098 [0.8443; 2.5406]
20	1.8399 [0.8430; 3.0874]	2.0559 [0.9326; 3.4747]	1.6125 [0.8463; 2.5418]

This table illustrates the expected cumulated capital distributions of a private equity, venture capital, and buyout fund. All calculations are based on quarterly simulated fund cash flows and are shown standardized, i.e., all calculations show expected capital distribution for $1 committed to the corresponding fund. Values in brackets give the 80 percent confidence interval of the cumulated capital distributions.

distributions that range between $0.54 and $2.71 after the first 10 years of the fund's lifetime with a probability of 80 percent. Thus, the simulation methodology also enables an investor to attach probabilities to future outcomes.

In the context of cash flow projections, the model can also incorporate and respond to the actual capital drawdown and distribution experience of a fund. The model can be updated each period with actual data, allowing it to adjust for current events. Additionally, the model can easily be adapted to changing investment environments. This flexibility is particularly helpful for an investor analyzing the impact of varying market conditions on future cash flows. For example, an investor can reflect the forecast of an unfavorable exit environment for private equity funds in the model by lowering the long-run multiple m or the parameter α that governs the speed at which capital distributions occur over time.

RISK MANAGEMENT

More generally, the model can also be used for risk management purposes. The model constituents allow, as a by-product, ex-ante calculations of the expected risk and return profile of a private equity fund. These calculations can be carried out with the performance measures commonly employed in the private equity industry such as the IRR. Table 28.4 provides an illustrative example for this methodology. The calculations are based on the estimated model parameters shown in Table 28.2 and are carried out by a Monte Carlo simulation approach with 100,000 iterations.

Table 28.4 provides various risk and return measures. The results show that the ex-ante expected IRR of a private equity fund amounts to 11.05 percent per year with a volatility of 8.16 percent and that the probability of incurring a loss—Prob(IRR$ < 0 percent)—is equal to 1.42 percent. Differences in the risk and return profiles can be found by comparing the venture capital and buyout segment. As expected, venture capital funds have a higher expected return than buyout funds. This higher expected return is also accompanied by a slightly higher level of risk, as indicated by the higher standard deviation of the IRR. However, venture funds interestingly show a lower probability of incurring a loss: Prob(IRR$ < 0 percent).

Table 28.5 illustrates how the model can be used to carry out a sensitivity analysis for the risk and return profile of private equity funds. The base case scenario in column 1 is constructed by using the estimated model parameters for the overall sample mature funds. Columns 2 and 3 show how uncertainly in the long-run multiple m can affect the risk and return profile of this fund. The best-case (worst-case) scenario in column 2 (3) is constructed by using the base case parameter m plus (minus) three times the standard error of the estimated value. The results illustrate that a lower value of m than expected can substantially decrease expected returns and increase the risk of the fund. For example, the probability of incurring a loss now amounts to 12.98 percent under the worst-case scenario with an expected IRR of only 6.14 percent.

Table 28.4 **Risk and Return Profile of Venture Capital Versus Buyout Funds**

	Internal Rate of Return (in % per year)		
	Private Equity Overall (%)	*Venture Capital (%)*	*Buyout Funds (%)*
Mean	11.05	11.27	9.77
Median	9.43	9.80	8.67
25th Quantile	5.91	6.68	5.33
75th Quantile	14.25	14.29	12.70
Standard Error	8.16	7.60	7.29
Probability of a Loss Prob(IRR < 0)	1.42	0.50	2.10
Average IRR given a Loss	−1.13	−0.84	−1.24

This table illustrates the risk and return profile of private equity, venture capital, and buyout funds. All calculations are based on the model parameters shown in Table 28.2 and are carried out by using quarterly simulated fund cash flows.

Table 28.5 **Sensitivity Analysis for the Risk and Return Profile of a Private Equity Fund**

	Internal Rate of Return (in % per year)		
	Base Case Scenario (%)	*Worst Case Scenario (%)*	*Best Case Scenario (%)*
Mean	11.05	6.14	15.79
Median	9.43	4.64	13.72
25th Quantile	5.91	1.61	9.66
75th Quantile	14.25	8.30	18.78
Standard error	8.16	33.70	13.18
Probability of a Loss Prob(IRR < 0)	1.42	12.98	0.14
Average IRR given a Loss	−1.13	−1.72	−1.39

This table provides a sensitivity analysis for the risk and return profile of a private equity fund. Column 1 shows the base case, which is constructed by using the estimated model parameters for the total sample of mature funds. Columns 2 and 3 show how the results change by altering the long-run multiple m. The Worst Case Scenario (Best Case Scenario) corresponds to the case when m is equal to the base case parameter plus (minus) three times the standard error of the estimator. All calculations are based on quarterly simulated fund cash flows.

A similar analysis can also be carried to study the impact of the other model parameters on the risk and return profile of a private equity fund. This short risk management application underlines that an investor can employ the model presented to measure the sensitivity of the IRR (or any other ex–post performance measure) to changes in the drawdown or distribution schedule in a clear and concise way. Additionally, the model is dynamic in the sense that risk and return figures can be evaluated for the entire lifetime of a fund. To illustrate this point, Figure 28.3 shows how the expected IRR of a private equity fund will develop over time. The development of the expected IRR in Figure 28.3 corresponds to the typical pattern of private equity fund returns. In the early years, private equity funds will show low or negative returns. The bulk of the capital distributions usually come in the later years as the companies mature. This increases the IRR over time. The effect of this timing on the fund's interim returns is known as the J-curve of fund IRRs.

PORTFOLIO MANAGEMENT

Besides its risk management applications, the model can also be used in the portfolio management context. It can, for example, be applied to analyze the optimal mix of venture capital and buyout funds in an investor's portfolio. The major obstacle is that standard portfolio theory requires estimating correlations between asset classes, which is impossible to carry out given that returns can only be measured by the IRR. This problem can be resolved with the model by following a

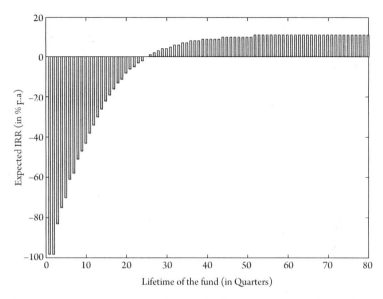

Figure 28.3 Expected IRR over the Lifetime of a Private Equity Fund. This figure shows the development of the expected IRR over the lifetime of a fund. Calculations are based on the parameters of all N = 203 sample mature funds.

novel approach. This approach allows considering several nontraded alternative investments in the portfolio optimization process, such as venture capital and buyout funds. The general idea behind this approach is to use the model to first generate cash flow patterns that have exactly the same correlation as the observable fund cash flows. This produces cash flow–based IRRs that can be calculated for venture capital and buyout funds. In a second step, a Monte Carlo simulation is then applied to produce pairs of comparable cash flow–based IRRs of the venture capital and buyout funds. Using these results, correlations between the venture capital and buyout funds can be calculated and used for portfolio optimization purposes in the standard way.

Table 28.6 shows an application of this idea. To carry out this analysis first requires estimating the correlation between the cash flow of the venture capital and buyout fund. This gives a correlation between the capital distribution of 0.41 and a correlation between the capital drawdowns of 0.60. Thus, capital drawdowns and capital distribution of the venture capital and buyout segment are highly positively correlated. Despite this relatively high correlation on the cash flow level, the correlation of the IRRs is very low at 0.10. This is due to the fact that venture capital and buyout funds have somewhat different cash flow timings.

Table 28.6 shows the resulting minimum variance and maximum Sharpe ratio portfolios for an investor who combines venture capital and buyout funds in his portfolio. The results show that the minimum variance portfolio consists of 48 percent invested into venture capital and 52 percent invested into the buyout segment. The maximum Sharpe ratio portfolio is somewhat riskier with 56 percent invested in the venture capital segment.

Table 28.6 **Optimal Portfolios of Venture Capital and Buyout Funds**

Optimal Portfolios	Portfolio Proportions		Performance		
	Venture Capital (%)	Buyout Funds (%)	Return IRR (per year) (%)	Risk IRR (per year) (%)	Sharpe Ratio
Minimum Variance Portfolio	48	52	10.49	5.52	0.99
Maximum Sharpe Ratio Portfolio	56	44	10.61	5.58	1.01

This table shows the optimal portfolios for an investor who combines venture capital and buyout funds in a portfolio. The Maximum Sharpe Ratio Portfolio is constructed by assuming a constant riskless rate of return of 5 percent per year.

Summary and Conclusions

This chapter presents a novel model for the cash flow dynamics of private equity funds that shows its possible applications in the risk and portfolio management area. The model differentiates itself from previous research in the area of venture and private equity fund modeling in the sense that the model of a fund's capital drawdowns and distributions is based on observable economic variables only. A theoretical model analysis shows that this model is flexible and reproduces the different drawdown and distribution patterns that can be observed for real-world private equity funds. Furthermore, the economic relevance of the model is underlined by the empirical analysis performed. Overall, the model fits the historical fund data nicely. At the same time, the main model parameters are easy to understand, and the model is straightforward to implement. Several applications of the model to questions in the risk and portfolio management area that cannot be handled using standard techniques have been shown in this chapter. Although the chapter focuses on private equity funds, the model can be extended to other alternative asset fund types. By altering the input parameters, the model can be used to represent funds that invest in other alternative assets such as real estate and infrastructure.

Discussion Questions

1. Discuss the main obstacles in applying standard risk and portfolio management techniques in the private equity area.
2. Explain the stale and managed pricing phenomenon discussed in the private equity literature. What is the influence of these effects on private equity returns that are based on the fund's disclosed net asset values (NAVs)?
3. Briefly summarize the two components of the model for the cash flow dynamics of private equity funds presented in this chapter.
4. Explain how the model for the cash flow dynamics of private equity funds can be applied in the risk and portfolio management context.

References

Buchner, Axel, Christoph Kaserer, and Niklas Wagner. 2010. "Modeling the Cash Flow Dynamics of Private Equity Funds: Theory and Empirical Evidence." *Journal of Alternative Investments* 13:1, 41–54.

Buchner, Axel, Christoph Kaserer, and Niklas Wagner. 2011. "Private Equity Funds: Valuation, Systematic Risk and Illiquidity." Working Paper, Technical University of Munich.

Burgel, Oliver. 2000. "UK Venture Capital and Private Equity as an Asset Class for Institutional Investors." Research Report, British Venture Capital Association.

Cochrane, John H. 2005. "The Risk and Return of Venture Capital." *Journal of Financial Economics* 75:1, 3–52.

Diller, Christian, and Christoph Kaserer. 2009. "What Drives Cash Flow Based European Private Equity Returns?—Fund Inflows, Skilled GPS and/or Risk?" *European Financial Management* 15:3, 643–675.

Kaplan, Steven, and Antoinette Schoar. 2005. "Private Equity Performance: Returns, Persistence and Capital Flows." *Journal of Finance* 60:4, 1791–1823.

Ljungqvist, Alexander, and Matthew Richardson. 2003a. "The Cash Flow, Return and Risk Characteristics of Private Equity." Working Paper, National Bureau of Economic Research.

Ljungqvist, Alexander, and Matthew Richardson. 2003b. "The Investment Behavior of Private Equity Fund Managers." Working Paper, New York University.

Malherbe, Etienne 2004. "Modeling Private Equity Funds and Private Equity Collateralized Fund Obligations." *International Journal of Theoretical and Applied Finance* 7:3, 193–230.

Phalippou, Ludovic, and Oliver Gottschalg. 2009. "The Performance of Private Equity Funds." *Review of Financial Studies* 22:4, 1747–1776.

Rhodes-Kropf, Matthew, and Charles Jones. 2004. "The Price of Diversifiable Risk in Venture Capital and Private Equity." Working Paper, Harvard University.

Takahashi, Dean, and Seth Alexander. 2002. "Illiquid Alternative Asset Fund Modeling." *Journal of Portfolio Management* 28:2, 90–100.

29

Venture Capital

PASCAL GANTENBEIN
Henri B. Meier Professor of Financial Management, Head of
Department of Financial Management, University of Basel,

RETO FORRER
Research Associate, Department of Financial
Management, University of Basel

NILS HEROLD
Research Associate, Department of Financial
Management, University of Basel

Introduction

Many entrepreneurial businesses require substantial capital in the startup phase. The period needed until a firm can bring its products to the market and generate revenues can take years, particularly in high-tech sectors involving scientific research and a complex development process. Often the founders do not have sufficient resources to finance the startup phase on their own. Thus, they need external financing, which, by nature, is mostly equity capital. Because startup firms face uncertain future prospects and lack a strong track record, they are unlikely to receive debt financing. Thus, venture capitalists are investors specialized in funding young businesses. They help close the gap when conventional financing is inapplicable.

From an economic point of view, the availability of venture capital is crucial for a nation's ability to sustain growth opportunities, transform intellectual property into economic wealth, and strengthen its competitiveness. Hellmann and Puri (2002) document that venture capital financing contributes to a professionalization of startup companies in various areas. Moreover, Hellmann and Puri (2000) explore the role of venture capital financing for developing Silicon Valley startup companies and find it to be linked to a faster time to market. Kortum and Lerner (2000), who evaluate the impact of an increase of venture capital activity within a specific industry on patent rates in the United States, find evidence for a strongly positive impact of venture capital on innovation.

From an investment perspective, the inherent uncertainty associated with early-stage investments is characteristic of venture capital. Investments in startup firms entail a distinct area of conflict among the involved players because of the potential for large returns while possessing high probabilities of losses. While many venture projects eventually do not succeed, a small number of projects achieve annual returns in excess of 100 percent. This vast spectrum of possible outcomes forces venture capitalists to undertake careful due diligence and selection. Thereby, venture capitalists not only face downside risk but also a risk of missing good investment opportunities. For example, Bessemer Venture Partners, one of the oldest venture capital firms in the United States, apparently is well aware of this fact. The firm lists its top 50 exits on the company webpage as well as an "anti-portfolio" with amusing descriptions of missed investment opportunities that include companies such as Apple, eBay, FedEx, Google, and PayPal.

Based on that perspective, the present chapter focuses on the investment profile of the organized venture capital market as a subset of the private equity market. Venture capitalists typically look for businesses that provide new and innovative products. Hence, they mostly operate in high-tech sectors such as information technology, software, energy, or life sciences. Because of this, the industry sector is a common criterion in classifying venture capital investments.

The remainder of the chapter is organized as follows: The next section provides an introduction to the structure of the organized venture capital market, including the players and their relationships in the investment process. The second section focuses on the financial economics of venture capital, providing the basics of evaluating returns and risks of venture capital as well as a comprehensive discussion of performance-related literature. The third section takes a closer look at special features that are relevant to investors with an exposure to the venture capital market. The final section summarizes and concludes the chapter.

The Organized Venture Capital Market

The venture capital market can be characterized by its financing stages, relationship between fund managers and investors, and investment process. The subsequent part explains the properties of the market and the fundamentals of venture capital funding.

VENTURE CAPITAL FINANCING STAGES

Venture capital, as a subset of private equity, refers to equity stakes in young and innovative private companies with high potential for future growth. It serves as a way of funding specific stages in a firm's life. Particularly, venture capital comprises seed, startup, and expansion financing.

Seed financing supplies financial resources for an initial concept before a business reaches the startup phase. In this initial process, the business plan is developed and verified. The founders often first use their own resources and get support from friends and families to finance the initial research and development (R&D). However, external private investors are also important for young companies. These business angels or angel investors often bridge the equity gap that founders face at this stage and bring in their knowledge and network. By contrast, venture capital funds typically come into play after the launch of a business. They pool money from investors and finance promising young companies with high growth potentials to achieve a return for their investors. Thus, before investing, venture capital funds often perform a more profound due diligence than business angels.

In the subsequent phases, funds are used to set up the company, to facilitate initial production and marketing activities, and to initiate commercial manufacturing and sales. In contrast to investments in the earlier stages, later-stage venture financing is provided for the expansion of an operating business and, therefore, comprises risk capital for relatively mature companies. In this phase, firms may break even. Beyond that, bridge or mezzanine financing helps for the transition from a private to a publicly listed company or for its sale. Sahlmann (1990) provides a detailed description of the various stages of venture capital investing.

VENTURE CAPITAL PARTNERSHIPS AND THE INVESTMENT PROCESS

Besides funding the businesses, venture capitalists get actively involved in portfolio companies by providing advice, motivation, knowledge, and access to networks. Where possible, venture capital funds are mostly structured as limited partnerships. In such a structure, the general partners manage the fund while the limited partners (e.g., institutional investors such as endowments, corporate and public pension funds, or insurance companies) provide most of the capital.

The *limited partnership agreement* specifies the compensation of the general partners. They typically earn an annual management fee defined as a percentage of the committed capital (approximately 1 to 3 percent). They also receive a share (typically around 20 percent) of realized capital gains ("carried interest") in order to align their interest with that of the investors. The limited partnership usually is a closed-end vehicle with a fixed lifetime of about 10 years and an option to extend the fund's life by a few more years. If investors commit to provide equity capital to the fund, this committed capital can then be drawn down over a certain period of time for investments in a specific field.

Unlike investment corporations, limited partnerships are typically not taxed at the level of the structure. Instead, income is only taxed at the individual level, i.e., at that of the general partner and the limited partners. Therefore, from a tax perspective, this type of structure for pooling funds of different investors is more favorable than an investment corporation.

Often the financing rounds are syndicated. This means that multiple venture capital funds simultaneously invest in a target company to share the risks and to reduce the uncertainty about the firm value. A typical structure in biotech ventures, for instance, involves a minimum of five venture capital funds with each having a maximum share of 20 percent of the target firm's capital. Deli and Santhanakrishnan (2010) contend that venture capital funds provide substantial human capital in addition to financial capital. Apparently, this value-added support is limited in a single fund structure, whereas, by syndication, more expertise is brought together. If several independent observers agree that the company is an attractive investment, this will lead to a superior selection of investments.

In exchange for investing their money in the portfolio company, the securities venture capitalist usually receives convertible preferred stocks. These instruments force the firm to make fixed payments to the holders of these securities before any other dividends are paid out to common stockholders. The convertibility feature gives the venture capitalist the incentive to maximize the firm's market value, as it offers the right to convert the financial claims into common shares.

The limited partners do not have the right to withdraw their capital during the fund's life. Therefore, their investment is illiquid during the term of the fund. Furthermore, they are not permitted to play an active management role but exercise their control rights through covenants (e.g., restrictions on how much fund capital can be invested in one company, on the types of securities, or on debt at the fund level). Value creation achieved in the company leads to capital gains for venture capitalists, but it can only be realized once the investment in the company is exited through an acquisition by a third party or an initial public offering (IPO). At the end of the fund's life, cash and securities are distributed to the investors.

Financial Economics of Venture Capital

This section discusses the basic properties of venture capital as an asset class. It provides an overview of the relevant empirical findings on the risk and return characteristics as well as on risk premia, excess returns, and sensitivities in particular. A key question here is to which extent the asset class of venture capital can be integrated into the framework of modern portfolio theory.

RISK AND RETURN OF VENTURE CAPITAL INVESTMENTS

The venture capital industry has seen considerable growth in terms of committed capital as well as investment volumes over the past three decades. Throughout this time, the media repeatedly reported stories of projects with annual returns in excess of 100 percent adding to a widely held belief of venture capital as a highly performing asset class. The dotcom bubble in the 1990s clearly made its contribution to this when investments, capital commitments, and exit volumes reached all time highs. However, from an investment perspective, one needs to evaluate the asset class based on the initial cohort of investments or funds—and then the picture turns blurry. There still is no comprehensive historical performance account for venture capital and the evaluation of returns and performance is anything but trivial. Evidence from empirical research may seem to be contradictory at times because of the different methodologies and approaches. Hence, starting with a discussion of some basic properties is worthwhile.

First, estimators of risk and return of venture capital may refer to either *entrepreneurial firms* or to *venture capital funds*. Both approaches are common and reasonable. In terms of measurement, however, the evaluation of firm-level risk and return always rests on valuations that are only observed occasionally, e.g., in case of financing rounds, acquisitions, or IPOs. Clearly, these events tend to occur more often in case of well-performing companies. However, valuation events occur more frequently at times of high valuations. As a result, the timing of valuation events is endogenous causing a sample selection bias. Korteweg and Sorensen (2010) call this a dynamic sample selection problem and find that controlling for it lowers the estimated returns and increases the riskiness of entrepreneurial investments.

Conversely, fund returns are based on investment portfolios and therefore are evaluated on the cash flows distributed to the limited partners. Since investors generally invest across partnership structures, they are exposed to the venture capital flows on a fund level. This fact is particularly important in regard to the link between fund performance and fund properties, a field that has attracted considerable attention in the past decade. However, the returns are typically earned over a period of 10 years (sometimes longer), which makes deriving comparable measures of returns for shorter time periods difficult. Over the investment period, funds report their projects based on net asset values (NAVs). These values are based on accounting profits, which ultimately may or may not turn into positive cash flows to limited partners. Thus, performance evaluations based on samples including funds without a liquidation history may be distorted. Returns therefore are typically upward biased, although the opposite can be observed. Consequently, funds raised in recent years should not be included in empirical studies. Because of this situation, analyzing the performance of young funds is practically impossible. Furthermore, a problem similar to the sample selection bias arises because unsuccessful funds typically do not raise follow-on funds but will rather disappear.

Fund returns for venture capital are usually measured as the annualized internal rate of return (IRR) and as a profitability index (PI). The IRR represents an average return per period, whereas the PI is a measure for excess return over the entire investment period. The latter is defined as the present value of the cash flows received by the investors divided by the present value of the paid-in capital. Typically, some index return serves as the discount rate (e.g., the S&P 500 and NASDAQ indices for US funds). A PI above one is interpreted as an outperformance and can be translated into a cumulative alpha. However, doing so implicitly assumes a beta of one. Thus, unless investment risks for the asset class and the index are truly equivalent, this procedure is prone to substantially distort the comparability of excess returns. The IRR measure also has its shortcomings. Besides the well-known problems of this measure, comparing IRRs across venture capital funds can be particularly problematic due to the fact that it disregards both fund size and investment period.

Because general partners earn fees that are often substantial, investors should be interested in the net-of-fee performance. Phalippou and Gottschalg (2009) find that private equity fund returns outperform the S&P 500 index gross of fees but underperform the index net of fees. Furthermore, venture capital returns are heavily skewed, i.e., a relatively small number of investments and funds perform extremely well, while median returns are considerably lower than average returns. Therefore, one has to be careful in interpreting historical returns and expected returns. Moreover, compared to other asset classes, venture capital investments are highly illiquid because of a lack of an active secondary market and the investment of capital for a long period of time.

Finally, data availability is an important limiting factor for the evaluation of venture capital performance. Only a few commercial databases provide relevant information while academic researchers, in general, do not have access to detailed fund-level performance data. Therefore, academic studies evaluating performance drivers occasionally use the fraction of venture investments successfully exited by IPO or merger and acquisition (M&A) transactions as a proxy for performance.

THE RETURN OF VENTURE CAPITAL FUNDS

Kaplan and Schoar (2005) find a median IRR (cash-flow-based) net of fees for venture capital funds of 13 percent, a mean return of 17 percent and returns at the 25th and 75th percentiles of 3 percent and 23 percent, respectively. All of these return calculations are size weighted based on committed capital. Additionally, using the total return of the S&P 500 as a benchmark, the authors calculate a PI referred to as public market equivalent (PME) and find a median of 0.92, an average of 1.21 and 0.55 for the 25th percentile and 1.4 for the 75th percentile, respectively. Thus, the data show a wide dispersion in fund returns and skewness to the right with more than half of the funds underperforming the S&P 500 (net of fees). Assuming a beta of one, Kaplan and Schoar translate the average PME of 1.21 into a cumulative alpha (risk-adjusted excess return) of 21 percent over the life of the fund. They further analyze returns by vintage year (1980 to 1997) and find significant time-series variations. Funds raised in much of the 1980s performed relatively poorly with single digit IRRs and PMEs below one. Starting from 1988, funds had higher IRRs and PMEs above one. However, the authors do not explicitly address issues in regard to the timing of cash flows or the risk profiles of funds and portfolio companies.

Using the same dataset as Kaplan and Schoar (2005), Jones and Rhodes-Kropf (2003) find that venture capital funds exhibit a mean IRR of 19.3 percent (again, size weighted based on committed capital) and annual alphas, based on a Fama and French three-factor model (Fama and French, 1992, 1993) close to 5 percent (1.17 percent on a quarterly basis). But because of the high standard errors, these returns are not significantly different from zero. The authors report cross-sectional standard deviations of annualized IRRs of nearly 58 percent, which indicates a wide return distribution across funds.

Ljungqvist and Richardson (2003) refer to the records of one of the largest institutional investors in private equity in the United States. Although the sample is relatively small and only related to a single investor, the data allow the authors to account for the timing of cash flows. They find a median IRR for venture funds of 17.5 percent and a mean IRR of 14.1 percent. Returns at the 25th and 75th percentiles are at the levels of 6.6 percent and 26.9 percent, respectively. The authors further calculate an average PI of 1.15. Hence, the distribution of returns shows a left skewness. By focusing on the timing of cash flows, Ljungqvist and Richardson report that venture capital funds, on average, take nine years (since the first closing) to break even. Additionally, they find that at the end of its fourth year, the average private equity fund (both venture and nonventure) has cumulatively drawn down about 73 percent of its committed capital. Nevertheless, the speed of drawing down committed capital shows substantial variations across funds.

Phalippou and Gottschalg (2009) address several biases in the performance evaluation attributable to sample selection, accounting values (reported NAVs), fees, and the weighting of funds by the present values of invested capital. They find that, after these adjustments, the effective returns are substantially lower. Using the S&P 500 and NASDAQ indices as benchmarks, the authors report an average PI of 0.88 and 0.87, respectively, for venture funds. Accordingly, limited partners, on average, have lost about 12 percent of their invested capital. Furthermore, to capture the underlying venture capital fund risks, Phalippou and Gottschalg estimate the industry and size-matched costs of capital to calculate PIs. Using their measure, the average PI further decreases to 0.77, which corresponds to an alpha of about −6 percent per year. These results document a low average performance for investors and raise the question of why limited partners are willing to invest in venture capital at all.

Phalippou and Gottschalg (2009) discuss three possible explanations for investing in venture capital. First, inexperienced funds with a low initial performance may improve due to learning. By investing from the very beginning, limited partners occasionally obtain the right to participate in follow-on funds the general partners may establish. Second, investors may overrate the asset class by giving too much weight to a few successful investments. Third, due to side benefits, as explained by Ljungqvist and Richardson (2003), investors may not have the sole objective to maximize asset returns.

In a study about the returns of entrepreneurial investments in nonpublicly traded equity in the United States, Moskowitz and Vissing-Jorgensen (2002) conclude that investors obviously are willing to allocate substantial amounts of capital to private equity despite the fact that the asset class, on average, exhibits returns no higher than those of public equity markets, yet with a worse risk-return profile. They discuss issues including high-risk tolerance, additional pecuniary and nonpecuniary benefits, the preference for skewness, and overoptimism, i.e., misperceptions about the probability of failure, as possible explanations for their findings.

Finally, Phalippou and Zollo (2005) use an approach that Agarwal and Naik (2004) previously applied to hedge funds and link the observed performance to optionlike risk factors, namely out-of-the-money European call and put options on the S&P 500 composite index. They maintain that venture funds, similar to hedge funds, are likely to have optionlike payoffs. Phalippou and Zollo also find a significant correlation with call options and conclude that private equity funds (they do not report separate results for venture funds) bear significant right-tail risk, i.e., their performance is high at times of high stock market returns and it is low at times of low stock market returns but with a lower sensitivity in the latter situation.

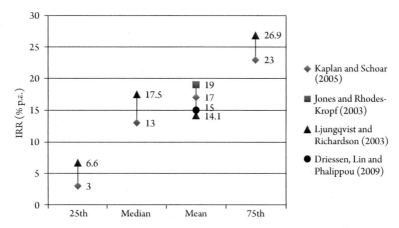

Figure 29.1 IRR of Venture Capital Funds. This figure presents estimates for venture capital fund returns. It indicates ranges for IRRs based on the median and mean IRRs as well as the IRRs at the 25th and 75th percentiles. Methodologies and datasets are not identical across the studies. Kaplan and Schoar (2005) use a dataset of Thomson Venture Economics and calculate IRRs net of fees and size-weighted returns based on committed capital. The same data source is used in Jones and Rhodes-Kropf (2003) as well as in Driessen et al. (2009). The results of Jones and Rhodes-Kropf are statistically not significant. Ljungqvist and Richardson (2003) use the records of a large institutional investor in the United States.

Figures 29.1 and 29.2 summarize the literature findings previously discussed. Figure 29.1 shows venture capital fund returns (IRRs) estimated in the various academic studies and figure 29.2 presents the values for fund performances (PIs).

RISK AND RISK-ADJUSTED EXCESS RETURNS

Benchmarking fund returns relative to indices such as the S&P 500 or the NASDAQ index in order to measure simple excess returns assumes a beta equal to one. However, this approach is only an approximation and leads to distorted performance measurement unless the indices have the same systematic risk. Since Jensen (1968), a common practice in financial economics is to estimate alpha and beta by time-series regressions. However, as Driessen, Lin, and Phalippou (2009) point out, in the context of a nontraded asset class, a time-series estimation of alpha and beta is generally not possible. The common approach in such situations is to estimate parameters from a cross-section analysis, assuming that all invest-ments entail identical risk.

Cochrane (2005) evaluates the alphas and betas of venture-backed companies based on gross returns calculated from valuations as observed at financing or exit events (IPO and acquisition). Because valuation events are more likely to occur for well-performing companies, overcoming the selection bias is crucial in this setup. Addressing selection bias requires defining a parametric probability

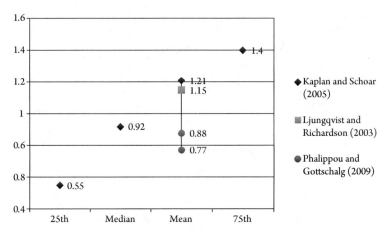

Figure 29.2 Profitability Indices for Venture Capital Funds. This figure presents estimates for venture capital fund performance. It indicates ranges for PIs based on the median and mean PIs as well as the PIs at the 25th and 75th percentiles. Methodologies and datasets are not identical across studies. Kaplan and Schoar (2005) use a dataset of Thomson Venture Economics and take the S&P 500 as benchmark. Phalippou and Gottschalg (2009) use the same data source. They benchmark to the S&P 500 (0.88) but also calculate an industry and size-matched cost of capital to evaluate performance (0.77). Ljungqvist and Richardson (2003) use the records of a large institutional investor in the United States and the S&P 500 as a benchmark.

structure of the underlying return process (return distribution) and the selection of projects. Cochrane assumes log-normal distributions of returns and models the probability of getting a new round of financing as an increasing function of value. In a CAPM framework, he finds a mean log return of 15 percent, a mean arithmetic return of 59 percent, an arithmetic alpha of 32 percent, and a beta of 1.9. Although being corrected for sample selection bias, the alpha seems very high. Cochrane documents that the timing of valuation events is endogenous, i.e., controlling for the selection problem substantially decreases expected returns. He further finds that investments in later financing rounds are less risky and less rewarding, i.e., mean returns, alphas, and betas all decline for later rounds. While the first finding is technical but highly relevant for empirical studies, the latter is an important refinement to consider when assessing the risk and return characteristics of venture capital.

Korteweg and Sorensen (2010) use a more recent version of Cochrane's dataset and also analyze gross returns from valuations at financing rounds and exit events. They, too, work in a parametric framework and estimate the alpha and beta of venture-backed companies both with a one-factor market model and a Fama and French three-factor model. In each case, they find a large exposure to market risk with an average beta of 2.8 in the first and 2.3 in the latter case. Arithmetic monthly alphas are between 3.3 and 3.5 percent. Specifically, the authors find the largest alphas for seed investments, while later-stage investments exhibit the lowest alphas but substantially higher exposure to market risk. Furthermore, in the period from 1987 to 1993, arithmetic monthly alphas were low with a mean of 1.5 to 1.6 percent but then increased in the dotcom boom from 1994 to 2000 to a mean of 5.8 percent. By contrast, the period from 2001 to 2005 has seen negative alphas with a mean of −2.6 to −2.7 percent.

Hall and Woodward (2007) estimate alphas and betas of venture investments in a capital asset pricing model (CAPM) framework using a nonparametric approach, i.e., they do not rely on a probability structure for the underlying returns. They explicitly distinguish between returns earned by general partners, limited partners, and founders and find that limited partners earned an annual risk-adjusted excess return of about 7 percent with a substantial time variation of the alpha. Hall and Woodward further estimate a beta of about 1.3.

Driessen et al. (2009) estimate the risk and abnormal returns of private equity funds. They observe that many venture funds paid large cash distributions when stock markets boomed in the late 1990s. But when market returns were lower in the period from 2001 to 2003, cash distributions also declined. They estimate a beta of 3.2 for venture funds (after fees), which confirms the strong dependence of fund returns on market performance. Furthermore, the authors report a mean IRR of 15 percent for venture funds but find an annual alpha of −15 percent. In other words, venture funds entail large negative risk-adjusted returns for the limited partners. They argue that investors possibly underestimate the risk associated with venture funds.

Figure 29.3 gives an overview of the academic findings on risk and risk-adjusted excess returns discussed in this section. It shows the estimated alphas and betas of venture capital investments.

The results by Driessen et al. (2009) challenge the perception of venture capital as a well-performing asset class. In general, the estimation of parameters from historical data is difficult and academic research apparently shows mixed results in regard to the return and risk of venture capital. In particular, performance measures are highly sensitive to risk corrections and the calculation of returns.

Further, venture capital entails further constraints to portfolio management such as limited investment decisions, illiquidity, and the questionable use of average returns to form expectations. In regard to the first point, limited partners' decision options typically comprise the selection of a fund but neither of the single entrepreneurial companies nor of the share taken in these companies. This limits the investors' control over the risk-and-return profile of their venture capital exposure. Moreover, investments in venture capital funds are highly illiquid and investors are typically unable to continuously rebalance their portfolios in order to meet their needs.

Finally, one can expect that the fund managers' skills are relevant to the fund's outcome. If skills have a major impact on performance, one could observe performance persistence, i.e., general partners with well-performing funds will likely have well-performing funds in future periods. This situation, however, clearly sets a constraint on the relevance of industry statistics because return expectations then become conditional on the skills of the general partners. Limited partners, therefore, aim to invest together with highly skilled general partners. Establishing

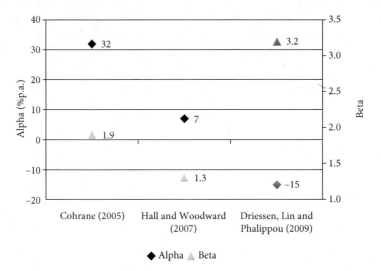

Figure 29.3 Risk and Risk-Adjusted Excess Return. This figure presents estimates for alpha and beta of venture capital–backed companies as well as venture capital funds. Methodologies and datasets are not identical across studies. Cochrane (2005) evaluates gross returns calculated from valuations as observed at financing or exit events assuming log-normal distributions of returns. Hall and Woodward (2007) likewise estimate alpha and beta of venture investments but use a nonparametric approach. They explicitly calculate returns earned by limited partners. In contrast, Driessen et al. (2009) estimate alpha and beta for venture capital funds.

a good relation with well-performing fund managers can be seen as a real option because the limited partner obtains the right to invest in future funds. This link between partnership characteristics and fund performance will be discussed in more detail in the next section of the chapter.

Special Features of Venture Investing

In venture capital investing, various issues typically not known from traditional asset classes have been identified to be crucial for investors. In particular, these issues concern the roles of the general partners and the limited partners as well as the question of performance persistence. This section also addresses the nature of cyclicality in the venture capital industry.

PARTNERSHIP CHARACTERISTICS

General partners actively search, select, and monitor portfolio companies. Therefore, funds are sometimes called "smart money." One would expect that smartness pays off, i.e., that general partners with superior screening and monitoring skills can add more value to their investment and outperform the industry.

If so, fund performance also depends on luck. Instead, the relationship between partnership characteristics and fund returns is of particular interest. Unfortunately, the extent to which partnership characteristics can be observed for the purpose of econometric analyses is quite limited in practice.

Kaplan and Schoar (2005) use committed capital, i.e., fund size and the sequence number of the fund as explanatory variables for fund performance, and report that larger and later funds exhibit a significantly higher performance. The two variables size and sequence do not directly characterize the general partners, but they can be interpreted as measurable proxy variables for skill and experience. However, in a specification including fixed effects for the general partners, Kaplan and Schoar find that larger funds have higher returns in the cross-sectional view, but, if a given general partner raises a larger fund, its performance declines. The authors observe a similar but statistically insignificant effect for the sequence number. Furthermore, the relationship between fund size and performance seems to be concave, i.e., larger funds display a higher performance, but if funds become very large, performance declines. Phalippou and Gottschalg (2009) likewise conclude that performance increases with fund size and that the relationship between performance and fund sequence is positive although not always significant. By contrast, they do not find evidence of a concave relationship between performance and fund size.

Nahata (2008) evaluates the impact of reputation, measured as the cumulative market value of IPOs backed by specific venture capitalists combined with the respective venture capitalists' shares of aggregate investments in the industry. According to his observation, reputable venture capitalists are more likely to bring their investments to successful exits (IPOs). Hochberg, Ljungqvist, and Lu (2007) focus on the performance impact of networks arising from the syndication of venture capital investments. They contend that networks affect the ability to select promising companies and to add value to these companies. Their evidence indicates that better networked venture capital firms show a significantly better fund performance.

IPOs and M&As as shares of fund outcomes may also serve as proxies for performance, although actual fund performance measures are preferred. Smith, Pedace, and Sathe (2010) evaluate the correlation between IPO and M&A percentages and fund performance (measured as IRR and total value to paid-in capital) and find a significant relationship but a rather low correlation. The authors also examine the performance impact of funds' abandonment practices. According to their evidence, funds that are more likely to abandon unprofitable investments at an early stage perform significantly better than funds that continue to support their investments.

Sorensen (2007) provides evidence that entrepreneurial firms with more experienced investors are more likely to go public. However, using a two-sided matching model (see Roth and Sotomayor, 1990), Sorensen is able to attribute the finding to two distinct effects, namely the value added by the venture capitalist and the sorting. *Sorting* means that more experienced venture capitalists invest in better companies, i.e., part of the performance directly results from the companies and not from the added value provided by the venture capitalist. Sorensen points out that, in contrast to rather experience driven added value from managing and monitoring skills or from networking effects and reputation, sorting arises from the matching between the venture capitalists and the companies. Hence, experienced venture capitalists have better deal flows because entrepreneurial companies prefer them, while less experienced venture capitalists are left with less attractive deals. Sorensen also finds that both effects are statistically significant. However, not taking account of the sorting results in a substantial overstatement of the performance affects the venture capitalists' skills.

PERFORMANCE PERSISTENCE

Academic research on the impact of fund characteristics on performance is closely related to research on performance persistence. In general, an important question is whether fund managers' performance is persistent over time. In the case of venture capital, the question is whether the performance of two successive funds is positively correlated. In this situation, well (poorly) performing funds would indicate that these general partners' follow-on funds are likely to perform well (poorly) too. Therefore, the evaluation of performance drivers now includes lagged performance as an independent variable, thus specifying an autoregressive relationship.

Kaplan and Schoar (2005) find evidence that persistence is large and statistically significant, i.e., that a fund's performance tends to be positively related to the performance of previously raised funds by the same venture capital firm. In a similar regression, Phalippou and Gottschalg (2009) also report strong and robust performance persistence. They further find that other characteristics such as size and sequence are not significant in explaining performance anymore once including past performance in the model.

Because of the evidence that partnership characteristics affect performance, the finding that performance is persistent may not be surprising. However, from the viewpoint of financial economics, performance persistence is puzzling and contradicts previous findings for mutual funds. Unlike for venture capital funds, past performance of mutual fund managers seems to have no or only little predictive power for future performance. Berk and Green (2004), however, contend that the lack of performance persistence with mutual funds does not imply that superior performance is due to luck, i.e., that differing abilities are of no relevance. They show theoretically that because investors at each point in time adjust their capital allocations to funds based on past returns, expected excess returns eventually equal zero, thus agreeing with empirical evidence. Thereby, Berk and Green assume that fund managers' skills are heterogeneous and affect performance, returns to scale for fund managers are decreasing and fees are constant, and investors rationally learn about fund managers' skills.

With respect to the venture capital industry, the question arises of whether limited partners adequately allocate their funds based on past performance and why general partners do not expand fund size or raise fees to capture excess returns and hereby eliminate performance persistence. Hochberg, Ljungqvist, and Vissing-Jorgensen (2010) question why general partners do not aggressively raise performance fees for follow-on funds. They argue that only current investors in a fund, but not potential outside investors, know whether past performance was due to skill or luck. If current investors refuse to reinvest, outside investors interpret this as a sign of low skills and the general partner will be unsuccessful in raising a new fund. This situation gives bargaining power to investors, prevents the fund managers from raising fees, and causes performance persistence. The authors find data supporting this hypothesis. In particular, they observe that performance is not predictable from returns publicly known at the time the follow-on fund is raised but is predictable from "soft-information" in the possession of current investors. Glode and Green (2008) maintain that the investors' learning about the fund managers' investment strategies gives them bargaining power. To prevent information spillovers that would increase competition and reduce returns, general partners need to retain investors and therefore share excess performance with the current limited partners.

Phalippou (2010) points out that Kaplan and Schoar (2005) measure performance of consecutive funds at the end of the funds' lifetime (or at the end of the sample period). Following this setup, he also finds strong correlation in fund performance. However, Phalippou reports that the time spread between the vintage years of consecutive funds is often small (the median is three years). He argues that only in case of a long time spread do investors effectively know the final past performance at the inception date of the follow-on fund. He finds performance persistence to be large and robust for small spreads (one to two years). But when the spread expands (three to five years), the coefficient decreases substantially and finally performance persistence disappears for large spreads (six years and more).

Phalippou (2010) also evaluates performance persistence using measures of past performance available at the time investors have to commit their capital (ex-ante performance) instead of final past performance. He finds a positive but weak and statistically insignificant relationship. Thus, at the time investors make their investment decisions past performance has no predictive power. If funds are separated into high and low performing funds, low performing funds show a significantly positive relationship, but no such relationship exists for high performing funds. Phalippou contends that this is consistent with an economy as described by Berk and Green (2004) but with investors differing in their degree of sophistication. Only investors of well performing funds use all available information at the inception date and adjust their capital allocations so that these funds exhibit less performance persistence.

HETEROGENEITY AMONG LIMITED PARTNERS

The discussion of performance persistence reveals the active role limited partners play in the venture capital industry. Since they control fund flows, one expects them to back the most promising partnerships. Theory suggests that limited partners base their investment decisions on past performance, thus giving rise to a strong flow-performance relationship, which, in turn, eliminates performance predictability (Berk and Green, 2004). The previous section indicates that limited partners actively control fund flows but obviously at varying degrees. Moreover, evidence suggests that fund flows are driven by limited partners' skills and are directly related to their success in the venture capital industry.

Lerner, Schoar, and Wongsunwai (2007) analyze differences in returns and investment strategies across classes of institutional investors that historically accounted for a large share of the committed capital in the venture capital market. They document average IRRs of venture funds for the entire industry (68.9 percent for early stage funds and 27.4 percent for later stage funds) as well as for eight classes of limited partners. In regard to the latter point, they find significant differences between endowments (95.4 percent, 35.9 percent), public pension funds (57.9 percent, 26.3 percent), corporate pension funds (36.9 percent, 21.3 percent), advisers (69.7 percent, 27.3 percent), insurance companies (47.2 percent, 26.0 percent), banks and finance companies (17.3 percent, 10.8 percent), and other investors (15.8 percent, 29.3 percent). These differences are robust when controlling for vintage year as well as for the type of fund. Yet, the authors point out that the return calculation is not size weighted, and thus the results rather than showing the final performance primarily indicate the ability to identify good funds.

To analyze the impact of investor sophistication, Lerner et al. (2007) further evaluate reinvestment decisions. They find that follow-on funds backed by endowments and public pension funds exhibit higher performance than follow-on funds in which these investors refuse to invest. This pattern does not apply to other institutional investors and indicates that endowments and public pensions are better at evaluating available information. The authors also analyze investments in young partnerships for which all limited partners can only refer to public information. Again, funds backed by endowments and public pension funds perform better. Along with the well-documented impact of general partners on fund performance, the limited partners' skills, i.e., their ability to evaluate information and to learn about the quality of partnerships, also affects performance in the venture capital industry.

VENTURE CAPITAL CYCLES

Besides the active role of industry participants and their impact on performance, the venture capital industry is strongly dependent on the overall economy and exhibits a cyclical pattern. Phalippou and Zollo (2005) estimate the impact of macroeconomic conditions at the inception, during the lifetime, and at the exit of investments on private equity fund performance. Their results indicate a strong procyclical performance. Notably, investing at economic troughs lowers performance, while high GDP growth and high public market performance during the lifetime of investments go along with higher fund performance. In the field of venture capital, cyclicality particularly refers to a high volatility of investment and exit volumes over time.

Figure 29.4 illustrates this strong cyclicality in the venture capital industry. It shows investment volumes, exits through venture-backed IPOs, and fund returns over time.

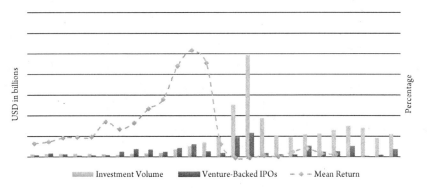

Figure 29.4 Volatility of Investment Amounts and Returns in the US Venture Capital Market. This figure shows investment volume, IPO offer amounts, and mean fund returns by vintage year for the US venture capital market from 1985 to 2010. Investment volumes and offer amounts for venture-backed IPOs are in billions of USD and taken from the NVCA Yearbook 2011. Returns are taken from the NVCA Venture Capital Returns Q4 2010 Benchmark Report provided by Cambridge Associates LLC. Returns are IRRs since inception and calculated net to the limited partners as well as dollar-weighted based on cash flows and ending NAVs. Cambridge Associates comments that meaningful returns for vintage years since 2007 cannot be produced because the funds are too young. Returns are plotted on the secondary axis (the dashed line is for the purpose of illustration only).

These movements in capital flows and performance can be explained by different factors. Gompers and Lerner (1998) examine the determinants of aggregated fundraising in the venture capital industry, in particular, the impact of industry performance (based on the market value of venture backed IPOs) on committed capital. In general, volatility in performance mirrors volatility in fundraising. However, once control variables are included, only the previous year's real GDP growth has a positive and significant impact on committed capital.

Kaplan and Schoar (2005) evaluate entries and exits of partnerships in the industry as well as fundraising activities of existing partnerships. They find a positive relationship between the number of partnerships started each year and both market returns (one-year lagged S&P 500 returns) and industry performance (one-year lagged aggregate venture capital industry returns). The same relationship applies to the amount of capital raised by first-time funds, i.e., new partnerships. They also report a negative correlation between the ability to start a follow-on fund and market returns at the time of the previous fund placement. Apparently, partnerships starting a fund at times of high market returns are less likely to establish a follow-on fund. Finally, Kaplan and Schoar examine the impact of fund entries on industry performance and find that periods with an increased number of entries exhibit negative performance. Yet, the impact is larger for new partnerships, while the number of entries barely affects established partnerships.

One has to be aware that changes in certain industry statistics may arise from either supply or demand for venture capital (Poterba, 1989). Thus, the evaluation of causal relations to explain variations in these industry statistics must isolate supply and demand effects in order to avoid biases. However, this is often problematic because prices cannot be observed and supply and demand effects are hard to disentangle (Hellmann, 1998). In any case, volatility is a given fact, which also raises the question of whether fundamentals or an overreaction to perceived investment opportunities cause booms. Sahlman and Stevenson (1985) analyze the venture capital and stock market boom and bust of the Winchester disk drive industry in the early 1980s. They conclude that market players acting myopically as well as by massive overfunding and unsustainable levels of valuation characterized the situation. The authors contend that market participants should have noticed that valuation levels were too high. Thus, volatility in the venture capital industry may reflect periods of overfunding caused by investors irrationally reacting to positive investment signals, followed by periods of low and likely insufficient funding.

Gompers and Lerner (2000) examine the relationship between inflows to the venture capital industry (committed capital) and the valuations of investments. They ask whether this relationship arises from changes in fundamentals that increase valuations and thus lead to higher inflows or whether it is due to inflows driving up the valuations. The authors find a strong positive relationship between inflows and valuations, i.e., valuations are higher at times with more committed capital. To check if larger inflows and higher valuations are due to better investment prospects, Gompers and Lerner examine the success rate of venture-backed firms over time. They conclude that the results are supportive of inflows driving up prices, which are likely caused by competition for a limited number of attractive investments. By contrast, Phalippou and Gottschalg (2009) find no evidence for such an effect.

Gompers, Kovner, Lerner, and Scharfstein (2008) build on the evidence that general partners' skills affect performance and examine how groups of venture capitalists with different levels of experience react to public market signals. The authors maintain that, if more experienced partnerships increase investments following a market boom, then changes in fundamentals cause volatility. In contrast, if less experienced investors are the most likely to increase investments, this relationship supports the overreaction view. They find that firms with the most industry experience are most responsive and conclude that volatilities in fundamentals are determinants of volatilities in investment activities.

The research findings discussed in this chapter provide no uniform conclusion about the causes of venture capital market volatility. But one can clearly see that better investment prospects come along with the potential of market overheating. However, disentangling the initial responses to perceived investment opportunities from potential feedback effects causing overreaction is challenging. Therefore, this aspect is an interesting field for future research.

Summary and Conclusions

Venture capitalists close the financing gap for innovative startup businesses when conventional financing is inapplicable. From an investment perspective, venture capital entails a distinct area of conflict between high risks of losses and potentially high returns. These high returns typically are well publicized and make venture capital an attractive asset class in the media.

However, the picture gets blurry if return expectations and risks are evaluated for the purpose of portfolio management. Furthermore, empirical analyses are methodologically demanding and typically lack comprehensive historical data. Academic studies reveal mixed results and indicate a wide dispersion of fund IRRs as well as considerable right skewness with means ranging from about 14 to 19 percent. Evaluating the performance of venture capital as an asset class is even more tedious because adequate risk corrections are crucial. Estimates of mean PIs for funds range from 0.77 to 1.21, largely depending on what risk correction is applied. Although popular, benchmarking to the returns of the S&P 500 and NASDAQ indices is problematic.

Alphas show similar methodological sensitivities. Cochrane (2005) finds an alpha of 32 percent for venture investments while Hall and Woodward (2007) arrive at 7 percent. Driessen et al. (2009) report an alpha for venture funds of −15 percent. Because evidence shows that the majority of venture funds may underperform public stock markets, the question is why investors are willing to engage in venture capital. Phalippou and Gottschalg (2009) discuss three possible explanations: learning effects and the right to participate in future funds, overestimation of the asset class, and objectives other than maximizing asset returns.

Besides risk and return that lie at the heart of modern portfolio theory, academic research has found further determinants of investment outcomes important to investors with an exposure to venture capital. In particular, these are the roles of the general partners and the limited partners. The general partners actively search, select, and monitor portfolio companies. Evidence suggests that their experience and skills in performing these tasks affect fund performance. Yet, Sorensen (2007) argues that two distinct effects associated with experience affect performance: the value added by the venture capitalist and the sorting. Besides the heterogeneity among partnerships, the limited partners also affect performance by controlling the fund flows through selecting the funds and their ability to evaluate information and learn about the quality of partnerships.

The impact of fund characteristics on performance is closely related to performance persistence, which means whether performance is correlated for two successive funds of the same venture capital firm. Although several studies find evidence for strong persistence, this is puzzling from the viewpoint of financial economics. The question arises of whether limited partners adequately allocate funds based on past performance to eliminate performance persistence. Phalippou (2010) finds that persistence seems to be tied to low-performing funds, i.e., investors of well-performing funds adequately adjust capital allocations so that these funds exhibit less performance persistence.

Finally, the venture capital industry is strongly dependent on macroeconomic conditions and is extremely cyclical. The industry has repeatedly seen periods of dramatic growth in performance and investment volumes followed by slumps. Kaplan and Schoar (2005) find a positive relationship between the number of partnerships started each year and lagged industry performance. Yet, periods with increased numbers of entries have a negative performance impact on the industry. Besides the interdependence of performance and fundraising activities, academic research is particularly concerned to find out whether fundamentals or an overreaction to perceived investment opportunities cause market booms. So far, this question has no clear answer. The possibility exists that better investment prospects come along with the potential of market overheating.

Discussion Questions

1. Discuss the advantages and disadvantages of investing in venture capital.
2. Many cases of venture capital investing involve general partners and limited partners. Why are such partnerships necessary, and what are their roles in the investment process?
3. In the field of venture investing, why is performance persistence investing considered to be puzzling?
4. During the financial crisis of 2008 and 2009, venture capital investments experienced a sharp downturn. Discuss the reasons for this economic cyclicality.

References

Agarwal, Vikas, and Narayan Y. Naik. 2004. "Risks and Portfolio Decisions Involving Hedge Funds." *Review of Financial Studies* 17:1, 63–98.

Berk, Jonathan B., and Richard C. Green. 2004. "Mutual Fund Flows and Performance in Rational Markets." *Journal of Political Economy*, 112:6, 1269–1295.

Cochrane, John H. 2005. "The Risk and Return of Venture Capital." *Journal of Financial Economics* 75:1, 3–52.

Deli, Daniel N., and Mukunthan Santhanakrishnan. 2010. "Syndication of Venture Capital Financing." *Financial Review*, 45:3, 557–578.

Driessen, Joost, Tse-Chun Lin, and Ludovic Phalippou. 2009. "A New Method to Estimate Risk and Return of Non-Traded Assets from Cash Flows: The Case of Private Equity Funds." Working Paper, National Bureau of Economic Research (NBER).

Fama, Eugene F., and Kenneth R. French. 1992. "The Cross-Section of Expected Stock Returns." *Journal of Finance* 47:2, 427–465.

Fama, Eugene F., and Kenneth R. French. 1993. "Common Risk Factors in the Returns on Stocks and Bonds." *Journal of Financial Economics* 33:1, 3–56.

Glode, Vincent, and Richard Green. 2008. "Information Spill-Overs and Performance Persistence in Private Equity Partnerships." Working Paper, Carnegie Mellon University.

Gompers, Paul A., Anna Kovner, Josh Lerner, and David Scharfstein. 2008. "Venture Capital Investment Cycles: The Impact of Public Markets." *Journal of Financial Economics* 87:1, 1–23.

Gompers, Paul A., and Josh Lerner. 1998. "What Drives Venture Capital Fundraising?" *Brookings Papers on Economic Activity: Microeconomics* 1998, 149–204.

Gompers, Paul A., and Josh Lerner. 2000. "Money Chasing Deals? The Impact of Fund Inflows on Private Equity Valuations." *Journal of Financial Economics* 55:2, 281–325.

Hall, Robert E., and Susanne E. Woodward. 2007. "The Quantitative Economics of Venture Capital." Working Paper, Department of Economics, Stanford University.

Hellmann, Thomas. 1998. "Comment on Paul A. Gompers and Josh Lerner, 'What Drives Venture Capital Fundraising?'" *Brookings Papers on Economic Activity: Microeconomics* 1998, 197–203.

Hellmann, Thomas, and Manju Puri. 2000. "The Interaction Between Product Market and Financing Strategy: The Role of Venture Capital." *Review of Financial Studies* 13:4, 959–984.

Hellmann, Thomas, and Manju Puri. 2002. "Venture Capital and the Professionalization of Start-Up Firms: Empirical Evidence." *Journal of Finance* 57:1, 169–197.

Hochberg, Yael V., Alexander Ljungqvist, and Yang Lu. 2007. "Whom You Know Matters: Venture Capital Networks and Investment Performance." *Journal of Finance* 62:1, 251–301.

Hochberg, Yael V., Alexander Ljungqvist, and Annette Vissing-Jorgensen. 2010. "Informational Hold-up and Performance Persistence in Venture Capital." Working Paper, Northwestern University.

Jensen, Michael C. 1968. "The Performance of Mutual Funds in the Period 1945–1964." *Journal of Finance* 23:2, 389–416.

Jones, Charles M., and Matthew Rhodes-Kropf. 2003. "The Price of Diversifiable Risk in Venture Capital and Private Equity." Working Paper, Graduate School of Business, Columbia University.

Kaplan, Steven N., and Antoinette Schoar. 2005. "Private Equity Performance: Returns, Persistence, and Capital Flows." *Journal of Finance* 60:4, 1791–1823.

Korteweg, Arthur, and Morten Sorensen. 2010. "Risk and Return Characteristics of Venture Capital-Backed Entrepreneurial Companies." *Review of Financial Studies* 23:10, 3738–3772.

Kortum, Samuel, and Josh Lerner. 2000. "Assessing the Contribution of Venture Capital to Innovation." *RAND Journal of Economics* 31:4, 674–692.

Lerner, Josh, Antoinette Schoar, and Wan Wongsunwai. 2007. "Smart Institutions, Foolish Choices: The Limited Partner Performance Puzzle." *Journal of Finance* 62:2, 731–764.

Ljungqvist, Alexander, and Matthew Richardson. 2003. "The Cash Flow, Return and Risk Characteristics of Private Equity." Working Paper, New York University.

Moskowitz, Tobias J., and Annette Vissing–Jorgensen. 2002. "The Returns to Entrepreneurial Investment: A Private Equity Premium Puzzle?" *American Economic Review* 92:4, 745–778.

Nahata, Rajarishi. 2008. "Venture Capital Reputation and Investment Performance." *Journal of Financial Economics* 90:2, 127–151.

Phalippou, Ludovic. 2010. "Venture Capital Funds: Flow-Performance Relationship and Performance Persistence." *Journal of Banking and Finance* 34:3, 568–577.

Phalippou, Ludovic, and Oliver Gottschalg. 2009. "The Performance of Private Equity Funds." *Review of Financial Studies* 22:4, 1747–1776.

Phalippou, Ludovic, and Maurizio Zollo. 2005. "What Drives Private Equity Fund Performance?" Working Paper, University of Amsterdam.

Poterba, James. 1989. "Venture Capital and Capital Gains Taxation." Working Paper, National Bureau of Economic Research (NBER).

Roth, Alvin, and Marilda Sotomayor. 1990. "Two-Sided Matching: A Study in Game-Theoretic Modeling and Analysis." Cambridge, UK: Cambridge University Press.

Sahlman, William A. 1990. "The Structure and Governance of Venture-Capital Organizations." *Journal of Financial Economics* 27:2, 473–521.

Sahlman, Wiliam A., and Howard H. Stevenson. 1985. "Capital Market Myopia." *Journal of Business Venturing* 1:1, 7–30.

Smith, Richard, Roberto Pedace, and Vijay Sathe. 2010. "Venture Capital Fund Performance: The Effects of Exits, Abandonment, Persistence, Experience, and Reputation." Working Paper, University of California.

Sorensen, Morten. 2007. "How Smart Is Smart Money? A Two-Sided Matching Model of Venture Capital." *Journal of Finance* 62:6, 2725–2762.

30

Socially Responsible Investing

HUNTER M. HOLZHAUER
Assistant Professor of Finance, Penn
State Erie, The Behrend College

Introduction

> Each time a man stands up for an ideal, or acts to improve the lot of others, or strikes out against injustice, he sends forth a tiny ripple of hope, and crossing each other from a million different centers of energy and daring, those ripples build a current that can sweep down the mightiest walls of oppression and resistance. Robert Kennedy speaking in 1966 to South African students. (Domini, 2001, p. 157)

Socially responsible investing (SRI) uses environmental, social, and corporate governance (ESG) criteria to generate long-term, competitive financial returns and positive societal impact (SIF, 2010). According to Sparkes (2002), SRI is unique in that it combines both financial goals and social responsibility. This distinction separates SRI from both traditional investing, which focuses solely on the financial return, and charitable giving, which does not require any financial return. Somewhere between these two opposing views of monetary beliefs lies the vast and rapidly changing field of SRI.

As SRI grows, it encompasses a broader range of ideals and investment strategies. The term most often used interchangeably with SRI is *corporate social responsibility* (CSR). Sparkes (2002) states that "CSR and SRI are two sides of the same coin." However, there is one important difference. SRI is a bottom-up approach focusing primarily on the power of the investor, while CSR is a top-down approach that requires more action from corporations than investors. Still, SRI and CSR share many of the same ideals for societal change.

Like CSR, SRI also encompasses several types of investing labels such as ethical investing, sustainable investing, responsible investing, impact investing, mission-related investing, values-based investing, and green investing (Sparkes, 2002; SIF, 2010). Although the specific ESG or CSR criteria for each investing style may differ widely, SIF points out that the screening policies for the leading SRI firms closely resemble one another in practice. This grouping of SRI firms is important because it allows for meaningful comparisons and measureable observations.

One obvious observation is that SRI in the United States is growing at a far faster pace than the broader universe of conventional investments. SRI assets have grown nearly 400 percent in the last 15 years from $639 billion in 1995 to $3.07 trillion in 2010. In comparison, total assets under management have only grown 260 percent over the same time period from $7 trillion to $25.2 trillion. Furthermore, no real growth has occurred in total assets under management since the beginning of the 2007 recession. However, SRI assets have increased by more than 13 percent during this same turbulent financial period. Thus, the SRI market share of total assets under management has grown by more than 3 percent over the past 15 years to 12.2 percent, or nearly one out of every eight dollars under professional management (SIF, 2010).

THE ORIGINS OF SRI

The origins of SRI can be traced back to the foundations of religious traditions. Both Judaism and Christianity provide ancient teachings on how to use money ethically, especially regarding usury. In 1139, the Catholic Church even imposed a universal prohibition on usury. In 1758, the Quakers were among the first to prohibit participation in the slave trade. Also during the 18th century, John Wesley, a founder of the Methodist Church, outlined several of the basic tenets of social investing in his sermon "The Use of Money," stating "Having, first, gained all you can, and, secondly saved all you can, then 'give all you can'" (Wesley, 1771, p. 1). More specifically, Wesley's sermon discourages profiting in several unethical business practices such as gaming, unfair lending, the distillation of liquor, and even environmentally toxic businesses such as tanning, which pollutes local water sources.

Hence, the greatest attribute of SRI is that it allows money to be used as a form of voting for individual belief systems. In this way, almost all religious faiths, such as Judaism, Christianity, Islam, Hinduism, and Buddhism, discourage using certain products. Four of the most common faith-based investment filters are alcohol, tobacco, gaming, and weaponry, which happen to be four of the most common SRI filters today (Domini, 2001).

THE MODERN AGE OF SRI

In 1928, Philip Carret founded the Pioneer Fund, then known as Fidelity Mutual Trust. The Pioneer Fund is credited as the first mutual fund to employ ethical screens for companies that made or sold alcohol and tobacco (Cory, 2004). However, the modern SRI movement really took off in the middle of the 20th century with trade unions targeting SRI goals with pension fund assets. In 1946, the United Mine Workers of America (UMWA) formed the multiemployer UMWA Welfare and Retirement Fund. The UMWA Fund invested heavily in medical facilities, financing numerous clinics and building eight hospitals in the Appalachia area. Other union examples include the International Brotherhood of Electrical Workers (IBEW) and International Ladies' Garment Workers' Union (ILGWU), both of which funded union-sponsored housing projects.

The 1960s and 1970s gave rise to a new age of accountability with the growth of both the civil rights movement and the antiwar movement. From these movements, the real influence of SRI began to emerge. In 1972, an infamous photograph was taken during the Vietnam War of a naked young girl running toward the photographer while screaming in agony from napalm burning her back. This picture burned into the minds of many Americans and sparked public outrage against Dow Chemical, the manufacturer of napalm, and other companies profiting from war. The strong opposition to the Vietnam War in the early 1970s spurred the creation of the Pax World Fund, an antiwar SRI fund, which avoided investments in weapon contractors. However, SRI soon began to play an even more influential role in history.

APARTHEID AND DIVESTMENT: A SOUTH AFRICAN CASE STUDY

The most influential example of SRI came during the 1980s with the boycott of South Africa's apartheid regime. The Afrikaner National Party instituted apartheid, a system where the majority is ruled by the minority through state-sanctioned racial segregation, after its electoral victory in 1948. The government initially enforced apartheid to ease the wealthier white population's concern about the growing black population. However, apartheid condemned most blacks in South Africa to lives of poverty with very limited opportunity for upward mobility.

International opposition against apartheid began to escalate after the state-sponsored 1960 Sharpeville massacre, which resulted in the deaths of 69 black protesters at the hands of the South African police. In 1963, the United Nations imposed a voluntary arms embargo against South Africa, which became mandatory in 1976 following the Soweto Uprising. The Soweto Uprising began with the protest of an estimated 20,000 students from Sowetan schools over the language requirements for their educational instruction. The uprising ended with approximately 700 students killed and 4,000 injured. After this uprising, Reverend Leon Sullivan, a board member for General Motors, created a code of conduct for practicing business in South Africa that became known as the Sullivan Principles. Reports tracking corporations' adherence to the Sullivan Principles provided evidence that US companies were not attempting to lessen workplace discrimination in South Africa. Following these reports, public outrage intensified and many colleges, universities, faith-based groups, and pension funds began divesting from companies doing business in South Africa. Investments in South Africa continued to slowly decrease until in 1986 when American and European governments agreed to ban new investment in South Africa. The subsequent decline in capital flow pressured a group of businesses, representing 75 percent of South African employers, to draft a charter calling for the end of apartheid. Apartheid did not officially end until 1994 when the apartheid regime was voted out of power. However, SRI efforts received much of the credit.

Several studies challenge the impact of divestment during the antiapartheid movement. Rudd (1979) argues that the exclusion of companies operating in South Africa did not significantly alter portfolio risk. Grossman and Sharpe

(1986) compare the returns of a value-weighted portfolio free of South African investments and an unrestricted New York Stock Exchange (NYSE) portfolio. They find that the screened portfolio outperformed the benchmark by 1.87 percent per year from 1960 to 1983.

Mukherjee, Hingorani, and Lee (1995) look at the costs of voluntary divesture before and mandatory divesture after the 1986 ban on new investment in South Africa. Not surprisingly, they find time-varying results. Specifically, they observe negative abnormal returns for the preban group and no significant abnormal returns for the postban group. The authors conclude that the preban group voluntarily bore the cost for their social actions. However, when a social act becomes mandatory, all firms share the cost, and investors are indifferent to such actions as long as the cost is relatively small.

Teoh, Welch, and Wazzan (1999) estimate the market effects of potentially important political events between March 1985 and October 1986. Specifically, they examine the impact on the largest South African firm, two stock-based indexes, and the dollar/rand exchange rate. They find no support for the common perception that the antiapartheid legislative and shareholder boycotts affected the financial markets adversely, despite the intense publicity of the boycotts and the large number of divesting companies.

Two reasons exist for this finding. First, the financial markets were not that heavily invested in South Africa in the first place suggesting little demand. Second, most stocks have perfectly elastic demand, which implies that a small change in quantity demanded will not significantly alter stock prices. Thus, with little original demand for South African investment, SRI is unlikely to change demand enough to impact the markets because it only represents a fraction of total assets (Entine, 2005). Apparently, South African divestment has a stronger perceived impact than an empirical one.

TOOLS OF THE TRADE

Domini (2001) describes three tools that individuals can use to participate in SRI efforts. The first SRI tool is shareholder activism, which allows shareholders to engage directly with management. The shareholder's right to participate in the governing of the company through proxy voting is of most concern. In this manner, shareholder activism can bring about specific business changes in a timely fashion. It can also help companies avoid future problems by allowing shareholders' concerns to be addressed as soon as possible.

The second SRI tool is community development, which directly connects the investor with those in need. The three main forms of community development are community development loan funds, community development banks, and community development credit unions. These community development programs not only help revive distressed communities but can also make a reasonable alternative to cash reserves.

The third SRI tool is screening, which is the primary method for selecting SRI assets. Screening strategies are simple filtering processes. However, when used effectively, screening can also create long-term change in corporate culture as evidenced by the South African boycotts. Of the three tools, screening is the only tool with considerable empirical research.

Review of Empirical Findings: SRI Performance

Research in SRI has changed drastically over the last 40 years. Moskowitz (1972, 1975) is among the first to publish in the SRI literature. In his comparison of the financial performance of screened and unscreened portfolios, he is among the first to suggest that screened portfolios might outperform unscreened portfolios. Moskowitz is also well known for his role in establishing the *Working Mother's* annual list of "The 100 Best Companies for Working Mothers" and *Fortune's* annual list of "The 100 Best Companies to Work for in America" (Moskowitz, 1996; Levering and Moskowitz, 1998), which are often used in SRI research. For example, Waddock and Graves (1997) find a strong link between *Fortune's* corporation reputation rankings and SRI rating data.

Furthermore, several studies analyze the performance effects of companies being announced in one of these prestigious lists and other lists such as *Fortune's* annual list of the "Most Admired Companies" and *Business Ethics'* annual list of "The 100 Best Corporate Citizens." These studies find evidence that CSR may lead to both satisfied employees and satisfied shareholders (Preece and Filbeck, 1999; Filbeck, 2001; Kurtz and Luck, 2002; Filbeck and Preece, 2003; Filbeck, Gorman, and Zhao, 2009; Edmans, 2011).

In honor of Moskowitz and his many contributions to SRI, the Center for Responsible Business awards the annual Moskowitz Prize to the most outstanding quantitative research in SRI. Sponsors of this prize are several of the most influential firms in SRI: Calvert Group, First Affirmative Financial Network, KLD Research & Analytics, Nelson Capital Management, Rockefeller Management, and Trillium Management. Since 1996, past winners have explored topics such as the costs of shareholder boycotts (Angel and Rivoli, 1997), impact of environment regulations on US pulp and paper companies (Repetto and Austin, 2000), effects of corruption ratings on price-to-book ratios (Lee and Ng, 2002), and financial benefits of corporate governance initiatives within the California Public Employees Retirement System (CalPERS) (Barber, 2007).

DOMESTIC STUDIES IN SRI PERFORMANCE

Orlitzky, Schmidt, and Rynes (2003) use meta-analysis to compile the earliest studies on SRI performance. Specifically, they review 52 studies from 1972 to 1997 examining the relationship between corporate social performance (CSP) and corporate financial performance (CFP). These studies use several different measures for CFP including stock market returns, earnings, earnings per share (EPS), price-to-equity (PE) ratio, return on equity (ROE), return on assets (ROA), return on sales (ROS), and many others. Across these studies, Orlitzky et al. find that CSP and CFP are positively correlated, this relationship is bidirectional and simultaneous, and reputation appears to be an important mediator of this relationship. They also find that CSP has a lower correlation with external market-based measures of CFP than accounting measures of CFP, which capture a firm's internal efficiency.

Dhrymes (1998) tests 17 SRI factors based on a CSR database and finds no consistent differences in returns for SRI firms compared to firms in the broader investment universe. Additionally, most of the recent studies of the performance of SRI funds find no significant difference in the risk-adjusted returns of SRI funds compared to conventional benchmarks (Hamilton, Jo, and Statman, 1993; Guerard, 1997; Goldreyer and Diltz, 1999; Statman, 2000, 2006; Stone, Guerard, Gultekin, and Adams, 2002; Schröder, 2004; Bauer, Koedijk, and Otten, 2005; Bello, 2005). These findings seem robust, especially considering that the studies use diverse testing methods to investigate different time periods within various countries.

Yet a few exceptions document evidence of an SRI factor. For example, several studies on the effects of environmental ratings show positive SRI factors. Russo and Fouts (1997) examine the performance of 243 stocks from 1991 to 1992. They find that a firm's environmental rating has a small, but significantly positive, impact on its ROA. Dowell, Hart, and Yeung (2000) agree that being "green" pays. In their analysis of the performance of S&P 500 manufacturing and mining companies from 1994 to 1997, the authors find that the firms with the highest environmental standards also tend to have higher market value. Dowell et al. further indicate that proactive firms can quickly increase their price-to-book (PB) ratios by adopting a higher environmental standard.

Derwall, Guenster, Bauer, and Koedijk (2005) analyze the performance impact of using environmental rankings as part of an active management strategy. Specifically, they rank equities using an ecoefficiency rating and construct two matched value-weighted portfolios, one portfolio with high-ranking environmental firms and another with low-ranking firms. The authors find that the high-ranking portfolios provide substantially higher average returns than the low-ranking portfolios from 1995 to 2003. Derwall et al. suggest that these findings may be indicative of mispricing in the stock market.

Similar to their previous work, Guenster, Bauer, Derwall, and Koedijk (2011) explore ecoefficiency and financial performance from 1997 to 2004. They show that lower ecoefficiency rankings lead to lower performance and valuation. However, higher ecoefficiency rankings do not lead to higher performance and valuation. Their findings suggest that managers do not face a tradeoff between ecoefficiency and financial performance.

A few studies on either corporate governance practices or diversification costs document a negative SRI factor. Gompers, Ishii, and Metrick (2001) analyze the corporate governance practices of 1,500 US companies in the 1990s. Specifically, they measure the degree to which 24 corporate governance practices, such as poison pill provisions, favor management or shareholders. The findings indicate that firms with corporate governance relationships favoring management tend to have lower PB ratios. They further show that firms in the top 10 percent of their corporate governance rankings significantly outperform the remaining firms, while firms in the bottom 10 percent significantly underperform. Gompers et al. (2011,

p. 36) conclude that reducing even one governance provision could decrease agency costs and add value to the firm, and that "the long-run benefits of eliminating numerous provisions would be enormous." These influential findings helped pave the way toward improved corporate governance practices.

Geczy, Stambaugh, and Levin (2006) use Bayesian analysis to measure SRI diversification costs from 1963 to 2001. Specifically, they construct optimal portfolios for mean-variance investors using a range of prior beliefs about model mispricing and manager skills. When comparing the optimal SRI fund to the optimal convention fund, they find imposing SRI constraints on mean-variance optimizing investors can result in a significant cost. They also report that SRI funds had a higher average expense ratio (1.3 percent) compared to conventional funds (1.1 percent). In a similar fashion, Adler and Kritzman (2008) document that SRI limitations on diversification can be costly. They find that the cost is highest for the most highly skilled managers with the most stringent constraints on their investment universes.

EVIDENCE FROM FIXED-INCOME FUNDS IN THE UNITED STATES

Derwall and Koedijk (2009) examine SRI in fixed-income securities by comparing SRI bond funds and SRI balanced funds with matched conventional funds from 1987 to 2003. The evidence shows that the average SRI bond fund performed similarly to its respective conventional fund, whereas the average SRI balanced fund outperformed its respective conventional fund by more than 1.3 percent per year.

Recent findings suggest that increasing environmental standards can lower a firm's cost of debt, which has obvious credit risk implications for bond investors. Bauer and Hann (2010), who examine the environmental profile of 582 US public corporations from 1995 to 2006, find that environmental concerns are strongly correlated with both a higher cost of debt financing and lower credit ratings. Therefore, lower environmental standards can affect the solvency of borrowing firms by increasing their exposure to costly legal, reputational, and regulatory risks.

INTERNATIONAL STUDIES IN SRI PERFORMANCE

The literature on international SRI performance is quickly approaching the level of literature on US SRI performance in terms of depth. However, the literature is not equally weighted among foreign countries. This is not surprising considering that the relative size of the SRI markets varies widely from country to country. Thus, the international research is examined in order based on the relative size of the SRI market within a country (or region) and its relative contribution to the SRI literature.

Evidence from SRI Funds in the United Kingdom
Eurosif (2010a) estimates that SRI assets under management in the United Kingdom increased by nearly 20 percent from January 2008 to January 2010 and

that these assets currently stand at £939.9 billion. Most notably, large pension funds in the United Kingdom have a major presence in the SRI market. UKSIF (2000) surveys 171 of the top 500 UK pension funds and reports two striking results. First, 59 percent of the funds (representing 78 percent of the assets surveyed) state that they incorporate SRI principles into their investment strategies. Second, only 14 percent of the funds (representing 4 percent of the assets surveyed) firmly state that they do not take into account SRI criteria. Taken together, these results clearly show that larger pension funds are more likely to employ SRI actions than smaller funds.

Initial empirical studies on SRI funds in the United Kingdom use benchmark comparisons and focus on whether an SRI factor or other factors such as fund size and age can explain performance (Luther, Matatko, and Corner, 1992; Luther and Matatko, 1994; Mallin, Saadouni, and Briston, 1995; Gregory, Matatko, and Luther, 1997). Luther et al. find weak evidence that 15 UK SRI funds outperform two broad-based stock market indices. Luther and Matatko improve on their prior work by including a small market index, which consequently improves SRI performance. They contend that a small market index is needed, considering that many SRI funds are more heavily weighted toward smaller firms with lower dividend yields. Luther and Matatko find that using a combination of a small market index and a larger broad-based index works best for their dataset. They conclude that the selection of an appropriate benchmark index is paramount.

The absence of an appropriate benchmark is a major weakness of these earlier studies. Mallin et al. (1995) avoid the difficulty of choosing an appropriate benchmark by using a matched sample approach. Specifically, they match 29 SRI funds in the United Kingdom from 1986 to 1993 with 29 conventional funds based on age and size. Their evidence shows that SRI funds outperform conventional funds on a risk-adjusted basis, which they suggest may be the result of a temporary phenomenon created by increased awareness of these SRI funds and subsequently increased demand.

One criticism of Mallin et al. (1995) is that they fail to control for the established size bias in the SRI funds addressed by Luther and Matatko (1994). In other words, although Mallin et al. control for fund size, they do not directly control for the size of the investments made by the funds. To overcome this size bias, Gregory et al. (1997) adopt a similar matched-pairs approach, but they include a size-adjusted performance measure. Matching 18 SRI funds in the United Kingdom from 1986 to 1994 to 18 conventional funds, they find no significant difference in the performance of either group of funds. Yet the findings of their cross-sectional analysis show that SRI funds underperform their respective benchmarks, possibly due to decreased investment options, decreased diversification potential, and increased monitoring costs. The results from the cross-sectional data also indicate that the age of the SRI fund is a far more important factor than the fund's size, indicative of a learning effect.

Finally, Gregory and Whittaker (2007) examine performance persistence for 32 UK SRI funds from January 1989 to December 2002. Similar to several previous studies, they find that SRI funds do not underperform compared to conventional funds. Their evidence also reveals that past "winner" SRI funds outperform past "loser" SRI funds at 36-month horizons on a risk adjusted basis. In other words, these results suggest that SRI investors could improve performance by investing in past "winners" and avoiding past "losers."

Evidence from SRI Funds in Continental Europe

Eurosif (2010a) shows that the total SRI assets under management in Europe increased from 2.7 trillion euros in January 2008 to 5 trillion euros by January 2010. The European market remains largely represented by institutional investors, who manage 92 percent of the total SRI assets under management. Eurosif (2010b) estimates European high net worth individual (HNWI) SRI assets under management to be approximately 729 billion euros as of January 2010. These SRI assets represent about 11 percent of the total European HNWI market, a 35 percent increase from 8 percent in January 2008. Eurosif also predicts that this share will increase to 12 percent by January 2012 with total HNWI SRI assets exceeding 1 trillion euros.

Kreander, Gray, Power, and Sinclair (2002) are among the first to research SRI funds outside of the United States and the United Kingdom. They use performance data of 40 European SRI funds from Belgium, Germany, the Netherlands, Norway, Sweden, Switzerland, and the United Kingdom for a three-year period from 1996 to 1998. Their results show that the SRI funds perform as well or better than the global benchmark, the Morgan Stanley Capital International World Index (MSCIWI). Similar to earlier UK studies, these findings are limited to the appropriateness of the chosen benchmark.

Kreander, Gray, Power, and Sinclair (2005) improve on their earlier work by incorporating the match-pair approach used in Mallin et al. (1995). In this study, they use performance data of 60 European funds from Germany, the Netherlands, Sweden, and the United Kingdom for a seven-year period from January 1995 to December 2001. The authors find no statistical difference in the performance of the 30 SRI funds compared to the 30 matched conventional funds.

Evidence from SRI Funds in Australia

As of 2010, the SRI market in Australia stands at $18.19 billion, which represents a 13 percent growth rate from $16.15 billion in 2009. Although this market is obviously smaller than SRI markets in the United States, the United Kingdom, and continental Europe, the Australian SRI market is experiencing a similar growth rate. Furthermore, the SRI market in Australia is larger than any other Asian-Pacific country (RIAA, 2010).

The empirical research on the performance of Australian SRI funds provides two different findings. First, Cummings (2000) finds no significant difference in the financial performance of Australian SRI trusts compared to three common market benchmarks. Second, Bauer, Otten, and Rad (2006) find similar results to the UK SRI studies by Gregory and Whittaker (2007) in that the performance of Australian SRI funds tend to be time varying. Specifically, Bauer et al. show that Australian SRI funds significantly underperform conventional funds from 1992 to 1996 as these SRI funds undergo a catchup phase. They also find that these SRI funds match the performance of conventional funds more closely from 1996 to 2003.

Evidence from SRI Funds in Japan

The SRI market in Asia lags behind the United States, Europe, and Australia. Sakuma and Louche (2008) report that Japan is the Asian country with the strongest SRI market. The SRI movement in Japan began in 1999 with the inception of four green investment funds and quickly grew to 34 SRI funds by January 2008. As of 2010, the value of Japanese SRI assets under management stood at $5.4 billion with most of the funds targeting individual investors. SRI funds represent less than 1 percent of the total Japanese mutual fund market, which is much smaller than the SRI market share in the United States and Europe. In fact, 60 percent of SRI funds in Japan are international equity funds (SIF-Japan, 2010).

Furthermore, Sakuma and Louche (2008) report that Japan has adopted a preference for positive screening rather than exclusion, which is not surprising considering that 80 percent of Japanese SRI funds use environmental screens. Although little empirical research exists on the performance of Japanese SRI funds, Jin, Mitchell, and Piggott (2006) find that SRI funds are costly and should only be included as an option in Japanese pension plans. Renneboog, Ter Horst, and Zhang (2008a) also support these results in a global SRI study, which is detailed in the next section.

GLOBAL STUDIES IN SRI PERFORMANCE

Several recent studies extend their samples to include a more global analysis. Schröder (2004) uses multifactor models and style analysis to assess 30 US funds and 16 German and Swiss funds. He surmises that SRI funds do not significantly underperform the benchmark portfolio. Schröder notes, however, that US SRI funds tilt toward blue chip stocks, whereas German and Swiss funds tilt toward smaller companies.

Bauer et al. (2005) use a multifactor attribution model to investigate the performance of 103 US, UK, and German SRI funds from 1990 to 2001. The multifactor model is based on the four-factor model created by Carhart (1997), which incorporates the three-factor model developed by Fama and French (1993) and a fourth momentum factor. Bauer et al. do not report a significant difference between SRI funds and conventional funds. Yet their findings suggest that UK SRI funds slightly outperform their respective index, whereas US and German SRI funds underperform their respective indices. The authors also find evidence of a learning effect similar to Gregory et al. (1997) in that older SRI funds outperform younger funds. Finally, Bauer et al. find evidence of a small size bias similar to Luther and Matatko (1994) in that SRI funds tend to be more heavily weighted toward stocks with low market capitalization.

Renneboog et al. (2008a) examine all SRI funds across the world and find that the conventional benchmarks outperform most of these SRI funds by more than 2 percent, suggesting a negative SRI factor. This finding holds true for the United States, the United Kingdom, and many continental European and Asian-Pacific countries. Only a few of these countries, such as France, Japan, and Sweden, significantly underperform on a risk-adjusted basis. Finally, similar to previous studies such as Geczy et al. (2006) and Adler and Kritzman (2008), Renneboog et al. show that social and corporate governance screens are costly and lead to lower risk-adjusted returns.

PERFORMANCE STUDIES OF SRI INDICES

Analyzing SRI indices compared to SRI investment funds has three important advantages. First, transaction costs do not have to be taken into account, which can distort the returns of investment funds. Second, analyzing SRI indices does not necessitate considering timing activities, which avoids many methodological problems mentioned in other studies. Third, the skill of the fund manager does not have to be considered, which allows for a more direct test of the performance of the SRI assets.

Evidence from the Domini Social Index

One of the most successful and most researched SRI indices is the Domini Social Index (DSI). The social research firm Kinder, Lydenberg, Domini & Co. (KLD) constructed the DSI in May 1990. From its inception through March 1999, the DSI has grown 470 percent compared to 389 percent for the S&P 500. This growth rate is impressive considering that KLD modeled the DSI primarily on the S&P 500. Of the original 400 stocks that represented the DSI, 257 were S&P 500 companies that passed screens eliminating companies associated with alcohol, tobacco, gambling, military contracting, nuclear power, South African involvement, environmental mismanagement, and poor employee relations.

KLD also included 143 companies in the DSI that were not listed on the S&P 500. Selection of these companies occurred in two stages. In the first stage, KLD selected 40 smaller-capitalization companies with high SRI rankings in product quality, corporate citizenship, and relations with women and minorities. In the second stage, KLD chose 103 larger-capitalization companies to provide better industry representation (Luck and Pilotte, 1993).

Using the first 17 months of DSI return data, Luck and Pilotte (1993) perform one of the first studies comparing the performance of the DSI to the S&P 500. Over this period, they find that the DSI earned a 7.56 percent higher cumulative return than the S&P 500. They investigate the source of DSI's outperformance using BARRA's PC performance analysis package (PAN). Luck and Pilotte attribute about half of this outperformance to DSI stock selection via screening, which creates several persistent biases relative to the S&P 500.

The most notable DSI bias is a size bias, which reflects findings in SRI fund research (Luther and Matatko, 1994; Bauer et al., 2005). The DSI size bias that results from screening is essentially twofold. Negative screening creates size bias by excluding larger-capitalization "value" stocks in the S&P 500, whereas positive screening creates size bias by including smaller-capitalization "growth" stocks outside the S&P 500. Although size bias has generally had a positive impact on DSI's return, Luck and Pilotte also point out that size bias has been detrimental to performance by underweighting a few traditional large-capitalization industries such as oil and tobacco.

Sauer (1997) finds time-varying results for DSI performance. First, he back-tests DSI data from January 1986 to April 1990 and finds that the DSI would have underperformed both the S&P 500 and a CRSP Value-Weighted Market Index on a risk-adjusted basis over this period. However, when combining the backtest results with DSI data from May 1990 to December 1994, Sauer finds that the DSI outperforms both benchmarks.

Using a more recent time frame, Statman (2000) analyzes the performance of the DSI from May 1990 to September 1998 and finds higher risk-adjusted returns than those of the S&P 500. Statman also analyzes 31 SRI mutual funds over the same period. He finds that their returns are inferior to both the DSI and S&P 500, but the SRI mutual funds performed better than mutual funds of similar size. In general, these studies find that the DSI performs better than both the S&P 500 and SRI mutual funds.

In contrast to these studies, DiBartolomeo and Kurtz (1999) investigate returns of the DSI from May 1990 to March 1999 and find that DSI's indus-try exposure explains much of its performance, suggesting the absence of an SRI advantage. Using an arbitrage pricing theory (APT) optimization model, the authors further show that their optimized DSI portfolio has monthly returns of 1.49 percent over this period, which are slightly less than the S&P 500 monthly returns of 1.55 percent.

Evidence from Other SRI Indices

Garz, Volk, and Gilles (2002), who examine the Dow Jones Sustainability Index (DJSI) from January 1999 to October 2002, find a small but significant level of risk-adjusted excess return of 2.1 percent compared to the DJ STOXX600 index. Schröder (2004) makes benchmark comparisons for 10 SRI indices, including the DSI and DJSI. The 10 SRI indices are comprised of four global indices, four US indices, and two European indices. Schröder's results indicate that only the Calvin index clearly underperforms the benchmarks, and that the *Financial Times* Europe-wide SRI index underperforms in one of the two models used. His find-ings suggest that at least eight of the 10 SRI indices do not suffer from a per-formance disadvantage compared to conventional assets. In a more recent study, Schröder (2007) makes benchmark comparisons for 29 SRI indices and finds similar results. He notes that many SRI indices have a higher risk relative to the benchmarks. Statman (2006) makes benchmark comparisons for four US SRI indices including the DSI. The evidence shows that these four indices generally outperform during the upswing of the late 1990s, but underperform in the down-turn of the early 2000s.

These results also seem to hold for faith-based indices. Kurtz and DiBartolomeo (2005) examine the performance of the KLD Catholics Value (CV) 400 Index, which was launched in 1998 using a broad index of stocks that represented the values of many Catholic investors. The authors show that CV investors can hold true to their values without sacrificing investment returns. They also note that the CV 400 shares many of the same performance attributes as other SRI indices. These characteristics include a higher beta, lower market capitalization, higher valuation ratios, and higher anticipated growth than the S&P 500.

PERFORMANCE STUDIES OF SIN STOCKS

Hong and Kacperczyk (2009) provide considerable evidence of investor avoidance in "sin" stocks such as alcohol, tobacco, and gambling stocks. Evidence from 1980 to 2006 finds that stocks in these sin industries have approximately 18 percent lower institutional ownership than stocks in other industries. Evidence from 1976 to 2006 reveals that sin stocks receive about 21 percent less analyst coverage, indicative of neglect. Finally, evidence from 1965 to 2006 indicates that sin stocks outperform other stocks by approximately 2 percent a year. The collective evidence strongly suggests that SRI funds pay a financial cost for not holding these investments.

Fabozzi, Ma, and Oliphant (2008) find similar results using a sample of 267 sin stocks across 21 national markets from January 1970 to June 2007. Moreover, they show not only that the average sin stock produces a return of 19 percent but also that every sin industry in their study produces returns in excess of 13 percent. The authors also provide strong support for the Vice Fund, which only invests in alcohol, tobacco, and gaming companies. From a return perspective, their support seems warranted. Since its inception in 2003, the Vice Fund has earned an annualized return in excess of 20 percent. Overall, Fabozzi et al. conclude that screening out sin stocks in an investment portfolio in an attempt to uphold social values is economically irrational.

Statman and Glushkov (2009) analyze stock returns from 1992 to 2007 by segregating stocks into three categories: high-ranking SRI stocks, conventional stocks, and sin stocks. They have two major findings. First, high-ranking SRI stocks outperform conventional stocks. Second, sin stocks also outperform conventional stocks. From these findings, the authors contend that the premiums of positive screening are essentially offset by the costs of negative screening. Setting moral contradictions aside, these findings suggest that investing in both high-ranking SRI stocks and sin stocks might improve returns.

Summary and Conclusions

Renneboog, Ter Horst, and Zhang (2008b), Hoepner and McMillan (2009), and Kurtz (2011) provide extensive reviews of the SRI literature. The prevailing finding is no evidence is available for either an SRI advantage or disadvantage over the long term. Furthermore, of the few studies that document outperformance for SRI assets, most attribute a large portion of the excess return to size bias. Size bias is primarily due to SRI assets tilting toward smaller capitalization. However, many indices, such as the DSI, purposefully exclude many large capitalization stocks in shunned industries, creating additional size bias. Finally, those assets reporting the highest abnormal returns over conventional assets are high-ranking SRI assets and sin stocks, but little theory explains these results.

Entine (2003) maintains that most of the SRI literature uses flawed data and pseudoobjective ratings. In particular, Entine (p. 1) labels the KLD ratings as "tainted by anachronistic, contradictory, idiosyncratic, and ideologically constructed notions of corporate social responsibility." Entine is not the first to critique SRI. Two of the most influential economists in history argue that free market economies are more productive and beneficial to their societies. The first to make this proclamation is Adam Smith (1904), who in 1776 published the *Wealth of Nations*. The second is the Nobel Prize–winning economist Milton Friedman (1970). Friedman clearly argues that business has only one social responsibility, which is to increase its profits. Although he is more against chief executive officers (CEOs) engaging in SRI activity than individual investors, Friedman (p. 32) maintains that SRI is "frequently a cloak for actions that are justified on other grounds rather than a reason for those actions."

Kempf and Osthoff (2008) are the first to test these assertions that SRI funds are really just wolves in sheep's clothing. They compare the holdings of SRI funds to conventional funds based on social and environmental standards from 1991 to 2004. They find that SRI funds are higher ranked than conventional funds with respect to every qualitative criterion. The authors also find no evidence that SRI funds increase their ethical rankings through window dressing strategies. Thus, contrary to the convictions of Entine (2003) and Friedman (1970), Kemp and Osthoff find that SRI funds are not conventional funds in disguise.

Nonetheless, Entine (2003) raises a valid point about the lack of theory supporting SRI outperformance. Most reasoning behind SRI outperformance centers on the benefits of screening. Camejo (2002) states that SRI screening not only reduces company-specific risk and liabilities but also helps identify firms with solid finances and effective management. Camejo's claims about screening may be true, but they necessitate SRI outperformance.

Moreover, modern portfolio theory (MPT) disputes claims of SRI outperformance. For example, MPT teaches that restricting the investment universe for any reason forces the investor into a suboptimal portfolio. In other words, SRI incurs a cost regardless of whether or not the market is efficient. If markets are efficient, SRI will incur a diversification cost. On the contrary, if markets are inefficient, SRI will interfere with active management strategies (DiBartolomeo and Kurtz, 1999; Kurtz, 2005).

Either way, SRI advocates might argue that this cost is likely mitigated by the vast number of stocks in the investment universe. In any case, a few major conclusions emerge for investors. First, advocates of SRI perceive that the positive benefits from SRI outweigh any mitigated cost. Second, advocates of MPT disagree. Third, this debate is far from over. As public interest in SRI undoubtedly continues to rise, SRI moves further and further from the fringe into the mainstream.

Discussion Questions

- Discuss two ways other than screening that an individual can participate in SRI.
- Discuss whether SRI funds and indices outperform conventional benchmarks.
- Do any financial theories support SRI? Explain.
- Do SRI stocks outperform sin stocks? Explain.

References

Adler, Timothy, and Mark Kritzman. 2008. "The Cost of Socially Responsible Investing." *Journal of Portfolio Management* 35:1, 52–56.

Angel, James, and Pietra Rivoli. 1997. "Does Ethical Investing Impose a Cost upon the Firm? A Theoretical Examination." *Journal of Investing* 6:4, 57–61.

Barber, Brad M. 2007. "Monitoring the Monitor: Evaluating CalPERS' Activism." *Journal of Investing* 16:4, 66–80.

Bauer, Rob, and Daniel Hann. 2010. "Corporate Environmental Management and Credit Risk." Working Paper, European Centre for Corporate Engagement (ECCE), Maastricht University.

Bauer, Rob, Kees Koedijk, and Rogér Otten. 2005. "International Evidence on Ethical Mutual Fund Performance and Investment Style." *Journal of Banking & Finance* 29:1, 1751–1767.

Bauer, Rob, Roger Otten, and Alireza T. Rad. 2006. "Ethical Investing in Australia: Is There a Financial Penalty?" *Pacific-Basin Finance Journal* 14:1, 33–48.

Bello, Zakri Y. 2005. "Socially Responsible Investing and Portfolio Diversification." *Journal of Financial Research* 28:1, 41–57.

Camejo. Peter. 2002. *The SRI Advantage: Why Socially Responsible Investing Has Outperformed Financially.* Gabriola Island, BC, Canada: New Society.

Carhart, Mark M. 1997. "On Persistence in Mutual Fund Performance." *Journal of Finance* 52:1, 57–82.

Cory, Jacques. 2004. *Business Ethics: The Ethical Revolution of Minority Shareholders.* New York: Springer.

Cummings, Lorne S. 2000. "The Financial Performance of Ethical Investment Trusts: An Australian Perspective." *Journal of Business Ethics* 25:1, 79–92.

Derwall, Jeroen, Nadja Guenster, Rob Bauer, and Kees G. Koedijk. 2005. "The Eco-Efficiency Premium Puzzle." *Financial Analysts Journal* 61:2, 51–63.

Derwall, Jeroen, and Kees Koedijk. 2009. "Socially Responsible Fixed-Income Funds." *Journal of Business Finance & Accounting* 36:1&2, 210–229.

Dhrymes, Phoebus J. 1998. "Socially Responsible Investing: Is It Profitable?" Working Paper, Columbia University.

DiBartolomeo, Dan, and Lloyd Kurtz. 1999. "Managing Risk Exposures of Socially Screened Accounts." Working Paper, Northfield Information Services.

Domini, Amy L. 2001. *Socially Responsible Investing—Making a Difference and Making Money.* Chicago: Dearborn Trade.

Dowell, Glen, Stuart Hart, and Bernard Yeung. 2000. "Do Corporate Global Environmental Standards Create or Destroy Market Value?" *Management Science* 46:8, 1059–1074.

Edmans, Alex. 2011. "Does the Stock Market Fully Value Intangibles? Employee Satisfaction and Equity Prices." *Journal of Financial Economics* 101:3, 621–640.

Entine, Jon. 2003. "The Myth of Social Investing. A Critique of Its Practice and Consequences for Corporate Social Performance Research." *Organization & Environment* 16:3, 352–368.

Entine, Jon. 2005. *Pension Fund Politics: The Dangers of Socially Responsible Investing.* Washington, DC: The AEI Press.

Eurosif. 2010a. "European SRI Study 2010." European Social Investment Forum (Eurosif). Available at http://www.eurosif.org/images/stories/pdf/Research/Eurosif_2010_SRI_Study.pdf.

Eurosif. 2010b. "High Net Worth Individuals and Sustainable Investment." European Social Investment Forum (Eurosif). Available at http://www.eurosif.org/research/hnwi-a-sustainable-investment/2010.

Fabozzi, Frank J., K. C. Ma, and Becky J. Oliphant. 2008. *Journal of Portfolio Management* 35:1, 82–94.

Fama, Eugene F., and Kenneth R. French. 1993. "Common Risk Factors in the Returns on Stocks and Bonds." *Journal of Financial Economics* 33:1, 3–53.

Filbeck, Greg. 2001. "*Mother Jones*: Do Better Places to Work Imply Better Places to Invest?" *Review of Financial Economics*, 10:1, 57–70.

Filbeck, Greg, and Dianna Preece. 2003. "*Fortune*'s Best 100 Companies to Work for in America: Do They Work for Shareholders." *Journal of Business Finance & Accounting* 30:5&6, 771–795.

Filbeck, Greg, Raymond Gorman, and Xin Zhao. 2009. "The 'Best Corporate Citizens': Are They Good for Their Shareholders?" *Financial Review* 44:1, 239–262.

Friedman, Milton. 1970. "The Social Responsibility of Business Is to Increase Its Profits." *The New York Times* September 13, 32.

Garz, Hendrik, Claudia Volk, and Martin Gilles. 2002. "More Gain Than Pain—SRI: Sustainability Pays Off." WestLB Panmure, November. Available at http://s3.amazonaws.com/zanran_storage/www.djindexes.com/ContentPages/10244444.pdf.

Geczy, Christopher C., Robert F. Stambaugh, and David Levin. 2006. "Investing in Socially Responsible Mutual Funds." Working Paper, The Rodney L. White Center of Financial Research, The Wharton School, University of Pennsylvania.

Goldreyer, Elizabeth F., and J. David Diltz. 1999. "The Performance of Socially Responsible Mutual Funds: Incorporating Sociopolitical Information in Portfolio Selection." *Managerial Finance* 25:1, 23–36.

Gompers, Paul, Joy L. Ishii, and Andrew Metrick. 2001. "Corporate Governance and Equity Prices." Working Paper, National Bureau of Economic Research.

Gregory, Alan, John Matatko, and Robert Luther. 1997. "Ethical Unit Trust Financial Performance: Small Company Effects and Fund Size Effects." *Journal of Business Finance & Accounting* 24:5, 705–725.

Gregory, Alan, and Julie Whittaker. 2007. "Performance and Performance Persistence of 'Ethical' Unit Trusts in the UK." *Journal of Business Finance & Accounting* 34:7&8, 1327–1344.

Grossman, Blake R., and William F. Sharpe. 1986. "Financial Implications of South African Divestment." *Financial Analyst Journal* 42:4, 15–29.

Guenster, Nadja, Rob Bauer, Jeroen Derwall, and Kees Koedijk. 2011. "The Economic Value of Corporate Eco-Efficiency" *European Financial Management* 17:4, 679–704.

Guerard, John B., Jr. 1997. "Is There a Cost to Being Socially Responsible in Investing?" *Journal of Investing* 6:2, 11–18.

Hamilton, Sally, Hoje Jo, and Meir Statman. 1993. "Doing Well While Doing Good? The Investment Performance of Socially Responsible Mutual Funds." *Financial Analysts Journal* 49:6, 62–66.

Hoepner, Andreas G. F., and David G. McMillan. 2009. "Research on 'Responsible Investment': An Influential Literature Analysis Comprising of a Rating, Characterization, Categorization, and Investigation." Working Paper, University of St. Andrews.

Hong, Harrison, and Marcin Kacperczyk. 2009. "The Price of Sin: The Effects of Social Norms on Markets." *Journal of Financial Economics* 93:1, 15–36.

Jin, Henry H., Olivia S. Mitchell, and John Piggott. 2006. "Socially Responsible Investment in Japanese Pensions." *Pacific-Basin Journal* 14:5, 427–438.

Kempf, Alexander, and Peer Osthoff. 2008. "SRI Funds: Nomen Est Omen." *Journal of Business Finance & Accounting* 35:9&10, 1276–1294.

Kreander, N., R. H. Gray, D. M. Power, and C. D. Sinclair. 2002. "The Financial Performance of European Ethical Funds 1996–1998." *Journal of Accounting & Finance* 1, 3–22.

Kreander, N., R. H. Gray, D. M. Power, and C. D. Sinclair. 2005. "Evaluating the Performance of Ethical and Non-Ethical Funds: A Matched Pair Analysis." *Journal of Business Finance & Accounting* 32:7&8, 1465–1493.

Kurtz, Lloyd. 2005. "Answers to Four Questions." *Journal of Investing* 14:3, 125–139.

Kurtz, Lloyd. 2011. "Bibliography." Center for Responsible Business, Haas School of Business, University of California, Berkeley. Available at http://sristudies.wikispaces.com/Bibliography.

Kurtz, Lloyd, and Dan DiBartolomeo. 2005. "The KLD Catholic Values 400 Index." *Journal of Investing* 14:3, 101–104.

Kurtz, Lloyd, and Chris Luck. 2002. "An Attribution Analysis of the 100 Best Companies to Work for in America." Presentation to Northfield Investment Conference, May 5–7, Fish Camp, California.

Lee, Charles M. C., and David T. Ng. 2002. "Corruption and International Valuation: Does Virtue Pay?" Working Paper, Cornell University.

Levering, Robert, and Milton R. Moskowitz. 1998. "The 100 Best Companies to Work for in America." *Fortune* January 12, 84–95.

Luck, Christopher, and Nancy Pilotte. 1993. "Domini Social Index Performance." *Journal of Investing* 2:3, 60–62.

Luther, Robert G., and John Matatko. 1994. "The Performance of Ethical Unit Trusts: Choosing an Appropriate Benchmark." *British Accounting Review* 26:1, 77–89.

Luther, Robert G., John Matatko, and Desmond C. Corner. 1992. "The Investment Performance of UK 'Ethical' Unit Trusts." *Accounting, Auditing and Accountability Journal* 5:4, 57–70.

Mallin, C. A., B. Saadouni, and R. J. Briston. 1995. "The Financial Performance of Ethical Investment Funds." *Journal of Business Finance & Accounting* 22:4, 483–496.

Moskowitz, Milton R. 1972. "Choosing Socially Responsible Stocks." *Business & Society* 1:1, 71–75.

Moskowitz, Milton R. 1975. "Profiles in Corporate Social Responsibility." *Business & Society* 13:1, 29–42.

Moskowitz, Milton R. 1996. "100 Best Companies for Working Mothers." *Working Mother Magazine* 19, 10–70.

Mukherjee, Tarun K., Vineeta L. Hingorani, and Sang H. Lee. 1995. "Stock Price Reactions to Voluntary versus Mandatory Social Actions: The Case of South African Divestiture." *Journal of Business Finance & Accounting* 22:2, 301–311.

Orlitzky, Marc, Frank L. Schmidt, and Sara L. Rynes. 2003. "Corporate Social and Financial Performance: A Meta-Analysis." *Organization Studies* 24:3, 403–441.

Preece, Dianna C., and Greg Filbeck. 1999. "Family Friendly Firms: Does It Pay to Care?" *Financial Services Review* 8:1, 47–60.

Renneboog, Luc, Jenke Ter Horst, and Chendi Zhang. 2008a. "The Price of Ethics and Stakeholder Governance: The Performance of Socially Responsible Mutual Funds." *Journal of Corporate Finance* 14:1, 302–322.

Renneboog, Luc, Jenke Ter Horst, and Chendi Zhang. 2008b. "Socially Responsible Investments: Institutional Aspects, Performance, and Investor Behavior." *Journal of Banking & Finance* 32:1, 1723–1742.

Repetto, Robert, and Duncan Austin. 2000. *Pure Profit: The Financial Implications of Environmental Performance*, Washington, DC: World Resources Institute.

RIAA. 2010. "Responsible Investment 2010." Responsible Investment Association Australasia (RIAA). Available at http://www.responsibleinvestment.org/wp-content/uploads/2011/06/RIAA-Benchmark-Report-20101.pdf.

Rudd, Andrew. 1979. "Divestment of South African Equities: How Risky?" *Journal of Portfolio Management* 5:3, 5–10.

Russo, Michael V., and Paul A. Fouts. 1997. "A Resource-Based Perspective on Corporate Environmental Performance and Profitability." *Academy of Management Journal* 40:3, 534–559.

Sakuma, Kyoko, and Céline Louche. 2008. "Socially Responsible Investment in Japan: Its Mechanism and Drivers." *Journal of Business Ethics* 82:1, 425–448.

Sauer, David A. 1997. "The Impact of Social-Responsibility Screens on Investment Performance: Evidence from the Domini 400 Social Index and Domini Equity Mutual Fund." *Review of Financial Economics* 6:2, 137–149.

Schröder, Michael. 2004. "The Performance of Socially Responsible Investments: Investment Funds and Indices." *Financial Markets and Portfolio Management* 18:2, 122–142.

Schröder, Michael. 2007. "Is There a Difference? The Performance Characteristics of SRI Equity Indices." *Journal of Business Finance & Accounting* 34:1&2, 331–348.

SIF. 2010. "2010 Report on Socially Responsible Investing Trends in the United States." Social Investment Forum (SIF). Available at http://ussif.org/resources/research/documents/2010TrendsES.pdf

SIF-Japan. 2010. "2009 Review of Socially Responsible Investment in Japan." Social Investment Forum Japan (SIF-Japan). Available at http://www.sifjapan.org/document /nenpo09_English.pdf.

Smith, Adam. 1904. *An Inquiry into the Nature and Causes of the Wealth of Nations*. London: Methuen and Co.

Sparkes, Russell. 2002. *Socially Responsible Investment: A Global Revolution*. Chichester,UK: John Wiley & Sons.

Statman, Meir. 2000. "Socially Responsible Mutual Funds." *Financial Analysts Journal* 56:3, 30–39.

Statman, Meir. 2006. "Socially Responsible Indexes: Composition, Performance, and Tracking Error." *Journal of Portfolio Management* 32:3, 100–109.

Statman, Meir, and Denys Glushkov. 2009. "The Wages of Social Responsibility." *Financial Analysts Journal* 65:4, 33–46.

Stone, Bernell K., John B. Guerard, Jr., Mustafa N. Gulekin, and Greg Adams. 2002. "Socially Responsible Investment Screening: Strong Evidence of No Significant Cost for Actively Managed Portfolios." Working Paper, Marriott School of Finance, Brigham Young University.

Teoh, Siew H., Ivo Welch, and C. Paul Wazzan. 1999. "The Effect of Socially Activist Investment Policies on the Financial Markets: Evidence from the South African Boycott." *Journal of Business* 72:1: 35–89.

UKSIF. 2000. "Pension Funds Want Fund Managers to Consider Financial Impact of Corporate Social Responsibility." UK Social Investment Forum (UKSIF). Available at http://www.uksif.org/45745745/uksif/publications/press_releases/273438.

Waddock, Sandra A., and Samuel B. Graves. 1997. "Finding the Link Between Stakeholder Relations and Quality of Management." *Journal of Investing*, 6:4, 20–24.

Wesley, John. 1771. "Sermon 50: The Use of Money." *Sermons on Several Occasions*. Available at http://new.gbgm-umc.org/umhistory/wesley/sermons/50/.

DISCUSSION QUESTIONS AND ANSWERS

Chapter 2. Modern Portfolio Theory

1. A market timer predicts a negative risk premium $\mu - R_f$ for the upcoming investment period. What should be the optimal allocation to the risky asset?

In this situation, Merton's optimal asset allocation applies. The negative numerator in the optimal allocation shows that the market timer will take a negative position (i.e., short) in the risky portfolio. The amount is determined by the variance and risk aversion. Intuitively, the graph is reversed from the standard case of Figure 2.1. Positive positions lie on a negatively sloped capital allocation line with intercept R_f. A negative position in the risky asset opens up mirroring a positively slope allocation line. This is where the market timer who forecasts a negative risk premium will locate her allocation according to Merton's formula.

2. When the risk-free borrowing rate R_B is higher than the lending rate R_L, explain why some investors may prefer P_2 to P_1 in Figure 2.1. Which investors are these likely to be?

Consider P_1 in Figure 2.1. A very risk-averse utility-maximizing investor has a steeply sloped indifference curve. Merton's allocation will occur to the left of P_1. Therefore, this investor will use the lending rate as she will buy some risk-free asset. However, for a more risk tolerant investor, the optimal allocation may occur to the right of P_1. This investor borrows at the risk-free rate. Consequently, the relevant CAL to the right of P_1 is drawn from the higher intercept R_B and has a lower slope. This lower sloped CAL can then intersect the lending CAL_2 for P_2. For a σ larger than this intersection point, the P_2 CAL_2 then dominates.

Another important implication of this transaction cost is that some investors may neither borrow nor invest because of the kink in the CAL at the portfolio P. One can show that the lowest risk aversion on the lending side ($w^* < 1$) is larger than the highest risk aversion on the borrowing side ($w^* > 1$). The transaction cost renders the risk-free capital market unappealing for this class of investors.

3. In the risk frontier of many assets, as in Figure 2.3, what is the link between the MVP's expected return and the risk-free rate?

A link exists between the MVP mean return and the risk-free rate. Consider a case where μ_{MVP} is below the risk-free rate. This situation could happen if the mean returns were estimates from a period with low returns. First, the investor would not invest in any efficient portfolio with mean returns between μ_{MVP} and R_f because this would imply a negative Sharpe ratio. Second, because the efficient frontier is a hyperbola, its asymptotes are drawn from the vertical axis at μ_{MVP}. Mathematically, an attempt to maximize the Sharpe ratio from a point R_f higher than μ_{MVP} results in an infinite slope. For the Sharpe ratio maximizing portfolio to make mathematical sense, R_f must be strictly below μ_{MVP}. Consequently, the Sharpe ratio maximization cannot deliver a sensible tangency portfolio to a market timer whose beliefs imply a μ_{MVP} below the risk-free rate. The only limitation in infinite positions would come from margin limits. This result has a dynamic economic interpretation. Portfolios very far up on the frontier have very large short weights on the assets with the lower mean returns. This short demand lowers their price, which in turn raises their expected return, until in equilibrium, the resulting MVP has a mean above the risk-free asset.

4.When combining an active portfolio P with a beta of 1 and the market portfolio to maximize the Sharpe ratio, the optimal weight in the active portfolio is:

$$w^* = \frac{\alpha_P / \sigma_{\varepsilon,P}}{\left[E(R_M) - R_f \right] / \sigma_M^2}$$

Discuss this result.

The above formula can be extended to portfolios with betas different from 1, but it becomes more complex and less intuitive. The optimal weight increases with the information ratio. However, the formula shows that the optimal weight is also decreasing with the reward to variance ratio offered by the market. Note that the optimal weight may be negative if the active portfolio's α is negative. Logically, the Sharpe ratio is then improved by short selling a portfolio with a negative α.

Typically, a quantitative manager has more than one portfolio or security with a nonzero α. The above formula extends to the optimal weight in each of these securities so as to maximize the Sharpe ratio. Further, if one assumes an index model whereby the idiosyncratic returns ε_i are uncorrelated with one another, the square of the information ratio of this portfolio can be shown to be the sum of the squared information ratios, $a_i / \sigma_{\varepsilon i}$ of each security.

5. Consider P_1 and P_2 in Figure 2.4. Find the Sharpe ratio for M. Why cannot P_1 help improve this Sharpe ratio? Find the Sharpe ratio for P_2. Is it better or worse than M's Sharpe ratio? Explain why P_2 can improve on the Sharpe ratio of M.

The market Sharpe ratio is $Sh(M) = 0.2$. The return for P_1 is set at the CAPM expected return of $0.04 + 1.2(0.04) = 0.088$. Therefore, by construction, the optimal weight w_1 in a portfolio of P_1 and M is 0. This is the CAPM setup where M already has the highest possible Sharpe ratio. P_2 has an alpha of 0.04, therefore an expected return of 0.128, which is the CAPM expected return plus the alpha. Its Sharpe ratio is 0.196 using Equation 2.2, which is lower than the market. However, because of its nonzero alpha, P_2 contributes to an improvement on the market Sharpe ratio. P_2's residual variance is $0.45^2 - (0.2)(1.2)^2 = 0.145$. The maximized Sharpe ratio at T is:

$$\sqrt{(0.04 + 0.04^2)/0.145} = 0.226.$$

6. Show that the precision of estimating the mean does not change with the sampling frequency. In contrast, show that the precision of estimating the standard deviation increases with the square root of the sampling frequency?

Assume that an investor obtains estimates (m,s) for the T annual data and (m_D, s_D) for the daily data. There are H days in a year. The confidence interval for the daily mean is:

$m_D \pm 1.96\, s_D/\sqrt{HT}$. Note that the sample size for the daily returns in HT. The bounds of this interval are known to be the 2.5 percent and 97.5 percent values on the distribution of the high frequency mean. This interval can be converted into an implied interval for the low frequency mean by using the aggregation result for the mean: $\mu = H\mu_D$ and the standard deviation: $\sigma = \sqrt{H}\sigma_D$. Multiplying each bound by H, the low frequency interval implied by the high frequency estimates is $Hm_D \pm 1.96\, s_D/\sqrt{T}$. This is exactly the same interval as before. The higher frequency sample yields no added precision to the estimation of the mean. Comparing t-values for the low and high frequency mean estimates will show that they are equal.

The aggregation of standard deviations is exact only when returns are not auto-correlated. Predominant positive autocorrelations could lead the low frequency standard deviation to larger than implied by the aggregation, and in turn, the interval implied by high frequency data to be narrower. In practice, the autocorrelations of financial asset returns are too small to modify the aggregation result. As an exercise, the reader can collect financial asset returns for various frequencies and calendar period and verify that higher frequency data do not yield more precise inference on the mean return.

Consider the standard deviation result. For simplicity, use the simple asymptotic distribution of the maximum likelihood estimator s, which is normally distributed with mean sigma and variance sigma squared over T. Write the low frequency confidence interval with sample size T. Write the high frequency confidence interval with sample size HT. Realize that its bounds are points on the distribution of the high frequency standard deviation, and therefore, must be multiplied by $\sqrt{H}$ to yield the implied interval for the low frequency standard deviation. The low frequency interval implied by the high frequency estimate is $\sqrt{H}$ narrower than the original low frequency interval. The implied interval indeed shrunk at a rate $\sqrt{H}$.

Chapter 3. Asset Pricing Theories, Models, and Tests

1. Discuss the advantages and the drawbacks of the Hansen-Jagannathan distance and cross-sectional R^2 for evaluating and comparing possibly misspecified asset pricing models.

The Hansen-Jagannathan (HJ) distance measures the degree of misspecification of an asset pricing model. Let m denote an admissible stochastic discount factor

(SDF) that prices the test assets correctly (i.e., $E[m(1+R)] = 1_N$) Let also $\mathcal{M}$ denote the set of all admissible SDFs and y be a candidate SDF. Hansen and Jagannathan suggest using $\delta = min_{m \in \mathcal{M}} (E[(y - m)^2])^{1/2}$ as a misspecification measure of y. In the literature, δ is often referred to as the unconstrained HJ-distance. They show that δ corresponds to the maximum pricing error that one can get from using y to price the test assets. If investors care about the pricing error of the mostly misspecified portfolio with unit second moment, the unconstrained HJ-distance represents an appealing measure of model misspecification. Additionally, when y depends on unknown parameters, the HJ-distance can be used as a statistical criterion function for estimating these parameters. A SDF can possibly price all the test assets correctly and yet take on negative values with positive probability. Such a SDF does not necessarily rule out arbitrage opportunities and using this SDF could be problematic in pricing assets outside of the payoff space such as derivatives on the test assets. To address this issue, Hansen and Jagannathan provide a second model misspecification measure (constrained HJ-distance):

$\delta_+ = min_{m \in \mathcal{M}^+} (E[(y-m)^2])^{1/2}$, where M^+ denotes the set of all positive SDFs. Unlike the unconstrained HJ-distance, δ_+ generally represents only a lower bound on the maximum pricing error. As a result, using δ_+ for comparing competing models could be problematic because a model with a smaller δ_+ may not necessarily be a model with smaller maximum pricing error. Therefore, it may not be a better model for pricing derivatives.

In the beta framework, the R^2 for the cross-sectional relation is a natural goodness-of-fit measure. The ordinary least squares (OLS) R^2 is more relevant if the focus is on the expected returns for a particular set of assets or test portfolios, but the generalized least squares (GLS) R^2 may be of greater interest from an investment perspective in that it is directly related to the relative efficiency of portfolios that "mimic" a model's economic factors. Furthermore, as emphasized by Kan and Zhou (2004), R^2 is oriented toward expected returns whereas the HJ-distance evaluates a model's ability to explain prices. Thus, the two measures need not rank models the same way and the choice between the two depends on the economic context.

2. Some studies suggest that the predictive power of different financial and macro variables for forecasting future stock returns should be evaluated only out of sample (i.e., using information only up to the time when the forecast is made). List several reasons that could justify the preference for out-of-sample over in-sample evaluation of predictive power.

Evaluating the statistical significance of different predictors in in-sample predictive regressions suffers from various problems. These problems include potential parameter instability and structural breaks over the sample, spurious evidence of predictability, nonstandard inference theory for highly persistent predictors and long-horizon predictive regressions, and limited practical value for investors and risk managers. Out-of-sample evaluation provides a more objective and appealing assessment of predictability although it may be less powerful in detecting useful conditioning variables. Both in-sample and out-of-sample evaluations are susceptible to data mining and statistical inference should be conducted using methods that guard against potential data snooping.

3. The SDF approach discussed in this chapter can be used for evaluating the performance of mutual and hedge funds. Describe briefly how the SDF approach can be implemented in practice for this task if mutual/hedge fund data are available.

The performance evaluation of mutual/hedge funds should start with constructing mutual/hedge fund portfolios that reflect different investment strategies. The asset pricing models used for evaluation should account for derivative-like features in fund returns, alternative asset classes such as commodities, real estate, currencies, and sovereign bonds. The evaluation is typically performed using the SDF approach and the HJ-distances described in answering question 1.

4. Despite the recent developments in asset pricing theory and practice, many statistical problems can still potentially compromise some empirical findings reported in the literature. Discuss some of the pitfalls in the empirical analysis of asset pricing models.

Some pitfalls in the empirical analyses of asset pricing models include using inference methods for correctly specified models when the model is likely to be misspecified as well as employing standard inference procedures in the presence of useless factors, highly persistent conditioning variables and a large number of test assets. The potential lack of invariance to data scaling and the possible (mis) interpretation of the prices of beta risk in the context of model selection should also serve as a warning against blindly applying and interpreting some existing methods in the literature.

Chapter 4. Asset Pricing and Behavioral Finance

1. Kahneman and Tversky postulate that the concept of representativeness explains why people are prone to underestimate regression to the mean. For example, in a regression of height of son on height of father, the estimated slope coefficient tends to be positive, but less than one. Nevertheless, people are prone to predict that sons will be as tall as their fathers, in effect treating the slope coefficient as one. Explain how representativeness might account for this prediction error, and then extend the analysis to explaining how representativeness might underlie the De Bondt-Thaler winner-loser effect.

Representativeness involves the overweighting of stereotypes by placing undue weight on the general characteristics of a population when evaluating members of that population. In the case of heights of sons, representativeness leads people to overweight the characteristic father's height, and to underweight if not ignore the other determinants of the height of a son. The estimated regression equation does imply that tall fathers tend to have tall sons and short fathers tend to have short sons. However, a slope coefficient that is less than one implies that the height of sons tends to be closer to the mean height in the entire population than the height of the father. In other words, regression to the mean occurs. People who rely on representativeness overestimate the heights of sons with tall fathers and underestimate the heights of sons with short fathers. This line of reasoning also applies to the winner-loser effect in which past three-year returns corresponds to the heights of fathers, and subsequent five-year returns correspond to the heights of sons.

Representativeness leads investors to stereotype past extreme losers as future extreme losers and past extreme winners as future extreme winners. Because long-term returns are mean reverting, investors who fail to account for regression to the mean will tend to overestimate the future returns of past winners and to underestimate the returns of past losers.

2. In the DSSW noise trader model, the younger generation possesses physical endowment but does not consume, while the older generation possesses no physical endowment but consumes. Portfolios consist of two securities, a risk-free security paying a fixed rate of interest r and a stock paying a certain dividend of r per share. The price of the stock is P per share, in units of endowment, and the price of the risk-free security is normalized to 1. Let W denote the value of investors' portfolios at the end of a period. Suppose one share of stock is available, which is perfectly divisible but because a perfectly elastic storage technology underlies the risk-free security. The supply of the risk-free security is also perfectly elastic. Let δ denote the net holdings of the risk-free security. Use the aggregate budget constraint to develop an equation that relates P to W and δ and to relate W to e. Then use these equations to describe what happens along a bubble in the DSSW framework. Analyze whether a bubble can occur if the risk-free asset were available in zero net supply, and if a bubble can grow without limit.

At the end of a period, portfolios consist of the stock, with value P, and the risk-free security, with value δ. Because there is only one share of stock and the price of the risk-free security is 1, W must equal the sum $P + \delta$. Therefore, $P = W - \delta$. Because only younger investors hold portfolios at the end of a period, and invest their entire endowments, W must equal e. These two equations together imply that $P = e - \delta$. Along a bubble, P grows. Given that $P = e - \delta$, P can only grow if δ declines. If P grows without limit, then δ must decline without limit. Negative δ connotes net borrowing. That is, along a bubble, younger investors must engage in unbounded borrowing. If the risk-free security were available in zero net supply, then $\delta = 0$, and therefore, $P = e$, in which case no bubble is possible. Nonzero net risk-free borrowing by the younger generation must have a physical counterpart in respect to the storage technology, meaning the drawdown of inventory of physical endowment stored in the past. Of course, this will increase the consumption of the older generation. However, the stock price P will only be able to increase to the extent that drawing down inventory is possible.

3. As Fama (1998) points out, instances of overreaction appear about as often as instances of underreaction. He suggests that this feature is consistent with market efficiency because the mean abnormal return is zero, with random fluctuations giving rise to nonzero deviations (anomalies) in both directions. Evaluate Fama's position.

There is a joke about an elderly trial lawyer, now retired, who is writing his memoirs. The lawyer reflects on his time as a young inexperienced attorney and recalls having lost many cases he should have won. He then reflects on his time as an older, experienced attorney and recalls having won many cases he should

698   DISCUSSION QUESTIONS AND ANSWERS

have lost. He concludes his memoir with the words, "Well, I guess you can say that on average justice was done!"

The joke, of course, is that justice was not done in either case described. By analogy, markets are not efficient if overreaction occurs as often as underreaction. The key issue is whether conditional on the situation at hand, one can predict overreaction but not underreaction and vice versa. If conditioning on past long-term returns and predicting future long-term returns, the prediction should be for overreaction. If conditioning on past short-term returns and predicting future short-term returns, the prediction should be for underreaction.

Fama singles out postearnings announcement drift as a true anomaly, which cannot be explained using the Fama-French three-factor model. This phenomenon combines both short-term momentum and long-term reversal.

4. Excessive optimism involves overestimating mean returns, while overconfidence involves underestimating return standard deviation. Suppose that excessive optimism and overconfidence are positively correlated in the investor population. In this respect, assume that bearish investors tend to be underconfident while bullish investors tend to be overconfident. Consider the change of measure associated with market sentiment. How will this positive correlation affect the shape of the sentiment function and the shape of the SDF, when graphed against consumption growth?

Excessively bullish, overconfident investors will attach too low a probability to unfavorable aggregate consumption growth. For very high aggregate consumption growth, overconfidence will lead them to attach too low a probability to very favorable aggregate consumption growth. These investors overestimate the probability of moderately favorable aggregate consumption growth. Excessively bearish, underconfident investors overweight the probabilities of tail events. What they underestimate is the probability of moderately unfavorable aggregate consumption growth.

The beliefs of the representative investor are generated as a Hölder average of the individual investors' probability density functions (pdfs). Because the bears' pdfs dominate in the left tail, and the bulls' pdfs dominate in the right tail, the bears will dominate the change of measure in the left tail and the bulls will dominate the change of measure in the right tail. Therefore, the log change of measure will be positive and declining in both the left tail and right tail. However, because the bears' log change of measure has the shape of a U, and the bulls' log change of measure has the shape of an inverted U, the combination will feature an oscillating pattern in the middle of the market log change of measure.

Because the SDF combines the fundamental component and sentiment, if sentiment is strong enough its shape will carry over to the SDF. In this case, the SDF will be declining in the tails but oscillate in the middle.

Chapter 5. Assessing Risk Tolerance

1. The Survey of Consumer Finance's financial risk tolerance question is widely used in the academic literature to measure the risk aversion level of households.

Why might this not be the best measure to use given how risk tolerance should normatively be measured?

Risk tolerance is based on the concavity of a household's utility function. The more concave a household's utility function, the greater is the level of risk aversion for that household. The more risk averse a household is, the more it must be compensated (via a risk premium) to invest in risky assets due to the uncertainty in asset payout. The Survey of Consumer Finance uses one question with four possible responses to measure the financial risk tolerance of households. The possible responses include willingness to accept no financial risk, average financial risk, above average financial risk, and substantial financial risk. This question does not measure willingness to accept variation in consumption. Therefore, questions that do measure such willingness may better explain investor behavior based on expected utility theory.

2. Most risk tolerance surveys contain questions that are not explicitly grounded in theory. Why is having a theoretical basis important when determining which type of questions should be included in a questionnaire?

The Arrow-Pratt measure is based on an investor's willingness to accept variation in consumption. The more variation in consumption a household is willing to accept, the greater is its risk tolerance. Under modern portfolio theory, if an investor is willing to accept greater variation in asset returns (which is tied to consumption), then he should be compensated with a higher expected return. Therefore, households that are more risk tolerant should be more heavily invested in equities. Questions based on prospect theory that measure loss aversion may also be useful in determining the extent to which a household is willing to accept losses. This information could help the household avoid shifting substantial allocations to cash during a down market and giving up an equity risk premium.

3. What is human capital and how is it measured? How should human capital and labor flexibility influence an optimal portfolio allocation?

Human capital is the stock of an individual's knowledge and skills that are productive in some economic context. It can be measured by calculating a person's present value of future cash flows. Human capital is typically more bond-like, and therefore when an individual's human capital is high, he should invest more heavily in equities. As age increases, the present value of future cash flows declines and the percentage allocated to fixed income should be increased. However, increasing the allocation to fixed income may be normatively justified if there is a strong positive covariance of return between an individual's human capital and the equity market. The ability of a household to vary labor supply allows it to invest a higher percentage of the portfolio in equities. This situation exists because labor market flexibility acts as a hedge against bad outcomes.

4. What role should investment horizon play, if any, when determining an optimal portfolio allocation?

Various scholars question whether observed prior return characteristics should guide household portfolio selection in the absence of a theoretical rationale for return predictability. Even with a high likelihood that stock returns are independent and identically distributed and time horizon is irrelevant, a rational, long-term investor will weigh the nonzero possibility that the future will resemble the past and favor equities. Strong evidence of observed mean reversion in historical equity returns exists in the financial literature. This evidence implies lower risk in equity investments to those with a long-run time horizon. As long as mean reversion persists, investors may be able to earn a time premium by having a long-run investment horizon.

Chapter 6. Private Wealth Management

1. Chris Wilson is conducting a situational profile of James Cho, her client. What should Wilson focus on in the profile?

A situational profile is the first step in understanding an individual client. Wilson's goal is to understand Cho and his circumstances that relate to managing his portfolio. She should consider both the financial and human characteristics of Cho's situation as well as his stage of life. The profile should describe the client's goals, preferences, and lifestyle. How Cho accumulated his wealth and his perceptions of wealth ultimately define his willingness to tolerate risk.

2. How may an individual's willingness to tolerate risk differ from his ability to tolerate risk?

The willingness to tolerate risk is related to an individual's psychological profile. It depends on both how the person's accumulated wealth and his perception of wealth. The ability to tolerate risk is more objective. It involves a person's financial assets, human capital, and financial requirements. Liquidity needs, spending requirements, and unique circumstances all influence an individual's ability to tolerate risk.

3. Compare and contrast traditional financial models with behavioral finance.

Modern portfolio theory, which is the foundation for traditional financial models, assumes that investors are risk averse. This assumption implies that investors expect to be appropriately compensated for taking on additional risk. Another component of traditional models is rational expectations, which means that investors' forecasts are unbiased and reflect available information about an investment's true worth. Traditional financial models also assume that investors view assets in terms of their entire portfolio and consider the risk/return implications of assets relative to other assets. The correlation of returns is important to the asset allocation decision.

In behavioral finance, individuals are loss averse, which means that they care more about loss (or avoiding loss) than about the volatility of assets returns. Investors also have biased expectations, which mean that they neither use relevant information nor learn from their mistakes. Behavioral finance recognizes that investors do not consider assets as they relate to the overall portfolio, but on a stand-alone basis, which is referred to as asset segregation.

4. Explain three constraints that are more relevant to individual investors than to institutional investors.

Three constraints that are more relevant to individual investors than to institutional investors are tax management, liquidity constraints, and time horizons.

- Tax management is more complex and individual specific. Individuals can engage in tax avoidance, reduction, and deferral. The issues are complicated and must be handled on an individual/family basis.
- Liquidity constraints are also individual specific. They may include college tuition payments, nursing home payments, and general spending requirements to maintain life style and entertainment needs.
- Time horizons vary and an individual may have more than one relevant period. For example, one time horizon might cover the period until children go to college and the second might cover the period between the children finishing college and the individual retiring.

The IPS is complicated, dynamic, and specific to the individual. Some constraints tend to be less important to individuals, such as legal issues, while others tend to be more important, such as tax issues.

Chapter 7. Institutional Wealth Management

1. Phil Johnson, President of Johnson Pharmaceuticals, has hired a consultant to help develop an IIPS for his company's defined benefit Plan. Johnson provides the consultant with the following relevant details:

- The company routinely maintains a profit margin of 15 percent and has virtually no debt. The average profit margin of the industry is 12.6 percent with a total debt-to-equity ratio of 0.5.
- The average age of the workforce is 40 years old. The industry average age is 47 years old.
- A total of 25 percent of the plans participants are currently retired. The industry average is 32 percent.
- The pension plan currently has $75 million in assets and is 15 percent overfunded.
- The actuarial required rate of return is 6 percent.
- The trustees want to maintain a 5 percent cash balance.
- Johnson wants to earn at least 7.5 percent per year so that future contributions can be minimized.

A. What should be used as the return objective?

The fund's assets have a required return of at least 6 percent to meet the actuarially determined growth in PBO. Johnson has requested a 7.5 percent return target to minimize future contributions. This secondary goal is reasonable to pursue, but is less important than the 6 percent base level established by the actuaries.

702 DISCUSSION QUESTIONS AND ANSWERS

B. What should be the fund's risk tolerance level? Provide three points of evidence for your answer.

The defined benefit plan for Johnson Pharmaceuticals can tolerate an above average risk level. This level is based upon the company's low average age, its low retired lives percentage, and its overfunded status.

C. Identify two specific constraints

The pension fund for Johnson Pharmaceuticals has a long time horizon with moderate to low liquidity needs. The company must maintain a minimum cash balance of 5 percent. Normal ERISA regulations apply to this company.

2. Phil Johnson returns to the consultant 10 years after the initial consultation. He wants a reassessment of the defined benefit plan given the following information:

- The profitability and debt position of Johnson Pharmaceuticals remain similar to 10 years ago.
- The average age of the workforce is now 52 years old.
- The percentage of retired lives is now 45 percent.
- The pension plan currently has $140 million in assets and is now 10 percent underfunded.
- The actuarial rate has been adjusted upward to 8 percent.
- The trustees have not altered the previous minimum cash balance mandate.
- Johnson wants to eliminate the underfunded status as quickly as possible with half of the shortfall being made up in a two $4 million dollar contributions—one occurring in one month and the second occurring one year from that contribution.

A. What should be used as the return objective?

The fund's assets now have a required return of at least 8 percent to meet the actuarially determined growth in PBO. Johnson's desire for rapid growth needs to be offset with the fund's risk tolerance.

B. What should be the fund's risk tolerance level? Provide three points of evidence for your answer.

The risk tolerance for Johnson Pharmaceuticals should now be adjusted to below average. This level is based upon its increased average age, increased percentage of retired lives, and underfunded status. The natural tendency is to increase the risk level to correct the underfunded status more quickly. However, this could worsen the underfunded status. A decreased risk tolerance is most appropriate.

C. Identify two specific constraints

The constraints for Johnson Pharmaceuticals have changed somewhat. The company still has a long time horizon although it has shortened due to the increased average age and the increase percentage of retired lives. Johnson Pharmaceuticals has moderate to low liquidity needs. It must maintain a minimum cash balance of 5 percent. Normal ERISA regulations apply to this company.

3. The Fisher Foundation was established by the estate of a wealthy industrial tycoon. Its sole purpose is to provide grants to improve literacy in low-income

demographics in Alabama. Its trustees are targeting a required return of 8 percent, which adds a 3 percentage point inflation adjustment on top of the 5 percent spending rule. The fund has assets totaling $75 million.

A. What should be the foundation's risk tolerance level?

The risk tolerance level for the Fisher Foundation is high because they have a time horizon that is presumed to be infinite. Further, the foundation is not contractually required to improve literacy levels in low-income demographics. This goal is their objective not their obligation.

B. What is the foundation's time horizon?

The time horizon for the Fisher Foundation is assumed to be infinite: The intention of the foundation is to exist in perpetuity and write grants to benefit low-income Alabamans.

4. The Eagle University Endowment was established with $75 million dollars. The endowment has two major goals: to build a $25 million dollar library and to provide scholarships to environmental science majors. The environmental science program is not reliant upon this endowment to remain viable. The endowment has opted to use a simple spending rule with a 5 percent spending rate. Those responsible for the endowment intend to adjust the required return by an allotment for education inflation, which they assume to be 5 percent.

A. What should be used as the return objective?

The return objective for the Eagle University Endowment should be 10 percent, which incorporates the 5 percent simple spending rule and the adjustment for 5 percent education inflation.

B. What should be the fund's risk tolerance level?

The risk tolerance should be above average due to the fact that the environmental sciences department does not rely on this endowment to remain viable. The long-term nature of an endowment also gives the endowment an ability to have high risk tolerance.

C. Identify two specific constraints.

The primary constraint that is unique to the Eagle University Endowment is the capital project. The Endowment's trustees need to maintain unusual liquidity until after that project is completed. They may even subdivide the assets into two pools: one to fund the capital project and the other to fund the long-term goals of the endowment, which enable a higher risk tolerance level.

5. Omaha Life, a regional life insurance company, provides all forms of life insurance coverage. The company's actuaries have calculated a 4.5 percent minimum return to meet its obligations. Omaha Life has $950 million in assets and $750 million in known liabilities.

A. What should be used as the return objective?

For Omaha Life's core holdings, the required return is at least 4.5 percent. These core holdings will comprise $750 million. The remaining $200 million of Omaha Life's assets can be allocated with the goal of maximizing the return potential. The firm will hopefully use this portion, called the surplus, to compete with other regional life insurance vendors by lowering premiums.

B. What should be the risk tolerance level?

The risk tolerance level for Omaha Life is low for the core holdings and moderate for the surplus holdings. They have a very low tolerance for loss in their core holdings because these assets must be used to satisfy insurance payment needs. They can accept higher risk in the surplus holdings because its purpose is not to meet immediate cash flow needs but rather to strengthen the insurance company's competitive position through maximizing the return potential.

C. Identify one constraint relative to Omaha Life's liabilities and one relative to its regulatory framework.

Omaha Life should pay special attention to matching the maturity of the assets in their core holdings with the assumed maturity of the liabilities they have estimated. This constraint will best enable them to meet their liabilities when they are due. The company should also pay special attention to maintaining its Asset Valuation Reserve. The AVR must be met to avoid a violation of their regulatory requirements.

Chapter 8. Fiduciary Duties and Responsibilities of Portfolio Managers

1. What are the proscriptive duties to which fiduciary portfolio managers may be bound?

Fiduciary portfolio managers are bound by twin proscriptive duties of loyalty and care. They must be loyal to the investors on whose behalf they are acting, while taking the proper care expected of such a fiduciary. Fiduciaries must avoid conflicts of interest or disclose such conflicts to their clients.

2. What are the fiduciary duties by which trust managers must abide?

Trust managers, as well as pension plan managers, are fiduciaries. As such, they must abide by all fiduciary duties. Specifically, they must also maximize the value of the assets they are managing within reasonable risk limits. This requirement usually means that trust managers must ensure that the assets are invested in diversified portfolios.

3. Are broker-dealers fiduciaries, and if so, what specific duties must they perform?

Broker-dealers, who do not offer active advice, are not fiduciaries, except in some states in the United States. They do, however, have to abide by other regulations that could subject them to quasifiduciary duties. These regulations include the suitability requirements that brokers must ensure are met when investing their clients' money. Suitability requirements require that brokers understand the kinds of risks that their clients are willing to tolerate. This requirement dictates the type of investments a broker is allowed to recommend or even purchase for their clients.

4. Should mutual fund managers be classified as fiduciaries? If so, what are the practical implications of being fiduciaries for their fee structure?

Because mutual fund managers are investment advisers, they are fiduciaries to their clients. They must avoid any appearance of a conflict of interest. Also, their fee structure must be reasonable. The courts, however, have made winning a lawsuit challenging the reasonableness of the fees almost impossible. These actions have not stopped many academic critics from trying to reform this area of the law.

5. What is soft dollar brokerage and why does it present a potential breach of fiduciary duties?

Soft dollar transactions occur when a broker pays a third party to provide an investment manager with research services. The investment manager then executes the portfolio's transactions with the broker at higher brokerage commissions. This type of arrangement could be a conflict of interest, but some scholars contend that it is a quality control mechanism.

6. Are hedge fund managers bound by fiduciary duties to their investors? Explain.

Hedge fund managers are currently unregulated by Federal laws and state laws allow them to contract out of the fiduciary duty obligation. As such, they are free to engage in certain financial and accounting strategies that would be considered breaches of fiduciary duties if initiated by mutual fund managers.

Chapter 9. The Role of Asset Allocation in the Investment Decision-Making Process

1. Compare and contrast the historic approach to the scenario approach in generating inputs to the asset allocation process.

Using the historic approach to generate inputs to the asset allocation process is a straightforward matter of presuming the risk-return relationships including standard deviations and correlations will persist into the future. Thus, an investor will use these risk-return relationships inputs into the asset allocation projection. By contrast, scenario forecasting entails assessing what the likely economic environment might look like over the next three to five years with respect to likely returns and risks. An investor also needs to determine the probability of occurrence for each of these scenarios over the forecast period.

2. How does the status of the secular market (bull or bear) affect the difficulty of implementing a TAA strategy?

During secular bull markets, cyclical bull markets last longer and show greater returns, while the bear markets have more limited downside risk and shorter duration. In contrast, during secular bear markets, cyclical bull markets are of shorter and limited duration and the bear markets are more severe and last longer. During the secular bear market, TAA activity has a greater margin for error in positioning and repositioning a portfolio. In short, the odds of success are greater in secular bear markets.

3. Describe how the risk premium approach provides perspective on the relative attractiveness of asset classes.

Risk premium valuation begins by first comparing the equity class return as measured by, for example, an earnings yield (earnings to price) over a longer period of time. It then entails looking at how that metric compares with a less risky asset such as Baa bonds or Treasury bills, which are generally considered to be a "riskless asset."

4. Compare the underlying "concept" driving the different technical indicators. Describe an example of each.

Market practitioners consider technical indicators to be "internal" because analysts develop such indicators from the internal action of the market. One major category of indicators falls under the heading of momentum, which assumes that underlying forces are favorable and propel the market higher by a growing consensus recognizing this favorable underpinning. The 200-day moving average of the S&P 500 is a good example of this category of indicators. In contrast, mean reversion assumes that stocks have an underlying value that represents a floor on the price of the stock or universe of stocks and will rebound from that price level. Volatility, as measured by standard deviation or the VIX indicator, is a good example of this category of indicators.

Chapter 10. Asset Allocation Models

1. Adopting the Markowitz assumptions means that investors either have quadratic utility or believe all investments follow a normal distribution. Markowitz acknowledges that neither of these assumptions is likely to reflect the preferences or beliefs of real investors. Identify and discuss one shortcoming of assuming quadratic utility and a normal distribution.

Quadratic utility implies that above some level of return, investors prefer less wealth. This implication is contrary to common sense and to Assumption 2 of the Markowitz model. Assuming investment returns are distributed normally simplifies the analysis because normal distributions can be completely described by only two parameters—the mean and variance. Although much research effort has been devoted to investigating the empirical distribution of stock prices, no consensus has emerged. The other problem with assuming some other distribution controls the evolution of prices is that no model as general as the Markowitz model has been proposed.

2. Investors who want to construct Markowitz mean-variance optimal portfolios face several challenges. List and discuss two of these challenges.

The first challenge in constructing Markowitz mean-variance optimal portfolios is estimating future correlations between assets. Historical correlations are available but they require assuming the future is going to be like the past. The second challenge is providing the portfolio construction algorithm with all relevant information. Illiquid assets such as private equity are attractive to an optimizer because they have low correlations with other assets. These assets could be modeled by reducing the expected return but the magnitude of such reduction is subjective in nature. The third challenge is that optimal portfolios are poorly diversified. Portfolio managers constrained by Prudent Investor Acts or ERISA must meet a standard of diversification that is rarely satisfied by mean-variance optimal portfolios. The fourth challenge is that small changes in estimated inputs cause large changes in the optimal portfolio weights. When investors rebalance to match the new allocations, they incur transactions costs.

3. The U.S. wealth portfolio is used to gain insight into how U.S. investors allocate their assets. Explain why the market value of the wealth portfolio's asset classes is a reasonable proxy for the collective optimal portfolio. Cite one example of why investors might be motivated to change their asset allocation.

When investors demand one asset class more than a second asset class, the price of the first asset class rises relative to the second. One example of how changes in preferences would be reflected in the aggregate wealth portfolio is to imagine that because prospects for stocks are better than bonds, investors prefer stocks over bonds. Investors would then sell bonds (lowering their market value) and buy stocks (increasing their market value). The relative market values, therefore, reflect how investors have allocated their funds.

4. The research presented in this chapter compares how U.S. investors have allocated their funds with how a Markowitz portfolio would allocate among the same asset classes. Identify and discuss two differences between the actual U.S. wealth portfolio and the Markowitz portfolio.

Between 1977 and 2010 the U.S. wealth portfolio averaged about 12 percent in "other liabilities" while the Markowitz portfolio placed substantially more in this asset class with every portfolio with more than a minimal amount of risk. In the U.S. wealth portfolio, equity averaged 11 percent while the Markowitz portfolios with more than a minimal amount of risk allocated nothing to this asset class. The U.S. wealth portfolio averaged about 7 percent in U.S. government Treasury bonds. The Markowitz portfolio was much more enthusiastic about this asset class, allocating about 30 percent to Treasuries in all but the riskiest portfolios.

5. Portfolio rebalancing is necessary to keep every portfolio as close as practical to its original risk-return specifications. Perold and Sharpe (1988) classify all rebalancing strategies into four types. Identify each of these four strategies and discuss how they behave in a trendless market.

The buy-and-hold strategy never rebalances. In a trendless market, the buy-and-hold strategy provides little return relative to other strategies. Constant mix strategies buy low and sell high, outperforming the buy-and-hold strategy. Constant proportion strategies are the opposite, buying high and selling low. Consequently, this strategy does poorly in trendless markets. Finally, option-based strategies are horizon-based and do poorly in a trendless market just as equity options require a premium and do not provide much expected return when the price of the underlying does not change.

Chapter 11. Preference Models in Portfolio Construction and Evaluation

1. What are the possible combinations of assumptions on individual's preferences and on the statistical distribution of asset (portfolio) returns that may justify a simple mean-variance approach to portfolio optimization such as in Equation 11.5?

The two such combinations of assumptions on individual's preferences and assumptions on the statistical process of portfolio/asset returns are: (1) when the investor has preferences described by a quadratic utility function, provided her wealth does not exceed the bliss point; and (2) when the investor has preferences described by negative exponential utility and the joint distribution of asset returns implies that terminal wealth has a log normal distribution. Otherwise, more generally, mean-variance preferences are either assumed to hold in an ad hoc way or can at best be interpreted as local (second-order Taylor) approximations to properly defined utility functions.

2. Why is computing the standard (small) risk measures CARA(W) and CRRA(W) in the case of mean-variance preferences impossible? Explain the source from which deficiencies stem.

Standard, ad hoc mean-variance preferences fail to derive from properly defined utility functions that map either terminal wealth or interim consumption in some utility index (welfare level). Trivially, because ad hoc mean-variance preferences are based on severing the link between wealth and utility, computing any functions, such as CARA(W) and CRRA(W) that depend on wealth, is impossible. Of course, exceptions to this general result exist: (1) when the investor has preferences described by a quadratic utility function, provided her wealth does not exceed the bliss point; and (2) when the investor has preferences described by negative exponential utility and the joint distribution of asset returns implies that terminal wealth has a log normal distribution.

3. Describe the intuition underlying Klibanoff, Marinacci, and Mukerji's (2005) smooth ambiguity-averse preferences. Explain how these smooth preferences can nest both Gilboa and Schmeidler's (1989) max-min type, multiple priors preferences and the standard subjective expected utility case.

Under Klibanoff, Marinacci, and Mukerji (KMM) preferences, the ambiguity of a risky act or decision is characterized by a set $\wp = \{P_1, ..., P_n\}$ of subjectively plausible cumulative probability distributions. Letting W denote the random variable distributed as P_j, $j = 1, ..., n$, based on her subjective information, the decision maker associates a distribution $(q_1, ..., q_n)$ over $\wp$, where q_j is the subjective probability of P_j being the true distribution of W. The resulting preferences have the representation $\sum_{j=1}^{n} q_j \zeta\left(\int u(W) dP_j\right)$, where is an increasing real-valued function, whose shape describes the investor's attitude towards ambiguity. The role ζ of is crucial. If ζ were linear, the criterion would simply reduce to (S)EU maximization with respect to the combination of the probabilities qs and possible distributions $P_j s$. When ζ is not linear, one cannot combine qs and $P_j s$ to construct a reduced probability distribution. A concave ζ will reflect ambiguity aversion, in the sense that it places a larger weight on poor expected u-utility realizations. When $\zeta(\cdot)$ becomes infinitely concave, MPP obtains as a limiting case.

4. Why is a dynamic model of risky asset returns such as a Markov switching model likely to bring out the power of smooth ambiguity preferences to improve realized performance?

Markov switching models are useful to model time variation in higher-order moments of terminal wealth or portfolio returns. Moreover, they often produce flexible semiparametric approximations to many kinds of densities, in which rich dynamics in the tails may be captured. Therefore, in back-testing exercises, the preferences attach the highest weights to forecasting the time variation in higher-order moments and/or in the tail of densities that may offer a superior chance to obtain effective realized performances under Markov switching models.

Chapter 12. Portfolio Construction with Downside Risk

1. Give several shortcomings of the Markowitz paradigm and provide a rationale to account for downside risk in portfolio optimization.

The Markowitz paradigm has several shortcomings. First, the Markowitz approach to portfolio optimization is static. Second, the approach is highly sensitive to its inputs. For example, taking expected returns and variances for granted, the Markowitz paradigm often gives rise to highly concentrated portfolios that provide disappointing performance ex-post. Third, the employed risk metric has been subject to some criticism because volatility treats both positive and negative deviations as risk. This characteristic is at odds with investors' risk perception that is mainly governed by downside events. Of course, in a world of normally distributed returns or for a quadratic utility investor, this distinction is meaningless. However, both assumptions are not sustained in practice.

2. Discuss several downside risk metrics.

The classical downside risk metric is value at risk (VaR), which is nothing but a quantile of the return distribution. While VaR represents a return threshold that is not breached with a relatively high probability, it is not informative with respect to potential dangers embedded in the tail of the return distribution. Addressing this question the conditional VaR gives the conditional expected return of the return distribution below a certain threshold. Likewise, lower partial moments seek to evaluate a return distribution below a given threshold. For example, semideviation gives the mean downside deviation from the mean of the return distribution, while the semivariance gives the variance arising from mere downside events. Going beyond mean-variance, the skewness metric also attempts to capture the tail behavior of the return distribution. Besides turning to other risk metrics in the classical optimization approach, one can also accommodate downside-averse risk preferences within the employed utility function. Finally, one can compute a return-distribution-free metric such as the maximum drawdown, which simply gives the maximum loss one could have suffered over a given period of time.

3. Describe the employed methodology of comparing different downside metrics in portfolio construction.

The effectiveness of the different downside risk optimizations is evaluated in two settings. The first setting assumes perfect foresight of expected returns in order to isolate the forecasting of risk and return. Because this knowledge is unavailable in practice, this assumption is dropped in the second setting to obtain a reasonable reality check. Judging the optimization outcome involves considering the degree to which one can exploit the spread between the benchmark and the optimal solution given perfect foresight of risk and return. Also, hit rates of whether the optimization is beating the benchmark in terms of downside risk are computed.

4. What are the main findings and implications of the empirical study presented in this chapter for portfolio management?

The main findings of the empirical tests for portfolio management suggest that some downside risk metrics allow for successful downside risk minimization of a European equity portfolio in the last two decades, even in the absence of perfect foresight. Conversely, metrics such as skewness are rather useless in that respect. Also, in many cases mean-variance optimization is quite close to the other strategies in terms of downside risk. Hence, European equity may still be too symmetric to drive a wedge between these different optimization procedures.

Chapter 13. Asset Allocation with Downside Risk Management

1. To diversify across risk factors may lead to better portfolio diversification and lower downside risk than allocating across asset classes. While to allocate across principal components would be a theoretically superior approach to risk factor diversification, practitioners typically prefer to use fundamental risk factors. Explain at least two challenges of principal component analysis and enumerate four of the key risk factors commonly used by practitioners.

Using principal component analysis involves several challenges. First, principal components are not easily "investable." A principal component may be presented as a linear combination of long/short weights on securities, but most investors have short-sale restrictions and other institutional constraints preventing them from directly investing in such long/short portfolios. Second, principal components can be highly unstable, which prevents strategic asset allocators from using them. Third, principal components are not always intuitive. Linking their behavior to observed macro variables is often difficult. In practice, asset allocators seek to diversify across the following risk factors: interest rates (duration), spreads, slope, equity risk, value, growth, momentum, currencies, liquidity, and volatility.

2. Duration represents a security's sensitivity to changes in interest rates, in other words, a security's exposure to the interest rate risk factor. Explain two ways to measure duration and recommend the preferred methodology.

A regression between a security's returns and changes in interest rates provides a "backward looking" estimate of duration. As an alternative, pricing models provide a current estimate of a security's duration based on its cash flows. Durations derived from pricing models provide a superior estimate because regression analysis ignores the fact that duration changes with the passage of time (by definition).

3. Discuss three reasons that risk factor decompositions often show a substantial allocation to the equity risk factor.

Risk factor decompositions can show a surprisingly high percentage of the portfolios risk is attributed to the equity risk factor. This high percentage can be explained by three components. First, most asset classes, such as real estate and private equity, contain indirect exposure to the equity risk factor. Second, the equity risk factor is more volatile than other risk factors, such as interest rates and spread. Third, equity risk correlates with other risk factors, especially in times of crises. The correlation between corporate spreads and equities during large market drawdowns provides a good example of the high correlation between equities and other risk factors in times of crisis.

4. Explain why the decision to hedge tail risk may change the asset allocation decision.

Just as people tend to drive faster with safer cars, hedging tail risk reduces exposure to large losses, and therefore may allow investors to invest a larger proportion of their portfolio in risk assets. To analyze the cost-benefit tradeoff of tail risk hedging, investors should take into account the increased risk premium earned from a larger allocation to risk assets.

5. Provide another example of an indirect benefit of tail risk hedging.

During liquidity/"risk off" crises, investors who are "long" a tail hedge may monetize their position to take advantage of opportunities to buy undervalued assets. During such crises, several distressed sellers are prepared to take substantial losses in order to meet their liquidity needs. This creates opportunities for those with substantial liquidity from in-the-money hedges.

Chapter 14. Alternative Investments

1. Alternative investments can offer exposure to risk-return profiles not replicable by traditional asset classes. Discuss why this is the case for hedge funds.

Hedge funds enjoy a much wider regulatory freedom than traditional asset classes. Therefore, hedge funds can invest in complex derivatives and can use short selling and high levels of leverage. Accordingly, the universe of available hedge fund strategies is large, allowing investing in very different return drivers.

2. What should be considered when including private equity in asset allocation models?

Private equity is an asset class with very low transparency. Reported returns differ substantially for different sources. Therefore, appropriate benchmarks need to be used in asset allocation.

3. Why is using the Markowitz approach inappropriate for asset allocation with alternative investments?

Return distributions of alternative investments exhibit significant higher moments (i.e., skewness and kurtosis). By contrast, the Markowitz approach only takes mean and variance into account and thus leads to suboptimal asset allocation results.

4. What are the performance consequences when including alternative investments in the asset allocation?

Portfolios with alternative investment have significantly higher expected returns and exhibit lower risk as measured by the standard deviation, LPM, CVaR, or MaxDD. Hence, such portfolios experience higher Sharpe ratios and portfolio returns.

Chapter 15. Measuring and Managing Market Risk

1. Identify and discuss at least three different types of market risk.

The different types of market risk include equity risk, interest rate risk, property risk, foreign exchange risk, commodity price risk, and liquidity risk.

- *Equity risk* relates to equity (stock) prices. Several fundamental risk factors drive equity risk including growth expectations, interest rates, risk premia, and others.
- *Interest rate risk* relates to any interest-sensitive instrument such as bonds. Driving forces underlying this risk are changes in the expected interest rate and interest rate structure.
- *Property risk* involves the risk associated with real estate prices.
- *Foreign exchange risk* is associated with movements in the exchange rate of two currencies. Driving forces are fundamental factors such as the relative movement of interest rates in the underlying currencies and the trade balance of the respective countries.
- *Commodity price risk* is associated with commodity prices. Driving forces include fundamental risk factors associated with the expected demand and supply of specific commodities as well as their extraction or production costs.

- *Liquidity risk* is associated with adverse price changes when selling or buying a financial asset. One factor influencing this risk is the depth of the market.

2. What is meant by the mean-variance framework? Under the i.i.d. assumption, how does the return variance of a portfolio evolve over time? How is this related to what is empirically observed?

Only two parameters are required to describe a distribution under the mean-variance framework: the mean (μ) and the variance (σ^2) or the square root of the variance, namely, the standard deviation (σ). For a normal distribution, these two parameters are sufficient to characterize the whole distribution. Under the assumption of independently and identically distributed (i.i.d.) returns over time, the variance σ^2 of an asset's return increases linearly over time, which implies that the standard deviation increases by the square root of the time interval. From an empirical perspective, the following stylized facts hold: (1) returns follow a leptokurtic distribution (i.e., they are more peaked and have fatter tails than a normal distribution); (2) returns are serially correlated, especially over short time intervals; and (3) return volatility is clustered over time (i.e., periods with low volatility follow periods with high volatility).

3. What is the market model and what is its relation to market risk? What is the Fama-French model? Discuss some recent empirical findings regarding the Fama-French model.

The market model assumes that a single asset's return depends linearly on the return of the market portfolio. Moreover, an idiosyncratic factor forces the return to deviate randomly from this linear relationship. The market model builds on the i.i.d. assumption because the distribution of the idiosyncratic risk is assumed to be constant but has no serial dependence over time. Also assumed is no cross-sectional dependence in the idiosyncratic risk. On the basis of this assumption, a stock's individual risk can be separated into two components: market risk and idiosyncratic risk.

The Fama-French three-factor model includes the market risk factor complemented by a size and value factor. Recent empirical findings based on expected returns extracted by the implied cost of capital corroborate the Fama-French model, especially concerning the value effect.

4. What is VaR? Who uses VaR, and what are some alternative risk measures?

VaR represents a critical loss value for a given probability p in the sense that the probability that the realized loss will be higher than the VaR is p%. An alternative called benchmark VaR is related to the concept of the tracking error or the expected tail loss.

5. Define liquidity risk and discuss whether it is a relevant component in the overall riskiness of a portfolio.

When liquidating an asset, the most important cost component is the spread (i.e., the difference between the achievable transaction price and the fair price of the stock). If market liquidity is relatively low, selling or buying an asset can influence the market price. From an ex-ante perspective, the size of the price impact is unknown. This situation refers to liquidity risk. Liquidity risk is not negligible and its impact varies depending on order size and a stock's liquidity.

6. Define model risk and explain whether this is mainly a pure statistical problem or a management problem.

Model risk refers to the problem that risk assessment is biased either because analysts apply inappropriate models for measuring the risk or the model calibration (i.e., parameter estimation) is defective. The second problem is mainly a statistical issue whereas the first problem is more a management problem. As risk management models become increasingly complex, senior management should have at least an understanding of the most important risk factors driving the risk position of their institutions.

Chapter 16. Measuring and Managing Credit and Other Risks

1. Identify the first methodology applied to estimate default in a prediction model and describe its weaknesses,

The first methodology used to estimate default in a prediction model was multivariate discriminant analysis (MDA). When applied to the default prediction problems, the two basic assumptions of MDA are often violated. These restrictive assumptions are: (1) the independent variables included in the model are multivariate normally distributed; and (2) the group dispersion matrices (or variance-covariance matrices) are equal across the failing and the nonfailing group. Moreover, in MDA models, the standardized coefficients cannot be interpreted in the same manner as the slopes of a regression equation and hence do not indicate the relative importance of the different variables.

2. Explain the benefits of using a logit methodology to develop default prediction models.

From a statistical point of view, logit regression seems to fit well the characteristics of the default prediction problem, where the dependent variable is binary (default/nondefault) and with the groups being discrete, nonoverlapping, and identifiable. The logit model yields a score between zero and one, which conveniently can be transformed in the probability of default (PD) of the client. Also, the estimated coefficients can be interpreted separately as the importance or significance of each of the independent variables in the explanation of the estimated PD.

3. Discuss the approaches that can be used to quantify operational risk under Basel II.

The Basel II rules on operational risk were first released in 2004 and then revised in 2010. These rules allow banks to measure operational risks using a Standardized or an Advanced Measurement Approach (AMA).

4. What is the difference between risk capacity and risk appetite? Why is distinguishing between the two concepts important?

Risk capacity (or risk tolerance) defines the minimum expected return and the maximum acceptable risk of the institution. Risk appetite describes the desired expected return and the desired acceptable risk. Distinguishing between risk capacity and risk appetite is important for several reasons. First, these two concepts differ substantially. Hence, confusing them could lead to generating uncertainty around what is possible and what is desired. Second, each concept has a specific time horizon. While risk capacity is a long-term statement, risk appetite should change frequently adapting to the market and economic situation.

5. What is the main objective of ERM?

Ideally, a good Enterprise Risk Management (ERM) framework should be able to summarize all risks into one metric: the optimal level of available capital.

6. How is risk appetite defined?

For a bank, risk appetite is defined as the maximum risk the bank is willing to accept in executing its chosen business strategy and to protect itself against events that may have an adverse impact on its profitability, capital base, or share price. In order to manage risk efficiently, quantifying risk appetite with the most appropriate and advanced tools is an extremely important factor in determining a bank's success.

Chapter 17. Trading Strategies, Portfolio Monitoring and Rebalancing

1. Discuss the main reasons for rebalancing assets in a financial portfolio.

Rational investors may want to trade in financial markets and adjust their financial portfolios for many reasons. For example, one reason concerns market price movements. With market movements, relative prices change and the portfolio proportions are modified in a direction that may not be optimal. Another reason for rebalancing assets concerns the modification of individual characteristics such as personal wealth, income, and preferences. These changes imply a revision in the investor's optimal portfolio. A third reason is new information, expectations, and learning, suggesting a revision of the optimal target portfolio. A fourth reason is the passing of time, making previous portfolio positions no longer optimal as in the case of portfolio insurance and life-cycle investments.

2. Explain the effects of fixed and proportional trading costs on optimal asset allocation.

In absence of transaction costs, the current portfolio could be immediately and continuously reset at the optimal level. In the case of proportional trading costs, the optimal portfolio is the result of an optimization, taking into account the goals of the investments (e.g., consumption, wealth, and returns) as well as the costs of implementing the trades. As a result, the optimal allocation is substituted by a no-trade region delimited by optimal boundaries. If the current portfolio is inside the region, no trade is required. If it pierces the boundaries, an immediate trade is made to keep the portfolio inside or at the boundaries. In the case of fixed costs, the breaking of a boundary implies a lump sum trade toward the (inner) optimal level. With fixed and proportional costs, the no-trade region contains the inner boundaries where the portfolio has to be reset as soon as it strays from the optimal region.

3. Discuss the problem of optimal rebalancing with respect to a given benchmark portfolio.

The distance from a given benchmark portfolio is measured by the tracking error volatility (i.e., the volatility of the difference between the current portfolio $w(t)$ and the benchmark $w^*(t)$). A high tracking error implies a cost in terms of suboptimal diversification. At the same time, the sale of the current portfolio and the purchase of the optimal one create costs in proportion of the absolute distance $|w(t + 1) - w(t)|$. Optimal rebalancing must find a tradeoff between the costs of erroneously tracking the target (measured by a parameter of "tracking error aversion") and the costs of trading it against current positions, measured by the market transaction costs. As in the case of absolute trading strategies, even in this case a no-trade region defines the optimal policy.

4. Describe the most popular rules of portfolio rebalancing and discuss the relative merits of each.

Several rebalancing rules are available for private and institutional investors. The simplest one is "time rebalancing," in which the portfolio managers rebalances toward a given target (e.g., constant mix portfolio) periodically (monthly, quarterly, or yearly). A different class is "fixed rebalancing," which is implemented whenever the distance (for each asset) between current portfolio and the target is (in absolute value) greater than a fixed percentage. "Proportional rebalancing" requires a trade when the relative distance between the portfolio and the target (in term of the target allocation) is (in absolute value) greater than a given percentage.

Another rule ("probability rebalancing") uses as a trigger the excess absolute return of each asset with respect to its volatility. According to the empirical analysis, no single rebalancing rule is superior to all the others and to buy and hold under all market regimes (up-down-no trend; high-medium-low volatility). Moreover, with high frequency monitoring (daily or weekly), the best results are obtained with large trigger parameters (e.g., 15 percent) but in the case of low frequency monitoring (yearly), narrow boundaries (e.g., 1 percent) are preferred. In general, fixed and proportional rebalancing seems to provide superior returns (also adjusted for risk) with respect to buy and hold as well as the popular time rebalancing.

5. Explain the functioning of two popular trading strategies, portfolio insurance and life-cycle investments, aimed at protecting the portfolio.

Portfolio insurance is a class of strategies in which the target portfolio is continuously adjusted in order to maximize the probability to achieve an investment value at or above a given floor level at time T. This strategy implies rebalancing the risky component of the portfolio in order not to jeopardize the stated goal. In the case of "constant proportion portfolio insurance," this component must be in proportion (in terms of the multiplier m) of the distance between the portfolio value and the floor value: the greater (shorter) the distance, the greater (lower) is the risky exposure. This implies a convex relationship between the portfolio value and the risky asset price as well as a "momentum" rebalancing rule suggesting to buy when the market goes up and to sell when the market goes down.

Life-cycle investment is a long-run strategy in which the investor must gradually reduce the risk exposure as long as he approaches the target date (usually retirement). Conventional wisdom suggests using the rule: $w^* = 100 - age$. The strategy could be implemented through periodic switches from more risky funds to safer portfolios or just investing in a target date fund with time-decreasing risk. The stated goal is not only to take profit from the long-term growth of stocks but also to preserve, over the lifetime, the investor's accumulated wealth, avoiding the unpleasant, last-minute surprises from adverse market movements. The rationale supporting the strategy is in a few "postulates" that fed a long and lively debate: the presence of a significant risk premium of stocks, the reduced long-run volatility of risky assets caused by mean reversion (so called time-diversification effect) and the human capital to be included as personal wealth in the analysis.

Chapter 18. Effective Trade Execution

1. Explain the advantages and risks of algorithmic trading.

Algorithmic trading (AT) identifies the usage of several trading instructions or algorithms that involve computer-based implementation. Basically, an algorithm is a set of decision rules and strategies employed to fulfill a specific trading goal or achievement. High frequency trading (HFT) is the natural evolution of AT and represents the fast implementation of trading algorithms. The basic advantage of AT and HFT is a general improvement of the liquidity and reduction of the transaction costs. Conversely, AT cannot be viewed as separate from market competition and fragmentation. In fact, the increased degree of competition among exchanges by lowering fees and introducing a competitive fee structure will determine the need to use AT to choose the best execution venue. A key driver is the latency reduction, which allows for the ability to capture profit opportunities within a very short time span and reduces the price risk associated with trades. The disadvantage of AT is given by the displacement of human actions in the trading activity. The use of fast computing schemes introduces an adverse selection effect because human-based traders can be evicted from the market. Another critical point is given by the strong investment needed to trespass the technological barrier formed by fast computers and colocation services in the proximity of exchanges.

2. Discuss the most useful instructions that are widely employed in high frequency trading and the role of flash orders.

Some of the key instructions employed in high frequency trading are given by the following:

- Fill or kill (FOK). This instruction ensures that either the order gets executed immediately in full or not at all.
- Immediate or cancel (IOC). This instruction inserts a rigid priority command such as any portion of the order that is not executed immediately is cancelled from the order book. Such instruction can be associated to both market and limit order.
- All or none (AON). With this instruction, the trader forces a 100 percent completion requirement on the order. This type of instruction may require some time before the full execution.

According to the time duration of presence on the order book, orders can be classified as:

- Good til date (GTD). In this case, the order is active until the end of the trading session at the prespecified date.
- Good til cancel (GTC). With this instruction, the order remains active until the user specifically cancels it.
- Good after time date (GAT). In this case, the order allows the trader to choose the time at which it becomes active. This type of order is useful when the trader needs to spread the order during a given period such as a day or a week.

Flash orders can be displayed only for a very limited amount of time and allow some type of traders to take advantage of National Market System (NMS) regulation to get the best possible price among all the trading venues. This type of order is under discussion because of the front running phenomenon associated to this practice.

3. Describe the role of transaction costs in conditioning the design of optimal trading strategies.

Broadly speaking, transaction costs can be of two types: implicit and explicit. Explicit transaction costs include commission and fees whereas implicit transaction costs are related with the execution opportunity and delay costs. These costs can also be classified according to fixed and variable or visible and transparent. In general, visible costs cannot be managed because they are associated with the commission and fees side, while nontransparent cost component can be managed according to the design of a proper execution strategy.

Wagner and Glass (2003) propose an expanded measure of transaction costs. The design of an optimal execution strategy basically implies a cost minimization procedure. In this context, the idea is to find the trade intensity that minimizes the price impact and the timing risk of trade execution. Almgren and Chriss (2000) illustrate the cost minimization process via the construction of the efficient trading frontier (ETF), which allows traders to choose the intensity according to the preferences of the trader/investor. Kissel and Glantz (2003) and Kissel and Malamut (2006) demonstrate the cost minimization strategy via a simple approach that explicitly identifies the timing risk and obtains the trade intensity as the solution of the cost minimization process.

4. Discuss the role of slicing an order.

Order slicing is a trading procedure that allows the splitting of a large order into a subset of smaller-sized orders with the goal of minimizing the price impact. This procedure can be applied to iceberg orders where a sequential slice of a large order allows making visible to the market only a fraction of the total order. When that fraction gets executed, the instruction allows making visible another portion of the order until when the full iceberg order gets completely executed. The slicing approach can be applied to multiple venues. In this case, the slicing can be released and funneled sequentially to each of the trading venue. The interesting aspect of the slicing approach is given by the possibility for the trader to keep under control the amount of the order to be issued to a specific or to multiple trading venues.

Chapter 19. Market Timing Methods and Results

1. Define the term asymmetries of returns.

Asymmetries in the returns correspond to identifying and exploiting investment opportunities where the risk/reward relationship is asymmetric, so that the potential profit is higher than the potential loss or the probability of a profit is higher than the probability of a loss of the same magnitude, or a combination of the above. Asymmetry can be analyzed into two basic directions: (1) by the frequency of positive versus negative returns and (2) by the magnitude of positive versus negative returns.

2. Identify and describe three factors that may affect implementing trading strategies.

Three basic factors that may affect implementing trading strategies are:

- *The mechanism of arbitrage.* Market timing strategies are implicitly grounded in the importance of exploiting arbitrage opportunities. Arbitrage opportunities emerge under the spectrum on the convergence to the long run or to the extreme price differential. However, the arbitrage opportunities are fewer in the extreme circumstances where all arbitrageurs are fully invested and the profits have to be shared by a pool of participants.
- *The role of leverage.* Leverage in quantitative funds is compulsory. Such funds tend to earn small steady gains that they can enhance through leverage.
- *The day-of-the-week effect.* Specific days of the week, specifically Monday, Wednesday, and Friday, have certain properties that help investors implement trading strategies. Those specific days are known as the weekend

effect or closedmarket effect (Monday-Friday), which are the days following holidays or weekends. The Wednesday effect confirms the existence of several trading patterns on trades, while returns exhibit predictive ability and returns from Wednesday to Wednesday are positively correlated. Returns on Fridays are slightly skewed to the right based on a substantial decrease in trading activity and liquidity. However, when arbitrageurs and investors do not participate in the market, this leads to high levels of volatility, which, in turn, could lead to creating opportunities for applying profitable arbitrage strategies.

3. Name two indicators based on empirical distributions that can be used to identify the market trend and indicate the main advantages of these indicators.

The two indicators that can be used to identify the market trend are the omega ratio and the stochastic dominance indicator. The main advantage of empirical distributions is the ability to identify trading strategies that are nonparametric in nature and to incorporate the entire set of data. The omega ratio employs all statistical moments (return, variance, skewness, and kurtosis) of the distribution and thus leads to a more precise evaluation of a strategy's "alpha." Stochastic dominance is defined as a ranking scale over possible outcomes between two assets taking into consideration their probability distribution function. The comparative advantage of stochastic dominance theory is the ability to use risk evaluation and create accurate results under the minimum possible quantity of information.

4. What is a pairs trading strategy?

A pairs trading strategy is a market neutral strategy that uses the concept of convergence/divergence of prices between related securities in formulating a long/short positions, where one security is perceived to be undervalued and the other security is viewed to be overvalued. The success of the strategy depends on the comovement of the underlying assets and the degree of mean reversion. Implementing the strategy requires simultaneously investing in a long and short position where investors take positions based on a timing signal. Identifying the long and short positions can be achieved through several methods. The original methodology followed by practitioners assumes that if a price divergence occurs by more than two historical standard deviations, then a trade unwinds.

Chapter 20. Evaluating Portfolio Performance: Reconciling Asset Selection and Market Timing

1. Using Carhart's (1997) multifactor model, why is neither using alpha suited to measure market timing skills nor using alpha with a quadratic term suited to measure asset selection skills?

Under the Carhart multifactor model, the alpha is calculated as $\alpha_{4F} = \overline{R} - R_f - \beta_1(\overline{R}_m - R_f) - \beta_2\overline{SMB} - \beta_3\overline{HML} - \beta_4\overline{UMD}$ (Equation 20.6). In the presence of market timing, the sensitivity coefficients β_1 up to β_4 vary over time as the portfolio manager performs active bets on the market returns, the size premium, the value premium or the momentum premium. By considering constant betas, this specification does not have the power to reflect a market timing behavior. Consequently, α_{4F} cannot market timing skills.

The Carhart model with market timing is calculated as $R_t = \alpha_{4F-TM} + R_f + \beta_1(R_{mt} - R_f) + \beta_2 SMB_t + \beta_3 HML_t + \beta_4 UMD_t + \gamma r_{mt}^2 + \varepsilon_t$ (Equation 20.21). If gamma is positive, then the global portfolio performance is equal to α_{4F-TM} + *correction for market timing*, where the correction is positive under all types of corrections proposed in the literature. Thus, a fund with neutral performance must have α_{4F-TM} + *correction for market timing* = 0, which induces $\alpha_{4F-TM} < 0$. Such a negative alpha does not mean that selectivity has been bad, as the portfolio manager exhibits no selectivity at all. Consequently, the alpha cannot be interpreted as the identifier of selectivity. Under this model, there is no possibility to disaggregate global performance and isolate market timing from asset selection skills.

2. Under the Treynor and Mazuy (1966) model, four adjustment methods have been proposed to integrate market timing and asset selection in a single, synthetic performance measure. Why are the three classical methods likely to leave a biased measure of performance?

The classical adjustment methods, namely the correction with market variance by Grinblatt and Titman (1994), the correction with market squared returns by Bollen and Busse (2004), and the correction with an option on the squared market return by Ingersoll, Spiegel, Goetzmann, and Welch (2007), all neglect the portfolio linear sensitivity to the market index, namely the portfolio beta, in the adjustment. Therefore, they implicitly consider that the passive portfolio corresponding to the active one has no directional exposure, thereby underestimating the impact of the option. Table 20.3 shows that the correction obtained with the option replication approach of Hübner (2010) has a much larger magnitude than the other ones for all cases.

3. Explain the reasoning underlying the replicating option adjustment method to the Treynor and Mazuy (1966) model and apply it to all possible patterns for the sign of the delta and the gamma.

Consider the case of positive market timing. Creating a self-financing investment strategy is possible consisting of buying a call option on the market index, creating a positive convexity in returns, and lending at the risk-free rate. The position involving a long call option written on this index has a positive delta and a positive gamma, and the delta of the position can be modified through the lending position. In principle, the possibility exists of finding an option whose time to maturity and moneyness match the sensitivities to the underlying index observed with the TM regression.

For a negative market timer, the positive beta—negative gamma position is replicated by a position involving a short put option with a positive delta and a negative gamma. If the portfolio is short the market (negative beta) with positive market timing (positive gamma), the replicating position involves going long on a put. Finally, a negative beta—negative gamma position induces a short call.

In case of a portfolio with no market direction (zero beta), the desired strategy involves a long straddle (long call + long put) to reproduce a positive gamma, and a short straddle otherwise.

4. Based on the empirical analysis of mutual funds in this chapter, discuss evidence that the intensity of market timing is related to portfolio performance.

Because the correction of alpha using the option replicating approach is rather large, a portfolio manager who chooses a large gamma will benefit from a large correction. As the intercept of the regression is not very negative, the sample results show a tendency to get an aggregate performance that is larger as the level of gamma increases. The left graphs of Figure 20.1 illustrate this pattern. As a matter of fact, the correlation between the gamma and the overall performance for positive market timers is positive and quite high (Table 20.5). Generally, this correlation is larger for positive than for negative market timers, especially when using daily data.

Chapter 21. Benchmarking

1. What is the objective of active portfolio management under benchmarking?

The objective of active portfolio management is to maximize the portfolio's expected return, or sometimes the investor's expected utility, subject generally to a more or less strict tracking error (TE) constraint. When the TE is tight, usually less than 5 percent on an annual basis, the portfolio beta measured against the benchmark is generally close to one.

2. Explain the terms "tracking error" and "information ratio."

The tracking error (TE) is the standard error (or volatility) of the random difference between the return on the managed portfolio and the return on a specified index or benchmark, computed over a given investment horizon. Some practitioners, however, define TE as the difference in returns between the portfolio and the benchmark. The information ratio (IR) is a measure of the relative performance of a portfolio with respect to its benchmark (i.e., its average excess return divided by its TE (defined as volatility)). IR generalizes the Sharpe ratio for which implicitly the benchmark is the riskless asset.

3. What is a symmetric incentive fee?

A symmetric compensation scheme implies that a manager receives a bonus if the portfolio return exceeds that of the benchmark, but is penalized if the opposite occurs. Asymmetric compensations generate bonuses only when the portfolio outperforms the benchmark and without penalties when the portfolio underperforms the benchmark.

4. Who is the principal and who is the agent in portfolio delegation?

The agent is the one who will make the actual portfolio decisions and therefore is the manager who will design and monitor the portfolio. The principal is the one who delegates the decisions to an agent, and therefore is the investor.

5. Explain whether benchmarking matters for asset prices.

The development of trading associated with passive investing implies an increased trading commonality among the constituents of frequently adopted benchmarks, as it has been actually observed (at least) in the United States since 1997. Such trading commonality induces increased systematic fluctuations in overall demand and in systematic market risk. Consequently, even well-diversified portfolios exhibit greater risk for all styles of portfolios, which, other things being equal, is detrimental to investors' welfare. The decrease in diversification benefits also implies lower, less appealing Sharpe ratios.

When a manager is rewarded according to fulcrum performance fees, the prices of the securities included in the benchmarks unambiguously increase and, consequently, the Sharpe ratios decline. This situation occurs because the managers are incentivized to tilt their portfolios towards benchmark securities. Under asymmetric schemes, however, the effects on prices and Sharpe ratios are more complex and ambiguous as the composition of the managers' portfolios depends crucially on their excess performance relative to their benchmarks and thus varies randomly.

6. What is an efficient index?

An efficient index is one that replicates an efficient portfolio. An efficient portfolio exhibits the lowest level of risk for a given expected return or yields the highest expected return for a given level of risk. In general, usual market indices are not optimal. The industry strives to propose and promote new benchmarks that may be optimal.

Chapter 22. Attribution Analysis

1. What are the potential pitfalls in the attribution model of Brinson et al. (1986) in interpreting the selection component as a measure of the manager's ability to select superior stocks?

The selection component in the attribution model of Brinson et al. (1986) reflects all deviations of the actual portfolio from the benchmark, regardless of the risk level. Because deviations from the risk level are usually associated with timing activities of the manager, the selection component gets polluted with components that should be measured as a timing effect.

2. If an investor's asset allocation has a major impact on the performance of the portfolio, why do various studies show that market timing does not work?

Market timing refers to the ability to anticipate future market movements. To use this skill, an investor needs proprietary information on the future state of the economy, which is information not yet priced into the market. Because market-wide information is usually public, obtaining such information is difficult and perhaps impossible, especially compared with obtaining security-specific information.

724   DISCUSSION QUESTIONS AND ANSWERS

3. What is the fundamental difference between timing as defined in the traditional Brinson model and characteristic timing as defined by Daniel et al. (1997)?

The Brinson model defines timing relative to a constant exposure to the risky asset classes, which is usually obtained from the investment plan. Daniel et al. (1997) define timing as changing the asset allocation relative to the previous period's exposure. The advantage of the method of Daniel et al. is that it better captures the time varying nature of risk premia.

4. The model of Daniel et al. (1997) controls for risk by creating characteristic-based benchmark portfolios. Similar to the Carhart (1999) model, the model uses size, book to market, and momentum as characteristics. Discuss the advantages and disadvantages of using the model developed by Daniel et al. versus Carhart.

The advantages of the Daniel et al. (1997) model over the Carhart (1999) model include: (1) adjusting for time-varying exposure to the underlying risk factors and (2) helping to identify the exact asset classes where outperformance has been achieved. The disadvantages of the Daniel et al. (1997) model over the Carhart (1999) model include: (1) requiring detailed data on portfolio holdings and (2) measuring risk exposure in discrete intervals based on the five categories for each characteristic.

5. Finance textbooks typically express concern about the existence of a unique solution for the IRR. Discuss whether this concern is justified for mutual funds and hedge funds.

The concern about the existence of a unique solution for the IRR is not justified for mutual funds and hedge funds. The rationale is because a unique IRR always exists when the portfolio values are positive, which is the case for both mutual funds and hedge funds.

Chapter 23. Equity Investment Styles

1. Contrast the key differences between determination of a stock's style and a fund's style.

A stock's style is determined by sorting on the basis of some predetermined ranking such as size and price to book (PB). However, more sophisticated methods of establishing growth-value orientation have gained prominence recently. There has been a move by index providers and academic studies to incorporate a wider range of variables in their determination of a stock's style in recognition of the fact that using a single valuation multiple indicates little about a stock's earnings history or potential. To establish whether a stock may be classified as a "growth" stock, some measure of growth or growth potential must be included. The subject (i.e., the stock) has no part to play in determining its designated style.

A fund's style is determined by its investment philosophy and investment process. The character of the portfolio and its inherent portfolio bias is determined by these factors, which in turn determine a fund's performance. A broader range of portfolio characteristics is now considered in the analysis of investment funds' styles. The behavioral aspect of investment management (i.e. where investors believe the best investment opportunities are to be found and how best to exploit these opportunities, should not be overlooked). The subject (i.e., the fund or fund manager) determines the style of the fund through portfolio selection and construction.

2. Discuss the ability to evaluate a growth fund without considering growth.

The key aim of a growth investor is to maximize fund returns by investing in companies with above average potential for earnings growth. There may be variations in how aggressively this aim is pursued but it is central to all growth funds. Growth investors do not search for stocks that are expensive on the basis of a valuation multiple. Instead, they search for stocks that meet their criteria in terms of growth potential and the price paid. The biggest risk for a growth fund is that the anticipated level of growth is not achieved and the premium rating of its stocks evaporates. With growth funds being the largest category of funds in the US equity market, classifying funds without considering growth is an anomaly. Prominent value investors such as Warren Buffet acknowledge that investors cannot determine value without considering growth and value. Value investors often describe their portfolio objectives as "growth and income." Therefore, evaluating either a growth or a value fund without taking account of growth is inadvisable.

3. Distinguish between RBSA and CBSA.

Both returns based style analysis (RBSA) and characteristics based style analysis (CBSA) give different information about a fund's portfolio. Yet, both still have a role to play in style analysis. The key difference is the type of information required to perform the analysis. In order to perform RBSA, only fund returns and relevant index returns are required as inputs to the style analysis model. In the case of CBSA, detailed portfolio holdings, or aggregate portfolio characteristics are required and this has been more difficult to acquire in the past. Comparative studies seem to favor CBSA over RBSA. However, the two approaches give different information and may be complementary.

The benefits of considering a fund from both perspectives should not be understated. Being aware of each model's strengths and weaknesses is useful to gain insights into a fund's true style characteristics. RBSA gives an indication of a fund's relationship to a range of indexes but only provides an "average" picture over a long time period. CBSA, based on portfolio holdings, shows what is actually held in a portfolio at a particular point in time. It shows a fund's preferred combination of income, growth, and valuation. RBSA plays a useful role for multisector funds where a single benchmark might be inappropriate. RBSA was initially popular because acquiring portfolio holdings was difficult and it only required returns data that was easier to obtain. The data required for CBSA analysis are more widely available today and there are a number of data providers who facilitate CBSA.

3. Discuss evidence associated with the outperformance of "otherwise equivalent benchmarks."

Otherwise equivalent benchmarks are benchmarks that represent the true investment universe of a fund. They possess the same risk-reward characteristics as the fund's underlying exposure. Many studies have highlighted the importance of identifying the right benchmark. If this cannot be achieved, then the quality of performance assessment must be questioned. Recent research underscores the importance of comparing like with like. Different benchmarks yield different outcomes even within the same study. Using actual portfolios rather than mimicking portfolios may capture constraints faced by fund managers and using actual investible indexes may be of more practical use than factor models, which may be difficult to replicate in practice.

Evidence associated with the outperformance of otherwise equivalent benchmarks is mixed. Some studies conclude that there may be some evidence of outperformance before fees are levied but these excess returns are swallowed up by investment costs. If a fund is outperforming its benchmark after fees, then it is adding value but the "average" fund is often found to underperform its benchmark once all costs are taken into account.

Chapter 24. Use of Derivatives

1. Discuss the main mistakes to avoid in options investing.

When investing in options, investors should avoid several mistakes. One mistake is to focus on buying inexpensive options. An inexpensive option does not necessarily indicate a good deal because the low price implies a low probability of success. If an investor only buys out-of-the-money options (with low prices), implicitly he expects a large move of the underlying asset.

Another mistake is to believe that good market timing is enough to realize a successful trade. This assumption is false because of volatility. Ignoring volatility implies the risk of paying too much to purchase options. The size of the move has to be large (or small) enough in order to reach at least the break-even point of the strategy.

A third mistake is to assume that investors should monitor all options contracts believing that this is the correct way to find out the best trades. On the contrary, an investor should work on a limited number of assets and use strategies and options combinations that are well understood. Compared to a direct investment in the underlying stock, an option investment is time consuming because it implies a deep analysis of the underlying asset to build a view (for example, by fundamental analysis or quantitative signals), but it also requires selecting the strike and the maturity of the contract, assessing the current level of implied volatility of the asset, and monitoring the liquidity of the contract.

A final mistake would be for an investor to restrict himself only to buying options. This strategy can provide comfort in that the investor knows the amount of maximum loss. Yet, such a focus ignores probabilities of success that favor the options seller.

2. Discuss good practices of options investing.

Several good practices should be followed when investing in options. The first good practice is to evaluate the current implied volatility level of the underlying asset. Such an analysis helps to determine if the price of the option is historically expensive for a given underlying asset. As a result, the investor can better determine if buying or selling options is preferable. Then, he is better able to choose a directional or neutral position.

Another good practice is to avoid focusing on the most recent price of an option contract. Three major risk factors (underlying price, volatility, and time) influence changes in the option premium. Moreover, because of the leverage, these changes in the option price could be large. Thus, the only important information is the current bid-ask spread given by market makers that reflects the current market's conditions. The last trade price reflects obsolete information in options trading.

A third good practice is to carefully identify an option's intrinsic and time values. When the investor is willing to buy volatility, he should purchase the option with the largest intrinsic value, because time is the enemy of long options positions. These contracts are in-the-money options with a higher probability of success, but with less leverage. By contrast, an investor should sell options for which the price is essentially time value (i.e., out-of-the-money options). Because higher volatility implies higher time value, when the volatility drops, option prices decrease and the seller has the opportunity to close on a winning trade.

3. What kind of information does the options market offer investors?

The options market reflects additional information about the positions of the players who engage in hedging, leverage, or short selling. Further, when an option is priced, traders need to anticipate future (or implied) volatility and possibly the levels of dividends because these parameters are the only ones that are not directly observable on the market. The displayed price translates market forecasts not contained in the cash market.

For stocks or indices, the significance of the implied volatility, its skew, and its term structure are useful information to represent the market's risk aversion. Low volatility suggests possible profit taking and a reason to reposition with calls to maintain a long exposure (strategy of cash extraction).

For an underlying asset, the slope of its skew (the difference between downside and upside implied volatility) gives the market's assessment of the risk of a stock. A high slope implies that the market expects higher downside movement than upside movement (i.e., a higher probability for a downward move). This slope, if normalized, may be used to compare one asset to another. This measure indicates a strategy that overweights or buys stocks with the lowest slope (meaning less downside risk) and underweights or sells assets whose risk is higher (higher slope).

4. What are the advantages to using futures in a portfolio?

Using futures in a portfolio has several advantages. First, with futures, an investor has the possibility to express bearish views and even generate profits from them. According to his expectations, the investor can then finely manage the exposure of his portfolio. Moreover, as listed derivatives, futures offer reactivity and possibilities of market timing with low transaction costs.

A second advantage of futures is that they work well with portfolio theory. For example, the capital asset pricing model (CAPM) helps investors to understand how a future position influences a given portfolio's performance and even how to calibrate a position (i.e., identify the appropriate number of contracts to buy or sell in order to have a suitable risk factor exposure). In particular, futures offer hedging possibilities without disinvesting the portfolio. In this way, an investor can protect his positions from a bearish movement while the selected stocks in the portfolio outperform the market's performance, demonstrating his stock-picking capacities.

Compared to options, an advantage of futures is the simplicity of the product. The dynamics of futures is similar to a cash product such as stocks or indices. The impact of a future's position is easy to understand and exposures to risk factors are stable over time. The maturity of a contract is usually not difficult to manage because there is no exercise feature, even if a position has to be rolled forward from time to time.

A final advantage of a futures contract is that it has no value implying no valuation problems when an investor wants to take a position. He only considers this investment according to his upward or downward expectations without worrying about losing money if the price movement is too strong or not strong enough.

Chapter 25. Performance Presentation

1. How similar or customized are performance presentations?

Performance presentations vary because some presentations contain common elements whereas others are customized to meet client needs. Presentations to prospective clients are very similar and tend to follow a common template or templates. This is due to compliance with voluntary standards such as the Global Investment Performance Standards (GIPS®) or to regulatory requirements. Reports to existing clients for their actual portfolios can be customized to client requests or needs. Typically, however, similar content and/or templates are used for existing clients on their actual portfolios. This has likely evolved over time and experience to assist in report scalability and comparability when using multiple investment managers. Further, the reporting content nucleus among clients is often similar.

2. Who contributes to the process of creating performance presentations?

Although the specific contributors depend upon the content and presentation, the following parties are typically involved in the process of creating performance presentations. Investment performance departments contribute heavily in performance and disclosures. Portfolio managers provide explanatory comments. An operations or accounting unit may provide trading and valuation statements. A graphics team may assemble the data. A department oriented to interact with prospective or existing clients, such as client service or marketing, may set the production and/or delivery schedules, while the legal or compliance department provides prerelease review and approval.

3. How prevalent is reporting time-weighted returns as compared to dollar-weighted returns?

Time-weighted returns continue to be most prevalent in investment performance reporting for most products. This is likely a by-product of their predominance in reporting to prospective clients and/or advertising requirements by regulators. Yet, dollar-weighted returns, such as the internal rate of return (IRR), which reflects a derived constant rate of return by equating a portfolio's ending values to its beginning value and the timing and size of intermediate cash flows, are more prevalent in alternative assets investing such as private equity and alternative structures where investment managers control investment capital flows and their timing.

4. Which performance metric matters more: portfolio absolute return, portfolio benchmark-relative return, portfolio peer-universe ranking, or portfolio risk-adjusted return?

The type of performance metric that matters more varies by client. Typically, no one single measure captures success completely. As such, some or all the metrics above are applied to a given portfolio. Measures such as book yield, net investment income, and realized gain/losses also measure success for such clients as insurance companies. For clarity, the relative importance of each and the time periods and frequency of gauging success should be identified in advance. For a traditional, actively managed portfolio with a three-year time horizon the performance metrics in typical order of importance would be as follows: portfolio benchmark-relative return, portfolio peer-universe ranking, and portfolio risk-adjusted return.

Chapter 26. Exchange Traded Funds: The Success Story of the Last Two Decades

1. Discuss how ETFs are superior and inferior to traditional open-ended index funds.

Researchers stress a cost advantage of ETFs over their mutual fund counterparts in terms of administrative fees but they also highlight that ETFs are subject to additional costs such as the bid-ask spread and the commissions paid to brokerage houses, which do not occur when investing in mutual funds. Empirical evidence reveals that ETFs generally do not outperform mutual funds and occasionally underperform them. A substitution effect also exists between ETFs and index funds when taking into account asset flows. That is, ETFs have attracted substantial funds at a cost to their mutual fund peers.

2. Can ETFs perfectly replicate the performance of the underlying indexes, and what are the factors that affect their tracking efficiency?

Researchers indicate that the perfect replication of the tracking index's performance is a nonevent for ETFs. This failure applies to all types of ETFs and to all ETF markets worldwide. Some factors that negatively influence the ability of ETFs to fully deliver the performance of the tracking indexes include expenses, nonfull replication strategies frequently pursued by ETFs, and nonreinvestment of dividends also called the cash drag effect. Other factors include taxes on dividends, bid-ask spreads, geographical proximity between ETFs and the underlying assets, and the nonoverlapping trading hours when considering international ETFs.

3. What is the relationship between the trading prices and NAVs of ETFs?

The literature shows that the equity-linked ETFs trade at slight and nonpersistent premiums or discounts to their NAVs. These gaps are usually easy to notice and can be vanished through efficient and profitable arbitrage techniques. Yet, researchers show that the premiums or discounts of ETFs invested in nondomestic indexes are more prominent and persistent due to frictions to arbitrage strategies derived from the nonoverlapping hours or other burdens raised by the local authorities. Premiums and discounts also seem to be persistent in the case of fixed-income ETFs.

4. Can the divergence between the trading prices and NAVs of ETFs be indicative of future returns? If so, how?

Regarding the relationship between premiums or discounts and future returns, research reveals that the performance of ETFs is positively affected by the contemporaneous premium or discount while the lagged premium exerts a negative influence on performance. These relationships also apply to fixed-income ETFs. The performance of ETFs can be predictable on the basis of information included in the deviation between the trading values and NAVs of ETFs.

Chapter 27. The Past, Present, and Future of Hedge Funds

1. During the 2007–2008 financial crisis, the question of contagion in the financial industry has received intense attention. Among others, the role of hedge funds in spreading contagion throughout the system has been widely discussed. Discuss whether hedge funds have increased the riskiness in the system and spread increased risks to other participants.

The events in 2007–2008 financial crisis dramatically affected financial markets and altered the structure of the financial system. Nevertheless, hedge funds have been much less affected than investment banks or insurance companies. A number of quantitative hedge funds most likely triggered the so-called quant crisis in August 2007. Sell orders for large positions within few funds affected market prices and eventually led to sell pressure for other funds. Although the quant crisis lasted for only five days, it was unrelated to the later events induced by the incidents in the subprime market.

Academic research finds that the number of participants in certain trades for positions considered to be return generating has increased significantly leading to so-called crowded trades. Crowded trades will increase correlation between certain types of hedge funds once prices get under pressure. This is consistent with academic research that finds increased correlations between different hedge fund types during crisis times.

Conversely, research shows that the correlation of hedge funds with other asset classes declines during crisis times. More recent research argues that the immediate impact of a crisis within the hedge fund industry for the rest of the financial industry largely depends on the state of the industry at that point in time. Probabilities of spillovers might be small during calm times, but will increase dramatically during crisis times.

2. Discuss some important aspects to consider for investing in hedge funds irrespective of their distinct characteristics.

Investors who are considering selecting hedge funds for their portfolios should undertake an operational due diligence irrespective of the nature of the hedge fund. They should place special attention on the organization, operations, and people of the fund and whether the hedge fund is capable of providing necessary information to investors. Hedge funds should have a proven track record of the performance they advertise to their prospective clients. This track record should be transparent in calculation and understandable for investors. With respect to their entire portfolio, investors should consider the correlation of the respective hedge fund with other hedge funds in their portfolio as well as with the rest of the portfolio such as equities, bonds, commodities, or real estate.

Finally, hedge fund investments require constant monitoring with respect to their risk and return as well as possible drift in style. Hedge fund managers alter their investments in order to profit from any perceived opportunity in the market and might thus change their investment style. Investors should analyze on an ongoing basis whether this style fits within their overall asset allocation.

3. Hedge fund return data differ from returns of other traditional asset classes such as bonds or stocks. How should investors account for this disparity in their investment process?

Hedge fund returns are not normally distributed as they exhibit negative skewness and positive excess kurtosis. Standard performance measures will therefore not correctly reflect the risk and return characteristics of the hedge fund or hedge fund portfolio. More advanced performance measures replace traditional measures of risk such as the standard deviation by more comprehensive risk measures. Risk perceived in hedge funds is better reflected by lower partial moments (LPMs) and by risk-adjusted performance measure such as the Omega and Sortino ratio or ratios based on drawdowns such as in the Calmar and Sterling ratio. In this way, excess returns are compared to the risk of a negative deviation below a predefined minimum acceptable rate of return or excess returns are compared to the maximum possible loss during a certain period of time. Such considerations are also better in line with the perception of hedge funds as absolute return investments (i.e., investments without a benchmark).

Investors should also consider the specifics of hedge fund data in their allocation decision. The statistical characteristics of hedge fund data result in a substantial allocation to hedge funds under Markowitz's optimization. Optimization considering higher moments or shortfall risk is now widely available. Research shows that portfolios including hedge funds resulting from such optimization approaches are superior to the standard mean-variance optimization with respect to the generated portfolio moments.

4. Name at least three biases that are present in hedge fund return data. Identify the source of each bias and discuss how each one affects implications drawn from such data.

Hedge fund return data are subject to several biases. The most important and well-known biases are survivorship bias, stale price bias, self-reporting bias, and backfill bias.

Hedge fund databases comprise data of hedge funds that are still operating (also called live funds) and funds that no longer report to the database (also called dead funds or graveyard). Survivorship bias can occur when funds cease reporting to databases and are no longer part of the respective dataset. The two main reasons for these dropouts are because the fund was liquidated and it simply stopped reporting performance. However, "graveyard" does not mean the fund has ceased operations and was liquidated but only that the fund stopped reporting. Funds might stop reporting simply because they reached their target size. Survivorship bias has received wide attention in the academic literature. Studies such as Fung and Hsieh (1997) and Brown, Goetzmann, and Ibbotson (1999) find significant survivorship of around 3 percent. Performance from hedge fund databases thus tends to be biased upwards.

Hedge funds often invest in illiquid assets and assets that are not marked to market resulting in serially correlated returns. This bias is referred to as *stale price bias*. Kat and Lu (2002) and Kat (2003) find significant autocorrelation in hedge fund returns. Geltner (1991, 1993) and Connor (2003) provide desmoothing techniques to delagging return data.

Self-reporting bias results from hedge funds voluntarily reporting to databases. Each fund decides for itself to which database it provides information on returns and other characteristics. Thus, different hedge fund databases may vary considerably concerning the constituents. Implications drawn on basis of one set of data might not hold for other sets of data. Fung and Hsieh (2009) find that only 7 percent of all funds are included in the four databases analyzed (HFR, Lipper/TASS, Barclays Global Investors, and CISDM). Agarwal, Fos and Jiang (2010) even find that only 1 percent of funds are included in all of the five databases in the sample (HFR, Lipper/TASS, Eureka, CISDM, and MSCI).

Once a hedge fund is included into a database, its historic returns are retrospectively added to the dataset. As hedge funds are more likely to start reporting their returns when they are positive, the overall performance of the database will be biased upwards upon the inclusion of additional funds to the database. This bias is called *backfill bias*.

Chapter 28. Portfolio and Risk Management for Private Equity Fund Investments

1. Discuss the main obstacles in applying standard risk and portfolio management techniques in the private equity area.

Traditional portfolio and risk management approaches fail to adequately describe the private equity asset class for two reasons. First, institutions invest in private equity predominantly through closed-end limited partnership funds that are illiquid. As such, public markets are unavailable to help set the valuations of these vehicles. The only observable variables are usually the cash flows of the funds. As a consequence, returns of private equity funds cannot be evaluated on the basis of standard time-weighted returns. Rather, returns of private equity funds have to be evaluated using other performance measures that cannot be taken into account directly in standard portfolio and risk management models, such as the internal rate of return (IRR) or cash multiples. Second, private equity funds have special cash flow structures that distinguish them from other asset classes. Private equity funds are raised every few years on a blind pool basis by professional management companies who invest, manage, and harvest the portfolio companies of the fund. At the onset of the partnership, investors commit capital that gets drawn over several years. Together with the illiquid nature of the private equity funds, the uncertain schedule of the capital drawdowns, and the unpredictable distributions of cash or securities to the investors of the fund increase the difficulty of accurately managing these partnership interests.

2. Explain the stale and managed pricing phenomenon discussed in the private equity literature. What is the influence of these effects on private equity returns that are based on a fund's disclosed net asset values (NAVs)?

Stale pricing is caused by the fact that the reported NAVs of the fund management do not readily incorporate all available information. Stale pricing leads to lag time differences between observable market valuations and valuations in private equity portfolios. Under these conditions, the reported NAVs will only occasionally reflect the true market values (i.e., the price at which the fund's assets could be sold in an open market transaction). Similarly, as private equity fund managers have considerable discretion in their valuations, reported NAVs might suffer from a managed pricing phenomenon. In this sense, fund managers may mark the values of their portfolios up or down only when doing so is favorable to them. The effects can cause biases in the returns that are measured by using NAVs.

3. Briefly summarize the two components of the model for the cash flow dynamics of private equity funds presented in this chapter.

Given the typical construction of private equity funds, the stochastic model of the cash flow dynamics consists of two components that are modeled independently. A first stochastic model is developed for the drawdowns of the committed capital, and a second stochastic model is developed for the distribution of dividends and proceeds. A mean-reverting square root process represents the rate at which committed capital is drawn over time. Capital distributions are assumed to follow a geometric Brownian motion with a time-dependent drift that incorporates the typical repayment patterns of private equity funds.

4. Explain how the model for the cash flow dynamics of private equity funds can be applied in the risk and portfolio management context.

The model has several possible applications in the risk and portfolio management area. First, an institutional investor can employ it for the purpose of liquidity planning. In this area, an investor can use the model to estimate expected future cash needed to meet capital commitments, as well as projected distributions that generate liquidity in the future. Second, the model can be used as a tool for many risk management applications. For example, an investor can measure the sensitivity of some ex-post performance measure, such as the internal rate of return (IRR), to changes in typical drawdown or distribution patterns. Third, the model can be employed in the portfolio management area to determine to optimal allocation between, for example, the venture capital and buyout segment.

Capture 29. Venture Capital

1. Discuss the advantages and disadvantages of investing in venture capital.

Investing in venture capital offers both advantages and disadvantages. On the positive side, these investments create an opportunity to achieve tremendous returns in case of successful startup firms. Some well-known companies such as Apple, Google, and Microsoft have generated huge capital gains for their early investors. Even apart from such exceptional cases, the average internal rates of return (IRRs) have been high compared to other investments. Furthermore, for investors seeking a more pronounced business involvement, venture capital investments enable them to support portfolio companies by providing advice, knowledge, and access to their networks.

On the negative side, investors may face several disadvantages. For example, venture capital investments involve a high degree of uncertainty regarding the outcome. Because such investments imply a high risk of losses, they require both a careful due diligence and a professional management of funds. Evidence shows that fund returns depend on the skills and experience of the general partners. However, participation in funds of established partnerships is typically restricted to the investors of former funds. Thus, investors newly seeking an exposure to venture capital may possibly face inferior return expectations. Additionally, empirical research provides no clear picture of performance due to the lack of data. Performance evaluations based on samples including funds without a liquidation history may be distorted. Moreover, the net-of-fee performance may be substantially lower than the gross performance. Finally, compared to other asset classes, venture capital investments are highly illiquid due to a lack of an active secondary market. Investors can realize capital gains only once the investment in the company is exited through an acquisition by a third party or an initial public offering (IPO). Hence, investors cannot continuously rebalance their portfolios in order to meet their needs.

2. Many cases of venture capital investing involve general partners and limited partners involved. Why are such partnerships necessary and what are their roles in the investment process?

The typical structure of venture capital investing is a limited partnership. The general partner (GP) manages the funds and gets compensated for his activities by a management fee and by carried interest on realized capital gains in case of a successful investment. In most cases, the general partner also holds a minority position of the capital (e.g., 5 percent). The limited partners (LP) are those investors who provide most of the capital. From an organizational perspective, the limited partners delegate some of the decision rights to the general partner in order to enhance the efficiency of the investment process. However, to align the interests of the general partner with those of the limited partners, the general partner also participates in the fund capital. In this regard, the limited partnership features the same advantages as corporations. However, unlike corporations, limited partnerships are not taxed on the level of the structure. Instead, income is only taxed on the individual level (i.e., at the level of the general partner and the limited partners). Therefore, from a tax perspective, this type of structure for pooling funds of different investors is more favorable than an investment corporation.

3. In the field of venture investing, why is performance persistence investing considered to be puzzling?

In the case of venture capital, performance persistence is seen to be a puzzle when comparing the persistence pattern to that of mutual funds. However, this phenomenon can be partly explained by the financial economics of venture capital investments. Empirical research documents that the performance of venture capital funds is persistent. That is, a fund's performance tends to be positively related to the performance of previously raised funds by the same venture capital firm. Given the relevance of the general partner for the investment policy, this result seems quite obvious. Nevertheless, this argument might be equally relevant for mutual funds where empirical findings suggest that past performance of fund managers has no or only little predictive power for future performance. The absence of performance persistence for most mutual funds is due to the continuous capital reallocations by investors. However, because of the illiquidity of venture capital investments as well as the lack of information, these reallocations do not seem to happen as quickly for venture capital funds. Evidence also suggests that only investors of well-performing funds use all available information and properly adjust capital allocations so that these funds exhibit less performance persistence than low performing funds. Because general partners may want to retain current investors, the general partners do not eliminate performance persistence by raising fees.

4. During the financial crisis of 2008 and 2009, venture capital investments experienced a sharp downturn. Discuss the reasons for this economic cyclicality.

The venture capital industry is strongly dependent on the overall economy. The industry exhibits a cyclical pattern in terms of capital volumes and the type of capital invested in startup firms as well as regarding the returns. This pattern occurs due to the strong economic sensitivity of young companies to growth in gross domestic product (GDP). Startup firms typically grow very quickly in a boom whereas in times of crises they might not even survive. Conversely, this pattern can be related to the financial economics of venture capital investing. If economic activity is in full swing, investors are overly optimistic. In troughs they tend to be more risk averse and would rather withdraw their money instead of investing it in new risky businesses. This situation translates into the observed cyclicality of money flows. As a result, the performance of venture capital investments is strongly procyclical. In other words, this is due to the volatile investment and exit volumes in the course of the business cycle and the shifting underlying economic outlook.

Chapter 30. Socially Responsible Investing

1. Discuss two ways besides screening that an individual can participate in SRI.

Besides screening, one way to participate in SRI is through shareholder activism, which allows shareholders to engage directly with management through proxy voting. In this manner, shareholder activism can bring about specific business changes in a timely fashion. It can also help companies avoid future problems by allowing shareholders' concerns to be addressed as soon as possible. Another way is through community development, which directly connects the investor with those in need. Community development has three main forms: community development loan funds, community development banks, and community development credit unions. These, community development programs can help revive distressed communities and can also serve as a reasonable alternative to cash reserves.

2. Discuss whether SRI funds and indices outperform conventional benchmarks.

The prevailing evidence is that SRI funds and indices do not outperform conventional benchmarks. Thus, neither a SRI advantage nor a SRI disadvantage exists over the long term. Of the few studies that document outperformance for SRI assets, most attribute a large portion of the excess return to size bias. Size bias is primarily due to SRI assets tilting towards smaller capitalization. However, many indices, such as the DSI, purposefully exclude large capitalization stocks in shunned industries, creating additional size bias. Finally, those assets reporting the highest abnormal returns over conventional assets are high-ranking SRI assets and sin stocks.

3. Do any financial theories support SRI? Explain.

Modern portfolio theory (MPT) disputes claims of SRI outperformance. For example, MPT states that restricting the universe of securities for any reason forces the investor into a suboptimal portfolio. In other words, SRI incurs a cost regardless of whether or not the market is efficient. If markets are efficient, SRI will incur a diversification cost. If markets are inefficient, SRI will interfere with active management strategies. SRI advocates might argue that the vast number of stocks in the investment universe is likely to mitigate this cost. The advocates' best support centers on the benefits of screening. Screening reduces company-specific risk and liabilities and helps identify firms with solid finances and effective management.

4. Discuss the empirical evidence on whether SRI stocks outperform sin stocks.

Evidence shows that sin stocks outperform SRI stocks. Hong and Kacperczyk (2009) show that sin stocks outperform other stocks by about 2 percent a year. Fabozzi, Ma, and Oliphant (2008) find that the average sin stock produces a return of 19 percent, and that every sin industry produces returns in excess of 13 percent. Since its inception in 2003, the Vice Fund has earned an annualized return in excess of 20 percent.

Index